New Perspectives

21st Edition

Computer Concepts

Introductory

Cengage

Australia • Brazil • Mexico • Singapore • United Kingdom • United States

***New Perspectives on Computer Concepts:* Introductory 21st edition**
June Jamrich Parsons

SVP, Product: Erin Joyner

VP, Product: Thais Alencar

Product Director: Mark Santee

Senior Product Manager: Amy Savino

Product Assistant: Ciara Horne

Learning Designer: Zenya Molnar

Content Manager: Christina Nyren

Digital Delivery Quality Partner: Jim Vaughey

Developmental Editor: Dan Seiter

VP, Product Marketing: Jason Sakos

Director, Product Marketing: Danaë April

Executive Product Marketing Manager: Jill Staut

IP Analyst: Ann Hoffman

IP Project Manager: Nick Barrows

Production Service: Lumina Datamatics Ltd.

Designer: Erin Griffin

Cover Credit: Kaveex/Shutterstock.com

For product information and technology assistance, contact us at **Cengage Customer & Sales Support, 1-800-354-9706 or support.cengage.com.**

For permission to use material from this text or product, submit all requests online at **www.copyright.com.**

Library of Congress Control Number: 2022938337

Student Edition: ISBN: 978-0-357-67462-8
Loose-leaf Edition: ISBN: 978-0-357-67464-2

Cengage
200 Pier 4 Boulevard
Boston, MA 02210
USA

Cengage is a leading provider of customized learning solutions with employees residing in nearly 40 different countries and sales in more than 125 countries around the world. Find your local representative at **www.cengage.com**.

To learn more about Cengage platforms and services, register or access your online learning solution, or purchase materials for your course, visit **www.cengage.com**.

Printed in the United States of America
Print Number: 01 Print Year: 2022

Table of Contents

Contents at a Glance

Introduction

Module 1

Module 2

Module 3

Module 4

Module 5

Module 6

Module 7

Module PY

Preface

New Perspectives on Computer Concepts

College graduates of the 21st century are expected to have a **broad base of knowledge** to intelligently address social, political, economic, and legal issues associated with rapidly evolving digital technology.

Today's students have a patchwork of knowledge, acquired from using various digital devices. *New Perspectives on Computer Concepts,* 21st edition, helps students build a cohesive framework that organizes this acquired knowledge and serves as a foundation for assimilating new concepts **essential to careers and lifestyles** in our digital world. This course is geared toward introductory students who are first learning about digital literacy and fundamentals of technology.

Updated. This edition has been newly **revised and updated** to increase learning effectiveness and to reflect the wide scope of digital devices in use today, with an enhanced focus on the connectivity that pervades modern life and the security necessary to protect it. Notable updates include the addition of digital assistants in the Introduction module, extensive revisions to the social network lab in Module 5, a new Issue feature in Module 6 about banned apps, updates to the Module 7 Issue and Lab features, a new Issue feature in Module 8 (Is Big Tech Too Big?), coverage of blockchain in Module 10, updates to the Technology in Context feature about politics in Module 10, and revised objectives for the Python programming module.

Targeted Learning Support. This award-winning textbook contains layers of targeted learning support for **active learning** that keeps students engaged and helps them succeed. Using the **MindTap digital platform**, students benefit from interactive feedback and collaborative opportunities.

Reading in the Discipline. Short paragraphs and a clear narrative style help students grasp concepts and learn **how to read technical material**.

Retention. What's the most effective study technique: Taking notes? Reviewing? According to researchers, students study most effectively by simply trying to recall the material they've read, seen, or heard. That's why this edition offers **continuous assessment**. Embedded QuickChecks on just about every page help students recall key concepts while reading and later while reviewing. QuickQuizzes and end-of-module reinforcement promote **successful learning outcomes**.

Hands-On. This edition contains plenty of practical information about how to use apps, manage files, create content, configure security software, and more. Try It! activities throughout the book show students how to **immediately apply concepts in real-world contexts**.

Flipped Classrooms. Flipping a course is easy with this textbook, which includes flipped class projects for **critical thinking**, cyberclassroom exploration, **collaborative group work**, multimedia integration, career building, and **globalization**. End-of-module features, such as Issues and Information Tools, offer additional topics for hands-on in-class activities.

A Fresh Approach to Social Media. Sure, students use social media, but are they familiar with underlying concepts, such as the **Social Media Honeycomb, geolocation, and sociograms**? Are they up to speed with Creative Commons and intellectual property concepts? Do they recognize **fake news**? And do they understand the relevance of **online identity, privacy, and reputation management**? Module 5 offers a fresh approach to social media that delves into concepts while also providing practical how-to tips.

Imaging Technologies. In an increasingly visual world, graphical imaging is becoming ever more sophisticated. Module 1 is packed with information about 360-degree video, stereoscopic graphics, and spherical imaging popularized by **GoPro cameras, YouTube 360, and virtual reality**.

The Latest Technology. Digital technology evolves at a fast pace. This edition keeps students up to date with **Raspberry Pi**, 3D printers, smart appliances, Lightning ports, USB-C, accelerometers, gyro sensors, magnetometers, macOS, **Windows 11**, virtual reality headsets, Microsoft Edge, **two-factor authentication**, ransomware, and more!

Hands-On Programming Module. Using Python provides highly interactive programming activities that **introduce students to the world of programming** without requiring any prior experience. Python is an easy-to-learn language that supports procedural and object-oriented programs.

Infographic Illustrations. Illustrations based on popular infographic visuals are carefully integrated into the learning path to provide **visual scaffolding** that is so important to understanding technical concepts.

Infographic-style illustrations

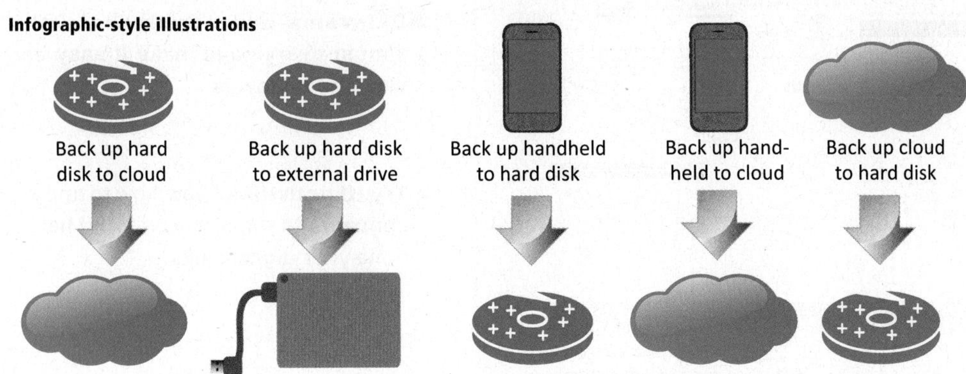

Student Resources: The Book

Whether you use the printed book or digital versions, New Perspectives learning materials give you the straight story on today's technology.

Easy to Read. Each module is divided into five **sections**, beginning with a **concept map** that provides a visual overview of topics. **FAQs** answer commonly asked questions about technology and help you follow the flow of the presentation.

Keeps You on Track. As you read each page, watch for **QuickChecks**. They'll help you gauge if you comprehend key concepts. And take some time to complete the **Try It! activities**. They bring concepts to the real world and help you hone your digital skills. **QuickQuizzes** at the end of each section provide a chance to find out if you remember the most important concepts. **End-of-module review** activities such as Key Terms, Interactive Situation Questions, and Interactive Summary questions are great for test prep.

Helps You Explore. The **Issue** section in each module highlights controversial aspects of technology. In the **Technology in Context** section, you'll discover how technology plays a role in careers such as film-making, architecture, banking, and fashion design. The **Information Tools** section helps you sharpen your digital research techniques. Check out the **labs** at the end of each module for some step-by-step exploration into your digital devices.

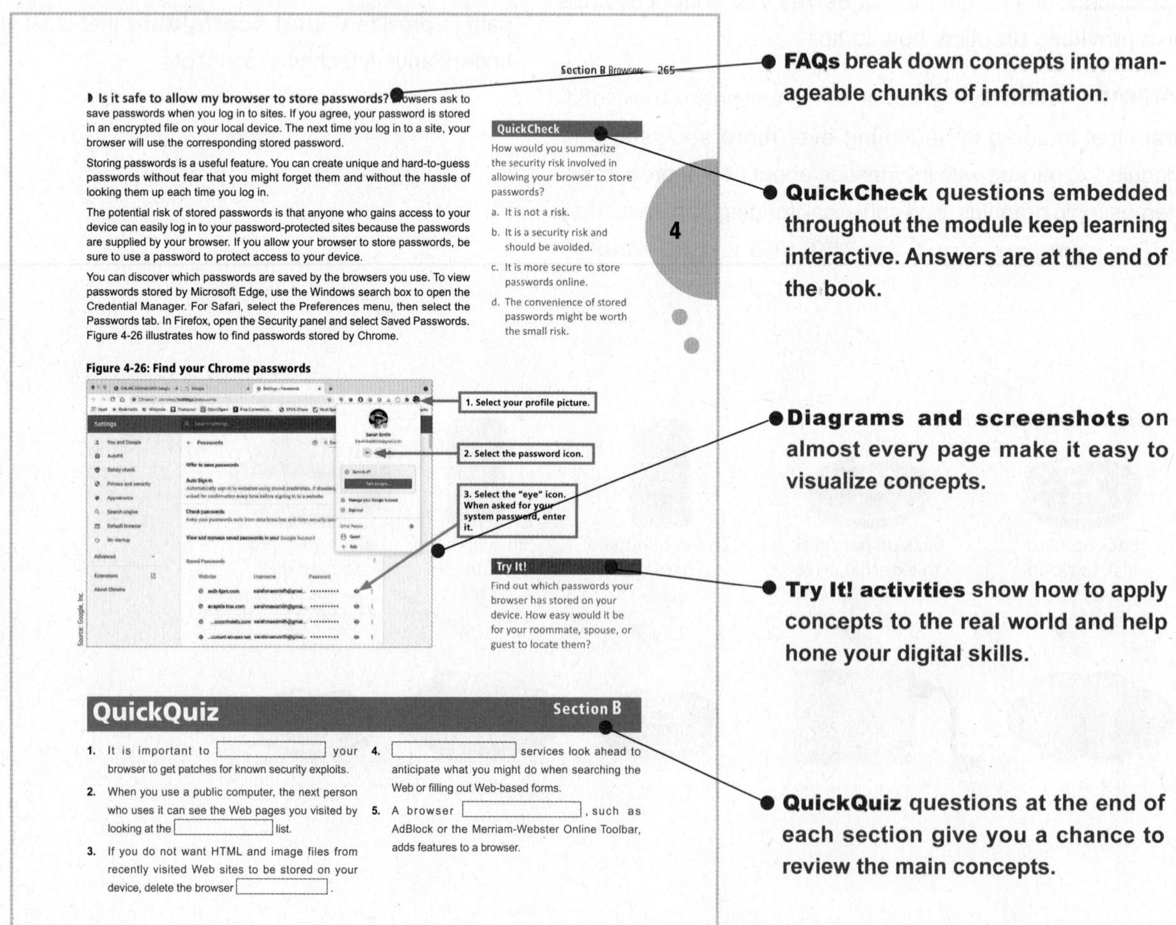
Section B Browsers 265

Is it safe to allow my browser to store passwords? Browsers ask to save passwords when you log in to sites. If you agree, your password is stored in an encrypted file on your local device. The next time you log in to a site, your browser will use the corresponding stored password.

Storing passwords is a useful feature. You can create unique and hard-to-guess passwords without fear that you might forget them and without the hassle of looking them up each time you log in.

The potential risk of stored passwords is that anyone who gains access to your device can easily log in to your password-protected sites because the passwords are supplied by your browser. If you allow your browser to store passwords, be sure to use a password to protect access to your device.

You can discover which passwords are saved by the browsers you use. To view passwords stored by Microsoft Edge, use the Windows search box to open the Credential Manager. For Safari, select the Preferences menu, then select the Passwords tab. In Firefox, open the Security panel and select Saved Passwords. Figure 4-26 illustrates how to find passwords stored by Chrome.

QuickCheck

How would you summarize the security risk involved in allowing your browser to store passwords?

a. It is not a risk.
b. It is a security risk and should be avoided.
c. It is more secure to store passwords online.
d. The convenience of stored passwords might be worth the small risk.

4

Figure 4-26: Find your Chrome passwords

1. Select your profile picture.
2. Select the password icon.
3. Select the "eye" icon. When asked for your system password, enter it.

Source: Google, Inc.

Try It!

Find out which passwords your browser has stored on your device. How easy would it be for your roommate, spouse, or guest to locate them?

QuickQuiz Section B

1. It is important to [ ] your browser to get patches for known security exploits.
2. When you use a public computer, the next person who uses it can see the Web pages you visited by looking at the [ ] list.
3. If you do not want HTML and image files from recently visited Web sites to be stored on your device, delete the browser [ ].
4. [ ] services look ahead to anticipate what you might do when searching the Web or filling out Web-based forms.
5. A browser [ ], such as AdBlock or the Merriam-Webster Online Toolbar, adds features to a browser.

FAQs break down concepts into manageable chunks of information.
QuickCheck questions embedded throughout the module keep learning interactive. Answers are at the end of the book.
Diagrams and screenshots on almost every page make it easy to visualize concepts.
Try It! activities show how to apply concepts to the real world and help hone your digital skills.
QuickQuiz questions at the end of each section give you a chance to review the main concepts.

Student Resources: Online

Digital versions of your textbook include multimedia and hands-on activities designed to enhance your learning experience.

MindTap. The digital version of this book is available in **MindTap**, a personalized online learning platform. In addition to the full text contained in the printed book, the digital version includes activities based on a learning path designed by your instructor that **guides you through the course**.

MindTap is a cost-effective alternative to a printed textbook. You can purchase access to MindTap from *www.cengagebrain.com*.

Jaimie Duplass /Shutterstock.com

Student Resources: Hone Your Technical Reading Skills

If you would like to improve the way you comprehend and retain the information found in technical books and documentation, read on.

Prepare. Your goal is to complete one section of a module. That's a sufficient amount of material for one session. **Look at the concept map** at the beginning of the section. It is designed to help you connect concepts in a Web of relationships, so they become more than random facts.

Divide and Conquer. Don't expect to read technical material in the same way you'd read a novel. Trying to read without stopping from the beginning to the end of a module, chapter, or section is likely to produce more confusion than confidence. Instead, **take it one page at a time**. Read the page and then pause. Imagine that you are going to teach that material to someone else. Then summarize the main points in your own words.

Take Notes. When you come across a fact that you want to remember, make a note. A study conducted by researchers at UCLA and Princeton University revealed that students who take lecture notes using a pen or pencil scored better on tests than students who took notes on their laptops. The same effect may come into play when taking notes as you read. Whether you make notes on screen or on paper, make sure to **use your own words**. That will help you understand the essence of a concept and retain it for future use.

Highlight. Use highlights to **mark passages you do not understand**. This advice may seem contrary to the idea of highlighting key concepts, but simply marking something in the book—or worse, copying and pasting passages from a digital book—does little to help you internalize a concept. Highlighting passages that you do not understand allows you to return to them after you've completed a section. You may find that the passage now makes sense. If not, you've marked a concept that will be a great question for your instructor.

Read the Pictures. The figures in this book are included to reinforce, explain, and **expand the information presented in the written narrative**. Concepts that may seem complex when explained in words can be much easier to understand when you see an illustration, screenshot, or photo. So, take some time with each figure to make sure you understand how it is related to the text that precedes it.

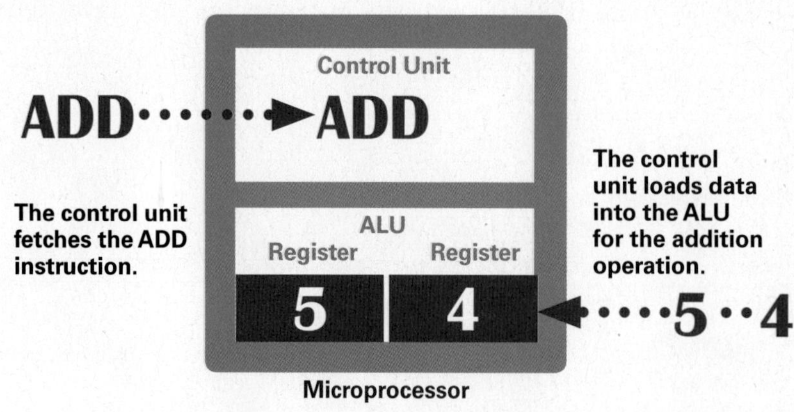
Control Unit
ADD
ADD
The control unit fetches the ADD instruction.
ALU
Register
Register
5
4
5
4
The control unit loads data into the ALU for the addition operation.
Microprocessor

Test Yourself. Researchers at Purdue University discovered that "practicing retrieval" through self-testing is one of the **most effective techniques for learning**. New Perspectives learning materials supply you with lots of opportunities to retrieve material. Make sure to use the QuickChecks, QuickQuizzes, Interactive Summaries, and Interactive Situation Questions. Additional resources, such as flashcards and module quizzes, are available with MindTap.

Be an Active Learner. The concepts you'll learn are not abstract theories. Most have practical applications for today's digital lifestyles. You'll find that concepts are much easier to remember if you can apply them and understand how they are relevant. The **Try It! activities** throughout every module show you how to apply concepts. The best learning strategy is to complete these activities as you encounter them. They'll give you a break from reading and help you to understand how all the practical and conceptual pieces fit together.

Get the Connections. The bubble diagrams supplied at the beginning of each section provide an overview of concepts and their linkages. After reading a section, you might want to **extend the concept maps** by adding more details. You can add another level of concepts. Also, think of additional relationships between the existing concepts and mark them with dotted lines.

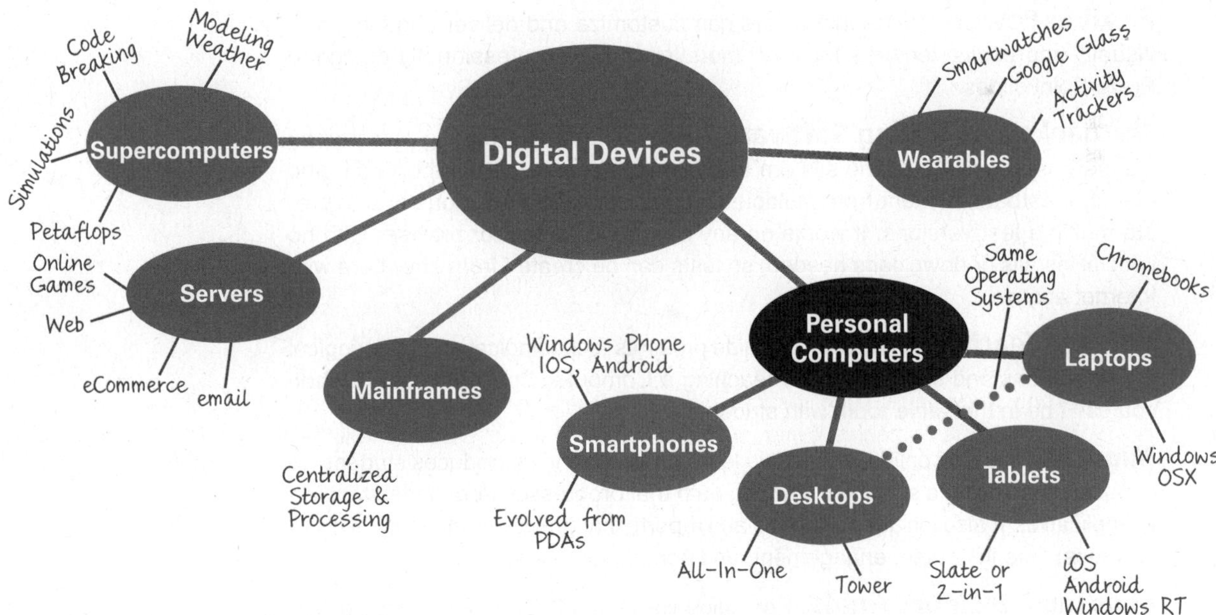

Corrections. Despite intensive attention to quality, occasional typos and other errata slip into the book. Corrections are posted to your student companion site, which you can access by logging in to your account at *login.cengage.com*.

Cengage Instructor Center

Additional instructor resources for this product are available online. Instructor assets include an Instructor's Manual, Educator's Guide, PowerPoint® slides, Solution and Answer Guide, and a testbank powered by Cognero®. Sign up or sign in at *www.cengage.com* to search for and access this product and its online resources.

Instructor's Manual. The Instructor's Manual offers the following comprehensive instructional materials:

- Module objectives
- Purpose and perspective of the module
- What's new in each module
- Module Outline
- Discussion questions and activities

Solution and Answer Guide. Your password-protected instructor resources provide answers to all the QuickChecks, Lab Assignments, Interactive Summaries, Interactive Situation Questions, Issue Try It! activities, and Information Tools Try It! activities.

Transition Guide. This guide highlights all of the changes in the text and in the digital offerings from the previous edition to this edition.

Flexible PowerPoints. Instructors can customize and deliver engaging and visually impressive lectures for each module with the professionally designed PowerPoint slides.

Testbanks and Testing Software. Cengage Learning Testing powered by Cognero is a flexible, online system that allows instructors to author, edit, and manage testbank content from multiple Cengage Learning solutions and to create multiple test versions. It works on any operating system or browser with no special installs or downloads needed, so tests can be created from anywhere with Internet access.

Guide to Teaching Online. This guide presents technological and pedagogical considerations and suggestions for teaching a Computer Concepts course when you can't be in the same room with students.

MindTap. This fully online, interactive learning experience introduces students to core concepts using a simplified learning path that progresses from understanding to application. It also includes analytics and reports that provide a snapshot of class progress, time in course, engagement, and completion rates.

MindTap Educator's Guide. This guide walks you through the unique activities in MindTap, where you'll find them, and how they're built for easier curriculum integration.

From the Author

So much has changed since the first edition of *Computer Concepts* was published in 1994! From year to year, the changes have been subtle, but looking back, it is clear that technology, students, and even education has progressed in amazing and sometimes unexpected directions. As digital technology continues to evolve, New Perspectives continues to keep pace, providing students with up-to-date content and cognitive tools that engage and ensure successful learning outcomes.

Many of today's students have substantially more practical experience with digital devices than their counterparts of twenty years ago, but even these experienced students may lack a cohesive framework for their knowledge.

The goal of *New Perspectives on Computer Concepts* is to bring every student up to speed with computer basics, and then go beyond basic computer literacy to provide students with technical and practical information that every college-educated person would be expected to know.

Whether you are an instructor or a student, we hope that you enjoy the learning experience provided by our text-based and technology-based materials.

Acknowledgments

The book would not exist—and certainly wouldn't arrive on schedule—were it not for the efforts of our media, editorial, and production teams. Grateful thanks to Dan Seiter for his developmental edit and tireless work on every detail of the project; Amy Savino and Christina Nyren for their leadership; Flora Emanuel and the team at Lumina for managing production; and our brilliant sales reps for encouraging instructors to adopt this book to enhance their introductory courses.

A special shout-out in this edition goes to my father, John X. Jamrich, who as a lifelong educator and president of Northern Michigan University showed me the value of helping students achieve their goals through education.

Additional acknowledgements go to the New Perspectives Advisory Committee members, reviewers, and students who have made a tremendous contribution to every edition of *Computer Concepts*. Thank you all!

June Jamrich Parsons

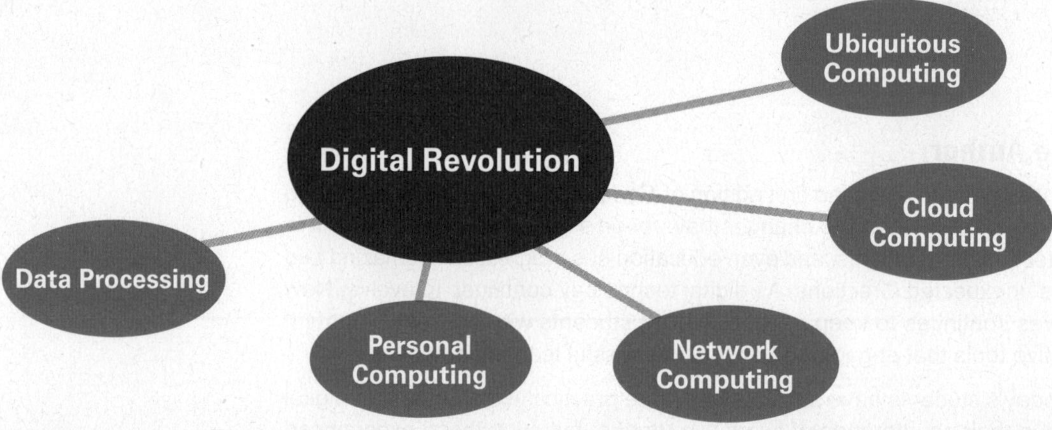

Introduction

Objectives

- Name the five phases of the digital revolution and place each on a timeline.
- Describe the digital devices that were popular during each phase of the digital revolution.
- List at least five characteristics of each phase of the digital revolution.
- Find two similarities and two differences between technology in the data processing era and technology in the cloud computing era.
- Explain the concept of convergence as it pertains to digital devices.
- Distinguish between virtual reality and augmented reality.
- Explain the relationship between the Internet of Things and ubiquitous computing.

You live in the information age:

a period in history when information is accessible and technology affects many aspects of everyday life, from the economy to politics and social relationships. The importance of information is not new. It has always been a powerful tool. Scrolls treasured by monks during the Middle Ages, scientific knowledge collected during the Renaissance, and intelligence data collected during the Cold War were all critical in shaping world events. The Information Age is unique because of its underlying technology, which is based on digital electronics. This introduction will help you put the technology that you use into the context of the digital revolution that continues to reinvent the Information Age.

Terminology

digital revolution
digital
digital content
user interface
computer terminal
centralized computing
data processing
personal computing
local software
computer network
Internet
Web
cloud computing
convergence
Web 2.0
social media
sharing economy
virtual reality
ubiquitous computing
augmented reality
Internet of Things
virtual assistant
voice as a user interface
autonomous vehicles

The Digital Revolution

The **digital revolution** is an ongoing process of social, political, and economic change brought about by digital technology, such as microchips, computers, and the Internet.

What is digital? **Digital** is a type of technology that represents written, visual, audio, and quantitative data as numbers, such as 1s and 0s. The word *digital* comes from the root *digit*. In the language of mathematics, a digit is the symbol used to write the numerals 0, 1, 2, 3, 4, 5, 6, 7, 8, and 9.

Like the agricultural revolution and the industrial revolution, the digital revolution offers advantages but requires adaptations. Digital innovations challenge the status quo and require societies to make adjustments to traditions, lifestyles, and legislation.

Digital devices were originally called *computer hardware* or *computing machines*. The programs and data they contain were referred to as *computer software*. The software that runs on today's smartphones and tablet devices has come to be known as *apps*.

The technology driving the digital revolution is based on digital electronics and the idea that electrical signals can represent data, such as numbers, words, pictures, and music. We often call this data **digital content**.

What is the significance of digital content? An interesting characteristic of digital content is that it can be easily duplicated with no loss of quality. Before digital technology, photocopies of paper documents usually looked blurred. Copying a movie on videotape reduced its quality, and every subsequent copy became progressively worse. Now, digital copies are essentially indistinguishable from originals, which has created new possibilities for content distribution on platforms such as Apple Music and Netflix.

Digital devices, including computers and smartphones, transformed our world. Without them, your favorite form of entertainment would probably be foosball, and you'd be listening to a bulky old Victrola instead of your sleek smartphone (Figure 1).

Intro

Figure 1: Is music cheaper today?

1922
For $1.00, you could purchase a record containing two songs.
That's $14.11 in today's money.
2022
On iTunes, one song costs $1.29.
Two songs cost only
$2.58 today.

Try It!

Music is less expensive today than it was back in 1922, but what about books? Can you find the price of a book during the 1920s and the price of an equivalent Kindle book today? Don't forget to convert the cost into today's dollars. (Search online for *inflation calculator*.)

Data Processing

Some historians mark the 1980s as the beginning of the digital revolution, but engineers built the first digital computers during World War II for breaking codes and calculating missile trajectories. In the 1950s, computers were marketed for business applications, such as payroll and inventory management.

What was computing like back then? In the first phase of the digital revolution, computers were huge, complex, and expensive devices that stored data on reels of magnetic tape. They existed in limited numbers and were primarily housed in big corporations and government agencies. Computers were operated by trained technicians. Each computer installation required specialized software. The thought that computers might someday be used by millions of people in their homes was only a glimmer of an idea in the minds of science fiction writers.

One drawback to computer use was the **user interface**, the mechanism for entering and viewing data. Back then, processing components for computers were housed in closet-sized cabinets. The main computer unit was separate from the devices used for input and output. Initially, data was entered on punched cards and results were printed on continuous form paper. Later, computers were accessed using the keyboard and display screen of a terminal. A **computer terminal** has little processing capability of its own, so it was simply used to enter data and view results produced by software that ran on the main computer (Figure 2).

This method of computing, in which a main computer holds all of the data and performs all of the processing, is called **centralized computing**. It was the main technology model used during the data processing era. Devices such as terminals and printers were connected to a centralized computer with cables, as shown in Figure 2.

QuickCheck

Data processing was characterized by _________.

a. centralized computing

b. primitive digital devices such as calculators and watches

c. standalone computers such as Apple IIs and IBM PCs

d. local software and data storage

Figure 2: Centralized computing

100%
processing performed on central computer

Enter
data that will be processed by central computer

0%
processing performed on terminals

View
data received from central computer

Try It!

A computer terminal, like the one shown below, is an input and output device that depends on a centralized "host" computer for processing and storing data. Can you identify similarities between these old-fashioned devices and the way today's digital devices interact with the Internet?

▸ Who had access to computers? During the antiestablishment era of the 1960s, the digital revolution was beginning to transform organizations, but ordinary people had little direct contact with computers.

As with many new technologies, computers were initially viewed with suspicion by consumers. IBM's corporate slogan "THINK" conveyed to some people a disturbing image of giant machine brains.

Computers seemed remote. They were housed out of sight in special facilities and were inaccessible to ordinary people. Computers also seemed impersonal. To uniquely identify an individual, computers used a sequence of numbers such as a Social Security number. The fact that computers tracked people by numbers, rather than by their names, alienated many students and workers.

In the 1960s, computers and punched cards became a symbol of the establishment. Students were uncomfortable with the use of punched cards for storing academic records (Figure 3). The leader of a protest on the University of California, Berkeley campus complained, "You're processed. You become a number on a set of file cards that go through an IBM machine."

Figure 3: Antiestablishment protests

In the 1950s and 1960s, data used by government and business computers was coded onto punched cards that contained the warning "Do not fold, tear, or mutilate this card." Similar slogans were used by protesters who were concerned that computers would have a dehumanizing effect on society.

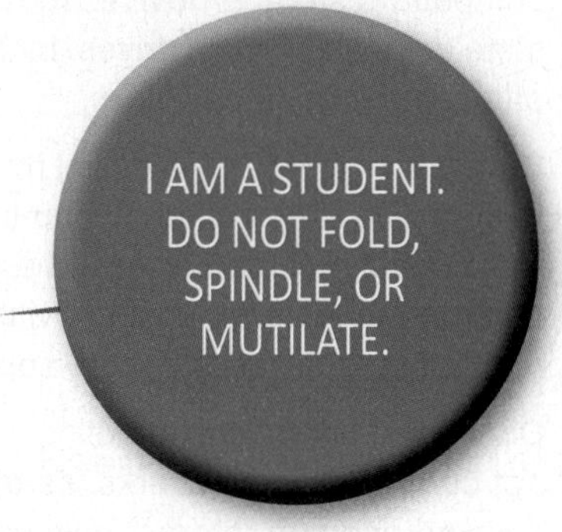

I AM A STUDENT. DO NOT FOLD, SPINDLE, OR MUTILATE.

Intro

▸ What is data processing? Throughout the first phase of the digital revolution, businesses adopted computers with increasing enthusiasm based on benefits such as cutting costs and managing mountains of data. Computers and data processing became crucial tools for effective business operations. **Data processing** is based on an input-processing-output cycle. Data goes into a computer, it is processed, and then it is output (Figure 4).

The data processing era lasted from the 1940s through the 1970s. Data processing installations still exist today, but other technologies emerged, making computing available to a more diverse group of users.

Figure 4: Data processing

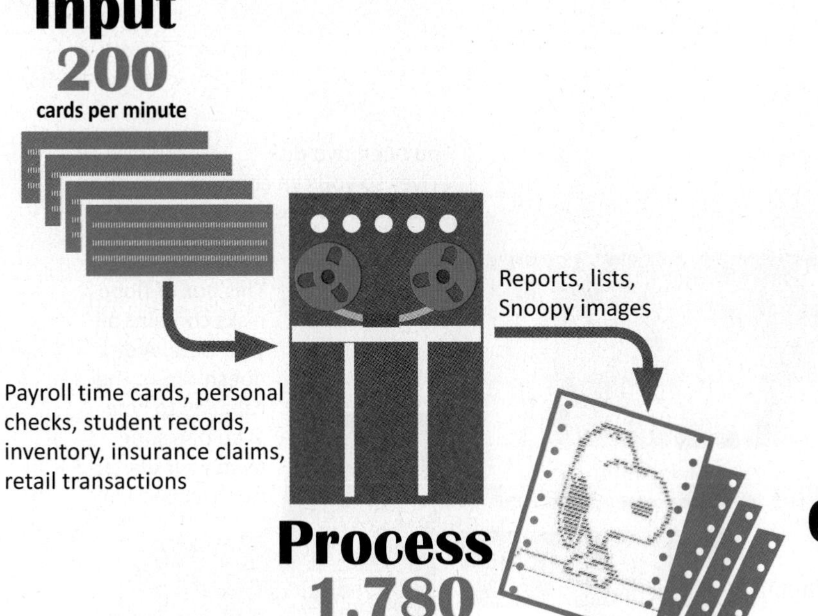

Try It!

Have you seen the classic film *Desk Set*, starring Spencer Tracy and Katharine Hepburn? It characterizes the public's attitude toward computers in the 1950s. Look for it on Netflix or Amazon Prime. What do you think caused such widespread technophobia?

Personal Computing

Digital devices were first available to consumers in the 1970s, when handheld calculators and digital watches hit store shelves. The first personal computers made their debut in 1976, but sales got off to a slow start. Without compelling software applications, personal computers, such as the Apple II and IBM PC, seemed to offer little for their $3,000 price tag. As the variety of software increased, however, consumer interest grew.

QuickCheck

Personal computing was characterized by ________.

a. software housed on a centralized computer

b. sophisticated software applications

c. storing data in the cloud

d. local software and data storage

▸ What is personal computing? The second phase of the digital revolution, **personal computing**, is characterized by standalone computers powered by local software. **Local software** refers to any software that is installed on a computer's storage device. Today, local software resides on hard disks, solid state drives, and flash drives. In the personal computing era, local software was often stored on floppy disks.

During this phase of the digital revolution, computers were used to enhance productivity. Writing, gathering numbers into uncomplicated charts, and scheduling were popular computer-based activities. Computers and videogame machines emerged as entertainment devices, and the game industry drove the development of ever faster and more sophisticated digital components.

During the personal computing phase of the digital revolution, computers were not connected to networks, so they were essentially self-contained units that allowed users to interact only with installed software. On the business front, centralized computer systems continued to run payroll, inventory, and financial software. Some managers used personal computers and spreadsheet software to crunch numbers for business planning.

Try It!

Imagine that there is no Internet. Take a look at your computer and make a quick list of programs that you'd be able to use in a world without the Internet.

If you had owned a computer back in the second phase of the digital revolution, it was probably a standalone machine with primitive sound capabilities. The display device looked like an old-fashioned television (Figure 5).

Figure 5: Personal computing circa 1985

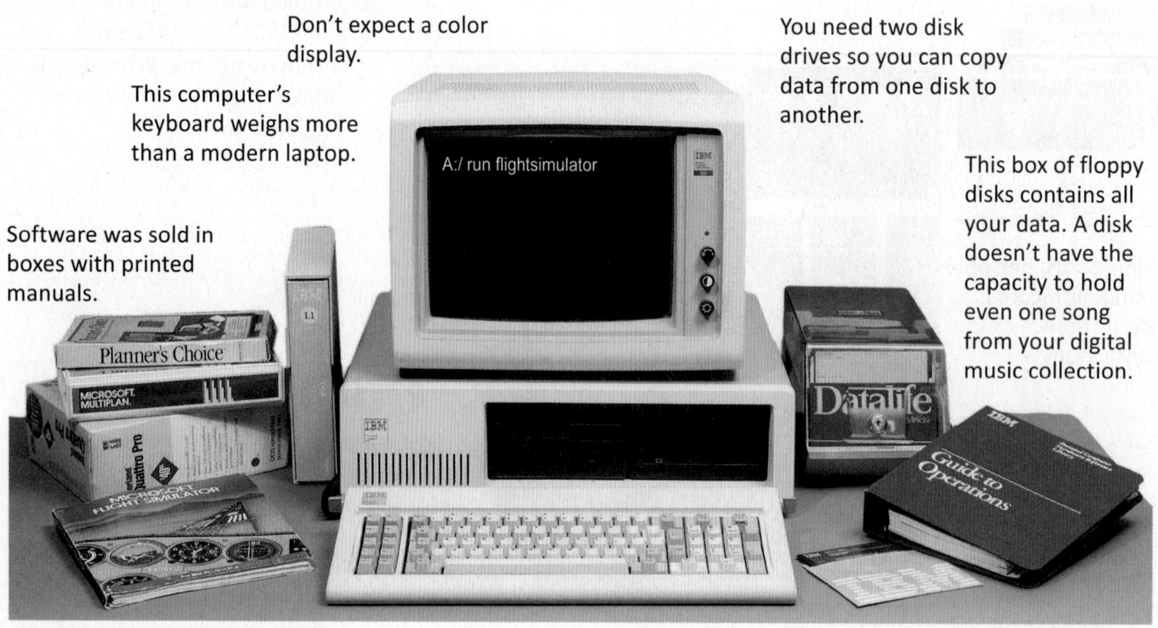
Don't expect a color display.
This computer's keyboard weighs more than a modern laptop.
Software was sold in boxes with printed manuals.
You need two disk drives so you can copy data from one disk to another.
This box of floppy disks contains all your data. A disk doesn't have the capacity to hold even one song from your digital music collection.
A:/ run flightsimulator
IBM
Planner's Choice
MICROSOFT MULTIPLAN
Quattro Pro
MICROSOFT FLIGHT SIMULATOR
Datalife
Guide to Operations

How extensive was computer use? In contrast to the corporate focus of the data processing phase, personal computing promised to put the power of digital devices in the hands of ordinary people. Computers were no longer a symbol of the corporate establishment. As a new generation of computing devices evolved, IBM's "THINK" slogan was upstaged by Apple's message: "Think Different."

The promise of populist computing, however, was not backed up with compelling reasons to invest in a computer. In 1982, fewer than 10% of U.S. households had a computer. Working on a standalone computer wasn't for everyone. People without an interest in typing up corporate reports or school papers, crunching numbers for accounting, or playing computer games weren't tempted to become active in the digital revolution.

Social scientists even worried that if personal computing became widespread, people would become increasingly isolated as they focused on computer activities rather than social ones. Although rudimentary email systems existed on centralized corporate computers, home computers were not connected, so there was no way to transmit email messages among them.

How long was the second phase of the digital revolution? Computer ownership increased at a gradual pace until the mid-1990s, and then it accelerated into the third phase of the digital revolution (Figure 6).

QuickCheck

What problem arising from personal computing worried social scientists?

a. Big corporations spying on customer behavior

b. Increasing isolation as people spent more and more time using a computer

c. Privacy

d. Piracy

Intro

Figure 6: Personal computer ownership (percent of U.S. households)

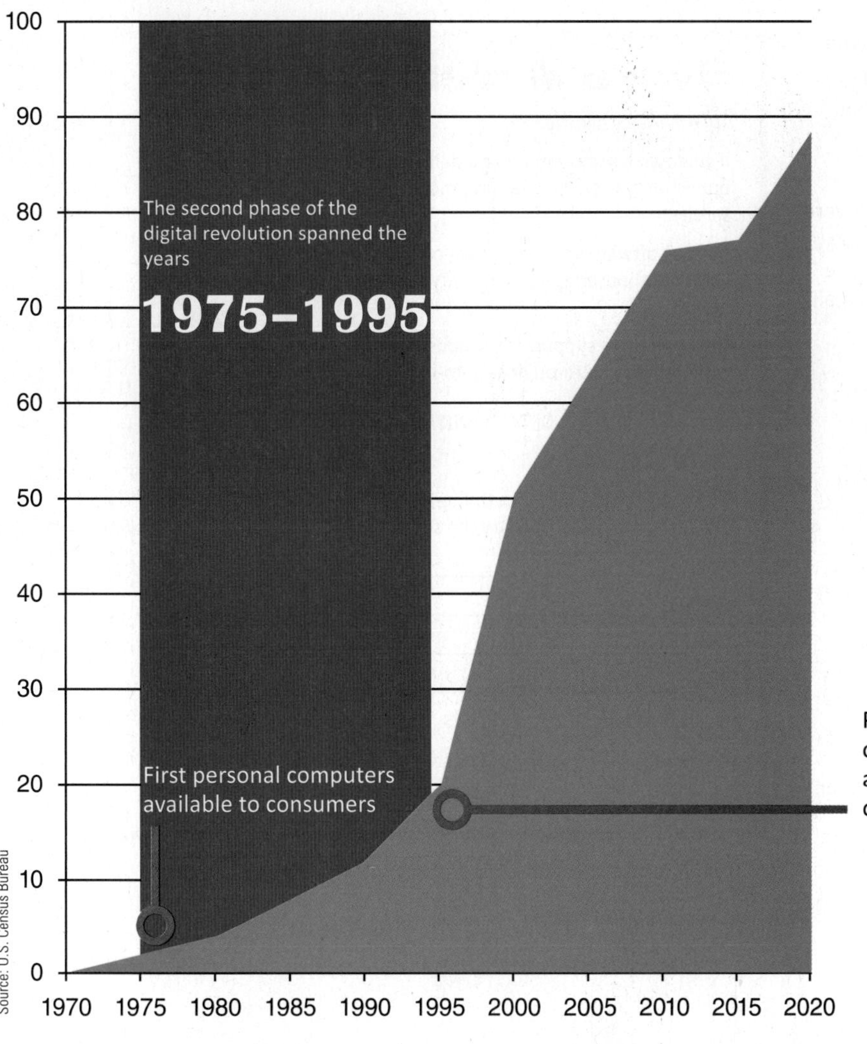

QuickCheck

During the second phase of the digital revolution, which one of the following was making news headlines?

a. A new band called The Beatles

b. The first space flights

c. Think Different

d. WikiLeaks

Network Computing

The third phase of the digital revolution materialized as computers became networked and when the Internet was opened to public use. A **computer network** is a group of computers linked together to share data and resources.

▶ **What kinds of networks were available?** Network technology existed before the Internet became popular, but these networks were mainly deployed to connect computers within a school or business. For the most part, these networks connected devices using cables; wireless networks were not available.

During this era, networks were complicated to set up and were often unreliable. Before the Internet opened to public use, online services such as CompuServe and America Online operated centralized computer networks that could be accessed by the public from dial-up modems.

▶ **What role did the Internet play?** The **Internet** is a global computer network that was originally developed as a military project and was later handed over to the National Science Foundation for research and academic use. When restrictions on commercial use of the Internet were lifted in the early 1990s, newly emerged ISPs offered fee-based Internet access. America Online, CompuServe, and other online services expanded to offer Internet-based chat and Web access. Excerpts from the AOL ad in Figure 7 may help you to appreciate the digital environment during this phase of the digital revolution.

Try It!

Internet connections were initially made over telephone lines with a device called an acoustic modem. You'll be surprised to see how these modems work. Search for a photo of one online. Could you use this type of modem with your smartphone?

Figure 7: Using an online service in the 1990s

Step 1: Mail in your application and wait to receive your software.

Step 2: Your software arrives on a floppy disk. Insert it in the disk drive and install it.

Step 3: Fire up the software and your modem to make a connection. If you have an acoustic modem, put your telephone handset into it.

Step 4: Download software, send email, post messages, and mingle with people from all over the world in online chat rooms.

Own a Modem?

Try America Online for FREE

If you own a computer and modem, we invite you to take this opportunity to **try the nation's most exciting online service**.

Build a software library by downloading selected files from a library of thousands—productivity software, games, and more!

Get computing support from industry experts at online conferences and through easy-to-use message boards.

DETACH AND MAIL TODAY

YES, I want to try America Online! Send me FREE software and a FREE trial membership to try the service.

Name: ______________________

Address: ______________________

City: ______________________

State: __________ Zip: __________

Disk type and size: ❑ 5.25 ❑ 3.5

❑ High Density ❑ Double Density

Source: *Wired*, May 1993

What about the Web? When historians look back on the digital revolution, they are certain to identify the Web as a major transformative influence. The **Web** (short for *World Wide Web*) is a collection of linked documents, graphics, and audio that can be accessed over the Internet.

A key aspect of the Web is that it adds content and substance to the Internet. Without the Web, the Internet would be like a library without any books or a railroad without any trains. Online storefronts, auction sites, news, sports, travel reservations, and music downloads made the Web a compelling digital technology for just about everyone.

QuickCheck

The Web and the Internet are not the same. Why?

a. The Internet is a communication network, but the Web consists of content that is distributed by the Internet.

b. The Internet consists of sites such as Twitter and Facebook, whereas the Web links devices such as iPods and computers.

So what was computing like during this phase? From 1995 to 2010, computing was characterized by the increasing use of laptops (Figure 8) and the following elements:

Sophisticated software. The network computing phase may have been the peak for productivity software. Computer owners amassed large collections of software, purchased in boxes containing multiple distribution CDs. Software such as Microsoft Office, Norton's Internet Security suite, and Corel Digital Studio required local installation and provided more features than most people had any desire to use. This trend reverses during the next phase of the digital revolution, when applications become simpler and more focused on specific tasks.

Stationary Internet access. Even as laptop computers began to displace desktop models, connecting to the Internet required a cable that effectively tethered computers to a nearby phone jack or cable outlet. In the next phase of the digital revolution, Internet access breaks free from cables and goes mobile.

Online communication. Email was the first widespread technology used to communicate over the Internet. Online services such as CompuServe and AOL pioneered chat rooms, which were primitive versions of Google Hangouts. Early forums and message boards were similar to Facebook timelines. A technology called Voice over IP allowed participants to bypass the telephone company to make phone calls over the Internet. That technology eventually developed into Skype and similar video chat services.

Multiplayer games. Sophisticated computer games reached a peak during the network phase of the digital revolution. Audio and visual hardware components improved to support video-realistic game environments, artificial intelligence opponents, and multiple players logging in remotely and chatting with other players over headsets. In the next phase, mobile devices become popular gaming platforms, but hardware limitations restrict the feature set.

Music downloads. During the network computing phase, an online business called Napster pioneered the concept of sharing and downloading music. Subscribers exchanged millions of music files, which they played through the speakers of their computers. The music was protected by copyright, however, making sharing and distribution illegal. This type of file sharing activity and rampant software piracy became one of the defining problems associated with the network phase of the digital revolution.

iTunes and other services for legally downloading music soon appeared, along with dedicated playback devices, such as the iPod. Video distribution over the Internet lagged behind until connection speeds increased in the next phase of the digital revolution.

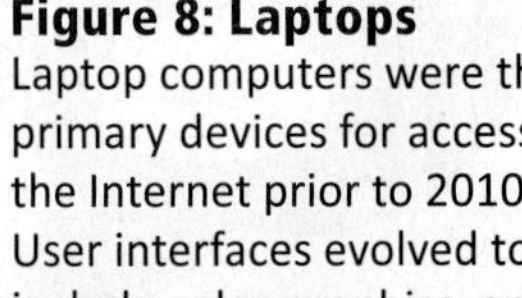

Figure 8: Laptops
Laptop computers were the primary devices for accessing the Internet prior to 2010. User interfaces evolved to include color, graphics, and mice.

Cloud Computing

Around 2010, the digital revolution eased into a fourth phase called **cloud computing**, which provided access to information, applications, communications, and storage over the Internet.

What did cloud computing change? Before cloud computing, most computers ran software based locally. For example, to use a word processor, you might fire up the latest edition of Microsoft Word, which you'd installed on your computer's hard disk. Prior to the cloud, you stored data locally, too. Email, documents, photos, and music all resided on your computer's hard disk or flash drive.

With cloud computing, all that changed. In the cloud, you can use your browser to access word processing applications that run from the Internet instead of software that you have installed on your local hard disk. You can use online applications to manage your email, create floor plans, produce presentations, and carry out a host of other activities. You can store your data in the cloud, too, making it available on any of your digital devices that connect to the Internet.

The cloud gets its name from diagrams like the one in Figure 9, which shows Internet-based applications, storage, and other services outlined by a cloud-like shape designed to help you visualize the idea that cloud services are "out there" somewhere on the Internet.

QuickCheck

Which characteristic of cloud computing most sets it apart from network computing?

a. Internet access

b. Sophisticated software

c. The migration of applications and data off local devices

d. File sharing

Figure 9: The cloud hosts applications, content, and services

Wait, this sounds familiar! If cloud computing sounds a bit like centralized computing, you're paying attention. The concept of applications and data residing somewhere other than on a local device is common to both centralized and cloud computing. The cloud concept reawakens the idea of monolithic computing facilities, as opposed to distributed architectures of the network era. The fact that your cloud-based data is not stored on devices under your direct control is a potential privacy and security concern, which is a topic for later modules.

▶ Are smartphones the signature device of the cloud computing era? The cloud itself is populated by commercial-grade high-speed computers and high-capacity storage devices. The consumer side is dominated by smartphones (Figure 10) and tablet computers. These handheld devices—a product of convergence—were the driving force for many cloud innovations.

▶ What is convergence? The expansion of cloud computing is due in part to **convergence**, a process by which several technologies with distinct functionalities evolve to form a single product. Convergence was important to the digital revolution because it created sophisticated mobile devices whose owners demanded access to the same services available from a full-size desktop computer. Those services became available in the cloud.

Your computer plays movies. Your cell phone has a camera. Your clock has a radio. Your watch functions as a communications device. You can store data on your iPod Touch. All these are examples of technological convergence.

Convergence worked its magic on cell phones, computers, portable media players, televisions, digital cameras, GPSs, watches, and ebook readers. Now you get features from all of them by purchasing a single digital device, such as a smartphone or tablet computer (Figure 11).

Figure 10: Smartphones
Cloud computing caters to smartphones and other mobile devices that are a product of convergence. They access and share data from the cloud using apps.

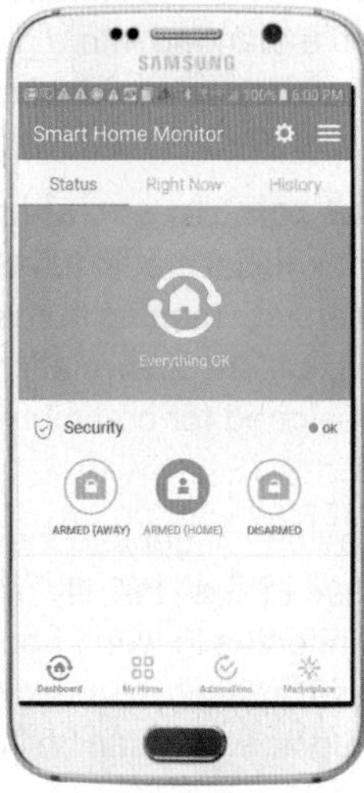

Figure 11: Smartphones are a prime example of convergence

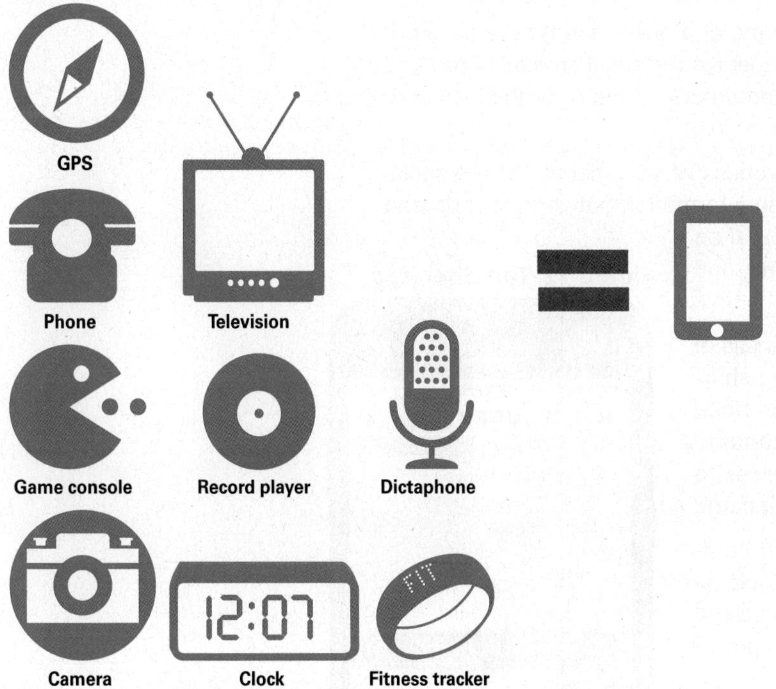

▶ Why do these devices need the cloud? Smartphones are portable. Compared to desktop and laptop computers, smartphones have small screens, lack a proper keyboard, and have limited space for storing apps and data. The cloud offers a convenient place to store data and applications. Think of the cloud as a repository for streaming videos, music, photos, and apps. With that concept in mind, you will begin to understand the cloud's importance to today's consumers.

QuickCheck

Which of the following instigated the move to cloud computing?

a. Social media

b. Mobile devices

c. Touchscreens

d. Music downloads

Did the cloud kill the Web? A 2010 *Wired* magazine cover announced "The Web Is Dead." That pronouncement was premature. The cloud consumed the Web but did not kill it. As a legacy technology from the networking era, the Web continues to be a global marketplace where Amazon, Alibaba, and other retailers sell directly to consumers.

That said, Facebook, Twitter, and Google Apps sent the Web in new directions. Once a collection of storefronts run exclusively by businesses and corporations, the Web expanded into a global hub where content was created by individuals, shared on social media sites, and uploaded to content sharing platforms. This grassroots Web of user-created content is sometimes referred to as **Web 2.0**.

What role do social media play in the cloud era? Facebook, Twitter, and other social media turned the worry of social isolation on its head; instead of computers decreasing human interaction, social media encourage interpersonal communications and relationships. **Social media** are digitally mediated applications designed for communication, social interaction, and consumer-generated content.

Many factors influenced the popularity of these sites, but one important factor is their ease of use. Initially offered as Web sites, there was no software to install and no updates to worry about. Getting started was as simple as registering your name and creating a password. Now, access to social media is also available from mobile apps, which can be installed on a smartphone or tablet with a single touch.

The connections that social media offer come at a price, and that price is not just monetary. Today's digital citizens surrender a substantial amount of privacy, exposing information that can be used by predators. Privacy, or the lack of it, may be the defining challenge of cloud computing.

Another challenge is the growing pervasiveness of advertising. Where social media was once a platform for exchanging information between friends and colleagues, intrusive advertising is now found on virtually every Web page, Facebook timeline, and Twitter stream.

Cloud-enabled apps? A key characteristic of the cloud computing era is globe-spanning sharing services. Cloud-based services such as Uber, Airbnb, and Etsy are part of the **sharing economy** in which consumers offer goods and services to other consumers through a shared digital platform.

These sharing services use the cloud to communicate and process data. The apps used by consumers may look simple (Figure 12), but behind the scenes an amazing amount of computer power handles the necessary data and logistics.

Try It!

In 2011, the United Nations declared that the Internet "is an indispensable tool for realizing a range of human rights...." Visit the Internet World Stats site to find out what percentage of the world's population has Internet access.

Figure 12: The Uber app

Ubiquitous Computing

Many computing technologies use data to represent things in the real world. Photos represent people. Maps show the location of places. Videos give us a glimpse of events. Game-based fantasy worlds and characters entertain us. **Virtual reality** (VR) creates a simulated three-dimensional world that's experienced with a headset (Figure 13).

Terminology

Ubiquitous computing is sometimes referred to as *pervasive computing*. The idea is not new. In the 1990s, Mark Weiser predicted that computers will "weave themselves into the fabric of everyday life until they are indistinguishable from it."

Figure 13: Virtual reality simulates the real world

Monstar Studio/Shutterstock.com

Photos, videos, and games are all conjured from data. None of it is tangible reality. Augmented reality, the Internet of Things, digital assistants, and automated vehicles are shaping a new digital era in which technologies bring computing beyond the screen and into the world of tangible objects. This fifth stage of the digital revolution, **ubiquitous computing**, is characterized by a focus on controlling and manipulating real-world objects instead of data.

What is augmented reality? **Augmented reality** (AR) superimposes data over the real world. AR applications can help you navigate through a city by displaying your route over a live view of surrounding streets and buildings. It is the technology that "paints" the first-down line on the field as you watch an NFL game.

Pokémon GO popularized augmented reality and provides a great example of how it works. It shows the real world in your vicinity as a pass-through image from your cell phone camera. Pokémon augments this reality with game characters that are superimposed on the camera image (Figure 14).

Figure 14: Pokémon Go is augmented reality

Matthew Corley/Shutterstock.com

What is the Internet of Things? The **Internet of Things** (IoT) connects sensors embedded in machines, clothing, and other objects to the Internet, where they can report data and receive commands. It provides a clear example of digital technology controlling objects in the real world.

You're probably familiar with smartphone-controlled IoT devices such as digital locks, smart LED lights, smoke alarms, and doorbell cameras. These devices send and receive signals to and from your phone using a Wi-Fi network, the Internet, or a cellular network.

A smart smoke alarm is an IoT device that not only contains sensors but also contains circuitry that connects to a home Wi-Fi network. That Wi-Fi network can establish communication with a smartphone to report its status and accept commands. If the device senses smoke when you are away from home, it sends an alarm to your phone. The phone can be used to remotely silence a false alarm—such as when your roommate burns a bagel in the toaster.

IoT devices can also be controlled by using a **virtual assistant**, such as Alexa, Cortana, Google Assistant, or Siri. This technology's **voice as a user interface** (VUI) lets you issue voice commands to turn on lights, play music, lock doors, search for answers, and monitor your home security system.

However, the Internet of Things also connects multiple devices so that they can communicate with each other. A smart thermostat is designed to control a home's heating and cooling systems. For example, if a faulty furnace outputs dangerous carbon monoxide (CO), an IoT smoke detector can sense a high level of CO and send a message to a compatible IoT thermostat to turn off the furnace (Figure 15).

Figure 15: The Internet of Things links devices with embedded sensors

Smoke detectors and thermostats send signals to each other and connect to a smartphone through a home network and the Internet.
Protect
nest
Upstairs
EMERGENCY
CARBON
MONOXIDE
BASEMENT

▶ What about autonomous vehicles? Self-driving cars and robots are related to the Internet of Things because they require sensor-equipped parts to communicate with each other. **Autonomous vehicles**, for example, navigate without human intervention using sensors to detect the surrounding environment, physical location, speed, and other parameters. They send data and receive commands from an onboard computer running sophisticated artificial intelligence software.

Autonomous vehicles are clear examples of ubiquitous computing—the use of digital technology to manipulate objects in the real world, instead of abstract data. You'll delve into some of these ubiquitous technologies in future modules. For now, try to guess the year in which you take your first ride in a self-driving car (Figure 16).

Figure 16: Autonomous vehicles exemplify ubiquitous computing

No hands!

Are there more changes to come? If we can learn one thing from the evolving Information Age, it is this: Change is inevitable. Where savvy consumers once gave up on slow GEO satellite Internet service, new LEO satellites may offer speedy access from remote areas. (GEO stands for "geosynchronous equatorial orbit"; LEO stands for "low Earth orbit.") Today, your favorite social media platform is Facebook; in the future, Facebook may go the way of CompuServe. Figure 17 summarizes changes through each era of the digital revolution.

Figure 17: The Information Age evolves

Expired	Tired	Uninspired	Desired	Admired
Data processing	Personal computing	Network computing	Cloud computing	Ubiquitous IoT
Big corporate and government computers	Desktop computers	Laptop computers	Smartphones and tablets	Digital assistants
Custom applications	Standalone applications	Software suites	Mobile apps and cloud-based apps	Embedded apps
CB radios	Dial-up Internet access	Cable and GEO satellite Internet	4G and Wi-Fi Internet access	5G and LEO satellite Internet
ARPANET	AOL and CompuServe	The Web and email	Social media	Augmented reality
Arcade games	2D action games	3D multiplayer games	Touchscreen microgames	Virtual reality
Printers	Keyboards	Mice	Touchscreens	Voice as a user interface

So what's the point? Learning about digital technology is not just about circuits and electronics, nor is it only about digital gadgets, such as computers and portable music players. Digital technology permeates the very core of modern life.

Understanding how this technology works and thinking about its potential can help you comprehend many issues related to privacy, security, freedom of speech, and intellectual property. It will help you become a better consumer and give you insights into local and world events.

As you continue to read this textbook, don't lose sight of the big picture. On one level, you might be simply learning about how to use a computer and software in this course. On a more profound level, however, you are accumulating knowledge about how digital technology applies to broader cultural and legal issues that are certain to affect your life far into the future.

QuickCheck

According to Figure 17, AOL and CompuServe were popular when ________.

a. data processing was the main digital technology

b. most people had dial-up Internet access and used desktop computers

c. smartphones and tablets were introduced

d. people stopped using cloud computing

QuickQuiz — Introduction

1. Data processing is based on an ________-processing-output cycle.
2. In the personal computing phase of the digital revolution, data and software were stored on ________ devices, such as hard drives.
3. The idea that several technologies evolve into a single device is called ________.
4. Two major technologies that defined the network computing era were the ________ and the Web.
5. ________ computing provides access to information, applications, communications, and storage over the Internet.

1 Digital Content

Module Contents

So many aspects of life today are digital: music, photos, movies, news, and communications. How can all this diverse "stuff" be accessed through one device, such as a laptop or a smartphone? It's all about digitization.

Try It! Apply what you learn.

- Compress files containing various types of data, including text, photos, music, and videos.
- Record audio files.
- Select an audio sampling rate and file format for high-quality sound in files that won't use up all your storage space.
- Convert audio files from one format to another.
- Use voice commands to control your digital devices.
- Select the best file format for digital images, such as photos and scans, taking into account which formats reduce image quality with lossy compression.
- Convert a paper document into a digital file that can be edited using word processing software.
- Work with RGB colors in decimal, hexadecimal, or binary notation.
- Use resolution to gauge the maximum size for an image.
- Use "photoshopping" techniques to enhance, colorize, clone, inpaint, clip, and merge photo images.
- Capture 360-degree images on your smartphone.
- Draw vector images for logos and infographics.
- Convert vector images into bitmaps.
- Render a 3D image from a wireframe.
- Use video editing software to combine video footage with a soundtrack.
- Select output settings for a video, including aspect ratio, resolution, bit rate, compression level, and file format.
- Transcode a video from one file format to another.
- View vector and bitmap images in a VR headset.

Gauge your level of expertise. The answers are in the module.

6

How do you write it in binary?

How do you write it in ASCII?

A sound wave is digitized by ___________ its height thousands of times per second.

Which type of compression makes files smaller without any data loss?

LOSSY

LOSSLESS

List **FIVE** bitmap graphics formats:

____

____

____

____

____

What is the basic unit of sound in speech synthesis?

#EE82EE

is the hexadecimal number for what color?

BLACK

GREEN

VIOLET

WHITE

Bike.svg

Bitmap or vector?

List two popular video codecs:

____

____

Adding light and shadows is part of what process that creates an image from a wireframe?

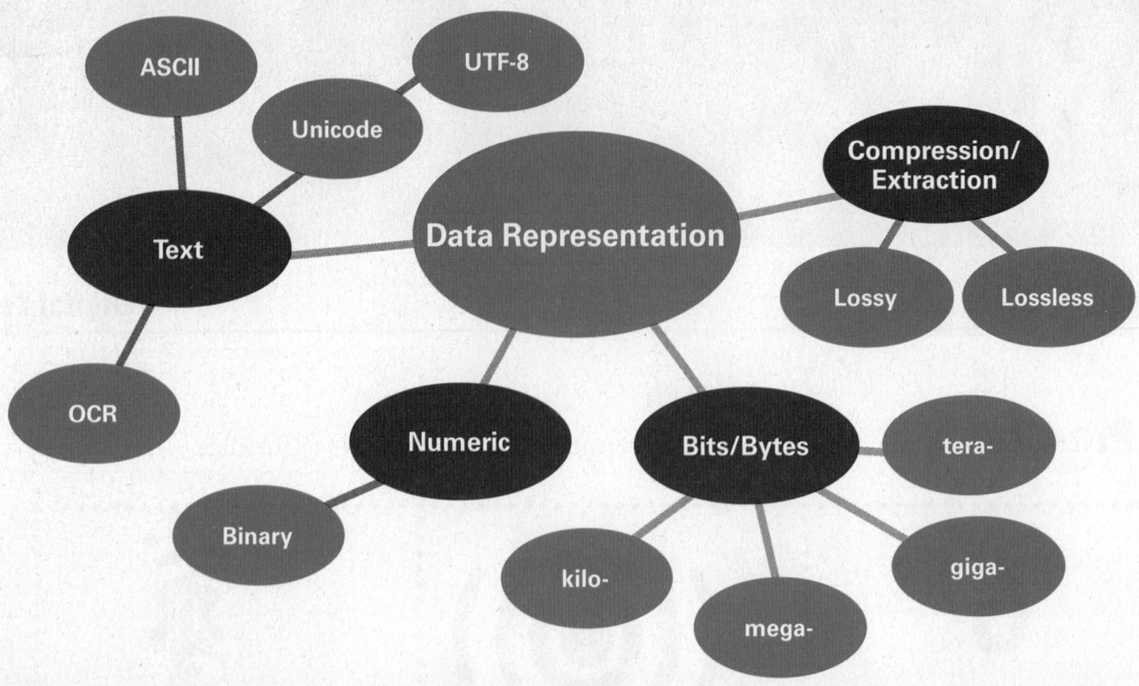

Section **A**

Digital Basics

Objectives

- List three technologies that digital devices use to physically store or transmit 1s and 0s.
- Write the numbers 1 through 10 in binary.
- Decipher ASCII text.
- Demonstrate how to use the terms *bit, byte, megabyte, megabit,* and *gigabyte* in the context of data storage and digital devices.
- Distinguish between data that would be represented by binary numbers and data that would be represented by ASCII or Unicode.
- Explain how OCR relates to ASCII and Unicode.
- Describe the difference between lossy and lossless compression.
- Demonstrate how to compress a file.

Text, numbers, music, videos, images, and speech; all of this "stuff" is digital content. The amazing aspect of digital technology is that it distills such diverse content into 0s and 1s and stores them as pulses of electricity. Understanding the data representation concepts presented in Section A will help you grasp the essence of the digital world and get a handle on all the jargon pertaining to bits, bytes, megahertz, and gigabytes.

Terminology

data
data representation
digital data
analog data
binary
digitization
bit
file
file name extension
file format
numeric data
binary number system
character data
ASCII
Extended ASCII
Unicode
UTF-8
ASCII text
delimiter
OCR
byte
kilobit
kilobyte
megabit
megabyte
gigabit
gigabyte
data compression
lossless compression
lossy compression

Data Representation Basics

Digital content, such as an ebook, document, image, music, or video, is a compilation of data. **Data** refers to the symbols that represent people, events, things, and ideas. Data can be a name, a number, the colors in a photograph, or the notes in a musical composition.

Is there a difference between data and information? In everyday conversation, people use the terms *data* and *information* interchangeably. However, some technology professionals make a distinction between the two terms. They define data as the symbols that represent people, events, things, and ideas. Data becomes information when it is presented in a format that people can understand and use. As a general rule, remember that (technically speaking) data is used by machines, such as computers; information is used by humans.

What is data representation? **Data representation** refers to the form in which data is stored, processed, and transmitted. Devices such as smartphones, portable media players, and computers store data in digital formats that can be handled by electronic circuitry. Today, digital data representation has replaced the analog methods previously used for storing and transmitting photos, videos, music, and text.

What's the difference between analog and digital? **Digital data** is text, numbers, graphics, sound, and video that have been converted into discrete digits such as 0s and 1s. In contrast, **analog data** is represented using an infinite scale of values. For a simple illustration of the difference between analog and digital, consider the way you can control the lights in a room using a traditional light switch or a dimmer switch.

A dimmer switch has a rotating dial that controls a continuous range of brightness. It is, therefore, analog. A traditional light switch, on the other hand, has two discrete states: on and off. There are no inbetween states, so this type of light switch is digital.

A traditional light switch is also **binary** because there are only two possible states. Technically, a digital device could represent data using more than two states. Some of the earliest computers represented numbers using the decimal system. Today, however, most digital devices represent numbers and other data using the binary system.

Terminology

The word *data* can be correctly treated either as a plural noun or as an abstract mass noun, so the phrases "The data are being processed" and "The data is being processed" are both correct usage. In this textbook, the word *data* is paired with singular verbs and modifiers.

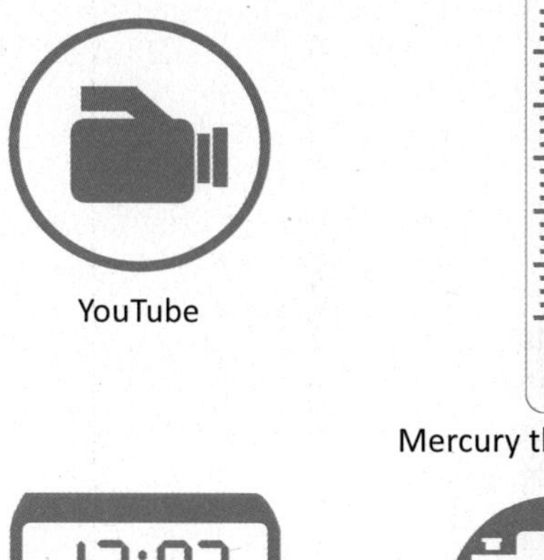

YouTube

LED clock

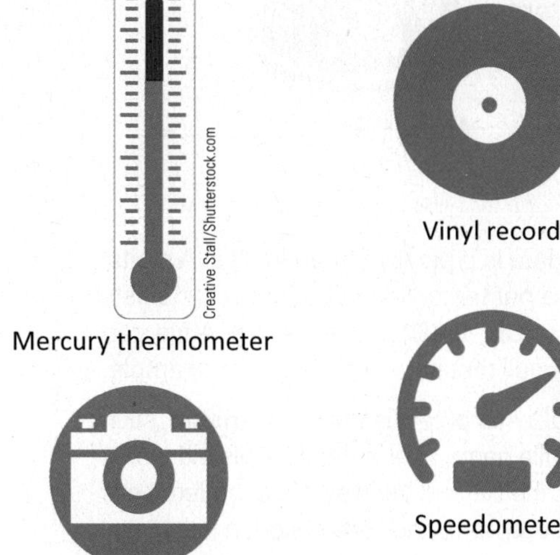

Mercury thermometer

Film camera

Creative Stall/Shutterstock.com

Vinyl record

Speedometer

QuickCheck

Which of the devices on the left illustrate analog data representation?

a. The speedometer and YouTube

b. The thermometer and the vinyl record

c. All but the speedometer

d. All but YouTube and the clock

How does digital data work? The process of converting information, such as text, numbers, photos, videos, or music, into digital data that can be manipulated by electronic devices is called **digitization**.

Imagine that you want to send a message by flashing a light. Your light switch offers two states: on and off. You can use sequences of ons and offs to represent various letters of the alphabet. To write down the representation for each letter, you can use 0s and 1s. The 0s represent the off state of your light switch; the 1s indicate the on state. For example, the sequence *on on off off* would be written as 1100, and you might decide that sequence represents the letter *A*.

The 0s and 1s used to represent digital data are referred to as binary digits. It is from this term that we get the word *bit—bi*nary digi*t*. A **bit** is a 0 or 1 used in the digital representation of data.

Digital devices are electronic, so you can envision bits flowing within these devices as pulses of light. But digital signals can take many forms, as shown in Figure 1-1.

QuickCheck

Digital devices work with bits in all of the following ways except:

a. voltage variations

b. light and dark spots

c. analog values

d. orientation of magnetized particles

Figure 1-1: Many ways to represent digital data

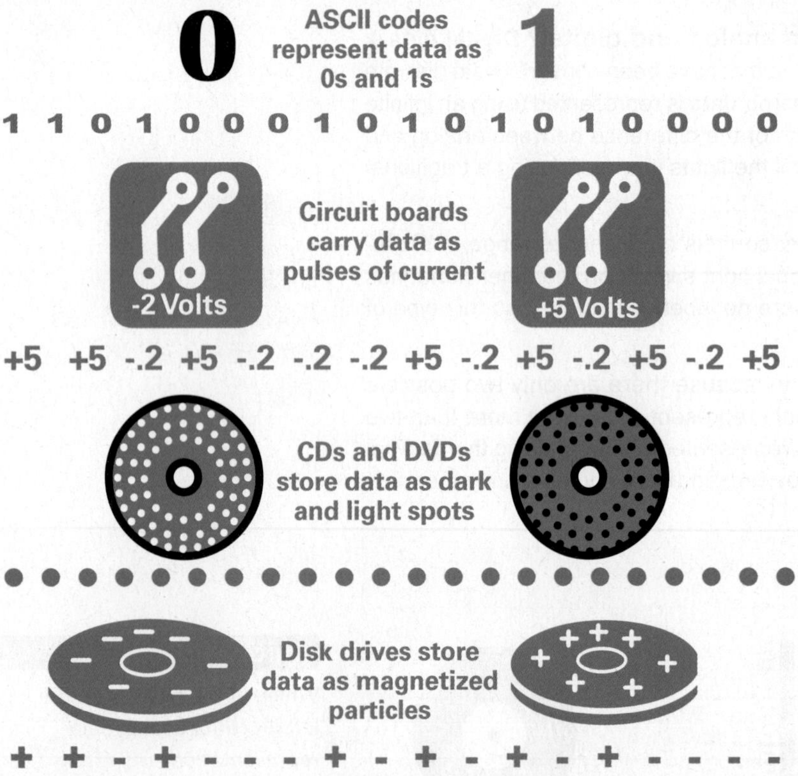

How is digital data stored? Digital data is typically stored in files. A digital file, usually referred to simply as a **file**, is a named collection of data that exists on a storage medium, such as a hard disk, CD, DVD, or flash drive. A file can contain data for a term paper, Web page, email message, or video, for example.

Every file has a unique name, such as MyPodCast.mp3. A **file name extension**, such as .mp3, can be appended to the end of the file name after a period. This extension indicates the **file format**—the type of data in the file and the way it is encoded. Let's take a look at how numbers, text, images, sound, and video are encoded into digital formats that become computer files.

Representing Numbers

Numeric data consists of numbers that can be used in arithmetic operations. For example, your annual income is numeric data, as is your age. That concept seems clear, but some data that looks numeric is represented differently. Social Security numbers, telephone numbers, street numbers, and similar data are not represented by numeric data. These "numerals" are not considered numeric data because they are never used in mathematical calculations. This numeric quirk is a key concept in the digital world and turns up when you work with spreadsheets, databases, and computer programming.

QuickCheck

Which one of the following is considered numeric data?

a. Driver license number J522-67-20-200-5

b. Telephone number 906-222-3450

c. The $28,995.00 cost of a car

d. The address 22 E. Main Street

1

How do digital devices represent numbers? Digital devices represent numeric data using the binary number system, also called base 2. The **binary number system** has only two digits: 0 and 1. No numeral like 2 exists in this system, so the number "two" is represented in binary as 10 (pronounced "one zero"). You'll understand why if you think about what happens when you're counting from 1 to 10 in the familiar decimal system. After reaching 9, you run out of digits. For ten, you have to use the digits 10—zero is a placeholder and the 1 indicates one group of tens.

In binary, you just run out of digits sooner—right after you count to 1. To get to the next number, you use 0 as a placeholder and 1 indicates one group of twos. In binary, then, you count 0 (zero), 1 (one), 10 (one zero), instead of counting 0, 1, 2 in decimal. If you need to brush up on binary numbers, refer to Figure 1-2.

Figure 1-2: Binary equivalent of decimal numbers

Decimal (Base 10)	Binary (Base 2)
0	0
1	1
2	10
3	11
4	100
5	101
6	110
7	111
8	1000
9	1001
10	1010
11	1011
1000	1111101000

QuickCheck

Figure 1-2 shows the binary equivalent for numbers 0 through 11 and 1000. What is the binary equivalent for the number 12?

a. 10111

b. 1100

c. 10000

d. 1111

The important point to understand is that the binary number system allows digital devices to represent virtually any number simply by using 0s and 1s. Digital devices can then perform calculations using these numbers. The ability to perform rapid and accurate calculations was the key feature of the first computers, and it now provides the foundation for online banking, ecommerce, and many other number-crunching applications.

Representing Text

Character data is composed of letters, symbols, and numerals that are not used in calculations. Examples of character data include your name, address, and hair color. Character data is commonly referred to as "text."

QuickCheck

Write out **Hi!** in Extended ASCII code. (Hint: Use an uppercase *H*, but a lowercase *i*.)

H

i

!

▶ **How do digital devices represent text?** Digital devices employ several types of codes to represent character data, including ASCII, Unicode, and their variants. **ASCII** (American Standard Code for Information Interchange, pronounced "ASK ee") requires seven bits for each character. For example, the ASCII code for an uppercase *A* is 1000001. ASCII provides codes for 128 characters, including uppercase letters, lowercase letters, punctuation symbols, and numerals.

Extended ASCII is a superset of ASCII that uses eight bits for each character. For example, Extended ASCII represents the uppercase letter *A* as 01000001. Using eight bits instead of seven bits allows Extended ASCII to provide codes for 256 characters. The additional Extended ASCII characters include boxes and other graphical symbols.

Unicode (pronounced "YOU ni code") uses 8, 16, 24, or 32 bits and provides codes for representing the alphabets of 154 modern and historical languages, as well as a variety of symbols and emojis.

UTF-8 is a variable-length Unicode standard that uses eight bits for common ASCII characters, but can use 16, 24, or 32 bits as necessary to represent the alphabets for Cyrillic, Greek, Hebrew, and other languages.

Take a look at the ASCII codes in Figure 1-3. Notice there is a code for the space character in addition to codes for symbols, numerals, uppercase letters, and lowercase letters.

Figure 1-3: ASCII codes

00100000	Space	00110011	3	01000110	F	01011001	Y	01101100	l
00100001	!	00110100	4	01000111	G	01011010	Z	01101101	m
00100010	"	00110101	5	01001000	H	01011011	[	01101110	n
00100011	#	00110110	6	01001001	I	01011100	\	01101111	o
00100100	$	00110111	7	01001010	J	01011101	]	01110000	p
00100101	%	00111000	8	01001011	K	01011110	^	01110001	q
00100110	&	00111001	9	01001100	L	01011111	_	01110010	r
00100111	'	00111010	:	01001101	M	01100000	`	01110011	s
00101000	(	00111011	;	01001110	N	01100001	a	01110100	t
00101001	)	00111100	<	01001111	O	01100010	b	01110101	u
00101010	*	00111101	=	01010000	P	01100011	c	01110110	v
00101011	+	00111110	>	01010001	Q	01100100	d	01110111	w
00101100	,	00111111	?	01010010	R	01100101	e	01111000	x
00101101	-	01000000	@	01010011	S	01100110	f	01111001	y
00101110	.	01000001	A	01010100	T	01100111	g	01111010	z
00101111	/	01000010	B	01010101	U	01101000	h	01111011	{
00110000	0	01000011	C	01010110	V	01101001	i	01111100	|
00110001	1	01000100	D	01010111	W	01101010	j	01111101	}
00110010	2	01000101	E	01011000	X	01101011	k	01111110	~

Why are there ASCII codes for numbers? While glancing at the table of ASCII codes in Figure 1-3, you might have wondered why the table contains codes for 0, 1, 2, 3, and so on. Aren't these numbers represented by the binary number system? Yes, the binary number system is used for representing numeric data, but these ASCII codes are used for numerals, such as Social Security numbers and phone numbers that are not used for calculations. For example, 475-6677 is a phone number; it is not a formula that means subtract 6677 from 475.

Where is digital text used? Digital text is everywhere. It is the foundation for all kinds of digital documents, Web sites, social media sites, games, and email. It is also the basis for ebooks designed for Kindles and other ebook readers.

Documents produced on a digital device are stored as a string of 1s and 0s and generally encoded as ASCII or UTF-8. Some kinds of documents simply contain this plain text, whereas other documents contain formatting codes to produce bold fonts, columns, and other effects.

What is plain text? Plain, unformatted text is sometimes called **ASCII text** and is stored in a so-called text file with a name ending in .txt. On Apple devices, these files are labeled "Plain Text." In Windows, these files are labeled "Text Document," like this:

Roller Coasters.txt Text Document 2 KB

ASCII text files can be created with text editors, such as TextEdit and Notepad. They are typically used for writing computer programs because executable program code cannot include formatting such as underlining and special fonts. They can also be used for creating Web pages.

Text files can usually be opened by any word processing software, regardless of the type of device. In that sense, they are universal. Figure 1-4 illustrates an ASCII text file and the actual binary code that is stored for it.

QuickCheck

If your address is 10 B Street, what are the first three bytes in ASCII?

a. 00110001 00110000 01000010

b. 00110001 00110000 00100000

c. 00110001 00110111 00100000

1

Figure 1-4: ASCII text files contain no formatting codes

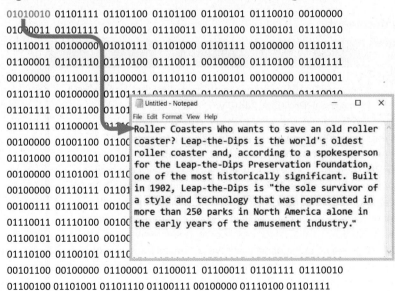

```
01010010 01101111 01101100 01101100 01100101 01110010 00100000
01000011 01101111 01100001 01110011 01110100 01100101 01110010
01110011 00100000 01010111 01101000 01101111 00100000 01110111
01100001 01101110 01110100 01110011 00100000 01110100 01101111
00100000 01110011 01100001 01110110 01100101 00100000 01100001
01101110 00100000 01101111 01101100 01100100 00100000 01110010
01101111 01101100 01101
01101111 01100001
00100000 01001100 0110
01101000 01100101 00101
00100000 01101001 0111
00100000 01110111 01101
00100111 01110011 0010
01110011 01110100 0010
01100101 01110010 0010
01110100 01100101 0111
00101100 00100000 01100001 01100011 01100011 01101111 01110010
01100100 01101001 01101110 01100111 00100000 01110100 01101111
```

Untitled - Notepad

File Edit Format View Help

```
Roller Coasters Who wants to save an old roller
coaster? Leap-the-Dips is the world's oldest
roller coaster and, according to a spokesperson
for the Leap-the-Dips Preservation Foundation,
one of the most historically significant. Built
in 1902, Leap-the-Dips is "the sole survivor of
a style and technology that was represented in
more than 250 parks in North America alone in
the early years of the amusement industry."
```

QuickCheck

What is the seventh byte in the Roller Coasters file?

a. Uppercase C (01000011)

b. Lowercase c (01100011)

c. Space (00100000)

d. Carriage return (00001101)

How does formatting get added to documents? ASCII text files contain no formatting. They have no bold, italics, underlining, or font colors. There are no margins, columns, bullets, headers, or page numbers.

Suppose you want the title of the Roller Coasters document to be centered and shown in a large, bold font, like this:

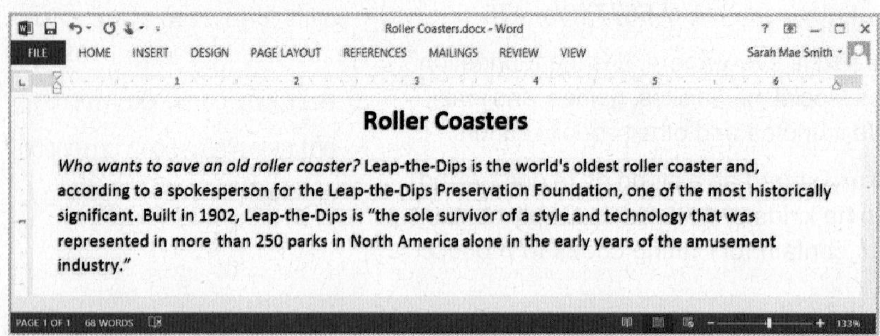

To create documents with styles and formats, formatting codes have to be embedded in the text. There are many techniques for doing so, and each one produces a unique file format. These formats can be opened by the software that produced them. Opening those files with other kinds of software requires conversion.

Microsoft Word produces formatted text and creates documents in DOCX format, whereas Apple Pages produces documents in PAGES format. Adobe Acrobat produces documents in PDF format. The HTML markup language used for Web pages produces documents in HTML format. Many ebooks are created using the EPUB format.

Formatting codes can be added to documents directly within the text stream, using some sort of **delimiter** to signal the beginning and end of the formatting command. When the document is displayed, the formatting codes are hidden. What do those hidden codes look like? Figure 1-5 gives you a behind-the-scenes look at the Roller Coasters document with all the embedded formatting codes revealed.

Terminology

A *delimiter* is a special character used to separate commands or formatting characters from the rest of the text in a file. Slashes // and angle brackets < > are commonly used delimiters.

Figure 1-5: Formatting codes within a document

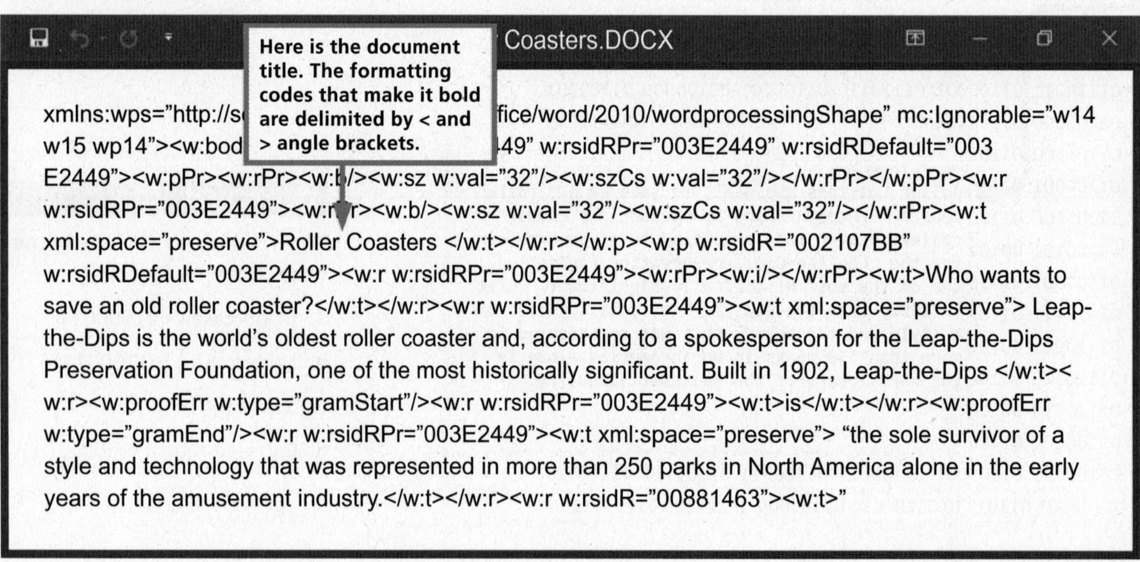

What happens when I scan a document? When using a scanner to digitize a document, you may have a choice between graphics formats and OCR. Graphics formats, presented later in the module, essentially capture a photo of the document. Individual letters and punctuation marks are not encoded as ASCII. A document scanned into a graphics format cannot be edited using a word processor.

OCR (optical character recognition) is a process that interprets individual characters during or after a scan. It assigns the appropriate ASCII code to each letter and outputs the document in a format that can be edited using word processing software. OCR software is available for most scanners and is handy when you have a printed copy of a document that you want to modify, but would prefer not to retype.

QuickCheck

Which one of the following would most likely require OCR?

a. A two-page bibliography of award-winning books from 1945 that you would like to annotate

b. An excerpt from a magazine article that you want to include in a term paper

c. A football poster containing the home game schedule

d. A page from a handwritten diary that you want to include in a historical biography

Bits and Bytes

All of the text and numeric data stored and transmitted by digital devices is encoded as bits. Terminology related to bits and bytes is extensively used to describe storage capacity and network access speed. As a digital-goods consumer, you'll want to have this terminology handy.

What is the difference between bits and bytes? Even though the word *bit* is an abbreviation for *binary digit*, it can be further abbreviated, usually as a lowercase *b*. A group of eight bits is called a **byte** and is usually abbreviated as an uppercase *B*.

Transmission speeds are expressed in bits, whereas storage space is expressed in bytes. For example, a cable Internet connection might transfer data from the Internet to your computer at 50 mega*bits* per second. In an iPad ad, you might notice that it can store up to 128 giga*bytes* of music, video, photos, and games.

Try It!

Scan a one-page document using a scanner or a multifunction printer. The default format for the scan is probably a JPEG or PNG graphic. Try using your scanner's OCR feature or a free online OCR service to convert the scan into a document that can be edited using word processing software.

What do the prefixes kilo-, mega-, giga-, and tera- mean? When reading about digital devices, you'll frequently encounter references such as 90 kilobits per second, 1.44 megabytes, 2.4 gigahertz, and 2 terabytes. *Kilo*, *mega*, *giga*, *tera*, and similar terms are used to quantify digital data, as shown in Figure 1-6.

Figure 1-6: Digital quantities

Bit	One binary digit	Gigabit	2^{30} bits
Byte	8 bits	Gigabyte	2^{30} bytes
Kilobit	1,024 or 2^{10} bits	Terabyte	2^{40} bytes
Kilobyte	1,024 or 2^{10} bytes	Petabyte	2^{50} bytes
Megabit	1,048,576 or 2^{20} bits	Exabyte	2^{60} bytes
Megabyte	1,048,576 or 2^{20} bytes		

Why such odd numbers? In common usage, kilo, abbreviated as K, means a thousand. For example, $50K means $50,000. In the context of computers, however, 50K means 51,200. Why the difference? In the decimal number system we use on a daily basis, the number 1,000 is 10 to the third power, or 10^3. For digital devices where base 2 is the norm, a kilo is precisely 1,024, or 2^{10}. Mega is derived from 2^{20} and giga from 2^{30}.

Terminology

What's a *kibibyte*? Some computer scientists have proposed alternative terminology to dispel the ambiguity in terms such as *kilo* that can mean 1,000 or 1,024. They suggest the following prefixes:

Kibi = 1,024

Mebi = 1,048,576

Gibi = 1,073,741,824

▶ When do I use bits and when do I use bytes? As a general rule, use bits for data rates, such as Internet connection speeds and movie download speeds. Use bytes for file sizes and storage capacities. Figure 1-7 provides some examples.

Figure 1-7: Bits or bytes?

56 Kbps

Kilobit (Kb or Kbit) can be used for slow data rates, such as a 56 Kbps (kilobits per second) dial-up connection.

104 KB

Kilobyte (KB or Kbyte) is often used when referring to the size of small text files.

50 Mbps

Megabit (Mb or Mbit) is used for faster data rates, such as a 50 Mbps (megabits per second) Internet connection.

3.2 MB

Megabyte (MB or MByte) is typically used when referring to the size of files containing photos and videos.

100 Gbit

Gigabit (Gb or Gbit) is used for really fast network speeds.

16 GB

Gigabyte (GB or GByte) is commonly used to refer to storage capacity.

QuickCheck

My iPhone has 128 ______ of storage space; I uploaded a high-resolution 128 ______ graphic; and I am going to download a small 8 ______ text file.

a. GB, MB, Mbps

b. MB, GB, KB

c. GB, MB, KB

d. Mbps, MB, GB

Compression

All those 1s and 0s can quickly expand the size of digital files. Whereas a "€" is simply one character in a printed document, it requires 16 bits when represented as ASCII and 16 bits when represented as Unicode. That "1" in "1st place" seems like it could be represented by a simple 1 bit, but it requires multiple bits when encoded. Numeric data also requires lots of bits. The number 10 is 1010 in binary and requires four bits.

To reduce file size and transmission times, digital data can be compressed. **Data compression** refers to any technique that recodes the data in a file so that it contains fewer bits. Compression is commonly referred to as "zipping." Many compression techniques exist. They can be divided into two categories: lossless and lossy.

▶ What is the difference between lossless and lossy compression? **Lossless compression** provides a way to compress data and reconstitute it into its original state. Character data and numeric data in documents and spreadsheets are compressed using lossless techniques so that the uncompressed data is exactly the same as the original data.

Lossy compression throws away some of the original data during the compression process. After the data is uncompressed, it is not exactly the same as the original. This type of compression is typically used for music, images, and videos because the human ear or eye cannot discern minor changes. Later in the module, you'll learn more about the compression techniques used to shrink the size of music, image, and video files.

QuickCheck

Which one of the following requires lossless compression?

a. A very large document that you intend to send as an email attachment

b. A photo of your class reunion that you intend to post on your Facebook page

c. An iTunes track saved to your iPod that you want to back up on your computer

How do I compress data? The software for compressing data is sometimes referred to as a compression utility or a zip tool. Most computers include software for compressing data, but tablets and smartphones may require a third-party app for working with compressed data.

On laptops and desktop computers, the compression utility is accessed from the same screen used to manage files. You can compress the data in a single file or you can combine multiple files to create a single zipped file that is reconstituted to the original files when unzipped (Figure 1-8).

Try It!

Experiment with compressing files to see how much they shrink. Try compressing a document, then try a graphic.

Figure 1-8: Compressing files

Source: Apple Inc.

Compressing files using Finder on a Mac

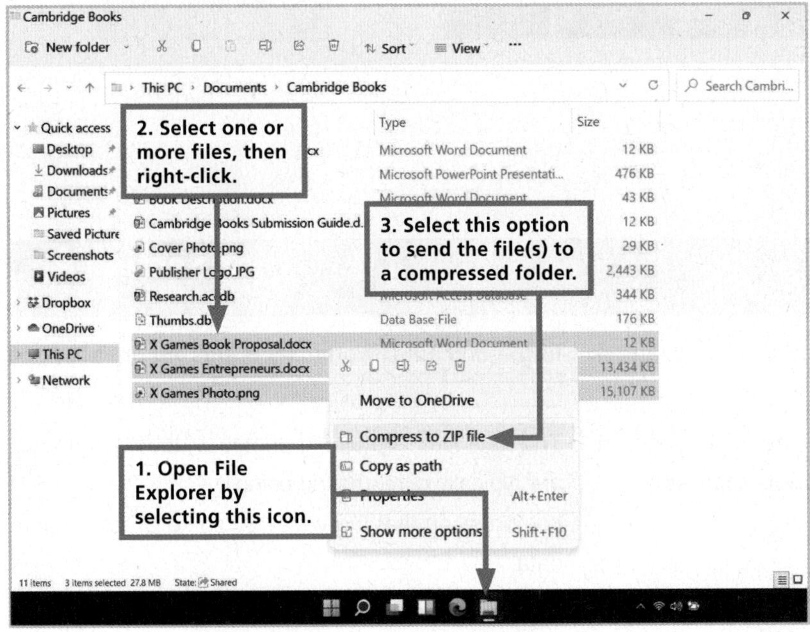

Compressing files using File Explorer on a PC

QuickCheck

Compression utilities can be used to accomplish all of the following except:

a. bundle two or more files into a single small file

b. enlarge a file to increase its resolution

c. zip a single file to decrease its size

d. extract a file to its original size and content

How do I return files to their uncompressed state? The process of reconstituting files is called extracting or unzipping. As with compression, most laptops and desktop computers include extraction and unzipping software; tablets and smartphones may require a third-party app.

Compressed files usually have .zip at the end of the file name and are represented with specialty icons. Compressed files may also end with .gz, .pkg, or .tar.gz. These files have to be extracted or unzipped before you can view the data they contain. The process is easy. To extract a file on a Mac, simply double-click the zipped folder. With Windows (Figure 1-9), use the Extract All option.

Figure 1-9: Extracting files in Windows

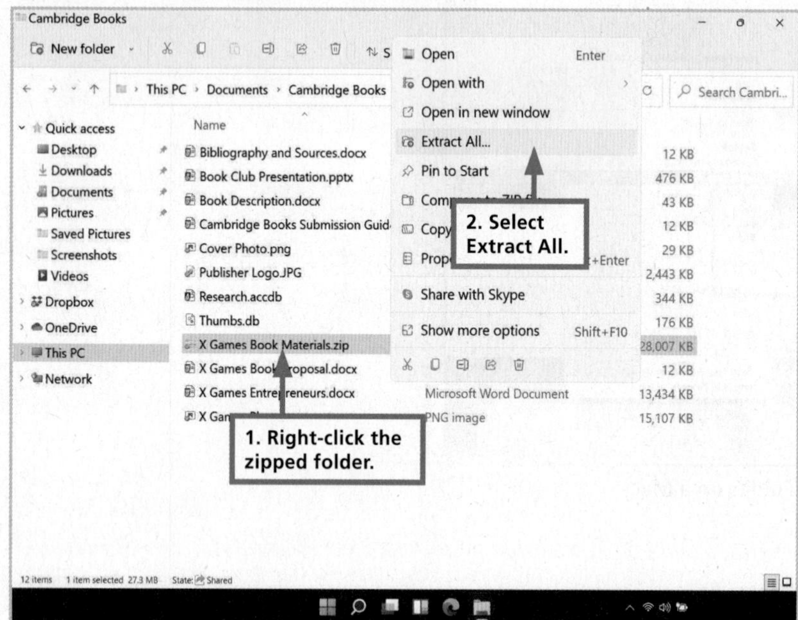

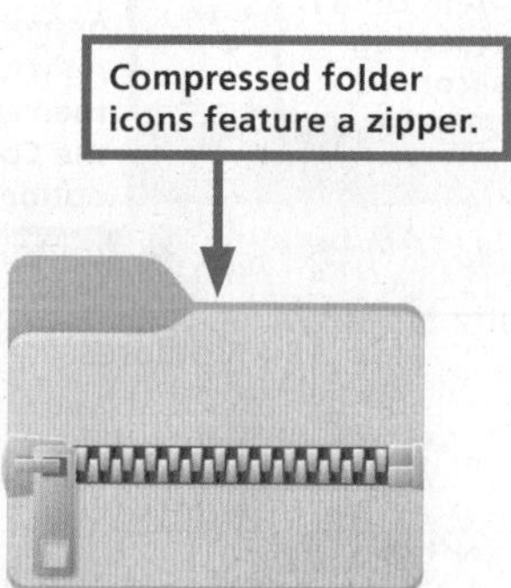

QuickQuiz

Section A

1. A(n) ______ is a 0 or 1 used in the digital representation of data.

2. Most computer data is encoded as UTF-8 or Extended ______ code to represent character data. (Hint: Use the acronym.)

3. Formatting codes can be added to documents using a(n) ______, such as slashes // and angle brackets< >.

4. In the computer world, TB is the abbreviation for ______.

5. The data files containing photos, videos, and music are typically compressed using ______ compression that throws away some of the original data.

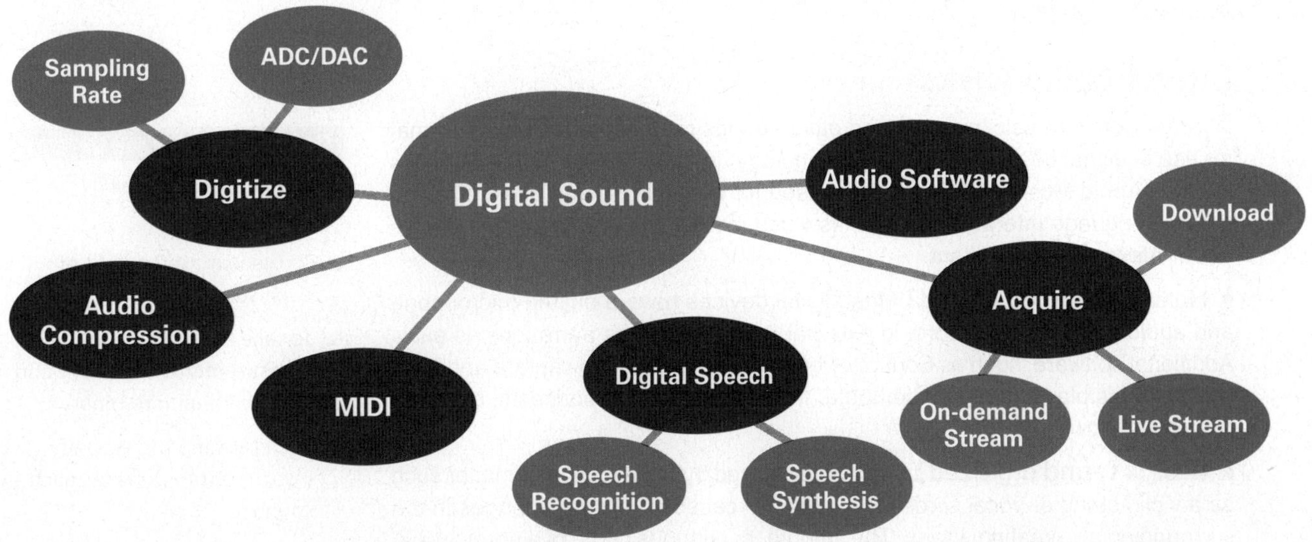

Section **B**

Digital Sound

Objectives

- Describe the process of digital sampling.
- Select the appropriate sampling rate for a digital audio recording.
- Identify digital audio files by their file name extensions.
- Convert digital audio files from one format to another.
- Explain why most audio files are compressed and how this affects sound quality.
- Decide when to download, live stream, or stream music on demand.
- Describe the difference between digital audio and MIDI.
- Explain how Siri and similar services work.

Music downloads were one of the first massively popular types of digital content, but audio technology plays a key role in other interesting applications. This section covers a wide-ranging selection of digital audio concepts and technologies that you're likely to find handy for personal and professional use.

Terminology

digital audio
analog-to-digital converter
digital-to-analog converter
sampling rate
audio compression
AAC
MP3
Ogg Vorbis
WAV
AAX
WMA
audio interface
digital audio extraction
download
live stream
on-demand stream
copy protection
digital rights management
synthesized sound
MIDI
MIDI messages
speech synthesis
speech recognition
phoneme
text-to-speech software

Digital Audio Basics

Digital audio is music, speech, and other sounds represented in binary format for use in digital devices. It is a key technology used by popular music services such as Apple Music and Spotify. It is used for audiobooks and plays a role in natural language interactions, such as voice messaging and speaking to your Siri or Alexa virtual assistant.

How do I record sound? Most digital devices have a built-in microphone and audio software, so recording external sounds, such as narrations, is easy. Additional software, such as Soundflower, might be required to capture and save sound that is playing on your computer from Internet radio, podcasts, or online television shows.

How is sound digitized? Sound is produced by the vibration of matter such as a violin string or vocal cords. This vibration causes pressure changes in the surrounding air, creating waves. The smooth, continuous curve of a sound wave can be directly recorded on analog media, such as vinyl records or cassette tape, but digital recordings are based on samples of a sound wave.

To digitally record sound, samples of a sound wave are collected at periodic intervals and stored as numeric data in an audio file. For example, when recording a voice message on your phone, the sound waves of your voice are sampled many times per second by an **analog-to-digital converter** (ADC). Those samples are converted into binary 1s and 0s, which are stored in an audio file. When the audio file is played, a **digital-to-analog converter** (DAC) transforms the digital bits into analog sound waves and outputs them through speakers. Figure 1-10 shows how a sound wave is digitally sampled.

QuickCheck

What is the purpose of sampling?

a. To measure the height of each sound wave

b. To take multiple height measurements of a wave and convert them into binary

c. To determine the type of instrument that makes each sound

d. To record a sound at the highest fidelity

Figure 1-10: Digitizing a sound wave

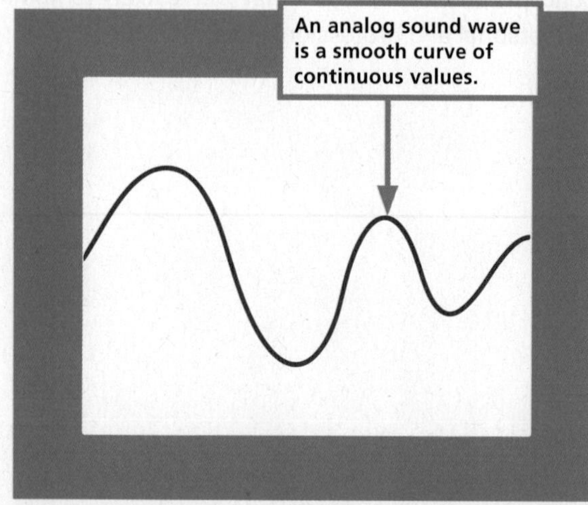
An analog sound wave is a smooth curve of continuous values.

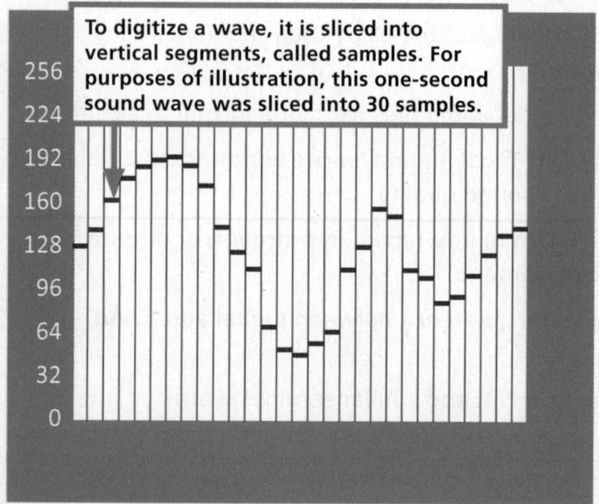
To digitize a wave, it is sliced into vertical segments, called samples. For purposes of illustration, this one-second sound wave was sliced into 30 samples.
256
224
192
160
128
96
64
32
0

Sample	Sample Height (Decimal)	Sample Height (Binary)
1	130	10000010
2	140	1000110
3	160	10100000
4	175	10101111

The height of each sample is converted into a binary number and stored. The height of sample 3 is 160 (decimal), so it is stored as its binary equivalent—10100000.

Does sampling rate affect sound quality? **Sampling rate** refers to the number of times per second that a sound is measured during the recording process. It is expressed in hertz (Hz). One thousand samples per second is expressed as 1,000 Hz or 1 kHz (kilohertz). Higher sampling rates increase the quality of the recording but require more storage space than lower sampling rates.

The standard sampling rate for most consumer audio is 44.1 kHz. To conserve space, voice-overs and narrations that do not require high-quality sound can be recorded with sampling rates of 11 kHz (11,000 samples per second). This rate results in lower-quality sound, but the file is about one-fourth the size of a file for the same sound recorded at 44.1 kHz (44,100 samples per second). Figure 1-11 illustrates how sampling rate affects sound quality and file size.

Try It!

Try recording a short narration. Does your digital device have a built-in microphone and recording software?

1

Figure 1-11: Sampling rate, sound quality, and file size

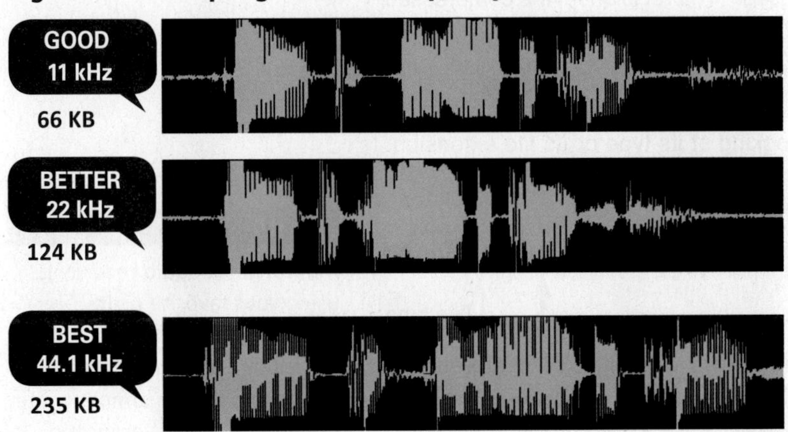

How much space is required to store an audio file? When sampling stereo high-fidelity music at 44.1 kHz, one second of music requires about 0.176 MB of storage space. Forty-five minutes of music—the length of a typical album—requires about 475 MB. You might wonder how audio files rack up so much space.

The height of each sound sample is saved as a 16-bit number for high-fidelity recordings. To achieve stereo effects, you must take two of these 16-bit samples. Therefore, each sample requires 32 bits of storage space. A sampling rate of 44.1 kHz records 44,100 32-bit samples per second. Here is the calculation:

$$32 \times 44{,}100 = 1{,}411{,}200$$

32	44,100	1,411,200
bits in one stereo sample	samples per second	bits (176,400 bytes) for each second of music

QuickCheck

In this calculation, the sampling rate is ______________.

a. 32 bits

b. 44.1 kHz

c. 1.4 Mbps

d. 2.8 Mbps

Is there any way to compress audio files? Regardless of sampling rate, digital audio file size can be reduced using audio compression techniques. **Audio compression** reduces the size of a sound file by removing bits that represent extraneous noise and sounds that are beyond the frequencies of normal hearing.

Most music for portable media players is stored in compressed audio file formats. These lossy formats reduce the size of audio files, but also reduce their quality. Sophisticated listeners can tell the difference, but most casual listeners are content with the quality produced by compressed files streaming from an iPod or a similar device. Files in compressed formats, such as MP3, don't get much smaller if you subsequently use general compression tools provided by Finder and File Explorer.

Files containing "raw" noncompressed audio can be compressed using the same general compression tools used for text and numeric data. For example, using lossless tools provided by Finder and File Explorer, you can compress a large audio file before attaching it to an email message. The recipient of the compressed files will have to unzip the file before listening to it, however.

QuickCheck

Audio compression is usually _______________.

a. lossy

b. lossless

c. raw

Digital Audio File Formats

You can recognize a digital audio file by looking at its type or its file extension. For example, Thriller.mp3 is an audio file, not a music video.

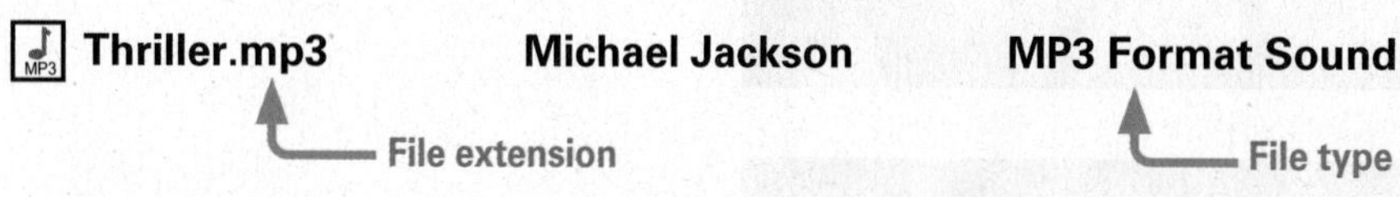

Which audio formats are most popular? Digital audio is stored in a variety of file formats. The table in Figure 1-12 provides an overview of the most popular digital audio formats, which include **AAC**, **MP3**, **Ogg Vorbis**, **WAV**, **AAX**, and **WMA**.

Try It!

Make a short audio recording using your favorite digital device. What are the default file format and sampling rate? If you record at a higher sampling rate, can you tell the difference in sound quality?

Figure 1-12: Popular audio file formats

Audio Format	Extension	Advantages	Disadvantages
AAC (Advanced Audio Coding)	.aac, .m4p, or .mp4	Very good sound quality based on MPEG-4; lossy compression; used for streaming Apple Music	Files can be copy protected so that use is limited to approved devices
MP3 (also called MPEG-1 Layer 3)	.mp3	Good sound quality; lossy compression; can be streamed over the Web	Might require a standalone player or browser plugin
Ogg Vorbis	.ogg	Free, open standard; lossy compression; used by Spotify; part of Google's WebM format	Slow to catch on as a popular standard
WAV	.wav	Good sound quality; supported in browsers without a plugin	Audio data is stored in raw, noncompressed format, so files are very large
AAX (Audible Enhanced Audio)	.aa, .aax	Used by Amazon to distribute audio books	.aa is lower quality than .aax; copying may be limited
WMA (Windows Media Audio)	.wma	Lossy or lossless compression; very good sound quality; used on several music download sites	Files can be copy protected; requires an add-on player for some devices

What are the best sources for digital music? There are several options for obtaining audio content, such as music, soundtracks, narrations, and sound effects.

Live recording is an option for obtaining digital sound files from concerts or lectures. For casual recording, Voice Memos and similar apps work well. Professional recordings require more sophisticated software and hardware tools. A device called an **audio interface** accepts input from a standalone microphone and feeds it into a computer.

Ripping CD tracks is handy for someone who inherits a stack of old CDs and wants to convert the music into a format that plays on a smartphone or other mobile device. *Ripping* is a slang term that refers to the process of importing tracks from a CD or DVD to your computer's hard disk. The technical term for ripping music tracks is **digital audio extraction**.

Downloading is popular for saving audio files on local devices. A **download** copies a file from a private network or Internet server to a local device. The file is transferred as a unit and cannot be played until the entire file has arrived.

Streaming offers yet another way of obtaining audio content. Unlike some digital content, such as photos, that must be accessed as a whole piece, audio content plays back over a period of time. Audio files can be acquired as a **live stream** or **on-demand stream** in addition to downloads (Figure 1-13).

Try It!

Find the names of two live streaming music services and the names of two on-demand streaming services.

1

QuickCheck

You've selected a music track on your smartphone, but there is a pause before it begins. This pause is associated with ___________.

a. downloading audio tracks

b. live streaming audio

c. on-demand streaming

Figure 1-13: Downloading and streaming

Download

A download transfers an audio file from a server to your local device.

You can play back the file even when your device is not online.

The file can be played with any compatible software or player.

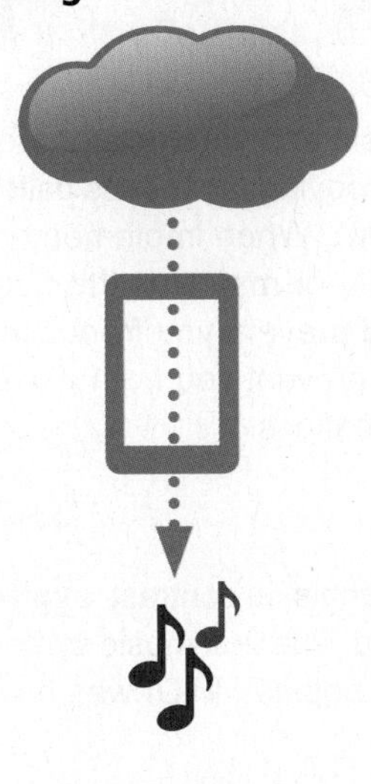

Live stream

A live stream sends media from a server to your local device, where it is played, but not stored.

This method is also known as Webcasting.

You have to be online while listening.

The content stream cannot be paused, stored, or rewound.

On-demand stream

An on-demand stream sends the media to your local device, where it is stored temporarily, or "buffered," until there is enough data to begin playback.

You can fast-forward to any point in the stream without waiting for the entire file to download.

◗ What type of software is required to work with digital audio files?

To play a digital audio file, you must use some type of audio software that works with the file's audio format.

General-purpose audio software and apps provide tools for recording, playing, and modifying audio files. They also provide tools for converting audio files from one format to another. Popular audio software includes Apple GarageBand, Windows Media Player, and Audacity (Figure 1-14).

QuickCheck

The term *ripping* applies to:

a. converting CD tracks to formats such as MP3 and AAC
b. downloading MP3 files illegally from the Internet
c. compressing AAC files with digital audio extraction

Figure 1-14: Audacity audio software

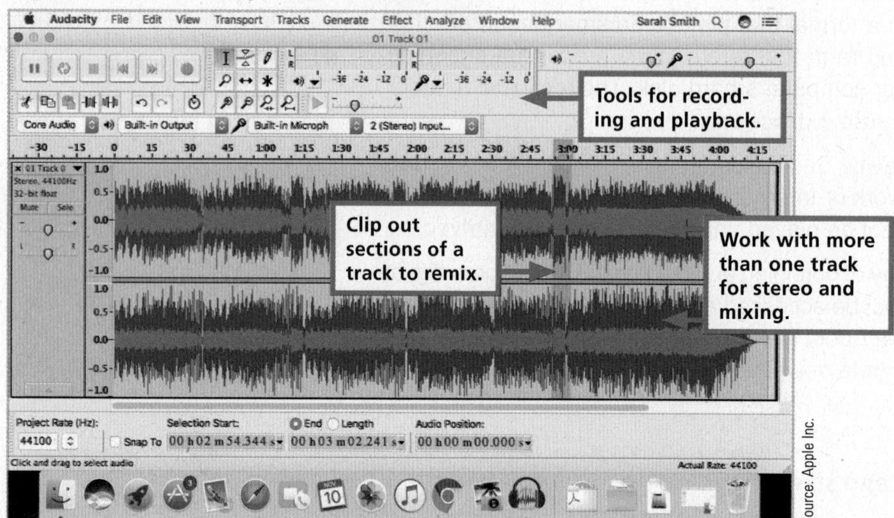

◗ Why can't I copy some music files? Music and video distributors may use various technologies to curtail unauthorized copying, a process called **copy protection** or **digital rights management** (DRM). When implemented, DRM technologies may prevent you from copying a file or may limit the number of copies you can make. These technologies could prevent you from converting files from one format to another. DRM may also prevent you from playing files on certain hardware or in certain geographical locations.

MIDI

Digital audio is a recording of real analog sound signals. In contrast, **synthesized sound** is an artificially created, or synthetic, sound. The first music synthesizers were analog. When digital synthesizers became popular, MIDI was developed as a way to control them.

◗ What is MIDI music? **MIDI** (Musical Instrument Digital Interface) specifies a standard way to store music data for synthesizers, electronic MIDI instruments, and computers. Unlike digital audio files, which contain digitized recordings of real performances, MIDI files contain instructions, called **MIDI messages**, specifying the pitch of a note, the point at which the note begins, the instrument that plays the note, the volume of the note, and the point at which the note ends. MIDI music is usually stored in .mid files.

What is the data representation for a MIDI message? As with all digital data, MIDI messages are distilled into a series of bits represented by 1s and 0s. A MIDI message might look like this:

1001	0001	01010100	0111000
Play note	Channel 1 designates piano	Note number 84 designates high C	Velocity 112 designates loud volume

What are the advantages and disadvantages of MIDI? MIDI files are much more compact than digital audio files. Depending on the exact piece of music, three minutes of MIDI music might require only 10 KB of storage space, whereas the same piece of music stored in a high-quality, noncompressed digital audio file might require 30,000 KB of storage space.

One of the main disadvantages of MIDI is that it cannot produce vocals. Another disadvantage is that the quality of MIDI music depends on the playback device, which stores a collection of synthesized sounds. MIDI music might sound great on a computer equipped with high-end MIDI equipment, but the same MIDI sequence might sound artificial on a handheld device.

QuickCheck

Which of the following files is likely to contain synthesized music?

a. Bongos.mp3

b. Screech.wav

c. Waltz.ogg

d. Sugar.mid

Who uses MIDI? Today, MIDI is primarily a tool used by studio musicians, performers, and composers. Musicians can input notes for several instrumental parts directly from a MIDI keyboard and create backup instrumentation for performances. One or two musicians with MIDI gear can sound like a large band.

Music composition software with MIDI support makes it easy to place notes on a screen-based music staff, then play back the composition on a MIDI keyboard or through the speakers of a digital device (Figure 1-15).

Figure 1-15: MIDI music composition

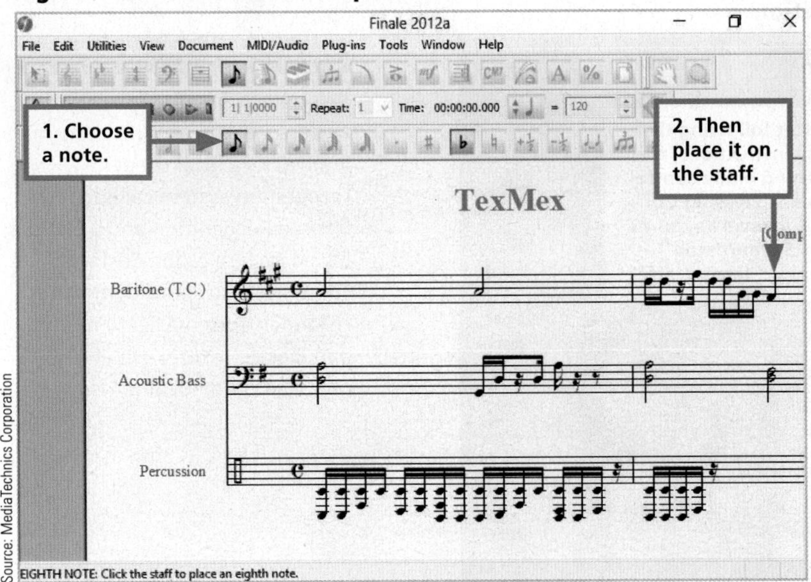

Source: MediaTechnics Corporation

Digitized Speech

Speech technologies are used to collect information from callers using telephone-based services such as Directory Assistance. They are the foundation for interactive voice response systems such as Google Voice Search, Siri, Alexa, and Cortana. Speech recognition enables people to control software with spoken commands, as well as dictate text into a word processing document. Speech technologies can also read a computer screen aloud, which unlocks access to computers and the Internet for individuals with visual disabilities.

What's the difference between speech synthesis and speech recognition? **Speech synthesis** is the process by which machines produce sound that resembles spoken words. **Speech recognition** (or voice recognition) refers to the ability of a machine to understand spoken words.

How does speech synthesis work? A basic sound unit, such as "reh" or "gay," is called a **phoneme**. Most speech synthesizers string together phonemes to form words. For example, the phonemes "reh" and "gay" produce the word *reggae*. Phonemes are usually derived from recordings of human voices reading specially prepared passages of text. **Text-to-speech software** analyzes the words in a section of text, finds corresponding phonemes, and combines them into sentences for output.

How does speech recognition work? On a personal computer or smartphone, a speech recognition system collects words spoken into a microphone that's connected to sound processing circuitry. This circuitry's analog-to-digital converter transforms the analog sound of your voice into digital data. This data is then processed by speech recognition software.

Speech recognition software analyzes the sounds of your voice and converts each word into groups of phonemes. Next, the software compares the groups of phonemes to the words in a digital dictionary that lists phoneme combinations along with their corresponding words. When a match is found, the software can display the word on the screen or use it to carry out a command. Most digital devices offer a way to use spoken commands (Figure 1-16).

QuickCheck

Which one of the following requires digital-to-analog conversion?

a. Speech synthesis

b. Speech recognition

c. Speaking to Siri

d. Voice dialing

Figure 1-16: Windows speech recognition

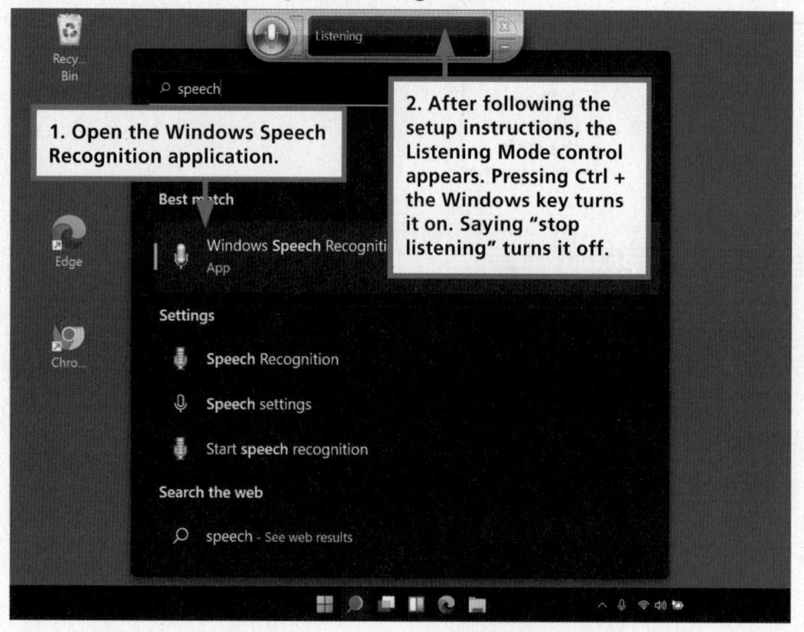
Listening
speech
1. Open the Windows Speech Recognition application.
2. After following the setup instructions, the Listening Mode control appears. Pressing Ctrl + the Windows key turns it on. Saying "stop listening" turns it off.
Best match
Windows Speech Recogniti
App
Settings
Speech Recognition
Speech settings
Start speech recognition
Search the web
speech - See web results
Recy... Bin
Edge
Chro...

Try It!

If you have a computer with the current version of Windows, it includes a local speech recognition system called Speech Recognition and a cloud-based system called Cortana. Try it! You can speak commands to launch apps, navigate menus, and dictate text for email messages and documents.

How does Siri work? Devices of the Speak & Spell generation had robotic voices and were not responsive to a wide variety of commands and queries. What makes modern technologies like Siri so much more versatile and lifelike? Figure 1-17 provides an overview.

Try It!

Are you wondering what a Speak & Spell is? Go to YouTube and search for "Speak & Spell" to see a demonstration.

Figure 1-17: How Siri works

The voices of Siri were created by live actors, but they couldn't record every possible response to user queries.

Instead they recorded the words and sentences from a script. Although the script may appear nonsensical, the sentences are rich in phonemes.

When the recordings are complete, a team of linguists analyzes and tags various speech components and loads them into a database. The process is called concatenative speech synthesis.

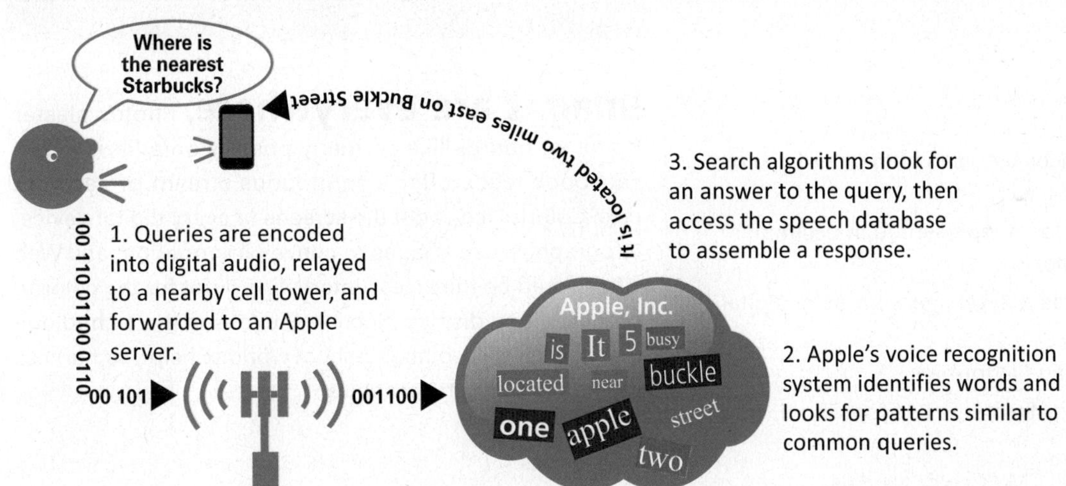

QuickQuiz Section B

1. ______ rate refers to the number of times per second that a sound is measured during the recording process.

2. Audio formats such as MP3, Ogg Vorbis, and AAC have good sound quality even though they use ______ compression.

3. The process of ripping tracks from an audio CD to a digital format is called digital audio ______.

4. ______ files store a series of instructions that specify which notes to play, their duration, and their volume.

5. The audio components for virtual assistants such as Siri are obtained by recording real voices and then applying ______ speech synthesis.

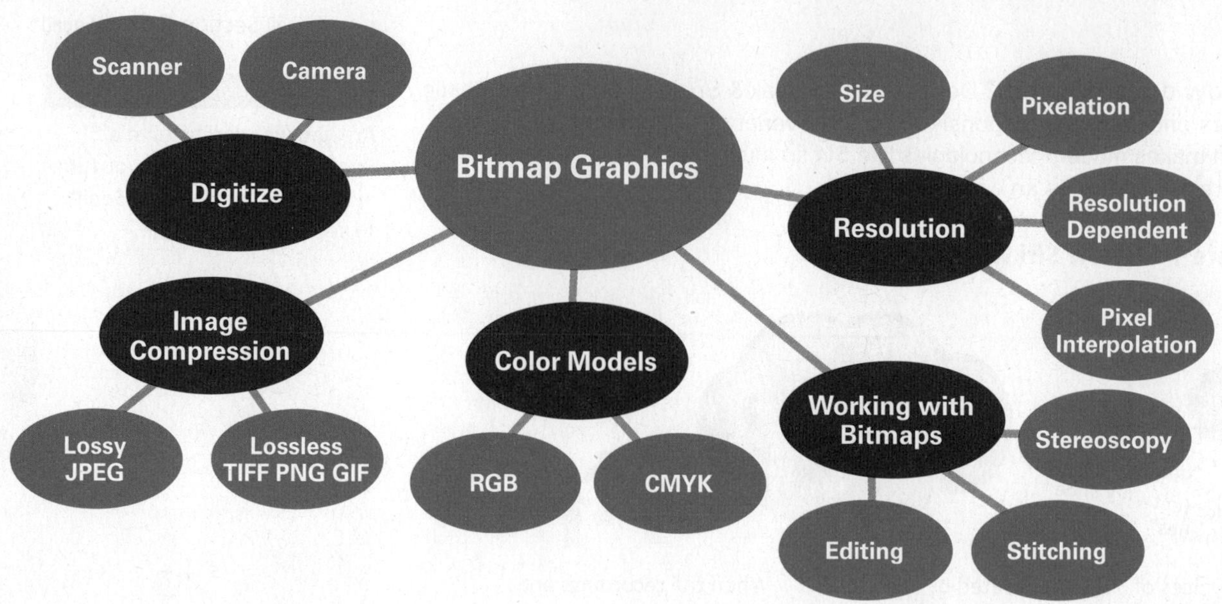

Section C Bitmap Graphics

Objectives

- Describe the differences between bitmap and vector graphics.
- Explain how pixel color is represented in decimal, hexadecimal, and binary.
- Describe how cameras and scanners produce digital images.
- List six popular bitmap file formats.
- Decide which graphics format to use for school, work, or personal projects.
- Describe the RGB and CMYK color models.
- Calculate the size of a bitmap file given its resolution.
- List the bitmap file formats that use lossless compression.
- Explain what a color histogram represents and how to use one.
- Explain how 3D images are created.
- Provide examples of image stitching.
- Describe two types of stereoscopic imaging.

Images are everywhere. Photos plaster Pinterest boards like so many posters on a Paris kiosk. Facebook feeds offer a continuous stream of vacation pics. Colorful icons dot the screens of every digital device. Infographics use images to convey information, and Web sites would be much less interesting if not for the colorful graphics they display. Section C explains the technology that powers this point-and-shoot world to help you harness the power of digital graphics.

Terminology

computer graphics
still images
motion graphics
bitmap graphic
pixel
scanner
CCD
photosites
BMP
RAW
TIFF
JPEG
GIF
PNG
RGB color model
color depth
True Color
image resolution
resolution dependent
pixelation
pixel interpolation
image compression
run-length encoding
image histogram
cloning
inpainting
digital compositing
clipping path
alpha blending
image stitching
stereoscopic imaging
stereo pair
stereogram
anaglyph

Bitmap Basics

As digital devices gained the ability to display images, two types of **computer graphics** evolved: bitmap and vector. These graphics can produce **still images**, such as photographs and diagrams, or **motion graphics**, such as videos and animations.

Computer graphics can produce two-dimensional flat images and stereoscopic images with visual depth that makes close-up objects appear near enough to grasp.

Despite their similarities, bitmap and vector images are quite different. Bitmap graphics may be the most common, but they are less flexible than vector graphics and cannot be used to model three-dimensional objects. To find out why, let's take a look at the characteristics of bitmaps.

Terminology

The term *3D* is used today to refer to a variety of commercial products that should be called stereoscopic. For example, those so-called 3D glasses with blue and red lenses are technically stereoscopic, not 3D. As you continue in this module, pay attention to the difference between 3D and stereoscopic.

1

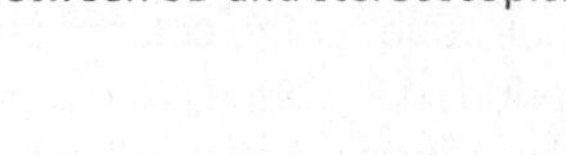

▶ What is a bitmap graphic? A **bitmap graphic**, also called a raster graphic or simply a bitmap, is composed of a grid of tiny rectangular cells. Each cell is a picture element, commonly called a **pixel**. Each pixel is assigned a color, which is stored as a binary number. Figure 1-18 illustrates these basic characteristics of a bitmap graphic.

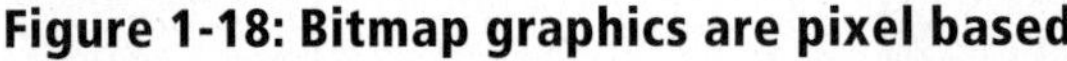

Figure 1-18: Bitmap graphics are pixel based

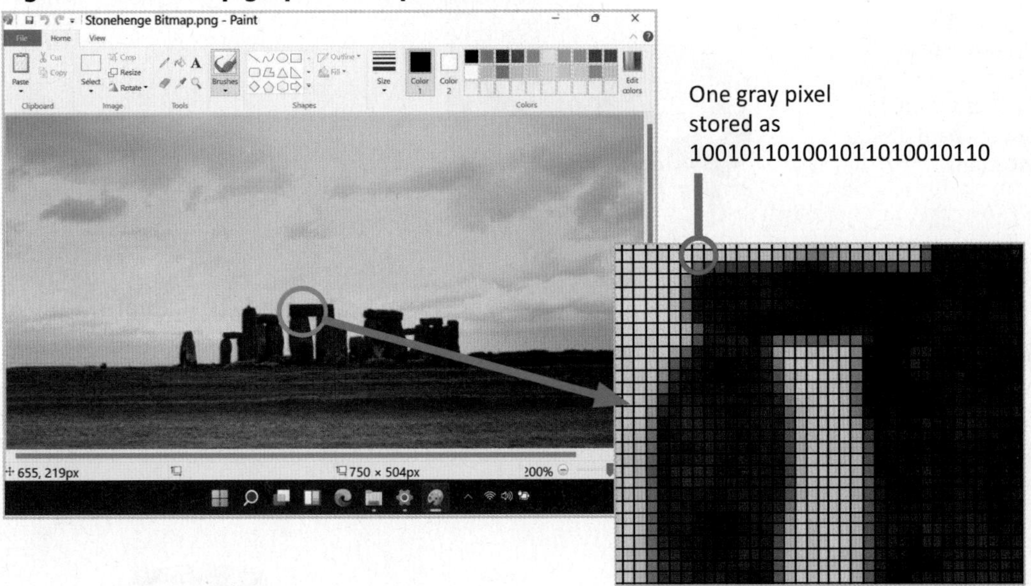

▶ Where would I encounter bitmap graphics? Bitmap graphics are used to create realistic images, such as photographs. You might also encounter bitmaps in the form of cartoons, images that appear in computer games, the desktop images displayed by your computer or smartphone, and photorealistic images derived from 3D graphical objects.

When you use a digital camera or camera-enabled cell phone, your photos are stored as bitmaps. A scanner also produces bitmaps. The photos you send or receive as email attachments are bitmaps, as are most Web page graphics.

QuickCheck

Bitmap graphics are based on:

a. codecs

b. pixels

c. rasters

d. vectors

How do I create bitmap images? You can create a bitmap graphic from scratch using the tools provided by graphics software—specifically a category of graphics software referred to as paint software. You might be familiar with paint software such as Adobe Photoshop, Apple Photos (included with Apple computers), and Microsoft Paint (included with Windows). Other alternatives, such as AutoDesk SketchBook, are available online and as downloads for smartphones and laptops.

Try It!

Check the features of the photo app on your smartphone. Which of the following does it provide?

Retouch

Crop

Special effects

Exposure adjustment

How do I convert a printed image into a bitmap? When you have a printed image, such as a photograph, a page from a magazine, or a picture from a book, you can use a **scanner** to convert the printed image into a bitmap graphic.

A scanner essentially divides an image into a fine grid of cells and assigns a digital value for the color of each cell. As the scan progresses, these values are transferred to your digital device and stored as a bitmap graphics file. Scanners, such as the one pictured in Figure 1-19, are inexpensive and easy to use.

Figure 1-19: Scan images
To scan an image, turn on the scanner and start your scanner software. Place the image face down on the scanner glass, then use the scanner software to initiate the scan. The scanned image is saved in memory and can then be saved on your computer's hard disk or in another storage location.

How does a digital camera capture bitmap images? The lens of a film camera captures the light from an image onto a light-sensitive roll of film, which is developed to produce a photographic print. In a digital camera, the lens focuses light from the image onto a small image sensor called a **CCD** (charge-coupled device). This technology is used in standalone digital cameras and smartphone cameras.

A CCD contains a grid of tiny light-sensitive diodes called **photosites**. The number of photosites depends on the size of the CCD. A one-half-inch square CCD can contain more than 500,000 photosites. Each photosite detects the brightness and color for its tiny piece of the image (Figure 1-20).

A CCD's photosites correspond to pixels. The more pixels used to capture an image, the higher its resolution, and the better the resulting picture. Cameras with larger CCDs produce higher-quality images. Some cameras contain multiple CCDs, which enhance the color quality of a camera's output.

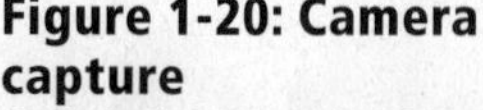

Figure 1-20: Camera capture
A digital camera's CCD converts the image captured by the camera lens into a grid of colored pixels, which are stored as bits.

What are the most common bitmap file formats? Cameras, scanners, and graphics software may offer a choice of bitmap formats, such as BMP, RAW, TIFF, JPEG, GIF, and PNG. Selecting the best graphics file format to use depends on what you intend to do with the image. Figure 1-21 summarizes popular bitmap formats and their uses.

Figure 1-21: Bitmap formats

	Bitmap Format	Use
	BMP, pronounced "bee-em-pee" or "bump," is the native bitmap graphics file format of the Microsoft Windows environment. Microsoft Paint, included as part of Microsoft Windows, creates BMP graphics files, as well as PNGs and JPEGs. The BMP format supports True Color and can be used for a wide variety of graphics applications, such as photographs, illustrations, and graphs. BMP files are often too large for email attachments. Their size makes BMPs undesirable for use on Web pages.	Graphical elements, such as buttons and other controls for graphical user interfaces
	RAW image formats contain the unprocessed pixel data generated directly by a digital camera's sensor. Up to 12 bits of data can be stored for each of the red, blue, and green values for a pixel, so RAW files are very large. Cameras that offer a RAW format usually supply software to convert RAW data to smaller JPEG or TIFF files.	Photographic images before they are stored in other formats
	TIFF (Tagged Image File Format), or TIF, is a flexible and platform-independent graphics file format supported by most photoediting software packages. Scanners and digital cameras commonly store bitmaps in TIFF format because it supports True Color and can be easily converted into other graphics file formats.	Desktop publishing and any projects that require high-resolution graphics; not supported by browsers
	JPEG (pronounced "JAY-peg"), which stands for Joint Photographic Experts Group, is a graphics format with built-in compression that stores True Color bitmap data very efficiently in a small file. The JPEG format is popular for Web graphics, smartphone photos, and for photos attached to email messages. When creating a JPEG or converting an image to JPEG format, you can control the level of compression and the resulting file size. The compression process eliminates some image data, however, so highly compressed files suffer some quality deterioration.	General use, such as desktop publishing or Web pages, where flexibility in file size is important
JPL/NASA	**GIF** (Graphics Interchange Format), pronounced "gif" or "jiff," was specifically designed to create images that can be displayed on multiple platforms, such as PCs and Macs. GIF graphics are limited to 256 colors, but the format supports simple animations. Once a popular format for Web pages, GIF is being replaced by JPEG and PNG.	Web graphics and simple animations
	PNG (Portable Network Graphics), pronounced "ping," is a graphics format designed to improve on the GIF format. A PNG graphic can display up to 48-bit True Color (trillions of colors). Unlike JPEG, PNG compresses bitmap files without losing any data, so compressed images retain the same high quality as the originals. PNG was developed as a public domain format without any restrictions on its use.	Web graphics and other general uses

1

Bitmap Data Representation

The fact that bitmap images are formed by a grid of pixels controls not only how those images are stored, but also how they can be modified. Color and resolution are key elements in bitmap data representation.

How does each pixel get a color number? Today's color display devices represent color using the **RGB color model**. The color displayed for a pixel is based on the intensity of red, green, and blue signals received by the screen's color elements.

Each red, green, and blue signal is assigned a value ranging from 0 to 255: 0 represents the absence of color, and 255 represents the highest intensity level for that color. A pixel appears white if the red, green, and blue signals are set to maximum intensity. If red, green, and blue signals are equal but at a lower intensity, the pixel displays a shade of gray. A pixel appears violet if it receives high red and blue signals and just a bit of green (Figure 1-22).

Terminology

The *CMYK* color model defines four color values: cyan, magenta, yellow, and black. It is a subtractive system, whereas RGB is an additive system. In CMYK, white is 00000000; but in RGB, 11111111 is white. CMYK is typically used for projects that require color printing.

Figure 1-22: RGB color

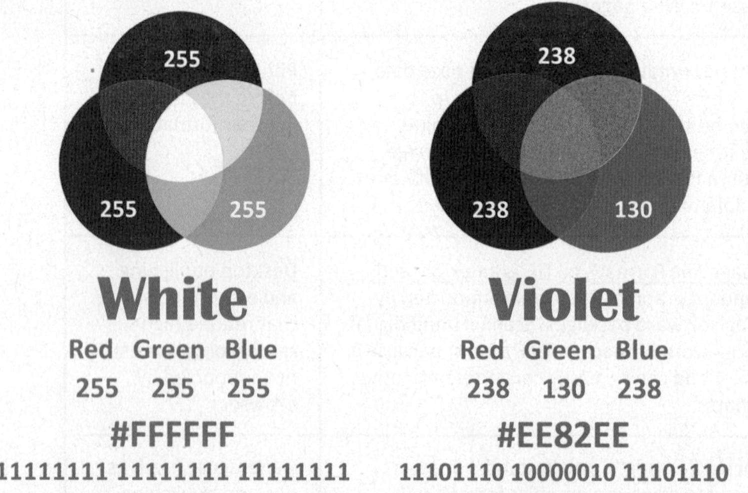

Look at the center where the circles intersect to see the color that is generated. Color numbers are shown in decimal, hexadecimal, and binary.

How are colors specified? Color values can be specified in decimal (base 10), hexadecimal (base 16), or binary (base 2). Even artists need to know their way around number systems! Decimal notation tends to be used within graphics software, and hexadecimal (hex) notation is common on the Web. Whichever notation is used, however, color data is ultimately represented as binary digits when it is stored and transmitted.

In decimal, a pixel color is specified with values such as Red 238, Green 130, and Blue 238. In hexadecimal, each pair of digits refers to a color value. For example, the hexadecimal number for violet is #EE82EE. That means EE(hex) = 238 Red, 82(hex) = 130 Green, and EE(hex) = 238 Blue. You can find lists of colors and their hexadecimal triplets on the Web. In binary, eight bits are used to represent the red value, another eight bits are used for the green value, and eight more bits are used for blue.

QuickCheck

To represent the color violet in Figure 1-22, the decimal value for green is 130. What are the equivalent hexadecimal and binary values for green?

a. 82 and 10000010

b. 255 and 11111111

c. EE and 11101110

How much data is required for each pixel color? With eight bits used to represent each color value, one pixel requires 24 bits. Because each R, G, and B can have 256 values, the number of possible colors is 16.7 million (256 x 256 x 256). The number of colors available in a graphic is referred to as **color depth**. Images that use 24 bits for each pixel have a color depth of 24, which is also called **True Color**.

How does resolution relate to image quality? The dimensions of the grid that forms a bitmap graphic are referred to as **image resolution**. The resolution of a bitmap is usually expressed as the number of horizontal and vertical pixels it contains. For example, a small graphic for a Web page might have a resolution of 150 x 100 pixels—150 pixels across and 100 pixels high.

High-resolution graphics contain more data than low-resolution graphics. With more data, it is possible to display and print high-quality images that are sharper and clearer than images produced using less data.

Can I shrink and enlarge bitmaps? Bitmap graphics are **resolution dependent** because each element is a discrete pixel. Imagine that a bitmap image and its grid come on a surface that you can stretch or shrink. As you stretch the surface, the grid maintains the same number of horizontal and vertical cells, but each cell becomes larger, the grid becomes more visible, and the image develops an undesirable jagged appearance referred to as **pixelation**. Simply stretching a bitmap to enlarge it doesn't produce high-quality results (Figure 1-23).

Figure 1-23: Pixelation
The enlargement of this balloon appears pixelated because it was a small part of a photo that had few pixels.

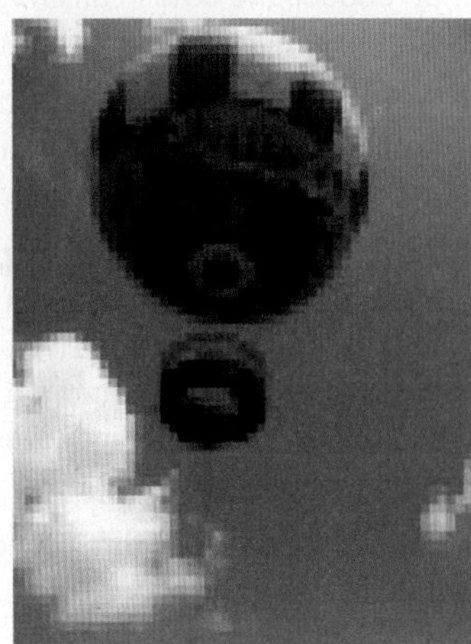

1

Can I change a bitmap's resolution? Graphics software offers options for changing the resolution of bitmap images. Suppose you reduce the resolution from 2160 x 1440 to 1080 x 720. The image grid becomes a quarter of its original size, but every fourth pixel was removed from the image, which typically reduces image quality.

If you attempt to enlarge a bitmap by increasing its resolution, your computer must somehow add pixels because no additional picture data exists. But what colors should these additional pixels become? Most graphics software uses a process called **pixel interpolation** to create new pixels by averaging the colors of nearby pixels.

For some images, pixel interpolation produces an enlargement that appears very similar to the original. Other images—particularly those with strong curved or diagonal lines—may appear pixelated.

Try It!
Open an image with Photoshop or similar graphics software. Check its size and its ppi. At 300 ppi, how large can the image be printed before its quality begins to deteriorate?

So how much resolution does a bitmap need to be printed as a poster? Graphics software, such as Adobe Photoshop, can help you gauge how large an image can be printed before the quality begins to deteriorate. The minimum resolution for printed output is 72 pixels per inch (ppi). Suppose that a photo taken with a smartphone has a resolution of 1936 x 2592. At 72 ppi, the photo can be printed up to a size of 26" x 36".

To print the same photo but with a better resolution of 150 ppi, the poster would be much smaller: about 12" x 17" as shown in Figure 1-24.

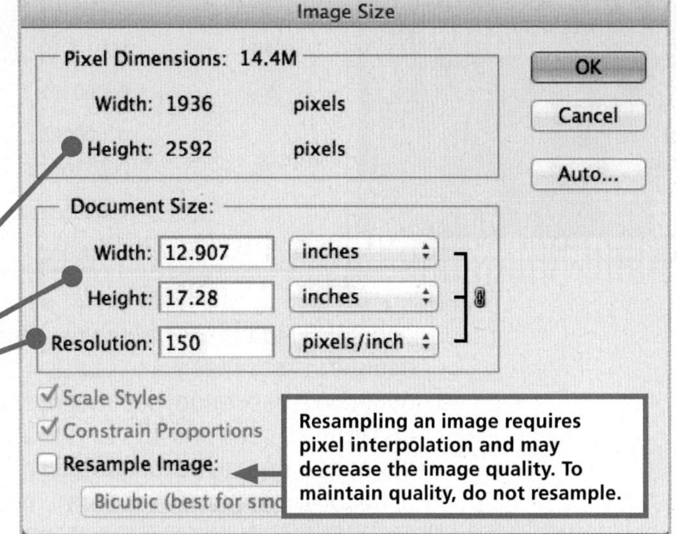

Figure 1-24: Image size
Check these specifications to determine maximum print size.

Image Compression

Bitmap files are big. An image with a resolution of 1936 x 2592 contains 5,018,112 pixels. Each pixel requires 24 bits, so the RAW image file could be as large as 120,434,688 bits (12,434,696 bytes or 12 megabytes). By any measure, that's a lot of data to store and move. Various image compression techniques can be used to shrink bitmap files.

QuickCheck

Run-length encoding is a type of ________.

a. bitmap digitization

b. RLE graphics format

c. lossless compression

d. pixelation

▶ **What is image compression?** **Image compression** refers to any technique that recodes the data in an image file so that it contains fewer bits. Many bitmap file formats automatically apply compression to an image when it is saved.

▶ **Which formats apply lossless compression?** TIFF, PNG, and GIF graphics formats offer lossless compression. Images stored in these formats do not lose any quality when compressed.

▶ **How does lossless compression shrink a file without throwing away data?** Various techniques exist for lossless image compression. As a simple example, consider a type of lossless compression called run-length encoding. **Run-length encoding** (RLE) replaces a series of similarly colored pixels with a binary code that indicates the number of pixels and their colors.

Suppose that a section of a picture has 167 consecutive white pixels, and each pixel is described by three bytes of data. RLE compresses this series of 167 bytes into as few as four bytes, as shown in Figure 1-25.

Figure 1-25: Run-length encoding

The data for the first 167 white pixels can be compressed as 10100111 11111111 11111111 11111111. The first byte is the binary representation of 167. The next three bytes are the code for white.

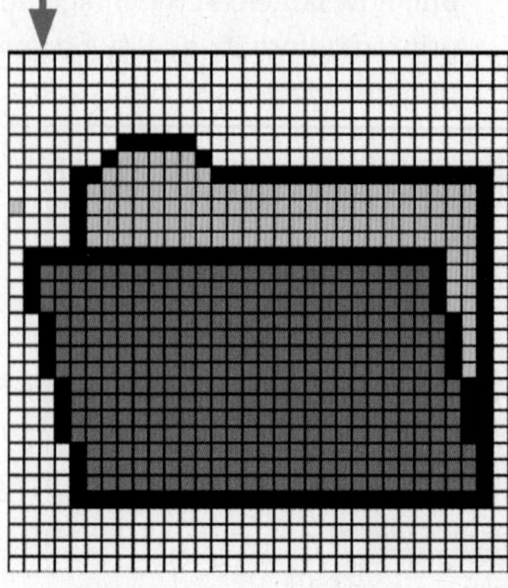

Number of Pixels (Decimal)	Number of Pixels (Binary)	Pixel Color	Pixel Color (Binary)
167	10100111	White	11111111 11111111 11111111
5	00000101	Black	00000000 00000000 00000000
26	00011010	White	11111111 11111111 11111111
1	00000001	Black	00000000 00000000 00000000
5	00000101	Yellow	11111111 11111111 00000000
1	00000001	Black	00000000 00000000 00000000
23	00010111	White	11111111 11111111 11111111
2	00000010	Black	00000000 00000000 00000000
7	00000111	Yellow	111111111111111100000000
18	00010010	Black	00000000 00000000 00000000
5	00000101	White	11111111 11111111 11111111
1	00000001	Black	00000000 00000000 00000000
25	00011001	Yellow	11111111 11111111 00000000
1	00000001	Black	00000000 00000000 00000000
1	00000001	White	11111111 11111111 11111111

QuickCheck

Is this the correct RLE for the row shown below?

a. Yes

b. No

00000001 11111111 11111111 00000000
00000011 11111111 11111111 11111111
00000001 00000000 00000000 00000000
00011001 11111111 11111111 00000000
00000001 00000000 00000000 00000000
00000001 11111111 11111111 00000000

Which formats apply lossless compression? JPEG files are compressed using lossy compression, so some quality is lost when the file is saved. When saving an image as a JPEG, you may be able to select a compression level. Take care with lossy compression to ensure that your image is not further compressed every time you save it (Figure 1-26).

Figure 1-26: JPEG compression

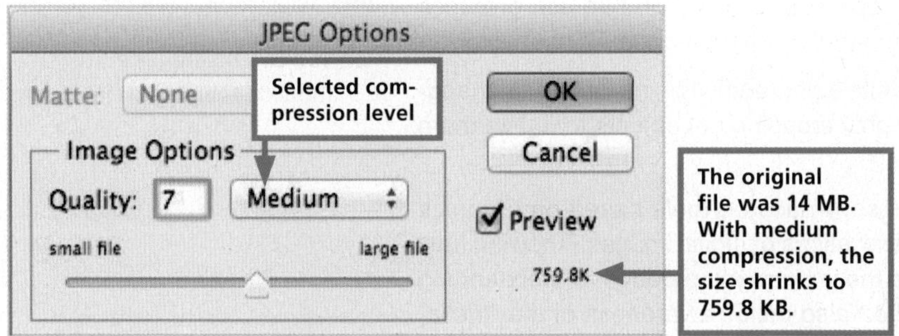

What happens during lossy compression? Lossy compression techniques discard some data from an image to shrink its file size. JPEG is a lossy version of run-length encoding that can be applied to images, such as photographs, that don't have large areas of solid color.

A True Color photograph might not have any adjoining pixels of the same color. Applying RLE to such a photo would not result in any compression whatsoever. JPEG preprocesses an image by tweaking the colors in adjoining pixels so that they are the same color whenever possible. After this preprocessing is complete, run-length encoding can be applied with more success.

For many images, lossy compression results in only a minor reduction in the sharpness of the image. The reduction in quality can be unnoticeable in many circumstances. Figure 1-27 illustrates a section of a noncompressed image and a section of that same image after JPEG compression has been applied. Can you see any difference?

Try It!

Open a JPEG image. Use the Save As command or Duplicate command to make a copy of the image with a name different from the original. As you save the copy, apply as much compression as possible. Close both files and then reopen them. Is there a visible difference in quality?

Figure 1-27: Compressed image quality

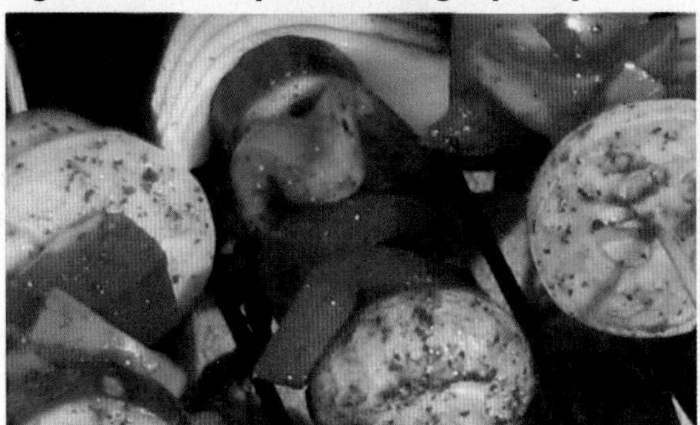

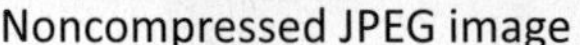
Noncompressed JPEG image

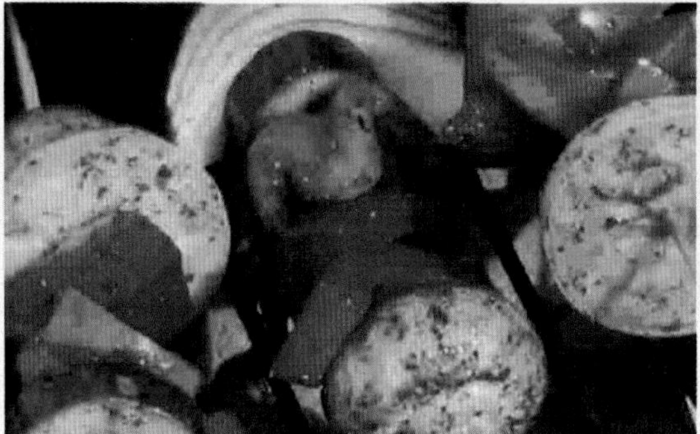
JPEG image with 35% compression

Can I compress images using general compression tools? The same compression tools used to shrink text and numeric data can be used with bitmaps. Images stored in file formats such as JPEG and PNG, which are automatically compressed, may not shrink much, whereas RAW files, BMPs, and noncompressed TIFFs may shrink quite a bit.

Modifying Bitmap Images

"Photoshopping" has become an everyday term for fixing up photos that are underexposed, are marred by red eye effects, or display an awkward object in the background. Photoshop software and a host of local and online apps make it easy to modify digital images.

What characteristics of a bitmap can I modify? Because bitmap graphics are coded as a series of bits that represent pixels, you can use graphics software to modify or edit this type of graphic by changing the color of pixels.

In the early days of digital imaging, primitive photoediting was limited to changing the color of individual pixels, or roughly cropping out objects to delete them or paste them elsewhere.

Today, photoediting software includes sophisticated tools based on graphics algorithms that produce amazing transformations of digital images. Knowing how to use the available toolset can improve the images you produce. Understanding the extent to which photos can be edited also builds awareness of the "tricks" that can be used to alter images in news stories and other information sources.

Noise reduction. In an image, "noise" refers to artifacts such as spots, dust, and scratches that may be produced when old photos are scanned. Some images have undesirable speckles resulting from low light conditions. Noise reduction tools can remove these noisy artifacts.

Image enhancement. A mediocre photo can benefit from image enhancement techniques that correct brightness, improve color saturation, and sharpen the focus. Beyond one-click enhancement tools, image editors provide an **image histogram** that can be used to adjust the brightness values for various ranges of dark, mid-range, or light pixels (Figure 1-28).

QuickCheck

When modifying a JPEG image, which of the following is true?

a. It is stored in a compressed format.

b. It cannot be modified until you unzip it.

c. You can no longer edit individual pixels in the image.

Try It!

Histograms can perform miracles! Open a photo using software such as Photoshop, Apple Photos, or Photo Gallery. Locate the histogram control and experiment to see what you can reveal in the shadows.

Figure 1-28: How image histograms work

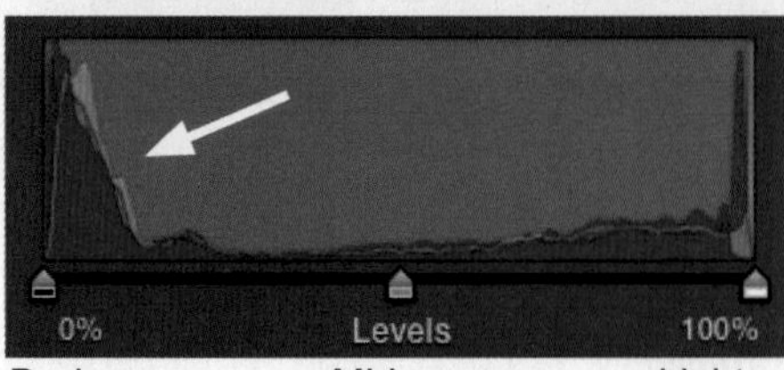

The histogram for the original photo shows lots of dark pixels (the buildings) and a few light ones (the sunset).

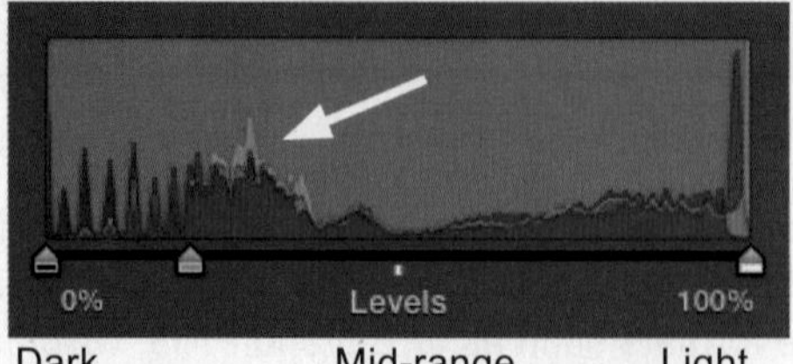

By sliding the Levels bar, more pixels become mid-range and the details of the buildings begin to emerge.

Selective color change. The mannequin at an online store displays a red dress, which is also available in other colors. How would it look in blue? The photographer did not have to take a photo of the dress in every color. Photoediting software can outline the dress in the original photo and then apply the new color. Similar algorithms are used to colorize black-and-white photos.

Correcting image distortion. The human eye compensates for perspective, but the camera does not. When a rectangular object in a photo appears distorted, reconstructing the straight edges is easy with photo editing software (Figure 1-29).

Figure 1-29: Correcting image distortion

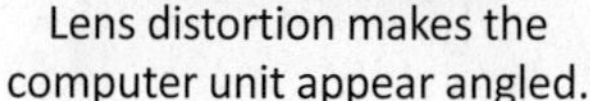

Lens distortion makes the computer unit appear angled.

Correcting image distortion straightens the sides.

Cloning. **Cloning** employs algorithms that pull pixels from one area of an image and then apply them to another area. Cloning can be used to remove small blemishes, as shown in Figure 1-30.

Figure 1-30: Erasing artifacts with cloning

Cloning works well to remove natural blemishes and photo artifacts, such as the white spot under the subject's eye.

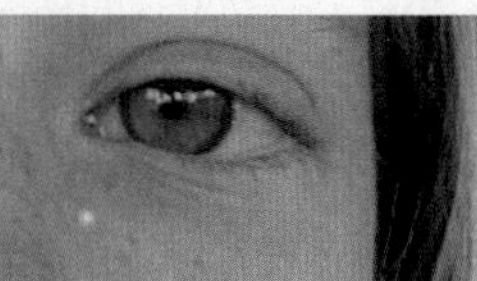

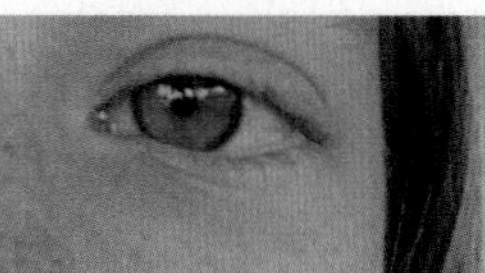

Inpainting. Reconstructing lost, unwanted, or deteriorated areas in a photo is called **inpainting**. Using information from nearby pixels, and taking into account the overall structure of the image, inpainting algorithms essentially scrub out designated areas and miraculously replace the missing pixels with a background or an object that fits with the rest of the image (Figure 1-31).

Figure 1-31: Inpainting with content-aware fill

The original photo includes a man in the foreground. Removing the man leaves a blank area.

Photoshop's Content-Aware Fill algorithm creates a background to fill the blank area.

Digital compositing. Have you seen the photo of a great white shark attacking a U.S. Air Force helicopter? That image and many more bizarre photos are a product of **digital compositing**, which assembles several images into one. Compositing is achieved using two tools: clipping paths and alpha blending.

A **clipping path** essentially cuts an object out of an image and knocks out the background to make it transparent. This object can then be superimposed on a different background. **Alpha blending** alters the pixel colors where the edges of the object and the background meet, so that the object appears to merge with the background (Figure 1-32).

Try It!

You can see digital compositing in action by going to YouTube and searching for **Content-Aware Fill**. If you have access to Photoshop, open a few of your own photos and see what kind of crazy composite you can create.

Figure 1-32: Digital compositing

A clipping path cuts out an object from the background.
The object is straightened and resized before being merged into the photo.

Panoramic and 360 Images

Photos are no longer limited to flat rectangles. They've gone beyond the box to become panoramic views, 360-degree images, and immersive photo spheres. These image formats are made possible by a technology called image stitching.

▸ What is image stitching? **Image stitching** (or photo stitching) creates a panoramic image by combining two or more separate photographs that have overlapping edges. The photos are captured from a fixed location. The photographer stands in one place and may rotate, but cannot step forward, back, or to the sides.

▸ What kinds of images does stitching produce? Stitching uses photos in standard bitmap formats, such as JPEG and PNG. The stitching process is based on sophisticated algorithms that match pixels near the edges of each image to determine how they fit together. Stitching connects the photos and produces various kinds of images called projections (Figure 1-33) that can be viewed on flat screens or with VR headsets.

QuickCheck

Image stitching knits photos into panoramic, cylindrical, and spherical images, but what technique is used to insert parts of one image into another image?

a. Cloning

b. Inpainting

c. Compression

d. Compositing

Figure 1-33: Image stitching

Rectilinear projections are viewed in a two-dimensional plane, typically as a long horizontal photo. These images can be produced using the panoramic feature of a digital camera.

Cylindrical projections produce a 360-degree image similar to the view from a merry-go-round. Images are captured from the front, back, and sides, and then stitched together.

Spherical projections include images from the 360-degree vertical view as well as the 360-degree horizontal panorama.

▸ Are special software and equipment required to capture photos for stitched images? A series of photos can be manually stitched together using software such as Autopano, PTGui, and AutoStitch, but many digital cameras take care of stitching automatically. Most smartphones include a camera app with a panoramic function for capturing a rectilinear projection. Panoramic functions are also available on most standalone digital cameras.

For producing 360-degree cylindrical projections with a smartphone, a third-party app might be required. Apps, such as Google Street View and Photo Sphere, guide photographers through the rotational process to capture a 360-degree view, which is then stitched together into a continuous image.

Special cameras are also available for capturing and stitching photos for cylindrical and spherical projections. These cameras typically use a fish-eye lens to capture a half-sphere (think of an upside-down cereal bowl) of images. Two of these fish-eye lenses can be linked to capture a full sphere of images.

Stereoscopy

Cylindrical and spherical projections can give viewers the sense of being immersed in a scene, but elements within the image remain flat and two-dimensional. Computer graphics technology can produce images with the illusion of depth that make some objects seem close enough to touch. These images are sometimes referred to as 3D, but technically they are stereoscopic.

▸ What is stereoscopic imaging? **Stereoscopic imaging** (or stereoscopy) is a graphical technique used to produce an illusion of spatial depth from flat, two-dimensional images. The technique dates back to the 1800s and the use of simple stereoscopes (Figure 1-34).

Figure 1-34: Stereoscopic imaging

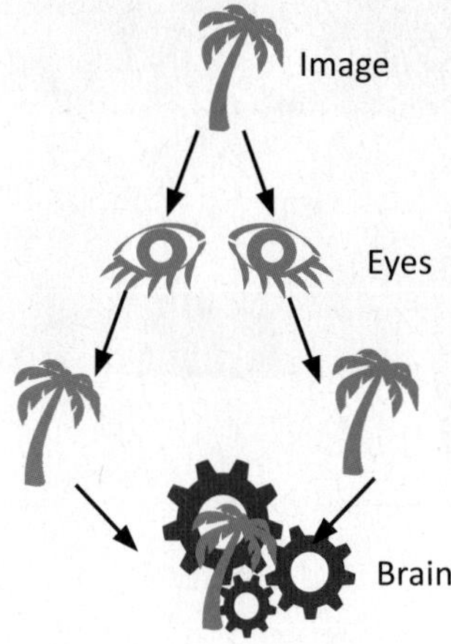

Because human eyes are spaced apart, they project two slightly different images onto the retinas. Those images are processed by the brain, which constructs an image of the world that corresponds to a three-dimensional environment with spatial depth.

Most cameras capture a photo using only one lens, so the image does not convey spatial depth. Two cameras, or a camera with two front-facing lenses, can produce two photos called a **stereo pair** that mimic the dual images captured by human eyes. Two images from a stereo pair displayed side by side are called a **stereogram**.

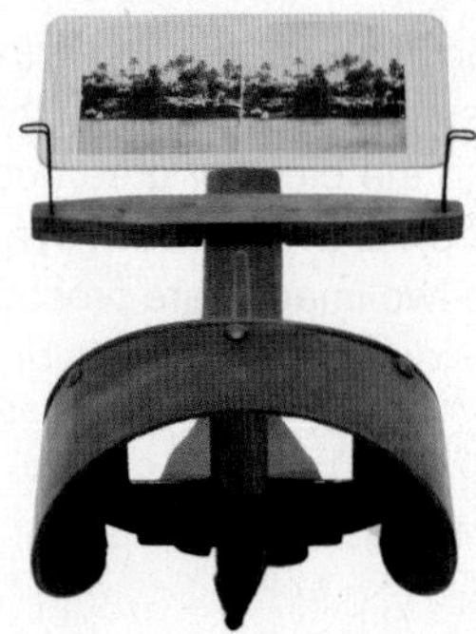

Simply looking at two similar photographs does not produce a 3D experience. Each image must be viewed with only one eye. A stereoscopic viewer, or stereoscope, provides this differentiation using lenses. Old-fashioned stereoscopic viewers placed images 5–11" away from the eyes and required a partition between the lenses to separate overlapping views.

▶ What's the modern version of stereoscopic imaging? Modern stereoscopic imaging uses digital images and viewers. Apps for capturing a stereo pair with a single lens camera are available, but somewhat tricky to use. As more cell phones sport dual front-facing cameras, creating stereo pairs becomes easier.

Some virtual reality headsets display images generated by mobile devices. A smartphone simply slides into the device where an app displays a digital stereogram (Figure 1-35).

QuickCheck

Name two techniques for creating stereoscopic images.

a. Anaglyphs and stereograms

b. Compositing and overlays

c. Blue and red

d. Steganography and depthing

Figure 1-35: Digital stereoscopy

VR headset stereoscope

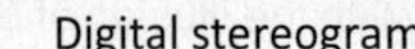

Digital stereogram

▶ What about those red and blue stereo glasses? An **anaglyph** is a graphic composed of two images, one that is tinted red and the other that is tinted blue. The two images are printed on top of each other to produce a stereoscopic effect (Figure 1-36).

Viewing anaglyph images requires red-green or red-blue glasses. Usually, the red lens on the left filters out blue and green, while the blue- or green-colored lens on the right filters out red. As a result each eye sees a slightly different image. The two images are processed in the brain to give the impression of three dimensions.

Figure 1-36: Anaglyphic image

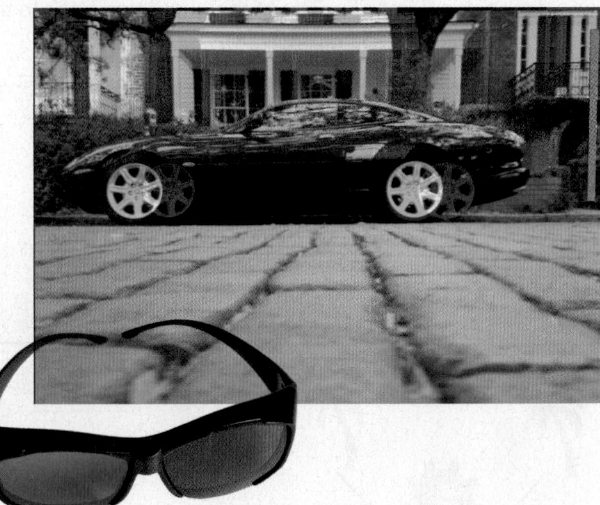

QuickQuiz

Section C

1. A digital camera captures images on the photosites of a(n) ______. (Hint: Use the acronym.)
2. A characteristic of bitmap graphics is that they are resolution ______, so that reducing the resolution also reduces the image quality.
3. Graphics stored in True Color format require ______ bits for each pixel.
4. Two images from a stereo pair displayed side by side are called a(n) ______.
5. The most popular True Color formats for Web graphics include ______ and JPEG. (Hint: Use the acronym.)

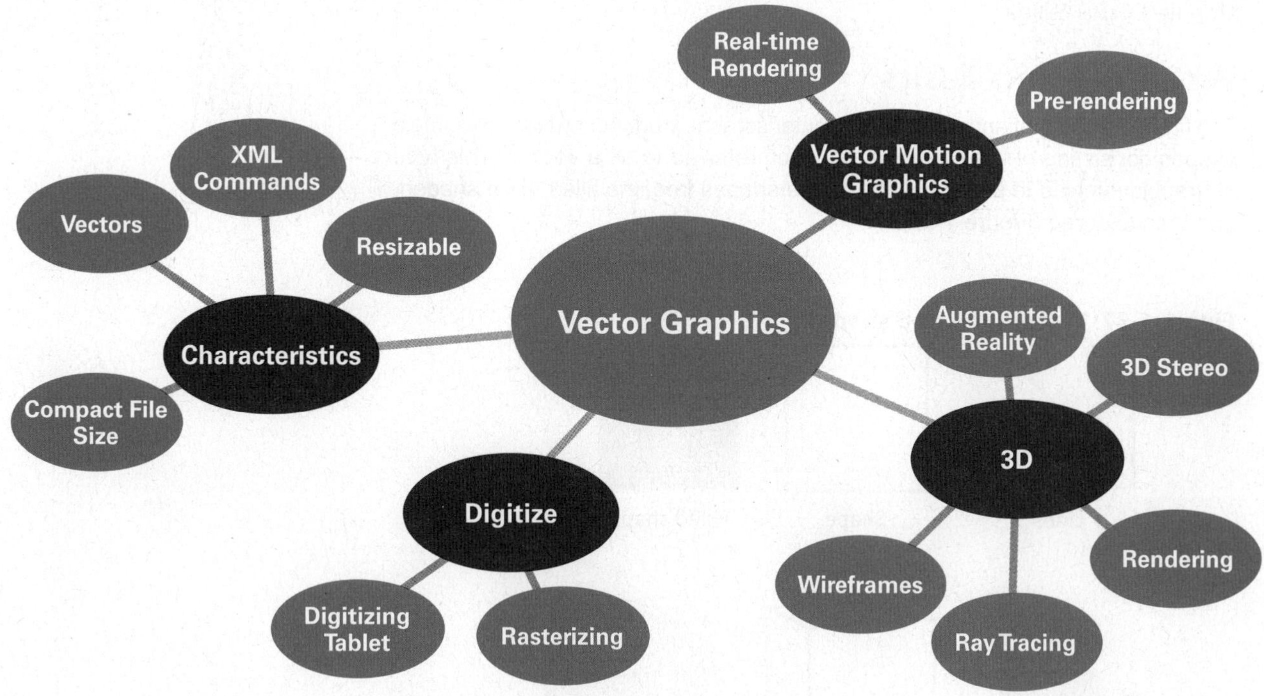

Section D

Vector Graphics

Objectives

- Identify vector graphics used on Web sites and social media.
- Based on the characteristics of vector graphics, determine when they are more suitable for a project than bitmaps.
- Draw simple vector shapes and outlines using drawing software.
- Convert a vector drawing into a bitmap.
- Explain the process of rendering a 3D wireframe into an image.
- Explain the process of animating vector graphics.
- Differentiate the roles CGI and VFX play in today's blockbuster films.
- Identify the key difference between rendering 3D graphics for computer games and creating special effects for movies.

If you've played any computer games recently or watched an animated movie, you've seen computer-generated graphics. This section begins with two-dimensional vector graphics. You'll find out how they differ from bitmaps and why you might want to use them. After covering the basics for two-dimensional graphics, the section progresses to static 3D graphics and concludes with a look at vector motion graphics for virtual reality videogames and instructional modules.

Terminology

vector
vector graphic
SVG
rasterization
3D graphics
wireframe
rendering
ray tracing
vector animation
frame
keyframe
pre-rendering
CGI
VFX
real-time rendering
game engine

Vector Graphics Basics

The first graphics that appeared on computer screens were not photos, but simple shapes consisting of lines and curves, each referred to as a **vector**. This type of graphic evolved in sophistication as the shapes became filled, then shaded, and then textured (Figure 1-37).

Figure 1-37: Vector lines and shapes

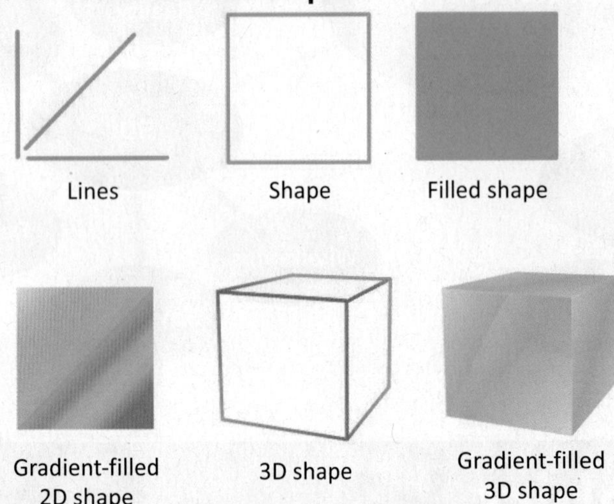

What is a vector graphic? A **vector graphic** consists of a set of instructions for creating a picture. Instead of storing the color value for each pixel, a vector graphics file contains instructions that a computer uses to create the shape, size, position, and color for each object in an image.

Vector drawing instructions are similar to those a drafting teacher might give students: "Draw a line of width 3 beginning at coordinates 20, 20 and extend the line to coordinates 20, 60. Color the line with #00BF00 (green)."

The command in "computerese" using an XML script would be:

```
<line x1 = "20" y1 = "20" x2 = "20" y2 = "60" stroke
= "#00BF00" stroke-width = "3"/>
```

Vector graphics include standard shapes such as circles and rectangles, so they don't have to be built from scratch. The green square in Figure 1-37 was created by specifying a rectangle beginning at coordinates 100,100 with a width of 400 and a height of 400, filled with #00BF00, like this:

```
<rect x = "100" y = "100" width = "400" height
= "400" fill = "#00BF00"/>
```

QuickCheck

Vector commands in the example at left are written using ________.

a. Flash

b. Basic

c. #00BF00

d. XML scripts

QuickCheck

What kind of shape would the following vector command create?

```
<circle cx = "100" cy = "100" r = "80" fill = "#FFFFFF" stroke =
"#00BF00" stroke-width = "10"/>
```

a. A green circle that's 100 wide with a black border

b. A white circle that has a radius of 80 and a green border

c. A white circle located at 100, 100 that has a black border

d. A green circle located at 100, 80 with a white border

1

How do vector graphics compare with bitmap images? Because vector graphics are based on commands, they have different characteristics than bitmap images, which are stored as a collection of colored pixels. The differences between the two are important when considering which is best for specific projects.

Vector graphics resize better than bitmaps. When you change the size of a vector graphic, the objects change proportionally and maintain their smooth edges. In contrast, bitmap graphics might appear to have jagged edges after they are enlarged, as shown in Figure 1-38.

Figure 1-38: Vector images do not pixelate when enlarged

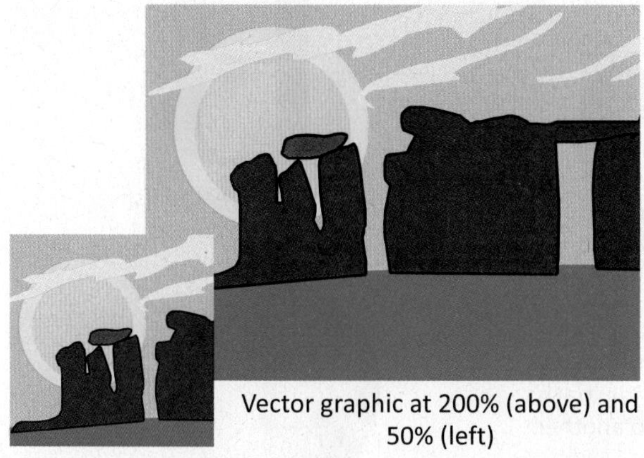

Vector graphic at 200% (above) and 50% (left)

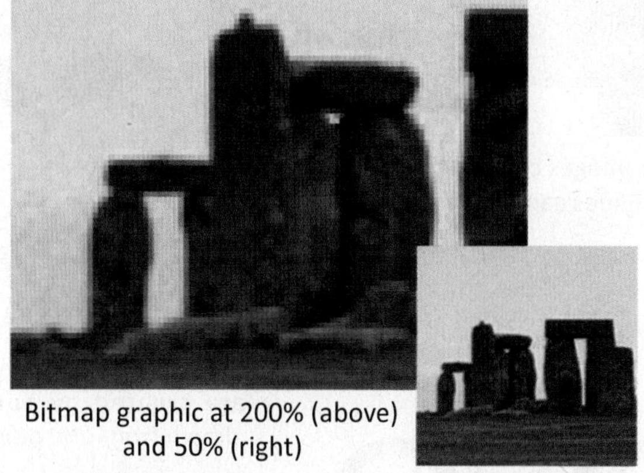

Bitmap graphic at 200% (above) and 50% (right)

Vector graphics usually require less storage space than bitmaps. The storage space required for a vector graphic reflects the complexity of the image. Each instruction requires storage space; the more lines, shapes, and fill patterns in the graphic, the more storage space it requires. The Stonehenge vector graphic used as an example in this module requires less than 4 KB of storage space. A True Color photograph of the same image requires 1,109 KB.

Vector graphics have a different visual quality than bitmap images. Many 2D vector images have a flat, cartoon-like appearance instead of the realistic appearance you expect from a photograph. This cartoon-like characteristic of vector images results from the use of objects filled with blocks of color.

It is easier to edit an object in a vector graphic than an object in a bitmap graphic. A vector graphic is like a collage of objects that can be layered over each other, but moved and edited independently. Figure 1-39 illustrates the difference between vector and bitmap graphics when you try to edit out parts of the Stonehenge image.

Figure 1-39: Vector objects are layered

Stones in this vector image are in a separate layer that can easily be removed.

A bitmap graphic is not layered, so without an inpainting algorithm, removing the stones leaves a hole.

Where are vector graphics used? Vector graphics are suitable for most line art, logos, simple illustrations, infographic elements, and diagrams that might be displayed and printed at various sizes. Vector graphics can include text, which is easily editable and scalable. Most modern fonts are created from vectors because they can scale smoothly to large sizes. Font effects for WordArt are based on vectors. Vector graphics are also used for floor plans, engineering diagrams, and spreadsheet charts because they are constructed from simple lines and shapes (Figure 1-40).

Figure 1-40: Vector images

Vector images created by combining shapes can look primitive.

More sophisticated vector images are created by outlining paths drawn from one point to another.

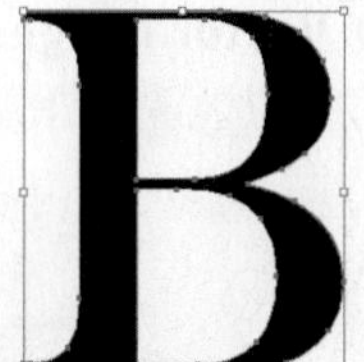

Fonts are also created using outlines and curves.

Gradients can be added to vector objects to create the illusion of three dimensions.

Combining circles and other simple shapes with outlined shapes produces clip art images.

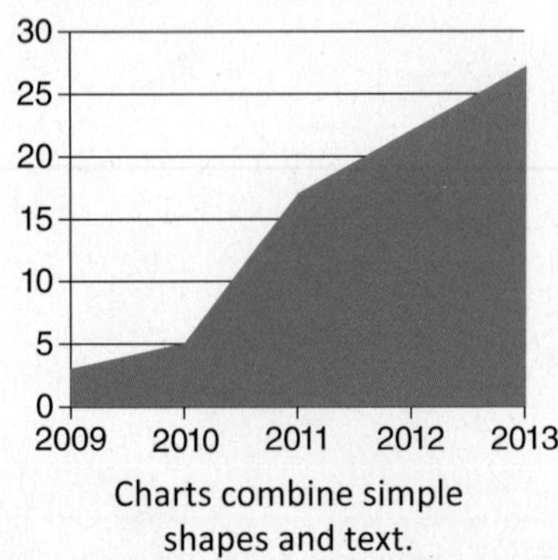

Charts combine simple shapes and text.

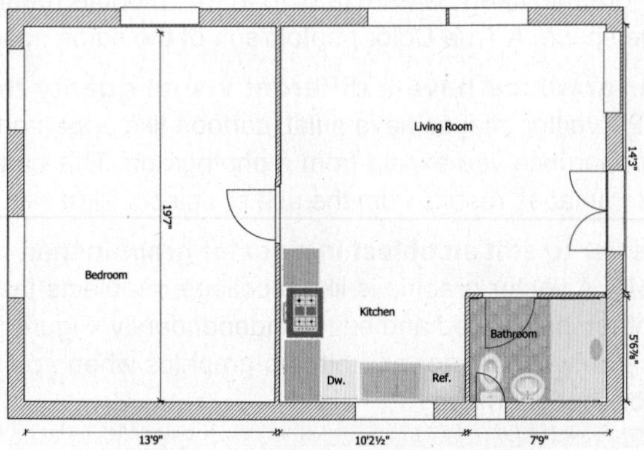

Floor plans merge shapes and text.

How can I identify vector graphics? It can be tricky to accurately identify a vector graphic just by looking at an on-screen image. Some have a flat, cartoon-like quality, but others can look fairly realistic. Also remember that not all bitmap graphics are photos. Bitmaps are used for on-screen icons, and a bitmap could consist of simple blocks of color that look like vector shapes.

For a more definitive identification, check the file type or extension. Vector graphics files have file extensions such as .wmf, .ai, .dxf, .eps, .swf, and .svg. **SVG** (scalable vector graphics) stores the commands for vector images as XML text files. It is the most popular format for Web-based vector graphics.

QuickCheck

Which format tends to require the least storage space?

a. Bitmap

b. Vector

c. Compressed bitmap

d. MIDI

Vector Tools

Neither scanners nor digital cameras produce vector graphics. Architects and engineers might use a digitizing tablet to turn a paper-based line drawing into a vector graphic. A digitizing tablet (sometimes called a 2D digitizer) is a device that provides a flat surface for a paper-based drawing and a pen or mouse-like puck that you can use to click the endpoints of each line on the drawing. The endpoints are converted into vectors and stored.

▶ What tools do I need to create vector graphics? Vector graphics are created from scratch with vector graphics software, referred to as drawing software. Popular drawing software includes Adobe Illustrator, LibreOffice Draw, and open source Inkscape. There are also numerous online vector drawing apps; just search for "vector drawing."

Vector graphics software provides an array of drawing tools that you can use to create objects, position them, and fill them with colors, gradients, or patterns. The software converts the items you draw into instructions that are stored, which can be later used to re-create your drawing. Figure 1-41 illustrates how to use drawing tools to create a vector graphic.

QuickCheck

Which of the following input devices is used to create vector images?

a. Camera

b. Scanner

c. Digitizing tablet

d. Gradients

1

Figure 1-41: Drawing vector shapes

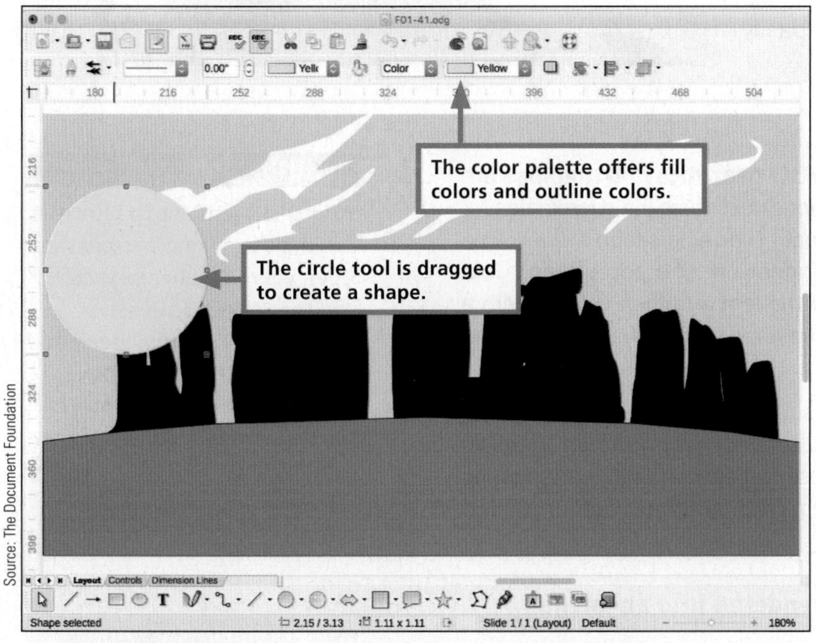

The color palette offers fill colors and outline colors.
The circle tool is dragged to create a shape.

Source: The Document Foundation

The clouds are created as a series of short line segments and filled with color.
The stones are created as a series of short line segments and filled with black.
The sun is two circles, each filled with a slightly different shade of yellow.

Try It!

You can find drawing tools such as Vectr and Draw SVG online, or use Adobe Illustrator if it is installed on your computer. Try drawing the sky, sun, clouds, and grass from the Stonehenge image in Figure 1-41. Save your work to use for another Try It! later in the module.

▶ Is it possible to convert a vector graphic into a bitmap? A vector graphic can be converted quite easily into a bitmap graphic through a process called rasterizing. **Rasterization** works by superimposing a grid over a vector image and determining the color for each pixel. This process can be carried out by graphics software, which allows you to specify the output size for the final bitmap image.

On a PC, you can rasterize a vector graphic by using the Print Screen (PrtSc) key to take a screenshot of a vector image. On a Mac, the Command-Shift-3 key combination takes a screenshot. It is important to rasterize images at the size you ultimately need. If you rasterize a vector image at a small size and then try to enlarge the resulting bitmap image, you will likely get a poor-quality pixelated image, such as the one in Figure 1-42.

Figure 1-42: Enlarged rasterized vector

After a vector graphic is converted to a bitmap, the resulting graphic no longer has the qualities of a vector graphic. For example, if you convert the Stonehenge vector graphic into a bitmap, the sun is no longer an object that you can easily move or assign a different color.

3D Graphics

▶ How do vector graphics relate to 3D graphics? **3D graphics** are based on vectors stored as a set of instructions describing the coordinates for lines and shapes in a three-dimensional space. The vectors form a **wireframe** that acts in much the same way as the framework of a pop-up tent. Just as you would construct the framework for the tent and then cover it with a nylon tent cover, a 3D wireframe can be covered with surface texture and color to create a graphic of a 3D object.

The process of covering a wireframe with surface color and texture is called **rendering**. The rendering process requires a computer to perform intensive calculations to determine the surface dimensions between vectors. Rendering outputs a bitmap image that can be displayed on the screen or printed (Figure 1-43).

Figure 1-43: 3D wireframe partially rendered into an image

Try It!

Turning a vector into a bitmap is as simple as taking a screenshot. Open your Stonehenge vector and then take a screenshot (PrtSc on a PC; Command-Shift-3 on a Mac). Next, try to move the sun on the screenshot. That simple task now requires digital compositing tools!

QuickCheck

Rasterization and rendering both produce a ___________.

a. bitmap

b. vector

c. 3D graphic

d. wireframe

For added realism, the rendering process can take into account the way that light shines on surfaces and creates shadows. The technique for adding light and shadows to a 3D image is called **ray tracing**.

Before an image is rendered, the artist selects a location for one or more light sources. The computer applies a complex mathematical algorithm to determine how the light source affects the color of each pixel in the final rendered image. Figure 1-44 shows the image from the previous figure rendered with an additional light source and ray tracing.

Figure 1-44: Ray tracing adds highlights and shadows

Software for creating 3D graphics includes Autodesk AutoCAD, open source Blender, and Trimble SketchUp. This software provides tools for drawing a wireframe and rotating it to any angle. It provides rendering and ray tracing tools, along with an assortment of surface textures that can be applied to individual objects.

▶ Can 3D images go stereo? A 3D vector image may have a three-dimensional appearance, but as a single image, it cannot convey visual depth. As with bitmap photos, 3D renderings require two images for a stereoscopic effect.

A 3D rendered image can be modified to create a second rendering slightly offset from the original. When viewed with a VR headset, the two images converge into one.

Anaglyph techniques can also be applied to rendered images by tinting one image red, tinting the other image blue, and then combining both images (Figure 1-45).

Figure 1-45: 3D anaglyphs

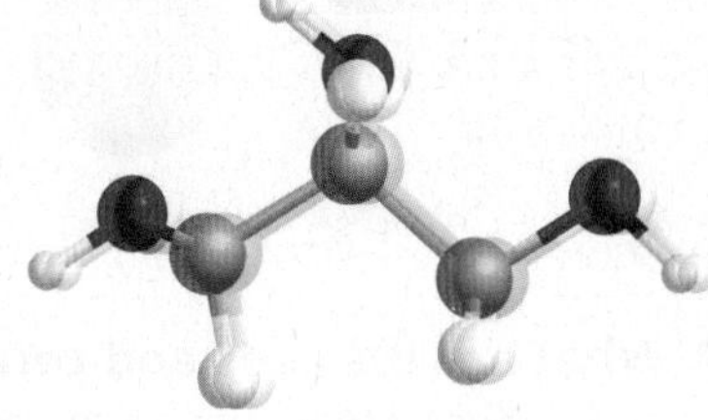

▶ What about augmented reality? Augmented reality adds computer-generated vector objects to a view of the real world. For example, in smartphone-based games such as Pokémon GO, game characters are computer-generated 3D graphics. A smartphone camera captures an image of the real world, and then a game character is rendered onto that image. The composite image is output to the smartphone screen (Figure 1-46).

Figure 1-46: Vectors augment reality

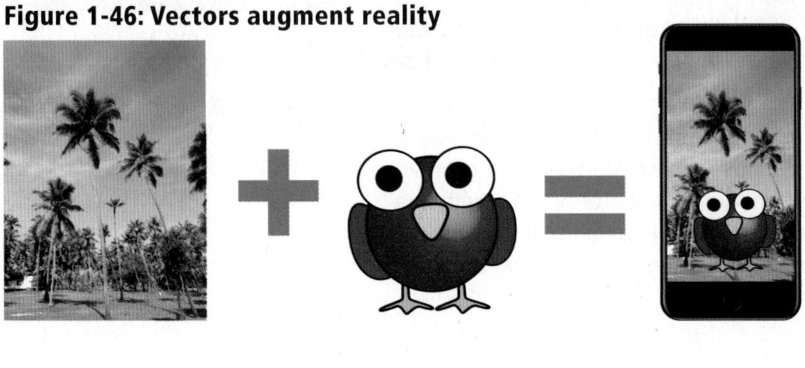

Animated Vector Graphics

From simplistic bouncing Web page icons to sophisticated interactive virtual reality, vector graphics can be set in motion. The key characteristic of vector graphics is that they are rendered from wireframes into solid objects. For animated sequences, the rendering process can occur ahead of time. Other applications, such as videogames and virtual reality, require rendering to occur in real time. Let's find out why this is the case.

How are vector animations created? A **vector animation** is a type of motion graphic in which a series of vector images is displayed sequentially to convey the illusion of movement. Each image is called a **frame**. The process of assembling frames for a vector animation is based on techniques pioneered for hand-drawn animations in classic cartoons.

In traditional hand-drawn animation, a chief artist draws each **keyframe** that marks the beginning and end points of action. For an animation of a bouncing ball, the first keyframe depicts the ball in its original position. A second keyframe shows the ball as it reaches the floor. Once keyframes are complete, a team of assistants creates a series of inbetween images—24 of these images for each second of animation.

For vector-based computer animation, the animation artist creates keyframes of vector objects. Graphics software creates inbetween images by moving the objects along paths specified by the artist. The software then renders each image to give it substance, color, and texture. After rendering, each frame has become a bitmap image. All the images are combined into a single file, creating essentially a digital movie (Figure 1-47).

Figure 1-47: Vector objects are animated and rendered into bitmaps

QuickCheck

How many keyframes are needed to create the bouncing ball animation shown at left?

a. 1

b. 2

c. 3

d. 6

What are the pros and cons of pre-rendering? The process of rendering vector-based frames and packaging them into a digital video file is called **pre-rendering**. The advantage of pre-rendering is that the time-consuming process of rendering and assembly can be done ahead of time using a computer with a fast processor. The resulting file can be distributed and viewed on less powerful devices, such as smartphones.

Pre-rendering is used to create special effect sequences for films, as well as full-length animated movies. In the film business, these pre-rendered clips are referred to as **CGI** (computer-generated imagery). Integrating CGI with live-action footage is called **VFX** (visual effects). Notable examples of VFX include the realistic but totally CG Thanos character in *Avengers: Infinity War* and all of the backgrounds and animals in *The Jungle Book*.

Try It!

Head over to YouTube and search for "The Jungle Book VFX Breakdown" and "Avengers: Infinity War VFX Breakdown" to see the way that incredible VFX footage was created for these films.

How do vector animations handle interaction? Pre-rendered files are not interactive. They play sequentially from beginning to end. Creating videogames and interactive educational modules that allow viewers to manipulate objects requires a different rendering technique.

Real-time rendering fills in wireframe objects and generates a bitmap image as the action unfolds. Rendering happens in real time as the computer turns the vector instructions into points of light on the screen.

For videogames, each frame is rendered while the game is played (Figure 1-48). When manipulating an instructional 3D model, rendering takes place as students point, click, and swipe displayed objects.

Figure 1-48: 3D real-time rendering

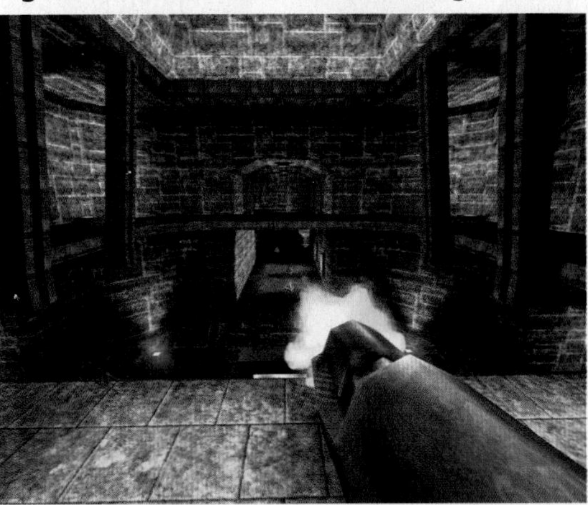

Source: OpenArena

1

Real-time rendering deals with an incredible number of bits. To give you a handle on the immensity of the processing power required to render the real-time images for computer games, consider a classic game like *Doom* that is displayed on a screen set at 1,600 x 900 resolution. At this resolution, the screen contains 1,440,000 pixels (1,600 multiplied by 900). If the game is presented in 24-bit color, each frame of the animation requires 34,560,000 bits.

To display 60 frames per second, the computer must handle 2,073,600,000 bits of data every second just to render the image frames. Additional data is processed to control character movement and game play.

How does real-time rendering relate to virtual reality? Most interactive virtual reality visuals are generated from 3D vector graphics and displayed on VR headsets. Stereoscopic rendering produces the sense that some objects are closer than others. Each object in a vector scene can have defined properties that allow it to be manipulated by players within a game engine.

What's a game engine? A **game engine** is graphics software that allows developers to create interactive videogames and educational modules. One of the most popular motion graphics tools is the Unity game engine. Introduced in 2005, its popularity continues to grow because it produces games and educational modules for multiple platforms, including mobile devices, Web browsers, and desktop computers. Additional tools include the Unreal Engine, developed by Epic Games for the Unreal action game, and Godot, a development environment for non-programmers.

Try It!

Can you find at least three popular games that were created using the Unity game engine?

QuickQuiz — Section D

1. Vector graphics require more storage space than bitmaps, but vectors can be enlarged without becoming pixelated. True or false? ______
2. A process called ______ converts vector graphics into bitmap images.
3. Based on XML, ______ is a popular format for vector graphics on the Web.
4. A 3D image is based on an assemblage of vectors called a(n) ______.
5. The technique of adding light and shadows to a 3D image is called ray ______.

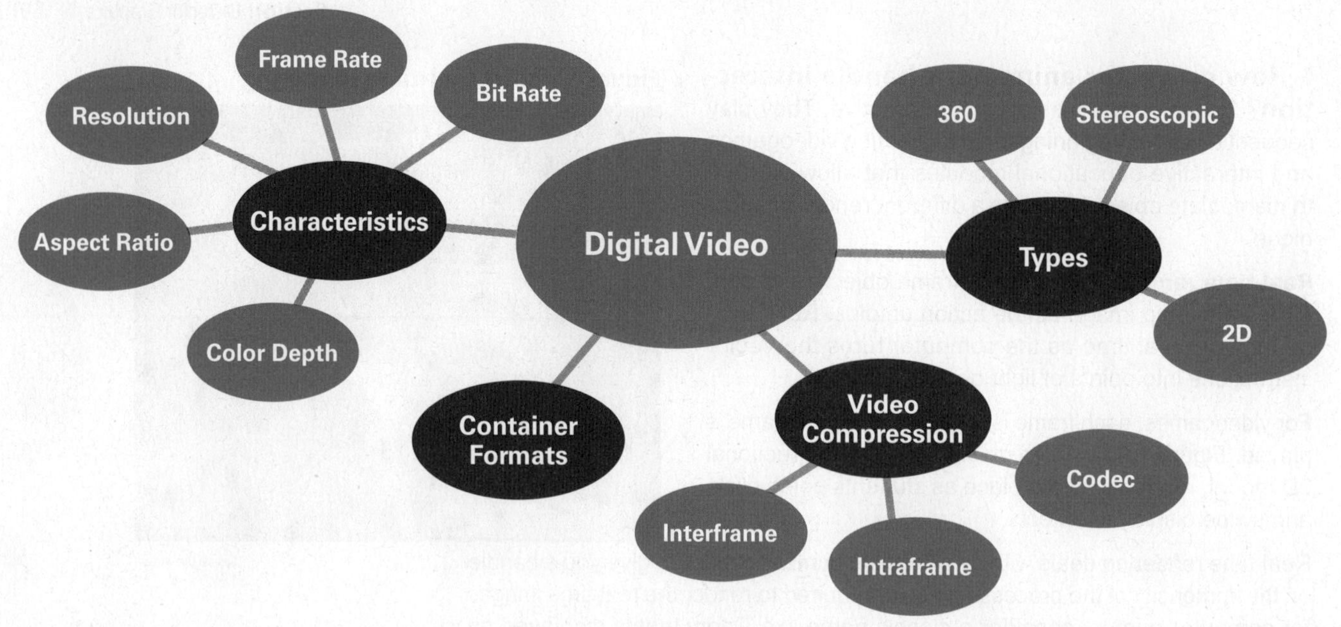

Section **E**

Digital Video

Objectives

- List devices and other sources that are commonly used to capture video footage.
- Describe the characteristics of five access options for digital video.
- List five factors that affect the size and quality of digital videos.
- Differentiate between interlaced and progressive scans.
- State the most commonly used aspect ratios on the following: iPhone screen, iPad screen, YouTube, and Windows laptop computer screen.
- Explain the purpose of a codec.
- Recognize digital video files by their file name extensions.
- List the video formats that are commonly used on the following: YouTube, iPhone, Android phone, television, and Web browsers.
- Explain the contents of a video container.
- List the variety of videos that originate as bitmap graphics.

Digital video is everywhere. It encompasses several technologies, including those that produce theater-quality movies, Snapchat shorts, and YouTube videos. In this section, you'll take a look at what you can do with affordable, easy-to-use video tools.

Terminology

digital video
frame rate
upconverting
progressive scan
interlaced scan
aspect ratio
bit rate
intraframe compression
interframe compression
compression ratio
codec
container formats
AVI
MOV
MPEG
WebM
ASF
VOB
Ogg Theora
transcoding

Digital Video Basics

A video is a series of still images projected at a rate fast enough to fool the human eye into perceiving continuous motion. Video technology for movies and television was exclusively analog until 1986, when Sony introduced a digital video format stored on videocassette tapes. In 1991, Apple introduced a digital video format for computers. Microsoft followed with a competing digital video format in 1992.

▸ What is digital video? **Digital video** is a type of motion graphics that uses bits to store color and brightness data for each video frame. The process is similar to storing the data for a series of bitmap images in which the color for each pixel is represented by a binary number.

▸ Where does digital video footage originate? Today, the most common source of digital video is smartphone cameras, but footage can be recorded with a webcam or camcorder, and it can be acquired from a DVD or a digital video recording device. Analog footage from Super 8 home movies, VHS videotapes, and other legacy sources can be digitized using video capture equipment.

Professional filmmakers in the motion picture industry use digital cinematography to capture moving images as bits, rather than on film. Digital video is a core technology for digital television, videoconferencing systems, and video messaging. Real-time video even allows people with hearing loss to use sign language over cell phones.

▸ What are the access options? YouTube, Snapchat, Instagram, Facebook, Comcast, Netflix, and Apple Music: the list of digital video suppliers goes on and on. These suppliers provide consumers with several options for accessing digital videos. Figure 1-49 explains these options.

QuickCheck

A digital video is essentially:

a. a series of bitmap images

b. a sequence of vector graphic frames

c. an on-demand pixel stream

d. an analog capture device

1

Figure 1-49: Accessing digital video

hugolacasse/Shutterstock.com

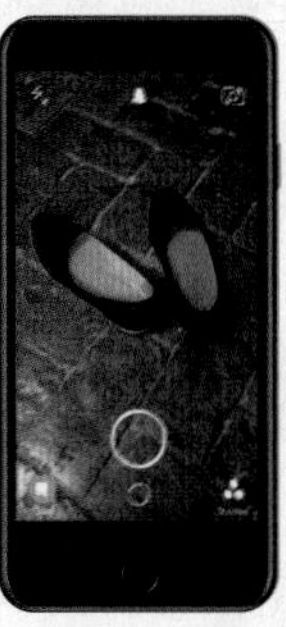

Broadcast	Download	On-Demand Stream	Short Live Stream	Real Live Stream
Pre-recorded	**Pre-recorded**	**Pre-recorded**	**Pre-recorded**	**Live, real-time**
Delivered at a set time; Internet not required	Obtained at any time; stored on consumer devices; Internet not required for viewing	Obtained at any time; not stored on consumer devices; requires Internet connection	Obtained only within a short time frame of recording; requires Internet connection	Delivered at a set time; requires Internet connection
Broadcast and cable television; movie theaters	Netflix movie download service	YouTube, Instagram, Facebook, Netflix, Amazon Prime Video	Snapchat	Periscope

What are the key properties of digital video? Most people can point a smartphone, shoot a few seconds of video, and upload it to YouTube, Facebook, or Snapchat. The quality of those videos, however, might be less than stellar. Achieving better quality and creating video for more widespread use requires a bit of background information.

The quality of digital video is based on several factors, including frame rate, resolution, color depth, bit depth, bit rate, compression technique, and file format.

What should I know about frame rate? Digital video displays bitmap images in rapid succession. Each bitmap image is referred to as a frame. The number of frames that are displayed per second is the **frame rate** (fps). Higher frame rates produce video that more smoothly simulates real motion. The standard frame rate for motion pictures was set in the 1930s before digital formats. Digital video can produce higher frame rates (Figure 1-50).

Figure 1-50: Video frame rates

6 Frame rate for the first 3D videogame

24 Standard frame rate for motion pictures

24 Standard frame rate for YouTube videos

48 Frame rate for *The Hobbit: An Unexpected Journey*

60 Frame rate for broadcast television

30–60 Acceptable frame rates for modern videogames

60 Maximum frame rate for YouTube videos

How does resolution affect video quality? Each frame is essentially a bitmap image with a resolution determined by the frame's width and height. A frame with 640 x 480 resolution contains 307,200 bits (multiply 640 by 480).

A video with a frame size of 640 x 480 will fill the screen of a device that has a similar screen size, mapping each pixel in the video frame to each pixel on the screen. Stretching the video to fit a larger screen requires pixel interpolation, which tends to reduce the quality of the image.

Modern projection devices and video playback software do an admirable job of **upconverting**, which is the digital video term for interpolation. As a rule, however, videos look sharpest when they are displayed at a resolution that is the same as the frame size.

QuickCheck

Suppose your computer screen has a resolution of 1920 x 1080, but you want to play a video with a resolution of 640 x 480. What happens?

a. The video won't play.

b. The video plays in a 640 x 480 window.

c. The video is upconverted to 640 x 480 resolution.

How is resolution expressed? Video resolutions can be expressed as width x height, as the horizontal resolution, or as the vertical resolution. Digital cinematography cameras capture video with a minimum resolution of 2048 x 1536. That resolution is also referred to as 2K because the horizontal resolution is about 2,000 pixels.

A resolution of 1920 x 1080 can also be expressed using its vertical resolution as 1080p. The "p" means **progressive scan**, in which the frame is drawn line by line in sequence from the top of the image to the bottom. An **interlaced scan** is a contrasting scanning technique that produces an image by drawing every other line, then going back and filling in the in-between lines. Digital video for computers typically uses progressive scanning, whereas digital television uses interlaced scanning (Figure 1-51).

Figure 1-51: Progressive or interlaced

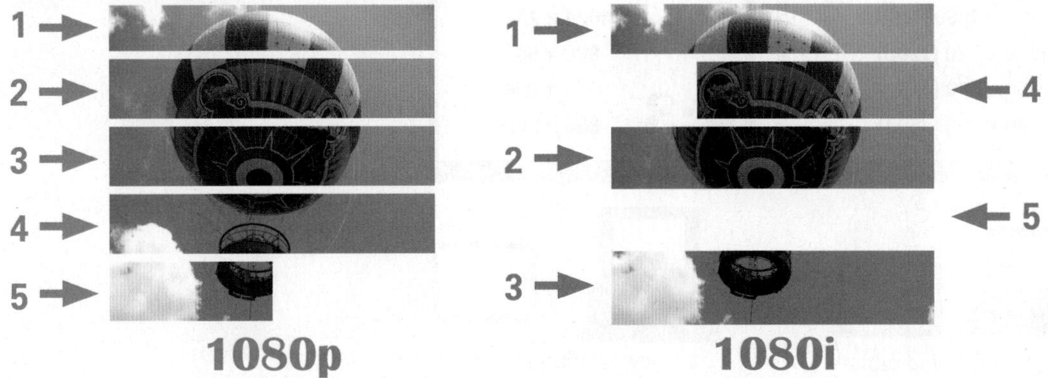

What about aspect ratio? Aspect ratio is the proportional relation between the width and height of an image or video frame. A 1:1 aspect ratio is a square. A 4:3 aspect ratio is slightly wider than high. Before widescreen cinema became popular in the 1960s, 4:3 was the standard aspect ratio for television and old movies. It was also the aspect ratio of early digital videos produced for 4:3 screens on the first generation of personal computers. iPads currently use the 4:3 aspect ratio.

Today's widescreen devices, such as laptops and smartphones, are designed for the 16:9 aspect ratio, which is recommended for most modern videos, including those uploaded to YouTube.

When 4:3 videos are displayed in a widescreen player, they are bordered by the black bars of a letterbox (Figure 1-52).

Figure 1-52: Letterboxes

The video on the left has a 16:9 aspect ratio that fits into the YouTube player window. The video on the right has a 4:3 aspect ratio. A letterbox creates black bars to fill the playback window.

How does resolution relate to aspect ratio? As long as the proportion of horizontal and vertical pixels remains the same, the aspect ratio is consistent. For example, a video frame with 1280 x 720 resolution has an aspect ratio of 16:9, as does a video with a resolution of 3840 x 2160. Both videos fit in a widescreen playback window, but the video with higher resolution offers a sharper, higher-quality image.

The math: Divide the horizontal by the vertical resolution. If the result is 1.7, then the aspect ratio is 16:9. If the result is 1.3, then the aspect ratio is 4:3. Try it yourself with the resolutions in Figure 1-53.

Figure 1-53: Aspect ratios for popular devices

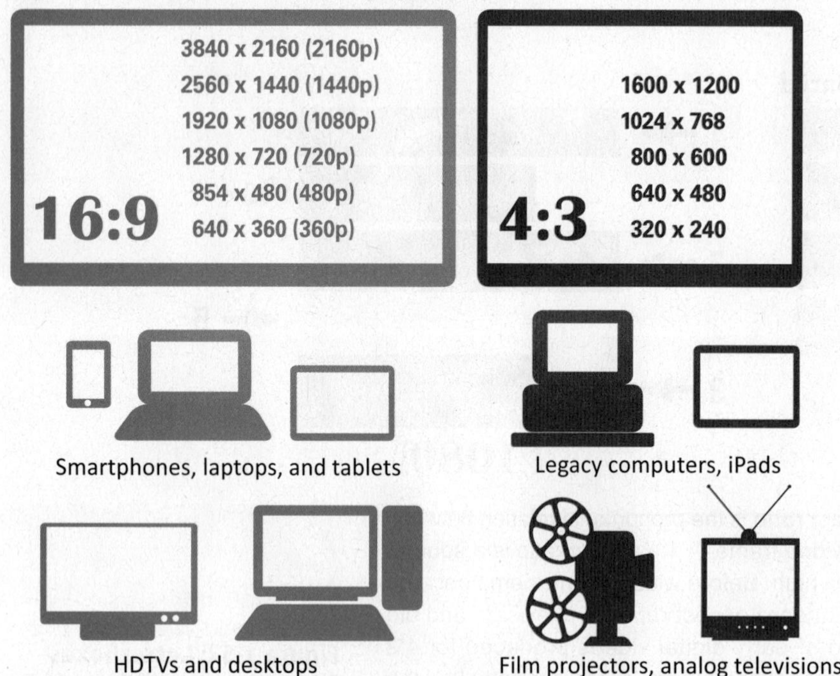

How does color depth affect video quality? Recall from earlier in the module that color depth refers to the number and variety of colors that can be used in an image. 24-bit color depth offers a palette of 16.7 million colors. A wide selection of colors produces realistic digital videos, but requires lots of space to store all the bits for every frame.

Let's use 1920 x 1080 as a typical resolution. The number of pixels in the frame is 2,073,600 (multiply 1920 x 1080). When each pixel requires 24 bits to define its color, 49,766,400 bits are required for the data in one frame.

Now take into consideration the video frame rate of 24 fps. How much data is required for one second of video? 1,194,393,600 bits! And for one minute of video? 71,663,616,000. That's more than 71 billion bits! You can see how the bits stack up for a two-hour movie by multiplying 71 billion by 120 minutes. A feature-length video requires an astounding 8,599,633,920,000 bits. Yes, more than eight trillion bits, or one trillion bytes.

QuickCheck

How big is the file that holds a two-hour noncompressed video?

a. 8 MB

b. 1 GB

c. 8 GB

d. 1 TB

Are digital devices powerful enough to handle all those bits? When working with digital video, you can't escape bit rates. You might have to specify a bit rate when you save a video, or when you convert a video from one format to another.

Bit rate is the number of bits that are processed during a specific unit of time, usually during one second. Bit rate can be expressed as bits per second (b/sec or bps), kilobits per second (Kbit/s or Kbps), and so on.

Bit rate becomes more important than file size for streaming video because it indicates how many bits must be transferred per second for the video to play smoothly without pausing to refill the buffer. To determine the bit rate for our 1920 x 1080 video, we have to find out how many bits are required for one second of video. We did that on the previous page, but here is the math:

1920 x 1080 x 24 x 24 = 1,194,393,600

resolution x color depth x fps = bits per second

1,194,393,600 bits per second would usually be expressed as 1.19 Gbps. That bit rate is far too high for today's network connections. A fast cable Internet connection maxes out at 50 Mbps, so it can handle megabytes of data each second, but not gigabytes of data.

The bit rate for this video must decrease or it will stutter and pause frequently as it is watched. To reduce the bit rate, digital videos can be compressed.

Video Compression

Okay, so video files are big. They can easily get too big to send as email attachments, post on Facebook, or stream without pauses. The size of a video file can be scaled down by reducing the resolution, specifying a destination, selecting a maximum file size, or choosing a bit rate (Figure 1-54).

Try It!

Open a video that you've captured with a smartphone, camera, or other source. Can you use compression and other techniques to whittle the video to a file that is less than 1 MB?

Figure 1-54: Making video files smaller and faster

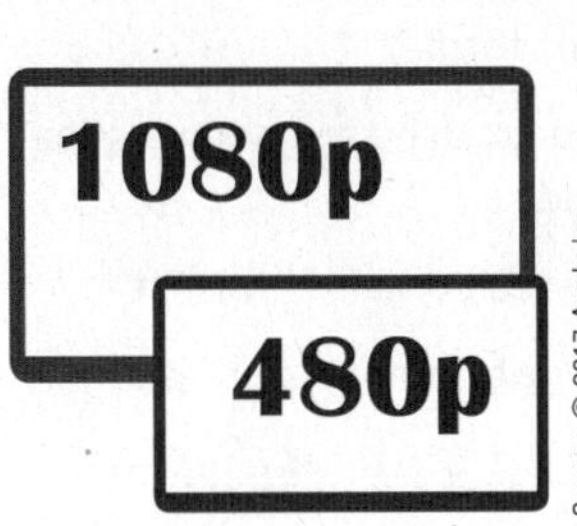

Reduce Resolution

Lower resolutions produce smaller file sizes and bit rates.

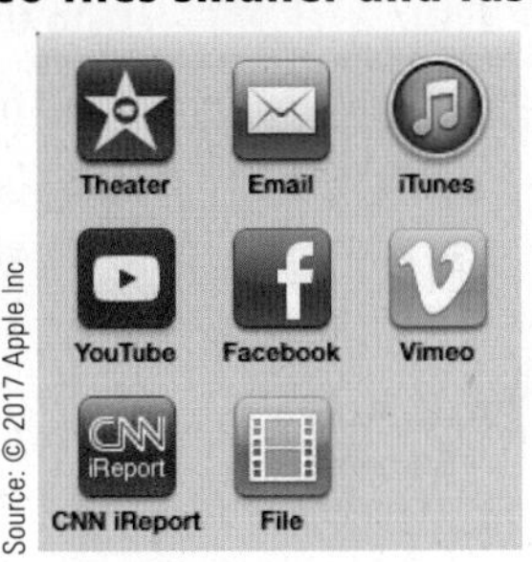

Specify Destination

Choosing a video service produces files sized appropriately for use.

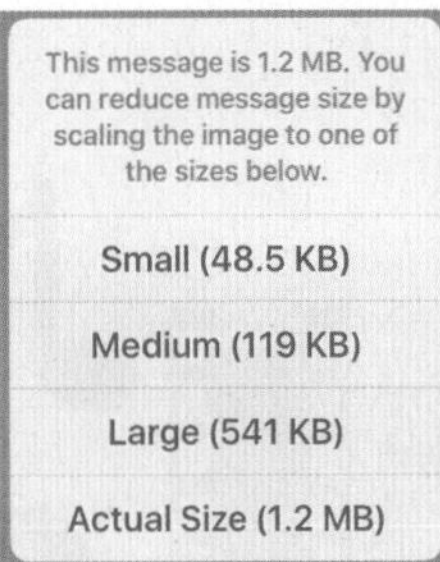

Select File Size

Smaller file sizes are achieved through compression that may reduce video quality.

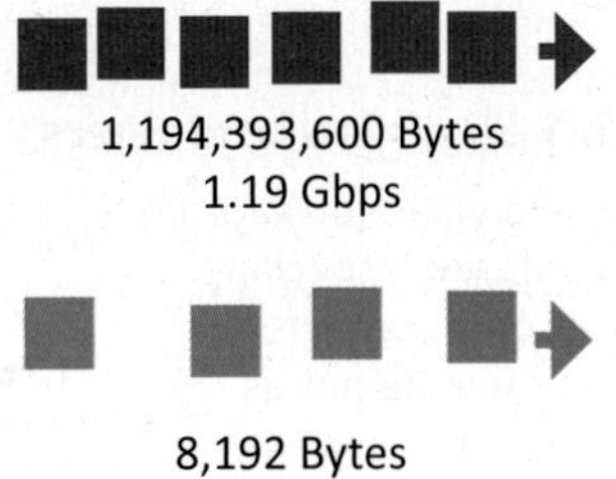

Choose Bit Rate

Compression can produce videos with lower bit rates that stream quickly, but quality might degrade.

How does video compression work? Compression removes some of the data from a video through techniques such as image compression and interframe compression.

Image compression. Earlier in the module, you found out how still images are compressed using lossy and lossless compression. This type of **intraframe compression** can be applied to each frame of a video. Suppose the data for each frame of a 1920 x 1080 video can be compressed by a factor of 10 from 49,766,400 bits to 50,000 bits. The resulting bit rate is 1.2 Mbps, which is suitable for most Internet connections.

Interframe compression. Two frames in a sequence often contain many similarly colored pixels, especially if the background remains unchanged. **Interframe compression** stores only the pixels that change color from one frame to the next. More sophisticated interframe compression uses motion compensation to track along with the camera, essentially following the camera movement to gain additional similarities between frames.

Video compression can be expressed as a **compression ratio**, which indicates the ratio of compressed data to noncompressed data. A video file with a high compression ratio, such as 35:1, has more compression, a smaller file size, and lower image quality than a file with a smaller compression ratio, such as 5:1.

QuickCheck

Which compression ratio produces the best-quality video?

a. 2:1

b. 5:1

c. 10:1

d. 35:1

Where does the compression come from? A **codec** (compressor/decompressor) is the software that compresses a video stream when a video is stored, and decompresses the file when the video is played.

Each codec uses a unique algorithm to shrink the size of a video file, so codecs are not interchangeable. A file compressed using one codec cannot be extracted and played using a different codec.

When creating videos, you should use one of the codecs included in popular video players. Popular codecs include MPEG, DivX, H.264, Theora, and Windows Media Video.

Video File Formats

Video files are stored in **container formats** that hold the compressed video stream and an audio stream. For example, the popular MP4 container format holds a video stream that was produced with the H.264 codec and an AAC audio stream (Figure 1-55).

QuickCheck

When people say they have H.264 video, they are referring to the:

a. file format

b. codec used to compress the video

c. video container format

d. video compression ratio

Figure 1-55: Video containers

Codecs and video formats are easily confused, especially because some containers have the same names as codecs. A codec, such as H.264, is software that compresses the video stream, whereas a container format, such as MP4, stores the video and audio streams.

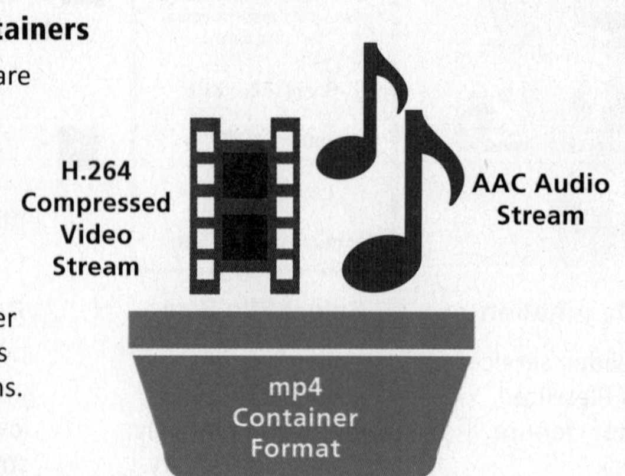

What are popular video container formats? Figure 1-56 describes some popular video container formats: **AVI**, **MOV**, **MPEG**, **WebM**, **ASF**, **VOB**, and **Ogg Theora**.

Figure 1-56: Video container formats

Format	Extension	Description and Use
MPEG (Moving Picture Experts Group)	.mpg, .mp4, .mpeg	Versions include MPEG-1, MPEG-2, and MPEG-4; used for downloaded and streaming Web video
WebM	.webm	Royalty-free, high-quality open format for use with HTML5
AVI (Audio Video Interleave)	.avi	A format sometimes used for storing digital clips from video cameras; used for legacy video on the PC platform
MOV (QuickTime Movie)	.mov	A legacy format for downloaded and streaming Web videos
ASF (Advanced Systems Format)	.asf, .wmv	Container format for Microsoft's Windows Media Video (WMV); supports downloads and streaming
VOB (Video Object)	.vob	Industry-standard format for standalone DVD players
Ogg Theora	.ogg	A non-proprietary container (Ogg) and video codec (Theora)

1

Can I change videos from one format to another? Digital videos can be converted from one file format to another through a process called **transcoding**. If you want to move a video into a different file format, you can check to see if your video editing software offers a conversion, export, or transcoding option. If not, you can find transcoding software on the Web. Transcoding can cause loss of quality, so avoid transcoding an already transcoded video file.

What tools are provided by video editing software? Basic video editing tools are used to arrange video clips, add a soundtrack, insert captions, select special effects such as fades between clips, and choose an output format (Figure 1-57).

Figure 1-57: Create a video

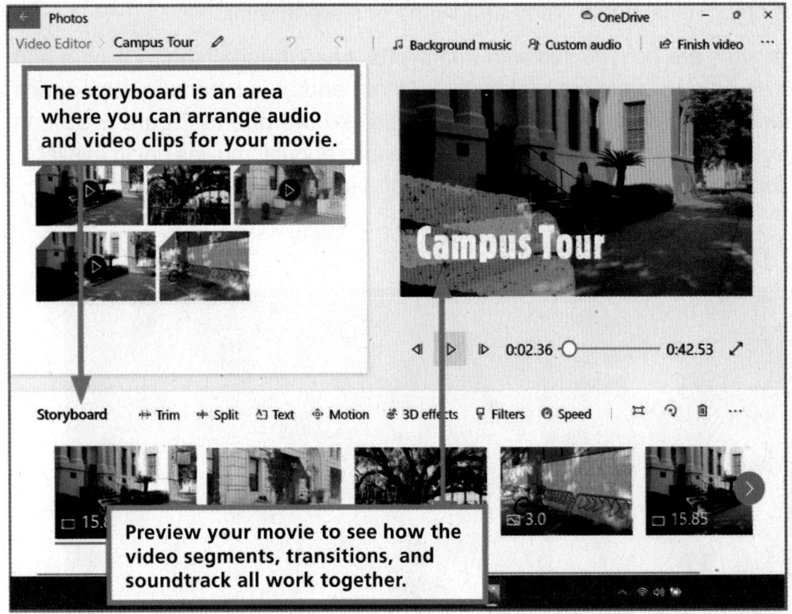

Try It!

Apply the skills you picked up from this module to combine video footage, music clips, narrations, and a still photo into a video that is about ten seconds in length. How can you share it with your classmates?

Digital Video Variations

Car chases, space battles, and marauding monsters can be exciting, but somehow a flat screen prevents viewers from making a closer connection to the action. Filmmakers, game developers, and educational technology specialists have a basket of techniques for going beyond 2D video to create immersive visuals. Technologies for 360-degree videos and stereoscopic movies are here today, along with tools aimed at consumers who want to experience, create, and share the adventure.

Try It!

You can view examples of 360-degree videos on Facebook and YouTube. When watching on a flat screen, try dragging the mouse or swiping to scroll the video around the fixed pivot point. You can also watch these videos with a VR headset, and as you rotate in place, the scene will shift.

▸ What is a 360-degree video? Movies are simply multiframe bitmaps that build on techniques used to create basic bitmap still images. Think back to the cylindrical projections of a 360-degree view or a spherical projection that can be constructed by stitching together a series of images filmed from a single pivot point. Those images were all stills—single frame photos.

Now imagine that instead of still frames, a photographer uses multiple video cameras to simultaneously film footage from all angles (Figure 1-58). A 360-degree video is a motion graphic that depicts continuous events happening within a 360-degree radius or sphere of a single pivot point.

Figure 1-58: A multi-camera rig to capture 360-degree videos

betto rodrigues/Shutterstock.com

▸ How about 3D movies? Movies that appear to have visual depth are commonly called "3D," but technically, they are stereoscopic. These movies create the illusion of visual depth using anaglyphs or stereograms.

When movies are constructed with anaglyphs, each frame contains a blue and red stereo pair. Viewers wear glasses with red and blue lenses to experience the effect of visual depth. Anaglyph movies like the one in Figure 1-59 can be projected on movie theater screens, but despite popular movies being available in this format, some moviegoers complain of headaches and eye strain.

Figure 1-59: Anaglyph movies

WARNER BROS / Ronald Grant Archive / Alamy Stock Photo

Can movies be created with stereograms? Displaying a pair of images side by side on a movie theater screen will not produce a stereoscopic experience. However, when projected in a VR headset, stereograms produce an amazingly realistic three-dimensional world.

Each frame of the video is divided vertically into two halves. The left half contains the image for the left eye. The right half contains the image for the right eye. When projected on the screens of a VR headset, these video frames produce the sensation of being within an unfolding three-dimensional movie (Figure 1-60).

Try It!

Enter your address in Google Maps, and then select Street View. Now that you understand graphics technology, how would you classify the type of graphics used for this app?

1

Figure 1-60: Stereographic video for VR headsets

Are stereoscopic movies virtual reality? Computer scientists define virtual reality as a computer-generated three-dimensional world that provides participants with seemingly real, direct, or physical interaction. Based on that definition, the underlying technology for virtual reality requires 3D motion vectors rendered in real time because the three-dimensional objects it produces can be moved and manipulated.

Today, however, the term *virtual reality* is applied to just about any motion graphics that are viewed through a VR headset, including vector-based pre-rendered animations, 360-degree videos, and stereoscopic movies. How this terminology sorts itself out in the future will depend on consumer awareness, marketing integrity, and technology development.

QuickQuiz Section E

1. The process of converting analog video signals into digital format is referred to as video ________.
2. A(n) ________ is the software that compresses a video stream when a video is stored, and decompresses the file when the video is played.
3. The "p" in 1080p stands for ________ scan.
4. MP4 is an example of a video ________ format.
5. Digital videos can be converted from one file format to another through a process called ________.

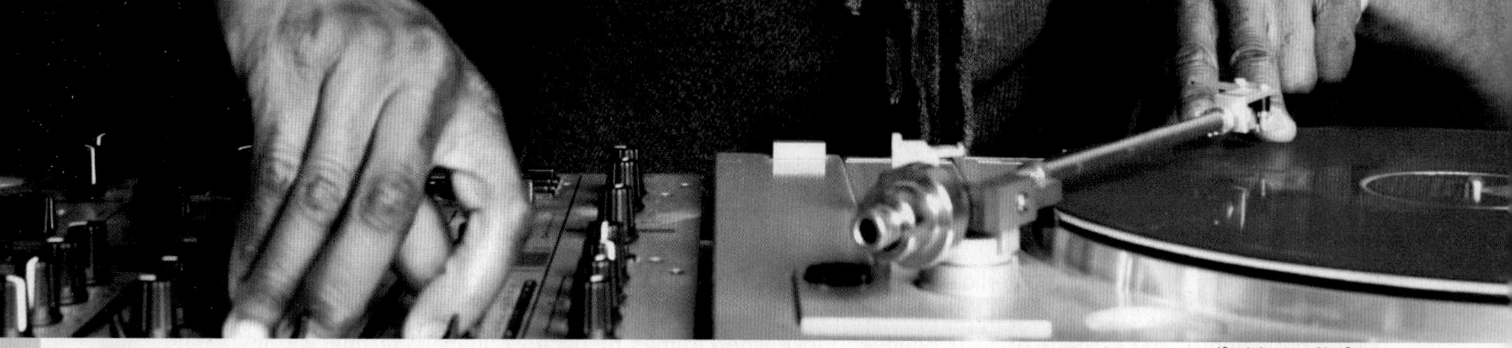

iStockphoto.com/Lise Gagne

Issue: What is Fair Use?

Fair use is the right to use portions of copyrighted material without the permission of the copyright holder for purposes such as review, criticism, or parody. Under certain circumstances, fair use is also a successful defense for practices such as time shifting, place shifting, and format shifting.

Exactly what constitutes fair use, however, is only sketched out in copyright law. The precise nature of fair use is shaped by court decisions covering situations and devices as diverse as vinyl records, printer toner cartridges, videotape recorders, and file sharing networks.

It seems incredible, but there once were no restrictions on copying sound recordings. "Record pirates" could legally copy and distribute, say, an Elvis Presley recording.

In 1971, the U.S. Congress passed the Sound Recording Act that prohibited copying music for commercial use. The law was not, however, aimed at prohibiting consumers from making copies for their own use.

"Specifically, it is not the intention of Congress to restrain the home recording, from broadcasts or from tapes or records, of recorded performances, where the home recording is for private use and with no purpose of reproducing or otherwise capitalizing commercially on it."

U.S. Judiciary Committee statement regarding the Sound Recording Act of 1971

Time shifting is the practice of recording music, videos, or other works for playback at another time. The legal precedent that gave consumers permission for time shifting was the landmark 1984 Betamax case in which Universal Studios attempted to hold Sony Corp. of America liable for copyright infringement by people who used video recorders to tape movies from their televisions. The U.S. Supreme Court sided with Sony and concluded that some instances of time shifting were legal.

The court's decision, however, was based on a definition of time shifting as "the practice of recording a program to view it once at a later time." Note the word *once*. The Betamax case did not offer legal precedent for copying and saving content for viewing multiple times.

The proliferation of computer networks and streaming media has made place shifting possible. Place shifting is the practice of transmitting a copy of a song or video to another device for playback. For example, you can view a cable television broadcast sent from your Wi-Fi equipped set-top box in your living room to your Wi-Fi equipped laptop out on the deck. Your network is transmitting a copy of the broadcast, a practice that is not explicitly allowed by copyright law in most countries. Therefore, unless a user agreement extends the basic rights granted by copyright law, place shifting would be considered a questionable practice.

So how about format shifting? Surely, it must be legal to rip tracks from a CD that you own and save them as an MP3 file that you can play on a digital device. Many consumers believe that they have a right to use a legally purchased song or video in any manner they please, short of redistributing it for profit.

Consumers are familiar with copyright restrictions on printed books and have an expectation that digital media can be legally used in parallel ways.

Readers expect to be able to carry a book with them to any location, read it at any time, use any type of reading light or reading glasses, loan the book to friends, and sell the book when they have finished using it.

Although it is convenient to focus on the "once I buy it, I can use it as I like" rationale, we tend to ignore situations in which our expectations about content use are more limited. For example, we do not expect that after attending a Justin Timberlake concert, we are entitled to a free MP3 of the performance. If we pay to see a movie at a theater, we don't then expect to download the movie or soundtrack for free when they are released.

Content suppliers, such as Apple Music and Netflix, allow their customers to stream music and videos to various devices. But even those services have restrictions. Savvy consumers always check the supplier's usage policy before subscribing to download and streaming services.

Try It! Do you know how to legally use music, movies, ebooks, and other media? Here's a chance for you to explore fair use and content usage policies.

1. Fair use is defined in Section 107 of U.S. copyright law. It includes four factors designed to determine whether a use is fair. Look up Section 107 of the U.S. Copyright Law. In your own words, what are those four factors?

2. The book *Grateful Dead: The Illustrated Trip* included concert posters and ticket images used without approval of the copyright holder. In a subsequent suit, courts decided the use was fair and transformative, based on a four-factor analysis. Look up the results of this case by searching for the article *Grateful Dead Posters' Re-publication Held to Be a Transformative, Fair Use* by Martine Courant Rife. In your own words, what did the court say about each of the four factors?

3. "Transformative use" means that you change a work enough to make it your own. Collages, music remixes, and video parodies can fall into this category. Find an example of a transformative work on YouTube and list the original works from which it is derived. In your opinion, what makes this a transformative work?

4. Digital content providers such as Netflix, Amazon, and YouTube each have their own rules about how you can use the content you purchase, rent, or subscribe to. To get an idea of a typical usage policy, search for *Amazon Prime Video Usage Rules*, and then answer the following questions:

    a. Are you allowed to stream more than one video at a time?

    b. Are you allowed to stream the same video to two devices at the same time?

    c. Are you allowed to stream videos to any digital device?

    d. Are you allowed to save rented content to a handheld device so that you can watch it after the viewing period has ended?

5. Because digital music is so accessible, it can be easily added to video footage as a soundtrack. Suppose you've purchased a Beyoncé song on iTunes. You want to use the song as a soundtrack for a video that you plan to post on YouTube. Would using the song in that situation be considered fair use? Would it be transformative? To find out, check YouTube's Web pages about using music in YouTube videos.

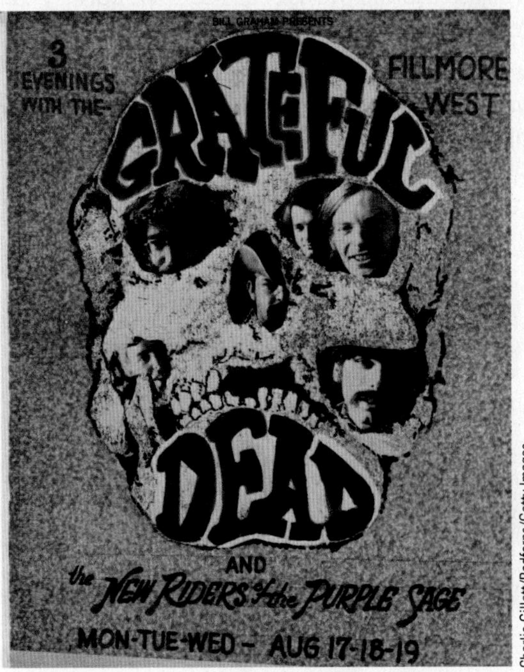

Charlie Gillett/Redferns/Getty Images

What Do You Think?

Issue

1. What would you change about the Fair Use Doctrine to make it more fair?
2. In your opinion, do services such as Amazon Prime Video provide consumers with enough flexibility for accessing content?
3. Have you heard of situations in which someone appeared to follow fair use guidelines, but was still charged with copyright infringement?

aaltair/Shutterstock.com

Information Tools: Photo Forensics

Digital tools make it easy to manipulate images. Many of the photos we see in magazines, in newspapers, and online have been adjusted to improve color and contrast. But they can also be altered in ways that are intended to deceive viewers.

Some images are obviously fake. Just about everyone is familiar with tabloid cover photos with a celebrity's head pasted onto another person's body, and cosmetic ads airbrushed beyond believability.

Krone

European Pressphoto Agency

A photo of a family in the war-torn city of Aleppo, Syria, was altered to make the background appear more dramatic. The altered photo is shown at left above.

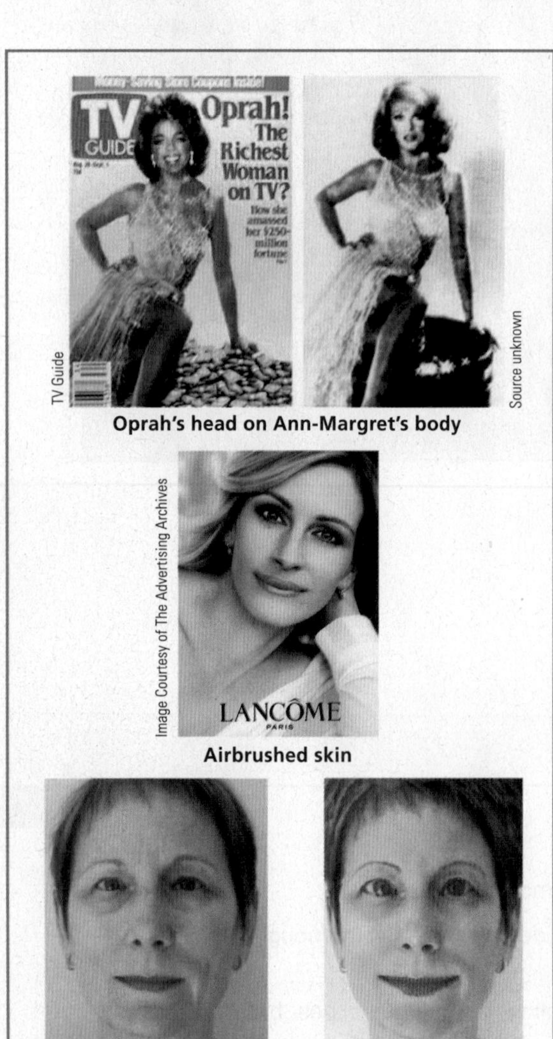

TV Guide

Source unknown

Oprah's head on Ann-Margret's body

Image Courtesy of The Advertising Archives

Airbrushed skin

Before

After

According to researchers, most people can identify clumsy photo fakes by looking for body parts that seem out of proportion and cloned areas that repeat themselves within the image.

Savvy consumers understand that the faces and bodies depicted in ads are not always realistic, but they have different expectations about photojournalism and the photos published about world events.

Photos in mainstream news outlets affect our views and opinions of real events. Yet photographs that record these events are sometimes manipulated to improve composition or convey a message.

Although detailed photographic analysis is beyond the ability of most readers, many photo fakes are eventually unmasked. Before you base opinions on a dramatic photo or use an image to substantiate your own research, check Internet resources to make sure the photo is not a known fake.

To spot a fake photo, look for:

- Body parts that seem out of proportion
- Remnants of body parts, scenery, or objects removed from a photo
- Areas of lighting that seem brighter or darker than they should be
- Light and shadow that are not consistent for all objects in the photo
- Parts of the background or crowd that seem to be cloned duplicates

Try It! "If you can change photographs, you can change history." That quote from Hany Farid, a computer scientist specializing in digital forensics, contains a warning about the perils of digital photo manipulation. Here's your chance to find out how to uncover photo forgeries.

1. Search for "photo tampering throughout history" to see some surprising examples about doctored photos, beginning with an iconic image of Abraham Lincoln. Look through the photo gallery and select the five photos you think are the most misleading, then explain why.

2. It is surprisingly easy to edit digital photos using today's sophisticated graphics software. To see how it works, check out the YouTube video "How to Remove Anything from a Photo on a Smartphone." Summarize the tools and processes used in the demonstration.

3. A Web site called TinEye bills itself as a reverse image search engine. Given any image, TinEye can find out where it came from and how it is being used. TinEye even finds modified versions of the image. Click the link for "How to use TinEye" and look at the examples to see the results that TinEye can produce. Then, upload an image of your own (or use an image that you select from the Web) to see what TinEye finds. Take a screenshot of your results. (Use the PrtSc or Print Screen key on a PC; use Command-Shift-3 on a Mac.)

4. Exif (Exchangeable image file format) data can reveal information that helps to verify or unveil a photo's origins. Specialized software is needed to view all the Exif data, but operating system utilities display some of the data. Select a photo stored in JPEG format and view its tags. On a PC, right-click the image, select Properties, then select the Details tab. On a Mac, click File, click Get Info, then expand the More Info section. Which of the following are revealed?

   a. Date taken
   b. Date modified
   c. Camera brand and model
   d. Photographer
   e. Place taken

5. When the eye cannot discern whether a photo is real or fake, photo detectives turn to computer science, mathematics, and physics to find answers. The same equations that are used to create light and shadows in 3D rendered images can also be used to analyze the shadows in a suspicious photograph. Dartmouth College researcher Hany Farid conducted an analysis of a suspicious shadow in a frame of the 1963 Zapruder film of President Kennedy's assassination. Locate his research paper. What did he conclude? Was the film a fake or real?

United Archives Gmbh/Alamy Stock Photo

Technology in Context: Film

In 1895, eager Parisians crowded into a busy cafe to watch the first public presentation of an exciting new invention—the Cinematograph. The 10-minute film, mostly scenes of everyday life, was a smashing success and ushered in the motion picture era. Early films were short, grainy, grayscale, and silent, but technology quickly improved. In the New York debut of *The Jazz Singer* (1927), Al Jolson spoke the first words in a feature film: "Wait a minute, wait a minute. You ain't heard nothin' yet!"

Even before "talkies" and Technicolor, filmmakers sought ways to escape the bounds of reality through special effects. As early as 1925, directors such as Willis O'Brien used stop-motion photography to animate dinosaurs, giant gorillas, and sword-wielding skeletons. Special-effects technologies—miniatures, blue screens, puppets, Claymation, 3D, and composite shots—were used with varying degrees of skill over the next 50 years. Films such as Stanley Kubrick's masterpiece, *2001: A Space Odyssey* (1968), and George Lucas's original *Star Wars* (1977) stretched these technologies to their limits, but audiences demanded even more spectacular, yet "realistic," effects.

In 1982, Disney released *TRON*, a movie about a programmer who becomes trapped in the depths of a computer where programs are human-like creatures that serve every whim of an evil Master Control Program. The movie included the first primitive attempts at computer-generated footage—30 minutes of computer-generated imagery (CGI) created by two Cray X-MP supercomputers.

CGI uses rendering techniques to create a 3D scene from a 2D image, a camera angle, and a light source. Sophisticated algorithms determine how textures, colors, and shadows appear in the rendered scene. Camera angles can be changed at will, and fantastic effects can be created by bending or stretching the image, manipulating light, creating textures, and adding movement to the scene.

Rendered scenes can be set in motion with computer animation techniques. Manual animation requires a painstaking process called inbetweening, in which an artist draws a series of incrementally different images to produce the illusion of movement. Computers can easily generate inbetween images and free up human animators for more challenging work.

A captivating animation special effect called morphing was first seen on the big screen in James Cameron's *The Abyss* (1989), and was later used in *Terminator 2* (1991) and other movies. Like inbetweening, morphing starts out with animators defining the morph's start and end points—for example, in *Terminator 2*, the liquid metal face of the T-1000 robot and actor Robert Patrick's face. The start and end points are rendered into digital images, and then the computer generates the inbetween images. Human animators tweak the images by inserting small discrepancies for a touch of less-than-perfect realism in the final footage.

Although the process might sound simple, morphing complex objects realistically and believably takes a tremendous amount of time and computer power. The five minutes of morphing sequences in *Terminator 2* took special-effects company Industrial Light & Magic a year to create.

© Disney/Pixar/Photofest

Memorable computer-generated scenes from classic blockbusters include the breathtaking aerial scenes in *Spiderman*, a furry blue monster called Sully careening downhill in *Monsters, Inc.*, the endless army of Uruk-hai marching down the valley toward Helm's Deep in *The Lord of the Rings: The Two Towers*, and Princess Merida unfurling her wildly curly locks in *Brave*.

Spiderman's acrobatic swing through Manhattan was generated with three professional rendering products: Maya, Houdini, and RenderMan. The Uruk-hai were created with MASSIVE, a custom program that gave each computer-generated warrior a unique sequence of actions. To individually animate each of Sully's 2,320,413 blue hairs, animators developed software called Fizt, a dynamic simulator.

Animation took another leap forward when Pixar's team of artists and engineers developed a computer program called Taz to realistically depict Princess Merida's flowing, curly hair.

Rendering, morphing, and other special effects require sophisticated computer systems. Pixar Animation Studios, the company that provided the technology behind *Toy Story*, *Up*, *Ratatouille*, *WALL-E*, and many other feature-length animated films, uses a cluster of computers called a renderfarm.

The film *Toy Story* took more than 800,000 computer hours to produce using the renderfarm. That might seem like a long time; but if Pixar animators had used a single-processor computer, it would have taken 43 years to finish the job!

Other CGI variations are being used for increasingly sophisticated effects. Special-effects guru John Gaeta developed "bullet time" and image-based rendering for *The Matrix* (1999). Bullet time produces reality-defying action sequences that slow time to a tantalizing crawl and then crank it back up to normal speed as the camera pivots rapidly around the scene. The effect requires a computer to meticulously trigger a circular array of more than 100 still cameras.

Films such as *Sky Captain and the World of Tomorrow* (2004) and *Sin City* (2005) took green screen special effects to a new level. Filmed entirely indoors on a sound stage, these movies used a technique called compositing that layers two or more video clips over each other and merges them into one image. Actors were filmed against a green background screen. During post-production, video editing software removed the background and layered in scenery created with CGI or from real footage on location.

Sin City is also notable as one of the first fully digital live-action motion pictures. It was filmed in full color with high-definition digital cameras. The footage was converted to black and white, and then color was reintroduced digitally with the use of a DLP Cinema projector.

Until 2013, movies were distributed on film, but Paramount Pictures led the switch to digital. Now studios deliver most films on hard drives or through an Internet download. For the dwindling number of theaters without digital projection equipment, digital footage can be output to film and reproduced using legacy techniques.

Motion capture suits were put to award-winning use for Peter Jackson's *The Lord of the Rings*. The actor who played Gollum was outfitted with sensors that tracked the position of his head, arms, and legs. The collected data was later used by animators to create the 3D animated Gollum seen on the screen. Motion capture was further refined for *Avatar*, which used digital technology to capture the actors' facial expressions.

Sophisticated animation and rendering techniques now come close to producing realistic human figures. Animations were once clearly two-dimensional and far from lifelike, but CGI renderings are becoming more difficult to distinguish from real actors.

What might happen in the future is the subject of *Simone* (2002), starring Al Pacino as a washed-up director who is given a hard disk containing code for a computer-generated movie star. Pacino uses her as the leading lady in a string of hits, all the while keeping her identity secret. According to reviewer Leigh Johnson, it becomes clear that Simone, a virtual computer-generated image, is more authentic than the people watching her. It is one of the film's main themes, expressed by Pacino's character: "Our ability to manufacture fraud now exceeds our ability to detect it."

The issues surrounding computer-generated actors are just emerging. Not only do they blur the line between reality and fiction, but they also raise puzzling questions for actors and their agents, directors, and programmers. It is possible to create CGI doubles for long-dead actors, such as Marilyn Monroe and James Dean, but who controls their use and profits from their work? Can aging actors sign contracts for use of their "young" CGI counterparts? Would it be legal and ethical for programmers to create and market virtual characters based on real actors or a compilation of the best traits of popular stars? As is often the case, new technologies present issues along with their benefits—issues you might want to consider the next time you watch a movie.

Flipped Class Projects

Critical Thinking

Copyright laws are changing as digital sound, image, and video technologies evolve and become easier to use. Although the courts seem to clearly hold that it is illegal to copy media for profit, they are not as clear about the acceptability of modifications. For example, video editing software makes it relatively simple for people to clip out parts of movies they find to be objectionable to themselves or their children. Should it be legal to do so for personal use? What if an organization wanted to rent out such edited copies? What if a specialized video player was set up so that it would edit and display the revised version on the fly? After you consider your own opinion, you might check the Web to see the latest information about this issue.

Group Project

Work with a group of four students to research three Web-based music download or streaming sites. Create one PowerPoint slide for each site. The slide should give a basic overview of the site, including its name, URL, music file format, price, pros, and cons. For the final slide in the presentation, create a table comparing the features and prices of each site.

Cyberclassroom

Each person on your team should email a photo in JPEG format to the other members of the group. The photo can be one you've taken or one you find on the Web. If you get your photo from the Web, make sure there are no restrictions on using it for a personal project, and note the Web site's URL so you have a record of your source. When you receive the photos from your teammates, be creative and use Photoshop or similar photo editing software to create a composite image that contains elements from all the photos. Submit your original photo and your composite photo to your instructor.

Multimedia Project

Use Windows Voice Recorder or similar software to record an original 15-second radio ad for your favorite music or video streaming service. Be sure to use an efficient sampling rate. Submit the text of your script along with the audio file containing your ad.

Resume Builder

Artists routinely create a portfolio containing examples of their best work. How can you apply the portfolio concept to your job search? Suppose you've decided to create a multimedia portfolio that showcases your talents. Describe what you'd like your portfolio to contain, indicating which of the items you currently have and which you'd like to create and add in the future. Also, describe the format for each item: photo, document, scan, audio, or video.

Globalization

The United States has been accused of exporting its culture and values through films and television. Sometimes referred to as "Coca-Colonization," the mass exportation of American culture is expected to increase as more and more people have access to the Internet. But is digital distribution a two-way street? What can you find out about the importation of cultures to the United States (or your country)? Incorporate your findings into a two-page paper. Make sure you cite specific examples and offer your ideas on how technology aids or discourages cross-cultural interchanges. Include a list of references on a third page.

Key Terms

3D graphics 56
AAC 32
AAX 32
alpha blending 48
anaglyph 50
analog data 19
analog-to-digital converter 30
ASCII 22
ASCII text 23
ASF 67
aspect ratio 63
audio compression 32
audio interface 33
AVI 67
binary 19
binary number system 21
bit 20
bit rate 65
bitmap graphic 39
BMP 41
byte 25
CCD 40
CGI 58
character data 22
clipping path 48
cloning 47
codec 66
color depth 42
compression ratio 66
computer graphics 39
container formats 66
copy protection 34
data 19
data compression 26
data representation 19
delimiter 24
digital audio 30
digital audio extraction 33
digital compositing 48
digital data 19
digital rights management 34
digital video 61
digital-to-analog converter 30
digitization 20
download 33
Extended ASCII 22
file 20
file format 20
file name extension 20
frame 58
frame rate 62
game engine 59
GIF 41
gigabit 26
gigabyte 26
image compression 44
image histogram 46
image resolution 43
image stitching 48
inpainting 47
interframe compression 66
interlaced scan 63
intraframe compression 66
JPEG 41
keyframe 58
kilobit 26
kilobyte 26
live stream 33
lossless compression 26
lossy compression 26
megabit 26
megabyte 26
MIDI 34
MIDI messages 34
motion graphics 39
MOV 67
MP3 32
MPEG 67
numeric data 21
OCR 25
Ogg Theora 67
Ogg Vorbis 32
on-demand stream 33
phoneme 36
photosites 40
pixel 39
pixel interpolation 43
pixelation 43
PNG 41
pre-rendering 58
progressive scan 63
rasterization 56
RAW 41
ray tracing 57
real-time rendering 59
rendering 56
resolution dependent 43
RGB color model 42
run-length encoding 44
sampling rate 31
scanner 40
speech recognition 36
speech synthesis 36
stereo pair 49
stereogram 49
stereoscopic imaging 49
still images 39
SVG 54
synthesized sound 34
text-to-speech software 36
TIFF 41
transcoding 67
True Color 42
Unicode 22
upconverting 62
UTF-8 22
vector 52
vector animation 58
vector graphic 52
VFX 58
VOB 67
WAV 32
WebM 67
wireframe 56
WMA 32

Interactive Summary

Section A: __________ data is processed, stored, and transmitted as a series of 1s and 0s. Each 1 or 0 is called a(n) __________. A series of eight 0s and 1s, called a(n) __________, represents one character—a letter, number, or punctuation mark. Data becomes __________ when it is presented in a format that people can understand and use. Digital signals are represented by two different __________, such as +5 volts and +.2 volts. Digital data can also take the form of light and dark spots etched onto the surface of a CD or the positive and negative orientation of __________ particles on the surface of a hard disk. __________ data consists of numbers that might be used in arithmetic operations. It can be represented digitally using the __________ number system. __________ data is composed of letters, symbols, and numerals that are not used in arithmetic operations. Computers represent this type of data using __________, Unicode, or UTF-8. Data is quantified using terms such as __________ or kibibyte (1024 bytes), and prefixes such as __________ or mebi (1,048,576), and giga or __________ (1,073,741,824). To reduce file size and transmission times, digital data can be compressed. __________ compression provides the means to compress data and reconstitute it into its original state. __________ compression throws away some of the original data during the compression process. Files created with a compression utility usually have __________ at the end of the file name and are represented with special icons. These files have to be __________ or unzipped before you can view the data they contain.

Section B: Music, voice, and sound effects can all be recorded and stored on a computer as __________ audio. To digitally record sound, __________ of the sound are collected at periodic intervals and stored as numeric data. High-quality sound is usually sampled at 44.1 __________, and each stereo sample requires 32 bits of storage space. To conserve space, radio-quality recordings of speaking voices are often recorded at lower sampling rates. Digital audio file formats include WAV, AAC, WMA, AAX, Ogg, and MP3. Most portable media players work with MP3 format or with the __________ format, used for streaming Apple Music. These media files can be acquired as a download, __________ stream, or on-demand stream. MIDI music is __________ sound that is artificially created. A series of MIDI __________ specify the pitch, volume, and duration of notes that sound like various musical instruments. MIDI files are typically much smaller than digital audio files for similar musical passages. However, MIDI music tends to lack the full resonance of symphony-quality sound that can be achieved with digital audio. Speech __________ is the process by which machines, such as computers, produce sound that resembles spoken words. Speech __________ refers to the ability of machines to "understand" spoken words.

Section C:

A bitmap graphic is composed of a grid of tiny rectangular cells called ________. The color of each cell is stored as a(n) ________ number. Popular bitmap graphics formats include BMP, TIFF, GIF, JPEG, RAW, and PNG. Both scanners and cameras produce images in bitmap format. Digital display devices represent colors using the ________ color model. Although colors are ultimately represented as bits when a graphic is stored or transmitted, color values can be specified in binary, ________, or decimal. Color ________ refers to the number of colors available for use in an image. The dimensions of the grid that forms a bitmap graphic are referred to as its ________. It is possible to change the resolution and/or the file size of a bitmap graphic; but because bitmaps are resolution ________, these changes can reduce image quality. For example, enlarging a bitmap requires your computer to fill in missing pixels, which often results in a jagged or ________ image. Image compression shrinks the size of a graphics file. ________ compression is used for images stored in JPEG format, but ________ compression is used for PNG, GIF, and TIFF files. Photoediting software includes tools, such as an image ________, that adjusts brightness values for various ranges of pixels. Algorithms for ________ scrub out designated areas of an image and replace the missing pixels. Clipping paths and alpha blending are useful for digital ________ when you want to assemble parts of several photos into one image. Panoramic and 360-degree images can be assembled using image ________ to match the edges of a sequence of photos. Stereoscopic effects can be achieved with a photo pair or by creating a(n) ________ with red and blue coloration.

Section D:

Unlike a bitmap graphic, created by superimposing a grid of pixels over an image, a vector graphic consists of a set of instructions for creating a picture. Vector graphics are stored as a collection of ________ and their corresponding sizes, colors, and positions. The big advantage of vector graphics is that they can be enlarged without becoming ________. Vector graphics are created by using ________ software. A vector graphic can be converted into a bitmap by a process called ________. Once converted, however, the resulting graphic loses the object-editing qualities it had in its vector state. The most common vector graphics format for the Web is ________. 3D graphics are stored as a set of instructions that contain the locations and lengths of lines that form a(n) ________ for a 3D object. This framework then can be covered by colored, patterned, and textured surfaces. This process, called ________, produces a bitmap image of the 3D object. ________ tracing adds highlights and shadows to the image. 3D graphics can be ________ to produce animated special effects for movies. Real-time ________ is required for 3D computer games and virtual reality.

Section E:

Footage for digital videos can be supplied from a digital source, or from a(n) ________ source that requires conversion. In addition to standalone digital cameras, digital footage can also be obtained from cameras embedded in handheld devices and from ________ built in above a computer screen. Video resolution varies, but 1080p is common. The "p" stands for ________ scan. Most videos today have a widescreen aspect ratio of ________. Most videos are output in a compressed format using intraframe and ________ compression. Software, such as MPEG, DivX, Theora, and H.264, that compresses the video stream is referred to as a(n) ________. A compression ________, such as 5:1, indicates the degree of compression. Video and audio streams are combined into the final video file and stored using a(n) ________ format, such as AVI, MOV, or WebM. So-called 3D movies are technically ________ in their use of anaglyphs or stereograms.

Interactive Situation Questions

1. At work, no one can find the digital version of a 20-page document that needs to be revised. You save the day by using a scanner and ______ software to digitize the paper document.

2. Suppose you are creating an English-as-a-Second-Language Web page and you want to add links to sound files that pronounce English phrases. Would it be better to store the files in MP3 or MIDI format? ______

3. Imagine that you're a musician and you are asked to synthesize some upbeat music for a modern ballet. For this project, you would most likely work with ______ music.

4. Suppose you visit a Web site that allows you to enter sentences, and then it reads the sentences back to you. The site even gives you a choice of a female or male voice. You assume that this site uses speech ______ technology.

5. You have an old photograph that you want to incorporate in a brochure for your antiques business. To convert the photo into digital format, you use a(n) ______.

6. Imagine that you are preparing a series of bitmap graphics for a Web site. To decrease the download time for each graphic, you can use a compressed format such as GIF, PNG, TIFF, or ______.

7. You've taken a photo with a high-resolution digital camera and you want to send it as an email attachment. You decide to ______ it to reduce the image to a more manageable size.

8. Suppose you are designing a logo for a client. You know the design will undergo several revisions, and you understand that the logo will be used at various sizes. You decide it would be best to use drawing software to create the logo as a(n) ______ graphic.

9. After you finish arranging video clips and adding a soundtrack, you can select a video file format and a compression technique. For example, you might store the video in WebM container format and use the H.264 ______ to compress the file.

10. You uploaded a video to YouTube, but it's got black bars on the side. If you want to get rid of them, you'll have to re-output your video and change its ______.

Lab: The Digital World with Eyes Shut

The digital world is very visual. Email demands to be read. Web sites are full of text. Social media feeds are constantly changing. Pinterest and Flickr are all about photos. And a lifetime is not long enough to view all the videos on YouTube. But what would this digital world be like if you could not see it? Can speech synthesizers and voice recognition tools change the visual experience into an auditory one? In this lab, you'll have an opportunity to set up a screen reader, activate voice recognition, and experience the digital world with your eyes closed.

Requirements:

For this lab, you'll need a Windows computer, an Apple computer, an iPhone 4s or newer, or an Android phone. The instructions are generalized; they provide helpful guidelines, but not specific steps. You may have to explore a bit to find all the tools needed to complete the assignment, but that is all part of the learning experience. You might find this lab goes more smoothly if you work with a partner.

Assignment:

❶ Activate voice commands on your device.

On a Mac, select the Apple menu, then choose System Preferences, Accessibility, and Voice Control. Enable Voice Control. Click the Commands button to see a list of voice commands that you can use.

On a PC with Windows, locate the Speech Recognition utility. If setup is required, select a microphone, then continue with the setup (choosing Disable document review). You can access a tutorial by searching online for "Windows Speech recognition."

On an iPhone, access Settings, then select Siri. Make sure Siri is on. Hold the Home button to open Siri (or hold your iPhone up to your ear if you've enabled Raise to Speak).

On an Android phone, access the Settings menu, select My device, then choose Voice control. Turn voice control on, then select it to find out what kinds of commands you can say.

❷ Try these activities and make notes on the results:

Does your device respond when you ask "What time is it?"

Can you launch the camera app and take a photo using voice commands?

Can you issue a voice command to get to the desktop, Start screen, or Home screen?

Can you dictate an email message or text message using only voice commands?

❸ Activate the screen reader for your device.

On a Mac, select the Apple icon, then choose System Preferences, Accessibility, and VoiceOver. Enable VoiceOver. (Leave the Accessibility window open so that you can disable VoiceOver when you complete the lab.) Take a few minutes to step through the VoiceOver training.

On a PC with Windows, enter Narrator in the Windows search box. Start the Narrator.

On an iPhone, select Settings, then select Accessibility. Turn on VoiceOver.

On an Android phone, select Applications, Accessibility, and TalkBack. Turn TalkBack on. Listen carefully to the instructions; you have to tap twice to select any screen options.

❹ Close your eyes and try a very simple activity, such as starting a browser, going to Wikipedia, or searching for information about wolves. Describe your experience.

❺ With your eyes open, explore the Web to locate any additional information or settings that might make navigation with eyes shut easier. Describe what you find.

❻ Reset your device to its usual speech mode.

Hint: On Windows, hold down the Windows key, Ctrl, and Enter to turn off the narration.

2 Digital Devices

Module Contents

The availability of digital devices is mind-boggling. How do you know which devices are right for your lifestyle and career? The first step is making sense of digital hardware.

Try It! Apply what you learn.

- Identify chips on the system board of any digital device.
- Identify components of a digital device, such as display, system unit, storage devices, input devices, output devices, and expansion ports.
- Safely clean and maintain a digital device.
- Operate portable devices using best practices to prolong battery life and battery lifespan.
- Take stock of your digital devices and maintain a list of their serial numbers.
- Shop for digital devices based on a usage plan.
- Interpret computer ads and specifications in order to make smart purchasing decisions.
- Find the processor specifications for digital devices that you own.
- Determine the RAM capacity of your digital devices.
- Understand when you might need to flash ROM and how to do it safely.
- Select the most effective storage devices for transporting, archiving, and backing up files.
- Use cloud storage safely and securely.
- Back up important data files.
- Use backup tools such as recovery drives, the Copy command, File History, Time Machine, and disk images so that you can restore a digital device after an incident that wipes out main storage.
- Use expansion ports to connect peripheral devices.
- Determine the resolution settings of your screen display.
- Correctly follow procedures to unplug devices such as USB drives.
- Determine if a digital device is equipped for Bluetooth connectivity.
- Describe the role of various sensors used in digital devices, the Internet of Things, and autonomous vehicles.

Pre-Check

Gauge your level of expertise. The answers are in the module.

This acronym stands for:

________ ________
________ ________

What's the most popular type of battery in today's digital devices?

What two components are crucial if you play lots of computer games?

Smith1979/Shutterstock.com

Which device uses iOS?

3.2

Processor speed is measured in ________.

GB

GHz

Gigaflops

Gbps

What's the name of the set of instructions that loads the operating system into RAM?

What kind of processing is like a pizza oven conveyor belt?

Identify this port.

A bit-for-bit backup of every sector on a hard disk is called a disk ________.

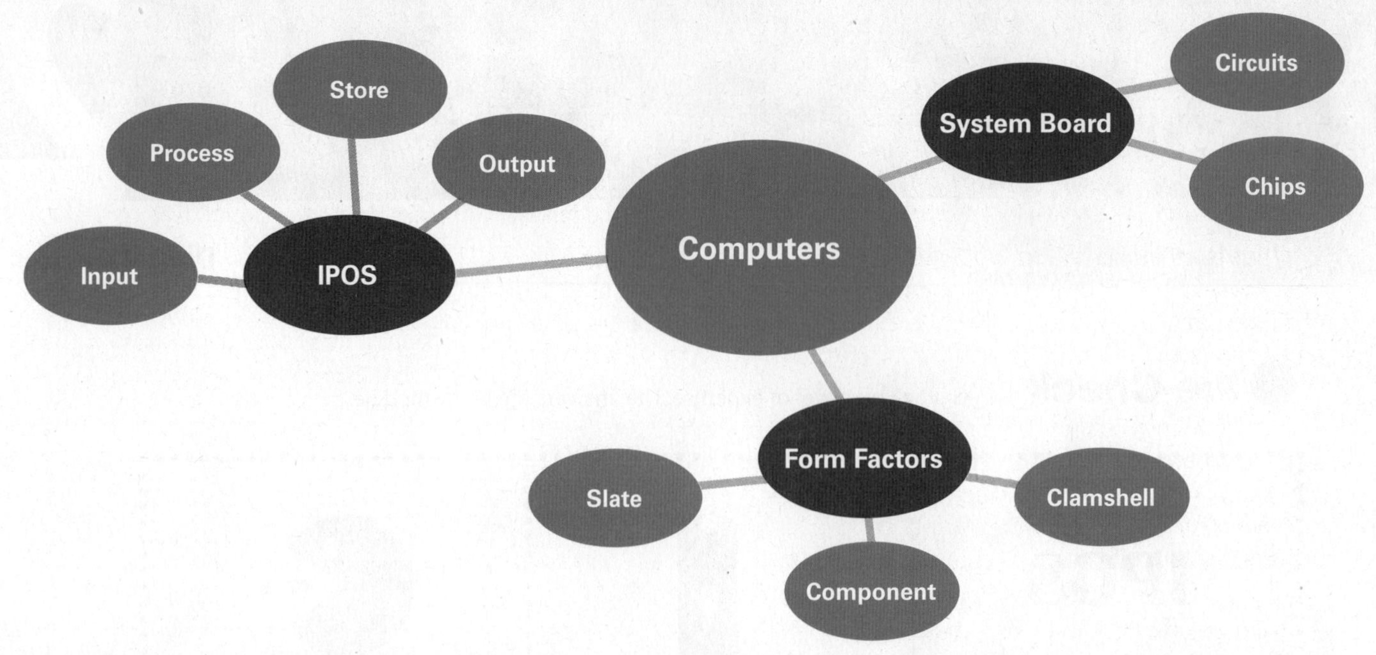

Section A

Device Basics

Objectives

- Draw a diagram showing the IPOS model of activities characteristic of computers.
- Describe the stored program concept and why it distinguishes computers from other simpler and less versatile digital devices.
- State which of the following are application software and which are system software: iOS, Windows, Microsoft Word, Android, PowerPoint.
- List three terms that are commonly used alternatives for "integrated circuits."
- Explain why semiconductors are the materials used for integrated circuits.
- Identify the microprocessor on a system board.
- Identify the components of a typical device that has a component, clamshell, or slate form factor.
- List four mistakes to avoid when cleaning a digital device.
- Describe what to do if liquid is spilled on a device.
- Explain how to care for a touchscreen.
- List six steps to take to increase battery life and lifespan.

What's inside all these digital devices that we use? Whether you're operating your trusty laptop or figuring out how to safely clean your smartphone screen, it is useful to have some background about the components of digital devices and how they work. Section A looks at digital devices from the outside in, first focusing on characteristics common to all digital devices, and then drilling down to circuits and chips.

Terminology

computer
input
output
process data
central processing unit
microprocessor
memory
storage
computer program
software
stored program
application software
app
system software
operating system
development tools
integrated circuit
semiconductors
system board
form factor
system unit
oleophobic
lithium ion
discharge rate

Computers

Pixar's huge server array that renders 3D animated movies and the tiny iPhone you can hold in your hand have more in common than you might think. These devices, along with mainframes, desktops, tablets, ebook readers, and game consoles, are all based on computer technology. Understanding the classical definition of a computer provides a useful picture of what all these devices have in common.

What is a computer? Most people can formulate a mental picture of a computer, but computers do so many things and come in such a variety of shapes and sizes that it might seem difficult to distill their common characteristics into an all-purpose definition. At its core, a **computer** is a multipurpose device that accepts input, processes data, stores data, and produces output, all according to a series of stored instructions.

Input is whatever is typed, submitted, or transmitted to a computer. **Output** is the result produced by a computer. Input and output can be handled by components contained within the computer or by add-ons, such as keyboards and printers, that are attached to the computer with cables or connected wirelessly.

Computers **process data** by performing calculations, modifying documents and pictures, drawing graphs, and sorting lists of words or numbers. Processing is handled by the computer's **central processing unit** (CPU). The CPU of most modern computers is a **microprocessor**, which is an electronic component that can be programmed to process data.

Computers store data and the software that processes data. Most computers have temporary holding areas called **memory** in addition to long-term **storage** housed on hard disks or flash drives. Figure 2-1 illustrates the IPOS (input, process, output, store) activities characteristic of computers.

Figure 2-1: The IPOS model defines computers

Terminology

The word *computer* has been part of the English language since 1613; but if you look in a dictionary printed before 1940, you might be surprised to find a computer defined as a person who performs calculations. Prior to 1940, machines designed to perform calculations were usually referred to as calculators and tabulators, not computers. The modern definition and use of the term *computer* emerged in the 1940s, when the first electronic computing devices were developed.

QuickCheck

Where does sorting fit into the IPOS model?

a. Input

b. Process

c. Store

d. Output

What's so significant about a computer's ability to store instructions? The instructions that tell a digital device how to carry out processing tasks are referred to as a **computer program**, or simply a program. These programs form the **software** that sets up a computer to do a specific task. When a computer "runs" software, it performs the instructions to carry out the task.

The first computers were "programmed" to perform a specific task by connecting wire circuitry in a certain way. Changing tasks meant rewiring the circuits. The term **stored program** means that a series of instructions for a computing task can be loaded into a computer's memory. These instructions can be replaced easily by a different set of instructions when it is time for the computer to perform another task. This ability to switch programs makes computers multipurpose devices (Figure 2-2).

QuickCheck

The stored program concept turns computers into ____________.

a. calculators

b. smartphones

c. multipurpose devices

d. software

Figure 2-2: Stored programs make computers versatile machines

The stored program concept allows you to use a computer for one task, such as word processing, and then easily switch to a different type of computing task, such as editing a photo or playing music. It is the single most important characteristic that distinguishes computers from other simpler and less versatile digital devices, such as digital clocks, calculators, and cameras.

What kinds of software do computers run? Computers run three main types of software: application software, system software, and development tools (Figure 2-3). A computer can be *applied* to many tasks, such as writing, number crunching, video editing, and online shopping. **Application software** is a set of computer programs that helps a person carry out a task. Application software for mobile devices is usually referred to as an **app**.

Whereas application software is designed to help a person carry out a task, the primary purpose of **system software** is to help the computer system monitor itself in order to function efficiently. An example of system software is a computer **operating system** (OS), which is essentially the primary controller for all the activities that take place within a computer.

Development tools are used for creating software applications, Web sites, operating systems, and utilities. Examples of development tools include computer programming languages, such as C++, and scripting languages, such as HTML.

Figure 2-3: Software categories

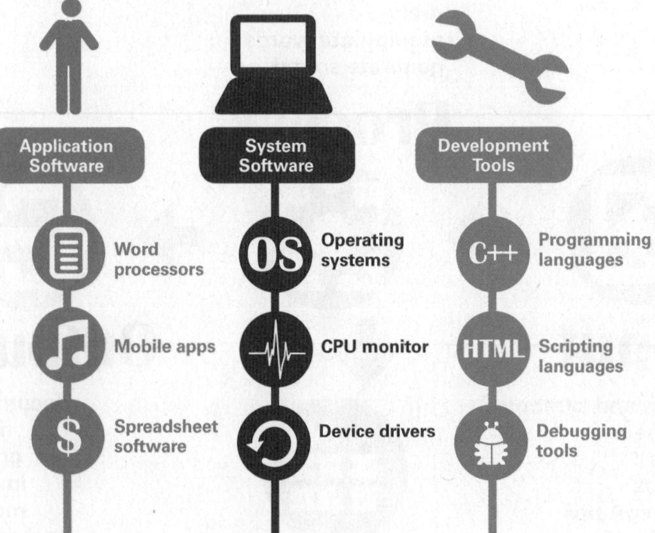

Circuits and Chips

The first computers were closet-sized devices filled with wires, vacuum tubes, transistors, and other bulky components. As digital electronics evolved, components became smaller and smaller. Open up a digital device. You won't see clumps of wires and gears. Instead, you'll see small circuit boards and integrated circuits. These tiny components are the essence of digital electronics.

QuickCheck

In Figure 2-4, the fiery bit ______________.

a. represents an electrical fault
b. is heading toward a resistor
c. is a low-voltage signal
d. represents a 0

2

What are digital electronics? Digital electronics represent data bits as electrical signals that travel over circuits in much the same way that electricity flows over a wire when you turn on a light switch. To represent data, such as 01101100, high-voltage signals are used for 1 bits, and low-voltage signals are used for 0 bits. All the calculations performed by digital devices take place in a maze of electronic circuitry (Figure 2-4).

Figure 2-4: A simple circuit

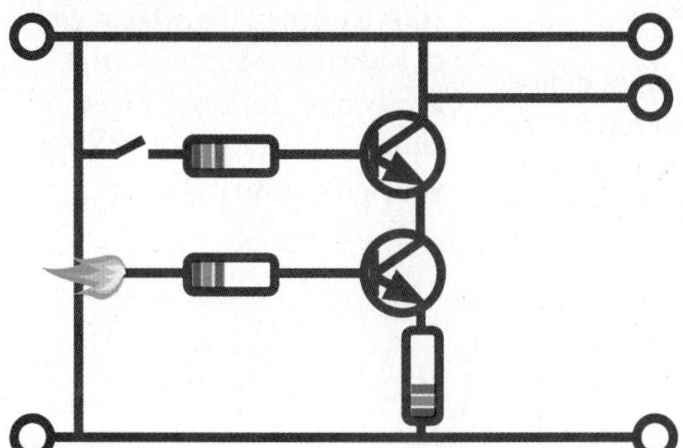

This little circuit is composed of electrical pathways (lines), transistors (circles), and resistors (rectangles). The electronics for digital devices require millions of similar circuits. Today, this circuitry is condensed into integrated circuits.

What's an integrated circuit? An **integrated circuit** (IC) is a set of microscopic electronic components etched onto a thin slice of semiconducting material. The terms *computer chip*, *microchip*, and *chip* are commonly used to refer to integrated circuits. Some integrated circuits are devoted to collecting input, while others might be devoted to processing tasks, output, or storage. The first computer chips contained fewer than 100 miniaturized components, such as resistors and transistors. The chips for today's digital devices contain billions of transistors.

QuickCheck

There is an abundant supply of materials for fabricating semiconductors because:

a. They are made from purified silicon (sand).
b. They are basically insulators made from wood.

Semiconductors, such as silicon and germanium, are substances with properties between those of a conductor (like copper) and an insulator (like wood). To fabricate a chip, the conductive properties of selective parts of the semiconductor can be enhanced to essentially create miniature electronic pathways and components, such as transistors, as shown in Figure 2-5.

Figure 2-5: Computer chips are made from semiconductors

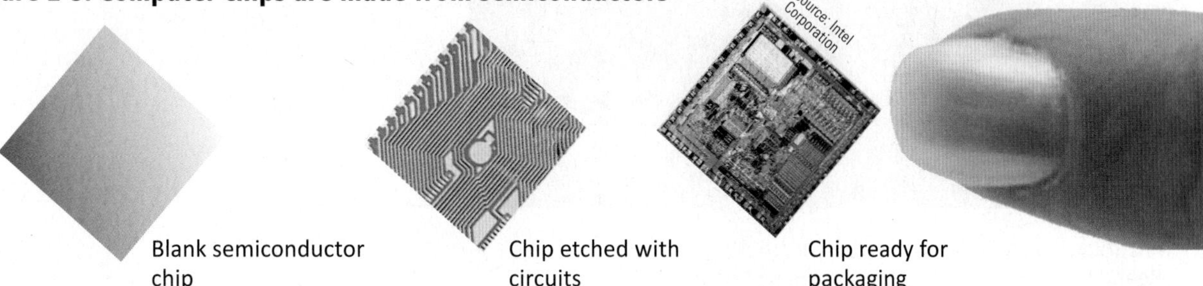

Blank semiconductor chip

Chip etched with circuits

Chip ready for packaging

Aren't chips black? Integrated circuits are packaged in protective carriers that vary in shape and size. Figure 2-6 illustrates some chip carriers, including small rectangular DIPs (dual in-line packages) with caterpillar-like legs protruding from a black, rectangular body, and pincushion-like LGAs (land-grid arrays).

Figure 2-6: Chips are housed in ceramic packages

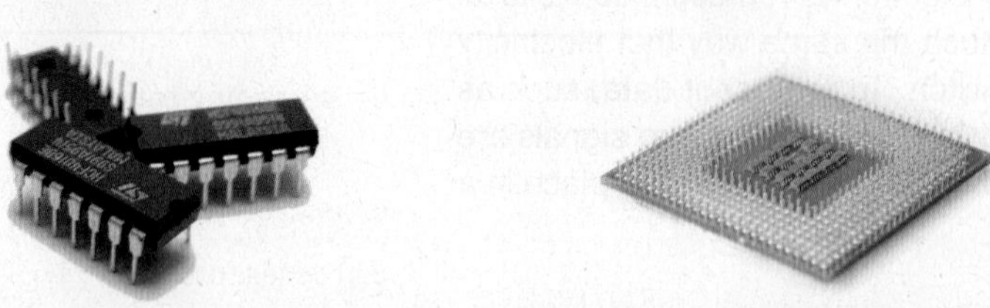

DIPs have two rows of pins that connect the chip to a circuit board.

An LGA is a square chip package, typically used for microprocessors, with pins arranged in concentric squares.

Maniacpixel/Shutterstock.com

How do chips fit together? The electronic components of most digital devices are mounted on a circuit board called a system board, motherboard, or main board. The **system board** houses all essential chips and provides connecting circuitry between them. Figure 2-7 illustrates the main chips on the front and back sides of a laptop system board.

Try It!

The chips on a circuit board have identifying numbers that you can look up online. Suppose you've opened the system unit of a Microsoft Surface tablet and you're looking at a chip labeled Samsung LPDDR4X. Can you find out what it does?

Figure 2-7: A system board holds chips and other components

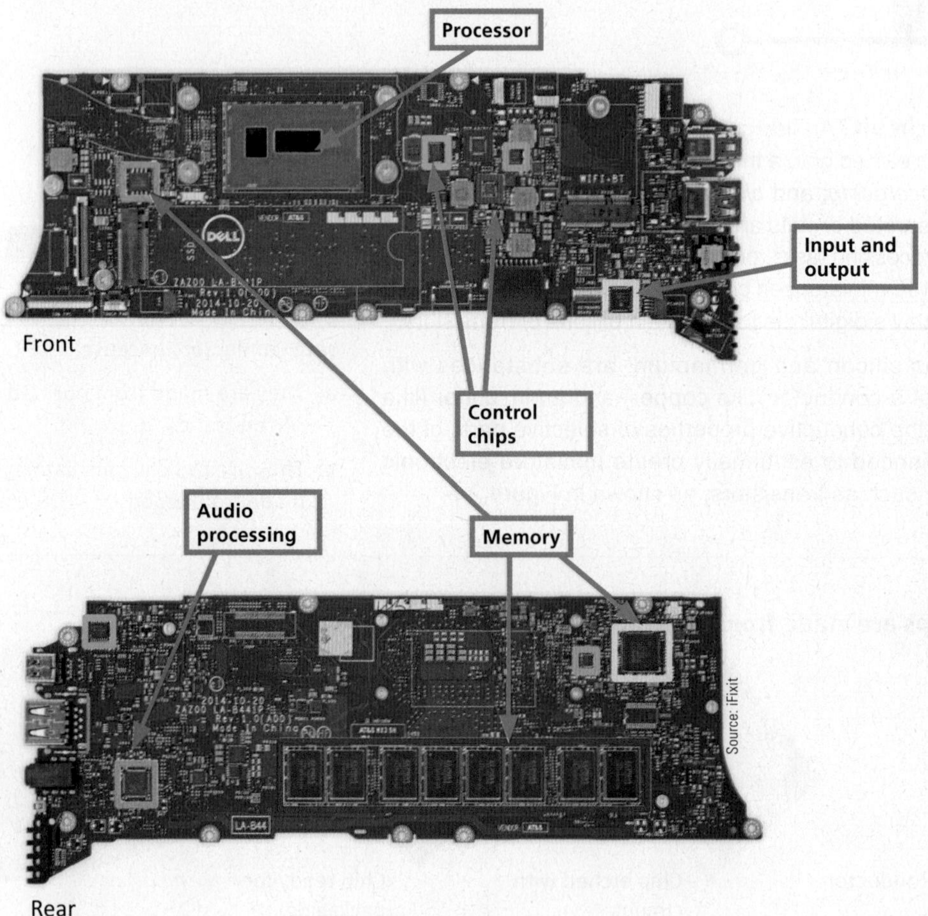

Source: iFixit

Components

When you acquire a new digital device, your first step is to locate the power button and all the other hardware components. The devices you use today have a fairly predictable collection of features, depending on the device's form factor.

What is a form factor? In the computer industry, the term **form factor** refers to the size and dimensions of a device or components, such as circuit boards and system units. The term **system unit** is tech-speak for the part of a digital device that holds the system board. It can apply to the body of a smartphone or laptop, as well as to the tower unit of a desktop computer. Digital devices are available in all sorts of form factors; some of the most popular include component, clamshell, and slate.

What are the features of a component system? A component device is composed of various standalone parts, such as a display unit, system unit, and keyboard. Components can be connected using cables or wireless signals. Most of the first personal computers were component systems. Today, this form factor is much less popular because of the effort required to assemble the components. Figure 2-8 illustrates the hardware features of a vintage component system.

QuickCheck

How many on/off buttons would you expect on a component system like the one in Figure 2-8?

a. One on the system unit

b. One for each wireless device

c. One on the system unit and one on the display device

2

Figure 2-8: A vintage component system

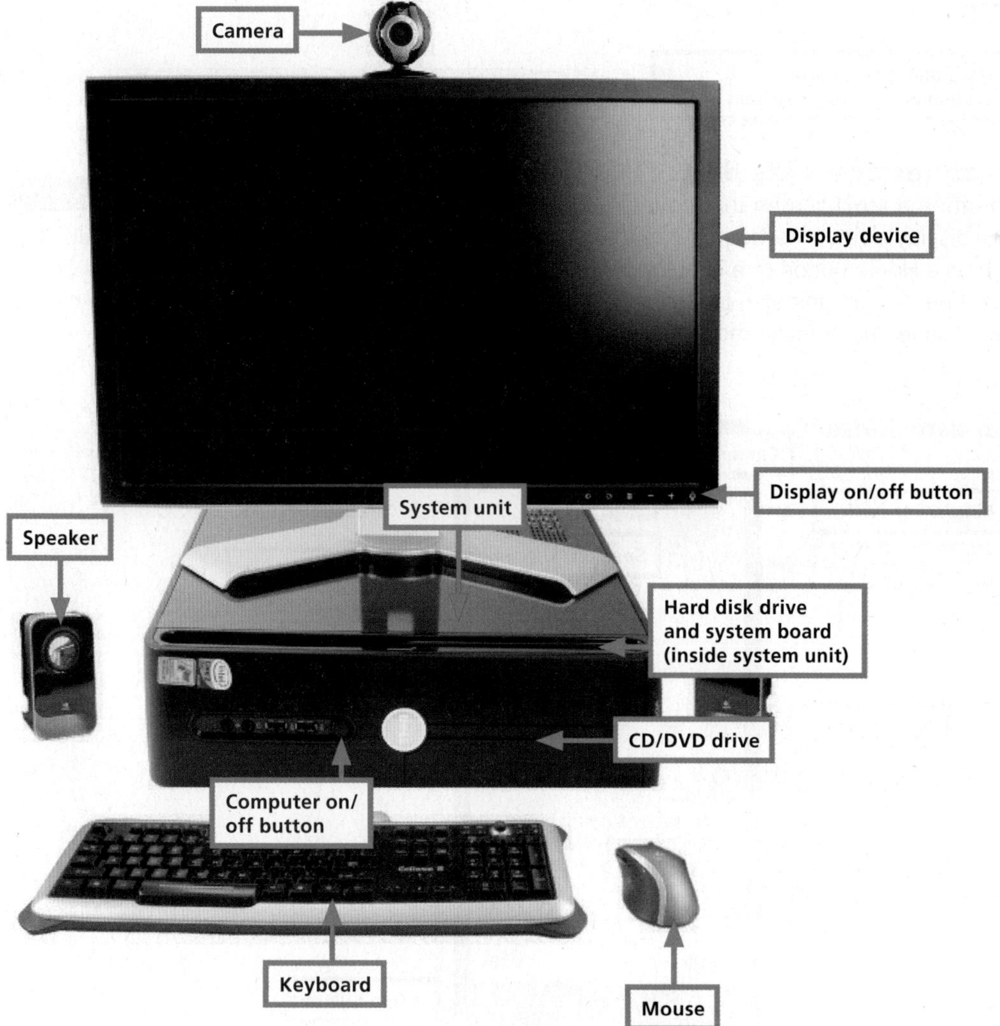

▶ What are the features of a clamshell device? Clamshell devices have a keyboard as the base and a screen on the hinged cover. The system unit on these devices contains all of the basic components required for input, processing, storage, and output (Figure 2-9).

Figure 2-9: A typical clamshell device

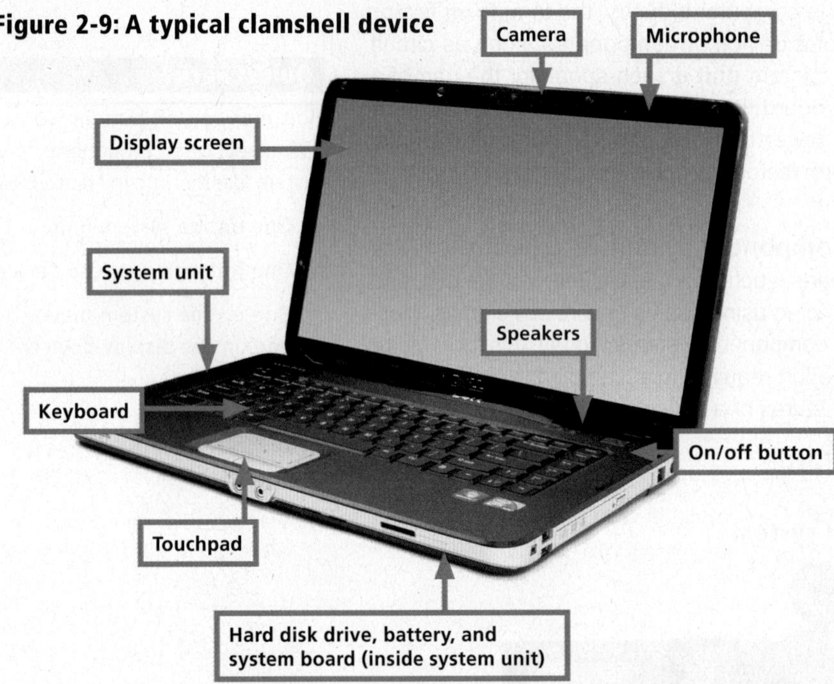

QuickCheck

How many components are housed on the top half of the clamshell device in Figure 2-9?

a. One

b. Two

c. Three

d. Four

▶ What are the features of a slate device? Devices configured in the slate form factor feature a touchscreen that covers most of the device's surface. The screen can display a virtual keyboard for text and numeric input. An additional control, such as a Home button or a circular control pad, is featured on some slate devices. The system unit also includes controls for commonly used features, such as volume and airplane mode (Figure 2-10).

Try It!

Check out the devices that you own. Can you find all of the components listed in the figures?

Figure 2-10: A typical slate device

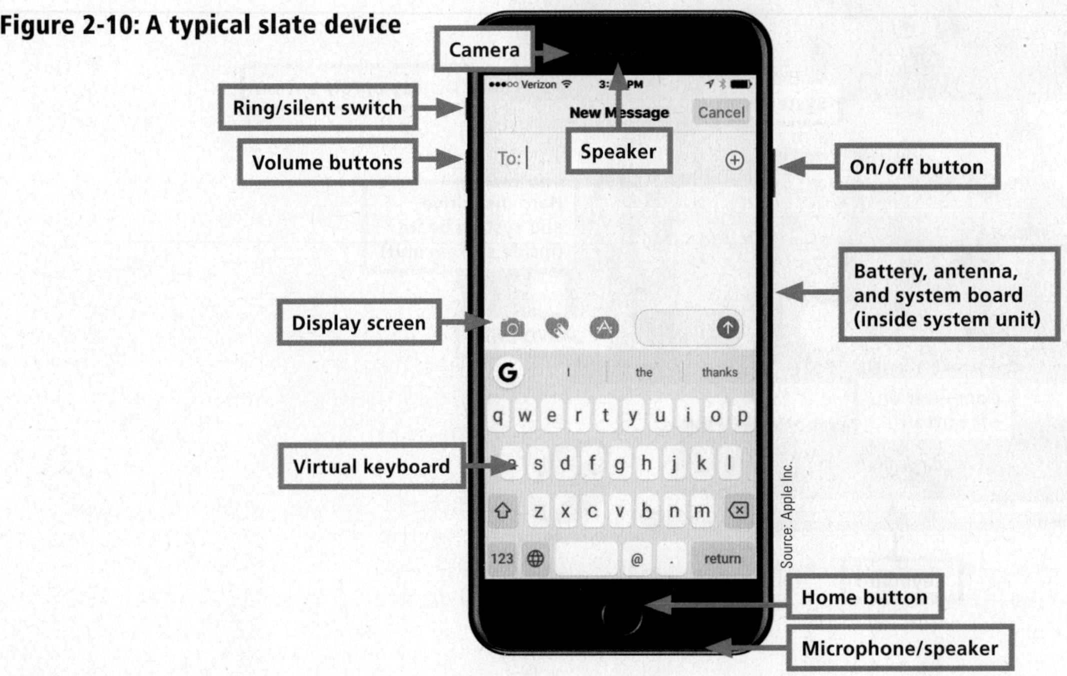

Maintenance

Digital devices can be costly. You can extend their life with a bit of regular maintenance. There are four components of digital devices that require maintenance: the system unit, keyboard, screen, and battery.

How do I start? Before you undertake any maintenance, turn the device off—that's *off*, not just asleep—and disconnect any power cables. Doing so will prevent random screen swipes or key presses from altering your device settings.

Which cleaning products are safe to use? The products you can use depend on the component you are cleaning. What might work well to scrub out stubborn stains on the system unit case could permanently cloud or scratch your touchscreen. Always follow the manufacturer's advice for cleaning procedures and products (Figure 2-11).

2

Figure 2-11: Cleaning guidelines

Don't use harsh cleaning products; follow manufacturer recommendations.

Never immerse a device in liquid; water and electronics don't mix.

Do not allow cleaning agents to drip on keyboards or touchpads.

Do not spray cleaning agents directly on the device; spray them onto a cleaning cloth.

What kind of maintenance does the system unit require? Basic system unit maintenance is simple. You want to keep the unit clean, prevent it from overheating, shield it from damage, and protect it from electrical surges (Figure 2-12).

Figure 2-12: Basic system unit maintenance

Dust with a clean microfiber cloth and disinfect with antibacterial wipes.

Use a low vacuum setting to remove dust from fan vents.

Use a protective case or carrying bag.

Only plug into a surge-protected outlet.

How can I safely clean and disinfect a touchscreen? Touchscreens collect fingerprints and are a breeding ground for bacteria, so it is a good idea to clean them periodically. Many touchscreens are made from Gorilla Glass, which is designed to resist scratching and cracking. Damaged screens can be replaced, but that can cost close to $100, so a few preventive measures may help you avoid costly repairs.

A plastic screen protector is the first line of defense against scratches and cracks. These films can be cleaned using water and a soft cloth, or a disinfecting wipe. When the screen protector gets grubby, simply peel it off and replace it with a new one.

QuickCheck

What is the first step for hardware maintenance?

a. Wipe it with a soft cloth.

b. Remove the screen protector.

c. Turn the device off.

d. Vacuum the fan vents.

Without a screen protector, you will have to carefully clean the screen itself. Many touchscreens have an **oleophobic** coating designed to repel the oils deposited by fingertips. When alcohol is used to clean these screens, each application degrades the coating. Non-alcohol wipes are available, or use eyeglass cleaner.

▶ What about my keyboard? Keyboards quickly build up grime, gather dust, and collect crumbs. To start the cleaning process, turn the keyboard upside down and shake it gently to dislodge debris. Most manufacturers suggest using an antibacterial wipe to clean key surfaces. Take a moment to test the cleaning product on a small unnoticeable spot, just to make sure it will not discolor the keys or leave a residue. Use cotton swabs to clean between the keys.

▶ What is the best way to clean up spills? Liquids and electronics don't mix. If you spill liquid on a device, turn it off immediately. With luck, that step will prevent electrical shorts that would permanently damage circuit boards. Once the device is off, you can assess the damage. If the spill is water, dry off the device, shake out the moisture, and set it in a warm, dry place where there is good air circulation. A fan or hair dryer *set on low* can help drive out moisture. Allow the device to dry for at least 72 hours.

Sticky spills are another matter. If the goo has penetrated the interior of the device, it is best to leave the cleanup to a professional. If you think the spill only affected the surface, you can wipe the device with clean water and allow it to dry for 24 hours (Figure 2-13).

Figure 2-13: Do not set liquids near a keyboard

QuickCheck

When liquid spills on a digital device, what should you do?

a. Shut off the device immediately.

b. Back up all your data before turning off the device.

c. Rinse the device with clear water.

d. Call *611.

▶ How do I maintain the battery for a device? You know how it goes. It happens to everyone. The battery on your device dies just when you really need it. Battery life is the time your device operates before it must be recharged. Battery lifespan is the amount of time a battery lasts until it must be replaced. Good maintenance extends the life of your battery and a device's lifetime, so your digital devices are ready when you need them.

Most of today's battery-powered digital devices contain a **lithium ion** (Li-ion) battery. Unlike batteries of the past, Li-ion batteries contain no toxic compounds and operate efficiently, but they are sensitive to heat.

Li-ion batteries can occasionally overheat, and in the worst case, they can explode. Most devices today contain circuitry to prevent heat-triggered damage, but smart consumers don't operate devices that are hot to the touch.

Batteries have a **discharge rate** at which they lose charge even when not in use. The discharge rate for Li-ion batteries is quite low—about 1.5% per month—so the batteries in your devices basically discharge only as they are used.

Device manufacturers often advertise battery watts per hour (Wh). A 60 Wh battery will last 60 hours if it expends 1 watt per hour. A typical laptop uses about 30 watts per hour, however, so a 60 Wh battery can power the device for two hours (60 Wh ÷ 30 watts = 2 hours).

Some applications require more battery power than others. Location-based apps that keep track of your whereabouts are constantly using extra power to check cell towers or Wi-Fi networks. Push applications, such as autoretrieving email, make your device continually check for new messages. To extend battery life, disable these kinds of apps when you are not using them. Figure 2-14 summarizes good practices for charging and using Li-ion batteries.

Figure 2-14: Extend the life of the batteries in your devices

1. Charge when the low battery indicator comes on.
2. Avoid totally discharging the battery.
3. Remove the device from the charger when it's fully charged.
4. If your device becomes hot while in use, turn it off.
5. Disable unused apps that constantly connect to the Internet.
6. Switch to airplane mode when in an area with no cell coverage.

QuickCheck

Suppose your smartphone has a battery rated at 5.2 Wh. When you use map guidance, the phone draws 1.3 watts per hour. How long can you travel before your phone runs out of juice?

a. One hour

b. Four hours

c. Eight hours

d. Ten hours

QuickQuiz — Section A

1. A computer is a multipurpose device that accepts input, processes ________, stores data, and produces output, all according to the instructions of a stored program.
2. An operating system is an example of ________ software.
3. A(n) ________ circuit is a set of microscopic electronic components etched onto a thin slice of semiconducting material.
4. Three form factors for digital devices are component, ________, and slate.
5. Touchscreens on many digital devices have a(n) ________ coating that resists fingerprints.

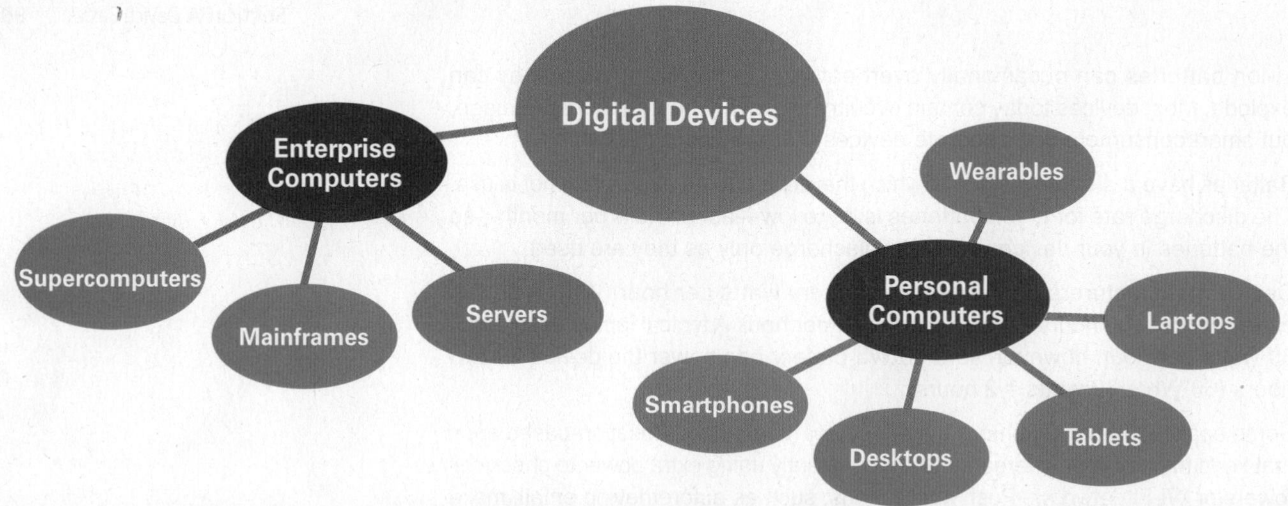

Section B

Device Options

Objectives

- List three types of computers that are commonly used in businesses, serve multiple simultaneous users, and offer very fast processing speeds.
- Draw a hierarchy chart showing the classifications of personal computers.
- Identify seven digital niche devices.
- List five activities that are important for consumers who are shopping for digital devices.
- List three pros and three cons that influence purchase decisions for each of the following: desktop, laptop, tablet, smartphone.
- Specify the operating systems that are common in each of the three major families of operating systems.

When shopping for a new device, the choices may seem overwhelming. Section B helps you sort out the devices that are on the market by function and price. It addresses the tricky issue of compatibility and other factors important to consumers.

Terminology

supercomputer
mainframe
server
personal computer
desktop computer
portable computer
laptop computer
Chromebook
tablet computer
slate tablet
2-in-1
smartphones
PDA
wearable computers
microcontrollers
compatible

Enterprise Computers

Figure 2-15: "Big" computers

AP Images/Mami Nagaoki/The Yomiuri Shimbun

Supercomputer

Source: IBM

Mainframe

dotshock/Shutterstock.com

Servers

At one time, it was possible to define three distinct categories of computers. Mainframes were housed in large, closet-sized metal frames. Minicomputers were smaller, less expensive, and less powerful, but they could support multiple users and run business software. Microcomputers were clearly differentiated from computers in other categories because they were dedicated to a single user and their CPUs consisted of a single microprocessor chip.

Today, microprocessors are no longer a distinction between computer categories because just about every computer uses one or more microprocessors as its CPU. The term *minicomputer* has fallen into disuse, and the terms *microcomputer* and *mainframe* are used with less and less frequency.

2

What are the most powerful computers? Today's most powerful computers include supercomputers, mainframes, and servers. These devices are generally used in businesses and government agencies. They have the ability to service many simultaneous users and process data at very fast speeds (Figure 2-15).

Supercomputers. A computer falls into the **supercomputer** category if it is, at the time of construction, one of the fastest computers in the world. Because of their speed, supercomputers can tackle complex tasks that just would not be practical for other computers. Typical uses for supercomputers include breaking codes, modeling worldwide weather systems, and simulating nuclear explosions.

Computer manufacturers such as IBM, Nvidia, and Fujitsu have in recent years held top honors for the world's fastest computer. Supercomputer speeds are measured in petaflops (PFLOPS). One petaflop is an astounding 1,000,000,000,000,000 (quadrillion) calculations per second. That's about 20,000 times faster than your laptop computer.

Mainframes. A **mainframe** computer (or simply a mainframe) is a large and expensive computer capable of simultaneously processing data for hundreds or thousands of users. Its main processing circuitry is housed in a closet-sized cabinet like the one shown at left; but after large components are added for storage and output, a mainframe installation can fill a good-sized room.

Mainframes are generally used by businesses and government agencies to provide centralized storage, processing, and management for large amounts of data. For example, banks depend on mainframes as their computer of choice to ensure reliability, data security, and centralized control. The price of a mainframe computer typically starts at several hundred thousand dollars and can easily exceed $1 million.

Servers. The purpose of a **server** is to "serve" data to computers connected to a network. When you search Google or access a Web site, the information you obtain is provided by servers. At ecommerce sites, the store's merchandise information is housed in database servers. Email, chat, Skype, and online multiplayer games are all operated by servers.

Technically, just about any computer can be configured to perform the work of a server. However, computer manufacturers such as IBM and Dell offer devices classified as servers that are especially suited for storing and distributing data on networks. These devices are about the size of a desk drawer and are often mounted in racks of multiple servers.

Personal Computers

A **personal computer** is designed to meet the computing needs of an individual. These computers were originally referred to as microcomputers. Personal computers provide access to a wide variety of computing applications, such as word processing, photo editing, email, and Internet access.

The term *personal computer* is sometimes abbreviated as PC. However, *PC* can also refer to a specific type of personal computer that descended from the original IBM PC and runs Windows software. In this book, *PC* refers to IBM PC descendants. It is not used as an abbreviation for personal computer.

Figure 2-16: Personal computers

Source: Apple Inc.

Desktop

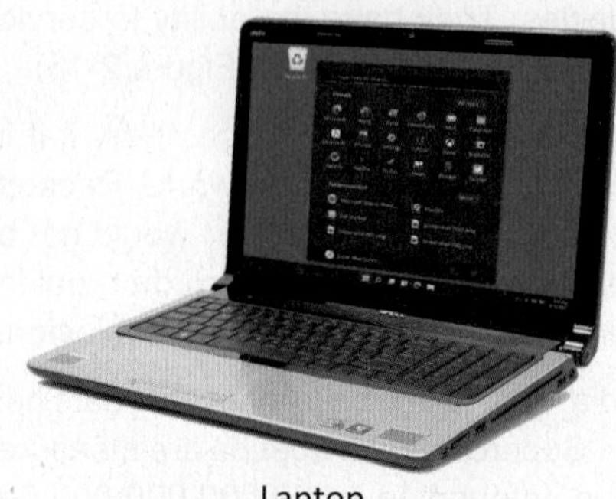

Laptop

Slate tablet

2-in-1 tablet

What are the options for personal computers? Personal computers can be classified as desktop, portable, or mobile devices. The lines that delineate these categories are sometimes a bit blurry, but the general characteristics of each category are described below and common configurations are shown in Figure 2-16.

Desktops. A **desktop computer** fits on a desk and runs on power from an electrical wall outlet. The keyboard is typically a separate component. A desktop computer can be housed in a vertical case or in a horizontal case. In some modern desktops, called all-in-one units, the system board is incorporated into the display device.

Desktop computers are popular for offices and schools where portability is not important. Their operating systems include Microsoft Windows, macOS, and Linux. The price of an entry-level desktop computer starts at $500 or a bit less.

Portables. A **portable computer** runs on battery power. Its screen, keyboard, camera, storage devices, and speakers are fully contained in a single case so that the device can be easily transported from one place to another. Portable computers include laptops, tablets, and smartphones.

Laptops. A **laptop computer** (also referred to as a notebook computer) is a small, lightweight personal computer designed like a clamshell with a keyboard as the base and a screen on the hinged cover. Most laptops use the same operating systems as desktop computers, with the exception of Chromebooks, which use Google's Chrome OS as their operating system.

A **Chromebook** is a special category of laptop, designed to be connected to the Internet for most routine computing activities. Chromebook owners use Web-based software and store all their data in the cloud rather than on a local hard disk. Chromebooks use a standard clamshell form factor, so they look very much like a laptop. Their sub-$300 price tags are attractive to consumers who primarily browse the Web and use Web-based apps.

Tablets. A **tablet computer** is a portable computing device featuring a touch-sensitive screen that can be used for input as well as for output. Popular tablet computers use specialized operating systems, such as iOS and Android. Some models support cell phone network data plans but require apps such as FaceTime or Skype for voice calls.

A **slate tablet** configuration is basically a screen in a narrow frame that lacks a physical keyboard (although one can be attached). The Apple iPad and Samsung Galaxy Tab are popular slate tablets. A **2-in-1** (or convertible tablet) can be operated using its touch-sensitive screen or with a physical keyboard that can be folded out of the way or removed.

Try It!

How many digital devices do you own? Which do you use most often? Make a list of your devices and their serial numbers, and tuck it away in a safe place in case one of your devices is lost or stolen.

2

Smartphones. Smartphones are mobile devices that have features similar to those of tablet computers, but they also provide telecommunications capabilities over cell phone networks. They can make voice calls, send text messages, and access the Internet. Unlike a basic mobile phone, smartphones are programmable, so they can download, store, and run software.

Smartphones are the most commonly used digital device in the world. A smartphone features a small keyboard or touchscreen and is designed to fit into a pocket, run on batteries, and be used while you are holding it in your hands (Figure 2-17).

Figure 2-17: Smartphones accept input from a touchscreen or microphone

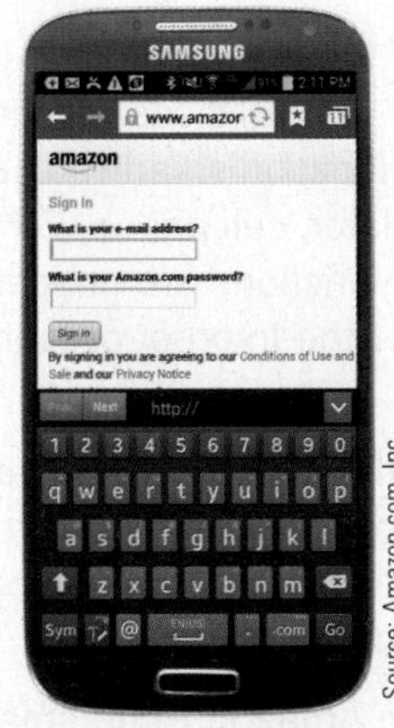

Source: Amazon.com, Inc.

Source: Apple Inc.

Source: Apple Inc.

Smartphones are equipped with built-in speech recognition that allows you to ask questions and control the device using spoken commands. Smartphones also include GPS capability so that apps are able to provide location-based services such as a route navigation map or a list of nearby restaurants.

Smartphones evolved from basic cell phones and PDAs. A **PDA** (personal digital assistant) was a handheld device used as an electronic appointment book, calculator, and notepad. Modern smartphones include a similar suite of applications, but they also have access to a huge variety of mobile apps that help you calculate tips, listen to your favorite music, and play entertaining games.

The operating systems for smartphones are similar to those used for tablet computers. iOS is used on the iPad and iPhone. The Android operating system used on Samsung tablets is also used for smartphones such as the Samsung Galaxy and Google Pixel.

Niche Devices

The list of digital devices is long. Many devices, such as fitness trackers, cameras, and handheld GPSs, are dedicated to specific tasks. Other devices perform a wider variety of tasks.

▶ What about other digital devices? Niche devices all have one thing in common: They contain a microprocessor. Some of these devices, such as smartwatches and fitness trackers, can be classified as **wearable computers**. Which of the devices in Figure 2-18 do you own?

Raspberry Pi. A full computer system unit that is just a tad larger than a deck of cards, the Raspberry Pi can be connected to a keyboard and screen for a full computer experience. These little powerhouses cost less than $50 and provide an inexpensive platform for experimenting with programming, robotics, and just about any creative computer application you can imagine.

Game consoles. Devices for playing computer games include Sony's PlayStation, Nintendo's Switch, and Microsoft's Xbox. They feature powerful processing capability and excellent graphics, but they are generally used for dedicated game playing and streaming videos rather than running application software.

Portable media players. Media players, such as the iPod Touch, revolutionized the music industry by providing consumers with a handheld device that can store and play thousands of songs. These devices are controlled by touchscreens or simple click-wheel mechanisms.

Smartwatches. Watches and clocks were some of the first devices to go digital. Mass produced in the 1970s with a price as low as $10, these watches were limited to time and date functions. Today's multifunction smartwatches can include a camera, thermometer, compass, calculator, cell phone, GPS, media player, and fitness tracker. Some smartwatch functions are onboard the device, whereas other functions require access to the Internet or to the wearer's smartphone.

Activity trackers. To monitor activity throughout the day, you can wear a fitness tracker. These devices, worn on the wrist or clipped to a pocket, monitor your steps and heart rate. They can calculate calories, graph your fitness achievements, and share information with your Facebook friends.

Smart speakers. Saying "Hey Alexa" activates an Amazon Echo smart speaker's virtual assistant that can carry out your verbal commands to control various devices or search the Internet. Apple's HomePod and Google's Nest are other examples of smart speakers that listen for your voice commands.

Smart appliances. Modern refrigerators, washing machines, and other appliances are controlled by integrated circuits called **microcontrollers** that combine sensors with processing circuitry. Microcontrollers can monitor energy efficiency, offer programmed start times, and may be controlled remotely from a smartphone or laptop.

Figure 2-18: Specialized devices

Raspberry Pi

Peter Kotoff/Shutterstock.com

Videogame console

Portable media player

Smartwatch

Fitness tracker

Ksander/Shutterstock.com

Smart appliances

Choosing a Digital Device

The process of selecting a digital device is all about choices, and there can be an overwhelming number of them. Do you want a tablet or a laptop? Do you need a super-light device? What size screen? Mac or Windows? Is the most powerful and most expensive processor necessary? Understanding the choices is the key to getting the right device at the right price.

QuickCheck

Which tasks tend to require the fastest processor?

a. Email and photo editing

b. Social media and Web browsing

c. Desktop publishing and video editing

d. Accounting and budgeting

2

How do I get started? Whether you are replacing an outdated device or adding to your digital collection, the following activities can get you started:

Consider how you plan to use your device.

Choose the type of device.

Decide on a budget and stick to it.

Select a platform.

Check out the device's specifications.

Why is it important to figure out how I'm going to use my new device? Some digital tasks require specific devices, processing power, storage capacity, and connectivity. Therefore, if you consider the usage guidelines in Figure 2-19, you're more likely to buy the right device and not have to purchase expensive upgrades later.

Figure 2-19: Usage guidelines

	Usage Plan	Purchase Recommendation
	You plan to use your computer for email and Facebook, browsing the Web, playing games, managing finances, downloading digital music, and writing school papers.	A mid-priced laptop with standard features might meet your needs.
	You're buying a new computer to replace an old one.	If you have a big investment in software, you should select a new computer that's compatible with the old one.
	You plan to work on accounting and budgeting for a small business.	Consider one of the business systems offered by a local or online computer vendor.
	You spend lots of time playing computer games.	Buy a computer with the fastest processor and graphics card you can afford, or consider a dedicated game console.
	You plan to work extensively with video editing or desktop publishing.	Select a computer system with a fast processor, lots of hard disk capacity, a large screen, and a graphics card loaded with memory.
	Someone who will use the computer has special needs.	Consider purchasing appropriate adaptive equipment, such as a voice synthesizer or one-handed keyboard.
	You plan to use specialized peripheral devices.	Make sure the computer you purchase can accommodate the devices you plan to use.
	Your work at home overlaps your work at school or on the job.	Shop for a computer that's compatible with the computers you use at school or work.
	You want to work with specific software, such as a 3D graphics tool.	Select a computer that meets the specifications listed on the software box or Web site.

What are the pros and cons of the most popular consumer devices?

The most popular digital devices are desktops, laptops, tablets, and smartphones. Figure 2-20 can help you choose the one that best meets your needs.

Figure 2-20: Choose the right device

Most power per dollar

Can make repairs and upgrade components yourself (except for all-in-one units)

Full-size keyboard with numeric keypad for data entry

Large screen for multiple windows and detail work

Adjustable placement of components means less strain on eyes, back, and wrists

Bottom line

The choice for dedicated gamers, serious designers, desktop publishers, and video editors

All components in one unit

Easier to move

Battery powered for portability

Energy efficient means low operating cost

Connects to Wi-Fi networks for Internet access

Lightweight models have higher price tags

Bottom line

Adequate for most digital tasks that are not dependent on cellular connections

The choice for students and on-the-go professionals who want to create content and be productive, in addition to consuming content

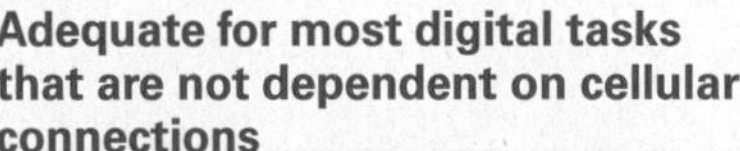

Small and easier to carry

Battery powered

Connects to Wi-Fi networks

Cellular data plans available for mobile Internet access

Convertible units with keyboards available for writing long documents and creating other content

Might not use software designed for desktop and laptops

Small screen limits multitasking

Bottom line

Great for consuming content, such as ebooks, music, and videos

Adequate for browsing the Web and managing social media

Works for some specialized tasks, such as business presentations

Cellular connection for voice and texting

Add a cellular data connection for Internet access

Connects to Wi-Fi networks

Longer battery life than tablets and laptops

Larger sizes offer bigger, easier-to-read screens

Bottom line

Great for communications and mobile apps

Adequate for watching occasional videos and for mobile access to social media

Not optimal for creating text-based content, but excellent for voice calls, texting, and Web browsing

QuickCheck

Which device is best if you want to consume and create content using a device that is portable?

a. Desktop

b. Laptop

c. Tablet

d. Smartphone

How important is compatibility? Suppose that you want to work on some assignments at home using the same software provided by your school lab. Maybe you want to transport data back and forth between your job and home. Or, perhaps your children want to use a computer at home that is similar to those they use at school.

Computers that operate in essentially the same way and use the same software are said to be **compatible**. They can also be described as having the same "platform." To assess whether two computers are compatible, check their operating systems. Computers with the same operating systems can typically use the same software and peripheral devices. Figure 2-21 provides an overview of popular platforms. You'll learn more about operating systems in a later module.

2

Figure 2-21: Compatibility is related to operating systems

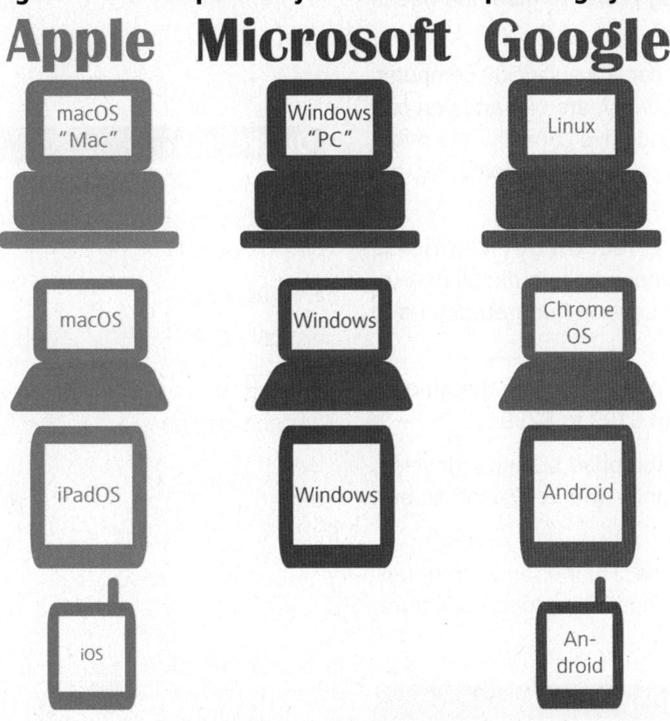

QuickCheck

Do Apple and Android tablets use the same software and apps as laptops?

a. Yes

b. No

Should I stick to one family of devices? As you can see from Figure 2-21, operating systems and the devices that use them are grouped into families. Apple produces macOS and iOS. The open source community produces Linux for desktops and servers; with the support of Google, it also produces Chrome OS and Android.

The operating systems within a family have similarities in the way they look and function. So if you are familiar with macOS on your laptop, then you might find it easier to work with an iPhone rather than an Android phone.

Working within an operating system family can have other benefits. For example, if you are storing your photos, documents, and other data in Apple's iCloud, you'll have easier access to them from devices running iOS, iPadOS, and macOS than from a device running Windows.

Finally, you might find that synching and backing up data between devices is easier if they have operating systems from the same family.

Terminology

Desktops and laptops that run Windows are sometimes referred to as *PCs*. Computers that run macOS are referred to as *Macs*.

▶ What can I expect to pay for a personal device? The price tag for a smartphone is $200–$900, whereas tablet computer prices range from $200 to $1,500. Desktop and laptop computers usually cost a bit more, with price points roughly grouped into three categories: above $1,200, $500–$1,200, and under $500.

Try It!

Visit the Dell Web site. What is the price of the least expensive desktop computer?

Computers priced above $1,200 contain one or more fast processors, a generous amount of RAM, and a copious amount of disk space. These computers contain state-of-the-art components and should not have to be replaced as quickly as less expensive computers. Computer game enthusiasts and anyone planning to work extensively with video editing, graphics, and desktop publishing are likely to require a high-end computer.

A majority of buyers select desktops and laptops that retail for between $500 and $1,200. These popular computers lack the flashy specifications of their state-of-the-art cousins but provide ample computing power to meet the needs of an average user.

In the computer industry, the equivalent of a compact car is a sub-$500 computer. The technology in these computers is usually one or two years old, and you can expect reduced processor speed, memory capacity, and drive capacity. You might have to replace a budget computer sooner than a more expensive computer, but it should be serviceable for typical applications.

QuickCheck

The majority of desktop and laptop buyers spend how much on a computer?

a. $100–$250

b. $250–$500

c. $500–$1,200

d. $800–$1,500

▶ What are the factors that have the biggest effect on device prices? A microprocessor is one of the most expensive components in a digital device. The newest, fastest microprocessor is likely to add several hundred dollars to the price tag.

Memory is another factor that affects price. For example, doubling the amount of memory in a smartphone could raise the cost from $199 to $299.

Large screens cost more to manufacture and raise the price of digital devices. An iMac—Apple's version of an all-in-one desktop unit—with a 27-inch screen costs $800 more than the 21-inch version.

For laptops, size and weight make a difference in price. Thinner and lighter laptops are priced higher, not necessarily because they cost more to manufacture, but because they are more desirable to consumers.

QuickCheck

Which one of the following statements is correct about computer classifications?

a. The speed of supercomputers is measured in petaflops, which makes them the ideal platform for ecommerce stores that are accessed by millions of people.

b. The fact that features of small tablets overlap with features of large smartphones is an example of how the lines between categories of computers can be a bit blurry.

c. The main distinction between desktop computers and laptops is the inclusion of processing circuitry in the display device.

d. Portable computers and desktops have similar characteristics when it comes to accessing cellular voice and data.

How can I make sense of all the jargon in computer ads? Computer ads are loaded with jargon and acronyms, such as RAM, ROM, GHz, GB, and USB. You're sure to spot lots of this computer lingo in ads like the one in Figure 2-22.

The remaining sections of Module 2 delve into specifications for digital components. You'll see how these components work and how they affect the way you work. By the end of Module 2, you should be able to understand the terminology in computer ads and use your knowledge to evaluate various digital devices.

2

Figure 2-22: Computer ads are full of jargon

Powerfully Light

Do everything you love.

- 11th Generation Intel Core i7 4.7 GHz processor
- 12 MB cache
- 16 GB DDR4 2666 MHz RAM
- 512 GB solid state drive
- 17.3" LCD display screen
- Intel integrated graphics
- Integrated speakers
- Integrated 1080p megapixel webcam
- 2 USB 3.2 Gen 1 USB ports
- 1 USB Type C port
- HDMI port
- MicroSD card reader
- Wi-Fi 802.11 ax, Bluetooth
- 53 Wh, 4-cell battery
- Windows 64-bit operating system
- Home/small business software bundle
- 2.7 pounds
- 1-year limited warranty

QuickQuiz Section B

1. Google and other Web service providers use banks of ________ to process and manage data.
2. Windows is the operating system used on desktop and laptop PCs. What is the equivalent operating system for Apple computers? ________
3. A(n) ________ computer is the only type of personal computer that must remain plugged into an electrical source during operation.
4. ________ are the most popular digital devices worldwide.
5. Compatibility is primarily controlled by a device's ________ system.

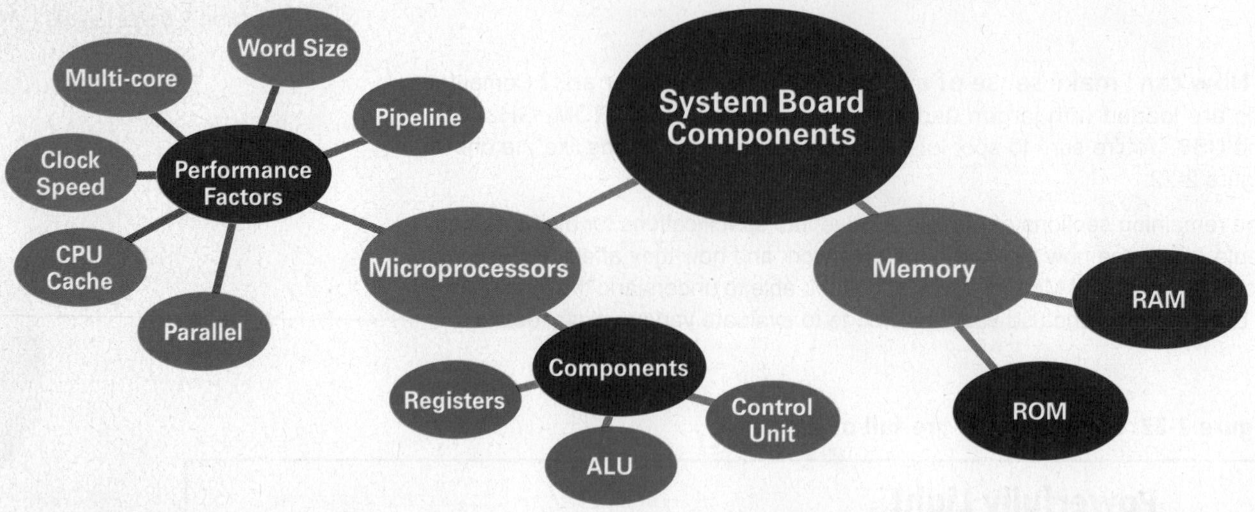

Section C

Processors and Memory

Objectives

- Distinguish between the x86 and ARM processor standards.
- Describe the significance of microprocessor instruction sets.
- Trace an instruction through RAM, the control unit, and ALU as it is processed.
- List seven factors that affect microprocessor performance.
- Use the pizza analogy to explain serial, pipeline, and parallel processing.
- Identify the terminology that pertains to RAM in consumer literature and technical specifications.
- List at least three items that would be found in RAM while you are using a digital device.
- List three events that occur during the boot process.
- Explain why digital devices have ROM in addition to RAM.
- List four reasons for flashing ROM.

Architecture. That's how techies refer to the inner workings of digital devices. Sure, you can use a digital device without understanding its architecture. But to intelligently discuss the opportunities and controversies of your digital world, you need more than a vague notion about microprocessors. Section C will help you keep your head above water when the talk gets technical.

Terminology

x86	control unit	pipeline processing	capacitors
ARM	instruction cycle	parallel processing	volatile
instruction set	instruction pointer	CPU cache	dynamic RAM
programming language	microprocessor clock	word size	virtual memory
machine language	gigahertz	CISC	ROM
ALU	multi-core processor	RISC	boot loader
registers	serial processing	RAM	

Microprocessors

A microprocessor is an integrated circuit designed to process instructions. It is the most important, and usually the most expensive, component of a digital device. The digital devices you use today likely include x86 or ARM microprocessors.

Which devices use x86 microprocessors? Intel Corporation is one of the world's largest chipmakers and supplies a sizeable percentage of the microprocessors that power desktops and laptops. In 1971, Intel introduced the world's first microprocessor—the 4004. Intel's 8088 processor powered the original IBM PC, and chips in Intel's 8086 family powered subsequent models of PCs manufactured by IBM and other companies.

The 8086 chip family set the standard for processors used in many of today's desktop and laptop computers, as well as servers. This standard is sometimes referred to as **x86** because it includes chip models that originally ended in 86, such as the 8086, 80286, and 80386.

Chipmakers no longer follow Intel's original numbering sequence, but x86 is still used when referring to the modern descendants of the 8086. These modern processors include Intel's Core i3, i5, and i7 microprocessors (Figure 2-23), as well as AMD's Radeon and Ryzen microprocessors. You'll find these chips in desktop and laptop computers that run Microsoft's Windows operating system.

QuickCheck

What does x86 mean?

a. It is the model of an Intel chip.

b. It designates low-power chips suitable for tablets and smartphones.

c. It is used to refer to a standard family of processors used in most Windows-based desktop and laptop computers.

d. It means the chip was manufactured by Intel.

Figure 2-23: Intel processors for desktops and laptops

Which devices use ARM microprocessors? Whereas processors based on x86 technology are inside just about all desktop and laptop computers that run Windows, processors based on **ARM** technology dominate in Apple's ecosystem. You'll also find them in most tablet computers and smartphones from other manufacturers.

ARM technology was originally designed by ARM Holdings, a British technology company founded by Acorn Computers, Apple Inc., and VLSI Technology. Today, ARM processors are designed and manufactured by companies that include NVIDIA, Samsung, Qualcomm, and Apple.

ARM-based processors are energy efficient—an important characteristic for devices that run primarily on battery power. Most Android smartphones contain ARM processors. ARM processors are found in Apple's iPads and iPhones. As of 2021, Apple began using M1 ARM processors for its Mac laptops and desktops, too. Apple's M-class processors integrate a CPU, RAM, graphics, and input/output circuitry into a single chip.

QuickCheck

Which processor would you be likely to find in an iPhone?

a. Intel x86

b. ARM

c. Intel Core M3

d. 8088

2

Which microprocessor is best? The microprocessor that's best for you depends on your budget and the type of work and play you plan to do. The microprocessors marketed with the current crop of desktops and laptops can handle most business, educational, and entertainment applications. You'll want to consider the fastest processor offerings if you engage in processing-hungry activities, such as 3D animated computer games, desktop publishing, multitrack sound recording, and video editing.

What microprocessor is in my favorite device? If you know the make and model of a digital device, you can generally find processor specifications by searching online. For example, searching for *processor specifications iPhone 12* reveals that the phone contains an A14 Bionic processor. Although an online search might be required to find processor specifications for phones and tablets, desktops and laptops offer an easier way to discover what's inside (Figure 2-24).

Figure 2-24: Find the processor specifications for a desktop or laptop

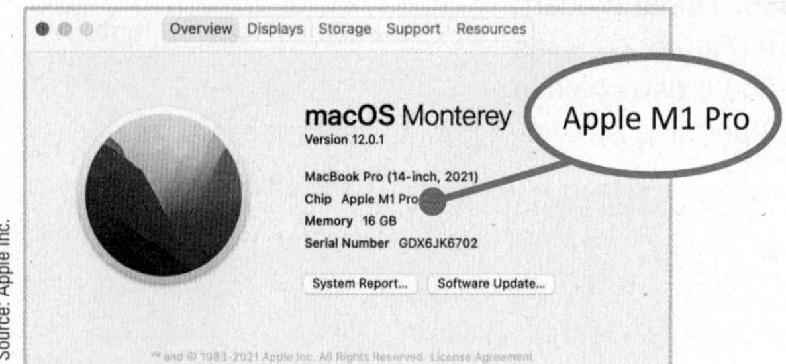

Source: Apple Inc.

On a Mac desktop or laptop, selecting the Apple icon and then choosing About This Mac displays processor specifications, along with memory capacity.

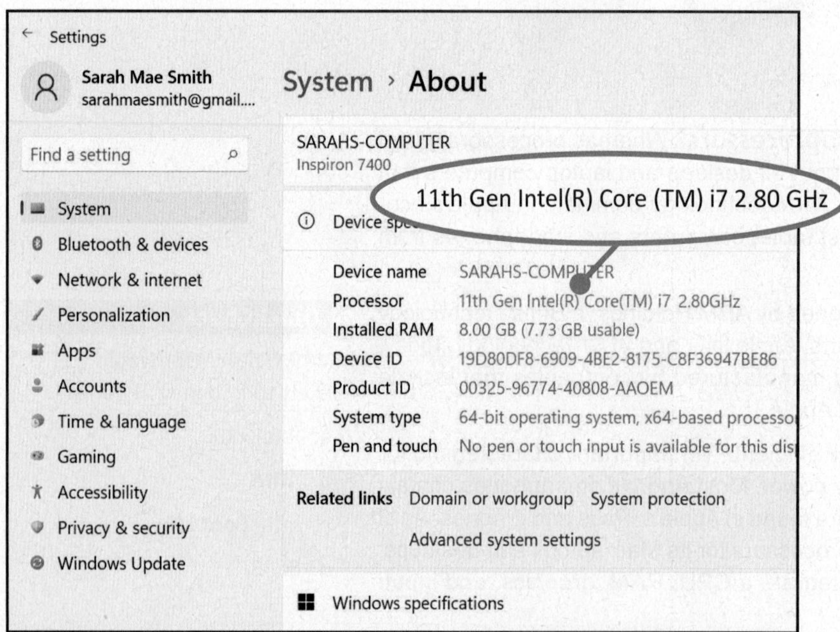

Windows 11 displays processor specs when you type "PC Info" in the Windows search box and then choose the option "About your PC."

Try It!

Find the processor specifications for your favorite desktop computer, laptop, or smartphone. How are the specs similar to or different from the processor specifications shown in Figure 2-24?

How Processors Work

To appreciate the microprocessor specifications in your digital devices, it is handy to have a little background on how processors work. This key technology is quite fascinating in its ability to perform an astounding variety of tasks based on a set of really simple instructions.

What is the significance of microprocessor instruction sets? Microprocessors are hard-wired to perform a limited set of activities. This collection of preprogrammed activities is called an **instruction set**. Instruction sets are unique to processor families. x86 processors use a different instruction set than ARM processors. That is one reason why a game designed to run on a smartphone with an ARM processor cannot directly run on your laptop with its Intel i7 processor.

What is in an instruction set? An instruction set contains a collection of instructions for actions that the circuitry in a microprocessor can perform. The ARM instruction set contains about 35 instructions, whereas the x86 set includes more than 100 instructions. Each instruction carries out a seemingly insignificant task, such as moving a number from computer memory into the processor or comparing two numbers to see if they are the same. Only when millions of these instructions are executed by the processor does a digital device seem to carry out any useful actions.

Are you talking about a computer program? Not exactly. Let's use a game like Fruit Ninja as an example. This game is written by programmers using a **programming language** such as C++, BASIC, COBOL, or Java. When we think of a computer program, we think of the long list of statements written in one of these programming languages.

Surprisingly, microprocessors can't directly understand these programming languages, so programs like Fruit Ninja have to be converted into **machine language** that corresponds to the microprocessor's instruction set. These machine language instructions are binary strings of 0s and 1s that can be processed by a digital device.

What are machine language instructions like? Machine language instructions are like baby steps. Take a look at the commonly used machine language instructions in Figure 2-25. It seems incredible that digital devices can carry out such a wide variety of tasks using such limited instructions.

Figure 2-25: Common commands from the x86 instruction set

Add	0000 0000
Input	0110 0011
Compare	0011 1100
Move	1010 0000
Multiply	1111 0110
Output	1110 1110
Subtract	0010 1100
Halt	1111 0100

QuickCheck

An instruction set is ________.

a. a set of commands, such as Print and Get, that programmers use to create software

b. the collection of preprogrammed activities that a microprocessor can perform

c. a command that is in binary format

d. the options that appear on a software application's main menu

2

▶ What happens inside a computer chip? A microprocessor contains miles of microscopic circuitry and millions of miniature components divided into different kinds of operational units, such as the ALU and the control unit.

The **ALU** (arithmetic logic unit) is the part of the microprocessor that performs arithmetic operations, such as addition and subtraction. It also performs logical operations, such as comparing two numbers to see if they are the same. The ALU uses **registers** to hold data that is being processed. As an analogy, registers are similar to a mixing bowl you might use to hold the ingredients for a batch of cookies.

The microprocessor's **control unit** fetches each instruction, in the same way you might get ingredients for cookies out of a cupboard or the refrigerator. Data is loaded into the ALU's registers, just like you add all the cookie ingredients to the mixing bowl. Finally, the control unit gives the ALU the green light to begin processing, just the way you flip the switch on your electric mixer to blend the cookie ingredients. Figure 2-26 illustrates a microprocessor control unit and its ALU preparing to add 5 + 4.

QuickCheck

When the control unit swings into action, which step comes first?

a. Perform arithmetic operations.

b. Load data into the ALU.

c. Fetch an instruction.

d. Execute the instruction.

Figure 2-26: The microprocessor's control unit and ALU

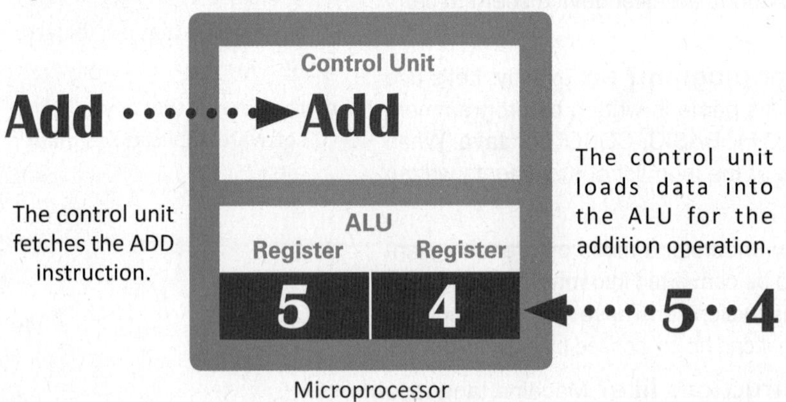

Control Unit
Add
Add
The control unit fetches the ADD instruction.
ALU
Register
Register
5
4
5
4
The control unit loads data into the ALU for the addition operation.
Microprocessor

QuickCheck

The processor in Figure 2-26 would use binary for the instruction and data. What is the binary machine language instruction for ADD? (Hint: Look back at Figure 2-25.)

a. 0000 0000

b. 0101 0100

c. 1110 1110

d. 1111 1111

▶ What happens when a computer executes an instruction? The term **instruction cycle** refers to the process in which a computer executes a single instruction. Some parts of the instruction cycle are performed by the microprocessor's control unit; other parts of the cycle are performed by the ALU. The steps in this cycle are summarized in Figure 2-27.

Figure 2-27: The instruction cycle

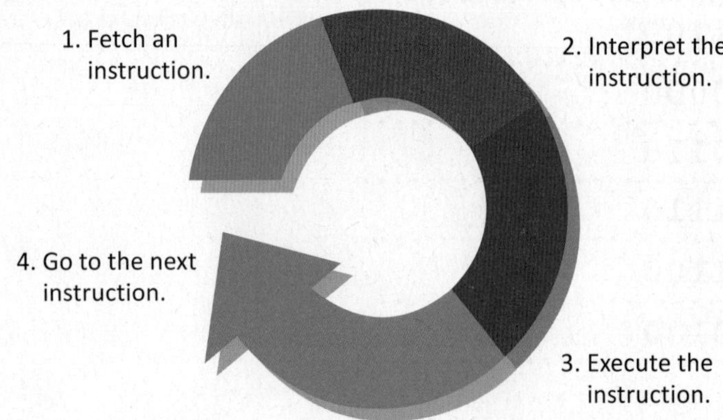

1. Fetch an instruction.
2. Interpret the instruction.
3. Execute the instruction.
4. Go to the next instruction.

2

▶ What role does the control unit play? The machine language instructions for a particular program are held in memory. When the program begins, the memory address of the first instruction is placed in a part of the microprocessor's control unit called an **instruction pointer**.

Figure 2-28 shows how the control unit can then go to the memory address (A) and fetch the instruction by copying data from that address into its instruction register (B). Next, the control unit interprets the instruction and executes it (C).

Figure 2-28: Processing an instruction

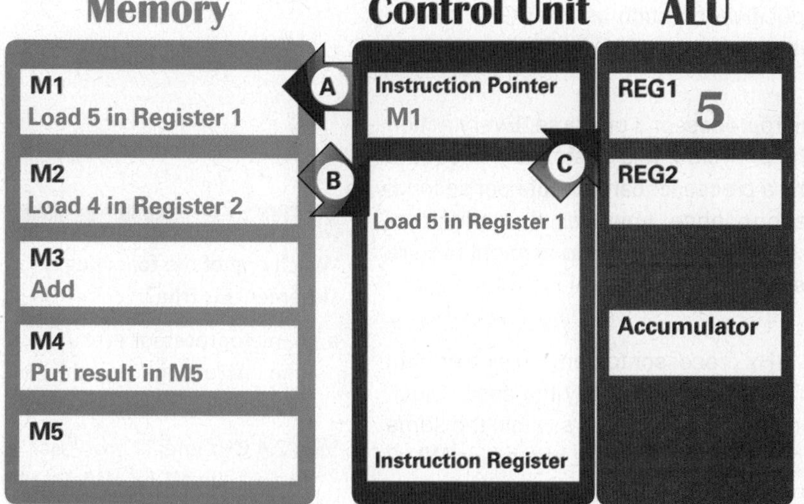

QuickCheck

In Figure 2-28, what happens next?

a. The control unit adds 2.

b. The instruction pointer changes to M2.

c. The processor checks register 2.

d. 5 is added to 4.

▶ When does the ALU swing into action? The ALU is responsible for performing arithmetic and logical operations. As shown in Figure 2-29, the ALU uses registers to hold data that is ready to be processed. When it gets the go-ahead signal from the control unit (A), the ALU processes the data and places the result in an accumulator (B). From the accumulator, the data can be sent to memory or used for further processing. When the computer completes an instruction, the control unit increments the instruction pointer to the memory address of the next instruction, and the instruction cycle begins again.

Figure 2-29: The ALU adds, subtracts, and compares

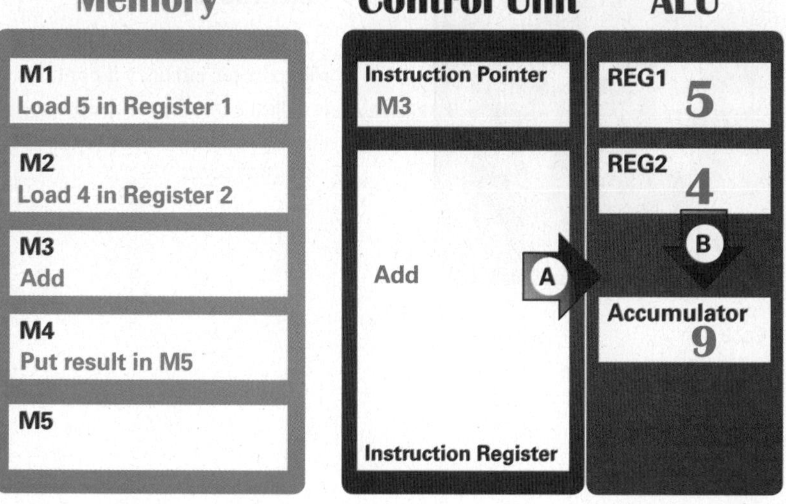

QuickCheck

When the processor has completed the instruction in M4, where is 9?

a. In the accumulator

b. In the control unit

c. In M5

d. In M5 and the accumulator

Performance

Now that you have some background on how microprocessors work, you can begin to appreciate what makes some microprocessors perform better than others. A microprocessor's performance is affected by several factors, including clock speed, number of cores, processing techniques, cache size, word size, and instruction set.

▶ What does GHz have to do with processor performance? A processor specification, such as 3.4 GHz, indicates the speed of the **microprocessor clock**—a timing device that sets the pace for executing instructions. Most computer ads specify the speed of a microprocessor in gigahertz. **Gigahertz** (GHz) means a billion cycles per second. A specification such as 2.13 GHz means that the microprocessor's clock operates at a speed of 2.13 billion cycles per second.

A cycle is the smallest unit of time in a microprocessor's universe. Every action a processor performs is measured by these cycles. It is customary to equate clock cycles with the number of instructions a processor can execute per second. There is not always a one-to-one correspondence, however. Some instructions are processed within one clock cycle, but other instructions might require multiple cycles. Some processors can even execute several instructions in a single clock cycle.

You might expect a computer with a 2.13 GHz processor to perform slower than a computer with a 3.4 GHz processor. This is not necessarily the case. Clock speed comparisons are only valid when comparing processors within the same chip family. A 2.13 GHz processor could outperform a 3.4 GHz processor. Why? Because factors other than clock speed contribute to the overall performance of a microprocessor.

▶ What's a multi-core processor? The "core" of a microprocessor consists of the control unit and ALU. A microprocessor that contains circuitry for more than one processing unit is called a **multi-core processor**. Having more cores usually equates to faster performance. A 2.4 GHz processor with two cores has the equivalent of 4.8 GHz performance (2.4 x 2). A 1.6 GHz processor with four cores has the equivalent of 6.4 GHz performance (1.6 x 4). Figure 2-30 illustrates a microscopic view of a processor with multiple cores.

QuickCheck

Which one of the following statements is true?

a. A microprocessor executes one instruction for each clock cycle.

b. A 2.4 GHz Intel i5 processor is faster than a 1.6 GHz Intel i7 processor.

c. Clock speed is the most important factor that affects processor performance.

d. A multi-core processor can outperform a single-core processor that has a faster clock speed.

Figure 2-30: Four cores of an Intel fourth-generation microprocessor

Terminology

The thin wafer of silicon and the microscopic circuitry it contains is called a *die*. Figure 2-30 illustrates a microprocessor die with four cores.

Can a microprocessor execute more than one instruction at a time? Some processors execute instructions "serially"—that is, one instruction at a time. With **serial processing**, the processor must complete all steps in the instruction cycle before it begins to execute the next instruction. To use an analogy, visualize a pizzeria with one small oven. The pizzas are instructions; the oven is the microprocessor. Pizzas (instructions) are processed one at a time.

Now, what if the pizzeria rigs up a conveyor belt through the oven? A pizza (instruction) starts moving along the conveyor belt into the oven; but before it reaches the end, another pizza starts moving along the belt. When a processor begins to execute an instruction before it completes the previous instruction, it is using **pipeline processing**.

A pizzeria might also have large ovens that hold multiple pizzas. Just as these ovens can bake more than one pizza at a time, **parallel processing** executes more than one instruction at a time. This efficient processing technology is possible with today's multi-core microprocessors.

Pipeline and parallel processing offer better performance than serial processing (Figure 2-31).

QuickCheck

Many of today's digital devices are capable of parallel processing because:

a. Their processors have multiple cores.

b. They have pipelining.

c. They can run more than one program at a time.

d. They have high GHz specifications.

2

Figure 2-31: Serial, pipeline, and parallel processing

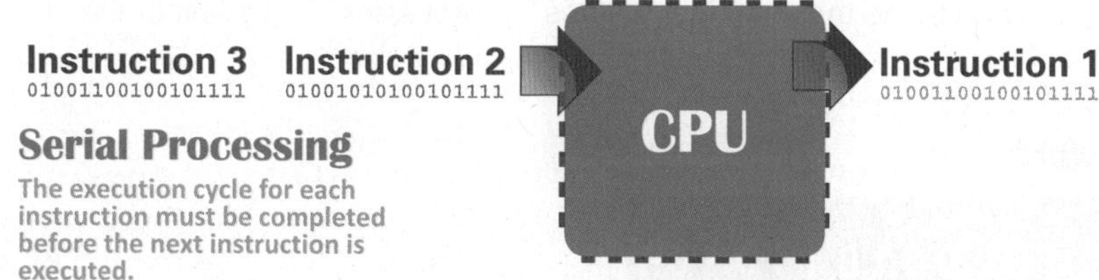
Instruction 3
0100110010010111 1
Instruction 2
01001010100101111
CPU
Instruction 1
01001100100101111
Serial Processing
The execution cycle for each instruction must be completed before the next instruction is executed.

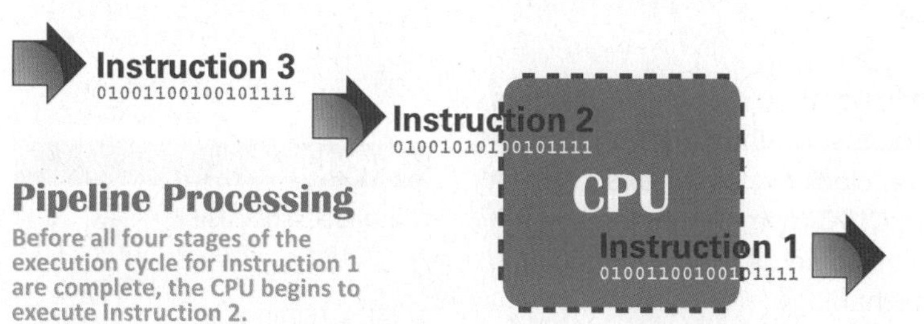
Instruction 3
01001100100101111
Instruction 2
01001010100101111
CPU
Instruction 1
01001100100101111
Pipeline Processing
Before all four stages of the execution cycle for Instruction 1 are complete, the CPU begins to execute Instruction 2.

Instruction 3
01001100100101111
Instruction 4
0010111010101010
Instruction 2
01001010100101111
CPU
Instruction 1
01001100100101111
Parallel Processing
The CPU executes multiple instructions at the same time.

How does cache size affect performance? **CPU cache** (pronounced "cash") is special high-speed memory that allows a microprocessor to access data more rapidly than from memory located elsewhere on the system board. A large cache can increase processing performance.

CPU cache is structured into several levels. Level 1 cache (L1) is the fastest, whereas Level 2 (L2) and Level 3 (L3) are slightly slower but still faster than accessing main memory or disk storage. Cache capacity is usually measured in megabytes.

What impact does word size have on performance? **Word size** refers to the number of bits that a microprocessor can manipulate at one time. It corresponds to the size of the registers used by the control unit and ALU. A processor with a 64-bit word size, for example, has registers that can process 64 bits at a time.

Word size controls the amount of memory that the processor can access. Processors with a 32-bit word size can access a maximum of 4 GB of memory, whereas processors with a 64-bit word size can potentially access many terabytes of memory.

A large word size gives processors the ability to handle more data during each processing cycle—a factor that leads to increased performance. Today's digital devices typically contain 32-bit processors or 64-bit processors. In a computer with a 32-bit word size, registers that hold data and those that hold instructions all have capacity for 32 bits (Figure 2-32).

Try It!

Take another look at the processor specifications for your favorite desktop or laptop computer. Can you tell if its processor has a 32-bit or 64-bit word size?

Figure 2-32: A register holds a 32-bit word

0 1 1 0 0 1 0 1 1 0 0 1 0 0 1 0 1 1 1 1 0 0 0 0 1 0 1 1 0 1 0 1

The bits in this 32-bit register could be an instruction or an item of data that is waiting to be processed.

How does an instruction set affect performance? As chip designers developed various instruction sets for microprocessors, they added increasingly complex instructions, each requiring several clock cycles for execution. A microprocessor with such an instruction set uses **CISC** (complex instruction set computer) technology. A microprocessor with a limited set of simple instructions uses **RISC** (reduced instruction set computer) technology.

A RISC processor performs most instructions faster than a CISC processor. It might, however, require more of these simple instructions to complete a task than a CISC processor requires for the same task.

CISC technology is the basis for most x86 processors. RISC technology is the basis for ARM processors. With that information, you can now understand why ARM was originally an acronym for Advanced RISC Machines.

QuickCheck

x86 processors use ____________.

a. RISC technology

b. CISC technology

c. ARM technology

Random Access Memory

RAM (random access memory) is a temporary holding area for data, application program instructions, and the operating system. RAM can be packaged in a chip carrier that is wired to the system board or it can be located on small circuit boards that plug into the system board.

Try It!

Find out how much RAM is in your favorite digital device. If you're working with a laptop or desktop, you can access RAM specs the same way you found the processor specifications.

2

How much RAM does a device need? When purchasing a digital device, you may have a choice of RAM capacity. Higher RAM capacity adds to the expense of a device. RAM capacity is expressed in gigabytes. Today's desktop and laptop computers typically feature 8 to 32 GB of RAM. Handheld devices usually have 2 to 12 GB of RAM.

But my smartphone has 64 GB, right? Your smartphone has RAM, but not 64 GB. The specifications for smartphones that describe "memory" capacity are not referring to RAM, but to another kind of storage that is more permanent. You'll learn more about this type of storage in the next section. For now, let's focus on RAM and why it is such an essential component of your favorite digital devices.

Why is RAM so important? RAM is the "waiting room" for the microprocessor. It holds raw data waiting to be processed as well as the program instructions for processing that data. RAM also holds the results of processing until they can be moved to a more permanent location such as an internal drive, flash drive, or cloud storage.

In addition to data and application software instructions, RAM holds operating system instructions that control the basic functions of a computer system. These instructions are loaded into RAM every time you turn on a digital device, and they remain there until you turn off the device (Figure 2-33).

Figure 2-33: RAM holds the elements for current tasks

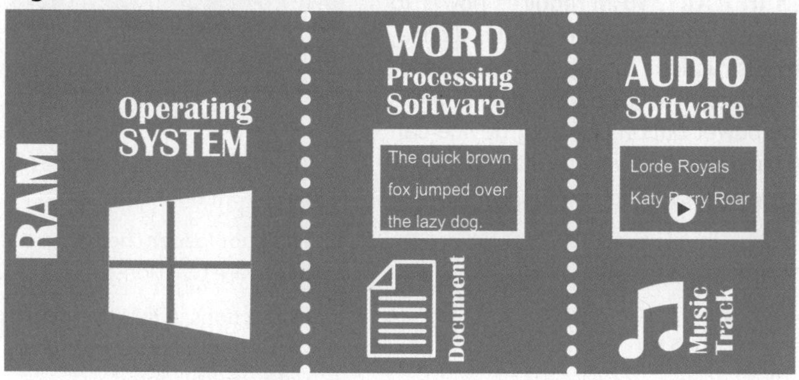

How does RAM work? In RAM, microscopic electronic parts called capacitors hold the bits that represent data. You can visualize the capacitors as microscopic lights that can be turned on or off. A charged capacitor is "turned on" and represents a "1" bit. A discharged capacitor is "turned off" and represents a "0" bit. A RAM address on each bank helps the computer locate data, as needed, for processing.

Unlike disk storage, most RAM is volatile, which means it requires electrical power to hold data. If the device is turned off, if the battery runs out of juice, or if a desktop computer is accidentally unplugged or experiences a power failure, all data stored in RAM instantly and permanently disappears. This type of RAM is technically classified as dynamic RAM (DRAM), but it is commonly referred to simply as RAM. A technical specification such as DDR4 refers to double data rate fourth generation dynamic random access memory.

QuickCheck

The programs and data in RAM disappear when ___________.

a. the device goes to sleep

b. the device is turned off

c. you close a program

d. the battery gets low

▶ Can a device run out of memory? Suppose that you want to work with several programs and large graphics at the same time. Will your device eventually run out of memory? The answer is probably not. If a program exceeds its allocated space, the operating system uses an area of the hard disk or other storage medium as **virtual memory** to store parts of programs or data files until they are needed.

By selectively exchanging the data in RAM with the data in virtual memory, your computer effectively gains almost unlimited memory capacity. Too much dependence on virtual memory can decrease performance, however, especially if virtual memory is located on a relatively slow mechanical device, such as a hard disk drive.

Read-only Memory

ROM (read-only memory) is a type of memory circuitry that is housed in a single integrated circuit on the system board. Whereas RAM is temporary and volatile, ROM is more permanent and non-volatile. The contents of ROM remain in place even when the device is turned off.

▶ Why do digital devices have ROM? When you switch on a digital device, there is a waiting period while the device gets ready for use. While you are waiting, ROM is performing its role to "boot" the device. The boot process varies from one kind of device to another; but in general, it begins when you press the power button and ends when the device is ready to use.

ROM contains a small set of instructions and data called the **boot loader**. The boot loader instructions tell a digital device how to start. Typically, the boot loader performs self-tests to find out if the hardware is operating properly and may also verify that essential programs have not been corrupted. It then loads the operating system into RAM.

▶ Why isn't the boot loader stored in RAM? RAM requires power to hold data. When a device is off, RAM is empty. When you turn on the device, RAM is still empty and doesn't contain any instructions for the microprocessor to execute. ROM, on the other hand, holds data even when the power is off. As Figure 2-34 shows, when you press the power button (A), your device can immediately access the instructions in ROM and proceed with the startup routine (B). Only when the startup is complete can you access apps and data (C).

Figure 2-34: Why the wait?

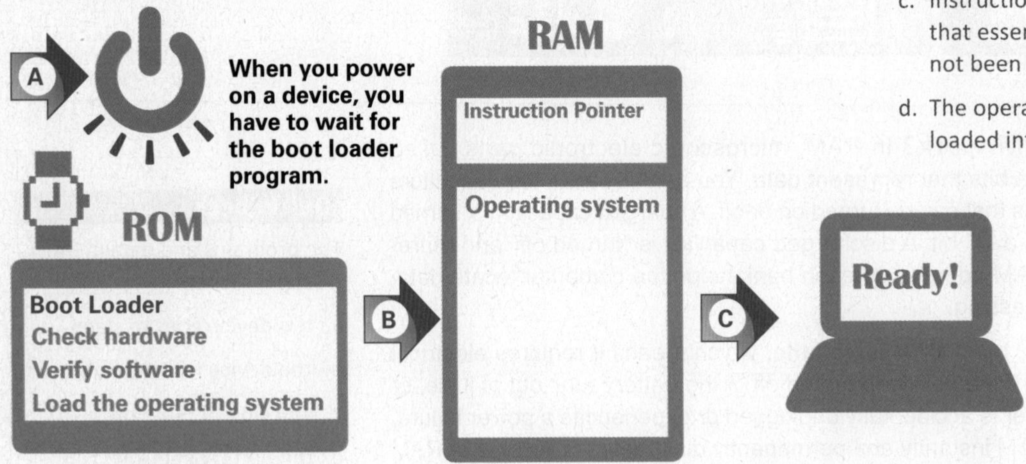

Terminology

A ROM chip, along with its instructions, is commonly referred to as *firmware* because it is a combination of hardware and software.

QuickCheck

While you are waiting for a digital device to boot, all of the following occur except:

a. The microprocessor fetches data from the ALU.

b. The boot loader checks hardware functions.

c. Instructions in ROM verify that essential programs have not been corrupted.

d. The operating system is loaded into RAM.

Can I change the contents of ROM? The process of changing the contents of ROM is sometimes called "flashing" because it is similar to the way a camera flash helps the camera capture an image. There are several reasons that you might want to change the contents of ROM and boot loader instructions.

Repair. Electrical surges and other hardware problems might corrupt the contents of ROM, which would prevent the device from powering on properly. Flashing the ROM to restore the boot loader instructions might correct the problem.

User modification. The boot loader may limit the programs that can be downloaded and run on a device. Flashing the ROM with a modified boot loader can bypass these limitations. The process is sometimes called "jailbreaking" on iOS devices and "rooting" on Android devices. These ROM modifications may cause more problems than they solve and may void the device's warranty.

Forensics. Tricky criminals may hide incriminating data in ROM, or they may alter the boot loader so that it deletes incriminating files when the device is powered on by an unauthorized person. Investigators may want to examine the BIOS for hidden data, and they may have to flash the BIOS to restore it to a non-destructive state.

Updates. Device manufacturers offer updates to the boot loader as necessary to patch security weaknesses. Such updates are performed by running a program supplied by the manufacturer. Be sure to back up your device before flashing, and carefully follow instructions for this procedure. If the flash fails, your device will not start until you get the ROM chip replaced. After a successful update (Figure 2-35), your device should boot normally.

Terminology

There are many types of non-volatile memory, such as EEPROM and NAND, but for convenience the term ROM is used for all of them. Technically, the contents of ROM cannot be changed. The EEPROM and NAND chips that hold the boot loader programs for modern computers can be changed by flashing.

2

Try It!

What does Apple have to say about jailbreaking iPhones and iPads? You can find out by conducting an online search for *support apple jailbreak*.

Figure 2-35: ROM update

The ROM chip containing the boot loader is located on the system board.

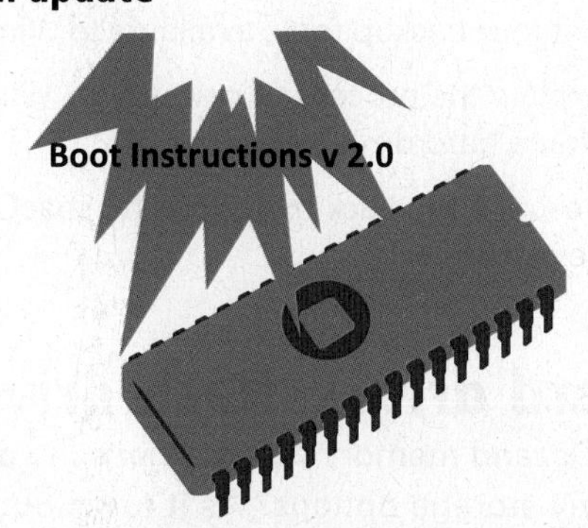

The process of flashing erases the contents of ROM and replaces it with a new set of instructions.

QuickQuiz — Section C

1. A laptop with an Intel Core i7 microprocessor operates at a speed of 3.4 ________. (Hint: Use the abbreviation.)
2. ARM and ________ are two distinct families of microprocessors.
3. The two main parts of a microprocessor include the ________ and the control unit.
4. Because RAM is ________, it cannot retain data in a device that is turned off.
5. The instructions for loading the operating system into RAM when a device is first turned on originate in ________. (Hint: Use the acronym.)

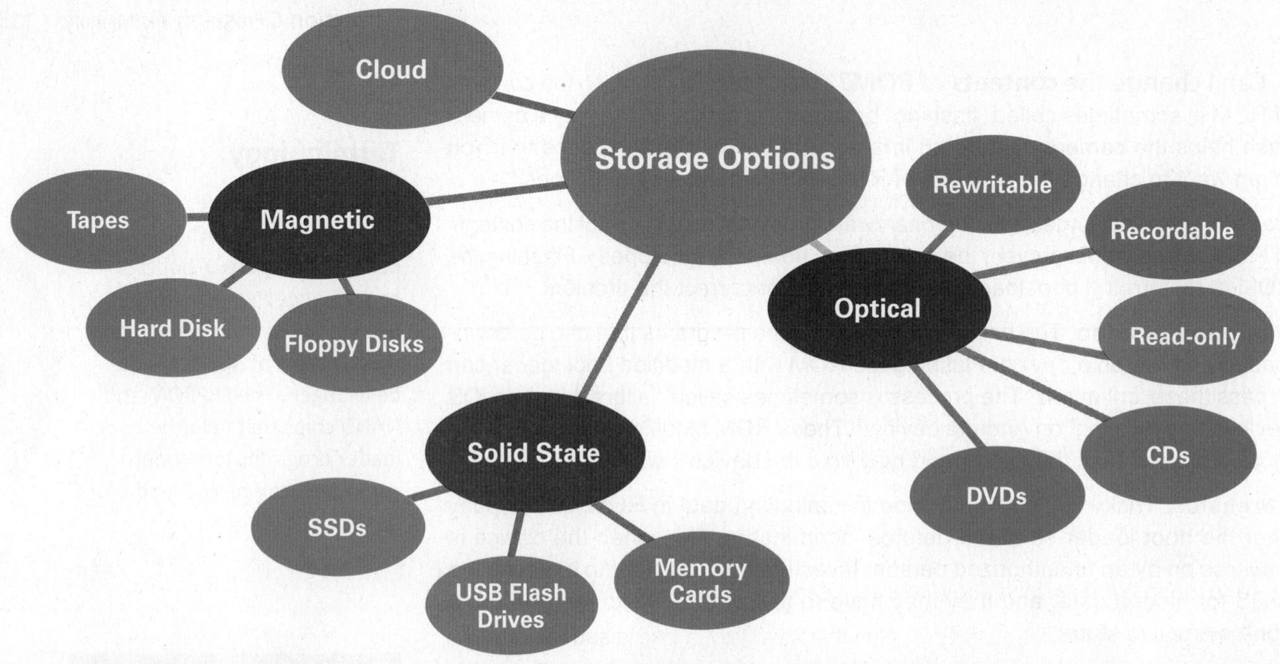

Section D

Storage

Objectives

- List five criteria for comparing storage options.
- Describe the relationship between storage and memory.
- Identify the technology used for hard disk drives, DVDs, USB drives, and other storage accessories.
- Interpret the storage specifications given for digital devices.
- State the advantages and disadvantages of devices that use magnetic storage technology.
- Name two types of optical storage media.
- Explain the significance of ROM, R, and RW for optical storage.
- List three commonly used solid state storage devices.
- Evaluate whether to use local or cloud storage for various projects.
- List at least four common backup pairings.
- List four backup tools available to Windows users.
- Explain the process of restoring a Windows computer after a hard drive failure.
- Describe the backup options for macOS and iOS devices.

Hard drives, flash drives, SSDs, CDs, DVDs, and memory cards. What's the point of having so many storage options? As it turns out, none of today's storage technologies are perfect. In this section, you'll find guidelines that can make you a smart storage technology buyer and owner. The storage technologies you'll learn about are used in a variety of devices—from digital cameras to player pianos—so an understanding of storage technology can be useful even outside the boundaries of personal computing.

Terminology

local storage
magnetic storage
hard disk drive
hard disk platter
read-write head
head crash
access time
SATA
data transfer rate
CDs
DVDs
optical storage
read-only
recordable
rewritable
solid state storage
non-volatile
memory card
card reader
solid state drive
USB flash drive
remote storage
cloud storage
backup
recovery drive
file synchronization
disk image

Storage Basics

Storage is the term used for the components of a digital device designed to hold data permanently. Unlike RAM, storage is non-volatile and retains data even when the device is powered down. Storage is used to save documents, photos, and playlists. It also houses software and the operating system.

Today's digital devices may use local storage and remote storage, but they are not interchangeable. To find out what gets stored where, let's look at local storage first, then expand into remote storage.

Which local storage technology is best? **Local storage** refers to storage devices and media that can be directly attached to a computer, smartphone, or appliance. Local storage options include hard drives, CDs, DVDs, flash drives, solid state drives, and memory cards.

Most digital devices have some type of local storage that is permanently available as you use the device. Built-in storage can be supplemented by removable storage, such as flash drives and memory cards.

Each of these local storage options has its advantages and disadvantages. If one storage system were perfect, we wouldn't need so many storage devices for our digital gear! To compare local storage options, it is useful to review their durability, dependability, speed, capacity, and cost (Figure 2-36).

Figure 2-36: Evaluating storage options

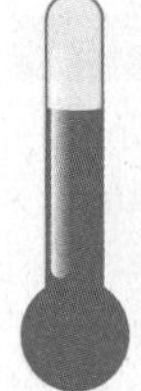

Durability

Resistance to damage from handling and environmental factors such as dust, humidity, heat, and cold. Can be measured in lifespan or in write cycles (the number of times data can be written and revised).

Available when needed; not subject to breakdown, malfunction, network outages, or service interruptions. Can be measured by mean time between failures (MTBF is the time a device is expected to function before failing).

Speed

The rate at which data can be stored or accessed. Faster is better. Can be measured by data transfer rate (the number of megabytes per second that are read or written by the storage device).

The amount of data that can be stored, usually measured in gigabytes (GB) or terabytes (TB).

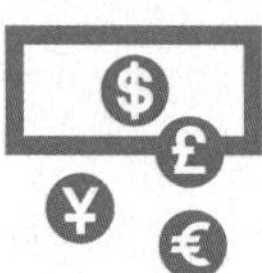

Cost

The price of the storage device and media, usually expressed per gigabyte (GB).

How much storage do I have? The amount of local storage available on a digital device depends on the capacity of each storage device and the amount of data that is currently stored. Available storage space is sometimes referred to as "free space." The process of finding the amount of free space depends on the device. Figure 2-37 can get you started.

Figure 2-37: Are you running out of storage space?

macOS (Macs)

1. Right-click the Macintosh HD icon.

2. Select Get Info.

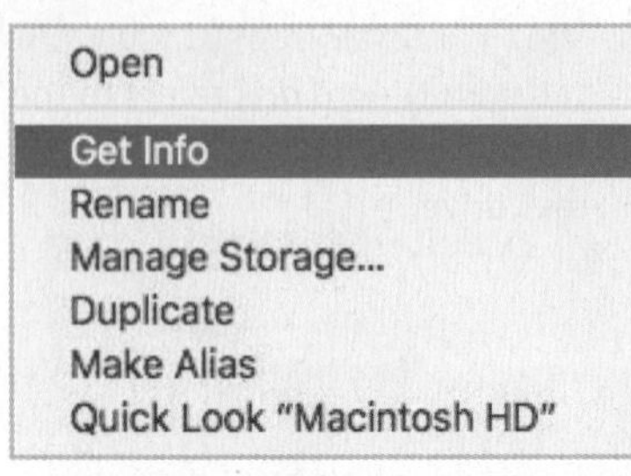

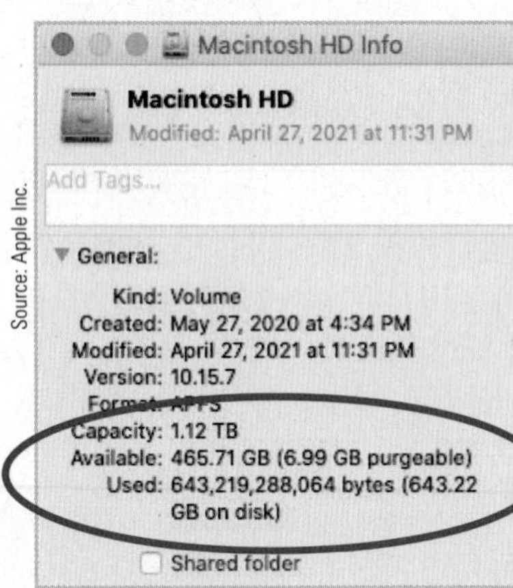

Source: Apple Inc.

Windows (PCs)

1. Enter **storage** in the Windows search box, then select the "Storage settings" option.

2. Select a storage device, such as C:.

Try It!

How close are you to running out of storage space on your favorite digital device? Check now to find out. For laptops and desktops, follow the steps in Figure 2-37. For iOS tablets and phones, select Settings→General→About. For Android devices, select Settings→More→Storage.

How do storage technologies work? You can think of your computer's storage devices as having a direct pipeline to RAM. Data gets copied from a storage device into RAM, where it waits to be processed. After data is processed, it is held temporarily in RAM, but it is usually copied to a storage medium for more permanent safekeeping.

As you know, a computer's processor works with data that has been coded into bits that can be represented by 1s and 0s. When data is stored, these 1s and 0s must be converted into some kind of signal or mark that's fairly permanent but can be changed when necessary.

Obviously, the data is not literally written as "1" or "0." Instead, the 1s and 0s must be transformed into something that can remain on a storage medium. Exactly how this transformation happens depends on the storage technology. For example, hard disks store data in a different way than CDs. Three types of storage technologies are commonly used for personal computers: magnetic, optical, and solid state.

Terminology

The process of storing data is often referred to as *writing data* or *saving a file* because the storage device writes the data on the storage medium to save it for later use.

The process of retrieving data is often referred to as *reading data*, *loading data*, or *opening a file*.

Magnetic Storage Technology

Those big reels of tape that you see on computers in classic science fiction movies are an example of magnetic storage technology used on data-processing era mainframe computers. The first personal computers used cassette tapes for storage, though floppy disk storage was soon available. Today, magnetic storage technology is the foundation for the hard disk drives in desktop computers, laptops, and enterprise servers.

What is magnetic storage technology? **Magnetic storage** represents data by magnetizing microscopic particles on a disk or tape surface. The particles retain their magnetic orientation until that orientation is changed, providing permanent but modifiable storage for data.

Data stored magnetically can be easily changed or deleted simply by changing the magnetic orientation of particles on the disk surface. This feature of magnetic storage provides lots of flexibility for editing data and reusing areas of a storage medium containing unneeded data.

How does a hard disk drive work? A **hard disk drive** (often abbreviated as HDD) contains one or more platters and their associated read-write heads. A **hard disk platter** is a flat, rigid disk made of aluminum or glass and coated with magnetic iron oxide particles.

The platters rotate as a unit on a spindle, making thousands of rotations per minute. Each platter has a read-write head that hovers just a few microinches above the surface. A **read-write head** mechanism in the disk drive magnetizes particles to write data, and senses the particles' polarities to read data (Figure 2-38).

Terminology

You might hear the term *fixed disk* used to refer to hard disks. You often see the terms *hard disk* and *hard disk drive* used interchangeably, though technically *hard disk* refers to the platters sealed inside the hard disk drive.

2

Figure 2-38: Orienting particles on a hard disk

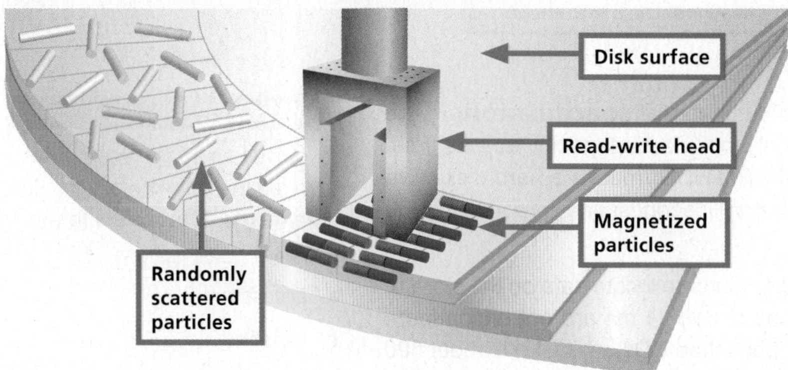

Before data is stored on a hard disk, particles on the disk surface are scattered in random patterns. The disk drive's read-write head orients them in a positive (north) or negative (south) direction to represent 0 and 1 bits, respectively.

QuickCheck

What is the purpose of a read-write head?

a. It pulls particles up as data is read.

b. It etches a track on the disk surface.

c. It orients particles north or south depending on if they represent 0s or 1s.

What are the advantages of hard disk drives? Hard disk drives can be installed inside a device or attached externally for additional storage capacity or backup. Hard disk technology has three advantages. First, it provides lots of storage, with capacities ranging from 40 GB to 8 TB. Second, it provides fast access to files. Third, hard disk drives are economical. The cost of storing 1 gigabyte of data is about two cents.

What's the downside of hard disk storage? Data stored on magnetic media can be unintentionally altered by magnetic fields, dust, mold, smoke particles, heat, and mechanical problems with a storage device. Over time, magnetic media gradually lose their magnetic charge. Some experts estimate that the reliable lifespan of data stored on magnetic media is about three years. They recommend that you refresh your data every two years by recopying it.

The read-write heads in a hard disk drive hover a microscopic distance above each platter. If a read-write head comes into contact with the platter, the **head crash** is likely to damage the platter and corrupt the data contained on it. The causes of a head crash are explained in Figure 2-39.

Figure 2-39: What causes a head crash?

Dropping a device may cause the read-write head to bounce off the surface of the platter, scraping off particles that represent data.
If dust particles or other contaminants seep into the drive case, they may come to rest on a platter where the read-write head will crash into them.

What should I know about hard disk drive specifications? The specifications for a hard disk drive commonly include its capacity, access time, and speed. For example, "2 TB 8 ms 7200 RPM HDD" means a hard disk drive with a 2 terabyte capacity, an access time of 8 milliseconds, and a speed of 7,200 revolutions per minute.

Access time is the average time it takes a computer to locate data on the storage medium and read it. Hard disk access times of 6 to 11 ms are not uncommon. Hard disk drives have much faster access times than CDs, which take about 500 ms to spin up to speed and find data.

Hard disk drive speed is sometimes measured in revolutions per minute (rpm). The faster a drive spins, the more rapidly it can position the read-write head over specific data. For example, a 7,200 rpm drive is able to access data faster than a 5,400 rpm drive.

You might see the term *SATA* included in technical specifications for hard disk drives. **SATA** refers to Serial Advanced Technology Attachment, which is the interface that transfers data from the drive to the main circuit board.

When comparing hard disk drives to other storage technologies, data transfer rates can be useful. **Data transfer rate** is the amount of data a storage device can move per second from the storage medium to RAM. Higher numbers indicate faster transfer rates. Hard disk drive transfer rates are typically 100-200 megabytes per second (expressed as MBps or MB/s).

QuickCheck

If you see an ad for a computer with a 6 ms hard drive, you can assume that 6 ms refers to the drive's ___________.

a. access time

b. capacity

c. rotational speed

d. data transfer rate

Try It!

Check online. What's the average price for a 2 TB hard drive?

Optical Storage Technology

CDs (compact discs) and DVDs (digital video discs) may seem outdated, yet they remain useful for archival storage because they can provide a permanent home for collections of documents, music, and photos that you might not trust to less robust storage technologies.

How does optical technology work? CDs and DVDs are classified as optical storage, which represents data as microscopic light and dark spots on the disc surface. An optical drive contains a laser that directs a beam of light toward the underside of the disc. Reflected light is collected by a lens and converted into 0s and 1s that represent data.

How do CD and DVD technologies differ? A single optical drive typically handles CDs and DVDs, but the costs and capacities of these discs vary (Figure 2-40).

QuickCheck

Optical storage devices read and record data using ________.

a. a read-write head

b. a laser lens

c. dark and light spots

d. electron microscopes

2

Figure 2-40: Optical storage options

CD
650 MB 15¢

CD (compact disc): Designed to hold 74 minutes of recorded music, then adapted for computer storage with capacity for 650 MB of data. Later improvements in CD standards increased the capacity to 80 minutes of music or 700 MB of data.

DVD
4.7 GB 25¢

DVD (digital video disc): Designed with the capacity to hold a feature-length film. A single-sided DVD offers 4.7 GB (4,700 MB) of data storage. A double-layer DVD has two recordable layers on the same side and can store 8.5 GB of data.

What's the significance of ROM, R, and RW? Optical technologies are grouped into three categories:

Read-only (ROM). CD-ROMs and DVD-ROMs are mass produced. Their contents cannot be changed; their lifespan is estimated to be 100 years.

Recordable (R). Data can be written on a recordable disc by consumer devices, but once written, the data cannot be changed. Lifespan: 100 years.

Rewritable (RW). Data can be written on the disc and later changed. The estimated lifespan of data is about 30 years.

How durable are optical discs? Optical discs are not disrupted by humidity, fingerprints, dust, magnets, or spilled soft drinks. Some optical discs have an estimated lifespan of at least 30 years, while other types of optical discs can probably hold data securely for up to 100 years. When using optical technology for archival purposes, the archive should include an optical drive as well as the media containing data. The drive that recorded the data will have the best chance of reading it as the years go by.

Terminology

Writing data on a CD or DVD is often called *burning* because the laser essentially burns a pit in the disc.

QuickCheck

Which optical technology performs most similarly to a hard disk drive?

a. RAM

b. ROM

c. R

d. RW

Solid State Storage Technology

If you're a typical digital device owner, you use solid state storage every day. You carry a flash drive and you might swap memory cards in a camera or tablet. The main storage for your smartphone is also based on solid state technology, as is the storage for many of today's laptops.

What is solid state storage? **Solid state storage** (sometimes called flash memory) stores data in erasable, rewritable circuitry, rather than on spinning disks or streaming tape. Each data bit is held in a gate-like circuit that can be open or shut.

Very little power is required to open or close the gates, which makes solid state storage ideal for battery-operated devices, such as digital cameras and media players. Once the data is stored, it is **non-volatile**—the circuits retain data without the need for an external power source.

Solid state storage provides fast access to data because it includes no moving parts. This storage technology is very durable—it is virtually impervious to vibration, magnetic fields, or extreme temperature fluctuations. It is also dependable. With no mechanical parts, it is less likely to fail than a hard disk drive.

When should I use memory cards? A **memory card** is a flat, solid state storage medium commonly used to transfer files from digital cameras and media players to computers. The term *memory card* might lead you to believe that it is similar to random access memory (RAM). However, these cards are non-volatile and classified as storage because they retain data even when they are disconnected from computers and other devices.

A **card reader** is a device that reads and writes data on memory cards. Common memory card formats include SD cards and microSD cards, which come in a variety of capacities and speeds. Those specifications are displayed on the card's casing, as shown in Figure 2-41.

QuickCheck

In what way are memory cards and RAM similar?

a. They are volatile.

b. They are non-volatile.

c. They are for temporary storage.

d. They are solid state.

Try It!

Check the device you are currently using. Does it have a built-in card reader?

Figure 2-41: Solid state memory cards

toozdesign/Shutterstock.com

Memory cards are available in several speeds and capacities.

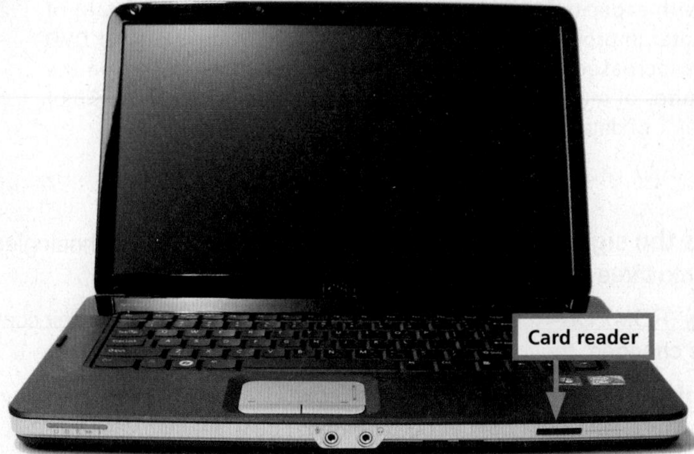

Many digital devices are equipped with a card reader for transferring data to and from solid state memory cards.

Do I need a solid state drive? A **solid state drive** (SSD) is a package of flash memory that can be used as a substitute for a hard disk drive. An SSD is installed inside the system unit and is not meant to be removed except for servicing. Some solid state drives are about the same size as a microprocessor chip; others are about the size of a small deck of cards (Figure 2-42).

Figure 2-42: Solid state drives

15¢ cost per GB

SSDs are widely used as the main storage device in smartphones and tablet computers. Many laptops and some desktop computers also include an SSD instead of a hard disk drive.

What should I know about USB flash drives? A **USB flash drive** is a portable storage device that plugs directly into a computer's system unit using a built-in USB connector. Also called thumb drives, pen drives, jump drives, keychain drives, or UFDs, USB flash drives are small and so durable that you can literally carry them on your key ring. USB flash drives have capacities ranging from 128 MB to 2 TB.

The data transfer rate of a USB flash drive depends on the USB version. USB 3.1 Gen 1 rates can reach 5 Gbps, rivaling hard disk drive speed. USB 3.2 Gen 2x2 speeds are four times faster.

QuickCheck

Which of the following is a good substitute for a hard disk drive?

a. An SSD

b. A memory card

c. A USB flash drive

d. A DVD-RW

Cloud Storage

You probably use several digital devices. Suppose you stored class notes on your laptop, but you've left it at home. Imagine if you could access those notes from your phone. Cloud storage can make that happen.

What is cloud storage? Storage that is built into a digital device or that can be plugged directly into a device is classified as local storage. In contrast, **remote storage** is housed on an external device that can be accessed from a network. Remote storage may be available on a home, school, or work network. It can also be available as an Internet service, in which case it is called **cloud storage**.

Cloud storage is provided to individuals by services such as Apple iCloud, Microsoft OneDrive, Google Drive, and Dropbox. The basic concept is that files can be stored in a subscriber's cloud-based storage area and accessed by logging in from any device. In a simple implementation, cloud storage functions just like a local drive (Figure 2-43).

Figure 2-43: Dropbox is in the cloud but accessed like a local drive

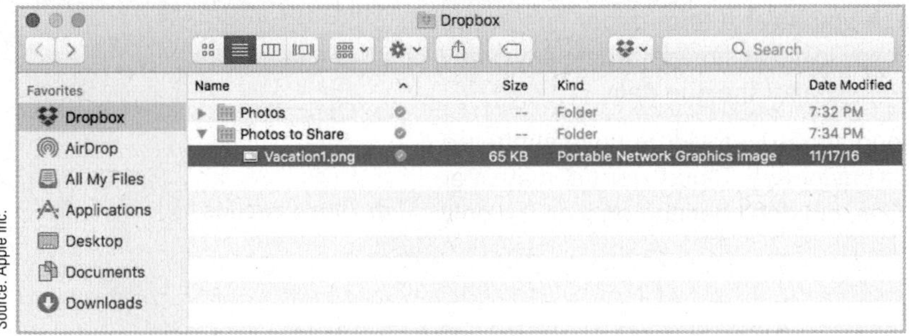

Source: Apple Inc.

Some cloud implementations offer a synchronization feature that automatically duplicates files stored on a local device by also saving them in the cloud (Figure 2-44).

Figure 2-44: Cloud synchronization

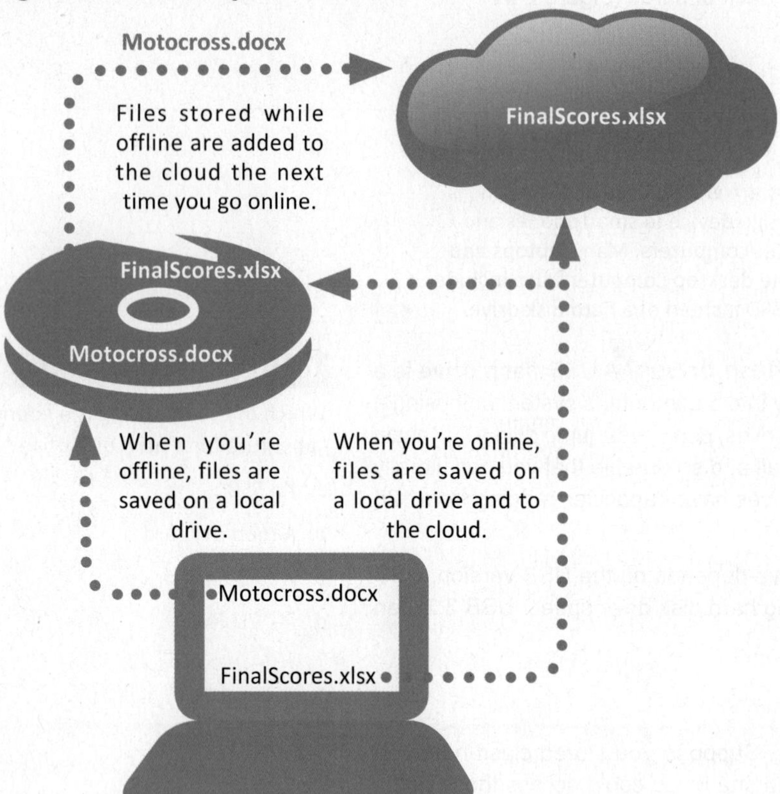

Motocross.docx
FinalScores.xlsx
Files stored while offline are added to the cloud the next time you go online.
FinalScores.xlsx
Motocross.docx
When you're offline, files are saved on a local drive.
When you're online, files are saved on a local drive and to the cloud.
Motocross.docx
FinalScores.xlsx

▶ **What should I know about cloud storage?** The term *cloud storage* refers to a set of technologies for transporting, synchronizing, and managing data stored on banks of high-performance hard disk drives housed in the service provider's data center.

Most cloud services offer a generous amount of free storage space, so the price is right. If you regularly use several digital devices and want to access your files from all of them, then cloud storage is an excellent solution. Also, if you procrastinate about backing up your devices, files stored in the cloud remain there even if a local device malfunctions. That being said, cloud storage has several drawbacks.

Security and privacy risks. The more places your data is stored and the more networks on which it travels, the more susceptible it becomes to intercepts from hackers and government spying agencies. Carefully consider what you store in the cloud.

Service outages. When a cloud storage site has an outage, all the data stored there becomes temporarily inaccessible. If you have a term paper due in two days, it would be best not to trust the only copy to cloud storage, where a two-day outage could make your files inaccessible until after the due date.

Discontinuation of service. Some cloud storage providers have shuttered their storage services with little warning to customers. Cloud storage may offer a convenient option for backing up your files, but don't depend on it as the only backup.

QuickCheck

Cloud services generally use what type of storage devices?

a. Magnetic

b. Optical

c. Flash

d. Cloud circuits

Backup

Storage devices fail. Cloud storage services go dark. When they do, the data they contain might not be recoverable. To protect your data, you need backups. Do you have them? Do they contain the files you'll need to resume work without a hitch?

What do I really need to back up? A **backup** is a copy of one or more files that is made in case the originals become damaged. Although the best practice might seem to be "back up everything," that is not always practical.

Your files are often scattered—some on a local hard disk, others on USB drives, some on your phone, and even others on cloud storage. Simply copying all of your files from one device to another or to the cloud requires lots of space and lots of time. Plus, there are some sticky technical issues that make it difficult to actually get a complete backup. To understand the problem, consider what a typical hard disk contains (Figure 2-45).

Try It!

How many GB of data would be stored in a backup of the entire contents of your desktop or laptop computer? (Hint: Figure 2-37 showed you how to check the amount of space that is used on a local hard disk.)

2

Figure 2-45: What can you afford to lose?

Operating system: The operating system is required to start your device, but a backup copy might not run if it is unauthorized.

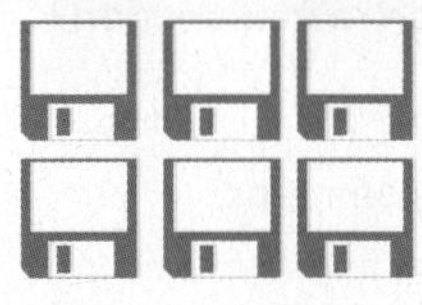

Software: Most devices are populated with preinstalled software, and you've probably downloaded and installed many additional apps. If these are wiped out when a storage device fails, the process of downloading and reinstalling them can be time consuming.

Data files: Your documents, photos, music, videos—all the goodies that you've created and gathered—can be difficult or impossible to reconstruct from scratch.

Settings, accounts, and profiles: How much time did you spend customizing your home screen, entering contacts, choosing passwords, and setting preferences for your favorite apps? No one wants to have to do that all over again!

Then what should I do? The best advice is this: Know what's important and ensure that current versions exist on more than one storage device. The easiest pairings of devices for backups are illustrated in Figure 2-46.

Figure 2-46: Backup pairings

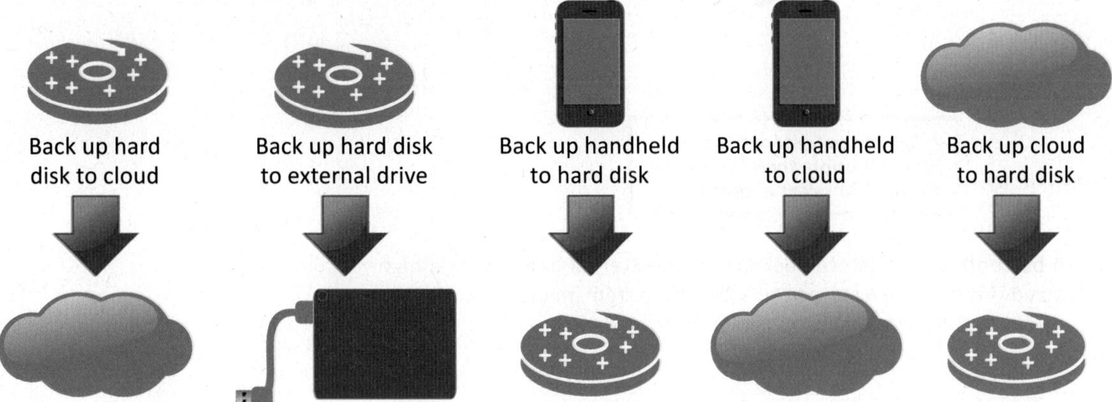

What tools do I need for backups? The tools you'll need depend on what you are backing up and where you are putting the backups. If you are a typical consumer with a laptop and a smartphone, you will need a cloud storage account, an external hard disk drive, synchronization software, a blank USB flash drive, and backup or disk imaging software.

I've got a Windows PC. What should I do? Windows users have access to several backup tools and will need to use more than one of them.

Recovery drive. A **recovery drive** (or system repair disc) contains parts of the operating system necessary to boot your computer and diagnose system problems after a hard drive failure or software malfunction. Files for creating a recovery drive are usually preinstalled on the hard disk drive, but they won't do you any good there when the hard disk fails. Follow the manufacturer's instructions to move the recovery files to a blank USB flash drive, which you can store until it is needed.

Copy command. As you are working on important projects, make copies of essential files. You can store the copies on the same device as the originals using versioning techniques, such as adding "v2" and "v3" to the file names of versions. And for safety, periodically copy a version to a USB drive or to cloud storage. You can manually create copies of your data files using the Copy option in Windows File Explorer.

File History. Data file backup can be automated using File History, which is included with Windows 8.0 and subsequent versions. File History uses **file synchronization** to make copies of files from your Documents, Music, Pictures, and Videos folders, along with any files that were created or modified while OneDrive was offline. File History is useful if a data file goes missing, but it requires the System Image Backup option for system files, software, and settings. File History is relatively easy to set up (Figure 2-47).

QuickCheck

Which backup tool can be used to boot a Windows computer after a hard drive malfunction?

a. A recovery drive

b. The Copy command

c. File History

d. A cloud drive

Figure 2-47: Activate File History

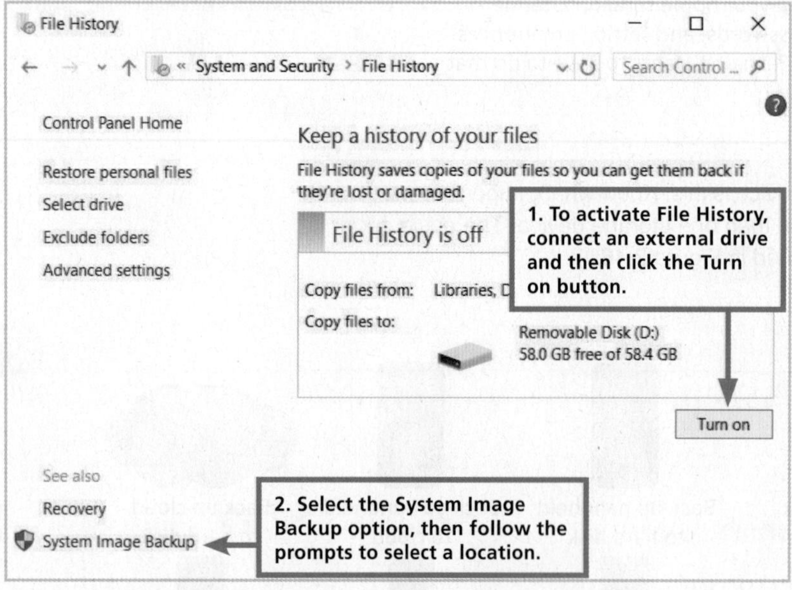

File History can be configured to store backups on an external hard drive, a high-capacity USB flash drive, or a cloud storage service. The system image requires more space than is available on most USB flash drives.

System image. A **disk image** is a bit-for-bit copy of the data from all sectors of a hard disk. Windows includes a disk imaging option called System Image that creates an exact clone of the original disk, including the operating system, your software, and all your settings. Be sure to select the System Image Backup option in the File History window to activate it.

▶ If my computer's hard drive fails, how do I proceed? First, a new hard drive has to be installed. Then, as shown in Figure 2-48, (A) use the recovery drive to boot the computer. Then, (B) attach the backup drive containing your system image. Respond to the prompts displayed on the screen to copy the system image to the new hard disk. After the system image is installed, recover your files by using the File History utility.

Figure 2-48: Restoring Windows after a hard disk crash

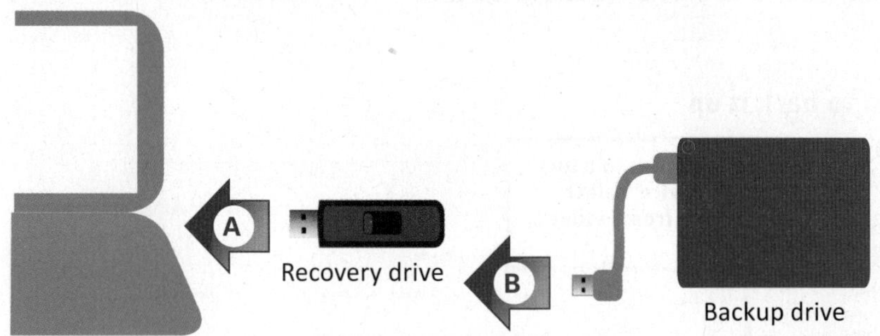

QuickCheck

In Figure 2-48, what is stored on the USB flash drive?

a. All the files that the user has backed up
b. Parts of the operating system needed to boot the computer
c. A system image
d. A synchronized backup

▶ I have a Mac. What's my best backup option? macOS offers a comprehensive file synchronization utility called Time Machine, which backs up the entire hard disk, including system files, applications, accounts, preferences, email messages, music, photos, movies, and documents. Make sure that Time Machine is set to run in the background at all times while your computer is turned on.

If you need to restore a single file, you can open Time Machine, choose a file, and then select the Restore option. To restore an entire backup, make sure the backup drive is connected and hold down the Command and R keys as the computer starts. Figure 2-49 illustrates Time Machine.

Figure 2-49: Time Machine backups

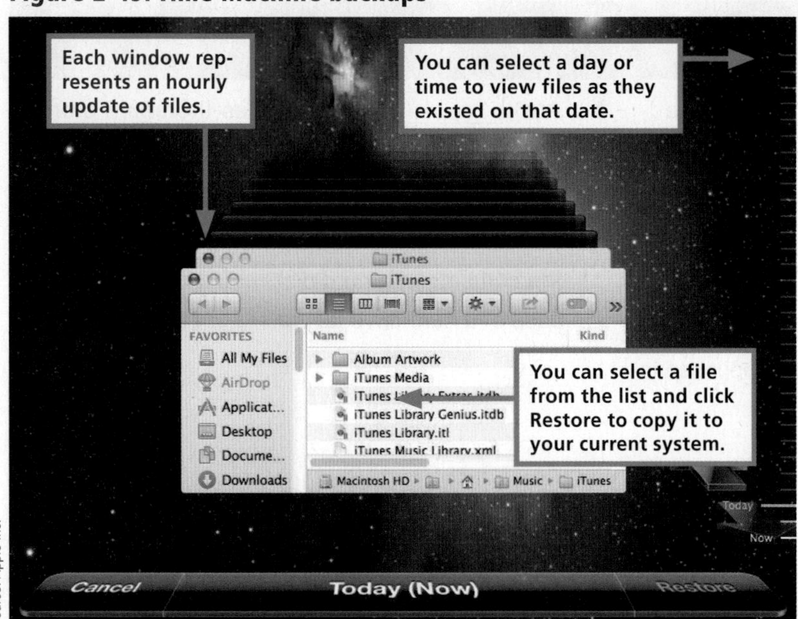

What about backing up my smartphone and tablet? Many Android devices include backup software, which is usually accessible from the Settings icon. Generally, backups from Android devices are stored in the cloud on Google servers. If your Android device accepts SD cards, you may also be able to make backups of individual files.

Owners of iOS devices can back up to a local computer using Finder, iTunes, or iCloud. The process is usually referred to as synchronization because it updates the files on the backup device with newer versions of files found on the smartphone or tablet.

To activate iCloud backup, you can access Settings for your iOS device, tap your account name, tap iCloud, and then select iCloud Backup. Slide the iCloud Backup button to On. To sync to a local drive using Finder, simply connect the device to a desktop or laptop using a USB cable and then choose the iPhone icon (Figure 2-50).

Figure 2-50: Sync your iPhone or iPad to back it up

Synching is usually initiated by tethering your handheld device to a desktop or laptop computer using a USB cable.

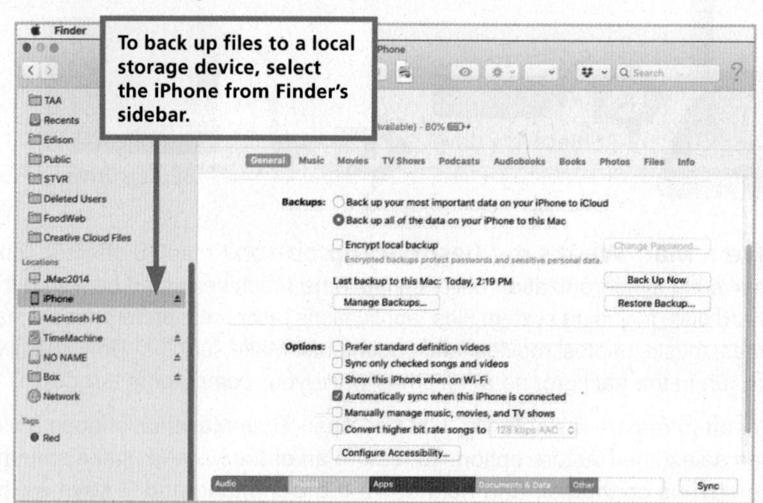

QuickQuiz

Section D

1. A magnetic storage device uses a read-________ head to magnetize particles that represent data.
2. Today, ________ storage technology, such as CDs and DVDs, is used for archiving data.
3. Cloud storage, such as OneDrive and iCloud, is classified as ________ storage as opposed to local storage.
4. A(n) ________ uses the same storage technology as a USB flash drive but is not designed to be removable. (Hint: Use the acronym.)
5. A disk ________ is a bit-for-bit copy of the contents of a hard disk, created as a backup in case of a hard drive failure.

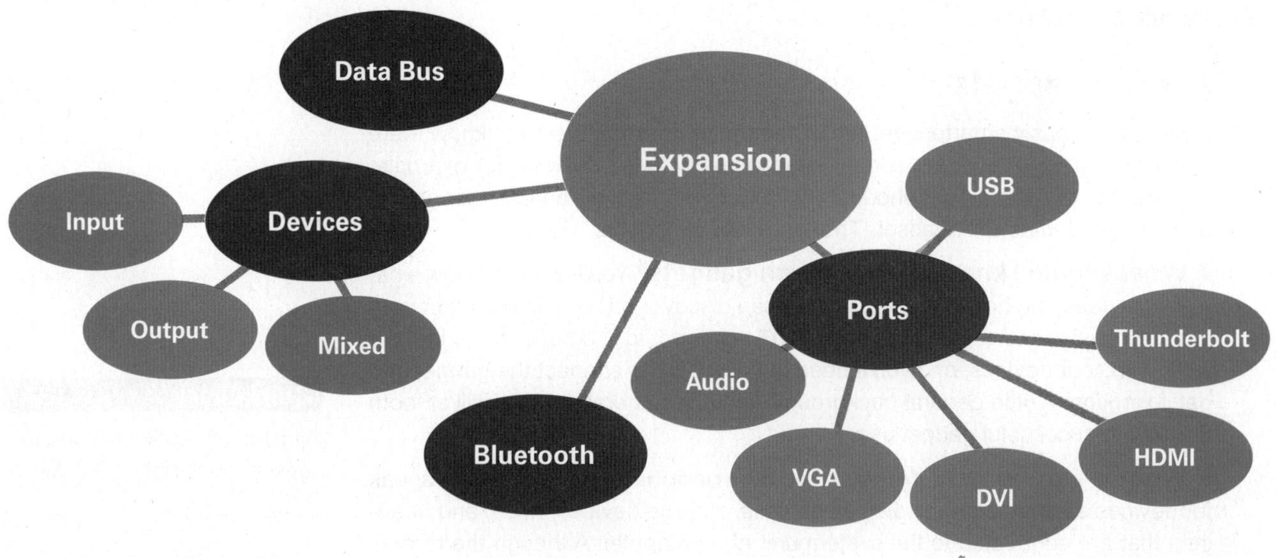

Section E

Input and Output

Objectives

- Categorize devices as input, output, or mixed.
- Diagram the path of data from external devices to the CPU.
- Identify common expansion ports and connectors, such as USB, VGA, HDMI, DVI, DisplayPort, Thunderbolt, and Ethernet.
- State which types of devices should not be unplugged without notification.
- List at least three examples of devices that might be connected using Bluetooth.
- Explain the purpose of a device driver and why one might have to be installed or updated manually.
- List four factors that affect display quality.
- Explain the role of a GPU and list the applications for which one is most useful.
- Explain how resolution settings affect the size of objects and text on the screen.
- Identify which printing tasks are best fulfilled by a dot matrix, laser, or 3D printer.
- Describe the function of the three most popular IMU sensors used by the Internet of Things.
- List five types of sensors that provide input to autonomous vehicles.

Gadgets. Those fitness trackers, VR headsets, credit card readers, and other gadgets are basically input and output devices. Section E focuses on the technology that makes it possible to expand a host device by connecting input and output devices, such as displays and printers. The section winds up with a look at the amazing array of sensors that collect data for the Internet of Things and self-driving vehicles.

Terminology

peripheral device
expansion ports
data bus
hot-plugging
USB hub
Bluetooth
device driver
LCD
response rate
dot pitch
screen resolution
touchscreen
virtual keyboard
resistive technology
capacitive technology
integrated graphics
dedicated graphics
graphics processing unit
ink jet printer
laser printer
additive manufacturing
smart sensors
sense-plan-act algorithms
accelerometer
gyro sensor
magnetometer
lidar

Add-on Gadgets

If you have a basic smartphone, tablet, laptop, or desktop, then you know there is a tempting list of add-on gadgets to accompany these devices: for example, that fine set of AirPod headphones, a Fitbit activity tracker, an external optical drive, or an Oculus VR headset. There are lots of options.

▶ **What should I know about add-on gadgets?** You'll want to know what a gadget does and how well it works. You can discover relevant information from product reviews and customer ratings. You'll also want to find out if the gadget will work with your devices, and you'll need to know how to connect the gadget and get it working. A little general background about peripheral devices will smooth the way to successful gadget use.

▶ **What is a peripheral device?** The term **peripheral device** is tech-speak for devices such as printers, display devices, storage devices, mice, and headsets that are connected to the system unit of a computer. Although the term is falling out of use, it still pops up here and there, so it is worth knowing. Some modern nontechnical terms for peripheral devices include *gadgets*, *add-ons*, and *accessories*. Peripheral devices are classified as input, output, or mixed devices, as shown in Figure 2-51.

QuickCheck

Which of the following are not considered peripheral devices?

a. RAM and CPU

b. Speakers and headsets

c. Hard disk drive and memory cards

d. Touchscreen and keyboard

Figure 2-51: Peripheral devices

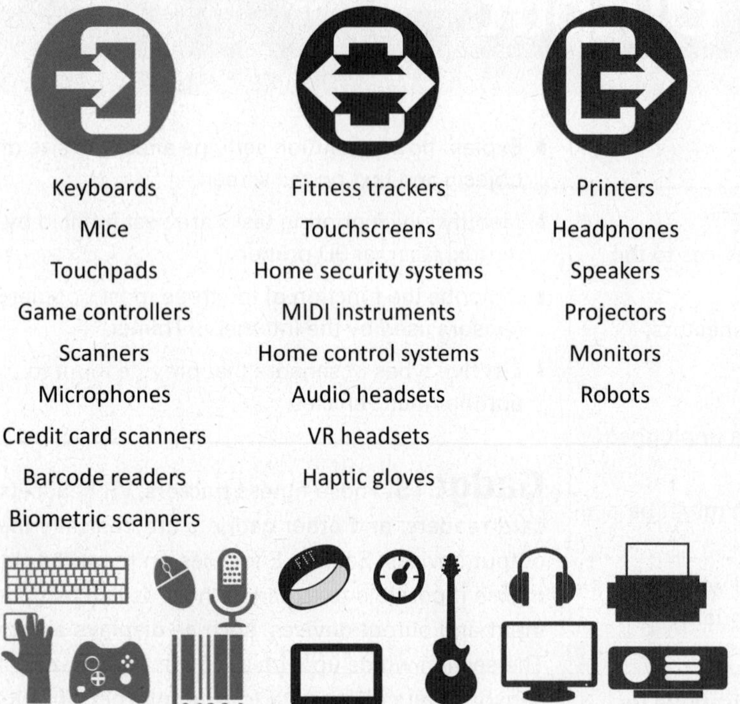

▶ **What can I connect to my devices?** Many gadgets, such as earbuds, work with a wide variety of devices, including smartphones, smartwatches, tablets, laptops, and desktops. Other gadgets are designed to work only with iPhones, for example. When shopping for gadgets, read the specifications and make sure they include your device.

▶ **What about connections?** Add-on gadgets can connect to laptops, desktops, and handhelds using a cable or a wireless connection. Let's take a look at commonly used connectors so that you can identify them on your devices.

2

Expansion Ports

Like an ocean liner's portholes, many digital devices have ports in the system unit that can be opened or closed. A computer port can be opened to allow data to flow to and from various add-on devices. Because these ports expand the options for input, output, and storage, they are commonly called **expansion ports**. When you plug in a USB flash drive or insert a memory card, you are using an expansion port.

How do expansion ports relate to the rest of the circuitry in a device? All of the components on the system board are connected by circuitry. The main circuits that carry data are called the **data bus**. These circuits carry data at lightning speeds as pulses of electrical voltages.

The part of the data bus that runs between the microprocessor and RAM is called the local bus or internal bus. This is the fastest part of the data bus because it has to keep up with the data demands of the microprocessor.

The part of the data bus that stretches from RAM to various expansion ports is called the expansion bus. This part of the bus has several branches to accommodate data traveling to and from various ports (Figure 2-52).

Figure 2-52: The expansion bus

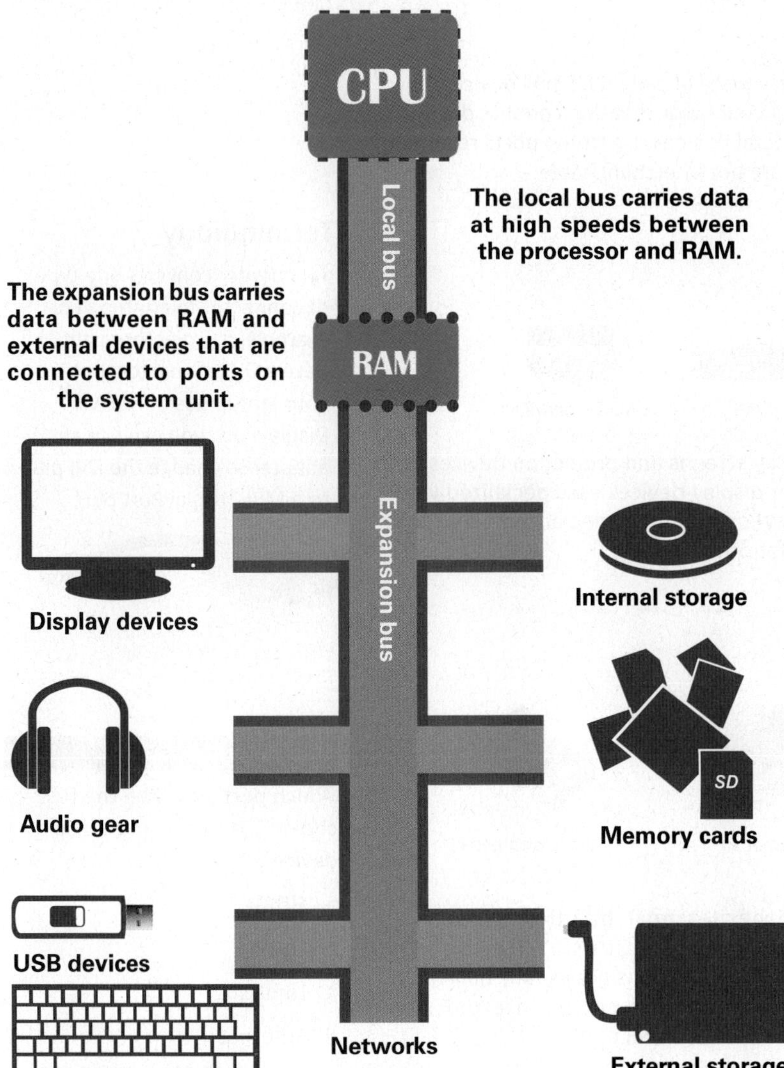
CPU
Local bus
The local bus carries data at high speeds between the processor and RAM.
The expansion bus carries data between RAM and external devices that are connected to ports on the system unit.
RAM
Expansion bus
Display devices
Internal storage
Audio gear
SD
Memory cards
USB devices
Networks
External storage

QuickCheck

How does data flow from an external storage device to the processor?

a. Data first travels on the expansion bus, and then switches to the data bus.

b. Data begins on the internal bus, and then ends up on the local bus.

c. Data from the expansion bus reaches RAM, and then it is transferred to the processor.

d. Data starts on the network bus, is processed in the CPU, and then is sent to RAM.

What should I know about expansion ports? When making a connection between a peripheral device and a computer, the cable must connect to the proper expansion port. Ports are sometimes marked by tiny symbols that are difficult to see. You'll want to be able to identify ports by their size and shape.

From Section D, you are already familiar with the storage ports used for memory cards. You'll also want to be able to identify general-purpose, video, audio, and network ports (Figure 2-53).

Try It!

Take a look at your laptop or desktop computer. Can you make a list of all its ports?

Figure 2-53: Expansion ports

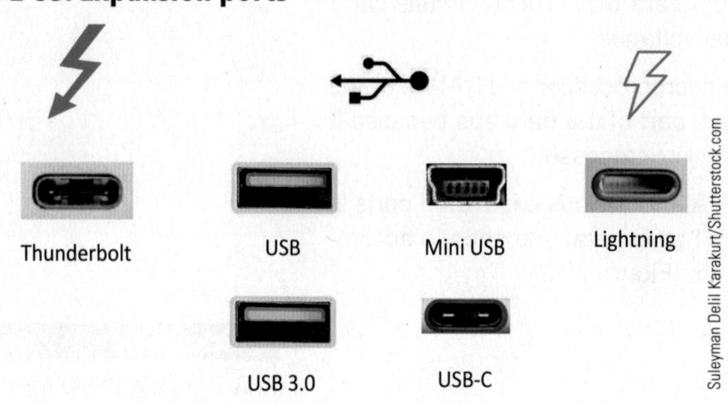

General-purpose ports are used to connect a variety of gadgets. Small devices, such as smartphones, might use a single Lightning connector that does double duty as a recharging cable and a connector for peripheral devices. Lightning ports resemble USB-C ports, but their cables are not interchangeable.

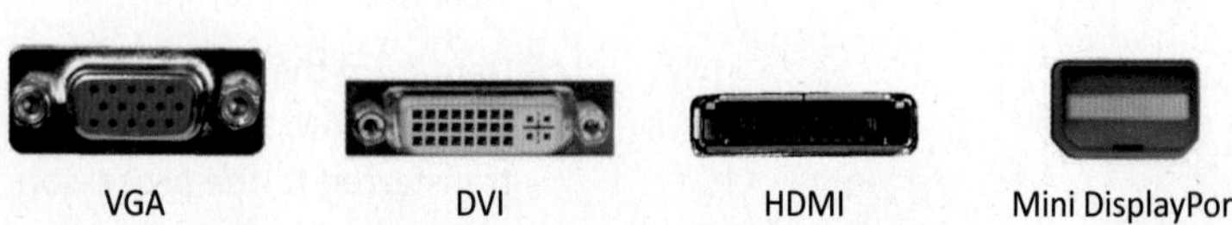

Some display devices, such as external display screens and projection devices, are designed to connect to USB ports, but other display devices use specialized video ports, such as HDMI, DVI, VGA, and DisplayPort. Using a specialized video port leaves USB ports free for other gadgets.

Terminology

An *adapter* converts one type of connector to another. For example, a projector might have a DVI connector; but if your laptop has only a Mini DisplayPort, you can use an adapter to change the DVI plug to a Mini DisplayPort plug.

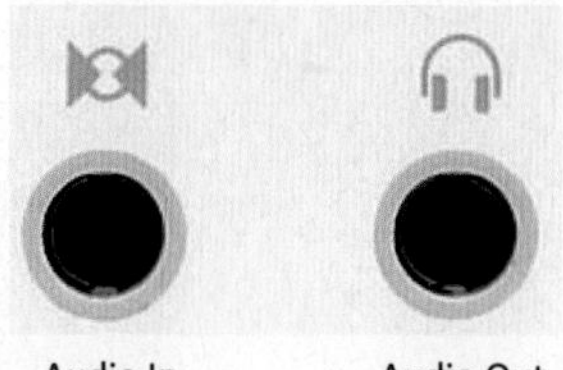

Most devices have at least one Audio Out port for a headset or earbuds. There may be an additional Audio In port for connecting a microphone.

An Ethernet port handles wired network connections. Wireless network connections are usually built in, but an antenna can be inserted in a USB port.

QuickCheck

Which port would be the first choice for connecting a display device?

a. HDMI

b. USB

c. Lightning

d. Ethernet

What is hot-plugging? When a peripheral device is connected or disconnected while the host device is operating, it is called **hot-plugging**. Although it is unnecessary to turn devices off before disconnecting them, some devices should not be disconnected while in the middle of data transfers. Before unplugging a device, such as a USB flash drive, your computer might require notification. Figure 2-54 shows how to safely remove a USB drive.

QuickCheck

When you're ready to put your laptop in your backpack, which of the following do you need to eject?

a. A printer that's connected with a USB cable

b. A USB flash drive

c. The mouse

d. The DVI port

Figure 2-54: How to safely eject USB flash drives

With Windows, use the File Explorer folder icon to view the flash drive icon. Right-click it, then select Eject. You can remove the flash drive when its name disappears from the list or the Safe to Remove Hardware message appears.

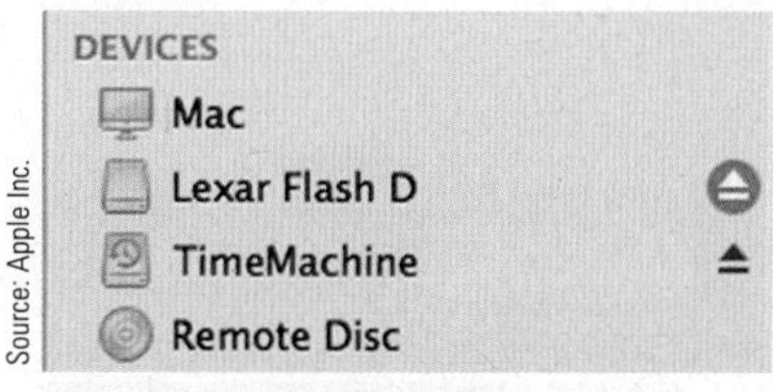

Source: Apple Inc.

With macOS, use Finder to view the flash drive icon. Select the round Eject icon. It is safe to remove the flash drive when its listing disappears.

Try It!

Do you have any devices connected to your computer that require notification before they are removed? (Hint: Use one of the methods in Figure 2-54 to find out.)

What if I run out of USB ports? If you want to connect more devices than the available number of USB ports, you can use a USB hub. A **USB hub** is an inexpensive device that turns one USB port into multiple ports. It also saves wear and tear on USB ports caused by repeatedly inserting and removing USB devices (Figure 2-55).

Figure 2-55: A USB hub is handy for connecting lots of gadgets

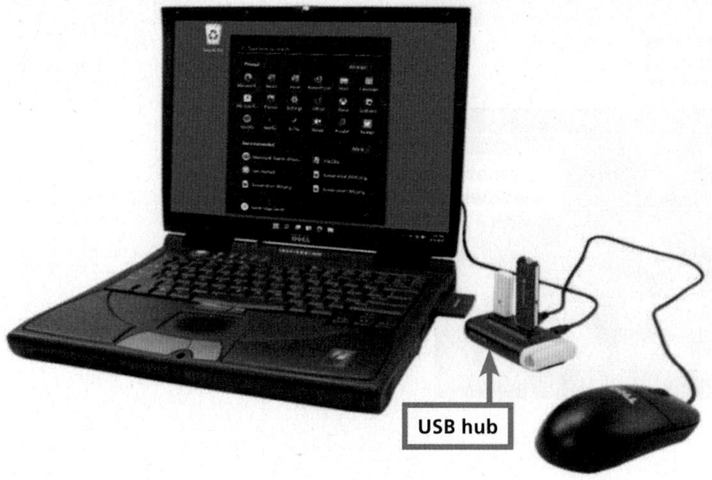

Bluetooth

Increasingly, gadgets are going wireless. Instead of exchanging data through a cable, devices can send signals through the air—no cable required. A common wireless technology for connecting peripherals is **Bluetooth**.

◗ **What kinds of devices use Bluetooth?** You'll find Bluetooth options for connecting wireless keyboards and mice to laptops and desktops. The connection between your phone and your car uses Bluetooth.

Bluetooth is a low-power technology, so it is ideal for mobile devices that don't have big batteries. Bluetooth is used to connect wireless headsets to smartphones. And if you're into fitness, then your fitness tracker may transmit data to your phone or computer using Bluetooth technology.

◗ **What are the range and speed of Bluetooth?** Bluetooth devices must be within 30 feet of each other. The peak data transmission rate is 3 Mbps, which is suitable for sending small bursts of data rather than large files. Compared to wired connections, Bluetooth is quite slow (Figure 2-56).

QuickCheck

Which of the following would be least likely to connect through a Bluetooth port?

a. A wireless headset

b. An external hard drive

c. A keyboard

d. A game controller

Figure 2-56: Data transfer rates of popular connection technologies

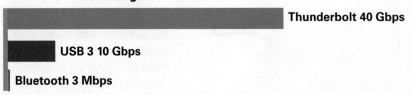

◗ **Can I tell if a device is equipped with Bluetooth?** Bluetooth is built into many smartphones, tablets, laptops, and desktops, but there is no corresponding physical port on the system unit. Look for the Bluetooth logo on the Windows taskbar or the Mac menu bar (Figure 2-57). For handheld devices, check Settings. If a device is not equipped with Bluetooth, you can plug a Bluetooth antenna into a USB port.

Try It!

Does your favorite device have Bluetooth? Look for the Bluetooth icon or settings to find out.

Figure 2-57: Does this device have Bluetooth?

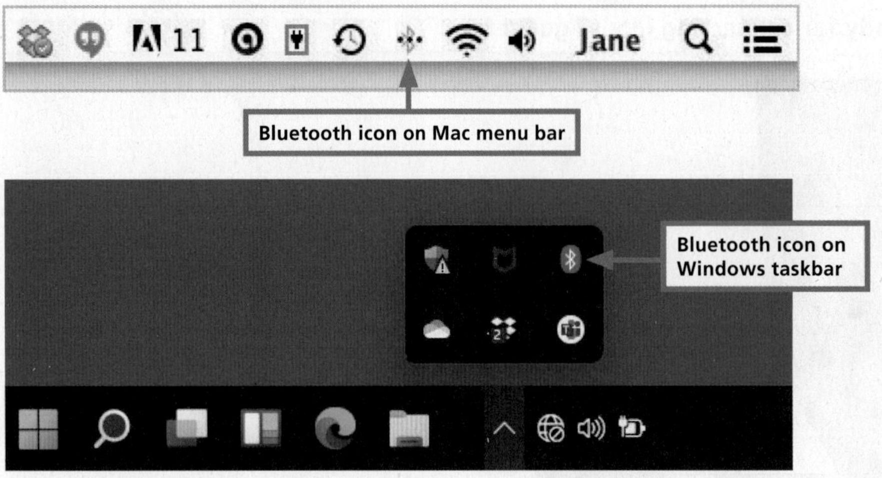

Device Drivers

Many gadgets have associated software. For example, there's an iPhone app for your fitness wristband that graphs your progress and shares it with your training buddies. These applications help you get the most out of your gadgets. In addition to application software, devices also require a type of software called a device driver.

▶ **What's a device driver?** A **device driver** is software that helps a peripheral device establish communication with its host device. For example, the device driver for an HP printer sets up data streams from RAM to the printer and makes sure that the data is formatted in a way that the printer can work with.

▶ **When do I have to install device drivers?** Operating systems include built-in drivers for standard expansion ports. This feature, sometimes called Plug and Play, makes it relatively easy to connect devices without manually installing device drivers. When you connect a new peripheral device, the operating system looks for an appropriate driver. If the device is unable to use a standard driver, you'll be prompted to install the device driver supplied by the peripheral device manufacturer.

▶ **Where do I get device drivers?** Device drivers, updates, and instructions for installing them can be downloaded from the manufacturer's Web site.

▶ **When do I need a device driver update?** Device drivers work directly with the host device's operating system. A printer or other connected gadgets might work perfectly—until the operating system gets an update. Then some device drivers might stop working correctly and the devices they control could malfunction.

In addition to checking cables, trying a different port, and rebooting, one of the first steps in troubleshooting a malfunctioning peripheral device is to access the manufacturer's Web site and look for a driver update. Updated driver downloads are usually available from the Support link (Figure 2-58).

QuickCheck

Suppose that the printer connected to your computer's USB port stopped working right after an operating system update. Which of the following would most likely fix the problem?

a. Install a new ink cartridge.

b. Plug the printer into a surge protector.

c. Connect the printer to a Bluetooth port.

d. Update the printer driver.

Figure 2-58: Device driver updates are available online

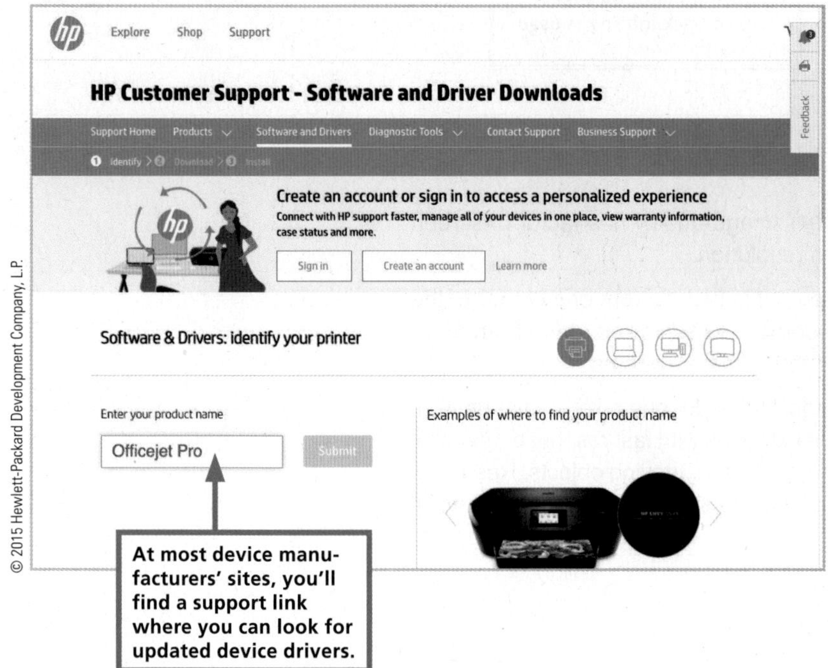

Display Devices

A computer display device that simply displays text and images is classified as an output device. Touchscreens, however, can be classified as both input and output devices because they accept input and display output.

What are my options for display devices? Standalone display devices, sometimes called monitors, are popular for desktop computers. Display devices for laptops, tablets, and handheld devices are built into the system units, but these devices may also accept an external monitor. Most of today's display devices are based on LCD technology.

LCD (liquid crystal display) technology produces an image by filtering light through a layer of liquid crystal cells (Figure 2-59). The advantages of LCD screens include display clarity, low radiation emission, portability, and compactness. The source of the light that filters through the LCD is referred to as backlighting.

QuickCheck

The liquid crystal cells used in display devices do not directly emit light, so ____________ is necessary.

a. backlighting

b. conversion

c. RGB

d. battery backup

Figure 2-59: LCD displays

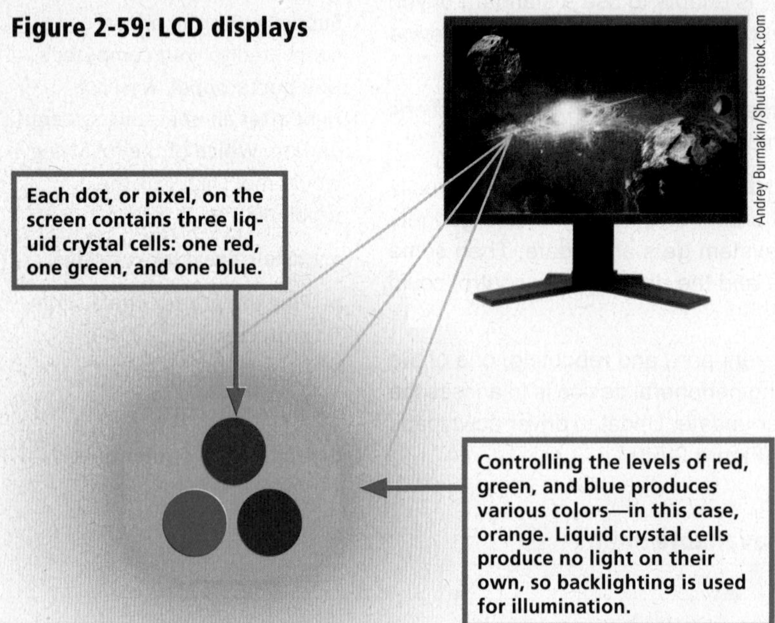

Each dot, or pixel, on the screen contains three liquid crystal cells: one red, one green, and one blue.
Controlling the levels of red, green, and blue produces various colors—in this case, orange. Liquid crystal cells produce no light on their own, so backlighting is used for illumination.
Andrey Burmakin/Shutterstock.com

What factors affect image quality? Image quality is a factor of screen size, response rate, dot pitch, and screen resolution.

Screen size. Screen size is the measurement in inches from one corner of the screen diagonally across to the opposite corner. Screen sizes range from 1" for smartwatches to 60" or more for home entertainment systems.

Response rate. **Response rate** is the time it takes for one pixel to change from black to white and then back to black. Display devices with fast response rates display a crisp image with minimal blurring or "ghosting" of moving objects. Response rate is measured in milliseconds (ms). For gaming systems, a response rate of 5 ms or less is desirable.

Dot pitch. The crystals that form an image on the screen are spaced in a grid. **Dot pitch** (dp) is the distance in millimeters between like-colored crystals (Figure 2-60).

QuickCheck

Which of these 4-inch smartphone displays would produce the sharpest image quality?

a. Dp = .26 mm

b. Dp = .50 mm

c. Dp = .08 mm

d. Dp = .06 mm

Figure 2-60: Dot pitch

0.26 mm
A small dot pitch produces the sharpest image.

Screen resolution. The number of horizontal and vertical pixels that a device displays on the screen is referred to as **screen resolution**. Your smartphone, for example, might have a resolution of 2532 x 1170. Another way to express resolution is pixels per inch (ppi). Your smartphone's 6.1-inch screen would have a resolution of 460 ppi.

▶ **Should I set my computer on its highest resolution?** Most displays have a recommended resolution at which images are clearest and text is crispest. On laptops and desktops, however, you can change the resolution. In Windows, you can right-click the desktop and select Display settings. In macOS, use the Apple icon to open System Preferences and choose Displays.

At higher resolutions, text and objects may appear smaller, but the desktop appears more spacious. The two screens in Figure 2-61 help you compare the same display set at two different resolutions.

Try It!

What is the current setting for the resolution on your laptop or desktop? Is it the highest possible resolution?

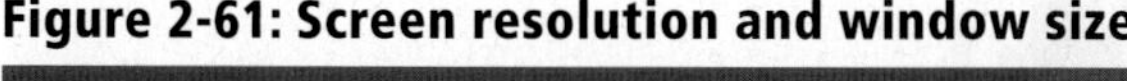

Figure 2-61: Screen resolution and window size

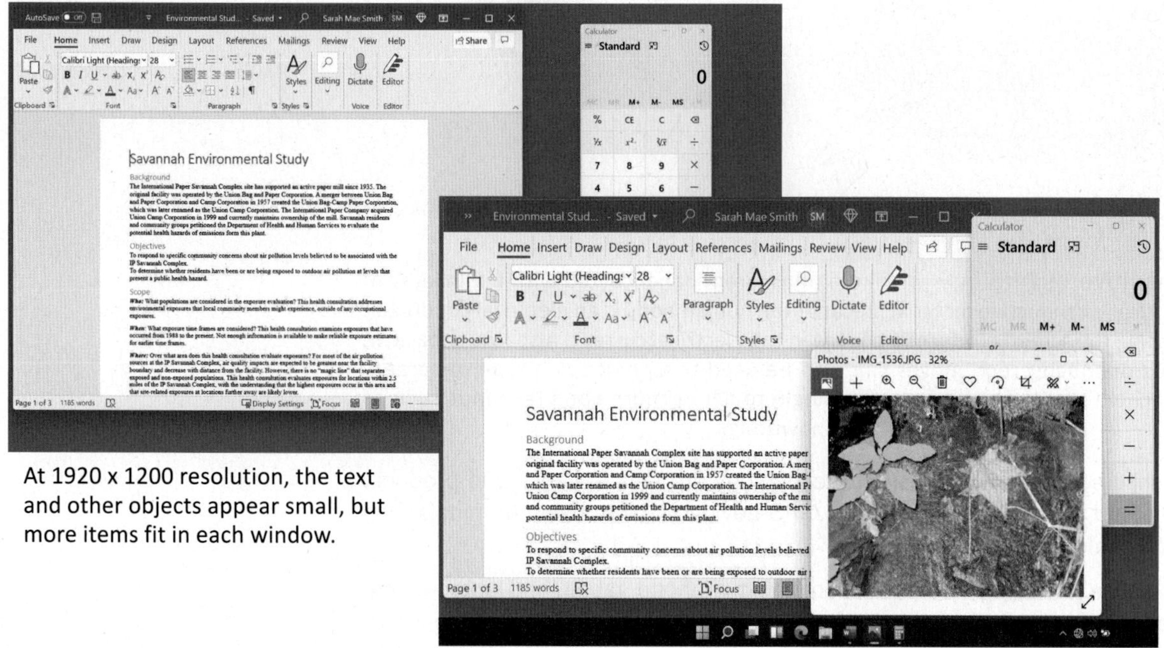

At 1920 x 1200 resolution, the text and other objects appear small, but more items fit in each window.

At 1280 x 768 resolution, the text and other objects appear large, but less text appears in the document window.

How does a touchscreen work? Tablet computers, handheld devices, retail store self-checkouts, and ATMs display output and collect input from a **touchscreen**. Touchscreens display menus, scroll bars, and other controls. They can also display a **virtual keyboard** for devices that are not connected to a physical keyboard.

Touch events, such as taps, drags, and pinches, are sometimes called gestures. The coordinates for a touch event are processed in essentially the same way as a mouse click. For example, if you touch your iPad screen at the location of a button labeled Calendar, the area you touch generates coordinates and sends them to the processor. The processor compares the coordinates to the image displayed on the screen to find out what is at the coordinates, and then responds—in this case, by opening your appointment calendar. The two most commonly used touchscreen technologies are resistive and capacitive (Figure 2-62).

QuickCheck

It was a cold day and you tried to use your smartphone while wearing gloves, but your gestures were ignored. The touchscreen on that device probably uses ___________ technology.

a. capacitive

b. resistive

c. virtual

Figure 2-62: Touchscreens

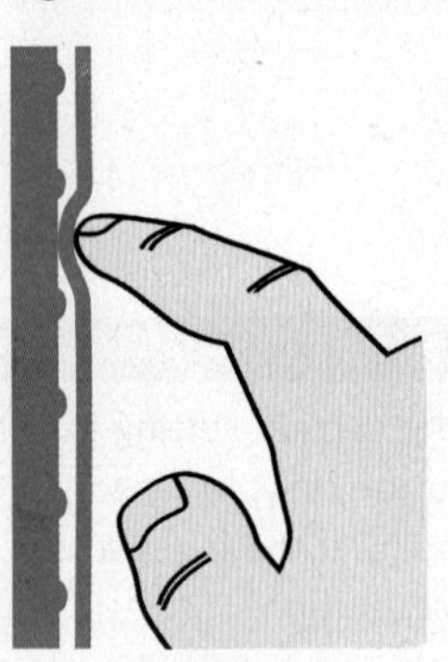

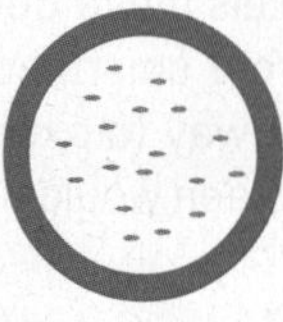

Screens built with **resistive technology** contain a base panel and a flexible top layer separated by a small space. Pressing slightly on the top layer brings it into contact with the base layer, and the point of contact is collected and passed to the processor. Resistive technology is not susceptible to dust or water, but it can be damaged by sharp objects.

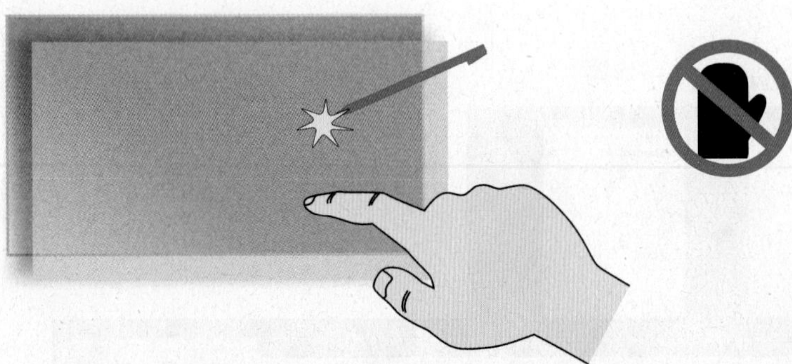

Capacitive technology contains a transparent panel coated with a thin layer of electrically conductive material. Because the human body is an electrical conductor, touching the screen produces a change in the electrical current. A special capacitive stylus or touchscreen gloves can also be used to operate this type of screen. Capacitive screens can interpret a single touch or more complex input such as handwriting.

Touchscreens based on resistive technology are less expensive to produce. They tend to be used for handheld GPS devices, point of sale terminals, and digital camera displays.

Capacitive technology is predominant on smartphone, tablet, and laptop touchscreens. That's why you can't operate your smartphone when wearing your woolen mittens or when your fingers are wet.

What is a GPU? Display devices require graphics circuitry to generate and transport the signals for displaying an image on the screen. One type of graphics circuitry, referred to as **integrated graphics**, is built into a computer's system board. A second option, called **dedicated graphics**, is graphics circuitry mounted on a small circuit board called a graphics card (or video card) like the one in Figure 2-63.

Figure 2-63: Graphics card

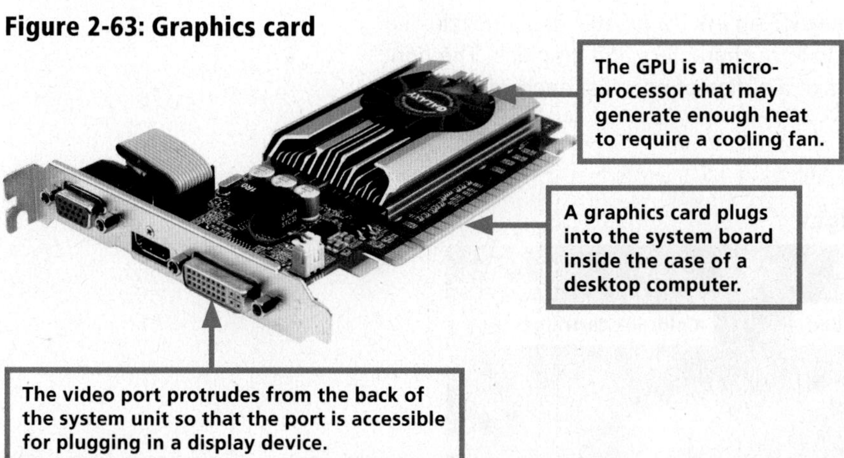

The GPU is a microprocessor that may generate enough heat to require a cooling fan.
A graphics card plugs into the system board inside the case of a desktop computer.
The video port protrudes from the back of the system unit so that the port is accessible for plugging in a display device.

A **graphics processing unit** (GPU) is an integrated circuit that contains processing circuitry and video memory. A GPU stores screen images as they are processed but before they are displayed. A fast GPU and lots of video memory are the keys to lightning-fast screen updating for fast action games, 3D modeling, and graphics-intensive desktop publishing (Figure 2-64).

Figure 2-64: Integrated vs. dedicated graphics

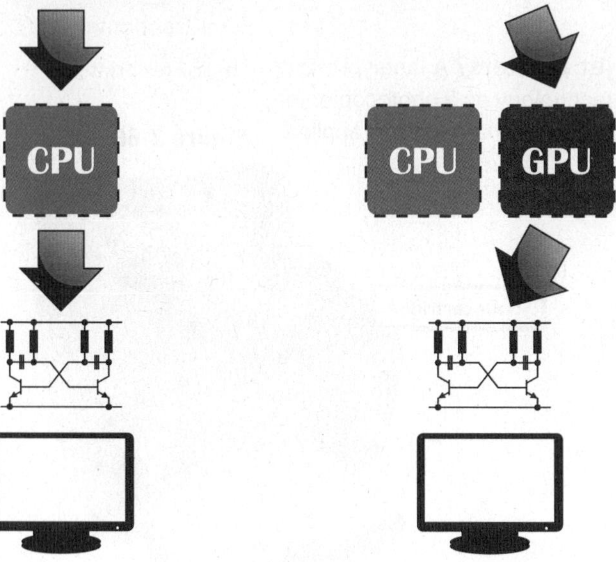

In a device with dedicated graphics, image data is processed by the GPU, freeing the CPU for other tasks.

Printers

The importance of printers has declined as digital distribution becomes more prevalent and cloud-based print services become more popular. Yet a printer can come in handy for creating printed documents, handouts, posters, and photos. Today's best-selling multifunction printers use ink jet or laser technology and can also serve as scanners, copiers, and fax machines.

▶ **How does an ink jet printer work?** An **ink jet printer** has a nozzle-like print head that sprays ink onto paper to form characters and graphics. The print head in a color ink jet printer consists of a series of nozzles, each with its own ink cartridge (Figure 2-65).

Figure 2-65: Ink jet CMYK cartridges

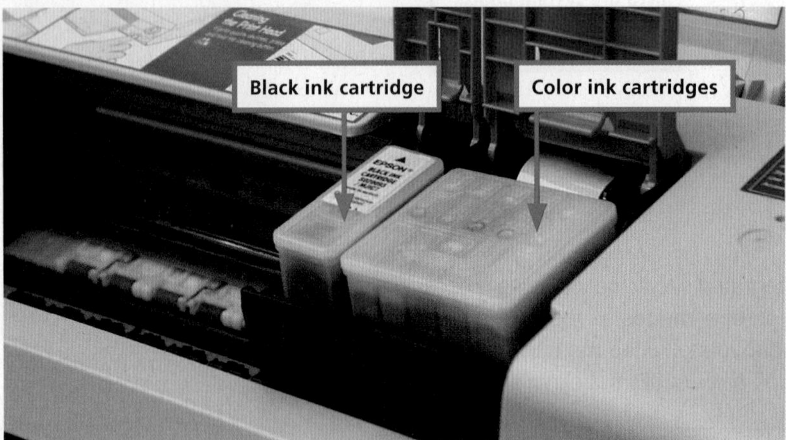

Most ink jet printers use CMYK color, which requires only cyan (blue), magenta (pink), yellow, and black inks to create a printout that appears to contain thousands of colors.

Ink jet printers outsell all other types of printers because they are inexpensive and produce both color and black-and-white printouts. They work well for most home and small business applications. Ink jet technology also powers many photo printers, which are optimized to print high-quality images produced by digital cameras and scanners.

QuickCheck

Which type of printer is slower but less expensive to operate?

a. Laser printer

b. Ink jet printer

▶ **How do laser printers compare to ink jet printers?** A **laser printer** like the one shown in Figure 2-66 uses the same technology as a photocopier to paint dots of light on a light-sensitive drum. Electrostatically charged ink is applied to the drum and then transferred to paper. A laser printer prints faster than an ink jet printer, but laser technology is more complex than ink jet technology, which accounts for the higher price of laser printers.

A basic laser printer produces only black-and-white printouts. Color laser printers are available, but they are somewhat more costly than basic black-and-white models. Laser printers are often the choice for business printers, particularly for applications that produce a high volume of printed material.

Figure 2-66: Laser printer

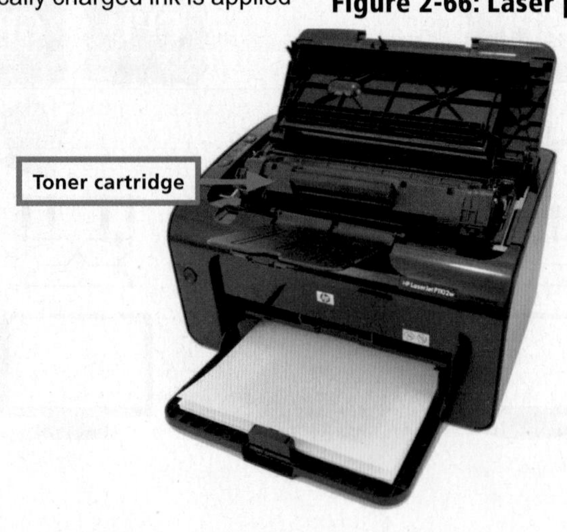

▶ **What about 3D printers?** The technology that deposits ink on paper is the foundation for 3D printers that deposit layers of plastic, resin, or metal to build a three-dimensional object. 3D printing is technically called **additive manufacturing**.

Consumers can use 3D printers to produce small toys, ornaments, and even simple electronic devices. These printers have been used to create wearable items, such as shoes, and replacement parts for household appliances.

An important industrial use for 3D printers is prototyping new products, such as automobile headlights, smartphone cases, firearms, and even full-scale bicycles.

Additive manufacturing is used to produce hearing aids and other medical devices that are custom fit or in other ways unique. Dental laboratories use 3D printing to produce crowns, bridges, and other dental appliances.

▶ **How do 3D printers work?** There are several additive manufacturing technologies, but most consumer-grade 3D printers use a technology called filament deposit modeling (FDM) that melts a coiled filament and deposits it in layers that harden and form an object (Figure 2-67).

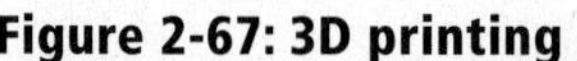

Figure 2-67: 3D printing

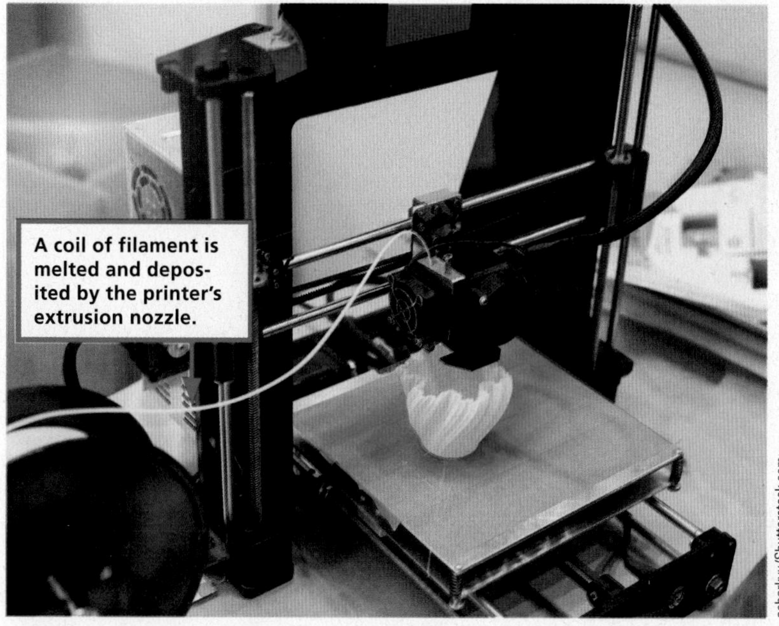

A coil of filament is melted and deposited by the printer's extrusion nozzle.
asharkyu/Shutterstock.com

▶ **What are the filaments made from?** Several types of filament are available. Polylactic acid (PLA) filament is versatile, and biodegradable because it is made from corn starch. Acrylonitrile butadiene styrene (ABS) filament is more durable and heat-resistant, making it suitable for printing objects that need to withstand some wear and tear. Polycarbonate (PC) filament is even sturdier and is used primarily for items that will be needed in high-impact situations. Filaments cost about $10 per pound.

▶ **What controls the printout?** A 3D printed object is based on a 3D model that is essentially a 3D vector graphic. The model can be created using graphics software or it can be derived from a 3D scan of a real object. Models are often stored in the STL file format. Several Web sites offer collections of STL files for 3D printing.

The Internet of Things

The utopian vision for the Internet of Things (IoT) is a busy hive of **smart sensors** that work behind the scenes to collect data and use it to improve just about everything. All types of "things" equipped with smart sensors can monitor our homes, cars, and workplaces. They can also monitor our habits and physical fitness and communicate with each other while doing so.

▶ What are the basic features required for IoT devices? IoT devices require some way to communicate with other sensors and devices. That communication is handled by network technology, which is covered in the next module.

IoT devices may include a microprocessor and memory if the device must process data, make decisions, or initiate an activity. A basic IoT circuit board contains one or more sensors, a power source, a transmitter, and an antenna (Figure 2-68).

Figure 2-68: Anatomy of an IoT device

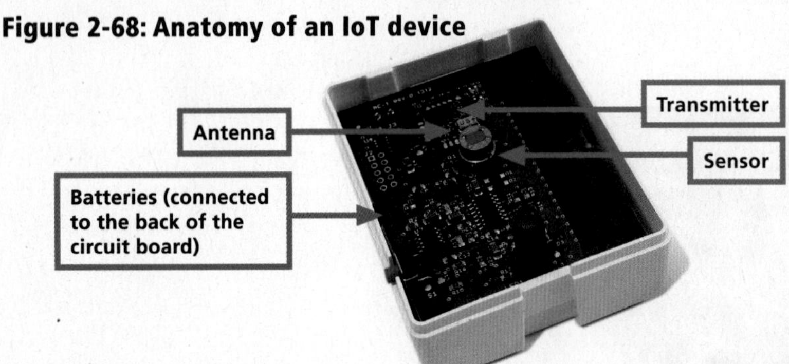

▶ What types of smart sensors are available? The most popular IoT sensors send alerts based on data they collect (Figure 2-69).

Figure 2-69: Sensors

"A window on your house just broke."
"Your dog is barking."
"The club is busy (noisy)."

Sound

"Your basement floor seems to be wet."
"Your swimming pool needs more chlorine."
"Your plant needs water."

Water

"Your dog is out of your yard."
"Your car is not in your driveway."
"You hiked a 2.5-mile circuit."

GPS

"Your front door isn't locked."
"Your doorbell just rang."
"Your child just got home from school."

Contact

"A person or animal approached your cabin last night."
"Your cat is at the litter box."

Motion

"You've walked 10,000 steps today."
"The baggage handlers just dropped your suitcase."

Accelerometer

"It's 10 pm; your porch light isn't on."
"Do you want to dim the lights?"
"Your UV exposure has reached the limit."

Light

"Your oven is on."
"Your apartment is unusually hot."
"It's below zero; remote start your car."

Temperature

What are the most popular sensors? Many smartphones, VR headsets, and automobile internal navigation systems incorporate three sensors: an accelerometer, a gyroscope, and a magnetometer. Figure 2-70 illustrates an IMU (inertial measurement unit) that packages these sensors into a single unit.

Figure 2-70: IMU sensors

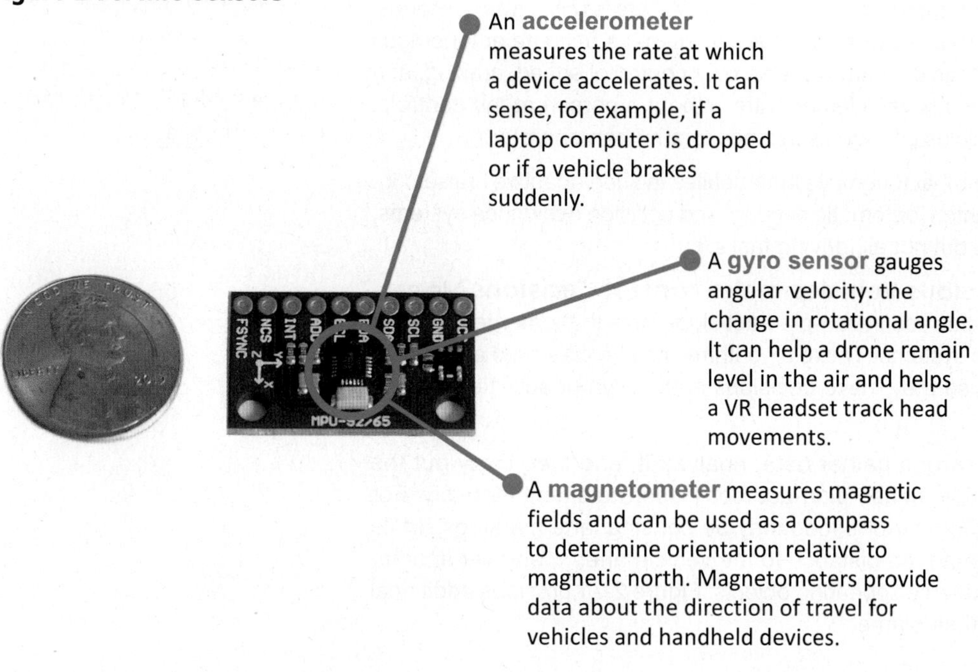

An **accelerometer** measures the rate at which a device accelerates. It can sense, for example, if a laptop computer is dropped or if a vehicle brakes suddenly.
A **gyro sensor** gauges angular velocity: the change in rotational angle. It can help a drone remain level in the air and helps a VR headset track head movements.
A **magnetometer** measures magnetic fields and can be used as a compass to determine orientation relative to magnetic north. Magnetometers provide data about the direction of travel for vehicles and handheld devices.
FSYNC
NCS
INT
ADO
SCL
SDA
GND
VCC

Where can I get IoT devices? Smart sensors are available in electronics stores, hardware stores, and online. Sensors can be purchased individually or in packages. Popular home monitoring packages, such as Apple's HomeKit, include cameras, thermostats, light bulbs, water sensors, door locks, and air quality sensors.

Do sensors have security risks? Sensors themselves are not generally a security risk, but the data they collect can be used for unauthorized purposes.

A smart thermostat can be used legitimately by a homeowner to remotely track and adjust the temperature of a house or apartment. With approval, data from the thermostat might even be collected by the local power company and used to gauge usage levels.

Because the thermostat communicates using a wireless network, the signal is subject to interception. An unauthorized person might monitor the signal to determine when a homeowner leaves the house (heat is turned down), arrives home (heat is turned up), or goes on vacation (heat remains down for several days).

When considering smart sensors, take care to understand where their data can be stored, who can access the data, and who can control the device. To maximize security, select sensors that store data locally or on a secure site. In addition, confirm that all data is encrypted before it is transmitted and stored, and ensure it can be controlled only by you.

QuickCheck

Which one of the following aspects of smart sensors on the IoT would be the least likely to pose a security risk?

a. Anonymized data

b. Data transmitted without encryption

c. Data stored on a Web site

d. Temperature sensors supplied by your electric service provider

Autonomous Vehicles

There are drones in the sky, Roombas crisscrossing the floor, and cars speeding down the highway in Supercruise mode. The technology that allows these vehicles to operate autonomously or semi-autonomously requires an array of sensors communicating with an onboard computer.

Try It!

Autonomous vehicles, such as self-driving cars, have limitations. Can you discover what type of pre-mapping is required before a Google car takes to the road?

▶ Exactly what is an autonomous vehicle? Cars, trucks, trains, drones, planes, and machines that are usually piloted by humans become autonomous as the vehicles, rather than the humans, take over control of speed, braking, and steering. Fully autonomous vehicles operate without a person at the controls. Semi-autonomous vehicles provide assistance to a human operator.

Features available in semi-autonomous automobiles include adaptive cruise control, in-lane steering control, automatic parking, and collision avoidance systems, which take over some, but not all, driving tasks.

▶ How do autonomous vehicles make control decisions? In general, autonomous vehicles use sense-plan-act algorithms that emerged with the development of robotic systems. These algorithms may be classified as artificial intelligence (AI) because they make decisions and carry out activities without human intervention.

Sense-plan-act algorithms gather data, analyze it, and then carry out the required actions. Multiple sense-plan-act loops operate simultaneously. For example, in a self-driving car one loop may be sensing lane markings, while another loop is monitoring the distance to the vehicle ahead, and yet another loop is watching for suddenly appearing objects. Figure 2-71 provides additional details pertaining to sense-plan-act.

Figure 2-71: Sense-plan-act algorithms for self-driving cars

Sense. Sensors on the vehicle gather raw data about the nearby environment and the status of the vehicle itself. Environmental data comes from sensing nearby vehicles, people, animals, and other objects, as well as the roadway itself. Vehicle status data includes speed, direction, angle, and altitude.

Sensor data is delivered to an onboard computer, where software quickly processes the input to identify road hazards and navigational points.

Brake?

Reduce Speed?

Honk?

Change Lanes?

Plan. Based on its interpretation of sensor data, the onboard computer applies a series of rules to determine the best course of action. For example, if radar data indicates that the vehicle ahead is slowing down, the computer must decide whether to adjust the speed or change lanes. The decision is based on rules such as "If the vehicle ahead slows down gradually, and the left lane is clear, then move to the left lane."

Act. After the computer determines a course of action, it sends signals to the vehicle's control systems. A signal to the car's steering system can initiate a lane change. Signals could also be sent to the car's throttle or braking system to achieve a change in speed.

2

◗ What kinds of sensors keep an autonomous vehicle on the road?

Lidar (light detection and radar) is a key input for the computer algorithms that steer an autonomous vehicle, but radar, sonar, infrared, GPS, cameras, and internal navigation systems also supply essential data (Figure 2-72).

Figure 2-72: Autonomous vehicle sensors

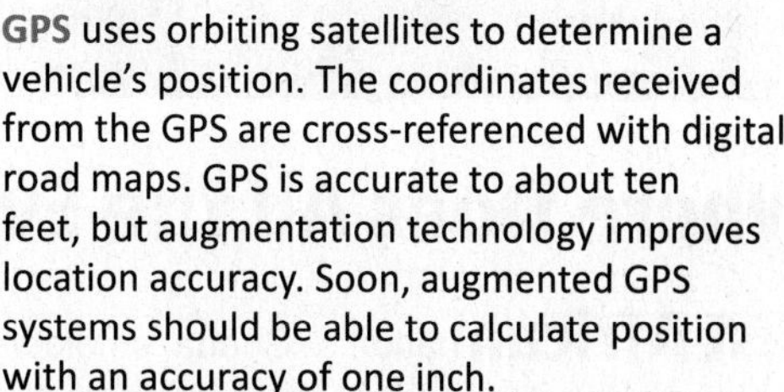

Lidar systems determine distance to obstacles using laser range finders. This device calculates the distance to objects based on the time it takes for the laser beam to reach an object and return. The range for this device is about 650 feet (200 meters), and 360-degree Lidar arrays can gather millions of data points per second to map objects in a 65-foot radius of the vehicle.

GPS uses orbiting satellites to determine a vehicle's position. The coordinates received from the GPS are cross-referenced with digital road maps. GPS is accurate to about ten feet, but augmentation technology improves location accuracy. Soon, augmented GPS systems should be able to calculate position with an accuracy of one inch.

Infrared sensors can be used to sense the heat signatures of pedestrians and animals, particularly when it is dark.

Radar adds more data about the nearby environment. Radar, which uses sound waves, does a good job of sensing metallic objects, but does not sense pedestrians and other non-metallic objects. It is primarily used to track nearby vehicles. Radar is currently used in adaptive cruise control systems to maintain a safe distance to the car in front.

Internal navigation systems (INS) include gyroscopes and accelerometers that continuously calculate position, orientation, and speed of the vehicle. These systems can monitor position if GPS signals are temporarily blocked by the structures in a dense urban area.

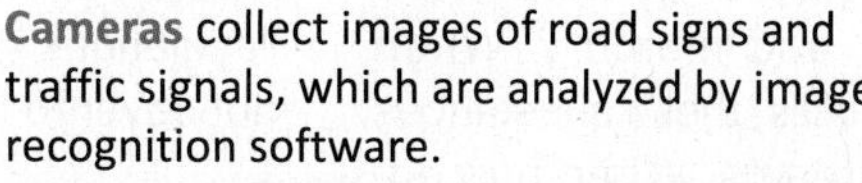

Cameras collect images of road signs and traffic signals, which are analyzed by image recognition software.

QuickQuiz Section E

1. The [   ] bus carries data from an external device to RAM.
2. [   ] is a slow wireless technology used to connect devices within a radius of about 30 feet.
3. A(n) [   ] handles image data, freeing the CPU for other processing tasks. (Hint: Use the acronym.)
4. The two most common technologies used for touchscreen displays are resistive and [   ].
5. The most commonly used general-purpose technology for connecting gadgets to laptop and desktop computers is a(n) [   ] port. (Hint: Use the acronym.)

Aurora Photos / Alamy stock photo

Issue: Where Does All the Ewaste Go?

In the West African nation of Ghana, smoldering piles of discarded computers and monitors ring a mucky river, polluted beyond recovery. Teenage boys play soccer in a toxic haze. When their break is over, they get back to work smashing monitors, ripping out the innards, and tossing the plastic cases onto a smoking pyre of oozing plastic.

In Guiyu, China, thousands of women huddle over primitive stoves "cooking" circuit boards to retrieve trace amounts of gold. Toxic fumes from the cooking process cloud the air; a toddler showing symptoms of lead poisoning plays listlessly with the carcasses of discarded mice and cell phones.

It is called ewaste, e-garbage, or technotrash—all unwanted and outdated computers, monitors, printers, cell phones, disk drives, disks, CDs, and DVDs. According to the Global E-waste Monitor, more than 50 million metric tons of ewaste are discarded worldwide every year. About 7 million tons of that total are discarded by U.S. consumers. More than 10 million tons are discarded in China.

Some illegal ewaste originates in legitimate recycling centers...

Computers and other electronic gear contain toxic substances such as lead, cadmium, and mercury. When discarded equipment is buried in landfills, these substances can leach into groundwater and streams. When burned, electronic components can emit toxic dioxin.

Ewaste is a global problem. As countries struggle to deal with discarded electronic components, an alarming amount of ewaste is shipped to developing countries where villagers, working for pennies a day, are exposed to toxic chemicals as they attempt to reclaim resalable metals from discarded equipment. Throughout the emerging world, ugly ewaste dumps defile the landscape and have yet unknown health effects.

Where does all this ewaste originate? Every country generates ewaste, but the bulk of it comes from prosperous, technology-forward countries such as the United States, Great Britain, Germany, Japan, France, and China. Despite laws that ban ewaste transhipping, loopholes allow discarded but working electronics to be shipped as "donations." Tons of donations arrive every day in port cities, such as Hong Kong, where they follow a shadowy route to unregulated workshops and dump sites.

Some illegal ewaste originates in legitimate recycling centers, where consumers assume electronic components will be handled in environmentally friendly ways. Many recycling centers do not process materials on site. Instead, they ship the ewaste to third parties. Without careful monitoring, that ewaste can be diverted to offshore locations where it piles up, waiting to be disassembled by backstreet laborers ungoverned by environmental protection regulations.

Developed countries have strict environmental regulations designed to prevent toxic substances from polluting air, land, and water. Proper disposal is expensive, however. In countries with high labor costs and stringent environmental regulations, the value of compounds retrieved from ewaste does not cover the cost of extraction.

The high cost of properly processing ewaste makes gray market options attractive. Ewaste can be handled more cost-effectively in emerging countries where environmental regulations are ignored, wages are pitiful, and workers are not covered by health and safety laws.

So, who is responsible for ewaste sweatshops and pollution? Is it consumers in developed countries who deposit unwanted gear at recycling stations that don't carry out the recycling process in-house, or is it the recycling firms that ship ewaste to third parties? Is it the firms that ship ewaste to emerging countries or the governments that can't close the loopholes on ewaste transhipping?

Perhaps the responsibility lies with emerging countries that are unable to control ewaste sweatshops and ignore the resulting environmental and human casualties.

Wherever the blame lies, consumers who are aware of the problem can become more responsible in the way they dispose of unwanted gear to keep it out of landfills at home and offshore.

Try It! Delve into the ewaste issue and explore the steps you can take to minimize the number of electronic components that end up in landfills and toxic waste dumps.

1. Which countries are taking steps to properly manage ewaste? Select five countries of your choice, and then use resources such as the Global E-waste Statistics Partnership to discover how much ewaste is generated per capita, how much ewaste is formally collected, and whether the country has national legislation governing the disposal of ewaste.

2. An environmental advocacy group, Basel Action Network, secretly planted tracking devices in electronic items donated to recycling centers in the EU. The project is summarized in a report called "Holes in the Circular Economy: WEEE Leakage from Europe." Read the key findings of the report and watch the video on YouTube. What is the circular economy and how is it related to ewaste?

3. Many computers, mobile phones, and other electronic components pile up in landfills because their owners are unaware of potential environmental hazards and simply toss them in the garbage. Use Web sites such as Earth911.com, or search for *recycling computers* and add your city name, as in *recycling computers Chicago*. Where is the nearest drop-off location for old laptop computers? Would you be charged a fee, and if so, how much?

4. Before donating or discarding a computer, you should erase all the data it contains. Simply deleting files is not sufficient to prevent data from being recovered. Search online for information about deleting or "wiping" the data from a hard drive. What are three ways you can securely prevent access to the data on a hard disk?

5. You might wonder if your digital devices are environmentally friendly. The Global Electronics Council rates specific digital devices as bronze, silver, or gold. Connect to the EPEAT site (*www.epeat.net*), select a product category, and then fill in the fields to find the rating for at least one digital device. Hint: Choose Select All for the EPEAT Tier.

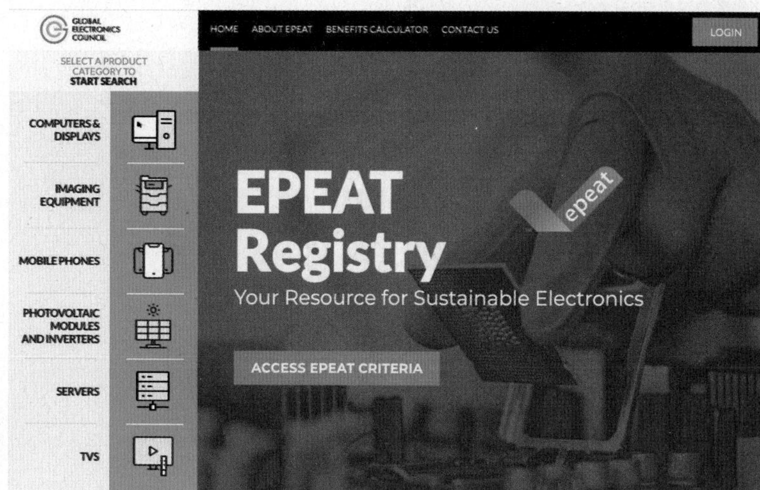

Source: epeat.net.

What Do You Think?

Issue

1. Have you ever thrown away an old computer or other electronic device?
2. Do you research products before purchasing them to find out if they are environmentally friendly throughout their life cycle?
3. Would it be fair for consumers to pay a recycling tax on electronic equipment that they purchase?

Mark Graves/Shutterstock.com

Information Tools: Finding the Right Stuff

You're looking for information. Where you start depends on how you plan to use the information. The sources you need for a class research paper often differ from information sources for personal use.

Information sources can be roughly divided into two categories: those that serve academic audiences and those that serve consumers.

Find these sources using Google Scholar and academic databases/directories such as DOAJ.

Scholarly and Academic Sources

- Written by experts
- Intended for academic or professional readers
- Peer-reviewed by other experts before publication
- Contain original research, theoretical analysis, or best practices
- Carefully documented by footnotes or endnotes
- Published by academic publishers, professional associations, or university presses
- Include academic books, academic journals, papers, conference proceedings, dissertations, textbooks, and monographs in printed or digital format

Use these sources for class papers, theses, essays, and dissertations.

Find these sources using Google, Google News, and commercial Web sites.

Consumer-Level Sources

- Written by reporters, bloggers, or practitioners
- Intended for the general public
- Possibly reviewed by an editor before publication
- Sometimes open to public comment after publication Like
- Printed or displayed in color with included photos
- Often published in for-profit publications that include advertising
- Include trade books, magazines, encyclopedias, press releases, trade journals, blogs, news sites, and online forums

Use these sources for product information, troubleshooting, news, and topic overviews.

Help!

Can't access what you need for a research project? Here are some common problems encountered by students, and solutions that help you find the resources you need for a paper that earns you an A.

Problem: Web search engines, such as Google, sometimes miss many of the articles most relevant for a college-level research project because articles are often locked behind paywalls or firewalls that don't allow search engine access. **Solution:** Go directly to a journal's Web site and search there.

Problem: Many scholarly journals display only abstracts to the general public; viewing the full text of articles requires a subscription or download fee.

Solution: Use your library's online database to locate articles that are included in the physical collection. You might have to go to the library to read the articles or ask for the full article from inter-library loan.

Problem: Access to academic search engines and databases, such as LexisNexis, requires subscriptions.

Solution: Your school might provide registered students with free access to journal databases if you log in from a computer on the school network or from within the library.

Try It!

Research about computers and technology relies on information from a broad base of sources. Let's explore these sources by comparing what they offer. Some searches will produce information suitable for academic projects, such as term papers, while other searches tend to produce information suitable for personal use, such as how to troubleshoot your smart thermostat.

To record the results of this comparison, write down (or screen capture) one example that you get from each source, and then describe an academic project or personal use for which that information would be suitable. As an example, suppose that you search for *Internet of Things or IoT* using Google Scholar and one of the results is:

Internet of Things: Evolution and technologies from a security perspective
R Ande, B Adebisi, M Hammoudeh, J Saleem - Sustainable Cities and ..., 2020 - Elsevier
In recent years, IoT has developed into many areas of life, including smart homes, smart cities, agriculture, offices, and workplaces. Everyday physical items such as lights, locks, and industrial machineries can now be part of the IoT ecosystem. IoT has redefined the. ...
Cited by 27 - Related articles - All 5 versions

This information is academic and could be a suitable source for a term paper about Internet of Things security in a computer science course. Okay, now see what you can do with the following sources.

1. Check Wikipedia for general information about IoT.
2. Search for a book about IoT at Amazon Books.
3. Search for conference proceedings about IoT at the ACM Digital Library.
4. Search an open access database such as DOAJ (see sidebar) for a recent paper about the Internet of Things.
5. Search an academic database (see sidebar) for an abstract about the Internet of Things.
6. Search Science.gov for a full text article about the Internet of Things.
7. Search an online computer magazine, such as *Wired*, for a recent article about IoT.
8. Use a search engine, such as Google or Bing, to locate a recent press release about IoT.
9. Search Amazon Electronics for IoT sensors and customer reviews.
10. Search a technology news site (see sidebar) for the latest industry news about the Internet of Things.

COMPUTER AND TECHNOLOGY ACADEMIC DATABASES

- DOAJ (Directory of Open Access Journals)
- Science.gov
- Microsoft Academic Search
- IEEE Xplore
- ACM (Association for Computing Machinery) Digital Library

TECHNOLOGY NEWS SITES

- HuffPost Tech
- Engadget
- TechCrunch
- Ars Technica
- Google News Technology
- WSJ Tech
- CNET News
- Tom's Hardware

Bettmann/Getty Images

Technology in Context: Military

In *Engines of the Mind*, Joel Shurkin writes, "If necessity is the mother of invention, then war can be said to be its grandmother." The military, an early pioneer in computer and communication technologies, continues to be the driving force behind technologies that have revolutionized everyday life.

During World War II, the U.S. military initiated a classified research program called Project PX to develop an electronic device to calculate artillery firing tables; by hand, each table required weeks of grueling calculations.

Project PX produced ENIAC (Electronic Numerical Integrator And Computer), one of the first general-purpose electronic computers. When ENIAC was completed in 1946, the war was over, but ENIAC's versatile architecture could be used for other calculations, such as designing hydrogen bombs, predicting weather, and engineering wind tunnels. ENIAC's technology evolved into the computers used today.

Bettmann/Getty Images

After Project PX, the military continued to support computer research. Like most large corporations, the military used mainframe computers to maintain personnel, inventory, supply, and facilities records. This data was distributed to terminals at other locations through rudimentary networks.

Because all data communication flowed through the mainframe, a single point of failure for the entire system was a possible risk. A malfunction or an enemy "hit" could disrupt command and control, sending the military into chaos. Therefore, the armed forces created the Advanced Research Projects Agency (ARPA) to design a distributed communications system that could continue operating without a centralized computer.

The result was ARPANET, which paved the way for the data communications system we know today as the Internet. ARPANET was activated in 1967, but the .mil domain that designates U.S. military Web sites was not implemented until 1984.

The U.S. Department of Defense (DoD) currently maintains several data communications networks, including SIPRNet, a classified (secret-level) network, and NIPRNet, which provides unclassified services. The DoD's public Web site provides official information about defense policies, organizations, budgets, and operations.

Computers and communications technology have also become an integral part of high-tech flight operations. U.S. Apache helicopters, for example, are equipped with computer-based Target Acquisition Designation Sights, laser range finder/designators, and Pilot Night Vision Sensors.

Networks are also crucial for combat operations, and a new generation of communication tools is evolving for soldiers deployed to battlefields. Networked communication devices offer immediate situational awareness by providing critical information such as orders, imagery, graphics, and maps. The U.S. Army's Nett Warrior program is essentially a secure smartphone carried by a soldier that displays the locations of friendly troops and facilitates text messaging when spoken communication is not possible.

An enhancement to the Nett Warrior handheld device is a head-mounted Integrated Visual Augmentation System (IVAS) based on Microsoft's HoloLens technology. Like a virtual/augmented reality headset, IVAS goggles and a head-mounted camera provide infrared and night-vision displays of surrounding territory as well as GPS mapping with overlays of routes and troop locations.

IVAS goggles can display information on how to repair combat vehicles and how to apply first aid to injured personnel. IVAS also acts as a weapons site, enabling soldiers to literally "shoot from the hip" instead of targeting through the site of a shoulder-mounted weapon.

IVAS goggles are used for combat training as well as on the battlefield. Using a combination of virtual and augmented reality, the goggles display scenarios similar to those in first-person shooter games, placing virtual enemy fighters around corners in settings based on real-world locations. IVAS training is a major step beyond previous arcade-style simulations. Intertwined evolution of civilian computer games and military training simulations is likely to continue.

"Live" military training is dangerous—weapons are deadly and equipment costs millions of dollars. With computer-generated simulations, however, troops can train in a true-to-life environment without physical harm or equipment damage.

Flying an F-16 fighter, for example, costs thousands of dollars an hour, but flying an F-16 simulator costs only a few hundred dollars per hour. The military uses simulators to teach Air Force pilots to fly fighter jets, Navy submarine officers to navigate in harbors, and Marine infantry squads to handle urban combat.

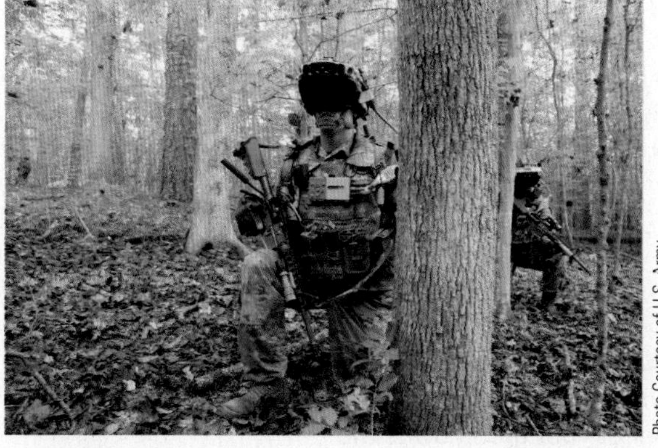
Photo Courtesy of U.S. Army

The U.S. Navy also seeks help from civilian developers—even college students. In the annual International RoboBoat competition, a $20,000 prize is awarded for the best-designed ships that can operate without crews in harsh environments or dangerous situations.

The Internet of Things has not escaped notice by the military. The Internet of Military Things (IoMT) is a concept that integrates environmental sensors, robots, drones, vehicles, munitions, armor, and biosensors to collect data from surrounding terrain, control equipment, and monitor soldiers' biometrics.

The next time you see a small drone swooping over a park or hovering for a bird's-eye view of a real estate listing, you can trace the technology to military research. Military optionally manned vehicles (OMVs) are used for air and underwater reconnaissance—situations that are often dangerous for on-platform troops.

Today, a growing cadre of computer and communications specialists is needed to create and maintain increasingly complex military systems such as the Defense Department's Distributed Common Ground System (DCGS) for sharing surveillance imagery and intelligence.

In the past, armies depended primarily on their infantry divisions, but today's high-tech armies also depend on database designers, computer programmers, and network specialists. Even previously low-tech military jobs, such as mechanics and dietitians, require some computer expertise. Happily, new recruits are finding military computer systems easier to learn based on their knowledge of civilian technologies, such as the Internet and computer games.

Although most citizens recognize that an adequate national defense is necessary, the cost of defense-related equipment, personnel, and cutting-edge research remains controversial. In a 1961 speech, President Dwight Eisenhower warned, "We must guard against the acquisition of unwarranted influence, whether sought or unsought, by the military-industrial complex."

Some socially motivated citizens and pacifists tried to withhold tax dollars from the military-industrial complex that Eisenhower cautioned against. In retrospect, however, military funding contributed to many technologies we depend on today.

For example, detractors tried to convince the government that Project PX was doomed to failure; but without ENIAC research, computers might not exist today. Skeptics saw no future for the fruits of ARPANET research; but it led to the Internet, which has changed our lives significantly.

Flipped Class Projects

Critical Thinking

For many years, personal computers were desktop models designed around four main components: system unit, monitor, keyboard, and mouse. Today, more than half the devices we use are slate form factors without physical keyboards. Some industry analysts speculate that the move away from physical keyboards signals a fundamental change in the use of digital devices. Whereas computers were once seen as tools for producing, they are now becoming tools for consuming. How significant is a physical keyboard to the creative and productive use of digital devices? What kinds of evidence would help to support your opinion?

Group Project

For this project, work in groups of three or four. The group should select a trending digital device, such as a fitness wristband, a smartwatch, a home security system, or a just-released smartphone. If a member of your group owns the device, that's a plus. Create promotional materials for a tradeshow booth featuring your device. You might include a product photo, a list of specifications, and a short instruction manual. If time permits, your instructor might ask your group to present your sales pitch or a demonstration to the rest of the class.

Cyberclassroom

Work in pairs to set up a cloud-based storage location where you can share files. Experiment with the following scenarios to find out what happens:

1) Two people access the same file at approximately the same time; neither person changes the file contents.

2) While one person is modifying a file, another person tries to access the file but does not try to modify it.

3) While one person is modifying a file, a second person attempts to access it and change it.

Multimedia Project

Imagine that you are a high school teacher and you have to design materials to teach a unit on how microprocessors work. To kick off the unit, create a 30- to 60-second video showing the control unit, registers, and ALU and how an instruction like ADD 9 + 2 would be processed. Be creative and make it interesting!

Resume Builder

Use the Web and other resources to learn about the digital devices and other technologies used in your career field. Format the information you find in a style similar to the Technology in Context section of each module in this textbook. Be sure to select two photos to accompany your narrative and include a list of relevant citations for your sources.

Globalization

Digital device ownership is growing worldwide and providing access to productivity tools and a global communications infrastructure. For this project, look for statistics and graphs showing the increase in device ownership around the world over time. How does it compare to telephone, television, and radio ownership? Are any aspects of this data unexpected or surprising? Gather your graphs and analysis into a two- to three-page executive summary.

Key Terms

Interactive Summary

Section A: A computer is a multipurpose device that accepts input, processes data, stores data, and produces output, all according to a series of stored __________ . The __________ processing unit of most modern computers is a(n) __________ . The instructions that tell a computer how to carry out a task are referred to as computer __________ , which are distributed as software. Computers run three main types of software: __________ software, system software, and development tools. An example of system software is a computer __________ system, which is essentially the primary controller for all the activities that a digital device performs. Digital devices are constructed using tiny electronic components that represent data bits as electrical signals. The system unit houses the system board, which contains several __________ circuits made from semiconducting materials. Computers come in three popular form factors: component, __________ , and slate. Many of today's digital devices operate on battery power supplied by __________ ion batteries. Battery life and lifespan can be extended by following good battery management practices.

Section B: Today, there are many computer categories. A(n) __________ is the category for the world's fastest computers. __________ computers are large, expensive devices capable of simultaneously processing data for thousands of users. Computers used by Google and Web service providers are classified as __________ . Personal computers come in several varieties. A(n) __________ computer fits on a desk, runs on power from an electrical wall outlet, and can be housed in a horizontal case or vertical case. Three categories of portable computers include tablets, smartphones, and clamshell style __________ computers. Selecting a digital device requires consumers to select a platform based on form factor and operating system. macOS is the operating system that runs on Apple laptops and __________ computers. The operating system for iPhones is __________ . The __________ operating system from Microsoft runs on laptop and desktop PCs. The open source community produces Linux for desktops and servers. This family of operating systems also includes Chrome OS, and __________ , which is popular for tablets and smartphones.

Section C: The microprocessor is a(n) __________ circuit, which is designed to process data based on a set of instructions. Desktop computers running Windows contain a microprocessor based on the __________ standard. Most tablets and smartphones contain processors based on __________ technology. A microprocessor's circuitry is designed to perform a limited number of tasks contained in its __________ set. During processing, an instruction is loaded into the processor's __________ unit. Data is loaded into registers in the processor's __________ where arithmetic and logic operations are performed. Microprocessor performance can be measured by its __________ speed. Other factors affecting overall processing performance include word size, cache size, and instruction set complexity. Most digital devices contain only one microprocessor chip, but today's multi-__________ processors contain circuitry that supports parallel processing. Computers contain various kinds of memory.

Random _____ memory is a special holding area for data, program instructions, and the _____ system. It stores data on a temporary basis until the processor makes a data request. RAM is different from disk storage because it is _____, which means that it can hold data only when the computer power is turned on. Computers also contain read- _____ memory, which is a type of non-volatile memory that provides a set of "hard-wired" instructions, called the _____ loader, that a computer uses to boot up.

Section D: Today's digital devices use a variety of storage technologies. _____ storage technologies, such as hard disks, store data as particles oriented north or south. A hard disk drive provides multiple _____ for data storage that are sealed inside the drive case to prevent airborne contaminants from interfering with the read-write heads. Hard disks are less durable than many other types of storage, so it is important to make a copy of the data they contain. _____ storage technologies store data as a series of dark spots and light spots on the surface of CDs and DVDs. Storage technologies, such as CD- _____, are used for distributing software and music, but you cannot alter the disc's contents. _____ technology allows you to write data on a CD or DVD, but you cannot delete or change that data. Rerecordable or _____ technology allows you to write and erase data on a CD or DVD. _____ state storage technologies, such as USB flash drives, store data by activating electrons in a microscopic grid of circuitry. A backup is a copy of one or more files that have been made in case the original files become damaged. A good backup plan allows you to restore a device's operating system, software, data files, settings, accounts, and profiles in case of a massive hardware failure or virus infection. Personal computer backups are typically recorded on _____ hard drives, USB flash drives, network servers, and online storage services. An easier way to get a backup of important data files is to use the _____ command to make duplicates and store them on a USB drive. Backup utilities such as File History and Time Machine use a technique called file _____ to make sure that files on two devices are the same. A disk _____ is a bit-for-bit copy of the data from all sectors of a hard disk.

Section E: Inside a digital device, a data _____ connects the processor to RAM, and connects RAM to a series of expansion _____. There are three technologies commonly used for general-purpose ports: Thunderbolt, Lightning, and _____. For video devices, the most common ports are VGA, DVI, _____, and Mini DisplayPort. Peripherals can be inserted or removed while the host device is on, but storage devices should not be removed without notification. To connect additional peripherals when all USB ports are full, it is possible to use a USB _____. Some peripherals can be connected wirelessly using _____ technology. The software that helps a peripheral device establish communication with its host device is called a device _____. Most devices include a(n) _____ crystal display. Image quality for a display device is a factor of screen size, response rate, dot _____, and resolution. Touchscreens use either _____ or capacitive technology to process gestures. Display devices receive images from graphics circuitry. A(n) _____ and special video memory can enhance graphics processing and free the main processor for other tasks. For printed output, most personal computer owners select _____ jet printers, though _____ printers are a popular option when low operating costs at high volume are important. The Internet of _____ is a technology that links smart sensors. Some of these sensors can also be found in smartphones and autonomous vehicles. A(n) _____ can sense if a laptop computer is dropped or if a car brakes suddenly. A(n) _____ sensor measures angular velocity. A(n) _____ can be used as a compass for navigation and map displays. Autonomous vehicles use sensor data as input to sense-plan- _____ algorithms processed on an onboard computer.

Interactive Situation Questions

1. Suppose you're reading a computer magazine and you come across the ad pictured to the right. By looking at the specs, you can tell that the microprocessor was manufactured by which company? [ ]

2. The capacity of the hard disk drive in the ad is [ ] GB and the memory capacity is [ ] GB.

3. Your friends are chatting about a low-cost laptop that "runs Google." You figure that they are actually talking about a device called a(n) [ ] that runs Google's Chrome OS as its operating system.

4. Looking over the specs for a new tablet device, would you expect it to have a RISC or CISC processor? [ ]

5. At the beginning of an update for your smartphone, you notice a warning: "Make sure your device is connected to a wall outlet and do not turn the device off until the update is complete." You suspect that the update is going to [ ] the ROM boot loader to fix a security vulnerability.

6. You've decided to archive your vast photo collection on DVDs. You want the longest possible lifespan. When you go to purchase blank DVDs, you see that some are marked DVD-R, whereas others are DVD-RW. Which should you choose? [ ]

7. You're working on a group project. Each person has to access a dataset for creating several graphs. You'll be compiling the graphs into a final report. Rather than emailing graphs back and forth, you suggest using Dropbox, a(n) [ ] storage service where members of the group can access a shared folder.

Sup-R Game Desktop Model EEXL

- Intel® Core™ i7
- 6 GB Tri-Channel DDR4
- 500 GB SATA (7200 rpm)
- 21.5" HD widescreen monitor
- NVIDIA® GeForce™
- Creative Sound Blaster® X-Fi Titanium
- Altec Lansing speakers
- Gigabit Ethernet port
- 3-year limited warranty
- Windows 11

$549

8. After purchasing a new Windows computer, your first step is to get all your backup tools in order, beginning with a(n) [ ] drive that you can use to boot your computer in case of a hard drive failure.

9. One of the ports on your laptop is rectangular and the inside of it is blue. It is a(n) [ ] port.

10. You need an external keyboard for your Android device, and thankfully you can add a wireless one because it has [ ] capability.

11. Suppose that you volunteer to produce a large quantity of black-and-white leaflets for a charity organization. It is fortunate that you have access to a(n) [ ] printer with low operating costs.

Lab: What's Going on in There?

The microprocessor clock is ticking. Data bits are flying in and out of RAM and zooming over the data bus to a storage device. All that seems invisible, but wait! You can get an idea of what's going on inside the system unit. Who needs to know? You might. If you suspect your computer has a virus. If you think your computer might have been compromised by a botnet. If your computer seems sluggish. Windows and macOS include monitoring utilities that provide all kinds of information about your computer's status.

Requirements:

For this lab, you'll need a desktop or laptop computer running either Windows or macOS. The instructions are generalized; they provide helpful guidelines, but not specific steps. As you complete the assignment, answer each question. Submit your answers in the format specified by your instructor.

Assignment:

❶ Open your computer's monitoring utility.

On a Mac, select the Applications folder from the dock. Select the Utilities folder, then select Activity Monitor. Use the View menu to select All Processes.

On a PC with Windows, launch Task Manager. It might be necessary to select More Details.

❷ Examine your computer's CPU usage.

On a Mac, select the CPU button; on Windows, select the Performance tab.

CPU utilization is expressed as a percentage of total processing capability. If CPU utilization exceeds 10% when you are not using software, it might signal a security breach. Temporary spikes are normal; when you are playing 3D games or using compute-intensive software, the usage could remain above 70%.

What is the current CPU utilization on your device?

❸ Check processes.

On a Mac, processes are listed on the CPU tab; on Windows, select the Processes tab.

A process corresponds to a program. Any programs that are currently running put a load on the CPU.

What is the process with the highest CPU usage? Do you recognize the program associated with this process? If not, look it up online.

❹ Check for malware.

Some processes are launched by the operating system rather than application software. If you don't recognize a process, you can find out if it is legitimate by checking online.

Select a process with an unusual name and search for it online. What is its name, and what does it do?

❺ Check memory.

On a Mac, select the Memory tab; on Windows, remain on the Processes tab.

As you know, RAM holds the operating system, programs, and data, but the amount of stuff that's actually in RAM is pretty surprising.

Find the listing for Kernel_task (Mac) or System (Windows). That process is part of the operating system. How much memory is it using?

What is the name of the software application that uses the most memory?

❻ Check storage.

On a Mac, choose the Disk tab; on Windows, remain on the Processes tab.

Programs send data to storage even when you are not in the process of manually saving files. Some programs create autorecovery files as temporary backups, and Web pages write cookies.

Find a process that is writing data to disk even when you are not actively using it. What is the name of that process and what is its purpose?

3 Networks

Module Contents

Networks let us reach out to the world. But they also let the world into our personal space. In this module you'll explore how to create and use networks that don't expose your darkest secrets.

Try It! Apply what you learn.

- Choose when to use wired connections and when to use wireless connections.
- Check the signal strength of a wireless connection.
- Find your router's IP address.
- Find the private IP address for your device.
- Differentiate between IPv4 and IPv6 addresses.
- Obtain a domain name.
- Find the owners of domain names and IP addresses.
- Find the address of your DNS server and change it if necessary.
- Check the speed of your Internet connection and compare it to the speed advertised by your ISP.
- Determine the latency, jitter, and packet loss on your Internet connection and gauge whether it affects the quality of streaming services.
- Use Traceroute to troubleshoot a slow Internet connection.
- Select an Internet service provider.
- Reduce your security risks when connecting to Wi-Fi hotspots.
- Construct a local area network that allows devices to share files and an Internet connection.
- Configure and secure a router for a local area network.
- Piece together a small IoT network for home monitoring.
- Access files from other devices on a LAN.
- Activate file sharing and use permissions to limit how your files can be used.
- Obtain files from Internet-based services, such as FTP, Dropbox, and BitTorrent.

3

Networks

Gauge your level of expertise. The answers are in the text.

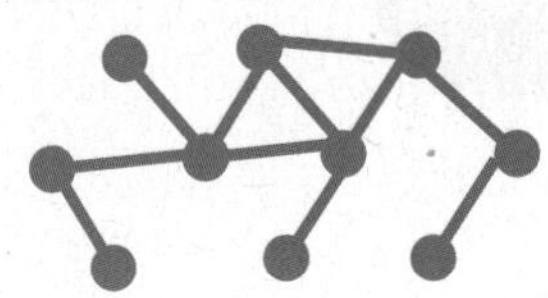

What type of network topology does the diagram above illustrate?

____

Before speeding over the Internet, files are divided into:

____

The major problem with GEO satellite Internet access is excessive:

______________.

List five types of fixed Internet access:

____

____

____

____

____

Which is more secure:

WEP or WPA

LTE

Broadband or narrowband?

www.course.com

What's the top-level domain?

TCP/IP **WPA2/WEP**

Which one is the Internet protocol stack?

To protect the files on your computer when connecting to a Wi-Fi hotspot, what should you turn off?

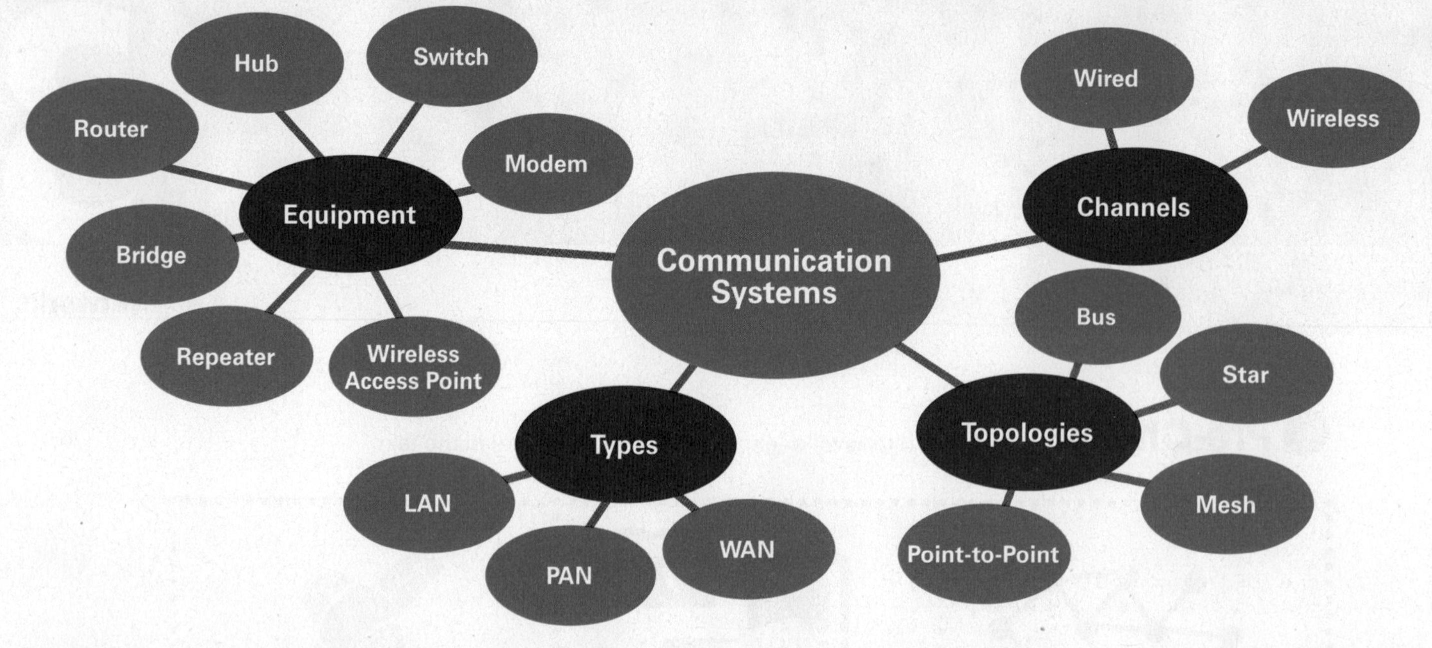

Section A

Network Basics

Objectives

- Replicate Shannon's diagram of a general communication system, including all nine labels.
- Give two examples of PANs, LANs, and WANs.
- List four examples of wired channels used for networks.
- State the two wireless channels most commonly used for communication networks.
- List two advantages and four disadvantages of wireless channels.
- State what differentiates broadband from narrowband.
- Draw a diagram showing how data from a smart thermostat could travel over several networks with different topologies.
- Compare and contrast mesh and star topologies based on dependability, security, capacity, expandability, control, and monitoring.
- List two examples of DTEs and two examples of DCEs.
- Explain the difference between a modem and a router.
- List five tasks that are handled by communication protocols.

Networks are everywhere. They are an indispensable part of our lives. When there are outages, things go haywire. When there are slowdowns, we get frustrated. What do you need to know about networks? The building blocks in Section A will get you started.

Terminology

communication network
PAN
LAN
WAN
communication channel
wired channels
wireless channels
RF signals
transceiver
microwaves
bandwidth
broadband
narrowband
topology
point-to-point topology
star topology
mesh topology
bus topology
node
DTE
DCE
router
modem
communication protocol
handshaking
protocol stack
error correction

Communication Systems

You use many networks for communication, research, and entertainment. Some networks are large and some are small. The largest networks offer little control to consumers. Smaller networks that you set up can be completely under your control, but they are also your responsibility. Networks can be classified in many ways; as a network user, you'll want to keep in mind the idea of control and how it affects your privacy and security.

QuickCheck

In Shannon's model, signals traveling along a communication channel can be disrupted by ______________.

a. a source

b. a transmitter

c. a receiver

d. noise

What is a network? A network links things together. A **communication network** (or communication system) links together devices so that data and information can be shared among them.

In 1948, Claude Shannon, an engineer at Bell Labs, published an article describing a communication system model applicable to networks of all types. His diagram illustrates the essence of a network, so it is a good place to begin this module. Shannon's model (Figure 3-1) is relatively easy to understand.

Figure 3-1: Components of a basic communication system

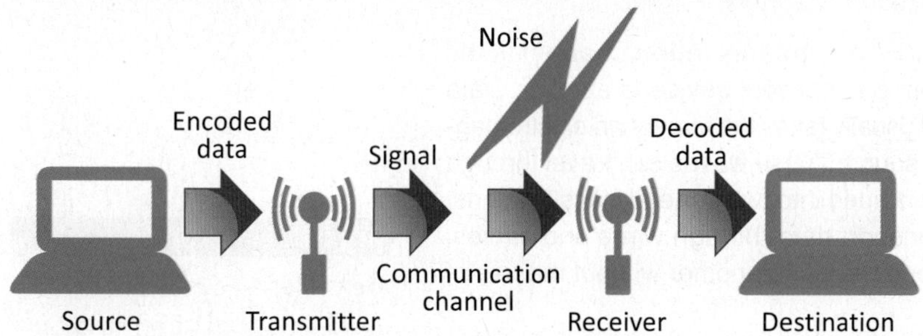

How are computer networks classified? Networks can be classified according to their size and geographic scope, as shown in Figure 3-2.

Figure 3-2: Network classifications

PAN (personal area network)

PANs connect smart devices or consumer electronics within a range of about 30 feet (10 meters) and usually without the use of wires or cables. The reference to *personal* indicates that the network serves a single individual, rather than multiple users. A PAN could be used to sync data from a handheld device to a desktop computer, ship data wirelessly to a printer, or transmit data from a smartphone to a wireless headset.

LAN (local area network)

LANs are data communication networks that connect personal computers within a very limited geographical area—usually a single building. School computer labs and home networks are examples of LANs. Wi-Fi networks that you can access in airports, coffee shops, and other public places are LANs. The in-house networks operated by most businesses are also LANs.

WAN (wide area network)

WANs cover a large geographical area and usually consist of several smaller networks, which might use different computer platforms and network technologies. The Internet is the world's largest WAN. Other public WANs include telephone systems, cable television systems, and satellite-based communication systems.

▶ Why is geographic scope important? Localized networks normally include a small number of computers, which can be connected using basic equipment. As the area of network coverage expands, the number of devices grows, specialized devices are sometimes required to boost signals, and the diversity of devices requires sophisticated management tools and strategies.

▶ What about the Internet of Things? The Internet of Things (IoT) is an evolving concept that may be difficult to classify as a PAN, LAN, or WAN. The IoT has the potential to become a global collection of smart devices transmitting to other devices over the Internet. Today, smart devices are more often grouped into small local pods that report to a centralized device, which in turn exchanges data with local networks and the Internet.

QuickCheck

A university that offers wireless Internet access to students in classrooms is operating what type of network?

a. PAN

b. LAN

c. IoT

d. WAN

Communication Channels

Do you suppose it is easier for a snooper to secretly access your computer when your device is connected to a Wi-Fi hotspot or cabled to a LAN? Some connections are more secure and more dependable than others, so it pays to understand the ins and outs of communication channels.

▶ What is a communication channel? A **communication channel** is the medium used to transport information from one network device to another. Data transmitted over a communication channel usually takes the form of an electromagnetic signal—waves of light, electricity, or sound. These waves can travel through the air or through cables, so channels are divided into two general classifications: wired and wireless. **Wired channels** transport data through wires and cables. **Wireless channels** transport data from one device to another without the use of cables or wires.

▶ What are the options for wired channels? Wired channels include twisted pair wires used for telephone landlines, coaxial cables used for cable television networks, Category 6 cables used for LANs, and fiber-optic cables used for high-capacity trunk lines that provide main routes for telephone, cable, and Internet communications (Figure 3-3).

Try It!

Are you using a network right now? Is it wired or wireless? If it is wired, can you identify the type of cable that connects your computer to the rest of the network?

Figure 3-3: Network cables

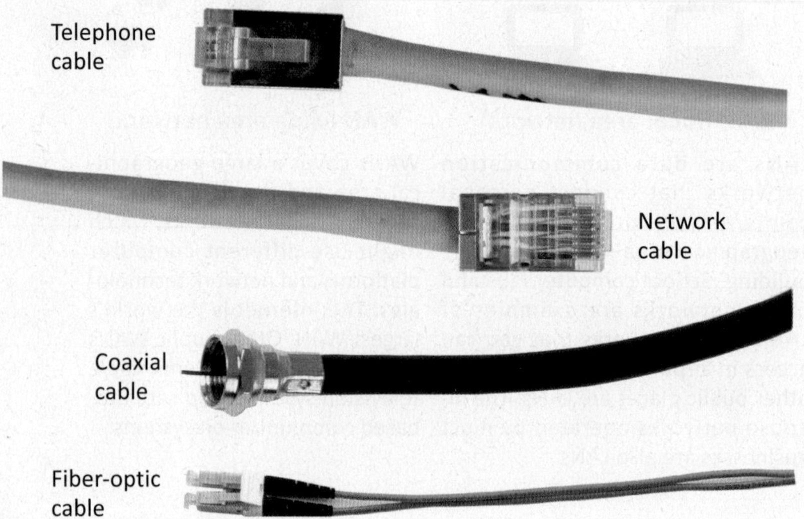

3

What are the advantages of wired channels? Before wireless technologies became available, local area networks were exclusively wired. Today, wired connections are used less frequently for home, school, and business networks. They remain the network technology of choice, however, for segments of the Internet and local area networks that require fast and secure connectivity.

When you set up a wired connection, you don't have to worry about hackers intercepting your data from the sidewalk outside your house, or your neighbor stumbling across personal files when your wireless signal reaches past your property line. Yes, there are ways to tap into a wired network, but they require physical access to the cable or fairly sophisticated snooping equipment. The advantages of wired channels are summarized in Figure 3-4.

Figure 3-4: Advantages of wired channels

Cables can be shielded against interference and encased in protective casings for installations that are outdoors and underground.

Wired connections are dependable. Their carrying capacity and speed are not affected by airborne interference from rain, snow, or electrical devices.

Wired connections are more secure than their wireless counterparts because a device can join a wired network only if it is physically connected by a cable.

QuickCheck

Data traveling on a wired channel tends to be more secure than data traveling on a wireless channel. True or false?

a. True

b. False

What are the disadvantages of wired connections? The cables that offer speed and security for a wired connection are also the main weakness of this type of connection. The disadvantages of wired channels include cost, lack of mobility, and installation hassles. Figure 3-5 provides more details.

Figure 3-5: Disadvantages of wired channels

In WANs, wired installation can be costly because cables have to be suspended from poles or buried underground. They can be damaged by weather events and digging in the wrong place. Repairs to underground cables require heavy equipment to locate, access, and fix the break.

LAN devices connected by cables have limited mobility. Desktop computers tend to be better candidates for wired connections, whereas laptops, tablets, and handheld devices can retain their mobility when they are not tethered to a cable.

Cables are unsightly, tend to get tangled, and collect dust. Running cables through ceilings, walls, and floors can be challenging. Cables can also carry electrical surges that have the potential to damage network equipment.

QuickCheck

Which of the following situations is most suitable for a network that connects most devices with cables?

a. A university campus

b. A bank branch office

c. A private home

d. A coffee shop

▶ What are the options for wireless channels? The most widespread wireless channels for communication networks are radio signals and microwaves.

▶ How do radio signals transport data? Most wireless channels transport data as **RF signals**, commonly called radio waves. RF channels are typically used for Bluetooth connections and Wi-Fi networks. It is also the technology used to carry voice and data between a smartphone and a cell tower. RF signals are sent and received by a **transceiver** (a combination of a transmitter and a receiver) that is equipped with an antenna (Figure 3-6).

Terminology

RF stands for radio frequency.

Figure 3-6: Transceiver-equipped devices

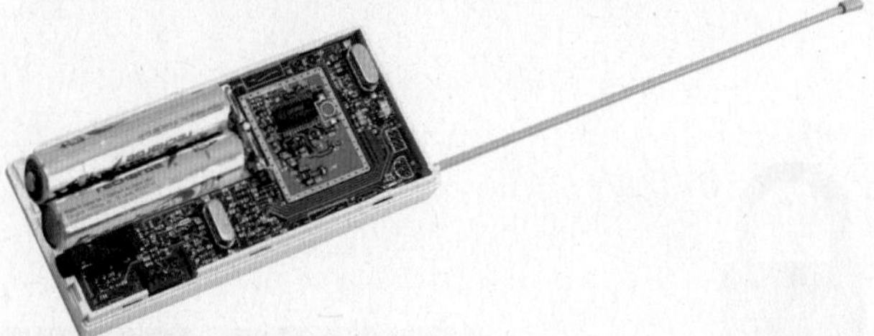

Devices used with wireless connections are equipped with transceivers that include a transmitter for sending data and a receiver for collecting data. A transceiver has an antenna, which may be visible or may be housed out of sight within a device's system unit.

Terminology

Although we use the term *wireless connection*, there is no physical connection between wireless devices in a network. Their connection is conceptual in the sense that data can travel between "connected" devices.

▶ How do microwaves transport data? **Microwaves** (the waves themselves, not your oven!) provide another option for transporting data wirelessly. Like radio waves, microwaves are electromagnetic signals, but they behave differently. Microwaves can be aimed in a single direction and have more carrying capacity than radio waves. However, microwaves cannot penetrate metal objects and work best for line-of-sight transmission when a clear path exists between the transmitter and receiver.

Microwave installations usually provide data transport for large corporate networks. They are also used to transmit signals between towers in cellular and wide area wireless installations.

▶ What are the advantages and disadvantages of wireless? The main advantage of wireless connections is mobility. Wireless devices are not tethered to network cables, so battery-operated laptops, tablets, and smartphones can be easily moved from room to room, or even outdoors. With wireless networks, there are no unsightly cables, and power spikes are much less likely to run through cables to damage equipment. The main disadvantages of wireless channels are speed, range, security, and licensing.

QuickCheck

What type of wireless channels are most typically used for networks in homes and coffee shops?

a. RF

b. Coax

c. Microwave

d. WiMAX

▶ Why is wireless slower than wired? Wireless signals are susceptible to interference from devices such as microwave ovens, cordless telephones, and baby monitors. When interference affects a wireless signal, data must be retransmitted, and that takes extra time.

▶ What limits the range of a wireless connection? The range of a wireless signal can be limited by the type of signal, the transmitter strength, and the physical environment. Just as radio stations fade as you move away from their broadcasting towers, data signals fade as the distance between network devices increases. Signal range can also be limited by thick walls, floors, or ceilings.

As signal strength decreases, so can speed. A weak signal usually means slow data transfers. You can get a rough idea of signal strength for your desktop, laptop, tablet, or smartphone by checking the network signal strength meter (Figure 3-7).

Figure 3-7: Wireless network signal strength meter

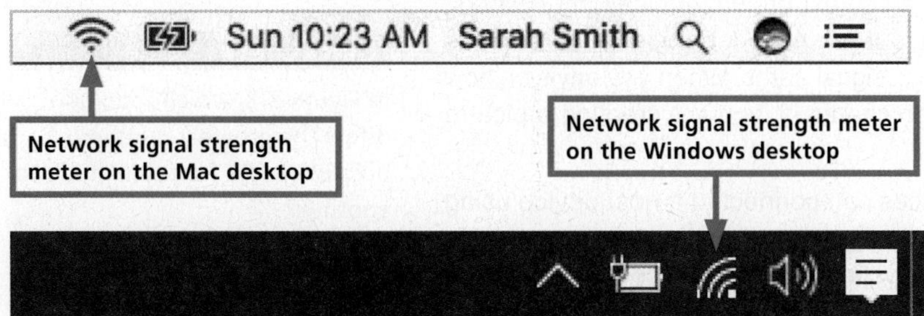

Try It!

Your digital devices may connect to various networks with differing signal strengths. Check the wireless signal strengths for any devices you have handy.

3

▶ What's the problem with wireless security? Wireless signals float through the air and penetrate walls. The signals that carry your wireless data can be accessed from outside your premises. Someone outside of your house, for example, could secretly join your network, access files, and piggyback on your Internet connection. To make wireless data useless to intruders, it should be encrypted. Later in this module, you'll learn how to use encryption to secure data sent over wireless connections.

▶ How does licensing affect wireless connections? Government agencies, such as the Federal Communications Commission (FCC), regulate signals that are sent through the air. To broadcast at most frequencies, including those used by radio and television stations, a license is required.

Wireless connections use unlicensed frequencies that are available for public use. These frequencies include 2.4 GHz and parts of the 5 GHz and 6 GHz spectrums. 2.4 GHz signals are subject to more interference from other devices, but have a wider range than 5 GHz or 6 GHz signals.

▶ What's bandwidth? Network channels must move data and move it quickly. **Bandwidth** is the transmission capacity of a communication channel. Just as a four-lane freeway can carry more traffic than a two-lane street, a high-bandwidth communication channel can carry more data than a low-bandwidth channel. For example, the coaxial cable that brings you more than 100 channels of cable TV has a higher bandwidth than your home telephone line.

The bandwidth of a channel that carries digital data is usually measured in bits per second (bps). For example, your wireless LAN might be rated for an average speed of 27 Mbps. The bandwidth of a channel carrying analog data is typically measured in hertz (Hz). For instance, the copper wires that carry voice-grade telephone signals are often described as having a bandwidth of 3,000 Hz.

In 2004, the FCC defined **broadband** as networks that are capable of downloading at least 25 megabits of data per second (25 Mbps) and uploading at least 3 megabits per second (3 Mbps). Channels slower than 25 Mbps are classified as **narrowband**. Broadband capacity is essential for networks that support many users and those that carry lots of audio and video data, such as streaming music and movies.

Terminology

Hz is an abbreviation for hertz, which refers to the number of times a wave oscillates, or peaks, per second. Telephone signals are transmitted in the 1,200 Hz range. A wireless network that transmits at 2.4 GHz has a wave that peaks 2.4 billion times per second.

QuickCheck

You have a choice of network connections. Which one of the following is broadband?

a. A 56 Kbps phone link

b. A 1,200 Hz landline

c. A 50 Mbps cable connection

d. A 1.2 Mbps satellite link

Network Topology

A spider weaves a web by making silky connections between leaves, branches, and other surfaces. Most spiderwebs have a structure, and the same can be said for communication networks. The topologies of the networks you use have an effect on their dependability, security, and scope.

▶ What is network topology? In the context of communication networks, **topology** refers to the structure and layout of network components, such as computers, connecting cables, and wireless signal paths. When you envision how devices are connected by communication channels, you are creating a picture of the network's topology.

Module 2 explained how peripheral devices can connect to a host device using expansion ports, USB cables, or Bluetooth. These connections are an example of **point-to-point topology**. When connecting several devices, two network topologies are popular. **Star topology** connects multiple devices to a central device. **Mesh topology** connects multiple devices to each other, either as a full mesh or as a partial mesh. The less popular **bus topology** connects devices in a linear sequence. Figure 3-8 illustrates these network topologies.

QuickCheck

In Figure 3-8, which topology offers the greatest number of possible paths from one node to another?

a. Star

b. Full mesh

c. Partial mesh

d. Bus

Figure 3-8: Network topologies

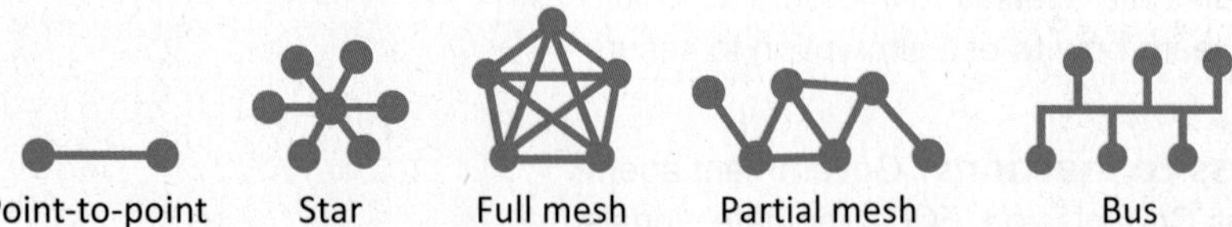

▶ Can a network use more than one topology? Data can flow over multiple networks that have different topologies. As shown in Figure 3-9, data from a fitness wristband connects to a laptop via a point-to-point connection (A). The laptop is part of a home network configured as a star (B). The home network connects to an Internet service provider, so it is part of a larger star network (C). Finally, the data is passed to the Internet, which has a mesh topology (D).

Figure 3-9: Multiple topologies

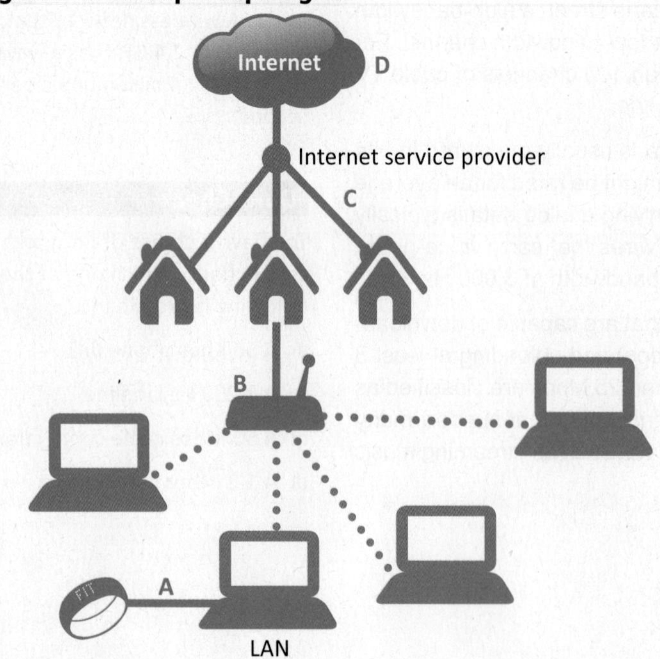

Which topology is best? Every topology has strengths and weaknesses, so there is no best network topology. Figure 3-10 compares strengths and weaknesses of the two most popular network topologies based on dependability, security, capacity, expandability, control, and monitoring.

Figure 3-10: Star or mesh?

Dependability

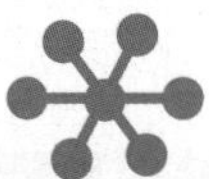

If the central point fails, data cannot flow anywhere on the network. If one of the other devices fails, however, the rest of the network remains operational.

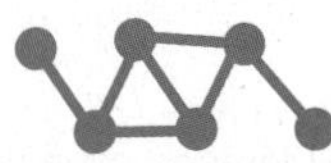

There is no central point of failure; redundant paths between devices can be used to bypass failed devices.

Security

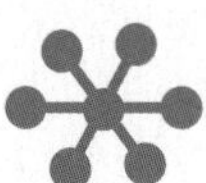

Data that travels on a star pathway makes only one intermediate hop between the sender and destination. The threat area for any transmission encompasses only three devices and two channels.

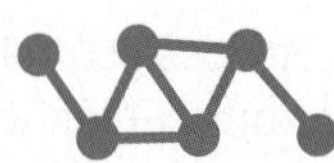

Within a mesh, data might travel through several devices and over multiple channels. Each leg presents a potential security risk. The chance of a security breach rises as the number of devices and channels increases.

Capacity

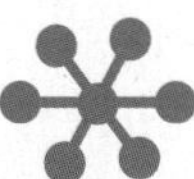

Star topologies are limited by the amount of data that can be handled by the central device.

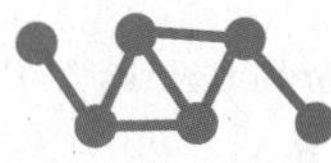

Mesh topologies offer higher capacities because data can be transmitted from different devices simultaneously.

Expandability

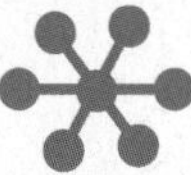

Expandability is limited by the number of devices that can be attached to the central device within its immediate area of wireless coverage or maximum cable length.

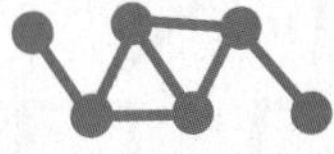

The network can be expanded infinitely. As new devices are added, the network continues to repeat the signal as necessary until it reaches the farthest devices.

Control

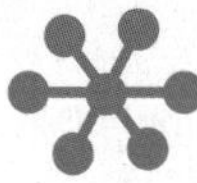

Setup and updates are primarily done on the central device, which also can be used to shut down the entire network.

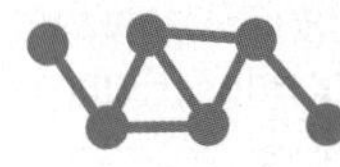

Setup is more complex, as each device must be configured to send, receive, and forward network data. There is no central point at which the network can be shut down.

Monitoring

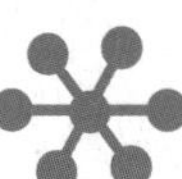

All data passes through a central point, which is relatively easy to monitor for legitimate or illicit purposes.

Data does not pass through a central point, making data more challenging to monitor.

Network Nodes

Communication networks connect all kinds of devices: from smartphones to satellite dishes, from computers to cell towers, and even between tiny sensors and RFID tags. Any device in a network is called a **node**. You are familiar with network nodes such as laptops, smartphones, tablets, desktops, and peripheral devices. There are many other nodes that you don't interact with directly, yet they ultimately control how smoothly your Netflix movie streams and whether your email arrives at its destination.

What should I know about network nodes? Devices on a network are classified as DTEs or DCEs. **DTE** stands for data terminal equipment. A DTE can be any device that stores or generates data. When connected to a network, your laptop is a DTE, as are your smartphone, tablet, and fitness tracker. The servers that house Web sites, handle email, offer cloud storage, and stream videos are also DTEs. Your own DTEs are under your control, and some servers are open to public access.

QuickCheck

When you connect a cell phone to a network, it is considered a(n)______________.

a. DTE

b. DCE

c. SPT

d. TCP

DCE stands for data communication equipment. These devices control the speed of data over networks, convert signals as they jump from cables to wireless, check for corrupted data, and route data from its origin to its destination. The most well-known DCEs are routers and modems.

How does a router work? You probably have a DCE in your home network. A **router** is a device that controls the flow of data within a network and acts as a gateway to pass data from one network to another. Routers are used to direct traffic over major Internet trunk lines, and they are commonly used to route data from home networks to the Internet (Figure 3-11).

Figure 3-11: Routers

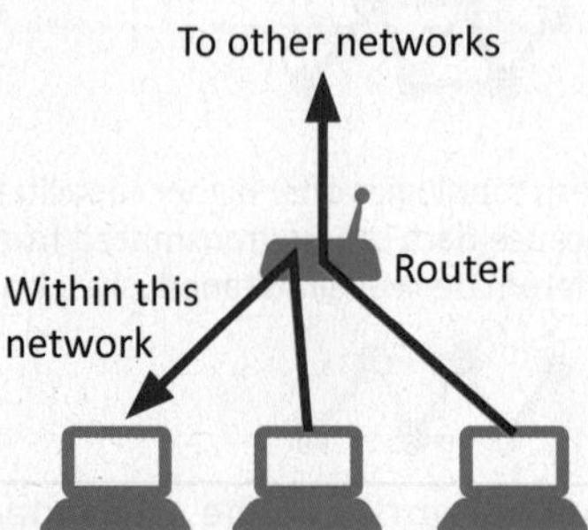

How does a modem work? A **modem** contains circuitry that converts the data-carrying signals from a digital device to signals that can travel over various communication channels. The kind of modem you use depends on whether you are connecting to a dial-up, wireless, cable, satellite, or DSL Internet service. A modem is usually supplied by your Internet service provider (Figure 3-12).

QuickCheck

A typical home network with Internet access would have ____________.

a. a single DTE

b. multiple DCEs, but no DTEs

c. a modem and a router

d. multiple routers

Figure 3-12: Modems

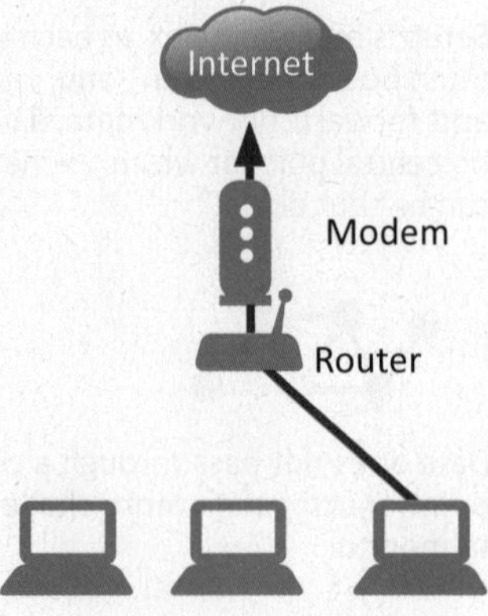

▸ What about other DCEs? DCEs perform all sorts of tasks. Suppose you want to extend the range of your home network out onto your balcony. What if your Internet provider wants to streamline network traffic in a neighborhood where lots of subscribers stream HD movies? DCEs such as repeaters, switches, and hubs can get the job done (Figure 3-13). These functions can sometimes be combined into a single device, such as a cable modem that also functions as a router.

Figure 3-13: Network devices

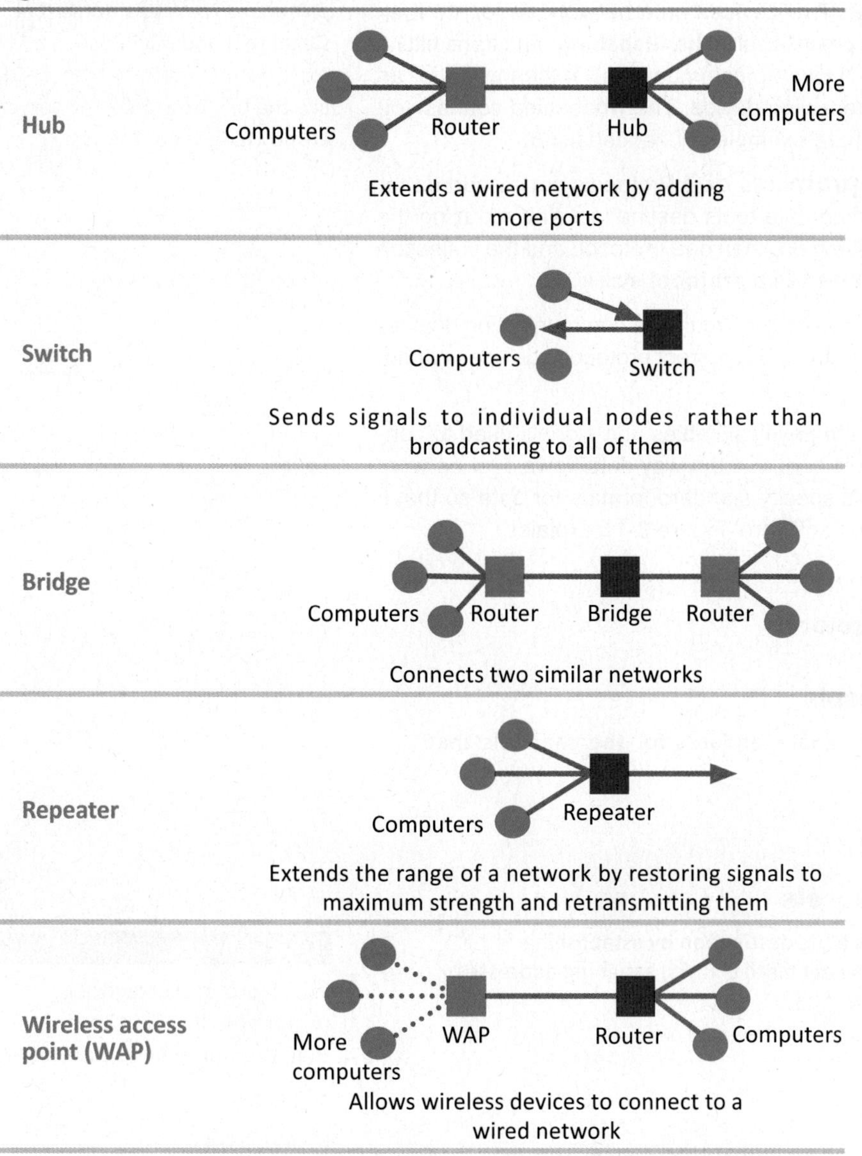

Hub
Computers
Router
Hub
More computers
Extends a wired network by adding more ports
Switch
Computers
Switch
Sends signals to individual nodes rather than broadcasting to all of them
Bridge
Computers
Router
Bridge
Router
Connects two similar networks
Repeater
Computers
Repeater
Extends the range of a network by restoring signals to maximum strength and retransmitting them
Wireless access point (WAP)
More computers
WAP
Router
Computers
Allows wireless devices to connect to a wired network

QuickCheck

To extend the reach of your wireless network out onto your balcony, which of the following devices would be best?

a. A hub

b. A router

c. A repeater

d. A gateway

3

Communication Protocols

A protocol is a set of rules for interacting and negotiating. In some respects, it is like the hand signals used by pitchers and catchers during baseball games. Before the ball is thrown, the pitcher and catcher use hand signals to negotiate the speed and style of the pitch. Similar to the way pitchers and catchers use signals, networks use communication protocols to coordinate data transfer.

Try It!

People use many verbal and nonverbal communication protocols. Think of a nonverbal signal that you might use in a restaurant to indicate that you'd like the bill. How does the server acknowledge your request?

What is a communication protocol? In the context of networks, a **communication protocol** refers to a set of rules for efficiently transmitting data from one network node to another. Two devices on a network negotiate their communication protocols through a process called **handshaking**. The transmitting device sends a signal that means "I want to communicate." It then waits for an acknowledgment signal from the receiving device. The whooshing sounds you hear as two fax machines connect are examples of handshaking.

What can communication protocols do? Protocols set standards for encoding and decoding data, guiding data to its destination, and reducing the effects of interference. Networks use more than one protocol, and the collection of protocols for a network is referred to as a **protocol stack**.

Communication protocols are provided by the circuitry of communicating devices and by communications software. Without the correct protocols, devices cannot communicate over a network.

Some protocols set standards for the physical cables and signals used to connect network nodes. Other protocols deal with the way data flows over network channels. And even more protocols specify standard formats for data so that it can be accessed by communication software. Figure 3-14 explains.

Figure 3-14: Communication protocols

Physical protocols

Specify cable and signal standards for the channels that carry data

Transport protocols

Make sure data gets to its destination by establishing standards for dividing data into chunks, assigning addresses, and correcting errors

Arrival protocols

Convert data into standard formats that can be used by applications, such as email, Web browsers, and Skype

QuickCheck

Which protocol category is responsible for the standards that attempt to block junk mail?

a. Physical

b. Transport

c. Arrival

How can a network detect if a signal has been corrupted? **Error correction** is one of the responsibilities of communication protocols. Remember from Module 1 that text, numbers, sound, images, and video all are represented by bits. Suppose that some of those bits are garbled in transmission. Did that email say to meet at 29:00? Did your music track stop halfway through? Without error checking, the data you receive may not be reliable or complete.

Digital networks—those that transmit digital signals—can be easily monitored to determine if interference has corrupted any signals. At its most primitive level, digital equipment is sensitive to only two frequencies—one that represents 1s and one that represents 0s.

Suppose that a 0 is sent as −5 volts and a 1 is sent as +5 volts. What if, during transmission, some interference changes the voltage of a 1 bit from +5 volts to +3 volts?

To correct the corrupted bit, the receiving device realizes that +3 volts is not one of the two valid voltages. It guesses that a 1 bit (+5 volts) was actually transmitted and cleans the signal by reestablishing its voltage to +5 (Figure 3-15).

Figure 3-15: Error correction

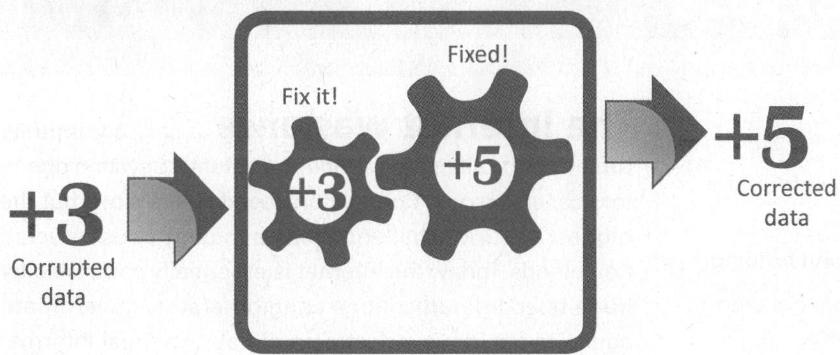

3

QuickQuiz Section A

1. A(n) ____________ area network connects smart sensors and digital devices within a range of about 30 feet.
2. The communication ____________ used for networks include copper cables, coaxial cables, radio signals, and microwaves.
3. Networks that upload at least 25 Mbps are classified by the FCC as ____________.
4. Modems and routers are examples of ____________ that control the flow of data within a network and act as a gateway from one network to another. Hint: Use the acronym.
5. Communication ____________ set standards for physical channels, transporting data, and correcting errors.

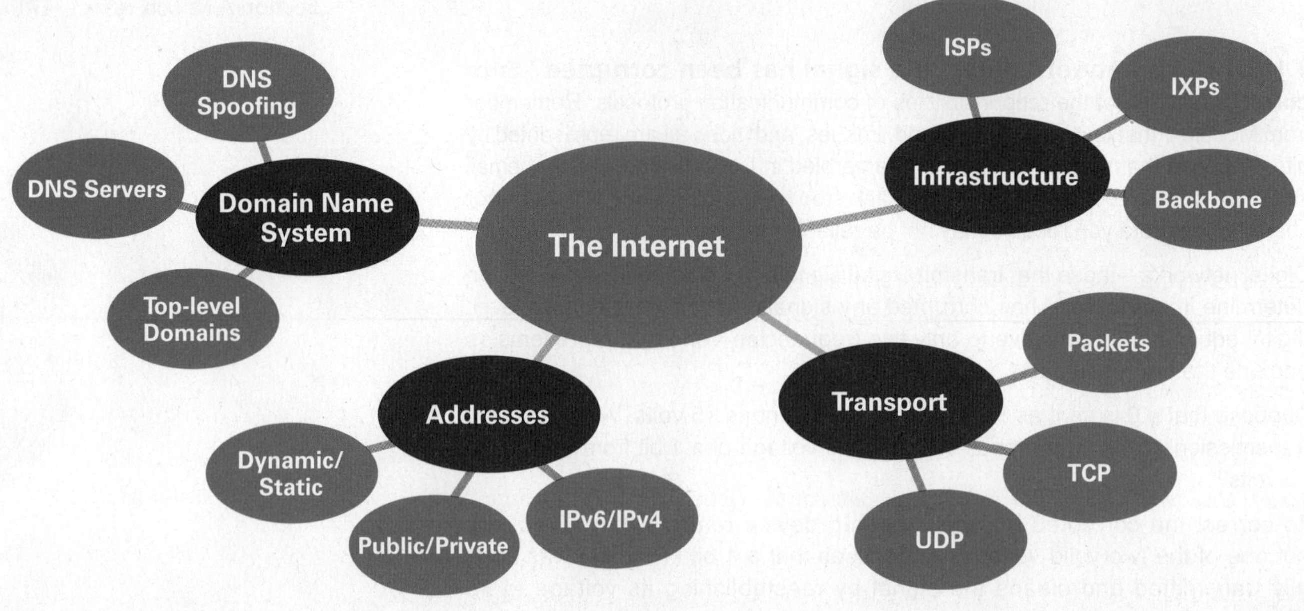

Section B

The Internet

Objectives

- Briefly describe how the Internet developed from the ARPANET.
- Explain the state of Internet governance and funding.
- Draw a diagram showing the interrelationship among the three tiers of Internet service providers.
- Describe how packets are created and how they are carried on packet-switching networks.
- State the roles of TCP, IP, and UDP.
- Identify IPv4 and IPv6 addresses.
- Explain the differences between static addresses and dynamic addresses.
- Draw a diagram illustrating how a router deals with private and public IP addresses.
- List at least five top-level domains.
- Explain the role of the domain name system and why it is one of the Internet's vulnerabilities.

The Internet was once a cozy community run by nonprofit organizations and volunteer system operators called sysops. Connection speeds were slow, but the biggest security challenge was avoiding virus-infected downloads. Today, the Internet is essentially controlled by huge telecommunications conglomerates, government agencies tap into every stream of data, and real information is difficult to sort out from a hailstorm of ads. How did the Internet evolve into what it is today, and what makes it "tick"? Section B gives you a glimpse of what happens on the Net.

Terminology

ARPANET
exabyte
Internet governance
ICANN
Internet infrastructure
Internet backbone
Internet service providers
Internet exchange points
packet
circuit switching
packet switching
TCP
UDP
communication port
IP
IPv4
IPv6
static addresses
dynamic addresses
DHCP
private IP address
public IP address
NAT
domain name
domain name system (DNS)
top-level domain
domain name servers
DNS spoofing

3

Background

The Internet has its roots in a U.S. Department of Defense project that transitioned first into a nonprofit civilian operation, and then to a burgeoning commercial enterprise. We use the Internet without a second thought to communicate, create, and consume content. Yet the Internet also offers profound ethical, security, privacy, and legal challenges. To understand these challenges and the controversies surrounding them, you need a good understanding of basic Internet technology.

How did the Internet get started? The history of the Internet begins in 1957 when the Soviet Union launched Sputnik, the first artificial satellite. In response to this display of Soviet expertise, the U.S. government resolved to improve its scientific and technical infrastructure. One of the resulting initiatives was the Advanced Research Projects Agency (ARPA).

ARPA swung into action with a project designed to help scientists communicate and share valuable computer resources. The **ARPANET**, created in 1969, connected computers at UCLA, the Stanford Research Institute, the University of Utah, and the University of California at Santa Barbara (Figure 3-16).

Figure 3-16: The ARPANET, 1969

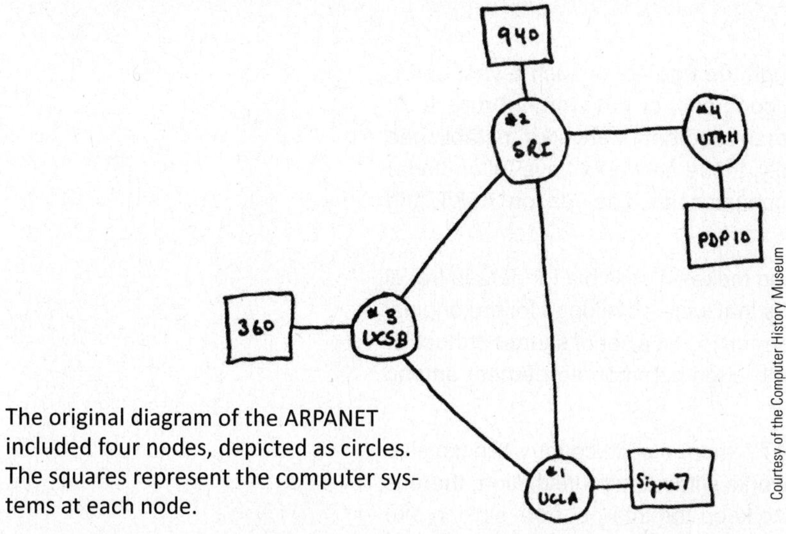

The original diagram of the ARPANET included four nodes, depicted as circles. The squares represent the computer systems at each node.

In 1985, the National Science Foundation (NSF) used ARPANET technology to create a larger network, linking not just a few mainframe computers but entire LANs at each site. Connecting two or more networks creates an internetwork, or internet. The NSF network was an internet (with a lowercase *i*). As this network grew throughout the world, it became known as the Internet (with an uppercase I).

How did the Internet become so popular? Early Internet pioneers used primitive command-line user interfaces to send email, transfer files, and run scientific calculations on Internet supercomputers. Finding information was not easy, and access was limited to a fairly small group of educators and scientists.

In the early 1990s, software developers created new user-friendly Internet access tools, and Internet accounts became available to anyone willing to pay a monthly subscription fee.

QuickCheck

The ARPANET was ___________.

a. a network used by the Soviet Union's space program

b. essentially a pilot program for what later became the Internet

c. created by the National Science Foundation

How big is the Internet? Connecting an estimated 50 billion devices and more than 4 billion users, the Internet is huge. Although exact figures cannot be determined, it is estimated that the Internet handles many exabytes of data every day. An **exabyte** is 1.074 billion gigabytes, and that's a nearly unimaginable amount of data. Visualizing such a vast network is difficult. Visualizations like the one in Figure 3-17 highlight locations with the most Internet activity.

Figure 3-17: There are many ways to visualize the Internet

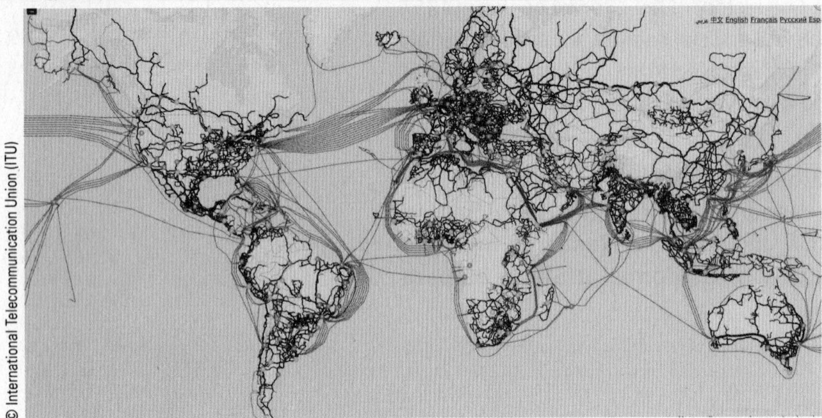

Try It!

How can you visualize the vast scope of the Internet? Do a Web search for *Internet visualizations* to see how scientists and artists have depicted the scope of the Internet throughout time.

Who operates the Internet? Although the Internet is such a vast entity, in theory no single person, organization, company, or government runs it. At one time, the Internet was composed of many regional networks, established in countries throughout the world. Gradually, these networks have fallen under the control of large telecommunications companies, such as Verizon, AT&T, and NTT Communications.

The glue that holds the Internet together and makes it possible for data to travel across borders is a set of standard protocols that were developed for the original ARPANET. In this respect, **Internet governance** is just a set of shared protocols, procedures, and technologies that evolve through common agreement among network providers.

Who supervises Internet standards? Although each country can develop laws, policies, and regulations for the networks within their jurisdiction, there is one crucial administrative task necessary to keep the Internet from sinking into chaos. Every Internet node—each server, each computer, and each piece of data communication equipment—must have a unique address in order to send and receive data.

The organization that supervises Internet addressing is **ICANN**, the Internet Corporation for Assigned Names and Numbers. ICANN is a not-for-profit private sector organization operated by an international board of directors. Its advisory committee has representatives from more than 100 nations, and public comments pertaining to ICANN policies are accepted at its Web site.

Control of Internet address assignments is a powerful tool. It provides the means to block users from accessing specific network nodes. Local governments exercise this power within their jurisdictions to shut down servers that violate copyrights and distribute inappropriate content. The power to globally shut down access to a server, however, only rests with ICANN. You will discover more about the key role of Internet addresses later in this section.

QuickCheck

The primary role of ICANN is to ______________.

a. run the Internet
b. provide funding for the Internet
c. supervise Internet address assignments
d. make sure that every country in the world gets equal access to the Internet

3

Internet Infrastructure

The Internet is not one huge communication network, but rather a network of networks. The way these networks fit together is referred to as the **Internet infrastructure**. Internet networks are organized into tiers. As a consumer, you are subject to the fees, policies, and technologies of the tiers that provide your Internet service.

What are the components of the Internet? The Internet is structured as a hierarchy of networks. Tier 1 networks are at the top of the hierarchy, followed by Tier 2 and Tier 3 networks. Across the globe, approximately 15 Tier 1 networks, such as AT&T, Tata Communications, Verizon, and NTT Communications, form the **Internet backbone**, a system of high-capacity routers and fiber-optic communication links providing the main routes for data speeding across the Internet. Routers on the Internet backbone store routing tables that calculate and track the most efficient routes for data to travel from point A to point B.

The Internet backbone is configured as a mesh network that offers redundant routes for data transport. The backbone's mesh infrastructure is probably the basis for the myth that the Internet originated as a Department of Defense project to create a network that could survive nuclear attacks.

Networks that form the Internet are maintained by **Internet service providers** (ISPs) that supply routers and other data communication equipment, as well as physical and wireless channels to carry data. ISPs exchange data at **Internet exchange points** (IXPs).

Consumers generally connect to Tier 2 or Tier 3 networks. Use the infographic in Figure 3-18 to become familiar with the Internet's infrastructure and its terminology; pay attention to the arrangement of network tiers and points where data moves between them.

QuickCheck

The Internet backbone _______.

a. became the ARPANET in 1985

b. is composed of Tier 1 networks

c. has IXPs where data can get sidetracked

d. is operated by the NSA

Figure 3-18: Internet infrastructure

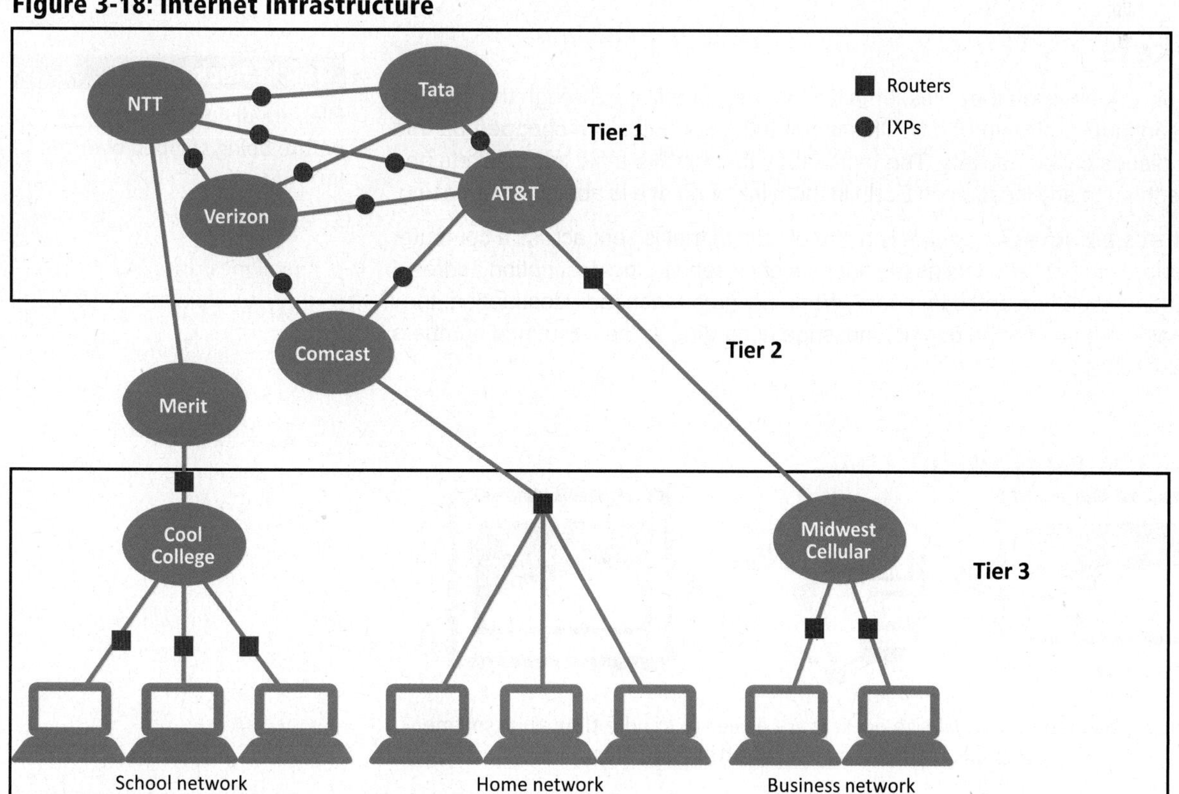

▶ Who pays for the Internet? The Internet is not free. ISPs make a substantial investment in equipment infrastructure. The largest providers each have close to 200,000 miles of cables installed across continents and under the ocean floor. ISPs also own and maintain millions of dollars' worth of data communication equipment.

In addition to infrastructure expenses, ISPs are subject to data transport fees, especially when shipping data up through higher tiers. To offset expenses, ISPs charge consumers for access. Figure 3-19 explains the Internet fee structure.

Figure 3-19: Internet fee structure

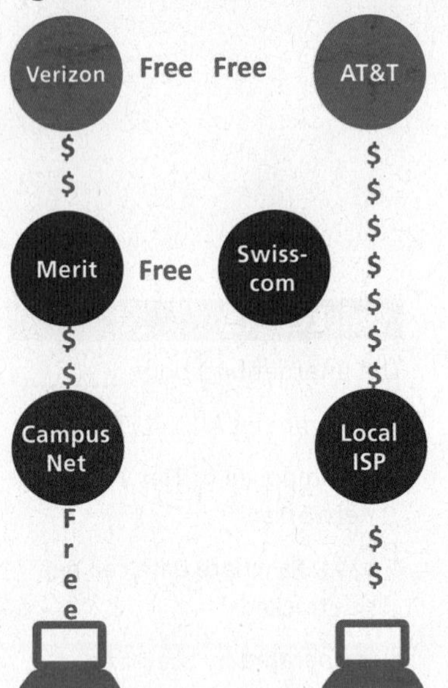

Tier 1 service providers exchange data with other Tier 1 providers on a no-cost basis.

Tier 2 service providers exchange data on a no-cost basis with other Tier 2 providers, but they pay fees to connect to the backbone through Tier 1 providers.

Tier 3 service providers connect to Tier 2 or Tier 1 providers and pay transit fees for the data exchanged.

Consumers either pay fees directly or their access is subsidized by an organization or government.

QuickCheck

Which ISP tier is not subject to transport fees from other tiers?

a. Tier 1

b. Tier 2

c. Tier 3

Packets

Most people envision their files, email, and other data flying through the Internet as a continuous stream of bits. This is not the case. Files are chopped up into small pieces called packets. The technology that breaks a file into packets and routes them to any location on Earth in the blink of an eye is absolutely amazing.

▶ What's a packet? A **packet** is a parcel of data that is sent across a computer network. Each packet contains the address of its sender, the destination address, a sequence number, and some data. When packets reach their destination, they are reassembled into the original message according to the sequence numbers (Figure 3-20).

QuickCheck

Files are divided into ______ before being shipped over the Internet.

a. packets

b. email messages

c. bits

d. tiers

Figure 3-20: Data packets

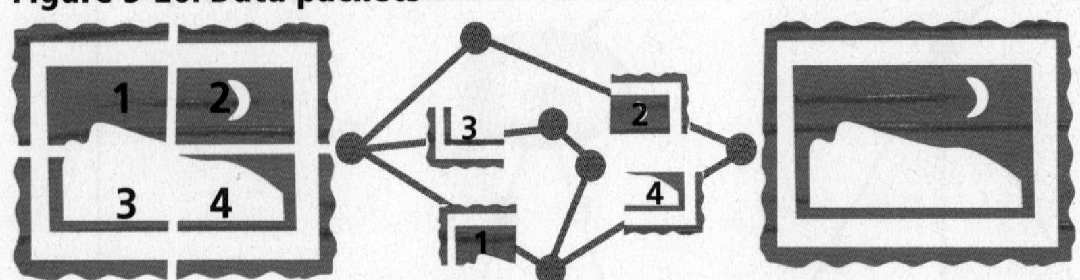

Messages divided into equal-size packets are easier to handle than an assortment of small, medium, large, and extra large files.

Why not just send an entire message? Some communication networks use a technology called **circuit switching**, which essentially establishes a dedicated, private link between one device and another. Landline telephone systems use circuit switching technology to link two callers. Unfortunately, circuit switching is rather inefficient. For example, when someone is on hold during a phone call, no communication is taking place, yet the circuit is reserved and cannot be used for other communication.

A more efficient alternative to circuit switching is **packet switching**, which divides a message into several packets that can be routed independently to their destination. Packets from many different messages can share a single communication channel or circuit.

Packets are shipped over the circuit on a first-come, first-served basis. If some packets from a message are not available, the system does not need to wait for them. Instead, the system moves on to send packets from other messages. The end result is a steady stream of data (Figure 3-21).

Terminology

The telephone network is sometimes referred to as the *public switched telephone network (PSTN).*

Figure 3-21: Circuit-switching and packet-switching networks

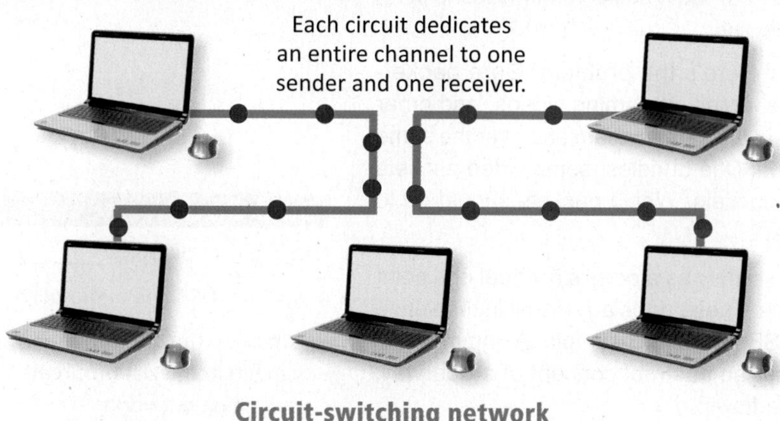
Each circuit dedicates
an entire channel to one
sender and one receiver.
Circuit-switching network

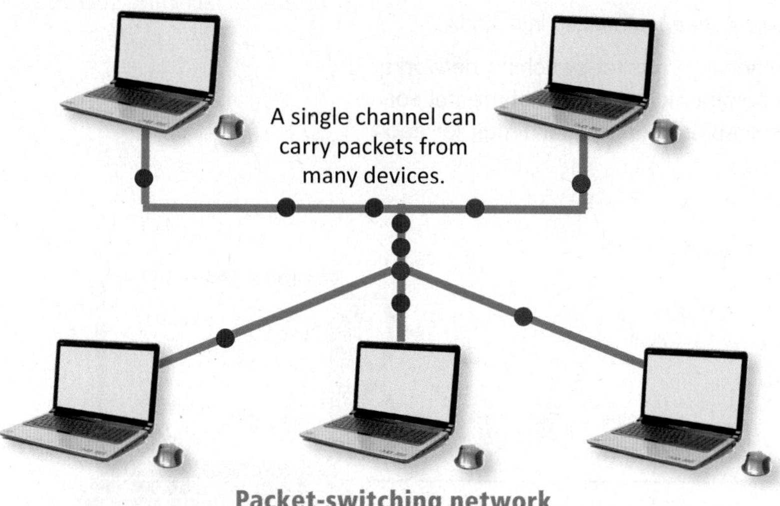
A single channel can
carry packets from
many devices.
Packet-switching network

Packet-switching networks (bottom) provide a more efficient communication system than circuit-switching networks (top).

QuickCheck

Which of the following dedicates a communication channel to each data transmission?

a. The Internet

b. Packet-switched network

c. Circuit-switched network

d. FedEx

Internet Protocols

How are packets created? One of the core Internet protocols, **TCP** (Transmission Control Protocol) is responsible for dividing files into chunks, adding headers containing information for reassembling packets in their original order, and verifying that the data was not corrupted while in transit (a process called error checking). When data is sent over the Internet using TCP, it will reliably reach its destination. TCP is built into applications that transmit data from one digital device to another.

How are packets transported? TCP is also responsible for establishing a connection, transferring packets, and closing the connection when the transmission is complete. Most of the data that flows over the Internet is under the control of TCP.

An alternative transport protocol, **UDP** (User Datagram Protocol) is faster than TCP but does not perform error checking and cannot reorder packets if they are received out of order. UDP, therefore, is suitable for applications in which a bit of lost data is not critical, such as streaming video and music, and Internet-based multiplayer games and voice calls. UDP and TCP both use communications ports to shuttle data into and out of a network device.

QuickCheck

Which data transport protocol includes robust error checking?

a. TCP

b. UDP

c. ARPANET

d. Circuit switching

What is a communications port? Here's the problem: On a packet-switching network, packets for Web pages, email, streaming videos, and other downloads may arrive at your digital device in the same stream and over the same channel. The packets may not arrive in neat little bundles; some video packets could arrive interspersed with Web page packets. Which packets should go to the browser and which to the Netflix player?

A **communication port** (usually referred to simply as a *port*) is a virtual end point for data entering and leaving a digital device. These ports are virtual in the sense that they are not physical ports, as are USB ports, for example. A communication port is not a physical circuit, but rather an abstract concept of a doorway, an opening, or a portal through which data flows.

Ports work in conjunction with Internet addresses. Computers can have up to 65,535 ports. Typically about 10–20 ports are in use and open for various types of data. Data originating from the Web, for instance, uses port 80, whereas streaming video uses port 554. When ports are open, data is allowed to flow freely. Closing ports can block data, and that strategy is used by firewalls to prevent unauthorized intrusions.

Ports create simulated end-to-end connections on packet-switching networks. So although the devices on two ends of a communication channel are not connected by a single dedicated circuit, ports create a conceptual circuit for each type of data, as shown in Figure 3-22.

QuickCheck

Communication ports ______.

a. include USB and audio ports

b. simulate the dedicated circuits that exist on circuit-switching networks

c. are designed to increase the download speed of video data

d. do not recognize packets

Figure 3-22: How communications ports work

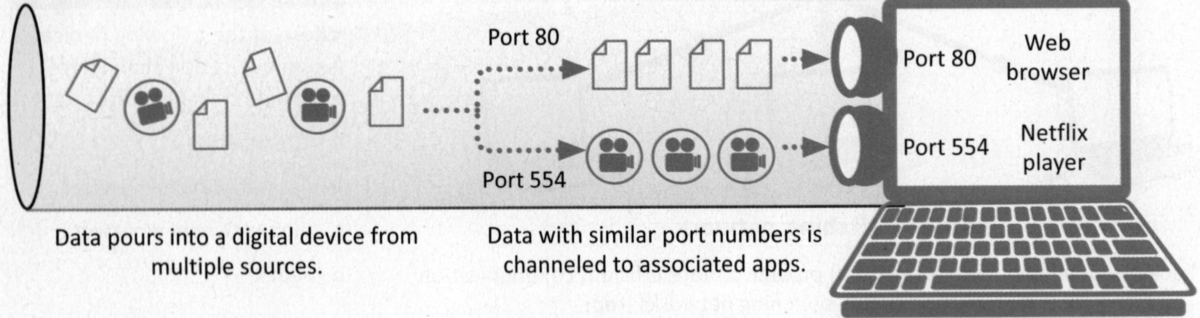
Port 80
Port 554
Port 80
Web browser
Port 554
Netflix player
Data pours into a digital device from multiple sources.
Data with similar port numbers is channeled to associated apps.

Internet Addresses

You might have heard that Internet addresses are running out. Does that mean some people will be unable to get online? Will people have to share addresses? Networks use several kinds of addresses to determine where packets originate and where they are headed. To find out how Internet addresses might affect your online access, read on.

Terminology

Internet Protocol is often referred to as *TCP/IP* (pronounced "T-C-P-I-P").

3

▶ **Exactly what is an Internet address?** Although most people are accustomed to entering something such as *www.wikipedia.org* to access Internet locations, those "www" addresses are not the underlying address used to transport data to its destination. Internet addresses are controlled by **IP** (Internet Protocol), which—along with TCP—is part of the Internet protocol suite. IP defines two sets of addresses: IPv4 and IPv6.

▶ **What is the difference between IPv4 and IPv6?** **IPv4**, which stands for Internet Protocol version 4, is the Internet address standard that has been used since the early 1980s. IPv4 uses 32-bit addresses to uniquely identify devices connected to the Internet. In binary, IPv4 addresses are written as:

11001111 01001011 01110101 00011010

For convenience, 32-bit binary addresses are usually written in decimal as four sets of digits separated by periods:

207.75.117.26

Using 32 bits, IPv4 offers about 4 billion unique addresses. In 2011, that supply of addresses was completely allocated. Yes, IP addresses can be recycled when the original assignees no longer want them, but the demand far outstrips the number of addresses coming up for recycling. Another set of addresses was needed.

IPv6 (Internet Protocol version 6) uses 128 bits for each address, producing billions and billions of unique Internet addresses. An IPv6 address is usually written as eight groups of hexadecimal digits, like this:

2001:48a8:800:1192:198:110:192:54

Don't worry, there are enough IPv6 addresses for the foreseeable future, even with the anticipated influx of 2 billion new Internet users and the Internet of Things adding hundreds of devices each second.

▶ **Does every Internet user need an IP address?** It is more accurate to say that every *device* on the Internet needs an IP address. Many, but not all, devices on the Internet have permanently assigned IP addresses, called **static IP addresses**. As a general rule, routers and computers on the Internet that act as servers use static IP addresses.

ISPs, Web sites, Web hosting services, and email servers that always need to be found at the same address also require static IP addresses. There is an emerging trend for individuals to request static IP addresses for their home networks, and a static address might be useful for remotely communicating with sensors and other devices in the Internet of Things.

QuickCheck

An IP address that contains 84a3 would be a(n) ________________.

a. IPv4 address

b. IPv6 address

c. corrupted address

d. static address

What happens when a device doesn't have a static IP address? IP addresses can be temporarily allocated so that a device uses an address only while it is actively online. When the device is turned off or its Internet connection is disabled, the address can be recycled to another device. The next time the device is turned on, it will be assigned a different IP address. Internet addresses that are temporarily assigned are called **dynamic IP addresses**.

In practice, dynamic IP addresses do not change very often. Today, most consumers have always-on Internet connections that remain active as long as the router that connects to the Internet remains powered on. Turning a computer off or on does not affect the IP address stored in the router. Customers who access the Internet using Comcast XFINITY or AT&T Internet, for example, could have the same IP address for weeks or months.

How do devices get IP addresses? IP addresses can be assigned by a network administrator, but more commonly they are automatically assigned by **DHCP** (Dynamic Host Configuration Protocol). Most devices are preconfigured to receive an IP address by sending a query to the network device acting as the DHCP server. That device could be a router for a local area network or a DHCP server from your ISP. IP addresses get a bit tricky because a device can have a public IP address and a private IP address.

What is a private IP address? Let's suppose that your laptop is connected to your school network. The DHCP server for the school assigns a dynamic IP address to your laptop when you log in. That address, which probably begins with 10, 172, 192, FD, or Fc00, is classified as a private IP address because it works only within the school network.

A **private IP address** can be allocated by any network without supervision from ICANN. However, the address cannot be used to send data over the Internet; it is not routable. Figure 3-23 demonstrates how to find your private IP address.

QuickCheck

When connected to a network, your computer can receive an address from ____________.

a. DHCP

b. packets

c. IPv4

d. the CPU

Try It!

Find your IP address. Is it in the range of private addresses listed in Figure 3-23?

Figure 3-23: Find your private IP address on a Windows computer

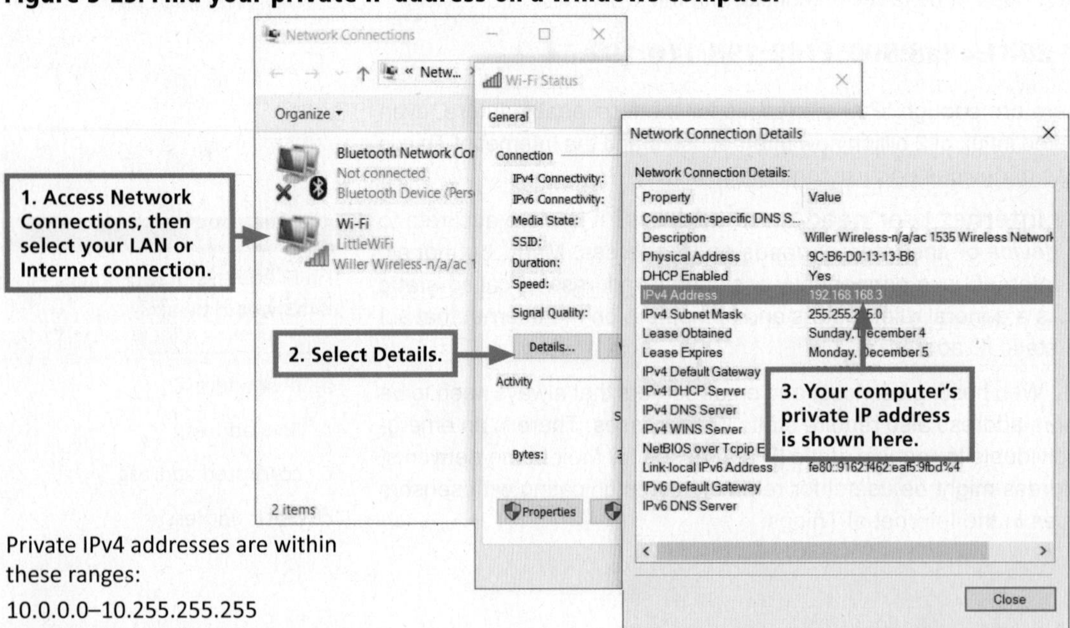

Private IPv4 addresses are within these ranges:

10.0.0.0–10.255.255.255

172.16.0.0–172.31.255.255

192.168.0.0–192.168.255.255

▸ If my private IP address can't be routed over the Internet, how does my data get anywhere? Here is where your local router plays a crucial role. Any network you use to access the Internet—a campus network, your home network, or a Wi-Fi hotspot—has a router that connects to the Internet. The router has a **public IP address** that is routable over the Internet. Figure 3-24 explains how public and private IP addresses work.

Try It!

What is your public IP address? You can find it with a Web search for *What's my IP*. Compare your public IP address to your private address.

3

Figure 3-24: Routing data using private and public IP addresses

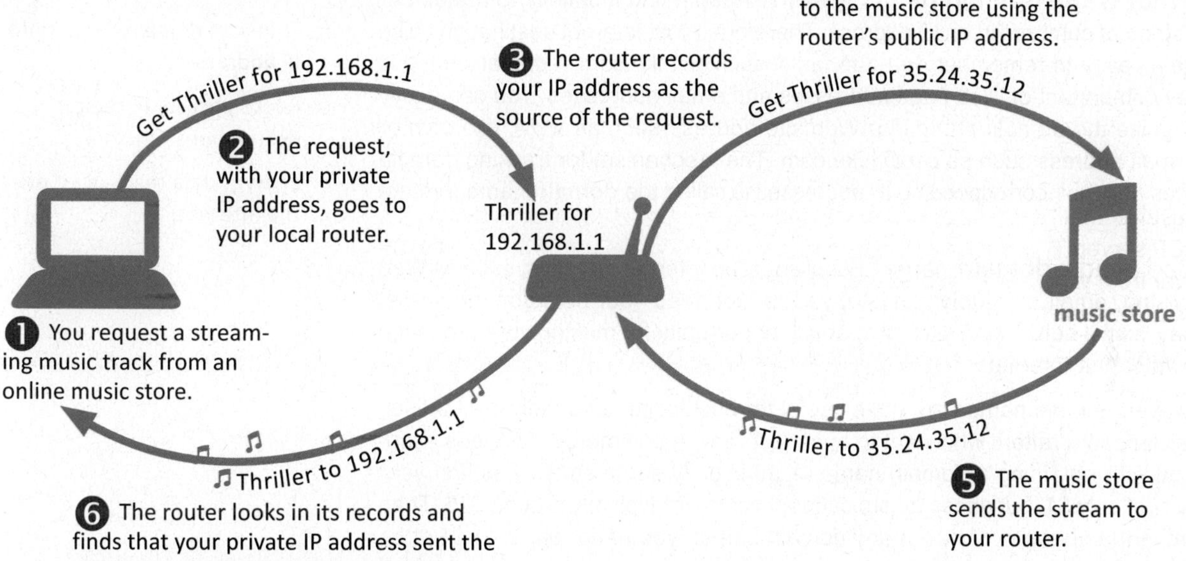

❶ You request a streaming music track from an online music store.
Get Thriller for 192.168.1.1
❷ The request, with your private IP address, goes to your local router.
❸ The router records your IP address as the source of the request.
Thriller for 192.168.1.1
❹ Your request is forwarded to the music store using the router's public IP address.
Get Thriller for 35.24.35.12
music store
❺ The music store sends the stream to your router.
Thriller to 35.24.35.12
Thriller to 192.168.1.1
❻ The router looks in its records and finds that your private IP address sent the request to the music store, so the music stream is forwarded to your computer.

▸ Does using a private IP address make me anonymous? No, the router's network address translation table keeps track of your activities, so your footprint across the Internet can be traced back to you. However, a private IP address can protect you from some threats. For example, a hacker who randomly enters IP addresses looking for unauthorized access will never find your private IP address because the only address that is visible to the public is the address of your local router. This security technique is usually referred to as **NAT** (network address translation).

That being said, private IP addresses cannot protect your devices from many other attacks. Clicking corrupted links or downloading infected files sends packets and makes a path in the network address translation table that can allow malware into your device.

QuickCheck

A local network's router uses an address __________ table to keep track of private IP addresses.

a. IP
b. routing
c. translation
d. dynamics

Domain Names

If the Internet has an Achilles' heel, it is the domain name system. When a wide swath of the Internet goes dark, when you hear about massive outages, or when you struggle to get to a Web site that seems to have disappeared, the domain name system is probably at fault. The ability of governments to censor information by blocking sites is also made possible by the domain name system. And if there is an Internet kill switch, you can bet that the domain name system will be involved.

QuickCheck

What's the purpose of the domain name system?

a. Hand out IP private addresses.

b. Translate domain names into IP addresses.

c. Route packets to their destinations.

d. Encrypt data that is sent over the Internet.

What is the domain name system? People find it difficult to remember the string of numbers in an IP address. Therefore, most Internet destinations also have an easy-to-remember **domain name**, such as nike.com. A domain name is a key component of Web page addresses and email addresses. You can easily recognize the domain name in a Web site address such as *www.nike.com* or an email address such as ceo@nike.com. The mechanism for tracking domain names and their corresponding IP addresses is called the **domain name system (DNS)**.

Do I need a domain name? For client-style Internet activities, such as Web browsing, email, and downloading, you do not need your own domain name. Today, social networking sites give ample opportunity for making your presence known on the Internet.

However, domain names are quite useful for businesses and individual artists, musicians, or crafters who want to engage in online commerce. The fees associated with obtaining a domain name might initially seem small. The first year may cost only $1, but prices for subsequent years are typically around $15. Then there is the question of how many domain names you need; one might not be enough. You might need domain names with more than one extension, such as .com or .club.

ICANN is the top-level authority for supervising domain name requests. Rather than going directly to ICANN, domain names can be obtained from several domain registrars and hosting services that provide Internet-based server space for Web sites (Figure 3-25).

Figure 3-25: Choose your own domain name

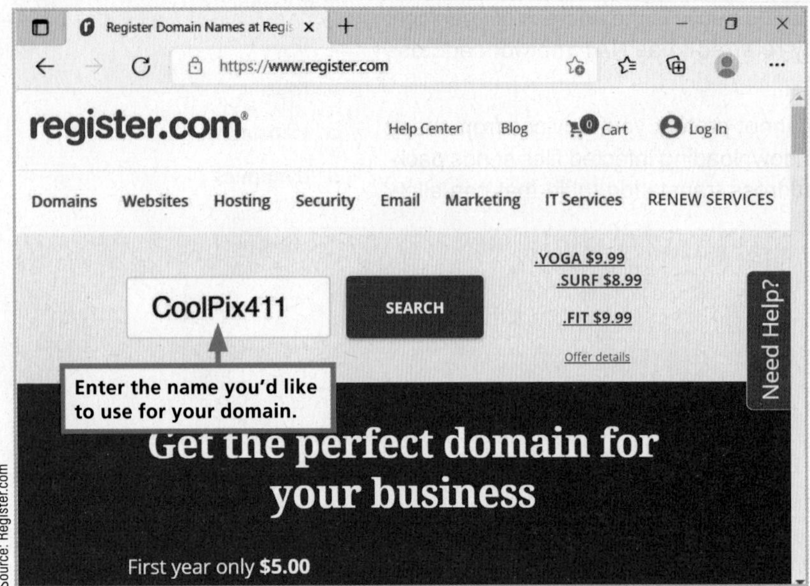

Source: Register.com

What is a top-level domain? A domain name ends with an extension that indicates its **top-level domain** (TLD). For example, in the domain name msu.edu, the top-level domain .edu indicates that the computer is maintained by an educational institution. Country codes also serve as top-level domains. Canada's top-level domain is .ca, the United Kingdom's is .uk, Australia's is .au, and the European Union uses .eu as a top-level domain.

Historically, businesses used the .com domain, while nonprofit organizations used .org. Educational institutions used .edu. The .net domain was usually used by communication companies.

Businesses generally obtained domain names with all applicable top-level domains (e.g., nike.com, nike.org, and nike.net) to prevent their use by competitors or fake businesses. Businesses also tried to acquire domain names with similar sounding names or those that are common misspellings of their corporate names.

Today, there are hundreds of additional top-level domains, such as .biz, .co, and .fit. Obtaining all the TLDs for a business name is not practical. Even within a sector such as education, .edu has been joined by .academy, .education, .guru, .institute, .training, and .university.

QuickCheck

What is the top-level domain in *www.nike.com*?

a. www

b. nike

c. .com

d. "dot"

How does the domain name system work? Scattered around the world are several **domain name servers** that maintain lists of all domain names and their corresponding IP addresses. In addition, frequently used domain names are stored by ISPs, educational institutions, organizations, and Internet companies such as Google.

When new domain names are added, these lists are updated. New domain names may take several days to propagate to all of the lists, which is why new Web sites can be accessed only by their IP addresses for the first few days they are in operation. A Web site can be accessed by its domain name once the name is added to the domain name server lists.

Suppose you want to look at the newest selection of Nike athletic shoes. You enter *nike.com* in your browser's address bar. Your browser must find the IP address that corresponds to nike.com before it can connect you to the site. Your browser queries a domain name server to get the IP address, a process that generally happens without noticeable delay (Figure 3-26).

Figure 3-26: How does the domain name system work?

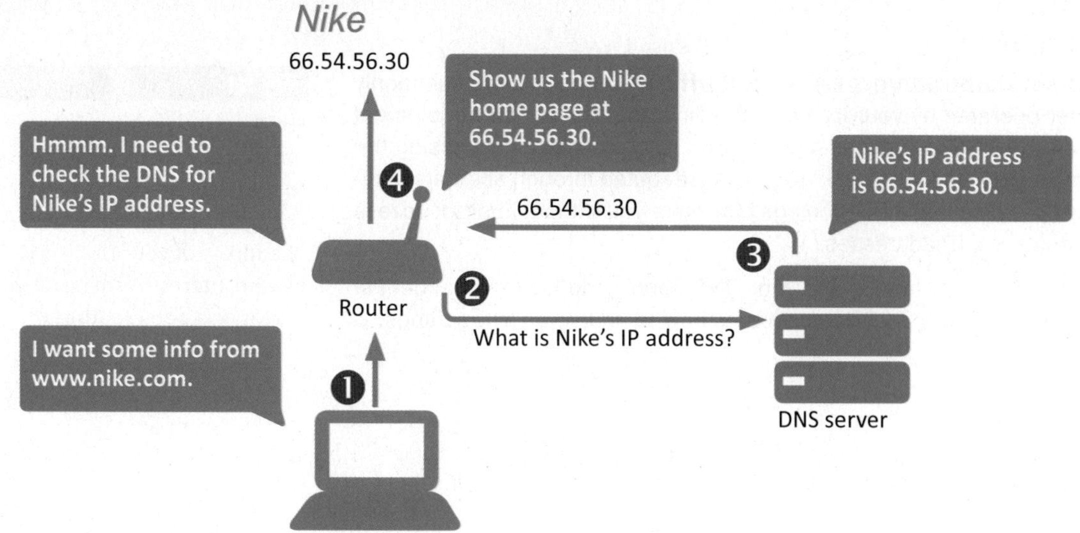

Can I discover the IP address and owner of a domain name? You might want to vet a Web site to assess the legitimacy of its owner. Access to information in the domain name database is provided by ICANN and various online apps. You can use a WHOIS lookup to find the IP address that corresponds to a domain name. Or you can look up an IP address to find its domain name and owner.

There are limitations, however. Large corporations tend to use a hosting service such as Akamai Technologies, which essentially operates its own DNS system with IP addresses and domains sheltered under its domain. A WHOIS lookup for Nike.com, for example, produces the IP address for Akamai Technologies and the address for Nike remains hidden. For smaller firms, WHOIS lookups continue to work, though ICANN is considering eliminating these lookups because they can be a potential security risk.

Try It!

If you want to know who owns a domain name or an IP address, use a Web site such as SecurityTrails or TraceMyIP to enter a domain name or IP address. Give it a try. Who owns 104.19.168.36?

So what makes the DNS one of the Internet's weaknesses? Altering the DNS records can change the destination of email, browser connections, and download requests. Unauthorized changes to the DNS are called **DNS spoofing**.

Hackers use DNS spoofing so that queries for legitimate sites are directed to fake sites. Some governments use DNS spoofing to redirect searches from culturally or politically inappropriate sites to government-approved sites. Figure 3-27 illustrates what happens when unauthorized changes are made in the DNS.

QuickCheck

Each record in the domain name system ______________.

a. represents a correspondence between a domain name and an IP address

b. protects domain names from DNS spoofing

c. routes packets over the Internet

d. has a spoofed IP address that is easy for hackers and governments to change

Figure 3-27: DNS spoofing

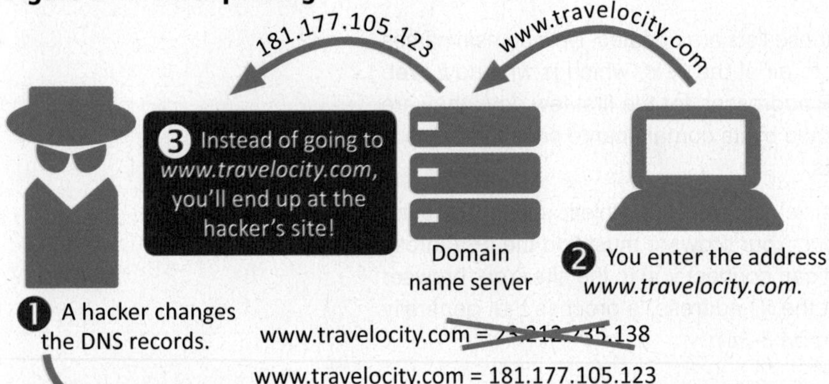

Can domain name servers be turned off? Yes, though more commonly a DNS server operated by your ISP will go offline as a result of an equipment failure. When the DNS you're using goes down, the process of accessing the Internet can get very slow while DNS requests are routed through alternate servers. It is even possible that a DNS outage can leave you without Internet access unless you enter raw IP addresses.

It is a good idea to know how to find your DNS server and how to change it in case of an outage. Figure 3-28 demonstrates how to find your DNS settings.

Try It!

For security, you should periodically check your DNS to make sure it hasn't been changed by a hacker. What is the IP address of your DNS? Is it a private address residing on your router or a public address?

3

Figure 3-28: Find your DNS settings

Windows

1. Use the Windows search box to open Network Connections.
2. Right-click your network, then select Properties.
3. Select Internet Protocol Version 4 (TCP/IPv4).
4. Select Properties. If the DNS server address is obtained automatically, your device is likely using your ISP's DNS. You can override the automatic settings as shown at right.

Obtain DNS server address automatically
Use the following DNS server addresses:
Preferred DNS server: 8 . 8 . 8 . 8
Alternate DNS server: . . .

macOS

1. Click the Apple menu and select System Preferences.
2. Select Network. Select the Advanced button, then select DNS. The DNS server is listed in the DNS Servers window.
3. To add an alternative DNS server, select the + button, then enter the IP address of the server.

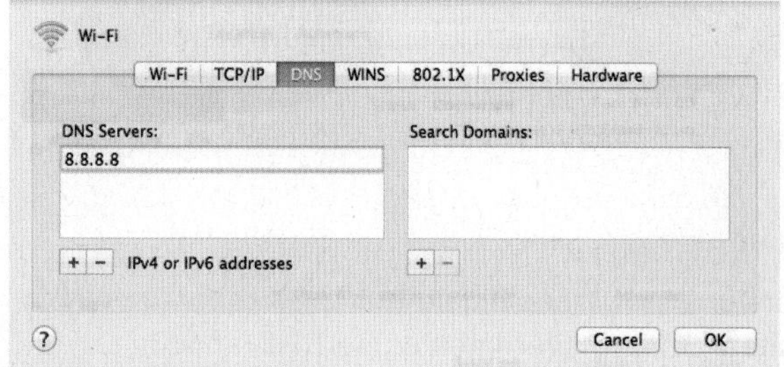

Source: Apple Inc.

What can I use as an alternative DNS server? Surprisingly, you might be able to bypass DNS outages, blocks, and hacks by changing your DNS server. Errors in the domain name tables may be limited to the domain name server that you are using. Connecting to a different domain name server might restore full access. In addition, when you are traveling—especially overseas—a local DNS server might be closer and quicker.

Keep the numbers in Figure 3-29 handy in case you need to change your domain name server. Write them down, or store them locally on your device. Remember, if your domain name server has an outage, you won't be able to use domain names to search the Internet for a solution.

QuickCheck

Which of the following would not be a reason to change your DNS server?

a. When the DNS server that I'm using goes down
b. When I'm traveling and other DNS servers are closer
c. If I suspect that my DNS server has been hacked
d. If I need to find the owner of a domain name

Figure 3-29: Public domain name servers

Google's public DNS
8.8.8.8 2001:4860:4860::8888
8.8.4.4 2001:4860:4860::8844

OpenDNS
208.67.222.222
208.67.220.220

QuickQuiz — Section B

1. The Internet _____ is a system of high-capacity routers and fiber-optic communication links.
2. The Internet uses _____ switching technology to route data from many different messages over a single communication channel.
3. _____ and UDP are two of the main protocols used to transport data over the Internet.
4. The Internet's supply of _____ addresses ran out in 2011.
5. _____ IP addresses are not routable over the Internet.

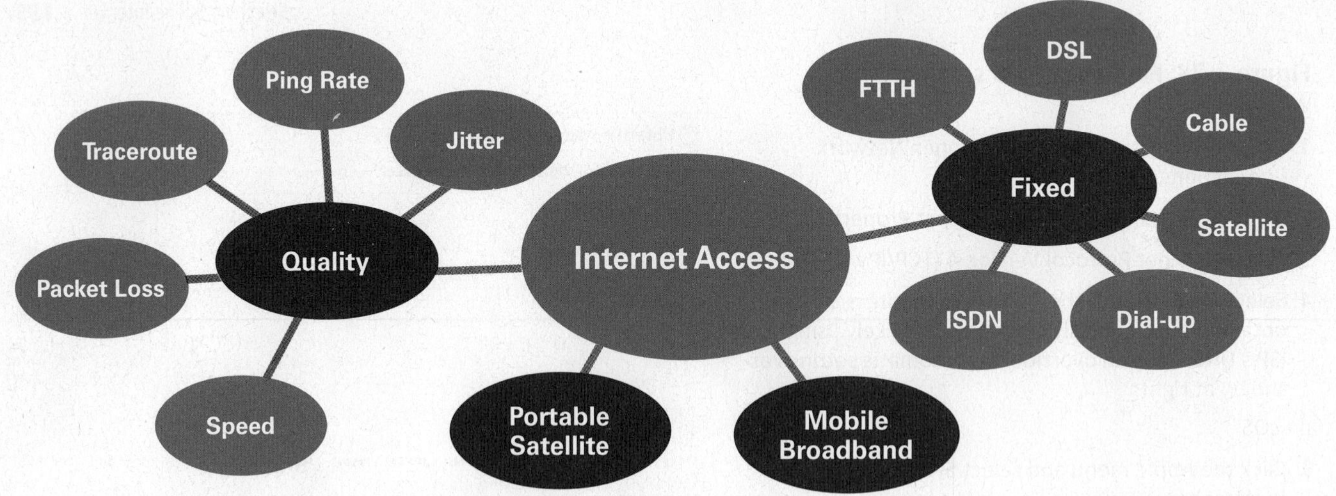

Section C

Internet Access

Objectives

- List acceptable speeds for the following: basic Skype video calls, streaming standard-definition movies, and viewing YouTube videos.
- Explain the significance of asymmetric Internet connections.
- Define latency and state the type of Internet service that it affects most negatively.
- List online activities that are most affected by jitter and packet loss.
- Name three tools that you can use to troubleshoot an Internet connection.
- Explain the pros and cons of fixed, portable, and mobile Internet access.
- Rank each type of Internet service according to speed, then rank them according to dependability.
- Draw diagrams of the infrastructures for cable, dial-up, DSL, satellite, mobile broadband, and Wi-Fi hotspot Internet services.
- Discuss why mobile Internet access is globally the most popular way to connect to the Internet.

A human rights violation. That's what the United Nations had to say about laws in France and England that penalize copyright violators by banning them from the Internet. Whether or not you agree that Internet access is a human right, there is little doubt that global network access is increasingly required to participate in activities ranging from politics to education to dating. As you read Section C, consider which of the access technologies are likely to be available in various regions of the globe.

Terminology

connection speed
bandwidth cap
bandwidth throttling
asymmetric connection
symmetric connection
Ping
latency
jitter
packet loss
Traceroute
fixed Internet access
portable Internet access
mobile Internet access
cable Internet service
dial-up
voiceband modem
ISDN
DSL
FTTH
satellite Internet service
mobile broadband
tethering
mobile hotspot
Wi-Fi hotspot

Connection Basics

With online access becoming an essential component in our daily lives, sociologists have been tracking Internet "haves" and "have-nots." According to the Statista Global Consumer Survey, an estimated 99% of American adults have Internet access. Worldwide, about 50% of the population has Internet access. Not all of these connections are fast and dependable. Let's take a look at what makes a good Internet connection.

How fast is the Internet? Data travels over the Internet at an incredible speed, but that speed varies. Some Internet services are faster than others. Speed is affected by the amount of traffic flowing over the connection. It slows down when usage is heavy. Slowdowns also occur as a result of faulty routers and when hackers launch denial-of-service attacks that overwhelm server capacity.

It is relatively easy to check the speed of your Internet connection by running a few online tests. Figure 3-30 shows results from testing speed in a metropolitan area. Is this connection suitable for streaming movies, playing online games, and conducting video chats?

3

Figure 3-30: Is your connection fast enough?

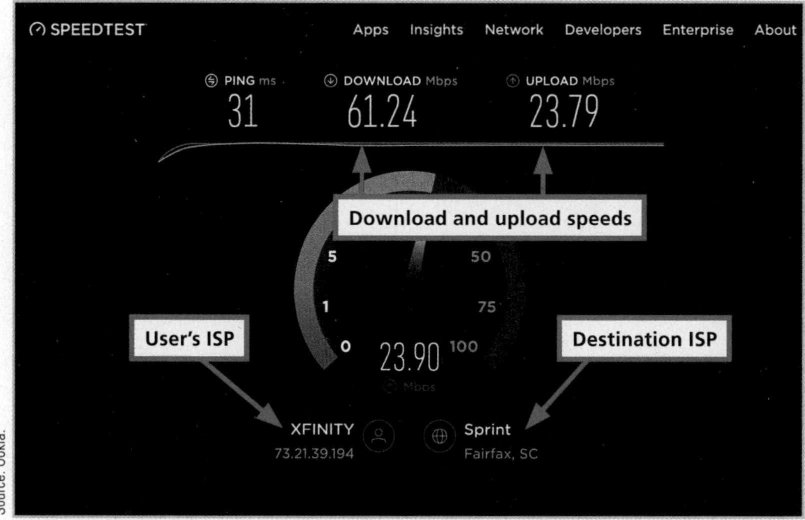

This speed test measured the rate of data flowing between an Xfinity customer in Columbia, SC and a Sprint server in Fairfax, SC.

Try It!

What is the speed of your Internet connection right now? Connect to a Web site such as *Ookla's Speedtest* or *the Bandwidth Place* and run a speed test to find out.

What does connection speed measure? Speed is the distance something travels in a specified amount of time. The speed of a car, for example, is measured in miles (distance) per hour (time). What we casually refer to as "connection speed" has little to do with distance. The most common measurement of **connection speed** is the amount of data that can be transmitted in a specified time. Technically, it is a measure of capacity. But let's use nontechnical terms and call it speed.

The speed test in Figure 3-30 produced a download speed of 61.24 Mbps because it was able to move 61 megabits of data down from a server to the user's computer in one second. The upload speed at which data is transferred from the computer to a server was only 23.79 Mbps. With this connection, downloading a two-hour SD-quality movie would take about 2 minutes. Uploading a 4 MB photo would take less than 1 second.

QuickCheck

Would the connection used for the speed test in Figure 3-30 be classified as broadband?

a. Yes, it is synchronous.

b. Yes, the upload and download speeds qualify as broadband.

c. No, its upload speed of 23.79 Mbps is not fast enough.

d. No, its average speed is only 9.79 Mbps.

How much speed do I need? For email, browsing the Web, and streaming videos, 0.5 Mbps (500 Kbps) speeds are adequate. However, other activities require higher speeds, as shown in Figure 3-31.

Figure 3-31: Connection speeds required for popular Internet activities

Service	Recommended Download	Recommended Upload
Skype video calling and screen sharing	300 Kbps	300 Kbps
Skype video calls (HD)	1.5 Mbps	1.5 Mbps
Skype three-person group calling	2 Mbps	512 Kbps
Netflix minimum required speed	.5 Mbps	—
Netflix SD-quality movie	3 Mbps	—
Netflix HD-quality movie	5 Mbps	—
Netflix Ultra HD-quality movie	25 Mbps	—
YouTube basic videos	500 Kbps	—
YouTube movies, TV shows, and live events	1 Mbps	—
Amazon Prime Video (SD)	8 Mbps	—
Amazon Prime Video (HD)	5 Mbps	—
Netflix and Amazon 4K Streaming Video	15–25 Mbps	—

QuickCheck

In the table at left, why are there recommended upload speeds only for Skype?

a. Skype doesn't use uploads.

b. Skype requires two-way communication, whereas the other services use most of the bandwidth only for downloads.

c. Skype is the slowest service of those listed.

d. Amazon, YouTube, and Netflix offer different levels of service, so the upload speed cannot be specified.

Why are upload and download speeds different? ISPs control connection speeds based on the service plan you've selected. Your **bandwidth cap** is the top speed allowed by your plan. During peak times, ISPs can place further limits on speed, a process called **bandwidth throttling**.

When Internet upload speed differs from download speed, you have an **asymmetric connection**. When upload and download speeds are the same, you have a **symmetric connection**.

Most Internet connections are asymmetrical, with upload speeds considerably less than download speeds. Asymmetric connections discourage subscribers from setting up Web and email servers that would transmit lots of outgoing data. For most users, however, an asymmetric connection is sufficient, but download speeds of less than 1.5 Mbps may not provide the full Internet experience.

What is Ping? **Ping** is utility software designed to measure responsiveness. Ping rate indicates how quickly data can reach a server and bounce back to you. Ping was named after the sound that a submarine's sonar makes when it bounces off an undersea object.

Technically, Ping measures latency. **Latency** is the elapsed time for data to make a round trip from point A to point B and back to point A. Latency is measured in milliseconds (ms). A millisecond is a thousandth of a second, so data transmitted on an Internet connection with 100 ms latency makes a round trip in one-tenth of a second.

Terminology

Download and upload speeds are sometimes referred to as *downstream speeds* and *upstream speeds*, respectively.

What is an acceptable ping rate? Latency generally averages less than 30 ms (milliseconds) within North America, but increases to about 70 ms for transatlantic transmissions. If you want to play online multiplayer games, it is best to have less than 100 ms latency. Good-quality video streaming and videoconferencing require latency rates of 200 ms or less.

Speed and latency are not the only factors that affect your Internet experience. Even if your connection gets good marks on speed tests, jitter and packet loss can degrade the quality of online activities.

3

What are jitter and packet loss? **Jitter** measures the variability of packet latency. Network traffic and interference can delay some packets and create erratic data flow. If the variation between packets exceeds 5 ms, Internet voice and video call quality is likely to be poor.

Packet loss refers to data that never reaches its destination or gets discarded because it arrives too late to be of any use. Packet loss of less than 2% is required for acceptable streaming, gaming, Skype, and voice calls. Too many lost packets during an online gaming session can cause the game to stutter or stall. And if packets don't arrive in the correct order, your game character might seem to act randomly for a few seconds. An Internet quality test can measure jitter and packet loss, producing results similar to those shown in Figure 3-32.

Figure 3-32: Check the jitter and packet loss on your connection

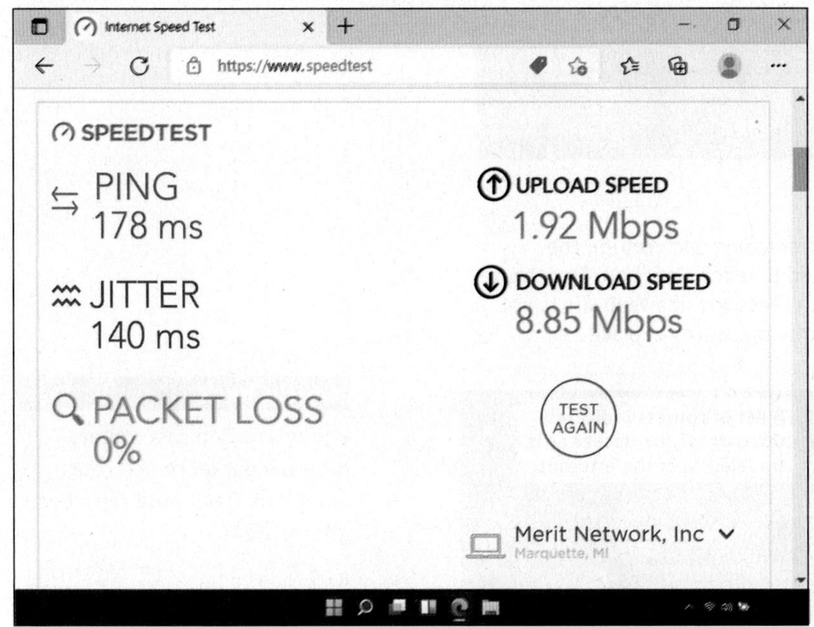

QuickCheck

The connection in Figure 3-32 gets a grade of D for bad performance. What are the problems?

a. The speed is too low and packet loss is too high.

b. The ping rate is too low and packet loss is too high.

c. The ping rate and the jitter rate are too high.

d. The ping rate is too high, but the jitter rate is too low.

Can I troubleshoot an Internet connection? Suppose your Internet connection seems unusually slow one day. Or, perhaps you cannot access a favorite Web site. You wonder, "Is the problem on my computer, with my ISP, or somewhere else on the Internet?" To find out, you can use **Traceroute**, a network diagnostic tool that lists each router and server your data encounters as it travels over the Internet.

Traceroute sends three packets of data to a specified destination. It records the address of each router along the way and the elapsed time for each "hop." When a connection is inoperable, the packets will not reach their destination and they will become lost. Figure 3-33 illustrates how to use Traceroute and how to interpret its results.

Figure 3-33: Where does your data travel?

On a Mac, open the Utilities folder, then select Terminal. Enter the command traceroute followed by any domain name, like this:

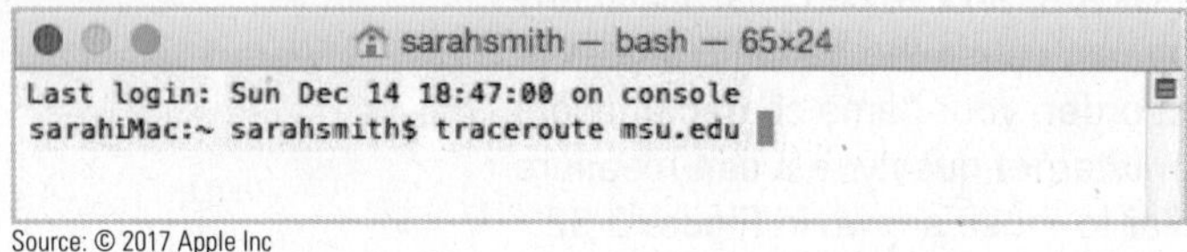

Source: © 2017 Apple Inc

On a PC, enter cmd in the Windows search box to open the Command Prompt window. Enter the command tracert followed by any domain name, like this:

```
Command Prompt
Microsoft Windows [Version 10.0.19042.1052]
(c) Microsoft Corporation. All rights reserved.

C:\Users\sarah>tracert msu.edu
```

Traceroute results appear as a list, showing each router, the router's IP address, and the elapsed time for each hop. Traceroute may produce a "Request timed out message" if a Web site is not operational or has defensive security measures in place.

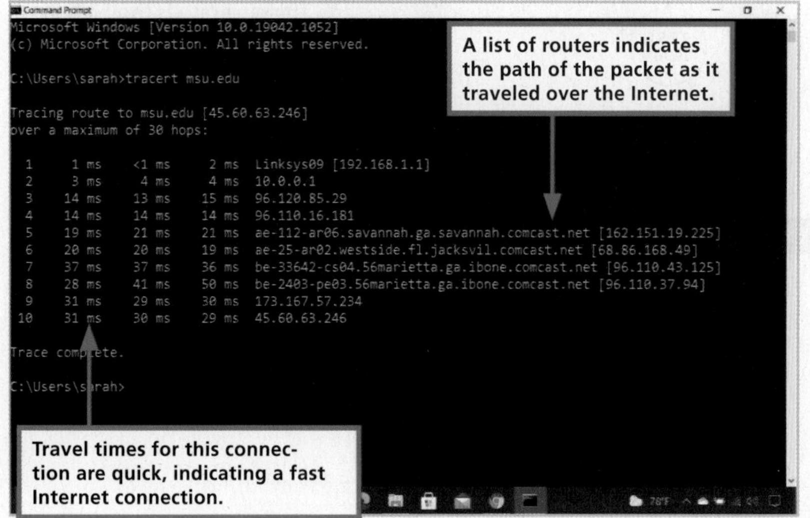

Try It!

Find out how many hops your data makes before it arrives at *www.wired.com*. What was the slowest leg of the trip? (Hint: Mac users may need to add -I after the traceroute command word.)

QuickCheck

How many Comcast routers did each packet pass through when this Traceroute report was generated?

a. 1

b. 4

c. 10

d. 16

What else affects the speed of my connection? Your Internet connection can be affected by outages and traffic. In Section B, you found out what can happen when a DNS server goes down. Service disruptions can also occur at ISPs, cloud storage sites, email servers, and other Internet-based services. You can use online tools such as downdetector.com and downrightnow.com to check the status of various Internet services.

What are my Internet connection options? Although public Internet access is available in many locations, such as coffee shops and libraries, most consumers like the convenience of having their own Internet connection. Depending on your geographical location, you may have several options for connecting to the Internet. Before we look at the most popular Internet access options such as cable Internet service and cellular broadband, consider the pros and cons of the three classifications of Internet connections in Figure 3-34.

Try It!

Are any service disruptions occurring right now? Connect to a Web site monitoring service such as downrightnow to find out.

Figure 3-34: Internet connection options

Fixed Internet Access

Fixed Internet access links your computer to an ISP from a stationary point, such as a wall socket or roof-mounted antenna. This service is dependable and relatively cost effective. You can't take it with you, so when you're away from home, you must depend on public access points.

Cable, DSL, ISDN, Fixed LTE, Satellite, Fiber-to-the-home

Portable Internet Access

Portable Internet access allows you to easily move your access device, as in the case of vehicle-mounted satellite dishes that can be deployed when the vehicle is parked. This service is primarily used in situations where mobile and fixed access are not available.

Mobile satellite

Mobile Internet Access

Mobile Internet access allows you to use the Internet while you are on the go, such as using a cell phone to collect your email while you are traveling by train or querying Siri while riding in a car. These services usually require a data plan.

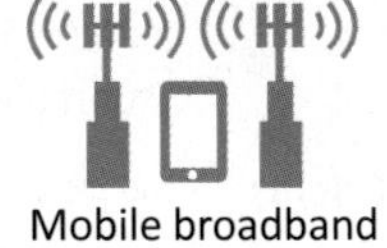

Mobile broadband

QuickCheck

A local ISP advertises a modem that you can carry to any location and plug in to access the Internet. This device would be used for __________ Internet access.

a. fixed

b. portable

c. mobile

d. cable

Cable Internet Service

The gold standard of fixed Internet access is **cable Internet service**, which is offered by the same companies that supply cable television. Cable service is a luxury enjoyed by developed countries; emerging nations cannot afford its expensive infrastructure, and device owners may not be able to afford the high cost of monthly subscriptions.

How does cable Internet service work? The cable television system was originally designed for remote areas where TV broadcast signals could not be received with a roof-mounted antenna. These systems were called community antenna television, or CATV. The CATV concept was to install one or more large, expensive satellite dishes in a community, catch TV signals with these dishes, and then send the signals over a system of cables to individual homes.

With cables branching out from a central location, the topology of a CATV system happened to also work as the infrastructure for a digital data network. Now, in addition to carrying signals for cable television, the CATV infrastructure also carries Internet data. When your cable TV company becomes your Internet provider, your computer becomes part of a neighborhood network linked together by the cable company's wiring (Figure 3-35).

Figure 3-35: Cable television infrastructure

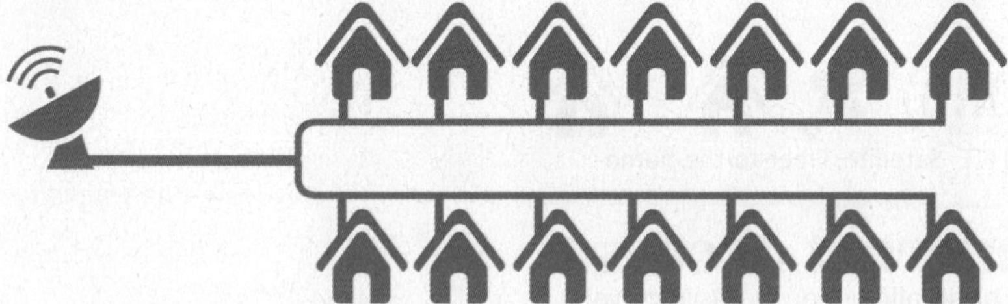

How does the system transport data? The cable modem supplied with your subscription converts signals from your computer to signals that can travel over the cable infrastructure. CATV coaxial and fiber-optic cables have plenty of bandwidth to carry television signals for hundreds of channels in addition to digital data. CATV cables provide bandwidth for television signals, incoming data signals, and outgoing data signals (Figure 3-36).

Figure 3-36: TV and data streams on one cable

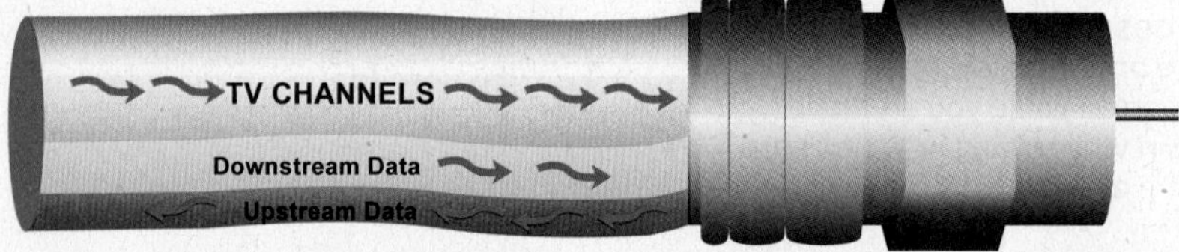

How fast is cable Internet service? Most cable Internet service is asymmetric, with upload speeds considerably slower than download speeds to discourage subscribers from setting up public Web servers. Service plans range from economy packages offering speeds of 25 Mbps to an expensive 400 Mbps package. Your actual speed may be less than the advertised speed due to traffic from other subscribers in your neighborhood.

QuickCheck

Which one of the following is most likely to affect the actual speed of your cable Internet connection from day to day?

a. Your ISP service plan

b. Weather

c. High traffic from other users

d. Watching TV shows

Telephone Network Internet Service

Some people limp along with narrowband access to the Internet, which is frustratingly slow. Telephone companies offer four types of service: dial-up, ISDN, DSL, and FTTH. Only one of these technologies is considered broadband. Are the other three of any use at all?

▶ What is a dial-up connection? A **dial-up** connection is a fixed Internet connection that uses a voiceband modem and the telephone company's circuit-switched network to transport data between a computer and an ISP. A **voiceband modem** converts digital signals from a computer into audible analog signals that can travel over telephone landlines. A modem transmits a 1070 Hz tone for a 0 data bit and a 1270 Hz tone for a 1 data bit (Figure 3-37).

3

Figure 3-37: A voiceband modem changes voltages to audio tones

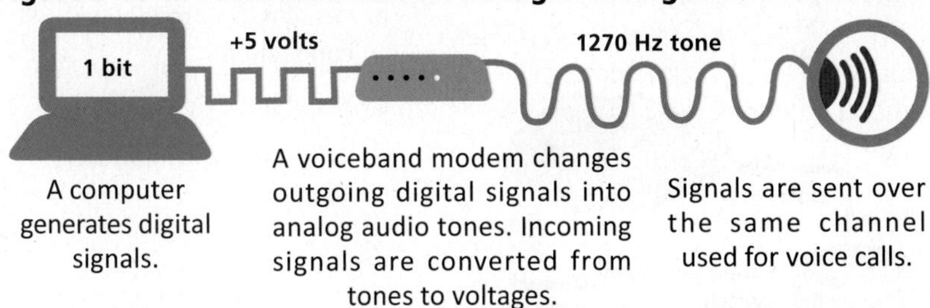

1 bit
+5 volts
1270 Hz tone
A computer generates digital signals.
A voiceband modem changes outgoing digital signals into analog audio tones. Incoming signals are converted from tones to voltages.
Signals are sent over the same channel used for voice calls.

▶ How does a dial-up connection work? The dial-up voiceband modem places a regular telephone call to the ISP. When the ISP's computer answers the call, a dedicated circuit is established between the modem and the ISP. The procedure is similar to placing a voice call and someone at the ISP answering the phone.

The circuit remains connected for the duration of the call to carry data between the computer and the ISP. As data arrives at the ISP, a router sends it out over the Internet (Figure 3-38).

QuickCheck

Dial-up connections use a voiceband modem to convert signals from ______________.

a. analog to digital

b. tones to pulses for outgoing signals, and voltages to binary digits for incoming signals

c. digital to analog

d. digital to analog for outgoing signals, and analog to digital for incoming signals

Figure 3-38: Dial-up infrastructure

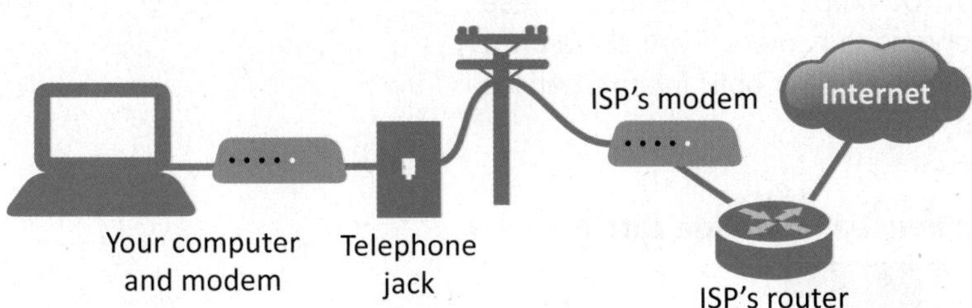

▶ How fast is dial-up service? The maximum speed of a dial-up connection is 56 Kbps, so it is not classified as broadband. Actual data transfer speeds are affected by factors such as the quality of your phone line and connection. In practice, the top speed for downloads is about 44 Kbps. For uploads, the data rate drops to 33 Kbps or less—that's kilobytes, not megabytes!

Dial-up service is the Internet connection of last resort for people who live in remote areas where landlines are the only communication services.

How about ISDN? **ISDN** stands for Integrated Services Digital Network. It essentially divides a telephone line into two channels: one for data and one for voice. The data channel uses packet switching and sends data in digital format, unlike dial-up, which uses analog tones to carry data. With data rates of 128 Kbps, ISDN was only briefly popular in the United States, though in Europe it still has an active base of users.

What is DSL? **DSL** (digital subscriber line) is a high-speed, digital, always-on, Internet access technology that runs over standard phone lines at speeds that range from 5 to 25 Mbps.

How does DSL work? A DSL modem converts computer signals into high-frequency data signals. Voice and data signals travel over telephone lines to the telephone company's local switching station. There, voice signals are routed to the regular telephone system and data signals are routed to the Internet (Figure 3-39).

QuickCheck

When using a DSL connection, can you expect similar upload and download speeds?

a. Yes, if it is an asymmetrical connection

b. Yes, if it is a broadband connection

c. Yes, if it includes ISDN

d. Only if it is a symmetric connection

Figure 3-39: DSL data path

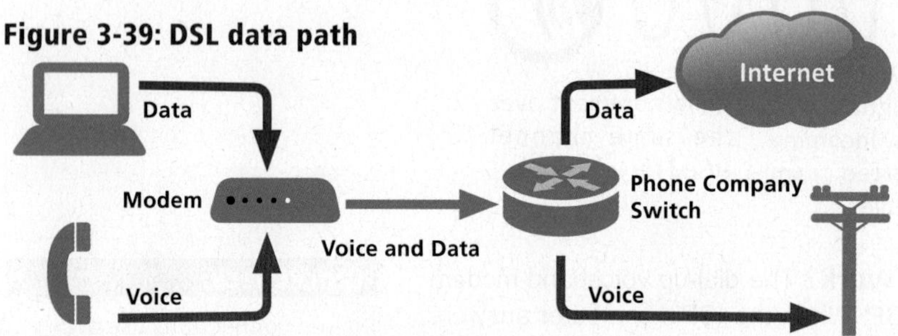

What about a fiber Internet connection? As communication companies install more and more fiber-optic cables, an increasing number of consumers have this high-speed Internet option. **FTTH** stands for fiber-to-the-home. It is the use of high-capacity fiber-optic cables, rather than coaxial cables or twisted pair wires, to connect homes to broader municipal networks.

As telephone companies upgrade their infrastructure with fiber-optic cables, they are able to offer access speeds ranging from 100 Mbps to 1,000 Mbps. These speeds are available only in areas where fiber runs to homes. If you see a crew laying orange cable carriers like the one in Figure 3-40, fiber-optic Internet service might soon be available in your neighborhood.

Figure 3-40: Fiber-optic cables are often housed in orange carriers

QuickCheck

What is the fastest type of Internet access plan that you might get from a telephone company?

a. Dial-up

b. FTTH

c. DSL

d. ISDN

Satellite Internet Service

Communications satellites seem so retro. They settled into orbit during an era when your grandparents watched *The Jetsons* and the United States rushed to catch up to the Soviet Union's spaceflight program. Yet, at one point in time, satellites used for continent-to-continent telephone communications appeared to be a natural fit with the emerging Internet. Unfortunately, those satellites had a fatal flaw that reduced their suitability for today's Internet. Has that problem been solved? Read on to find out.

▶ What is satellite Internet service? **Satellite Internet service** is a means of distributing broadband asymmetric Internet access by broadcasting signals to a satellite. In many rural areas, satellite Internet service is the only alternative to a slow dial-up connection.

Prior to 2020, the communications satellites providing Internet service were in geosynchronous equatorial orbit (GEO) 22,000 miles above the Earth's surface. Signals traveling from Earth to a satellite have a latency of 1,000 to 1,400 ms. That's a delay of about 1 second or more.

Geosynchronous latency might not pose much of a problem for general Web surfing and downloading files, but it can become a showstopper for interactive gaming, and for video chat, automated stock trading, and similar services that require quick response.

▶ Is there faster satellite Internet service? Yes. Low Earth orbit (LEO) satellites circle 2,000 miles above the Earth. Because they are much closer than GEO satellites, latency is reduced to about 40 ms—similar to a cable Internet connection.

▶ How does satellite Internet service work? Figure 3-41 illustrates how data from a customer's computer (1) is converted into signals by the customer's modem (2) that are carried by cable to a personal satellite dish (3) and broadcast to a communication satellite (4). Signals are rebroadcast from the satellite to a groundstation (5) that forwards them to the Internet (6).

Figure 3-41: Your data travels into space and back

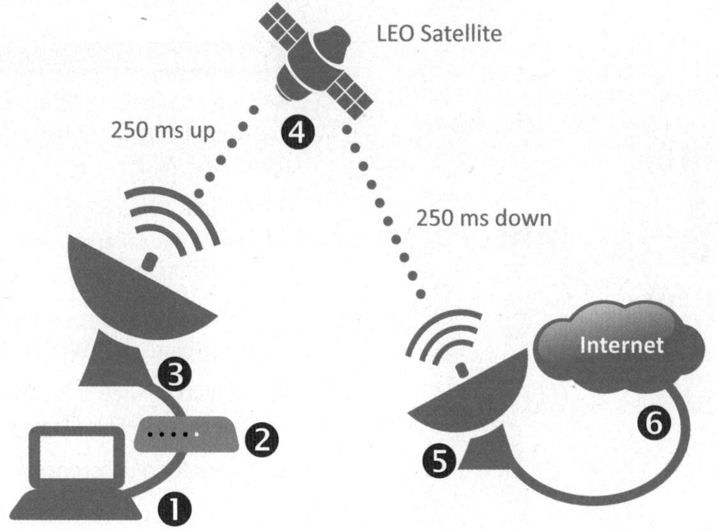

QuickCheck

What is the main problem with GEO satellite Internet service?

a. Speed

b. Latency

c. Traceroute

d. Cost

Mobile Broadband Service

Mobile broadband delivers voice, data, and text messages by means of a cellular tower that transmits and receives signals. The defining characteristic of mobile broadband is that you can use it while in motion. As you reach the edge of a cellular tower's range, your signal is seamlessly handed off to the next tower within range.

Mobile broadband is available on smartphones, cellular-equipped tablets and laptop computers, cellular smartwatches, and even some IoT devices. The most popular device for accessing mobile broadband is a smartphone.

◗ What's the difference between a mobile connection and Wi-Fi?

Smartphones support both cellular and Wi-Fi connections. Cellular connections require a service plan from a cell phone carrier, such as Verizon. Those service plans may distinguish between voice, data, and text for billing purposes.

When using a cellular connection, voice calls, texts, and data travel through a cellular tower. The minutes you use for voice calls, the number of texts you send, and the amount of data you transfer are tracked as part of your cellular plan. Fees may apply depending on the type of cellular plan you've selected. The upside is that you have mobile broadband coverage, so you can be a passenger in a moving car and carry out a phone conversation or stream music without interruption.

Wi-Fi connections can be supplied through a home network or a network located in a coffee shop, airport, or other business. When using a Wi-Fi connection, voice calls, texts, and data travel from a local area network to the Internet. Using Wi-Fi, voice calls do not count as minutes in your cellular plan, text messages are not tracked by your cellular carrier, and data transfers do not count against your cellular data limit. Wi-Fi is not mobile broadband, however, because you must remain within range of the Wi-Fi network for the duration of your call or streaming activity. Wi-Fi signals have a range of about 150 feet indoors and 300 feet outdoors. Unlike the cellular system, Wi-Fi has no standard for handing off signals when you move out of range (Figure 3-42).

Figure 3-42: The difference between cellular and Wi-Fi

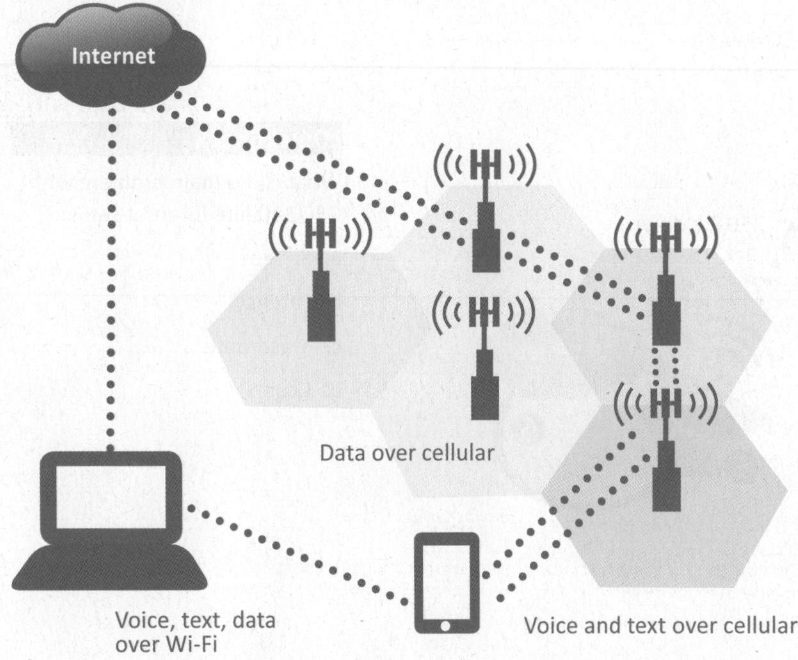

QuickCheck

What is the main difference between using a cellular service and using Wi-Fi?

a. Cellular service requires the use of a local area network, but Wi-Fi does not.

b. Cellular service is mobile broadband, but Wi-Fi is not.

c. Cellular service is for voice, whereas Wi-Fi is for data.

d. There is no difference.

▶ How fast is mobile broadband service? Mobile broadband has evolved through several generations. The most recent of these generations is 5G.

3G (third generation) service was available in the United States beginning in 2001. Common protocols included CDMA, which reached maximum download speeds of 4.9 Mbps, and GSM EDGE, with 1.6 Mbps speeds.

4G (fourth generation) technologies include LTE, which has typical download rates of 150 Mbps and upload rates of 50 Mbps. The range of 4G signals is about 10 miles.

5G (fifth generation) networks can carry data at ten times the speed of a 4G network and with much lower latency. 5G signals have a very short unobstructed range of about 1,500 feet. Instead of massive cell towers beaming signals over a broad area, 5G uses localized small cells with discreet transceivers mounted on nearby buildings and utility poles. For the near future, 4G and 5G will work together to provide coverage in cities, towns, and rural areas.

Mobile broadband speed decreases at the edges of coverage. It can be reduced by obstacles such as trees, hills, walls, and even metal roofs. Electromagnetic interference from speakers, microwave ovens, and other electrical devices can reduce speeds, too. Rain, snow, and high humidity can also reduce speeds.

▶ Can I access mobile broadband with my laptop? A mobile broadband device can provide Internet access from a laptop or desktop computer. Most of today's smartphones include a **tethering** feature that connects wirelessly with other digital devices. Figure 3-43 demonstrates how to set up tethering to create a **mobile hotspot**. Just remember that data sent over the tethered connection accumulates toward your monthly data usage total.

QuickCheck

Which of the following is true about LTE?

a. It is 3G technology.

b. It is not affected by weather like earlier mobile technologies were.

c. It is slower than a 5G network.

d. It uses circuit-switched networks for data.

3

Figure 3-43: Create a network with your cell phone

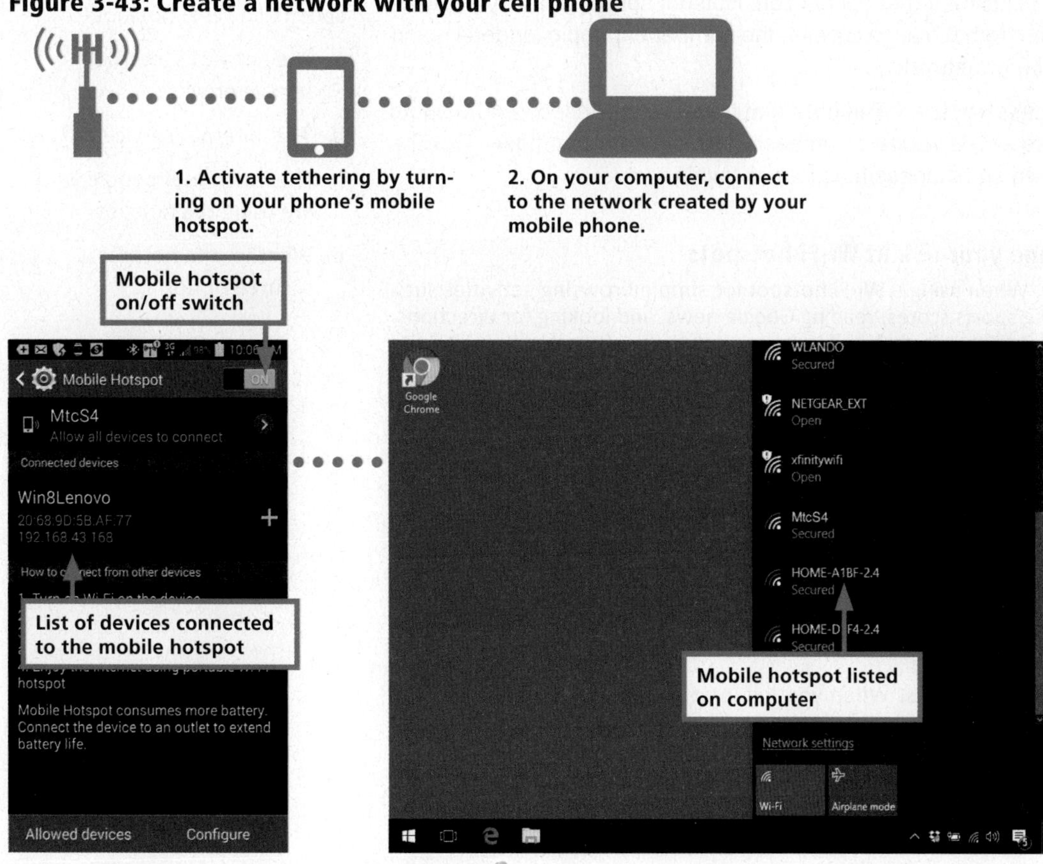

Wi-Fi Hotspots

Wi-Fi hotspots are everywhere. Pull out your smartphone in any coffee shop, airport, hotel lobby, or university building and you'll likely find more than one network that serves as an Internet on-ramp. But public Wi-Fi hotspots are fraught with security risks, so it pays to know how they work.

How do Wi-Fi hotspots work? A **Wi-Fi hotspot** is a wireless local area network, usually operated by a business, that offers Internet access to the public. The network has an Internet connection and a device called an access point that broadcasts Wi-Fi signals within a range of about 150 feet. Any and all devices with Wi-Fi capability can detect the signal (Figure 3-44).

Figure 3-44: Behind the scenes of a coffee shop Wi-Fi hotspot

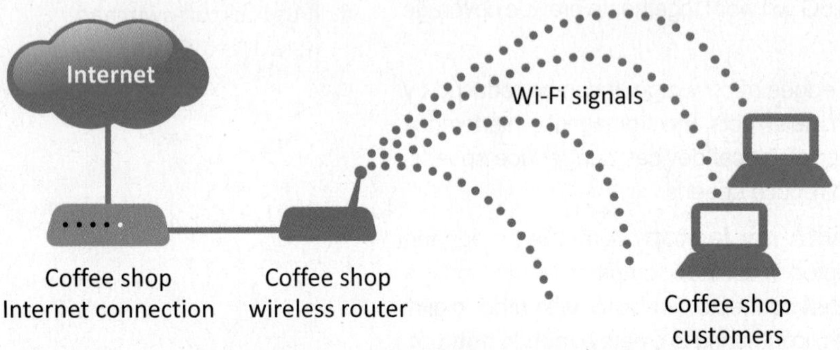

How fast is hotspot access? The speed of a hotspot is related to the speed of the Wi-Fi network and the service that connects it to the Internet. A hotspot that goes through a 1 Mbps DSL line will be slower than a hotspot that goes through a 50 Mbps cable Internet connection. Hotspot speed can vary depending on your distance from the access point, the number of people logged in, and interference from other networks.

Is hotspot access secure? The data that travels over unsecured hotspots is not encrypted, so eavesdroppers can easily tap into data that flows over the network. Figure 3-45 summarizes hotspot risk levels.

QuickCheck

Which of the following is most likely to affect the maximum speed of a Wi-Fi hotspot?

a. The hotspot's Internet service provider

b. Your Internet service provider

c. The number of people who are using the hotspot

d. Whether the hotspot is secured or not

Figure 3-45: Gauge your risk at Wi-Fi hotspots

Browsing. When using a Wi-Fi hotspot for simple browsing activities such as checking sports scores, reading Google news, and looking for directions, your security risk is fairly low if you have antivirus software running on the device you use to access the hotspot.

Using secure sites. Your security risk is low when you are accessing secured Web sites that have addresses beginning with HTTPS. These secured sites, which are used for activities such as online banking, accessing medical records, and making credit card purchases, encrypt the data that you enter to keep it safe from eavesdroppers.

File sharing. Eavesdroppers might be able to access the files on your computer if you have file sharing turned on. When using public networks, you should turn file sharing off. You can do so manually if your operating system does not offer that option when you connect.

Using unsecured sites. When you log in to unsecured sites while using public Wi-Fi hotspots, a wireless eavesdropper could potentially snag your user ID and password information, then use it later to access your accounts. Logging in to your Webmail account, for example, could be risky if your user ID and password are transmitted over an unsecured connection.

How do I access a Wi-Fi hotspot? The network utility on your computer or phone automatically senses a Wi-Fi network and adds it to the list of available connections. You can then connect using your network utility. Some Wi-Fi hotspots can be accessed simply by starting your browser and accepting the license. Other networks require you to enter a password, which you can obtain from the hotspot manager.

Select public networks with care. Hackers create networks that have names similar to those of legitimate hotspots. Those networks are not usually secured. Network utilities indicate unsecured hotspots in various ways. Microsoft Windows displays a shield icon for hotspots that are not secured.

If you mistakenly connect to a non-secured network, any passwords you enter or data you transmit could fall into the hands of a hacker. You can view a list of available networks and connect to one, as shown in Figure 3-46.

QuickCheck

In Figure 3-46, what tells you that the HolidayInn-FREE! network is not secured?

a. The misspelled SSID

b. The word *FREE!*

c. The shield icon

d. The number of bars

Figure 3-46: Access Wi-Fi hotspots securely

Look for a list of nearby Wi-Fi hotspots using the Wireless icon on the desktop or home screen.

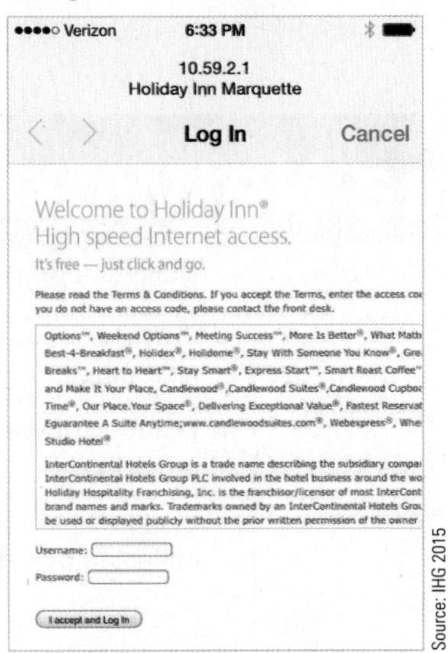

Some Wi-Fi hotspots display an access screen when you start a browser while within range of the hotspot.

QuickQuiz — Section C

1. A specification such as 10 Mbps that we commonly refer to as "connection speed" is technically a measurement of __________.

2. An Internet connection can be fast and have an acceptable ping rate but still have poor quality due to excessive __________ and packet loss.

3. A utility called __________ reports the path of packets over the Internet.

4. The problem with GEO satellite Internet service is excessive __________.

5. The defining characteristic of mobile broadband is that you can use it while in __________.

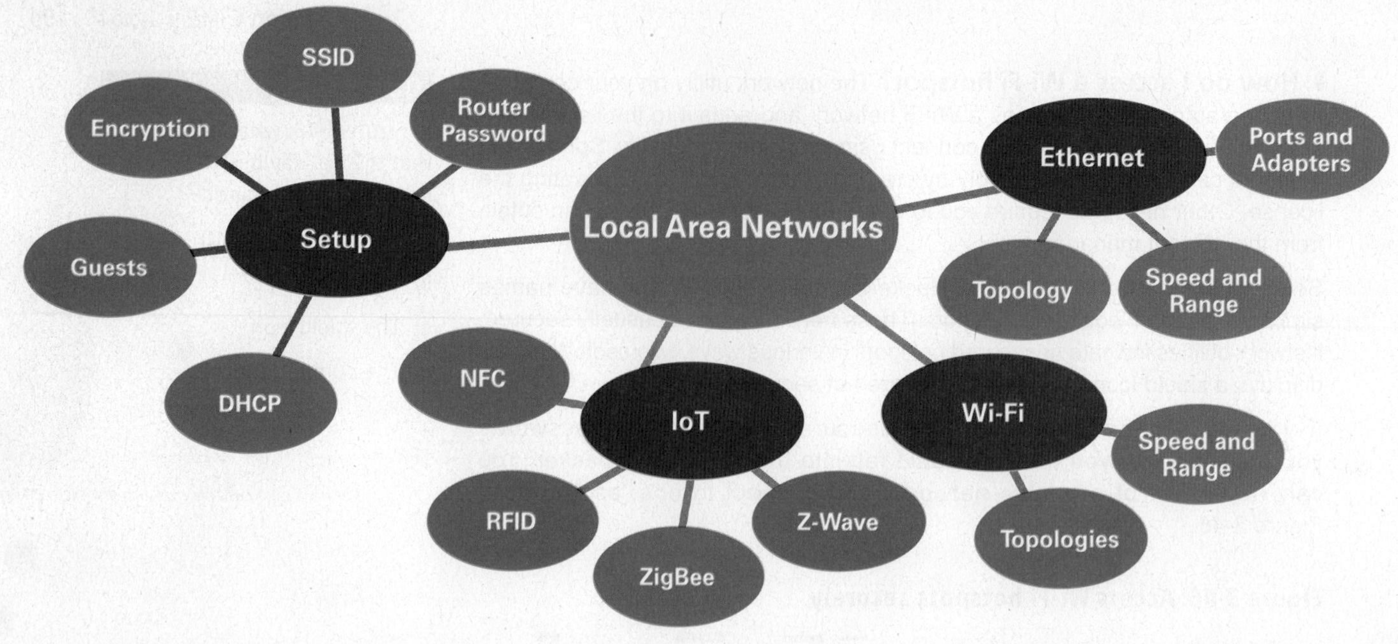

Section D Local Area Networks

Objectives

- Diagram the components and connections in a typical home LAN.
- Explain the roles of MAC addresses and IP addresses in local area networks.
- List five advantages of Ethernet wired network standards.
- Explain the pros and cons of wireless mesh networks as compared to centralized wireless networks.
- Compare the speeds and ranges of Ethernet and Wi-Fi.
- List five steps for securely configuring a wireless router.
- State the purpose of an SSID.
- List four types of wireless encryption.
- Identify tools that can be used to monitor network activity
- Provide two example scenarios for using RFID tags and NFC tags.
- List three low-power wireless standards used for IoT networks.
- Evaluate potential security exposure for data that is collected by IoT networks.

A network of your own. What was once a technology enjoyed only by huge corporations and government agencies can now be yours. Although the cloud offers apps, storage, and connectivity, keeping some of your data local offers security that is not available at remote sites. For passing data between your own devices and collecting data from wearables and home monitoring systems, your own network can become a safe little data fortress. Section D guides you through the basics of local area networks, including how to set them up.

Terminology

AirDrop
network interface controller
MAC address
Ethernet
IEEE 802.3
Ethernet adapter
Wi-Fi
IEEE 802.11
Wi-Fi adapter
dual-band
MU-MIMO
WAN port
SSID
wireless encryption
WEP
WPA
WPS
wireless encryption key
Guest network
RFID
NFC
Bluetooth LE
ZigBee
Z-Wave

LAN Basics

In the early years of personal computers, networks were scarce. Most personal computers functioned as standalone units, and computing was essentially a solitary activity in which one person interacted with one computer. Some computer engineers, however, had the foresight to anticipate that personal computers could be networked to provide advantages not available with standalone computers.

What are the characteristics of LANs? Local area networks are often referred to as LANs. They are designed to provide connectivity for devices within a limited area, typically within the premises of a home, office building, business, or school.

LANs use many of the same network technologies as the Internet, just on a smaller scale. They have a topology. They use communication protocols to ship packets. They require communication channels such as cables or wireless signals. They also include data communication equipment such as routers and modems. Figure 3-47 illustrates a LAN that you can easily build.

Figure 3-47: Build this LAN

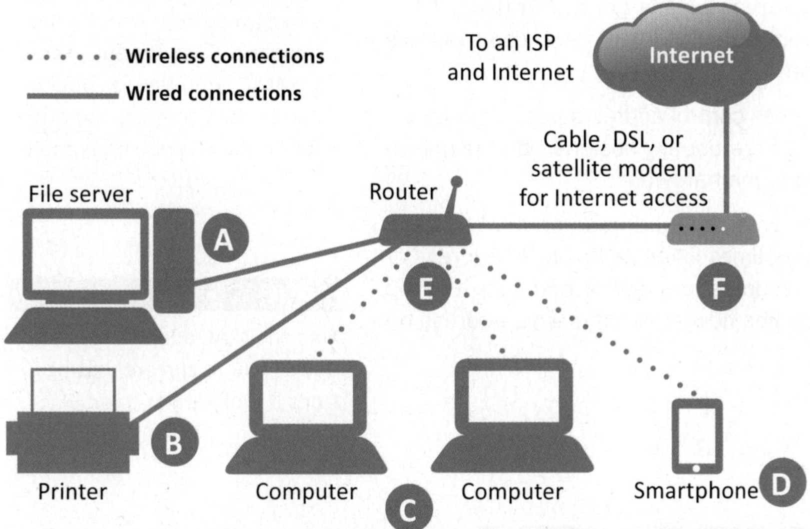

The plan for your network hinges on a centralized router that supports wired and wireless connections.

A Connect a computer to a wired connection for maximum speed. Use it for online games or as a file server where you store and back up your data.

B Connect a printer to a wired or wireless connection so that all devices on the network can access it.

C Connect computers wirelessly so you can use them in various rooms.

D Connect your smartphone and you'll be able to use the LAN's Internet connection instead of your expensive data plan.

E The router is the centerpiece of your network. Most wireless routers support five wired devices and a maximum of 255 wireless devices.

F All the devices in your LAN can access the Internet if you connect the router to a modem supplied by an ISP.

QuickCheck

In the LAN depicted in Figure 3-47, all the network data goes through the ________.

a. modem

b. printer

c. router

d. Internet

Do I need a LAN to share files? Not necessarily. If you have two devices within about 30 feet of each other, you might be able to transfer files using Bluetooth. The Windows operating system has a Share feature that uses a Bluetooth connection to transmit files between two nearby computers. macOS provides a tool called **AirDrop** for making a point-to-point connection between two computers.

Bluetooth is generally used to connect only two devices that are quite close to each other. To connect multiple devices, you'll want to use a LAN.

Are LANs regulated by the government? LANs can use wired or wireless connections. Wired connections are unregulated because the signals traveling through a wire are unlikely to interfere with broadcasts to radios, televisions, or other networks.

Most wireless LANs use the 2.4 GHz, 5.0 GHz, and 6.0 GHz unlicensed frequencies so that they can be set up without applying to the FCC for permission. The few unlicensed frequencies are crowded, however, and neighboring networks that are forced to use the same frequencies pose security risks.

Are my devices equipped to access LANs? The circuitry that enables a device to access a LAN is called a **network interface controller** (NIC). NICs are built into the circuit boards of most digital devices. NICs are also available as add-on circuit boards and USB devices.

NICs contain a **MAC address** (media access control address) used to uniquely identify devices on LANs. MAC addresses are usually assigned by the manufacturer of digital devices and embedded in the hardware.

A MAC address functions in conjunction with an IP address on a LAN. Each device on a LAN has a MAC address (sometimes listed as the Wi-Fi address or physical address). DHCP assigns an IP address to a device and links it to the device's MAC address. Figure 3-48 illustrates how to find the MAC address on various devices.

QuickCheck

Which frequencies are unlicensed?

a. Wireless frequencies

b. Radio frequencies

c. Internet frequencies

d. 2.4, 5.0, and 6.0 GHz

Terminology

The term *MAC address* has nothing to do with Apple's Mac computers. Both PCs and Macs have MAC addresses, as do smartphones, routers, and other data communication equipment.

Try It!

Find the MAC address for the device you're currently using. Does it look similar to an IP address?

Figure 3-48: Find the MAC address

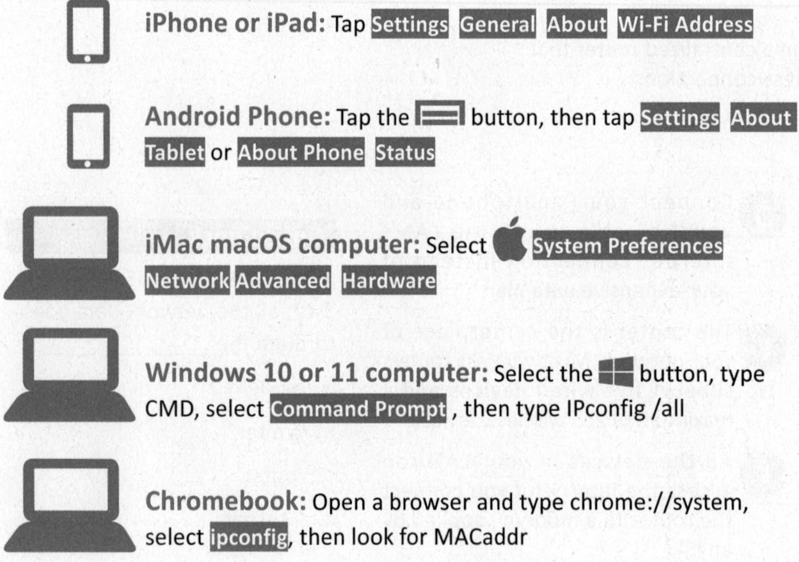

iPhone or iPad: Tap Settings General About Wi-Fi Address
Android Phone: Tap the button, then tap Settings About Tablet or About Phone Status
iMac macOS computer: Select System Preferences Network Advanced Hardware
Windows 10 or 11 computer: Select the button, type CMD, select Command Prompt, then type IPconfig /all
Chromebook: Open a browser and type chrome://system, select ipconfig, then look for MACaddr

Ethernet

The first computer networks were configured with wired connections. These networks used a variety of topologies and protocols, but a technology called Ethernet emerged as the dominant standard and became a key element in large and small computer networks.

What is Ethernet? Ethernet is a wired network technology that is defined by IEEE 802.3 standards. It was first deployed in 1976 and is now used for wired connections in just about every local area network.

Why is Ethernet so popular? Ethernet's success is attributable to several factors:

Easy. Ethernet is relatively easy to understand, implement, manage, and maintain.

Secure. The wired connections in an Ethernet LAN are more secure than wireless LAN technologies.

Inexpensive. As a nonproprietary technology, Ethernet equipment is available from a variety of vendors, and market competition keeps prices low.

Flexible. Current Ethernet standards allow extensive flexibility in network configurations to meet the needs of small and large installations.

Compatible. Ethernet is compatible with popular Wi-Fi wireless technology, so it is possible to mix wired and wireless devices on a single network.

How does Ethernet work? Ethernet was originally a bus topology in which computers were all strung along a cable like birds on a power line. Today's Ethernet LANs are usually arranged in a star topology with computers wired to central switching circuitry that is incorporated in modern routers. Data sent from a computer on the network is transmitted to the router, which then sends the data to the network nodes (Figure 3-49).

Terminology

IEEE is the Institute of Electrical and Electronics Engineers, a professional organization that develops technical standards in areas such as electronics and networking. These standards are grouped and numbered. Many IEEE LAN standards begin with the number 802.

QuickCheck

Ethernet and Wi-Fi are compatible network standards.

a. True

b. False

Figure 3-49: Ethernet topology

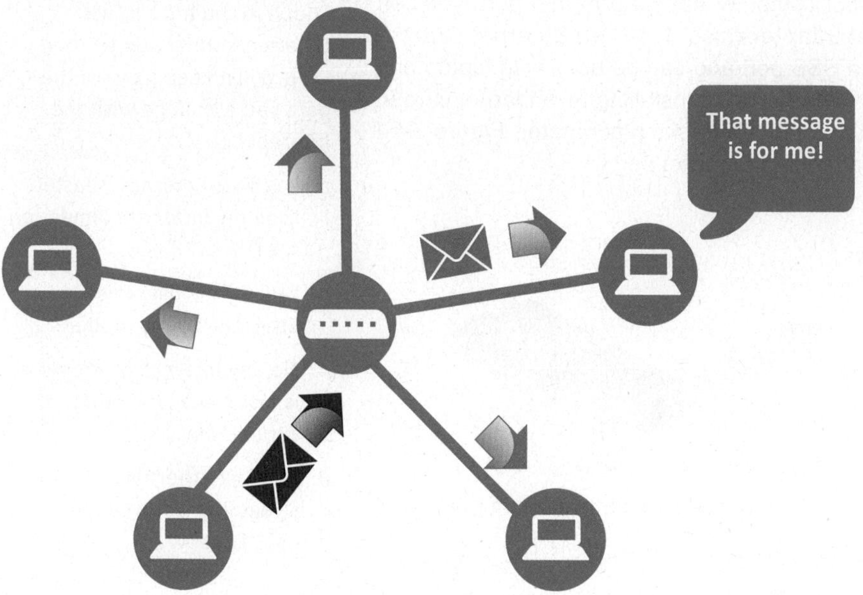

The central router handles all the traffic within the Ethernet. The router receives data and then broadcasts it to all of the nodes. The data is accepted only by the device to which it was addressed.

How fast is Ethernet? The original Ethernet standard carried data over a coaxial cable at 10 Mbps. Ethernet encompasses a family of LAN technologies that offer various data transmission rates, as shown in Figure 3-50. Today, most personal computers and LAN equipment work with Gigabit Ethernet.

Figure 3-50 Ethernet standards

Ethernet Standard	IEEE Designation	Speed
10BaseT Ethernet	IEEE 802.3i	10 Mbps
Fast Ethernet	IEEE 802.3u	100 Mbps
Gigabit Ethernet	IEEE 802.3z	1,000 Mbps
10 Gigabit Ethernet	IEEE 802.3ae	10 Gbps
40/100 Gigabit Ethernet	IEEE 802.3ba	40 or 100 Gbps

How can I tell if a device is Ethernet ready? Many computers have a built-in Ethernet port located on the system case. The port looks very similar to an oversized telephone jack (Figure 3-51).

Figure 3-51: Does your computer have an Ethernet port?

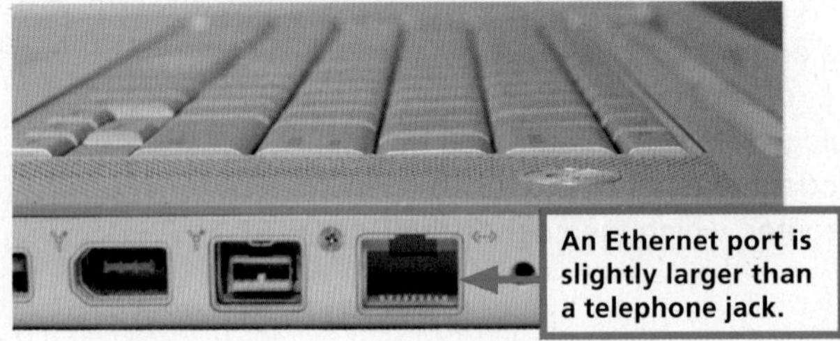

An Ethernet port is slightly larger than a telephone jack.

Try It!

Check your computer. Does it have an Ethernet port for wired network connections?

What if a computer doesn't have an Ethernet port? If you want a wired network connection but your computer has no Ethernet port, you can purchase and install an **Ethernet adapter** (also called an Ethernet card). A USB Ethernet adapter plugs into a USB port and can be used with laptop and desktop computers. You also have the option of installing an Ethernet card in an expansion slot inside the system unit of a desktop computer. Figure 3-52 illustrates two types of adapters for adding Ethernet ports.

Figure 3-52: Ethernet adapters

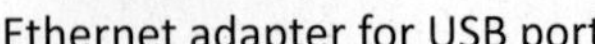

Ethernet adapter for USB port

Ethernet adapter for expansion slot

QuickCheck

Suppose you have a Fast Ethernet connection to your LAN. Will it keep up with the data you exchange with the Internet?

a. Yes, Fast Ethernet is faster than my Internet connection speed.

b. Yes, my ISP uses Fast Ethernet for my modem.

c. No, my Internet connection is faster than my Ethernet connection.

d. No, Fast Ethernet makes streaming video pause occasionally.

Wi-Fi

Wi-Fi refers to a set of wireless networking technologies defined by **IEEE 802.11** standards. A Wi-Fi device transmits data as radio waves and is compatible with Ethernet, so you can use the two technologies in a single network.

How does Wi-Fi work? You can set up Wi-Fi in two ways. One option is to use wireless mesh topology in which devices broadcast directly to each other (Figure 3-53).

Figure 3-53: Wireless mesh configuration

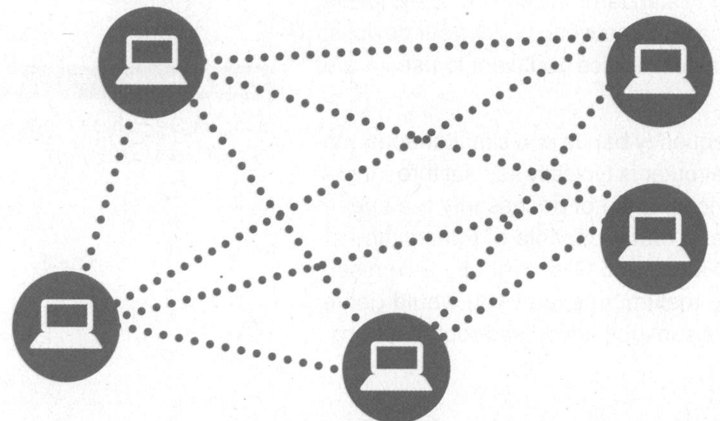

Wireless mesh networks are conceptually simple but provide few security safeguards. This type of connection is best limited to occasional use when you want to temporarily connect two computers to share a few files.

A second option for Wi-Fi networks is a star topology in which a centralized broadcasting device—a wireless access point—coordinates communication among network devices. Technically, the centralized device is a wireless access point, but that function is built into most routers (Figure 3-54).

Figure 3-54: Wireless star configuration

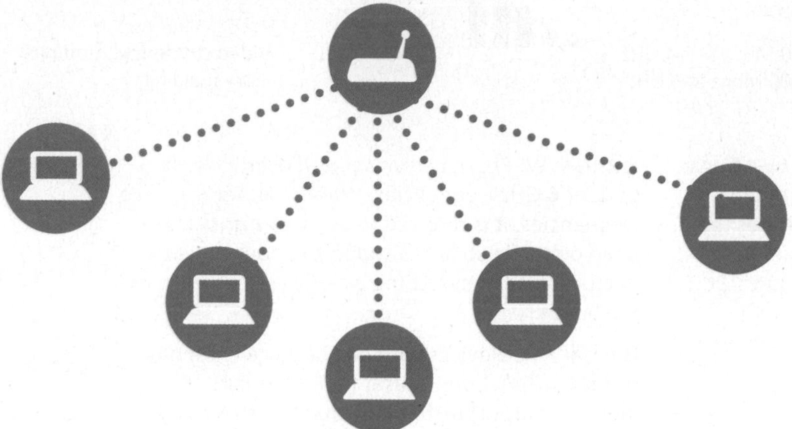

The most common wireless network technology uses a centralized device to handle data that travels from one device to another.

3

Terminology

Wireless mesh networks are sometimes called *peer networks* or *ad-hoc networks*. Wireless networks that depend on a router are sometimes called *wireless infrastructure networks* or *managed networks*.

QuickCheck

Which Wi-Fi infrastructure is more similar to Ethernet?

a. Wireless mesh

b. Wireless star

How can I tell if a device is Wi-Fi ready? Today, Wi-Fi capability is included with just about every desktop, laptop, tablet, and smartphone. Don't worry if your device has no visible antenna for transmitting and receiving data; the antenna is likely integrated into the case. Older equipment without Wi-Fi can be outfitted with a **Wi-Fi adapter** that plugs into a USB port or an internal expansion slot.

What is the range of a Wi-Fi network? Wi-Fi signals may reach up to 300 feet (90 meters) from the router. Thick cement walls, steel beams, and other environmental obstacles can drastically reduce this range.

How fast is Wi-Fi? Wi-Fi speed depends on the Wi-Fi standards of your router and your network devices. Current Wi-Fi standards include 802.11ac (Wi-Fi 5) and 802.11ax (Wi-Fi 6). When setting up a Wi-Fi network, check your devices. The router you select should support the fastest device you want to use on the network.

Routers can transmit data over different frequency bands and simultaneously to multiple devices. The advertised speed of a router is typically its total throughput capacity on all frequencies and to all devices. It is not necessarily the speed available for a single device. For example, a router capable of transmitting at 600 Mbps at 2.4 GHz frequency and 1300 Mbps at 5 GHz might be advertised as having a speed of 1900 Mbps, but the maximum speed you would get is 1300 Mbps. Figure 3-55 can help you make sense of advertised router speeds.

QuickCheck

Are Wi-Fi actual speeds faster than Ethernet actual speeds?

a. Yes.

b. No.

c. Some Wi-Fi speeds are faster than 10BaseT Ethernet.

d. Only 802.11ac Wi-Fi is slower than Ethernet.

QuickCheck

In Figure 3-55, how many of the routers are dual-band?

a. 0

b. 1

c. 2

d. 3

Figure 3-55: Wireless router options

Advertised speed	Max speed per user	Bands	Range	MU-MIMO	Uses
600 Mbps	600 Mbps	600 Mbps at 2.4 GHz		None	Browsing, email, voice chat
1900 Mbps 2x2	1300 Mbps	600 Mbps at 2.4 GHz 1300 Mbps at 5 GHz		2x2	Online gaming, simultaneous music downloads
1900 Mbps 4x4	1300 Mbps	600 Mbps at 2.4 GHz 1300 Mbps at 5 GHz		4x4	Video streaming, multiple-story buildings

Speed: Router speed can be designated by a single number or a combination of numbers. A router specification such as 600+1300 Mbps indicates the speed for each frequency. This router would be able to supply 1300 Mbps to a single user, not 1900 Mbps.

Bands: Wi-Fi can be transmitted over 2.4 GHz, 5 GHz, or 6 GHz frequencies. When a router uses two frequencies, it is referred to as **dual-band**. Dual-band offers flexibility to support various network devices and can overcome interference on either of the bands.

MU-MIMO: Devices with one or more antennas use **MU-MIMO** (multi-user multiple-input multiple-output) technology that transmits signals simultaneously to multiple devices. A router with two channels is designated as 2x2. A 4x4 router can broadcast simultaneously to four devices using two frequency bands. Adding channels does not increase the speed to each device.

Set Up Your Own Network

Having your own network is great. You can access the Internet from multiple devices, share files, and download apps to your smartphone without maxing out your data plan. But LANs can be a security risk. Here's how to set up your own safe and secure LAN.

▶ **What's the general procedure for setting up a network?** The basic steps for setting up a LAN are:

1. Plug in the router and connect it to your Internet modem.
2. Configure the router.
3. Connect wired and wireless devices.

▶ **How do I connect the router to my Internet modem?** Use a cable to connect the router's **WAN port** to the Internet modem's Ethernet port (Figure 3-56).

Figure 3-56: Connect the router to the Internet modem

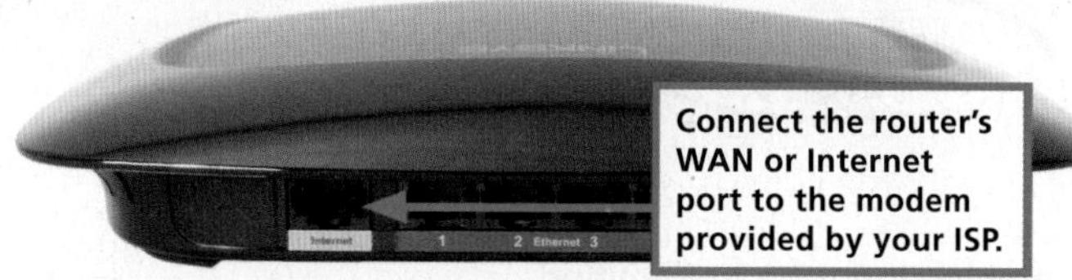

Connect the router's WAN or Internet port to the modem provided by your ISP.

▶ **How do I set up a router?** A router has no screen or keyboard of its own; to access the router's configuration software, you'll use a computer and connect to the router using a browser. Instructions are included with the router.

Change the password. The first step is to change the router password. All routers are shipped with a standard password. Your router can be accessed and controlled by anyone who enters that password until you've created a secure password, as shown in Figure 3-57.

Figure 3-57: Change your router's password

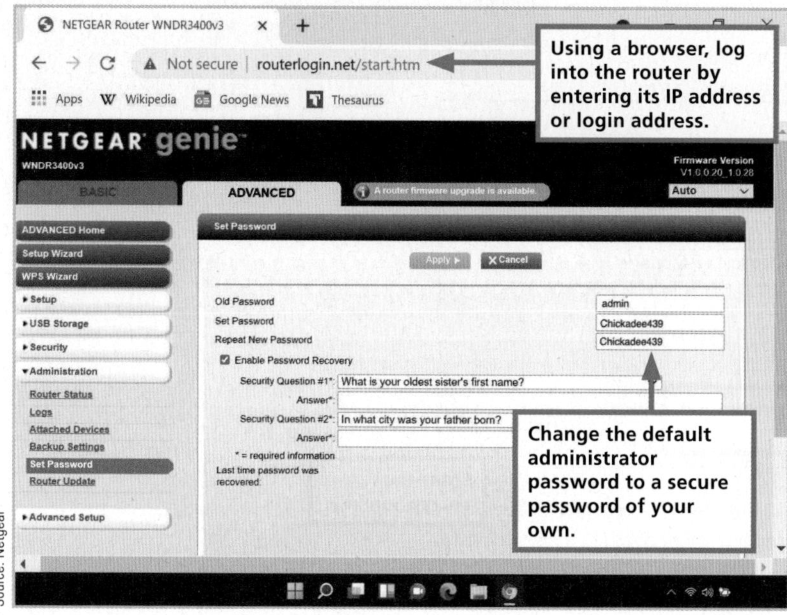

Source: Netgear

Create an SSID. After changing the router password, you can create an SSID for your network. An **SSID** (service set identifier) is the name of a wireless network. In areas where there are overlapping wireless networks, such as in a city or on a college campus, SSIDs help you log in to the right network, rather than a network run by a hacker who will try to suck important information off your computer as soon as you connect.

At the same time you change the router password, you can decide whether or not you want to broadcast the SSID. When SSID broadcasting is turned on, any wireless device passing by can see that a network exists. Go ahead and broadcast the SSID, as shown in Figure 3-58. You can use encryption to secure the network.

Try It!

Check your computer. What is the SSID for the network you're currently using? (Hint: Click the Wi-Fi icon to see a list of networks.)

Figure 3-58: Create an SSID

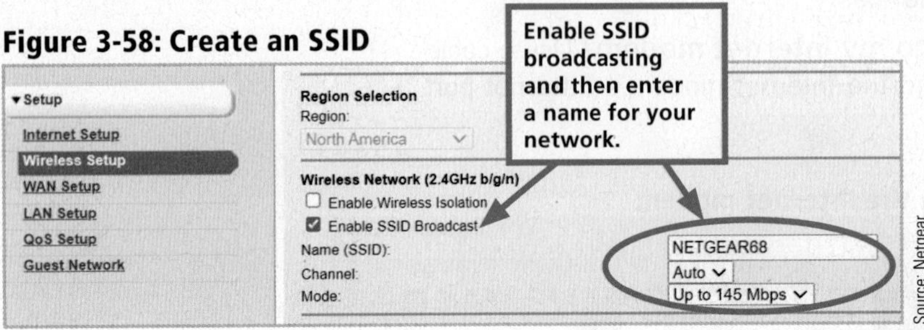

Source: Netgear

Activate encryption. Wireless encryption scrambles the data transmitted between wireless devices and then unscrambles the data only on devices that have a valid encryption key. **WEP (Wired Equivalent Privacy)** is the oldest and weakest wireless encryption protocol. **WPA** (Wi-Fi Protected Access) and related protocols, WPA2 and PSK, offer more security. Use the strongest encryption that is available.

When setting up encryption, you'll create a **wireless encryption key** (sometimes referred to as a network security key or password). The key is similar to a password. Any devices that connect to your secure LAN must have this key unless you've configured your router for **WPS** (Wi-Fi Protected Setup). With WPS on the router, devices can connect using an autoconnect feature. Figure 3-59 illustrates how to activate wireless encryption.

QuickCheck

What is the most effective encryption technology?

a. SSID

b. WEP

c. WPA

Figure 3-59: Activate encryption

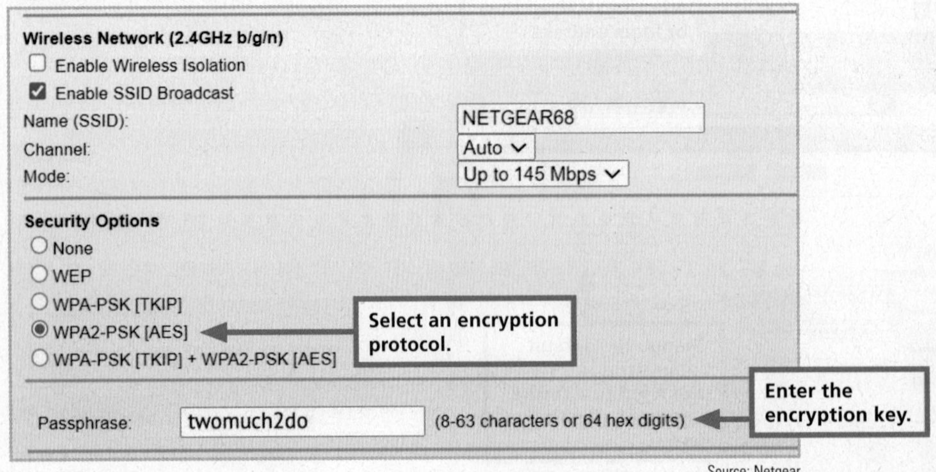

Source: Netgear

Configure the Guest network. A **Guest network** is essentially a second network that you can configure on your LAN's router. Guest networks allow visitors to access the Internet through your LAN, but don't allow them to access other resources on your network, such as your data files. Some routers come preconfigured with a Guest network. You should be sure to check your router's settings to verify that they meet your security requirements.

You can view Guest network settings using your router's configuration software. Your Guest network will have its own SSID and security settings. You may be allowed to change these settings, or the router manufacturer may have designated permanent settings.

If the Guest network is secured, it should have its own unique encryption key or password, which you'll have to supply to your visitors. Leaving the Guest network unsecured makes access open to anyone—not a good idea. Even when secured, a Guest network offers a potential security risk, so it should be disabled when you are not expecting visitors.

Activate DHCP. Each workstation requires a unique address for sending and receiving data. When you configure your router to act as a DHCP server, it will automatically assign an address to each device that joins your network. Figure 3-60 illustrates how to set up DHCP.

Try It!

Does the network you usually use have a Guest network? How can you tell?

Figure 3-60: Activate DHCP

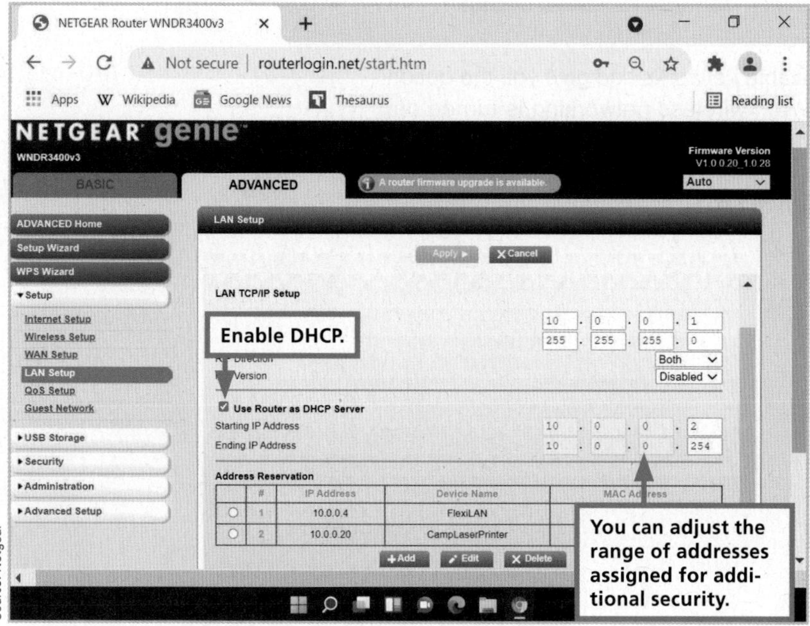

Source: Netgear

QuickCheck

If you have four wireless devices connected to your network and you do not want any interlopers to join, you can configure _______ to assign only four IP addresses.

a. SSID

b. WEP

c. DHCP

d. the Guest network

How do I connect devices to a LAN? Simply connect wired devices to the router using a network cable. Routers automatically sense wired devices and allow them to initiate a connection. A password is not needed for wired devices because the signals do not travel through the air where they are easy to intercept.

A wireless router is constantly broadcasting its SSID. Wireless devices, such as smartphones, laptops, and tablets, sense the router's signal and add the SSID to a list of nearby networks. The first time you connect to a secured network, you must enter the encryption key. Your device remembers the key for future logins.

Laptops and tablets running Windows display a list of nearby networks and their security status. Figure 3-61 illustrates the process of connecting to a secured network from a device using Windows 11.

Figure 3-61: Connecting to a LAN with Windows 11

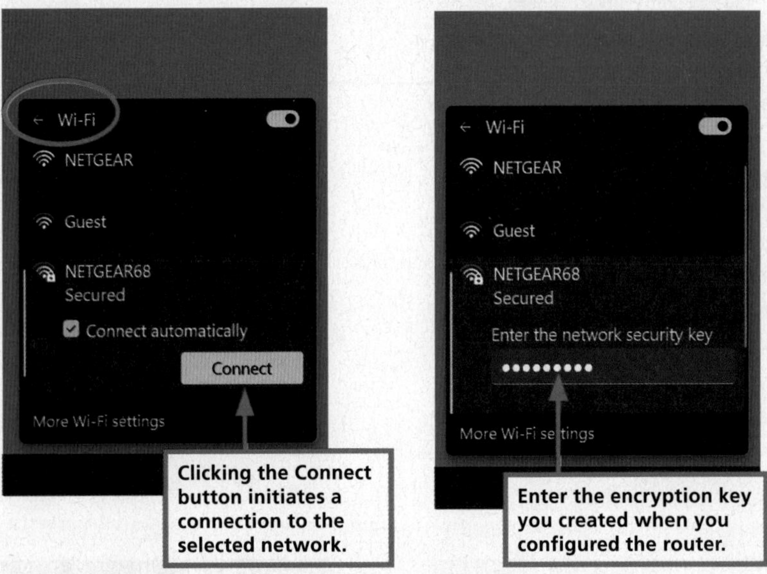

Like PCs, Macs automatically sense available networks and give you the option of connecting to them. Make sure that Wi-Fi wireless networking is turned on, then enter the encryption key when asked for the password (Figure 3-62).

Figure 3-62: Connecting to a LAN with macOS

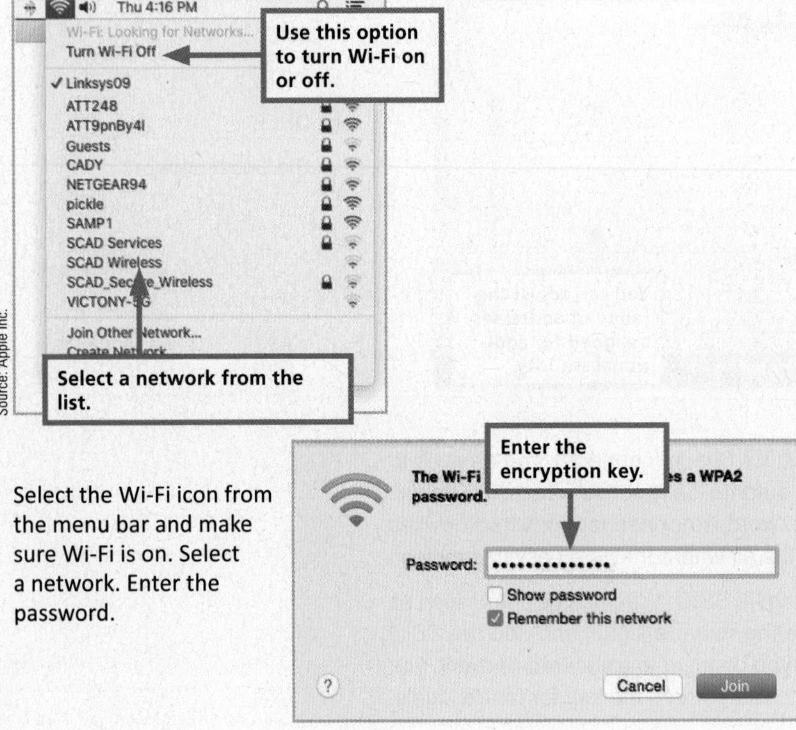

Select the Wi-Fi icon from the menu bar and make sure Wi-Fi is on. Select a network. Enter the password.

3

Network Monitoring

If your data isn't moving and you have no Internet access, the problem could be on your LAN. When your network has stopped sending and receiving packets, you might be able to correct the problem by turning off your router and Internet modem, waiting a few seconds, and then turning them on again.

▸ How do I monitor network activity? On Macs, you can view the number of incoming and outgoing packets using the Activity Monitor (Figure 3-63).

Figure 3-63: Mac network monitoring

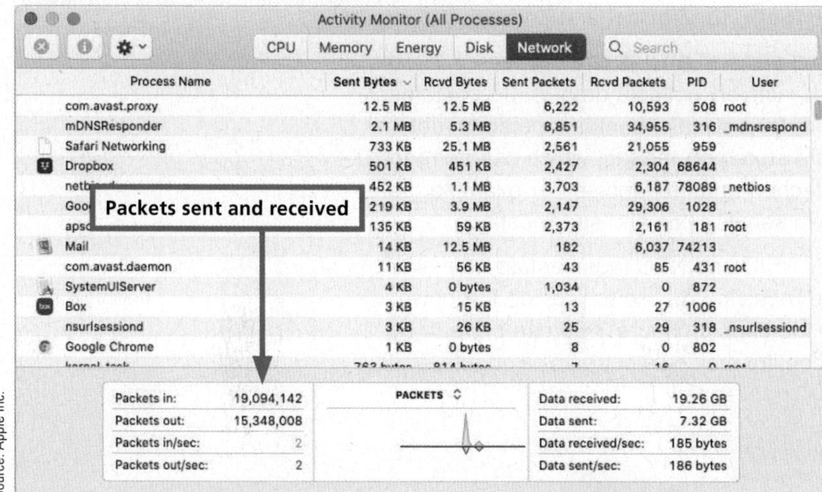

Source: Apple Inc.

On a PC, the Resource Monitor provides information about incoming and outgoing packets. It shows the incoming and outgoing activity for each connection, but does not offer a summarized total (Figure 3-64).

Figure 3-64: Windows Resource Monitor

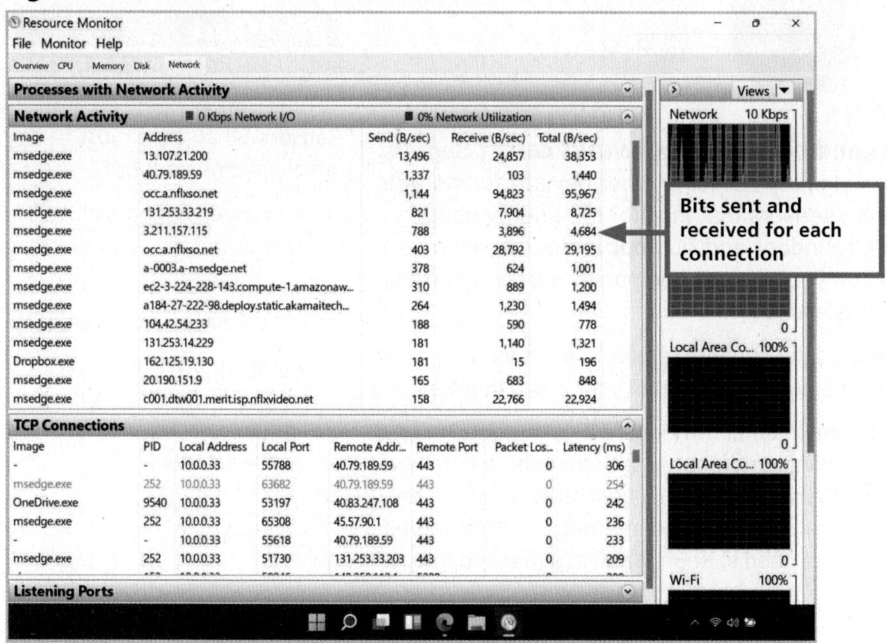

IoT Networks

Those plants you're growing indoors need constant attention. Would you like a text message when they need water? The Internet of Things connects active sensors and passive tags to communication networks, making it easier to remotely monitor places and things.

Terminology

RFID stands for radio-frequency identification. RFID tags have a range of about 300 feet (100 meters). *NFC* stands for near field communication. NFC tags have a range of just four inches (10 cm).

▶ Do IoT networks use Wi-Fi technology? Most sensors use battery power to collect data and to transmit it. Extended battery life is possible only if these activities consume small amounts of power. Wi-Fi is fairly power hungry, so it is not an optimal IoT technology. Existing wireless technologies such as **RFID** and **NFC** offer potential solutions. Additional low-power, short-range technologies developed specifically for IoT networks include **Bluetooth LE**, **ZigBee**, and **Z-Wave**.

▶ What's the difference between a sensor and a tag? A sensor, such as a thermometer or heart rate monitor, actively collects data. A tag contains passive data. An RFID tag in a passport, for example, contains personal data, such as the name and birth date that are stored on the tag, which can be read electronically. An NFC tag might be attached to merchandise, for example, so that you can tap it with your cell phone to see its price and specifications.

Tags can be battery powered, but many RFID and NFC tags contain no power source of their own and depend on the receiving device to provide the power for data exchange. Data from tags like the ones in Figure 3-65 can be read by network devices and used for identification, for making electronic payments, and for tracking things or people.

Figure 3-65: RFID and NFC tags

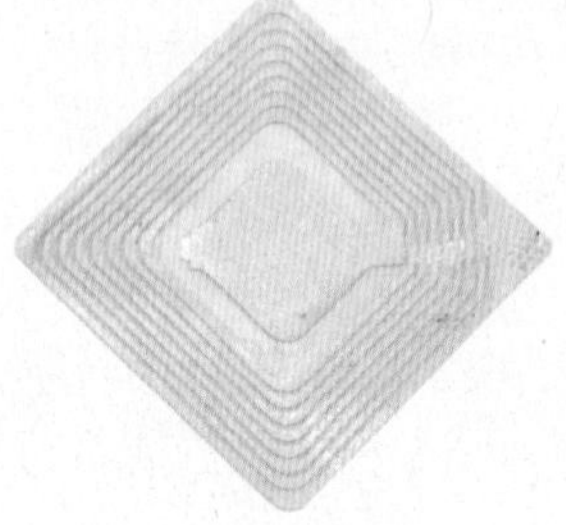

▶ What kinds of sensor input and output do networks carry? Sensors can use networks to transmit the data they collect to other devices for storage and output. For example, data from sensors that monitor the energy usage of your air conditioning unit relative to indoor and outdoor temperatures might be stored on your home network, on your electric company's server, or on the sensor manufacturer's cloud storage service.

Networks also provide a way to access the sensors remotely, such as when you use your smartphone at work to adjust the temperature of your home thermostat.

▶ How do IoT networks work? The Internet of Things is a flexible technology with many different applications and configurations. As an example, a common configuration for home monitoring is to link sensors to a base station, which can then ship data to routers in local area networks and the Internet. Sensors can be linked in a star topology or, if the sensors need to share data, in a mesh topology.

QuickCheck

If you are putting together an IoT network of home control sensors, what is the most efficient configuration?

a. Sensors equipped with Wi-Fi to transmit data to a Web site

b. Sensors with IP addresses to communicate with your LAN

c. ZigBee or Z-Wave sensors that send results to a base station, which communicates with your LAN's router

d. RFID tags and a dedicated RFID reader

How do sensors communicate with an IoT network? IoT sensors can be wired to a base station, but more typically they are equipped with some type of communication device that allows them to wirelessly send and receive signals. Digi XBee chips use radio signals to transport data wirelessly. Devices like the one shown in Figure 3-66 can easily pair with sensors in small form factor packages.

Figure 3-66: XBee transmitter

QuickCheck

Suppose you want to collect data from your fitness wristband. What is the most secure way to get that data to your laptop?

a. Use a USB cable to plug the band directly into your laptop.

b. Collect the data at a ZigBee base station, which will relay it to your LAN, where you can access it from your laptop.

c. Transmit the signal to your laptop using unencrypted Wi-Fi.

3

Are IoT networks secure? Data passing over IoT networks can seem trivial, but is it? Do you care if anyone else knows that your fitness wristband recorded lots of activity between midnight and 3:00 am last Saturday? As the IoT collects more and more data about our personal lives and the machines that run factory and power-grid infrastructures, security becomes crucial.

Secure IoT networks encrypt data transmissions, store data in encrypted format, password-protect access to base stations, and expose the least possible amount of data to the public Internet. As you begin to collect wearable devices and home monitoring sensors, think carefully about the security of the data they collect, transport, and store.

QuickQuiz — Section D

1. The key device at the center of a LAN is a(n) [____].
2. In addition to an IP address, devices on a LAN have a physical [____] address that uniquely identifies them.
3. The dominant standard for wired LANs is [____].
4. Technologies such as WEP, WPA, and PSK are examples of [____] that can be used on wireless networks.
5. ZigBee, Z-Wave, and RFID are low-power wireless technologies that transport data on [____] networks.

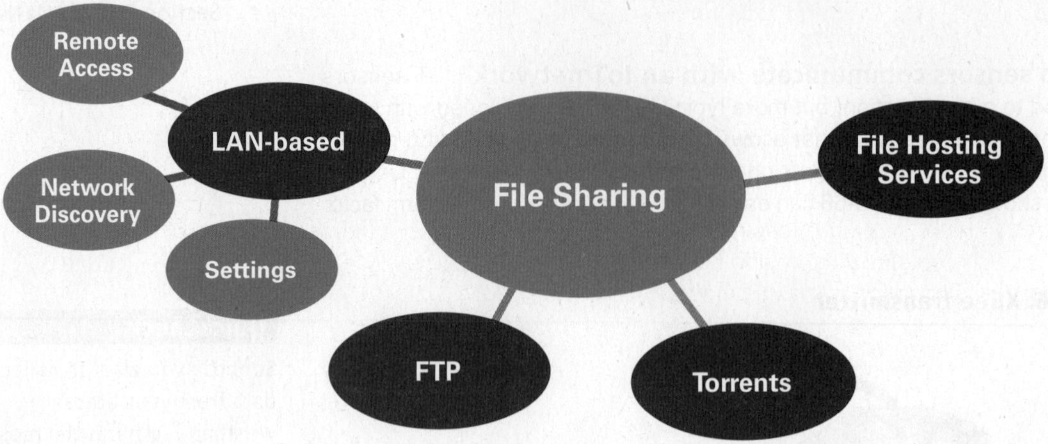

Section E

File Sharing

Objectives

- List seven factors that control your ability to share files.
- State the names of the utilities you use to view a list of files on Macs and on Windows.
- Explain the purpose of network discovery.
- List three precautions you can take when working with shared files.
- Define the three types of permissions that can be assigned to shared files.
- Describe at least two situations in which FTP would be a useful technology.
- List two factors that have a negative effect on files stored in the cloud.
- Draw a diagram that explains how torrents work.
- Discuss the legal issues that pertain to file sharing technologies, such as Napster and BitTorrent.

Digital defenses? One of the ways we invite trouble into our digital lives is by careless file sharing. This convenient technology for exchanging photos, documents, music, and videos can be the weak link in our chain of digital defenses. When was the last time you checked your file sharing settings?

Terminology

file sharing
network discovery
permissions
FTP
file hosting services
BitTorrent

File Sharing Basics

Networks provide access to all types of files. From Snapchats to feature-length movies, from magazine articles to full-length novels, and from sound effects to symphonies, a wide variety of files exist on local networks and on the Internet.

You may spend lots of time downloading files to your local devices, but there are also times when you want to provide access to files you have stored locally or in the cloud. File sharing makes this magic happen.

◗ **What is file sharing?** **File sharing** allows files containing documents, photos, music, and more to be accessed from devices other than the ones on which they are stored. Sharing can take place within a LAN or across multiple networks, including the Internet.

File sharing is a limited version of remote access that allows access to files, but it does not provide access to commands that launch programs or change settings on the remote computer.

◗ **How does file sharing work?** Given permission, you may open, view, edit, copy, and delete files stored on a remote device. The remote file will open with software that is running on your device, but will remain stored on the remote computer.

Your ability to share files with other devices on a network depends on several factors, which are listed in Figure 3-67.

Figure 3-67: File sharing depends on these factors

Which devices your computer can discover

Whether other network devices can discover your computer

Whether you are allowed to access files on other computers

Whether you allow other computers to access files on your computer

Which files you allow others to access

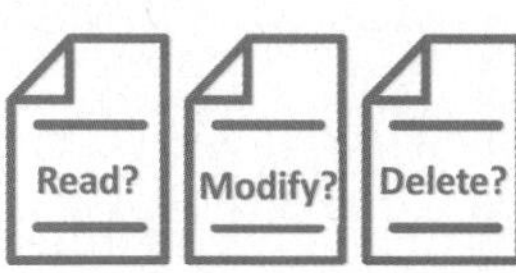

What you are allowed to do with files on other computers

What you allow others to do with the files they can access

Accessing LAN Files

Let's begin with a simple scenario. You've set up a home network and want to use one computer on the network to access files from another connected computer.

◗ How can I see all of the devices that are connected to my network?

To see a list of devices on your network, you can use your operating system's file management utility, such as Finder or File Explorer (Figure 3-68).

Figure 3-68: Find other computers on a LAN

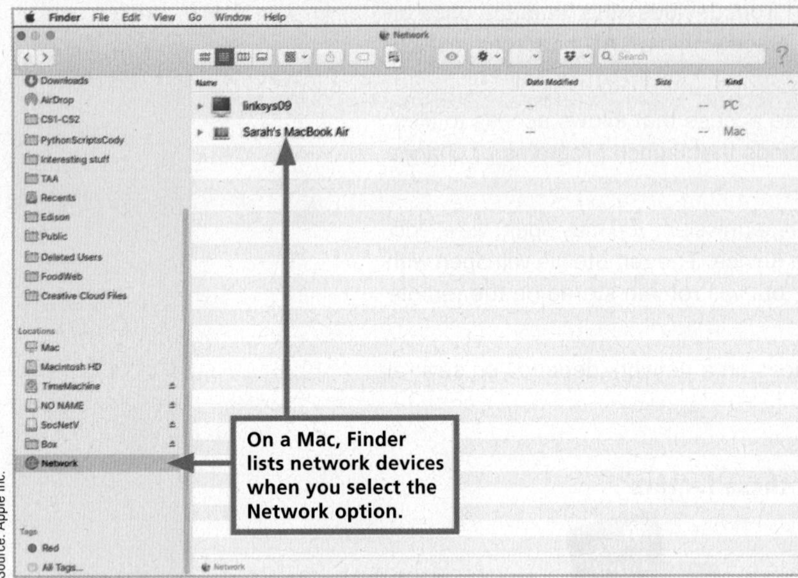

macOS Finder

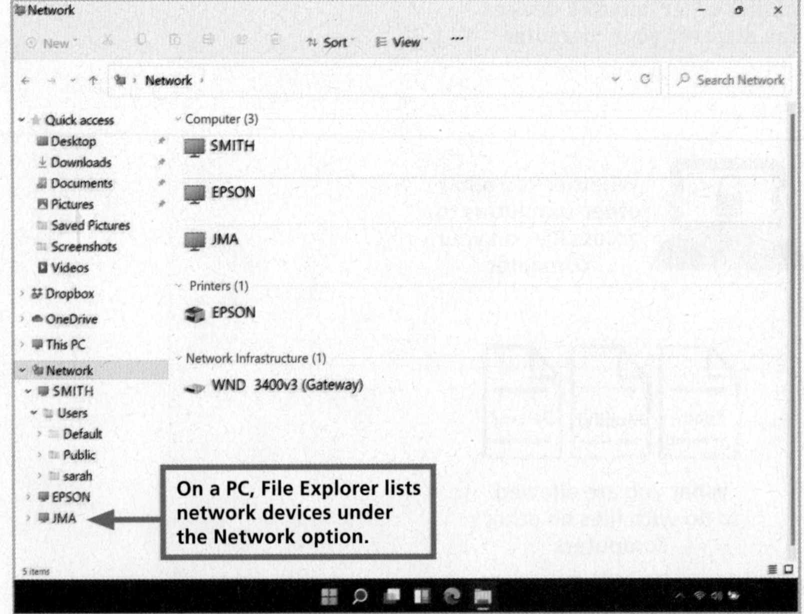

Windows File Explorer

QuickCheck

How many devices are set to discovery mode on the Windows network shown in Figure 3-68? (Hint: EPSON is a printer!)

a. 0

b. 1

c. 2

d. 3

Try It!

Check your computer. Are any network devices visible?

What if other network devices aren't listed? The network utilities provided by operating systems such as Windows and macOS automatically detect other devices when network discovery is turned on. **Network discovery** is a setting that affects whether your computer can see other devices on a network, and whether your computer can be seen by others.

When network discovery is turned on, your computer can see other computers on a LAN and those computers can see yours. When network discovery is off, the name of your computer will not appear in the list of network devices displayed on other computers. Network discovery works in different ways on different devices.

Mobile devices. The operating systems on mobile devices may not offer a way to see other devices on a network or to broadcast their presence on a network.

Macs. macOS devices, such as iMacs, have no user-modifiable network discovery settings, but offer file sharing settings instead. If file sharing is on, then network discovery is enabled.

Windows. PCs running Microsoft Windows offer a network discovery setting that allows users to turn network discovery off or on. When using public networks, this setting should be off (Figure 3-69).

QuickCheck

When network discovery is on, ________________.

a. you can see the SSIDs of all the available networks
b. all of the files on your computer are automatically shared
c. your computer will look for and list all the other computers on the local network
d. your computer will broadcast its name so that computers on the Internet can share your files

Figure 3-69: Network discovery settings in Windows

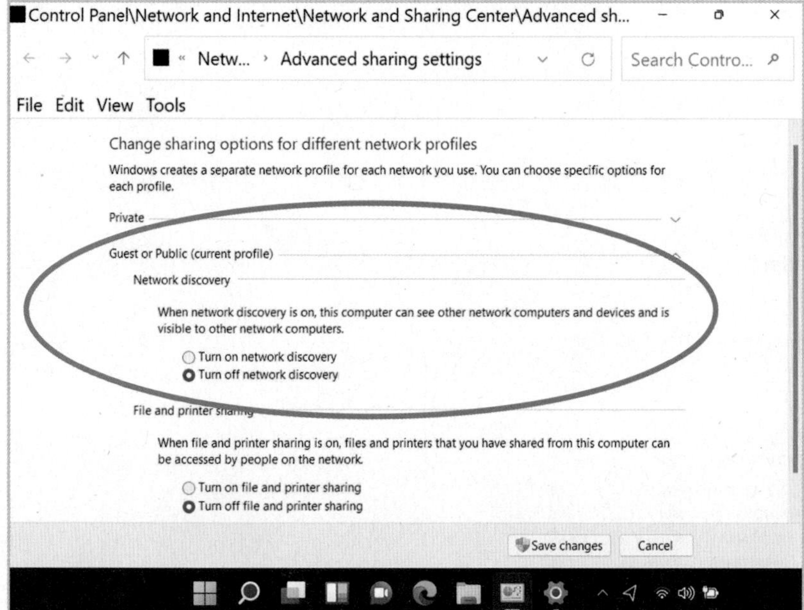

When using a public network, such as a Wi-Fi hotspot, turning network discovery off hides your computer from other users connected to the network. One caveat: The network administrator can see your device using router utilities even when network discovery is off.

Try It!

If your computer runs Windows, find out if network discovery is turned on. How do you think that setting affects the devices you were able to see in the previous Try It! exercise?

▶ How do I access files located on other computers? Folders on some computers require a valid password for access. Your file sharing user ID and password are usually the same as the password you use to log in to your computer.

Assuming that you have permission to access files on a network device, you can access files just as if they were on your own computer. Select the device that holds the files. Open the folder that contains the file, then select the file you'd like to access (Figure 3-70).

QuickCheck

One way to ensure that only valid users can access shared files is to ________________.

a. require a password

b. check the MAC address

c. only accept IP addresses

d. require encryption

Figure 3-70: Accessing files stored on other computers

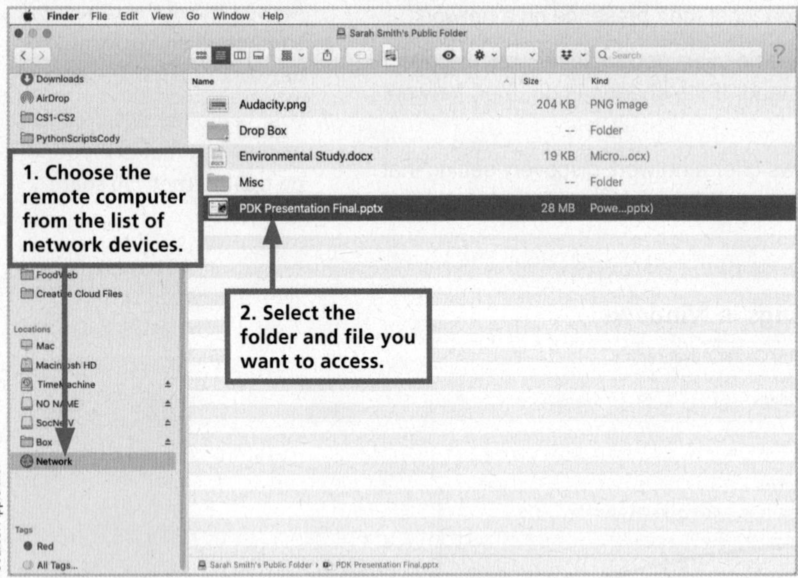

macOS Finder

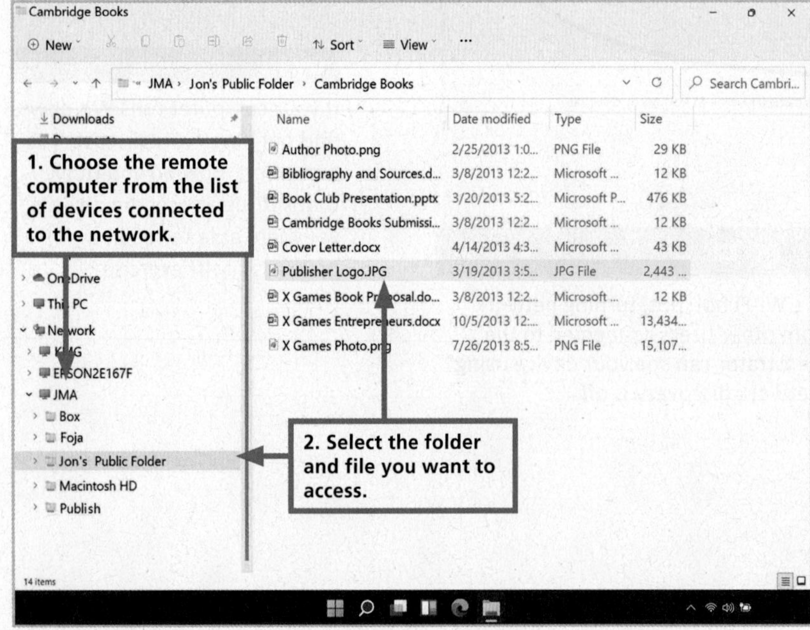

Windows File Explorer

Sharing Your Files

There are occasions when you'd like to share files stored on your computer with other people who are using your network. You may have guests who want to copy some of your sports photos, or you might want to transfer files from an old computer to a new one. Once computers can see each other on a network, sharing files can be easy—but take care to do it securely.

How secure is file sharing? File sharing poses security risks that have several dimensions. Shared files are subject to misuse, inadvertent modifications, and intentional alterations by those who have access to them. In addition, security holes in file sharing routines are notorious for providing Internet-based hackers with unauthorized access to computers.

If you don't need to share files, turn off file sharing globally. If you want the convenience of sharing files, limit what you share and who you share it with by following the tips in Figure 3-71.

Figure 3-71: Get smart about file sharing

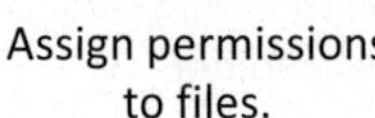

Assign permissions to files.

Limit sharing to specific people.

Remove sharing from files you no longer want to share.

What are permissions? **Permissions** specify how shared files can be used.

Read and write permission (full control) allows access for opening, viewing, modifying, and deleting files.

Read permission (also known as view-only) allows authorized people to open a file and view it, but they are not allowed to modify or delete it.

Can I control how files are modified? You can control who modifies a file, but not what they do to it. Once a shared file is bestowed with read and write permission, it can be modified so much that it is unrecognizable. If you are not checking shared files frequently, you may be surprised by what some of those files contain. You can see the potential problem. Read and write permission is not to be given without considerable thought.

One important consideration about file sharing is whether to provide access to the original file or to a copy of it. Your decision depends on the reason for sharing the file.

As a general guideline, do not offer read and write access to the original version of a file. Instead, make a copy of the file and designate the copy as shared with read and write permissions. If the file gets modified in some bizarre way, you will have a version of the original file that was not shared or modified.

Terminology

Permissions are also referred to as *user rights* or *privileges*.

QuickCheck

Suppose you would like to allow friends to access some photos, but you don't want them to make changes. What permissions would you assign?

a. Read

b. Read and write

c. Write

d. Admin

▶ **How do I share files from a Mac?** The first step is to turn on file sharing, then select the folders you'd like to share. You can designate an entire folder or a single file for sharing. To share one file, right-click it and select Get Info to access the Sharing & Permissions options. Use System Preferences to turn on file sharing and designate folders to share, as shown in Figure 3-72.

Figure 3-72: Sharing files from a Mac

❶ Access System Preferences from the Apple menu. There, you can select Sharing to turn on file sharing.

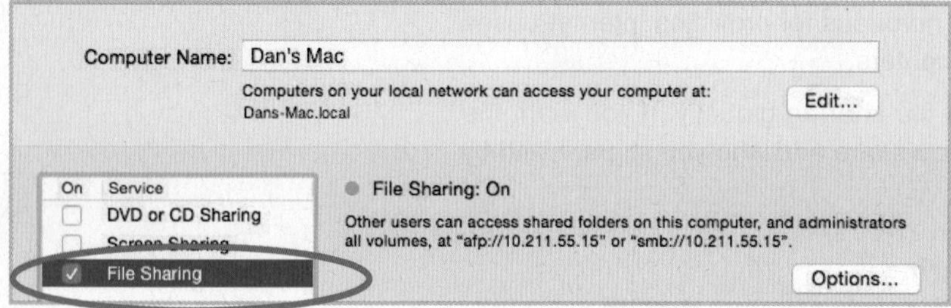

❷ Add folders to the Shared Folders list, then specify who can have access and the permissions they are allowed.

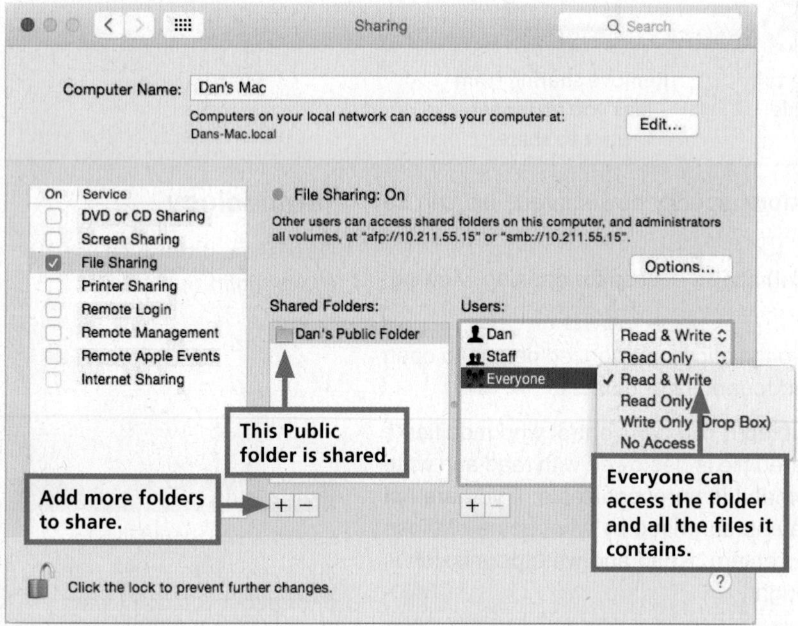

QuickCheck

What kind of files should Dan store in his Public folder?

a. Original files

b. Files he would prefer not to share

c. Copies of files that he doesn't mind being altered

d. Files that he doesn't want deleted

Try It!

If you're using a Mac, check to see if file sharing is turned on. Which folders are shared?

How do I share files from a PC? On a PC using Windows, the first step is to use the Control Panel's Network and Sharing utility to make sure that network discovery is on and then turn on file sharing.

Windows File Explorer includes a Share tab that's used to select folders or files you want to share. The Share tab also lets you specify permissions (Figure 3-73).

QuickCheck

Which operating system offers a way to designate individual files as shared?

a. macOS

b. iOS

c. Android

d. Windows

Figure 3-73: Sharing files from Windows

1. Access Windows Advanced Sharing Settings. Turn on network discovery and then turn on file and printer sharing.

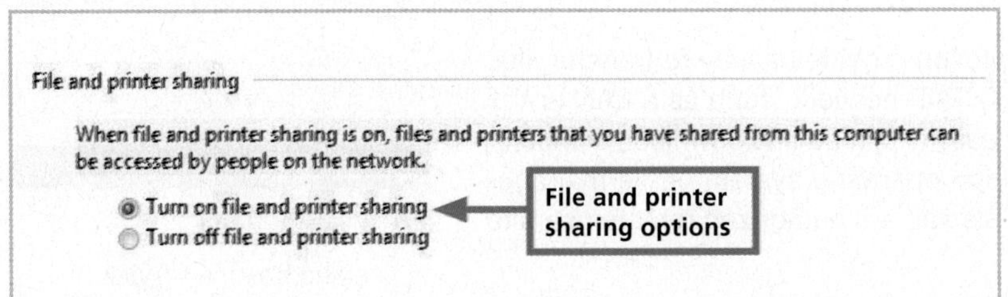

2. In File Explorer, you can select a folder or file that you want to share. Right-click the file and use the "Give access to" option to specify users and permissions.

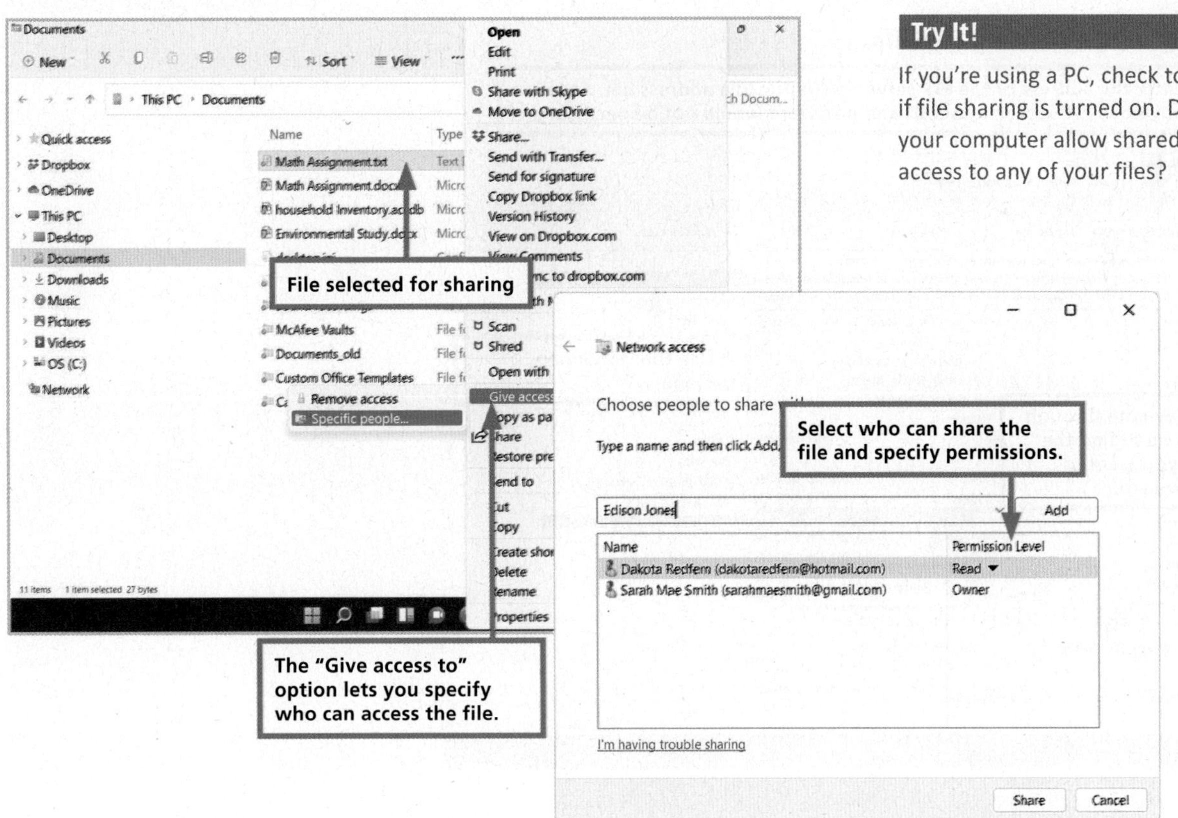

Try It!

If you're using a PC, check to see if file sharing is turned on. Does your computer allow shared access to any of your files?

Internet-Based Sharing

As more and more activity moves to the cloud, companies that provide cloud services have increased their interest in encouraging consumers to use those services. Cloud storage and sharing services are commonly hyped as being more convenient and more secure than local options, but many consumers are wary of cloud security, not to mention the rampant advertising that accompanies many of the free cloud storage services.

The concept of pulling files from remote servers traces back to a protocol called FTP. Newer technologies now power Dropbox and similar services. So what are they all about?

▶ **What is FTP?** **FTP** (File Transfer Protocol) provides a way to transfer files from one computer to another over any TCP/IP network, such as a LAN or the Internet. The purpose of FTP is to make it easy to upload and download computer files without having to deal directly with the operating system or file management system of a remote computer. FTP also allows authorized remote users to change file names and delete files.

▶ **How can I access FTP servers?** You can access FTP servers with FTP client software, such as FileZilla. Addresses of FTP servers usually begin with ftp://. To use FileZilla to download a file, enter the address of the FTP server, then select folders and files, as shown in Figure 3-74.

QuickCheck

FTP is ___________.

a. a cloud hosting service

b. a file sharing protocol

c. LAN-based secure file sharing

d. a permission-free file sharing service

Figure 3-74: FTP using FileZilla

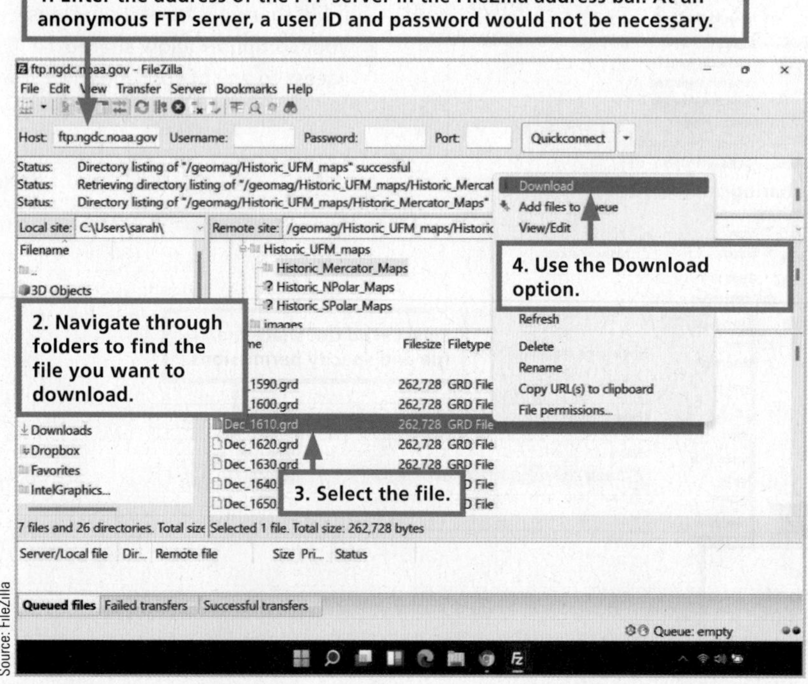

1. Enter the address of the FTP server in the FileZilla address bar. At an anonymous FTP server, a user ID and password would not be necessary.
2. Navigate through folders to find the file you want to download.
3. Select the file.
4. Use the Download option.
Source: FileZilla

What about Dropbox? Dropbox and similar **file hosting services** store files in the cloud. Those files can be shared when multiple users are allowed access to the same folders (Figure 3-75).

Figure 3-75: Dropbox file sharing

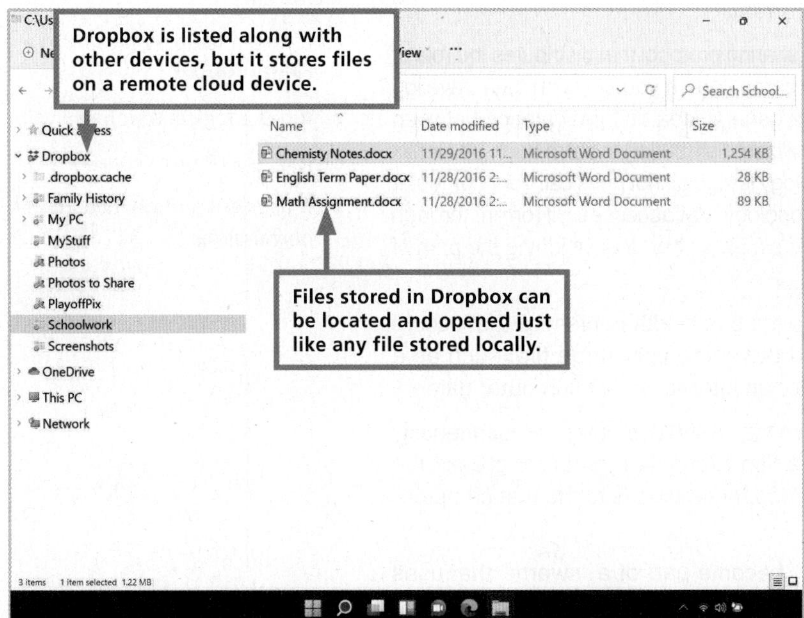

Dropbox can be installed as an app on a local device, but can be configured to store your files in the cloud. Those files can be accessed just as if they were stored locally.

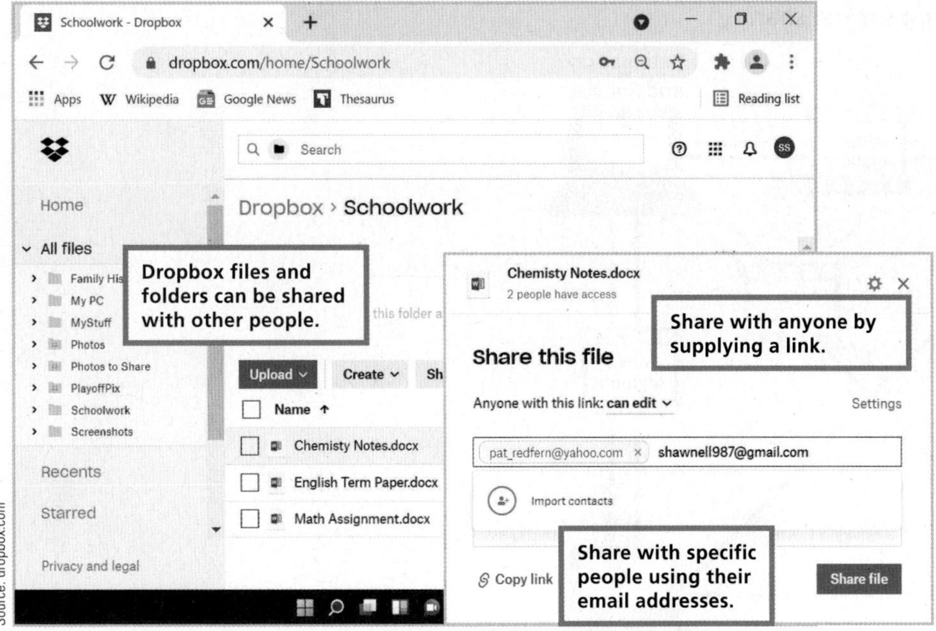

You can also access and share your Dropbox files using a browser.

Torrents

In the late 1990s, an online service called Napster burst onto the national scene when college students became aware that it provided free access to thousands of music downloads. Napster ran into some copyright infringement difficulties, but the concept of sharing files over the Internet spurred development of sophisticated, distributed protocols such as BitTorrent.

QuickCheck

What is unique about BitTorrent?

a. It doesn't supply files from a central server.

b. It has a logical topology.

c. It uses FTP protocols.

d. It uses encryption instead of permissions.

▶ What is BitTorrent? **BitTorrent** is a file sharing protocol that distributes the role of a file server across a collection of dispersed computers. If you envision data traveling over a mesh rather than a star, you'll have a general idea of the difference between a distributed file sharing system and a centralized distribution system such as Netflix Downloads. However, BitTorrent's mesh topology is logical, not physical. Your computer is still physically a part of a LAN with a star topology that accesses BitTorrent through a router. BitTorrent's logical mesh topology is simply a way of envisioning the path of data.

A BitTorrent network is designed to reduce the bandwidth bottleneck that occurs when many people attempt to download the same very large file, such as a feature-length film, application software, or an interactive 3D computer game.

▶ How does BitTorrent work? Suppose that 1,000 computers simultaneously request the newly released sequel to the film *Star Wars*. A server breaks the movie file into pieces and begins to download those pieces to the first computer that requested the movie.

As more computers request the file, they become part of a "swarm" that uses peer-to-peer technology to exchange movie segments with each other. After the server has downloaded all the segments to the swarm, its job is complete and it can service other requests. The swarm continues to exchange movie segments until every computer in the swarm has the entire movie (Figure 3-76).

Figure 3-76: Torrent peering for file sharing

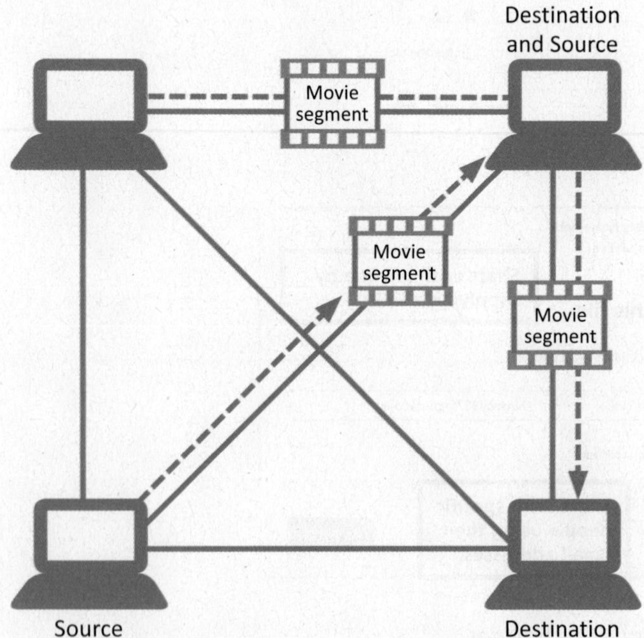

Every user who downloads from a torrent is automatically uploading to other users.

How do I use BitTorrent? When you want to download a musical album, movie, software, or ebook rather than stream it, BitTorrent may be able to provide the necessary content and technology.

BitTorrent client software is currently available from several Web sites. After installing the client, you can use it to download from any BitTorrent-enabled site by clicking the file you want. The BitTorrent client handles the entire file swapping procedure. After getting the entire file, good etiquette requires clients to remain connected to the swarm so that they can "seed" file pieces to others.

Are BitTorrent and similar file swapping networks legal? File sharing originated on Internet-based file servers, which held huge collections of popular music stored as digital MP3 files that could be easily downloaded and played on a computer or transferred to CDs. Free distribution of music without the copyright holder's permission is illegal, and file sharing server operators quickly encountered the legal ramifications of their computers' shady dealings.

Peer-to-peer file sharing networks and distributed technologies such as BitTorrent have legitimate uses for distributing music, images, videos, and software with the approval of copyright holders. For example, a bundle of ten *Doctor Who* episodes is available via BitTorrent with the approval of the BBC. The technology itself is not illegal; it is the use of the technology that is subject to legal scrutiny.

Is BitTorrent safe? Because BitTorrent files are assembled from little segments that come from a jumble of computers, they would seem to be bad candidates for distributing malware. Intelligent hackers would realize that their malicious code could easily be chopped up, too, and that pieces of it might not be delivered. Yet, BitTorrent files have become a source of adware and spyware. If you use BitTorrent, make sure your computer is protected with a security software suite that offers good spyware protection.

3

QuickCheck

BitTorrent would not be classified as a(n) ____________.

a. distributed network
b. peer-to-peer network
c. file sharing network
d. secure network

QuickQuiz — Section E

1. When network ____________ is on, your computer can see other devices that are connected to a LAN.
2. Read and ____________ permission allows a shared file to be opened, viewed, modified, and deleted.
3. File ____________ has to be turned on before any files on your computer can be accessed by other devices on a network.
4. ____________ client software, such as FileZilla, provides a way to upload and download files from an Internet-based server to a computer on a LAN.
5. Torrents exchange segments of files over a distributed network using a logical ____________ topology.

Vectomart/Shutterstock.com

Issue: Do We Want Net Neutrality?

It all started in October 2007, when the FCC accused Comcast of slowing and in some cases blocking Internet traffic from BitTorrent. Comcast claimed that it was attempting to even the playing field for the average Internet user, whose online speeds were languishing due to file sharing traffic from a minority of its customers.

Comcast's ability to adjust some users' bandwidth for the benefit of other users might seem beneficial until you consider that ISPs could manipulate Internet speeds to give preferential access to certain sites and services while slowing access to others. That practice could essentially give ISPs the power to deny access to sites based on business, political, or other values.

Today's action at the FCC could begin the dismantling of the open Internet as we know it...

Senator Edward J. Markey

What if your ISP institutes a system whereby you have to pay extra for high-bandwidth data, such as movie downloads? You might be thinking, "There ought to be a law against that!" That is exactly the opinion of net neutrality supporters.

The term *net neutrality* was created by Columbia media law professor Tim Wu in a 2003 paper *Network Neutrality, Broadband Discrimination*. Although the term *net neutrality* is relatively new, its roots can be traced to pre-1860 telegram technology. Back then, standard telegrams were routed equally, without discrimination, and without regard to their contents, source, or recipient. Telegraphs were end-to-end neutral networks. Because telegraph and—later—telephone networks were considered to be public utilities, or common carriers, they were not allowed to give preferential treatment to one customer over another. The Federal Communications Commission (FCC) was formed to regulate common carriers and ensure equal access and fair prices.

As the Internet evolved into a massive communication network, the FCC began to regard it as a common carrier that should fall under the FCC's umbrella of influence. The first step would be to ban ISPs from slowing or blocking traffic indiscriminately. In 2010, under the banner of net neutrality, the FCC issued the Open Internet Order, a set of regulations designed to "preserve the Internet as an open platform enabling consumer choice, freedom of expression, end-user control, competition, and the freedom to innovate without permission."

Shortly after the Open Internet Order, Comcast was back in court again to contest the FCC's right to regulate the Internet. The court ruled in favor of Comcast, based on the fact that the FCC's jurisdiction did not extend to the Internet.

Yet the FCC persisted. In 2014, FCC chairman Tom Wheeler proposed a compromise form of net neutrality that would allow ISPs to offer "faster lane" options at a premium rate to content providers such as Netflix, Facebook, and Amazon. That proposal absolutely confused the issue; the FCC's proposed version of net neutrality was not neutral at all.

Opponents of this new non-neutral neutrality pointed out that, considering the finite amount of bandwidth available on the Internet, users outside the proposed "faster lanes" would have their bandwidth squeezed while the added cost of fast-lane services would be passed directly on to the consumers of such services.

In 2015, Wheeler changed tactics and the FCC passed a net neutrality order. That order was reversed in 2017 under then FCC chair Ajit Pai. In 2018, more than 20 states sued the FCC in an attempt to reinstate the 2015 net neutrality policies. The court did not reinstate the 2015 net neutrality order, but ruled that states could implement their own net neutrality laws. As you can see, this issue has bounced back and forth between regulation and deregulation.

The net neutrality controversy boils down to simple ideology: Should the government regulate the Internet or not? On the one hand, regulation could prevent abusive business practices on the part of ISPs. On the other hand, if the Internet were to fall under the regulatory control of the FCC, where would the regulation end? The FCC currently regulates telephone and cellular service. It imposes a variety of taxes and fees that add to your monthly bill. Would similar taxes and fees be added to your monthly Internet service? And would FCC Internet monitoring add yet more points where the government can collect data on the activities of its citizens?

Try It! Net neutrality has become a political issue, and organizations with vested interests add to the confusion with misleading information. Here's a chance for you to explore the current status of net neutrality and to read arguments both for and against regulating ISPs.

1. Search online to find recent articles about net neutrality. What is its current status?
2. The Communications Act of 1934 was passed before there were computers or the Internet. Search online to find the full text version of the 1934 act and read the first two paragraphs. Explain why this act could be interpreted to apply to the Internet.
3. Shortly after the Internet went public, the U.S. Congress passed the Telecommunications Act of 1996. It defined two different but complementary services: "information services" and "telecommunications services." Explain the difference between these two services. How do these definitions relate to Title I and Title II of the Telecommunications Act? Classify the following as an information service or a telecommunications service: Amazon, Facebook, Comcast, Verizon, Twitter, Google.
4. Many ISPs and media companies have published written statements about their stance on net neutrality. What do you guess are the positions of Amazon, Mozilla, Netflix, Comcast, and the Electronic Frontier Foundation? Find the net neutrality statements of these companies online. Do they take the positions you expected? Why, or why not?
5. Search online for one article that supports net neutrality and one article that opposes it. Summarize the two positions.

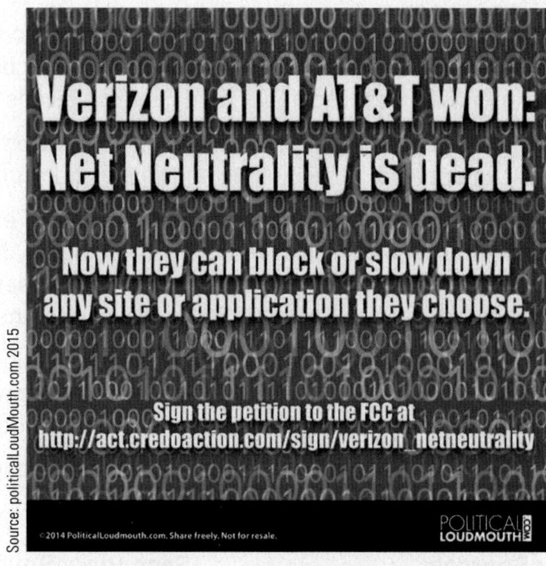

Source: politicalLoudMouth.com 2015

What Do You Think?

Issue

1. Do you support the idea that Internet traffic should flow freely?
2. Do you believe that the U.S. government should regulate the Internet as a common carrier?
3. Were you aware of the net neutrality controversy?

Skaljac/Shutterstock.com

Information Tools: Fact Checking

These days, you have to be a skeptic. Bloggers have opinions that are not always based on facts. Scam artists say anything to get your money. Fake news sites are proliferating. Just because an article shows up in Google results doesn't mean its contents are factual. Even reputable journalists sometimes make mistakes.

Before you form an opinion, make a decision, or take action based on what you read, see, or hear, you can easily use your computer or smartphone to verify facts and look up background information.

Search Google. You can use Google or a similar search engine to find information from all corners of the Web. You can search for information in specific formats, such as videos, images, and news reports. Check out Google Scholar for links to authoritative information in peer-reviewed journals, theses, and other professional publications. Remember that you can formulate searches such as *Define DNS spoofing* to learn the meaning of technical terms and find the meaning of acronyms.

Search within sites. Rather than conducting a wide-ranging Google search, you can go to a specific Web site and search within it. Search Wikipedia for definitions and topic overviews. Search news sites for articles and video footage about current events. Start at *www.snopes.com* or *www.factcheck.org* to identify email scams.

When you check facts or use them in your own research papers, primary sources tend to be more reliable than secondary or tertiary sources. How can you tell the difference?

Primary Sources

Original material such as speeches, interviews, letters, photos, email messages, tweets, artwork, diaries, laws, database reports, and accounting records

Example: A video of Apple's CEO announcing a new music product for the iPhone and iPad

Secondary Sources

Reviews, critiques, panel discussions, biographies, and other sources that analyze, summarize, or otherwise repackage information from primary sources

Example: An article on Google News that describes Apple's new music product

Tertiary Sources

A list or compilation of material that pertains to a topic; from sources that include bibliographies, dictionaries, almanacs, indexes, timelines, and inventory lists

Example: A Wikipedia article that presents a timeline of Apple products

Fact-Checking Tips

- **Two sources are better than one.** Cross-check facts between two or more sites.
- **Use common sense.** Claims that seem outlandish require extra verification.
- **Understand your priorities.** For example, you can go to YouTube and view the trailer for *Live Free or Die Hard*. That might be fun, but it might not be relevant for a term paper on cyberterrorism.
- **Use primary sources when possible.** Go to the original text of a speech, check the product manufacturer's Web site, or watch the video clip.
- **Use reputable sources.** The Web contains billions of documents; few of them follow strict journalistic standards for accuracy. Check the author's credentials, look at the general quality of the Web site, and make sure the information is up to date.
- **Maintain a list of the sites you frequently use for fact checking.** You can create a Fact Check folder in your browser's Bookmarks or Favorites list.
- **Nail down your search terms.** When using voice search on your mobile phone, think about an exact set of keywords before you launch Speak Now.

Try It! Fact checking can be fun and it can lead you to all sorts of intriguing factoids as well as to substantive information. Practice your fact-checking skills by completing the following activities:

1. In any given time period, there are controversies that tend to generate false or misleading information that is spread on social media, on news media, and by word of mouth. Identify a controversy that is currently trending. Summarize the opposing viewpoints that underlie the controversy. Specify the major stakeholders on each side of the controversy. Provide an example of a statement made by each of these stakeholders.
2. Fact-checking Web sites operated by Snopes, The Washington Post, PolitiFact, and FactCheck.org provide analyses of controversial statements. Find a statement that is analyzed by four fact-checking sites. Do they all come to the same conclusion about the truth or falsehood of the claim?
3. As controversies escalate, stakeholders sometimes misrepresent their opponents by taking quotations out of context or providing incomplete quotations. Find an example of this kind of misrepresentation. Summarize the example by providing the misleading quotation, its source, the actual quotation, and its source. Explain how you found the example.
4. Fact-checking organizations have been accused of bias in the stories they choose to fact-check and in the way they present conclusions about the veracity of information. This bias is often very subtle. A fact-checking organization may choose to fact-check only one side of an issue, for example, by only checking false claims made by liberals. Another sign of bias is editorializing within the analysis—for example, by using exaggerated wording such as "liar," "whopper," and "bizarre" to describe people or the statements that they make. Examine an analysis from your favorite fact-checking organization. Can you find evidence of bias? Explain why or why not.
5. Suppose you're gathering information for a term paper about the emergence of the Internet, and you come across the following short article posted on Facebook. Internaut Day could be an interesting addition to your report; but before you include material from this article, you should do a fact check. Go online and find answers to the questions in the diagram below.

Happy Internaut Day!

skaljac/Shutterstock.com

This year's calendar will feature a new U.S. national holiday recognizing the day the Internet was invented. Circle August 23rd. That is the date when then Vice President Al Gore threw the switch that opened the Internet to public use.

a. Was the Internet invented on August 23rd?

The Internet has become an indispensable part of everyday life. In declaring this new national holiday, the President stated, "The Internet is not a luxury, it is a necessity."

b. Is this an accurate quote from a U.S. president?

Few people would disagree, especially those who call themselves internauts. An "internaut" is a person who possesses a thorough knowledge of how to use the Internet and its history. The word, a combination of Internet and astronaut, first appeared in a 1999 article about response rates to information posted on the Web.

c. Is there such a thing as an internaut?

A group of hardy internauts has been petitioning presidents, from Nixon to Obama, for national recognition of this special day.

d. What's wrong with including Nixon here?

e. Is Internaut Day a U.S. national holiday?

The hashtag #internautday has become a rallying point for Internet enthusiasts and was instrumental in garnering more than five million digital signatures on the petition to institute a national Internaut Day.

Jenkedco/Shutterstock.com

Technology in Context: Education

The first educational application of computers emerged in the 1960s, when huge mainframes with clunky interfaces introduced students to computer-aided instruction (CAI). Based on operant conditioning research by B. F. Skinner and Ivan Pavlov—remember dogs salivating when a bell rings?—CAI uses basic drill and practice: The computer presents a problem, the student responds, and the computer evaluates the response.

Studies in the 1970s indicated that programmed instruction systems, such as Programmed Logic for Automated Teaching Operations (PLATO), improved test scores, but students soon became bored with the monochrome display and found the regimented drill format boring.

Courtesy of the University of Illinois at Urbana-Champaign Archive

Educators know that students have diverse learning styles and are equipped with varying degrees of background knowledge about a topic. Computers, with all their processing power, should be able to provide individualized instruction.

With promising breakthroughs in artificial intelligence during the 1980s, deploying computers for individualized instruction seemed within easy grasp. The problem, however, was more complex than first expected. Forty-some years later, individualized instruction in the form of adaptive learning has yet to mature.

Simulations have become a popular educational tool. There are educational simulations that mimic real-world situations through narrative descriptions, 2D graphics, or virtual reality. There are also game simulations that educate within an entertaining environment. Flight simulators are an example of real-world simulations, whereas Battlefield 1942 is a first-person shooter game based on historic World War II battles. The line between the two types of simulations is blurred. Is Guts and Bolts an anatomy simulation or a game for designing bizarre organisms?

In the 1990s, when laptops began appearing in classrooms, most educators assumed that equipping every student with a computer would lead to easy gains in academic achievement. The validity of this assumption is nuanced and research does not provide a clear answer. Technology seems to help some students with some subjects and some skills, but it also seems to provide distractions that may affect students' ability to focus.

In elementary schools with laptops or tablet devices in the hands of every child, students may spend up to 50% of class time on their digital devices. Students use their devices to interact with computer-scored workbooks, learn from educational apps, research topics on the Internet, and take standardized tests. The amount of time spent with digital devices has some parents concerned that their children are missing out on valuable in-person interactions with other students and their teachers.

Classroom technology has had a significant influence on K-12 teaching. Learning management systems (LMSs) provide teachers with handy tools for tracking student progress and grading. These tools have also become instrumental in standardizing curricula by providing lesson plans and learning content.

The U.S. Department of Defense Education Activity (DoDEA) operates K-12 schools in U.S. military bases throughout the world. It is important that the curricula for all schools are synchronized so that students in families who are transferred or deployed arrive at a new school where instruction picks up seamlessly at the same place it left off in the previous school. Using a standard LMS-based curriculum provides this continuity.

In higher education, computer use by both students and instructors is widespread. Colleges offer campus-wide Wi-Fi service with Internet access so that laptop-toting students can easily take notes in class, contact instructors via email, use the Internet as a research resource, and run educational software.

Another educational use of computers can be seen in distance education (DE), which is also referred to as remote learning, distance learning, elearning, and virtual learning. Historically, distance education meant correspondence study or courses delivered by radio or television, but the meaning has been broadened to encompass any educational situation in which students and instructors aren't in the same place.

Most DE courses today require students to have access to a computer and an Internet connection. DE courses are offered to K-12 students, college students, military personnel, businesspeople, and the general public.

Many students who choose DE courses do so because they want to learn at their own pace, at a convenient time, and in a location close to home. Parents who deal with the realities of child care, working professionals who cannot relocate to a college town, and students with physical disabilities find distance education handy.

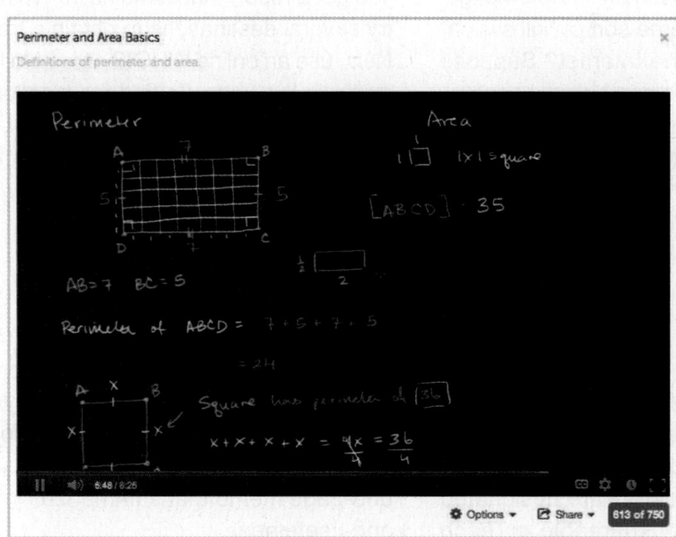

Source: Khan Academy

Distance education has the potential of increasing the pool of students for a by making it financially feasible; for example, an advanced Kanji course could be offered at a Midwestern university with only ten on-campus Japanese majors if enough distance education students can boost enrollment.

The Internet hosts a wide variety of DE courses, both credit-earning and noncredit. Online courses can be presented to a small group of enrollees or to huge numbers of students. The trend toward massive open online courses (MOOCs) gained momentum in 2011 when 160,000 students enrolled in an online course in artificial intelligence offered by Stanford-based Sebastian Thrun and Peter Norvig. MOOCs are currently offered by Udacity, edX, and Coursera. They are "open" to enrollments by almost anyone; students do not have to be formally admitted to a university to participate. Courses are offered by instructors from Stanford, MIT, and other prestigious schools, so they attract students from all over the world.

Some DE courses are offered in real time, whereas other online courses are posted on the Web and can be accessed at any time. Khan Academy, with its distinctively colorful instructional "chalkboard," is representative of this type of any-time access online course. Its video lessons (below) cover a wide range of topics.

The 2020 COVID-19 pandemic tested the limits of distance education. As schools and colleges shut down in-person instruction, online instruction appeared to offer a solution that would allow learning to continue.

School districts quickly cobbled together resources for virtual learning, using videoconferencing, online learning platforms, and educational apps. Teachers who were not trained on digital platforms struggled to quickly learn how to use them. Students were unprepared for the responsibility of directing their own learning. As the pandemic came to an end, there was consensus that for most younger students, the experience with virtual learning was a failure. However, the experience has provided new insight into the effective use of technology at all levels of in-person and virtual learning.

Computers and the Internet have opened opportunities for lifelong learning. Prospective students can use a search engine to find non-credit courses and tutorials for a wide range of topics, including pottery, dog grooming, radio astronomy, desktop publishing, and drumming. Some tutorials are free, and others charge a small fee.

In a society that promotes learning as a lifelong endeavor, the Internet has certainly made it possible for students of all ages to pursue knowledge and skills just by using a computer and an Internet connection.

Flipped Class Projects

Critical Thinking

After completing this module, you should have a comprehensive view of how the Internet works. Based on this knowledge, does it seem possible that there is some sort of "kill switch" that could turn off large swaths of the Internet? Suppose there was a period of extreme political unrest in your country. Would it be conceivable that your country's leader, or perhaps a group of technologically savvy insurgents, could shut down the Internet? Think about the question on your own for a bit, then check online for additional opinions. Does your government have an official statement on this issue?

Group Project

The purpose of this project is to explore file sharing within your school network. Work in groups of three or four, with at least two computers equipped with Wi-Fi in your group. Begin by checking which files and folders are designated as shareable. Make only one folder shareable on each computer, and be sure that it contains no files that would reveal personal information. Next, turn on network discovery (PCs only) and file sharing. Can the computers see each other? Why, or why not? Are the computers able to share files? Discuss why file sharing is or is not possible within the network you are using.

Cyberclassroom

Students sometimes hesitate to state their opinions or ask questions in class. Can network technology offer more opportunities for interaction? For this project, work in groups of five to research three technologies that can be used as classroom response systems, also known as "clickers." Set up one of these systems and try it among the five people in your group. How would you rate it for increasing the quality of your classroom experience?

Multimedia Project

Run Traceroute from your computer to various domains until you get a report that contains 10–15 hops. You might have to try several destinations to obtain a trace that is not too long. Next, use an online WHOIS search to find the location of each router in the trace. To find the location, copy the IP address into the WHOIS search box. Finally, use a Google map to create a visual track of the packets from your computer to their destination.

Resume Builder

Bluetooth technology can be used to exchange electronic business cards. Suppose you're working in the technology department of a corporation and your boss asks you to research the value of this concept for the company's sales representatives. After completing your research, write a one-page memo that summarizes your findings about cost and usefulness.

Globalization

The model for telecommunications in most technologically advanced countries depends on large telecommunication corporations for telephone and Internet access. The infrastructure costs are huge. Can you envision ways in which people in technologically underdeveloped countries could benefit from inexpensive network technologies? Jot down your initial thoughts, then search the Web for additional ideas. Write a one-page executive summary that describes your opinion.

Key Terms

AirDrop 202
ARPANET 173
asymmetric connection 188
bandwidth 165
bandwidth cap 188
bandwidth throttling 188
BitTorrent 224
Bluetooth LE 212
broadband 165
bus topology 166
cable Internet service 192
circuit switching 177
communication channel 162
communication network 161
communication port 178
communication protocol 170
connection speed 187
DCE (data communication equipment) 168
DHCP (Dynamic Host Configuration Protocol) 180
dial-up 193
DNS spoofing 184
domain name 182
domain name servers 183
domain name system (DNS) 182
DSL (digital subscriber line) 194
DTE (data terminal equipment) 168
dual-band 206
dynamic IP addresses 180
error correction 171
Ethernet 203
Ethernet adapter 204
exabyte 174
file hosting services 223
file sharing 215
fixed Internet access 191
FTP (File Transfer Protocol) 222
FTTH (fiber-to-the-home) 194
Guest network 209
handshaking 170
ICANN 174
IEEE 802.3 203
IEEE 802.11 205
Internet backbone 175
Internet exchange points (IXPs) 175
Internet governance 174
Internet infrastructure 175
Internet service providers (ISPs) 175
IP (Internet Protocol) 179
IPv4 (Internet Protocol version 4) 179
IPv6 (Internet Protocol version 6) 179
ISDN (Integrated Services Digital Network) 194
jitter 189
LAN (local area network) 161
latency 188
MAC address 202
mesh topology 166
microwaves 164
mobile broadband 196
mobile hotspot 197
mobile Internet access 191
modem 168
MU-MIMO (multiple-user, multiple-input multiple-output) 206
narrowband 165
NAT (network address translation) 181
network discovery 217
network interface controller 202
NFC 212
node 168
packet 176
packet loss 189
packet switching 177
PAN (personal area network) 161
permissions 219
Ping 188
point-to-point topology 166
portable Internet access 191
private IP address 180
protocol stack 170
public IP address 181
router 168
RF signals 164
RFID 212
satellite Internet service 195
SSID (service set identifier) 208
star topology 166
static IP addresses 179
symmetric connection 188
TCP (Transmission Control Protocol) 178
tethering 197
Traceroute 190
transceiver 164
top-level domain 183
topology 166
UDP (User Datagram Protocol) 178
voiceband modem 193
WAN (wide area network) 161
WAN port 207
WEP (Wired Equivalent Privacy) 208
Wi-Fi 205
Wi-Fi adapter 206
Wi-Fi hotspot 198
wired channels 162
wireless channels 162
wireless encryption 208
wireless encryption key 208
WPA (Wi-Fi Protected Access) 208
WPS (Wi-Fi Protected Setup) 208
Z-Wave 212
ZigBee 212

Interactive Summary

Section A: Networks can be classified by geographical scope as PANs, ______, and WANs. The cables and signals used to transport data from one network device to another are a communication ______. Wired channels include twisted pair wires, ______ cables used for cable television, and ______ -optic cables used for high-capacity trunk lines. Wireless channels use ______ signals and microwaves. Government agencies regulate some wireless ______. The transmission capacity of a channel is referred to as ______. Channels that are capable of downloading at least 25 Mbps are classified as ______. Networks can be configured in various ______, such as star, mesh, point to point, or bus. Any device in a network is referred to as a(n) ______. Data ______ equipment includes computers. Data ______ equipment includes modems and routers. Additional DCEs include hubs, switches, bridges, repeaters, and ______ access points. Networks use physical, transport, and arrival communication ______ to set the rules for efficiently transmitting data and handling errors.

Section B: The Internet is based on a U.S. government project called ______. Today, the Internet is a collection of networks, tied together by common ______. Tier 1 networks form the Internet ______, a system of high-capacity routers and fiber-optic communication links arranged in a(n) ______ topology. Networks that form the Internet are maintained by ______ that offer access to consumers. Before data travels over the Internet, it is divided into ______ by a protocol called ______, which also reassembles the data when it reaches its destination. Every device on the Internet uses an IP address. ______ addresses are 32 bits long, whereas ______ addresses are 128 bits long, providing billions and billions of possible addresses. Addresses are assigned by ______ servers. IP addresses that are temporarily assigned are called ______ addresses, whereas permanent ones are called ______ addresses. ______ IP addresses cannot be routed over the Internet and are usually assigned to devices within LANs. Because it is difficult to remember IP addresses, the ______ name system allocates easy-to-remember names, such as nike.com. ______ -level domains include .com and .edu. The servers that track these names are a vulnerable point in Internet security.

Section C: The speed and quality of Internet connections vary. For email and browsing the Web, speeds of [ ] Mbps are acceptable, whereas Skype video calls require 1.5 Mbps connections. Your bandwidth [ ] is the top speed allowed by your Internet access plan. You can use [ ] to check the latency of an Internet connection. You can use online tools to check for packet loss and [ ], which is the variability in packet latency. Another utility called [ ] reports the path that your data takes to reach its destination. Options for [ ] Internet access include cable, DSL, ISDN, satellite, and fiber-to-the-home. [ ] access options include mobile satellite. [ ] Internet access is available from cellular services. [ ] Internet service offers dependable connections over coaxial and fiber cables. The fastest offering that uses the telephone network is [ ]. GEO satellite Internet service suffers from high rates of [ ]. Mobile broadband service is offered by cell phone companies. Public Wi-Fi [ ] offer yet another Internet access option, though users have to be vigilant about security.

Section D: Local area networks use many of the same network technologies as the Internet, only on a smaller scale. Devices that access LANs are equipped with a network interface [ ] that contains circuitry for wireless or wired connections. Devices also have a physical [ ] address, in addition to the IP addresses acquired from a DHCP server. The most popular wired technology is [ ]. The most popular wireless technology is [ ], which can be configured as a(n) [ ] or star topology. Setting up a LAN and configuring its router is uncomplicated. The first step is to change the standard [ ] to one that is secure. Next, create a(n) [ ] that uniquely identifies the network by name. It is also important to activate wireless [ ] to prevent wireless signals from being intercepted during transmission. A limited-access [ ] network can be created for visitors to use. By activating [ ], the router will be able to assign IP addresses to each device that joins the network. To connect to a secure LAN that is protected by encryption, an encryption [ ], or password, is required. LANs can be used to access data collected by IoT devices and the networks that tie these devices together. Technologies such as RFID, NFC, Bluetooth LE, ZigBee, and Z-Wave offer [ ] -power links, essential for battery-powered devices that can't expend excess amounts of energy transmitting data.

Section E: File sharing allows files containing documents, photos, music, and other data to be accessed from computers other than the one on which they are stored. To access files on a LAN, network [ ] allows your computer to see other devices and permits other devices to see your computer. Sharing the files on your computer poses a security risk, but it is possible to specify [ ] for how your shared files can be used. File sharing is also possible across networks, as when you download files from Internet servers. One technology used for this purpose is [ ], which provides a way to transfer files over any TCP/IP network. Another file sharing protocol called [ ] distributes the role of a file server across a collection of dispersed computers.

Interactive Situation Questions

1. You're setting up an Ethernet wired network using a router. To access the router and its configuration software, you open your [ ] and type the router's IP address.

2. You're trying to figure out if your computer has a built-in Ethernet port. You see the port pictured to the right. Is that the port you should use for your Ethernet plug? Yes or no? [ ]

3. You're shopping for a new router and are attracted by the advertising for a 600N model. Upon examining the specifications, you see that the router transmits 300+300, so you know it is using [ ] broadcast channels.

4. You arrive at work and one of your co-workers tells you that the router is down. Is it correct to surmise that your workstation will not be able to access other workstations, but will be able to access the Internet? Yes or no? [ ]

5. You have a small network in your house that uses a wireless router. For the past week, you've seen an SUV parked outside, and its occupant seems to be using a laptop computer. The first step you should take to discover if this person has hacked into your network is: a) knock on the car window and ask; b) call the police; or c) use your router utilities to check who is connected to your network. [ ]

6. You've set up a network using some new equipment and a few old Wi-Fi adapters given to you by your roommates. One of the adapters is equipped only for WEP, whereas all the other adapters support WPA2. Your roommate tells you that in order to use all the adapters, you'll have to disable wireless encryption. Is your roommate right? [ ]

7. You're accustomed to using Dropbox to share files over the Internet; but at your new job, files are stored on an FTP server. This is not a problem. You know that you can access work files using FTP [ ] software such as FileZilla.

8. You've got class notes and you don't mind sharing them with your roommates, but you'd prefer that they don't change the files. You can keep your notes intact if you assign [ ] permission to those files.

9. Suppose you're connected to a Wi-Fi hotspot. When you use File Explorer, you see the names of other computers listed under Network. Oops! You must have network [ ] turned on.

10. You're expecting visitors who will be demanding Internet access. Before they arrive, you can activate a Guest network that has its own [ ] and a different password from the one used with the network where you store all your files.

Lab: Hack Your Net

Hackers and government snoopers love networks. Data flows freely. Most of it is not encrypted. Networks are a paradise for anyone who wants to peer into our private lives. But what do these snoopers actually find, and how much data must they sort through to find anything valuable? Let's take a look at the data flowing on your LAN and the data that's exchanged over the Internet.

Requirements:

For this lab, you'll need a computer running macOS or Microsoft Windows. Your computer should be connected to a Wi-Fi network. The instructions are generalized; they provide helpful guidelines, but not specific steps. You may have to explore a bit to find all the tools needed to complete the assignment, but that is all part of the learning experience.

There are two versions of this assignment: one for computers running Windows and one for computers running macOS. The Windows version begins on this page. The macOS version begins on the next page.

Windows Assignment:

❶ Open Task Manager's Performance tab to view Wi-Fi activity.

The easiest way to open Task Manager is by typing its name into a search box on the Start menu or Home screen. You can also open Control Panel and access Task Manager from there.

Once open, select the Performance tab and use the More Details link, if necessary, to display the graph and network statistics.

Arrange your desktop into two windows: one with Task Manager and one with a browser. Now navigate to several Web sites and note what happens in Task Manager.

What are typical speeds for sending and receiving data on your network?

❷ Monitor Wi-Fi throughput.

Continue watching the Wi-Fi graph when you are not using the browser. Why do you think there is Wi-Fi activity even when you are not actively using network services?

❸ Switch to the Processes tab.

The Network column of the Processes tab displays the applications that are active. Can you determine which applications are sending and receiving data over the network even when you are not actively using network services?

❹ Return to the Performance tab and select the Open Resource Monitor link. Select the Network link.

This set of monitoring tools gives you another view of the data that's traveling to and from your computer. Look at the list for Processes with Network Activity.

Do the active processes here match the processes you identified in Step 3?

❺ Monitor TCP connections.

Expand the list of TCP connections, if necessary, by selecting the ⌄ button. The Remote Address column displays the IP addresses of servers that have sent packets to your computer.

Type a few of these IP addresses into a browser address bar. Where do they lead?

❻ Open the Command Prompt window and enter the command netstat -e.

To open the Command Prompt window, you can enter cmd in the Windows search box. When the window opens, enter netstat -e.

The netstat command displays the number of bytes sent and received. It also displays the number of packets you've sent and received.

Unicast packets are simple TCP packets of data. Non-unicast packets are broadcast or multicast to multiple network nodes—typically from DHCP queries and Windows services.

You can see that snoopers have to examine lots of packets to find specific data. Record the number of unicast packets your computer has sent and received.

Lab: Hack Your Net

macOS Assignment:

❶ Open Activity Monitor's Network tab to view network activity.

The easiest way to open Activity Monitor is to select the Applications folder from the dock, select the Utilities folder, then select Activity Monitor.

Once the Activity Monitor window is open, select the Network button.

Arrange your desktop into two windows: one with Activity Monitor and one with a browser. Now navigate to several Web sites and note what happens in Activity Monitor.

The graph uses red for sent packets and blue for received packets. Data transport speeds are listed as "Data received/sec" and "Data sent/sec."

What are typical speeds for sending and receiving data on your network?

❷ Monitor network activity.

Continue watching the graph when you are not using the browser. Why do you think there is activity even when you are not actively using network services?

❸ Look at the process chart above the graph.

The Sent Bytes and Rcvd Bytes columns of the chart list active processes and show when they send or receive data.

Can you determine which applications are sending and receiving data over the network even when you are not actively using network services?

❹ Get ready to use the Netstat command by selecting the Applications folder and then selecting Terminal. At the prompt, type netstat -lb | head. (Be sure to use the | key, not the ! mark.)

Look at the beginning of the report. The columns contain the following data:

- Proto: The protocol, which is TCP or UDP.
- Rec-Q and Send-Q: Data that is queued up for sending or receiving.
- Local Address: The origin of outgoing packets.
- Foreign Address: The source of incoming packets. The address ends with its protocol; https indicates a secure Web protocol.
- (state): ESTABLISHED is an active connection. A socket is CLOSED. A CLOSE-WAIT socket is in the process of closing.
- rxbytes and txbytes: The number of bytes received by or transmitted from the foreign server.

For three of the foreign addresses, use an IP address lookup to see if you can associate them with your recent online activity.

Answer the following questions:

1. How many foreign addresses are listed?
2. What is the IP address of the server that is sending the most bytes?
3. What is the protocol of the server you identified in item 2?
4. Can you identify the domain name of the most active foreign server using an IP lookup? If so, what is it?

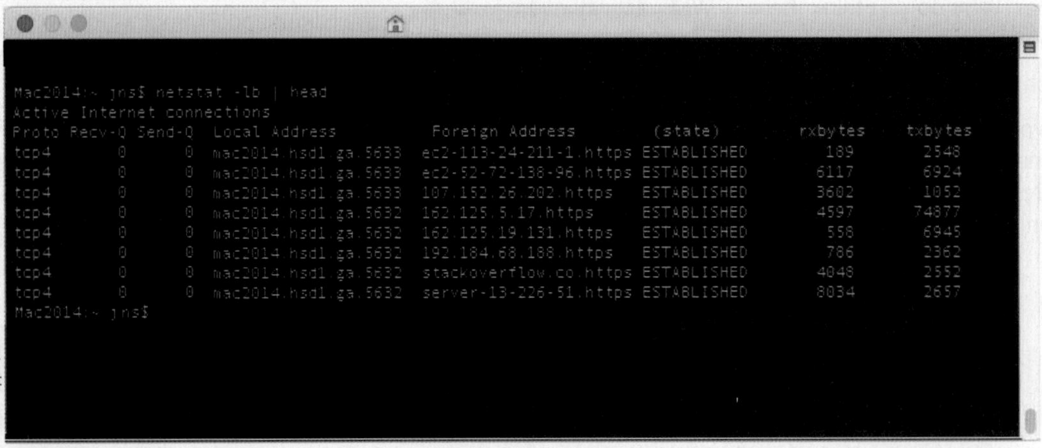

```
Mac2014:~ jns$ netstat -lb | head
Active Internet connections
Proto Recv-Q Send-Q  Local Address          Foreign Address        (state)         rxbytes    txbytes
tcp4       0      0  mac2014.hsdl.ga.5633   ec2-113-24-211-1.https ESTABLISHED         189       2548
tcp4       0      0  mac2014.hsdl.ga.5633   ec2-52-72-138-96.https ESTABLISHED        6117       6924
tcp4       0      0  mac2014.hsdl.ga.5633   107.152.26.202.https   ESTABLISHED        3602       1052
tcp4       0      0  mac2014.hsdl.ga.5632   162.125.5.17.https     ESTABLISHED        4597      74877
tcp4       0      0  mac2014.hsdl.ga.5632   162.125.19.131.https   ESTABLISHED         558       6945
tcp4       0      0  mac2014.hsdl.ga.5632   192.184.68.188.https   ESTABLISHED         786       2362
tcp4       0      0  mac2014.hsdl.ga.5632   stackoverflow.co.https ESTABLISHED        4048       2552
tcp4       0      0  mac2014.hsdl.ga.5632   server-13-226-51.https ESTABLISHED        8034       2657
Mac2014:~ jns$
```

Extra Credit Lab: Hack Your Net Part II

But what's in those packets? You were able to use utilities to see the number of packets flowing into and out of your computer. But what is a packet, exactly? What would a hacker see by using a packet sniffer to tap into your wireless communications? What do those government snoopers gather with their sophisticated surveillance? In this extra credit lab, you'll get a glimpse of the packet landscape.

Requirements:

For this lab, you'll need a computer running macOS or Microsoft Windows. Your computer should be connected to a Wi-Fi network. This part of the lab requires you to download and install software; make sure that you have permission to do so. You will need administrative privileges, so you must be logged in as an administrator.

Assignment:

1 Download and install the free Wireshark packet sniffer application.

Make sure you obtain the download from a trusted site!

The official Wireshark site is *www.wireshark.org*.

There are versions of Wireshark for Windows and for macOS. Be sure to download the correct version.

2 Verify that you are logged in using an administrator account, then start Wireshark.

3 Set up a capture.

When the Welcome screen appears, use the "interface" pull-down menu to select Wired or Wireless, depending on the type of network connection you are using.

Click the Start option by selecting the blue fin icon on the menu bar.

4 View the capture report.

The capture report is displayed in three sections, as shown in the figure below.

Selecting one of the packets in the Packet List displays details in the Packet Details and Packet Bytes sections.

The Packet Bytes section contains a capture of what is contained in your packets. That's what snoopers see!

5 Take a screenshot of your Wireshark window.

If you're using Windows, press the PrtSc key, then start Paint and paste the screenshot into the Paint window. On a Mac, use Command-Shift-3 to capture the screen to your desktop. Save your screenshot with the file name *Module3XtraLab* followed by your name.

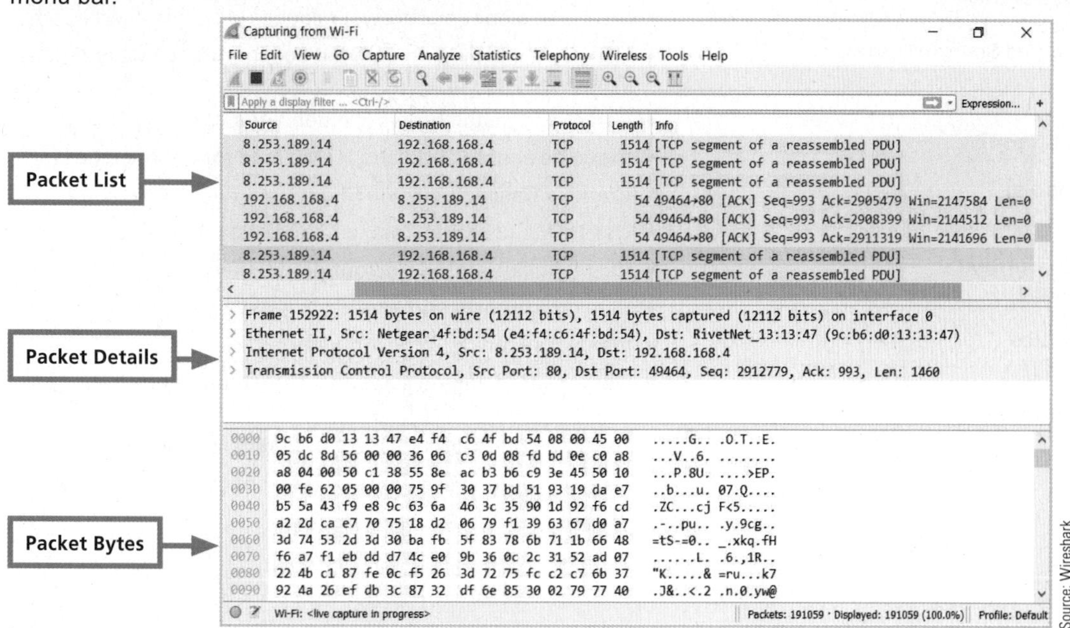

Source: Wireshark

4 The Web

Module Contents

The Web is a platform for free speech, if you don't mind it being tracked by advertisers, recorded by government snoopers, and stored indefinitely by search engines. Learn how to navigate the Web without leaving a trail.

Try It! Apply what you learn.

- Identify text and graphics links on Web pages.
- Manipulate URLs in the address box to recover from bad links.
- Shorten URLs for use in social media posts and short messages.
- Expand short URLs to see where they originate before clicking them.
- Designate a default browser.
- Choose a home page for your browser.
- Customize your browser's predictive services and tabs.
- Set bookmarks on the browser toolbar.
- Determine if your browser is storing passwords.
- View and clear your browser cache.
- Use private browsing to avoid accumulating evidence of Web sites visited.
- Select and install browser extensions.
- View the source code and HTML tags for a Web page.
- Create a Cascading Style Sheet for a Web site.
- Use HTML to create, test, and post a basic Web page.
- View cookies stored on your digital devices.
- Block third-party cookies.
- Identify secure HTTPS connections.
- Use a search engine's advanced search options to formulate queries.
- Manage your search history to maintain privacy.
- Use appropriate citations for Web content incorporated in your own work.

4
The Web

Pre-Check

Gauge your level of expertise. The answers are in the module.

On a Web page, this pointer indicates a(n)

____

This browser icon means

____

This is an example of a(n)

____

Third parties use these to display targeted ads based on your browsing activity.

____

Google uses this icon for

____

Web source documents end with one of these extensions.

____

____

List three search operators:

____

____

____

When you see this icon in the browser address box, what protocol is being used?

____

What type of Web encryption uses two keys?

____

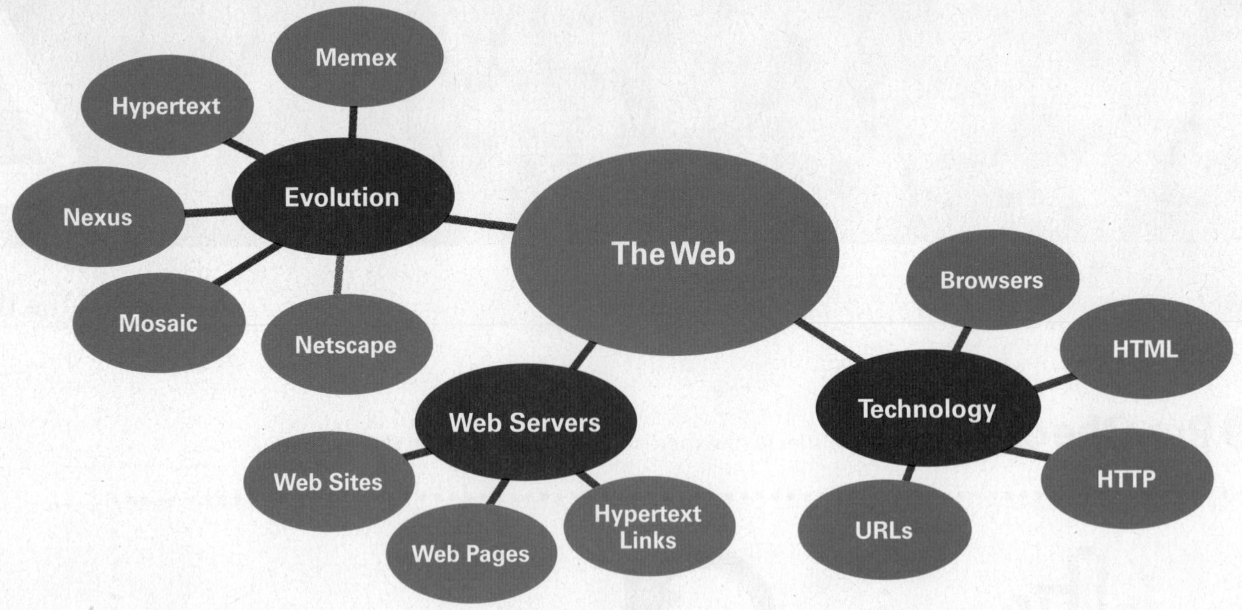

Section A Web Basics

Objectives

- List six essential technologies that are the foundation of the World Wide Web.
- Summarize the key events in the emergence of the modern Web.
- Draw a diagram showing the hierarchy of the following: Web server, Web sites, Web pages, hypertext links.
- Describe a situation in which bidirectional hypertext links would improve your online research experience.
- Give an example of the URL for a Web site home page, one for a Web page that is stored in a folder, and one for a Web page that is produced based on a query.
- State four rules for correctly typing URLs.
- Define the term *linkrot.*
- Describe a situation in which you might use a short URL service.
- Explain the difference between a URL and a domain name.

There were visionaries who dreamed of some way to link libraries of knowledge and navigate through them with the ease of floating down a lazy river. Those visionaries never imagined the tsunami of information that's awash on today's Web. To help you navigate all that the Web has to offer, this module begins with the basics: hypertext, Web content, and URLs.

Terminology

World Wide Web	Web site	hypertext links	URL
Web browser	Web server	unidirectional links	linkrot
hypertext	Web page	bidirectional links	short URLs

Web Overview

The Web is not the Internet. Just as cellular towers are different from the text messages you send over them, the Internet is different from the Web. The Internet is a global data communications network. The Web is just one of the many technologies that use the Internet to distribute data.

▶ **What are the key elements of Web technology?** The **World Wide Web** (usually referred to simply as *the Web*) is a collection of HTML documents, images, videos, and sound files that can be linked to each other and accessed over the Internet using a protocol called HTTP.

The Web is accessed from desktop computers, laptops, tablets, and smartphones using software commonly called a browser. A **Web browser** is client software that displays Web page elements and handles links between those pages. Popular browsers include Microsoft Edge, open source Mozilla Firefox, Google Chrome, and Apple Safari. Figure 4-1 lists the essential Web technologies that you'll explore in this module.

Terminology

The process of accessing a Web site is sometimes referred to as *surfing the Web* and visitors are called *Web surfers*.

4

Figure 4-1: Essential Web technologies

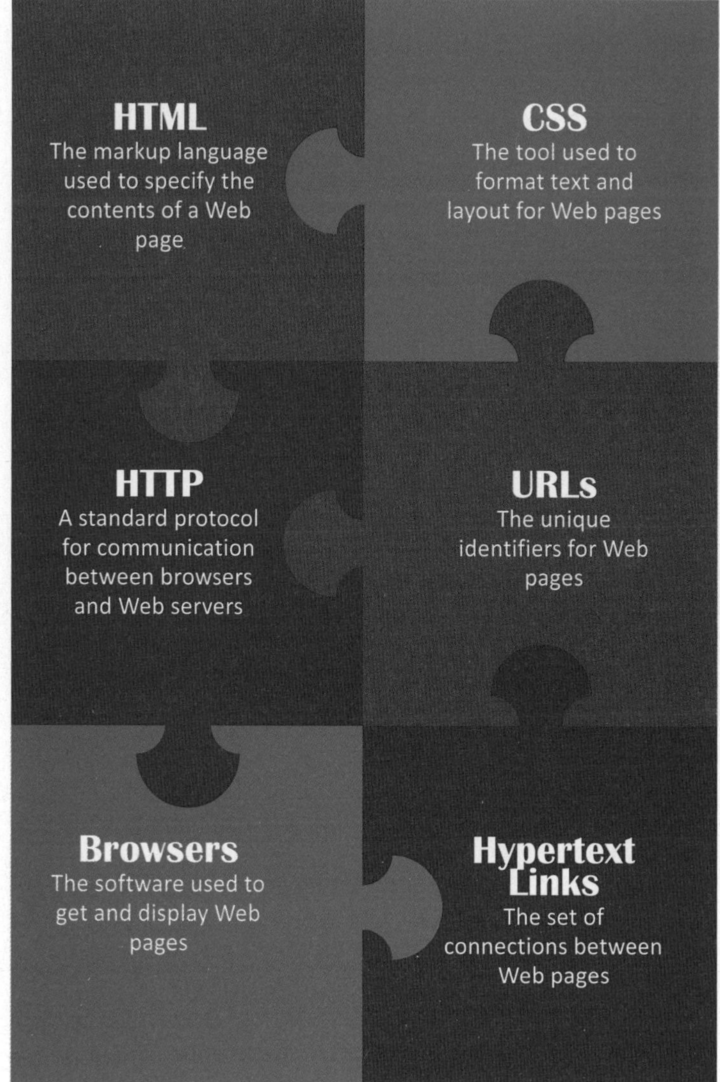

HTML
The markup language used to specify the contents of a Web page
CSS
The tool used to format text and layout for Web pages
HTTP
A standard protocol for communication between browsers and Web servers
URLs
The unique identifiers for Web pages
Browsers
The software used to get and display Web pages
Hypertext Links
The set of connections between Web pages

QuickCheck

Content is the main emphasis for which of the following?

a. The Internet

b. The Web

c. CSS

d. URLs

Evolution

According to MIT researcher Matthew Gray, in June 1993 there were a total of 130 Web sites containing linked documents. By January 1996, there were 100,000 Web sites. Today, there are more than a hundred million active Web sites and new sites appear every day. The remarkable story of such explosive growth began more than half a century ago.

How did the Web evolve? In 1945, an engineer named Vannevar Bush described a microfilm-based machine called the Memex that linked associated information or ideas through "trails." By following trails from one document to another, readers could track down ideas from within an extensive library of information. Bush's Memex was hypothetical, however; the microfilm readers and analog computers of the time were not suitable for such a complex task.

The idea of linked documents resurfaced in the mid-1960s when Harvard graduate Ted Nelson coined the term **hypertext** to describe a computer system that could store literary documents, link them according to logical relationships, and allow readers to comment on and annotate what they read. Nelson sketched the diagram in Figure 4-2 to explain his idea of a computer-based "web" of "links."

Figure 4-2: Ted Nelson's sketch of Project Xanadu

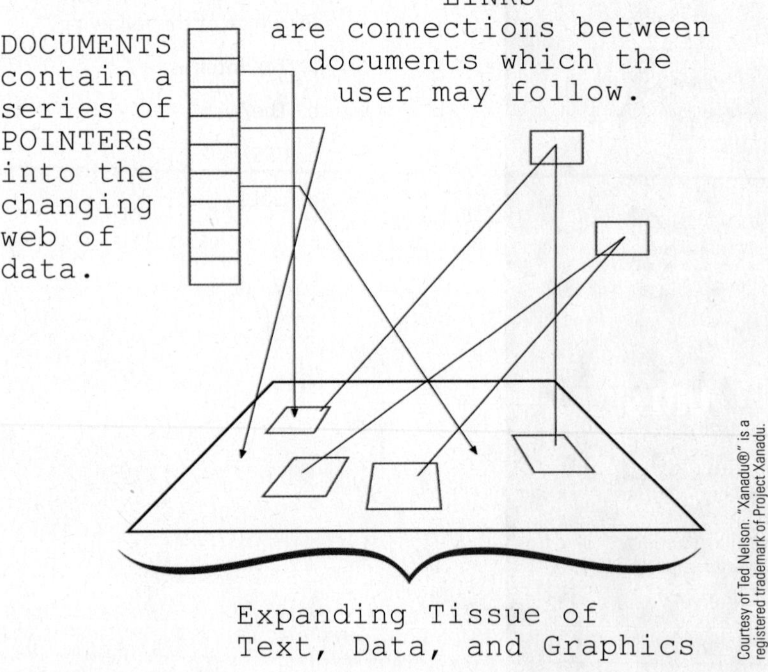

Ted Nelson sketched his vision for Project Xanadu in the 1960s. Notice his use of the terms *web* and *links*, which are now familiar to everyone who uses the World Wide Web.

QuickCheck

What do the rectangles in Figure 4-2 represent?

a. The Web

b. The Internet

c. Web sites

d. Linked documents

Fast-forward to 1990 when a British scientist named Tim Berners-Lee developed specifications for URLs, HTML, and HTTP—the foundation technologies of today's Web. Berners-Lee also created Web browser software originally called WorldWideWeb but later renamed Nexus (Figure 4-3).

Figure 4-3: The first Web browser

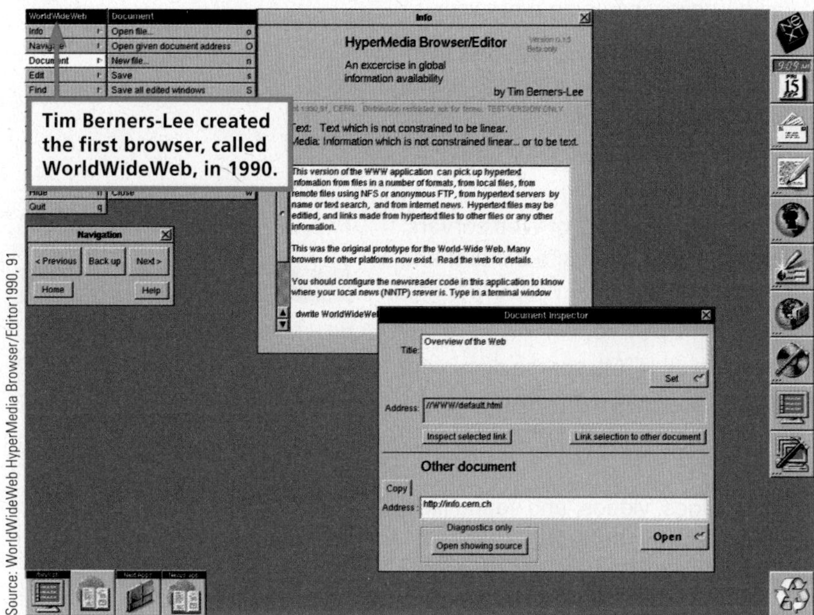

Source: WorldWideWeb HyperMedia Browser/Editor1990, 91

Nexus ran on NeXT computers and was not available to the huge installed base of IBM PCs. In 1993, Marc Andreessen and his colleagues at the University of Illinois created Mosaic, a browser that ran on several computing platforms, including Windows. Andreessen later formed his own company and produced a browser called Netscape (Figure 4-4), which put the Web into the hands of millions of consumers.

Figure 4-4: The browser that popularized the Web

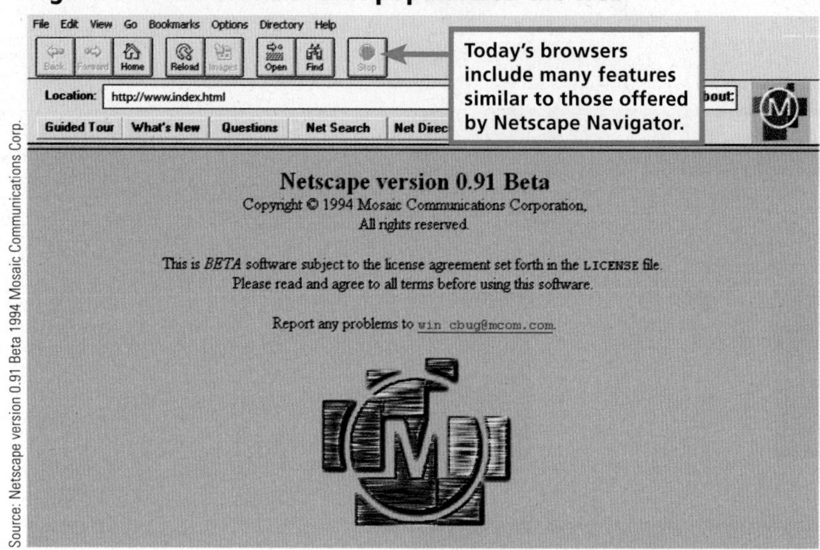

Source: Netscape version 0.91 Beta 1994 Mosaic Communications Corp.

Netscape Navigator was the first browser in widespread use. Can you recognize elements of the Netscape window that are similar to elements of the browser you use today?

Web Sites

Web sites are the cyberspace equivalent of shops and offices in a city's commercial district. A home page serves as the Web site's doorway and links to all the Web pages that the site offers.

▶ What is a Web site? A **Web site** typically contains a collection of related information organized and formatted so it can be accessed using a browser.

You are probably familiar with informational Web sites such as HowStuffWorks.com, CNN.com, ESPN.com, and Wikipedia.org. Web sites can also offer Web-based applications, such as Google Docs, and social networking, such as Facebook. Another popular category of Web sites includes ecommerce stores such as Amazon, eBay, and Etsy.

The activities that take place at Web sites are under the control of Web servers. A **Web server** is an Internet-based computer that stores Web site content and accepts requests from browsers. One server can host multiple Web sites, and some Web sites are spread across multiple servers.

▶ What is a Web page? A **Web page** is based on an HTML source document that is stored as a file on a Web server. The source document contains the text for a Web page interspersed with coding for how to display text and any additional visual or auditory elements.

The content of Web pages can incorporate text, images, videos, and sound files, as well as elements pulled on the fly from databases (Figure 4-5).

QuickCheck

How many Web sites are stored on a Web server?

a. None

b. One

c. A maximum of 10

d. One or more

Figure 4-5: Web servers collect Web page content from many sources

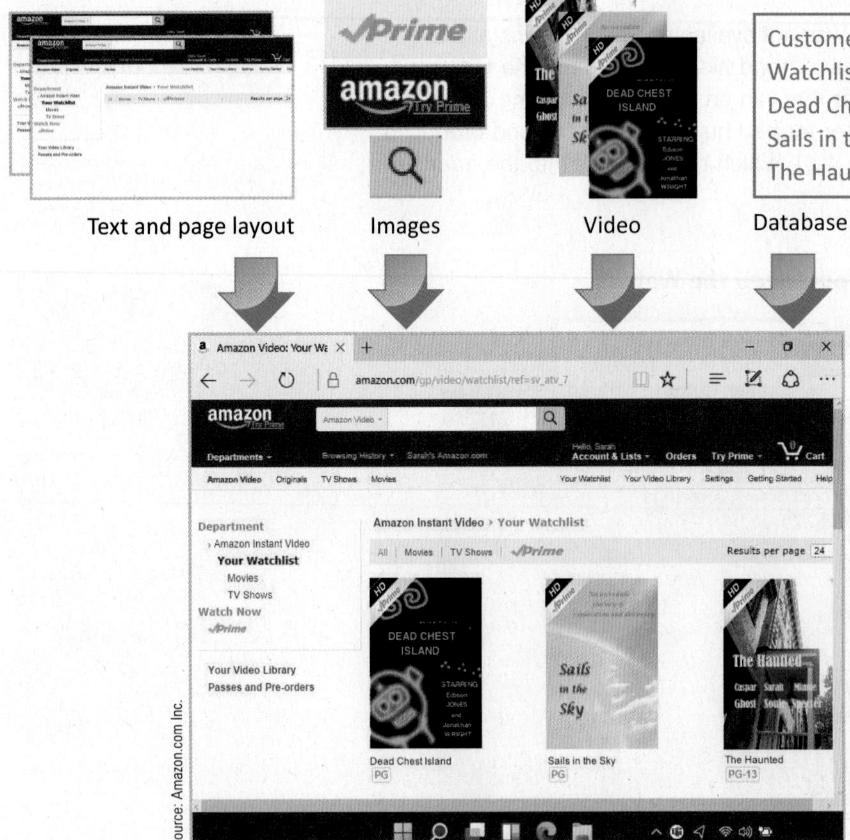

4

Hypertext Links

Most of us have used the Web so much that we've become conditioned to the way it works. We rarely stop to consider how it might be improved. But the way hypertext links function might have been quite different if Ted Nelson's vision of the Web had come to fruition.

▶ **What are hypertext links?** Web pages are connected by **hypertext links** (commonly referred to simply as *links*). For example, a syllabus can contain links to other documents, such as lecture notes or an assigned reading.

Links are commonly indicated by underlined or colored text, but a photo, button, tab, or other object on a Web page can act as the source of a link. On conventional screens, the mouse pointer changes to a hand when it rolls over a link (Figure 4-6). On touchscreens, users often have to experiment with tapping and swiping to discover links.

QuickCheck

Where did the term *hypertext* originate?

a. From Ted Nelson

b. From Microsoft

c. From IBM

d. From a science fiction novel

Figure 4-6: Finding the links

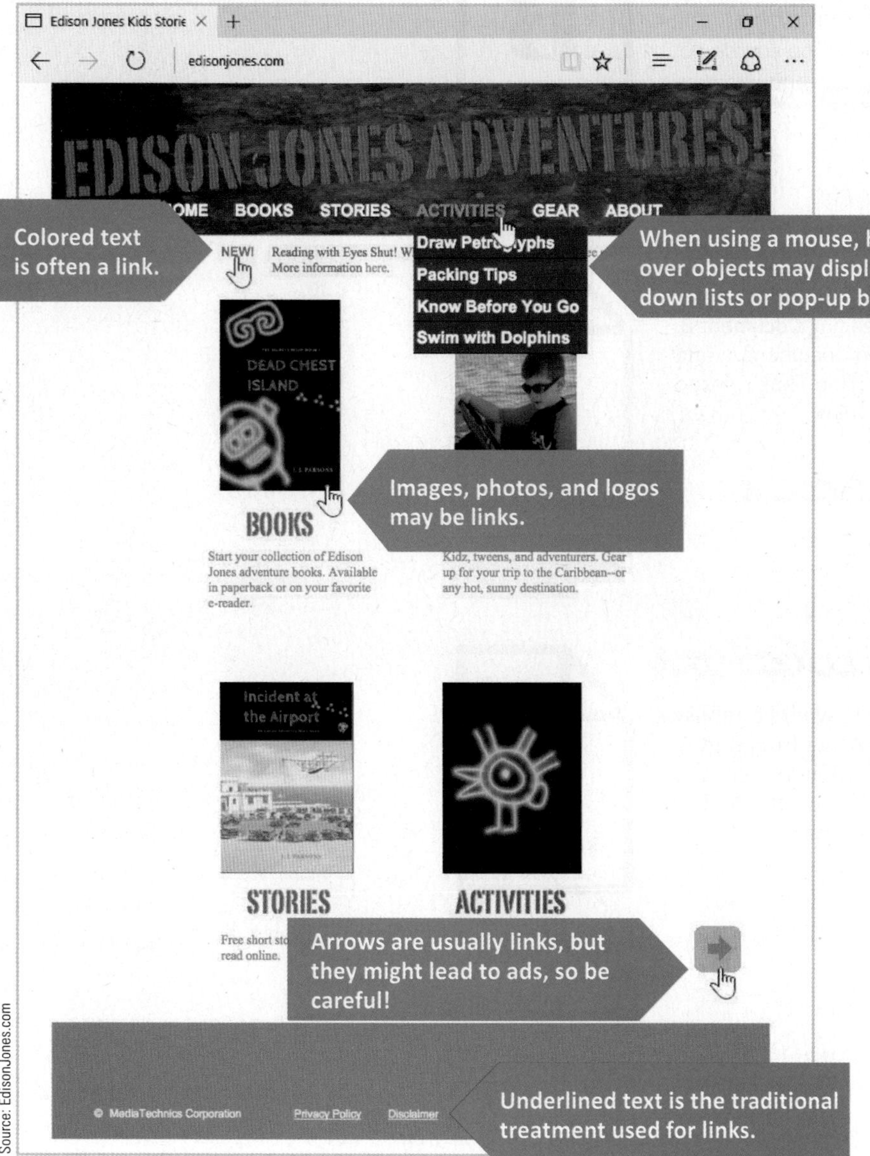

Source: EdisonJones.com

Try It!

Connect to Wikipedia and look up *India*. What kinds of links do you find on that page?

How do links work? In today's Web, Web pages have **unidirectional links**—so Document A links to Document B, but not vice versa. Unidirectional links were a key factor in simplifying early Web prototypes so that they could be feasibly implemented. However, this type of link limits the ability to trace back to related material.

Bidirectional links connect two documents using a two-way link that can be followed from either document. A Web with bidirectional links, such as that envisioned by Ted Nelson's Project Xanadu, was too complex to successfully construct. Figure 4-7 illustrates the difference between unidirectional links and bidirectional links.

QuickCheck

Today's Web uses ___________ links.

a. bidirectional

b. unidirectional

c. A/B

d. X

Figure 4-7: Unidirectional and bidirectional links

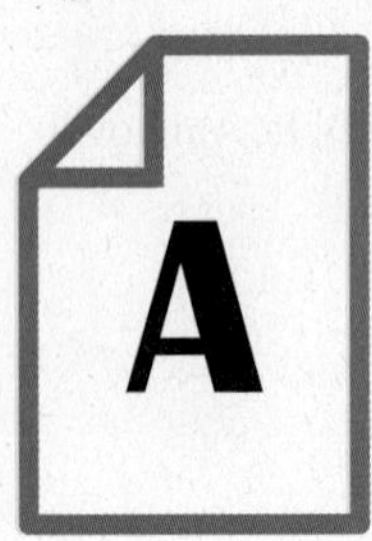

Document A contains a link to Document B. When reading Document A, you can easily follow the link to the related material in Document B.

But the link from Document A to Document B is unidirectional. When you are reading Document B, there is no link to Document A, and you may never find that related material.

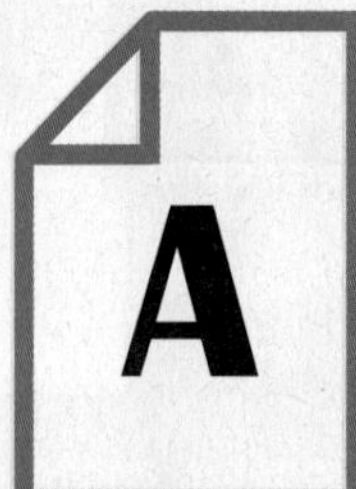

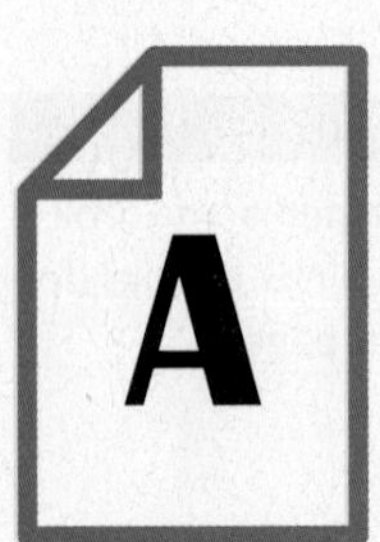

Bidirectional links would establish links from A to B and from B to A. Regardless of which document you viewed first, a link would exist to the other document.

URLs

URLs identify Web sites and Web pages. They offer clues about what pages contain. Or do they? URLs can be long and complex. They can also be shortened to disguise what they contain. The security of your digital devices may depend on your understanding of URLs and their components.

What are the components of a URL? Every Web page has a unique address called a **URL** (Uniform Resource Locator, pronounced "you are ELL"). For example, the URL for the Cable News Network (CNN) Web site is *https://www.cnn.com.* Most URLs begin with http:// or https://.

The pages for a Web site are stored in folders on the Web server. The names of folders and subfolders that hold a Web page are reflected in the URL. For example, the CNN site might store entertainment news stories in a folder called Showbiz. The URL for that folder would be *https://www.cnn.com/showbiz/*.

The file name of a specific Web page always appears last in the URL. Web page files usually have an .htm or .html extension, indicating that the page was created with Hypertext Markup Language. The main page for a Web site is usually called Index.html. Figure 4-8 identifies the parts of a URL.

4

QuickCheck

What is typically the name of the file that holds the main page for a Web site?

a. Main.html

b. Movies.html

c. Index.html

d. Site.html

Figure 4-8: URL components

https://www.cnn.com/showbiz/movies.htm

https://	www.cnn.com	/showbiz/	movies.htm
Web protocol	Web server name	Folder name	File name and extension

Do all URLs reference pages? Some URLs contain a search string rather than the name of an HTML document. Suppose you are at the CNN site and want to find the latest music news. Entering *music* in the search box produces an address that includes a question mark and a query string. The Web page that's displayed is a result of the search (Figure 4-9).

Figure 4-9: A URL can contain a query string

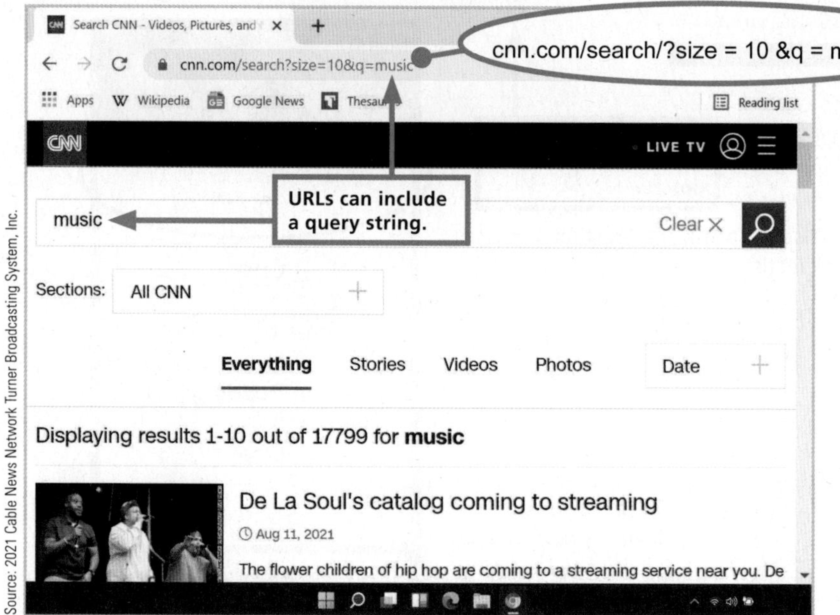

Try It!

Connect to Amazon.com and search for *Mountain Bikes*. Is there a question mark in the query string?

▸ What are the rules for correctly typing a URL? When typing URLs in the browser address box, there are a few rules to remember:

- A URL never contains spaces, even after a punctuation mark, so do not type any spaces within a URL. An underline symbol is sometimes used to give the appearance of a space between words in a file name—for example, *www.detroit.com/top_10.html*.
- When typing a URL, the http:// or https:// can be omitted, so *www.cnn.com* works just as well as *https://www.cnn.com*.
- Be sure to use the correct type of slash—always a forward slash (/).
- Duplicate the URL's capitalization exactly. Some Web servers are case sensitive. On these servers, typing *www.cmu.edu/Info.html* (with an uppercase *I*) will not locate the Web page that's stored on the Web server as *www.cmu.edu/info.html* (with a lowercase *i*).

Try It!

Can you connect to the CNN Web site without using https:// in the address? Can you connect without using www?

▸ Are links URLs? No, but a link contains the URL that points to another Web page. Before linking to a page, for security reasons, you might want to preview the URL for the page. Figure 4-10 shows how.

Figure 4-10: Look before you click

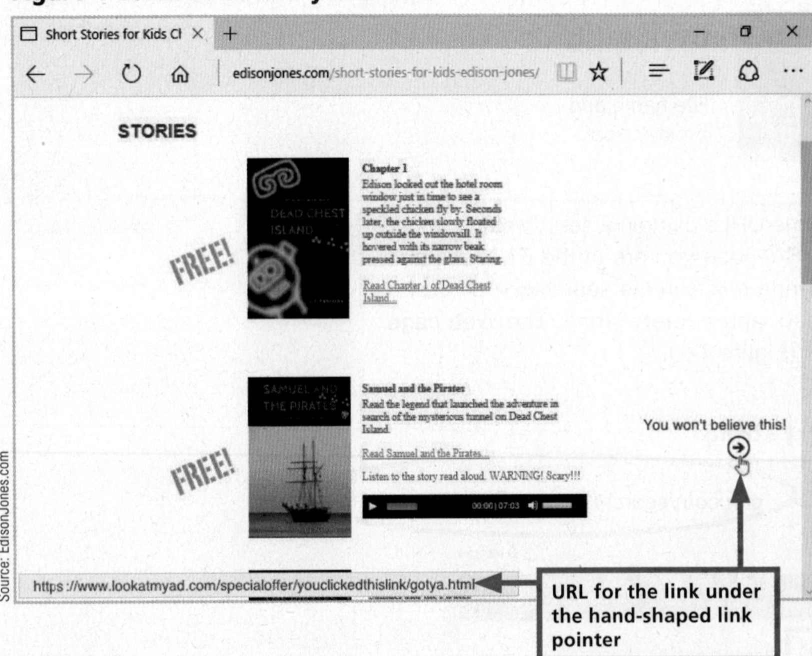

When using a mouse, hovering over a link displays a link preview that indicates where the link leads.

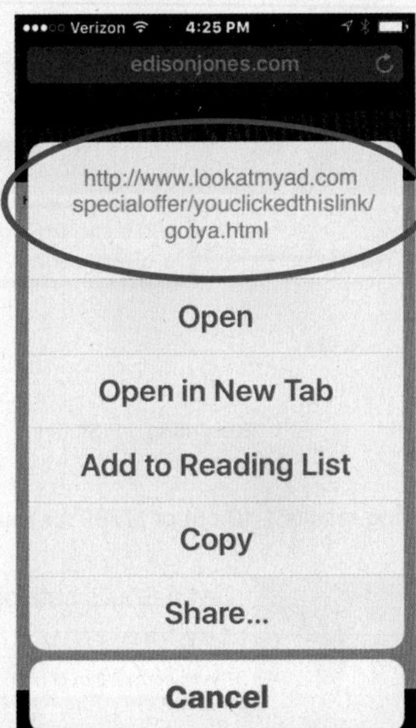

On a touchscreen device, pressing and holding a link may display the URL.

How are URLs related to domain names? URLs contain a domain name. For example, the URL *https://www.nike.com/fitness* contains the domain name nike.com. Some domain names are based on the name of the business or organization that operates the Web site. But many domain names and Web site URLs provide no indication of a site's real owner. To discover that information, you can use a WHOIS search, as explained in Module 3.

Can I manipulate URLs? When you click a link, your browser links to the URL and displays the associated Web page. Sometimes links lead to pages that are no longer available, a situation known as **linkrot**. Links that no longer work are called broken links or dead links. If you reach a dead link, you can sometimes manipulate the URL to locate similar material that remains on the Web site. Figure 4-11 illustrates the technique.

QuickCheck

Bikes.com is an example of a ___________.

a. URL

b. hypertext link

c. domain name

d. Web page

4

Figure 4-11: Getting past linkrot

www.bleacherreport.com/articles/nfl/injuries/new-helmets.htm

www.bleacherreport.com/articles/nfl/injuries/

When a Web page no longer exists at the specified URL, edit the link in the address box by backtracking to the first slash. Press the Enter key. The modified link may take you to a list of content similar to the original link.

www.SavannahBookFestival.com/events/2023/calendar.htm

www.SavannahBookFestival.com/events/2024/calendar.htm

You can also experiment with changing words or numbers in a URL—a technique that often works for locating materials for a different date or page number.

Try It!

Can you connect to *https://www.sec.gov/news/pressrelease/2016-500.html*? What happens if you change the URL in the address bar to end with 50, instead of 500?

Why are URLs so long? When visiting Web sites, glance at the address bar from time to time. Many of the URLs are long and complex. Here's a long URL that's the Web page for a short article about UV clothing:

http://www.edisonjones.com/kid-gear-swim-shop/sun-safety-uv-clothing-kids.html

Is there any way to shorten URLs? Long URLs can be a problem. The longer they are, the easier it is to make a typing error. Also, long URLs consume too many characters in short messaging applications such as Twitter.

Several services, such as Bitly and TinyURL, create **short URLs**. You can request a short URL by entering the normal URL at one of these services. The service will generate a short URL. The original URL and the short URL are stored in a translation table on the service's server. Figure 4-12 illustrates how short URLs work.

Figure 4-12: Shorten that URL

1. Copy and paste the full URL into the box provided by a short URL service such as TinyURL.
2. The service produces a short URL.
3. The short URL is stored on the server along with the full URL.
4. Links to the short URL are directed to the server, which forwards the link to the full URL.

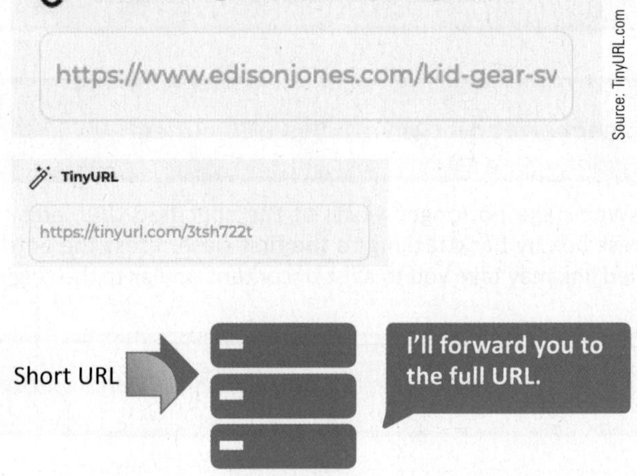

Why use a short URL? Suppose you want to share an article or video with your friends on Twitter. Just find the Twitter icon and click it, right? Twitter automatically shortens the URL to 22 characters.

Sure, that works on Twitter and a few other social media sites, but what if you want to share something from a site without Share links to social media sites? You can copy the link and obtain a short URL before pasting it into an email message or social media post.

Posting a short URL takes up less space in a Tweet or post. Also, if you expect that recipients might manually type the URL, they will make fewer mistakes when typing a short one.

Try It!

Use TinyURL or Bitly to create a short URL for an article or video you've found on the Web. Mail the link to yourself. Test the link. Does it produce the article or video you specified?

Do short URLs expire? Short URL services may lead consumers to believe that all short URLs will last forever, but they last only as long as the service maintains its servers. If a service ceases operations, the short URLs maintained on its servers will no longer work.

Short URLs are sometimes used to disguise the real address of a Web site that is illegitimate. This practice has resulted in short URL services being blocked by Web hosts and ISPs. When URL services are blocked, the short URLs on their servers will not work.

You should be aware that short URLs may lead to questionable Web sites and scams. Never click a short URL link in an email message if you are not certain it leads to a legitimate site. As shown in Figure 4-13, several sites, such as checkshorturl.com and getlinkinfo.com, provide ways to check the actual destination of a shortened URL before you click it.

Try It!

Can you discover where the short URL *https://tinyurl.com/y7rvussm* goes without actually visiting the site?

Figure 4-13: Expand that URL

Source: CheckShortURL.com

Online services such as checkshorturl expand short URLs and display the original, full URL.

QuickQuiz Section A

1. The World Wide Web is one of the many technologies that uses the [__________] infrastructure to distribute data.
2. The basis for Ted Nelson's original idea for [__________] was to use bidirectional links to navigate between digital documents.
3. A(n) [__________] symbol in a URL indicates a query.
4. In the URL *https://www.musicwire.com/bit.htm*, the [__________] name is musicwire.com.
5. *Https://bit.ly/MY67dd93B* is an example of a(n) [__________] URL.

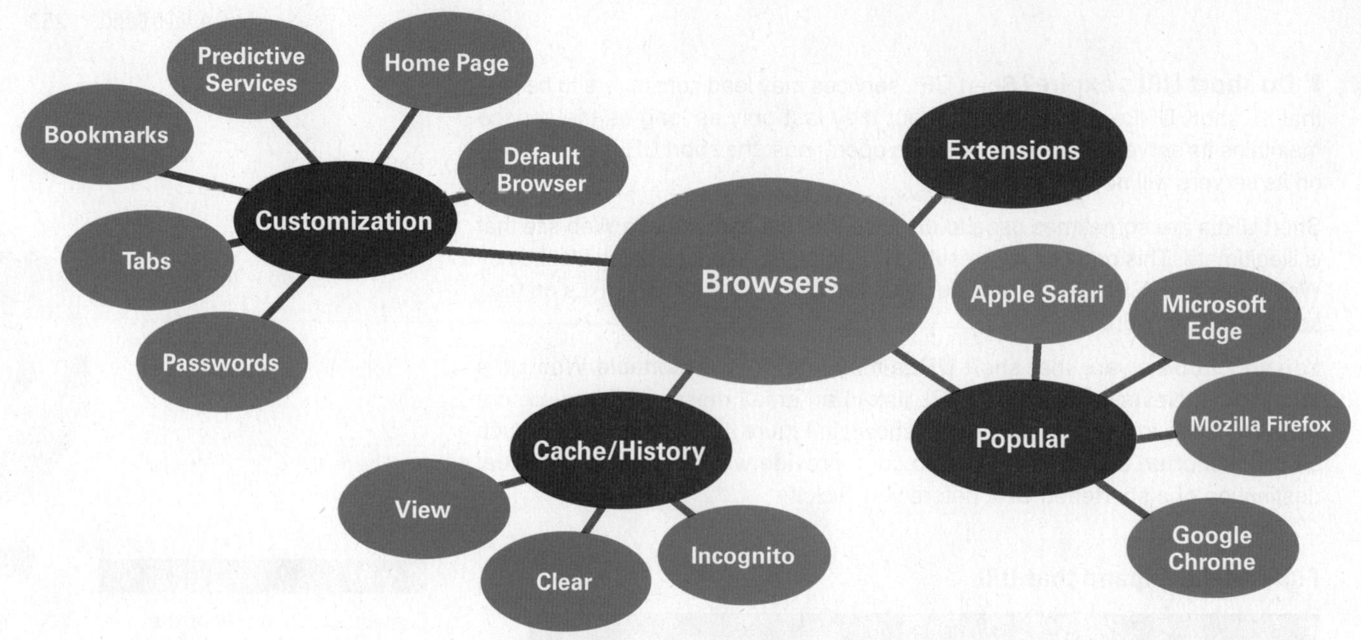

Section B Browsers

Objectives

- Identify the following elements of a browser window: address box, refresh and home buttons, back and forward buttons, tabs, and settings menu.
- List four popular browsers.
- State the difference between the default browser and the browser home page.
- Explain the purpose of predictive services.
- Provide an example of a browser extension.
- Describe what is in a browser cache and how it can affect your privacy.
- Describe what is in a browser's History list.
- Explain how private browsing works.
- Summarize the potential problem with allowing your browser to store passwords.

Go incognito. After you read Section B, you might want to put dark glasses on your browser so you can navigate the Web in private without accumulating a trail of Web sites, images, and ads that trace your Web activity.

Terminology

default browser
browser home page
predictive services
bookmarks
browser tabs
browser extension
browser cache
History list
private browsing

Browser Basics

Web browsers are the all-purpose tool for accessing the Web and everything it has to offer. They are used on all personal computer platforms. What's surprising is that the essential elements of browsers for small-screen devices, such as smartphones, are so similar to those for large-screen devices, such as desktops and laptops.

◗ What's in the standard browser window? The essential elements of a browser include an entry area for URLs and searches, navigation controls to move from one page to another, a refresh button, a home button, a settings menu, and a display area for Web page content. Additional elements, such as tabs, facilitate the browsing experience. Figure 4-14 illustrates essential browser elements and several additional features common to browsers on full-screen and mobile devices.

Terminology

The address box originally was used only for entering URLs. Today, the trend is to also use it for entering search terms. The address box is sometimes called an *Omnibox* to reflect its dual use.

Figure 4-14: Essential browser elements

Source: Google, Inc.

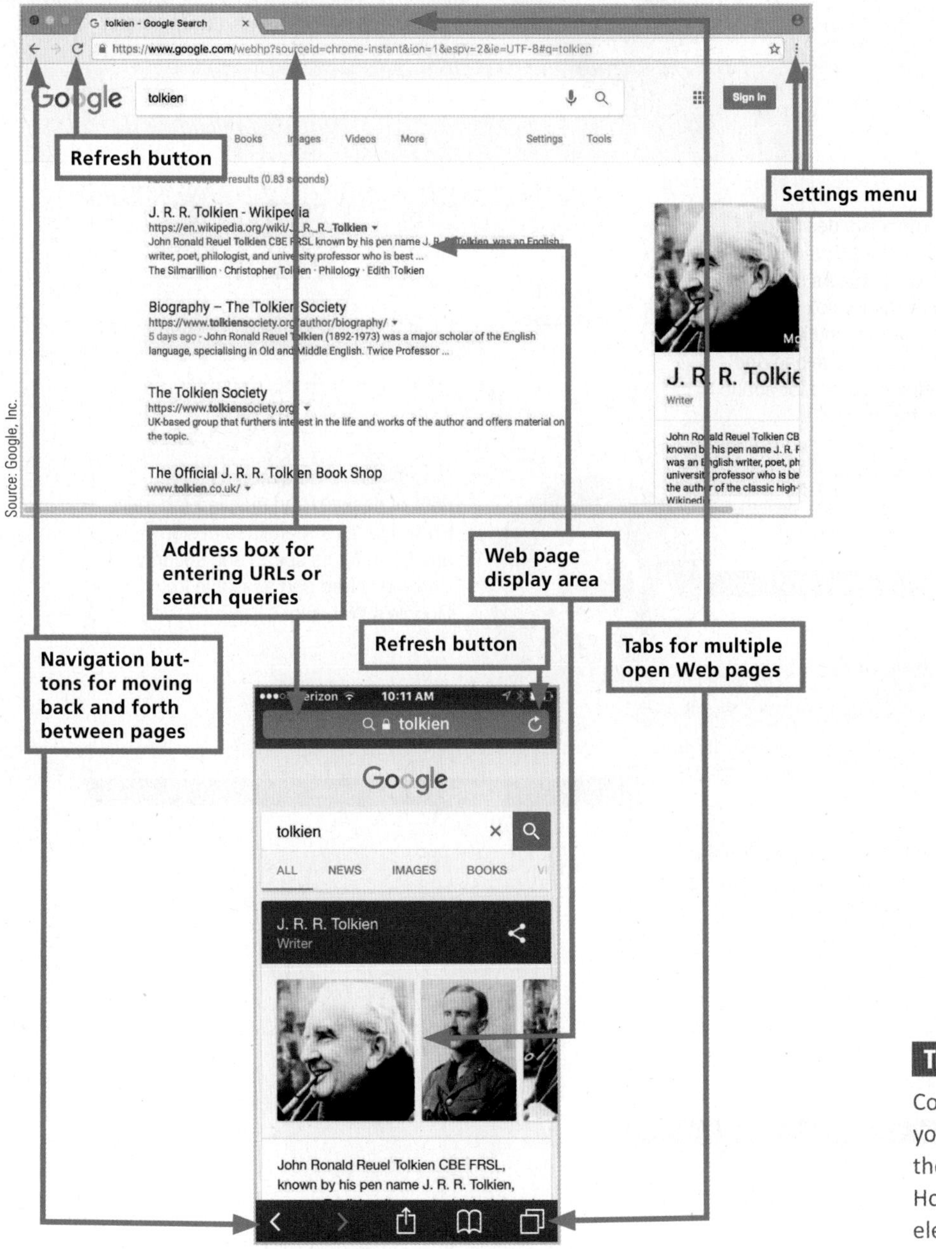

Try It!

Compare the browsers that you use on mobile devices to those you use on your laptop. How many of the user interface elements are similar?

What are the most popular browsers? Today's popular browsers are Apple Safari, Google Chrome, Microsoft Edge, and Mozilla Firefox. In Figure 4-15, compare the placement and design of the address bars and navigation controls of these popular browsers.

Figure 4-15: Popular browsers

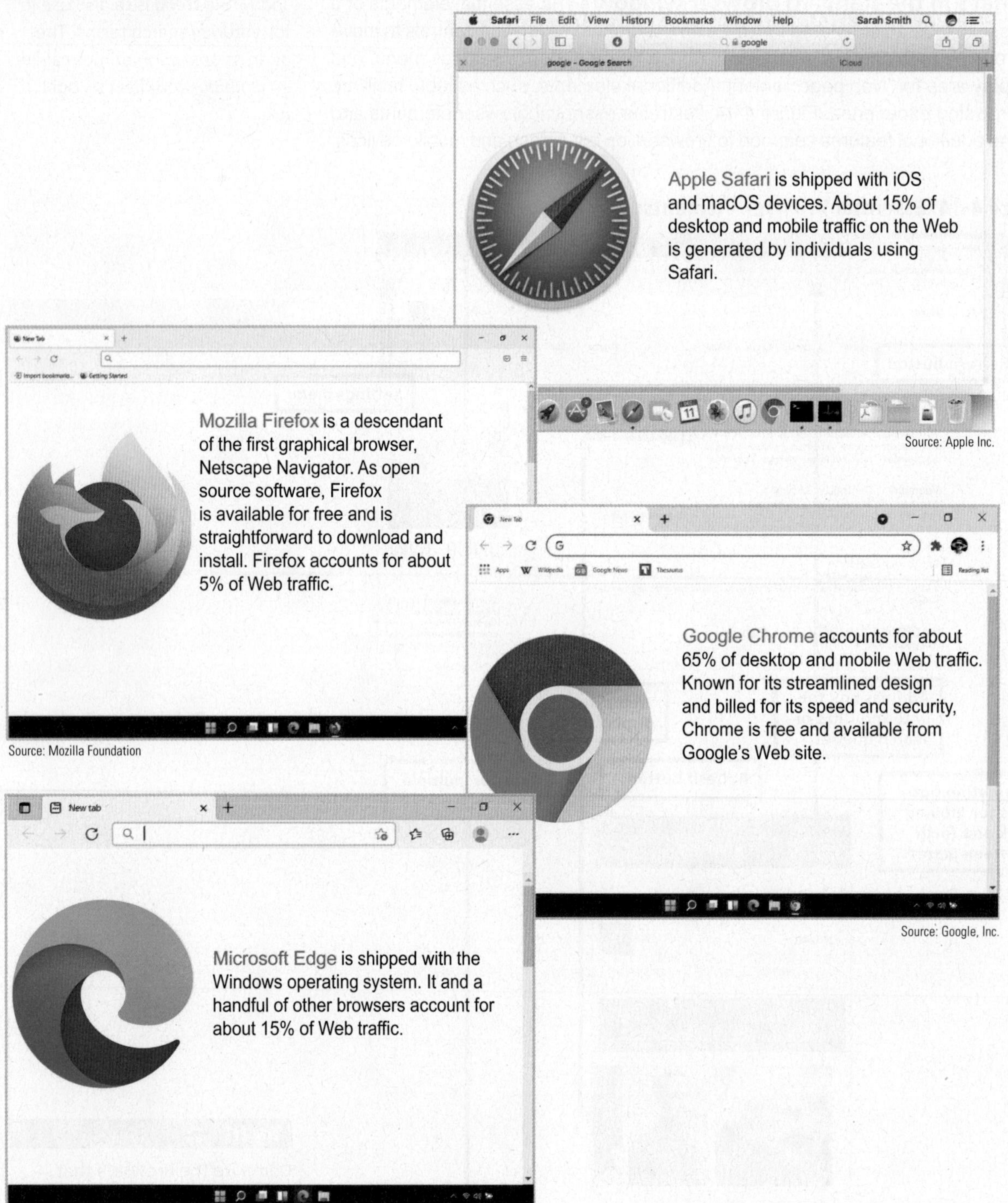

Apple Safari is shipped with iOS and macOS devices. About 15% of desktop and mobile traffic on the Web is generated by individuals using Safari.
Source: Apple Inc.
Mozilla Firefox is a descendant of the first graphical browser, Netscape Navigator. As open source software, Firefox is available for free and is straightforward to download and install. Firefox accounts for about 5% of Web traffic.
Source: Mozilla Foundation
Google Chrome accounts for about 65% of desktop and mobile Web traffic. Known for its streamlined design and billed for its speed and security, Chrome is free and available from Google's Web site.
Source: Google, Inc.
Microsoft Edge is shipped with the Windows operating system. It and a handful of other browsers account for about 15% of Web traffic.

When should I upgrade my browser? It is a good idea to upgrade when a new version of your browser becomes available. Because most browser updates are free, you can get up-to-date functionality simply by spending a few minutes downloading and installing an update.

The most important reason to upgrade is for increased security. As hackers discover and take advantage of security holes, browser publishers try to patch the holes. Upgrades normally contain patches for known security exploits, although new features might sometimes open new holes.

New versions of browsers also reflect changes in operating systems and specifications for the HTML used to create Web pages. To take advantage of the latest innovations and to experience Web pages with all the bells and whistles intended by their designers, an updated browser is recommended.

Is it possible to use multiple browsers? It is allowable to have more than one browser installed on a device, and you can open any installed browser and use it to surf the Web. Only one browser can be designated as the **default browser**, which is automatically used when you click a link in an email message or PDF file, for example.

You can add browsers and change which browser is used as the default. Suppose that your device is equipped with Microsoft Edge, but you'd prefer to use Chrome or Firefox. There is no need to delete Microsoft Edge. After you download and install an additional browser, you can set it as your default browser using the browser's Settings menu, as shown in Figure 4-16.

QuickCheck

Which of the following is not a reason to upgrade your browser?

a. To improve security

b. To keep up with new Web technologies

c. To get a free one

Try It!

How many browsers are installed on the device you use most frequently? What is the default browser?

Figure 4-16: Make Chrome your default browser

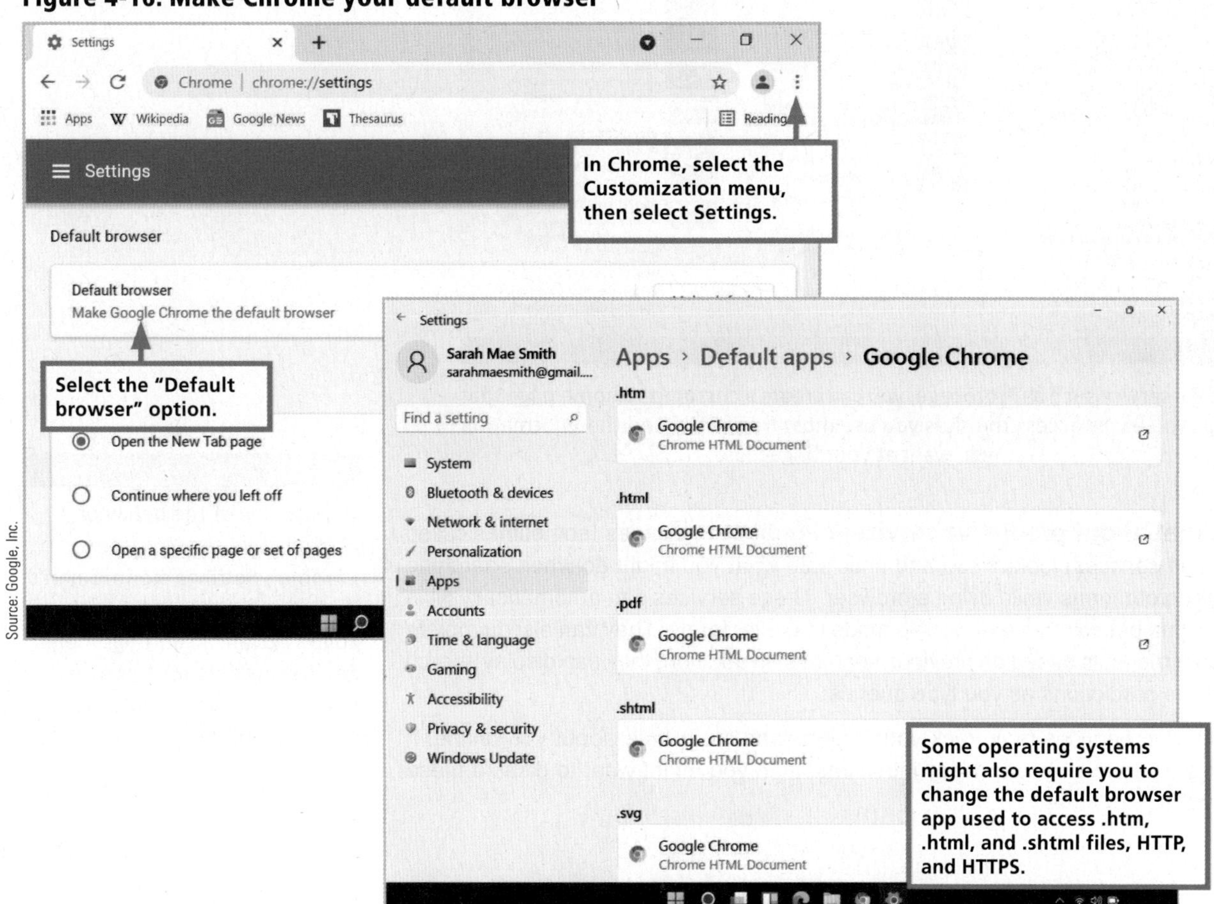

Customization

Stop for a moment and think about how many hours a day you spend using a browser for research, entertainment, and communication. Why settle for a plain vanilla interface when you can streamline your Web experience by customizing your browser? You can change your home page, customize bookmarks and favorites, control tab behavior, select predictive services, adjust password settings, and more.

▶ **What should I set as my home page?** The **browser home page** is the first page displayed when the browser starts. Set the home page to a site that works as a doorway to your Web world. If your primary use of the Web is seeking information, then a search engine site, such as Google, makes a good home page. If you prefer to land amidst your online friends, then Facebook makes a good home page. If you're a newshound, point your home page to Google News, CNN, or Fox News. You can also use services such as Protopage, My Yahoo, or uStart to design your own start page, like the one in Figure 4-17.

Try It!

Which Web site is designated as your browser's home page? Would you prefer a different one?

Figure 4-17: Create your own home page

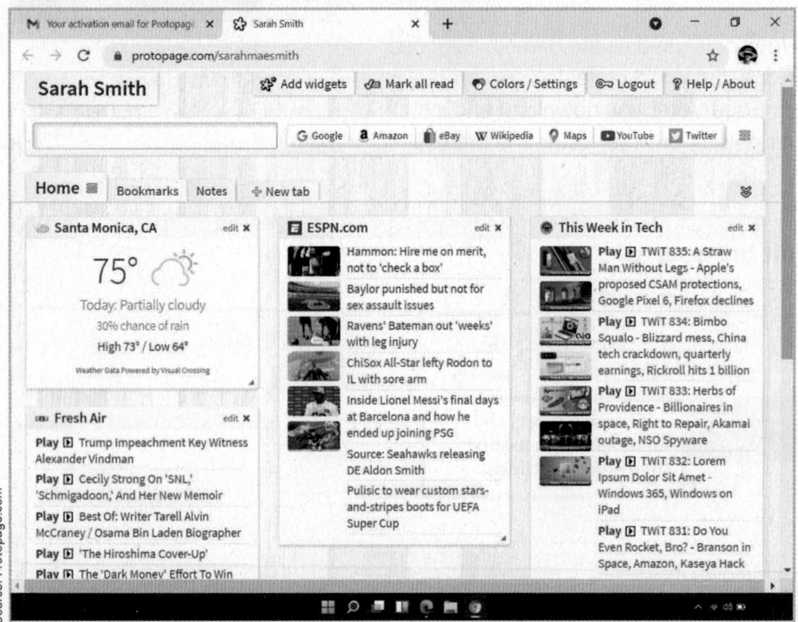

Using a service such as Protopage, you can create a customized home page that helps you easily access the sites you use most frequently and the information you want at your fingertips.

▶ **What about predictive services?** **Predictive services** (sometimes called *preload services*) look ahead and anticipate what you might do when searching or filling out forms while using a browser. These services can automatically fill in form data based on entries you've made to earlier forms. They can also complete search requests based on previous searches. In addition, they can display search and site predictions as you type queries.

Predictive services may track your actions and store data about you online. If you are nervous about privacy intrusions, then you might want to disable these services.

Try It!

You can adjust the behavior of predictive services from Chrome's Settings menu, Safari's Preferences menu, Microsoft Edge's Advanced Settings menu, and Firefox's search box. Are predictive services turned on in your browser?

How do I customize bookmarks and favorites? **Bookmarks** (or Favorites, as they are called in some browsers) link to pages that you use frequently. When the browser is configured to show bookmarks, they appear on the browser toolbar and are fairly easy to access.

Consider creating bookmarks to your favorite social networking and informational sites. Set a bookmark to your favorite music service, or create a bookmark to quickly check the caloric content of the food you eat. Perhaps a bookmark to an online thesaurus can help improve your writing (Figure 4-18). One caution: Create bookmarks for sites that help, not hinder. That addictive cat video site? Don't bookmark it if the site becomes a distraction.

4

Figure 4-18: Customize your Favorites toolbar

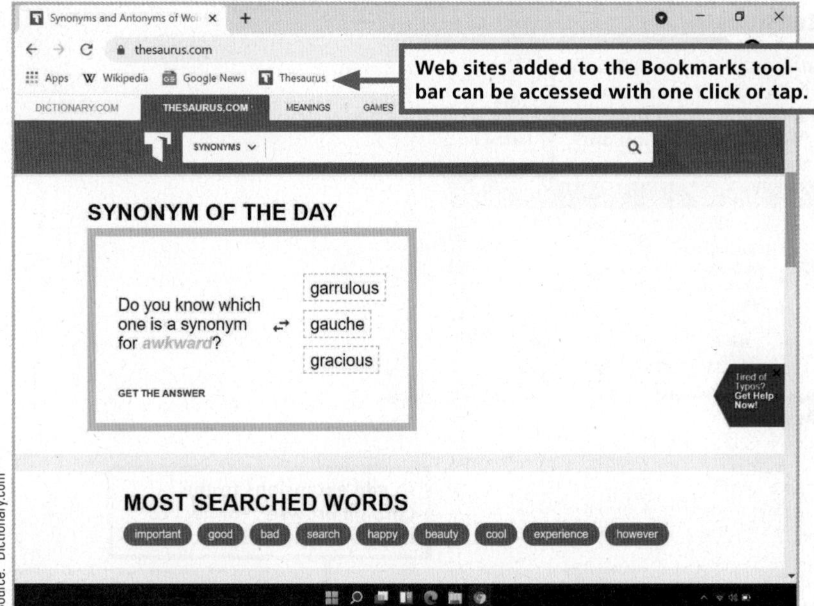

Try It!

Take a look at your browser's Favorites or Bookmarks toolbar. Does it contain sites you access often?

QuickCheck

Which one of the following cannot be customized?

a. Tabs

b. Predictive services

c. The home page

d. The Close button

Can I control tabs? **Browser tabs** allow your browser to queue up multiple Web pages so that you can easily switch between them. Your browser's Settings menu allows you to specify whether to use tabs or a new browser window. Each tab holds a Web page, and simply clicking the tab displays the corresponding page.

An alternative to tabs is opening new pages in separate browser windows—a process that allows you to see multiple pages at the same time, rather than switching among them (Figure 4-19).

Figure 4-19: Display multiple sites as tabs or separate windows

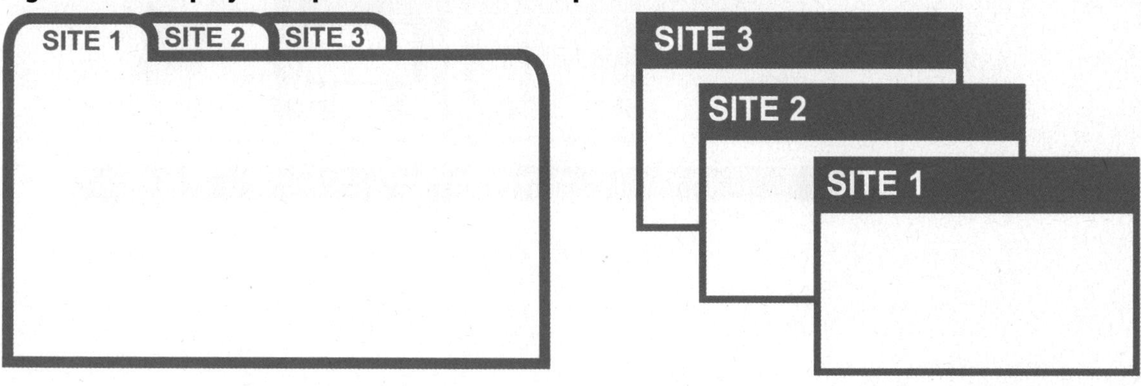

What is an extension? A **browser extension** adds features to a browser. For example, one very popular extension called AdBlock removes advertisements from Web pages. Extensions are similar to apps because they provide you with a tool to accomplish a task. Unlike apps, which are accessed from a desktop or home screen, extensions are available only when using your browser.

Extensions for work, play, security, and accessibility are available online. To find them, search for the name of your browser followed by the word "extensions," like this: *Chrome extensions*.

How do I manage extensions? Browsers provide a list of installed extensions and provide tools for disabling, enabling, or deleting them, as shown in Figure 4-20.

Try It!

Search online for a list of extensions that are available for your browser. If you don't have AdBlock, you might consider downloading it from a reputable source, such as the Chrome Web Store.

Figure 4-20: Find your browser's extensions

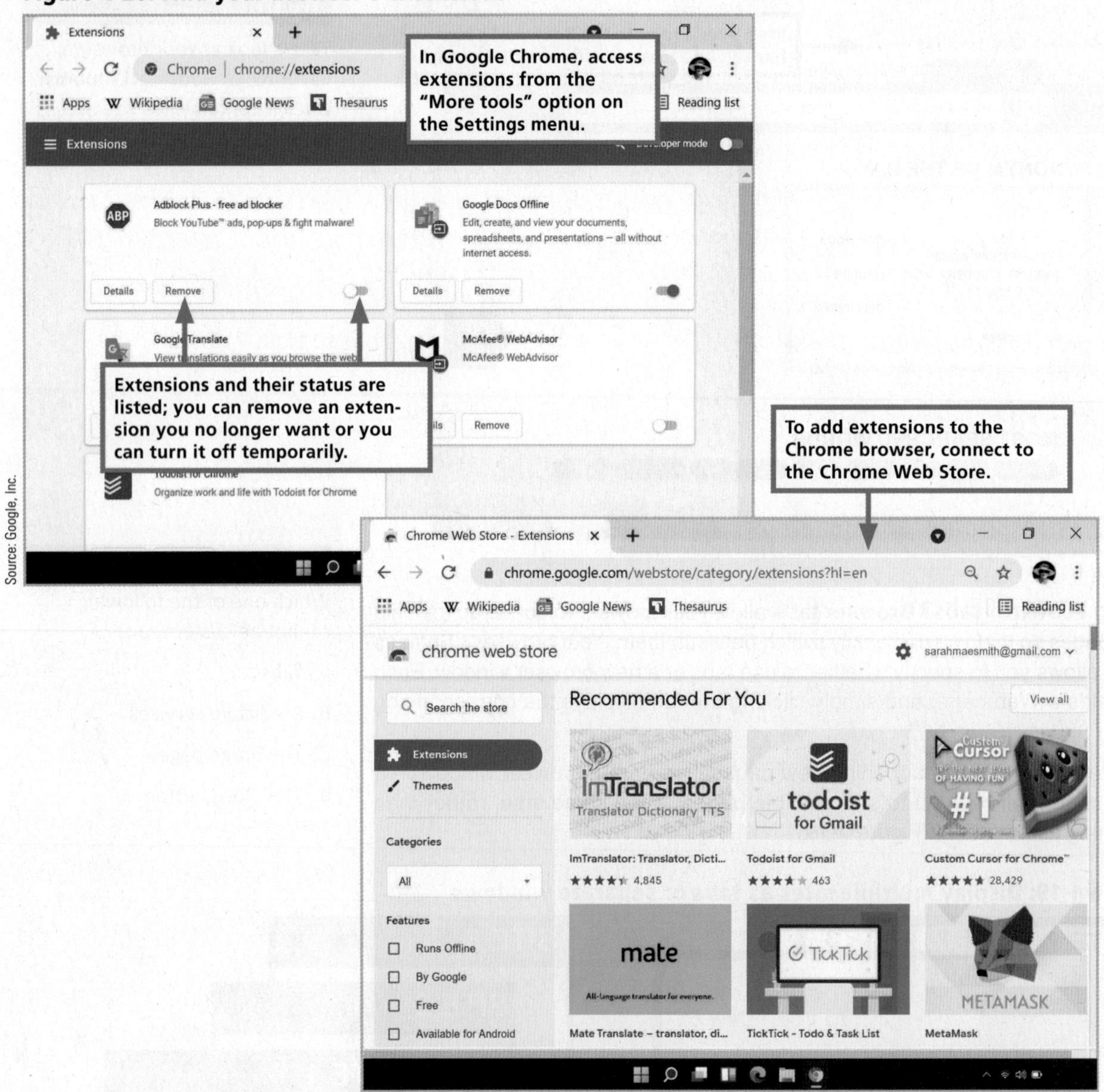

4

What else can I customize on my browser? Your browser provides lots of built-in customization tools. Here are some handy options that might be available with your browser:

- Change the color of the tabs, address bar, and Favorites or Bookmarks bar.
- Select a different font or font size.
- Adjust the zoom level.
- Specify whether to display the Favorites or Bookmarks bar.
- Show or hide the status bar that shows the destination URL for Web page links.
- Set what happens when you open your browser: open a specific page, open a set of pages, or continue where you left off the last time you closed the browser.
- Control the browser tabs by specifying if new tabs should become active, selecting shortcut keys for switching between tabs, and showing or hiding Web site icons in tabs.
- Select your default language and indicate if you'd like an automatic translation for material that is not in your selected language.
- Spell check your queries.
- Specify the destination for downloaded files.
- Select accessibility options, such as providing live captions for audio and video.
- Tighten security by identifying fraudulent Web sites and preventing automatic use of your computer's camera and microphone.
- Ensure your privacy by reducing the ability of sites to track your footprints as you navigate the Web.

Figure 4-21 highlights some of the customization settings for the Google Chrome browser.

Try It!

Access the customization settings for your browser to make sure they reflect the way you access the Web.

Figure 4-21: Browser customization settings

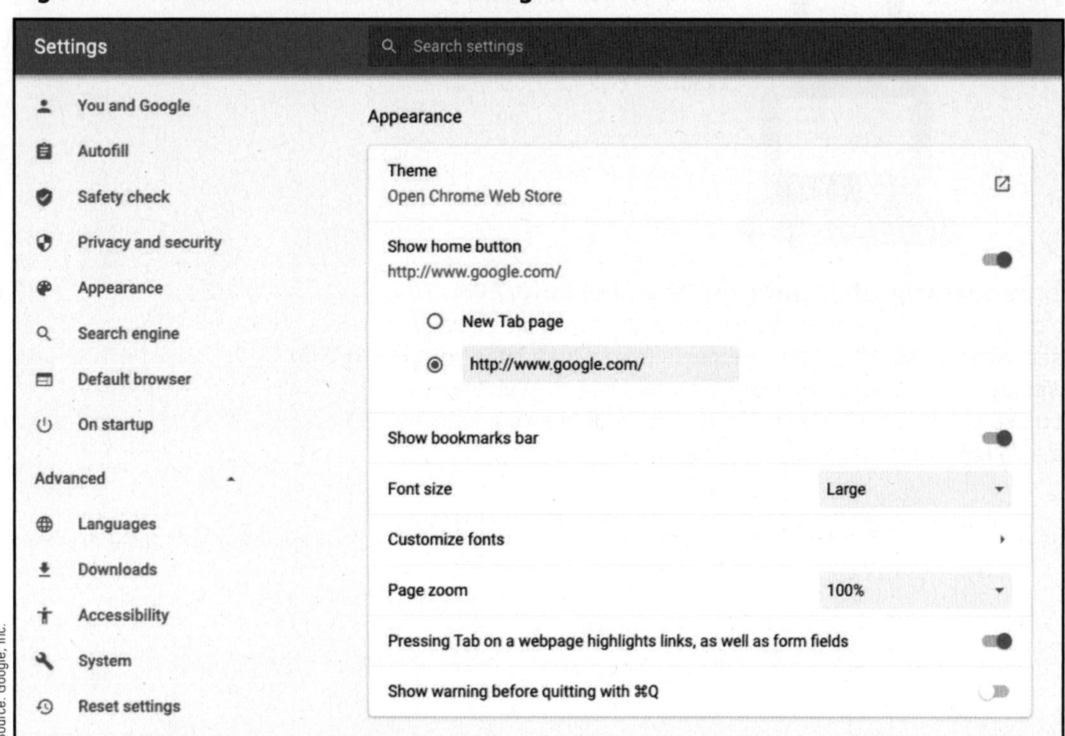

Source: Google, Inc.

Browser Cache

Browsers pull HTML documents, images, and other Web page elements to your local device—and not just the main elements of a page. All those funky ads are pulled down, too. It is somewhat troubling that these elements may remain in a Web cache on your device, leaving a trail of digital bread crumbs to the Web sites you've visited.

What is a browser cache? When your browser fetches pages and graphics to form a Web page, it stores that material on your device in temporary files referred to as a **browser cache**, Web cache, or browser data.

A browser cache comes in handy if you switch back and forth between pages or sites. Rather than fetch the entire page and all its graphics again, your browser can simply load them from the local cache (Figure 4-22).

QuickCheck

Which of the following would you not expect to find in a browser cache?

a. Passwords

b. Image files from Web pages

c. Images from ads

d. HTML documents

Figure 4-22: Your browser cache in action

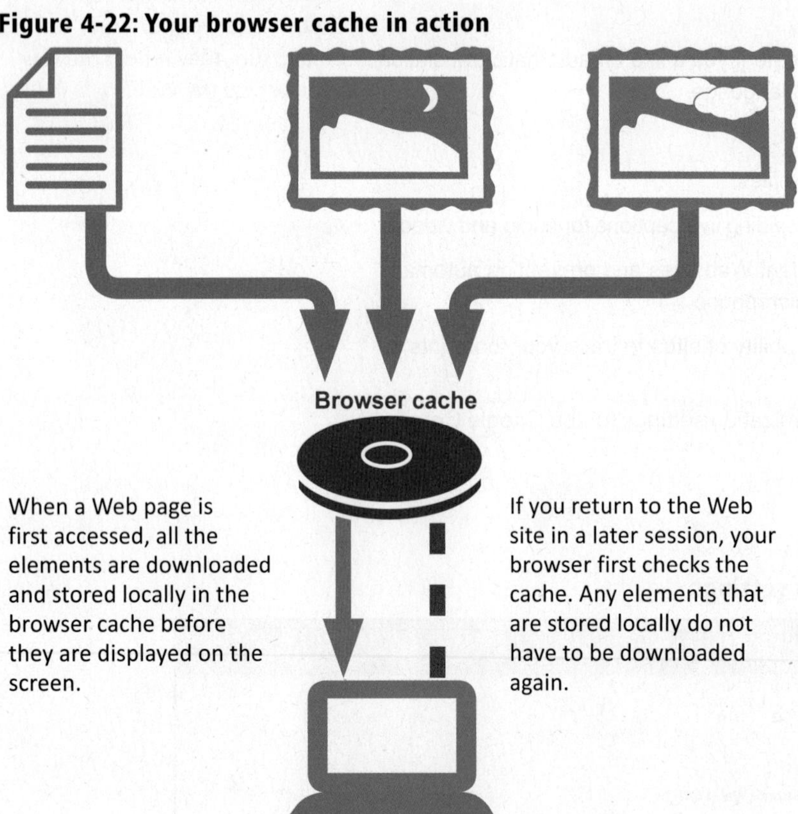

Browser cache
When a Web page is first accessed, all the elements are downloaded and stored locally in the browser cache before they are displayed on the screen.
If you return to the Web site in a later session, your browser first checks the cache. Any elements that are stored locally do not have to be downloaded again.

How does a browser cache affect my privacy and security? Files can remain in the Web cache for days or weeks, depending on your browser's settings. Because a browser cache stores Web page elements from all the sites you've visited, anyone with access to your device can view this trail of Web sites. In addition, when you use a public or lab computer, the next person who uses the computer may be able to see the cache of your Web activity.

▶ Can I see what's in a browser cache? Your browser maintains a **History list** of the Web sites you've visited. This list displays Web pages, but not the video, audio, or link components that form the page. Those components are stored in a folder somewhere on a local storage device.

If you use more than one browser, each one has its own cache. With modern browsers, the files in the cache are likely to be stored in a compressed format, making it difficult to view their contents.

Although you may not be able to view the actual cache files, you can remove them by deleting the contents of the History list.

Figure 4-23 illustrates options for clearing the Safari browser cache.

Figure 4-23: Clear the Safari browser cache

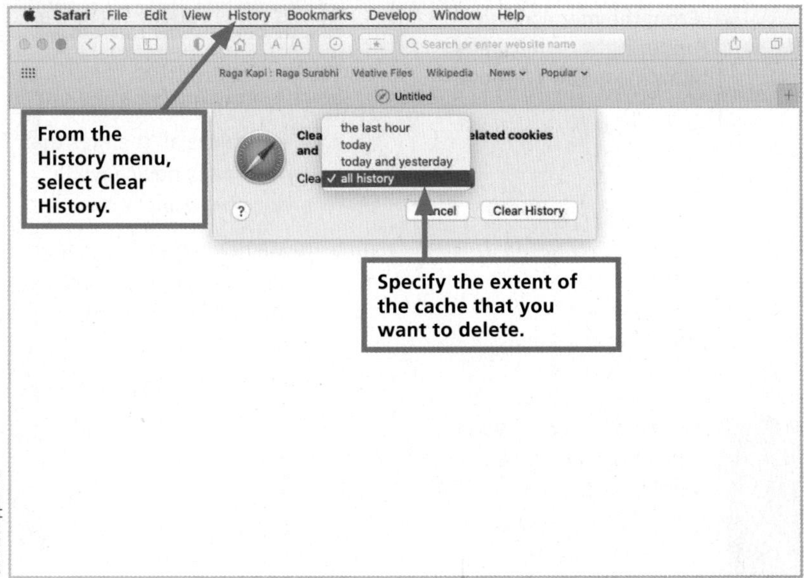

Source: Apple Inc.

The Chrome browser provides more options for clearing items in the cache. Figure 4-24 illustrates.

Figure 4-24: Clear the Chrome browser cache

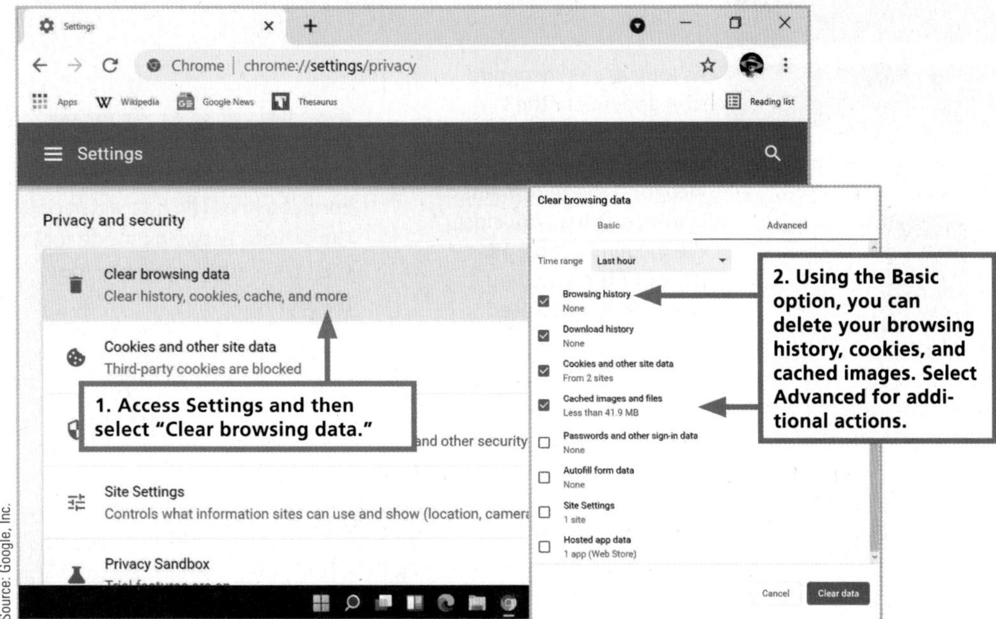

Source: Google, Inc.

Is there a way to browse without using the cache? Today's browsers offer **private browsing** modes, in which traces of your activity are not maintained in the History list or browser cache. Microsoft browsers call this mode InPrivate Browsing. Google Chrome calls it incognito mode. In Safari and Firefox, it is called Private Browsing.

Although private browsing accumulates no trail of Web activity on your local device, it does not prevent external sources, such as advertisers and government snoopers, from tracking your activity. Use private browsing when you prefer not to leave a trail that can be seen by others who gain access to a device that you have recently used. Figure 4-25 demonstrates how to enter incognito mode in Google Chrome.

Figure 4-25: Go incognito!

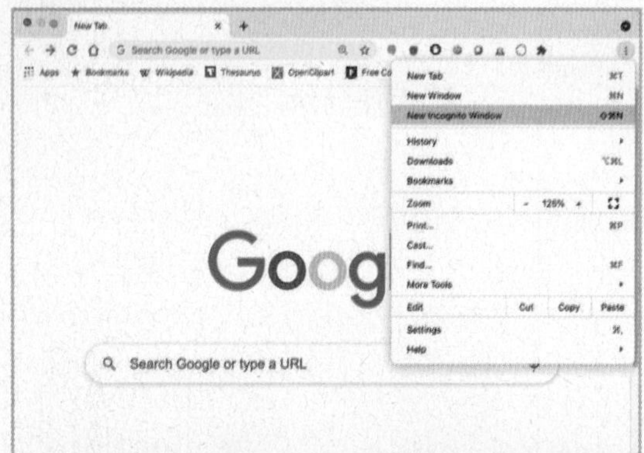

From the menu in the upper-right corner, select New Incognito Window.

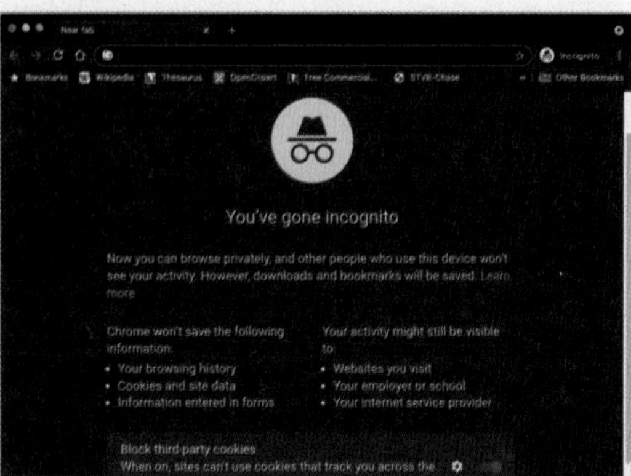

Google Chrome displays the incognito home screen.

Incognito icon

As long as the incognito icon appears in the address bar of the browser window, incognito mode remains in effect. When you close the incognito tabs, all traces of the sites you visited will be deleted.

Source: Google, Inc.

QuickCheck

What can you expect when private browsing is turned on?

a. It will delete all the files that arrive on my device while private browsing is on.

b. It will delete the browser cache, history, and cookies when I exit private browsing mode.

c. It will keep my Web activities hidden from advertisers and government snoopers.

Try It!

Do you go incognito? Make sure you know how to activate the private browsing mode for the browser that you use most frequently.

▶ Is it safe to allow my browser to store passwords? Browsers ask to save passwords when you log in to sites. If you agree, your password is stored in an encrypted file on your local device. The next time you log in to a site, your browser will use the corresponding stored password.

Storing passwords is a useful feature. You can create unique and hard-to-guess passwords without fear that you might forget them and without the hassle of looking them up each time you log in.

The potential risk of stored passwords is that anyone who gains access to your device can easily log in to your password-protected sites because the passwords are supplied by your browser. If you allow your browser to store passwords, be sure to use a password to protect access to your device.

You can discover which passwords are saved by the browsers you use. To view passwords stored by Microsoft Edge, use the Windows search box to open the Credential Manager. For Safari, select the Preferences menu, then select the Passwords tab. In Firefox, open the Security panel and select Saved Passwords. Figure 4-26 illustrates how to find passwords stored by Chrome.

QuickCheck

How would you summarize the security risk involved in allowing your browser to store passwords?

a. It is not a risk.

b. It is a security risk and should be avoided.

c. It is more secure to store passwords online.

d. The convenience of stored passwords might be worth the small risk.

4

Figure 4-26: Find your Chrome passwords

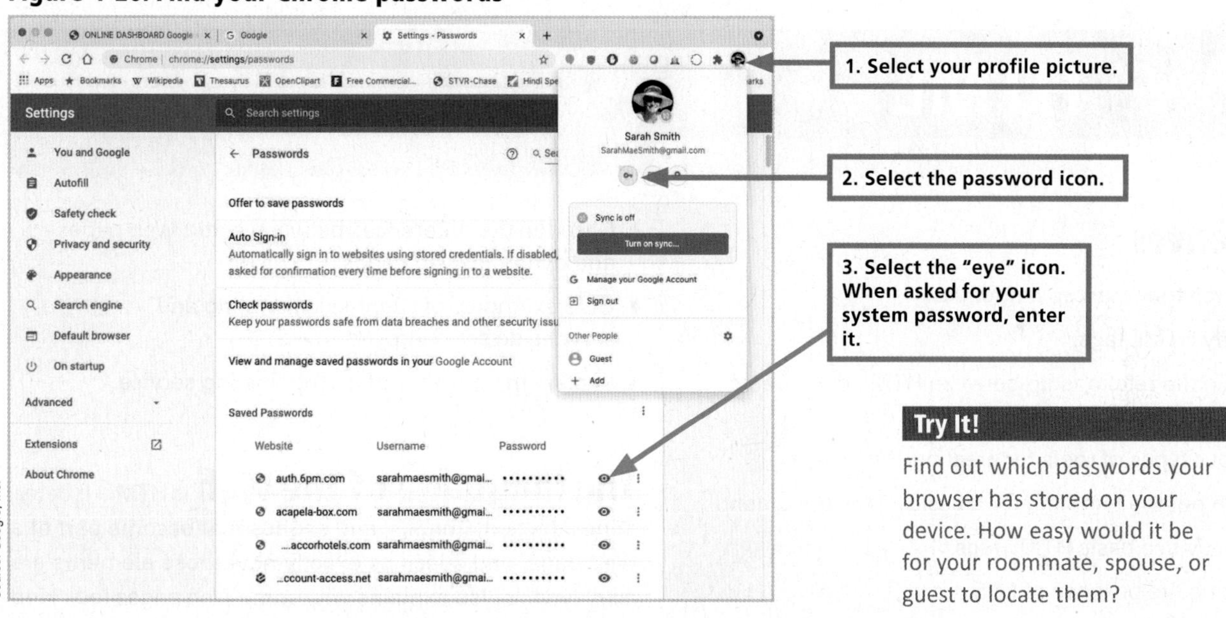

Try It!

Find out which passwords your browser has stored on your device. How easy would it be for your roommate, spouse, or guest to locate them?

QuickQuiz — Section B

1. It is important to ______ your browser to get patches for known security exploits.

2. When you use a public computer, the next person who uses it can see the Web pages you visited by looking at the ______ list.

3. If you do not want HTML and image files from recently visited Web sites to be stored on your device, delete the browser ______.

4. ______ services look ahead to anticipate what you might do when searching the Web or filling out Web-based forms.

5. A browser ______, such as AdBlock or the Merriam-Webster Online Toolbar, adds features to a browser.

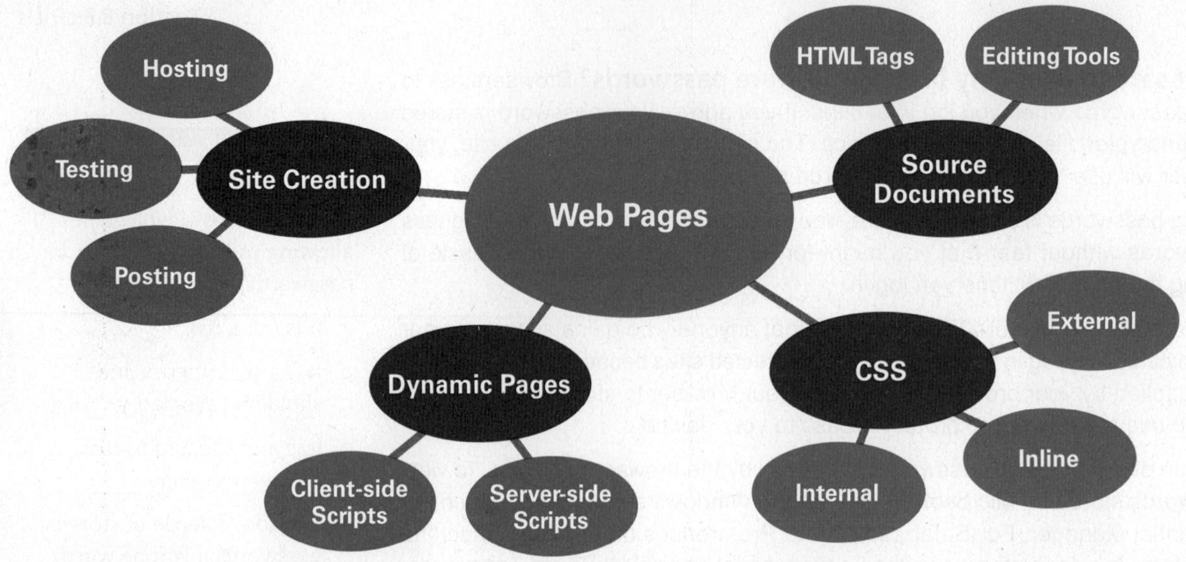

Section C HTML

Objectives

- Describe four markup languages.
- Identify HTML tags.
- Explain the relationship between HTML documents and Web pages.
- List four types of tools for creating Web pages.
- Sketch out the template for a basic HTML document.
- Correctly use basic HTML tags.
- Describe the purpose of CSS.
- Differentiate inline CSS from internal and external CSS.
- Describe the differences between static Web pages and dynamic Web pages.
- Give examples of client-side scripting and server-side scripting.
- Explain the purpose of a Web hosting service.

The language of the Web is HTML. It determines the text, images, and sounds that become part of a Web page, and specifies exactly how those elements are displayed. It also explains why some Web pages look kind of funky in one browser but picture perfect in others. The language of the Web, it seems, is open to interpretation.

Terminology

HTML5
markup language
HTML tags
HTML document
source document
HTML conversion utility
online HTML editor
local HTML editors
CSS
style rules
inline CSS
internal CSS
external CSS
static Web page
dynamic Web page
client-side scripts
server-side scripts
Web hosting service

4

HTML Basics

HTML is the foundation for professionally designed corporate Web sites, but a little knowledge of HTML can come in handy for your everyday interactions online. You can use HTML tags to enhance blog posts, and some Web sites allow HTML for reader comments.

What should I know about HTML? Tim Berners-Lee developed the original HTML specifications in 1990. These specifications have been revised several times by the World Wide Web Consortium (W3C). The current version, **HTML5**, was introduced in 2010.

HTML is a set of elements for creating documents that a browser can display as a Web page. It is called a **markup language** because authors "mark up" documents by inserting special instructions called **HTML tags** that specify how the document should appear when displayed in a browser.

HTML is a member of a family of markup languages. You may see references to these languages as you work with Web site design. Figure 4-27 summarizes the markup language family tree.

Figure 4-27: Markup language family tree

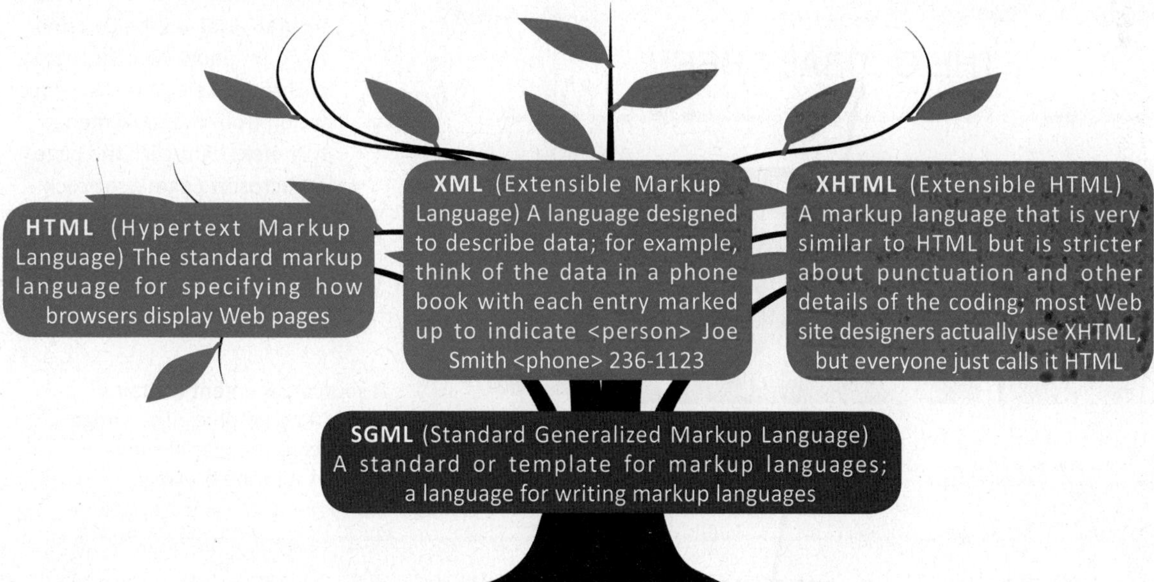

How do HTML tags work? HTML tags are incorporated into an **HTML document**, which is similar to a word processing file but has an .htm or .html extension. HTML tags such as <h1> and <p> are enclosed in angle brackets and embedded in the document. The <h1> tag specifies a heading; the <p> indicates a new paragraph.

Most tags are inserted as pairs. The start tag and end tag enclose the content like this:

<h1> THE GLOBAL CHEF </h1>

HTML tags are instructions for the browser. When your browser displays a Web page on your computer screen, it does not show the tags or angle brackets. Instead, it attempts to follow the tags' instructions. When displayed in a browser, the <h1> tag for THE GLOBAL CHEF might produce this:

THE GLOBAL CHEF

QuickCheck

The HTML tag <h1> specifies the ________.

a. style of text used as headings

b. title of an HTML page

c. beginning of an HTML document

d. format for images

▶ So HTML documents look a lot different from Web pages, right?

Exactly. An HTML document is like a screenplay, and your browser is like a director who makes a screenplay come to life by assembling cast members and making sure they deliver their lines correctly.

As the HTML "screenplay" unfolds, your browser follows the instructions in an HTML document to display lines of text on the screen in the right color, size, and position.

If the screenplay calls for a graphic, your browser collects it from the Web server and displays it. Although the HTML screenplay exists as a permanent file, the Web page you see on the screen exists only for the duration of the "performance."

An HTML document is sometimes referred to as a **source document** because it is the source of the HTML tags used to construct a Web page. Figure 4-28 illustrates the difference between an HTML source document (bottom) and the Web page it produces (top).

QuickCheck

The text for a Web page and the HTML tags are stored in ________.

a. a source document

b. a file with a .web extension

c. a browser

d. an HTML tag

Try It!

Open your browser and connect to any Web page. Can you find your browser's option to view the source HTML? (Hint: In Safari, look on the Develop menu for Show Web Inspector. In Chrome, select the Developer option from the View menu. In Firefox, right-click the page. In Microsoft Edge, right-click a blank part of the page and select View page source.

Figure 4-28: HTML source document

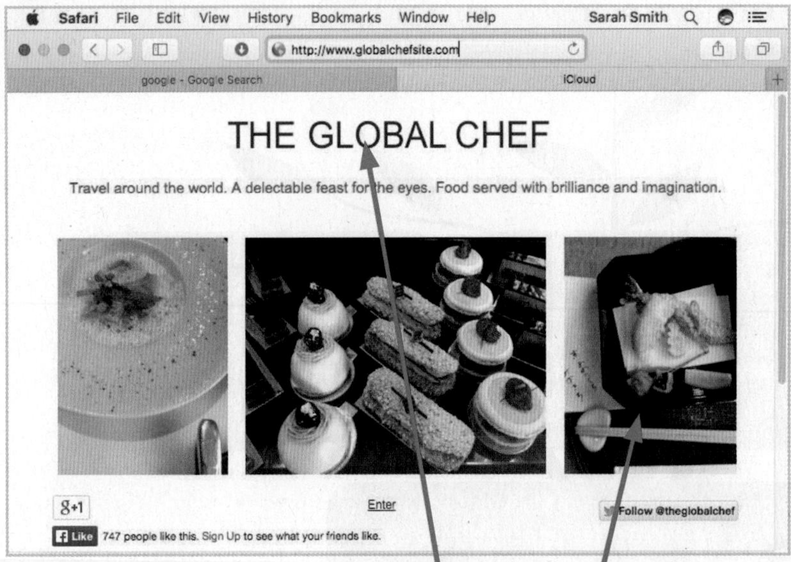

A source document contains text but no graphics. The <img> tag links to the graphic and displays it in the browser.

```
<div style="margin: 4.32px 2.16px 4.32px 2.16px;"><p style="line-height:54px;margin-top:0px;margin-
bottom:11.25px;" class="Style1">THE GLOBAL CHEF</p></div></div></div>

<div style="margin: 2.16px 2.16px 2.16px 2.16px;"><p style="line-height:17px;margin-top:0px;margin-
bottom:14.58333px;" class="Style2">Travel around the world. A delectable feast for the eyes. Food
served with brilliance and imagination.</p></div></div></div>

<div style="position:relative"><img src="London.jpg" style="left:56px;top:236px;height:232px;width:174
px;z-index: 3;position: absolute;"></div></div>

<div style="position:relative"><img src="Paris.jpg" style="left:248px;top:236px;height:232px;width:309p
x;z-index: 4;position: absolute;"></div></div>

<div style="position:relative"><img src="Tokyo.jpg" style="left:576px;top:236px;height:232px;width:175p
x;z-index: 5;position: absolute;"></div></div>

<div style="position:relative"><div class="shape_6" style="left:371px;top:487px;height:32px;width:4
8px;z-index: 6;position: absolute;"><div style="margin: 4.32px 2.16px 4.32px 2.16px;"><p style="line-
height:14px;margin-top:0px;margin-bottom:11.25px;" class="linkStyle_3"><a href="choose-the-course.
html" class="linkStyle_6">Enter</a></p></div></div></div>
```

4

HTML Editing Tools

There is an extensive toolset available for creating Web pages. Once you're aware of the options, you can select the tools that best suit your project and your ability as a designer.

▶ What tools are available for creating Web pages? You can create files for Web pages with an HTML conversion utility, online HTML editor, local HTML editor, or text editor.

HTML conversion utility. An **HTML conversion utility** creates an HTML document from a conventional document, spreadsheet, or other text-based file. For example, you can work with Microsoft Word to create a standard DOCX file, and then use Word's Save As Web Page option or the Transform option to convert the document into HTML format. The HTML conversion process occasionally produces an unusual result, however, because some of the features and formatting in your original document might not be possible within the world of HTML.

Online HTML editor. A second option for Web page authors is to use an **online HTML editor**, such as WordPress or Google Sites. Working with these tools is straightforward—select a template, choose a color scheme, enter titles and other text, upload graphics, and add links to other pages (Figure 4-29).

Figure 4-29: Using Google sites to create Web pages

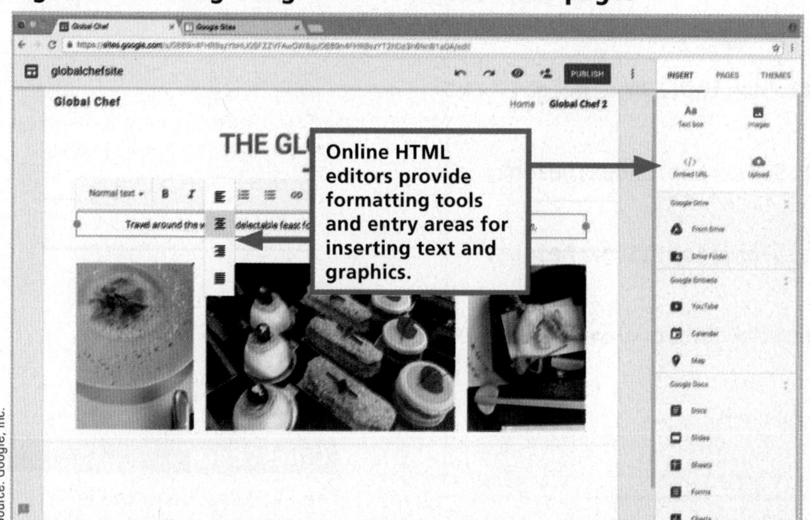
globalchefsite
PUBLISH
INSERT
PAGES
THEMES
Global Chef
THE GL
Online HTML editors provide formatting tools and entry areas for inserting text and graphics.

Source: Google, Inc.

Locally installed HTML editor. Two more options for creating Web pages include **local HTML editors** and comprehensive Web development software. Some of these tools offer professional features for managing extensive corporate Web sites, while others are geared toward creating smaller personal sites. Popular Web development products include Adobe Dreamweaver CC and open source Atom.

Text editor. HTML documents can be created with a basic ASCII text editor, such as Windows Notepad or TextEdit. With these tools, you start from scratch, with a blank page, and enter HTML codes along with the text that you want to include in the Web page. Although Web designers rarely use these tools to create entire Web sites, text editors can be useful for troubleshooting HTML documents. Text editors also offer a great way to learn HTML basics that you may be able to use for formatting online comments and posts.

QuickCheck

Documents created with word processing software _____.

a. can be posted to the Web as DOCX files

b. cannot be used on the Web

c. can be converted to HTML files for the Web

d. contain HTML tags

▶ What are the parts of an HTML document? The framework for an HTML document consists of two sections: the head and the body. The head section begins with <!DOCTYPE html> and <head> tags. It may also include information that defines global properties, including the Web page title that appears in the browser title bar and information about the page that can be used by search engines.

The body section of an HTML document begins with the <body> HTML tag. This section of the document contains text, HTML tags that format the text, plus a variety of links to graphics, sounds, and videos. Figure 4-30 contains basic HTML for a Web page. You can use it as a template for creating your own pages.

Figure 4-30: HTML document template

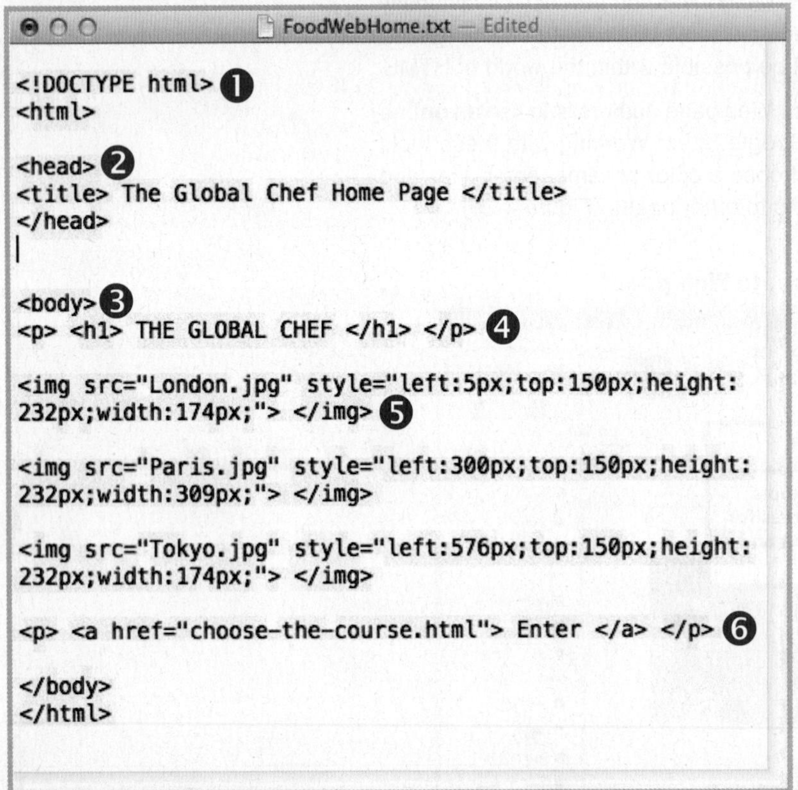


```
<!DOCTYPE html> ❶
<html>

<head> ❷
<title> The Global Chef Home Page </title>
</head>

<body> ❸
<p> <h1> THE GLOBAL CHEF </h1> </p> ❹

<img src="London.jpg" style="left:5px;top:150px;height:
232px;width:174px;"> </img> ❺

<img src="Paris.jpg" style="left:300px;top:150px;height:
232px;width:309px;"> </img>

<img src="Tokyo.jpg" style="left:576px;top:150px;height:
232px;width:174px;"> </img>

<p> <a href="choose-the-course.html"> Enter </a> </p> ❻

</body>
</html>
```

❶ An HTML document begins with the DOCTYPE and html declarations.

❷ The <head> tag contains the page title.

❸ The body section contains text and links to images.

❹ Headings are formatted with the <h1> tag and can be set off with the <p> tag.

❺ Images are linked to pages with the <img> tag.

❻ Links to other Web pages are coded using the <a href> tag.

QuickCheck

The head section of the HTML document in Figure 4-30 does not contain ________.

a. the title

b. the DOCTYPE declaration

c. the <html> declaration

d. image links

How do I specify the text and graphics for a Web page? In the body section of your HTML document, you can enter text and HTML tags to mark sections of text that should appear in different styles. You can also specify the images you want to appear on the page, and you can create clickable links to other Web pages. The table in Figure 4-31 provides a list of basic tags that you can use to create your own HTML documents.

Figure 4-31: Basic HTML tags

HTML Tag	Use	Example
<b> <i>	Bold or italicize text	<b> Hello </b>
<h1> <h2> ... <h6>	Change font size; h1 is largest	<h1> Chapter 1 </h1>
<h1 style="color: ">	Change font color	<h1 style="color:green"> Fir Trees </h1>
<hr/>	Include a horizontal line (no end tag)	Section 2 <hr/>
** **	Line break (no end tag)	This is line one. This is line two.
<p>	Paragraph break	<p>It was the best of times, it...of comparison only. </p>
<ol> <ul> <li>	Numbered list <ol>; bulleted list <ul>; list items <li>	<ol> <li> First item</li> <li> Second item</li> </ol>
<a href="URL">	Link to another Web page	<a href="www.news.com/today.htm"> Click here </a>
<img src="File">	Include an image	<img src="Photo.jpg">
<table>, <tr>, <td>	Create tables, table rows, and cells	<table>

Which HTML tags can be used in blog posts and comments? Most blogging platforms allow authors to insert HTML tags to format blog posts. Some social media sites also allow readers to insert basic HTML tags, such as <b> and <i>, in comments.

To discover if HTML tags are allowed in a specific online venue, check its Help link or perform a Web search such as *Goodreads HTML*, as shown in Figure 4-32.

Figure 4-32: Using HTML on social media 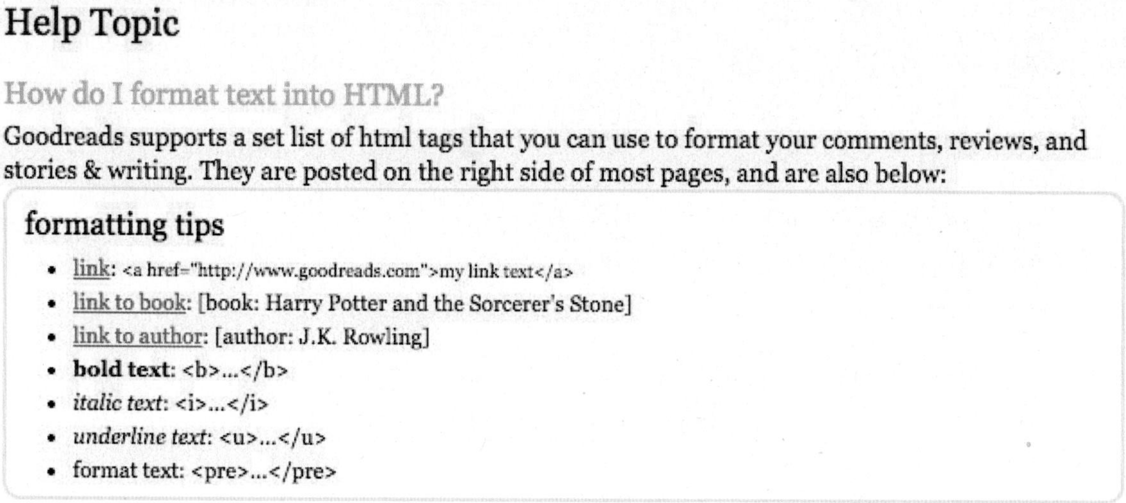

Help Topic

How do I format text into HTML?

Goodreads supports a set list of html tags that you can use to format your comments, reviews, and stories & writing. They are posted on the right side of most pages, and are also below:

formatting tips

- link: <a href="http://www.goodreads.com">my link text</a>
- link to book: [book: Harry Potter and the Sorcerer's Stone]
- link to author: [author: J.K. Rowling]
- **bold text**: <b>...</b>
- *italic text*: <i>...</i>
- *underline text*: <u>...</u>
- format text: <pre>...</pre>

CSS

A Web page displayed in a browser may look simple. The page might contain some blocks of text, a handful of photos, some text links, and a few navigation buttons. With your knowledge of HTML, you can probably envision the source document for such a page. But that document is usually accompanied by CSS. What's that all about?

▶ What is CSS? **CSS**, which stands for Cascading Style Sheets, is a set of detailed style specifications for an HTML document. These specifications are called **style rules**, which include settings for font colors, font sizes, background colors, borders, text alignment, link formats, and margins. There are three types of style sheets:

Inline. Style sheets can be intermixed within an HTML document, but the use of an **inline CSS** is avoided by professional designers.

Internal. An **internal CSS** is included within the header of an HTML document. It places all the formatting elements where they can be edited without hunting through the entire document.

External. With an **external CSS**, style rules are placed in a separate file with a .css extension. CSS files can be manually created with a text editor. HTML editors generally create external CSSs automatically. For Web sites with more than one page, an external CSS is the recommended approach.

The advantage of external CSS is that all of the pages for a Web site can be controlled by a single style sheet. If you decide, for example, to change the color of the heading font, you make only one change to the style sheet and it will be applied to every page on the site.

▶ What does a style rule look like? CSS style rules have a selector and a declaration block. The selector indicates an HTML element to which you want to apply a style rule. The declaration specifies the styles. Here is a style rule for displaying Heading 1 text in purple 10-point font.

```
h1 {color: purple; font-size: 10 px;}
```

A CSS containing several styles for a Web site might look like Figure 4-33.

QuickCheck

Professional Web designers should avoid using ________ CSS.

a. inline

b. internal

c. external

Figure 4-33: Use a CSS to set font colors

```
body
{
font-family: arial; } ❶
h1 {
   color: purple; text-align: center;} ❷
a:link {
   color: purple; } ❸
a:visited {
   color: blue; } ❹
```

❶ Set the font to Arial for the entire Web page.

❷ Set the Heading 1 font color to purple and the alignment to centered.

❸ Set the font color of text links to purple.

❹ Set the font color of visited text links to blue.

QuickCheck

Based on the CSS in Figure 4-33, what is the color for visited links?

a. Purple

b. White

c. Blue

d. Black

How does external CSS work? Let's suppose you have a Web site containing five pages. You have five HTML documents—one for each page. At the top of each page is the heading "THE GLOBAL CHEF." You want the browser to display that text in purple and centered in the browser window. Figure 4-34 illustrates how to link the CSS to the five Web pages.

Figure 4-34: Use one CSS for multiple Web pages

❶ Create a CSS called SiteStyle.css and define the h1 style like this:

h1 {color: purple; text-align: center;}

SiteStyle.css

```
body
{
font-family: arial; }
h1 {
  color: purple;
  text-align: center;}
a:link {
  color: purple; }
a:visited {
  color: blue; }
```

❷ Link each of the HTML documents to the CSS by placing a <link> tag within the <head> area of the HTML document like this:

<head> <link rel="stylesheet" type="text/css" href="SiteStyle.css">

Page5.html, Page4.html, Page3.html, Page2.html, Page1.html

```
<head> <link
rel="stylesheet"
type="text/css"
href="SiteStyle.css">

<h1> "THE GLOBAL
CHEF"
</h1>
```

❸ Define the heading text in all HTML documents as Heading 1 like this:

<h1> "THE GLOBAL CHEF" </h1>

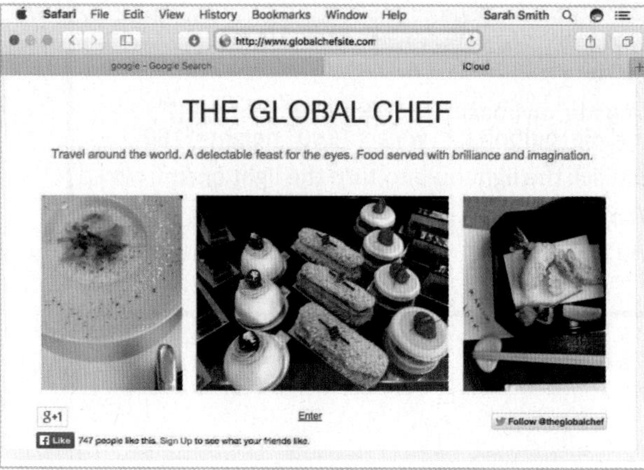

❹ When any of the five Web pages are displayed in a browser, the Heading 1 font will be purple and centered.

QuickCheck

The name of the file that contains the CSS in Figure 4-34 is called ______________.

a. Page 1

b. Style Sheet

c. SiteStyle.css

d. "THE GLOBAL CHEF"

4

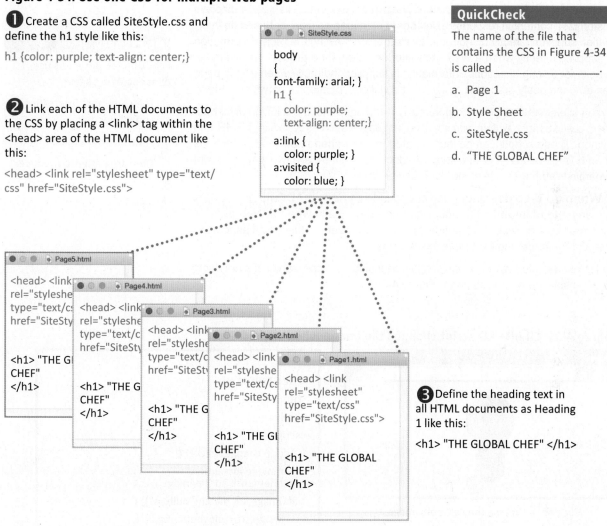

Dynamic Web Pages

Using HTML and CSS, Web designers can create a **static Web page** that displays the same information, regardless of who accesses it. The page will have the same content and format for all visitors. In your experience, however, Web sites can display customized pages that show products you're shopping for, tunes from your favorite musicians, and driving directions for your next road trip. These dynamic Web pages require an additional layer of technology.

How do Web pages become dynamic? A **dynamic Web page** displays customized content in response to keyboard or mouse actions, or based on information supplied directly or indirectly by the person viewing the page. Information is supplied directly when a Web site visitor searches for a product, for example, or asks for driving directions. Information is supplied indirectly when a Web page can autonomously grab data based on the visitor's location or browsing history.

Dynamic elements can be incorporated in Web pages with the addition of instructions, called scripts, written with scripting languages such as JavaScript, PHP, and Python. These scripts can be incorporated into the <head> or <body> sections of an HTML document or in a separate document. There are two ways to script dynamic Web pages: client-side and server-side.

When do Web designers use client-side dynamics? **Client-side scripts** are embedded in an HTML document and run locally when a Web page is displayed by a browser. Client-side dynamics are used to customize aspects of the user interface and for simple interactions.

A classic example of a client-side script is changing the appearance of a graphical object displayed on a Web page (Figure 4-35).

QuickCheck

Why do Web designers use dynamic Web pages?

a. They are more interesting and interactive.

b. They are more secure.

c. They are easier to produce.

d. They are faster than static pages.

Figure 4-35: Client-side script changes the image when clicked

Clicking or tapping the lightbulb image...

...runs the script to change the image.

```
<!DOCTYPE html>
<html>
<body>
<script>
function changeImage() {
  var image=document.
  getElementById('myImage');
  if (image.src.match("bulbon")) {
    image.src="pic_bulboff.gif"; }
  else {
    image.src="pic_bulbon.gif"; }}
</script>
<img id="myImage" onclick="changeImage()"
src="pic_bulboff.gif" width="100" height="180">
<p>Click the light bulb to turn the light on/off.</p>
</body>
</html>
```

When do Web designers use server-side dynamics? **Server-side scripts** run on Web servers rather than on your local device. The server typically accesses information from a database and uses that information to create customized Web pages on the fly.

A common use of server-side scripting is online shopping. Figure 4-36 illustrates how an online store uses server-side scripts to display a customized list of products when you search for *Mountain Bikes*.

Figure 4-36: Server-side scripts can create Web pages on the fly

The site initially displays a generic home page.

Entering a search initiates a server-side script.

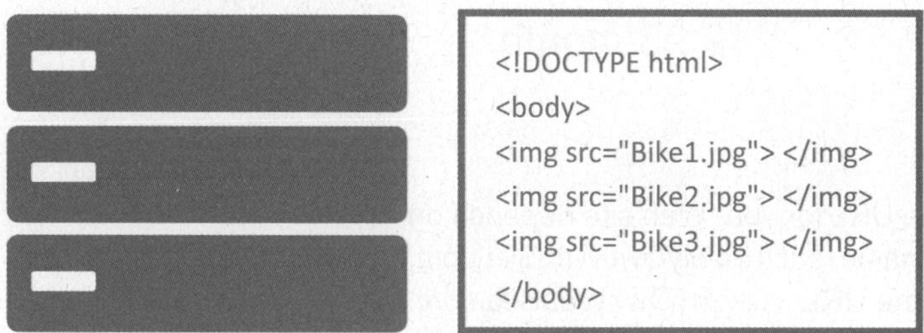

The script looks for mountain bikes and generates an HTML page, which is sent to the local browser.

The browser displays the page that was created on the fly by the server-side script.

QuickCheck

In Figure 4-36, what generated the Web page?

a. A database

b. An HTML document

c. A query

d. A server-side script

Site Creation

Whether you work with a text editor or another authoring tool, HTML documents should be saved in files with .htm or .html extensions. Creating a Web page is not the end of the publishing process. The steps for establishing a Web site include selecting a hosting service, choosing a domain, posting Web pages, and testing pages in various browsers.

▶ **What is a hosting service?** Getting a Web site up and running is uncomplicated and inexpensive. You need a hosting service, a URL, and a set of Web pages for your site.

A **Web hosting service** is a company that provides space on a server to house Web pages. Web hosting services such as GoDaddy, Amazon Web Services, HostGator, and Google offer a variety of hosting plans. Figure 4-37 illustrates the types of plans available from a typical hosting service.

Figure 4-37: Plan options from a typical hosting service

Starter	Standard
1 GB storage space	Your own domain
Site management tools	100 MB Web space
Supported by ads selected by the hosting service	Site management tools
	Ads
Free	$5.95/month

Enhanced	Ecommerce
Your own domain	Merchandise database
No ads	Credit card processing
1 GB Web space	Secure connection
Site management tools	Site management tools
$10.95/month	$19.95/month

▶ **What are the choices for URLs?** The URL for your Web site depends on its domain. You can obtain your own domain name, such as MyOwnWebSite.com, and then your site can be accessed using the URL *www.MyOwnWebSite.com*. Once you have your own domain name, you can use it with any hosting service. Another option is to use a subdomain of your hosting service. For example, a Web site created with Google Sites could use Google's domain name combined with a name that you choose for your site—for example, *sites.google.com/site/MyOwnWebSite*.

▶ **How do I post pages?** When pages are created locally using a text editor or local HTML editor, those pages must be uploaded to your hosting service. A mechanism for doing so is usually provided by your hosting service. If not, you can use FTP to upload files.

Pages that are created online using tools from your hosting service just need to be "published," which specifies that they become publicly accessible.

QuickCheck

What is the purpose of a Web hosting service?

a. Storing documents offline

b. Supplying a server platform for Web sites

c. Providing Internet service

d. Providing access to the Web

What does testing involve? Basic Web page testing involves trying every text link to make sure that it leads to the intended destination. In addition, it is important to test every navigation link to ensure that visitors can easily reach every page of your site.

It is an unfortunate fact that today's browsers are not completely standardized. They render some HTML tags differently. Effects that work on some browsers may look odd and behave very differently on others.

An additional problem involving fonts can affect how pages are displayed. A browser generally uses the fonts installed on the local device when displaying Web pages. Suppose our example Web site, The Global Chef, uses an unusual font such as American Typewriter. When its pages are displayed on devices without the American Typewriter font, a substitute font will be used; that font might make the page look quite different from the intended design (Figure 4-38).

To uncover problems that might be caused by browser compatibility, careful designers test new and revised sites using each one of the popular browsers.

Try It!

Connect to the same Web page using two different browsers; one can be on a mobile device, such as a smartphone. What are the major differences in the way the page is displayed?

Figure 4-38: Available fonts may affect Web page appearance

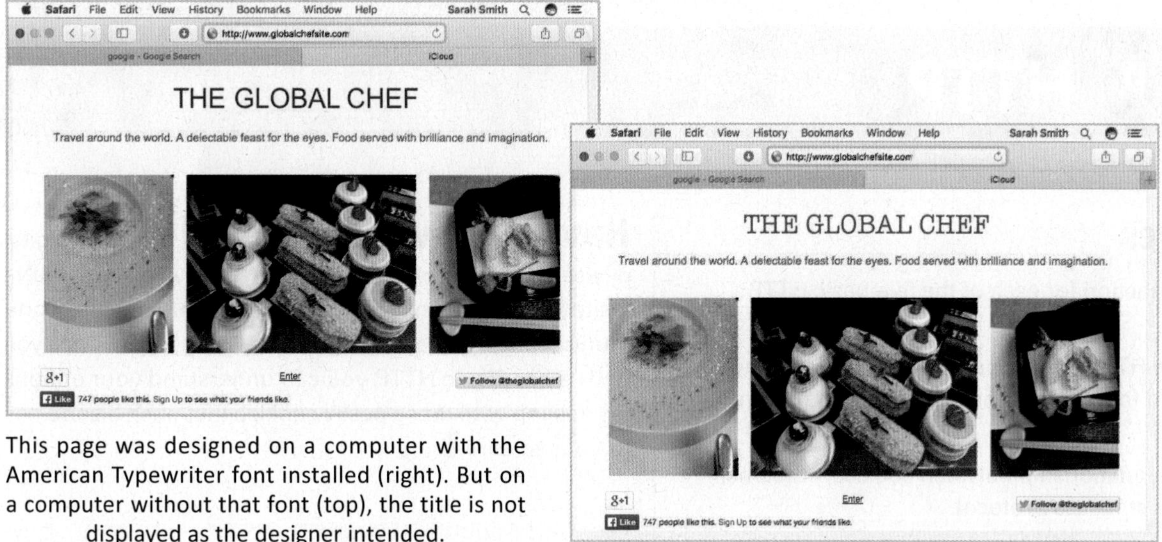

This page was designed on a computer with the American Typewriter font installed (right). But on a computer without that font (top), the title is not displayed as the designer intended.

QuickQuiz — Section C

1. A Web server sends a(n) ________ document to a browser, which then displays it as a Web page.
2. Notepad and TextEdit can be used to manually enter HTML ________ into a document.
3. <a href> is used to create ________ in an HTML document.
4. CSS stands for Cascading ________ Sheets.
5. Dynamic Web pages are created with ________ written in languages such as PHP and JavaScript.

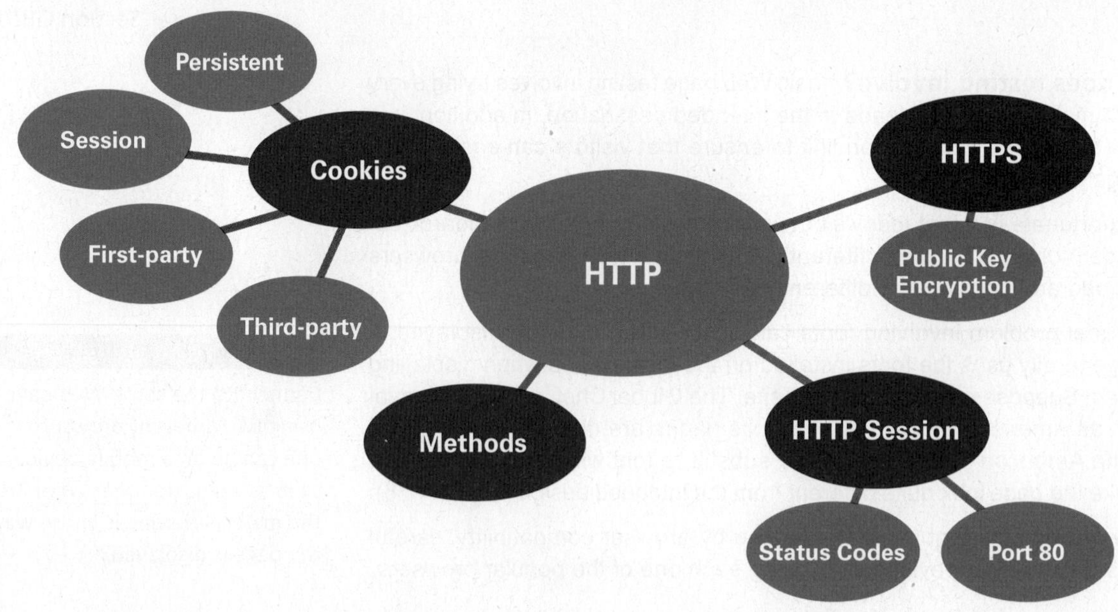

Section **D**

HTTP

Objectives

- State the function for each of the five basic HTTP methods.
- Identify the HTTP status codes for requests that are fulfilled and for requests that ask for a nonexistent URL.
- Explain the relationship between cookies, sessions, and HTTP's stateless protocol.
- List four reasons that Web sites use cookies.
- Describe the difference between session cookies and persistent cookies.
- Summarize the reasons for blocking third-party cookies but not blocking first-party cookies.
- Identify when your browser is displaying a secure site where it is safe to enter passwords, financial information, and other personal data.
- Explain how public key encryption works.

Have you ever wondered why your digital devices are littered with cookies from every Web site you've visited? Blame it on HTTP, the protocol that handles communications between browsers and Web servers. Once you have a handle on HTTP, you can understand your options for dealing with those pesky cookies that push bizarre ads to your screen.

Terminology

HTTP	HTTP status code	first-party cookie	public key encryption
HTTP methods	cookie	third-party cookie	
HTTP session	session cookies	cross-site tracking	
stateless protocol	persistent cookies	HTTPS	

HTTP Basics

You can think of HTTP as the system that browsers use to communicate with a Web server and ask for HTML documents. HTTP is responsible for transporting Web pages, whereas HTML is responsible for the way Web pages look when displayed by a browser.

QuickCheck

One of the key transport technologies for Web pages is ________________.

a. HTML

b. HTTP

c. BitTorrent

d. Chrome

4

▶ How does HTTP work? **HTTP** is a communication protocol that works with TCP/IP to get the elements for Web pages to a local browser. A set of commands called **HTTP methods** helps your browser communicate with Web servers.

GET is the most frequently used HTTP method. GET is used to retrieve text and image files necessary for displaying a Web page. GET can also be used to pass a search query to a Web server (Figure 4-39).

Figure 4-39: How GET requests data from a Web server

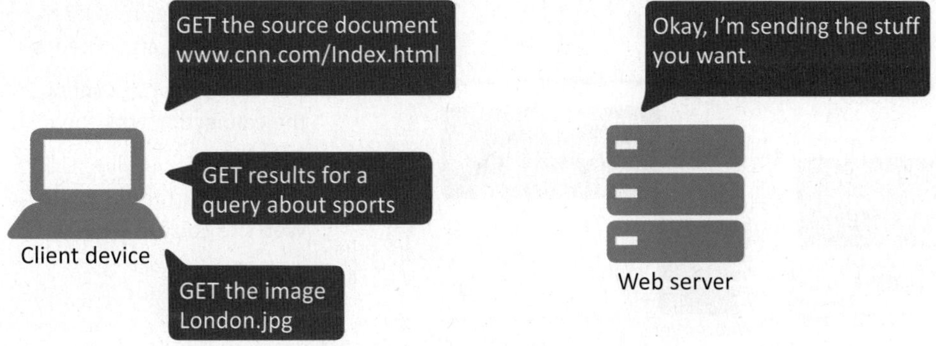

The set of methods for HTTP is not very large. As with many aspects of the digital world, amazingly complex activities are carried out by seemingly simple elements. The most commonly used HTTP methods are listed in Figure 4-40.

Figure 4-40: HTTP methods

Method	Function
GET	Requests data from a specified source
POST	Submits data to a specified source
HEAD	Requests the HTTP header only for requested data
PUT	Uploads data to a specific Web address
DELETE	Removes a specified resource
OPTIONS	Fetches a list of methods supported by the server

QuickCheck

Which HTTP method does a browser use to request an HTML source document?

a. GET

b. POST

c. HEAD

d. OPTIONS

What is an HTTP session? HTTP uses port 80 for communications between a client device and a server. The exchange takes place within a session. An **HTTP session** is a sequence of transactions most commonly used to request data from a Web server and fetch the files needed to display a Web page in a browser window.

At the end of a session, the connection is closed. Because the server does not "remember" its state from one session to the next, HTTP is called a **stateless protocol**. Figure 4-41 illustrates typical HTTP sessions.

Figure 4-41: HTTP sessions

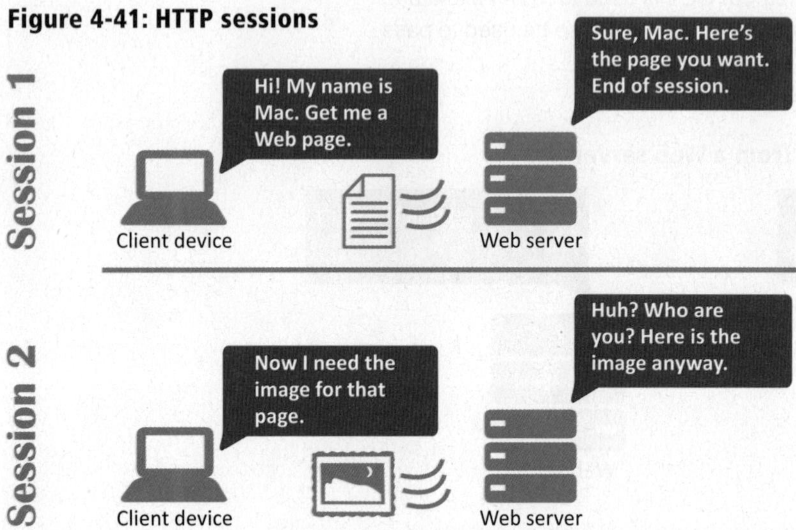

QuickCheck

What happens at the end of an HTTP session?

a. The Web server goes offline.

b. The Web server asks the browser what else it needs.

c. The Web server discontinues the connection with the browser.

d. The browser forgets which Web site you are viewing.

What if an element cannot be found? A Web server's response to a browser's request includes an **HTTP status code** that indicates whether the browser's request could be fulfilled. The status code 200 means that the request was fulfilled—the requested HTML document, graphic, or other resource was sent.

While surfing the Web, you might have encountered the "404 Not Found" message. Your browser displays this message when a Web server sends a 404 status code to indicate that the requested resource does not exist (Figure 4-42).

Figure 4-42: An HTTP 404 status code

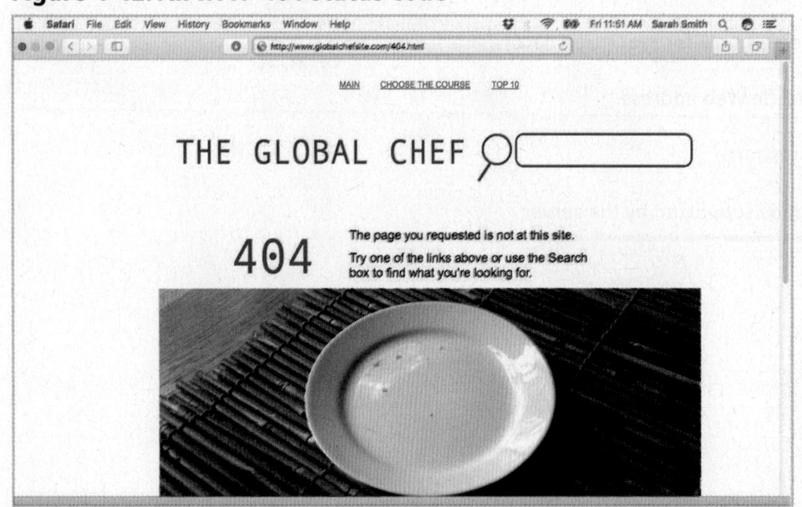

Try It!

Designers have been creative with 404 pages. Search online for *best 404 Web pages* to see some fun examples.

Cookies

Cookies—the kind associated with the Web—have a bad reputation. They are affiliated with marketing exploits that track your browsing behavior by recording products you've viewed, merchandise you've purchased, and Web sites you've visited. You can take control of cookies once you understand why they are used and how they work.

Terminology

HTTP cookies are also referred to as *Web cookies* and *browser cookies.*

▶ What is a cookie? A **cookie** (technically an HTTP cookie) is a small chunk of data generated by a Web server and stored as a text file in memory or on disk. Cookies can be stored on any devices—desktop computers, laptops, tablets, or smartphones—on which you use a browser.

Cookies provide a way for Web sites to store information on a client device for later retrieval. Web sites use cookies to:

- Monitor your path through a site to keep track of the pages you viewed or the items you purchased.
- Gather information that allows a Web server to present ads targeted to products you previously purchased at that Web site.
- Collect personal information you submit to a Web page, and retain it for the next time you visit the Web site.
- Verify that you have logged in to a site using a valid user ID and password, if necessary.

▶ Why do Web sites need to use cookies? In many respects, cookies are the solution for problems caused by HTTP's stateless protocol, which maintains no record of the pages you visit at a Web site.

QuickCheck

When a Web server cannot determine if a series of requests comes from the same browser, the protocol is ______.

a. stateless

b. a 404 error

c. HTML

Suppose that you use your browser to visit a popular online music store. You search for your favorite bands, listen to some sample tracks, and put a few albums in your shopping cart. Because HTTP is a stateless protocol, each time you connect to a different Web page at the site, the server regards it as a new visit. Therefore, HTTP by itself cannot record your path through a Web site. Cookies, however, enable the server to keep track of your activity and compile a list of your purchases.

▶ What's in a cookie? A cookie can contain any information that's collected by the host site, such as a customer number, Web page URL, shopping cart number, or access date. It may also contain an ID number that is assigned by the server or by a JavaScript. Figure 4-43 illustrates the contents of a typical cookie.

Figure 4-43: Cookie contents


```
"domain": ".amazon.com",
"expirationDate":
  2043165173.969223,
"hostOnly": false,
"httpOnly": false,
"name": "session-token",
"path": "/",
"secure": false,
"session": false,
"storeId": "0",
"value": "oH3JSTye7MX5OYLxKPdZCxY-
  RPLOj3GAb42bWfdUPv8f-
  nXBwSIG6rFt7RVY/
  uWxPUB453CMBR2d65uoEjJ-
  kA1HcqBYbmRhJ1perKUghJF/
  dYLU2Ylv3HqYBrasNH8Yvsjj-
  tjwWysyGvLvWW7U9pFcauCs-
  0GYjSC4V9ugYNJ4UOsryW7+iE
  K+H0AuAg3A/zctXp00Ysodb20
  3NvgdY72obobXhgio4vMxVjoi
  PlnoucjzOWRZa+iJXas2JjLj",
"id": 3
```


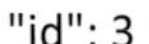

QuickCheck

Why does the cookie in Figure 4-43 refer to Amazon.com?

a. The cookie is stored on the Amazon.com Web server.

b. The cookie was set by Amazon.com.

c. The cookie transfers a Web page to Amazon.com.

How long do cookies remain on a device? There are two kinds of cookies: session cookies and persistent cookies.

Session cookies. Some cookies are stored in memory and are deleted when the browser is closed. These **session cookies** are never stored on a disk or other permanent storage medium.

Persistent cookies. Cookies that are stored on a device after a session ends are referred to as **persistent cookies.** These cookies remain on a device until they expire or are deleted. Some persistent cookies are programmed to time out after a designated date. When one of these cookies reaches the end of its predefined lifetime, your Web browser simply erases it. Some persistent cookies have no expiration date or expire on a date far into the future, so they tend to accumulate in the main storage area of digital devices.

What's the problem with cookies? A **first-party cookie** is set by the domain that hosts a Web page. A **third-party cookie** is set by a site other than the one you connected to. Third-party cookies are often set by Web sites that have affiliations with wide-ranging ad-serving companies able to combine cookie data from multiple sites, a practice called **cross-site tracking**. This tracking can be used to create profiles of your browsing habits. These profiles are used to generate targeted ads for products that might appeal to your interests.

Profiles compiled by ad aggregators are not always accurate. But regardless of their accuracy, those profiles generate ads and other offers that pop up in your browser window with maddening frequency. Figure 4-44 explains how third-party cookies are used to create profiles.

Terminology

Persistent cookies are also called *permanent cookies* or *stored cookies.*

Try It!

Connect to an informational Web site, such as *www.huffpost.com*, and look at the ads that are displayed. Do the ads seem to be generic, or do they seem to be based on personal data about you?

Figure 4-44: Third-party cookies track and profile

1 Suppose you connect to GlobalChef.com. It sets a cookie that's called a first-party cookie because it came from a site that you deliberately accessed.

2 GlobalChef.com also displays an ad from FatBusters.com. FatBusters is part of an ad network called WeSeeU. The ad sets a cookie for WeSeeU.com. That cookie might seem innocent, but just wait.

3 Next, you visit Sports.com, where there is an ad for SlimSlurp, another member of the WeSeeU ad network. Now your device is accumulating WeSeeU cookies.

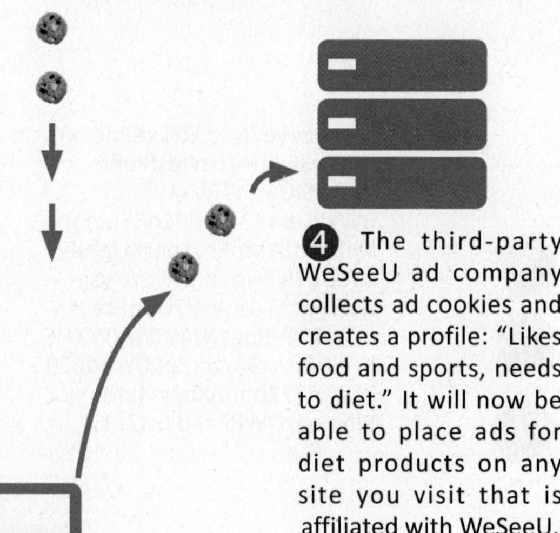

4 The third-party WeSeeU ad company collects ad cookies and creates a profile: "Likes food and sports, needs to diet." It will now be able to place ads for diet products on any site you visit that is affiliated with WeSeeU.

QuickCheck

The cookies in Figure 4-44 are ____________.

a. stateless

b. session

c. persistent

d. second-party

▶ Is it possible to see the cookies stored on a device? You can view a list of cookies stored on your device. Some parts of cookies are generally encrypted, so you cannot tell exactly what they contain. You can, however, see where the cookies are from. Cookies from domains such as adnxs.com, doubleclick.com, fetchback .com, 33across, and ad.360yield.com are likely to contain tracking information that is shared with advertisers.

Periodically, you can take a look at your accumulated cookies to gauge the amount of tracking information that is building up. For instructions about locating cookies, refer to your browser documentation. Figure 4-45 shows how to find cookies stored by Google Chrome.

Try It!

Look at the cookies stored on your device. Can you identify any that appear to be set by advertisers?

Figure 4-45: How to view cookies

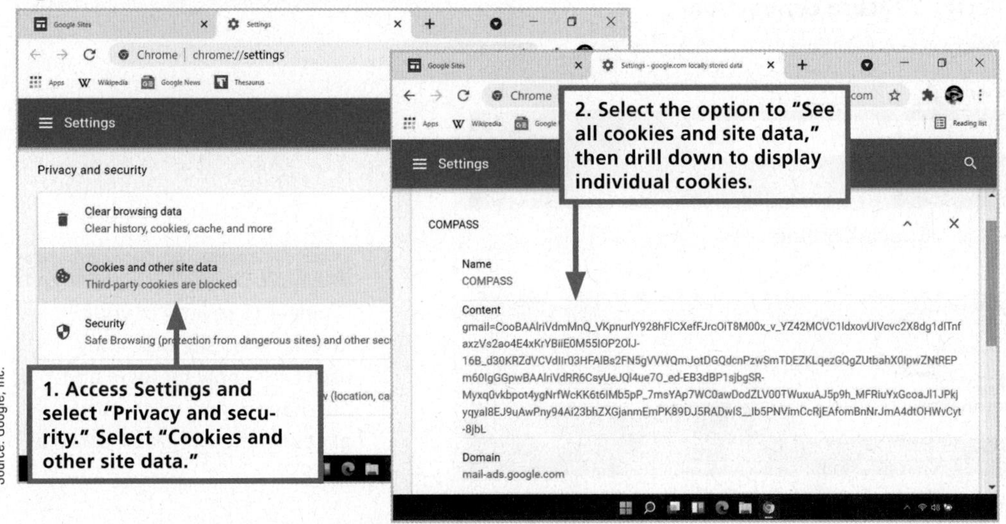
1. Access Settings and select "Privacy and security." Select "Cookies and other site data."
2. Select the option to "See all cookies and site data," then drill down to display individual cookies.
Privacy and security
Clear browsing data
Cookies and other site data
Security
COMPASS
Name
Content
Domain
mail-ads.google.com
Source: Google, Inc.

▶ Can I block cookies? Blocking all cookies drastically changes your Web experience. When you don't allow sites to set cookies on your device, those sites cannot keep track of your preferences or purchases.

Rather than turning off all cookies, you may prefer to turn off third-party cookies. Doing so should eliminate much of the profiling that is produced by cookies. Blocking cookies does not eliminate ads, however. You'll still see ads in your browser window, but they will be more generalized. Figure 4-46 illustrates the procedure for blocking third-party cookies in Google Chrome.

QuickCheck

Blocking first-party cookies ________________.

a. prevents profiling

b. makes it difficult to use online shopping carts

c. secures your device from fraud

d. prevents snoopers from discovering the Web sites you've visited

Figure 4-46: How to block third-party cookies

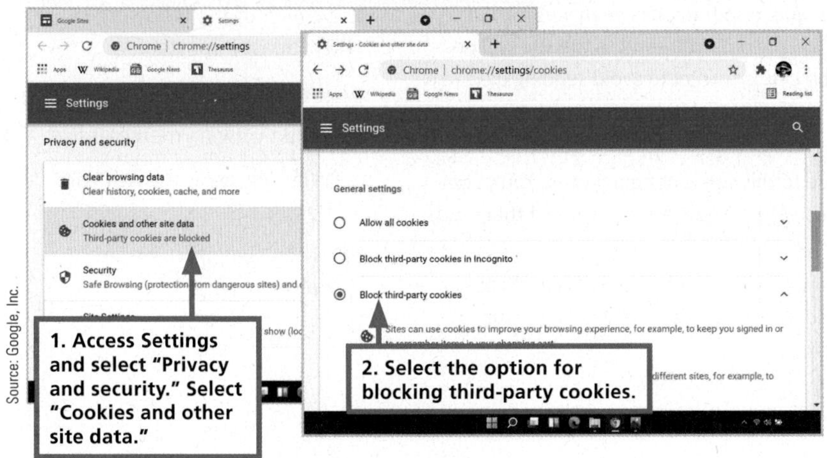
1. Access Settings and select "Privacy and security." Select "Cookies and other site data."
2. Select the option for blocking third-party cookies.
General settings
Allow all cookies
Block third-party cookies in Incognito
Block third-party cookies
Source: Google, Inc.

HTTPS

When you see https:// in the address box, pay attention. It is important.

▶ Is HTTP secure? No. HTTP transports unencrypted data between your device and a Web server. Your login passwords, credit card numbers, and other personal data are not secure on an HTTP connection. The data you transmit to a Web server can be secured, however, if it is sent over an **HTTPS** (HTTP Secure) connection, which encrypts the data stream between client devices and servers.

Currently, most Web sites use HTTPS, but when submitting personal data, you can verify that it will be transmitted by HTTPS if the URL in the address box begins with https:// or displays a lock icon (Figure 4-47).

Figure 4-47: How to verify a secure connection

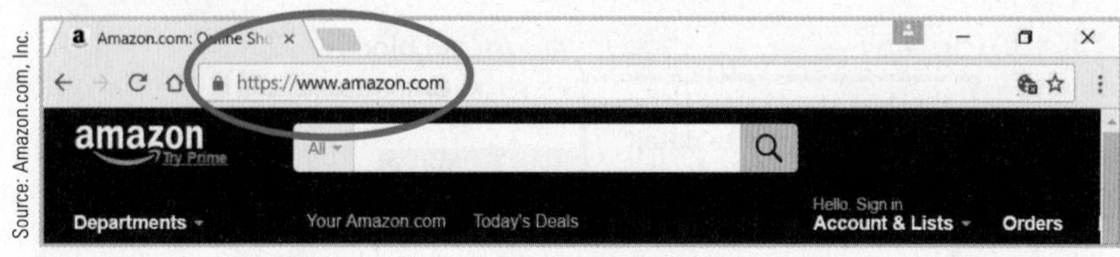

Source: Amazon.com, Inc.

Google Chrome

Source: Amazon.com, Inc.

Microsoft Edge

Try It!

Connect to several of your favorite Web sites. Do they use HTTPS only for login and purchase pages, or are other pages on the site transmitted as HTTPS?

▶ How does HTTPS work? Sites that use HTTPS are required to present an SSL certificate to the browser. This certificate helps the browser verify that the site is not pretending to be another site. Your browser may indicate the status of the SSL certificate. Figure 4-48 shows the SSL certificate icons Google Chrome displays to help you decide if a connection is secure and if it is safe to enter personal data.

Figure 4-48: SSL certificate icons

Icon	What It Means
🔒	The site's certificate is valid and its identity has been verified by a trusted third-party authority. The data you send to the site will be encrypted. Confirm that the URL is correct to avoid sending data to a fake site.
ⓘ	The site is using HTTP, not HTTPS, to exchange data with your browser. Data that you send to this site is not encrypted. You might try changing http:// to https:// in the address bar to see if there is a secure version of the site.
⚠	Google Chrome has detected problems with the site's certificate. Avoid using the site. If you decide to proceed, realize that your private information is at risk.

Source: Google, 2017

QuickCheck

For which of the following is HTTPS least important?

a. When logging in

b. When viewing merchandise

c. When providing credit card details

d. When signing up for an online service

How does HTTPS encryption work? HTTPS is based on HTTP and a public key encryption technology called SSL/TLS. **Public key encryption** is a very clever process that requires one key to encrypt data, but a different key to decrypt it. The encryption key can't be used to decrypt the message, so if that key falls into the hands of a third party, it cannot decrypt the data. Figure 4-49 explains how it works.

Figure 4-49: Public key encryption

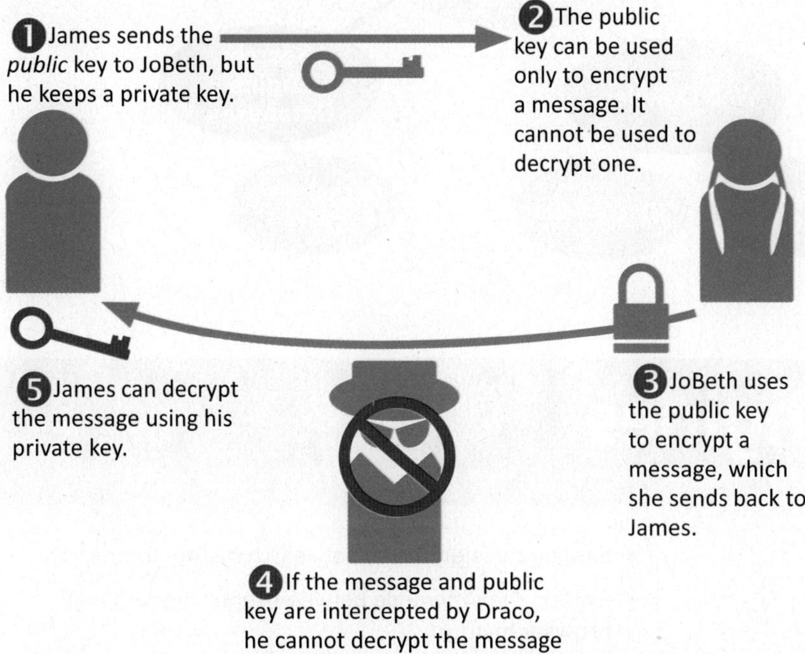

1 James sends the *public* key to JoBeth, but he keeps a private key.
2 The public key can be used only to encrypt a message. It cannot be used to decrypt one.
3 JoBeth uses the public key to encrypt a message, which she sends back to James.
4 If the message and public key are intercepted by Draco, he cannot decrypt the message because he does not have the private key.
5 James can decrypt the message using his private key.

QuickCheck

How does HTTPS protect data transmitted from Web pages to Web servers?

a. Public key encryption

b. Ad blocking

c. Setting cookies

d. Switching to a stateless protocol

QuickQuiz — Section D

1. HTTP is a(n) ______ protocol, so it cannot tell if a series of sessions were initiated by a single source or multiple sources.
2. A(n) ______ -party cookie is not set by the domain that houses the Web page displayed by the browser.
3. A(n) ______ cookie is deleted when you close your browser.
4. When a browser request is fulfilled, the Web server sends an HTTP ______ code, such as 200.
5. HTTPS uses ______ key encryption, which requires two keys: one to encrypt data and the other to decrypt it.

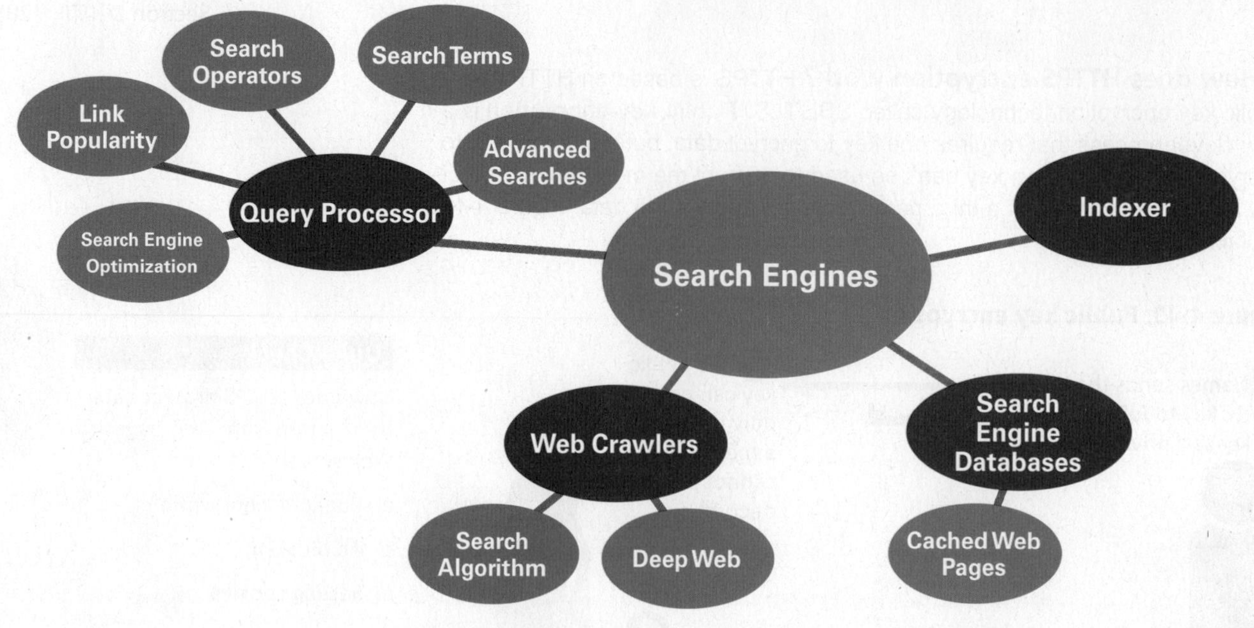

Section E

Search Engines

Objectives

- List three popular search engine Web sites.
- List the four components of a search engine.
- Explain how Web crawlers traverse the Web to collect pages for search engines.
- Provide at least three examples of the deep Web.
- Explain the difference between cached pages and live pages.
- Explain the function of a search engine indexer.
- List the steps executed by a query processor to respond to a query.
- State five techniques that can be used for search engine optimization.
- Give examples of queries using search operators such as AND, OR, NOT, quotation marks, asterisks, and range dots.
- Explain the significance of search history to privacy.
- Explain the difference between search history and browser history.
- Describe general guidelines for when fair use applies to content that you might incorporate in your own work.

The Web encompasses hundreds of millions of pages stored on servers scattered all over the globe. To use this information, you have to find it. Like most people, you probably depend on search engines to wade through the tsunami of information stored on the Web. In Section E, you'll find out how Web search engines work so that you can use them more efficiently.

Terminology

Web search engine
Web crawler
deep Web
dark Web
search engine indexer
query processor
link popularity
search engine optimization
sponsored links
search terms
search operator
search history

Search Engine Basics

According to Google, the Web has billions of unique pages and it continues to grow. We depend on search sites, such as *www.google.com*, to quickly locate specific pages. But behind the fairly straightforward act of entering a search query, there is mind-boggling technology. Let's see how it works.

What is a Web search engine? A **Web search engine** (commonly referred to simply as a search engine) is a computer program designed to help people locate information on the Web by formulating queries consisting of one or more words called keywords or search terms.

In response to a query, the search engine displays results, or "hits," as a list of relevant Web sites, accompanied by links to source pages and short excerpts containing the keywords (Figure 4-50).

Figure 4-50: Search engine results

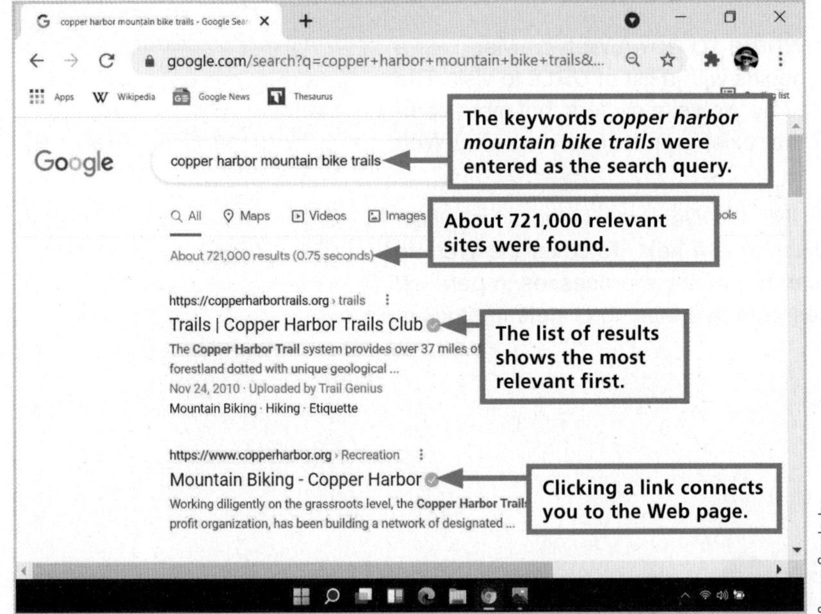
copper harbor mountain bike trails
The keywords *copper harbor mountain bike trails* were entered as the search query.
About 721,000 results (0.75 seconds)
About 721,000 relevant sites were found.
Trails | Copper Harbor Trails Club
The list of results shows the most relevant first.
Mountain Biking - Copper Harbor
Clicking a link connects you to the Web page.

Source: Google, Inc.

Try It!

The Web is constantly changing. Search for *copper harbor mountain bike trails* and compare the results of your search to the results in Figure 4-50.

What is the difference between a search engine and a search engine site? Search engines are found at Web sites, such as *www.google.com*, *www.yahoo.com*, and *www.bing.com*. Search engines can also be accessed from mobile apps on a tablet device or smartphone.

It is easy to think of *www.google.com* as a search engine; but to be precise, it is a Web site that offers access to a search engine. A search engine is the program that works behind the scenes to gather, index, find, and rank information from the Web.

Some sites, including Google, use their own proprietary search engines, but other sites use third-party search technology. For example, Microsoft's Bing search engine is the underlying technology used for Yahoo! searches.

How do search engines work? A search engine contains four components:

Web crawler: Combs the Web to gather data that's representative of the contents of Web pages

Indexer: Processes the information gathered by the crawler into a list of keywords and URLs stored in a database

Database: Stores billions of index references to Web pages

Query processor: Allows you to access the database by entering search terms, and then produces a list of Web pages that contain content relevant to your query

Let's take a look at each of these components to find out how they affect your ability to mine information from the Web.

What is a Web crawler? A **Web crawler** (also referred to as a Web spider) is a computer program that is automated to methodically visit Web sites. Web crawlers can be programmed to perform various activities as they visit sites, but in the context of search engines, Web crawlers download Web pages and submit them to an indexing utility for processing.

How does a Web crawler know where to go? A Web crawler uses a search algorithm to traverse the Web. It begins with a list of URLs to visit. The URLs on this list may have been submitted by Web site owners, but more commonly they are collected from the links that exist on previously crawled Web pages.

After copying the material at a specified URL, the Web crawler looks for hypertext links and adds them to the list of URLs to visit next. To cover the Web as efficiently as possible, a Web crawler can run multiple processes in parallel. Sophisticated algorithms keep processes from overlapping or getting stuck in loops (Figure 4-51).

QuickCheck

What does a search engine use to organize the data pertaining to Web pages?

a. An indexer

b. A query processor

c. A Web crawler

d. An HTML viewer

Figure 4-51: Crawling the Web

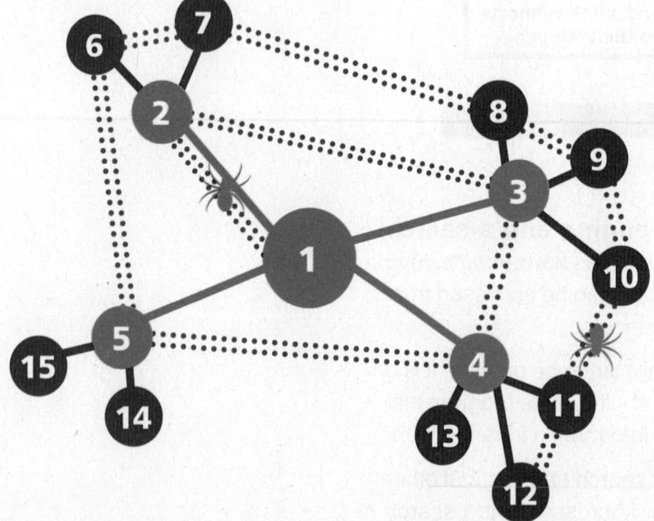

The crawler begins by making a list of all the sites that are directly connected to site 1. It crawls to each of those sites and adds links from those sites to its list of sites to crawl.

How much of the Web does a Web crawler cover? High-performance Web crawlers can visit hundreds of millions of Web pages a day. Those pages, however, only constitute a fraction of the Web. Researchers estimate that the most extensive search engines cover no more than 70% of the Web. Each search engine seems to focus on a slightly different collection of Web sites. The same search entered into different search engines can produce different results, so it is sometimes worthwhile to try alternative search engines.

Web crawlers generally do not gather material from the **deep Web** (also called the "invisible Web"), which encompasses pages that require password-protected logins and pages that are dynamically generated with server-side scripts.

The potential volume of dynamically generated pages, such as all the possible pages that Amazon.com could generate from its inventory database, is just too great to feasibly index. To access information related to online merchandise or library catalogs, you might have to go directly to the merchant's or library's Web site and use its local search tools.

Search engines also do not index the **dark Web** (or darknet), which is a part of the deep Web accessible with special software that encrypts searches and anonymizes users. The dark Web has a reputation for illicit content and activities.

How frequently do Web crawlers revisit sites? When you query a search engine, you want the results to be up to date so that you don't waste time trying to link to pages that have changed or have been deleted. Search engines use various algorithms to refresh their indexes.

The number of times a search engine's crawler visits a Web page varies, depending on several factors such as how often the page tends to change and its popularity. Obscure pages might be visited only once a month, whereas the pages at a news site would be visited daily.

Search engine results are based on the material on a Web page when the crawler last visited it. Content can change by the time you link to a page, but you can look at the cached page to see the exact page indexed by the crawler (Figure 4-52).

Figure 4-52: Cached pages

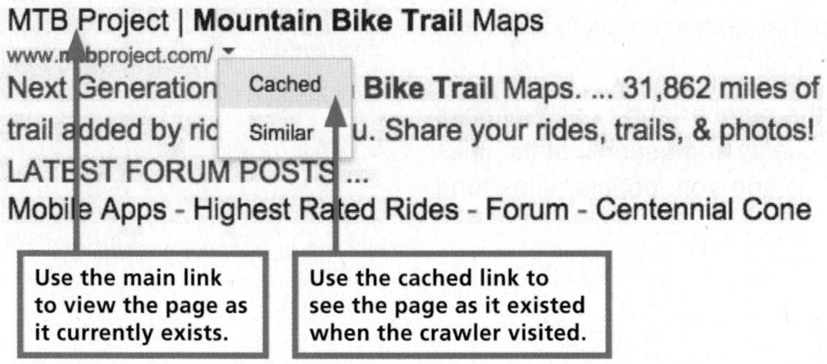

MTB Project | **Mountain Bike Trail** Maps
www.mtbproject.com/
Next Generation Cached Bike Trail Maps. ... 31,862 miles of trail added by ric Similar u. Share your rides, trails, & photos!
LATEST FORUM POSTS ...
Mobile Apps - Highest Rated Rides - Forum - Centennial Cone

Use the main link to view the page as it currently exists.

Use the cached link to see the page as it existed when the crawler visited.

How do search engine indexers work? A **search engine indexer** is software that pulls keywords from a Web page and stores them in an index database. The purpose of the indexer is to make pages easier to find based on their contents. For example, a Web page at a mountain biking site might contain information about bikes, gear, riding, and trail maps. Keywords that might help catalog this page for future access include *mountain*, *bike*, *trail*, *directions*, *gear*, *Michigan*, *bikepacking*, and *bunny hop*.

QuickCheck

Which of the following would not be considered part of the deep Web?

a. Library of Congress catalog record for a book
b. Facebook posts
c. A syllabus in the Blackboard learning management system
d. An article on CNN entertainment news

Try It!

Use Google to search for *Noquemanon Trail*. Are there any differences between the current page and the cached page?

4

What does a query processor do? A search engine's **query processor** looks for your search terms in the search engine's indexed database and returns a list of relevant Web sites. Google's query processor handles more than 60,000 queries per second. On some days, the total number of Google queries exceeds 6 billion! Each query is processed in less than a second. What happens in that second is summarized in Figure 4-53.

Figure 4-53: Query processing

1. Get the user's query.
2. Streamline the query by deleting "stop" words such as *a* and *the* and recognizing search operators AND OR NOT.
3. Add synonyms to the query.
4. Search for the query string in the 100 million GB index.
5. Rank each document for relevance based on frequency of terms, popularity of links, and proximity of query terms.
6. Display an ordered list of results.

What determines the order of results? A query processor is likely to find millions of pages that contain words matching the query. The order in which those pages are listed depends on the search engine's ranking algorithm. Google keeps this algorithm a closely guarded secret so that Web site developers can't manipulate pages to get better placement.

The underlying ranking algorithm is based on the number and quality of links to a page. **Link popularity** is a measure of the quality and quantity of the links from one Web page to others. Pages with links to and from popular sites tend to get high relevancy ratings (Figure 4-54).

Figure 4-54: Which sites rank first?

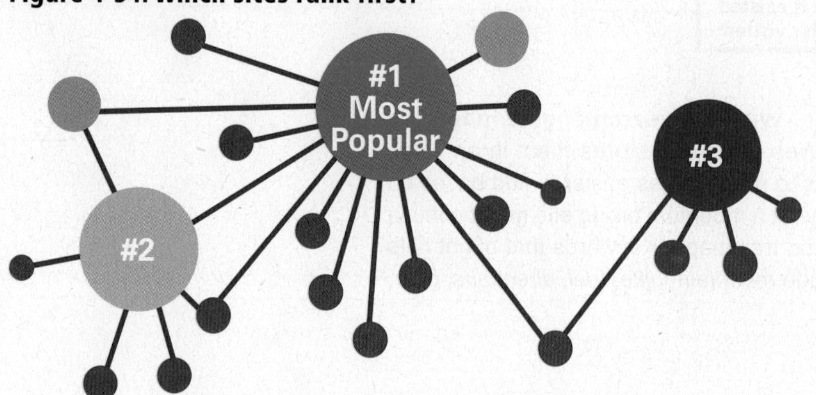

QuickCheck

What does a search engine use to rank pages before they are displayed?

a. An algorithm

b. An indexer

c. A Web crawler

d. The links to keywords

Try It!

Can you find the popularity ranking and other metrics for your favorite Web sites? Go to Alexa Site Info (*www.alexa.com/siteinfo*) and paste the URL for bicycling.com in the search box. What do the metrics tell you about this site's popularity?

Can a search engine be manipulated to give a high ranking to a page? A series of techniques called **search engine optimization** (SEO) can affect the ranking and visibility of Web pages. Search engine companies, such as Google, Yahoo!, and Bing, provide guidelines for optimizing Web sites and the pages they contain. Figure 4-55 summarizes some of these SEO techniques.

Figure 4-55: SEO techniques

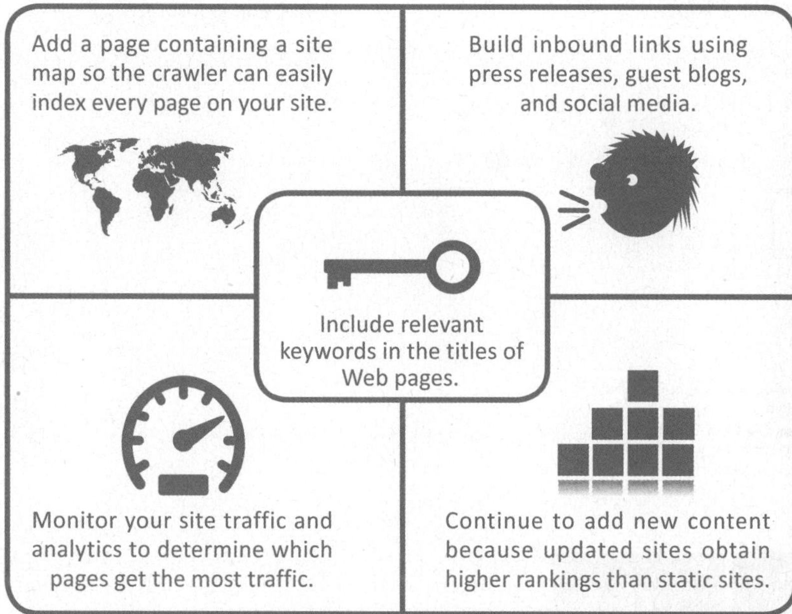

Add a page containing a site map so the crawler can easily index every page on your site.
Build inbound links using press releases, guest blogs, and social media.
Include relevant keywords in the titles of Web pages.
Monitor your site traffic and analytics to determine which pages get the most traffic.
Continue to add new content because updated sites obtain higher rankings than static sites.

What are sponsored links? Some search engines accept paid ads, sometimes called **sponsored links**, which are bumped to the top positions on the results list. Other search engines also accept paid ads but place them in a clearly marked area (Figure 4-56).

Figure 4-56: Sponsored links

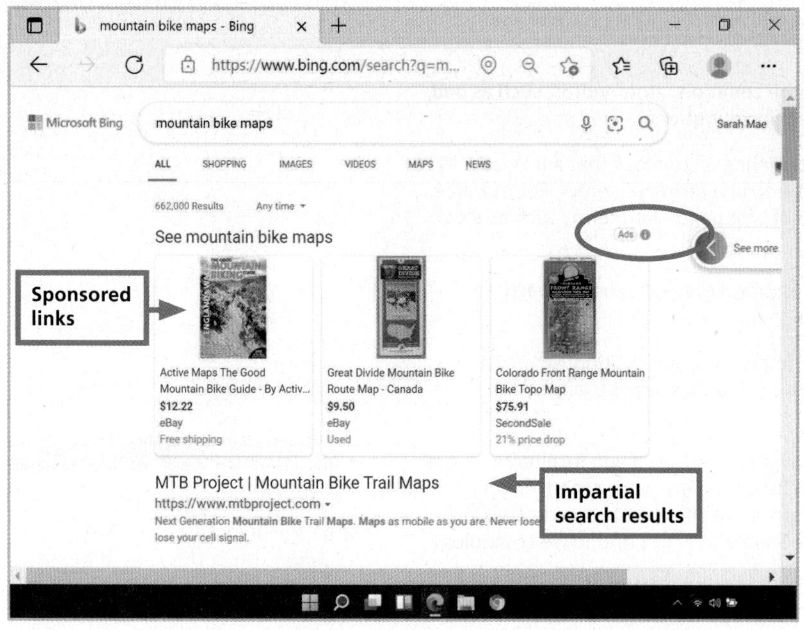

QuickCheck

Search engine optimization ________.

a. helps Web sites get higher search engine rankings
b. makes Web sites load faster
c. blocks ads and spam
d. is not encouraged by major search engine sites

4

Try It!

Search for *mountain bike maps* in Google, and then run the same search in Bing. What are the similarities and differences in the way these sites handle sponsored links?

Formulating Searches

Basic queries consist of a few keywords. When these basic queries don't produce useful results, you can try advanced query techniques.

How do I formulate a basic search? Most search engines work with keyword queries in which you enter one or more words, called **search terms**, related to the information you want to find. For example, if you're interested in Batman comics, you can type *Batman* (Figure 4-57).

Terminology

The words you enter for your search can be referred to as *queries, search criteria, search terms*, and *keywords*.

Figure 4-57: Basic queries

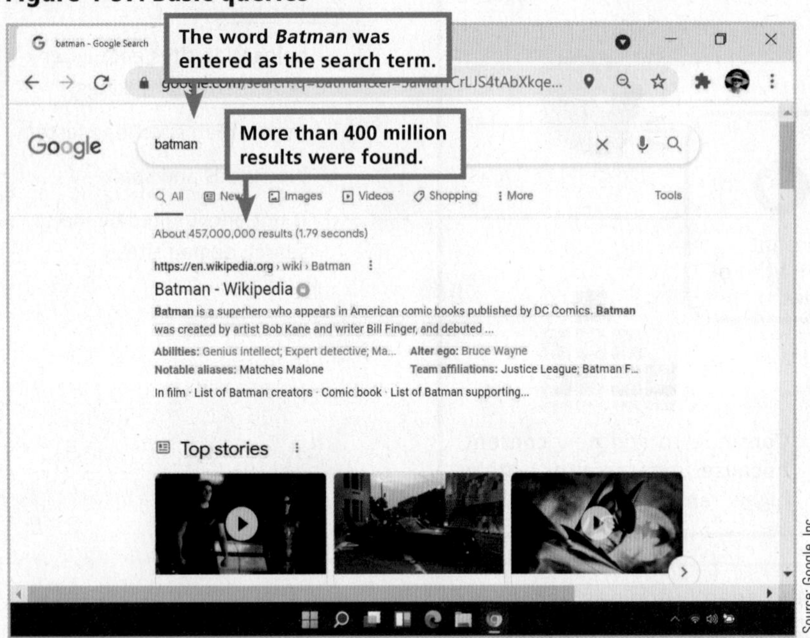

When formulating queries, keep the guidelines from Figure 4-58 in mind.

Figure 4-58: Tips for effective queries

- **Case.** Most search engines are not case sensitive, so you don't have to use the Shift key when entering proper nouns.
- **Stop words.** Search engines generally ignore common "stop" words, such as *and*, *a*, and *the*, so don't bother to include them in your query.
- **Stemming.** The top search engines use stemming technology that automatically looks for plurals and other variations of the search terms you enter. For example, if you enter *diet*, the search engine also looks for pages with terms such as *diets*, *dietary*, and *dietician*.
- **Order.** A search for *time machine* produces different results than a search for *machine time*.
- **Location.** If your search engine is able to determine your location, your results might be affected. Most search engines give you an option to change your location or hide it.
- **Context.** Search engines build on your previous searches. If you formulate several Batman-related searches and then search for *dark night*, your search engine might assume that you are looking for information about the Batman movie *The Dark Knight* instead of astronomy information. Google uses this predictive technology unless you clear your Web history.

Try It!

Enter the query *nearby restaurants* into any search engine. Does the search engine seem to know your location?

How do I get more targeted results? Narrowing a search can reduce the number of results and produce a more targeted list. It may seem counterintuitive, but entering more words in a query produces fewer, more targeted results.

Whereas the short query *Batman* produces more than 400 million results, a query for *Orson Welles Batman hoax* produces a few thousand results.

What are search operators? A **search operator** is a word or symbol that describes a relationship between search terms and helps you create a more focused query. Figure 4-59 provides a quick overview of how to use search operators when formulating searches.

4

Figure 4-59: Search operators

Operator	Description
AND	When two search terms are joined by AND, both terms must appear on a Web page before it can be included in the search results. *Batman AND movies* Result: Pages about Batman movies
OR	When two search terms are joined by OR, either one or both of the search words could appear on a page. *Batman OR Catwoman* Result: Pages about Batman and pages about Catwoman
NOT	The search term following NOT must not appear on any of the pages found by the search engine. *Batman NOT Catwoman* Result: Pages about Batman, but no pages about Catwoman
" "	To search for an exact phrase, enter it in quotes. *"Dynamic Duo"* Result: Pages that contain the exact phrase *Dynamic Duo*
*****	The asterisk (*) is sometimes referred to as a wildcard character. It allows a search engine to find pages with any derivation of a basic word. *Bat** Result: Pages about bats, batters, Batman, batteries, etc.
..	Google lets you use two dots to specify a range of numbers, dates, episodes, or prices. *Batman episodes 5..8* Result: Pages about Batman episodes 5, 6, 7, and 8

Try It!

Which one of the following searches returns the most targeted (fewest) results?

racing shell gear

"racing shell" gear

racing shell -gear

racing OR shell OR gear

Is it possible to filter results by file type? Some search engine sites offer separate searches for academic works, images, videos, news, maps, and blogs. Look for links to these specialized searches at your favorite search engine sites (Figure 4-60).

Figure 4-60: Filter searches for images, videos, or other criteria

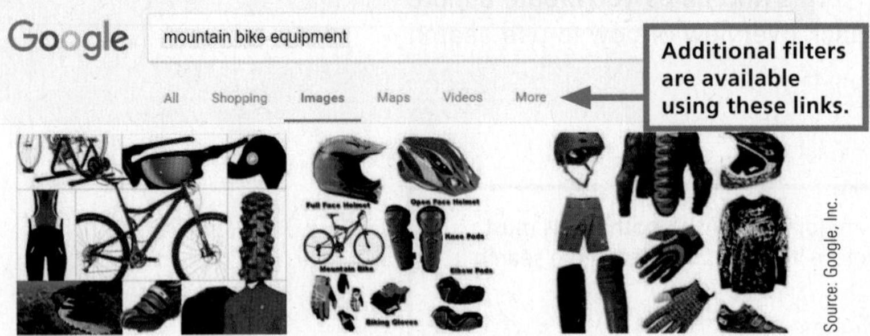

What is an advanced search? Many search engines provide ways to make your searches more precise and obtain more useful results. You might be able to use advanced search options to limit your search to material written in a specific language or stored in a specific file format. You might be able to specify a date and stipulate whether to look for your search terms in the title, URL, or body of the Web page (Figure 4-61).

Figure 4-61: Google advanced search

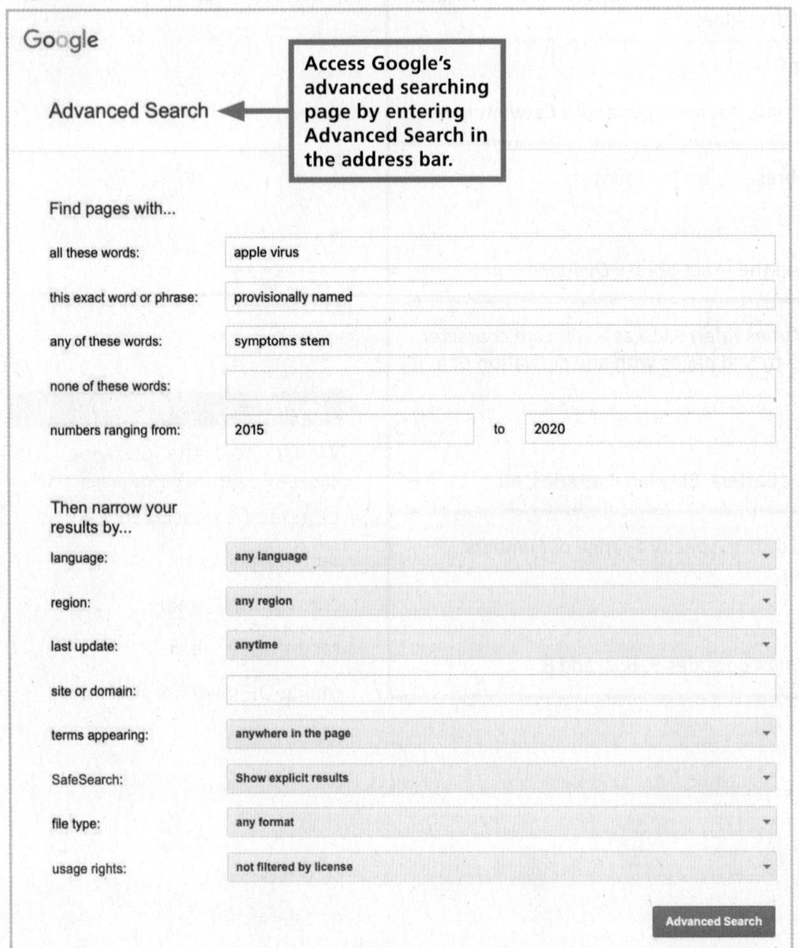

Try It!

What results would you expect based on the advanced search in Figure 4-61? Try the query to find out if you guessed correctly.

Search Privacy

It is troubling that browsers store a list of sites you've visited and cache the files for those sites. And then there are cookies that can be used to profile your browsing activities. Yet another intrusion into your privacy is the data stored in query logs maintained by search engines.

Do search engines keep records of queries? Considering that a major search engine can receive billions of queries every day, the surprising answer to this question is "yes." Search engines at major sites such as Google, Bing, and Yahoo! save massive numbers of searches made by site visitors. Industry analysts believe that some sites retain user queries for at least 30 days and that at least one search engine site has retained every search ever made at the site.

In 2006, AOL provided researchers with a database of 20 million queries made by site visitors. Figure 4-62 illustrates a small section of this database for queries made by users interested in Batman.

Figure 4-62: Should search engines retain users' queries?

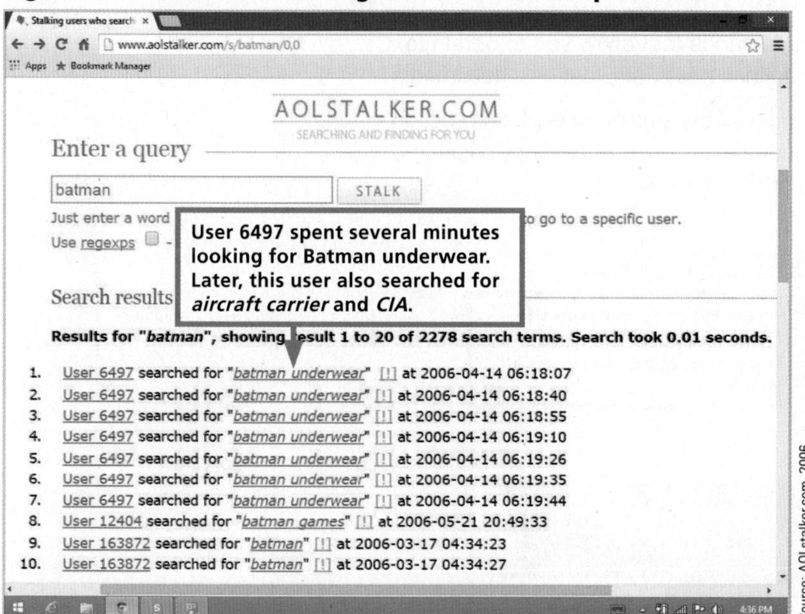

Source: AOLstalker.com, 2006

What kind of information does a search engine store? Your **search history** contains a list of queries that you've made in a specific search engine. It is not the same as your browser history, which is a list of Web sites you've visited and is maintained by your browser. Search history is stored in server logs on the search engines' computers. In its Privacy Policy, Google provides the example of a server log shown in Figure 4-63.

Figure 4-63: What's in a search engine server log?

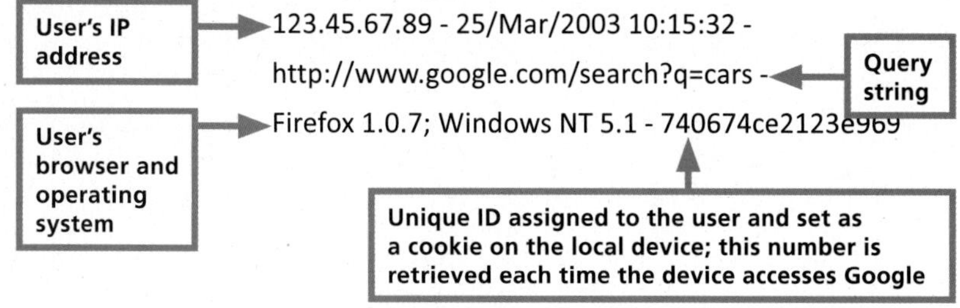

QuickCheck

Which one of the following is stored on search engine computers?

a. Browsing history

b. Browser cache

c. Search history

d. Search settings

Can I access my search history? Check your search engine's privacy policy to find out if it offers access to your search history. Your Google search history can be viewed and deleted by entering *Google My Activity* in the search bar of any browser. Your search history is accessible only if you have a Google account and are logged in.

What can I do to keep my searches confidential? For Google users, go to *Google My Activity* and turn Web & App Activity off. Yahoo! users can control search history settings from the Search History option on the Settings menu. Bing users can find settings on the History page at *www.bing.com/profile/history*.

Anonymizer sites, such as *www.torproject.org*, act as relay stations to forward your searches to Google or other search engines without leaving a trail back to a cookie or an IP address. Tor also offers a browser that runs on a distributed network to cloak queries. Although law-abiding citizens may have nothing to hide, the increasingly invasive tracking and advertising at many Web sites is leading many Web surfers to use anonymizer tools that offer privacy.

Try It!

Are your search queries being tracked? Use the information supplied on this page and additional online resources to find out.

Using Web-based Source Material

Most browsers provide Copy and Save commands that allow you to obtain text and images from a Web page, which you can then paste into your own documents.

How do I save the source? To keep track of the source for each text section, you can highlight the Web page's URL in the Address box, use the Copy command, and then paste the URL into your document (Figure 4-64).

Figure 4-64: Copy the URL along with source material

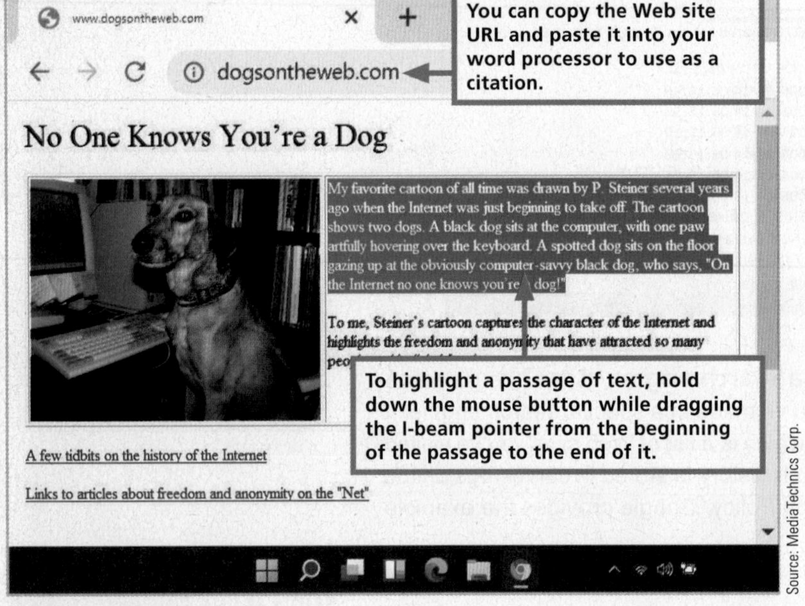

Source: MediaTechnics Corp.

How do I cite sources? Presenting someone else's work as your own is plagiarism. If you copy text, pictures, or other works from a Web page, be sure to credit the original author. Information that identifies the source of a quotation or excerpted work is called a citation. Written documents, such as reports and projects, generally include footnotes, endnotes, or in-line citations formatted according to a standard style, such as MLA, APA, or Chicago.

When compiling the citation for online sources, be sure to provide sufficient information so readers can locate the source. Also, include the date when you accessed the source and the full URL. According to APA style, a citation to a Web-based source should provide a document title or description; the author's name, if available; the date of publication, update, or retrieval; and a URL.

Do I need permission to use material? In the United States, the Fair Use Doctrine allows limited use of copyrighted material for scholarship and review without obtaining permission. For scholarly reports and projects, for example, you can use a sentence or paragraph of text without obtaining permission if you include a citation to the original source.

Photos and excerpts from music and videos can be used within the context of critique, but their use purely as decorative elements for a document or Web page would, in most cases, not be considered fair use.

Some Web sites clearly state allowable uses for material. Look for a link to Terms of Use. For example, the YouTube Web site contains a collection of videos submitted by amateurs and semi-professionals, who retain the copyright to their materials. The Terms of Use section of the site allows the public to access, use, reproduce, distribute, create derivatives of, display, and perform user-submitted works within the YouTube platform. Even with such broad terms of use, however, it is essential to cite the original source of the material if you incorporate it in your own work.

How do I get permission? To obtain permission to use text, photos, music, videos, and other elements you find on the Web, contact the copyright holder by email, and explain what you want to use and how you plan to use it. You can often find contact information on the Web site—if not for the copyright holder, at least for a Web site administrator who can direct you to the copyright holder.

4

QuickCheck

When you incorporate Web-based material in research papers, why is it not necessary to get permission from the source?

a. Because the Fair Use Doctrine allows it.

b. Because the material is not copyrighted.

c. Because it is on the Web.

d. Because your school library has a deal with the content owner.

QuickQuiz — Section E

1. A search engine's ________ pulls keywords from a Web page and stores them in a database.
2. When you enter search terms, the search engine's ________ processor looks for the terms in the search engine's database.
3. *AND*, *OR*, and *NOT* are examples of search ________.
4. Most search engines keep track of users by assigning a unique ID number, which is stored in a(n) ________ on the hard disk of the user's device.
5. To keep track of the Web pages where you obtained information or images, you can highlight the Web page's ________, copy it, and then paste it into a list of sources. (Hint: Use the acronym.)

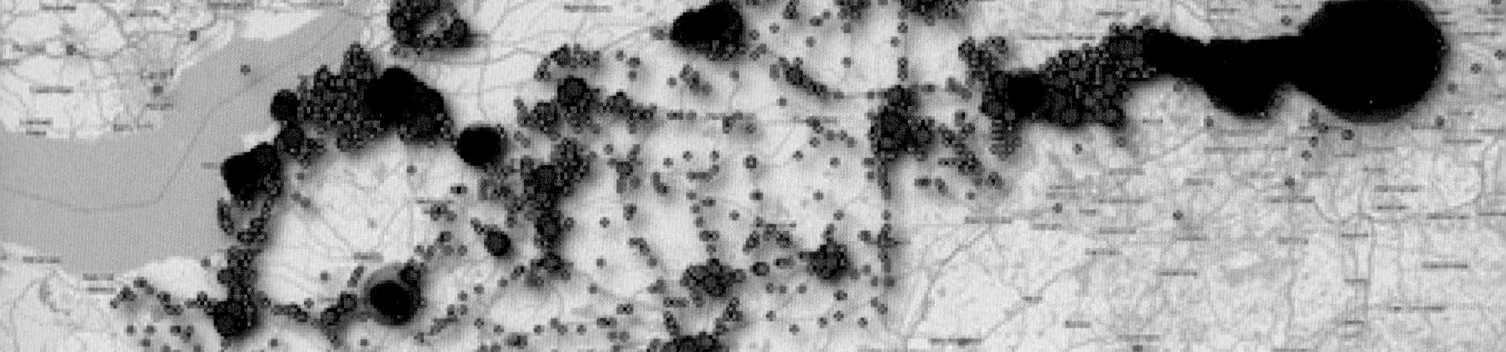

Courtesy of Alasdair Allan and Pete Warden

Issue: Who Is Tracking You?

In the movie *Harry Potter and the Prisoner of Azkaban*, Harry acquires a magical item called the Marauder's Map, which shows the location of every teacher and student at the Hogwarts School of Witchcraft and Wizardry.

In the context of Harry Potter, tracking technology seems fun, but real-life tracking technologies have a dark side, which privacy advocates fear might be misused by governments, corporations, and possibly criminals to monitor the daily activities of ordinary people.

According to the EFF (Electronic Frontier Foundation), "Tracking is the retention of information that can be used to connect records of a person's actions or reading habits across space, cyberspace, or time."

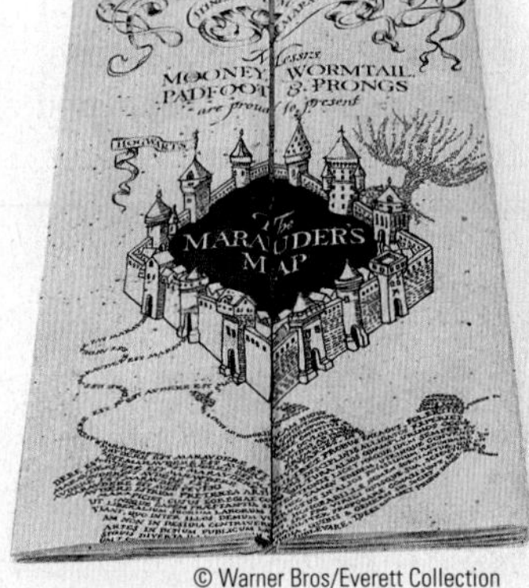

© Warner Bros/Everett Collection

Two broad categories of tracking are behavioral tracking and locational tracking. Behavioral tracking accumulates information about what you do: the Web sites you visit, the merchandise you purchase online, and the people with whom you correspond. Locational tracking records your physical location: where you live and work, where and when you shop, and the route you take to get to school.

Tracking made headlines in 2011 when security experts Pete Warden and Alasdair Allan discovered that iPhones collected and stored date-stamped information that triangulated the phone's location. A simple software application called iPhone Tracker could retrieve this data and display it on a map.

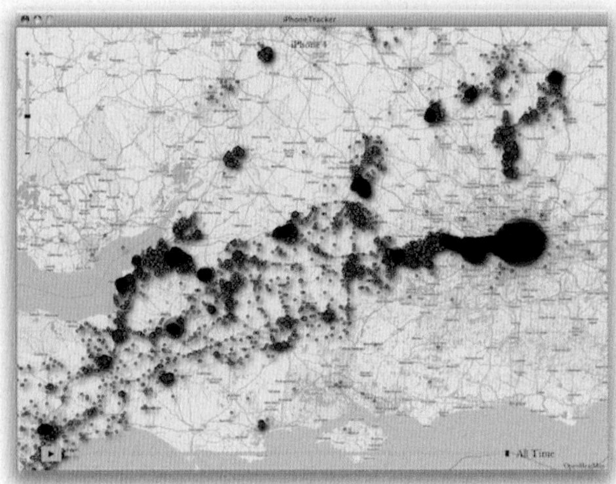

The iPhone tracking story spread like wildfire over the mainstream media, blogs, and social networks. Privacy advocates pointed out that government agencies, disgruntled spouses, parents, and criminals could easily trace a person's whereabouts.

In 2020, location tracking hit the headlines again when tracking apps were considered as a possible way of controlling the COVID-19 pandemic. Privacy organizations such as Human Rights Watch questioned the efficacy, equity, and even the constitutionality of government-mandated location tracking.

The technology that makes it easy for a cell phone to track your movements can be incorporated into other handheld devices and tucked into vehicles, identification badges, pet collars, clothing, and even tiny chips that can be implanted under the skin. Tracking is controversial, especially when it occurs without the consent or control of the trackee.

Privacy advocates want strict protocols for collecting, using, storing, and distributing location information. They face opposition, however, from government officials who would like to explore ways that location technology can be used to track criminals, prevent terrorism, and control the spread of diseases.

Commercial interest in tracking technology for marketing and advertising is also high, and consumers seem willing to give up some privacy for the convenience offered by location-based services, such as Yelp and Foursquare.

The outcome of conflicting interests will determine if location-tracking technology can be implemented in such a way that the rights and privacy of individuals are protected.

Try It! Locational tracking is kind of creepy. The idea that someone can pinpoint where you regularly use your digital devices is a little unsettling, but knowing that someone might be tracking your movements as you travel from home to school, to the mall, to the doctor, and to the movies might give you more than a moment of concern. Explore tracking technologies to arm yourself with knowledge that can help protect your privacy.

1. As an experiment, make sure that location services are turned on for one of your digital devices, and track your activities for one day. If possible, print out a map. After you collect your tracking data, write a short summary describing how this data could be used to your benefit, or how it might infringe on your privacy.The following instructions will help you turn tracking on for various devices:

   Android smartphones. Go to Settings and make sure Location service is on. Turn on Google Location Reporting and Location History. After you've tracked for a day, view your location history on a map by connecting your device to *maps.google.com/locationhistory*.

   iPhones. Go to Settings, Privacy, Location Services, and turn Location Services on. Then, scroll down to System Services, turn on all settings, and select Significant Locations to turn it on. After you've tracked for a day, view the track by accessing Significant Locations and looking at its History options.

   Laptops. You can install free tracking software such as FollowMee GPS Tracker (*www.followmee.com*) and Prey (*preyproject.com*). Or, sign up for iCloud and install the FindMyiPhone app on any macOS or Windows device.

2. Your smartphone might be tracking your location. In addition, some apps might be storing data related to your whereabouts. Review the settings on one of your digital devices to ensure that they reflect the level of location privacy you prefer. Describe what you think is an ideal level of privacy for people with a lifestyle similar to yours.

3. The location of digital devices can be pinpointed using three different, but complementary, technologies: GPS, cell-tower triangulation, and WPS. Use Wikipedia and other online resources to explore these technologies. How would you describe each technology?

4. Tracking usually happens behind the scenes, often without a user's knowledge or approval. However, information that people intentionally post online can also be used to track their locations. Think about the information that you post on your social networking and media sharing sites. How might that information be used to determine your location or track your movements?

What Do You Think?

Issue

1. Do you worry about behavioral tracking based on your Internet use?
2. Do you have a device that can track your physical location?
3. Under what circumstances do you think tracking is justified?

Z-River/Shutterstock.com

Information Tools: Citations

You can use other people's ideas in your own research papers and presentations, but you must cite the source for any information that is not common knowledge. A citation is a formal reference to a published work, like this:

"It Can't Happen Here." *Encyclopædia Britannica. Encyclopædia Britannica Online*. Encyclopædia Britannica, 2011. Web. 13 Sep. 2014. <http://www.britannica.com/EBchecked/topic/297133/It-Cant-Happen-Here>.

A collection of citations is called a bibliography.

Use an approved citation style, such as MLA, APA, or Chicago. Several Web sites, such as the Purdue University Online Writing Lab, include detailed style guides.

Papers on technology topics frequently contain material from books, magazines, journals, news reports, press releases, and court decisions. Make sure you understand the citation data that you need to collect for each of these formats, both in print and online.

Articles from Print Sources

Author, article title, periodical title, date of publication, page numbers

Books

Author, book title, edition, publisher, place and date of publication, ISBN

(If referencing a section of a book, note page numbers, chapter title, and chapter author, if applicable.)

Journals

Same information as a periodical with the addition of the volume and issue numbers

Legal Decisions

Case name; the volume, abbreviation, and page reference for the legal reporter where the case was reported; the date of the case

Web Pages

Author, title of Web page, title of Web site, complete URL, date of publication (sometimes there will not be a publication date; some citation styles use "n.d." in this case), sponsoring organization (look for it on the copyright line at the bottom of the page), date visited

A publication might have several unique identifying numbers. Stay alert so that you use the correct one.

ISBN (International Standard Book Number): A unique number given to a book or monograph

DOI (Digital Object Identifier): A unique number assigned to journal articles and other online documents

LCCN (Library of Congress Control Number): A unique number assigned to each publication in the Library of Congress

Desktop software such as EndNote, RefWorks, Cite This For Me, and Zotero can help you create and manage all the citations for your bibliographies.

Mobile apps such as Cite It Now and Bookends read bar codes on book covers and accept manual entries to automatically create citations on the go.

Try It! Let's go beyond the basics and work with some advanced citation tools. Use any word processor and create a document called Citation Project [Your Name], then complete the following steps:

1. Suppose that you'd like to include information from press releases in a research paper. How should you format the citations? Use a search engine to look for *How do I cite a press release*. Next, search for a recent press release from Apple. Create a citation for the press release and save it in your Citation Project document.

2. Some academic directories/databases provide citation information for the resources they list. BibTeX, illustrated at right, is a common format. Open an academic directory of technology articles, such as Microsoft Academic, ACM Digital Library, or Google Scholar. Search for "privacy" and select a recent article related to mobile phone privacy. Look for the Cite, Bib, or BibTeX icon, and then click it. Notice that each element of the reference is clearly labeled. Copy the BibTeX data and paste it into your Citation Project document; you'll find out how to format this citation data in the next steps.

Be sure to collect data for the article itself, not simply the directory that lists the article.

3. Microsoft Word includes a built-in bibliography manager that helps you format citations. To access the citation feature, select References, choose the MLA style, then click Insert Citation. Fill in the form to create an MLA citation for the BibTeX data you found in Step 2.

4. You can use free Web-based citation formatters, such as BibMe, Citation Machine, Cite This For Me, or EasyBib, to format citations in MLA, APA, or other approved styles. Connect to a Web-based citation formatter, choose Online Journal as the source, select the MLA citation style, then enter the BibTeX data you collected in Step 2. Paste the formatted citation into your Citation Project document.

When using automated citation formatters based on ISBNs or DOIs, look carefully at the citation that is produced to ensure that it contains all required citation information.

5. For some books, Web sites, and journal articles, you can use their ISBN, URL, or DOI instead of manually entering the citation data. Connect to a Web-based citation formatter, such as one of those listed in Step 4. Enter the ISBN 978-0316380508 to search for the citation. Produce the MLA citation, copy it, then paste it into your Citation Project document.

6. DOIs are an alternative to ISBNs for identifying academic articles. Enter the DOI 10.1145/2818717 in any browser to connect to the source document. Add the citation to your Citation Project document.

BibTeX Citation

```
@article{Aditya15,
title = {Brave New World: Privacy Risks for Mobile Users},
author = {Paarijaat Aditya and Bobby Bhattacharjee and Peter Druschel and Viktor Erdelyi and Matthew Lentz},
journal = {ACM SIGMOBILE Mobile Computing and Communications Review},
volume = {18},
number = {3},
pages = {49-54},
issn = {1559-1662},
month = {1},
year = {2015},
note = {http://www.odysci.com/artcle/1010113021738527},
url = {http://portal.acm.org/citation.cfm?id=2721896.2721907},
doi = {10.1145/2721896.2721907},
```

© Lynn Barry/MIT Media Lab

Technology in Context: Fashion Industry

Fashion is big business. Worldwide, this industry generates more than $1 trillion in annual revenue. Competition is tough as designers, manufacturers, and retailers compete for customer dollars.

In the fashion industry, trends change quickly. As the saying goes, "Today's style is tomorrow's markdown." Fashion industry players look for every competitive advantage. It is no surprise that technology plays a major role in this glitzy industry.

Fashion begins with designers, such as Miuccia Prada, John Galliano, and Marc Jacobs. Their runway extravaganzas set off fashion trends that eventually work their way to retail stores. Fashion runways went high-tech in 1999 when lingerie manufacturer Victoria's Secret produced a Webcast watched by over 1 million viewers. Bravo television's *Project Runway* show has been one of the top iPod downloads. Fashion podcasts and blogs abound on the Web, as do fashion sites packed with news about the latest trends.

Although runway fashions are often conceived with a sketch and stitched by hand, designs are adapted for the ready-to-wear market by using computer-aided design (CAD) tools, such as pattern-making software.

Garments are constructed by sewing together sections of fabric that form arms, fronts, backs, collars, and so forth. The set of templates used to cut fabric sections is called a pattern. Pattern-making is a tricky 3D challenge because flat pieces of fabric eventually become garments shaped to conform to curved body contours. Pattern-making software helps designers visualize how flat pieces fit together and drape when sewn. Once a pattern is complete, pattern-making software automatically generates a set of patterns for each garment size.

Fashion requires fabric, and computers play a major role in fabric design and manufacturing. Computer software, such as ArahWeave, lets fabric designers experiment with colors, yarns, and weaves while viewing detailed, realistic on-screen samples.

Most of today's weaving mills use computerized machinery that directly accepts digital input to control threads and patterns. Networks tie looms to CAD stations and to the Internet. Fabric designs can be stored in XML format, transmitted to a fabric manufacturer over the Internet, and used directly by computerized weaving machines.

Fabrics that can alert the wearer to conditions in their surroundings are currently being developed. Two students at the Tisch School of the Arts designed a shirt that can detect carbon monoxide. Microcontrollers change the color of the shirt's thermochromatic fabric to alert wearers of harmful pollutants in their vicinity.

Clothing production, warehousing, and shipping are also highly automated. Benetton's high-tech facility in Castrette, Italy, can produce over 110 million garments per year. Its automated distribution center handles 120,000 boxes of merchandise daily. RFID tags—sometimes called smart labels—can be attached to individual garments or to packing boxes as an important tool for controlling inventory.

© Lifetime Television/Everett Collection

RFID technology uses an inexpensive, tiny computer chip with a built-in antenna and the capacity to store between 64 and 128 bits of data about a garment—its SKU number, size, model, dye lot, manufacturing date, and so on. Tags can be attached to a garment or its label. An RFID reader that can retrieve data from tags is used to track merchandise from the manufacturing plant through the distribution chain to the retailer.

RFID tags have become popular for all types of merchandise. Businesses that use them can save time and money. For example, RFID tags can reduce the time it takes to do a physical inventory by a factor of 10. Privacy advocates, however, are worried because these tags remain active even after you bring your merchandise home. Could a thief circle your house with an RFID scanner to find out what's inside? Could a stalker follow your movements by tracking the RFID tag embedded in your sweater?

Next time you buy a garment, check to see if an RFID tag is attached. It would normally be sewn into a seam and may carry a warning such as "Remove before wearing."

© Lynn Barry/MIT Media Lab

Online shopping has become routine, but one drawback of catalog and online ordering is the cost associated with restocking returned merchandise. Can an online customer find out how a garment will fit and look before ordering it?

A company called TrueFit has accumulated a database containing millions of detailed garment specifications that help consumers select the correct garment size based on their body measurements, actual garment measurements, and customer reviews. Some fashion brands offer digital showrooms where shoppers can photographically try on apparel to see how it looks.

No discussion of fashion and technology would be complete without highlighting wearable technology. MIT's Media Lab has been a hub of wearable technology development. One student project integrated a webcam, a battery-powered projector, and an Internet-enabled mobile phone so that wearers could use hand gestures in 3D space to conjure up information from the phone and project it on any surface.

Some wearables have even emerged from the laboratory and onto store shelves.

Originally popular with Secret Service agents, jackets produced by SCOTTeVEST include pockets for a cell phone, MP3 player, and iPad, along with built-in wiring to connect these devices into a personal area network (PAN). Available in both men's and women's sizes, the jackets can now be purchased by civilians.

At the more extreme end of the wearable technology spectrum and sometimes reminiscent of technology found in science-fiction books and movies, solar panels that can be used for charging smartphones and other mobile devices are starting to illuminate the more fashionable side of wearables. Designer Pauline van Dongen's Wearable Solar clothing incorporates traditional fabrics and materials such as wool and leather with high-technology solar cells strategically hidden in the garment to create an aesthetically pleasing and functional high-tech fashion statement.

And then there is Nadi X, yoga clothing containing sensors that assess your body position and produce subtle pulses to guide you into the correct yoga poses.

Even more extreme and futuristic, invisibility cloaks made from smart fabrics and metamaterials are beginning to blur the line between camouflage and invisibility. Using technologies that bend light around a special fabric, companies such as HyperStealth Biotechnology Corp. have developed products that they call "active camouflage." One promising camouflage technology uses fractals to create repeated patterns with the ability to change color. Whether this technology becomes more popular on the runway or in the military is yet to be determined.

With a growing emphasis on the use of technology in fashion design and manufacturing, fashion degree programs at colleges and technical schools have added courses such as computer-aided fashion design, computer-based pattern drafting, pattern grading and computer-aided drafting, and wearable computers.

Flipped Class Projects

Critical Thinking

Your browser can track the Web sites you've visited and save Web page files in its cache. The search engine you use can store a record of your search queries.The U.S. government seems to be recording all of the data that flows over the Internet. Advertisers track your Web activities using cookies. How much do these privacy intrusions bother you? Which seem the most disturbing? Have you taken steps to curb these intrusions, or in your opinion is tracking no big deal?

Group Project

The purpose of this project is to hone your search skills. Work in groups to develop a set of five questions for a Web scavenger hunt. The questions should have concrete answers and should not be easy to locate with a basic Wikipedia query. Exchange your group's question set with another group, then see which group finds all the answers first.

Cyberclassroom

The use of digital devices in the classroom is controversial. In some classrooms, digital devices are welcomed and incorporated into activities. In other classrooms, digital devices are seen as a distraction. Compile a list of your personal observations about the way digital devices are used in classes by you and the students around you. Be prepared to share your observations in a class discussion.

Multimedia Project

Surf the Web to select a home page that needs improvement. Take a screenshot of the original page. Use an online Web page authoring tool, such as Simbla, Webflow, or Google Sites, to create an improved home page. Consider a design that works both on a full-size screen and on the screens of mobile devices. Also consider how the design works with a mouse or touchscreen. Take a screenshot of your makeover and save it as Home Page Makeover [Your Name]. Make a list of the changes you made. Submit the original page, the makeover page, and the list of changes to your instructor.

Resume Builder

Many companies have a Web site that provides information on their products and services. Use a search engine to locate a company in your career field. Suppose you are a recruiter for that company and you'll be attending a series of college career fairs. Create a one-page information flyer that you can hand out to prospective recruits. The flyer should include:

- The company's name, URL, and physical location(s)
- A brief description of the company's mission, products, and services
- Instructions on how to submit a resume electronically

Globalization

We're accustomed to seeing Web pages in English. But for many people, English is not their native language. Explore online resources to find the current percentage of Web pages that are published in languages other than English. Also explore to find the number of Web users who are not English-language natives. As a supplemental activity, use Advanced search to find a Web page in a language such as Arabic or Chinese, and use Google Translate to view the same page in English. Record your impressions about Web access across the spectrum of human languages.

Key Terms

bidirectional links 248
bookmarks 259
browser cache 262
browser extension 260
browser home page 258
browser tabs 259
client-side scripts 274
CSS (Cascading Style Sheets) 272
cookie 281
cross-site tracking 282
dark Web 289
deep Web 289
default browser 257
dynamic Web page 274
external CSS 272
first-party cookie 282
History list 263
HTML conversion utility 269
HTML document 267
HTML tags 267
HTML5 267
HTTP 279
HTTP methods 279
HTTPS 284
HTTP session 280
HTTP status code 280
hypertext 244
hypertext links 247
inline CSS 272
internal CSS 272
link popularity 290
linkrot 251
local HTML editors 269
markup language 267
online HTML editor 269
persistent cookies 282
predictive services 258
private browsing 264
public key encryption 285
query processor 290
search engine indexer 289
search engine optimization 291
search history 295
search operator 293
search terms 292
server-side scripts 275
session cookies 282
short URLs 252
source document 268
sponsored links 291
stateless protocol 280
static Web page 274
style rules 272
third-party cookie 282
unidirectional links 248
URL 249
Web browser 243
Web crawler 288
Web hosting service 276
Web page 246
Web search engine 287
Web server 246
Web site 246
World Wide Web 243

Interactive Summary

Section A: The Web, one of the Internet's hottest attractions, is a collection of document, image, video, and sound files that can be linked and accessed over the Internet via the [ ] protocol. The Web is an interlinked collection of information, whereas the [ ] is the communications system used to transport Web information. The Web evolved from a concept called [ ], which describes a collection of literary documents linked according to logical relationships. In 1990, Tim Berners-Lee developed the technologies used for today's Web. An Internet-based computer that stores and distributes Web files is called a Web [ ]. It can host one or more Web [ ] such as *www.wikipedia.org* or *www.facebook.com* containing HTML [ ] documents, which can be accessed and displayed using client software called a Web [ ]. Each Web page has a unique address called a(n) [ ].

Section B: Today's popular browsers include Microsoft Edge, Google [ ], Apple Safari, and Mozilla Firefox. The browser that starts automatically when clicking links in email messages is called the [ ] browser. Browsers can be customized in many ways—for example, by adding [ ] for pages you use frequently. Browser [ ] such as AdBlock and toolbars add functionality to browsers. Browsers can also store user IDs and [ ] to make logging in to Web sites more convenient. Browser users can decide whether or not to turn this feature on even though it is a slight security risk. When browsers download HTML documents, images, and links for a Web page, they are stored in a browser [ ]. Browsers also store a list of the Web sites you've visited in the [ ] list. Turning on [ ] browsing stores these items only temporarily and deletes them when the browser is closed.

Section C: The current version of HTML is ________, which was introduced in 2010. HTML is an example of a(n) ________ language that uses HTML ________, such as <h1> and <p>, to specify the format for text and images. A similar language, called ________, is used to describe data by inserting tags that represent database fields. An HTML document is also called a(n) ________ document, which can be viewed from within a browser. Several online and local tools are available for creating HTML documents. An HTML document consists of two parts: the head and the ________. The specifications for text styles in Web pages can be included in ________ style sheets. These can be ________, internal, or external. A link to an external CSS document can be inserted in the ________ section of an HTML document. Using HTML and CSS, Web designers can create a(n) ________ Web page that displays the same information regardless of who accesses it. Designers can also use client-side and server-side scripting to create ________ Web pages featuring animations or content that is customized for a specific user. Web sites can be posted on Web ________ services, where they can be thoroughly tested before being open for public access.

Section D: HTTP is the Web's communications ________ that works with TCP/IP to deliver elements of Web pages to a local browser. A browser communicates with a Web server using HTTP ________ such as GET and POST. An HTTP ________ is a sequence of transactions that typically include a browser request and the server's response. HTTP ________ codes such as 200 and 404 indicate whether the server was able to fulfill the browser's request. HTTP is a(n) ________ protocol, which cannot detect if a sequence of sessions originate from the same source. To compensate, Web servers use cookies, which store a small file of data on the user's device. Cookies can be collected during subsequent sessions to keep track of pages viewed and items purchased. ________ cookies remain on the local device after a session ends. Cookies can be set by the domain that hosts a Web site. Additional cookies can be set by advertisers that have a presence on the site. These ________-party cookies can be blocked using browser settings. HTTP is not a secure transport protocol, so financial transactions and personal data should be submitted to Web servers using a more secure protocol that displays ________ in the browser address bar. This technology uses ________ key encryption to scramble the data while it is in transit.

Section E: To sift through the massive amounts of information available on the Web and locate pertinent information about a topic, Web surfers utilize programs called search ________. These special programs have four major components. A Web ________, also called a Web spider, is automated to methodically visit Web sites and gather Web pages. A search engine ________ culls keywords from the gathered pages and stores them in a(n) ________. The search engine's query ________ accepts one or more words called search ________, looks them up in the database, and produces a list of relevant Web sites. There are a number of ways to narrow searches and produce more targeted results, such as using ________ operators or putting exact phrases in ________. The order in which Web sites are returned in response to your query is dependent on relevancy criteria, such as keyword matches and ________ popularity.

Interactive Situation Questions

1. You are mentoring two elementary school students who are creating their first Web page. They've asked you to recommend some tools for the task. Which one requires less knowledge of HTML tags: Notepad or Microsoft Word? ______

2. Suppose you visit a Web site that has eye-catching pages. You want to know how these pages were formatted, so you use one of the options on your browser's menu to take a look at the HTML ______ document.

3. Embedded in an email message is a link to *https://bit.ly/40Lm3320*. You can assume that this is a ______ URL.

4. You'd prefer not to have the search engine you use maintain accumulative records of your searches. You can block ______ from a specific search engine site, and that setting will force the search engine to assign a different ID number to you for each session.

5. Some of your relatives are afraid that their credit card numbers might get stolen from a merchant's server by a hacker. Is it correct to tell them that they can best avoid these potential rip-offs by using a secure connection, such as HTTPS? Yes or no? ______

6. You're conducting a research project that requires you to visit sites that include lots of pop-up ads and other junk that you don't want accumulating in your browser cache. You remember that you can turn on ______ browsing to delete all that junk when you end your session.

7. You think that your browser is secured so your Web activity won't be tracked, but now you discover that you can't check out at Zappos.com. Ooops! Looks like you have blocked all ______.

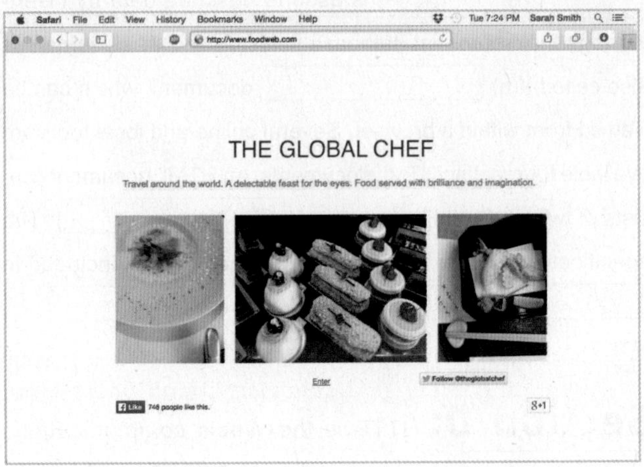

8. You've designed your first Web site and it looks great. But you know that the design is only the beginning of the process of developing a Web site. To make sure that your pages get the best ranking and most visibility, it is important to consider techniques for search engine ______.

9. Your Web pages should all have a similar design based on heading styles, fonts, and colors. Using an external ______ keeps the design consistent for all the pages on your site.

10. Suppose that you want to add some simple interaction to your site by changing the color of buttons when they are clicked. You can accomplish this goal using ______-side scripting.

Lab: Design Your Home Page

HTML can be fun. Really! The basics of HTML and CSS are not complicated, and this lab will give you an opportunity to design a customized Web page.

Requirements:

For this lab, you'll need a computer running macOS or Windows. Your computer should be connected to the Internet. The instructions are generalized; they provide helpful guidelines but not specific steps. You may have to explore a bit to find all the tools needed to complete the assignment, but that is all part of the learning experience.

Assignment:

❶ Connect to an online HTML editor, from a site such as *www.jsfiddle.net* or the *W3Schools Online Code Editor.*

You might be happiest with an HTML editor that allows you to save your work, so look for a Save button before you begin. When this book was published, both jsFiddle and W3Schools offered great tools for HTML and CSS.

❷ Enter the outline for a basic HTML document using the template in Figure 4-30.

❸ Modify the template to add your name as an h1 heading at the beginning of the body section of the document.

The HTML code will look something like this:

```
<p><h1> Sarah Smith </h1></p>
```

❹ Make sure the editor is able to show you what your Web page will look like when displayed in a browser.

If you are using jsFiddle, click the Run button and look for your results on the right side of the screen. If you are using W3Schools, select the Run button.

❺ Next, locate a photo that you like on the Wikimedia site and copy its URL.

To copy the URL, right-click the photo and select Copy Image URL.

❻ Return to the HTML editor and enter the tags to insert the image. Make sure you include the quotation marks. The HTML should look something like this:

```
<img src="http://name_of_photo.jpeg" style="left:56px;top:236px;height:232px;width:174px;position: absolute;
> </img>
```

You can play around with the numbers for left, top, height, and width until the image is positioned where you want it to be.

Add two more images positioned artistically on the page.

❼ Add a hypertext link under the photos that leads to your favorite Wikipedia page. Your link should look something like this:

```
<p> <a href="https://en.wikipedia.org/wiki/Astronomy">
I love Astronomy! </a> </p>
```

❽ Next, turn to the CSS tab or work area and enter the code to center the h1 style for your name and display it in the color and size of your choice. Here is a sample:

```
body
{ font-family: arial; }
h1 { color: purple; text-align: center; font-size: xx-large}
```

❾ Finally, select colors for the link and add the code to the CSS, like this:

```
a:link { color: green; }

a:visited { color: blue; }
```

❿ Save your work in a format that you can submit to your instructor. Depending on the HTML editor you used, you may:

- Take a screenshot using the PrtSc key (Windows) or Command-Shift-4 (Mac).
- Save a file locally and email it to your instructor.
- Save the URL and submit it to your instructor.
- Copy the text of your HTML and CSS, then paste it into a text editor, such as Notepad or TextEdit. Submit that document to your instructor.

5 Social Media

Module Contents

They're personal, global, and disruptive. Social media are a unique part of 21st-century life. Have you mastered them, or are you struggling to find your social media niche?

Try It! Apply what you learn.

- Create effective social media profiles that reflect your identity and uniqueness.
- Use social networking tools to convey your personal "brand."
- Enable or disable location services as necessary for geosocial networking.
- Interpret a sociogram or adjacency matrix to evaluate connections in a social network.
- Use tools provided by your social media services to discover if you've been tagged in photos or videos.
- Assign a Creative Commons license to your original work before posting it.
- Evaluate whether your use of copyrighted media would be considered fair use, a derivative use, or a transformative use.
- Identify and use basic blogging tools to create blogs and interact with bloggers.
- Evaluate a blog to determine if its information is accurate and reliable.
- Use Twitter to tweet, retweet, and read messages using @ mentions and # hashtags.
- Use tabs on Wikipedia articles to access Talk pages, edits, and revision history.
- Use Wikipedia information appropriately in your academic setting.
- Set up forwarding between Webmail and local mail accounts.
- Use online chat, VoIP services, and mobile communication apps.
- Manage your online reputation to ensure that it is not hijacked by impersonators, identity thieves, or cyberbullies.
- Monitor third-party social media apps to limit the amount of your social data that is gathered by off-site entities.

5

Social Media

Pre-Check

Gauge your level of expertise. The answers are in the module.

This image is a generic ____________ for a social media account.

In the context of social media, this symbol is called a(n)

____

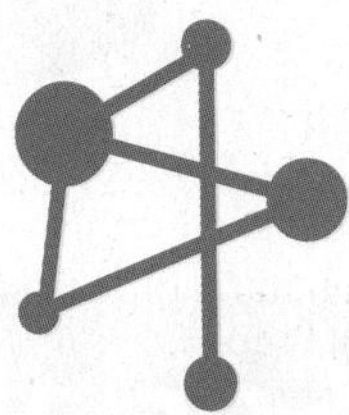

What is the name of this analytical tool that depicts social networking connections?

____

List 3 email protocols

____

____

____

What does this symbol mean?

____

NPOV

What social media platform requires editors to adhere to this standard?

____

What can't you create if you see this icon?

____

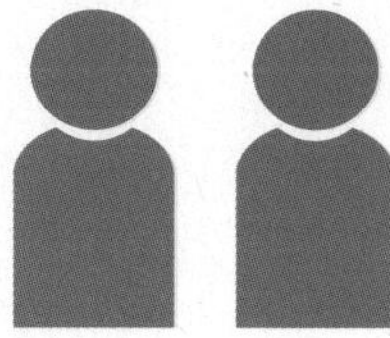

Your online twin is called a(n)

____

What is the meaning of this Creative Commons license icon?

____

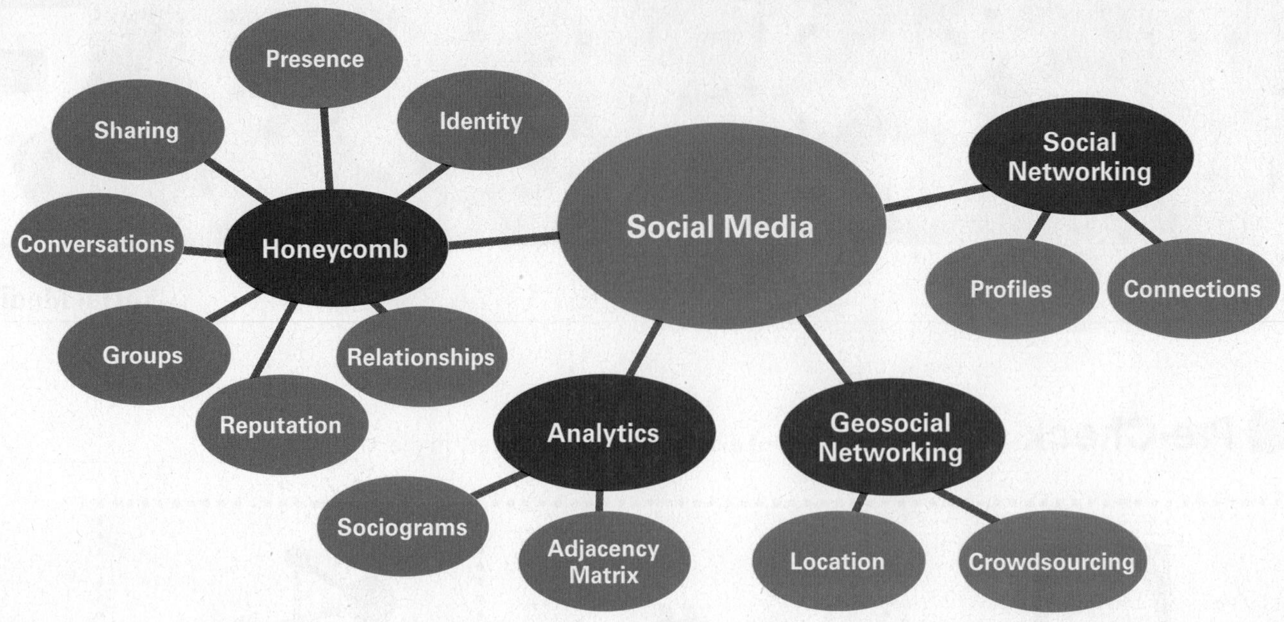

Section A Social Networking

Objectives

- Use the Social Media Honeycomb to differentiate among various social media.
- Provide at least two examples of social networking, geosocial networking, content communities, and online communication.
- Trace the history of social networking services.
- List the three elements of a social media profile.
- Provide three examples of crowdsourcing.
- Describe four technologies that can be used to locate mobile and stationary devices.
- Interpret the analytics displayed by a sociogram.
- Explain how Six Degrees of Separation applies to social networking.
- Provide examples of the inferences that might be drawn from an adjacency matrix.

The social media landscape is vast. From megasites such as Facebook to emerging niche services such as Caffeine, social media have spread across the globe. They now soak up hours of screen time and spill over into other media outlets such as news, television, and movies. Section A offers some structures for selecting and categorizing social media services, and then focuses on social networking and surprising linkages that put the concept of Six Degrees of Separation to the test.

Terminology

social media
Social Media Honeycomb
social networking service
online services
online identity
social media profile
geosocial networking
social discovery
crowdsourcing
GPS trilateration
cell tower triangulation
hotspot triangulation
IP address lookup
geocoding
geotagging
sociograms
sociogram nodes
sociogram edges
two-way edges
one-way edges
binary adjacency matrix

The Social Media Mix

Across the globe, billions of people participate in social media, using services such as Facebook, Twitter, Snapchat, Pinterest, YouTube, Wikipedia, Yelp, and Flickr. The variety of social media offerings is immense, and trying to take part in all of them would be a daunting task. So choices have to be made. Let's look at the social media mix available to you.

▶ What are social media? **Social media** are online services that facilitate communication and interaction among people who want to share information about their lives, issues, and events using a multimedia mix of text, pictures, video, and audio.

Classifying social media provides a general structure for comparisons and helps you to understand their benefits. Various classification schemes have been proposed for social media. For example, one way to classify social media is by their focus. In such a classification, a professional social media service such as LinkedIn would be placed in a different category from friends-and-family services such as Facebook and TikTok.

Social media are sometimes categorized by the type of content that they support. Text-based services, such as Blogger and WordPress, would be classified differently from image and video services, such as Flickr and YouTube.

The **Social Media Honeycomb** provides a visual model for classifying and comparing various social media services. Each hexagon in the honeycomb represents a social media building block. Look at the honeycomb in Figure 5-1 and think about how strongly the characteristics in each hexagon apply to your favorite social media site.

Figure 5-1: The Social Media Honeycomb

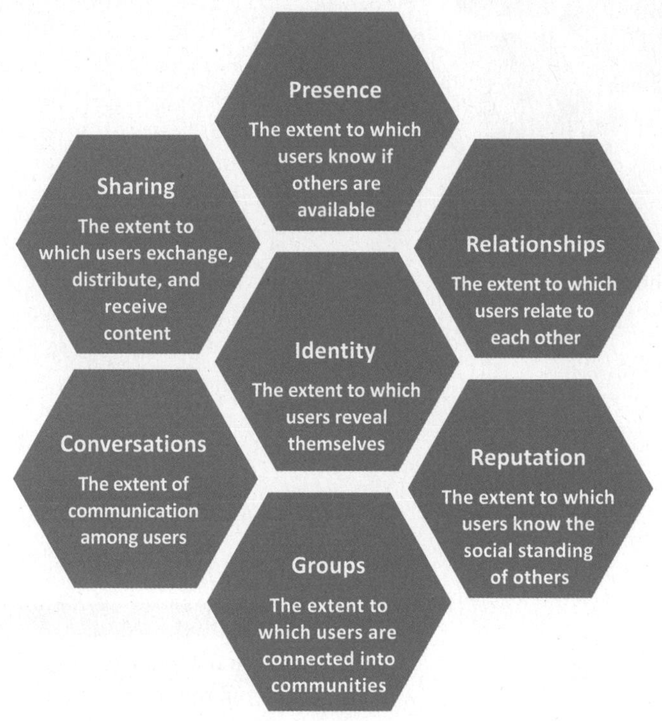

Source: Kietzmann, Hermkens, McCarthy, and Silvestre

5

QuickCheck

Which hexagon in the Social Media Honeycomb characterizes Facebook "Likes"?

a. Relationships

b. Sharing

c. Reputation

d. Conversations

◗ How does the honeycomb help me compare social media services?

Each social media service emphasizes a different set of social interactions. Services such as LinkedIn emphasize identity but do not encourage conversations among users. Facebook and similar services tend to emphasize relationships among users, with a secondary emphasis on conversations, identity, presence, and reputation. In the social media honeycombs shown in Figure 5-2, darker hexagons indicate factors with more emphasis.

Figure 5-2: Social media services emphasize different social factors

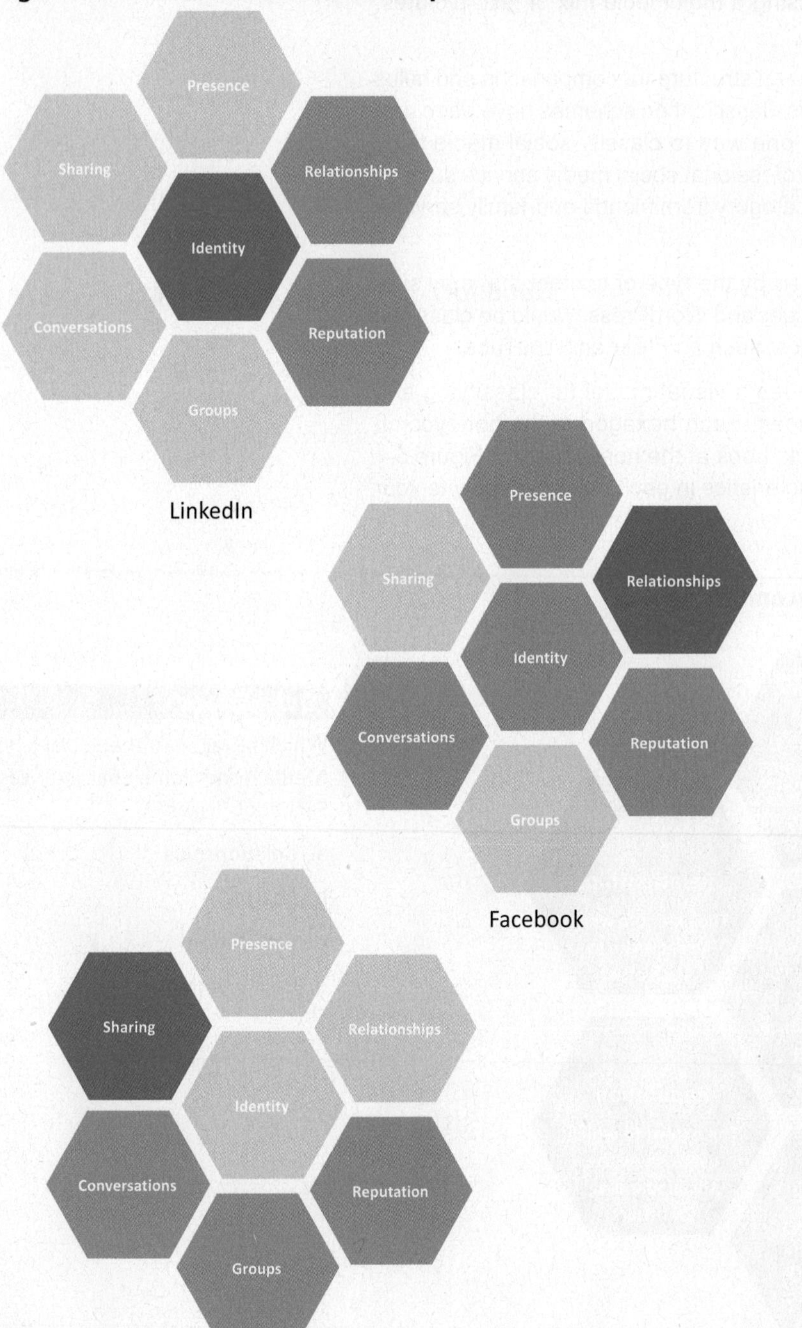

QuickCheck

Which of the Social Media Honeycombs in Figure 5-2 would be most similar to the honeycomb for Flickr?

a. LinkedIn

b. Facebook

c. YouTube

Try It!

Sketch out a honeycomb and color in the social factors that are emphasized by Twitter.

What are the most popular social media services? New social media services pop up every day, or so it seems. Some are in the spotlight briefly, while others have more staying power. In this module, social media are categorized into four groups: social networking, geosocial networking, content communities, and online communications. Figure 5-3 offers a brief overview of these categories and lists some of the most popular services in each one.

Figure 5-3: Popular social media services

Social Networking	Geosocial Networking	Content Communities	Online Communication
Good for: Creating an online presence Connecting with friends and family	**Good for:** Locating places, people, and events	**Good for:** Sharing user-generated media and topical information Ratings Spreading a message	**Good for:** One-to-one, real-time communication Asynchronous messaging
Examples: Facebook Classmates.com LinkedIn Twitter Tumblr Nextdoor	**Examples:** Yelp Foursquare Swarm Nearby Zillow Google Maps OpenTable Meetup	**Examples:** YouTube Flickr Pinterest Instagram Wikipedia Reddit Blogger WordPress TikTok	**Examples:** Email Snapchat Skype Chat WhatsApp Zoom

Social Networking Evolution

Let's turn our focus from the broad spectrum of social media to the specific category of social networking. Today's social networking landscape is dominated by Facebook, but social media were born in a rapidly changing environment, and they are likely to continue to evolve as consumer preferences change. It may seem as if social networking sprang up overnight when Facebook went online, but that is not the case.

Try It!

Social networks come and go. Are the ones listed in the first column of Figure 5-3 still popular? Which social networking services are your favorites?

▶ **What are social networking services?** A **social networking service** revolves around personal profiles and interconnections among subscribers who want to share information about themselves.

▶ **What was the first social networking service?** Social networking can be traced back to **online services**, such as CompuServe, Prodigy, and America Online (AOL), that were not part of the Internet. The popularity of those services decreased as a new generation of Internet-based services emerged. The timeline in Figure 5-4 traces the evolution of social networking services.

Figure 5-4: Social networking services timeline

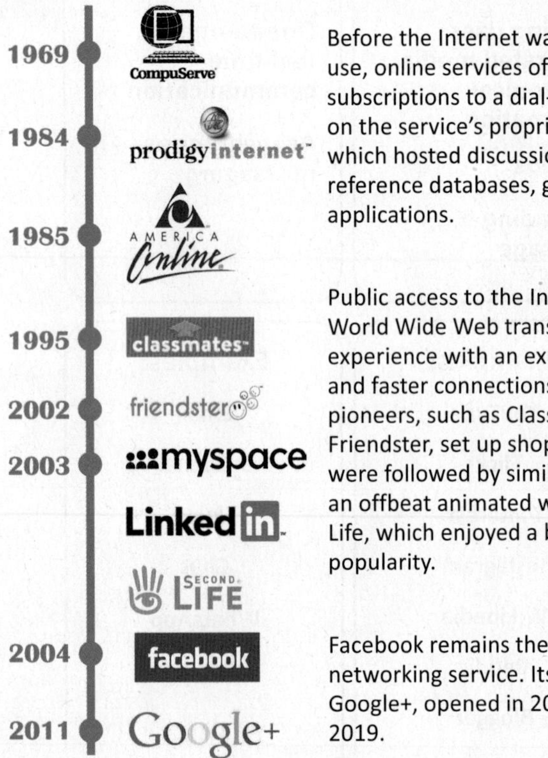

Before the Internet was opened to public use, online services offered fee-based subscriptions to a dial-up network housed on the service's proprietary computers, which hosted discussion groups, email, reference databases, games, and software applications.

Public access to the Internet and the World Wide Web transformed the online experience with an expanding user base and faster connections. Social networking pioneers, such as Classmates.com and Friendster, set up shop at Web sites. They were followed by similar services, including an offbeat animated world called Second Life, which enjoyed a brief period of wild popularity.

Facebook remains the most popular social networking service. Its main competitor, Google+, opened in 2011, but shut down in 2019.

▶ **How are social networking services likely to evolve?** When it comes to the online social scene, history tells us that nothing lasts forever. Consumer tastes change, and a site with billions of users today can all too quickly become old news. A report from the research division of the asset firm Piper Jaffray indicates that the popularity of Facebook among teens decreases every year.

Teen preferences for simpler social media platforms such as Instagram, TikTok, and Snapchat may be a glimpse of the future in which a young demographic seeks easy-to-use, smartphone-based communication platforms, while career-minded individuals maintain LinkedIn profiles.

QuickCheck

The first generation of social networking services ________.

a. offered free access

b. was not part of the Internet

c. was launched by Facebook

d. became popular with the launch of mobile devices

Social Networking Basics

Each social networking service has its own focus and terminology. "Friends" on one service are called "followers" or "connections" on other services. "Likes" might be called "endorsements." When joining a social network, one of your first steps should be to get a handle on its terminology, which will help you learn how to use its features.

▶ **What should I know about social network profiles?** A person's presence on a social media service is referred to as an **online identity**. Each online identity is encapsulated in a profile. A **social media profile** is the set of information provided to friends, contacts, and the public. A basic profile generally includes a user name, an image, and a few lines of descriptive text. Figure 5-5 illustrates profiles from several popular social networking services.

Terminology

Online identities are also called *personas* and *avatars*.

5

Figure 5-5: Social media profile elements

A Twitter profile can include a photo and a tagline. Bill Gates sets a good example, using his tagline to provide potential followers with information about the topics he tweets about.

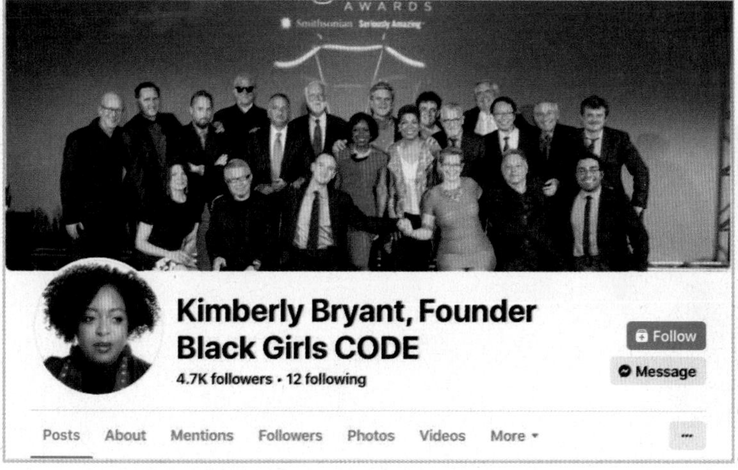

Facebook profiles help to build an online identity. Here, Kimberly Bryant highlights her organization, Black Girls CODE.

Try It!

Visit your favorite social networking service and look at the profiles for at least three people. Which of those profiles seems most effective?

What are the common elements of social networks? Reflect back on the social media characteristics presented in the honeycomb diagram in Figure 5-1. Social networking services tend to emphasize identity and relationships. Most social networking sites offer elements similar to those in Figure 5-6.

Figure 5-6: Anatomy of a social network account

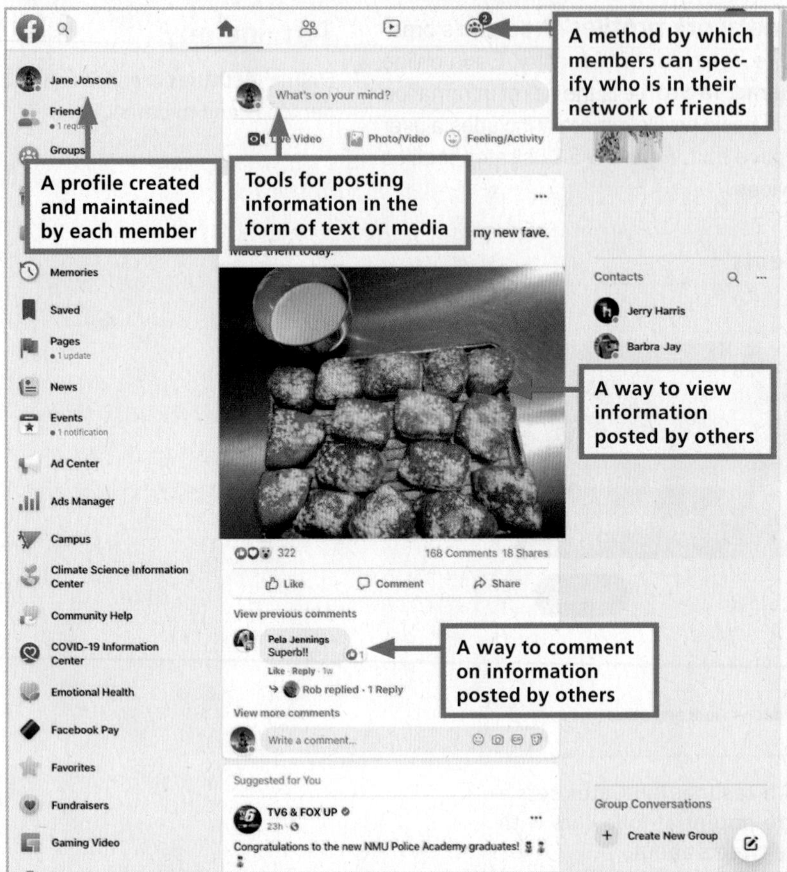

Source: Facebook

Presence
Sharing
Relationships
Identity
Conversations
Reputation
Groups

Social networking sites focus on identity (the user's profile) and relationships (friends and connections).

Geosocial Networking

Your smartphone's GPS can pinpoint your location. Although it presents some security and privacy issues, judicious use of location-based services can expand your social circle.

What is geosocial networking? **Geosocial networking** provides a platform for users to carry out interactions based on their current locations. Some of the most popular and well-designed geosocial networking services include Yelp, Foursquare Swarm, and Google Maps. Social networking services, such as Facebook and Twitter, also offer geosocial features.

Geosocial networking services can help you find the nearest popular restaurant, pinpoint the location of your friends' favorite biking trails, get special deals from nearby merchants, and leave feedback about business services and products. An emerging subset of geosocial networking called **social discovery** uses geolocation to locate people who are nearby and have similar interests. The basic activities offered by geosocial networking are summarized in Figure 5-7.

QuickCheck

Based on the Social Media Honeycomb, the key characteristics of social discovery are ________.

a. presence and reputation

b. identity and relationships

c. reputation and identity

d. sharing and conversations

5

Figure 5-7: Geosocial network activities

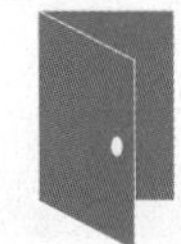

Check in

Registered users open the app or otherwise sign in to indicate they want to interact.

Locate

Using automatic geolocation technology or manually initiated location tracking, the user's current location is determined.

Search

Depending on the service, users can search for geotagged places, people, or events that are nearby.

Recommend

Crowdsourced ratings and recommendations are offered.

Map

Maps and directions to selected places, people, or events are provided.

What is crowdsourcing? When individuals contribute computer time, expertise, opinions, or money to a defined project, they are participating in **crowdsourcing**. For example, Yelp provides restaurant ratings compiled from user reviews. Amazon, Zappos, and other online merchants also collect and display customer reviews. Waze is a crowdsourcing app that collects real-time traffic information from subscribers and then uses that information to provide drivers with the optimal route to their destinations.

Crowdsourcing is often associated with geosocial networking because the focus of many crowdsourcing apps is on user reviews of places. Not all crowdsourcing apps are geosocial, however. As an example, Kickstarter is a crowdsourcing app that provides consumers with a platform for donating money to creative projects.

Crowdsourcing is based on contributions from groups of individuals, but it differs from collaborative work. For collaborative work, participants interact with each other to achieve a goal. Crowdsourcing does not require collaboration among participants. Contributions from each crowd participant are aggregated by the crowdsourcing platform. For example, the rating for Cathy's Cafe is not created by Yelp users chatting with each other until they agree on a three-star rating. Instead, reviewers submit independent reviews, which are consolidated by algorithms on the Yelp platform.

QuickCheck

Which one of the following would be considered crowdsourcing?

a. Skype conversations

b. A blog entry

c. A tweet

d. Facebook "Likes"

How does geolocation work? Most people are aware that mobile devices, such as smartphones, send out location signals that can be used to track the device. Desktop computers, laptops, and tablets without GPS or cellular service can also be located, though not with dependable accuracy. Figure 5-8 lists four ways that the location of a device can be determined.

Figure 5-8: Location technologies

GPS trilateration
This technology locates smartphones and other devices containing GPS chips. It is accurate to within a 16-foot radius.

Cell tower triangulation
Cellular telephone companies monitor the position of mobile phones relative to nearby cell towers. If a phone is turned on and within range of three towers, a process called cell tower triangulation can determine the position of a device to an area of about three-quarters of a mile.

Hotspot triangulation
This technique can gauge the location of a Wi-Fi router based on its signal strength relative to nearby routers. Desktop and laptop computers connected to the router can be assumed to be operating within a circle of about 50 feet.

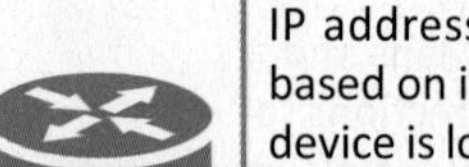

IP address lookup
IP addresses can provide a rough estimate of a device's location based on information in the WHOIS database. The country in which a device is located can be determined with 99% accuracy. However, the accuracy of pinpointing the region or city dwindles to about 50%.

Try It!

Check the location settings on any handy digital device. Are they set to allow geosocial networking?

What should I keep in mind about geolocation? Location-aware apps may use more than one type of location service. The location services settings for a digital device can be used to enable or disable location tracking for each individual app.

Geosocial networking depends on geolocation, so your participation requires an accurate assessment of your location. If you want to be found, activate all available location services by making sure GPS, cellular, and Wi-Fi are turned on. If you don't want to be found, make sure that all of those location services are turned off.

What is geotagging? Presenting information about what's nearby requires places and landmarks to be tagged with their location. Restaurants featured on Yelp, for example, must have a street address or longitude and latitude available in a machine-readable format that can be interpreted by the geosocial networking service's search engines. Geotagging and geocoding provide the necessary geographical information.

Geocoding is the process of determining the coordinates of a specific place, such as the street address or the longitude and latitude of Cathy's Cafe. **Geotagging** is the process of adding location data to photos, Web sites, HTML documents, audio files, blog posts, and text messages. Standard formats for geotagging and geocoding ensure that location data can be read by the computer programs operated by geosocial networking services.

QuickCheck

A service that displays the location of a post office on a map is using ________ data.

a. geotagged

b. geocoded

c. social media

d. crowdsourced

5

Social Network Analytics

The now infamous game Six Degrees of Kevin Bacon is based on a notion that any Hollywood actor can be linked to Kevin Bacon in six steps through the actors' roles in various films. The Six Degrees of Separation concept originated in a 1929 short story by author Frigyes Karinthy, whose characters devised a game of figuring how to most quickly relay a letter between any two people on Earth based on links between their personal acquaintances. Today, tools let us map and analyze social networks. What do they tell us?

How are social networks mapped? Social networks are not exclusively online. Everyone has face-to-face networks of family, friends, and acquaintances, who in turn have their own networks of social connections. You may envision these networks as points connected by lines. Sociologists use social network diagrams called **sociograms** to depict connections between people.

The circles in these diagrams are referred to as **sociogram nodes**. The lines connecting nodes are referred to as **sociogram edges**. **Two-way edges** exist when two people consider each other to be friends. **One-way edges** exist when a relationship is not reciprocal, such as a Twitter follower who does not follow back. What do the connections in Figure 5-9 tell you about the relationships between characters in *The Lord of the Rings*?

Figure 5-9: Anatomy of social networking

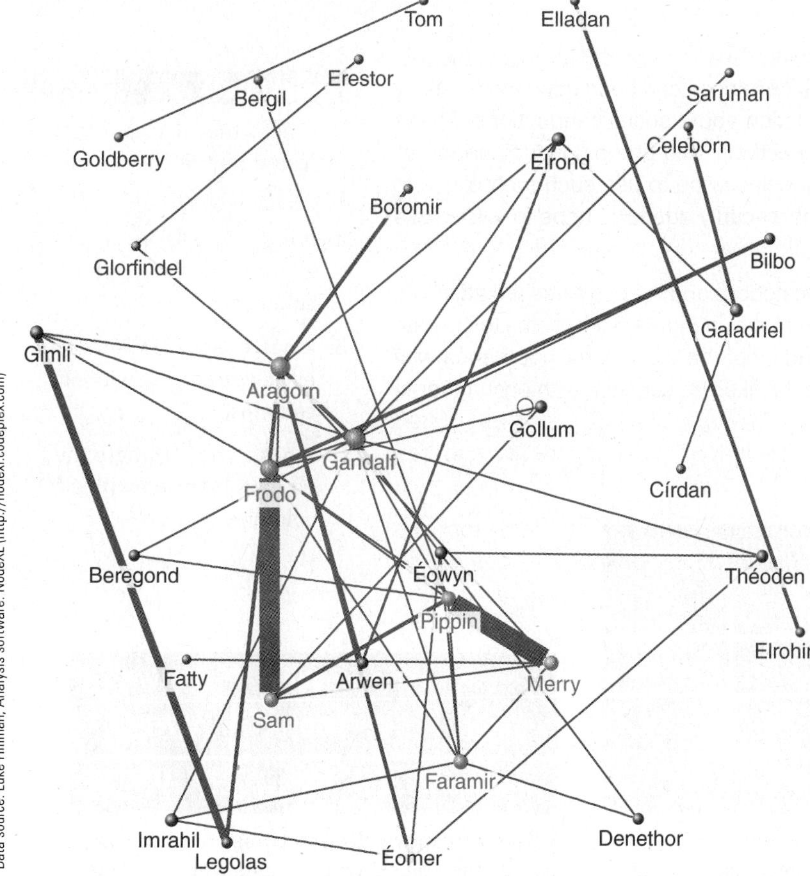

The thickness of connecting lines (edges) indicates connection strength. Node colors indicate which characters are most important.

QuickCheck

In a sociogram, edges indicate ________.

a. connections
b. the boundaries of relationships
c. individuals with few friends
d. 3D connections

Try It!

Do the most important characters in Figure 5-9 appear to have the most "friends"?

Is it possible to sort through the complexity? Sociograms can get extremely complex, which makes connections difficult to trace and analyze. An alternative method for depicting social connections is with an adjacency matrix.

A **binary adjacency matrix** is simply a set of cells containing a 0 if there is no connection between two people and a 1 if there is a connection. The adjacency matrix in Figure 5-10 depicts the relationships between some of the elves and hobbits of Middle Earth as a sociogram and as an adjacency matrix.

Figure 5-10: Hobbits and elves

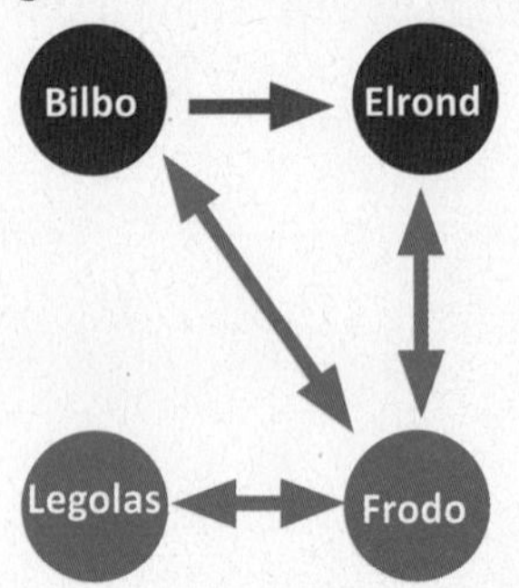

In this sociogram, Bilbo considers Elrond his friend, but Elrond does not consider Bilbo to be his friend.

	Bilbo	Elrond	Frodo	Legolas
Bilbo	—	1	1	0
Elrond	0	—	1	0
Frodo	1	1	—	1
Legolas	0	0	1	—

The intersection of dark blue cells in the adjacency matrix contains a 1 to show that Bilbo considers Elrond his friend. Can you find the cell that indicates Elrond does not consider Bilbo to be his friend?

What else does the matrix reveal? Matrices can be manipulated visually and mathematically to reveal more information about social connections. These manipulations can expose pathways, connections, and groupings that lead to all sorts of revelations. Law enforcement agencies hope to use such techniques to uncover criminal organizations, and national security agencies hope to follow links to identify members of terrorist groups.

Suppose we rearrange the matrix so the two hobbits and the two elves are adjacent. The results are interesting. The rearranged matrix in Figure 5-11 seems to indicate that the hobbits chose each other as friends, but the elves were not friends with other elves. Therefore, the elves would not be likely to conspire with each other to overthrow Middle Earth or to save it.

QuickCheck

How does the adjacency matrix indicate that the elves are not friends?

a. It has a zero (0) where the elf rows intersect with elf columns.

b. It has a dash (-) where the elf rows intersect with elf columns.

c. It has a one (1) where the elf rows intersect with elf columns.

Figure 5-11: Inferred connections

	Bilbo	Frodo	Elrond	Legolas
Bilbo	—	1	1	0
Frodo	1	—	1	1
Elrond	0	1	—	0
Legolas	0	1	0	—

In the rearranged matrix, the two hobbits are adjacent, as are the two elves. Color blocks illustrate the general relationships between hobbits (red) and between elves (green).

	Hobbits	Elves
Hobbits	100%	75%
Elves	50%	0%

This matrix shows the percentage of connections within each block, with hobbits well connected, but elves not connected to each other.

How do analytic tools apply to online social networks? Sociograms and other analytic tools help us understand the quality and quantity of our personal social networks. The concept of one-way edges is important, for example, in understanding that although you may receive status updates directly from the President of the United States and the First Lady, you are not likely to enjoy a similar link in the other direction—they are probably not going to read your Facebook posts.

Social network analytic tools also uncovered a very odd phenomenon. Does it seem like most of your friends have more friends than you have? It turns out that is the case with more than 80% of Facebook users. This phenomenon is referred to as the class size paradox because it is related to the reason students feel that they are always in larger than average classes. The explanation is that people tend to choose popular classes and friends, and such popularity does indeed mean that the classes are larger and your friends have more friends than you have. Figure 5-12 offers additional interesting facts about Facebook friends.

Figure 5-12: Facebook friend facts

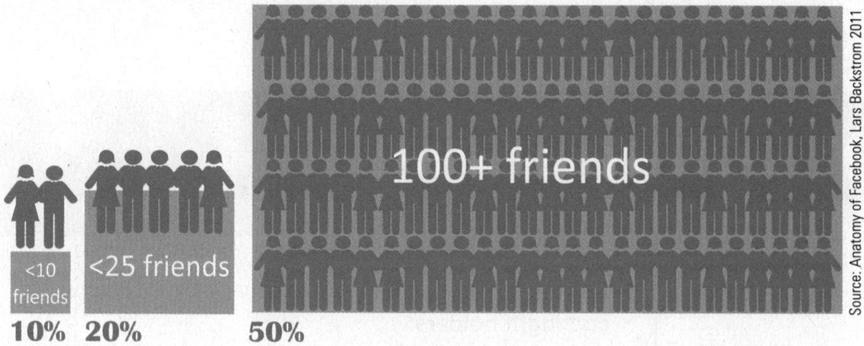

So how many degrees of separation are there on social networks? In 2001, a professor at Columbia University set out to track the path of more than 50,000 email messages forwarded from senders to intermediaries. The messages finally wended their way to one of 19 designated people with undisclosed email addresses. The average number of intermediaries turned out to be six—an amazing confirmation of the Six Degrees of Separation theory.

Researchers studying Twitter connections, however, found the average degree of separation was less than 4. The majority of Facebook users have between 2.9 and 4.2 degrees of separation.

QuickCheck

If you are a typical Facebook user, your friends have ______ you have.

a. more friends than

b. fewer friends than

c. the same number of friends as

QuickQuiz — Section A

1. The Social Media [ ] uses hexagons to depict characteristics of social media.
2. Algorithms at Yelp, Amazon, and Zappos depend upon [ ] to produce ratings based on user reviews.
3. Cellular services can determine the location of a mobile device using cell tower [ ].
4. A(n) [ ] depicts connections between people as nodes and edges.
5. A(n) [ ] matrix is a social media analytic tool arranged as a table.

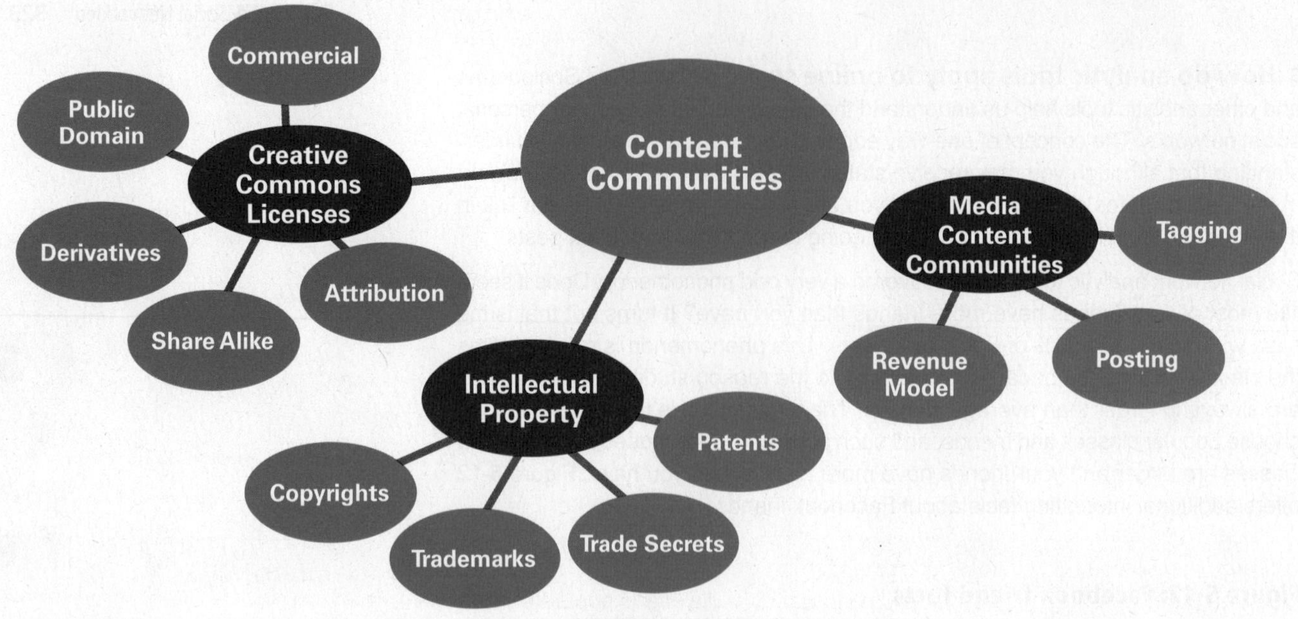

Section B Content Communities

Objectives

- Use the Social Media Honeycomb to identify the primary characteristics of content communities.
- Draw a timeline of the emergence of content communities, including significant dates.
- Explain the concept of viral media.
- Explain where content is stored and how that may affect privacy.
- Describe the financial model for most content communities and how that model may affect the future of these communities.
- State the difference between formal tagging and informal tagging.
- List four types of intellectual property.
- Identify which types of intellectual property are typically encountered in content communities.
- List the six rights that are exclusively exercised by copyright holders.
- List the five rights that can be granted under a Creative Commons license.
- List the four factors that characterize fair use.
- State the difference between a derivative work and a transformative work.

Content communities struggle with the divide between what is shared and what is owned. One side champions shared ownership; the other side believes that personal property is associated with ownership rights. Bridging the gap is an organization called Creative Commons. If you have not yet used its services, the information at the end of this section can get you started.

Terminology

content communities
bulletin board systems
viral
metadata tag
formal tagging
intellectual property
trademark
copyright
public domain
Creative Commons license
copyleft
fair use
derivative work
transformative work

5

Evolution

Back before the Internet, the creative world was controlled by a small set of gatekeepers who influenced popular culture. Music moguls decided which bands to promote. Hollywood studios selected the films that were produced. The editors at publishing houses filtered the books and magazines that went to print.

Today, those gatekeepers can be bypassed because online content communities so effortlessly distribute books, photos, videos, and music. Popularity no longer depends on endorsement by an elite band of critics, but instead by a democratic vote of "Likes" from everyday folks. Where this democratization of culture leads is anyone's guess. The availability of tools to create and distribute digital media removed the old gates but erected new barriers to talent based on the sheer volume of media that competes for screen time.

▶ What is a content community? Many social media sites, such as Wikipedia, YouTube, and Flickr, were designed as repositories for user-generated content. These social media sites are sometimes called **content communities**. Although it can be said that just about every social media site is populated with user-generated content, content communities emphasize the content itself, unlike social networking sites that revolve around user identities.

Content communities may focus on text-based information, or their focus may be on other media, such as photos, music, or video. Content communities typically have the characteristics listed in Figure 5-13.

QuickCheck

Which one of the following would not be considered a content community?

a. Skype

b. Flickr

c. YouTube

d. Instagram

Figure 5-13: Content community characteristics

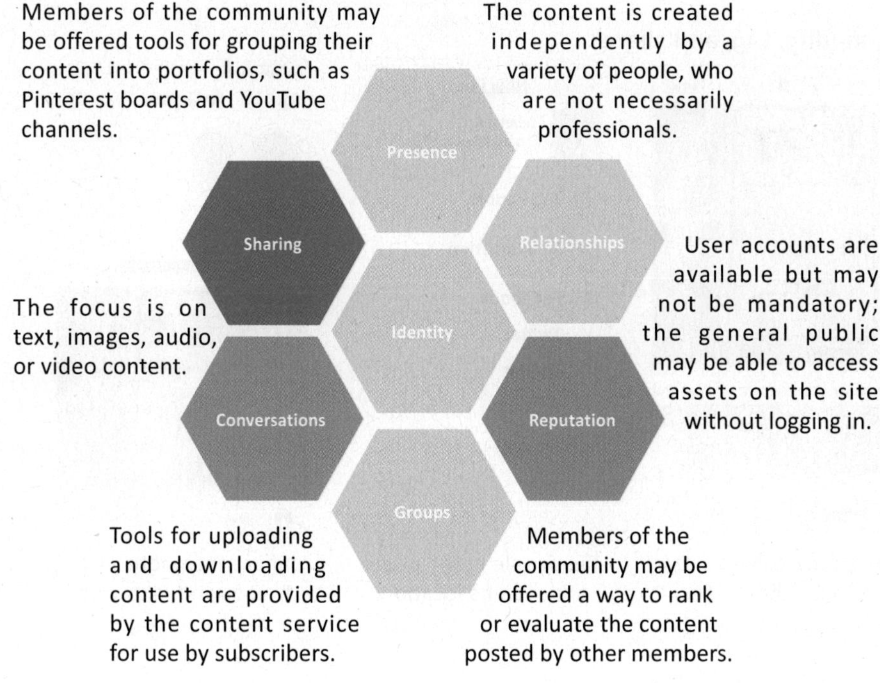

Members of the community may be offered tools for grouping their content into portfolios, such as Pinterest boards and YouTube channels.
The content is created independently by a variety of people, who are not necessarily professionals.
Presence
Sharing
Relationships
User accounts are available but may not be mandatory; the general public may be able to access assets on the site without logging in.
The focus is on text, images, audio, or video content.
Identity
Conversations
Reputation
Groups
Tools for uploading and downloading content are provided by the content service for use by subscribers.
Members of the community may be offered a way to rank or evaluate the content posted by other members.

When did content communities originate? The **bulletin board systems** (BBSs) of the 1970s contained user-generated content and could be considered forerunners of today's content communities as well as today's social networks. Bulletin boards were popular for about 20 years before other efforts to gather and archive meaningful collections of online content emerged.

One of the first online content communities was Project Gutenberg. Started in 1991 by Michael S. Hart and now supervised by a nonprofit organization, Project Gutenberg's mission is to preserve literary works, particularly those with expired copyrights. Initially, volunteers manually entered the text from printed books; however, today, books are digitally scanned.

In 2001, another text-based collaborative appeared. An online encyclopedia called Wikipedia was launched, and a community of contributors quickly formed around it.

In 1999, the Webshots community became one of the first social media sites for sharing photos online. Competing communities such as Flickr and Photobucket soon followed. Video content communities launched with the founding of YouTube in 2005, and that same year the world saw the first instance of an online video that went **viral**. SlideShare opened in 2006, offering an archive of PowerPoint-style slide presentations.

Pinterest, founded in 2010, revived interest in photo sharing communities, with its use of "boards" containing a collection of related items, such as photos of fashions, home decor, or book covers. Mobile photo sharing became popular in 2010, when Instagram made it simpler to snap, modify, tag, and share photos taken with the smartphone app shown in Figure 5-14.

QuickCheck

Which type of content community came first?

a. Bulletin board systems
b. Wikipedia
c. Flickr
d. Instagram

Terminology

In the context of social media, *viral* refers to videos, music tracks, blog posts, and other media elements that quickly infiltrate popular culture via social media.

Figure 5-14: Instagram snap, modify, tag, and share

Start the Instagram app and snap the photo.

Use tools to edit and retouch the image.

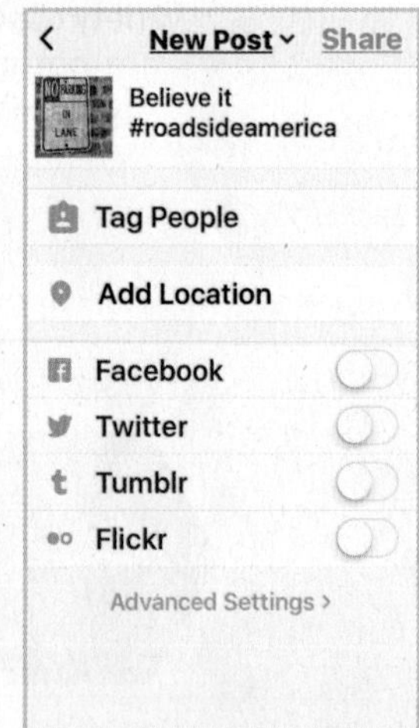

Tag people in the photo and map its location.

Share the photo with friends and followers.

Media Content Communities

Media content communities are so popular that almost everyone with an Internet connection has logged in to take a look at videos from YouTube and images from sites such as Flickr. Many people participate in these communities by posting media. Others become unknowing participants when they are the subject of photos and videos posted by others.

How do media content communities work? Media content communities specialize in user-generated images, videos, animations, and audio. Posted content can be accessed using a general search engine, such as Google, or an internal search engine provided by the community site. Community members who post content can specify whether it is available to the public or to a limited list of members. Unlike wikis, where editing the source content is encouraged, the media in content communities are not usually modified by other members.

The technological core of media content communities is server-based content management software and an associated database, which stores content and information about that content. Once media are posted to a server, they may remain there indefinitely.

Some media communities incorporate advertising as a source of revenue both for content creators and for operational income. The fact that content communities have few options for generating revenue may lead to their eventual demise if advertising revenue cannot sustain operational costs for server space and administrative personnel.

How do I post content to a media community? Although many content communities allow open access to media, most require registration before files can be uploaded. Content communities offer basic tools for uploading media files from a computer, and most offer apps that handle uploads from mobile devices. Figure 5-15 illustrates how to upload a photo to Flickr from a computer.

QuickCheck

The photos and videos that are posted to content communities are stored ______.

a. as apps

b. in torrents

c. in a wiki

d. on Web servers

Figure 5-15: How to upload a photo to Flickr

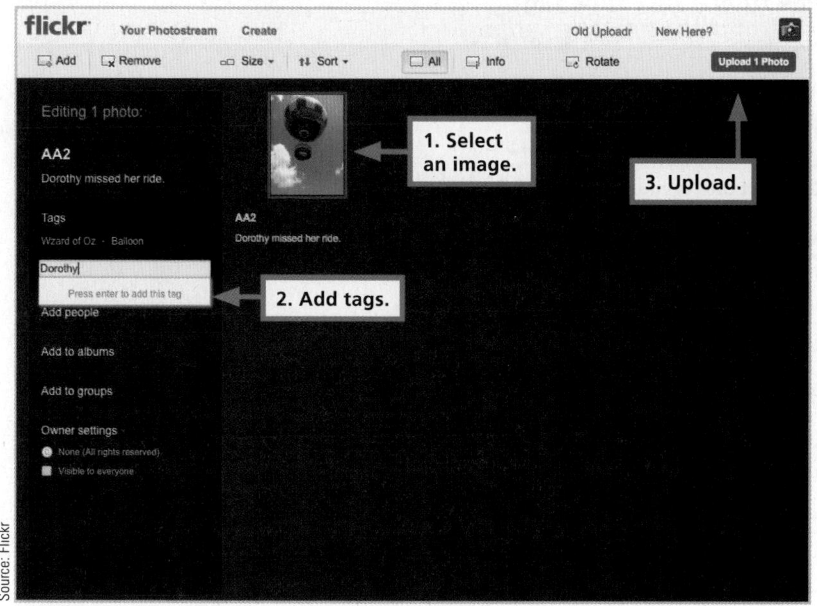

Source: Flickr

Try It!

If you don't have an account on a content community, subscribe to one now and find out if it is easy to upload content.

What should I know about tagging media? A **metadata tag** is a keyword that describes information, such as the content of a media element. In the context of content communities, tags are used to describe people and places in photos and videos.

Unlike documents and other text-based information, media elements contain no text that can be used for indexing, identification, or searching. Tags make it possible to search for photos or videos using keywords, such as *dogs*, *beach*, *sun*, *water*, and *driftwood*. Audio file tags help to locate tracks based on musicians' names, record labels, recording dates, and so on.

Informal tagging simply requires content creators to assign one or more keywords to a media element. The format for entering tags depends on the community. Some require a comma between tags, whereas others separate tags with a space.

Formal tagging methods add information to a tag according to a set of tagging standards. These standards make it possible to create generalized media search engines that can locate media from multiple locations.

Dublin Core schema is an example of a formal tagging standard. It can be used for digital resources as well as for physical media such as CDs, books, and phonograph records.

Have I been tagged? Suppose that an acquaintance takes an unflattering photo of you and posts it on Facebook with your name as one of the tags. If you are not friends with the poster, you may never see the post, but wouldn't you want to know about it?

Facebook and several other social media services provide ways to discover if you've been tagged. On Facebook, you can access your activity log and look at the activities that you are tagged in. If you find a photo in which you'd rather not be identified, you can choose to remove the tag yourself or ask the poster to remove the entire photo (Figure 5-16).

QuickCheck

What is the primary advantage of formal tagging methods?

a. They protect privacy.

b. They cannot be hacked.

c. They are machine-readable standards.

d. They limit the tag words that can be used to describe a media element.

Try It!

Check your social media sites. Which of them notify you when you've been tagged?

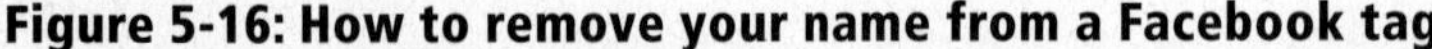

Figure 5-16: How to remove your name from a Facebook tag

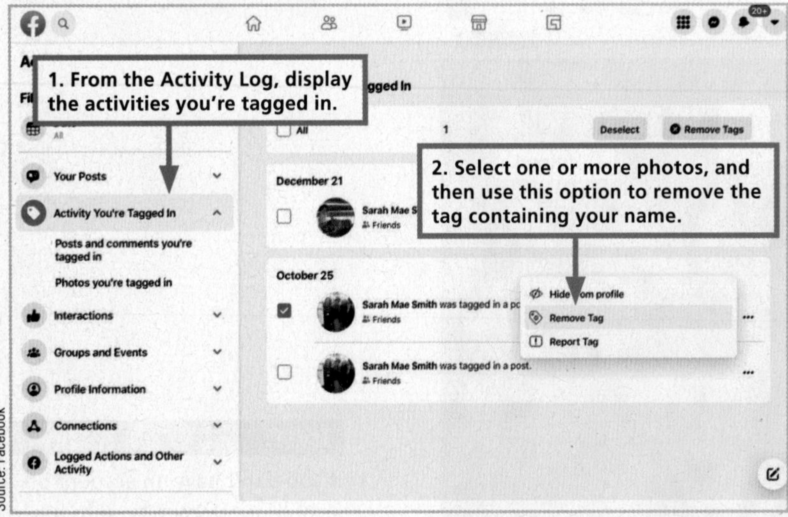

Intellectual Property

Content communities put all types of media at your fingertips. You have access to photos, stories, reports, videos, animations, and music, all in digital formats that you can copy, modify, and incorporate into your own works. But just because you can access this media doesn't necessarily mean that it is legal or ethical to use it. Conscientious citizens of content communities know how, when, and where it is okay to use the media created by other community members.

QuickCheck

The works in most content communities are classified as what types of intellectual property?

a. Trademark and patent

b. Copyright and trademark

c. Patent and trade secret

d. Copyright and patent

▶ What is intellectual property? People are creative. They produce beautiful art. They invent useful machines. They write captivating novels. All of the creations that materialize from the mind or intellect are considered **intellectual property**. Inventors, artists, writers, and other creative individuals are the owners of their intellectual property. Like other property, intellectual property is protected by various laws and regulations.

There are four categories of intellectual property: patents, trademarks, copyrights, and trade secrets. Some of the media in content communities can be classified as trademarks, but most of it is copyrighted material.

▶ What should I know about trademarks? A **trademark** is any word, name, symbol, or design used in commerce to identify and distinguish the goods of one company from those of another. Twitter's little blue bird is a trademark, as is Facebook's stylized "f" logo. Trademarks occasionally display a ® or TM, but those marks are sometimes not visible. You should assume that all company logos are trademarks that are legally protected from misuse by law.

Many companies with an online presence, such as a Web site, provide information about the acceptable use of their trademarks. Before including a company's logo on your Web site, in a blog, or as part of a Pinterest board, check the company's policy on the use of its trademark. You may find, for example, that it is acceptable to use Facebook's Like button on your Web site, but that it is not permissible to mash up a banner image for your site that combines your name with the Facebook logo (Figure 5-17).

Figure 5-17: Use trademarks according to policy

Source: Facebook

Acceptable use

Unacceptable use

▶ How much stuff is copyrighted? **Copyright** is a form of legal protection that grants the author of an original work an exclusive right to copy, distribute, sell, and modify that work. Copyright applies to "works" such as photos, books, articles, plays, dance performances, videos, animations, sound effects, musical compositions, and audio recordings.

Just about everything available on content communities is protected by copyright. It is not necessary for the work to carry a copyright notice, nor is it required that the work's creator register the work to obtain copyright protection. Any original work automatically becomes copyrighted as soon as it is created, and the rights in Figure 5-18 can only be exercised by the copyright holder.

Figure 5-18: Copyright holder exclusive rights

Reproduce the Work

Prepare Derivative Works

Distribute Copies of the Work

Perform the Work

Display the Work Publicly

Transfer Ownership of the Work

▶ Is it legal to use copyrighted works? The copyright holder has total control over how a work may be used. The default protections make it illegal for anyone else to copy, distribute, perform, display, or license the work, or to prepare derivatives of it. That means it would be illegal, for example, to copy a photo from a content community and publish it as a Facebook post or as an illustration for a magazine article without the copyright holder's permission.

Copyright holders can give permission for the use of their work. They can agree to the content community's Terms of Use that allow works to be reposted within that community. They can place a work in the public domain, or they can license the work.

▶ When does a work become part of the public domain? **Public domain** refers to the status of works with expired copyrights or whose creators have forfeited their copyright. The works of Shakespeare, for example, are in the public domain. You can perform one of Shakespeare's plays or publish an anthology of his works. However, the 1996 film *Hamlet* directed by Kenneth Branagh is a new instance of the work and is protected by copyright.

In the United States, copyrights do not expire until 70 years after the author's death, and various loopholes allow for extensions. Legal specialists sometimes have difficulty determining if a work has reverted to the public domain. Even when a work seems very old, it is best not to assume that it is in the public domain.

QuickCheck

You should not use a photo that you find on the Web if ________.

a. the work is in the public domain

b. you've obtained permission from the copyright holder

c. the work has a license that allows your use

d. the author retains all copyrights

Creative Commons

A nonprofit organization called Creative Commons (CC) has done content communities a welcomed service by providing a set of standardized licenses that copyright holders can use to extend the rights to use their works to others.

◗ **What is a Creative Commons license?** A **Creative Commons license** is based on five rights that copyright holders can grant or deny to others (Figure 5-19).

Figure 5-19: Creative Commons license rights

Attribution. When the work is used, the copyright holder must be given credit for the work in a citation or another appropriate manner.

Share Alike. New works based on the original must be distributed under the same license as the original work.

No Derivatives. The work must not be changed when it is redistributed or shared.

Public Domain. All rights are granted for reuse or the work has been placed in the public domain.

Noncommercial. The work may not be used for commercial purposes.

Creative Commons rights can be combined for a variety of licenses.

Try It!

Which CC license would you assign to the photos and videos that you create?

How do CC licenses work? Copyright holders can assign any combination of CC rights to create a license. For example, a photographer who posts a photo on Flickr might offer a CC BY-ND license, which means it has a Creative Commons license allowing the photo to be used as long as there is a credit line attributing the photographer (BY) and the photo is not modified to create a derivative work (ND).

The Share Alike right is sometimes referred to as copyleft. The term *copyleft* was chosen to convey the idea that it is the opposite of copyright. Whereas copyright is designed to limit the use of a work, **copyleft** is designed to make a work freely available for distribution and modification under the condition that all derivative works use the same license. Works and their derivatives with a copyleft license cannot be later licensed in a way that would restrict their use.

Before using any work that you find at a content community, check for a Creative Commons license. You'll usually find it in the tags for a photo.

Can I assign a CC license to my own work? When you create a work, it is automatically protected by copyright and you have exclusive rights to its distribution, modification, and sale. If you would like to release some of those rights to make the work easier for others to use and share, you can assign a Creative Commons license. Figure 5-20 explains how to assign CC licenses to various types of media.

QuickCheck

Look back at the CC licenses in Figure 5-19. Which one would be considered a copyleft license?

a. BY NC SA

b. BY ND

c. BY

d. BY NC

Figure 5-20: How to assign CC rights

1. Connect to the Creative Commons license chooser at *creativecommons.org/choose.*

2. Choose the rights you want to grant to others.

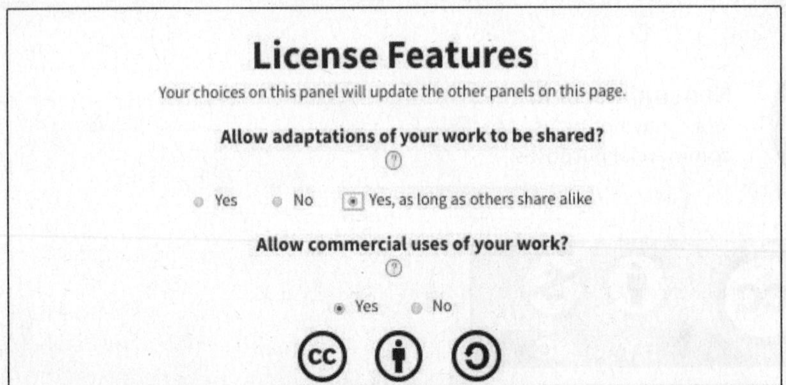

3. Place the license where it can be easily accessed.

Type of Work	Where to Place License
Web page, Web site, or blog	At the Creative Commons site *creativecommons.org/choose/*, select a license, copy the HTML code provided, then paste it onto a Web page or blog.
Image	Reference the CC license you've selected in the image caption or in the image tag.
Presentation	Reference the CC license you've selected on the title slide or the last slide. Add a link, if possible, to the license.

What about fair use? Earlier modules touched on the concept of **fair use**, which allows for the limited use of copyrighted material without obtaining permission from the copyright holder. United States copyright regulations include four factors that characterize fair use:

1. **The purpose and character of the use.** The use of copyrighted materials without permission is more likely to be "fair" when the materials are transformed and used for a purpose different from that of the original work.
2. **The nature of the copyrighted work.** Guidelines for fair use of photos may differ from guidelines for music, videos, or written works.
3. **The amount of the copyrighted work that is used.** Quoting a paragraph from a book is more likely to be fair use than reproducing an entire chapter.
4. **The effect on the value of the copyrighted work.** Uses that deprive the copyright holder of income are not generally considered fair use.

Is a transformative work different from a derivative work? Yes. A **derivative work** modifies a copyrighted work but does not substantially change its content or purpose. Translations, adaptations, musical arrangements, dramatizations, reproductions, condensations, and similar modifications would all be considered derivative.

Mashups that combine two or more music tracks into a single recording are usually regarded as derivative works because they are intended for the same uses as the original recordings. Derivative works are not fair use, and they require permission directly from the copyright holder or from an applicable license, such as CC BY.

A **transformative work** repackages a copyrighted work to add new meaning or produce a work that is used for a purpose different from the original work. Parodies, for example, are considered transformative. Cutting up magazine covers to create a collage to hang on a wall would also be considered a transformative use.

Transformative works are considered fair use; they can be produced and distributed without the copyright holder's permission.

Although the differences between derivative and transformative works may seem clear, in practice copyright holders are free to sue anyone who produces a work that is based on their copyrighted works. The courts are the ultimate decision makers in copyright infringement cases. If you want to safely incorporate the works of others into your own work, use only works that have a CC BY or CCØ license.

5

QuickCheck

Suppose that you create a YouTube video and add a music track from a recent hit film. Would your work be considered transformative?

a. Yes, I've created a new, original work.

b. Yes, the copyrighted sound track is just part of the new work.

c. No, I'm not going to make any money from it.

d. No, the sound track is used in my work for the same purpose as in the original work.

QuickQuiz — Section B

1. A media element goes ______ when it quickly infiltrates popular culture and is accessed by millions of people around the globe.
2. Content communities form around user-______ content.
3. Dublin Core is an example of a formal ______ standard.
4. The Twitter bird logo is an example of a company ______ that is protected from misuse by law.
5. A Creative Commons license designated as CC BY ______ does not allow derivative works.

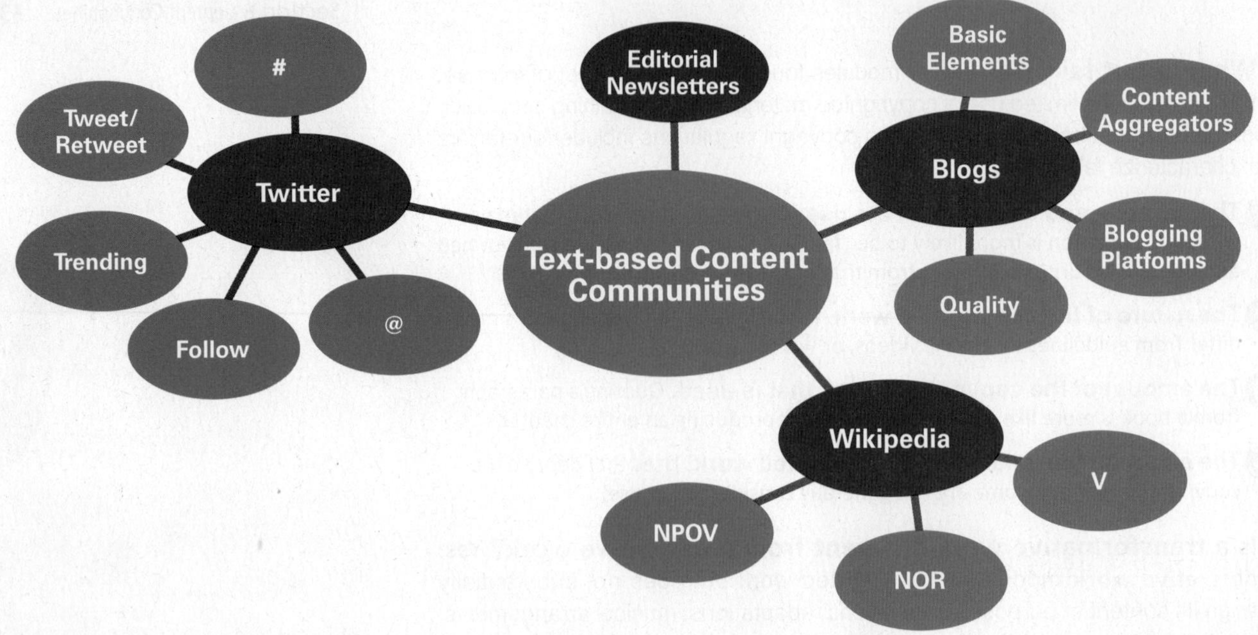

Section C

Blogs and More

Objectives

- Identify the major elements of a blog page.
- List examples of at least two blogging platforms.
- Discuss why blogs could be considered a disruptive technology.
- List five questions that help to evaluate the quality of information presented in a blog.
- Give examples of six ways in which Twitter has expanded its focus to go beyond personal status updates.
- Identify the major elements of a Twitter page.
- Describe the characteristics of a wiki.
- Explain how Wikipedia articles are written and edited.
- Explain the meaning of NPOV, NOR, and V in the context of Wikipedia.
- Identify the elements of a Wikipedia article.
- Identify the purpose of each Wikipedia tab.

Blogs, newsletters, tweets, and wikis. The major text-based content communities offer up a mountain of content. Some of it is accurate and dependable; some of it is downright false. Even more of it is misleading in subtle ways. In this section, you'll explore the origins of this text-based content and how to tell the good from the bad.

Terminology

blog
blogging platform
content aggregator
blogosphere
editorial newsletter platforms
tweets
microblogging service
@username
retweet
promoted tweet
Twitter stream/timeline
follow
follower
follow back
@mention
#hashtag
DM
trending
wiki
NPOV
NOR
V

5

Blogs

The democratization of culture is not limited to art; it spills over into the mainstream news media. Today, blogs provide alternative news sources that offer a greater diversity of topics and opinions than pre-Internet gatekeepers such as Reuters, Associated Press, and CNN. The ease of broadcasting information has become a major disruptive force with no clear outcome in sight.

▶ **What is a blog?** A **blog** (short for Web log) is a sequence of informational articles posted in reverse chronological order and displayed on a scrollable Web page. Blogs are generally maintained by a person, a company, or an organization.

▶ **What are the basic elements of a blog?** Blog entries are text based, but they can get visually fancy with lots of photos and videos. Basic blogs have a standard set of elements illustrated in Figure 5-21.

Figure 5-21: Anatomy of a blog

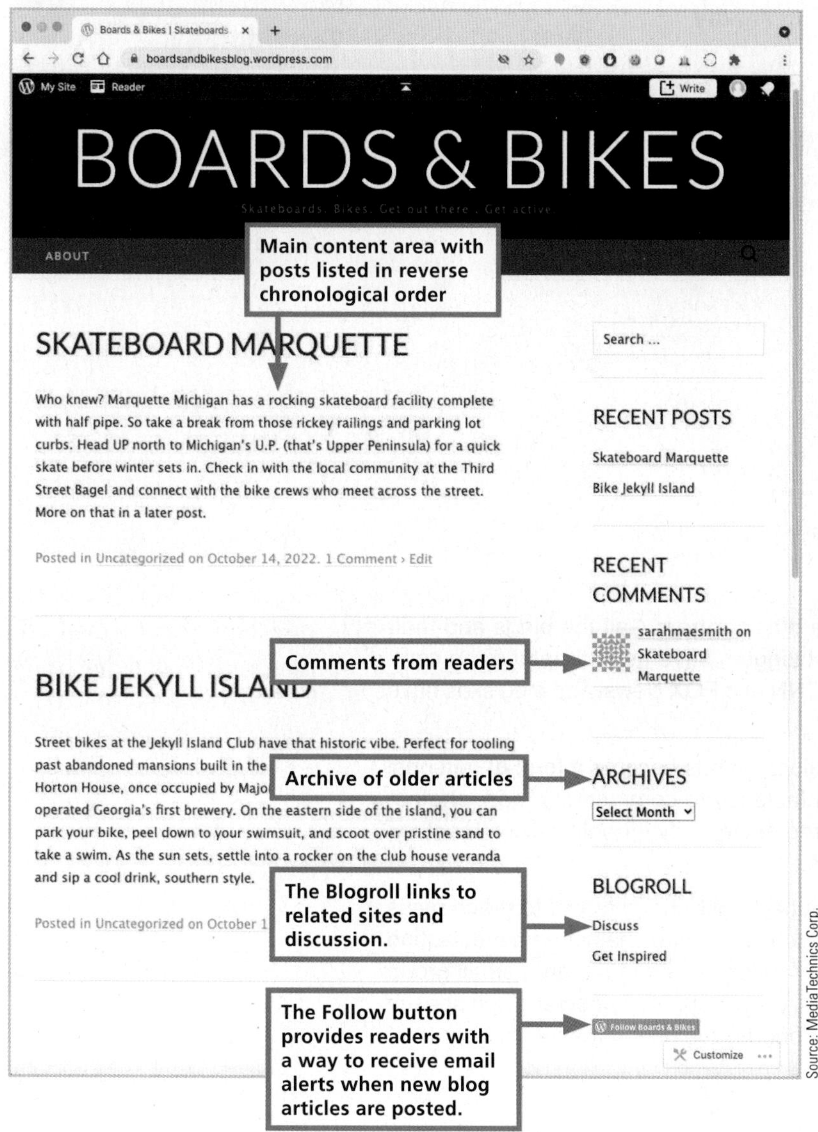

QuickCheck

If you subscribe to WordPress, how would you get email alerts for new blog posts?

a. By making a comment

b. By subscribing to the archive

c. By joining the blogroll

d. By selecting the Follow button

How can I become a blogger? Popular blogging platforms include Blogger, WordPress, Wix, and Medium. A **blogging platform** provides tools for creating blogs. It may also provide a Web site where blogs can be posted for access by the public.

Bloggers may post to a subdomain, such as *https://medium.com/@sarah*, offered by the blogging platform. Bloggers who want a dedicated domain name, such as *www.edisonjones.com*, can use a Web hosting service, such as HostGator or GoDaddy. These hosting services offer blogging plug-ins for authoring and managing blog posts.

How can I find and access blogs? You can find blogs by going to Blogger, WordPress, and Medium or by simply launching an online search such as *Skateboard Blogs*. You can use a **content aggregator** to set up a "feed" that monitors your favorite blogs, collects the latest posts, and displays them (Figure 5-22).

Try It!

How would you discover if there are any skateboarding blogs on WordPress?

Figure 5-22: Setting up a "feed" using Feedly

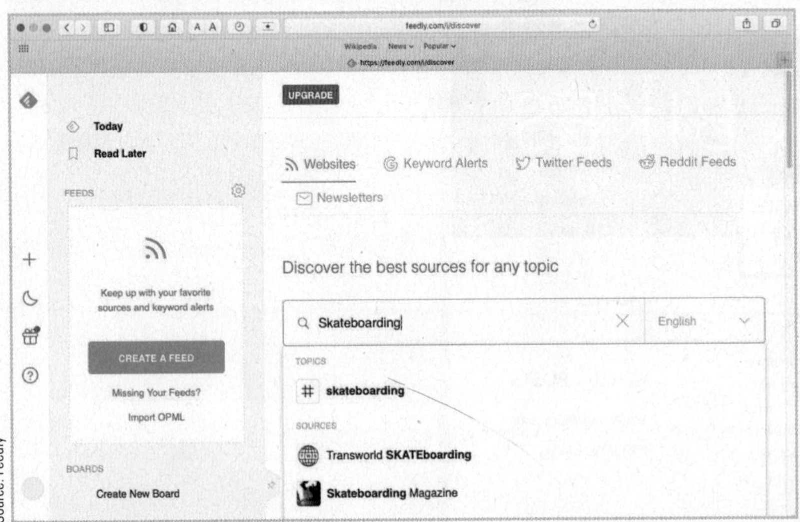

Source: Feedly

Terminology

Blogger (uppercase *B*) is the name of Google's blogging platform. A *blogger* (lowercase *b*) is a person who blogs. Bloggers are sometimes referred to as *influencers*.

How significant are blogs? The **blogosphere**—all the blogs and their interconnections—is influential. Some bloggers have been tapped to be commentators for headline news shows on CNN and FOX News. Top blog sites have millions of monthly readers.

Many blogs are open to the public, so blogging has become a form of personal journalism. Bloggers can chase down facts, write commentary, post photos, and offer opinions. Blogs have been used extensively for political commentary, celebrity publicity, and technology news.

Blogs and other Internet-based news outlets have the potential to reach mass audiences. Totalitarian governments, which can control mainstream media, find it more difficult to silence a multitude of freelance bloggers than a small group of professional journalists. In that respect, blogs support democratic free speech values and have the potential to disrupt oppressive governments.

Blogging also offers an alternative source of news and information, reducing the audience for mainstream news outlets. The fact that blogs and many Internet-based news outlets offer free access has disrupted print-based news media by reducing sales and forcing major newspapers to shutter operations. Industry analysts are concerned that if this trend continues in the years ahead, few reliable mainstream news outlets will remain.

But blogs themselves may be on the endangered list. Some readers find it inconvenient to periodically connect to their favorite blogs. Many bloggers offer subscriptions to their blog content in the form of a newsletter that is sent directly to a subscriber's email address. As a spin-off, **editorial newsletter platforms** such as Substack and Review offer tools for creating and sending content directly to subscribers' inboxes.

QuickCheck

News media consider blogs to be a(n) ___________ technology.

a. disruptive

b. old-fashioned

c. cutting-edge

d. failed

5

▸ Who is responsible for blog content? Professional journalists and the media companies they represent are guided by a code of ethics that encourages seeking truth, reporting it, minimizing harm, resisting outside influences, and maintaining accountability. It is true that not all professional journalists live up to these standards, but the standards do exist.

Bloggers, who may not have journalistic training or the supervision of responsible corporations, may have a less rigorous approach to accuracy and accountability. They might not take steps to verify information, and they might not understand the significance of intellectual property.

Overall, the information provided by blogs tends to be less reliable than information from the mainstream media. However, many reliable and professional blogs exist. As with other online and offline materials, readers are ultimately responsible for evaluating the quality of information in a blog. Figure 5-23 offers some tips for evaluating blogs.

Figure 5-23: How to evaluate blogs

Who is the blogger? Look for information about the blogger's expertise at sites other than the blog.

What are the blog's readership and Alexa rating? Popular blogs tend to be more reliable because they are subject to scrutiny by many readers.

Are comments substantive and supportive? Blogs that generate negative comments and corrections may not contain accurate information.

How extensive is the blog's archive? Well-established blogs may remain active for many years, so look at the blog's track record and make sure it contains recent posts.

QuickCheck

Who is ultimately responsible for evaluating the material presented in a blog or newsletter?

a. The blogger

b. The mainstream media

c. The government

d. The reader

Try It!

Connect to Phil Plait's Bad Astronomy blog. What information about the blogger's background can you find in the blog and elsewhere on the Web? Based on that information, would you consider this blogger reputable?

Microblogs

Michael Brown's death, the Hudson River plane crash, the Osama bin Laden raid, and the Boston Marathon bombings are some of the breaking news stories that appeared first on Twitter, a social media service that relays information from the mundane to the extraordinary.

◗ **What was the original idea behind Twitter?** Twitter was modeled as a Web-based version of the text messaging services offered on mobile phones. Just as those services were limited to 140 characters, Twitter messages, called **tweets**, initially carried such a limit. Now expanded to 280 characters and associated videos, Twitter is an example of a **microblogging service** because a Twitter message is basically a short blog post.

Twitter originated as a social networking service where participants could keep track of what their friends were doing based on trivial status updates such as "I'm heading to my bio class" or "Just saw Peter at the Laundromat." As the service evolved and the participants' circles of influence mushroomed, Twitter's focus expanded to include topics of more substance, in addition to a continuing stream of personal updates. Some examples of Twitter's expanding influence include the following:

A platform for breaking news. In 2008, NASA researchers used Twitter to announce an exciting discovery from the Phoenix Mars mission: "Are you ready to celebrate? Well, get ready: We have ICE!!!!! Yes, ICE, *WATER ICE* on Mars! w00t!!! Best day ever!!" Tweets have since evolved into one of the main sources for news.

Citizen journalism. In 2021, Taliban fighters seized control of Afghanistan, throwing the country into chaos. Citizen journalists chronicled the throngs of desperate people crowding the road to the airport and futile protests staged against the Taliban's treatment of women, journalists, and those who refused to recognize the new, fundamentalist government.

Celebrity watching. Twitter illustrates and reinforces the power of celebrity. Oprah Winfrey had more than 100,000 followers on the day she opened her Twitter account. Ellen DeGeneres's selfie at the 2014 Oscars became one of the most popular tweets of all time.

Online presence. Companies from McDonald's to Starbucks have established corporate Twitter accounts where product information can be quickly disseminated to customers. Corporate presence on social media sites is a requirement of doing business in the digital age.

Public opinion. Twitter users can be quick to comment about breaking events and controversies, though their opinions may be based on information gleaned from a mere 280 characters of information. Principles of justice, such as being innocent until proven guilty, can be forgotten as Twitter users rush to tweet reactions to trending controversies.

Social organizing. Twitter's ability to quickly disseminate information makes it a desirable platform for social organizing. Hashtags such as #blacklivesmatter, #metoo, #prolife, and #bluelivesmatter have been instrumental in organizing protests, rallies, and virtual meetups. Twitter and other social media have also been used, however, by government authorities to identify protesters.

Try It!

Access Twitter and look at the list of trending topics. How many of these would you classify as substantive? Next, try conducting an online search for *Most popular Twitter handles.* Examine the list and guess how many are not self-promotional.

QuickCheck

Technically, Twitter is most similar to ____________.

a. blogs

b. Flickr

c. email

d. crowdsourcing

What's the basic Twitter vocabulary? Twitter has a vocabulary all its own, and some of its terminology has spilled over to other social media. Figure 5-24 presents Twitter jargon in the context of a Twitter page.

Figure 5-24: Twitter terminology

Source: 2015 Twitter

@username: A unique identifier for each Twitter account holder

Tweet: A message consisting of 280 or fewer characters of text plus optional photos/videos

Retweet: A tweet that is forwarded from one Twitter user to others

Promoted tweet: Tweets that contain paid advertising and are labeled to distinguish them from noncommercial tweets

Twitter stream/timeline: A list of tweets; a user's Home timeline shows the user's own tweets and tweets from anyone the user is following

Follow: Specifying a Twitter user whose tweets you want to receive

Follower: A Twitter user who follows your tweets

Follow back: When Twitter users mutually follow each other (e.g., Keysha follows Joe, and then Joe follows Keysha back)

@mention: A person who is referred to in a tweet with a Twitter username preceded by an @ symbol (e.g., mentioning @BillGates in a tweet broadcasts it to your followers and places it in Bill Gates' Mentions tab)

Reply: A message sent in reply to a tweet; automatically addressed to the source of the original tweet preceded by the @ symbol

#hashtag: A hashtag, such as #ipadgames, specifies a keyword that can be used to find and group tweets by topic, both in Twitter and across other social media; clicking a hashtag in a tweet displays other tweets with that hashtag (a directory of hashtags can be found at *www.hashtags.org*)

DM: Direct, private email-like messages sent by Twitter users to any of their followers

Trending: Twitter hashtags that are popular for a period of time

Try It!

Access Twitter and make sure that you can identify examples of each term in Figure 5-24.

5

How substantive is the information on Twitter? There is no doubt that tweets shape the social dialogue. Mainstream news organizations use tweets as a source of breaking news and as indicators of public opinion. Although socially significant discussions occasionally appear in the list of trending topics, a casual review of trending topics and popular Twitter handles seems to reveal a breathtaking number of tweets that have little social relevance.

Researchers have found Twitter to be a fascinating topic of study. Notable efforts include a study of trending topic classifications conducted by Northwestern University, and a project called Truthy that traced the spread of memes. There was also a University of Pennsylvania study of cardiovascular disease commentary, and a study conducted by the Pew Research Center that examined Americans' use of social media for political activism.

QuickCheck

Twitter pioneered the use of the ________ symbol to group messages pertaining to a topic.

a. @

b. !

c. RT

d. #

Wikis

The content communities that attract attention today serve up user-generated videos and images. However, some of the oldest and most productive content communities are built upon text-based wikis.

What is a wiki? A **wiki** is a collaborative Web application that provides tools for contributors to post, read, and modify content. For example, one contributor might write and post an article about wolves. That article can be read and modified by others. Changes to an article are tracked, allowing the community to view changes, leave changes in place, or revert back to earlier content.

Wiki software runs on a wiki server and provides a set of tools for creating and editing content. Content is stored in a database on the wiki server, along with a list of changes to the content. Popular wiki software, such as MediaWiki, is open source, so all users are free to create and host a public or private wiki. The world's most popular wiki is Wikipedia.

How does Wikipedia work? Wikipedia is an online encyclopedia. It uses MediaWiki software to manage millions of articles in 285 languages. Wikipedia receives about a billion page views per day as people from all over the world seek factual information about the arts, geography, history, science, society, and technology. Wikipedia is organized by topics, such as Wolves, Egypt, Origami, Tolkien, London, American Revolution, and Skateboards.

Wikipedia pages can be accessed, viewed, and edited anonymously by the general public without subscription or registration. Participants are encouraged to register with the Wikipedia community and become "Wikipedians." These editors not only contribute new material and updates but also monitor pages to ensure that they retain high-quality contents, adhere to Wikipedia standards, and are not subject to vandalism.

What are Wikipedia standards? Wikipedia endeavors to provide non-biased, accurate, and verifiable information. Content creators and editors are encouraged to filter material through a sieve of strict standards known to insiders as **NPOV**, **NOR**, and **V**. Figure 5-25 explains these standards.

Figure 5-25: Wikipedia content policies

NPOV **Neutral point of view:** Content for Wikipedia articles should be phrased and presented in neutral language and with unbiased intent.

NOR **No original research:** Articles should be based on existing recognized knowledge. Personal views and original research are not appropriate.

V **Verifiability:** Readers must be able to verify all content against reliable external sources based on citations included within the text and listed at the conclusion.

QuickCheck

In an attempt to keep articles unbiased, Wikipedia has a(n) ____________ policy.

a. NPOV

b. NOR

c. RS

d. V

What are the elements of a Wikipedia article? Wikipedia articles vary in length but contain the set of standard elements that are shown in Figure 5-26.

Figure 5-26: Wikipedia page elements

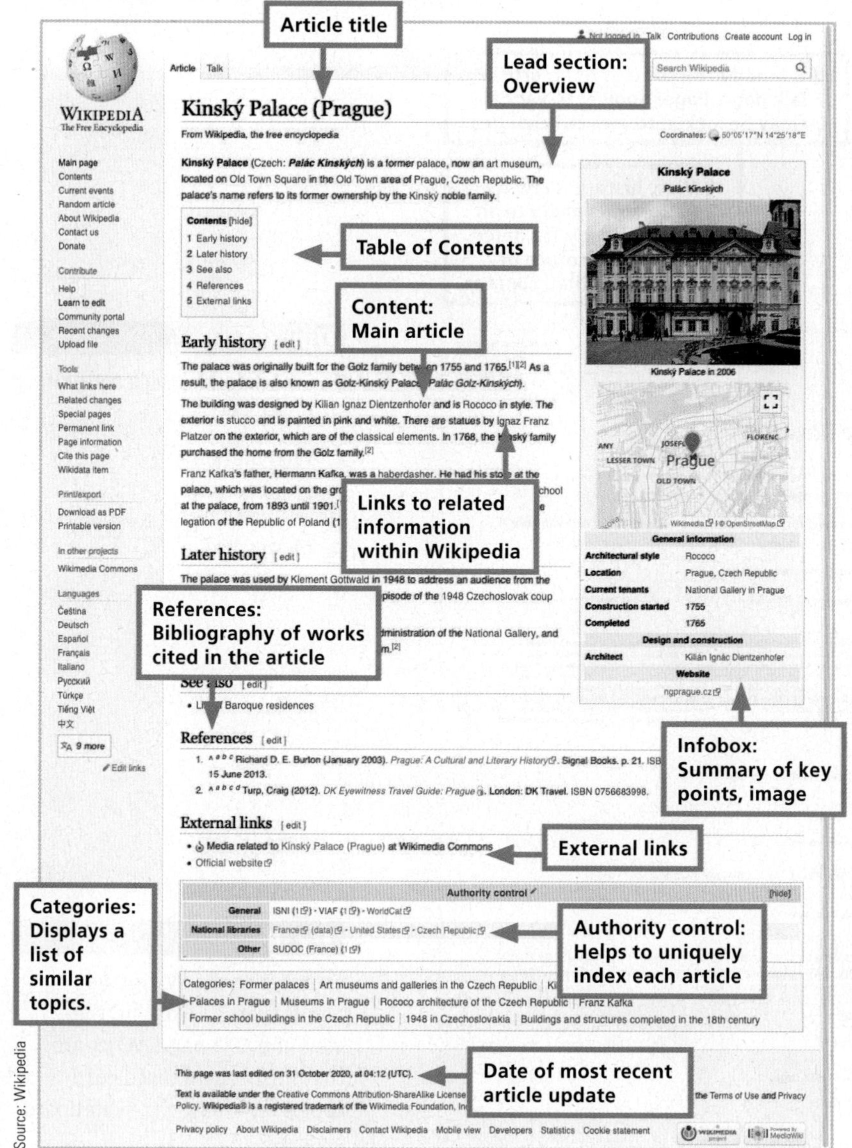

Source: Wikipedia

Try It!

Pull up a Wikipedia page and identify each of the sections listed in Figure 5-26.

Try It!

See how to contribute content to Wikipedia by connecting to the Wikipedia article *Help: Introduction to Editing with VisualEditor.*

▶ What's on the other Wikipedia tabs? Most Wikipedia users focus on the main topic page displayed on the Article tab; however, valuable information can be found on other tabs. For example, it is possible to edit the text of an article from the Edit tab using wiki markup or HTML, as shown in Figure 5-27.

Figure 5-27: Wikipedia tabs

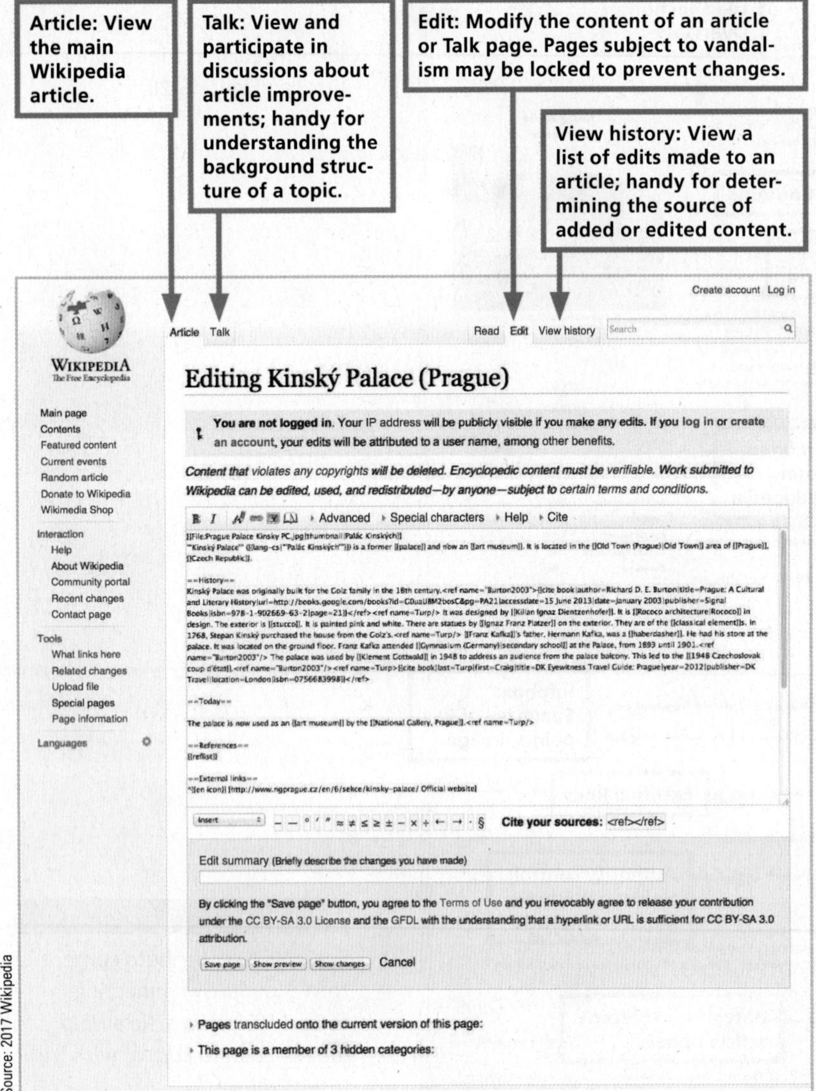

Source: 2017 Wikipedia

QuickCheck

The markup language for editing Wikipedia articles is ________.

a. Wiki markup

b. Java

c. MediaWiki

d. Kinsky

Try It!

Connect to the Wikipedia page about skateboards and then view the Talk page. What are the most recent discussion topics regarding the skateboard article?

▸ What should I know about using Wikipedia information? Because Wikipedia articles can be edited by anyone at any time, the accuracy and reliability of Wikipedia information are controversial. Some articles contain errors and omit important data. Occasionally, articles are deliberately falsified. Older Wikipedia articles tend to be more accurate than new articles because they have been through more editing cycles. Older articles, however, may not be up to date.

In some academic settings, Wikipedia is not regarded as a reliable source of information. Figure 5-28 lists some guidelines for its use in academia.

5

Figure 5-28: Wikipedia academic usage guidelines

  Do not quote Wikipedia directly; do not list Wikipedia articles in bibliographies; work with original sources.

 Cross-check before using facts from Wikipedia articles.

 Follow links in citations or use Google to locate original sources before including information in research papers.

 Never "lift" citations from the references section of a Wikipedia article; use citations only if you have examined the source document.

 Be sure to use sources beyond Wikipedia to research topics in sufficient depth.

 Before submitting papers, articles, and other academic work, check the sourcing guidelines provided by instructors or editors who will review your work.

QuickQuiz — Section C

1. WordPress and Blogger are examples of blogging ________.
2. A(n) ________ aggregator sets up a feed that monitors your favorite blogs, collects the most recent posts, and displays them.
3. The ________ symbol specifies a Twitter topic.
4. A collaborative Web application that provides tools for contributors to post and modify content is called a(n) ________.
5. Wikipedia articles are not supposed to refer to original ________ (NOR).

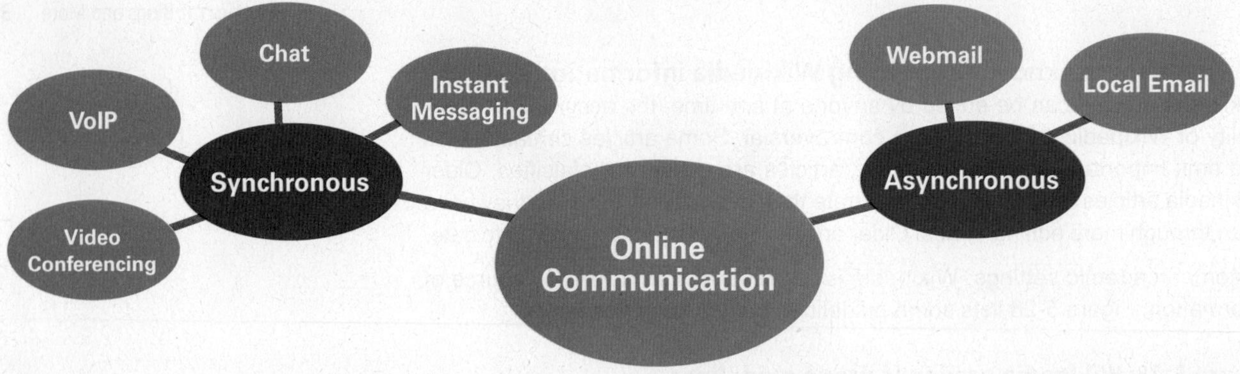

Section D Online Communication

Objectives

- Classify communications technologies as synchronous, asynchronous, public, or private.
- Interpret the information in an email header.
- List the pros and cons of Webmail and local mail.
- Explain how the term *store-and-forward* relates to email.
- Differentiate between IMAP and POP.
- List four steps that help to reduce the security risk of accessing email on a public computer.
- Explain the circumstances under which a person might want to forward email between a Webmail account and a local account.
- Describe the evolution of online chat.
- Name four services that use VoIP technologies.
- List some of the security and privacy problems associated with videoconferencing systems.

When you think of social media, email and Skype might not immediately come to mind. And yet, what could be more social than corresponding with friends or chatting with them in real time? Social media offer plenty of choices for communicating. Section D presents communication technologies in a handy, purpose-oriented structure.

Terminology

synchronous
asynchronous
email
email message
email system
email server
message header
Webmail
local email
store-and-forward
POP3
IMAP
SMTP
instant messaging
VoIP

Communication Matrix

The Internet offers many tools for communicating and collaborating; more are appearing every day. These tools can be classified into a four-cell matrix, as shown in Figure 5-29.

Figure 5-29: Communication matrix

Public Asynchronous	Public Synchronous
Blogs Microblogs (Twitter) Forums and discussion groups Public social media posts	Chat rooms Live streaming video
Private Asynchronous Email Text messaging service (SMS) Multimedia messaging service (MMS) Private social media posts	**Private Synchronous** Voice over IP (Skype) Videoconferencing (Zoom) Instant messaging (ICQ, AIM)

5

▸ How are synchronous and asynchronous communications different? Think about email and Skype. You use them differently because one is synchronous and the other is asynchronous.

Synchronous. When communication is **synchronous**, interchanges happen in real time while all parties are online. Synchronous communications have the advantage of immediacy. They can convey your thoughts as you speak and events as they happen. Telephone calls are synchronous, as are video conferences and live streaming video.

Asynchronous. When communication is **asynchronous**, messages are held until the recipient is ready to view them. Asynchronous communication offers convenience because information can be gathered whenever you want it. That information can, however, be out of date by the time you obtain it. Email is an example of asynchronous communication.

▸ What is significant about public or private communications? There are times when you want to communicate with certain people, and there are times when you want to reach a wider audience. Networks offer opportunities for both public and private communications.

Public. Public communications can be accessed by individuals unknown to the person who created a message. The word *posting* is associated with this type of communication because it is similar to posting a billboard, sign, or poster. Public communication platforms, such as Twitter and blogs, are useful for disseminating information to a wide audience.

Private. Communications for which you specify one or more recipients would be classified as private. Text messaging is a popular type of private communication. A limited audience can be an advantage or a disadvantage, depending on what you hope to accomplish with your message. Be aware, however, that private messages can be forwarded by recipients, so they do not necessarily remain private.

QuickCheck

Email is an example of ____________ communication.

a. synchronous

b. asynchronous

c. mediated

d. public

Email

An estimated 300 billion email messages speed over the Internet each day. You can access email using Webmail, local mail, or both. Which system you use has implications for your security and privacy.

QuickCheck

The message header in Figure 5-30 indicates that the message originated ________.

a. from a Yahoo! account

b. from a Facebook user

c. from a Hotmail account

d. from a POP mail server

▶ **Exactly what is email?** The term **email** can refer to a single message or to the entire system of computers and software that transmits, receives, and stores email messages. An **email message** is an electronic document transmitted over a computer network to a specific recipient

The computers and software that provide email services form an **email system**. At the heart of a typical email system is an **email server**—a computer that essentially acts as a central post office for a group of people. Email servers run special email server software, which provides an electronic mailbox for each person, sorts incoming messages into these mailboxes, and routes outgoing mail over the Internet to other email servers.

Email messages have a standard format that consists of a message header and the message body. The **message header** contains the sender and recipient addresses, date, and subject line. When you view an email message, this information is a simplified version of a more complex header that contains a huge amount of routing information, which traces the path of the message and reveals how it was treated by various servers. If you want to know exactly where a message originated or why a message was returned to sender, check the header (Figure 5-30).

Try It!

Open one of your own email messages and take a look at the header. Can you locate any information indicating security checks on the sender?

Figure 5-30: Email message headers

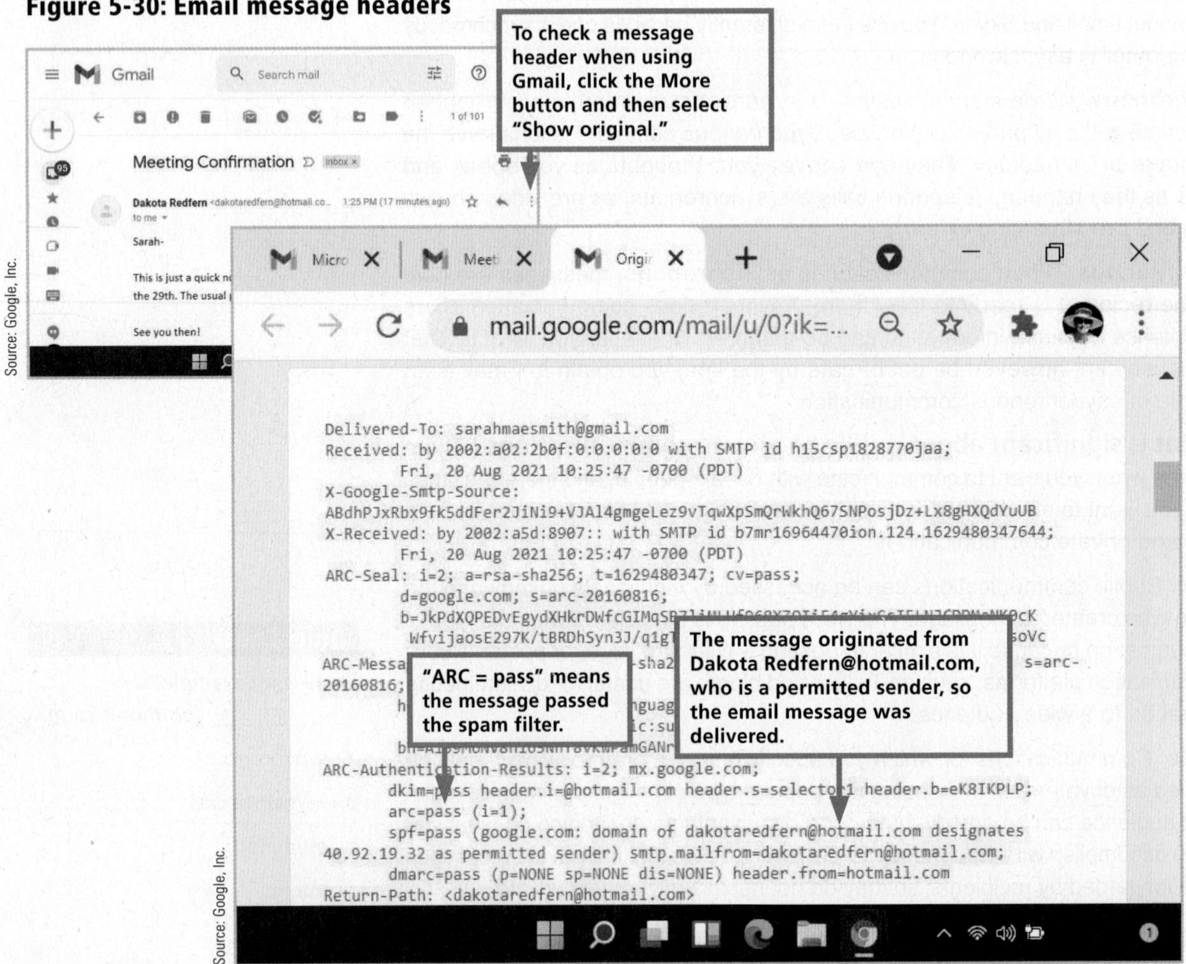

How does Webmail work? **Webmail** is typically a free service accessed using a browser. In a classic Webmail configuration, incoming messages are stored in an inbox on the Web. When you want to read or send mail, use a browser to go to your email provider's Web site and log in. The controls for reading, composing, and managing messages are all presented in the browser window. While reading and composing mail, you generally must remain online (Figure 5-31).

Try It!

An email address is frequently used to verify your identity when subscribing to social media services. But that email address may easily fall into the hands of marketers. You can use a "junk" email address or work with a service such as 10 Minute Mail to obtain a temporary email address that lasts only long enough to subscribe to a service, receive the confirmation email, and click the verification link. Check it out!

Figure 5-31: Webmail

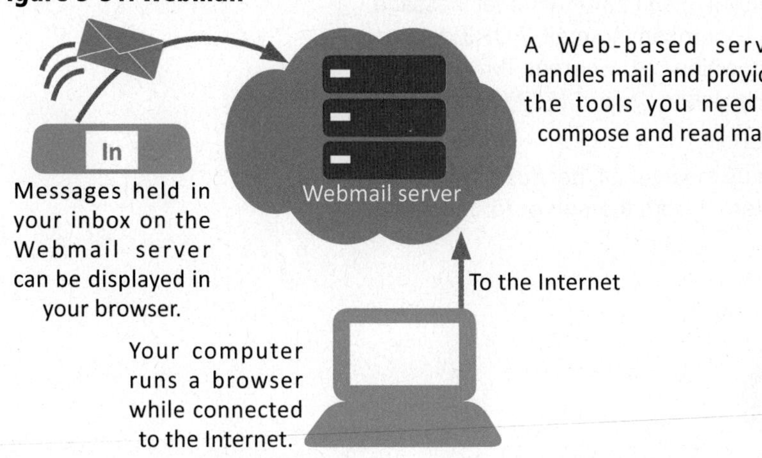

A Web-based server handles mail and provides the tools you need to compose and read mail.
In
Webmail server
Messages held in your inbox on the Webmail server can be displayed in your browser.
To the Internet
Your computer runs a browser while connected to the Internet.

What are the pros and cons of Webmail? Webmail accounts are handy. They offer several advantages, but they also have a few disadvantages that require consumer awareness.

Affordable. Most Webmail is free. In addition to your primary account, you can establish additional accounts to use as throwaways for online activities that require registration, but that you don't intend to continue using.

Access from any device. Webmail can be accessed from any device that has a browser. With smartphones and tablets, as well as laptops and desktops, just open a browser and log in to your Webmail account.

Access anywhere. Webmail is ideal for people who travel, because messages can be accessed from any computer connected to the Internet.

Security risks. Your email messages are stored on Web servers that can be targets for hackers and are monitored by government agencies. Accessing email from a public computer is handy when traveling, but it can be a security risk. To reduce the risk, you should:

- Reboot the computer before logging in to your email account.
- Avoid entering sensitive information, such as your credit card number, in case your keystrokes are being monitored by malicious software lurking on the public computer.
- Be sure to log off when your session is finished.
- Log out and shut down the computer.

Advertising. Free Webmail is supported by advertising, so expect to see advertisements. Today's sophisticated ad servers can search the contents of an incoming message looking for keywords and then use them to display targeted ads in your browser window.

How does local email work? When you use **local email**, an Internet-based email server stores your incoming messages until you launch your email client and get your mail. Messages are then downloaded to a folder on a local storage device that serves as your email inbox. This telecommunications technique is sometimes referred to as **store-and-forward**.

Try It!

Do you customarily use Webmail or do you use a local email client?

Using your email client, you can read your mail at your leisure. You can also compose new mail and reply to messages. This outgoing mail can be temporarily stored in an outbox or it can be sent immediately.

The protocols **POP3** (Post Office Protocol version 3) and **IMAP** (Internet Message Access Protocol) can be used to manage your incoming mail. POP3 deletes messages from the server after they are downloaded, whereas IMAP leaves messages on the server until you specifically delete them. **SMTP** (Simple Mail Transfer Protocol) handles outgoing mail.

Keep these protocols in mind when setting up local email, because the server you specify for outgoing mail might be different from the server for incoming mail (Figure 5-32).

Figure 5-32: Local email

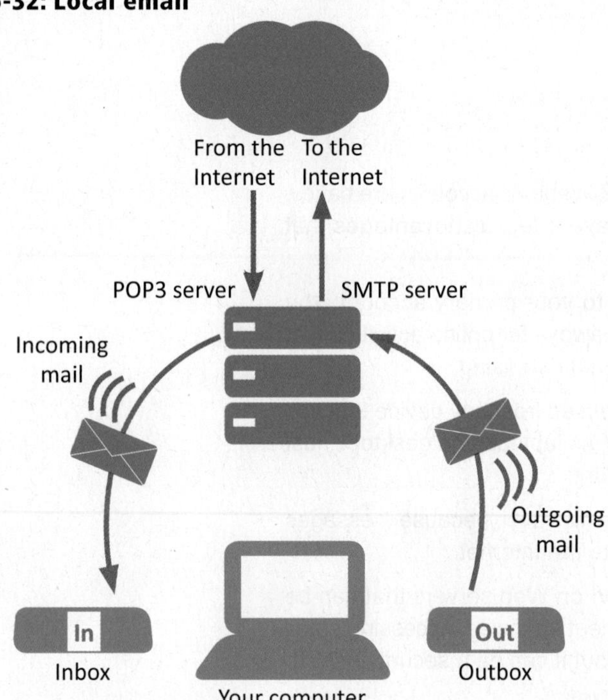

What are the advantages of local email? Local email has the following advantages:

Offline access. Because local email stores your inbox and outbox on your computer, you can compose and read mail offline. You are required to go online only to transfer outgoing mail from your outbox to the email server, and to receive incoming messages. This feature is useful if you have a very slow connection or sporadic Internet access.

Control. When you use POP3 to collect your mail, your messages are transferred to your computer's hard disk, where you can control who has access to them. With this control, however, comes the responsibility for maintaining backups of your important email messages.

QuickCheck

Which server handles outgoing mail?

a. POP

b. IMAP

c. SMTP

d. LOCAL

How do I set up local email? To set up local email, the first step is selecting a local email client. Macs include an email client called Mail. Microsoft Outlook is one of the most popular email clients for Windows.

After installing an email client, you can configure it for the email service you're using. Your email provider can supply the information needed for this task. That information can include the following:

- Your email user ID, which is the first part of your email address (e.g., in LiuChan@gsu.edu, the user ID is LiuChan)
- Your email password, if required to access the email server
- An address for the outgoing (SMTP) server, such as mail.viserver.net or smtp.charter.com
- An address for the incoming (POP3 or IMAP) server, such as mail.gsu.edu or pop.media.net
- Port numbers for incoming and outgoing servers, which are usually Port 110 (incoming) and Port 25 or 587 (outgoing)
- Whether the connection uses SSL security

Figure 5-33 displays basic information needed to set up a local email account.

QuickCheck

What happens on the server when mail is downloaded for the account in Figure 5-33?

a. The messages in Sarah's inbox are deleted.

b. Sarah's outgoing mail is blocked.

c. The messages are forwarded to an online account.

d. The messages remain on the server.

5

Figure 5-33: How to set up local mail

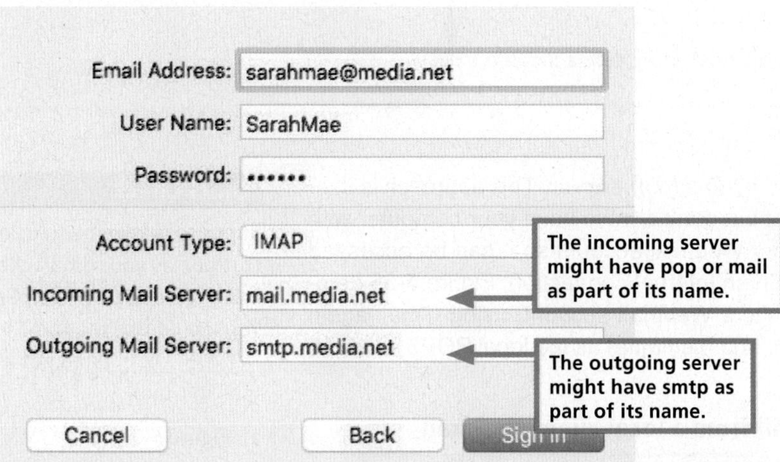

What about email apps for mobile devices? Webmail and local email services, such as Gmail, Apple Mail, Windows Mail, and Microsoft Outlook, are available as mobile apps. Downloading an email app to a mobile device places the necessary client software on your smartphone or tablet.

When an email app opens, it collects the most recent messages from your inbox on the email server. These messages are temporarily copied to your device so that you can read them. The original copy of the message is retained on the email server.

When you delete messages and mark them as read while using a mobile app, IMAP protocols generally perform the same actions on the email server. Deleting a message using a mobile app deletes the message from the server. Some email apps provide menu options for customizing this synchronization. Be sure to understand the synchronization settings for your mobile app so you don't mistakenly delete messages you might later want to access from another device.

Can I use both local email and Webmail? Yes. You can mix and match Webmail and local mail in various ways.

Use local email software to access messages sent to your Webmail account. This approach is useful if you want to compose mail offline or if you prefer the interface of a local email client such as Outlook compared to the interface offered by Webmail services, such as Gmail.

Once you've created a Gmail account, for example, you can access Settings to enable POP/IMAP mail and then forward your mail to your local client (Figure 5-34).

Figure 5-34: How to forward mail from Gmail to a local client

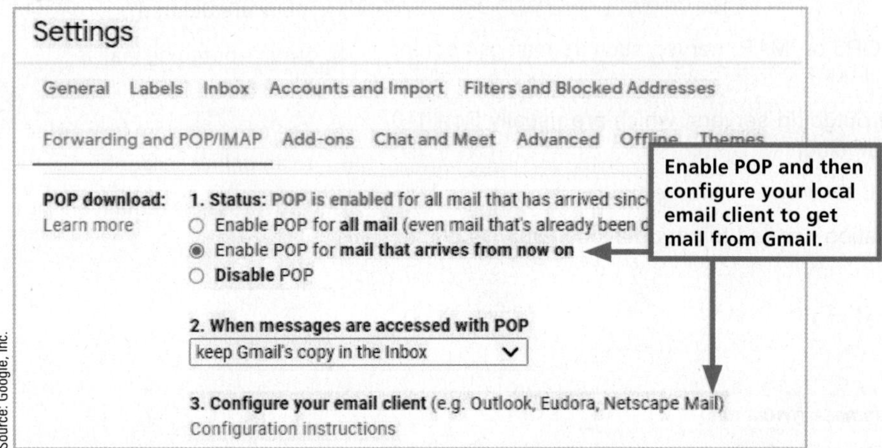

Source: Google, Inc.

Use Webmail to collect messages from a POP server. This approach is useful if you have a local email account but don't always have your computer with you. Your local mail is copied to your Webmail account so it can be accessed when you log in to any computer with an Internet connection. Figure 5-35 demonstrates how to forward local mail to a Webmail account, using Gmail again as an example of a Webmail service and Media.net as the local POP3 account.

QuickCheck

Suppose you've been using Outlook as your email client but decide to switch to Gmail. You would use the tools in ______________ to get all your mail in Gmail.

a. Figure 5-34

b. Figure 5-35

Figure 5-35: How to forward mail from a local client to Gmail

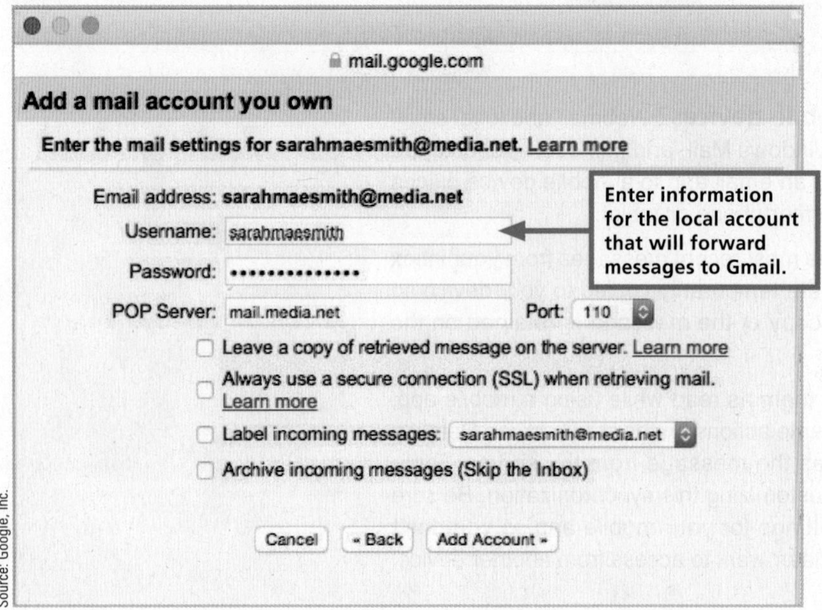

Source: Google, Inc.

Try It!

If you use Webmail, take a moment to check your forwarding settings and make sure your mail is not copied to an unauthorized location. Is mail forwarded to any local or online accounts?

Online Chat

When email might take too long, and when you want to establish two-way communication, online chat services offer just the technology you need. The concept of shipping synchronous text, voice, or video over the Internet has its roots in instant messaging.

▶ What is instant messaging? **Instant messaging** (IM) is a synchronous, real-time technology for two or more people to type messages back and forth while online. It has the vibe of a phone call except that instead of talking, the parties are typing. With some IM systems, both parties can see messages character by character as they are typed. More typically, however, the recipient does not see the message as it is typed but must wait until it is completed.

Instant messaging technologies were available on local area networks even before the Internet was open to the public. As the Internet grew, online services, such as Yahoo!, MSN, AOL, and Excite, developed IM systems. Initially, all these systems were proprietary. This meant that messages could not be sent from one service's IM client to a different service's client. Eventually, some IM systems were able to interoperate.

IM technology offers a degree of anonymity because typed messages have no associated voice or video. This anonymity led to the popularity of chat rooms, where individuals could discuss a variety of topics without fear of being identified and without necessarily taking responsibility for their statements.

Today, consumer preferences have shifted to audio and video communications platforms, but IM is still quite popular for customer service at ecommerce sites, where customers can ask questions about merchandise and services as well as get help and support (Figure 5-36).

Figure 5-36: Online chat

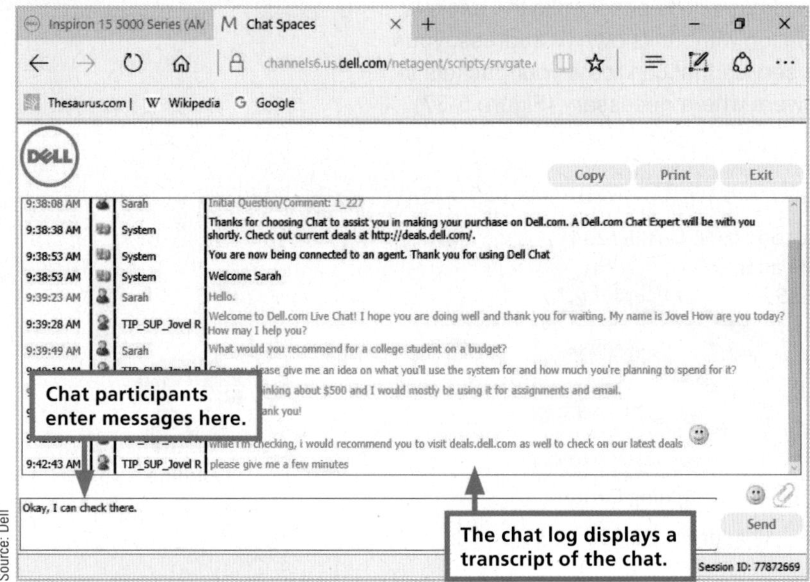

Source: Dell

QuickCheck

Which of the following is not a characteristic of instant messaging?

a. Asynchronous

b. Text-based

c. Two-way communication

d. Similar to chat rooms

Voice and Video Over IP

A soldier Skypes home from a faraway country to spend a few precious moments talking with his spouse. Proud parents use FaceTime to give the grandparents a first peek at a newborn baby. College students keep in touch from all over the globe without incurring long-distance charges. Communication today is far different from the handwritten letters and expensive long-distance telephone calls of 20th century technology.

▶ What is Voice over IP? **VoIP** (Voice over Internet Protocol) is a technology that uses a broadband Internet connection instead of telephone landlines to place voice and video calls. Today's VoIP systems use a variety of communication protocols. Some of these protocols are open standards, while others, such as those used by Skype, Google Hangouts, Zoom, and FaceTime, are proprietary. Therefore, consumers have several options when choosing a system to install and use.

VoIP technologies are ideal for instant, synchronous communications, and video calls are currently "the next best thing to being there," to borrow the tagline from old Bell telephone ads. VoIP is also the underlying technology for business teleconferencing applications such as GoToMeeting and WebEx.

Voice and video calls can be made between various devices, including laptops, desktops, tablets, and smartphones. On mobile devices, VoIP uses the data stream, not the voice stream. Communications are easiest when the person initiating a call and the person receiving a call use the same VoIP software and service. Callers are generally online, but some services can route calls to landlines.

▶ How do today's VoIP systems work? Software converts voice communications and video images into data packets using digitizing techniques similar to those presented in Module 1.

An IP address is attached to each packet. If you are calling a friend with computer-based VoIP, for example, your friend's IP address will be attached to the packets. If you are calling a landline or other destination without its own IP address, your VoIP packets will carry an IP address of a service that can route your packets to their destination using landlines or cell towers where necessary (Figure 5-37).

Try It!

Which VoIP clients are available on your digital devices? Do you tend to use them on one of your devices or several of them?

Terminology

VoIP is also referred to as *Internet telephony*.

QuickCheck

What type of addresses are used to transport VoIP packets?

a. TCP

b. IP

c. SMTP

d. POP3

Figure 5-37: VoIP to landlines

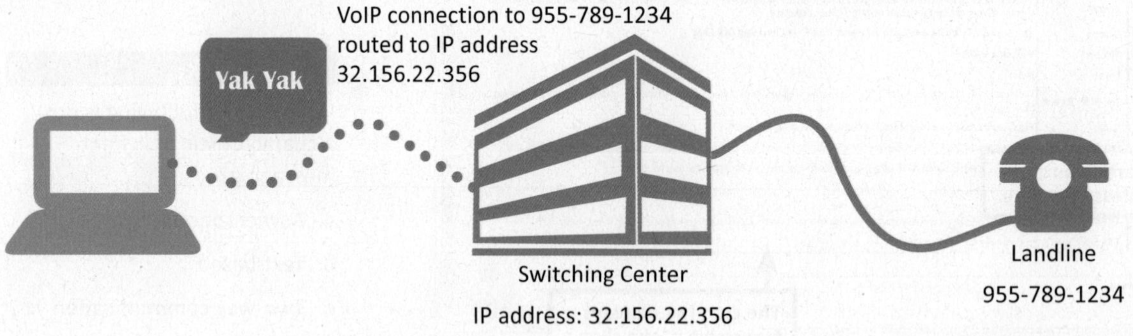

5

What about videoconferencing? During the COVID-19 pandemic, videoconferencing went mainstream. In response to stay-at-home lockdowns around the world, many segments of society turned to online videoconferencing. Schools held virtual classes. Doctors held telemedicine consultations. Businesses embraced teleworking. Families reached out using Zoom and FaceTime. Politicians held virtual legislative sessions, and charitable organizations held online fundraisers.

The need to use this virtual lifeline, however, has not been without controversy. A government investigation of one videoconferencing service revealed that promised end-to-end encryption had not been implemented. Thousands of videoconferences that were thought to be private were found freely viewable and unsecured on the Web.

More than 500,000 accounts from one videoconferencing service were harvested by hackers and posted on the dark Web. Meetings have been disrupted by "zoombombing," a phenomenon perpetrated by agitators who join a meeting and harass legitimate participants with hateful messages and indecent images.

When privacy risks and security breaches are revealed, the companies that provide videoconferencing services typically respond with program patches and updates.

Videoconferencing systems have become essential tools, but the controversies surrounding security and privacy illustrate the need to exercise caution when using them (Figure 5-38).

Figure 5-38: Exercise caution when videoconferencing

Source: Zoom Video Communications, Inc.

QuickQuiz Section D

1. In the communication matrix, email is an example of private, [ ] communication.
2. Information in an email [ ] tracks the path of a message from the sender to the recipient.
3. Local email uses protocols such as POP3 and [ ] to manage incoming mail.
4. The concept of shipping synchronous text, voice, or video over the Internet has its roots in [ ]. (Hint: Use the acronym.)
5. VoIP, Skype, and FaceTime are examples of [ ] communications because both parties are online at the same time.

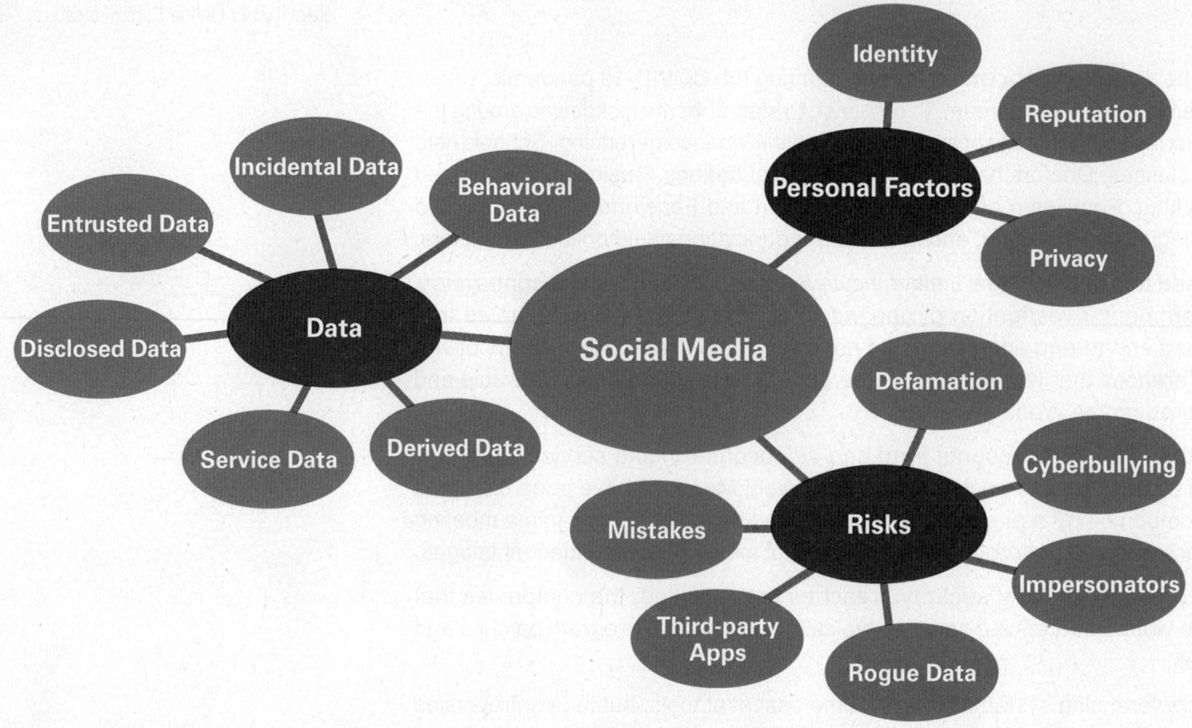

Section E Social Media Values

Objectives

- List the elements that constitute an online identity.
- Describe four ways in which sockpuppets are used for purposes of deception.
- List three situations in which the use of an online pseudonym is justified if allowed by the social media service.
- Explain why using a generic profile image should be avoided.
- Differentiate between an online identity and an online reputation.
- List five factors that can ruin an online reputation.
- List four techniques for dealing with cyberbullies.
- State the difference between an impersonator and a doppelganger.
- List at least five reputation management practices.
- Explain how an online presence can become a threat to an individual's privacy.
- Define each of the six types of social media data.
- List four potential problems with third-party social media apps.

Social media offer a sea of content that ranges from commonplace to momentous. Much of the information that floats through these communities is light entertainment, but some of it profoundly affects people's lives. Although laws and regulations influence online behavior, there is also a set of evolving ethics regarding online self-governance. You'll find out more about this topic in this section.

Terminology

sockpuppets
generic profile image
tagline
online reputation
defamation
cyberbullying
impersonation
doppelgangers
privacy
personally identifiable information
privacy policy

5

Identity

Self-identity is the way we view and define ourselves as unique individuals. That identity, however, may not be the one we strive to project in our social media profiles. Some scholars worry that social media encourage individuals to construct facades that depict identities they hope are acceptable to others, rather than identities that reflect who they really are. You should exercise caution when constructing an online identity, because social media personas are globally public. Creating an online profile that reflects your identity requires careful attention.

What constitutes a social media identity? An online identity consists of far more than a photo and a brief autobiographical sketch. The elements that constitute a social media identity include a biographical profile, the set of people who form connections, and the information supplied as posts. All these elements create a social media identity and offer clues to an individual's offline identity.

How important are first impressions? Whether you're connecting with former classmates, collaborating with colleagues, or climbing the career ladder, people looking for you online first encounter your social media profile—and the impression it conveys influences subsequent interactions. For example, a user name carries lots of information. A familiar name can convey a favorable first impression, whereas a wacky pseudonym might be a turnoff.

How prevalent are pseudonyms? The terms of use policies for some social media services require participants to use their real names, whereas other services permit pseudonyms. Regardless of the terms of service, online identities are not always genuine, and it is important to remain aware of that fact. User names such as BumbleBee532 and CrossWalkTrekker are obviously pseudonyms. But user names such as BillGWillis or ShenikaLouisaEspinosa that seem legitimate also could be fakes.

Some fake identities are created by people who prefer not to use their real names. Spammers control armies of fake avatars that want to be your friends so they can carry out a variety of identity exploits. False identities are used for nefarious purposes by cyberbullies, criminals, and stalkers. The use of **sockpuppets**—any online identity created and used for purposes of deception—is widespread (Figure 5-39).

QuickCheck

Which of the following is not likely to be part of a person's social media identity?

a. An avatar

b. A profile

c. Sockpuppets

d. Posts

Figure 5-39: Sockpuppet primer

Photka/Shutterstock.com

Sockpuppet: A false identity used for purposes of deception such as:

- To circumvent a suspension or ban from an online group
- For surreptitious self-promotion
- For criminal identity theft
- To stuff online ballot boxes

Try It!

Take a quick look at your Facebook friends and your contacts on other social media platforms. Do most of them use their real names?

What about anonymity? The principle of anonymity was expressed by former Supreme Court Justice John Paul Stevens: "Anonymity is a shield from the tyranny of the majority. It thus exemplifies the purpose behind the Bill of Rights, and of the First Amendment in particular: to protect unpopular individuals from retaliation—and their ideas from suppression—at the hand of an intolerant society."

There are legitimate reasons for people to conceal their identities. Political dissidents, victims of abuse, and corporate whistleblowers, for example, may not be able to safely interact online under their real names. However, with a little detective work on the contents of posts, photo locations, and IP addresses, real identities can be uncovered.

If you decide to conceal your offline identity by using an online pseudonym, be careful not to tread on someone else's legitimate identity.

Try It!

Take a moment to look at your public profile for one of your social media sites. Do you think it conveys an image that is representative of your identity?

How significant is a profile photo? Most social media sites provide a **generic profile image** for users who do not upload a personal photo. Users who retain the generic image tend to be newcomers or spammers. Members of online communities may ignore friend requests and comments that come from accounts without a custom image. Figure 5-40 lists some things to consider when selecting a profile image.

Figure 5-40: Image guidelines

Toranico/Shutterstock.com

What are you wearing?

Toranico/Shutterstock.com

What is your facial expression?

Toranico/Shutterstock.com

What are you holding?

Toranico/Shutterstock.com

What are you doing?

Kzenon/Shutterstock.com

Who are you with?

What does a tagline reveal? Most social media profiles include a short, publicly viewable **tagline**. In LinkedIn, this tagline is called a Headline; on Facebook, it is called a Bio. Along with the profile photo, a tagline establishes the first impression of an online persona. Taglines not only reveal biographical information but also can offer insights into a person's personality. Taglines are not dependable, however. They can be total fiction.

When creating a tagline, be aware that it is part of your public first impression. Consider your wording carefully. Tailor it to the site and to your audience, but give it some personality to convey your uniqueness.

What about detailed biographical information? Detailed biographical information is generally viewable only by designated connections, depending on the user's privacy settings. Biographical information can include details about a person's education, work experience, residences, family, skills, expertise, and volunteer work. Providing these details helps the social media service to recommend groups or individuals with similar interests. This information can also be abused by advertisers and identity thieves, so be cautious about the information you reveal.

QuickCheck

Using a generic image rather than one of your own tends to __________.

a. label you as a newcomer

b. make it easier to get friends

c. give your opinions more authority

d. keep your personal data private

Reputation

When a prospective employer asks for access to your social media accounts, is it time to panic, or do you have a well-managed set of sites that you don't hesitate to share with the world? "Starting today you are a brand." That is the advice of Tom Peters, author of *In Search of Excellence*. Nowhere is this statement more true than online. Your online identity requires careful nurturing and constant vigilance. Maintaining your online reputation ensures that it is an accurate reflection of your offline identity as well as your online presence.

5

How important are online reputations? An **online reputation** is the impression that is generated by an online persona. It relates to the way a person perceives the online identities of others, as opposed to the way those people define themselves.

An individual's online reputation may be used to evaluate whether to accept friend requests and whether a person's tweets are worth following. It can also help to gauge the authority of a person's comments, ratings, and posts.

Online reputations can affect real life. A good online reputation can lead to job offers, collaborative projects, and other opportunities. A bad online reputation can have disastrous consequences. Examples are scattered across the digital landscape. A job applicant's embarrassing vacation photos on Classmates.com. A high school student's Facebook page defaced by cyberbullies. An offensive tweet made by a high-profile athlete. Inappropriate photos sent as text messages by a prominent politician.

What can ruin an online reputation? According to executive coach Steve Tobak, "Everything you do on the Internet is like a tattoo you get late at night that can never ever be erased." Many factors can have a negative effect on an individual's online reputation.

Mistakes. An individual may inadvertently post messages, comments, photos, or personal details that are incorrect or unwise, or that can be misinterpreted. Such posts can affect public opinion by damaging the poster's reputation.

Defamation. Communicating false statements that damage the reputation of another individual is referred to as **defamation**. In most countries, defamation is illegal.

Cyberbullying. Using information technology, such as the Internet, to deliberately harm or harass someone is called **cyberbullying**. The intent of cyberbullying is often to damage the reputation of the targeted person. Recommended techniques for dealing with cyberbullying include not responding, deleting posts, blocking the perpetrator, and saving screenshots in case you decide to notify authorities.

Impersonation. Deliberately using the name or avatar of another person without consent and with the intent to harm, defraud, or intimidate is called **impersonation**. Impersonators can be prosecuted for carrying out reputation-damaging activities, such as posting inflammatory comments.

Doppelgangers. Online **doppelgangers** are two or more online personas with the same name or user name. The personas of doppelgangers are sometimes mistaken for each other, and their reputations may become intertwined.

Try It!

Use Google to search for your name. Try entering your first and last names, then enter your first, middle, and last names. Do you have any doppelgangers?

What factors contribute to a person's online reputation? Online reputation encompasses many factors that affect the perception of an online identity. It includes the user profile, list of friends, list of followers, posts, comments, mentions, photo tags, and blog entries at social media sites. It also includes personal Web sites, Web pages, publications, and other original works that may exist online. Further, it may include data that tracks online activity, such as purchases and downloads.

Some of the data that contributes to an online reputation is created and managed by the person who controls the online persona. Other data is posted by friends and connections. Yet other data, such as credit scores and shopping activity, is compiled by third parties. Figure 5-41 summarizes the elements of an online reputation.

Figure 5-41: Anatomy of an online reputation

User Profile
Profiles may explicitly state a reputation, such as "avid skier" or "award-winning author."

Media Presence
Elements of an online reputation are derived from multiple sources, so it includes social media accounts, blogs, and Web sites.

Comments
The comments that individuals append to other peoples' posts, tweets, and blogs contribute to building a reputation within the group of participants.

Contacts
People tend to interact with those who share their interests. An individual's contacts and group associations contribute to the way that individual is regarded by others.

Google Results
When someone uses Google to search for an individual, the first page of search results forms an impression that may be perceived as the individual's reputation.

Popularity
The popularity of blogs and Web sites as measured by Alexa and other rating services indicate a person's relevancy.

Expertise
Many reputations are built on knowledge and expertise that are displayed in various online forums, social media, and offline sources.

Images
Whether posted by you or by others, images provide clues about a person's age, ethnicity, personality, and lifestyle. Viewers form opinions based on those images.

Posts
Words, pictures, and videos that individuals post about themselves are evaluated by others to form an impression that becomes an online reputation.

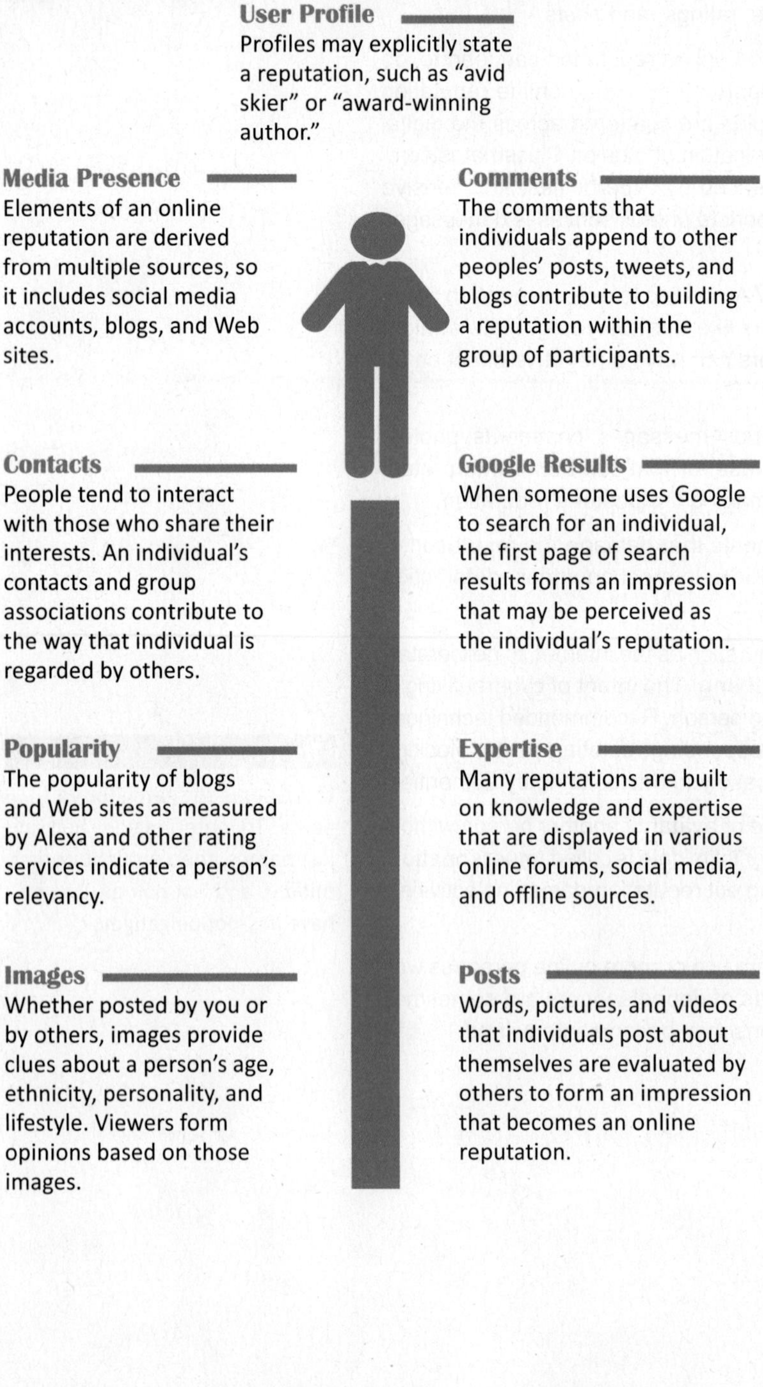

QuickCheck

How does an online identity differ from an online reputation?

a. Your online identity is how you see yourself, but your online reputation is how others see you.

b. Your online identity is more extensive than your online reputation.

c. Your online reputation is established at social networking sites, whereas your online identity is produced offline.

d. They are both the same.

5

What are best practices for managing online reputations? The key to managing your online reputation is vigilance. Just as you learn to use social media tools for connecting to friends and colleagues, it is important to learn how to use the evolving set of tools for understanding and managing your online reputation. Figure 5-42 explains the basic tools and techniques for reputation management.

Figure 5-42: Reputation management best practices

Cultivate your roster of friends. Don't be tempted to bump up your numbers by accepting invitations from random avatars operated by spammers.

Search for your name and make note of any results that might damage your reputation.

Use Google Alerts to keep informed of information that is posted about you.

Adjust settings within your social media accounts so that you are notified when you are tagged in photos and videos.

Don't let your online identities languish. Add posts regularly.

Check all your social media sites periodically to make sure they have not been compromised by identity thieves.

Maintain a consistent user name and identity across sites—especially those that are open to the public.

Remove posts, comments, photos, and blog entries that don't portray your desired online image.

Push enough positive information to the top of your Google search results to obscure any negative content that relates to you.

Separate your professional sites from your personal sites and keep posts appropriate to each.

Consider buying domain names that contain your real name.

Establish accounts on all the popular social media sites so that others cannot impersonate you there.

Maintain civil discourse. Democracies promote free speech, but there are legal and cultural limits. You must be alert, within all of your networking circles, for the norms regarding speech that is acceptable and speech that is not.

Try It!

Which of the items listed in Figure 5-42 are most likely to help improve your online reputation?

Privacy

It was 1890, and journalists using a new technology called photography were snapping sensationalistic photos and publishing them without the consent of the photo subjects. This breach of ethics prompted two young attorneys to call for laws that would keep pace with new technology. One of these attorneys was appointed to the Supreme Court in 1916. Justice Louis Brandeis became a staunch defender of privacy rights and defined the legal precedents for today's privacy laws.

◗ **Exactly what is the right to privacy?** In the words of Justice Brandeis, **privacy** is the "right to be let alone." Commonly held expectations of privacy include freedom from intrusive surveillance and the expectation that individuals can control their own **personally identifiable information** (PII) to limit when they can be identified, tracked, or contacted.

Privacy is different from security, though the two overlap. Security refers to the way we protect ourselves and our property. Privacy is our ability to control access to our personal information and activities. Security is the lock on your front door. Privacy is the curtains on your bedroom window.

◗ **Why is privacy important?** You may think that you have nothing to hide and so privacy rights are unimportant. You may be happy to share the details of your life with friends and even with the general public. But ask yourself this: Would you be willing to give your social media passwords to any stranger who asked for them? If you answered no, then privacy is important to you.

It is somewhat ironic that you need a password to access your social media accounts, even though the information they hold can be accessed without passwords by marketing agencies, third-party app developers, government agencies, and various data collection programs.

Although the United States Constitution does not explicitly define privacy as a right, wording in that document infers the importance of privacy. According to many legal scholars, the importance of privacy goes beyond individual rights and is a foundational concept of freedom and democracy.

In the *Harvard Law Review* article "What Privacy Is For," Julie E. Cohen states: "... privacy is an indispensable structural feature of liberal democratic political systems. Freedom from surveillance, whether public or private, is foundational to the capacity for critical self-reflection and informed citizenship. Second, privacy is also foundational to the capacity for innovation.... A society that values innovation ignores privacy at its peril, for privacy also shelters the processes of play and experimentation from which innovation emerges."

◗ **What is a privacy policy?** Most social media services have a written **privacy policy** that states how PII data is handled, including how it is accessed and how long it is stored. Privacy policies can be several pages long, and they are worth reading to discover if your expectations of privacy correspond to the privacy protections offered by the service. Even if you don't read the entire policy, try to determine how your data may be used by third parties such as advertisers. Also check to see if your posts, photos, and other media remain your own, or if they become the property of the social media service.

Privacy policies change, and the changes usually offer fewer privacy protections. When you receive a privacy policy change notification, check your account settings. As a result of changes, data that was previously private may have become public.

QuickCheck

The right to privacy is _________.

a. explicitly guaranteed by the U.S. Constitution

b. the same as personal security

c. a commonly held expectation

d. described by the privacy policies of online communities

Where can users access privacy settings? Privacy settings are usually included along with general account settings and accessed from the menu bar or account icon. Figure 5-43 illustrates privacy settings available for Facebook users.

Figure 5-43: Check your privacy settings regularly

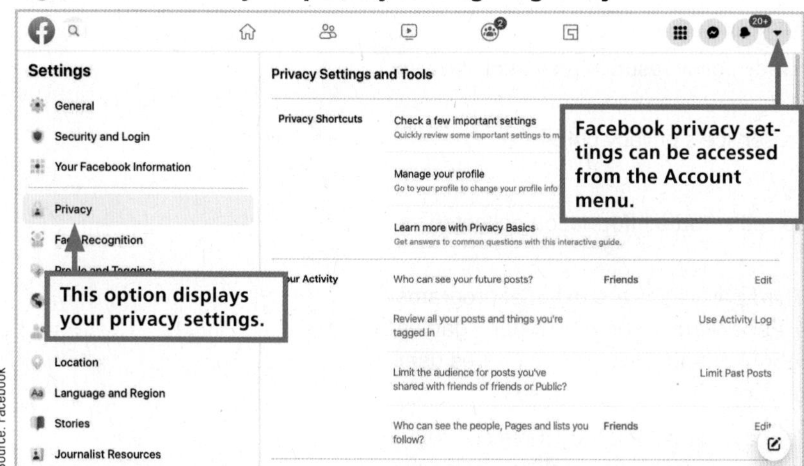

Are there levels of privacy? Some data is suitable for general publication, while other data is suitable for colleagues. Yet another set of data may be suitable for friends, while some data is confidential. Key steps in maintaining online privacy include awareness of the different types of data collected by social media services and the level of privacy appropriate for each type. Computer security expert Bruce Schneier devised the taxonomy of social media data in Figure 5-44.

Figure 5-44: Taxonomy of social media data

Service data	The data you give to a social media service when registering to use it. Such data might include your legal name, your age, and your credit card number.
Disclosed data	Information that you post on your own pages. Such information can include blog entries, photos, messages, and comments.
Entrusted data	Information that you post on other people's pages. This information includes the same items as disclosed data, but you don't have control over the data once you post it.
Incidental data	Information that other people post about you. As with entrusted data, you do not have control over it.
Behavioral data	Data about you that is collected by the social media service based on your habits, site usage, post contents, and connections.
Derived data	Data about you that is derived from all the other data. For example, if lots of your friends self-identify as gay, your derived data might profile you as gay, too.

QuickCheck

According to the table in Figure 5-44, the information that other people post about you is ______.

a. service data

b. disclosed data

c. entrusted data

d. incidental data

Try It!

For each type of data in the table in Figure 5-44, consider whether you have the means to control it through privacy settings or other methods.

How does personal information go rogue? Data "gone rogue" escapes its appropriate privacy setting and somehow goes public. An item of PII such as a photograph or a Facebook post can become publicly accessible when users explicitly make it so, either by choice or by mistake. PII can also become public through the actions of others. The most common causes of rogue data include:

- A user changes the global privacy setting to Public.
- A user designates an item as public when it is posted.
- Changes in the social media service's privacy policy result in previously private information becoming public.
- A user ignores changes in the social media service's privacy policy.
- Posted information is reposted publicly.
- Third-party social networking applications redistribute information collected as the user works with an app.

How risky are social media apps? Third-party apps are external programs that interact with social networking services. For example, some third-party games allow you to share your winnings with Facebook friends. WhatsApp shares user phone numbers and activity data with Facebook-affiliated companies.

Hundreds of third-party social media apps are available, and they have one thing in common: All of them collect information from social media profiles, including personal data and contact lists.

The following aspects of third-party apps may affect your privacy:

- Collected data might not be transmitted over secure channels.
- An excessive amount of personal data could be collected.
- Data about your contacts might be collected.
- The collected data may not be subject to the same privacy policies as the social networking service it accesses.

The amount of information accessed by third-party apps depends on your privacy settings and the access you grant when signing up to use the app (Figure 5-45).

QuickCheck

What is the risk of using third-party social media apps?

a. They have lots of errors.

b. They access the data in users' social media accounts.

c. They change users' profile data.

d. They cannot be removed.

Figure 5-45: Apps may require access to your social media profiles

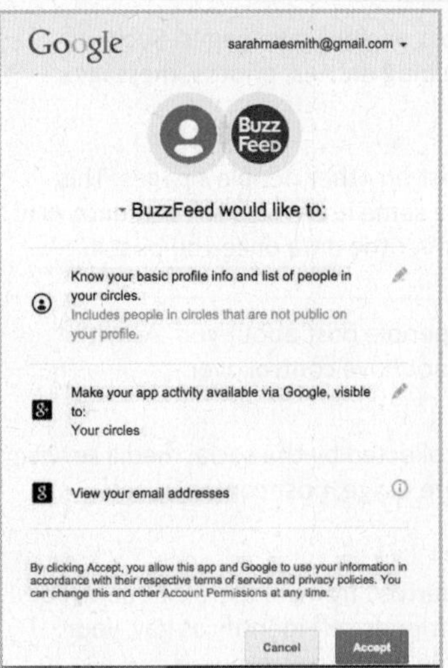

Before installing a third-party app, be aware of the information that it will collect from your social media accounts.

▶ Can I monitor social media apps? Once permission to use a third-party app has been granted, that permission remains in effect until you cancel it. Major social networking services with associated third-party apps provide information about the apps that are permitted to access a user's account. Be sure to check this setting for your social media accounts and disable any apps that you are no longer using (Figure 5-46).

Figure 5-46: Manage your third-party apps

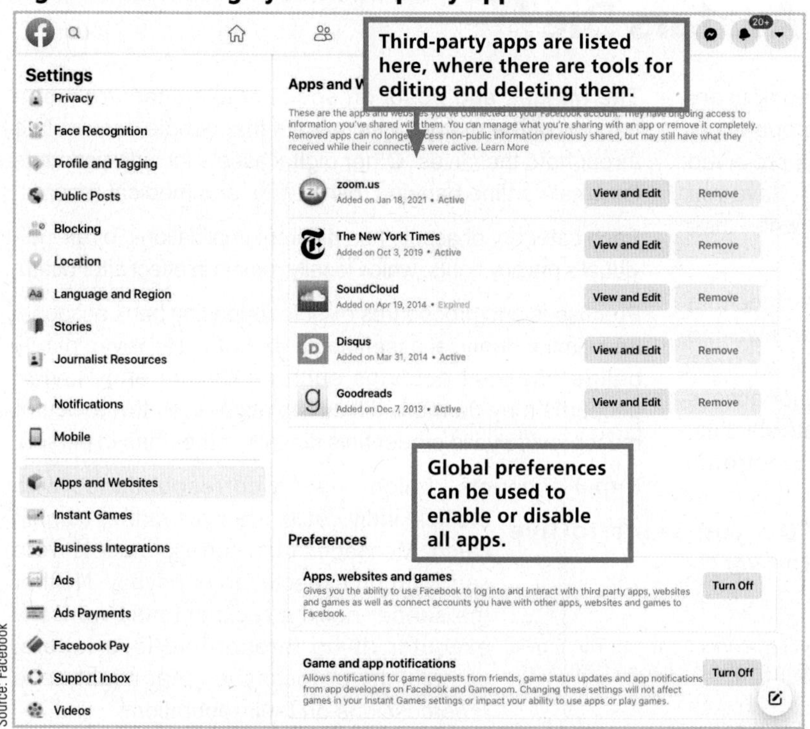

Access Facebook's third-party app settings from the Account menu located in the upper-right corner of the Facebook toolbar.

QuickQuiz — Section E

1. A(n) ________ is a false identity used for purposes of deception.
2. Online ________ are the way in which people define themselves on social media sites and other Internet-based venues.
3. The intent of ________ is usually to damage a person's online reputation through harassment.
4. Personally ________ information consists of details that can be used to find, track, or contact an individual.
5. Data that a subscriber gives to a social media service when registering is called ________ data.

Frenzel/Shutterstock.com

Issue: When Do Online Avatars Die?

30 million. That's the number of Facebook users who died during the service's first eight years in operation. The number of deceased Facebook members is projected to outnumber the service's living avatars by 2030. Have you ever wondered what happens to online avatars when their owners pass away?

Consider the case of a 15-year-old high school student in Virginia who tragically committed suicide. His parents wanted to access their son's social media accounts to look for clues that might explain his motivation. Their request for access was denied. Facebook's denial was based on state statutes, federal laws, and language in the 1986 Electronic Communications Privacy Act that protects the privacy of minors.

As a result of the ensuing controversy, the Virginia Legislature passed HB 1752, or the Virginia Digital Assets Law. This law allows parents or legal guardians of minors to access their children's social media accounts. According to the official summary, this bill "Provides that the personal representative of a deceased minor has the power to assume the deceased minor's terms of service agreement with an Internet service provider, communications service provider, or other online account service provider for the purposes of consenting to and obtaining the disclosure of the minor's digital assets."

The Virginia law focuses on the rights of minors and their parents, but who has rights to an adult's digital data after death?

The estate of a deceased person includes personal effects such as clothing and household implements. It may also include financial assets and real estate. An executor is an individual whose responsibility is to dispose of these personal effects. The ability of an executor to access the digital assets of a deceased person depends on a myriad of state and federal laws as well as the policies of various social media services. The terms of use for most social media sites are nontransferable, which means that account access and use cannot be transferred from a deceased person to an executor.

"Do you want to live forever?"

Valeria asks Conan in the movie *Conan the Barbarian* (1982)

The images and posts on social media sites are just a fraction of the many digital assets that people accumulate throughout their lives. Other digital assets include accounts for email, online banking, bill paying, and medical records.

Each category of assets has different implications for an individual's privacy rights, which legally remain in effect after death.

Processes and procedures exist for releasing bank accounts and similar financial assets to an executor. However, purely online financial holdings such as Bitcoin and PayPal accounts may be more difficult to access, as the executor must provide valid credentials digitally rather than in person.

Email accounts, which contain correspondence with multiple individuals, are even further complicated. Messages from correspondents were sent with an expectation of privacy. Neither the sender nor the recipient may want the executor rifling through old love letters, complaints, or messages that might have repercussions on their reputations.

As with other aspects surrounding estate planning, a fully executed will is the key to ensuring that real and digital assets are handled in a specific way and by specified people. Some people may wish their online avatars to live forever, whereas others may wish to exercise their right to be forgotten.

Facebook will memorialize deceased members' accounts when provided with proof of death. A memorialized account cannot be modified and logins are not allowed. The account can, however, accept messages, and content that was posted before the account holder's demise continues to be accessible.

Individuals may not live forever, but their social media avatars can continue to exist in cyberspace. Online identities can be frozen in time, surrounded by posts and images accumulated over a lifetime and now set as a permanent, unalterable record of a person's activities, friends, and accomplishments. It makes you think: What kind of digital legacy are you leaving behind?

Try It! Who can go through your digital belongings after you die? There's never a good time to think about your demise, but no one is immortal. Keeping an eye on your digital reputation includes specifying your wishes for the disposition of your digital assets even after you are no longer around to manage them.

1. Visit one of the social networking sites that you frequently use. Search for its policy about access to the accounts of deceased members. Briefly describe the policy and explain if you are satisfied with its terms. If the site offers user-modifiable settings, are the default settings appropriate or would you choose to change the settings?

2. The afterlife has not been ignored by resourceful developers. Projects such as Replika, LifeNaut, and Eterni.me have attempted to create immortal digital avatars based on real people. Use online resources to explore this "immortality technology." Report your findings by summarizing the current state of the art and describing some of the platforms that are currently available.

3. Search online for *state laws on digital passing*. Find your state in the list, and read its associated laws and proposals. Read about your state's policy regarding digital property in the event of death. Write a brief summary of the laws and/or proposals in your state.

4. One of the first things that you can do when creating your own digital legacy is to compile a list of your digital assets and accounts. Visit a Web page such as "How to Safeguard Your Digital Legacy" at *Deathwithdignity.org* to get some tips on how to accurately compile an inventory of your digital assets. Then, make your own list. You don't need to be specific—for security, do not include bank names, account numbers, or passwords. Instead, refer to these confidential items generically as "my bank account," "my computer password," and so on.

5. Document how you want your online accounts handled in the event of your own death, and decide who will handle your accounts. Also think about and determine a place where you would store your list of digital accounts and assets, including by whom and how your accounts should be handled.

Frenzel/Shutterstock.com

What Do You Think?

Issue

1. Have you ever thought about what happens to the social media accounts of people who are deceased?
2. Do you know who might have access to your social media accounts if you meet an untimely death?
3. Are memorialized accounts a good idea?

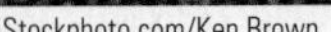
iStockphoto.com/Ken Brown

Information Tools: Media Attribution

You can copy music, photos, and video clips for use in reports, on your blog, on YouTube, and on your Facebook page. If you are not creating a transformative work or a critical work that would be covered by fair use, what steps must you take to use "borrowed" content correctly?

As a general rule, assume that all images and media are copyrighted. Media elements on the Web are covered by the same copyrights as works in print and in other formats. When using copyrighted media, you should seek permission and provide attribution that identifies the copyright holder. Permission and attribution are not the same:

- **Permission** means obtaining rights for a specific use, such as on a Web site.
- **Attribution** means acknowledging the person who holds the copyright, usually by including a tagline under a media element or a citation in a bibliography.

You can obtain permission by asking the copyright holder. Most media sharing sites provide links to copyright holders. Supply the copyright holder with information about the item you want to use and how you intend to use it.

You might not have to contact the copyright holder for permission if the media element is covered by a license. Look for a license or rights link near the media element or a site-use policy near the bottom of a Web page.

You can place your photo attribution in a small font directly under the photo or on its side, or you can include it in the bibliography. Video and music attributions should be placed near the "Play" link or in a bibliography.

The copyright holder might specify the text you should use for the attribution (e.g., "Courtesy of IBM" or "Jerry Harris Photography").

If the wording for an attribution is not specified, then you should include the following:

- Copyright holder's name
- License type, such as "with permission" or "Creative Commons"
- URL (optional)

The easiest media elements to use legally have a Creative Commons license for Attribution (BY).

These licenses specify whether the element can be used for personal or commercial use, and they only require you to provide an attribution crediting the source.

For academic work, such as term papers and theses, you must include attributions for any media elements that you use, even though academic work falls under the umbrella of fair use. As with citations for quoted and paraphrased material, media attribution helps to establish the legitimacy of your work.

Courtesy of NASA

Courtesy of Creative Commons

Try It!

The more you learn about copyright, citations, and attributions, the more complex these topics seem. Here's your chance to track down a few more concepts pertaining to media citations and then summarize what you've learned. For this project, create a document called Module 5 Media Project.

1. Photographers occasionally give permission to use images that are not free from other copyright and legal restrictions. For example, if a photographer takes a photo of a painting, it is considered a derivative work and it is subject to the painting's copyright. Link to the Shutterstock photo site and search for photos of the Mona Lisa. Can you find any photos of the actual painting? Why do you think this is the case?
2. Some museums and libraries allow personal, educational, and noncommercial use of digital images and other media. What is the policy for personal and educational use of digital versions of works from the Smithsonian American Art Museum's collection?
3. Media elements that include images of identifiable people are open to complex legal issues, depending on the subject, the subject's age, and the element's intended use. To be on the safe side, photos or videos that contain images of identifiable people should be used only if the license includes a model release. Link to Shutterstock and Flickr and search for images of businesspeople. Which site provides clear information about model releases?
4. Go to Flickr and enter *pyramids* in the search field, then select the options for "Creative Commons–commercial use allowed." Select an image with a BY attribution license that can be used commercially. Download the smallest resolution and paste the image into your Media Project document. Add the appropriate attribution under the pyramids photo in your Media Project document.
5. Fill in the following table to summarize what you've learned about media attributions and citations.

Situation	Is This Use Correct? Why or Why Not?
You use a photo from an online magazine in a research paper without seeking permission, and you do not attribute the source.	
You use a photo from an online magazine in a research paper without seeking permission, but you do attribute the source.	
You use a photo from an online magazine in a poster for an event without seeking permission, but you do attribute the source.	
You use a photo from an online magazine in a poster for an event after getting permission to do so, and you follow the photographer's instructions for attribution.	
A photo from Shutterstock is royalty free, so you use it on your Facebook page.	
You use a photo from the Smithsonian American Art Museum for a background in an app that you sell on iTunes.	

Eddie Gerald/Alamy Stock photo

Technology in Context: Journalism

In the ancient world, news spread by word of mouth, relayed by bards and merchants who traveled from town to town—in essence, they were the first reporters to broadcast the news. The news business is all about gathering and disseminating information quickly. Technology has played a major role in news reporting's evolution from its bardic roots to modern 24-hour news networks and Web sites.

Johann Gutenberg's printing press (ca. 1450), the first technological breakthrough in the news business, made it feasible to publish news as printed notices tacked to walls in the town square. As paper became more economical, resourceful entrepreneurs sold broadsheets to people eager for news, and the concept of a newspaper was born. The first regularly published newspapers appeared in Germany and Holland in 1609, and the first English newspaper, the *Weekly News*, was published in 1622.

But the news spread slowly. In the early 1800s, it took four weeks for newspapers in New York to receive and publish reports from London. With the advent of the telegraph in 1844, however, reporters from far-flung regions could wire stories to their newspapers for publication the next day. The first radio reporters in the 1920s offered live broadcasts of sports events, church services, and variety shows. Before the 1950s, black-and-white newsreels shown in movie theaters provided the only visual imagery of news events, but within a few years, viewers could watch the news at home on their televisions.

Technology has benefited print journalism, too. For decades, typesetters transferred reporters' handwritten stories into neatly set columns of type. Today, reporters use computers and word processing software to tap out their stories and run a preliminary check of spelling and grammar.

Stories are submitted by computer network to editors, who also use word processing software to edit stories to fit time and space constraints. The typesetting process has been replaced by desktop publishing software and computer to plate (CTP) technology. Digital pages produced with desktop publishing software are sent to a raster image processor (RIP), which converts the pages into dots that form words and images. After a page has been RIPed, a platesetter uses lasers to etch the dots onto a physical plate, which is then mounted on the printing press to produce printed pages. CTP is much faster and more flexible than typesetting, so publishers can make last-minute changes to accommodate late-breaking stories.

Personal computers also added new dimensions to the news-gathering process. Reporters were once limited to personal interviews, observation, and fact gathering at libraries, but they can now make extensive use of Internet resources and email. Web sites and online databases provide background information on all sorts of topics. Other resources include social media, where reporters can monitor public opinion on current events and identify potential sources.

Erik S. Lesser/The New York Times/Redux Pictures

Most major networks maintain interactive Web sites and social media accounts that offer online polls designed to collect viewers' opinions. Although online poll respondents are not a representative sample of the population, they can help news organizations gauge viewer opinions and determine whether news coverage is comprehensive and effective.

A 2019 Muck Rack study identified Twitter as the most popular type of social media used by journalists. Watching Twitter trends helps journalists stay on top of breaking events, supplies information on the competition's reporting, and provides journalists with ideas for news stories.

Email has changed the way reporters communicate with colleagues and sources. It is often the only practical method for contacting people in remote locations or distant time zones, and it is useful for communicating with reluctant sources, who feel more comfortable providing information under the cloak of anonymous Gmail or Yahoo! accounts. Vetting email sources—verifying credentials such as name, location, and occupation—can be difficult, however, so reporters tend not to rely on these sources without substantial corroboration.

For broadcast journalism, digital communications play a major role in today's live, "on the scene" television reporting. Most news organizations maintain remote production vans, sometimes called satellite news gathering (SNG) trucks, that travel to the site of breaking news, raise their antennas, and begin to broadcast. These complete mobile production facilities include camera control units, audio and video recording equipment, and satellite or microwave transmitters.

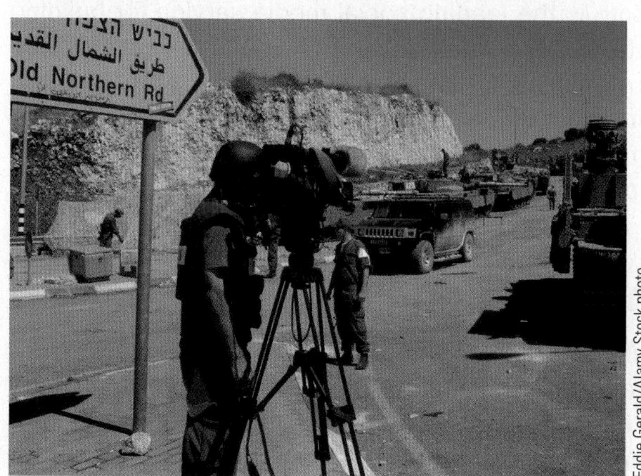

Eddie Gerald/Alamy Stock photo

A memorable tour de force in SNG was the brainchild of David Bloom, an NBC reporter embedded with the U.S. Army 3rd Infantry Division during Operation Iraqi Freedom. In 2002, he helped modify an M-88 tank recovery vehicle into a high-tech, armored SNG vehicle. The $500,000 Bloommobile featured a gyrostabilized camera that could produce jiggle-free video as the tank blasted over sand dunes at 50 mph. Tragically, Bloom died while covering the conflict. However, viewers vividly remember his exhilarating reports as the Bloommobile raced down desert roads, trundled along with Army supply convoys, and narrowly escaped enemy fire.

On-the-scene reporting no longer requires a truck full of equipment, however. Citizen journalists who are on the spot during news-making events simply use their smartphones to shoot and email footage to media Web sites, such as CNN.com and FOXNews.com. During the tragic 2008 terrorist attacks in Mumbai, eyewitness accounts and updates flooded social networking sites such as Facebook and Twitter. The first images of the attacks spread through social networking sites minutes before they appeared on mainstream news channels.

One drawback of point-and-shoot journalism is that the video quality usually isn't as crisp as images filmed with studio cameras. News organizations with high standards were once hesitant to use this lower-quality video, but they have found that viewers would rather see a low-quality image now than a high-quality image later. To many viewers, a few rough edges just make the footage seem more compelling—more like you are there.

Social media have radically altered the financial models that support news organizations. Newspaper readership is in steep decline while revenue from advertising is also dropping. News organizations attempting to move online are forced to compete with free news gathered by automated aggregators such as Google News and online news sites including *HuffPost* and *Reuters*.

The availability of free news on the Internet has had a devastating effect on newsroom jobs. Journalism graduates face a tough job market as news organizations scramble to restructure their business models. Today, many journalism graduates are finding employment at online startups and in related industries that require research and intelligence-gathering skills.

Computers, the Internet, and communications technology make it possible to instantly broadcast live reports across the globe, but live reporting is not without controversy. Reporters and amateur journalists who arrive at the scene of a disaster with microphones, cameras, or smartphones in hand have little time for reflection, vetting, and cross-checking, so grievous errors, libelous images, and distasteful video footage sometimes find their way into news reports.

According to Jeff Gralnick, former executive producer for ABC News, "In the old days, we had time to think before we spoke. We had time to write, time to research, and time to say, 'Hey, wait a minute.' Now we don't even have the time to say, 'Hey, wait a nanosecond.' Just because we can say it or do it, should we?"

Technology has given journalists a powerful arsenal of tools for gathering and reporting the news, but it has also increased their accountability for accurate, socially responsible reporting.

Flipped Class Projects

Critical Thinking

There's a cartoon that has become a social media meme. Two pigs are chatting. The first pig says, "Isn't it great? We have to pay nothing for the barn." The second pig replies, "Yeah! And even the food is free." This cartoon is frequently linked to a quote that goes something like this: "If you're not paying for it, you're not the customer; you're the product being sold." What do these statements imply about social media? What are specific ways that social media users become a product that is being sold?

Group Project

Work with a group of three or four students to research a new social media service. If possible, install it on your devices and try it out. On the basis of your trial run, make a list of the service's advantages and where there is room for improvement. Discuss the target audience for the service and how easy or difficult the service is to use. Also consider if use of the site poses privacy concerns. Collaborate with your group to write a review of the service that you can present to the rest of the class.

Cyberclassroom

In a small group, discuss the use of social media as a tool in education, specifically thinking about how it can be used effectively for on-campus students. Is its best use for communication or instruction? Can you share personal experiences of when social media have been used effectively for education or examples of attempts to use them that have fallen short?

Multimedia Project

Create an original work, such as a photo, video, or audio track. Select a Creative Commons license for the work using the license chooser located at *creativecommons.org/choose*. Post the work along with its license on a social media site.

Resume Builder

LinkedIn is the leading social media service for building a professional online image. If you don't have a LinkedIn account, sign up for one and begin building a profile. If you already have a LinkedIn account, revisit it, consider the information you've collected from this module, and revise your profile as necessary.

Globalization

Social media are used across cultures, but the specific sites that rank highest differ by country and region. Search the Web for usage statistics for social networking sites. For example, Alexa (*www.alexa.com/topsites/countries*) provides data that ranks Web sites by country. What are the most popular services in the United States, England, and Australia? Which services are most popular in Japan, China, South Korea, and India? Can you find the services that are most popular in Russia and in Middle Eastern countries? What about African countries, such as Botswana and Kenya? Are similar services popular in Mexico, Brazil, and Colombia? Based on the information you find, what can you conclude about social media usage differences around the world? Gather statistics and create a graph to support your conclusions.

Key Terms

Interactive Summary

Section A: Social media are online services that facilitate communication and __________ among people who want to share information about their lives, issues, and events. Social media can be characterized using the Social Media __________, which contains elements such as identity and presence. Social networking is a type of social media that revolves around personal __________ and interconnections among contacts, friends, and followers. Social networks evolved from online __________ such as CompuServe and America Online. A person's presence on a social media service is referred to as an online identity. __________ networking services provide a platform for users to carry out interactions based on their current locations. Many of these services incorporate __________ features for reviews and ratings. User locations can be determined by __________ trilateration, cell tower triangulation, hotspot triangulation, and IP address lookup. Destination locations are identified by __________ or geocoding. Social networks can be mapped using tools such as __________ that depict relationships as nodes and edges. Another useful tool called an adjacency __________ depicts social relationships in table format.

Section B: Content communities are social media sites that focus on sharing user-__________ content. These communities originated as pre-Internet __________ board systems. Media content communities specialize in images, videos, animations, and audio rather than text-based content. The technological core of content communities is server-based content __________ software and an associated database. Once media are posted to a server, they may remain in the database indefinitely. To facilitate indexing, identification, and searching, content can be assigned __________ tags. Media elements are the __________ property of their creators. Some media, such as corporate logos, are protected by __________, but most of the media at content communities are protected by copyright. Copyright is a form of legal protection that grants the author of an original work a(n) __________ right to copy, distribute, sell, and modify that work. A copyright holder can forfeit the copyright and place the work in the public __________. A copyright holder can also choose to license the work. A Creative __________ license allows a work to be used by others under specified conditions that include attribution (BY), __________ (SA), no derivatives (ND), and noncommercial (NC). A(n) __________ work modifies a copyrighted work but does not substantially change its content or purpose. A(n) __________ work repackages a work to add new meaning or produce a work that is used for a purpose different from the original work.

Section C: Text-based content communities form around blogging and wiki platforms. A(n) __________ created on a platform such as WordPress or Medium contains a series of entries on one or more topics and may include photos or other media. Subscription services make it easy to follow specific blogs. The information published on blogs may not be as reliable as mainstream information sources. __________ services, such as Twitter, offer a platform for messages similar to those in blogs but with limited length. Tweets, for example, are limited to 280 characters. Twitter jargon has infiltrated into other social media platforms. For example, the __________ symbol is universally used to identify and tag topics, whereas the __________ symbol is used to indicate user names in mentions and replies. A(n) __________ is a collaborative Web application that provides tools that contributors can use to post, read, and modify content. The best-known example is Wikipedia, an online __________ that can be accessed, viewed, and edited anonymously by the general public. To maintain quality standards, Wikipedia is supervised by volunteer editors who encourage __________ point of view, no original research, and verifiability.

Section D: Online communications tools can be classified as __________, in which all parties are online at the same time, and __________, in which messages are held until the recipient is ready to view them. Communication can also be characterized as public or private. Email is a communication service provided by email servers that provide an electronic __________ for each subscriber, sort incoming messages, and route outgoing messages to recipients. __________ is a type of email service that stores messages on a server and requires a browser to access those messages. Using a browser to access mail is handy, but doing so may pose security risks when mail is accessed from public computers. Local email is a store-and-__________ technology that holds messages on a server until they are downloaded by email client software such as Microsoft Outlook. Local mail uses IMAP or __________ protocols to manage incoming mail and __________ to manage outgoing mail. Mobile email apps use a locally installed client to temporarily download messages to the local device and use __________ protocols to synchronize the local and server-based mailboxes. Local mail and Webmail can be used interchangeably when appropriate forwarding settings are enabled. Synchronous text-based communication characterizes instant __________ and online chat. Synchronous voice and video communications are handled by __________ technologies on platforms such as Skype, Google Hangouts, Zoom, and FaceTime.

Section E: An online __________ is a collection of elements that reflect an individual's self-perception. The core of that identity is an online __________ that commonly consists of a user name, image, and short biographical tagline. The use of __________ as user names is widespread, though it is banned on some social media sites. An online __________ is the impression that is generated by an online persona. It relates to the way that others perceive an online identity. Factors such as mistakes, defamation, cyberbullying, impersonation, and the existence of doppelgangers have the potential to damage an online reputation. Best practices for monitoring and managing online reputations include setting up Google __________, removing detrimental posts and photos, creating separate personal and professional sites, and maintaining civil discourse. __________ is freedom from intrusive surveillance and the expectation that individuals can control their personally __________ information. Most social media services provide settings that can limit the extent to which personal information is disseminated. There are six types of social media data: service, __________, entrusted, incidental, behavioral, and derived.

Interactive Situation Questions

1. Your friend complains that a lot of her Facebook friend requests are refused. To help her find out why, the first step is to check her __________ and make sure she's replaced the generic photo with one of her own.

2. When you prefer not to be tracked by a geosocial networking app, use the __________ services setting to turn off the tracking feature for the app.

3. If you want your social media contacts to know when they are included in photos that you've posted, you can add their names to the photo __________.

4. You've found the perfect photo on Flickr to include in a paper you're writing about recycling. The photo has a CC BY-ND license, which means that you can use the photo if you credit the photographer, but you cannot make __________.

5. Your friend wants to create a __________, so you recommend a platform such as WordPress or Wix.

6. You're composing a tweet about politics and Barack Obama. To include a mention of Obama's name in the tweet, you need to use a(n) __________ symbol.

7. The Wikipedia article about the Tea Party movement contains a statement that doesn't seem correct. To find the origin of the statement, you might use the __________ tab.

8. Suppose that you have a local email account, but you want to switch to Webmail. You're worried that some people might continue to use your old email address, so you set up mail __________ from your local account to your Webmail account.

9. When it's time to look for your next job, having a good online reputation will be important. To keep tabs on information that might pertain to your online identity, you set up a Google __________.

10. When registering to use a new social media site, you hesitate because it collects __________ data including your name, phone number, and Apple account ID.

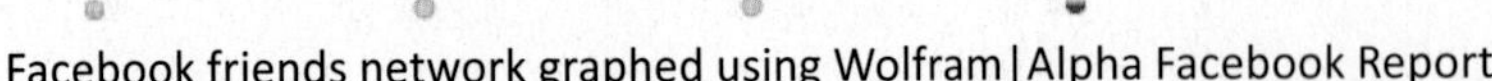

Facebook friends network graphed using Wolfram|Alpha Facebook Report

Lab: Social Network Analysis

Social analytics rock. They provide statistics about friends and contacts, connections, and links. They are used for contact tracing, literary analysis, and business analytics. Professor Robin Banerjee and colleagues at the University of Sussex developed an analytical tool for understanding patterns of acceptance and rejection among student groups.

Requirements:

For this lab, you'll need a computer with access to the Internet.

Assignment:

1. Connect to the Web site for Robin Banerjee's Sociogram Tools. Follow the link for "Sociogram Creator."

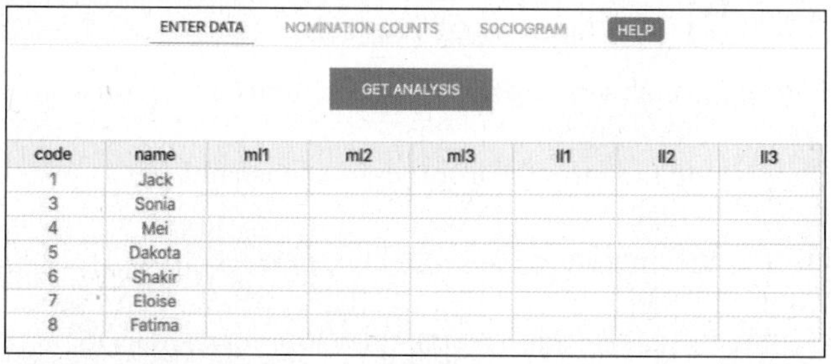

ENTER DATA NOMINATION COUNTS SOCIOGRAM HELP

GET ANALYSIS

code	name	ml1	ml2	ml3	ll1	ll2	ll3
1	Jack						
3	Sonia						
4	Mei						
5	Dakota						
6	Shakir						
7	Eloise						
8	Fatima						

Source: Robin Banerjee, *https://users.sussex.ac.uk/~robinb/socio.html.*

2. Use the matrix to enter 1 as the code for a student named Jack.

3. Enter the codes and names of the remaining seven students.

4. In the matrix, the headings ml1, ml2, and ml3 refer to the individuals that each student most likes. The headings ll1, ll2, and ll3 refer to the individuals that each student least likes. Jack most likes Eloise, whose code number is 7. Enter 7 in the ml1 column in Jack's row.

5. Complete the matrix as shown below.

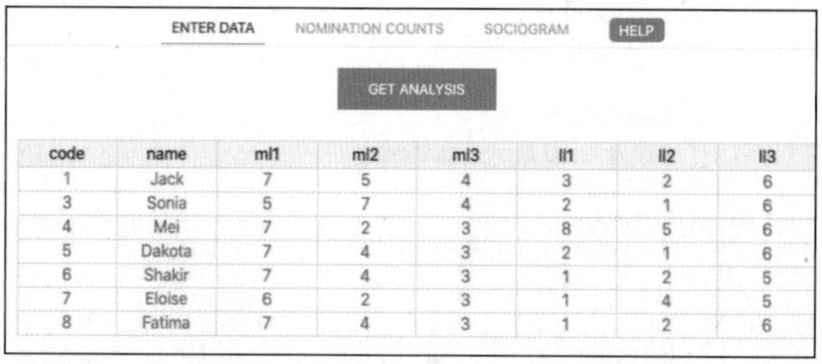

ENTER DATA NOMINATION COUNTS SOCIOGRAM HELP

GET ANALYSIS

code	name	ml1	ml2	ml3	ll1	ll2	ll3
1	Jack	7	5	4	3	2	6
3	Sonia	5	7	4	2	1	6
4	Mei	7	2	3	8	5	6
5	Dakota	7	4	3	2	1	6
6	Shakir	7	4	3	1	2	5
7	Eloise	6	2	3	1	4	5
8	Fatima	7	4	3	1	2	6

Source: Robin Banerjee, *https://users.sussex.ac.uk/~robinb/socio.html.*

6. Who do you think is the most popular student? The least popular? To find out, select the GET ANALYSIS button to view the sociogram.

7. Notice how the color coding indicates the most popular, rejected, and ignored students. Drag the ovals to position the most popular student in the center of the sociogram. Download the image and save it.

8. Use the matrix to create a sociogram for a group of real or fictional students. Download and save your final sociogram and write a short paragraph explaining what it indicates about the social interactions within the group.

Optional: Your instructor might specify that you create a sociometric survey to collect actual data for a sociogram. Your survey might collect data about friends, students, celebrities, or historic figures. The survey would consist of two questions:

Which three people would you most like to associate with?

Which three people would you least like to associate with?

6 Software

Module Contents

In the digital world, anything that is not hardware is software. The realm of software "stuff" includes apps, applications, operating systems, and files. Module 6 explores these diverse software elements.

Try It! Apply what you learn.

- Determine if a software app or application can run on a specific digital device.
- Understand the terms of a software license before accepting them.
- Identify the operating system that is installed on a digital device.
- Identify the key desktop elements in Windows, macOS, iOS, Android, and Chrome OS.
- Use a computer that has one or more virtual machines.
- Access and use Web apps.
- Find, download, and install mobile apps.
- Download and install local applications on PCs.
- Download and install local applications on Macs.
- Uninstall software.
- Use features of word processing software to enter text, improve your writing, and produce appropriately formatted output.
- Use spreadsheet software to create what-if analyses using formulas, functions, and relative or absolute references.
- Identify fields and records in a database table.
- Create a basic presentation that includes speaker notes.
- Select valid and meaningful names for files.
- Identify storage devices based on their names or device letters.
- Follow best practices for file management by organizing files into a sensible structure of folders.
- Send files to the trash, permanently delete them, and shred them.

Pre-Check

Gauge your level of expertise. The answers are in the module.

The operating system ______ remains in RAM while a device is in use.

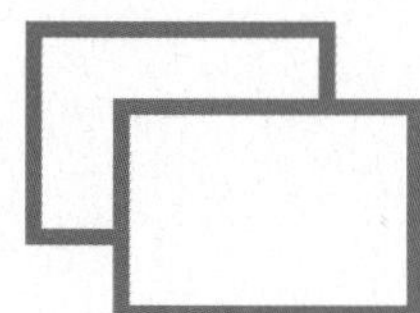

Two or more applications running simultaneously is an example of ______ .

Chrome OS is an example of a(n) ______ client.

macOS
Windows

A computer running more than one operating system is using a(n) ______ machine.

Software downloads for Macs are packaged as ______ files.

$B$6

In a spreadsheet, this is a(n) ______ reference.

1 2 3 4 5

What is the maximum length of a file name in macOS or Windows?

______

C:\

In Windows, this is the prompt for the ______ directory.

Name two file management utilities.

______

______

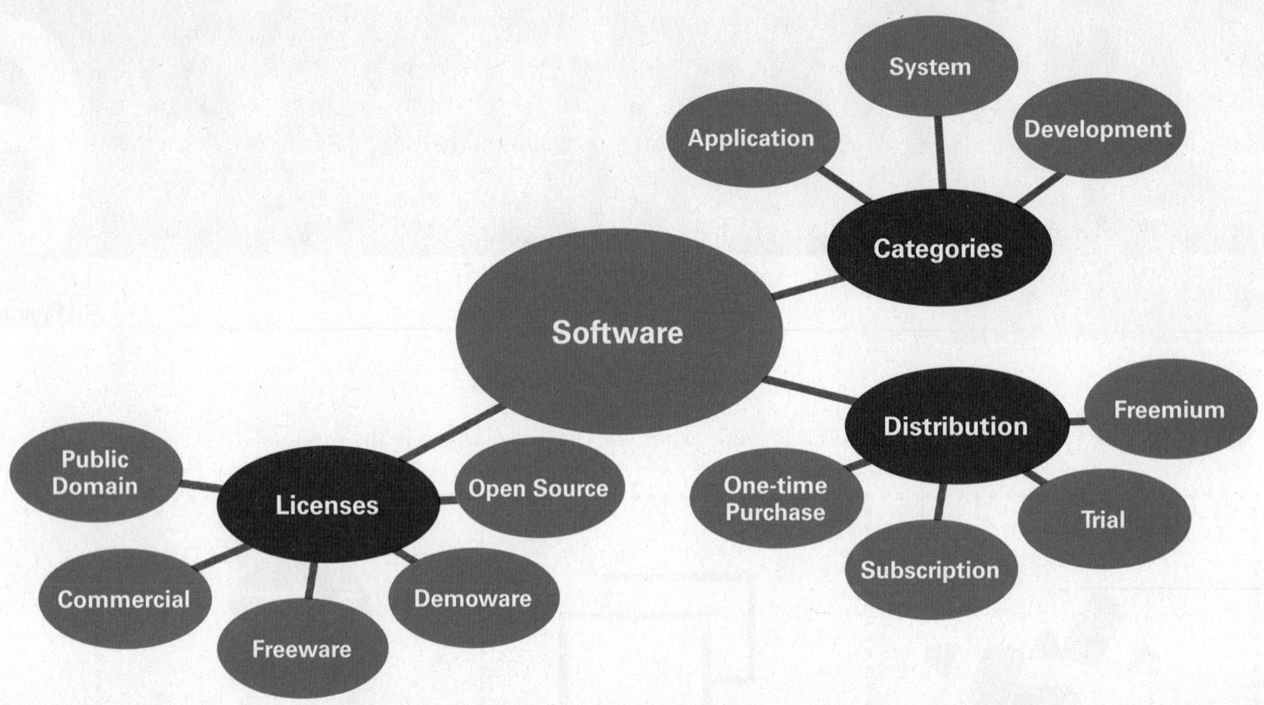

Section A **Software Basics**

Objectives

- Draw a hierarchical diagram that illustrates the three main categories of software and their subcategories.
- List the software that is considered essential for desktop, laptop, and mobile devices.
- Distinguish between software updates and upgrades.
- List five pricing models commonly used in the software industry.
- Explain why most software is licensed.
- Describe the difference between proprietary software and public domain software.
- Describe three types of commercial software licenses.
- Identify the key differences in licenses for freeware, demoware, and open source software.
- Name two popular open source software licenses.
- List four ways to avoid fake mobile apps.

You never actually buy software. Instead, you receive a license to use it. So how does that work? Section A begins with an overview of software essentials, and then it focuses on the way software is distributed and licensed.

Terminology

executable file
system requirements
software upgrade
software update
software license
EULAs
public domain software
proprietary software
commercial software
single-user license
site license
multiple-user license
freeware
demoware
product activation
hash value
open source software
BSD license
GPL
pirated software

Essentials

In the broadest meaning of the term, *software* refers to all the nonhardware components of a digital device. Those components include data files as well as files that contain program code. In common use, however, the term *software* is used for computer programs, such as operating systems, applications, and apps. Let's begin by looking at the software products that give digital devices such a diverse repertoire of functions.

▸ What are the main software categories? There are millions of software titles. When searching through this overabundance of choices for new software, it helps to have a framework of categories, such as the one in Figure 6-1.

Figure 6-1: Software categories

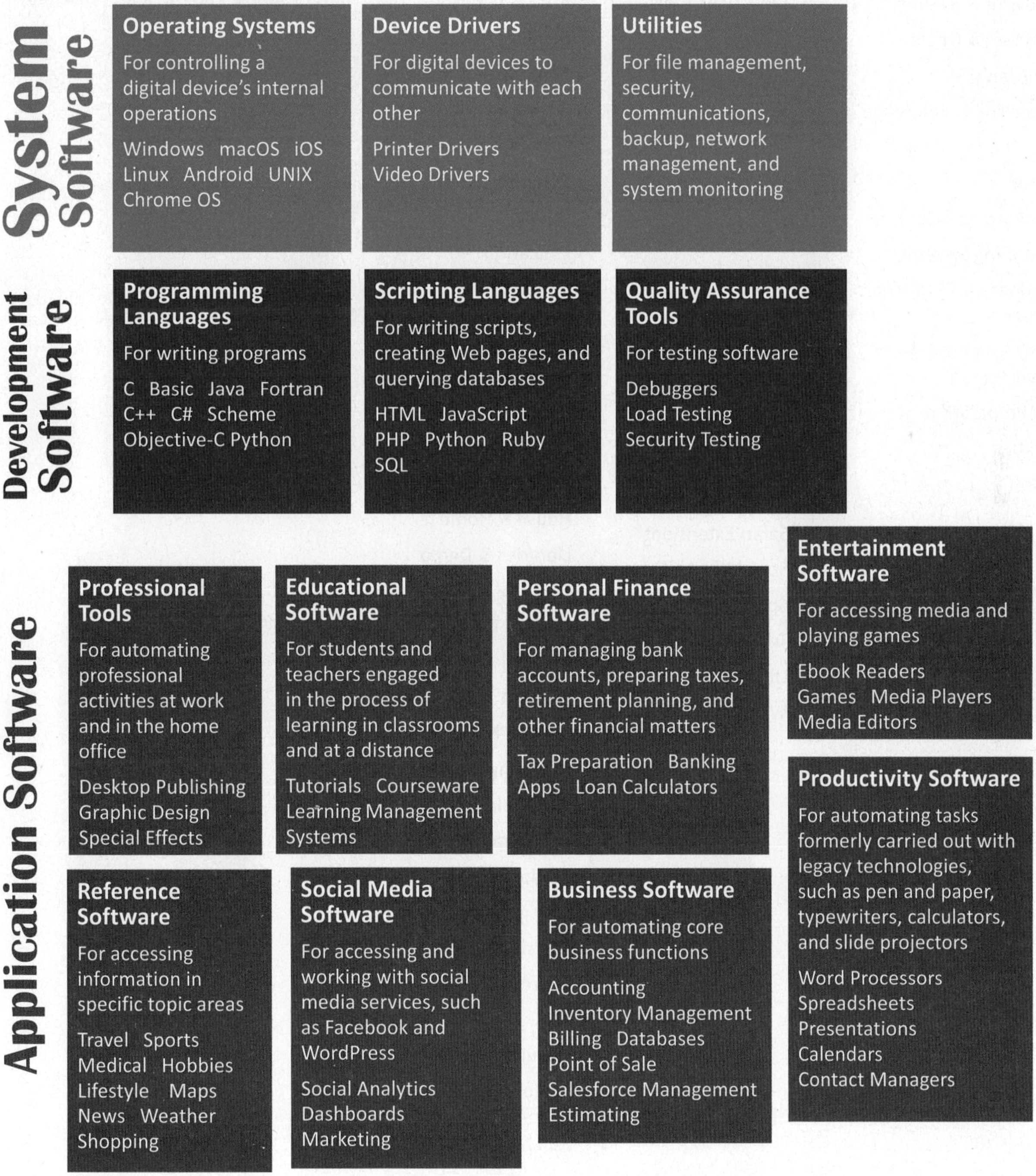

System Software

Operating Systems	Device Drivers	Utilities
For controlling a digital device's internal operations Windows macOS iOS Linux Android UNIX Chrome OS	For digital devices to communicate with each other Printer Drivers Video Drivers	For file management, security, communications, backup, network management, and system monitoring

Development Software

Programming Languages	Scripting Languages	Quality Assurance Tools
For writing programs C Basic Java Fortran C++ C# Scheme Objective-C Python	For writing scripts, creating Web pages, and querying databases HTML JavaScript PHP Python Ruby SQL	For testing software Debuggers Load Testing Security Testing

Application Software

Professional Tools
For automating professional activities at work and in the home office
Desktop Publishing Graphic Design Special Effects

Educational Software
For students and teachers engaged in the process of learning in classrooms and at a distance
Tutorials Courseware Learning Management Systems

Personal Finance Software
For managing bank accounts, preparing taxes, retirement planning, and other financial matters
Tax Preparation Banking Apps Loan Calculators

Entertainment Software
For accessing media and playing games
Ebook Readers Games Media Players Media Editors

Reference Software
For accessing information in specific topic areas
Travel Sports Medical Hobbies Lifestyle Maps News Weather Shopping

Social Media Software
For accessing and working with social media services, such as Facebook and WordPress
Social Analytics Dashboards Marketing

Business Software
For automating core business functions
Accounting Inventory Management Billing Databases Point of Sale Salesforce Management Estimating

Productivity Software
For automating tasks formerly carried out with legacy technologies, such as pen and paper, typewriters, calculators, and slide projectors
Word Processors Spreadsheets Presentations Calendars Contact Managers

◗ **Are software categories universal?** No. There is no universal standard for categorizing software, but various categorization schemes have many similarities. For example, Google Play uses a different set of categories from Apple's App Store and Amazon, and yet there are similarities. Look for similarities and differences in the software categories shown for the online merchants in Figure 6-2.

Figure 6-2: Software categories are not standardized

amazon

Accounting & Finance
Antivirus & Security
Business & Office
Children's
Education & Reference
Lifestyle & Hobbies
Music
Networking & Servers
Operating Systems
Photography & Graphic Design
Programming & Web Development
Tax Preparation
Utilities
Video

Business
Developer Tools
Education
Entertainment
Finance
Games
Graphics & Design
Health & Fitness
Lifestyle
Medical
Music
News
Photo & Video
Productivity
Reference
Safari Extensions
Social Networking
Sports
Travel
Utilities
Weather

Google play

Art & Design
Auto & Vehicles
Beauty
Books & Reference
Business
Comics
Communication
Dating
Education
Entertainment
Events
Finance
Food & Drink
Games
Health & Fitness
House & Home
Libraries & Demo
Lifestyle
Maps & Navigation
Medical
Music & Audio
News & Magazines
Parenting
Personalization
Photography
Productivity
Shopping
Social
Sports
Tools
Travel and Local
Video Players & Editors
Weather

Try It!

Based on the information in Figure 6-2, why do you think the categories used by the Apple App Store are more similar to Google Play's than to Amazon's?

▸ What are the most essential applications for desktop and laptop computers? Most digital devices come loaded with preinstalled applications. Some of these software applications are included because the software developer has made a deal with the device vendor; other applications are more essential.

Desktop and laptop computers require an operating system with a file manager that allows users to view and manipulate data files. A basic set of system utilities includes security and antivirus software, network management tools, a browser, and device drivers for the mouse, keyboard, display device, printer, and other peripheral devices. For application software, most desktop and laptop owners require an office suite containing productivity software for word processing, spreadsheet manipulation, slide show presentations, and scheduling.

▸ What are the essential applications for mobile devices? Mobile devices tend to be used somewhat differently from desktop and laptop computers, so the configuration of their software is slightly different.

Mobile devices require an operating system and utilities for adjusting system settings and accessing networks. Additional basic utilities include a browser, camera controls, and voice integration. Files tend to be stored and retrieved by each app, so users have little need for a utility that allows access to the file management system. Also, because mobile devices are used primarily to consume content rather than create it, an office suite is not at the top of the must-have list. Instead, mobile devices tend to be populated by entertainment apps, games, and social media services.

Figure 6-3 lists the core sets of software for desktops and laptops as well as for mobile devices.

QuickCheck

Which of the following would not be considered essential software for mobile devices, desktops, and laptops?

a. An operating system

b. An office suite

c. Network utilities

d. A browser

Figure 6-3: Essential applications

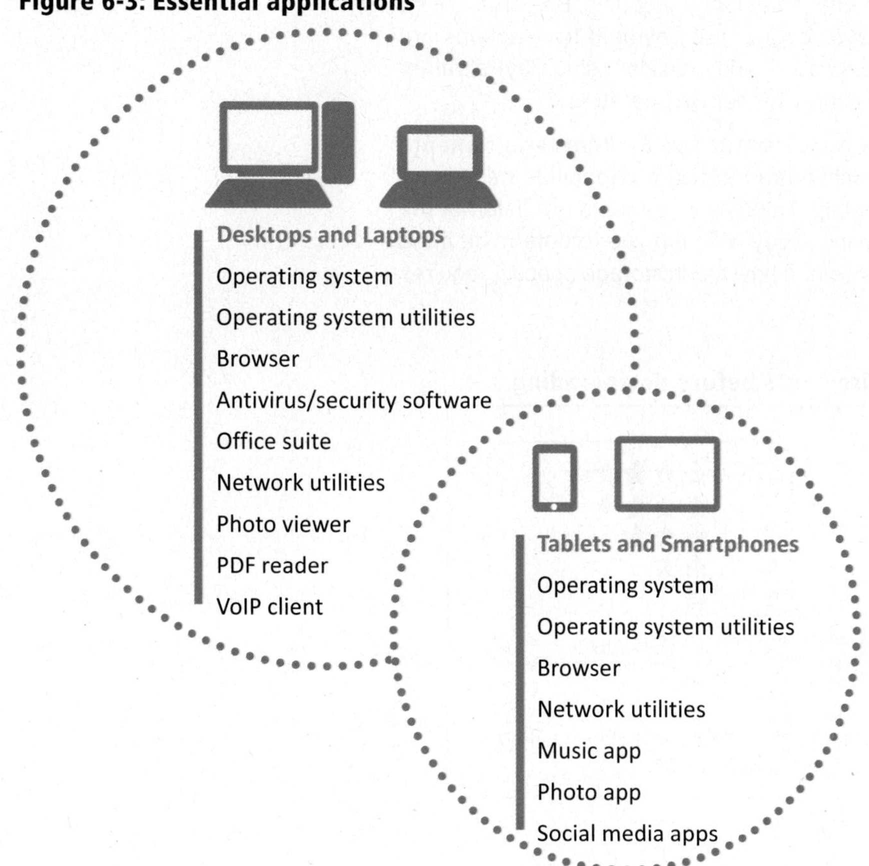

Distribution

Although there are offline sources for software, most consumers obtain software online, where it can be downloaded directly from the developer or from a software aggregator, such as an app store.

▶ What are the components of a typical software application? A software application may contain a single executable file or it may be composed of many separate files that work together. An **executable file** contains a computer program that is carried out step by step within the microprocessor. Executable files designed for PCs usually have an .exe file name extension, whereas executable files for Macs have .app extensions.

To prepare software for distribution, the distribution files are usually "zipped" or packaged into a single unit that can be easily downloaded over the Internet.

▶ What are the best sources for software? Software can contain viruses and other malware, so consumers should download new applications only from trusted sources. Although there is never a guarantee that an application is malware-free, the major app stores, such as Google Play and the Apple App Store, have policies in place that discourage harmful programming. Checking user comments and ratings at these sites is always a good practice that can help consumers avoid downloading risky apps and those that are not well designed.

Software download sites, such as CNET Downloads and FileHippo, offer applications from multiple developers. The focus of these software outlets is applications for desktop and laptop computers. A Google search for *free software* yields many sites, but be careful. Some of these sites are riddled with ads and spyware that will infect your device even if you do not download anything.

Software developers usually have a Web site for distributing software. Well-established developers tend to offer trustworthy products. Be careful when dealing with smaller vendors. Always confirm that payment transactions are processed over a secure HTTPS connection, and consider using PayPal rather than a credit card if you doubt the integrity of the site operators.

▶ How important are system requirements? **System requirements** specify the operating system and minimum hardware capacities necessary for a software product to work correctly. These requirements are listed at the download site and are worth reviewing. They will help you to determine if the software is compatible with your device and how much storage space it requires (Figure 6-4).

QuickCheck

Which of the following is not an executable file?

a. *Notepad.exe*

b. *Textedit.app*

c. *Spreadsheet.dat*

d. *Virus.exe*

Figure 6-4: Review system requirements before downloading

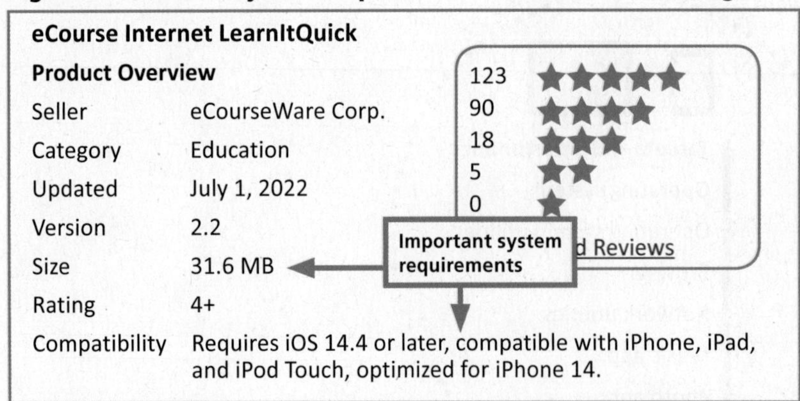

What payment options are available? Software can be obtained under a variety of pricing models. The availability of one or more of these pricing plans depends on the software vendor.

Free. Some software and apps are free to use without payment. Users of free products might be subjected to ads or in-app purchases, however.

One-time payment. Some software can be obtained through a one-time payment in which the consumer pays a set amount to license and use the software without an expiration date. The advantage of the one-time payment model is that there are no additional fees, and with the exception of a few updates, the software remains basically the same as when it was initially installed. There are no surprise changes to the way the software looks or works during its lifetime.

Subscription. The subscription pricing model is an established distribution method in which consumers pay a monthly or annual fee to use the software. Consumers benefit because updates and upgrades are usually included in the pricing. Consumers must remain alert while using subscription services. When a subscription lapses, the software may cease to function. Some vendors allow former customers to launch the software and view files but do not allow those files to be further modified. Credit card information is stored on the vendor's site and may be vulnerable to hacking.

Trial. A third type of pricing model offers consumers the use of a software product during a free trial period. The trial version may be fully functional or it may be limited in functionality. When the trial period ends, a one-time payment or paid subscription is required. This pricing model is common for software applications, such as antivirus utilities and productivity applications, that are preinstalled on new devices.

Freemium. Another popular pricing model for software provides free use of a stripped-down or basic version of the product but requires payment for upgraded features (Figure 6-5).

Terminology

An *in-app purchase* refers to buying goods or services from inside a mobile app. These purchases could be for a clue in a game, for a subscription, or for extra content. In-app purchases allow developers to make a profit while distributing a basic app for free.

6

Figure 6-5: The freemium model

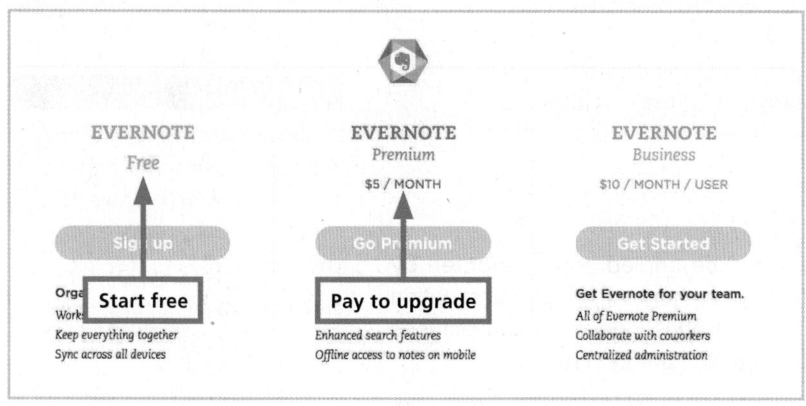

Try It!

Visit Microsoft's Web site to find out which pricing models are available for Microsoft Office.

What are updates and upgrades? Periodically, some software publishers release a new version or edition of a software product that is referred to as a **software upgrade**. An upgrade entirely replaces an older edition with a new one. Each edition carries a version number, such as 1.0 or 2.0. Upgrading software obtained with a one-time payment may involve a fee.

A **software update** (sometimes called a software patch) is a small section of program code that replaces part of the software currently installed. Updates are designed to correct problems and address security vulnerabilities. They are distinguished by revision numbers to the right of the decimal, such as 2.101. Software updates are usually free.

Software Licenses

Obtaining software is not the same as buying tangible goods, such as mittens, chairs, and shoes, that can be bought outright by consumers. Once they've been purchased, tangible goods can be used, altered, loaned to friends, resold, or given away. In contrast, a software "purchase" is actually a license agreement that may include certain restrictions. Some licenses are less restrictive than others, so their terms are factors to consider when selecting software.

▸ Why is software licensed? A **software license**, or license agreement, is a legal contract that defines the ways in which a computer program may be used. These licenses are sometimes referred to as **EULAs** (End User License Agreements). The reason software is licensed has to do with copyrights.

Like books and movies, software is a type of intellectual property. Software copyrights protect the rights of the person or corporation that developed the intellectual property. Most software displays a copyright notice, such as *© 2023 eCourse Corporation*, on one of its screens. This notice is not required by law, however, so programs without a copyright notice are still protected by copyright law.

Try It!

Open a few of your favorite applications and try to locate the copyright notices. Are they located in similar places?

A copyright grants the author of a software product an exclusive right to copy, distribute, sell, and modify that work. Purchasers do not have this right except under the circumstances listed in Figure 6-6.

Figure 6-6: When can software be legally copied?

The purchaser has the right to copy software from distribution media or a Web site to a device's internal storage medium in order to install it.

The purchaser can make an extra, or backup, copy of the software in case the original copy becomes erased or damaged—unless the process of making the backup requires the purchaser to defeat a copy protection mechanism designed to prohibit copying.

The purchaser is allowed to copy and distribute sections of a software program for use in critical reviews and teaching.

QuickCheck

Suppose you download a free app for your smartphone and the main screen contains no copyright notice. What should you assume?

a. The software is copyrighted.

b. The software is pirated.

c. The software has a virus.

d. The software is defective.

Without copyright protection, software would be copied and distributed by unauthorized parties without compensation to its authors. Although that situation might sound like it benefits consumers, it discourages innovation and reduces the incentives for technical support and upgrades in the long run.

Copyright protects a software product by imposing a set of restrictions on its use. The copyright holder may want to add or remove some of those restrictions, and a software license provides the means to do so.

Where can I find the license for a software product? Most legal contracts require signatures before the terms of the contract can take effect. This requirement becomes hard to manage with software—imagine having to sign a license agreement and return it before you can use a new app. To circumvent the signature requirement, software publishers use screen-based license agreements.

License agreements are displayed during the installation process. By clicking the I Agree button, you consent to the terms of the license agreement (Figure 6-7).

Figure 6-7: Viewing the license agreement

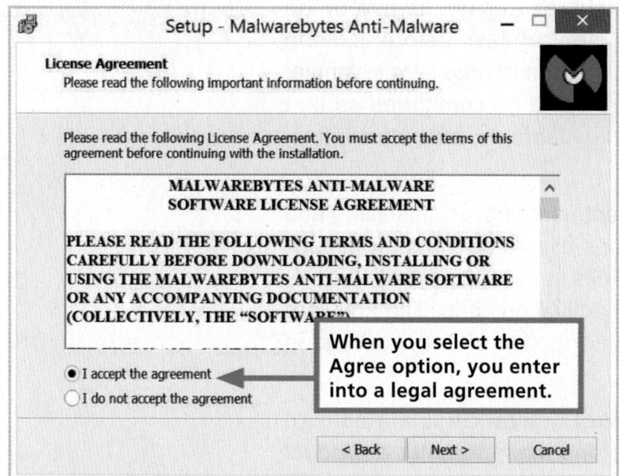

What are the most common types of software licenses? From a legal perspective, there are two categories of software: public domain and proprietary. **Public domain software** is not protected by copyright because the copyright has expired or the author has placed the program in the public domain, making it available without restriction. Public domain software may be freely copied, distributed, and even resold. The primary restriction on public domain software is that you are not allowed to apply for a copyright on it.

Proprietary software has restrictions on its use that are delineated by copyright, patents, or license agreements. Some proprietary software is distributed commercially, whereas some of it is free. Based on licensing rights, proprietary software is distributed as commercial software, freeware, demoware, or open source software.

What is commercial software? **Commercial software** is usually distributed from the software publisher's Web site or from an app store. Most licenses for commercial software adhere closely to the limitations provided by copyright law, although they might permit the software to be installed on multiple devices. A further restriction could permit the software to be used on only one device at a time.

Most commercial software is distributed under a **single-user license** that limits use to one person at a time. However, some software publishers offer volume licenses, such as site licenses and multiple-user licenses, to households, schools, organizations, and businesses.

A **site license** is generally priced at a flat rate and allows software to be used on all computers at a specific location. A **multiple-user license** is priced per copy and allows the allocated number of copies to be used simultaneously.

QuickCheck

Suppose your school's computer lab provides high-end architecture software that can be accessed from any lab computer, but a maximum of five students can use it at any given time. What kind of license does it have?

a. A single-user license

b. A site license

c. A multiple-user license

d. A pirated license

What about freeware? **Freeware** is copyrighted software that—as you might expect—is available for free. It is fully functional and requires no payment for its use. A freeware license permits you to use the software, copy it, and give it away, but the license does not permit you to alter or sell the software. Many utility programs, most device drivers, many mobile apps, and some games are available as freeware.

What is demoware? Some proprietary software is available as a trial version, sometimes called demoware. **Demoware** is distributed for free and often comes preinstalled on new devices, but it is limited in some way until you pay for it.

Demoware publishers can use a variety of techniques to limit the use of the software. It might remain functional for a set number of days before expiring and requiring payment. It might run for a limited amount of time—for example, 60 minutes—each time you launch it. Demoware could be configured so that you can run it only a limited number of times. Or key features, such as printing, might be disabled.

Demoware publishers usually take steps to prevent users from uninstalling and reinstalling the demo to circumvent time limitations. Users who want to unlock the full version of a demo can do so by following links to the software publisher's Web site and using a credit card to purchase an activation code. The software can then be restarted and used without further interruption after the activation code is entered.

How do activation codes work? **Product activation** is a means of protecting software from illegal copying by requiring users to enter a product key or an activation code before the software can be used. Activation is usually part of the software installation process, but it can also occur when demoware times out. Failure to enter a valid code prohibits the program from launching. A software publisher can validate a user's activation code by checking it against an online database or a hash value.

Checking an activation code against an online database ensures that the code you've entered has not been used before. If the code is a duplicate, then the license for that copy of the software is being used by someone else and you will have to call customer service to straighten out the problem.

A **hash value** is a unique number derived from encoding one or more data sets, such as names, serial numbers, and validation codes. Product validation can create a hash value based on your validation code and your device's internal serial number, effectively tying the software and its use to one specific device.

QuickCheck

The free apps you download from your mobile phone are _______________.

a. classified as freeware
b. activated with a hash value
c. designed to self-destruct if copied
d. licensed as commercial software

What is open source software? **Open source software** makes uncompiled program instructions—the source code—available to programmers who want to modify and improve the software. Open source software may be distributed free of charge or for payment in a compiled form, but it must always include the source code.

Linux is an example of open source software, as are programs such as Blender and FileZilla. LibreOffice—a full-featured productivity suite—is another popular example of open source software. You can search for open source applications at the SourceForge Web site.

Despite the lack of restrictions on distribution and use, open source software is copyrighted and is not in the public domain. It is not the same as freeware, which you are not supposed to modify or resell.

Two of the most common open source and free software licenses are BSD and GPL. The **BSD license** originated as the Berkeley Software Distribution license for a server operating system (Figure 6-8).

Figure 6-8: The BSD license

Copyright (c) 2022, [Publisher] All rights reserved.

Redistribution and use in source and binary forms, with or without modification, are permitted provided that the following conditions are met:

- Redistributions of source code must retain the above copyright notice, this list of conditions, and the following disclaimer.
- Redistributions in binary form must reproduce the above copyright notice, this list of conditions, and the following disclaimer in the documentation and/or other materials provided with the distribution.
- Neither the name of the Publisher nor the names of its contributors may be used to endorse or promote products derived from this software without specific prior written permission.

THIS SOFTWARE IS PROVIDED BY THE PUBLISHER AND CONTRIBUTORS "AS IS" AND ANY EXPRESS OR IMPLIED WARRANTIES, INCLUDING, BUT NOT LIMITED TO, THE IMPLIED WARRANTIES OF MERCHANTABILITY AND FITNESS FOR A PARTICULAR PURPOSE ARE DISCLAIMED. IN NO EVENT SHALL THE PUBLISHER AND CONTRIBUTORS BE LIABLE FOR ANY DIRECT, INDIRECT, INCIDENTAL, SPECIAL, EXEMPLARY, OR CONSEQUENTIAL DAMAGES (INCLUDING, BUT NOT LIMITED TO, PROCUREMENT OF SUBSTITUTE GOODS OR SERVICES; LOSS OF USE, DATA, OR PROFITS; OR BUSINESS INTERRUPTION) HOWEVER CAUSED AND ON ANY THEORY OF LIABILITY, WHETHER IN CONTRACT, STRICT LIABILITY, OR TORT (INCLUDING NEGLIGENCE OR OTHERWISE) ARISING IN ANY WAY OUT OF THE USE OF THIS SOFTWARE, EVEN IF ADVISED OF THE POSSIBILITY OF SUCH DAMAGE.

QuickCheck

The first clause of the BSD license permits what?

a. Breaking copy protection

b. Distributing the source code

c. Pirating

d. Modifying the copyright

What is unique about GPL licenses? The **GPL** (General Public License) was developed for a free operating system called GNU. The GPL is slightly more restrictive than the BSD license because it requires derivative works to be licensed. That means if you get a really cool computer game that's licensed under a GPL and you modify the game to create a new level, you have to distribute your modification under the GPL. You cannot legally market your modification under a commercial software license. There are currently three versions of the GPL. Their differences are of interest primarily to software developers.

When I accept a software license, what am I agreeing to?

Software licenses are often lengthy and written in legalese, but your legal right to use the software continues only as long as you abide by the terms of the software license. Therefore, you should understand the software license for any software you use (Figure 6-9).

Figure 6-9: Elements of a software license

Software License Agreement

Important - Read Carefully: This License Agreement ("Agreement") is a legal agreement between you and eCourse Corporation for the software product, eCourse GraphWare ("The SOFTWARE"). By installing, copying, or otherwise using the SOFTWARE, you agree to be bound by the terms of this Agreement. The SOFTWARE is protected by copyright laws and international copyright treaties. The SOFTWARE is licensed, not sold.

Grant of License. This Agreement gives you the right to install and use one copy of the SOFTWARE on a single digital device. The primary user of the device on which the SOFTWARE is installed may make a second copy for use on a portable device.

Other Rights and Limitations. You may not reverse engineer, decompile, or disassemble the SOFTWARE except and only to the extent that such activity is expressly permitted by applicable law.

The SOFTWARE is licensed as a single product; its components may not be separated for use on more than one device. You may not rent, lease, or lend the SOFTWARE.

You may permanently transfer all of your rights under this Agreement, provided you retain no copies, you transfer all of the SOFTWARE, and the recipient agrees to the terms of this Agreement. If the software product is an upgrade, any transfer must include all prior versions of the SOFTWARE.

You may receive the SOFTWARE in more than one medium. Regardless of the type of medium you receive, you may use only one medium that is appropriate for your single device. You may not use or install the other medium on another device.

Warranty. eCourse warrants that the SOFTWARE will perform substantially in accordance with the accompanying written documentation for a period of ninety (90) days from the date of receipt. TO THE MAXIMUM EXTENT PERMITTED BY APPLICABLE LAW, eCourse AND ITS SUPPLIERS DISCLAIM ALL OTHER WARRANTIES AND CONDITIONS EITHER EXPRESS OR IMPLIED, INCLUDING, BUT NOT LIMITED TO, IMPLIED WARRANTIES OF MERCHANTABILITY, FITNESS FOR A PARTICULAR PURPOSE, TITLE, AND NON-INFRINGEMENT, WITH REGARD TO THE SOFTWARE PRODUCT.

Try It!

Read the EULA in Figure 6-9 and answer the following questions:

Is the consumer buying the software or licensing it?

When does the license go into effect?

Under what circumstances is it legal to make copies?

Is it permissible to loan the software?

Is it permissible to sell the software?

Does the software publisher provide a warranty?

Fake and Pirated Software

Not all software is legitimate. *New York Times* investigators discovered hundreds of fake shopping apps in Apple's App Store, and similar apps lurk in the Google Play Store. Illegal copies of software are also sold. Consumers should be cautious when selecting apps to make sure they are legitimate.

What is a fake app? Fake apps masquerade as something they are not. For example, the Overstock Inc app is designed to fool consumers who are looking for the Overstock.com app. Fake apps may steal passwords, spread malware, and access personal social media data. Here are some tips to help you avoid fake apps:

- Carefully compare the name of the app publisher with the company that produces the company's legitimate Web site.
- Check reviews of the app. Legitimate apps have hundreds of reviews, and most of them should be favorable.
- Watch for spelling and grammar errors in the description of the app. Most fake apps are not professionally reviewed for spelling and grammar errors.
- Check the date. Apps for established companies rarely have recent publication dates, though they may have recent "updated on" dates.

What's the problem with illegal copies? Software that is illegally copied and sold is referred to as **pirated software**. It is not always easy to identify pirated software. Some unsuspecting consumers have inadvertently obtained pirated software, even when paying full price from a reputable source. Pirated software may not update properly and is not eligible for authenticated upgrades. The following characteristics could be signs of pirated software:

- Software sold at Web sites for prices well below retail
- Commercial software offered as a free download from a third-party Web site or Tor server
- Software sold in a clear CD-ROM jewel case with no accompanying documentation, license, registration card, or Certificate of Authenticity
- Software marked as "Academic" that requires no proof of eligibility
- Software marked as "OEM" or "For Distribution Only with New PC Hardware"

QuickQuiz — Section A

1. Device drivers and utilities are classified as [ ] software.
2. Most executable files for a PC have a(n) .[ ] extension, whereas executable files for Macs have an .app extension.
3. Software is a type of [ ] property and is therefore protected by copyright.
4. The [ ] pricing model provides free use of a basic version of the product, but upgraded features require payment.
5. A hash value can be created during the [ ] process to tie a software product to a specific device.

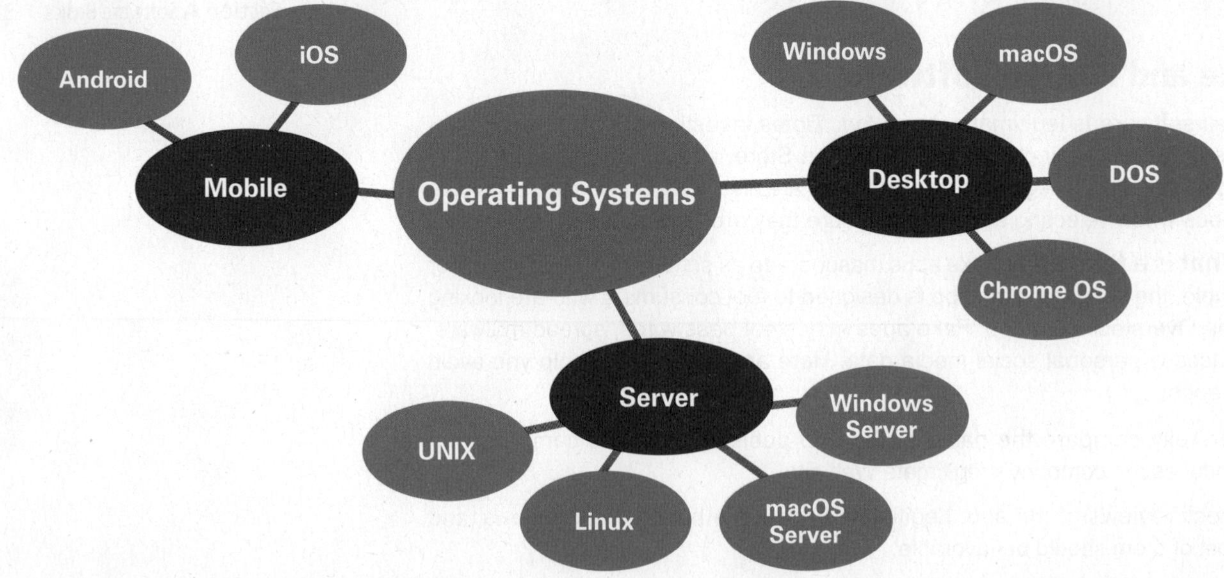

Section B Operating Systems

Objectives

- Describe three categories of operating systems.
- Explain the purpose of an operating system kernel.
- Name the operating system kernels that were used to develop Windows and macOS.
- List five digital device resources that are managed by the operating system.
- Define the terms *multitasking*, *multiprocessing*, and *multithreading*.
- Explain how memory leaks develop and why they are a problem.
- Give an example of a buffer that is managed by the operating system.
- Summarize the strengths and weaknesses of the Windows operating system.
- Summarize the strengths and weaknesses of macOS.
- List three ways in which iOS and Android are the same and two ways in which they differ.
- Explain why Chrome OS is considered a thin client.
- Give an example of a situation in which Linux would be a desirable operating system.
- Provide an example of a situation that would benefit from the use of a virtual machine.

An operating system is an integral part of virtually every digital device. It fundamentally affects how you can use a desktop, laptop, tablet, or smartphone. Can you run two programs at the same time? Can you connect the device to a network? Does the device run dependably? Does it accept touch input? To answer questions like these, it is helpful to have a clear idea about what an operating system is and what it does.

Terminology

user interface
desktop operating system
mobile operating systems
server operating system
kernel
resource
processes
multitasking
multithreading
multiprocessing
memory leak
buffers
Microsoft Windows
DOS
macOS
iOS
Android
Chrome OS
Linux
forked
thin client
Linux distribution
virtual machine

6

Operating System Basics

An operating system gives your digital device a personality. It controls key elements of the **user interface**, which includes the visual experience as well as the keyboard, mouse, microphone, or touchscreen that collects user commands. Behind the scenes, the operating system is busy supervising critical operations that take place within a device.

Are there different categories of operating systems? Consumers are familiar with operating systems such as Windows and iOS, but there are several others in widespread use. Operating systems can be categorized by the devices on which they are used (Figure 6-10).

Figure 6-10: Operating system categories

Desktop operating systems. A **desktop operating system** is designed for a desktop or laptop computer. The computer you use at home, at school, or at work is most likely configured with a desktop operating system, such as Microsoft Windows, macOS, or Chrome OS. Key characteristics of desktop operating systems include the following:

- Accommodate one user at a time, but allow multiple accounts
- Provide local area networking capability
- Include file management tools
- Run more than one application at a time
- Offer a graphical user interface designed for keyboard, mouse, and optional touchscreen or voice input

Mobile operating systems. Operating systems such as iOS and Android are classified as **mobile operating systems** because they are designed for use on smartphones, tablet computers, and ebook readers. Key characteristics of mobile operating systems include the following:

- Accommodate one user at a time
- Provide connectivity to wireless local area networks
- Offer a graphical user interface designed for touchscreen input
- Support voice input
- Include integrated cellular communications

Server operating systems. Computers that are deployed as Web servers, or as servers for files, applications, databases, or email, generally use a **server operating system** designed for distributed networks accessed by many simultaneous users. Linux, UNIX, Windows Server, and macOS Server are examples of popular server operating systems with the following characteristics:

- Accommodate multiple simultaneous users
- Include sophisticated network management and security tools
- Provide a utilitarian user interface

Where is the operating system? In some digital devices, such as smartphones and ebook readers, the entire operating system is small enough to be stored in ROM. For most other computers, the operating system program is quite large, so most of it is stored on a hard disk or SSD.

During the boot process, the operating system kernel is loaded into RAM. A **kernel** provides essential operating system services, such as memory management and file access. The kernel stays in RAM the entire time your computer is on. Other parts of the operating system, such as customization utilities, are loaded into RAM as they are needed.

QuickCheck

The operating system kernel provides essential services and remains __________ while the computer is on.

a. inactive

b. in RAM

c. off

d. mobile

▶ What does an operating system do? An operating system interacts with application software, device drivers, and hardware to manage a set of resources. In the context of digital devices, the term **resource** refers to any component that is required to perform work.

The processor is a device's main resource. RAM, storage space, and peripheral devices are also resources. While you interact with application software, the operating system is busy behind the scenes performing resource management tasks such as those listed in Figure 6-11.

Figure 6-11: Operating system resource management tasks

Manage processor resources to handle simultaneous input, output, and processing tasks

Manage memory by allocating space for all the programs and data that are in use during a computing session

Keep track of storage resources so that files and programs can be found and manipulated

Ensure that input and output proceed in an orderly manner by communicating with peripheral devices

Establish basic elements of the user interface such as the appearance of the desktop, menus, and toolbars

▶ How do operating systems manage processor resources? Every microprocessor cycle is a resource for accomplishing a task, such as executing a program instruction. Many activities—called **processes**—compete for the attention of a device's microprocessor. The microprocessor receives commands as software carries out tasks and while input arrives from the keyboard, mouse, and other devices. At the same time, data is being sent to output devices or over network connections.

To manage all these competing processes, an operating system must ensure that each process receives its share of attention from the microprocessor. You can check the processes that are being executed by using system utilities such as Task Manager (Figure 6-12).

Figure 6-12: View active processes

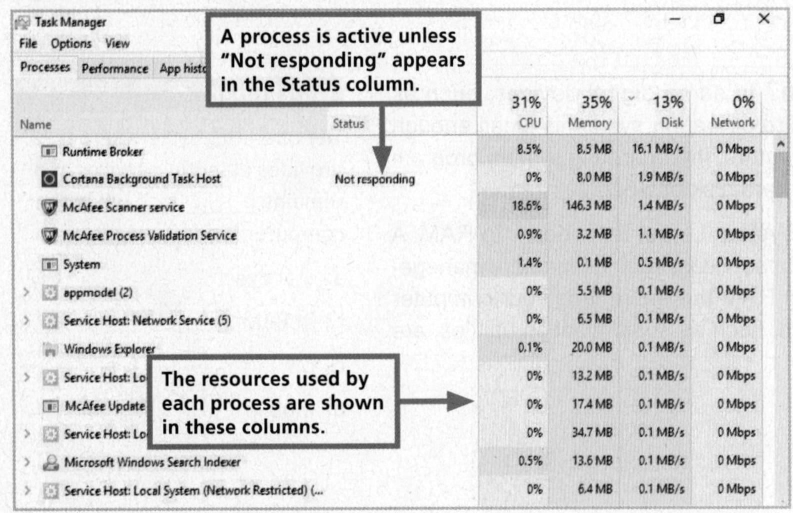

QuickCheck

In Figure 6-12, which process seems to be using the most memory resources?

a. Runtime Broker

b. McAfee Scanner service

c. Windows Explorer

d. Microsoft Windows Search Indexer

How do operating systems handle so many processes? During a typical session, a laptop computer might run an average of 50 processes. Ideally, the operating system should be able to help the microprocessor switch seamlessly from one process to another. Depending on the capabilities of the operating system and computer hardware, processes can be managed by multitasking, multithreading, and multiprocessing.

Multitasking. Most of today's popular operating systems offer multitasking services. **Multitasking** provides process and memory management services that allow two or more tasks, jobs, or programs to run simultaneously.

Multithreading. Within a single program, **multithreading** allows multiple commands, or threads, to run simultaneously. For example, one thread for a spreadsheet program might be waiting for input from you, while other threads perform a long calculation in the background. Multithreading can speed up performance on single- or multiple-processor devices.

Multiprocessing. Many digital devices include multi-core processors or multiple processors. An operating system's **multiprocessing** capability supports a division of labor among all the processing units.

How does an operating system manage memory? A microprocessor works with data and executes instructions stored in RAM—one of the most important resources for a digital device. When you want to run more than one application at a time, the operating system has to allocate specific areas of memory for each application.

Sometimes an application requests memory but never releases it—a condition called a **memory leak**. These leaks slowly drain available memory, eventually preventing other applications from accessing enough memory to function properly (Figure 6-13). Applications affected by memory leaks can crash, and the operating system might display error messages, such as "General Protection Fault" or "Program Not Responding." A device can sometimes recover from a memory leak if you access Task Manager (PC) or Activity Monitor (Mac) to close the non-responding application.

QuickCheck

What is the term used when two or more instructions from an application are running simultaneously?

a. Multitasking

b. Multithreading

c. Multiprocessing

d. Memory leak

Figure 6-13: During a memory leak, a program overruns its memory space

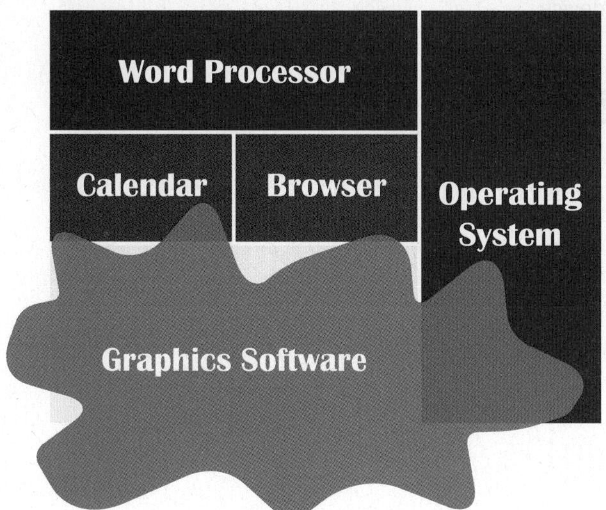

How does the OS keep track of storage resources? Behind the scenes, an operating system acts as a filing clerk that stores and retrieves files from various storage devices. It remembers the names and locations of all your files and keeps track of empty spaces where new files can be stored. Later in this module, you'll explore file storage in more depth and learn how the operating system affects the way you create, name, save, and retrieve files.

Why does the operating system get involved with peripheral devices? Every peripheral device connected to a computer is regarded as an input or output resource. Your computer's operating system communicates with device driver software so that data can travel smoothly between the computer and peripheral resources. If a peripheral device or driver is not performing correctly, the operating system makes a decision about what to do—usually it displays an on-screen message to warn you of the problem.

Try It!

Open any word processing software or email client and type as fast as you can. Can you type fast enough to overrun the keyboard buffer so that some of the characters you type are lost and not displayed on the screen?

An operating system ensures that input and output proceed in an orderly manner, using **buffers** to collect and hold data while the device is busy with other tasks. By using a keyboard buffer, for example, your computer never misses one of your keystrokes, regardless of how fast you type or what else is happening in your computer at the same time (Figure 6-14).

Figure 6-14: How buffers work

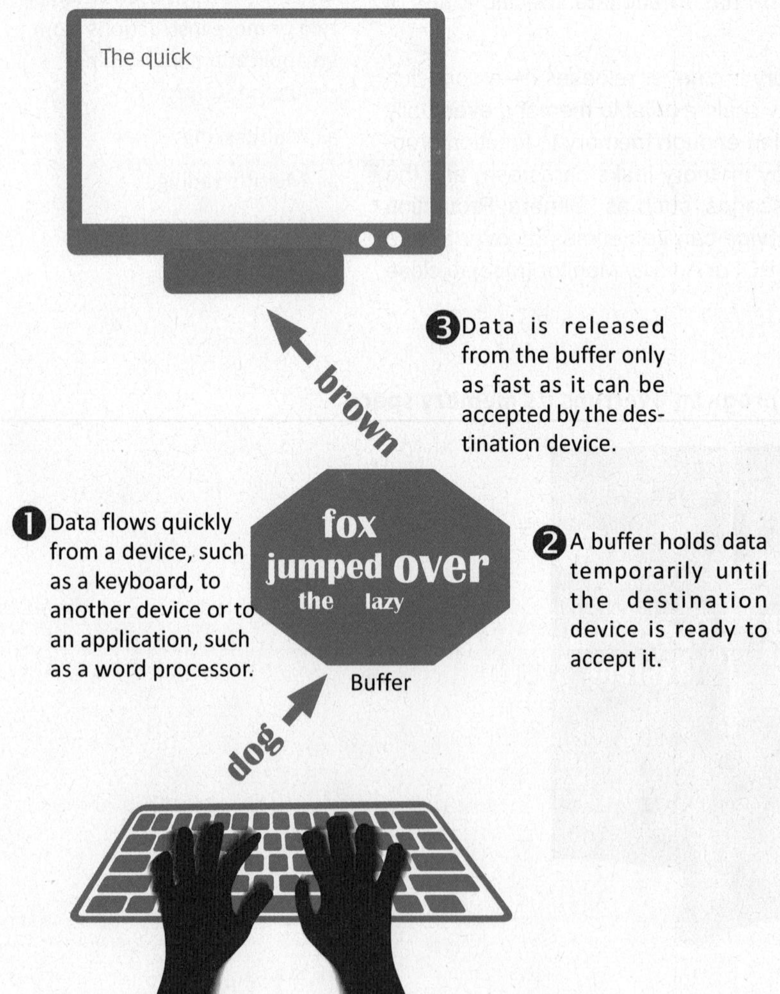
The quick
3 Data is released from the buffer only as fast as it can be accepted by the destination device.
brown
1 Data flows quickly from a device, such as a keyboard, to another device or to an application, such as a word processor.
fox
jumped over
the lazy
Buffer
2 A buffer holds data temporarily until the destination device is ready to accept it.
dog

Microsoft Windows

Microsoft Windows is installed on about 75% of the world's personal computers. Its screen-based desktop is populated with colorful icons used to launch applications, connect to Web sites, and organize files.

Why "Windows"? The Windows operating system got its name from the rectangular work areas displayed on its screen-based desktop. Each window can display a different document or application, which provides a visual model of the operating system's multitasking capabilities. Figure 6-15 illustrates the characteristics of the Windows desktop.

Figure 6-15: Windows 11 desktop elements

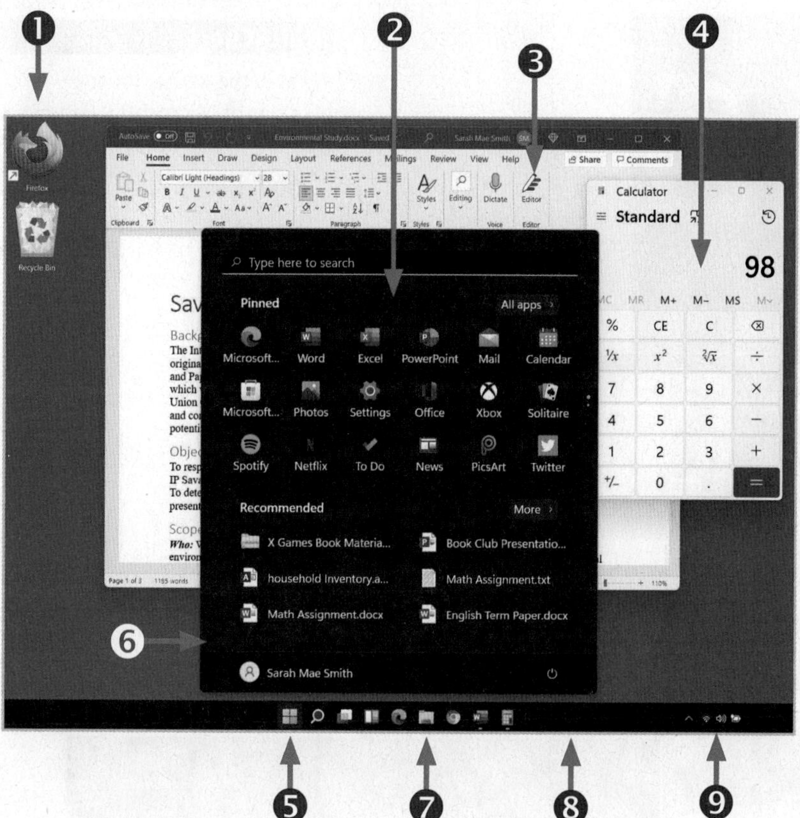

1. Desktop **icons** represent programs, folders, and data files.
2. **Pinned icons** provide quick access to apps.
3. An **application window** displays a program.
4. Another application window displays a calculator.
5. The Windows **Start button** opens the Start menu.
6. The **Start menu** provides access to frequently used applications and utilities.
7. Application icons are "pinned" to the taskbar.
8. The desktop **taskbar** contains the Start button, pinned icons, and the notification area.
9. The **notification area** displays status icons.

Try It!

Make sure that you can use the correct terminology to identify all of the elements on the Windows desktop.

QuickCheck

How many application windows are displayed on the Windows desktop in Figure 6-15?

a. 1

b. 2

c. 3

d. 4

▸ What do I need to know about the evolution of Windows?

Windows evolved from a Microsoft operating system called **DOS** (Disk Operating System) that was designed to run on early PCs with Intel or Intel-compatible microprocessors.

To create Microsoft Windows, developers used the DOS kernel but added a point-and-click graphical user interface. DOS was eventually dropped in favor of the NT kernel. Since its introduction in 1985, Windows has evolved through several versions. Although Windows 11, shown on the previous page, was the most recent version when this book was published, you might encounter some older computers that run Windows 7, Windows 8, or Windows 10 (Figure 6-16).

Try It!

If your device is running Windows, can you identify which version it is?

Figure 6-16: Windows 7, 8, and 10

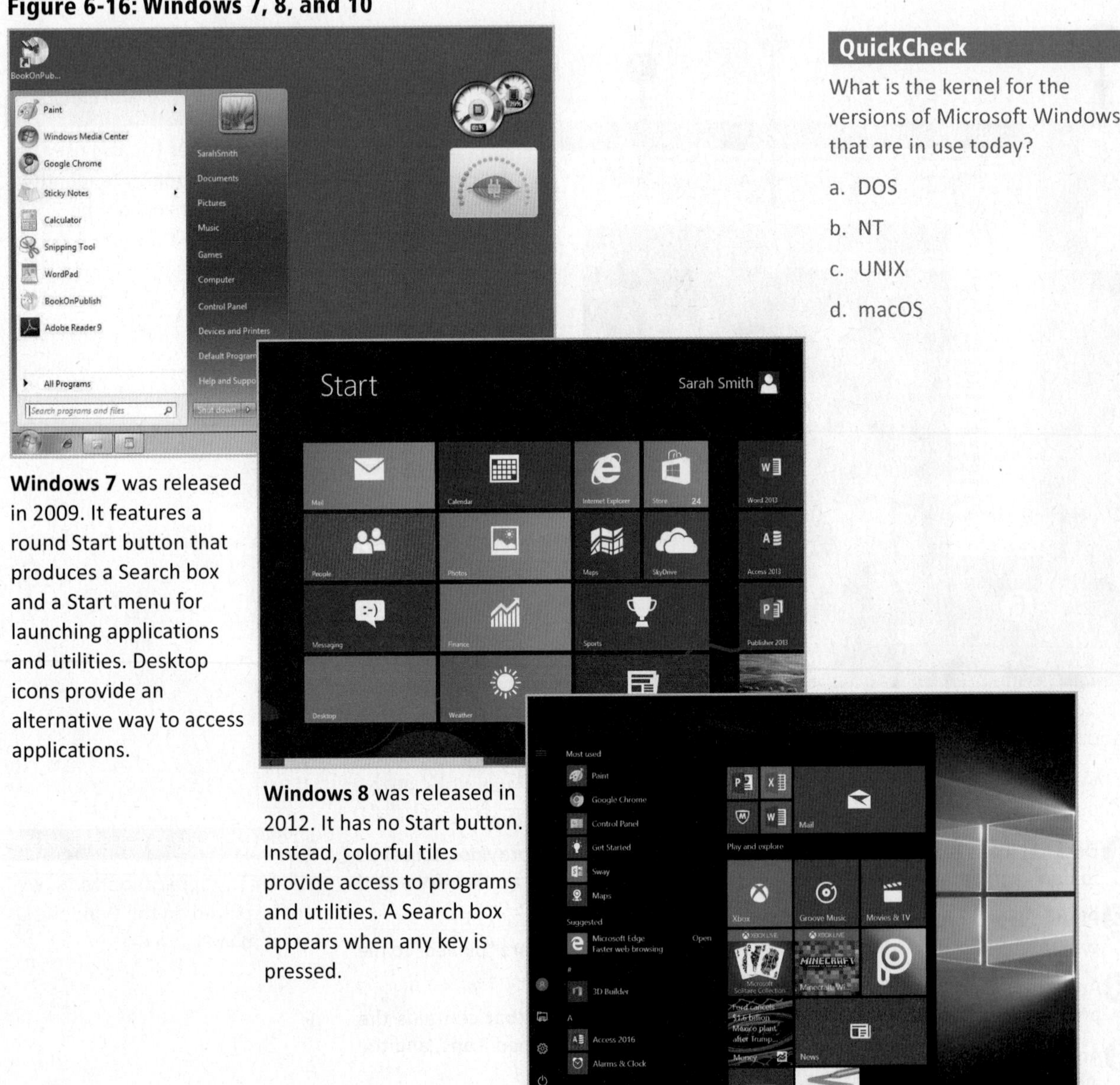

Windows 7 was released in 2009. It features a round Start button that produces a Search box and a Start menu for launching applications and utilities. Desktop icons provide an alternative way to access applications.

Windows 8 was released in 2012. It has no Start button. Instead, colorful tiles provide access to programs and utilities. A Search box appears when any key is pressed.

Windows 10 was released in 2015 after Microsoft decided to skip Windows 9. The Start button is again a prominent element of the taskbar. The desktop includes a Search box, a list of frequently used applications, and a set of tiles for accessing applications.

QuickCheck

What is the kernel for the versions of Microsoft Windows that are in use today?

a. DOS

b. NT

c. UNIX

d. macOS

▶ Does Windows run on tablets and phones, too? Microsoft offers several editions of Windows. The Home edition is designed for desktop, laptop, and tablet computers. Windows Pro and Windows Enterprise offer built-in tools for power users and businesses, such as encrypting the data on local drives, accessing a computer remotely, and managing networks.

Microsoft does not offer an operating system for mobile phones. Windows 11 can, however, be installed on tablet computers that are equipped with a SIM slot for cellular calling (Figure 6-17).

Figure 6-17: Windows 11 on a tablet with SIM card for cellular calls

▶ What are the strengths of Windows? The number and variety of programs that run on Windows are unmatched by any other operating system. For the best selection of software, especially for games and business software, Windows is the operating system of choice.

The Windows user community is also a strength. Comprehensive tutorials and troubleshooting guides can be found online, including a vast array of YouTube instructional videos. Microsoft's official site, *www.microsoft.com*, includes thousands of pages of searchable information.

Windows runs on third-party hardware from vendors such as Dell and Lenovo. Shoppers have lots of options for configuring a Windows device that meets their needs.

▶ What are Windows' weaknesses? Windows has been criticized for two major weaknesses: reliability and security. The reliability of an operating system is usually gauged by the length of time it operates without glitches. Windows tends to become unstable with more frequency than other operating systems.

Slow system response, programs that stop working, and error messages can be symptoms of a Windows malfunction. Rebooting usually clears the error condition and returns a computer to normal functionality, but the time wasted shutting down and waiting for a reboot adds unnecessary frustration to the computing experience.

Of the major desktop operating systems, Windows has the reputation for being the most vulnerable to viruses, worms, and other attacks. One reason for Windows' vulnerability is its huge user base, which makes it the biggest target for hackers. Although Microsoft is diligent in its efforts to patch security holes, its programmers are often one step behind the hackers; while users wait for patches, their computers are vulnerable.

macOS

In 1984, Apple Inc. introduced a computer "for the rest of us," designed for nonbusiness, non-IBM-PC users. The first Macintosh computers featured a desktop dotted with graphical icons that could be launched by clicking a mouse. That desktop evolved into the macOS that powers today's Macs.

▶ What's unique about macOS? As a desktop operating system, **macOS** features beautifully designed icons and multiple rectangular work areas to reflect multitasking capabilities. Characteristic features of the Mac desktop are shown in Figure 6-18.

Figure 6-18: macOS desktop elements

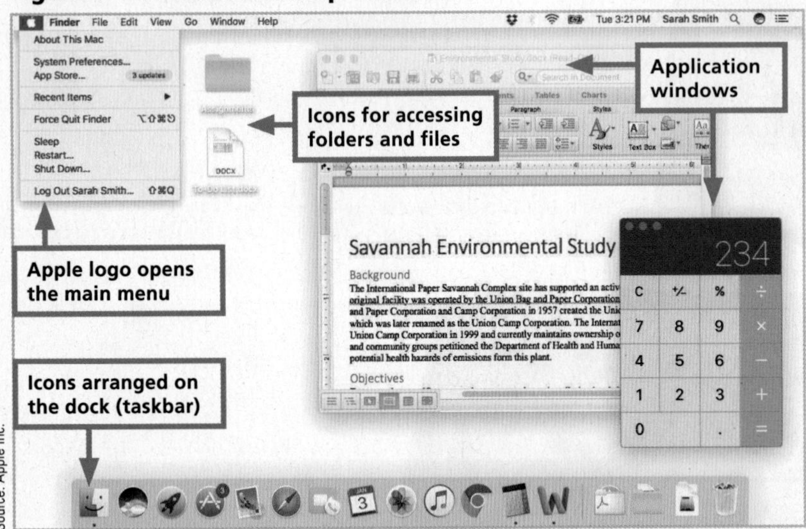

Source: Apple Inc.

Try It!

If you are using a Mac, identify which version of macOS is installed by clicking the Apple icon and selecting About this Mac.

▶ What do I need to know about the evolution of macOS? Like Windows, macOS has been through a number of revisions. The original Classic Mac OS was introduced in 1984 and designed for a line of Macintosh computers based on the Motorola 68000 microprocessor.

In 2001, Classic Mac OS was rewritten to run on Macintosh computers containing PowerPC microprocessors produced by IBM. The new Mac OS was designated Mac OS X. It was commonly called Cheetah, starting a tradition for easy-to-remember nicknames that continues today.

In 2006, Macintosh computers changed significantly with the switch from PowerPC to Intel processors and Mac OS X 10.4.4. In 2012, Apple released OS X 10.8 and officially dropped "Mac" from the operating system's name. With the release of Sierra in 2016, the operating system was renamed macOS. In 2020, Apple announced that Macs would use M-class processors with the Big Sur operating system (Figure 6-19).

Terminology

OS X is pronounced "oh es ten."

QuickCheck

Which came first: Mac OS or Windows?

a. Mac OS

b. Windows

Figure 6-19: macOS evolution

- 2001 Mac OS X 10.0 10.4 (Cheetah)
- 2006 Mac OS X 10.4.4 (Tiger Intel)
- 2007 Mac OS X 10.5 (Leopard)
- 2009 Mac OS X 10.6 (Snow Leopard)
- 2011 Mac OS X 10.7 (Lion)
- 2012 OS X 10.8 (Mountain Lion)
- 2014 OS X 10.9 (Mavericks)
- 2015 OS X 10.10 (Yosemite)
- 2016 macOS 10.12 (Sierra)
- 2017 macOS 10.13 (High Sierra)
- 2018 macOS 10.14 (Mojave)
- 2019 macOS 10.15 (Catalina)
- 2020 macOS 11 (Big Sur)
- 2021 macOS 12 (Monterey)

What are the strengths of macOS? macOS has a reputation for being an easy-to-use, reliable, and secure operating system. According to industry observers, Macintosh developers have always been in the lead when it comes to intuitive user interface design.

The operating system kernel of macOS is based on UNIX, a server operating system that includes industrial-strength memory protection features that contribute to a low incidence of errors and glitches. macOS inherited a strong security foundation from UNIX that tends to limit the number of security holes and the damage that can be done by hackers who manage to slip in.

Another factor that contributes to the security of computers running macOS is that fewer viruses are designed to target Macs because the user base is smaller than the Windows user base. Regardless of the relative security of computers running macOS, Mac owners should practice safe computing by applying software updates and OS patches as they become available, running security software, activating wireless network encryption, not opening suspicious email attachments, and not clicking links embedded in email messages.

The Apple ecosystem is yet another advantage of macOS. In the context of technology, an ecosystem is a family of devices, software, and services that work with one another. The Apple ecosystem includes computers running macOS and other devices such as iPhones, iPads, Apple Watches, and Apple TV.

Using devices in the Apple ecosystem, you can seamlessly share content. For example, an appointment made on an iMac computer automatically updates the calendar on your iPhone. With Apple's Handoff you can start an email message on your laptop and then complete it later on your iPhone (Figure 6-20).

Figure 6-20: Handoff in the Apple ecosystem

Use Handoff to continue tasks on your other devices

With Handoff, you can start work on one device, then switch to another nearby device and pick up where you left off.

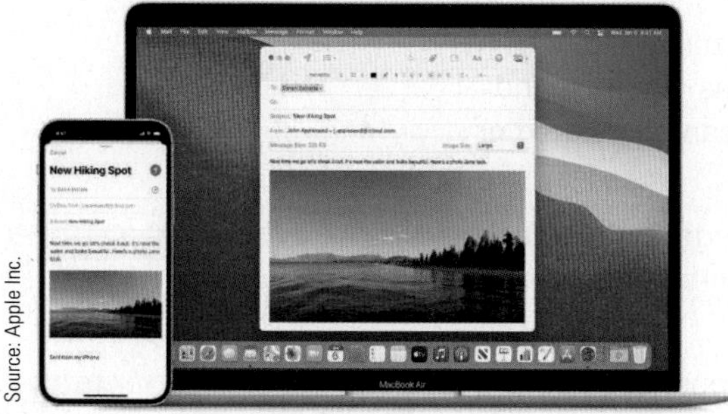

Source: Apple Inc.

What are the weaknesses of macOS? A decent collection of software is available for computers that run macOS, although the selection is not as vast as the Windows collection. Many of the most prolific software publishers produce one version of their software for Windows and another, similar version for macOS.

In contrast to the Windows platform, macOS runs only on devices from Apple. Shoppers are limited to the hardware devices offered by Apple, such as iMacs, Macbooks, and iPads. Hardware and configuration options are much more limited than those available for the Windows platform.

iOS

macOS is for desktop computers, but its cousin, iOS, powers mobile devices, such as iPhones, iPads, and iPods.

How is iOS related to macOS? **iOS** is a mobile operating system derived from the same UNIX code that is the basis for macOS. Both operating systems feature icons with a similar design aesthetic.

How does iOS work? iOS displays a home screen containing application icons. At the bottom of the screen, a dock holds icons for frequently used apps. Touching an icon launches its app. Pressing the physical or virtual Home button returns you to the home screen. The Settings icon leads to a variety of system utilities (Figure 6-21).

Figure 6-21: iOS is designed for mobile devices

Apps can be grouped into folders to save space on the Home screen. Touching and holding an app icon produces "Jiggle mode" in which icons vibrate to indicate they are in a modifiable state. From Jiggle mode, icons can be deleted or dragged on top of each other to put them into a folder.

iOS was the first operating system to offer routines to manage touchscreen gesture inputs, such as using your fingers to "squeeze" an on-screen graphic into a smaller size.

As a mobile operating system, iOS provides connectivity options, such as cell phone connections, as well as local networking. Although all iOS devices have Wi-Fi and Bluetooth capability, only iPhones and some iPads have cellular capabilities.

What are the limitations of iOS? iOS limits your selection of apps to those provided by the online Apple App Store, unless you make unauthorized modifications to the phone. Those modifications can also overcome other limitations, such as lack of access to the file system. Unlike full desktop operating systems, iOS does not include a file manager. The only way to access a data file is through the app that was used to create it.

You won't find a desktop with application windows on an iOS device. Each app fills the entire screen. Background processes, such as music, voice calls, and notifications, provide very limited multitasking capabilities.

QuickCheck

Which device does not use iOS?

a. iPhone

b. MacBook Air

c. iPad

d. iPod Touch

6

Android

Words such as *marshmallow, jellybean*, and *lollipop* might bring to mind sugary sweets, but they were also the nicknames for versions of the Android operating system.

What is Android? **Android** is a mobile operating system that is a popular platform for tablet computers, smartphones, and ebook readers. Android was developed by a consortium of technology companies and unveiled in 2007. It is an open source operating system under the project leadership of Google. As with other popular mobile operating systems, Android is designed for ARM processors.

How does the Android interface work? Android displays a home screen containing icons that represent software applications. Touching an icon launches the app.

Android devices have a screen-based home button that displays the home screen (Figure 6-22). In addition to touchscreen input, the Android OS supports voice input for Google searching, voice dialing, navigation, and other applications.

Figure 6-22: Android runs on smartphones and tablets

What are the key features of Android? The Android OS contains basic network and routing routines that allow Android devices to become Wi-Fi hotspots. For example, activating the Network utility on an Android-based smartphone transforms the phone into a router, and the phone's data connection can be used by a nearby desktop, laptop, or tablet computer to access the Internet.

Android provides access to the file system and provides a utility for viewing files stored internally or on external SD cards. A third-party file manager utility is required to manipulate files.

QuickCheck

Where can you find the home button on an Android device?

a. On the Start menu

b. On the system unit

c. Next to the Apple icon

d. At the bottom of the screen

Chrome OS

For consumers whose digital footprints rarely leave the cloud, there is an operating system that provides a secure platform. Sometimes described as a browser-based operating system, **Chrome OS** has limitations, but those limitations are not necessarily negative.

▶What is Chrome OS? Google launched an operating system called Chrome OS in 2009. Its kernel is based on an open source operating system called Linux, but Chrome OS itself is distributed under a proprietary license. This situation is common in the open source community where a product with an open source license is **forked**—meaning that the source code is developed and updated on two different paths by separate organizations. In the case of Chrome OS, the source code from a project called Chromium was appropriated by Google, modified with proprietary code, and then distributed under the Chrome OS license, which does not allow copying, modifications, or redistribution.

▶What are the pros and cons of Chrome OS? Chrome OS is an example of a **thin client** because it depends substantially on processing and storage provided by a remote computer—in this case, cloud-based servers. To get a sense of the Chrome OS world, visualize a browser as your desktop and imagine that your digital world is limited to only those online applications, communications, and storage locations that the browser can access.

As cloud services become more extensive, Chrome OS becomes less and less limiting. Unlike iPads, Chromebooks support multiple users. They provide very limited local storage space, however. Google claims that Chrome OS is very secure, but consumers understand that the security is equivalent to that provided by a browser and by cloud storage services.

▶Who uses Chrome OS? Currently, Chrome OS powers inexpensive clamshell-style devices called Chromebooks that are popular in educational settings and for light business use. Chromebooks boot very quickly to a basic desktop where apps are displayed in the Chrome browser (Figure 6-23).

QuickCheck

Why is Chrome OS considered a thin client?

a. Because it doesn't have many applications

b. Because it includes a browser

c. Because it depends on programs that run on remote Web servers

d. Because it runs on laptop computers called Chromebooks

Figure 6-23: Elements of Chrome OS

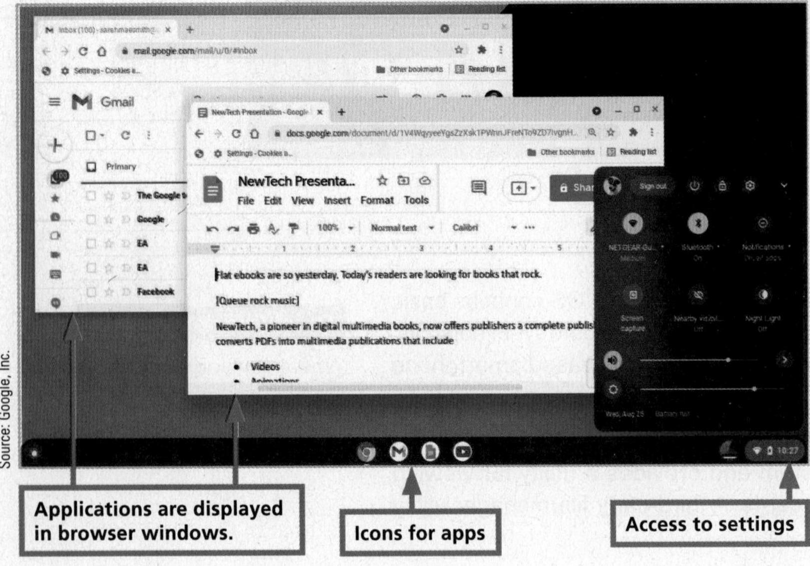

Source: Google, Inc.

Linux

When technology experts are in need of an operating system that is dependable, expandable, and versatile, they frequently turn to Linux. The Linux landscape offers a multitude of choices that might seem daunting to the uninitiated, but are prized by experts.

What is the origin of Linux? In 1991, a young Finnish student named Linus Torvalds developed the **Linux** (pronounced "LIH nucks") operating system. Linux was inspired by and loosely based on a UNIX derivative called MINIX, created by Andrew Tanenbaum. Linux is frequently used as an operating system for servers. It is not as popular for desktop applications as Windows or macOS.

What are the strengths of Linux? As an operating system, Linux is unique because it is distributed along with its source code under the terms of a GPL (General Public License), which allows everyone to make copies for their own use, to give to others, or to sell. This licensing policy has encouraged programmers to develop Linux utilities, software, and enhancements. Linux is primarily distributed over the Web.

One of the strongest aspects of Linux is the abundance of tools it provides for customization. Linux users can select from a long list of system utilities for file management, packaged to meet the needs of various businesses and industries. In addition to system utilities, Linux users can choose from a variety of desktops, each with its own set of icons and menus that create a unique user interface.

What are the weaknesses of Linux? Linux requires more tinkering than the Windows and macOS operating systems. The comparatively limited number of programs that run under Linux also discourages many nontechnical users. A collection of high-quality open source software is available for the Linux platform, but many of these applications are targeted toward business and technical users.

How do I get Linux? A **Linux distribution** (or "distro") is a download that contains the Linux kernel, system utilities, desktop user interface, applications, and an installation routine. Beginner-friendly Linux distributions include Arch, Fedora, Ubuntu, Debian, openSUSE, and Mint (Figure 6-24).

QuickCheck

The user interface for Linux is supplied as part of a(n) ________.

a. MINIX

b. device driver

c. kernel

d. distro

Figure 6-24: Linux Mint

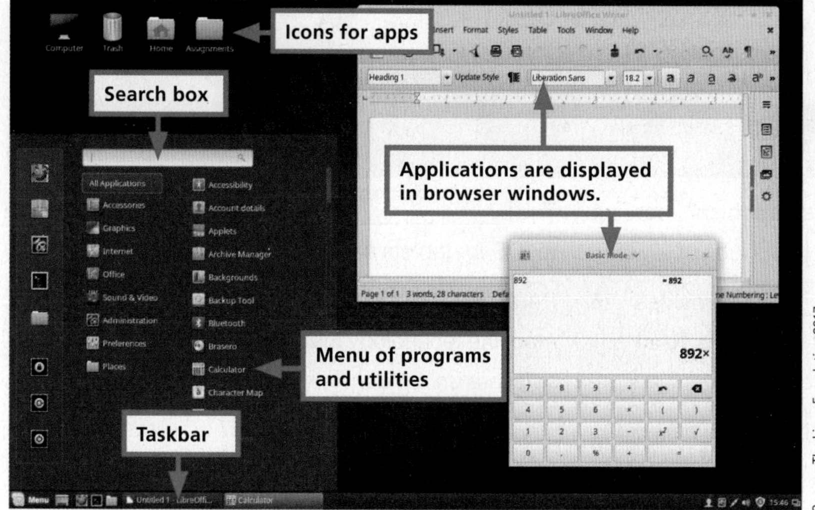

Source: The Linux Foundation 2017

Virtual Machines

We tend to think of an operating system as an immutable part of each digital device. PCs always run Windows, Macs always run macOS, and Samsung phones run Android. Is it possible to run Windows on a Mac and emulate an Android device on a desktop computer? Yes, it is possible using virtual machines.

Terminology

Virtual machine software is also called a *hypervisor*.

▶ **What is a virtual machine?** A **virtual machine** (VM) allows one computer to simulate the hardware and software of another. Each virtual machine has its own simulated processor, RAM, video card, input and output ports, and operating system. Each machine can run most software that's compatible with the virtual OS platform.

Popular virtual machine software such as VMware Fusion and Parallels Desktop create platforms where, for example, an iMac computer can run Windows. The iMac boots using its native macOS, but you can then launch a virtual machine that runs guest operating systems, such as Windows and Linux. The virtual machine's desktop appears in a window on the host desktop (Figure 6-25).

Figure 6-25: A virtual machine simulates one or more digital devices

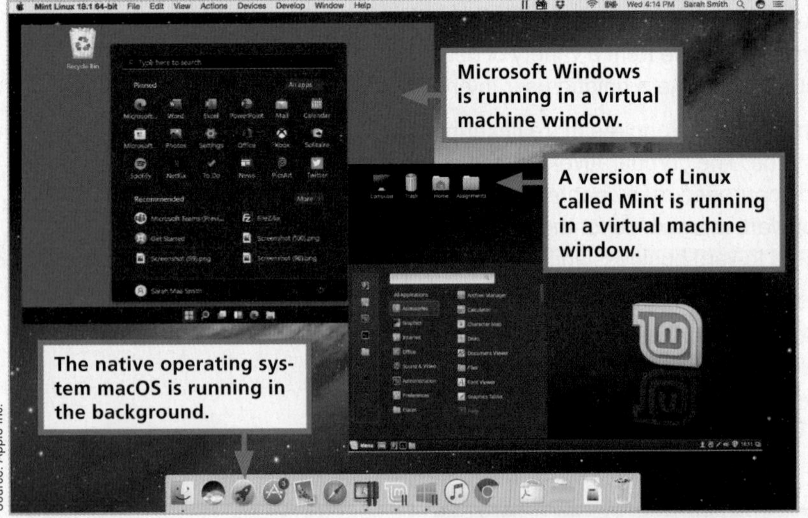

Microsoft Windows is running in a virtual machine window.
A version of Linux called Mint is running in a virtual machine window.
The native operating system macOS is running in the background.
Source: Apple Inc.

QuickCheck

_______ machine technology can be used to run two different operating systems on a single computer.

a. OS

b. Dedicated

c. Virtual

d. Windows

QuickQuiz

Section B

1. Microsoft Windows featured the first graphical user interface. True or false? [ ]

2. The operating system [ ] provides essential system programming and remains in RAM while the computer is on.

3. The operating system for iPads and iPhones is called [ ].

4. The [ ] operating system is an alternative to iOS for tablets and smartphones.

5. Parallels Desktop is an example of [ ] machine technology that can be used to run Windows software on a Mac.

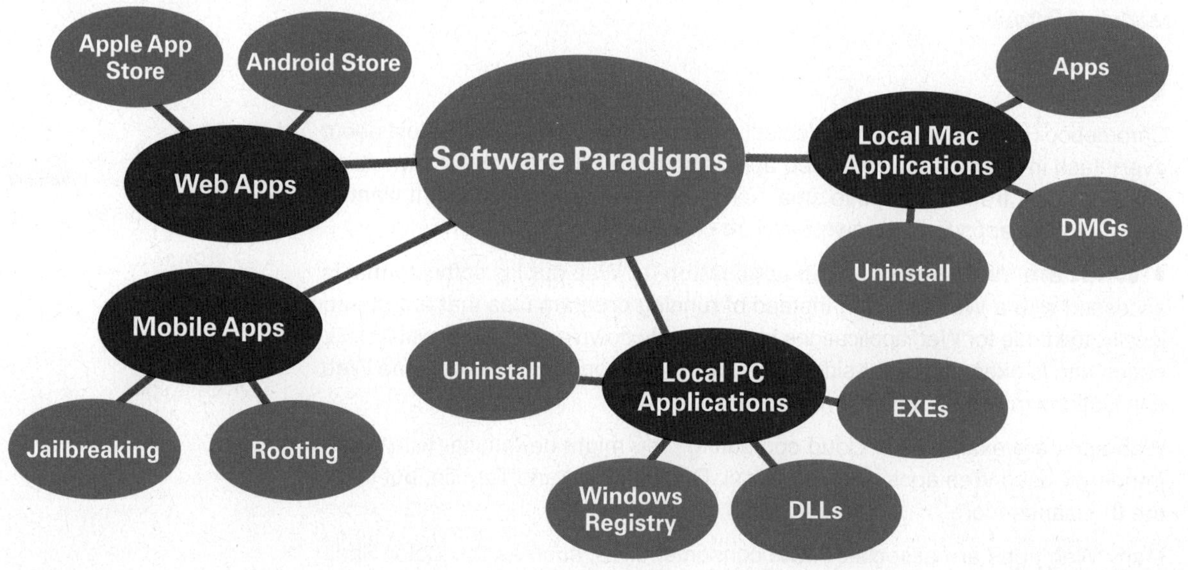

Section C Apps and Applications

Objectives

- Describe two ways in which Web apps differ from mobile apps.
- List four advantages and three disadvantages of Web apps.
- Describe the installation process for mobile apps.
- Explain why iPhone owners might want to jailbreak their devices.
- State whether the following file extensions are associated with PCs or Macs: .exe, .app, .dll, .dmg.
- List the seven activities that take place during the installation process for PC software.
- Describe the process for installing software on Macs.
- Summarize the different procedures necessary to uninstall software on PCs and Macs.

It is surprising how quickly you outgrow the standard set of apps that are preinstalled on your digital devices. When shopping for new apps and applications, you'll have your choice of software paradigms, which determine whether the software gets installed and takes up space on an internal storage device. Knowing the ins and outs of each paradigm will help you make the right software choices.

Terminology

Web application
mobile app
jailbreak
rooting
local application
application extensions
setup program
DMG
uninstall utility

Web Apps

Chromebook owners depend on Web apps for the software they use for just about every task in the digital world. Web apps also have advantages for owners of other devices, from desktops to smartwatches. Find out why you might want to seek out Web apps for your own software collection.

QuickCheck

Web apps require ____________.

a. a browser

b. a thin client OS

c. a mobile OS

d. installation

▶ **What are Web apps?** A **Web application** (or Web app) is software that is accessed with a Web browser. Instead of running program files that are stored locally, the code for Web applications is temporarily downloaded along with HTML pages and is executed client-side by the browser. Program code for some Web applications may also run on a remote server.

Web apps are examples of cloud computing. You might be familiar with some frequently used Web apps, such as Gmail, Google Docs, and Turnitin, but there are thousands more.

Many Web apps are associated with consumer sites, such as the Color Snap visualizer at the Sherwin-Williams Web site that uses a photo of your house to help you select paint colors. Other Web apps, such as the XE Currency Converter, have dedicated sites.

▶ **Do I have to install Web apps?** Most Web apps require no installation at all on your local computer or handheld device. Your device must, however, have a Web browser and an Internet connection.

To access a Web app, go to its Web site. You might have to register before your first use, and then log in using your registered user name and password for subsequent visits. Your browser will remain open while the app is in use (Figure 6-26).

Figure 6-26: Web apps run in a browser

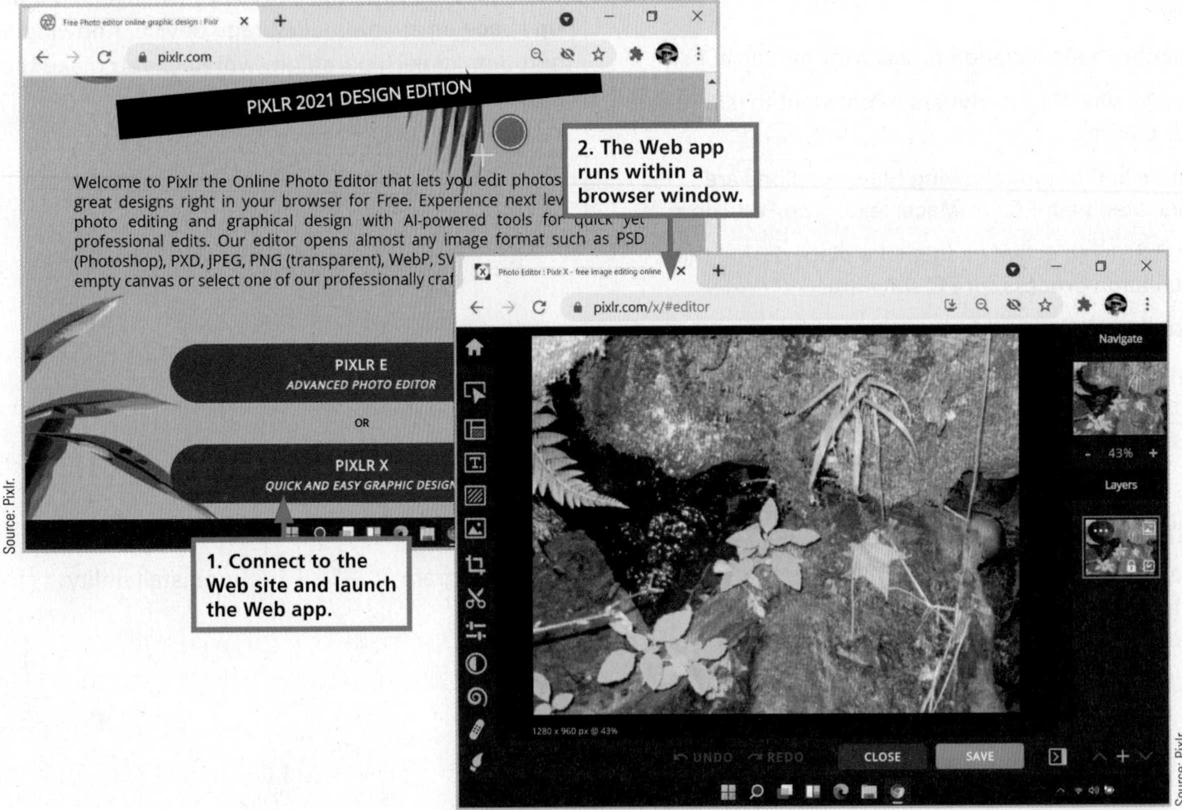

6

Who uses Web apps? Just about everyone. Web apps are particularly suited for consumer-level activities, such as basic word processing, spreadsheet creation, photo editing, audio recording, video editing, presentation design, and personal finance management. Although they may not yet provide features required by professionals, the sophistication of Web apps continues to increase.

As an extra bonus, many Web apps allow several people to collaborate on projects because the project files are stored on the Web and can be easily shared (Figure 6-27).

Figure 6-27: Web apps facilitate collaboration

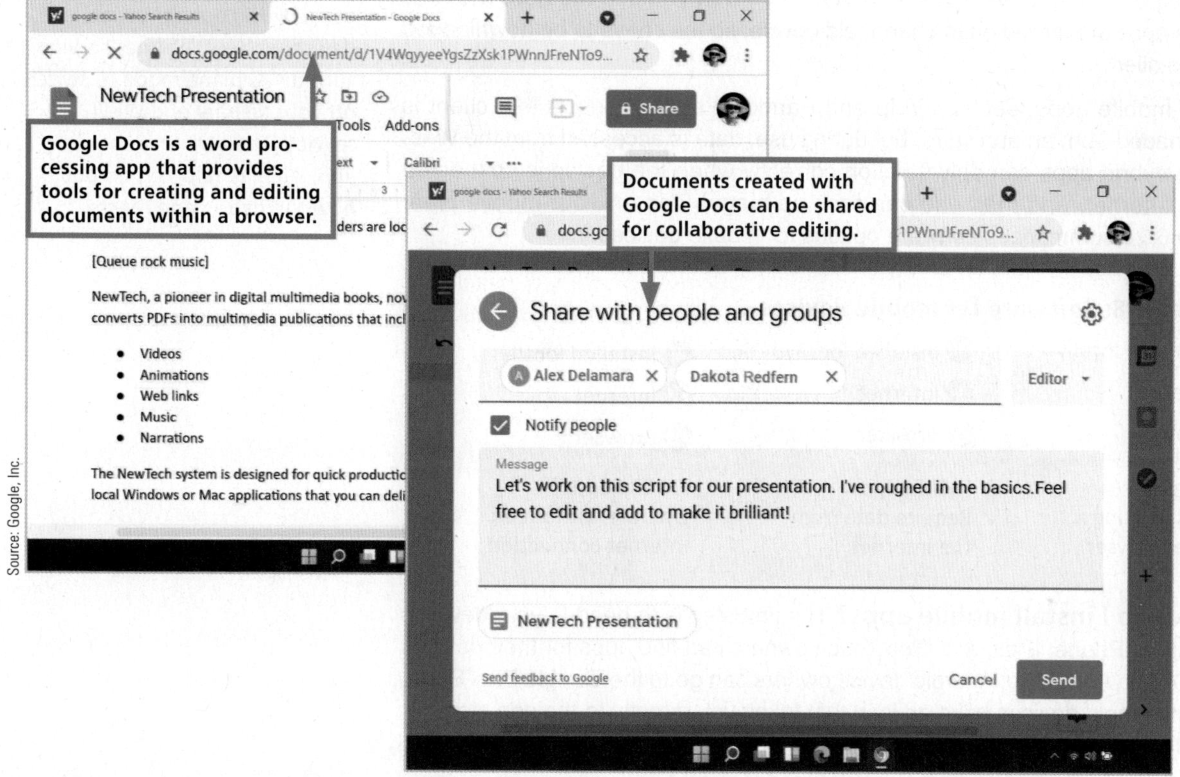

Source: Google, Inc.

What are the advantages and disadvantages of Web apps? Web apps are truly handy, but consider their advantages and disadvantages before entrusting them with your work:

- (+) You can access Web apps from any device that has a browser and an Internet connection, including full-size computers, smartphones, tablet computers, and enhanced media players.
- (+) Your data is usually stored on the app's Web site, so you can access data even when you are away from your main computer.
- (+) Web apps are always up to date; you don't have to install updates because the latest version is the one posted at the Web site where you access the app.
- (+) Web apps don't require local storage space, so you don't have to worry about them accumulating on your hard disk or SSD.

- (−) Web apps tend to have fewer features than applications that require installation.
- (−) If the site hosting the app shuts down, you will not be able to access the application or your data.
- (−) Your data might be more vulnerable to exposure or loss because it is out of your control. If possible, back up data to a local device or to an auxiliary cloud storage site.

Mobile Apps

Although just about every mobile device includes a browser, the current trend is not to use Web apps on mobile devices. Following Apple's lead, most mobile developers offer apps that are installed locally on a smartphone or tablet.

▸ What are mobile apps? A **mobile app** is designed for a handheld device, such as a smartphone, tablet computer, or enhanced media player. They are generally small, focused applications sold through an online app store.

▸ How do mobile apps differ from Web apps? Most handheld devices can use both Web apps and mobile apps. The difference between the two is that the program code for Web apps arrives only when you use the app, whereas mobile apps are stored on the handheld device, so they have to be downloaded and installed.

Some mobile apps, such as Yelp and Pandora, are hybrids. A thin client is downloaded from an app store, but during use, data is accessed from the Web. These hybrid apps can only function correctly when the device is connected to the Internet, and their use can rack up megabytes on your mobile plan. Figure 6-28 summarizes software options for mobile devices.

Try It!

What happens when you try to use a hybrid app on a mobile device without Internet service? Turn on Airplane mode to switch off your cellular and Wi-Fi service. Then try to launch an app, such as Yelp, to find out how the hybrid app reacts.

Figure 6-28: Software for mobile devices

Web apps	Hybrid apps	Mobile apps
⊗ Installed locally	⊕ Installed locally	⊕ Installed locally
⊕ Internet	⊕ Internet	⊗ Internet
⊕ Browser	⊗ Browser	⊗ Browser
Accessed using a mobile browser	Require data from the Internet	Operate without an Internet connection

▸ How do I install mobile apps? The first step is to head to your device's app store. iPhone, iPad, and iPod Touch owners can find apps for their devices at the Apple App Store; Android device owners can go to the Google Play Store. Most handheld devices have an icon that takes you directly to the app store for your device's platform.

At the app store, select an app and pay for it, if necessary. Touching the Download button retrieves the file and installs it automatically. The installation process places the app's program file on the storage device and creates an icon that you can use to launch the app.

QuickCheck

Apps such as Yelp and Pandora are hybrids that use a _______ and Web-based data.

a. browser

b. thin client

c. mobile OS

d. smartphone

▸ What is jailbreaking? iPads, iPhones, and iPods are only allowed to download apps from the official Apple App Store. Apps are available from other sources, but using them requires an unauthorized change called a **jailbreak** to the device's software. After downloading and installing the jailbreak software, your device will be able to install apps from a variety of sources other than the Apple App Store. The jailbreak lasts until you accept a software update from Apple. Updates wipe out the jailbreak software, forcing you to reinstall it.

▸ Can I jailbreak an Android device? Android phones are not limited to a single app store, so there is no need to jailbreak them to access more apps. There are various ways to make unauthorized modifications to any mobile device to overcome limitations imposed by mobile service providers. The process is called **rooting**, but most consumers have no need to root their mobile devices.

Local Applications

A **local application** is installed on a computer's hard disk. When it runs, the program code is copied into RAM, where it can be accessed by the microprocessor. Office suites, games, and professional software tools are common examples of local applications for desktop and laptop computers. Local applications do not require an Internet connection to run.

QuickCheck

The file used to launch an application on a PC has a(n) ________ extension.

a. .exe

b. .app

c. .dll

d. .html

6

▶ What's included in a typical software package? Software for Macs is usually stored in a single executable file with an .app extension. That file, however, is actually a package that contains other files and folders. The contents of an application's package can be viewed by right-clicking the .app file and selecting Show Package Contents.

Software designed for computers that run Microsoft Windows is commonly composed of multiple files. The main executable file has an .exe extension—for example, *Inkscape.exe*. Additional files required for Windows application software contain support modules called **application extensions** with file names that end in .dll, as shown in Figure 6-29.

Figure 6-29: PC software can be composed of many files

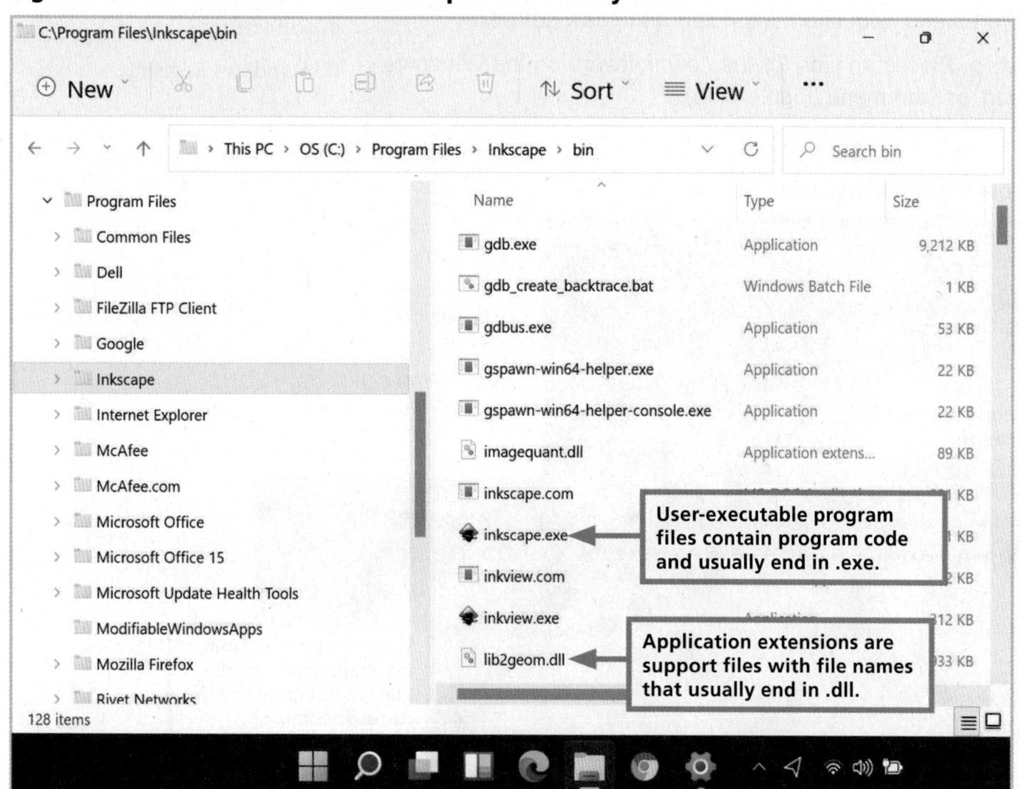

What is the process for installing software on PCs? Software for PCs contains a **setup program** that guides you through the installation process. The setup program simplifies installation because it handles a variety of behind-the-scenes technical details. During the installation process, the setup program usually performs the following activities:

- **Copy files.** Copies application files from distribution media (CDs or DVDs) or downloads files to specified folders on the hard disk or SSD.
- **Unzip files.** Reconstitutes files that have been distributed in compressed format.
- **Check resources.** Analyzes the computer's resources, such as processor speed, RAM capacity, and hard disk capacity, to verify that they meet or exceed the minimum system requirements.
- **Select device drivers.** Analyzes hardware components and peripheral devices to select appropriate device drivers.
- **Find players.** Looks for any system files and players, such as Microsoft Edge or Windows Media Player, that are required to run the program but are not supplied on the distribution media or download.
- **Update the Registry.** Updates necessary system files, such as the Windows Registry and the Start menu, with information about the new software.
- **Update the desktop.** Places an icon for the new software on the Windows desktop, Start screen, or Start menu (Figure 6-30).

Terminology

The *Windows Registry* is a database that keeps track of a PC's peripheral devices, software, preferences, and settings. When you install software on a computer running the Windows operating system, information about the software is recorded in the Registry.

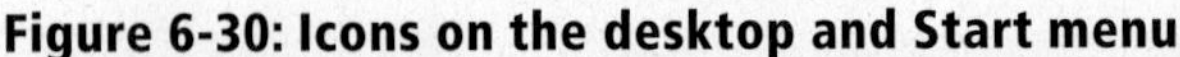

QuickCheck

When an application is installed on a PC, the application's name is added to the ____________.

a. EXE file

b. operating system

c. ZIP file

d. Windows Registry

Figure 6-30: Icons on the desktop and Start menu

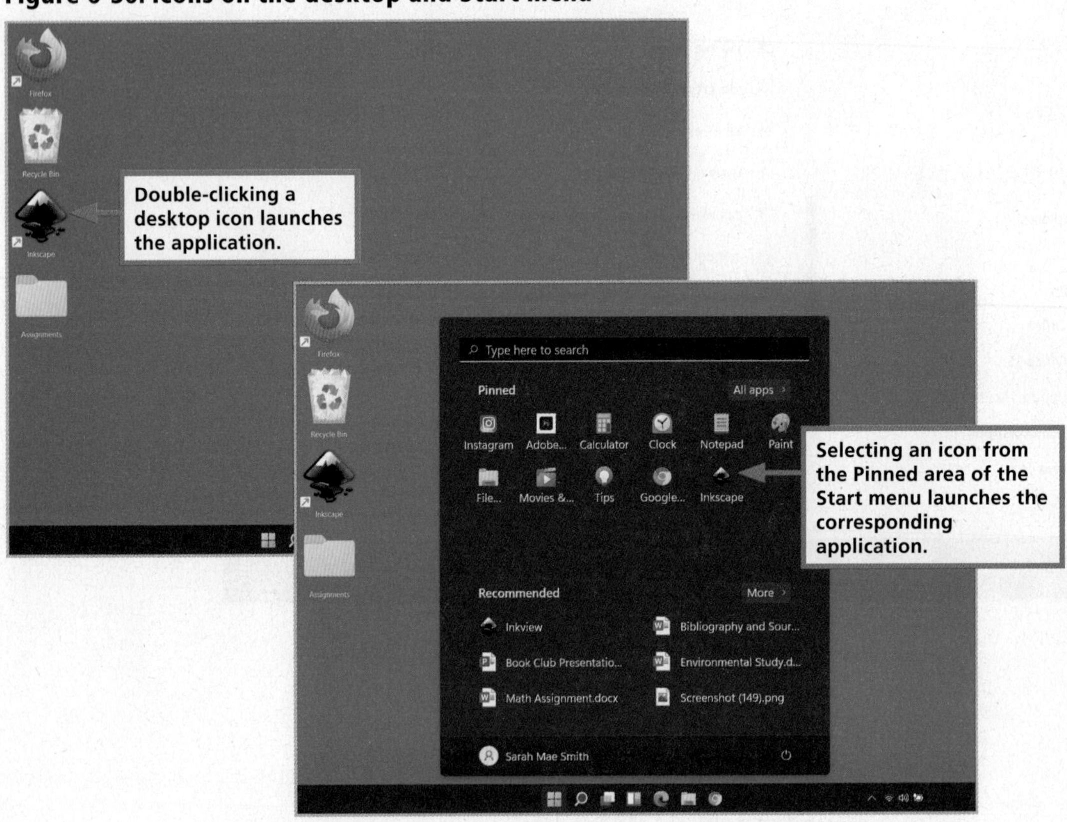

How do I download and install software on a PC? The EXE and DLL files for Windows application software are zipped to consolidate them into one large file, which is compressed to decrease its size and reduce the download time. As part of the installation process, this downloaded file must be reconstituted, or unzipped, into the original collection of files.

Downloaded files are generally stored in the Downloads folder. You can back up this folder periodically. If your computer's hard drive malfunctions, you can use these files to rebuild your software collection without having to download all of it again. Figure 6-31 maps out the process of downloading and installing local apps on a PC.

Try It!

If you are using a PC, open File Explorer by clicking the folder icon on the taskbar, then search for *.exe*. Can you identify the software applications that these EXE files launch?

6

Figure 6-31: Download and install software on a PC

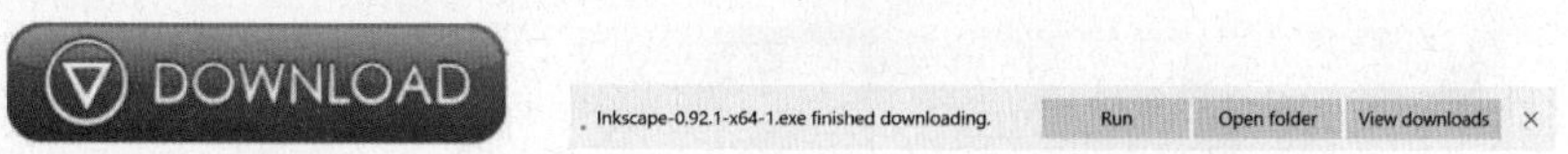

1. At the distribution Web site, read the installation instructions, then select the Download link.

2. If you are downloading from a trusted site and have antivirus software running, select the Run button.

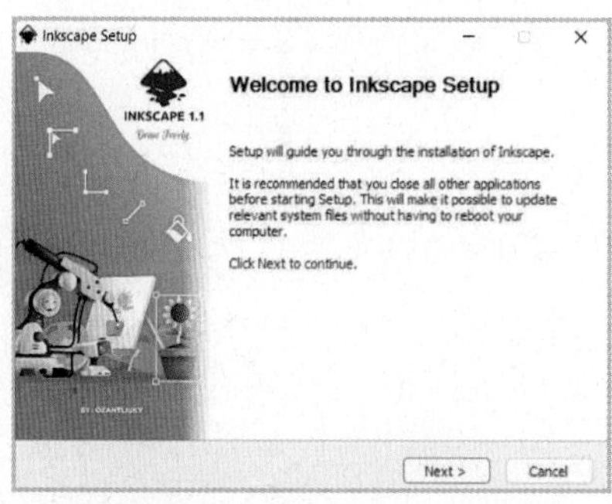

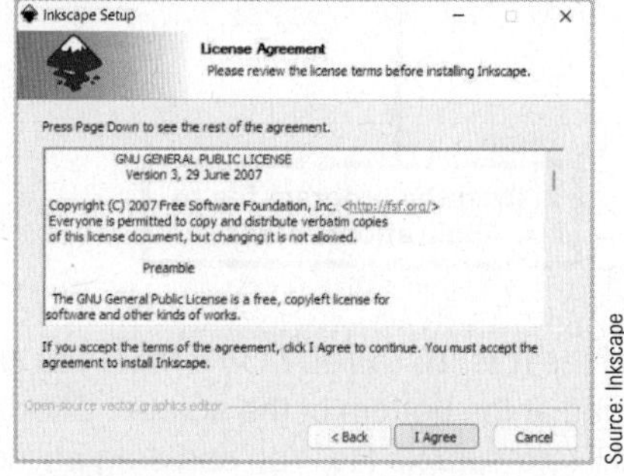

Source: Inkscape

3. Wait for the download to finish. The setup program included in the download starts automatically.

4. Read the license agreement and accept its terms to continue with the installation.

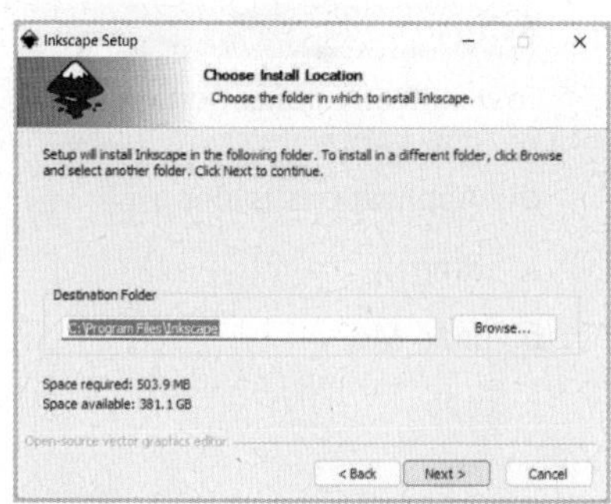

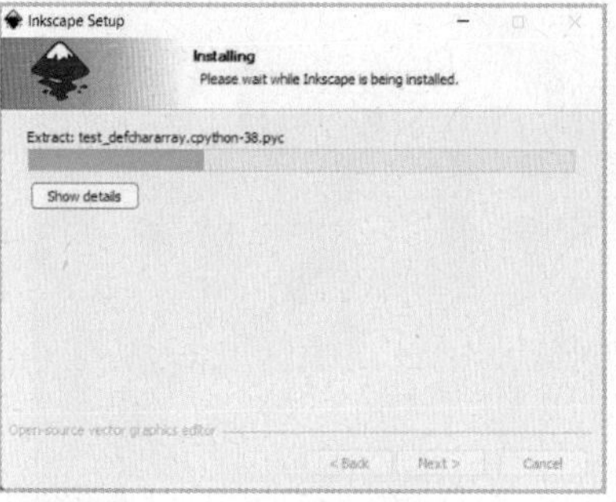

5. Select a folder to hold the new application. You can use the default folder specified by the setup program or a folder of your own choosing. You can also create a new folder during the setup process.

6. Wait for the setup program to uncompress the downloaded file and install the software in the selected directory. When the installation is complete, launch the software to make sure it works.

QuickCheck

When downloading software, why should you select Run only at trusted sites?

a. Because the download doesn't have to check for viruses

b. Because the setup program is going to run automatically; if it contains a virus, it could be transmitted

c. Because if you select Save, you might forget where the program is stored

d. Because the download is then transmitted over an HTTPS connection

How do I install software on a Mac? Mac software is straightforward to install. Downloads are ordinarily supplied as a **DMG** package commonly referred to as a "disk image." The DMG package has a .dmg extension. It contains the main APP file for the software, and it may also contain a Read Me file or other data files used by the application. Once the download is complete, open the DMG file from the Downloads folder and then drag the APP file to your Applications folder, as shown in Figure 6-32.

Try It!

If you are using a Mac, open Finder and then open the Applications folder. Can you identify the .app files for your software applications? Can you find DMG packages in your downloads folders? Hint: To display file extensions, select Finder, Preferences, Advanced, and then Show file extensions.

Figure 6-32: Install Mac software

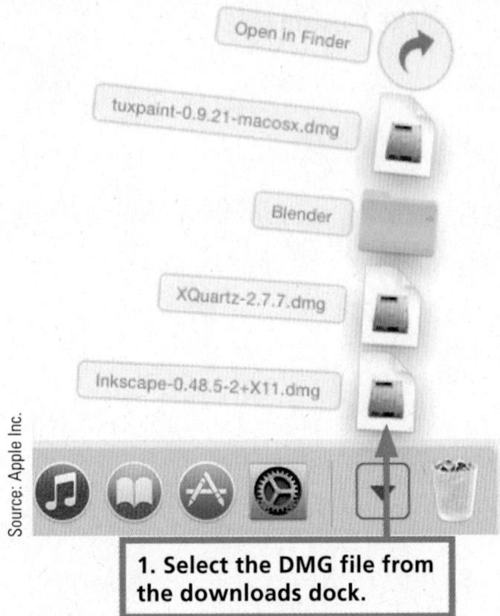

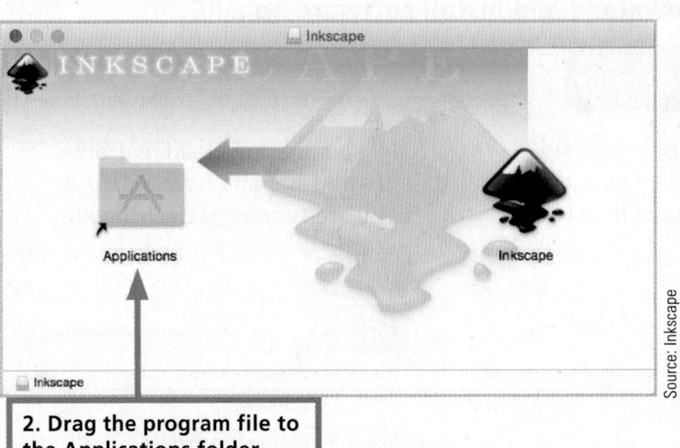

How do I access Mac software after it is installed? On a Mac, you can access most software from the Launchpad at the bottom of the screen. Clicking an icon tells the computer to start the APP executable file. You can drag an icon from the Launchpad to the Dock if you use it frequently (Figure 6-33).

Figure 6-33: Launch an application

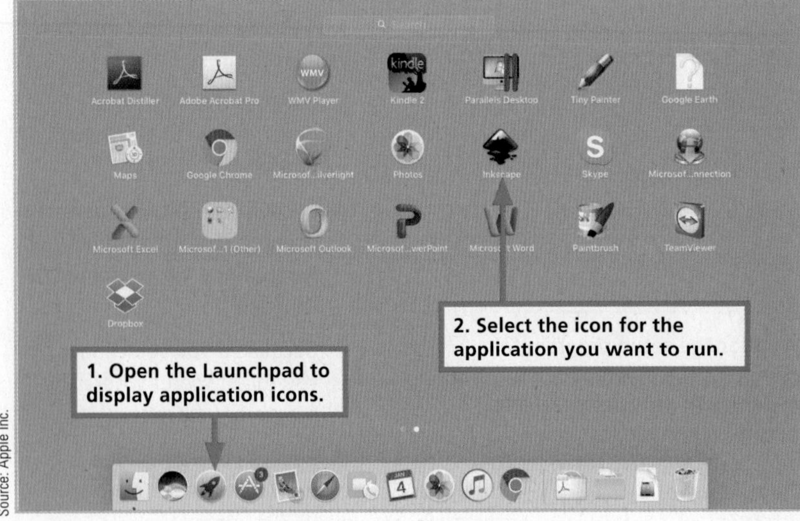

1. Open the Launchpad to display application icons.
2. Select the icon for the application you want to run.
Source: Apple Inc.

QuickCheck

To install an application on a Mac, drag the ________ file to the Applications folder.

a. .dmg

b. Read Me

c. .app

d. .exe

6

Uninstalling Software

When your smartphone or computer gets cluttered with unneeded demoware, unused applications, or outdated mobile apps, you can clean house.

How do I remove mobile apps? On an iPhone, press and hold the app icon until a menu appears, then select Remove App. On an Android device, go to Settings, and find the Applications Manager. Tap the program name, then select Uninstall.

How do I remove Mac software? Most Mac users simply use Finder to locate the program's APP file or folder and move it to the trash. Some Mac programs, such as those in the Adobe Creative Suite, include a more thorough uninstall routine, which is usually listed in the Utilities folder.

How do I get rid of PC software? Removing software from a PC is complicated by two factors. First, the process of installing software often sprinkles files into various folders, including the System folder, where they can be shared with other programs. Second, the Windows Registry must be updated when an application is removed.

Windows includes an **uninstall utility**, which deletes the software's files from various folders on your computer's hard disk. The uninstall routine helps you decide what to do with shared files that are used by more than one program. As a rule, you should leave the shared files in place. The uninstall utility provides access to the uninstall routine (Figure 6-34).

Figure 6-34: The uninstall utility removes software on a Windows PC

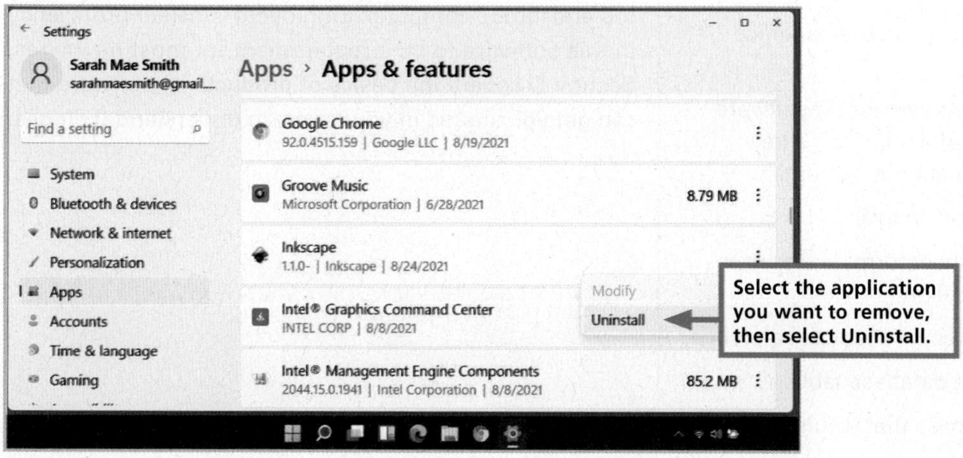

QuickQuiz — Section C

1. Most ________ applications require no installation and are accessed through a browser.
2. On a PC, a(n) ________ program guides you through the installation process.
3. Installing or removing a program from a computer running Windows requires an update to the Windows ________.
4. Software applications for Macs are usually distributed as files with ________ extensions.
5. To remove files from a PC, it is important to use the ________ utility to make sure the application's files are deleted from various folders where they were placed during installation.

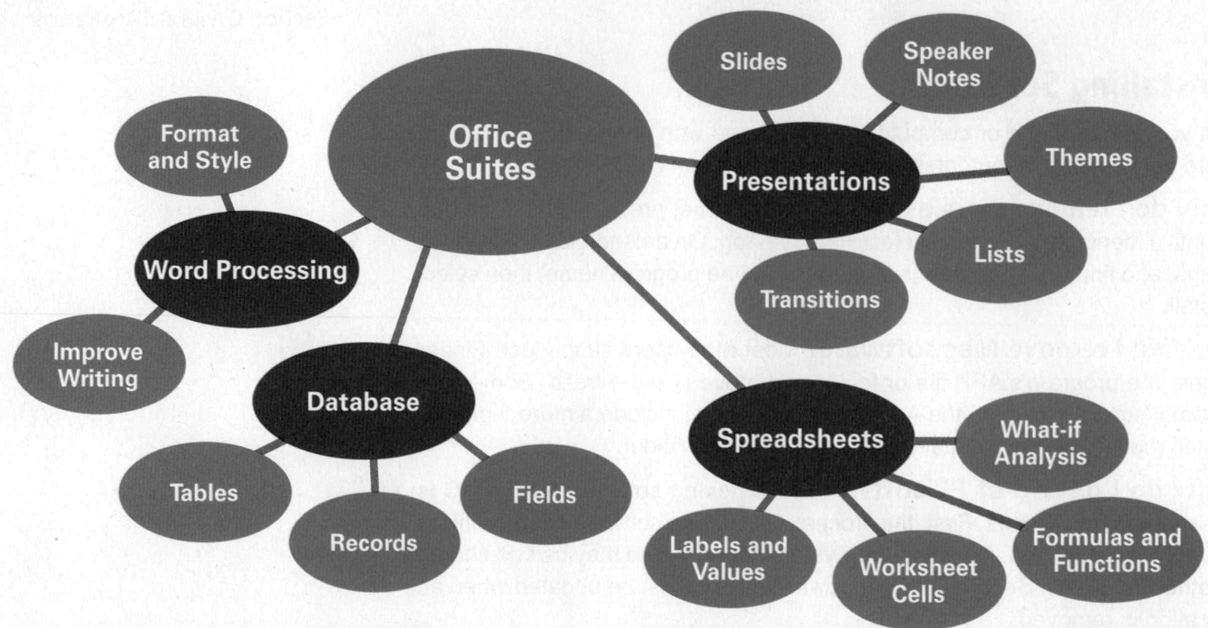

Section D Productivity Software

Objectives

- List three applications that are the core of an office suite.
- Describe three features of word processing software that help improve the quality of writing and three features that improve the format of documents.
- Provide an example of a what-if analysis.
- Give an example of a spreadsheet formula that uses mathematical operators and cell references.
- Describe a formula that requires an absolute reference.
- Identify fields and records in a database table.
- Provide an example of a database that would have two or more related tables.
- List five commonly used features of presentation software.

It's an essential set of applications for every desktop and laptop computer. Employers consider proficiency in this software to be a requirement for most new hires. Section D covers the basics of productivity software that can get you started in your quest to understand their use.

Terminology

productivity software
office suite
module
word processing software
word wrap
search and replace
thesaurus
grammar checker
readability formula
spelling checker
spelling dictionary
document formatting
page layout
header
footer
paragraph style
leading
paragraph alignment
fully justified
font
point size
style
spreadsheet
spreadsheet software
what-if analysis
worksheet
cell
value
label
formula
cell references
function
automatic recalculation
relative reference
absolute reference
database
database software
record
field
presentation software

Office Suite Basics

Office suites, such as Microsoft Office and Google Docs Editors, are popular with individuals and in business environments. They are sometimes referred to as **productivity software** because they offer features that really help get work done.

What is an office suite? An **office suite** is a collection of programs that typically include word processing, spreadsheet, and presentation modules. Suites may also include email and contact managers, calendars, and project management, database management, and drawing modules.

In the context of office suites, the term **module** refers to a component, such as a word processing module. Modules can be run as individual programs, but all of the modules in an office suite have a standard set of controls, enabling you to transfer your expertise on one module to the others.

What are the most popular office suites? Popular office suites include Google Docs Editors, iWork, LibreOffice, Microsoft Office, and Zoho Office Suite (Figure 6-35).

Figure 6-35: Office suites

Name	Modules	Platform
Google Docs Editors	Word processing, spreadsheet, presentation, drawing, forms	Online (Free)
iWork	Word processing, spreadsheet, presentation	macOS ($$)
LibreOffice	Word processing, spreadsheet, presentation, database, drawing	Windows, macOS, Linux (Free)
Microsoft Office	Word processing, spreadsheet, presentation, database, mail/calendar	Windows, macOS, Linux, iOS, Android ($$)
Zoho Office Suite	Word processing, spreadsheet, presentation, calendar, and more	Online (Free)

Word Processing

Whether you are writing a ten-page paper, generating software documentation, designing a brochure, or writing a dissertation, you will probably use the word processing module of an office suite.

▶ **How can software help me with my writing?** **Word processing software** replaced typewriters for producing many types of documents, including reports, letters, memos, papers, and book manuscripts. Word processing packages, such as Microsoft Word, iWork Pages, and LibreOffice Writer, give you the ability to create, spell-check, edit, and format a document on the screen before it is finalized.

A typical word processor window displays a work area, called a workspace, that represents a blank piece of paper. The window also includes controls for viewing and formatting the document (Figure 6-36).

Figure 6-36: Microsoft Word basics

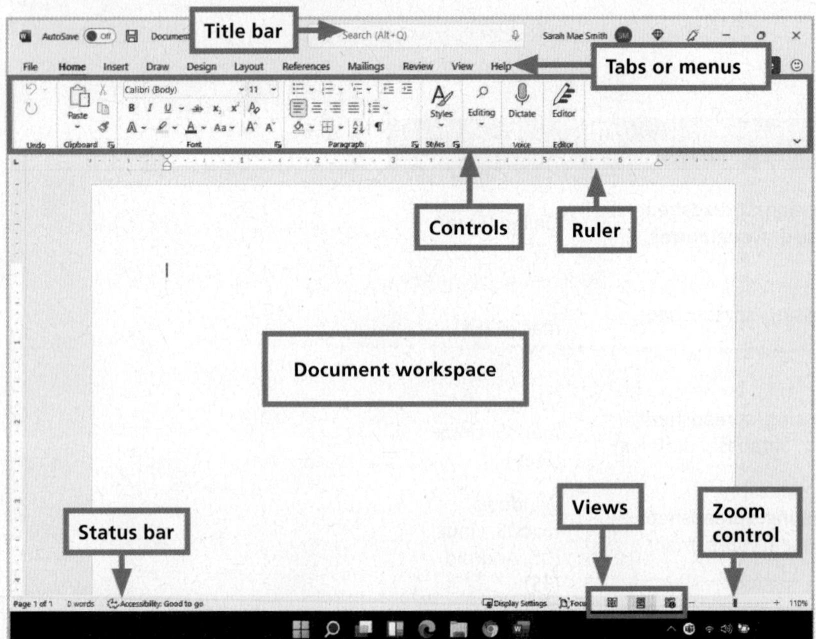

▶ **How does word processing software help me turn my ideas into sentences and paragraphs?** Word processing software facilitates the flow of ideas because it automatically handles many tasks that might otherwise be distractions. For example, you don't need to worry about fitting words within the margins. A feature called **word wrap** determines how your text flows from line to line by automatically moving words down to the next line as you reach the right margin.

Imagine that the sentences in your document are ribbons of text; word wrap bends the ribbons. Changing the margin size just means bending the ribbon in different places. Even after you type an entire document, adjusting the size of the right, left, top, and bottom margins is straightforward.

▶ **Can word processing software help me break bad writing habits?** You can use the **search and replace** feature to hunt down mistakes that you habitually make in your writing. For example, if you tend to overuse the word *typically,* you can use search and replace to find each occurrence of *typically* and then decide whether you should substitute a different word, such as *usually* or *ordinarily*.

QuickCheck

When using word processing software, it is not necessary to press Enter at the end of each line because ____________.

a. you might want to go back and make edits

b. word wrap automatically moves text to the next line

c. doing so activates search and replace

d. doing so would create double spacing

▸ Can word processing software improve my writing? Because word processing software is geared toward the writing process, it offers several features that can improve the quality of your writing.

Word processing software is likely to include a **thesaurus**, which can help you find a synonym for a word so that you can make your writing more varied and interesting. A **grammar checker** reads through your document and points out potential grammatical trouble spots, such as incomplete sentences, run-on sentences, and verbs that don't agree with nouns.

Your word processing software might also be able to analyze the reading level of your document using a standard **readability formula**, such as the Flesch-Kincaid reading level. You can use this analysis to find out if your writing level is appropriate for your target audience based on sentence length and vocabulary.

Most word processing software includes a **spelling checker** that marks misspelled words in a document. You can easily correct a misspelled word as you type, or you can run the spelling checker when you finish entering all the text. Some software even has autocorrecting capability; as you type, it automatically changes a typo (such as *teh*) to the correct spelling (*the*).

Although your software's spelling checker helps you correct misspellings, it cannot guarantee an error-free document. A spelling checker works by comparing each word from your document to a list of correctly spelled words stored in a data file called a **spelling dictionary**. If the word from your document is in the dictionary, the spelling checker considers the word correctly spelled. If the word is not in the dictionary, the word is counted as misspelled.

Spelling checkers can't tell if you misuse a word, such as if you use the phrase *pear of shoes* instead of *pair of shoes*. Also, spelling checkers flag many proper nouns and scientific, medical, and technical words because they are not included in the spelling checker's dictionary. Make sure you proofread, even after using a spelling checker (Figure 6-37).

Try It!

What is the reading level of a document that you've recently written? Use reading level analytics from your word processing software or use a Web app such as the Readability Test Tool.

6

QuickCheck

You can depend on your word processor's spelling checker to ______________.

a. flag words that are not in its dictionary

b. catch all your misspellings

c. identify words that you misuse

d. correct grammar errors

Figure 6-37: Check spelling and grammar

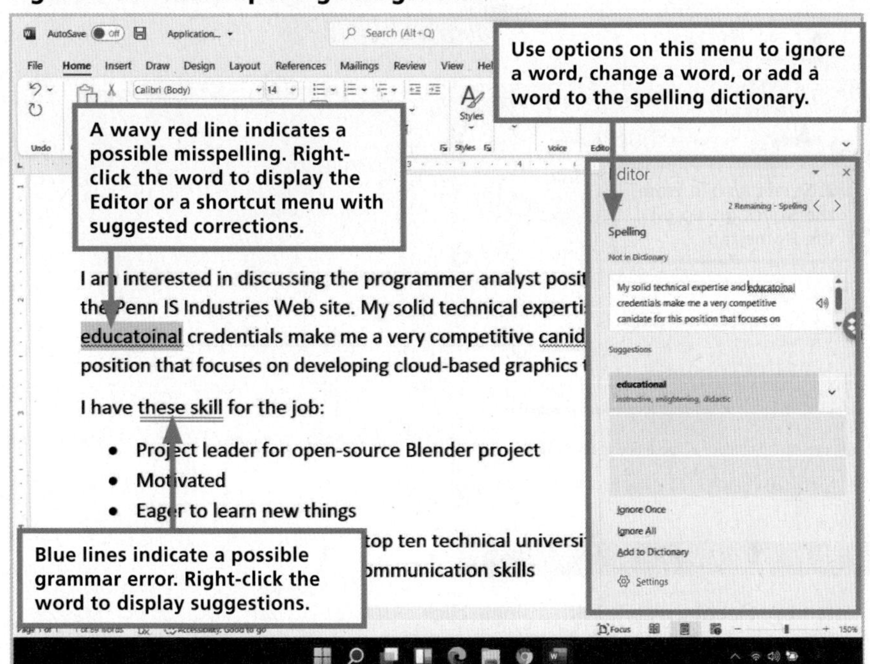

How do I get my documents to look good? The term **document formatting** refers to the way that all the elements of a document—text, pictures, titles, and page numbers—are arranged on the page.

The final format of a document depends on how and where you intend to use it. A school paper, for example, simply needs to be produced in standard paragraph format—perhaps double spaced and with numbered pages. A brochure, newsletter, or corporate report, on the other hand, might require more ambitious formatting, such as columns, headers, and graphics.

The look of your final document depends on several formatting factors, such as page layout, paragraph style, and font.

- **Layout and headers. Page layout** refers to the physical position of each element on a page. In addition to paragraphs of text, these elements might include margins, page numbers, **header** text that you specify to automatically appear in the top margin of every page, and **footer** text that you specify to automatically appear in the bottom margin of every page.
- **Styles and alignment. Paragraph style** includes the alignment of text within the margins and the space between each line of text. The vertical spacing between lines of text is called **leading** (pronounced "LED ding"). Most documents are single spaced or double spaced, but you can adjust line spacing in 1 pt. increments. **Paragraph alignment** refers to the horizontal position of text—whether it is aligned at the left margin, aligned at the right margin, or **fully justified** so that the text is aligned evenly on both the right and left margins.
- **Fonts.** A **font** is a set of letters that share a unified design. Font size is measured as **point size**, which is abbreviated as pt. One point is about 1/72 of an inch.

Instead of individually selecting font and paragraph style elements, word processing software allows you to select a **style** that lets you apply several font and paragraph characteristics with a single click (Figure 6-38).

QuickCheck

In the context of word processing, the term *leading* refers to ___________.

a. text that automatically appears at the top of each page

b. the feature that automatically moves text down when you reach the margin

c. the size of a font

d. the space between lines of text

Figure 6-38: Use styles for professional formatting

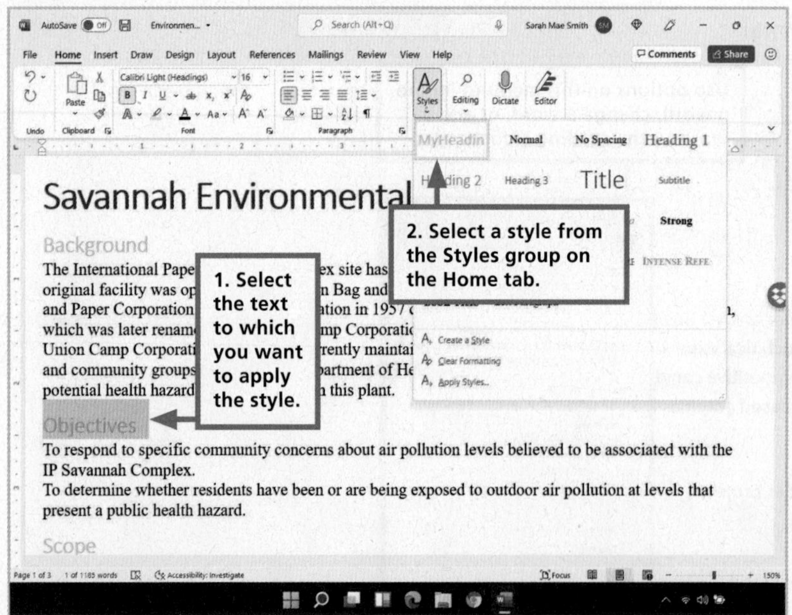

In this document, headings were formatted by selecting a style with a single click instead of individually selecting a font color, font size, and font style. Now if the heading style is changed to red, all the headings will automatically change color.

Spreadsheets

Spreadsheet software was initially popular with accountants who dealt with paper-based spreadsheets; they found the electronic version far easier to use and less prone to errors than manual calculations. Other people soon discovered the benefits of spreadsheets for projects that require repetitive calculations, such as budgeting, computing grades, tracking investments, calculating loan payments, and estimating project costs.

▶ What is a spreadsheet? A **spreadsheet** uses rows and columns of numbers to create a model or representation of a real situation. For example, your bank statement is a type of spreadsheet because it is a numerical representation of cash flowing into and out of your bank account.

▶ When do I need spreadsheet software? **Spreadsheet software**, such as Microsoft Excel, iWork Numbers, Google Sheets, and LibreOffice Calc, provides tools to create electronic spreadsheets. It is like a smart piece of paper that automatically adds up columns of numbers written on it.

Spreadsheet calculations are based on equations that you create or more complex built-in formulas. Spreadsheet software can turn data into colorful graphs. It also includes special data-handling features that sort data, search for data that meets specific criteria, and print reports.

Because you can experiment with different numbers, spreadsheet software is particularly useful for **what-if analysis**. You can use what-if analyses to answer questions such as "What if I get an A on my next two economics exams? But what if I get only Bs?" or "What if I invest $100 a month in my retirement plan? But what if I invest $200 a month?"

▶ What does a computerized spreadsheet look like? Spreadsheet software can be used to create an on-screen **worksheet**. A worksheet is based on a grid of columns and rows. Each **cell** in the grid can contain a value, label, or formula. A **value** is a number that you want to use in a calculation. A **label** is any text used to describe data (Figure 6-39).

QuickCheck

Is the worksheet in Figure 6-39 an example of a what-if analysis?

a. Yes

b. No

Figure 6-39: Microsoft Excel basics

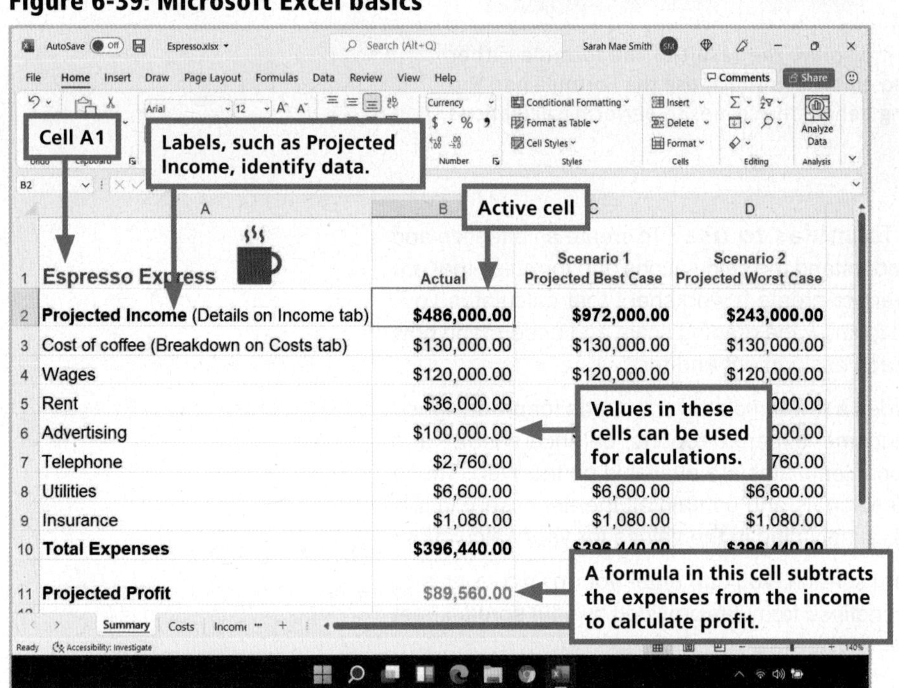

Are there formatting options? The labels and values on a worksheet can be formatted in much the same way as you would format text in a word processing document. You can change fonts and font size, select a font color, and select font styles, such as bold, italics, and underline.

How does spreadsheet software work? The values contained in a cell can be manipulated by formulas placed in other cells. A **formula** works behind the scenes to tell the microprocessor how to use the contents of cells in calculations. You can enter a formula into a cell to add, subtract, multiply, or divide numbers. More complex formulas can be designed to perform just about any calculation you can imagine. Figure 6-40 illustrates how a formula might be used in a spreadsheet to calculate savings.

Figure 6-40: How spreadsheet formulas work behind the scenes

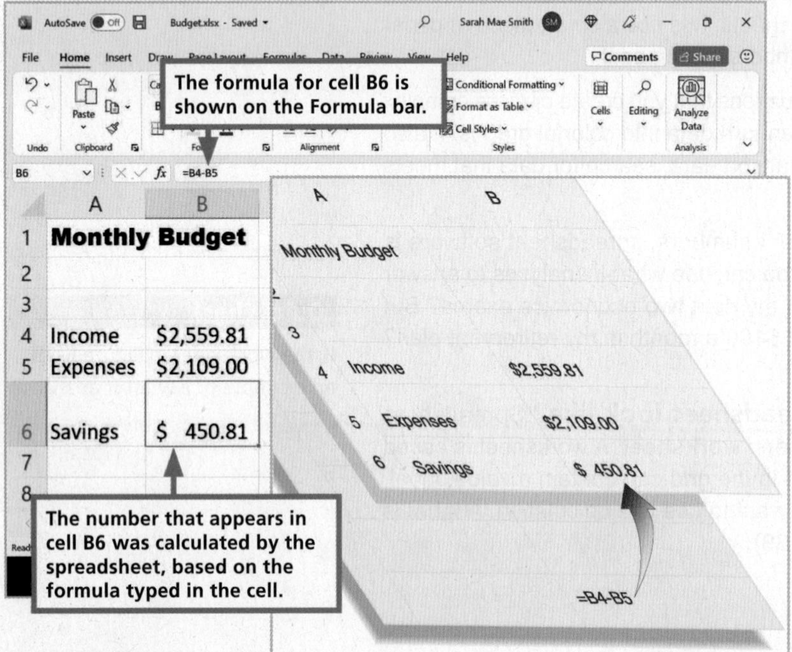

When a cell contains a formula, it displays the result of the formula rather than the formula itself. To view and edit the formula, use the Formula bar. You can think of the formula as working behind the scenes to perform calculations and then display the result.

QuickCheck

Where is the formula in Figure 6-40?

a. In cell A1
b. In cell A4
c. In cell B4
d. In cell B6

How will I know which formulas to use? To create an effective and accurate worksheet, you must understand the calculations and formulas that are involved. If, for example, you want to create a worksheet that calculates your final grade in a course, you need to know the grading scale and understand how your instructor plans to weight each assignment and test.

Most spreadsheet software includes a few templates or wizards for predesigned worksheets, such as invoices, income–expense reports, balance sheets, and loan payment schedules. Additional templates are available on the Web. These templates are designed by professionals and contain all the necessary labels and formulas. To use a template, simply plug in the values for your calculation.

When creating spreadsheets from scratch, you can enter your own formulas or you can select from a series of predefined formulas provided by your spreadsheet software.

What is the format for formulas? A formula, such as =A6-(B6*2), can contain **cell references** (such as A6 and B6), numbers (such as 2), and mathematical operators (such as the multiplication symbol [*], the division symbol [/], the addition symbol, and the subtraction symbol). Parts of a formula can be enclosed in parentheses to indicate the order in which the mathematical operations should be performed. The operation enclosed in parentheses—in this case, (B6*2)—should be performed first.

You can type the entire formula, or you can use pointer math, which adds cell references to the formula as you point to them. Figure 6-41 illustrates how to enter a formula into a cell.

6

Figure 6-41: Entering a formula

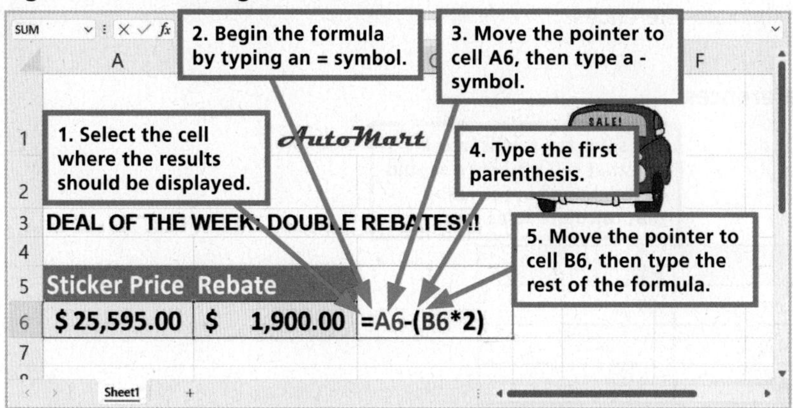

What is the process for entering functions? Spreadsheet software provides functions that are set up to perform common calculations, such as averages, loan payments, and comparisons. A **function** is a built-in preset formula. To use a function, select one from a list, as shown in Figure 6-42, and then indicate the cell references of any values you want to include in the calculation.

QuickCheck

In Figure 6-42, what information is entered for the Rate?

a. 5

b. The interest rate divided by number of annual payments

c. The Nper

d. PMT

Figure 6-42: Using built-in functions

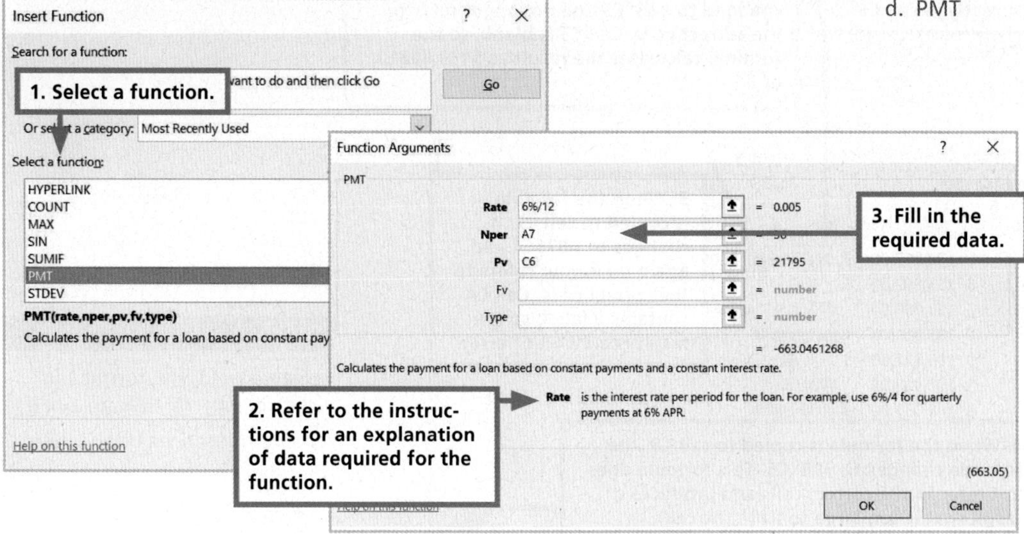

▸ What happens when I modify a worksheet? When you change the contents of any cell in a worksheet, all the formulas are recalculated. This **automatic recalculation** feature ensures that the results in every cell are accurate for the information currently entered in the worksheet.

Your worksheet is also automatically updated to reflect any rows or columns that you add, delete, or copy within the worksheet. Unless you specify otherwise, a cell reference is a **relative reference**—that is, a reference that can change from B4 to B3, for example, if row 3 is deleted and all the data moves up one row.

If you don't want a cell reference to change, you can use an absolute reference. An **absolute reference** never changes when you insert rows or copy or move formulas. Understanding when to use absolute references is one of the key aspects of developing spreadsheet design expertise. Figure 6-43 provides additional information about relative and absolute references.

Figure 6-43: Absolute and relative references

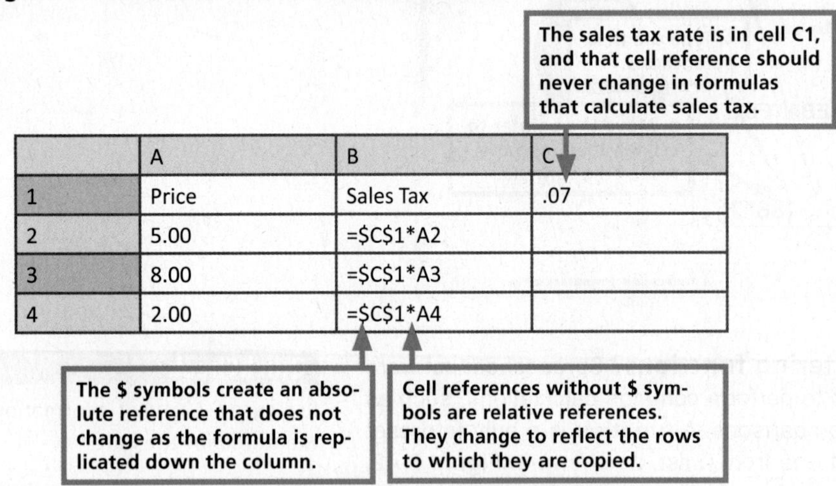

	A	B	C
1	Price	Sales Tax	.07
2	5.00	=$C$1*A2	
3	8.00	=$C$1*A3	
4	2.00	=$C$1*A4	

The sales tax rate is in cell C1, and that cell reference should never change in formulas that calculate sales tax.
The $ symbols create an absolute reference that does not change as the formula is replicated down the column.
Cell references without $ symbols are relative references. They change to reflect the rows to which they are copied.

What happens when a formula is not set up with the correct absolute references, and it is then copied or moved?

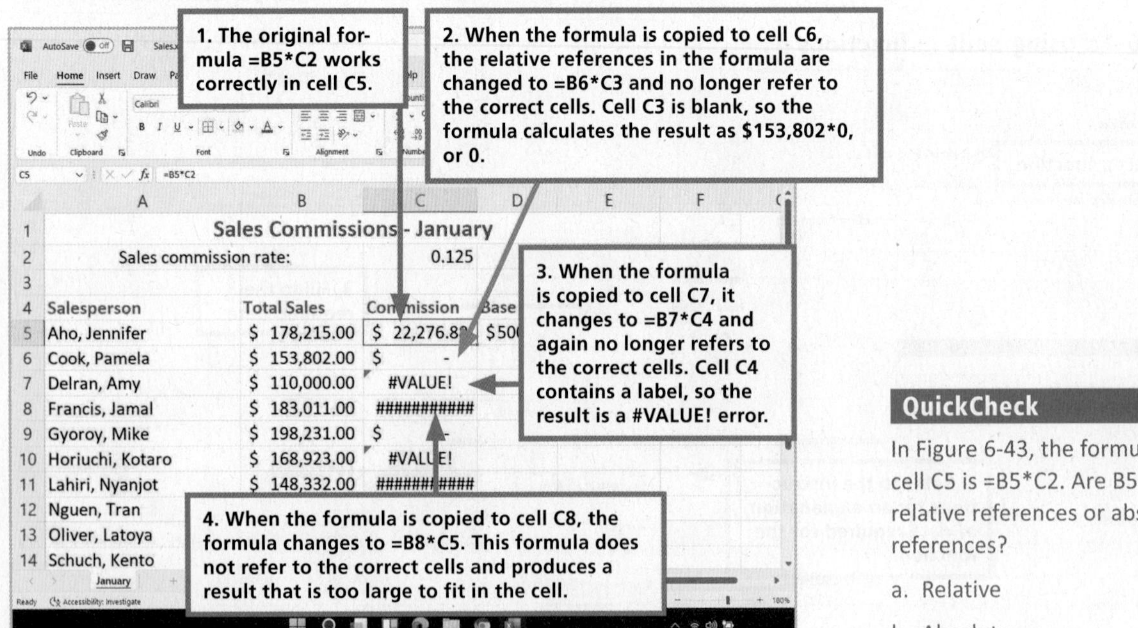

1. The original formula =B5*C2 works correctly in cell C5.
2. When the formula is copied to cell C6, the relative references in the formula are changed to =B6*C3 and no longer refer to the correct cells. Cell C3 is blank, so the formula calculates the result as $153,802*0, or 0.
3. When the formula is copied to cell C7, it changes to =B7*C4 and again no longer refers to the correct cells. Cell C4 contains a label, so the result is a #VALUE! error.
4. When the formula is copied to cell C8, the formula changes to =B8*C5. This formula does not refer to the correct cells and produces a result that is too large to fit in the cell.
Sales Commissions - January
Sales commission rate:
0.125
Salesperson
Total Sales
Commission
Aho, Jennifer
$ 178,215.00
$ 22,276.88
Cook, Pamela
$ 153,802.00
Delran, Amy
$ 110,000.00
#VALUE!
Francis, Jamal
$ 183,011.00
###########
Gyoroy, Mike
$ 198,231.00
Horiuchi, Kotaro
$ 168,923.00
#VALUE!
Lahiri, Nyanjot
$ 148,332.00
###########
Nguen, Tran
Oliver, Latoya
Schuch, Kento
January

QuickCheck

In Figure 6-43, the formula in cell C5 is =B5*C2. Are B5 and C2 relative references or absolute references?

a. Relative

b. Absolute

6

Databases

A database can contain any sort of data, such as a university's student records, a library's card catalog, a store's inventory, an individual's address book, or a utility company's customers. Databases can be stored on personal computers, network servers, Web servers, mainframes, and even mobile devices.

What is a database? The term *database* has evolved from a specialized technical term into a part of our everyday vocabulary. In the context of modern usage, a **database** is simply a collection of data that may be stored on one or more digital devices.

What is database software? **Database software** provides tools for entering, finding, organizing, updating, and reporting information stored in a database. Microsoft Access, Claris FileMaker, and LibreOffice Base are three examples of popular database software for personal computers. Oracle and MySQL are popular server database software packages.

How does a database store data? Database software stores data as a series of records, which are composed of fields that hold data. A **record** holds data for a single entity—a person, place, thing, or event. A **field** holds one item of data relevant to a record. You can envision a record as a Rolodex card or an index card. A series of records is often presented as a table arranged in rows and columns (Figure 6-44).

QuickCheck

In Figure 6-44, how many fields are in the database table?

a. 5

b. 7

c. 9

d. 11

Figure 6-44: Database elements

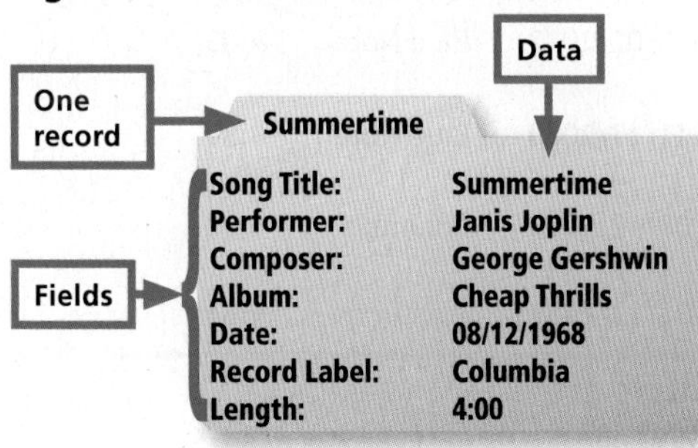

A single database record is similar to a Rolodex card or an index card. A series of records is usually depicted in table format.

A series of records in table format

Song Title	Performer	Composer	Album	Date	Label	Length
Take It Back	Norah Jones	Jones	Little Broken Hearts	05/01/2012	Blue Note	4:05
Even Though	Norah Jones	Jones and Harris	The Fall	11/17/2009	Blue Note	3:52
Summertime	Janis Joplin	Gershwin	Cheap Thrills	08/12/1968	Columbia	4:00
Summertime	Sarah Vaughan	Gershwin	Compact Jazz	06/22/1987	PolyGram	4:34

▶ Can a database hold different kinds of records? Some database software provides tools to work with more than one collection of records, as long as the records are somehow related to each other. For example, suppose MTV maintains a database pertaining to classic jazz music. One series of database records might contain data about jazz songs. It could contain fields such as song title, performer, and length.

Another series of records might contain biographical data about jazz performers, including the performer's name, birth date, and hometown. It might even include a field for the performer's photo. These two sets of records can be related by the name of the performing artist, as shown in Figure 6-45.

QuickCheck

Figure 6-45 shows a table of jazz performers and a table of jazz songs. How many databases do these tables represent?

a. 1

b. 2

c. 4

d. 8

Figure 6-45: Database records can be related based on common fields

Jazz Performers

Performer	Birth Date	Hometown
Ella Fitzgerald	04/25/1917	Newport News, VA
Norah Jones	03/30/1979	New York, NY
Billie Holiday	04/07/1915	Baltimore, MD
Lena Horne	06/30/1917	Brooklyn, NY

These two records are related by the Performer field. The relationship allows you to select Norah Jones from the Jazz Performers table and locate two of her songs in the Jazz Songs table.

Jazz Songs

Song Title	Performer	Composer	Album	Date	Label	Length
Take It Back	Norah Jones	Jones	Little Broken Hearts	05/01/2012	Blue Note	4:05
Even Though	Norah Jones	Jones and Harris	The Fall	11/17/2009	Blue Note	3:52
Summertime	Janis Joplin	Gershwin	Cheap Thrills	08/12/1968	Columbia	4:00
Summertime	Sarah Vaughan	Gershwin	Compact Jazz	06/22/1987	PolyGram	4:34

▶ How do I create a database? Database software provides tools for defining fields and entering records. Figure 6-46 shows a table you might use to specify the fields for a database.

Figure 6-46: Microsoft Access elements

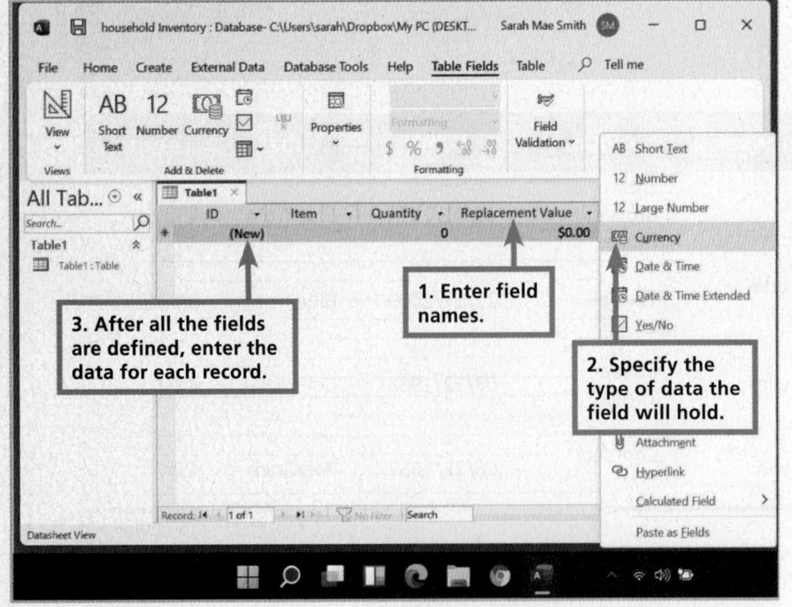

QuickCheck

How many fields are shown in Figure 6-46?

a. 0

b. 1

c. 4

d. 8

Presentations

Presentation software supplies the tools for combining text, photos, clip art, graphs, animations, and sound into a series of electronic slides that can be shown on a screen or projector (Figure 6-47).

Popular presentation software products include Microsoft PowerPoint, iWork Keynote, LibreOffice Impress, and Google Slides.

What are the best features of presentation software? Presentation software highlights include:

- Bulleted lists to summarize the points in your presentation
- Graphics to make your presentation visually interesting
- Transitions between slides to keep your audience's attention
- Speaker notes to help you remember what to say
- Themes and templates to give your slides a professional appearance
- Conversion routines to package presentations as PDF files and YouTube videos

Figure 6-47: Microsoft PowerPoint basics

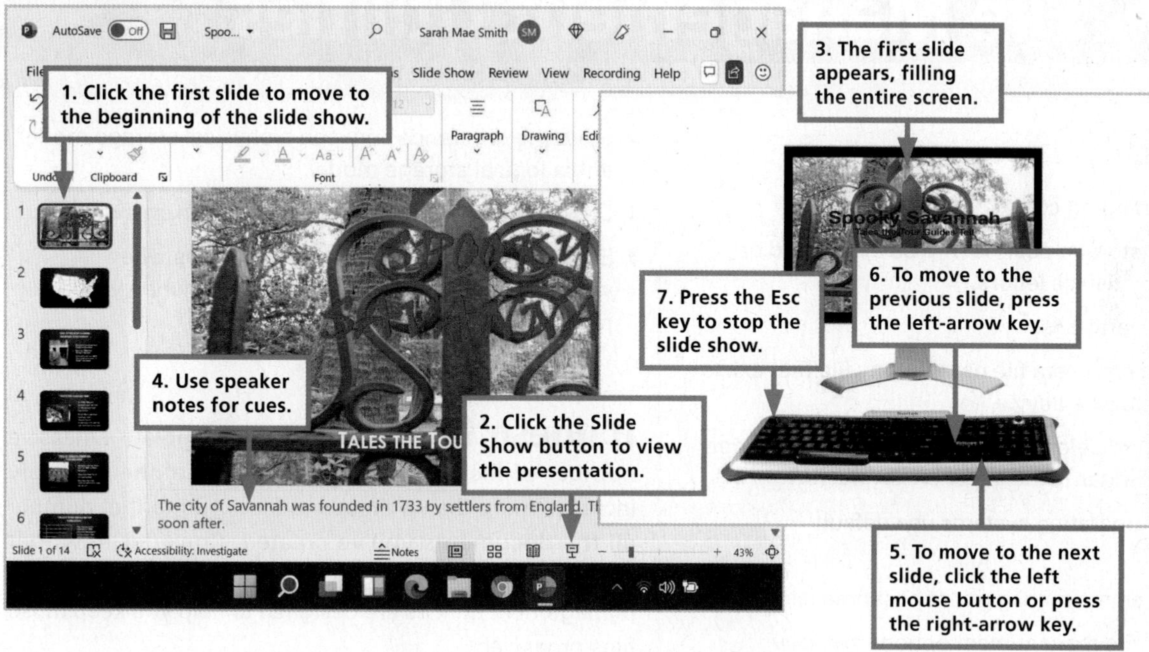

QuickQuiz — Section D

1. Word processing applications generally offer ________ style options including margins, leading, and alignment.
2. ________ software is useful for performing "what-if" analyses.
3. When entering formulas, you can use relative references and ________ references.
4. The information in a database is often represented as a(n) ________ with each row representing a record.
5. Each database record is composed of many ________.

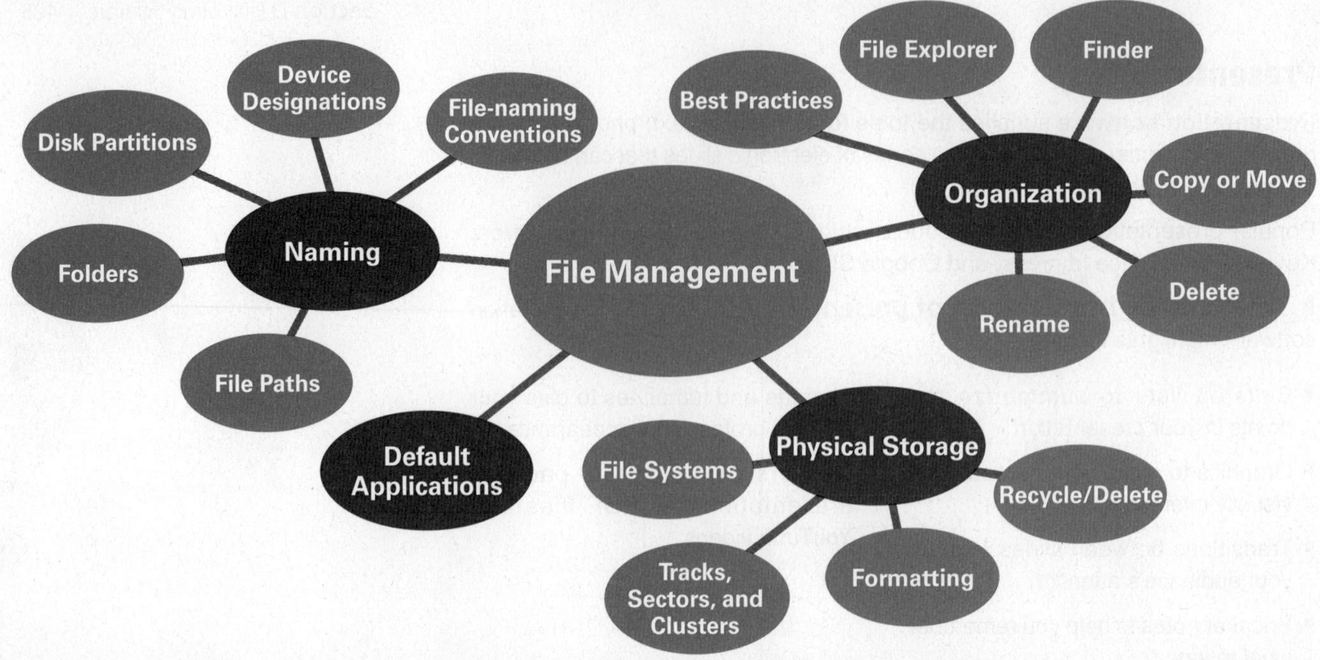

Section E File Management Utilities

Objectives

- List five file-naming conventions.
- Explain how storage devices on PCs are named or designated by device letters.
- Identify disk partitions.
- Write out the complete file path for any file that exists on a digital storage device.
- Identify the basic elements of Windows File Explorer and macOS Finder.
- Explain how operating systems use default applications.
- List at least ten file management best practices.
- Describe the file management options typically provided by application software.
- State the difference between a physical storage model and a logical storage model.
- Describe why an operating system uses an index file.
- Explain what the operating system does when you move a file to the Recycle Bin and when you permanently delete a file.

It doesn't take long to accumulate a massive number of files. Your photo collection alone probably includes more than a thousand files. Add to that number all the documents you've created. Consider how that collection of files might grow over the next five years. File management utilities are designed to help you keep those files organized!

Terminology

file-naming conventions
device letter
disk partition
directory
root directory
subdirectory
folder
file path
file management utilities
default application
logical storage model
physical storage model
formatting
tracks
sectors
file system
cluster
file shredder software

File Basics

Computer files in digital format offer a compact and convenient way to store documents, photos, videos, and music. Computer files have several characteristics, such as a name, format, location, size, and date. To make effective use of computer files, you'll need a good understanding of these file basics.

What's important about a file name? File names are the foundation for keeping files organized so that they can be easily located and so that old versions don't get mixed up with new versions. File names should be descriptive, and versioning must be clear. For example, if you anticipate several revisions to a report, add a version number, such as *Report v1.docx*, to the file name. Save the next version of the report as *Report v2.docx*. You then have the original version in case you want to retrieve some of the material it contains.

Are there rules for naming files? As you learned in Module 1, a computer file—or simply a file—is defined as a named collection of data that exists on a storage medium, such as a hard disk, cloud drive, or USB flash drive. When saving a file, you must provide a valid file name that adheres to specific rules, referred to as **file-naming conventions**. The conventions vary slightly from one operating system to another. However, because file sharing is so prevalent, the conventions in Figure 6-48 represent best practices for naming files on any platform.

Figure 6-48: File-naming conventions

Maximum length is 255 characters. Current versions of Windows and macOS support file names up to 255 characters long. In practice, some of the 255 characters are used for the file's drive letter, folder designation, and extension, so the name you assign to a file should be much shorter. A file name limitation of 255 characters gives you the flexibility to use descriptive file names, such as *Job Search Cover Letter Pixar*, so that you can easily identify what a file contains.

Avoid using symbols. If an operating system attaches special significance to a symbol, you cannot use it in a file name. For example, Windows uses the colon (:) character to separate the device letter from a file name or folder, as in C:Music. A file name that contains a colon, such as *Report:Summary*, is not valid because the operating system would become confused about how to interpret the colon. Avoid using the symbols * \ < > | " / : and ? in file names.

Do not use reserved words. Some operating systems also contain a list of reserved words that are used as commands or special identifiers. You cannot use these words alone as a file name. You can, however, use these words as part of a longer file name. For example, in Windows, the file name *Nul* would not be valid, but you could name a file something like *Null Set.exe*. The following words should not be used as file names: Aux, Com1, Com2, Com3, Com4, Con, Lpt1, Lpt2, Lpt3, Prn, and Nul.

Case is disregarded. Some operating systems are case sensitive, but those that you regularly work with on personal computers are not. A file named *Final Report* is the same as *FINAL REPORT* or *final report*.

Spaces are allowed. You can use spaces in file names. That's a different rule than for email addresses, where spaces are not allowed. You've probably noticed that people often use underscores or periods instead of spaces in email addresses such as Madi_Jones@msu.edu. That convention is not necessary in file names, so a file name such as *Letter to Edison Jones* is valid.

QuickCheck

Which file name would not be allowed when using Windows or macOS?

a. *Budget: Jan-March*

b. *MacBook Air*

c. *Navy Aux 540*

d. *Paint.exe*

▶ What are storage device designations? Files can be saved on internal storage devices as well as on external devices and in the cloud. Knowing the location of a file is the key to retrieving it. Every storage location has a name, such as C:, JacksHD, DropBox, Macintosh HD, or SanDiskUSB. The storage location name may identify the location of the device, its type, or its owner.

When working with Windows, storage devices can be identified by a **device letter**. The main hard disk drive is referred to as drive C. A device letter is usually followed by a colon, so C: is typically the designation for a hard disk drive. Removable storage devices are assigned drive letters when they are inserted. For example, Removable Disk (E:) might be the designation for a USB drive.

Drive letters are a legacy of DOS, which is why they remain in use in Windows but not on Macs. Macs do not use drive letters. Every storage device on Macs has a name. The main hard disk is called Macintosh HD. Figure 6-49 illustrates how devices might be designated on a PC.

Terminology

Storage locations are sometimes referred to as *storage volumes*. A volume can be an entire storage device, a storage medium, or a portion of a storage medium, such as a partition.

Figure 6-49: Storage device designations

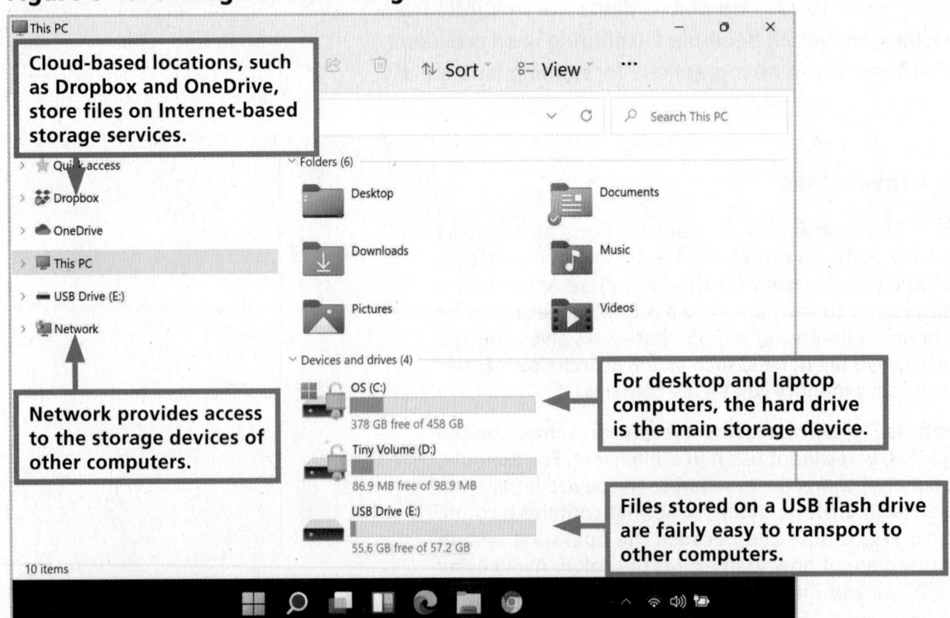

▶ What is a disk partition? A **disk partition** is a section of a hard disk drive that is treated as a separate storage unit. Most hard drives are configured with a single partition that contains the operating system, programs, and data. However, it is possible to create more than one hard disk partition, each with a separate name and device letter. Partitions are created, modified, and deleted using Disk Utility on Macs and Disk Management on PCs.

Based on the screenshot in Figure 6-49, the computer might appear to have two hard disk drives: C: and D:. However, in reality, it has one drive divided into two partitions. In such an arrangement, backing up files from C: to D: wouldn't offer protection in case of a hard disk failure because C: and D: are the same physical storage device.

Disk partitions help to separate programs from data files. For example, a PC might have one partition for operating system files and another partition for programs and data. This arrangement can speed up the process of disinfecting a computer that has been attacked by malicious software.

QuickCheck

Disk partitions C: and D: are generally used for __________________.

a. two USB drives

b. one hard drive

c. cloud storage locations

d. iOS devices

What is a folder? Every storage device has a **directory** containing a list of its files. The main directory is referred to as the **root directory**. A root directory can be subdivided into smaller lists. Each list is called a **subdirectory**. Each subdirectory is depicted as a **folder**.

Folders help you envision files as if they were stored in a filing cabinet. Each folder can hold related items—for example, a set of documents, sound clips, financial data, or photos for a school project. Windows provides a folder called Documents that you might use to hold reports, letters, and so on. You can also create and name folders to meet your needs, such as a folder called QuickBooks to hold personal finance data.

Folders can be created within other folders. You might, for example, create a Graduation folder within your Pictures folder to hold a collection of graduation photos and another folder named Fido to hold photos of your faithful canine companion.

A folder name is separated from a drive letter and other folder names by a special symbol. In Microsoft Windows, this symbol is the backslash (\). For example, the folder for your dog pics (within the Pictures folder on drive C) would be written as C:\Pictures\Fido. Other operating systems use a forward slash (/) to separate folders.

What is a file path? A computer file's location is defined by a **file path**, which on a PC includes the drive letter, folder(s), file name, and extension. Suppose that you have stored a JPEG file called *Yappy Hour* in the Fido folder on your hard disk. Its file specification is shown in Figure 6-50, along with a table of common file extensions.

QuickCheck

The list of files stored in a folder such as \Music is referred to as a ___________.

a. root directory

b. path

c. subdirectory

d. partition

6

Terminology

Modern operating systems may not display the slashes for a file path and instead use an alternative symbol, such as an arrow, triangle, or > symbol.

Figure 6-50: File paths

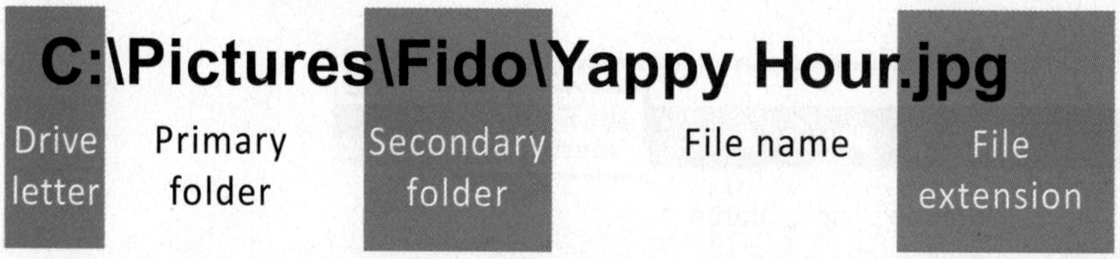

C:\Pictures\Fido\Yappy Hour.jpg

Drive letter | Primary folder | Secondary folder | File name | File extension

Type of File	Extensions
Text	.txt .dat .rtf .docx (Microsoft Word) .doc (Microsoft Word 2003) .odt (OpenDocument text) .wpd (WordPerfect) .pages (iWork)
Sound	.wav .mid .mp3 .m4p .aac
Graphics	.bmp .tif .wmf .gif .jpg .png .eps .ai (Adobe Illustrator)
Animation/video	.flc .swf .avi .mpg .mp4 .mov (QuickTime) .wmv (Windows Media Player)
Web page	.htm .html .asp .vrml .php
Spreadsheet	.xlsx (Microsoft Excel) .xls (Microsoft Excel 2003) .ods (OpenDocument spreadsheet) .numbers (iWork)
Database	.accdb (Microsoft Access) .odb (OpenDocument database)
Miscellaneous	.pdf (Adobe Acrobat) .pptx (Microsoft PowerPoint) .odp (OpenDocument presentations) .zip (WinZip) .pub (Microsoft Publisher)

File Management Tools

Operating systems provide file organization tools called **file management utilities**. Windows offers a utility called File Explorer, which is launched from the icon on the taskbar. macOS offers a utility called Finder, which is launched from the icon on the dock.

▸ What's in the file management utility window? File Explorer and Finder have many similarities. Although the icons are different, the general functions, features, and layouts are comparable. The examples in Figure 6-51 illustrate the components of File Explorer and Finder.

Figure 6-51: File management utility elements

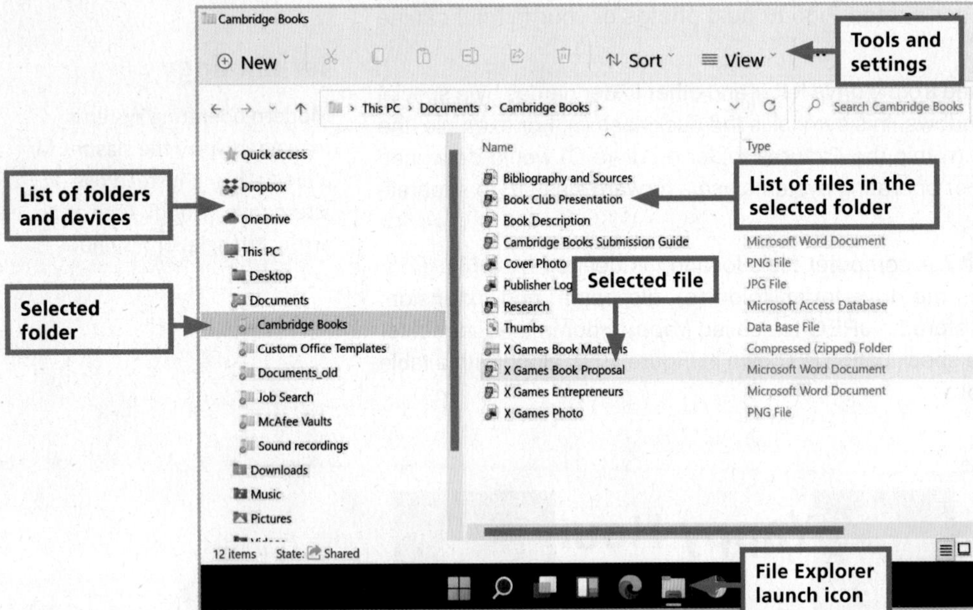

Windows File Explorer

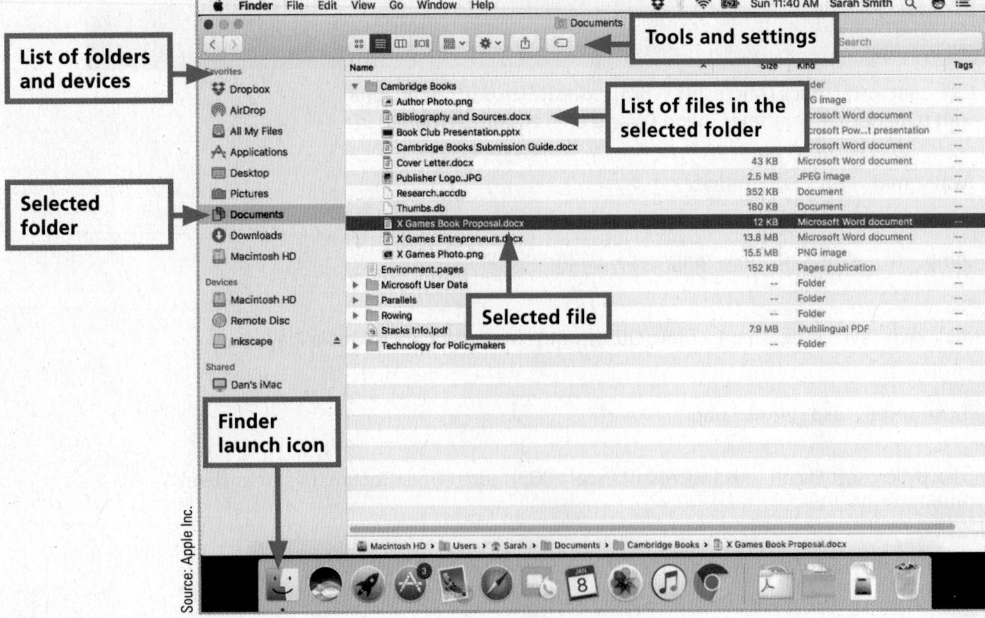

macOS Finder

Can I see file paths? Proficient computer users are adept at using file extensions and paths to keep files organized. To apply these tools, settings that display extensions and paths must be enabled in File Explorer and Finder, as shown in Figure 6-52.

Figure 6-52: Set file managers to display extensions and paths

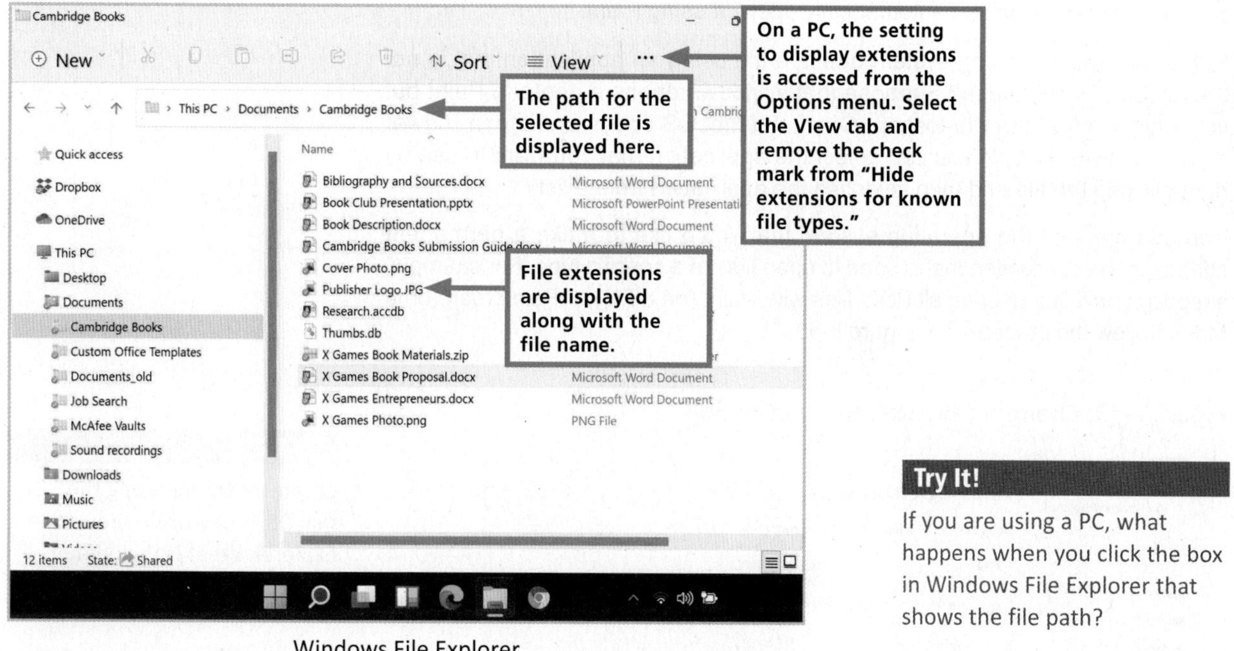

On a PC, the setting to display extensions is accessed from the Options menu. Select the View tab and remove the check mark from "Hide extensions for known file types."
The path for the selected file is displayed here.
File extensions are displayed along with the file name.

Windows File Explorer

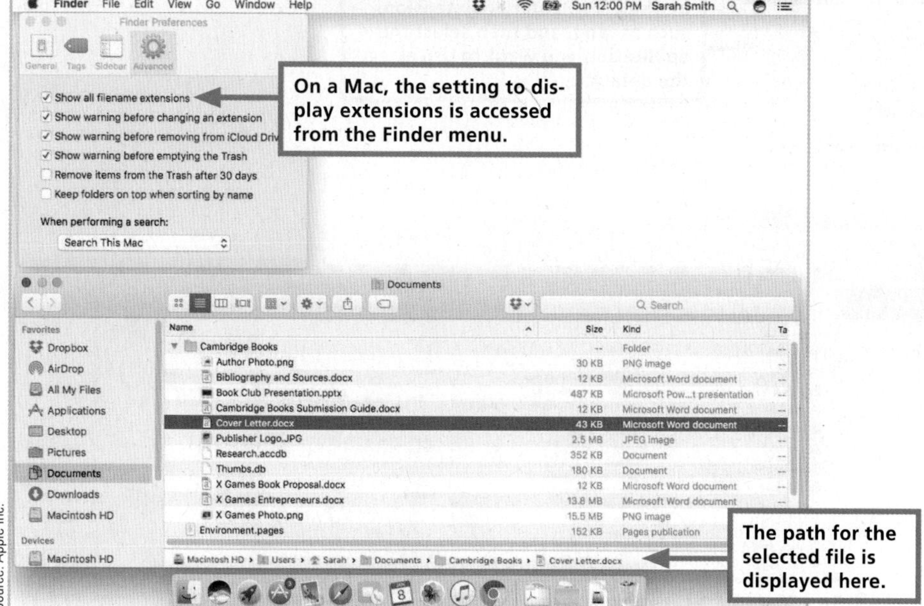

On a Mac, the setting to display extensions is accessed from the Finder menu.
The path for the selected file is displayed here.

macOS Finder

Source: Apple Inc.

6

Try It!

If you are using a PC, what happens when you click the box in Windows File Explorer that shows the file path?

What can I do with folders and files? File management utilities are useful for locating files and for viewing their contents. Selecting a data file by double-clicking it or tapping it opens the file and its corresponding software application. The software application associated with a specific file type is called a **default application**. For example, the Paint application might be the default application for all PNG files, so when you select a file such as *Sunset.png*, the operating system automatically opens it using Paint.

But what if the operating system opens a file using an application that is not the one you want to use? Suppose that Windows opens a photo in Paint but you want to view it in Photoshop. Or what if macOS opens a photo in Viewer instead of Photoshop? You can select the application that you want to use by right-clicking the file and then selecting the application from a list.

You can also tell the operating system that you'd like to make a permanent change in the application that is used to open files of a specific type. For example, suppose you'd like to open all PNG files with Paint (on a PC) or Paintbrush (on a Mac). Follow the procedure in Figure 6-53.

Figure 6-53: Changing the default application

On a PC, search for Default Apps and select it. Enter an extension, such as .png, and then select the application you want to use as the default.

On a Mac, right-click any program with the .png extension. Select Get Info. Use the Open With option to select the application you want to use as the default, then select the button labeled Change All.

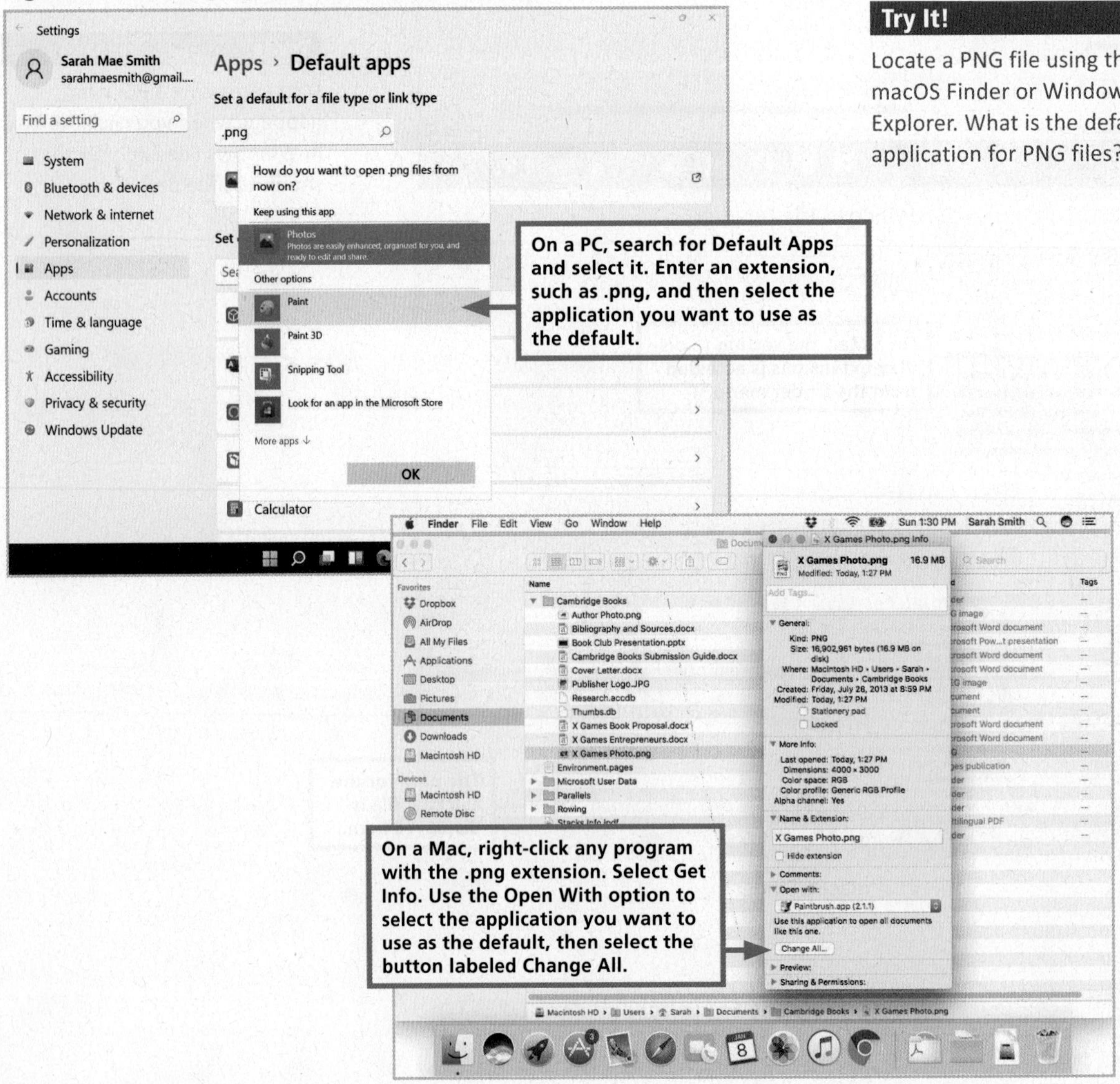

Source: Apple Inc.

Try It!

Locate a PNG file using the macOS Finder or Windows File Explorer. What is the default application for PNG files?

What else can I do with file management utilities? In addition to locating files and folders, file management utilities help you manipulate files and folders in the following ways:

- **Rename.** You can change the name of a file or folder to better describe its contents.
- **Copy.** You can copy a file from one device to another—for example, from a USB drive to the hard disk drive. You can also make a copy of a document so that you can revise the copy and leave the original intact.
- **Move.** You can move a file from one folder to another or from one storage device to another. When you move a file, it is erased from its original location, so make sure to remember the new location of the file. You can also move an entire folder and its contents from one storage device to another storage device or to a different folder.
- **Delete.** You can delete a file when you no longer need it. You can also delete a folder. Be careful when you delete a folder, because most file management utilities also delete all the files within a folder.

Can I work with more than one file or folder at a time? To work with a group of files or folders, you must first select them. You can accomplish this task in several ways. You can hold down the Ctrl key (Command key on the Mac) as you click each item. This method works well if you are selecting files or folders that are not listed consecutively.

As an alternative, you can hold down the Shift key while you click the first item and the last item you want to select. By using the Shift key method, you select the two items that you clicked and all the items in between. After a group of items is selected, you can use the same copy, move, or delete procedure that you would use for a single item.

What are personal folders? Windows and macOS offer a set of preconfigured personal folders, such as Documents and Music, for storing your personal data files. These folders may also appear in the Quick access list (PCs) or Favorites list (Macs). You can drag other folders to this list so that they can be accessed without clicking through several levels of folders (Figure 6-54).

Try It!

Use the macOS Finder or Windows File Explorer to experiment with selecting files using the Shift or Ctrl (Command) key.

Figure 6-54: Personalize your list of frequently used folders

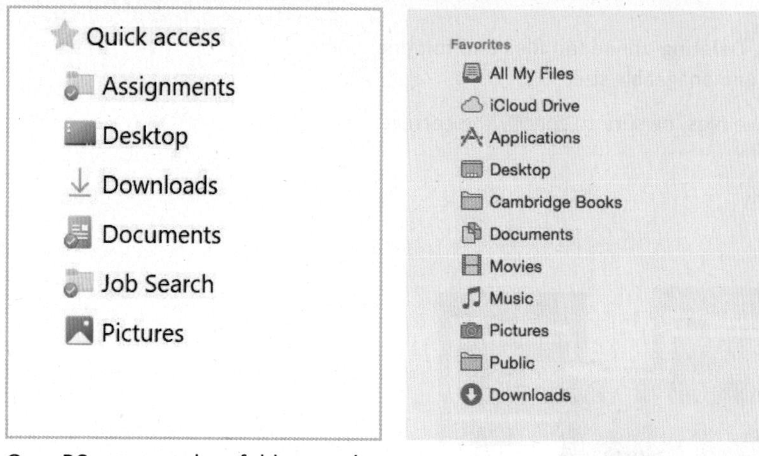

On a PC, you can drag folders to the Quick access area of File Manager. To remove a folder without deleting it, right-click it and then select Unpin from Quick access.

On a Mac, you can drag folders to the Favorites area of Finder. To remove a folder without deleting it, right-click it and select Remove from Sidebar.

▸ What are file management best practices? A file management utility provides tools and procedures to help you keep track of your program and data files. However, these tools are most useful when you have a plan for organizing your files and when you follow some basic file management guidelines. Consider the tips in Figure 6-55 for managing files on your own computer. When working with files on lab computers, follow the guidelines from your instructor or lab manager.

Figure 6-55: File management best practices

- **Use descriptive names.** Give your files and folders descriptive names, and avoid using cryptic abbreviations.
- **Maintain file extensions.** When renaming a file, keep the original file extension so that the file can be opened with the correct application software.
- **Group similar files.** Separate files into folders based on subject matter. For example, store your creative writing assignments in one folder and your art history notes in another folder.
- **Organize your folders from the top down.** When devising a hierarchy of folders, consider how you want to access files and back them up. For example, you can specify one folder and its subfolders for a backup. If your important data is scattered in a variety of folders, however, making backups is more time-consuming.
- **Consider using default folders.** You should use preconfigured personal folders, such as Documents and Music, as your main data folders. Add subfolders to these personal folders as necessary to organize your files.
- **Use public folders for files you want to share.** Use the public folders for files that you want to share with other network users.
- **Don't mix data files and program files.** Do not store data files in the folders that hold your software. Most software is stored in subfolders of the Program Files folder on Windows systems and in the Applications folder on Macs.
- **Don't store files in the root directory.** Although it is acceptable to create folders in the root directory, it's not a good practice to store programs or data files in the root directory of your computer's hard disk.
- **Access files from the hard disk.** For best performance, copy files from USB drives to your computer's hard disk before accessing them.
- **Follow copyright rules.** When copying files, make sure you adhere to copyright and license restrictions.
- **Delete or archive files you no longer need.** Deleting unneeded files and folders helps keep your list of files from growing to an unmanageable size.
- **Be aware of storage locations.** When you save files, be sure to specify the correct storage device and folder.
- **Back up!** Back up your folders and files regularly.

QuickCheck

When following best practices, whether you're using a PC or a Mac, you should not store files ________.

a. on the hard drive

b. in the root directory

c. with spaces in the name

d. in personal folders

Saving Files

Applications include menu options for opening and saving files. In fact, applications call the operating system's file management routines to get the job done. That is the reason the Save window provided by an application might look similar to the file management utility window.

What should I know about saving files? Applications generally provide a way to open files and save them in a specific folder on a designated storage device. Some applications also allow you to delete and rename files. To save a file, use the Save option provided by your application, specify a location for the file, and give it a name. Most applications allow you to create a new folder and add tags to a file during the save process (Figure 6-56).

Try It!

Use an application, such as Word, to save a file. Examine the Save window and compare it to the window for the file management utility (File Explorer or Finder) on your computer. Are they similar?

6

Figure 6-56: Creating folders and saving files with Microsoft Word

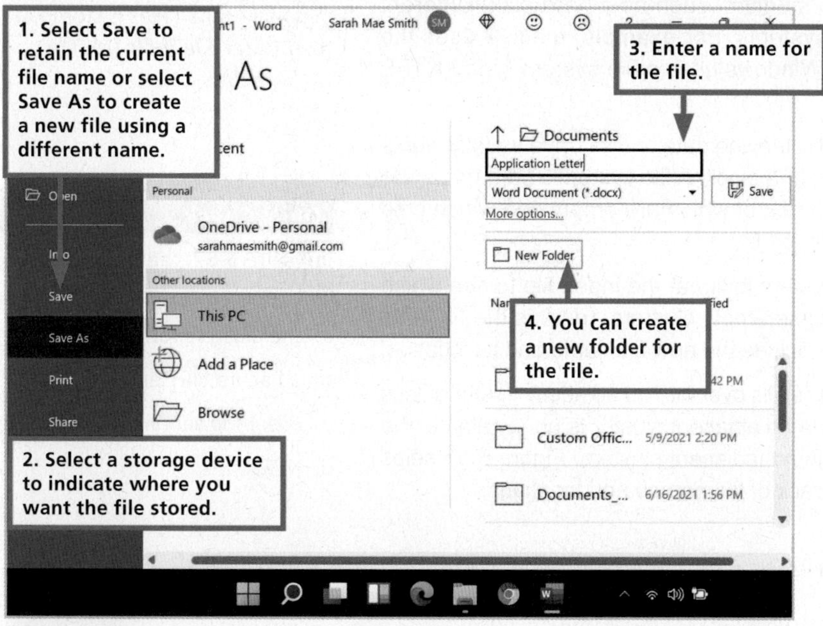

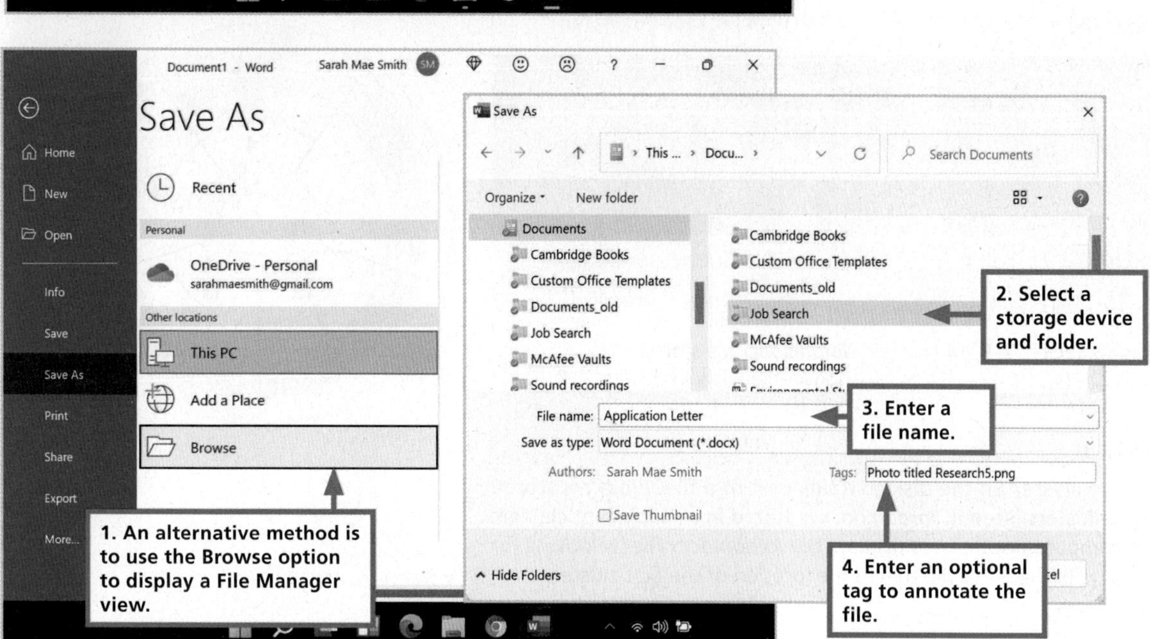

Physical File Storage

The structure of files and folders displayed in a file manager window is called a **logical storage model** because it helps you create a mental picture of the way files are organized in a hierarchy of folders. A **physical storage model** describes what actually happens on the disks and in the circuits. As you will see, the physical model is quite different from the logical model.

How is data stored? Before a computer can store a file, the storage medium must be formatted. The **formatting** process creates the equivalent of electronic storage bins. Magnetic and optical media are divided into circular **tracks** and then further divided into pie-shaped **sectors**. Solid state storage media are divided into units.

How does the operating system keep track of a file's location? The operating system uses a **file system** to keep track of the names and locations of files that reside on a storage medium, such as a hard disk. Different operating systems use different file systems. For example, macOS uses the Apple File System (APFS). Microsoft Windows uses a file system called NTFS (New Technology File System).

To speed up the process of storing and retrieving data, a disk drive usually works with a group of sectors called a **cluster** or a block. A file system's primary task is to maintain a list of clusters and keep track of which are empty and which hold data. This information is stored in an index file.

When you save a file, the operating system looks at the index file to see which clusters are empty. It selects one of these empty clusters, records the file data there, and then revises the index file to include the new file name and its location.

A file that does not fit into a single cluster spills over into an adjacent cluster unless that cluster already contains data. When an adjacent cluster is not available, the operating system stores parts of a file in nonadjacent clusters. Figure 6-57 helps you visualize how an index file keeps track of file names and locations.

Terminology

In NTFS, the index file containing metadata for all files is stored in the *Master File Table* (MFT).

QuickCheck

In Figure 6-57, the beige clusters illustrate _______________.

a. the clusters for *Jordan.docx*

b. adjacent clusters

c. *Pick.bmp* sectors

d. NTFS

Figure 6-57: How an index file works

Index File

File	Cluster	Comment
MFT	1	Reserved for MFT files
DISK USE	2	Part of MFT that contains a list of empty sectors
Bio.txt	3, 4	*Bio.txt* file stored in clusters 3 and 4
Jordan.docx	7, 8, 10	*Jordan.docx* file stored noncontiguously in clusters 7, 8, and 10
Pick.bmp	9	*Pick.bmp* file stored in cluster 9

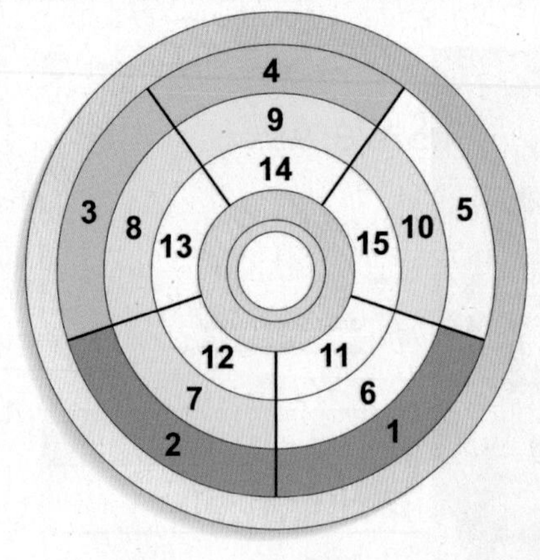

Each colored cluster on the disk contains part of a file. *Bio.txt* is stored in adjacent clusters (green). *Jordan.docx* is stored in nonadjacent clusters (beige). A computer locates and displays the *Jordan.docx* file by looking for its name in the index file to find the location of the first cluster.

What happens when a file is deleted? When you click a file's icon and then select the Delete option, you might have visions of the read-write head somehow scrubbing out the clusters that contain data. That doesn't happen. Instead, the operating system changes the status of the file's clusters to "empty" and removes the file name from the index file. The file name no longer appears in a directory listing, but the file's data remains in the clusters until a new file is stored there.

Can deleted files be undeleted? The Windows Recycle Bin and similar utilities in other operating systems are designed to protect you from accidentally deleting hard disk files you actually need. Instead of marking a file's clusters as empty, the operating system moves the file to the Recycle Bin folder. The deleted file still takes up space on the disk but does not appear in the usual directory listing.

Files in the Recycle Bin folder can be undeleted so that they again appear in the regular directory. In addition, the Recycle Bin can be emptied to permanently delete any files it contains.

What happens when I empty the Recycle Bin? When the Recycle Bin is emptied, the index file marks the clusters containing deleted files as "empty" and the file name is removed from all directory listings. The old data remains in the clusters, however, until it is overwritten by other files. Various third-party utilities can recover a lot of this supposedly deleted data. Law enforcement agents, for example, use these utilities to gather evidence from deleted files on the computer disks of suspected criminals.

To delete data from a disk in such a way that no one can ever read it, you can use special **file shredder software** that overwrites supposedly empty sectors with random 1s and 0s. This software is handy if you plan to donate your computer to a charitable organization and you want to make sure your personal data no longer remains on the hard disk.

QuickCheck

What happens when you delete a file and then empty the Trash (Mac) or Recycle Bin (PC)?

a. The clusters containing the file data are scrubbed clean.

b. The file is stuffed with 1s and 0s.

c. The file's clusters are marked "empty" but the data remains in them until it is overwritten.

d. The file is shredded.

6

QuickQuiz — Section E

1. File-naming ______ are a list of rules for creating valid file names.
2. A disk ______ divides a hard disk into two or more storage units.
3. Drive C:\ is also called the ______ directory.
4. A group of tracks and sectors used as a storage unit is called a(n) ______.
5. NTFS and APFS are examples of Windows and macOS file ______.

Source: IGN

Issue: What Happened to That App?

That app got banned. iPhone owners head to the Apple App Store to download apps for their phones. Samsung phone owners connect to the Google Play Store or the Galaxy Store for apps to enhance their devices.

These app stores offer millions of apps that generate billions of downloads. The apps also generate substantial profits for the stores, which take a percentage cut of all sales.

The companies that operate these app stores have good intentions. Here's what Apple has to say: "The guiding principle of the App Store is simple—we want to provide a safe experience for users to get apps and a great opportunity for all developers to be successful. We do this by offering a highly curated App Store where every app is reviewed by experts and an editorial team helps users discover new apps every day."

"We want to provide a safe experience for users..."

Apple App Developer Guidelines

Consumers have an expectation that apps marketed at app stores will be functional and secure. They expect the app to work as described. They expect the app to be free of creepy or offensive content. They do not want apps that sell personal data to marketers, contain malware, exploit minors, or promote unscientific medical practices.

Ensuring that millions of apps meet consumer expectations is not easy. Third-party developers from all over the world create apps and submit them to the app store's review process. During the review process, professional reviewers test the apps to make sure they comply with the app store's policy guidelines. The task is daunting. In a typical month, thousands of apps are submitted by developers hoping for approval.

According to Apple, about 40% of developer submissions are rejected, though many are subsequently approved after developers implement modifications required by the review process. But some apps are permanently rejected. Apps are banned if they contain objectionable content, if they collect or share personal data without permission, or if they are copycats of other apps.

The list of no-nos that are detailed in app review guidelines is long. Some of the criteria are subjective. The guidelines give app stores a lot of power over the apps that are published and those that are banned.

During the early days of the Apple App Store, its review process rejected the Google Voice app and banned several related apps that had previously been approved. Google appealed to the Federal Communications Commission, asking it to investigate whether Apple was colluding with its exclusive carrier, AT&T, to restrict user choice for wireless voice and text services. The issue was resolved in favor of Google, so now consumers are able to download Google Voice and similar VoIP apps.

More recently, Apple banned an app that was used by Hong Kong protesters to crowdsource the location of police forces. Regardless of its legitimate use to avoid streets on which conflicts might be taking place, authorities claimed that the app was being used to victimize people and property where there was no nearby police presence.

And then there was the Fortnite controversy. The popular game published by Epic Games was released on the Apple App Store and Google Play Store in 2018. Epic Games CEO Tim Sweeney was at the time an outspoken critic of the 30% revenue cut required by the stores. He also maintained that Apple's App Store was essentially a monopoly and anticompetitive.

In 2020, a new version of Fortnite was released. It included a 20% discount to gamers who used the in-game V-bucks currency. The discount was not made available to Fortnite users who purchased through the Apple or Google stores. Fortnite was immediately banned by Apple and Google. Lawsuits followed.

The controversies surrounding banned apps prompted companies such as Spotify and Blockchain to join Epic Games in forming the Coalition for App Fairness, which urges app stores to "recognize that every app developer, regardless of size or the nature of the developer's business, is entitled to fair treatment."

Try It!

Are app developers and consumers being exploited by the companies that operate app stores? Explore the issue by completing the Try It! activities. Your instructor can specify how to submit your findings.

1. To discover current information about your favorite app store, look online for answers to the following questions:

   a. Approximately how many apps are currently offered by the app store?

   b. What was the app store's revenue for the previous year?

   c. What percentage of a sale does the app store retain?

   d. How long does it take to approve or reject an app once it has been submitted for review?

   e. How many apps actually make money for the developer?

2. Take a look at an app store's review guidelines for developers to discover what is considered objectionable or inappropriate content. Describe the types of content that fall into this category. Provide examples of guidelines for this category that are subjective and could be the basis for banning apps that might not be harmful to consumers.

3. How successful is your app store at rejecting apps that contain malware? Search online to see if there have been recent warnings about apps that contain malware that was not discovered during the review process. Summarize what you find.

4. There is a YouTube video called *Fortnite 1984 Apple Parody Video*. Watch the original *Apple-1984* video and then watch the parody. Summarize the message of each video.

5. What is the current status of the Fortnite controversy? Explore online to find information about the original case, *Epic Games Inc. v. Apple Inc.* Explain how "in-app purchases" are relevant to the case. If the case has been resolved, what was the verdict? If the case has not yet been resolved, explain its current status.

6. The Fortnite case is representative of a growing sense that big tech companies are getting too big and wielding too much power over developers and consumers. In 2021, the European Commission found Apple in breach of EU antitrust law on the basis that the Apple App Store charged high commission fees and prohibited developers from informing consumers of alternative subscription and purchase options. What is the meaning of "antitrust"? How does that term relate to controversies about tech companies' app stores?

What Do You Think?

Issue

1. Have you downloaded an app that has later been banned?
2. Do you think that app stores are doing a good job of reviewing apps before publicly posting them?
3. Do you think that devices should be limited to obtaining apps from only one source?

Information Tools: Documentation Literacy

It wasn't too long ago that software arrived in a box that contained a CD and a lengthy printed manual. This documentation included a detailed description of every feature as well as tutorials and troubleshooting guides. Today, printed manuals have been replaced by a variety of online documentation. Finding and using it is a skill that is sometimes referred to as documentation literacy. You can use documentation like a pro by following a few easy guidelines.

Know what you are using. Make sure you know the name of the software that you are using, the software publisher, and the software version. To find this information on Macs, look at the About option on the software menu. On PCs, use the About option on the Help menu.

Use the Help menu. The Help menu is a great tool for learning how to use specific features of the software. From the Help menu you can expect to find:

- A searchable list or an index of help topics
- Links to online tutorials and help resources provided by the software publisher

Find the publisher's online documentation. An online user manual can include an overview of the software, information about system requirements, technical information about the software, and instructions for using each feature. Some documentation is very extensive; use the table of contents, index, and Search box to quickly find the information you seek. Don't spend too much time paging through a lengthy user manual. Your time might be spent more efficiently by looking elsewhere.

Check YouTube. When looking for a "getting started" tutorial or a walkthrough of how to use a specific software feature, YouTube is a good resource. You may also find software reviews that are helpful when deciding whether the software is worth downloading. Some software videos on YouTube are created by the software publisher, whereas others are created by unaffiliated users. Video tutorials tend to be accurate because they are recorded using the actual software. Their quality can vary, however. If multiple videos on the same topic are available, don't hesitate to bail out of a low-quality production. Product reviews posted on YouTube may be biased, so cross-check with other user reviews.

Use a search engine. For troubleshooting, a search engine may be your best resource. Entering a general search that includes the software product name, such as *LibreOffice help* or *Photoshop help*, usually yields results from the software publisher's online help resources.

Visit online forums. Popular software spawns user forums. Some are independent, whereas others are sponsored by the software's publisher. Independent forums are a good source of troubleshooting information—especially for problems that the software publisher would prefer to ignore. You can find forums by entering a query such as *LibreOffice user group* or *Photoshop discussion forum.*

Keep notes. Write down error messages. Enter the text of the error message in a search engine along with the name of the troublesome software product and your device's operating system. When you find a solution, pay it forward and post the fix on an appropriate online forum.

Evaluate before you implement. Not all of the information you find in user forums is accurate or up to date. Be especially careful when troubleshooting malware because some malware "fixes" introduce even more malware. Before implementing instructions for fixing a problem, cross-check the solution by searching further. Look for users who have successfully implemented the instructions. Also, make sure the instructions pertain to the software and operating system versions you are using. The information from moderated or software publishers' forums is more likely to be accurate than information from non-moderated forums.

Try It! As the amount of online information grows, more and more of it becomes outdated. When troubleshooting software, outdated information can be useless. Let's take a look at the assortment of software documentation available online.

1. Suppose that you are curious about Chromebooks. Would one be a useful addition to your digital device collection? Use a search engine to browse the Chrome OS discussion group on Reddit. Then browse the Community link of Google's Chromebook Help site. How would you characterize the discussion topics at each of these sites? How would you characterize the expertise of participants?

2. Suppose you are using a Chromebook and need to find its IP address. Watch at least three YouTube videos on the topic. For each video, record its URL and evaluate its quality.

3. What if you want to use your Chromebook offline to compose documents and spreadsheets? Is it possible to do so? What do you need to consider if you plan to edit documents using Google Docs and Google Drive offline? What is the most frequent problem that other people seem to have when attempting this? Use a search engine to locate information on this topic. Record what you find and where you find it.

4. A dynamic dashboard collects data from a spreadsheet and displays it in chart format, updating the charts on the fly as new data arrives. Locate an online tutorial about dynamic dashboards and attempt to follow the instructions to create one with graphs or tables from more than one data set. Record the URL for the tutorial. Submit your completed dashboard file along with a short rating and review of the tutorial. In your review, include information about the clarity and completeness of the tutorial.

5. Find the software publisher's documentation for an open source program called GIMP. What does the GIMP application do? Does the publisher's documentation include a tutorial or FAQs? Are there help groups?

6. Find tutorials and help resources for GIMP other than those supplied by the GIMP Web site. Give examples of at least three additional online GIMP resources. Can you locate instructions at any one of these sites for isolating an image from its background so that the "cut out" image could be overlaid on a different background? Write out the steps for doing so.

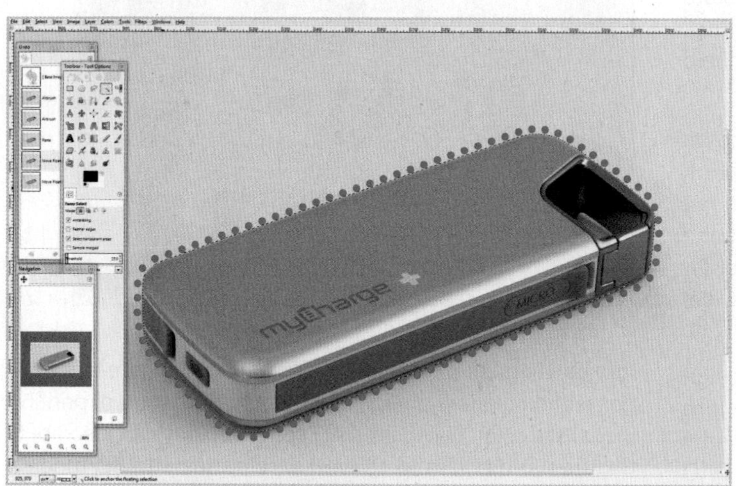

Source: MIDASoft Inc.

Technology in Context: Architecture and Construction

A cluster of workers in hardhats study a blueprint. Sun-bronzed laborers perch on a makeshift bench, munching sandwiches and waving to a group of carpenters hauling 2x4s onto a foundation. The sounds of hammers, shovels, and power tools fill the air from early morning through late afternoon. It is a typical construction site: an anthill of activity where a structure of some sort is eventually assembled—a house, a shopping mall, or a skyscraper.

Behind the scenes of this busy site, digital technology has added a high-tech flavor to construction projects with real-time interactive graphics, broadband wireless communications, distributed database management systems, wearable and vehicle-mounted computers, global positioning satellites, and laser-guided surveying systems.

Architects use computers to create blueprints. Contractors use computers for cost estimates and scheduling. Computers also appear on the job site, carried as handheld devices and embedded in construction equipment.

In the past, architects drew construction plans by hand on semitransparent film called vellum. To create a blueprint, they overlaid the vellum on special blue paper and then ran it through a machine that exposed it to intensified light and ammonia. Minor changes to a design were possible; but for major changes, architects often needed to create a new set of vellum drawings.

With the advent of computers and computer-aided design (CAD) software, architects realized they could be more productive—and make design changes more easily—by replacing their drafting tables with computers running CAD software. Using plotters with wide print beds, architects are able to produce computer-generated blueprints similar to those they created at a drafting table.

Initially, architects used CAD software to create 2D floor plans and elevations. Today, architects use 3D CAD software that offers a greatly expanded toolset. The HGTV series *The Property Brothers* works with a 3D rendering and animation company called Neezo Renders to create spiffy visualizations for home remodeling projects. Architects begin with a 2D floor plan and then use CAD tools to draw interior and exterior walls, ceilings, and roofs. Standard building materials, such as doors and windows, can be selected from a list of clip-art objects and dragged into position with a mouse. Electrical, plumbing, and framing schematics can also be added.

Any elements of the drawing can be displayed or hidden. For example, when discussing the design with an electrical contractor, an architect can hide the plumbing details. These 3D wireframe drawings with building, electrical, and plumbing elements included can be rotated and viewed from any angle.

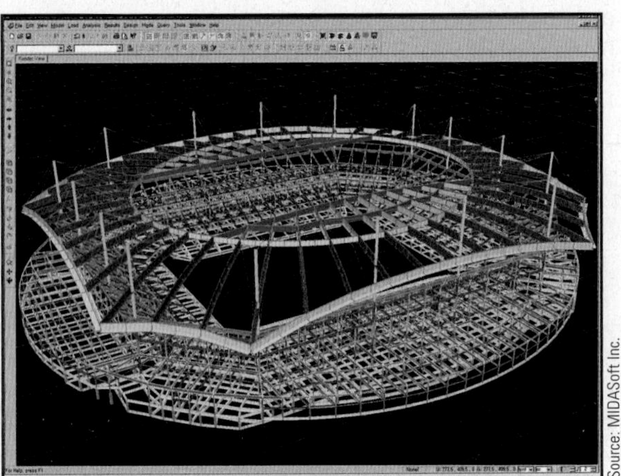

Source: MIDASoft Inc.

Inexpensive ink jet printers have replaced expensive first-generation plotters and give architects the option of printing in realistic color. Using 3D CAD software, they can also apply textures and colors to convert wireframes into 3D models that can be viewed from the inside or outside. Architects sometimes use an animated version of a 3D model for virtual reality walkthroughs.

After an architect has completed the building plans, a contractor estimates the project's price tag by calculating the cost of materials and labor. Computerized spreadsheets, such as Excel, are a popular tool for cost estimates. Large contracting firms often use commercial software specifically designed for construction estimates.

Contractors are also responsible for scheduling the tasks in a construction project, such as excavating the building site, erecting the foundation, constructing the frame, assembling the roof, adding wiring and plumbing, and doing interior finish work. Large construction projects, such as malls and government buildings, can involve thousands of tasks and many subcontractors.

Computerized scheduling tools, such as Gantt charts, PERT diagrams, and work breakdown scheduling software, make it possible to plan and track each construction phase and break a project down into a series of tasks. For each task, planners enter its estimated duration and how it relates to other tasks. For example, drywall work that requires eight days depends on interior framing, electrical work, and plumbing being finished first. Given information about all the tasks in a project, planning software can create a schedule showing both best-case and worst-case completion dates, and contractors can update the schedule based on actual construction progress.

At a high-tech construction site, computers can play several additional roles. A site supervisor can use a wireless handheld computer to view and update the construction schedule stored on a desktop computer at the contractor's main office. Rather than referring to a set of printed—and possibly outdated—plans, the supervisor can refer to up-to-date plans transmitted from the home office. A supervisor might even wear a hardhat-mounted computer that collects multimedia data, such as video and sound, to document site inspections. A voice-activated microphone records the supervisor's comments and adds them to the digital video, which can be uploaded to a database in the contractor's main office.

Digital devices also play a role in guiding bulldozers during site preparation by using construction software developed at Ohio State University that works with a global positioning system (GPS). A GPS receiver is mounted on a vehicle that traverses the site. GPS signals are collected and entered in the software program, which creates a map and a plan for site preparation. A wireless device mounted in each bulldozer's cab receives data from the software and displays it to the operator. The system allows construction crews to stake and grade a site with to-the-centimeter accuracy.

Computers embedded in robots are used extensively on large construction projects in Japan. These single-task robots perform specific jobs. For example, a concrete-task robot might lay forms, bend rebar for reinforcement, pour concrete, and screed the surface to a smooth finish. Other robots weld steel components, apply paint, or install tile. Single-task robots have been successful because they shield human workers from dangerous and difficult jobs, and tend to work faster and more consistently than humans. However, trained technicians are required to set up and monitor robot work.

It was once a summer tradition for college students to work in construction. Today, however, fewer students are attracted to those jobs, creating a labor shortage.

Construction robots might help fill the labor gap. For example, a robot that finishes drywall can be cost-effectively deployed at commercial construction sites. The robot, created by a construction robotics company, uses laser-light measuring devices to scan the walls and then activates a robotic arm to smooth the surface and apply drywall compound.

Potential barriers, such as union regulations, could discourage the use of construction robots. Some observers question how building trade union agreements might affect construction site robots. According to one supervisor's worst-case scenario, "Millwrights will want to set up the device, electricians will want to fix the electronic controls, equipment operators will want to run it, cement finishers will want to adjust it, and laborers will be expected to clean it."

The future of computer-powered robots at construction sites is still unclear, which illustrates the controversies that sometimes surround technology as it filters into society and the workplace.

Flipped Class Projects

Critical Thinking

Free content. Free software. Freemium pricing models. Viral popularity. Disappearing gatekeepers. These are the disrupters of the digital age. They affect software as well as digital content. But what is the endgame? Will these disrupters lead to a cultural renaissance or to a cultural dark age? Watch the Vimeo video titled "PressPausePlay." What are the two opposing viewpoints it presents? What is your perspective on the issue?

Group Project

Form a group with at least two of your classmates. Now imagine that your college (or business) has decided to negotiate with software publishers to offer students (or employees) a bundled software package at a greatly discounted price. Your group's job is to select the 15 software products for the bundle. Your group must make sure the software effectively meets the major needs of the students at your school (or employees in your workplace). Use Internet resources to look at the range of software available and make your selections. Make sure you take advantage of group members' expertise and experience with software products.

Cyberclassroom

Mobile apps used for educational activities are called mLearning apps. Do you use mobile flashcards? Have you downloaded a periodic table to your Android phone? Do you have a link to a reference portal or academic journal handy? Is your mobile device helping you to learn a second language? Do you have a stash of articles pertaining to your major field? Does your phone hold a list of assignments and due dates? Work in groups of two or three to share the mLearning apps that you use. Brainstorm ways you can use generic apps, such as Notes, Reminders, and Calendar, for mLearning.

Multimedia Project

Create an infographic that offers ten best practices for computer file management. You can base your infographic on the tips in Figure 6-55. To get started, browse the Web for some examples and ideas. You'll also find several free apps for creating infographics online, or use your favorite graphics software.

Resume Builder

Use the Web and other resources to compile a list of the software used in your current or future career field. Are there standard software products that job applicants need to know how to use? If so, what can you find out about those products on the Web? If your career field does not use any standard software products, explain why you think that is the case. Also, make a list of the software products you're familiar with. As you consider your school and career goals for the next year, list at least five additional software applications you would like to learn. Explain why they would be helpful.

Globalization

Computer games are big business. They are exported worldwide and accessed by communities of online players around the globe. For this project, gather information about the most internationally popular computer games. Try some of them yourself to see what they're all about. What effect, if any, would you expect these games to have on individual players living in the cultures of 1) industrialized countries, 2) Middle Eastern countries, and 3) developing countries? Summarize your ideas in one or two pages.

Key Terms

absolute reference 422
Android 401
application extensions 409
automatic recalculation 422
BSD license 387
buffers 394
cell 419
cell references 421
Chrome OS 402
cluster 436
commercial software 385
database 423
database software 423
default application 432
demoware 386
desktop operating system 391
device letter 428
directory 429
disk partition 428
DMG 412
document formatting 418
DOS (Disk Operating System) 396
EULAs 384
executable file 382
field 423
file management utilities 430
file path 429
file shredder software 437
file system 436
file-naming conventions 427
folder 429
font 418
footer 418
forked 402
formatting 436
formula 420
freeware 386
fully justified 418
function 421
GPL 387
grammar checker 417
hash value 386
header 418
iOS 400
jailbreak 408
kernel 391
label 419
leading 418
Linux 403
Linux distribution 403
local application 409
logical storage model 436
macOS 398
memory leak 393
Microsoft Windows 395
mobile app 408
mobile operating systems 391
module 415
multiple-user license 385
multiprocessing 393
multitasking 393
multithreading 393
office suite 415
open source software 387
page layout 418
paragraph alignment 418
paragraph style 418
physical storage model 436
pirated software 389
point size 418
presentation software 425
processes 392
product activation 386
productivity software 415
proprietary software 385
public domain software 385
readability formula 417
record 423
relative reference 422
resource 392
root directory 429
rooting 408
search and replace 416
sectors 436
server operating system 391
setup program 410
single-user license 385
site license 385
software license 384
software update 383
software upgrade 383
spelling checker 417
spelling dictionary 417
spreadsheet 419
spreadsheet software 419
style 418
subdirectory 429
system requirements 382
thesaurus 417
thin client 402
tracks 436
uninstall utility 413
user interface 391
value 419
virtual machine 404
Web application 406
what-if analysis 419
word processing software 416
word wrap 416
worksheet 419

Interactive Summary

Section A: Both ________ software and application software are essential for accomplishing tasks with a digital device. Today, most application software is distributed online or through app stores. The main executable file for PC software has a(n) ________ extension, whereas executable files for Macs have a(n) ________ extension. New versions of software are called ________ and are indicated by version numbers such as 1.0 and 2.0. A software ________ or patch is a small section of program code designed to correct problems and address security vulnerabilities. Software payment models include free, one-time purchase, ________, trial, and freemium. Software licenses, referred to by the acronym ________, can be divided into two main categories: public ________ and proprietary. ________ software is typically available directly from the publisher or an app store and may have options for site licenses as well as single-user licenses. Freeware is copyrighted software that is available free of charge. ________ is also available free of charge, but is limited in some way until you pay for it. Open ________ software may be sold or distributed free of charge, but the distribution must include the source code.

Section B: ________ operating systems—such as Windows, Chrome OS, and macOS—accommodate one user at a time, are capable of multitasking, and include a graphical user interface designed for keyboard and mouse input. Chrome OS is considered a thin ________ because it depends substantially on processing supplied by a remote computer. ________ operating systems, such as iOS and Android, are designed for smartphones and tablet computers. ________ operating systems, such as UNIX and Linux, are designed for hosting distributed networks. A single device can run more than one operating system as a(n) ________ machine. The operating system ________ remains in RAM while a device is in operation and manages the device's resources. Most operating systems have ________ capabilities that allow two or more processes to run simultaneously. ________ capabilities allow an operating system to run multiple simultaneous operations for a single program. ________ supports a division of labor among several processing units. Operating systems manage resources by monitoring processor cycles, allocating ________ space to programs, tracking stored files, and supervising data exchanges with peripheral devices. When an operating system fails to correctly track the allocation of RAM space to applications, a memory ________ may produce "Program Not Responding" error messages. Operating systems also manage ________ that collect and hold data from peripheral devices until a device is ready to accept it.

Section C: Software is available in several paradigms that affect how it is installed and used. __________ apps run in a browser and require no installation. Mobile apps are designed for smartphones and tablets. They are typically downloaded and __________ from an app store or Web sites, though owners with __________ devices must __________ the device to obtain apps from third-party sources. Local applications for PCs are installed using a(n) __________ program that copies files, checks resources, and updates the Windows __________. Software for Macs is distributed as __________ packages that are dragged to the Applications folder to complete the installation. To remove software that has been installed on a PC, Windows supplies a(n) __________ utility. To remove most applications from a Mac, the __________ file or folder can simply be dragged to the trash.

Section D: Office suites are sometimes referred to as __________ software because they offer features that really help get work done. Word __________ software assists you with composing, editing, designing, printing, and electronically publishing documents. When you want to change margins, headers, and footers, you can use __________ layout tools. To change the spacing between lines or the alignment of text, you can use tools to adjust __________ style. __________ software is like a smart piece of paper that automatically adds up the columns of numbers you write on it. You can use it to make other calculations, too, based on basic equations that you write or more complex, built-in formulas. Because you can experiment with different numbers, this type of software is particularly useful for __________ analyses. __________ software helps you store, find, organize, update, and report information located in one or more tables. Data is stored in __________, which form records. When two sets of records are __________, database software allows you to access data from both tables at the same time. __________ software supplies tools for creating a series of electronic slides that can be shown on a computer screen or projector.

Section E: Every file has a name and might also have a file extension. The rules that specify valid file names are called file-naming __________. These rules typically do not allow you to use certain characters or __________ words in a file name. A file's location is defined by a file __________, which includes the storage device, folder(s), file name, and extension. In Windows, storage devices are identified by a drive letter, followed by a(n) __________. Every storage device has a(n) __________ containing a list of files stored on the device. The top-level list of a device is referred to as the __________ directory, which can be subdivided into several smaller lists called subdirectories that are depicted as __________. Windows File Explorer and the macOS __________ are examples of file management utilities provided by operating systems. These utilities allow you to find, rename, copy, move, and delete files and folders. In addition, they allow you to perform file management activities with more than one file at a time. The way that data is actually stored is referred to as the __________ storage model. Before a computer stores data on a disk, CD, or DVD, it creates the equivalent of electronic storage bins by dividing the disk into __________ and then further dividing the disk into __________. This dividing process is referred to as __________. Each sector of a disk is numbered, providing a storage address that the operating system can track. Many computers work with a group of sectors, called a(n) __________, to increase the efficiency of file storage operations. When a file is deleted from a PC, the operating system changes the status of the file to "empty" and removes the file name from the __________ listing.

Interactive Situation Questions

1. Imagine that you've just paid for a year's subscription to highly rated antivirus software. You've installed the software, but it requires a(n) [________] code before it begins scanning for viruses.

2. Every time you want to edit a photo, your PC pulls up a Viewer application that has no editing capabilities. To avoid this frustration in the future, you have to change the [________] application that is associated with the JPEG and PNG file extensions.

3. Your friend has an iPhone that's loaded with all kinds of applications. But every time there's a software update, your friend grumbles about "redoing stuff." You guess that your friend's iPhone is [________].

4. Suppose that you've been hired to organize a professional skateboard competition. When you consider how you'll need to use digital devices, you realize that you must collect information on each competitor and keep track of every competitive event. With at least two types of related records, you'll probably need to use [________] software.

5. The screen below is likely to appear during the process of [________] a software application.

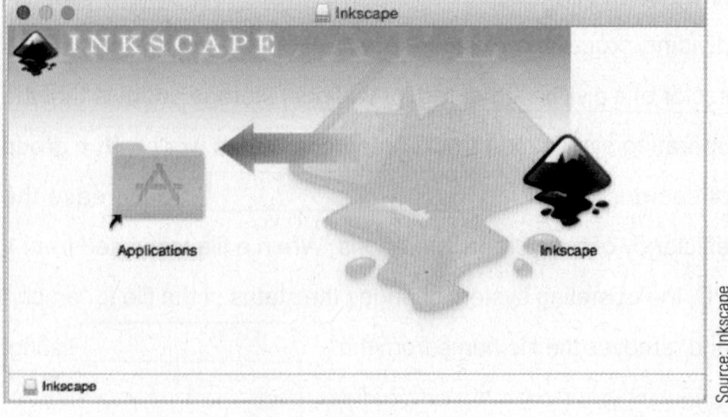

Source: Inkscape

6. While using several Windows programs at the same time, your computer displays an error message that refers to a program that is not responding. You recognize this message as one that might result from a(n) [________] leak and decide to close the nonresponding program using Task Manager.

7. Your friend wants to open a window on a Mac computer in order to run Microsoft Windows and play some games designed for the Windows platform. You tell your friend to create a(n) [________] machine using software such as Parallels Desktop.

8. Can you use a Windows application, create a document, and store it using the file name *I L*ve NY*? Yes or no? [________]

9. When specifying a location for a data file on your hard disk, you should avoid saving it in the [________] directory.

10. You have an old computer that you will donate to a school, but you want to make sure its hard disk contains no trace of your data. To do so, you use file [________] software that overwrites empty sectors with random 1s and 0s.

Lab: Organize Your Files Today!

Some day you have to get organized. That day is here. This lab is designed to help you evaluate your current file organization and make improvements that will increase your productivity and reduce the frustration of rifling through a jumble of unorganized files and folders.

Requirements:

For this lab, you'll need a desktop or laptop computer running Windows or macOS. The instructions are generalized; they provide helpful guidelines but not specific steps. You may have to do some exploring to find all the tools needed to complete the assignment, but that is all part of the learning experience.

Assignment:

❶ Examine your desktop computer, laptop, or cloud drive and total up your organizational points as described below:

Count the icons on your desktop. If you have fewer than 20, award yourself 1 point.

Check the root directory (Macintosh HD or Windows C:). Award yourself 1 point if there are only folders and no files there.

Examine the folders listed under your user name. Give yourself 1 point if you can identify the kinds of files that each one contains.

Open each of the folders listed under your user name. Award yourself 1 point if none of the folders is empty.

Open the Documents folder. Award yourself 1 point if you have fewer than 100 files (not counting folders) listed there.

If you use one set of folders for your personal data and another set of folders for school or work data, award yourself 1 point.

Open the folder that contains most of your photos. Give yourself 1 point if the photos are organized into subfolders according to date, subject, or other criteria.

Browse files on your storage device. If you don't seem to have unnecessary duplicates, give yourself 1 point.

If you can launch any program in fewer than 5 seconds, award yourself 1 point.

If files and folders that you use frequently are in your Quick Access or Favorites list, add another point to your score.

❷ Evaluate your score.

8–10 points: You're organized!

5–7 points: You're on the right track.

0–4 points: It is not too late to get organized.

❸ Make a backup of your data files. Do it.

If you have a backup, make sure it is current. If you have no backup, at least copy your data files to a USB flash drive. How much space does your backup require?

❹ Switch to Details view (PC) or List view (Macs).

For organizing files, the Details and List views provide the best visual picture of the folder hierarchy. After your files are in order, you may want to use a different view for everyday file access.

Use the View menu to experiment with various views. You may also explore the Sort options to see how they affect the arrangement of folders and files.

When you are finished exploring, return to the List view.

On a PC, select View and then select Details. Also use the Sort by option to select Type and Ascending, which lists all of the subfolders, followed by files.

On a Mac, select the List view and sort by Kind, which groups all of the subfolders together. Don't worry if the subfolders are not at the top of the list.

5 Organize your Quick Access or Favorites list.

On PCs running Windows 10 and 11, the Quick Access list is a handy location for the folders that you use most frequently. On earlier versions of Windows and on Macs, the Favorites list is the recommended location for preconfigured personal folders titled Desktop, Documents, Music, Pictures, Videos, and Downloads.

If the Quick Access or Favorites folder already contains the preconfigured personal folders, skip this step. Otherwise, locate your preconfigured folders and drag them to the Quick Access or Favorites list.

On a Mac, you'll find the preconfigured personal folders listed under Macintosh HD/Users/YourUserName. On a PC, you'll find these folders on drive C: under Users\YourUserName.

6 Add project subfolders to the Quick Access or Favorites list.

Folders in the Quick Access or Favorites area can be accessed with a single click. Consider the projects that you are currently working on and the folders that you access most frequently. Are there any additional folders that you would like to add to the Quick Access or Favorites list?

Drag additional folders to the Quick Access or Favorites list as necessary.

Tip: Don't let the Quick Access or Favorites list get too long or it will no longer be a quick way to access folders. When the number of folders in the list exceeds 20, it is time to remove folders that are less frequently used. To remove a folder, right-click it and select the Remove option or the Unpin option. Do not select the Delete option unless you want to move the folder and its contents to the trash.

7 Clean up your desktop.

The desktop should be reserved for files that you access on a daily basis. For example, the desktop is a good place for a To-Do list. You may also store frequently used programs there, though the Start menu and taskbar are preferable locations because they are always visible.

Remove any icons that are cluttering up your desktop.

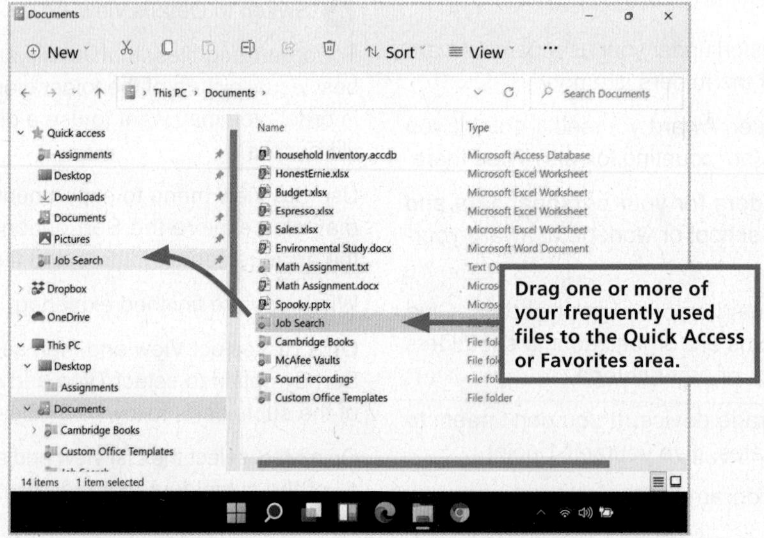

Lab: Organize Your Files Today! (cont.)

❽ Deal with shortcuts.

A shortcut (PC) or alias (Mac) is a link to a file, folder, or application. Shortcuts and aliases are useful for items that you want to access from multiple places but don't want to save as actual copies. For example, if you use the same photo for two projects, you might not want to duplicate the photo, but you might want a link for the photo to exist in more than one folder.

As another example, you might want to be able to launch an application from the desktop as well as from the taskbar or dock. You don't want two copies of the application, but a shortcut or alias will provide an icon that you can use.

Deleting a shortcut or alias only deletes the shortcut icon, not the file, folder, or application that it represents. You can identify shortcuts because their icons include an arrow.

Check your desktop and file listings for shortcuts or aliases by looking for icons, folders, and files that display arrows. If you do not need the shortcuts, remove them by right-clicking and selecting the Delete option (PC) or the Move to Trash option (Mac).

❾ Organize your Documents folder.

A well-organized set of folders has a logical hierarchical structure. For example, in the Documents folder, there can be subfolders for various types of documents. These folders can reflect various projects, assignments, classes, or jobs. The arrangement should reflect your work patterns.

To organize the files and subfolders in your Documents folder, do the following:

- Make sure that subfolders are clearly named. Rename folders if necessary.
- For folders that contain an excessive number of files, create additional subfolders and move files into them.
- Delete unneeded folders and files.

❿ Take a screenshot showing the subfolders in your newly organized Documents folder.

On a PC, press the Windows and PrtSc keys to capture the screen in memory. Next, launch the Paint program. When Paint is open, hold down the Ctrl key and press the V key to paste the image into Paint. Save the image using the File menu.

On a Mac, press Command-Shift-3 to capture the screen image on the desktop. Locate the image on the desktop, rename the image, and move it to an appropriate folder.

Source: Mozilla, 2021.

The Firefox shortcut on the desktop can be identified by its arrow. If it is removed from the desktop, the Chrome software will not be deleted.

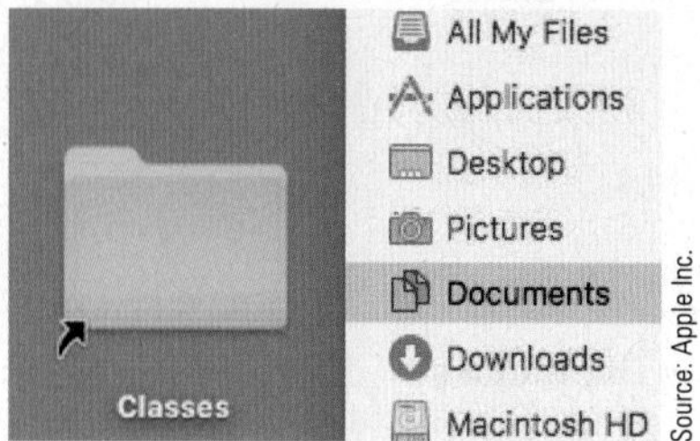

Source: Apple Inc.

The blue Classes folder on the desktop is an alias for the actual folder. Deleting the alias does not delete the actual folder or its contents.

7 Digital Security

Module Contents

As the rate of malicious attacks on digital devices expands, our level of privacy and security dwindles. What can you do to reinforce your digital defenses? Read on.

Try It! Apply what you learn.

- Encrypt an individual file or an entire storage volume.
- Adjust the login options on your digital devices to enhance security.
- Use two-factor authentication to enhance the security of your devices.
- Devise a personal strategy for creating strong passwords and maintaining them securely.
- Select, install, and configure antivirus software.
- Verify that antivirus software is actively scanning, and deal with virus alerts.
- Identify virus hoaxes.
- Close remote access features that might pose security risks.
- Take steps to be prepared if your device is infected with ransomware.
- Use an on-demand virus scanner as necessary to find and remove zero-day attacks.
- Discover which ports are open on your digital devices.
- Install, activate, and configure a personal firewall.
- Avoid Evil Twin exploits when using Wi-Fi hotspots.
- Watch for the signs of digital certificate hacks.
- Take steps to reduce the amount of spam you receive.
- Use spam filters to block unwanted email messages.
- Identify and avoid phishing, pharming, rogue antivirus, and PUA exploits.

7 Digital Security

Pre-Check

Gauge your level of expertise. The answers are in the module.

Current encryption standard:

____

$$\log_2 10^4$$

This formula calculates

________________.

Viruses have a unique

________________.

Malware that masquerades as a legitimate application:

____

One of the first cyberwar exploits:

____

0

An attack that exploits previously unknown hardware or software vulnerabilities:

____

A firewall is designed to defend against exploits entering a device through open

________________.

What kind of attack is this?

____

Computers under the secret control of a hacker form a(n)

________________.

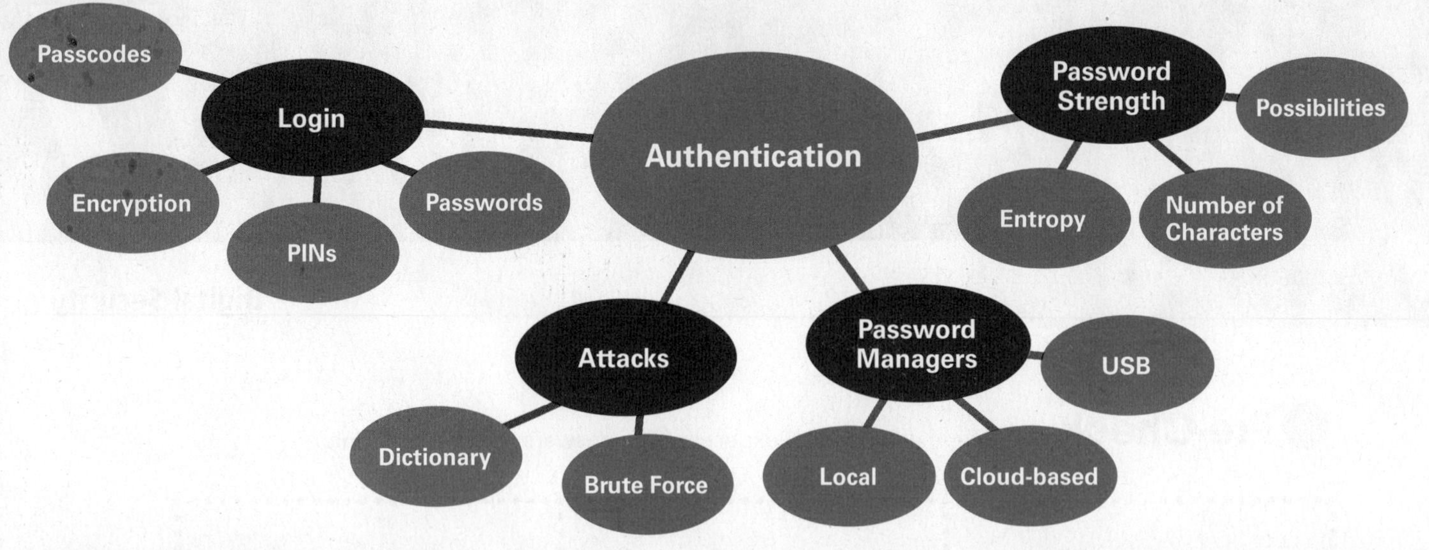

Section A

Basic Security

Objectives

- List five examples in which digital data is encrypted for security purposes.
- Compare and contrast PINs, passcodes, and passwords.
- Describe how two-factor authentication works when you log in to an account from a device you have never used before.
- Explain how encryption is linked to passcodes in some digital devices.
- Describe the advantages of encrypting an entire storage volume.
- Recite the basic rules for creating a strong password.
- List at least five characteristics of weak passwords.
- Recite the formula for calculating the number of possible passwords that can be generated using a four-digit PIN.
- Explain the concept of password entropy.
- Describe the advantages and disadvantages of local, cloud-based, and USB password managers.

Your smartphone is stolen. Your roommate is a busybody. A law enforcement agent wants to look at your files. Today, digital devices contain important and personal information. In the wrong hands, that information can compromise your privacy, ruin your credit rating, or even make you the target of legal action. Protecting physical devices and the data they contain is an important safeguard against identity theft and other security assaults.

Terminology

encryption	cryptographic algorithm	two-factor authentication	password entropy
plaintext	cryptographic key	strong password	password manager
ciphertext	AES	brute force attack	strength meter
decryption	user authentication	dictionary attack	

Encryption

Basic digital security depends on two techniques: encryption and authentication. These techniques are often combined to protect data from unauthorized access and to make data unintelligible if it is somehow hacked.

▶ **How does encryption work?** **Encryption** transforms a message or data file in such a way that its contents are hidden from unauthorized readers. An original message or file that has not yet been encrypted is referred to as **plaintext** or cleartext. An encrypted message or file is referred to as **ciphertext**. The process of converting plaintext into ciphertext is called encryption. The reverse process—converting ciphertext into plaintext—is called **decryption**.

Data is encrypted by using a cryptographic algorithm and a key. A **cryptographic algorithm** is a procedure for encryption or decryption. A **cryptographic key** (usually just called a key) is a word, number, or phrase that must be known to encrypt or decrypt data. A password, PIN, or passcode is typically used as the key to encrypt and decrypt data.

▶ **What can be encrypted?** Encryption is commonly applied to data packets sent over wired or wireless networks, bank card numbers and other personal data sent to ecommerce sites, email messages that contain confidential information, entire storage volumes for a digital device, and individual files that contain sensitive information.

▶ **How well does encryption protect files?** There are various encryption methods, and some are more secure than others. **AES** (Advanced Encryption Standard) is the encryption standard currently used worldwide. It is possible to crack AES, but the process is difficult and requires lots of computer power.

▶ **How can I encrypt files?** Methods for encrypting storage volumes are described later in this section. Individual files can be encrypted using encryption features built into applications such as word processing, spreadsheet, and database software. Encryption options, if available, can usually be found on the File menu. Figure 7-1 illustrates how to encrypt a file using Microsoft Word.

Terminology

A *password* is a series of characters that can contain letters, numbers, and symbols. A PIN (personal identification number) is typically four to six numeric digits, but it can be as long as 12 digits. *Passcode* is another term for a PIN because, technically speaking, PINs and passcodes contain only numbers. In common usage, however, the terms "passcode" and "password" are used interchangeably. When asked to create a PIN, passcode, or password, check the instructions to see if you need to include letters, numbers, or special characters.

Try It!

Use Microsoft Word or Apple iWork Pages to open a document. Find the encryption option on the application's menu and encrypt the document. Close the document, and then make sure that it can be opened only by providing the password.

Figure 7-1: How to encrypt individual files with Microsoft Word

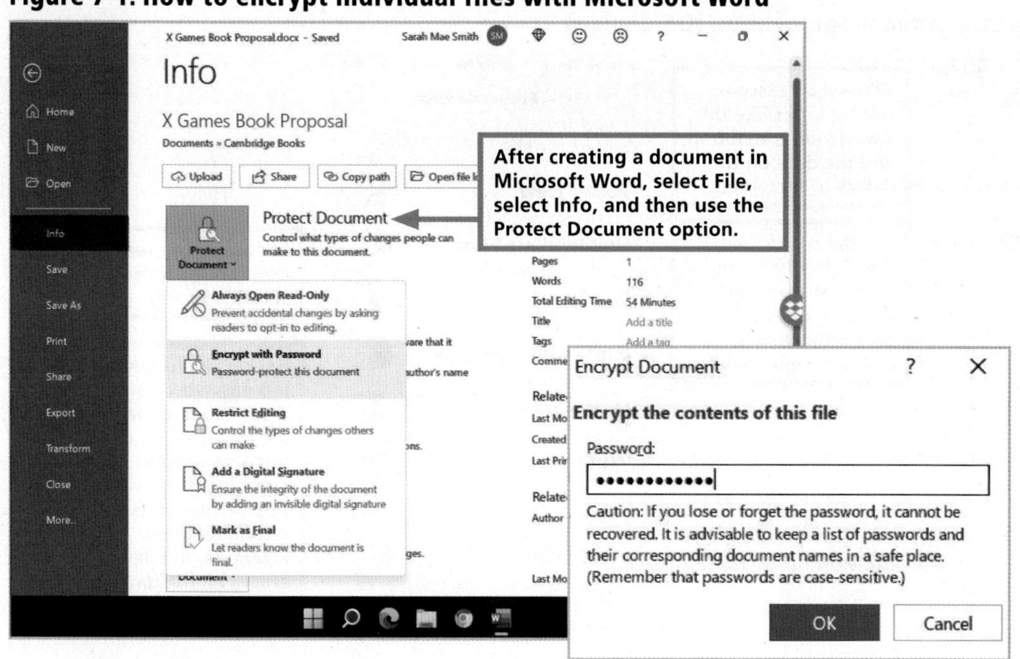

Authentication

In the context of digital security, **user authentication** is any technique used to verify or confirm a person's identity. Authentication techniques such as passwords, PINs, fingerprint scans, and facial recognition can prevent unauthorized access to the data on Web sites or stolen devices.

Two-factor authentication increases security by verifying identity based on two components, such as a password and a verification code. It is most useful for verifying logins initiated from a device that was not used previously to log in. After a valid password is entered, a verification code is sent to a secondary device, such as a mobile phone, known to belong to the user. The verification code is then entered, in addition to the password, as the second authentication component.

QuickCheck

Which one of the following would offer the most login security?

a. A 4-digit PIN.

b. An 8-letter password.

c. A 6-digit numeric passcode.

d. An 8-character alphanumeric code.

▶ What are the authentication options for iOS devices? iPhones and iPads can be "locked" to require a login password, PIN, or some other form of authentication each time the device is used. When an iOS device is locked, the contents of its storage volume are automatically encrypted. A hacker who manages to gain possession of a locked device cannot access its files without the proper authentication credentials. Even if the storage device is removed, the data it contains is meaningless because it is encrypted.

Authentication options for iOS devices include short passcodes, long alphanumeric passwords, facial recognition, and fingerprint scans. Refer to Apple Support for information about how exercising, swimming, cooking, and other activities might affect the ability of a device to reliably recognize fingerprints.

Try It!

If you have an iPhone, look at the password settings and consider whether you would like to secure your device with more than a basic passcode.

The standard iOS security setting establishes a six-digit numeric passcode. Short passcodes are not very secure. With six digits, 1 million passcodes are possible. Password hacking utilities can quickly try all of them in a matter of seconds. iOS can be set to erase a device after ten unsuccessful login attempts. When using a short passcode, the erase option offers much-needed protection.

Long alphanumeric codes are more difficult to hack than six-digit passcodes. To configure a longer code for an iOS device, use the Settings icon and select the Passcode option, as shown in Figure 7-2.

Figure 7-2: Login password management on iOS devices

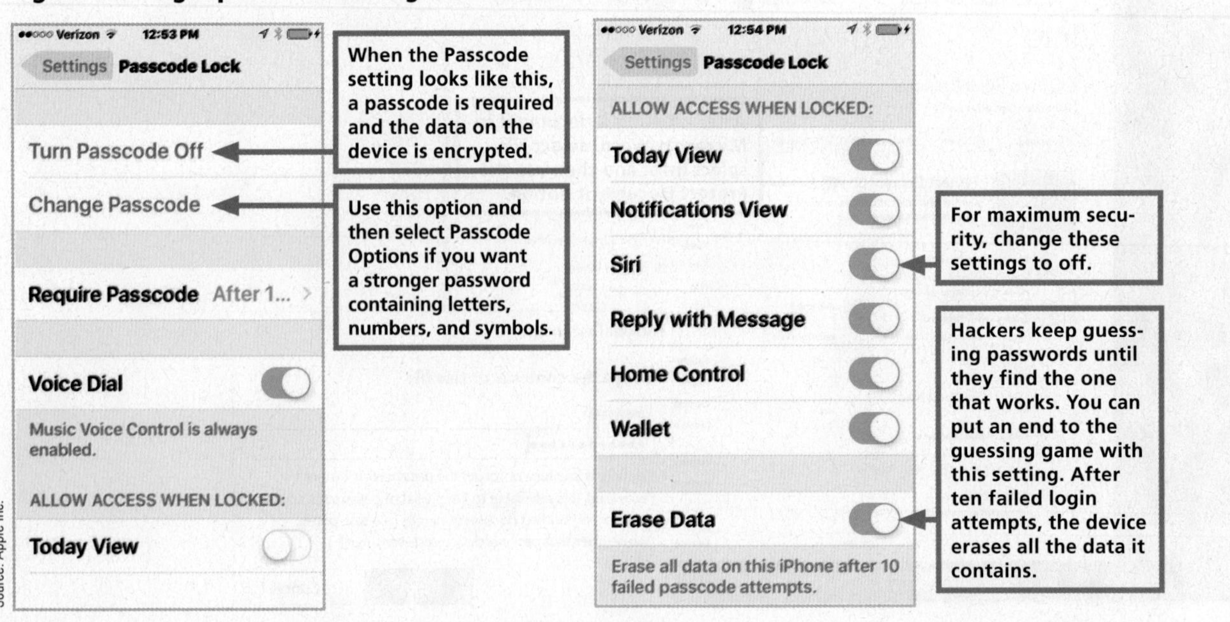

Source: Apple Inc.

▶ What are the authentication options for Android devices? Android devices have an overwhelming number of security settings, including PINs, passwords, facial recognition, voice recognition, and drawing a pattern on the screen. Setting a strong password provides the highest level of security.

Unlike iOS devices, Android devices do not automatically encrypt stored data. Configuring a password and activating encryption are two separate steps, as shown in Figure 7-3.

Figure 7-3: Login password management on Android devices

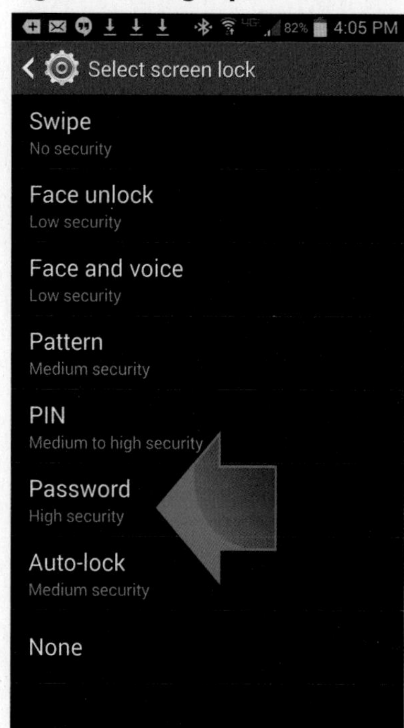

1 Android password options are accessed from the Settings menu by selecting the Lock Screen option and then selecting Screen lock. A strong password provides the best security.

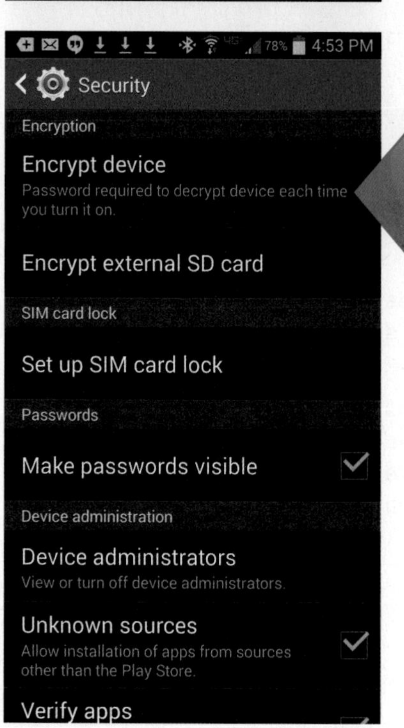

Source: Android 2017

2 To encrypt the files on an Android device, use the Security setting and select Encrypt device. When first activated, the encryption process may require up to an hour. Make sure your device is fully charged and plugged in during the process.

Try It!

If you have an Android phone, look at the password settings and consider whether you would like to secure your device with a longer password.

▶ What are the authentication options for Windows? Windows offers several sign-in options that can be configured using the Accounts option on the Settings screen. Figure 7-4 explains the authentication options and points out the critical security settings.

Try It!

If you have a laptop or desktop PC, look at the password settings and consider whether you should enhance the login security.

Figure 7-4: Login password management on Windows devices

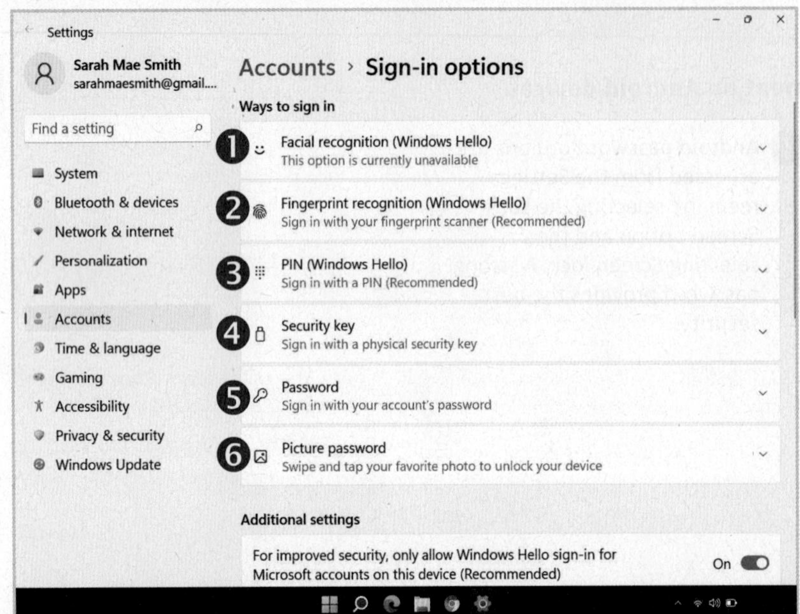

1. Facial recognition is possible with a computer equipped with a camera.
2. Fingerprint recognition requires a built-in or add-on fingerprint scanning device.
3. The Windows Hello PIN is a four-digit number that gives you a quick way to log in. For the best security, however, do not use a PIN instead of a longer password.
4. A security key is a device that connects to a USB port. This device provides an extra layer of security, but you must be careful not to lose it.
5. Windows password login uses the same password as for your Microsoft account, typically consisting of letters, numbers, and special characters.
6. You can set up a picture password on a touchscreen device by selecting an image and then drawing three gestures over it. Those three gestures allow you to log in.

▶ Is it possible to encrypt a Windows hard drive volume? Devices with Windows Pro and Enterprise editions can be encrypted using Microsoft's BitLocker or third-party utilities.

For Windows users who are working with the Home edition, Windows provides a Device Encryption option. As an alternative, individual file encryption can be used for critical files, as explained earlier in this module. Third-party software utilities that offer more comprehensive volume encryption capabilities include Symantec Encryption and GNU Privacy Guard.

What are the authentication options for macOS? Macs offer several password settings, which are accessed from the Security & Privacy preferences. A feature called Automatic Login allows access to a device without a password. For security, this feature should be disabled, as shown in Figure 7-5.

Figure 7-5: Login password management on Macs

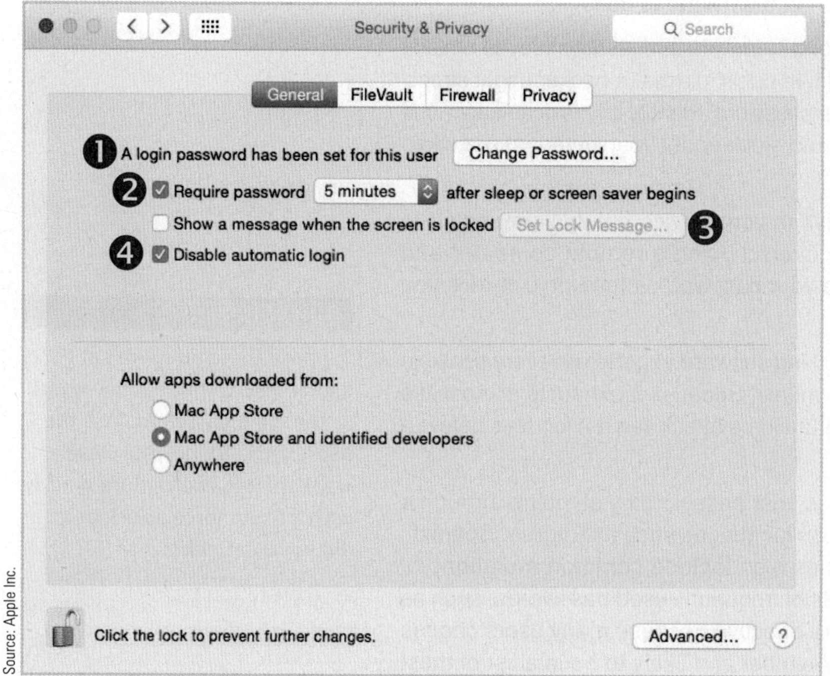

1. Use this option to change the password or disable the login password. If a password has not been set, check the option labeled *Disable automatic login*, and then create a password.
2. Users typically leave their digital devices in sleep mode rather than shutting them down, so devices that are lost or stolen are likely to be in sleep mode. Configuring a device to require a password when waking from sleep adds an important layer of security. For convenience, allow the device to awaken from short sleep periods without requiring a password.
3. Showing a message when the screen is locked can be useful if a device is lost. You can create a message to display your contact information so that the device can be returned if found.
4. When this option is not checked, no password is required to access the device. For security, make sure this setting is checked.

Is password authentication required before a macOS file volume can be encrypted? macOS devices include a utility called FileVault that automatically encrypts data stored locally. FileVault settings are accessed from the same Security & Privacy window used for password settings.

QuickCheck

Based on the settings in Figure 7-5, what happens when the device is awakened after it has been asleep for three minutes?

a. The device asks for a login password.

b. The device displays the "If found" message.

c. The display resumes without asking for a password.

d. The computer shuts down with a security warning.

Try It!

If you have a Mac laptop or desktop computer, look at the password settings and consider whether you should enhance the login security.

7

Passwords

Passwords protect digital devices from unauthorized access, and they protect user accounts at online banks, Web sites, and app stores. A **strong password** is difficult to hack. Conventional wisdom tells us that strong passwords are at least eight characters in length and include one or more uppercase letters, numbers, and symbols. These conventions create passwords that may be fairly difficult to crack, but they are also impossible to remember. What to do?

How can hackers get my password? Hackers and identity thieves employ a whole range of ways to steal passwords. In public places, a hacker might simply look over your shoulder as you type in your password. Identity thieves can easily find your password if you write it down on a note stuck under your keyboard or tucked inside your mobile phone case.

If a hacker doesn't have physical access to your device but it is connected to a network, your password can be discovered using a remote computer and software tools that systematically guess your password, intercept it, or trick you into revealing it.

A **brute force attack** uses password-cracking software to generate every possible combination of letters, numerals, and symbols. Because it exhausts all possible combinations to discover a password, a brute force attack can run for days before a password is cracked.

A **dictionary attack** helps hackers guess your password by stepping through a dictionary containing word lists in common languages such as English, Spanish, French, and German. These dictionaries also include common mutations of words, such as p@ssw0rd, and hundreds of frequently used passwords, such as qwerty and 12345. Dictionary attacks are effective because many users choose passwords that are easy for them to remember and likely to be in a list of most commonly used passwords (Figure 7-6).

QuickCheck

Suppose that you've lost a digital device that has a@rdvark as the login password. Will the hacker who found your device crack the password more quickly with a brute force attack or a dictionary attack?

a. A brute force attack

b. A dictionary attack

Figure 7-6: Commonly used passwords

12345	000000	buster	coffee	eeyore
abc123	money	dragon	dave	fishing
password	carmen	jordan	falcon	football
p@ssw0rd	mickey	michael	freedom	george
Pa55word	secret	michelle	gandalf	happy
password1	summer	mindy	green	iloveyou
!qaz2wsx	internet	patrick	helpme	jennifer
computer	service	123abc	linda	jonathan
123456	canada	andrew	magic	love
111111	hello	calvin	merlin	marina
a1b2c3	ranger	changeme	molson	missy
qwerty	shadow	diamond	newyork	monday
adobe123	baseball	matthew	soccer	monkey
123123	donald	miller	thomas	natasha
admin	harley	ou812	wizard	ncc1701
1234567890	hockey	tiger	Monday	newpass
photoshop	letmein	12345678	asdfgh	pamela
1234	maggie	apple	bandit	
sunshine	mike	avalon	batman	
azerty	mustang	brandy	boris	
trustno1	snoopy	chelsea	dorothy	

What makes a password susceptible to a dictionary attack? Many of the clever schemes users devise to create passwords are obvious to hackers and the programmers who create password-cracking tools. Weak passwords include the following:

- Words from a dictionary, including words that are in languages other than English
- Doubled words such as passpass or computercomputer
- Default passwords such as password, admin, system, and guest
- Words with a sequence of numbers at the end, such as Secret123 and Dolphins2022
- Words with symbol or numeric mutations, such as p@ssw0rd and V01dem0rt
- Sequences of numbers formatted as dates or telephone numbers, such as 01/01/2000 and 888-5566
- Any sequence that includes a user name, such as BillMurray12345
- Any sequence that uses conventional capitalization, such as Book34 and Savannah912

QuickCheck

Which password for Dave Meyers is most secure?

a. DaveBMeyers

b. Dave12345

c. Ih2gtg8pw

d. D@veMeyer$

7

What makes a password susceptible to a brute force attack? Brute force attacks methodically try every possible password until the correct one is found. Consider a simple guess-the-number game. You have a much better chance of guessing a number between 1 and 10 than guessing the correct number between 1 and 10,000. In the same way, a password selected from a universe of 10,000 possibilities is easier to crack than a password selected from a universe of 100 million possibilities.

The number of possible passwords depends on factors that include the size of the character set and the length of the password. Longer passwords and those consisting of a mixture of letters, numbers, and symbols are more difficult to crack. The general formula for calculating the number of possible passwords is:

$$\text{NumberOfCharacters}^{\text{PasswordLength}}$$

For example, suppose you are creating a four-digit numeric password for an iPhone. The character set consists of ten numerals on the keypad: 0, 1, 2, 3, etc. The password length is four digits. The number of possible passwords is:

$$10^4$$

NumberOfCharacters PasswordLength

10^4 is 10 x 10 x 10 x 10, which is equal to 10,000. Password-cracking software, with its ability to try more than a billion passwords per second, can run through all those possibilities within milliseconds.

How much safer is a five-digit password? The number of possibilities is 10^5, which is 100,000. That's a big increase over the possibilities for a four-digit password, but those possibilities are still easily handled by password-cracking software.

An eight-character password using uppercase letters, lowercase letters, numerals, and symbols has 6,095,689,385,410,816 possibilities. Running through all those possibilities would take a considerable amount of time. The difficulty of cracking such a password is a good start in providing enough entropy for a secure password.

Try It!

To make sure that you understand how to find the number of possibilities for a password, calculate how many possibilities exist for a password that is four characters long and uses only lowercase letters from the English alphabet.

What is password entropy? The number of possible passwords quickly becomes very large. Rather than discuss such huge numbers, security experts express password strength in terms of entropy. **Password entropy** is a measure in bits of a password's unpredictability. For example, the entropy of a four-digit iPhone passcode is 14 bits. For those of you interested in the math, entropy is calculated like this:

$$\log_2 10^4$$

10^4 = 10,000. $\log_2$ of 10,000 = 13.2877

Notice that the number of bits does not refer to the length of the password. An iPhone's passcode is four digits in length, but its entropy is rounded up to 14. The number 14 enumerates how many bits are needed to represent the number of possible passcodes in binary. For a four-digit passcode, the number of possible codes is 10,000. That's 10011100010000 in binary. Count the number of bits. There are 14, and that is the entropy (Figure 7-7).

Figure 7-7: Entropy for common password sizes

	Number of Characters	Length	Possibilities	Entropy
PIN	10	4	10,000	14-bit
Lowercase alphabetic password	26	8	208,827,064,576	38-bit
Lower and uppercase alphabetic password	52	8	53,459,728,531,456	46-bit
Alphanumeric-symbol password	94	8	6,095,689,385,410,816	53-bit
Long alphanumeric-symbol password	94	12	4.75920314814253E23	79-bit

Is all that math important? That math illustrates the principles underlying secure passwords. The takeaway about entropy is that passwords with higher entropy are more secure than passwords with low entropy. A 46-bit password, therefore, is far more secure than a 13-bit password.

Also, entropy is a theoretical concept. In the real world, security measures may be in place to prevent hacking tools from trying a continuous stream of passwords. Login routines at Web sites often restrict the speed at which passwords can be entered and the number of consecutive passwords that can be tried before the account is temporarily frozen and alternative authentication is required. Adjusting device settings to limit the number of login attempts is a wise security step.

QuickCheck

In Figure 7-7, why is the entropy for PINs 14 bits?

a. It is the number of possibilities.

b. It is the number of digits in the possibilities.

c. It is the number of bits when the possibilities are in binary.

d. It is 4 + 10.

▶ What is the recommended method for creating secure passwords?

The sophistication of password-cracking software and the processor speeds of today's computers pose challenges for consumers. Long, random passwords are most secure, but they are difficult to remember. It is possible to devise and remember a secure password for one or two sites, but the average consumer may have passwords for more than 50 devices and Web sites. Devising 50 unique, strong passwords and remembering which passwords correspond to which sites is just about impossible, or is it? Figure 7-8 offers some advice for creating passwords.

Try It!

Using the guidelines in Figure 7-8, create a secure multi-use password.

Figure 7-8: Password advice

Start with a phrase. Base your high-security password on the first letters of a phrase that generates a password containing numbers and proper nouns.

- Aim for a length of 8 to 12 characters because some sites limit password length.
- Use uppercase letters somewhere other than at the beginning of the password.
- Use numbers somewhere other than at the end of the password.
- Some sites do not allow symbols, so you may not want to use them in a password that will be modified for use on many sites.

Here is an example of a phrase that produces a fairly secure password:

I went to Detroit Michigan when I was 23 years old
IwtDMwiw23yo

Add the site name. By inserting the name of the site, every password will be unique and you will be able to remember the site on which it is used, like this:

I went to PayPal when I was 23 years old
IwtPayPalwiw23yo

Make a low-security password. A password achieves pretty good entropy when it is composed of four or more words. Create an everyday password using this method. Here is an example:

SpaBraidAmazonNuit

Be careful what you write. If you have to write down your passwords to remember them, keep them in a safe place that is not connected to your digital device. If your device is stolen, the passwords should not be located where they would also be stolen.

Use encryption. If you want to store passwords on your device, make sure to encrypt the file in which they are stored.

Use a password manager. If you feel more secure with a totally random and unique password for each of your logins, a password manager is an excellent option.

Password Managers

You hated memorizing facts in elementary school, and memorizing passwords is even less fun. Digital tools for managing passwords promise to shoulder the burden, but nothing is perfect, and password managers are not hacker-proof.

How does a password manager work? The core function of a **password manager** (sometimes called a keychain) is to keep track of passwords so users don't have to memorize them. Some password managers also have the ability to fill in forms with stored address and credit card data. Password managers are available as operating system utilities, browser extensions, and standalone utilities.

Most password managers can generate unique passwords composed of random letters, numbers, and symbols. These passwords have very good entropy and do not have to be memorized because they are stored and automatically retrieved by the password manager as needed.

When you initially register for an account with a Web site or app, the password manager may display the user ID you typically use; usually it is your email address. You are then asked if you would like to create a password or use an auto-generated password.

Password managers may display a **strength meter** that indicates password security—a feature that is useful if you create a custom password rather than using one generated by the password manager (Figure 7-9).

Figure 7-9: Password managers can generate strong passwords

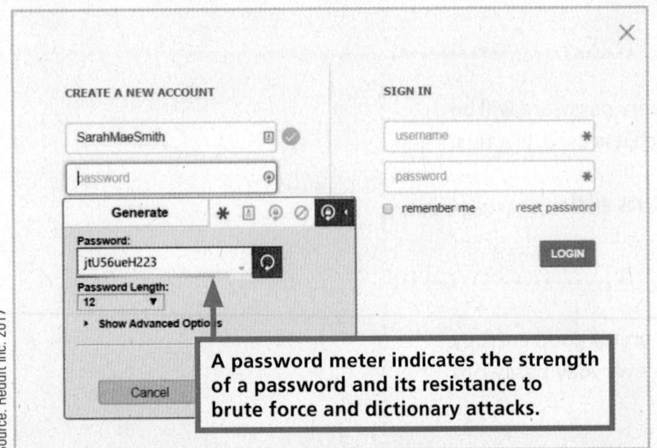

Does a password manager save time? A password manager stores a list of Web sites with corresponding user IDs and passwords in an encrypted file. Any time you reach a login screen for a known app or Web site, the password manager automatically supplies your user ID and password, saving you the time required to look them up.

The encrypted file that stores user IDs and passwords is protected by a primary password. That password has to be entered manually only once each time a device is turned on. The data stored by a password manager is secure unless the primary password is cracked. In that unfortunate situation, all of the passwords in the file are compromised and can be used by a hacker. In addition, if you forget the primary password, then you are locked out of all your password-protected accounts.

QuickCheck

The security of a password manager depends on ______.

a. the security of the primary password

b. the strength meter

c. a dictionary attack

d. a brute force algorithm

Is the data stored by a password manager secure? The vulnerability of a file protected by a single primary password is the security tradeoff for the convenience of delegating password security to password management software. The security of passwords created and preserved by a password manager also depends on where the password file is stored.

Local Storage. Passwords stored locally are tied to the device on which they are created. When a password manager is installed on a laptop, for example, the passwords are available only when using that device. The password file is encrypted, but if the device is stolen, hackers can take their time trying to crack the primary password.

Passwords stored locally are not available when using other devices. Suppose that you usually work with the Safari browser on your MacBook Air, and it stores your passwords; but if you use a public computer in a coffee shop, your passwords are not accessible from that device. This disadvantage of local storage encourages many consumers to try cloud-based password managers.

Cloud Storage. Some password managers can store the encrypted password file in the cloud. That file can be accessed from any device as long as the primary password is provided. Storing a file full of passwords in the cloud can be a security risk, however. Web-based password managers can be attractive targets for password thieves. By breaking into a single site, a password thief could harvest millions of passwords. When considering cloud-based password management tools, evaluate them carefully before trusting them with your valuable login data.

USB Storage. There are a few password managers available that store your passwords in an encrypted file on a USB drive. The passwords are available on any device with a USB port. For extra protection against intruders who might search your device for passwords, a flash drive that contains a password manager can be unplugged when you are not planning to visit password-protected sites. You can also remove the flash drive from your device when you're out so that your nosy roommate can't snoop through your digital files. When you remove the USB drive, your portable password manager leaves behind no traces of passwords. Losing the USB drive puts your digital life at risk, however, so consider connecting it to your key ring.

Try It!

If you were to use a password manager, would you store passwords locally, in the cloud, or on a USB drive? Why?

QuickQuiz Section A

1. PINs and passwords protect logins, but they can also be used to [ ] storage volumes.
2. User [ ] techniques include PINs, passwords, fingerprint scans, and facial recognition.
3. A(n) [ ] attack usually cracks passwords in less time than a brute force attack.
4. A term such as *46-bit* is used to indicate the strength, or [ ], of a password.
5. Password managers are available as operating system utilities, [ ] extensions, and standalone utilities.

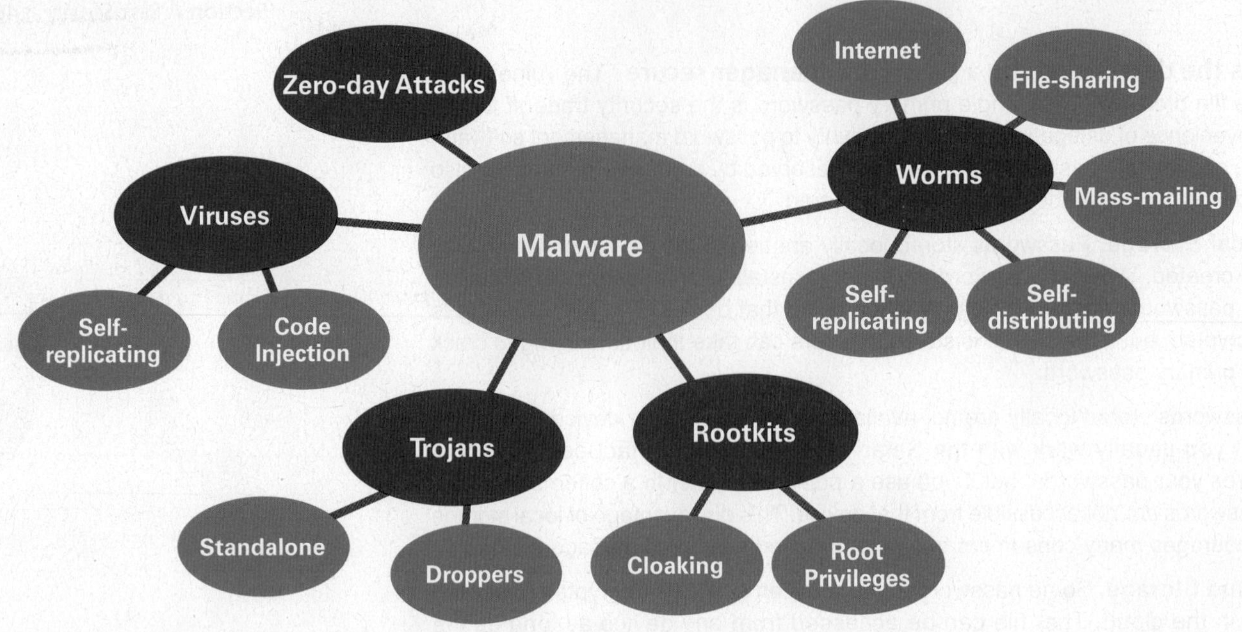

Section B Malware

Objectives

- List at least five examples of malware payloads.
- Describe the characteristics that differentiate computer viruses from other types of malware.
- Explain the purpose of a rootkit.
- Describe the characteristics of computer worms, including three common infection vectors.
- Explain the purpose of malware trojans and how they relate to droppers.
- List the two ways that antivirus software is able to detect viruses.
- Explain the three possible actions that antivirus software can take when a virus is detected.
- Explain the significance of false positives in the context of virus detection.
- Describe how to determine if an email warning about a virus is real or a hoax.

The days when viruses were the greatest threat to computers are long gone. Today, there are many other types of malicious software, or malware, that can wreak havoc on computer systems, networks, and even handheld devices. Windows computers have the highest risk of malware infections, but any digital device that receives email, accesses the Web, and runs apps is potentially vulnerable.

Terminology

malware
malware exploit
computer virus
code injection
side-loading
rootkit
computer worm
mass-mailing worm
Internet worm
file-sharing worm
trojan
dropper
antivirus software
virus signature
heuristic analysis
false positives
quarantined file
virus hoax

Malware Threats

Exploits against digital devices began as harmless stunts but quickly turned nasty. Simple pranks evolved into attacks that wiped out data on hard drives, wormed into networks, stole massive numbers of personal records, and hijacked access to segments of the Web. Malware is also a component of cyberwarfare attacks that pose a threat to national security.

▸ What are malware threats? **Malware** refers to any computer program designed to secretly enter a digital device. Malware can be classified by the way in which it enters a device or by the type of activity it carries out. Common classifications of malware include viruses, worms, and trojans.

Malware is created and unleashed by individuals referred to as hackers, crackers, or cybercriminals. Some malware is released as a prank. Other malware is designed to distribute political messages or disrupt operations at specific companies. In an increasing number of cases, malware is exploited for monetary gain. Malware designed for identity theft or extortion has become a very real threat to individuals and corporations.

Once malware infiltrates a device, its behavior depends on how it is programmed. The action carried out by malware code is referred to as a **malware exploit** or a "payload." Malware can be used for many types of exploits, such as deleting files, recording login keystrokes, opening access for intruders, and allowing remote control of a device. Figure 7-10 lists some malware exploits that affect consumers.

Terminology

Malware is also referred to as *malicious software*. The term *virus* is also used as an all-encompassing term for software that secretly invades a digital device.

Figure 7-10: Malware exploits

- Display irritating messages and pop-up ads
- Delete or modify your data
- Encrypt data and demand ransom for the encryption key
- Upload or download files
- Record keystrokes to steal passwords and credit card numbers
- Send messages containing malware and spam to everyone in an email address book or instant messaging buddy list
- Disable antivirus and firewall software
- Block access to specific Web sites and redirect a browser to infected Web sites
- Cause response time slowdowns
- Allow hackers to remotely access data stored on a device
- Allow hackers to take remote control of a device
- Link a device to others in a botnet that can send millions of spam emails or wage denial-of-service attacks against Web sites
- Cause network traffic jams

Try It!

Hackers are a common element of many TV shows and movies. With their fingers nimbly flying over the keyboard and streams of data scrolling on the screen, those hackers seem to accomplish their nefarious tasks in a matter of seconds. Is this realistic? To find out, watch the YouTube video *Hacker Breaks Down 26 Hacking Scenes from Movies and TV.*

Computer Viruses

The first computer virus designed to affect personal computers appeared in 1982 when the Apple II was at the height of its popularity. This virus, called Elk Cloner, was relatively harmless. It blanked the screen and displayed a short poem. From such innocent beginnings, viruses developed into a major threat, launching nasty attacks such as wiping out all the data stored on hard disks and overwriting the BIOS to make a computer unbootable.

▶ **What is a virus?** A **computer virus** is a set of self-replicating program instructions that surreptitiously attaches itself to a legitimate executable file on a host device. When the infected file is run, the virus code is loaded into RAM with the rest of the program. Once in RAM, the virus code is executed. When executed, the virus can replicate itself by injecting malicious code into other files. A common misconception is that viruses spread themselves from one device to another; they don't. Viruses can only replicate themselves on the host device.

In addition to replicating itself, a virus usually delivers a payload, which can be as harmless as displaying an annoying message or as devastating as trashing the data on your computer's storage device. It can corrupt files, destroy data, or otherwise disrupt operations. A trigger event, such as a specific date, can unleash some viruses. Viruses that deliver their payloads on a specific date are sometimes referred to as time bombs. Viruses that deliver their payloads in response to some other system event are referred to as logic bombs.

Today, viruses are a mild threat. They do not spread rapidly, and they are easily filtered out by antivirus software. They are interesting, however, because they illustrate the beginning of hacker culture and reveal the basic techniques that are still used to inject third-party code into legitimate data streams. **Code injection** is the process of modifying an executable file or data stream by adding commands, as shown in Figure 7-11.

QuickCheck

Computer viruses are characterized by their ____________.

a. ability to spread themselves to various devices

b. ability to self-replicate

c. severe level of threat

d. size

Figure 7-11: Code injection

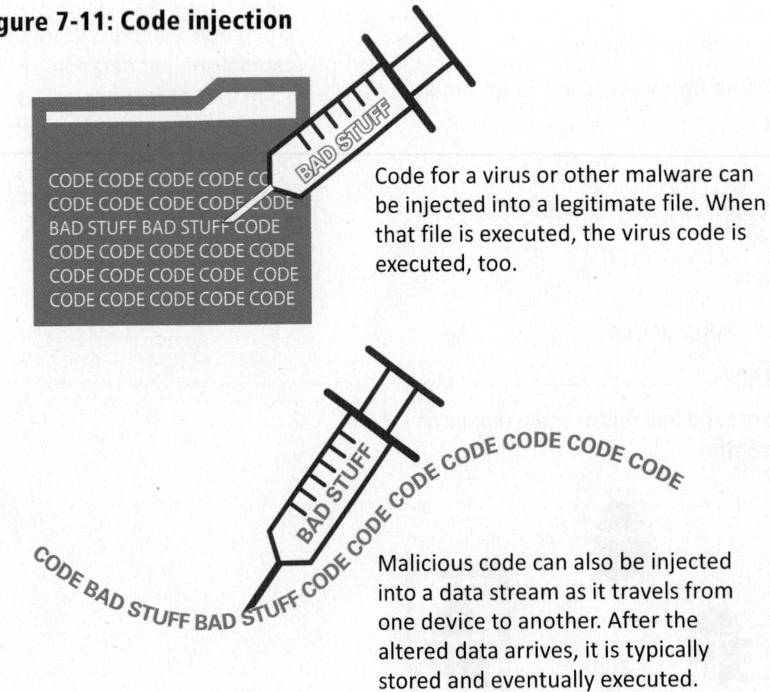
BAD STUFF
CODE CODE CODE CODE CODE
CODE CODE CODE CODE CODE
BAD STUFF BAD STUFF CODE
CODE CODE CODE CODE CODE
CODE CODE CODE CODE CODE
CODE CODE CODE CODE CODE
Code for a virus or other malware can be injected into a legitimate file. When that file is executed, the virus code is executed, too.
BAD STUFF
CODE BAD STUFF BAD STUFF CODE CODE CODE CODE CODE CODE CODE
Malicious code can also be injected into a data stream as it travels from one device to another. After the altered data arrives, it is typically stored and eventually executed.

7

How does a virus spread? Viruses spread when people exchange infected files on disks and CDs, as email attachments, and on file sharing networks, social networking sites, and download sites. They can also be inadvertently obtained from unauthorized app stores. Through a process called **side-loading**, an app from a source other than an official app store is installed on a device. Often these apps are altered versions of popular apps, which are placed on unofficial download sites. The app appears to be the same as the original legitimate app, but when downloaded, it may install a virus or other malware.

A key characteristic of viruses is their ability to lurk in a device for days or months, while quietly replicating themselves to other files on the device. As this replication takes place, you might not even know that your device has contracted a virus; therefore, it is possible to inadvertently spread infected files to other people's devices. Although viruses are no longer a top malware threat, virus-cloaking technology has become very sophisticated and is a key element of today's most serious security exploits. Viruses and other malware can cloak themselves using various techniques, such as rootkits.

What is a rootkit? Any code that is designed to hide the existence of processes and privileges is referred to as a **rootkit**. Rootkits were originally designed to allow "root" or administrative access to digital devices and computer systems. By changing system settings and then hiding those changes, hackers were able to become shadow administrators with access to all data on a device or network.

Modern rootkits are used to hide malicious code by replacing parts of the operating system with modified code. For example, a rootkit might subvert the operating system's master file table to hide evidence of the sectors in which a virus is stored. Some rootkits are even able to disable antivirus software to prevent it from detecting the existence of malware (Figure 7-12).

QuickCheck

A rootkit does not ________.

a. allow administrative access to digital devices

b. have the ability to hide malicious code

c. disable antivirus software

d. protect a device from hackers

Figure 7-12: Rootkits cloak malware

On this hard disk, a rootkit conceals a track that contains malware, so it is not visible to the file system.

Computer Worms

Initially, the spread of malware from computer to computer depended on humans to physically exchange infected floppy disks. In 1996, the distribution vector began to change as hackers devised malware that could spread on its own from one device to another. The first self-distributing malware infiltrated email address books to essentially mail copies of its code to other devices. By 2000, hackers were able to create malware that sent itself to huge numbers of IP addresses.

What is a worm? A **computer worm** is a small, self-replicating, self-distributing program designed to carry out unauthorized activity on a victim's device. Worms are usually standalone executable programs that can spread themselves from one device to another without any assistance from victims.

Worms can enter a device through security holes in browsers and operating systems, as email attachments, and when victims click infected pop-up ads or links contained in email messages. There are several common types of computer worms.

A **mass-mailing worm** spreads by sending itself to every address in the contacts list of an infected device. If a mass-mailing worm infects one of your devices, for example, your friends receive infected messages sent from your mail account. Thinking that the message is from a trusted source, your friends are likely to open the infected attachment, spreading the worm to their devices and then passing it on to their friends.

An **Internet worm** looks for vulnerabilities in operating systems, open communications ports, and JavaScripts on Web pages. These worms travel over communications networks as small bootstrap files that infiltrate digital devices. When a worm finds a host, it connects to a remote computer to download more comprehensive malware.

A **file-sharing worm** copies itself into a shared folder under an innocuous name. When the folder is distributed over a file sharing network or BitTorrent, the worm tags along and spreads to all the devices that participate in the share. Figure 7-13 illustrates how computer worms spread.

QuickCheck

What is the key difference between computer viruses and worms?

a. Viruses deliver more damaging payloads than worms.

b. Worms replicate themselves, but viruses do not.

c. Viruses are self-distributing, whereas worms are not.

d. Worms are standalone executable programs, whereas viruses have to piggyback on other executable files.

Figure 7-13: How a computer worm spreads

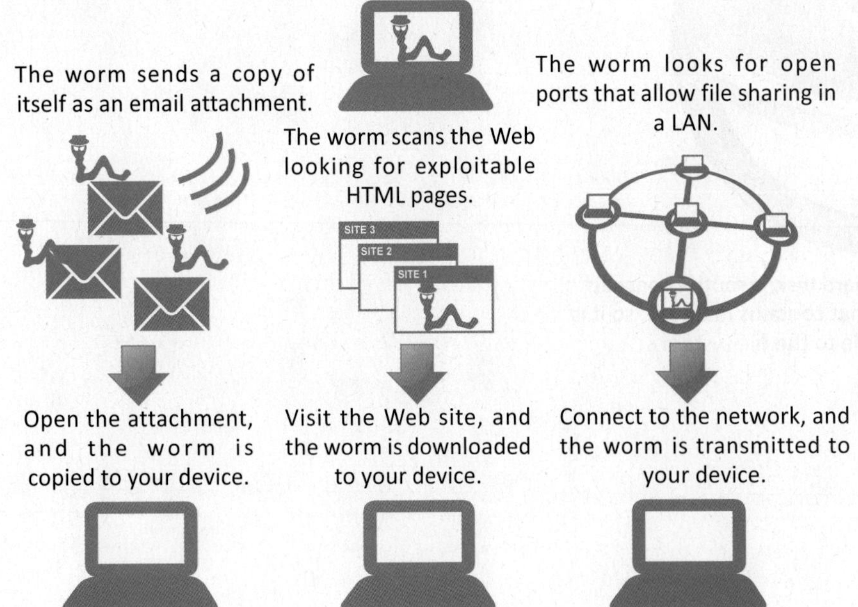

The worm sends a copy of itself as an email attachment.
The worm scans the Web looking for exploitable HTML pages.
SITE 3
SITE 2
SITE 1
The worm looks for open ports that allow file sharing in a LAN.
Open the attachment, and the worm is copied to your device.
Visit the Web site, and the worm is downloaded to your device.
Connect to the network, and the worm is transmitted to your device.

Trojans

Stuxnet is a notorious computer worm that damaged devices used in Iran's nuclear program. It is often identified as one of the first cyberwarfare tools. A file called Stuxnet.exe is unlikely to be downloaded, so malware developers depend on trojans to disguise malware as innocuous utility software and popular applications. Today, more than 80% of malware infections are trojans.

How do trojans differ from viruses and worms? A **trojan** (sometimes called a "Trojan Horse") is a computer program that seems to perform one function while actually doing something else. Unlike a worm, a trojan is not designed to spread itself to other devices. Also differing from viruses and worms, most trojans are not designed to replicate themselves.

Trojans are standalone programs that masquerade as useful utilities or applications, which victims download and install while unaware of their destructive nature. Trojans depend on social engineering—fooling users—to spread. Social engineering exploits are covered in detail in a later section of this module.

Trojans can contain viruses, code to take control of a device, or routines called droppers.

What is a dropper? A **dropper** is designed to deliver or "drop" malicious code into a device. It is similar to a setup program that unzips and installs software applications on Windows devices, except that droppers secretly install malware rather than legitimate software.

Droppers are commonly the first phase of a sophisticated malware attack. Most droppers contain compressed or encrypted malware files. When delivered, these files are uncompressed in memory to avoid detection. The uncompressed files are executed, sometimes to carry out a payload or to collect and install other malware components. Stuxnet famously used a dropper to initiate its attack (Figure 7-14).

QuickCheck

In the context of malware, a trojan's main purpose is to ____________.

a. disguise malware as legitimate software
b. replicate on a host machine
c. spread as quickly as possible
d. load additional malicious code

7

Terminology

There is a difference between a dropper and code injection. A *dropper* installs a malicious program on a device, and it works with an entire program. *Code injection* inserts a segment of malicious code into another program. It carries only a short segment of code rather than an entire program.

Figure 7-14: Stuxnet attacks nuclear centrifuges

1 A USB drive containing the Stuxnet dropper in disguise is inserted into a computer at a nuclear facility.

2 A security hole in Windows runs the dropper when the USB directory is viewed.

3 The dropper executes a second file containing a worm.

4 The worm spreads through the LAN, looking for a specific type of hardware device that Stuxnet is designed to destroy.

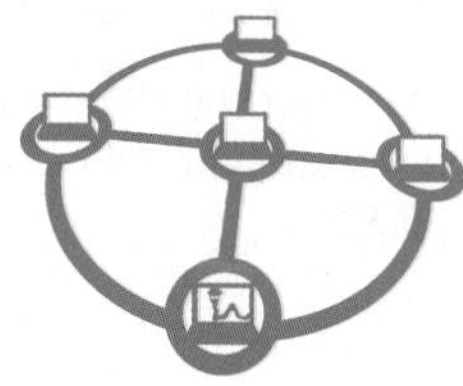

5 When the worm arrives at a target device, in this case a centrifuge, it downloads a more comprehensive file containing instructions for the payload.

6 The malware payload causes the nuclear centrifuges to fail.

Antivirus Software

Any data entering a digital device could be malware. Users have little hope of identifying files that contain malicious code. Avoiding known sources of malware, such as free file sharing services and offshore download sites, may reduce the risk of encountering malware; however, malicious code exists at legitimate Web sites, lurks in official app stores, and infiltrates trusted networks. The best defense against malware is antivirus software.

Try It!

What is the name of the antivirus software installed on each of your digital devices?

▶ **What are the most popular antivirus products?** **Antivirus software** is a type of utility software that looks for and eliminates viruses, trojans, worms, and other malware. It is available for all types of computers and data storage devices, including smartphones, tablets, personal computers, USB flash drives, servers, PCs, and Macs. Popular antivirus software includes Norton AntiVirus, Kaspersky Anti-Virus, Bitdefender Antivirus, Windows Defender, and Avast.

▶ **How does antivirus software work?** Modern antivirus software runs as a background process and attempts to identify malware that exists on a device or is entering a device as a download, email message, attachment, or Web page. The process of searching for malware is sometimes referred to as scanning or performing a virus scan. To identify malware, antivirus software can look for a virus signature or perform heuristic analyses.

▶ **What is a virus signature?** A **virus signature** is a section of program code that contains a unique series of instructions known to be part of a malware exploit. Although they are called virus signatures, the unique code may identify a virus, worm, trojan, or other type of malware.

Virus signatures are discovered by security experts who examine the bit sequences contained in malware program code (Figure 7-15). When discovered, virus signatures are added to a collection of virus definitions, which form a database that is used by antivirus software as it works to scan files that may harbor malware.

Figure 7-15: A virus signature

Virus

Michelangelo

Signature

bb00508ec3cd13730432

Erase hard drive boot sectors on March 6, Michelangelo's birthday

▶ **What is heuristic analysis?** Antivirus software can use techniques called **heuristic analysis** to detect malware by analyzing the characteristics and behavior of suspicious files. These techniques are especially useful for detecting new malware for which signatures have yet to be collected and added to the virus database.

One method of heuristic analysis allows the suspicious file to run in a guarded environment called a sandbox. If the file exhibits malicious behavior, it is treated like a virus and quarantined or deleted.

A second method of heuristic analysis involves inspecting the contents of a suspicious file for commands that carry out destructive or surveillance activities.

QuickCheck

What is the purpose of heuristic analysis?

a. To analyze virus signatures

b. To add virus signatures to the virus database

c. To detect virus-like commands or behaviors

d. To discover the time when malware might deliver its payload

How well does heuristic analysis work? Heuristic analysis requires time and system resources to examine files that arrive as downloads and email attachments. The process can slightly affect performance while the analysis is in progress.

Heuristics may produce **false positives** that mistakenly identify a legitimate file as malware. For example, a legitimate disk utility that contains routines for enhancing disk drive performance by deleting redundant files might be mistaken for a virus and prevented from being installed. Such a situation could be perplexing for users who download software, only for it to disappear upon arrival. Users who understand how antivirus software works should be able to quickly conclude that the legitimate application was mistakenly flagged as malware.

What happens when malware is detected? When antivirus software detects malware, it can try to remove the infection, put the file into quarantine, or simply delete the file (Figure 7-16).

Figure 7-16: Malware detected

Repair. Antivirus software can sometimes remove the malware code from infected files. This strategy is beneficial for files containing important documents that have become infected. Many of today's malware exploits are embedded in executable files and are difficult to remove. When malware cannot be removed, the file should not be used.

Quarantine. In the context of antivirus software, a **quarantined file** contains code that is suspected of being part of a virus. For your protection, most antivirus software encrypts the file's contents and isolates it in a quarantine folder so it can't be inadvertently opened or accessed by a hacker. Quarantined files cannot be run, but they can be moved out of quarantine if they are later found to have been falsely identified as malware.

Delete. Quarantined files should eventually be deleted. Most antivirus software allows users to specify how long an infected file should remain in quarantine before it is deleted. Most users rarely retrieve files from quarantine because it is risky to work with files that are suspected of harboring malicious code. There is no need, therefore, to delay deletion for more than a few days.

QuickCheck

Which one of the following is not a reason why antivirus software quarantines files?

a. It prevents users from inadvertently running suspected malware.

b. Uncontaminated files can be reinstated.

c. It prevents hackers from using it in exploits.

d. It sometimes takes days to analyze a file to determine if it is actually malware.

7

▶ How dependable is antivirus software? Today's antivirus software is quite dependable but not infallible. A fast-spreading worm can reach your digital device before a virus definition update arrives, and cloaking software can hide some viral exploits.

Despite occasional misses, however, antivirus software and other security software modules are constantly weeding out malware that would otherwise infect your device. It is essential to use security software, but it is also important to take additional precautions, such as making regular backups of your data and avoiding untrustworthy software distribution outlets.

▶ How do I ensure that my antivirus software is running? Antivirus software is an aspect of our digital lives that we tend to take for granted. We assume that it is installed and carrying out its work. However, antivirus software can be inadvertently disabled. Its configuration can be changed by malware that manages to infiltrate a device. It can expire at the end of a trial period or subscription. Ensuring that antivirus software is performing correctly may require periodic intervention from users.

Many antivirus products display an icon in the taskbar or notification area. The icon may offer a visual clue to indicate when the antivirus utility is active, scanning, or updating. Glancing at the icon can assure you that the software is running properly.

Some targeted malware attacks may alter the icons, however, leading you to believe that the antivirus software is active when, in fact, it has been disabled by a malware attack. As shown in Figure 7-17, opening antivirus software periodically to view its status is a good practice.

Try It!

Is your antivirus software actively scanning and up to date? Check it right now to find out.

Figure 7-17: Antivirus software is actively scanning

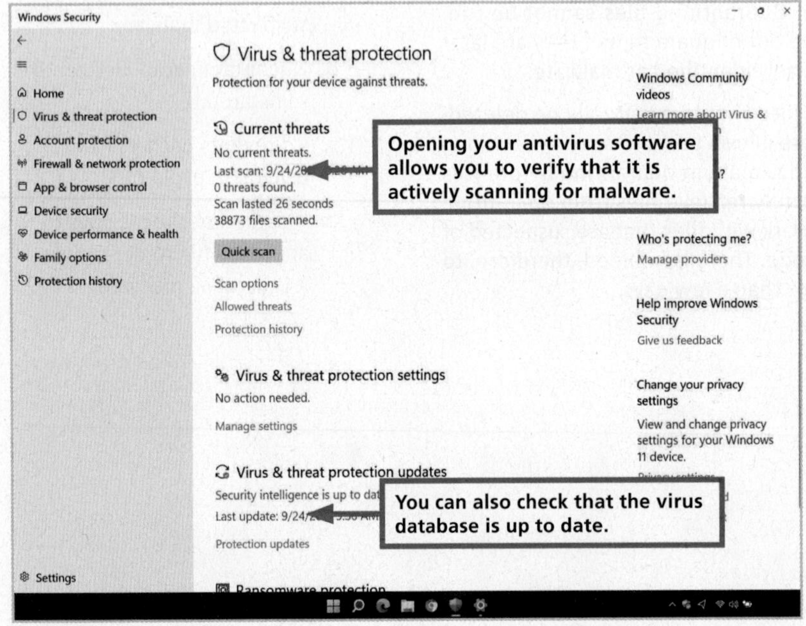

What configuration options are available? Once you have installed antivirus software, the best and safest practice is to keep it running full time in the background so that it checks every email message as it arrives and scans all files that attempt to install themselves or run. For the most extensive protection from malware, you should look for and enable the following features of your antivirus software:

- Start scanning when the device boots.
- Scan all programs when they are launched, and scan document files when they are opened.
- Scan other types of files, such as graphics, if you engage in some risky computing behaviors and are not concerned with the extra time required to open files as they are scanned.
- Scan incoming email and attachments.
- Scan incoming instant message attachments.
- Scan outgoing email for worm activity such as mass-mailing worms.
- Scan zipped (compressed) files.
- Scan for spyware and PUAs (potentially unwanted applications).
- Scan all files on the device's storage volume at least once a week.

Try It!

Is your antivirus software properly configured? Compare your settings to the recommendations listed on the left.

7

Where are the configuration settings? The location for configuration settings depends on the antivirus software. Usually, there is a Settings menu or a Preferences option. It is important to examine the settings after installing new antivirus software and after getting updates to make sure the desired level of protection is in place.

Also check for exclusions. If files, processes, and locations are excluded, they will not be scanned for malware. This feature is available to enhance performance from trusted sites, but it can be a doorway for malware exploits. For maximum protection, make sure that there are no exclusions listed in your antivirus software settings. Settings for Windows Security are accessed from the "Virus and threat protection" option (Figure 7-18).

Figure 7-18: Be sure to eliminate all exclusions

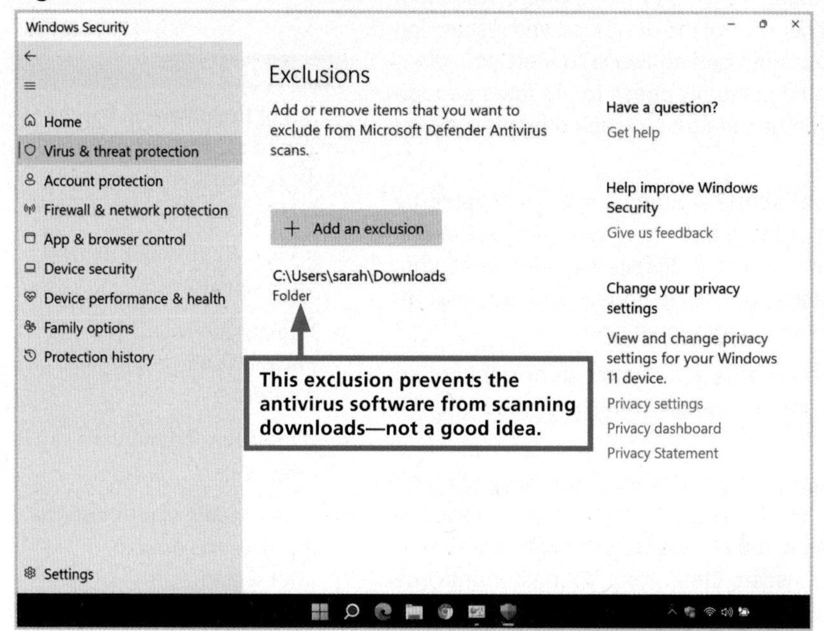

QuickCheck

What is significant about exclusions in antivirus settings?

a. They are usually zero-day attacks and won't be detected.

b. They are spyware exploits that antivirus software is not able to detect.

c. They define files and locations that the antivirus software will not scan.

d. They enhance the security of your device.

Do I need to take any action when a virus is detected? Most antivirus software displays an alert when malware is detected. Antivirus software automatically takes action to protect your device by attempting to repair the file, place it in quarantine, or delete it.

You do not have to take any action. However, the alert message is an important piece of information that may indicate you are connected to a malicious site or receiving email from an unreliable source that would be best avoided in the future (Figure 7-19).

Try It!

Has your antivirus software quarantined any malware recently? Check in the history, vault, or quarantine area to find out.

Figure 7-19: Malware security warning

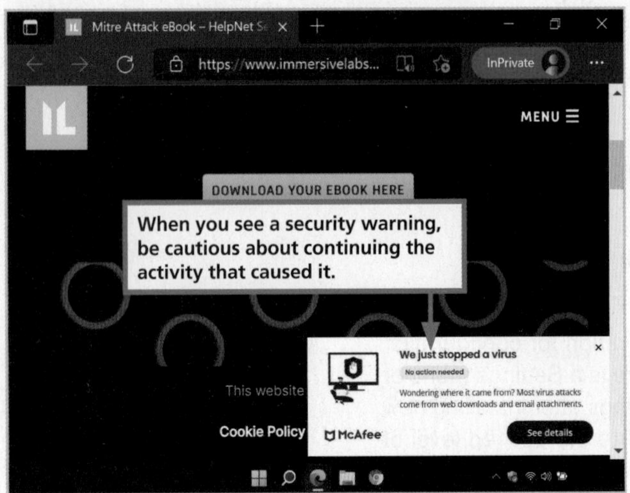

Source: Immersive Labs.

What is the best way to handle updates? Two aspects of your antivirus software periodically need to be updated. First, the antivirus program itself might need a patch or an update to fix bugs or improve features. Second, the list of virus signatures must be updated to keep up with the latest malware developments.

Antivirus program updates and revised virus definitions are packaged into a file that can be manually or automatically downloaded. Most antivirus products are preconfigured to regularly check for updates, download them, and install them without user intervention. If you would rather control the download and installation process yourself, you can configure your antivirus software to alert you when updates are ready. In any case, you should manually check for updates periodically just in case the auto-update function has become disabled by malware or if your subscription has expired.

What is the purpose of a manual scan? A manual scan is initiated by a user for the purpose of scanning one or more files. Manual scans are useful if you suspect that a virus has slipped into a device despite security measures. For example, a previously unknown attack might arrive undetected, but after an antivirus update, it can be detected by running a manual scan.

Manually scanning all the files stored on a device can slow performance, so schedule the scan for a time when you are not usually using your device, but it is turned on.

You can also run a manual scan of a specific file. For example, suppose you download an application and you want to make sure it is virus free before you install and run it. Depending on your antivirus software, you might be able to simply right-click the file name to start the scan. Otherwise, open your antivirus software and select the manual scan option.

QuickCheck

Which of the following is a reason to manually check for updates even if your antivirus software is set for auto-updates?

a. It is useful to check all the virus signatures.

b. It might indicate if your antivirus subscription has expired.

c. It indicates if a manual scan is necessary.

d. It can enable you to discover if a virus has arrived undetected.

7

What's a virus hoax? Some virus threats are very real, but you're also likely to get email messages about so-called viruses that don't really exist. A **virus hoax** usually arrives as an email message containing dire warnings about a supposedly new virus on the loose. It typically provides a link to download some type of detection and protection software. It may include removal instructions that actually delete parts of the operating system. And, of course, you are encouraged to forward this "crucial" information to your friends.

When you receive an email message about a virus or any other type of malware, don't panic. It could be a hoax. You can check one of the many hoaxbuster or antivirus software Web sites to determine whether you've received a hoax or information about a real threat.

These Web sites also provide security or virus alerts, which list the most recent legitimate malware threats. If the virus is a real threat, the Web site can provide information to help determine whether your device has been infected. You can also find instructions for eradicating the virus. If the virus threat is a hoax like the one in Figure 7-20, by no means should you forward the email message to others.

Figure 7-20: A typical virus hoax

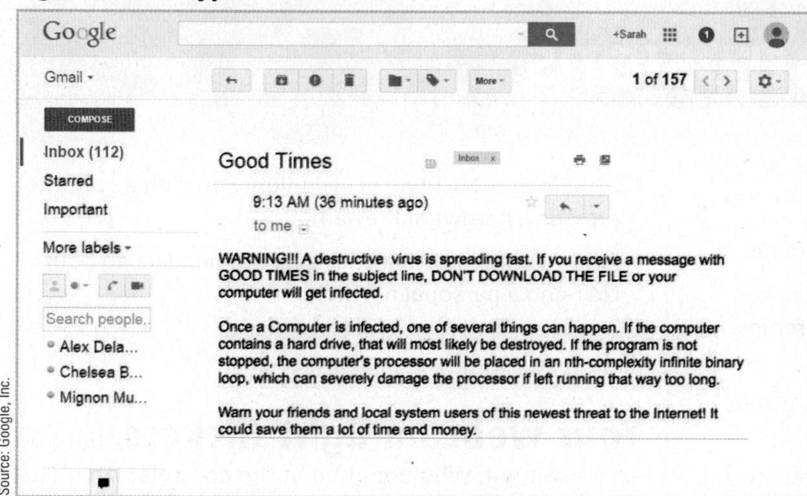

Source: Google, Inc.

QuickQuiz Section B

1. A(n) ______ is self-replicating, self-distributing malware.
2. Malware trojans often contain code that is called a(n) ______, which secretly installs malware.
3. Antivirus software can detect viruses by looking for signatures or by ______ analysis.
4. Antivirus software produces what is referred to as a false ______ when a legitimate program is mistakenly identified as a virus.
5. A virus ______ usually arrives as an email alert that warns against an imminent virus attack.

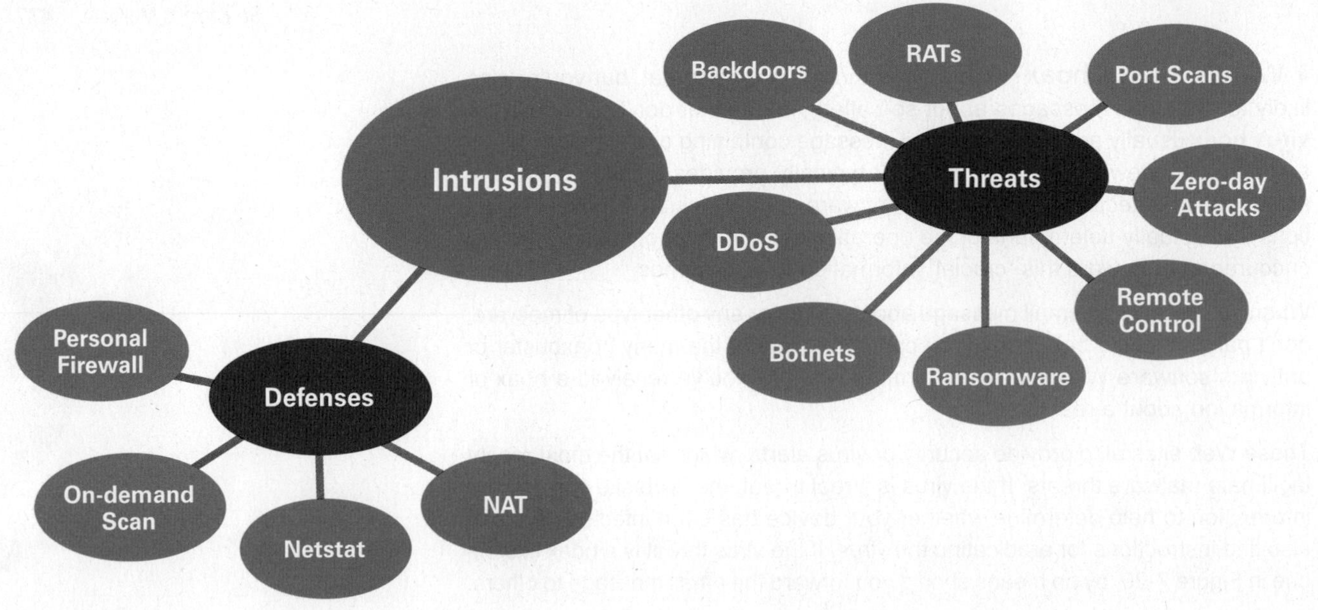

Section C Online Intrusions

Objectives

- Provide an overview that describes how an online intrusion takes place.
- Describe how RATs use backdoors to access remote devices.
- Describe the security vulnerabilities associated with legitimate remote access utilities.
- Summarize the types of threats posed by ransomware.
- Explain how a DDoS attack takes place.
- Describe the difference between an on-demand scan and on-access scanning.
- Summarize the significance of communications ports in online intrusions.
- Describe how a personal firewall works.
- Explain how NAT works in conjunction with a router to provide a hardware firewall.
- Explain why security experts recommend using both NAT and a personal firewall.

Your webcam light flickers, but you aren't using it. Who could be at the controls? An unauthorized person operating your digital devices by remote control constitutes a serious breach of privacy and security. Although a webcam's light signals its use, many other remote intrusions take place without any warning signs. Your digital device could be sending out thousands of spam emails without your knowledge. Section C explains how to defend against online intrusions.

Terminology

online intrusion
RAT
backdoor
ransomware
botnet
DDoS
zero-day attack
on-access scan
on-demand scan
port scan
firewall
personal firewall

Intrusion Threats

Unleashing viruses, worms, and trojans kept hackers busy for many years, and they gleefully watched their creations spread to devices throughout the world. But viruses and worms were ultimately unsatisfying because once an exploit was released, hackers had no way to interact with it or take control of infected devices. Inevitably, someone came up with the concept of malware that could connect back to a hacker's command and control center.

▶ What is the risk of online intrusions? An **online intrusion** takes place when an unauthorized person gains access to a digital device by using an Internet connection and exploiting vulnerabilities in hardware or software. Across the globe, millions of devices have been surreptitiously infiltrated by online intruders.

Every day, thousands of people discover that they are the victims of identity theft resulting from an intruder gaining access to their digital files. Thousands more realize that cameras on their devices are controlled by an unknown hacker. A growing number of devices are being remotely locked by extortionists who demand payment to supply an unlock code. All of these exploits are likely to have been carried out by online intrusions.

QuickCheck

How does an online intrusion usually begin?

a. With a virus alert

b. With a backdoor

c. With a worm or trojan

d. With a remote-controlled camera

An infiltrated device can be used as a launching platform for viruses and spam. Infiltrated devices can become part of a pornography network or an extortion ring. Hackers have even found ways to turn thousands of infiltrated computers into remote-controlled "zombies," link them together, and carry out coordinated attacks to disrupt online access to Microsoft, Bank of America, and other Internet businesses.

▶ What are the characteristics of online intrusions? Most online intrusions begin with malware. A worm or trojan infiltrates a device and sets up a backdoor that can be used for future access. That access can be used directly by a human to log in to the victim's device over the Internet. It can be used as a gateway for additional malware to infect a device. It can also be used as a conduit for commands issued from a hacker to a group of infected devices (Figure 7-21).

Figure 7-21: Anatomy of an online intrusion

❶ Malware, such as a worm or trojan, enters a digital device.

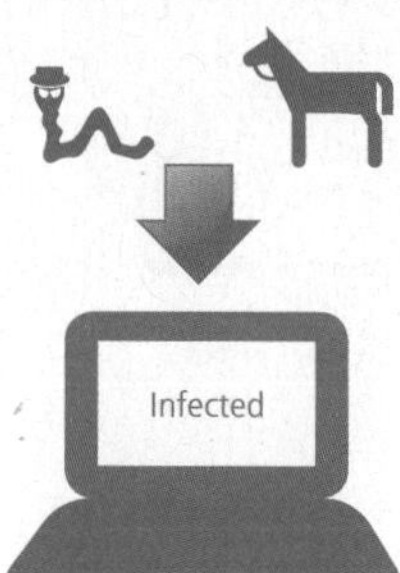

❷ The malware runs and creates a backdoor.

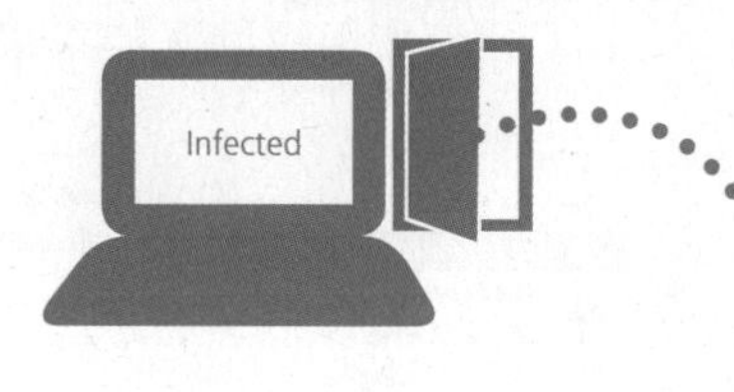

❸ The backdoor surreptitiously opens a communications link to a hacker.

❹ The hacker sends commands that run programs, search for confidential data, and remotely control devices.

Are there different types of intrusions? Yes. RATs, ransomware, and botnets are the most common types of online intrusions.

What is a RAT? A **RAT** (Remote Access Trojan) is malware that arrives in a trojan disguised as legitimate software and sets up a secret communication link to a hacker. RATs are the underlying technology for most online intrusions.

How do hackers take remote control of digital devices? A **backdoor** is an undocumented method of accessing a digital device. RATs create a backdoor to a victim's device that can be used by a hacker to send commands that take control of the device's camera, activate the microphone, or launch screen captures. Images and audio acquired by hackers are commonly posted on social media sites and used to extort money from victims who do not want their private activities made public.

Are legitimate remote access utilities a vulnerability? Features such as Windows Remote Desktop, TeamViewer, and macOS Screen Sharing are legitimate software utilities that allow users to access their computers from a remote location. These utilities are handy for travelers who want to read, modify, or copy files stored on a computer that was left at home or at work. Remote access utilities open a communication port—on Windows computers, it is TCP port 3389—that is ready to accept remote data and commands.

In theory, remote commands are accepted only from someone who has logged in with valid credentials. However, a poorly configured remote access utility might not request a login password, or it may allow access through a standard guest account.

To block unauthorized use of remote access utilities, they should be disabled when they are not needed. Unless you are traveling and expect to access files on a computer that you've left at home, make sure Screen Sharing (macOS) or Remote Desktop (Windows Pro) is turned off. Figure 7-22 shows how to configure the Screen Sharing setting on a Mac.

Try It!

Is remote access active on your desktop or laptop computer? Find out now and disable the feature if you do not currently need to use it.

Figure 7-22: Disable screen sharing in macOS

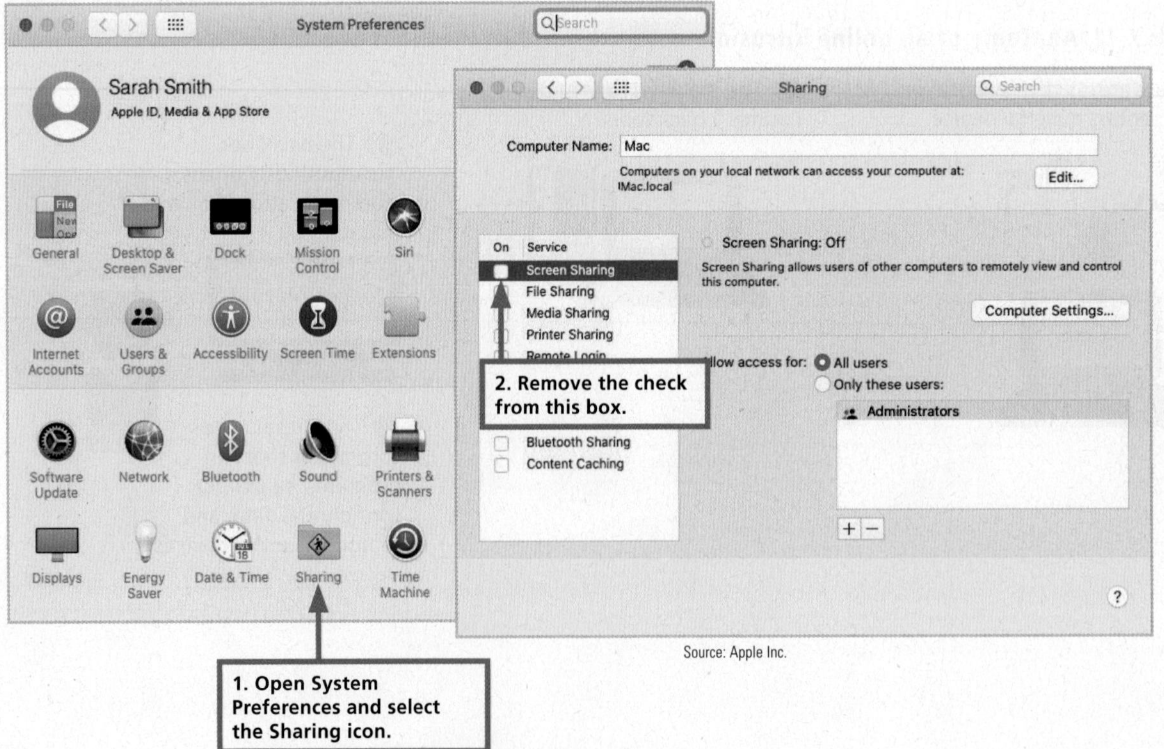

Source: Apple Inc.

What is ransomware? **Ransomware** locks a device and then requests payment for an unlocking code. You'll want to defend against ransomware attacks such as these:

Nemty: Arrives as an email love letter and threatens to publish personal data if the ransom is not paid.

Maze: Spreads by exploits that target security holes in commonly used software. Threatens to steal files.

Snatch: Forces Windows computers to boot into safe mode and then encrypts the user's hard drive.

VegaLocker: Disables login access and removes crucial data, such as backup files and restore points, before asking for a ransom payment.

Ransomware attacks tend to target businesses rather than individuals, but these exploits can target Android, Windows, and macOS devices as well as smart TVs. iPhones are not typically at risk from ransomware unless the phone was jailbroken and contains side-loaded apps.

Victims who pay the ransom don't always obtain the unlocking code. Once the scammers have their money, they may not bother to unlock the files. The FBI recommends that victims ignore the ransom demand, scrub the device, and restore files from a backup.

Ransomware is one of the fastest-growing threats to digital devices. Hackers launch new variants that may not be blocked by antivirus software until the virus database is updated. Anti-ransomware software that runs in addition to antivirus software may offer further defenses against files being encrypted and held for ransom.

Consumers can expect ransomware exploits of increasing sophistication. Attacks not only affect files on a device's main storage volume, they can affect USB drives, external hard drives, and any other storage devices connected at the time of the attack.

To prepare for a possible ransomware exploit, be sure to maintain current backups of your important data and disconnect the backup device when backups are not in progress. Taking these steps will help ensure that you'll be prepared if you ever encounter a ransomware exploit such as the one in Figure 7-23.

Figure 7-23: Ransomware demands

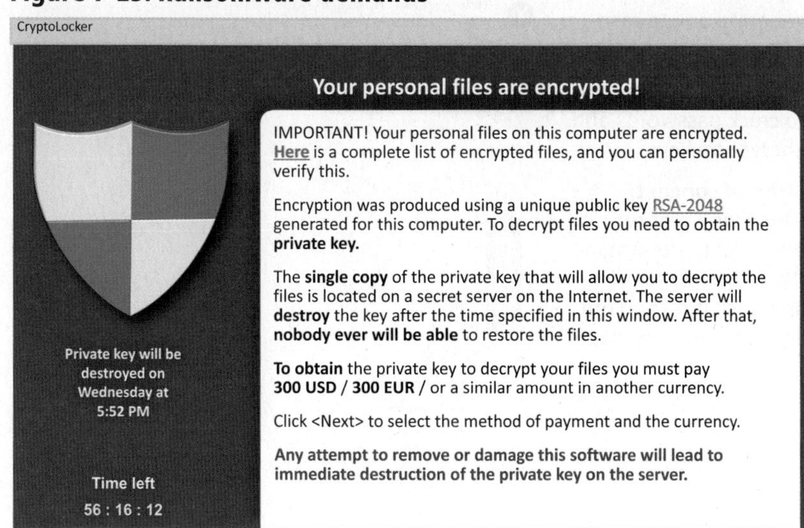

What is a botnet? Hackers who gain control over several computers can organize them into a client-server network known as a **botnet**. This network is hidden from the victims, who continue to use their devices as usual and are unaware of botnet activities that may be taking place behind the scenes. In addition to computers, botnets can contain just about any device that connects to the Internet, including smartphones, baby cams, DVRs, and IoT sensors.

A botnet has a command and control server that is operated by hackers. Infiltrated devices become network nodes, which carry out a variety of activities as directed by the server. Small botnets contain a few hundred devices. However, the world's largest botnets are estimated to contain more than 450,000 devices!

Botnets have been used to carry out massive **DDoS** (distributed denial-of-service) attacks designed to flood a legitimate Web site or an Internet router with so much traffic that it can no longer provide its intended service. DDoS traffic is generated by hundreds, thousands, or millions of botnet nodes harnessed to do the bidding of a botmaster.

In addition to their role in DDoS attacks, botnets are commonly used to generate email spam, carry out click fraud, generate Bitcoin digital currency, and crack encryption. Some DDoS attacks appear to be proof-of-concept exercises to test security measures of government agencies, financial institutions, and key infrastructure systems. Figure 7-24 provides more information about botnets.

Try It!

In 2020, a massive DDoS attack targeted cloud-based Amazon Web Services (AWS). Look for information about this attack online. What was the magnitude of the attack? What was the name of the malware?

QuickCheck

Botnets might carry out all of the following exploits, except ______.

a. RATs

b. DDoS

c. generating spam

d. cracking encryption

Figure 7-24: Anatomy of a botnet

A botmaster controls a network of victims' computers using IRC channels for communication.
The command and control server has no fixed IP address, so it can move to avoid detection.

Victims' computers receive commands from the botmaster to carry out various nefarious tasks.

Click fraud: Automated ad-clicking generates per-click revenue for botmasters.

DDoS: Floods an IP address with massive amounts of traffic.

Spam: Sends billions of spam emails per day.

Mine Bitcoins: Runs algorithms required to generate online cash.

Crack encryption: Runs brute force algorithms to crack passwords and encryption keys.

Proof of concept: Launches a test run designed to determine the effectiveness of an attack if carried out against a primary target.

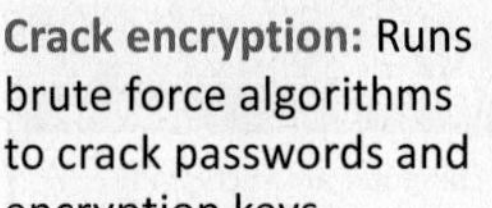

Zero-Day Attacks

Consumers are justifiably concerned that their digital devices are vulnerable to intrusions. Even with antivirus software in place, each year millions of consumers are victims of intrusions and ransomware. Consumers have to establish additional defenses.

▶ Does antivirus software protect devices from intrusions? Antivirus software can prevent some, but not all, intrusions. It has a good track record for blocking exploits that attempt to gain access using a trojan or worm, especially if a signature of the exploit exists in the virus database. New exploits, such as zero-day attacks, may not be caught by antivirus software, however.

▶ What is a zero-day attack? A **zero-day attack** exploits previously unknown vulnerabilities in software applications, hardware, and operating system program code. The name "zero-day" implies that the software developer has zero days notification of the vulnerability before it is used as the basis for a security exploit.

When a zero-day attack first appears, its signature does not exist in virus databases, and if the exploit is designed to also bypass heuristic filters, these attacks can infiltrate computers guarded by antivirus software.

▶ Is there any defense against zero-day attacks? Zero-day attacks are usually discovered rapidly by security experts who attempt to correct the vulnerabilities by issuing updates and security patches. Configuring applications for automatic updates ensures that security patches are applied as soon as they are available. Adobe Reader, Microsoft Windows, and Android OS account for a large portion of all zero-day attacks. It is vital that consumers promptly apply security updates to this software.

For zero-day exploits that slip through the antivirus net, an on-demand scan can be an effective remedy. Standard antivirus software is set for an **on-access scan**, which takes place in the background as Web sites are accessed and as files are opened. An **on-demand scan** can be launched manually at any time and examines every segment of code on a storage volume. On-demand scans with products such as Malwarebytes (Figure 7-25) can be used in addition to antivirus software as a second line of defense.

Figure 7-25: On-demand virus scan

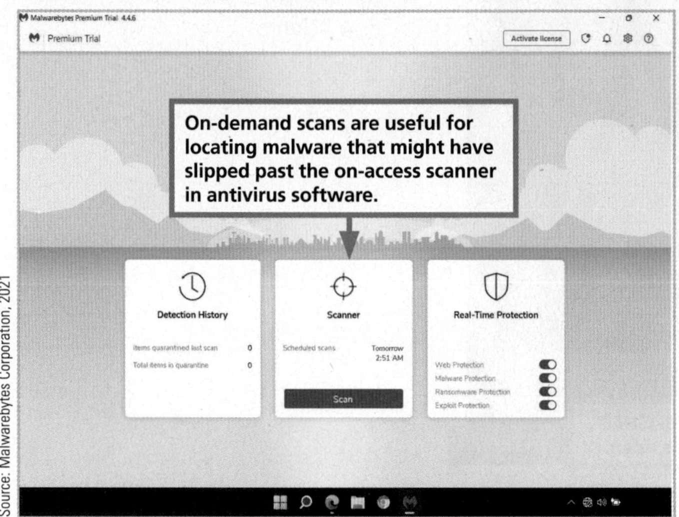

Source: Malwarebytes Corporation, 2021

QuickCheck

What is the significance of zero-day attacks?

a. They infect a device immediately upon arrival.

b. They take advantage of previously unknown vulnerabilities.

c. They have zero chance of being detected.

d. They make updates and patches unnecessary.

Terminology

On-access scans are also called real-time protection, background scanning, and autoprotect.

Try It!

Make sure automatic updates are enabled for your operating system and software such as Microsoft Office.

Netstat

Digital devices use communication ports for all kinds of tasks, such as connecting to networks, sending and receiving email, exchanging data with peripheral devices, and accessing the Web. These ports are exploited by hackers to access devices and plant malware. Hackers also use ports to communicate with devices in botnets. Preventing unauthorized communication to and from a digital device is an essential security precaution.

▶ How do hackers exploit communication ports? Hackers use a technique called port scanning to discover which ports are open on a device. A **port scan** pings a packet of data to the port. If a reply is received, the port is open.

Open ports correspond to various services. For example, suppose you've installed an online game—let's call it Warcraft Legends—that uses TCP port 6112 for the game client to communicate with the game server. A hacker pinging port 6112 would learn that the port is open. An exploit to penetrate a vulnerability of Warcraft Legends would likely be successful if directed through port 6112. In this way, open ports can be used to deliver malware.

Open ports are also used for communications between botnets and their controllers. Botnet malware opens ports on victims' computers. To communicate with the botnet commander, client bots might use port 6667, for example. Data collected by the bot's keylogger could be sent via port 6667 to the botmaster, and commands from the botmaster might be relayed to infected devices using the same port. Ports that exhibit unusual activity could be a sign of a botnet intrusion.

▶ Can I detect which ports are open? Network utilities such as Netstat produce a detailed list of open ports on a device. Although these utilities are useful diagnostic tools, their reports are lengthy and do not clearly separate ports needed by legitimate services from those used for nefarious purposes (Figure 7-26).

Figure 7-26: Netstat detects open ports

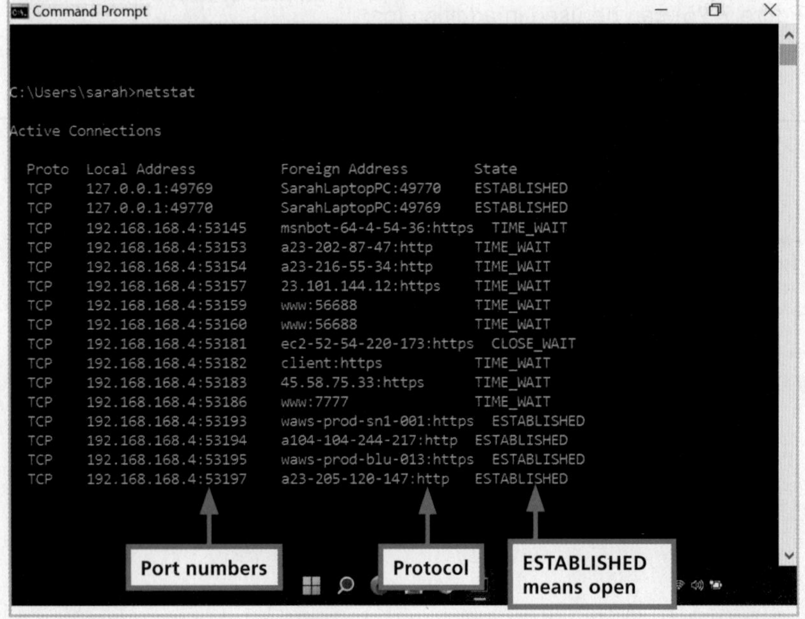

QuickCheck

In Figure 7-26, how many HTTP ports are not using a secure connection?

a. None

b. 2

c. 9

d. 16

Firewalls

Suppose that you could erect a digital wall that would block communication between your digital devices and the outside world. Although it would prevent unauthorized intrusions, it would also block email, and it would prevent access to the Web and a host of online communications services. What if you could drill holes through the wall for communications that you know are legitimate? That is the theory behind digital firewalls.

QuickCheck

Which of the following is true about multiple firewalls?

a. Multiple software-based firewalls tend to conflict with each other.

b. Activating multiple software-based firewalls provides added security.

c. A software-based firewall and a hardware-based firewall will reduce security.

d. Hardware firewalls should be disabled when a software-based firewall is installed.

7

▶ What is a firewall? A **firewall** is a device or software that is designed to block unauthorized access while allowing authorized communications. A **personal firewall** is a software-based deterrent against unauthorized port access. A network router can be deployed as a hardware-based firewall.

▶ How does a personal firewall work? A personal firewall uses a set of rules to block data or allow it to enter a digital device. Because firewalls offer a good level of defense against unauthorized intrusions, they should be installed and correctly configured on all digital devices that have network connections.

Firewalls are included in most security software products, and it is possible that more than one firewall might be available for use. Only one software-based firewall should be active, however, because firewalls have a tendency to conflict with each other.

Most personal firewalls are configured to block all communication unless an app and its corresponding communication port are on a list of allowed exceptions. When a new app attempts to establish a connection, users are notified and given a chance to allow or block the app. The recommended configuration for Windows Defender Firewall is shown in Figure 7-27.

Figure 7-27: Firewall configuration

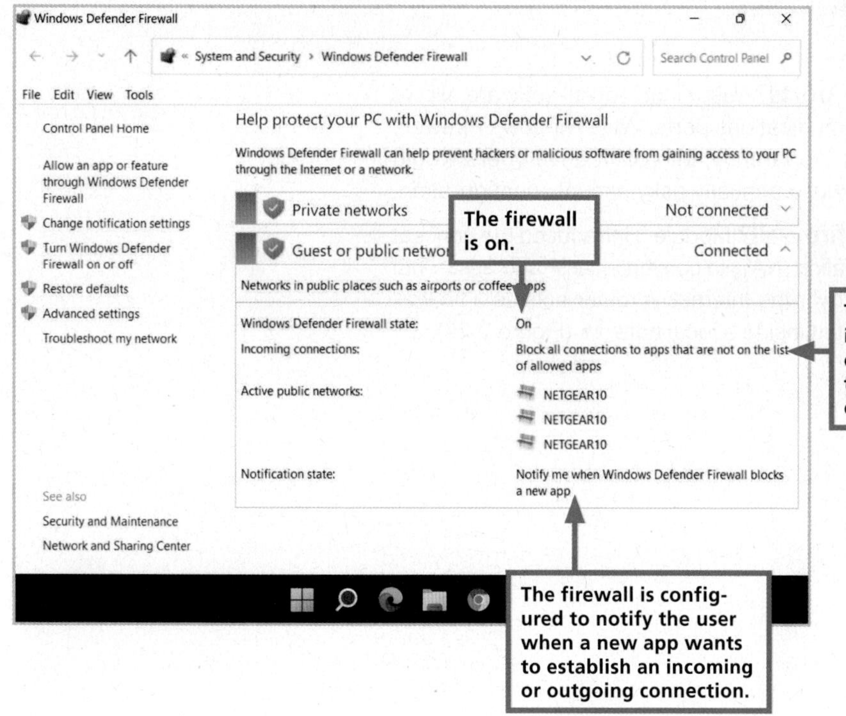

Which apps are allowed through a firewall? Firewalls contain a list of allowed apps. Users can view this list and modify it by adding or blocking apps. For example, Windows Firewall allows users to specify which apps are allowed on private networks and which are allowed on public networks (Figure 7-28).

Figure 7-28: Apps allowed through the Windows firewall

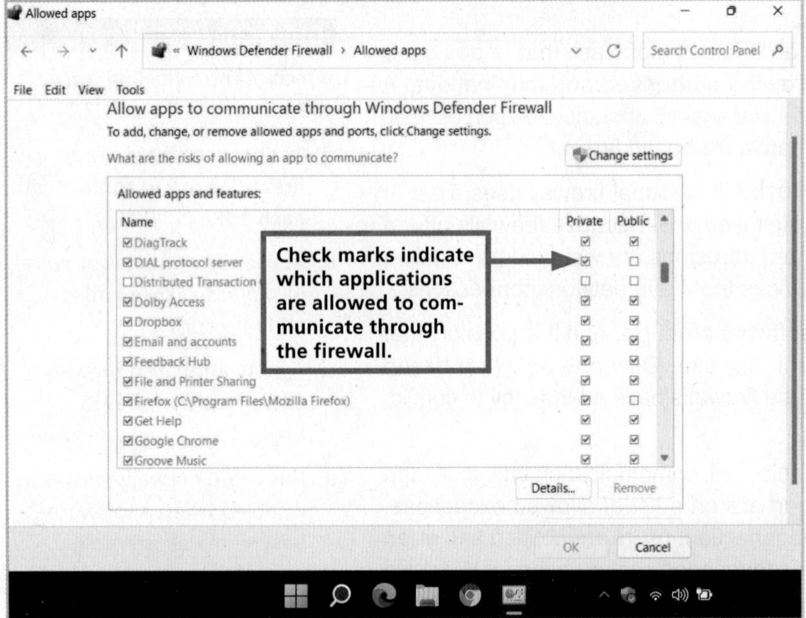

Applications that access the Internet require permission to communicate through the firewall. With permission, an app can open a port and use it to send and receive data.

Try It!

It is worth viewing the list of connections allowed by your firewall from time to time just to make sure there aren't any suspicious activities. Open the personal firewall on your digital device and check the configuration.

Are there firewall settings for ports? Yes, most firewall software allows users to open and close specific communications ports. With Windows Firewall, this process requires multiple steps. Apparently, Microsoft developers would prefer that consumers steer clear of this potentially risky security configuration.

How does a router become a firewall? Module 3 introduced the concept that routers use network address translation (NAT) to convert local IP addresses into routable IP addresses that can travel over the Internet. A router acts as a firewall to block connections that are not initiated inside a local network (Figure 7-29).

Figure 7-29: A router with NAT provides a hardware firewall

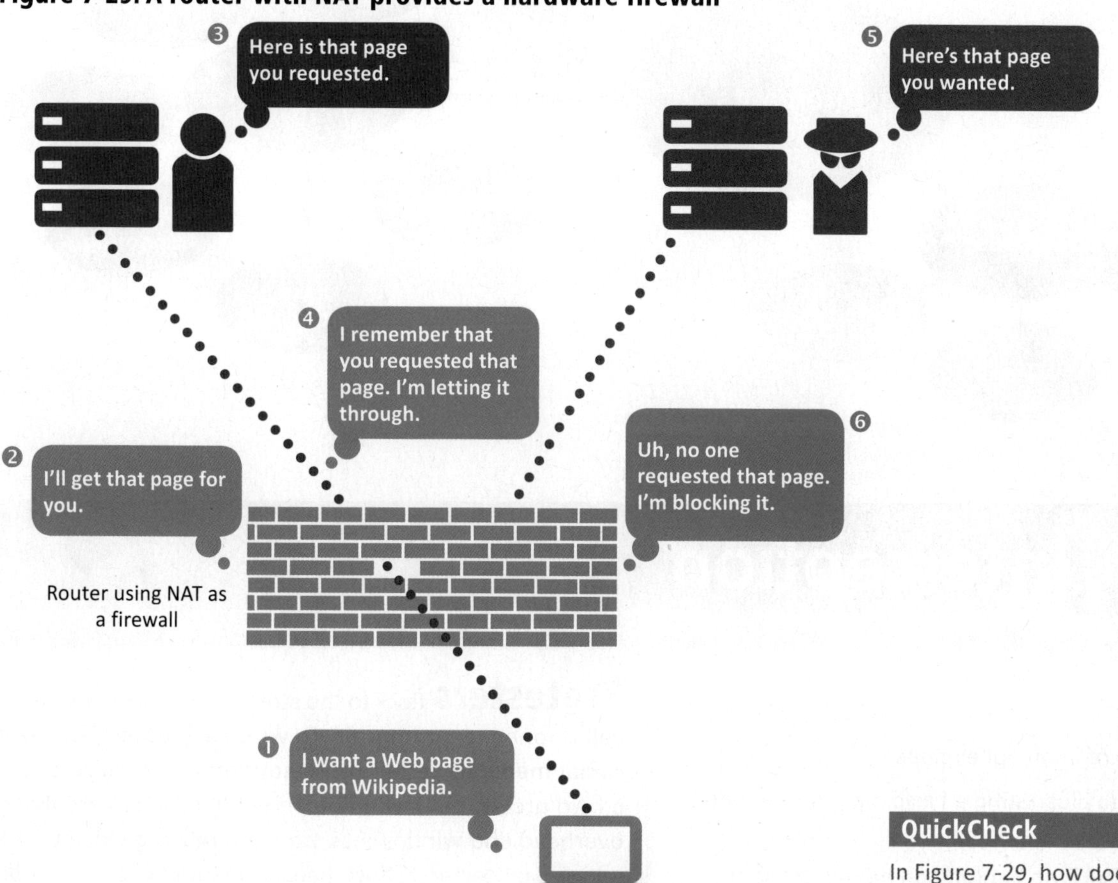

▶ **Do I need NAT in addition to a personal firewall?** Yes. NAT is a good line of defense against attacks that originate from the Internet, but it does not protect against threats that originate inside a network. Suppose that your laptop gets infected with a worm while you are using the laptop at a Wi-Fi hotspot. You then take your laptop home and connect it to your LAN. The NAT running on your LAN's router will not prevent the worm from spreading to other devices within your LAN, because NAT shields communications to and from the Internet, not between the devices connected within the local network.

QuickCheck

In Figure 7-29, how does the firewall know that the Web page from the blue server is legitimate?

a. It is using an open port.

b. It has the correct IP address.

c. It was requested by a computer within the LAN.

d. The browser marked it as "safe."

QuickQuiz — Section C

1. A(n) ________ access trojan is the underlying technology for most online intrusions.
2. Botnets are commonly used to carry out distributed ________ -of-service attacks.
3. A(n) ________ -day attack exploits previously unknown vulnerabilities in software applications, hardware, and operating systems.
4. A(n) ________ scan is used by hackers to discover which applications are using online communications.
5. A personal ________ uses a set of rules to block unauthorized access through open communications ports.

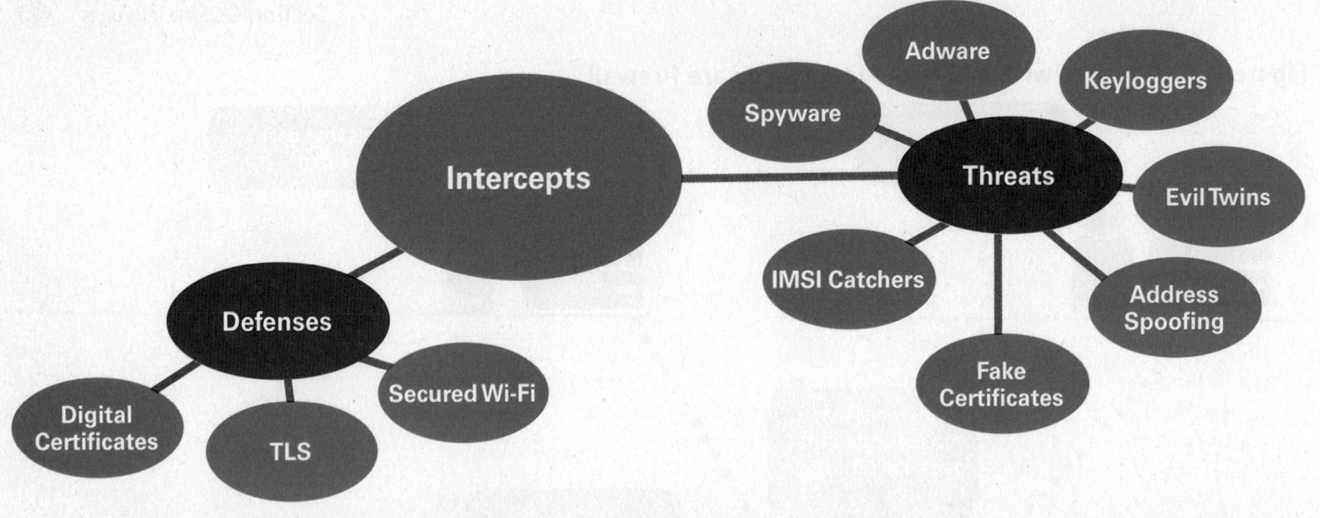

Section D

Interception

Objectives

- List four types of intercept exploits.
- Draw a diagram illustrating a basic man-in-the-middle exploit.
- Describe the Evil Twin exploit and how to avoid it.
- List four types of address spoofs.
- List the three important security components of a digital certificate.
- Describe or diagram how a digital certificate encrypts the connection between a client and a server.
- Explain how a fake digital certificate can defeat encryption.
- Describe how an IMSI catcher works.

Protesters flock to the streets. Organizers use their cell phones to communicate with each other. They use social media to gather more supporters. The size of the crowd grows, but law enforcement helicopters are flying overhead and windowless vans are moving close to the massed protesters. Those helicopters and vans might be deploying stingray devices to intercept cell phone communications, identify the protest leaders, and track their movements. This modern version of wiretapping is just one example of intercepts that can threaten your privacy and security.

Terminology

spyware
adware
keylogger
man-in-the-middle
Evil Twin
address spoofing
TLS
digital certificate
IMSI

Interception Basics

Networks are an integral part of our digital lives. Important information flows over Internet connections and mobile phone services. Consumers cannot, however, assume that those connections are secure, because a variety of exploits allow eavesdroppers to intercept data, email, text messages, and voice conversations that flow over communication infrastructures.

What types of interception exploits are threats? Interception exploits that are current threats to consumers include the following:

Spyware. Any software that secretly gathers personal information without the victim's knowledge is classified as **spyware**. Some spyware is designed for advertising and similar commercial purposes, whereas other spyware is designed with criminal intent to steal identities or take remote control of a victim's digital device.

Adware. A type of spyware called **adware** monitors Web browsing activity to supply ad-serving sites with data used to generate targeted ads. More than a nuisance, the data compiled by adware has the potential to become a record of an individual's habits and lifestyle.

Keyloggers. A common type of spyware called a **keylogger** records keystrokes and sends them to a hacker who sifts out user passwords to access the victim's accounts. Keyloggers are a common tool of identity thieves and industrial spies.

Man-in-the-Middle. In the context of cyber security, an eavesdropping exploit is referred to as a **man-in-the-middle** (MITM or MIM) attack. MITM attacks include Evil Twins, address spoofing, digital certificate hacks, and IMSI catchers.

How do MITM attacks work? The objective of an MITM attack is for a third party to intercept communications between two entities without their knowledge. The third party may passively monitor the communication or may actively modify the data before it reaches its destination. The person in the middle impersonates the other two entities to give the illusion that the two entities are communicating with each other, when in reality they are communicating with an intruder (Figure 7-30).

Figure 7-30: A basic MITM attack

In an MITM attack, two parties believe they are communicating directly with each other when they are actually communicating with a third party. Sue now thinks she should meet Joe at 1:00.

QuickCheck

The objective of most MITM attacks is to ______________.

a. monitor or alter communications

b. remotely control a victim's device

c. install unwanted data on a victim's computer

d. gather marketing data

Evil Twins

Public Wi-Fi hotspots are everywhere. They are operated by coffee shops, colleges, airports, hotels…and hackers. The next time you access a Wi-Fi hotspot, your activities could be monitored, intercepted, and altered by unauthorized third parties using an exploit called an Evil Twin.

▶ **What is an Evil Twin?** An **Evil Twin** is a LAN server that is designed to look like a legitimate Wi-Fi hotspot. Module 3 explained the basic security issues with Wi-Fi hotspots. Many hotspots are unsecured, require no login passwords, and carry data over unencrypted connections. When connecting to an unsecured Wi-Fi hotspot, you are blindly trusting that it is what it appears to be. The hotspot might be fraudulent, however. Hackers are skilled at creating fraudulent sites, referred to as Evil Twins, that resemble legitimate sites.

▶ **How does the Evil Twin exploit work?** To establish an Evil Twin, hackers set up a Wi-Fi hotspot complete with an Internet connection. The network is unsecured, so data that travels over the network is not encrypted, which allows the hacker to capture any information that users enter as they surf the Web, make purchases from online stores, log in to online banking services, and enter passwords at social media sites. Users may never suspect that their activities are monitored if hackers pass the data on to its legitimate destination after it is captured.

Evil Twins are difficult to detect. To avoid this exploit, refrain from entering sensitive data while using any questionable network, and avoid using unsecured networks. For example, when looking for Internet access at the Los Angeles airport, your digital device might list several networks that appear to be operated by the LAX Airport authority. In Figure 7-31, which of the Wi-Fi networks is most likely to be an Evil Twin?

QuickCheck

The attack vector for an Evil Twin exploit is a(n) __________.

a. Wi-Fi hotspot

b. email message

c. software download

d. PUP or PUA

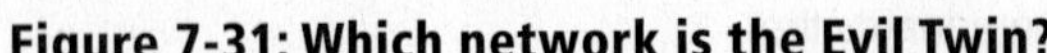

Figure 7-31: Which network is the Evil Twin?

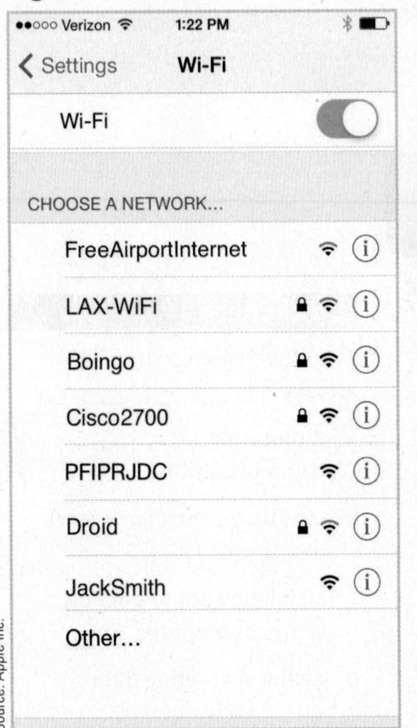

Source: Apple Inc.

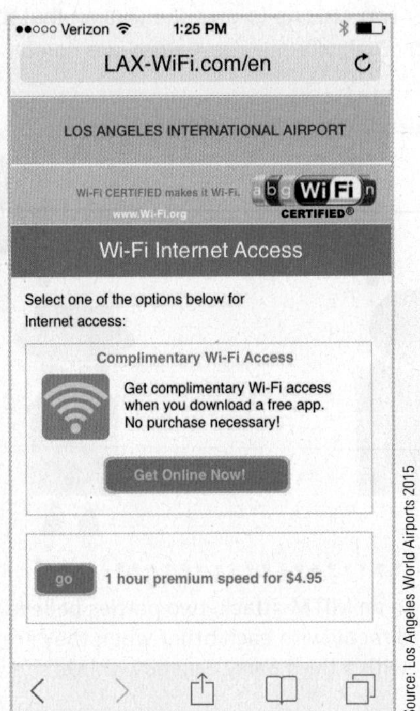

Source: Los Angeles World Airports 2015

Three public Wi-Fi services appear to be offered at the LAX airport: FreeAirportInternet, LAX-WiFi, and Boingo. The remaining Wi-Fi hotspots are operated by individuals using their phones as a tethering device. Of the three public Wi-Fi services, FreeAirportInternet is not secured; therefore, it is most likely to be an Evil Twin.

Address Spoofing

As the 25th anniversary of the Tiananmen Square protest approached, the Chinese government worried that online queries about the event might incite further unrest. The solution: tighten Internet censorship. For ordinary citizens using government-controlled ISPs, access to Google from within China was totally blocked. For academics using a privileged research and education network, Chinese censors deployed address spoofing exploits to route data through an intermediary site that allowed only politically correct queries to proceed.

What is address spoofing? Broadly speaking, **address spoofing** changes an originating address or a destination address to redirect the flow of data between two parties. In the context of security exploits, address spoofing can take place on various levels of communication (Figure 7-32).

Figure 7-32: Address spoofing is used for several black hat exploits

Email Address Spoof

Changes the sender's address. The spoofed address masks the source of spam.

IP Address Spoof

Modifies the source IP address of data packets used in a denial-of-service attack.

DNS Address Spoof

Changes the IP address that corresponds to a URL. The spoofed URL directs victims to a fraudulent Web site.

ARP Address Spoof

Changes the ARP (Address Resolution Protocol) routing table on a local area network. The spoofed address redirects traffic through a secondary, potentially malicious device.

How does address spoofing affect browsing? Just about every exchange of data on the Internet takes place between a client and a server. When using a Web app, for example, your browser connects to a server, such as *www.zoho.com*. When collecting Webmail, your browser might access *www.gmail.com*. When you want to enter a Google query, you connect to *www.google.com*.

On the Web, URLs correspond to IP addresses. When you use a browser to access *www.google.com*, it should connect you to a Google server with a valid IPv6 address such as 2607:f8b0:4007:804::1013. By spoofing Google's IP address, however, Chinese authorities were able to send users to a fake Google site. The fake site examined queries and blocked those that were destined for banned sites or contained controversial keywords.

QuickCheck

DNS spoofing changes the ______.

a. ARP address

b. IP address for a URL

c. sender's address

d. the URL

Digital Certificate Hacks

You can envision how an MITM attack can redirect data packets from a user's client device to a fake Web server. To make intercepted data useless to hackers, it would seem reasonable to encrypt it. Google offers end-to-end HTTPS encryption, for example, to scramble the text of queries made by users and the content of search results. Encryption should hide content from prying MITM attacks, but as Chinese users discovered, that is not always what happens.

◗ **Why is encryption vulnerable?** The current method of encrypting communication between a client and a server depends on a security protocol called **TLS** (Transport Layer Security) that checks a **digital certificate** to verify a server's identity and pass a public key to the client. The client then uses the public key to encrypt data that is sent to the server, as shown in Figure 7-33.

Figure 7-33: How digital certificates work

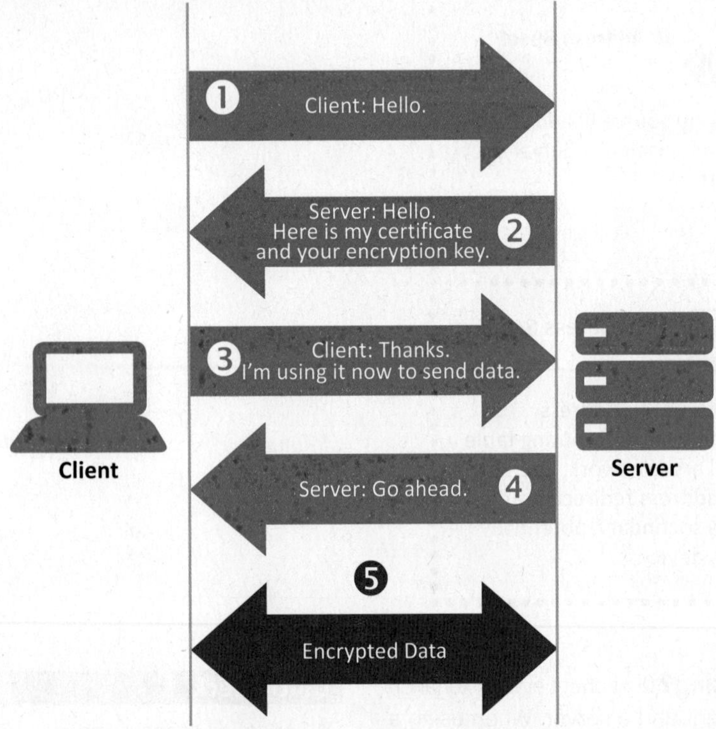
1 Client: Hello.
Server: Hello.
Here is my certificate
and your encryption key. 2
3 Client: Thanks.
I'm using it now to send data.
Client
Server
Server: Go ahead. 4
5
Encrypted Data

◗ **So what is the problem with TLS?** Digital certificates can be faked. Valid digital certificates are issued by official security authorities. These certificates are validated or "signed" by the certificate authority. A fake digital certificate contains the server's credentials and an encryption key, but it might not have a valid signature. Chinese censors, hackers, and government security agencies use fake certificates to snoop on supposedly secure communications.

◗ **How does a digital certificate hack work?** Consider what you know about MITM attacks, and imagine that by using DNS address spoofing, all the data from Chinese Internet users gets funneled through a government server.

QuickCheck

Digital certificates do not contain ________.

a. server identification

b. a public key

c. a certificate authority's signature

d. an ARP routing table

To screen the data and block out queries about the Tiananmen Square protest, for example, users are sent fake digital certificates. These certificates encrypt data, but the key is known to the government server. Encrypted Google queries and other data can then be decrypted by the government server, and only those queries that are politically correct are passed along to the real destination. Figure 7-34 illustrates how this works.

Figure 7-34: How fake digital certificates defeat encryption

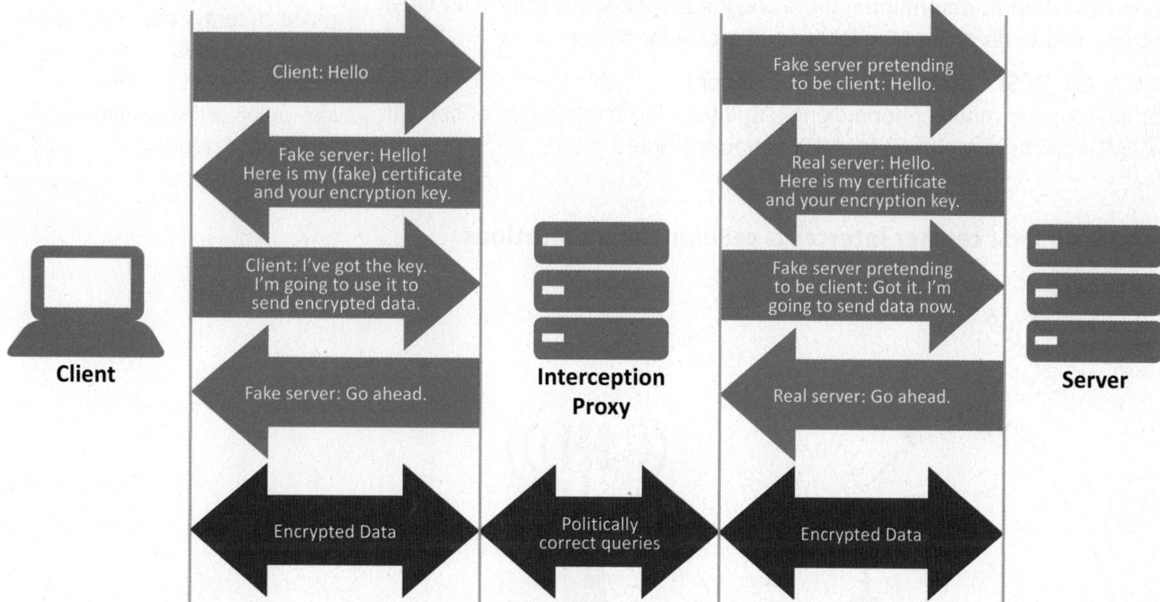

▸ Is there a way to stop MITM attacks that use fake digital certificates? Although most fake digital certificates contain the server's credentials and an encryption key, they may not contain a valid signature from a certificate authority. Most modern browsers flag Web sites that do not have a valid digital certificate. Users who pay attention to invalid certificate notifications, similar to those in Figure 7-35, should be aware that the server may be part of an MITM exploit.

Figure 7-35: Invalid certificate alert

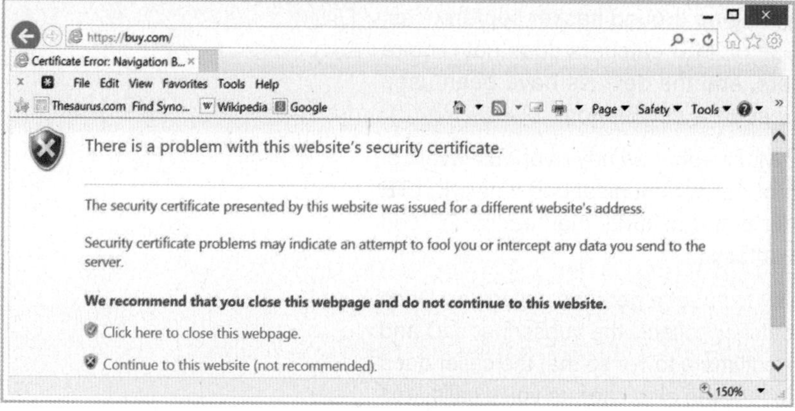

IMSI Catchers

While you drive through the streets of any city, your cell phone conversations, text messages, and Internet activity could be intercepted by fake cell towers. IMSI catchers are yet another MITM exploit.

▶ What is IMSI? **IMSI** is an acronym for International Mobile Subscriber Identity. It is a 64-bit number that uniquely identifies a cellular device. When a device connects to a cellular network, the IMSI is sent from the device to the tower. The tower uses the IMSI to determine if the device is a valid subscriber. The IMSI can also be used to determine the location of a cellular device.

▶ What is an IMSI catcher? An IMSI catcher is an eavesdropping device used for intercepting mobile phone signals and tracking the location of cellular devices. IMSI catchers are used for MITM attacks (Figure 7-36).

Terminology

IMSI catchers are sometimes called *stingrays* after the brand name of a well-known cellular surveillance device. They are also called *cell-site simulators* or *rogue base stations*.

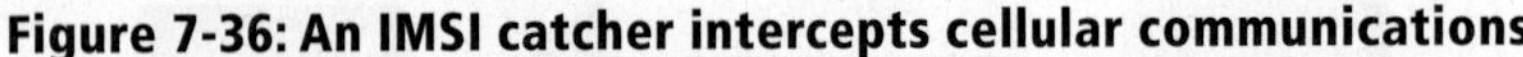

Figure 7-36: An IMSI catcher intercepts cellular communications

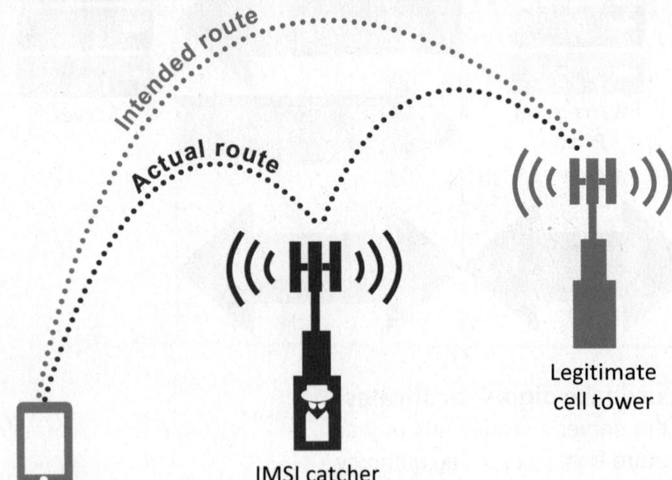

▶ Who operates IMSI catchers? IMSI catchers are operated by law enforcement agencies, criminals, and hackers. IMSI catchers are portable. They can be moved and quickly deployed, for example, during civil unrest when law enforcement agents want to intercept calls among protest organizers. Not surprisingly, IMSI catchers seem to spring up around hacker conferences, such as DEF CON and Black Hat. The use of IMSI catchers does not require cooperation from cellular service providers, and the devices have been used in some jurisdictions without a warrant or court authorization.

▶ How does an IMSI catcher work? Mobile phones have various levels of security, depending on the sophistication of the communications network. LTE and 5G cellular networks and devices offer better security than earlier 2G and 3G networks, but are not immune to IMSI attacks.

Sophisticated IMSI catchers have the ability to spoof a genuine cell tower. Once a mobile device has connected, the IMSI catcher collects the subscriber's ID and location before forwarding the signals to a legitimate tower so that the caller does not notice a disruption in service. IMSI catchers can also capture voice calls, text messages, and data streams that emanate from hijacked devices.

To bypass security, attackers can simply block the legitimate 3G, LTE, and 5G signals, forcing the target device to switch to a less secure 2G network. Once accomplished, the exploit proceeds to collect personal information before forwarding the call to a legitimate tower (Figure 7-37).

QuickCheck

IMSI catchers can force phones to use _________ in order to carry out an MITM attack.

a. a 2G connection

b. DNS spoofing

c. a fake digital certificate

d. a zero-day exploit

7

Figure 7-37: Anatomy of a basic IMSI catcher exploit

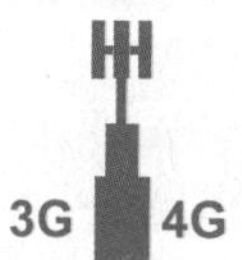

1 Disable 3G, LTE, and 5G service so that phones cannot authenticate the tower.

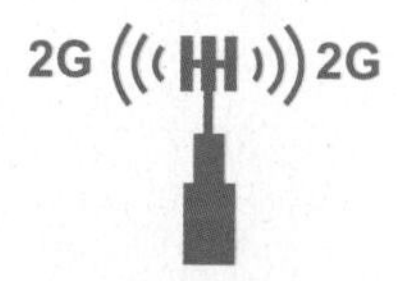

2 Broadcast a 2G signal, which phones are forced to use when no other service is available.

3 Connect phones to an IMSI catcher using unauthenticated 2G.

4 Collect a copy of the caller's ID, location, texts, and other data.

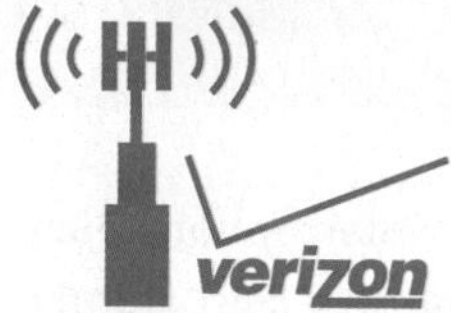

5 Pass the signal to a valid service provider so the caller does not notice a disruption in service.

▸ Are there warning signs that an IMSI catcher is intercepting calls?

Callers are rarely aware of IMSI catchers because calls and other services appear to proceed as normal. If you notice that the network indicator on a device switches to 2G, that could signify a connection controlled by an IMSI catcher. However, some of these interception devices spoof the indicator to make it display 3G, LTE, or 5G when the connection is actually 2G.

Savvy criminals and terrorists tend not to use mobile phones for illegal activities. Law-abiding citizens, too, should be mindful that their conversations may be intercepted.

QuickQuiz — Section D

1. An Evil Twin exploit usually takes place on an unsecured [ ] network.
2. Hackers and government agencies sometimes use [ ] address spoofing to set up an intermediary server to capture Web traffic.
3. A digital certificate depends on a security protocol called [ ].
4. Encryption is the best defense against MITM attacks. True or false? [ ]
5. Mobile phones are susceptible to an interception exploit that uses [ ] catchers.

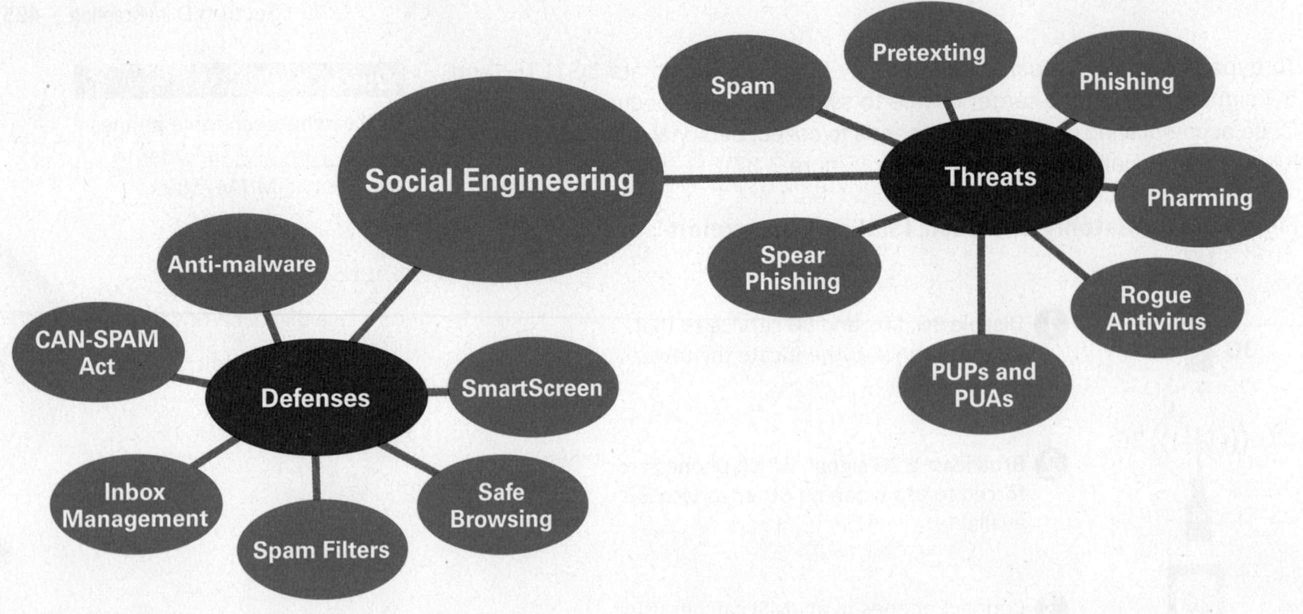

Section E Social Engineering

Objectives

- Create a diagram that illustrates the six elements of a social engineering attack.
- Describe advance fee fraud and the stranded traveler scam.
- List the three limitations placed on spam by the CAN-SPAM Act of 2003.
- List at least six best practices for avoiding spam.
- Describe the four types of spam filters.
- Explain the difference between phishing and pharming attacks.
- Explain the purpose of Safe Browsing.
- Describe how a rogue antivirus exploit works.
- Give two examples of PUAs.

Malware, intrusions, and interceptions. How do all these exploits end up on digital devices? Human psychology is an open book to scammers, who use it to prey on victims. No one—not even the most savvy consumer—is immune to the clever scams that arrive in email or lie dormant on the Web. Section E delves into the shady world of scammers and spammers to uncover their exploits and their weaknesses.

Terminology

social engineering
social engineer
clickbait
advance fee fraud
spam
CAN-SPAM Act
pretexting
spam filter
phishing
spear phishing
pharming
Safe Browsing
SmartScreen
rogue antivirus exploit
PUP
PUA

Social Engineering Basics

One of the most enterprising con artists of all time was a man named George Parker, who managed to sell the Brooklyn Bridge not once but several times to a succession of gullible buyers. Today, con artists have moved into cyberspace, where they devise a continuous barrage of scams to trick consumers into parting with passwords, cash, and control of their digital devices. As these scams become more sophisticated, they also become more difficult to detect. Avoiding them requires a set of security tools and constant vigilance on the part of consumers.

QuickCheck

Email scammers promise to deposit a large sum of money into your bank account if you pay them a small processing fee. Based on Figure 7-38, which of the following incentives are the scammers using?

a. Authority

b. Friendship

c. Scarcity

d. Reciprocity

What is social engineering? In the context of cyber security, **social engineering** (SE) is a deceptive practice that exploits human psychology by inducing victims to interact with a digital device in a way that is not in their best interest. **Social engineer** is a judgment-neutral term for a person who devises and carries out a scam in order to accomplish a goal, such as financial gain, unauthorized access, or service disruption. The target of a social engineering exploit is an individual or organization that may be tricked into participating in the scam.

A relatively harmless example of SE is **clickbait**, an eye-catching image with a teaser headline designed to entice people to click a provided link and satisfy their curiosity. Many clickbait links lead to harmless Web sites, but some lead to sites that contain malware.

SE attacks can be carried out using a variety of technologies, such as email, malware, fraudulent Web sites, SMS, and IRC. For each of these technologies, social engineers have developed effective techniques for tricking victims, including phishing, pretexting, and pharming. Social engineering attacks are multifaceted. Figure 7-38 offers an overview to help you visualize the elements of a social engineering attack.

Figure 7-38: Elements of a social engineering attack

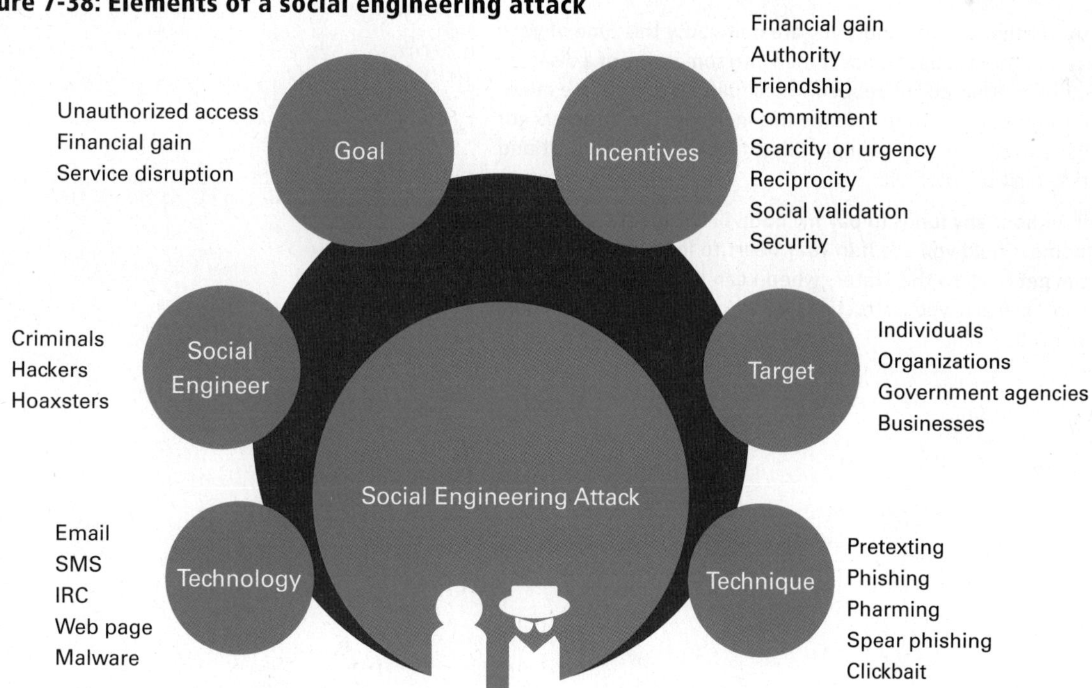

Diagram adapted from F. Mouton et al. Towards an Ontological Model Defining the Social Engineering Domain.

▶ **Why are people fooled by SE?** Social engineering attacks prey on human vulnerabilities, such as gullibility, ignorance, curiosity, greed, courtesy, indifference, and carelessness. The "bait" that is set forth in various social engineering scams is based on one or more incentives designed to compel individuals to participate in the scam.

One of the first examples of a social engineering email scam was **advance fee fraud**, in which a victim is promised a large sum of money in exchange for a bank account number from which a small advance fee is withdrawn. These scams prey on human greed and the hope that it is possible to "get rich quick" without any hard work. According to the FBI, a surprising number of people continue to be duped by these scams, which now often involve Bitcoin and other cryptocurrencies.

Most email-savvy consumers simply laugh at these preposterous messages and delete them, but other scams are much more insidious. For example, one widespread scam arrives as an "urgent" email message from a respected community member, such as a teacher, priest, or rabbi, who is traveling abroad, has been robbed, and needs a quick loan to return home. The message may, in fact, originate from a trusted person's account—one that has been hijacked by a hacker. Scams such as this one prey upon human kindness and the desire to help people who are in need (Figure 7-39).

Figure 7-39: Don't be fooled by the stranded traveler scam

FROM: **dbrownpastor@stmatthews.org**

TO: ManuellaAroyo@gmail.com

Need Assistance

Dear Manuella,

So sorry to bother you as I know you are quite busy this time of year. But my trip to the Philippines has turned into something of a disaster. Last night I was attacked and robbed. Thankfully, my injuries are minor and the hospital saw fit to release me this morning. The attackers got my wallet and phone, but I am glad that I locked my passport and airline ticket in the hotel safe.

I am left without any funds to pay my hotel bill or meet expenses to return home. Could you see it in your heart to loan me $2,000 just until I can get back to the States, when I can immediately pay you back? If so, I can give you instructions for wiring the money. It should not be difficult.

Sincerely,

Donald Brown

7

Spam

Spam is a nuisance and it accounts for approximately 50% of all email. Not only does spam clog up Internet bandwidth that could be put to better use, but it reduces individual productivity as users spend time separating useless and sometimes offensive messages from legitimate messages sent by friends, family, and colleagues. Some spam contains malicious attachments and links that lead to fake Web sites.

Try It!

How much spam do you get? Open the folder containing your junk mail and count the number of emails it contains. Then divide that number by the number of days of mail that is stored to calculate the average number of spam emails you receive each day.

Where does spam originate? **Spam** is defined as unsolicited messages that are usually sent in massive numbers using electronic mail systems. It is junk mail that recipients do not request or want. Spam includes advertisements from legitimate companies and from scammers attempting to trick victims into parting with their money or their personal information. Spam sent by scammers often uses spoofed email addresses or addresses of unfortunate victims whose computers are part of a botnet used to mass-mail spam.

Who gets spam? Everyone. Mass-mailing databases are quite inexpensive. Obtaining a million email addresses for a mass mailing costs less than $200. Databases used by spammers contain millions of email addresses. Some of these addresses are legitimately compiled from customer lists, but many more are harvested from social media sites, discussion forums, Web sites, and other online locations using email extractor software. Malware also harvests addresses for mass-mailing databases. Even more email addresses can be generated by appending the domain of a popular email service to names from a telephone directory (Figure 7-40).

Figure 7-40: Generating email addresses for a mass-mailing database

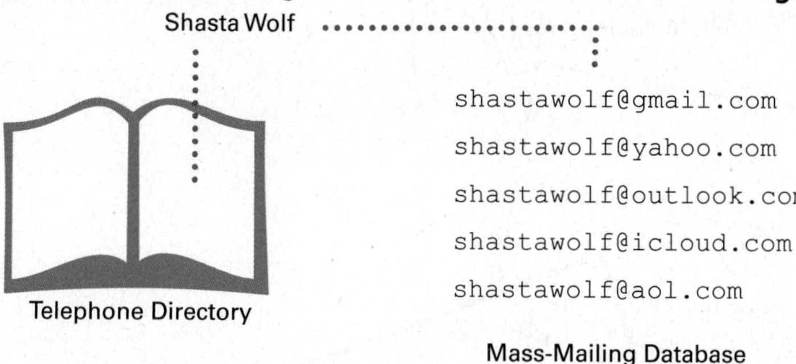

Isn't spam illegal? Most countries have laws that regulate spam, but legal measures seem to have little effect on the volume of unsolicited email messages. In 2003, the United States Congress passed an anti-spam law, the **CAN-SPAM Act** (Controlling the Assault of Non-Solicited Pornography And Marketing Act of 2003). Ironically, this act confirmed the legality of sending unsolicited email messages. The act attempted to regulate bulk email by requiring senders to do the following:

- Provide a visible means for recipients to opt out of further messages.
- Include accurate information in the "From" line, a relevant subject line, and a legitimate physical address of the sender.
- Avoid using harvested email addresses or false email headers.

The effectiveness of this law can be evaluated by looking at the content of your inbox and examining a few of the many unsolicited messages that continue to pile up in your email trash and junk mail folders.

QuickCheck

Which one of the following statements about spam is true?

a. Spam may originate from legitimate merchants as well as from hackers and scammers.

b. Spam is effectively regulated by the CAN-SPAM Act and similar legislation.

c. Spam accounts for a small percentage of the billions of email messages that flow over the Internet.

d. The primary destination of spam is computers linked in a botnet.

◗ **What are the most common email scams?** A high percentage of illegitimate spam contains stock market frauds, pretexting scams, advance fee fraud, phishing attacks, and ads for dubious products. **Pretexting** is a term describing spam that uses a false pretext to trick victims into participating. Spam messages like those in Figure 7-41 are examples of common pretexting exploits.

Figure 7-41: Lots of spam uses pretexting exploits

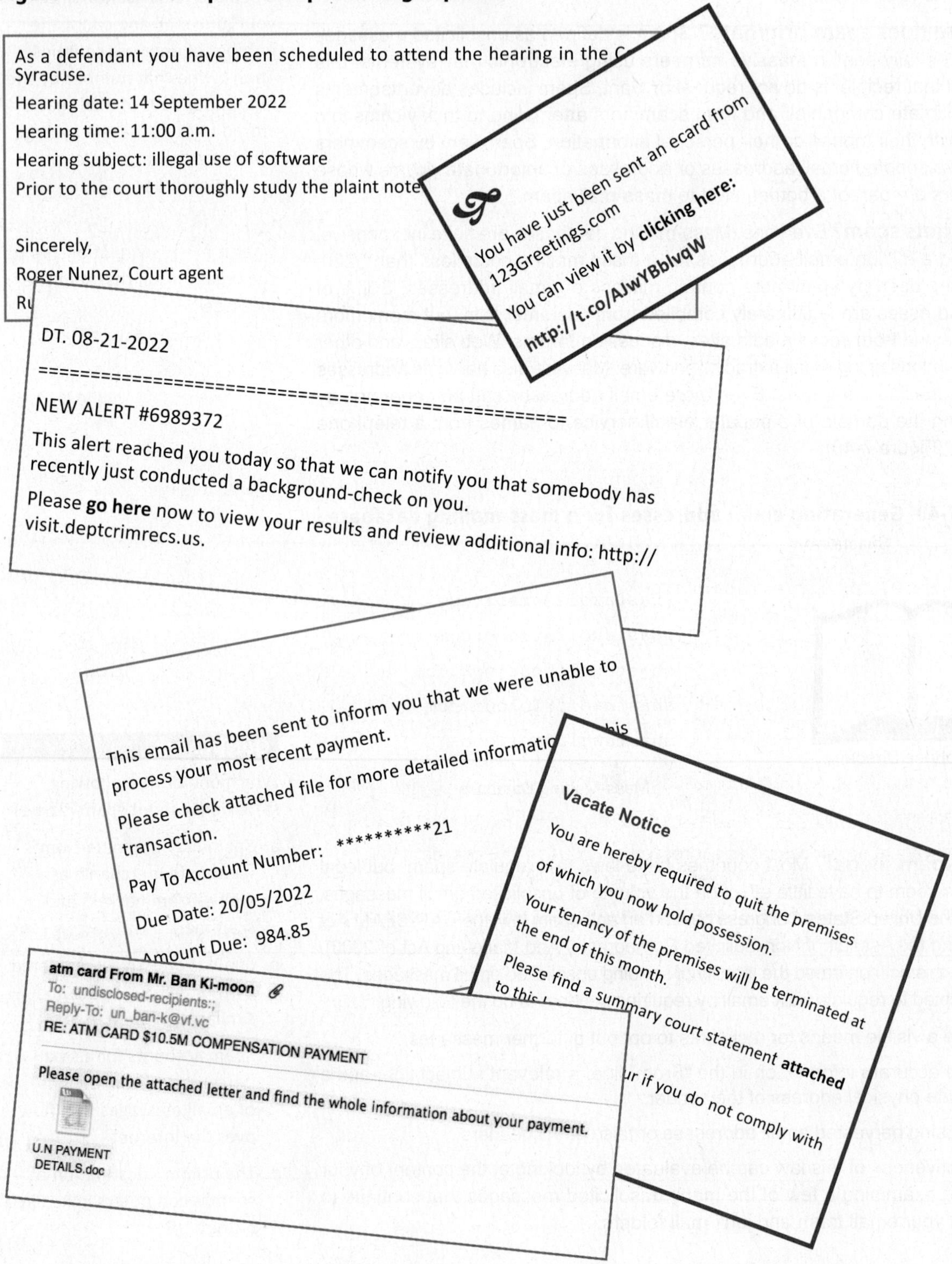

As a defendant you have been scheduled to attend the hearing in the C
Syracuse.
Hearing date: 14 September 2022
Hearing time: 11:00 a.m.
Hearing subject: illegal use of software
Prior to the court thoroughly study the plaint note

Sincerely,
Roger Nunez, Court agent
Ru

You have just been sent an ecard from 123Greetings.com
You can view it by **clicking here:**
http://t.co/AJwYBblvqW

DT. 08-21-2022
==
NEW ALERT #6989372
This alert reached you today so that we can notify you that somebody has recently just conducted a background-check on you.
Please **go here** now to view your results and review additional info: http://visit.deptcrimrecs.us.

This email has been sent to inform you that we were unable to process your most recent payment.
Please check attached file for more detailed informatio... his transaction.
Pay To Account Number: **********21
Due Date: 20/05/2022
Amount Due: 984.85

Vacate Notice
You are hereby required to quit the premises of which you now hold possession.
Your tenancy of the premises will be terminated at the end of this month.
Please find a summary court statement **attached** to this ... ur if you do not comply with

atm card From Mr. Ban Ki-moon
To: undisclosed-recipients:;
Reply-To: un_ban-k@vf.vc
RE: ATM CARD $10.5M COMPENSATION PAYMENT
Please open the attached letter and find the whole information about your payment.
U.N PAYMENT DETAILS.doc

Is it possible to block spam? Most ISPs and email services use filtering techniques to block spam coming from IP addresses and senders that are known to generate spam. These services also block messages sent in bulk that all contain the same wording. Spammers have developed techniques to bypass these barriers, and spam continues to make its way into consumer mailboxes.

Defending against spam requires careful inbox management. To reduce the amount of spam that lands in your online mailbox, consider the following recommendations:

- Share your primary email address only with people or businesses that you trust not to distribute it to others. Businesses sometimes share mailing lists with affiliates, and lists may fall into the hands of illegitimate spammers. Keeping your email address off one list can keep it from propagating to multiple lists.
- Never reply to spam. Mailing lists contain a high percentage of invalid addresses. Replying to a spam message marks your email address as valid, which only generates more unwanted mail.
- Do not click links in spam messages. If you are curious about where a link might lead, hover over it with the pointer and look at the destination URL. Links in spam often are designed to direct victims to fake sites where malware is waiting.
- Do not open attachments in email messages unless you are certain that the sender is trusted and the attached file is expected.
- Use a complex email address with a user name that would not be found in a telephone directory. For example, add a number or symbol to your name.
- Use a disposable email address in situations where an email address is required but you don't want to receive solicitations. Disposable email addresses are useful when registering to use Web apps and when signing up for merchant loyalty programs.
- When displaying your real email address—for example, on your Web site—disguise it by posting it as a graphic. You can create a graphic containing your email address by using graphics software such as Paint and saving it as a PNG file.
- Use an opt-out link only if the email originated from a reputable national company. Before clicking the opt-out link, hover over it to make sure it leads to a legitimate URL.
- Remember that if a deal seems too good to be true, it is probably a scam.
- Be suspicious of shortened URLs that do not reveal the genuine domain.
- Be wary of email messages addressed to "undisclosed recipients" or addressed to numerous recipients that you don't know.
- Be cautious of email messages addressed to your email user name rather than your real name.
- Use the spam filters provided by your email client.

Try It!

The next time you receive an outlandish spam email on your desktop or laptop, hover the mouse pointer over one of the links. DON'T CLICK THE LINK. Look at the destination address. Does it have any relationship to the organization that sent the message?

QuickCheck

A disposable email address is most useful for __________.

a. detecting infected email attachments
b. reducing the amount of spam that arrives at your main email account
c. evading mail extractors
d. opting out of legitimate URLs

7

How do spam filters work? A **spam filter** uses a set of rules to examine email messages and determine which are spam. Messages that are identified as spam can be blocked, deleted, or moved to a junk mail folder. There are four common types of spam filters:

- **Content filters** examine the content within a message for certain words or phrases commonly used in spam emails.
- **Header filters** review the email header for falsified information, such as spoofed IP addresses.
- **Blacklist filters** block mail that originates from IP addresses of known spammers.
- **Permission filters** block or allow mail based on the sender's address.

Blacklist and header filtering is usually performed by ISPs and email services, such as Google and Yahoo!. Email clients and Webmail services provide consumers with permission filters and content filters. Knowing how to use these filters is handy for blocking spam that can slip through filters operating upstream at your ISP or email service (Figure 7-42).

QuickCheck

Who typically sets up blacklist filters?

a. Consumers

b. Email clients

c. ISPs

d. Antivirus software

Figure 7-42: Gmail spam filters

The simplest spam filter blocks a specific sender based on that sender's email address. That technique works on unwanted mail from creepy individuals, but most spammers send mail from a spoofed address that is fraudulent. The spammer will never use the same address twice, so blocking it does little to curtail spam.

Suppose you're receiving a barrage of spam about "unbelievable stock deals." If the messages contain similar wording, you may be able to devise a content filter to block similar spam in the future. The trick is to create a specific filter rather than one that is general enough to block legitimate messages.

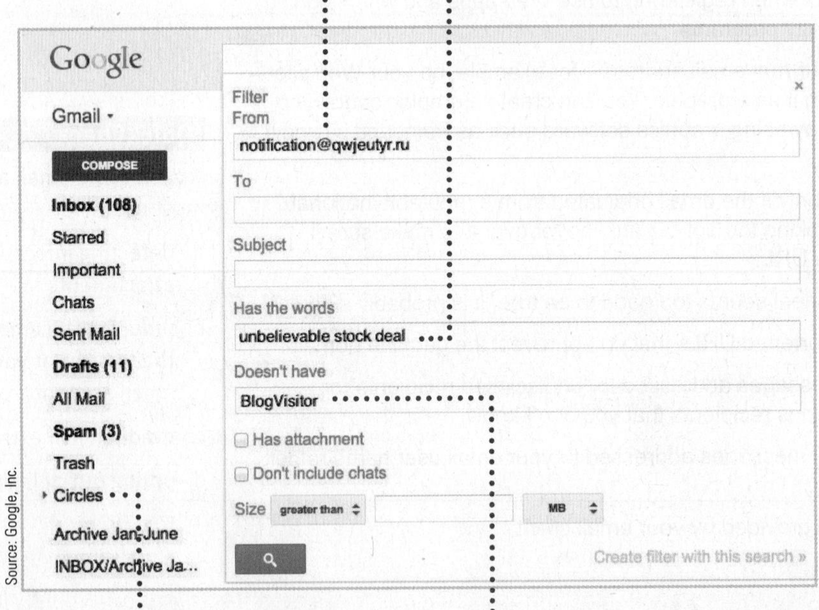

Some spam filters can be set up to allow email only from people who are included in your contacts list or address book. This technique introduces a problem, however, because email from new acquaintances who are not yet in your address book is blocked. When using a permission filter, it is important to periodically check the junk mail folder in case legitimate messages are there.

You can also use email filters to create "ham." In the world of email, ham is like a password that verifies the validity of a sender. For example, suppose you expect email from visitors to your Web site or blog. Tell your visitors to include a ham password, such as "BlogVisitor," in the subject line of their messages. Set your spam filter to require the password for any messages that don't originate from people who are in your contacts list.

Phishing

Phishing exploits are responsible for some of the most effective social engineering scams, including the exploit that caused a scandal during the 2016 U.S. presidential election. A look at some examples reveals how these attacks work.

Try It!

Take another look at the contents of your junk email folder. How many of the messages would you classify as phishing attacks?

7

▶ **What is phishing?** **Phishing** is an email scam that masquerades as a message from a trusted friend, legitimate company, or agency of authority, such as the IRS. The goal of a phishing scam is usually to obtain private information, including login passwords and bank card numbers.

Phishing scams often contain infected attachments or include links to fake Web sites infected with malware. Phishing email messages are typically the beginning of exploits that infect a device with malware, use keyloggers to collect personal information, set up a backdoor for intrusions, and link a device to a botnet.

Phishing messages are usually mass-mailed to millions of email addresses. A **spear phishing** attack is more targeted. It is typically sent only to members of a specific organization. The spear phishing email that caused such a scandal during the 2016 U.S. presidential election was sent to 100 of candidate Hillary Clinton's campaign workers. It contained a short URL that led to a hacker's site where additional exploits waited. Clinton's campaign manager clicked the link and unintentionally activated the spear phishing exploit, which gave hackers access to email messages and other files related to the campaign.

QuickCheck

Phishing attacks are a type of spam that ______________.

a. appears to originate from a trusted business
b. is sent to undisclosed recipients
c. spoofs the target's email address
d. contains an infected dropper

Some of the most common phishing attacks appear to originate from FedEx, UPS, DHL, or the U.S. Postal Service and pertain to package delivery services. Tax scams in messages headed with an official IRS seal are also prevalent, as are scams that use realistic logos of financial institutions, government agencies, and merchants (Figure 7-43).

Figure 7-43: Phishing attacks appear to originate from trusted businesses

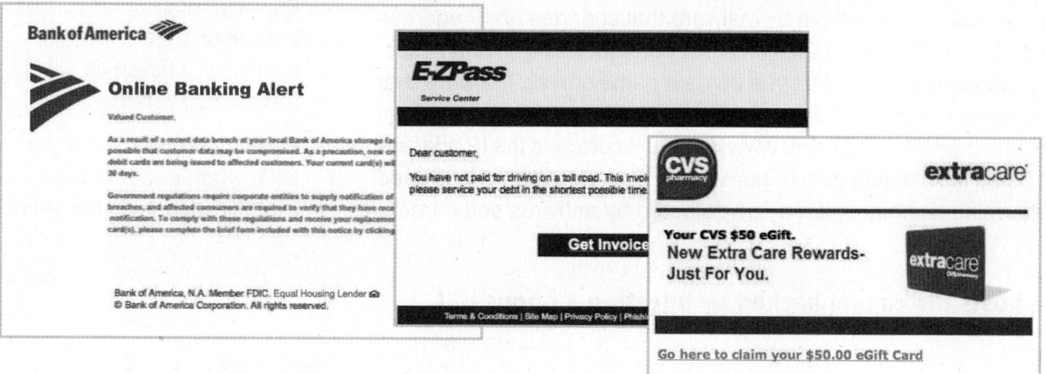

▶ **What is the best strategy for dealing with phishing attacks?** Phishing attacks are not always easy to identify. Their messages may appear to originate from trusted businesses. Although some phishing messages include misspellings and bad grammar, others contain no such errors. Phishing messages are more compelling than most spam, and the temptation to click the links they contain is strong.

Phishing exploits are a type of spam, and both require the same type of vigilance on the part of consumers: Take steps to keep your email address off mass-mailing lists, use spam filters, avoid opening attachments, and do not click links in email messages unless you are certain that they lead to a trusted source.

Pharming

Email is not the only source of social engineering attacks. The Web is host to its share of fraudulent sites and other scams. Using screenshots and graphics tools, for example, one can construct Web sites that closely resemble those of trusted online retailers. But how are consumers tricked into visiting these sites? That's the purpose of pharming exploits.

▶ What is pharming? **Pharming** redirects Web site traffic to fraudulent Web sites that distribute malware, collect personal data, sell counterfeit products, and perpetrate other scams. Fraudulent Web sites often have URLs that are similar to the legitimate sites they imitate. A basic exploit is to establish a look-alike site at a URL, such as *www.amzon.com*, that is a common misspelling of a legitimate online storefront. Careless consumers who leave out the "a" end up at the look-alike Web site.

Another pharming strategy is to use a URL that sounds like a legitimate merchant. For example, a gang of offshore scammers selling counterfeit Louis Vuitton handbags hoped consumers would think the URL *www.nordstrom-louisvuitton.net* was affiliated with Nordstrom department stores.

▶ How is pharming related to the domain name system? The most insidious pharming attacks are implemented by DNS spoofing, which was explained in Module 3. Hackers infiltrate a domain name system server to alter the IP address of a legitimate site and send visitors to a fraudulent site instead. Past pharming attacks have redirected URLs for Web sites such as The New York Times, Google Malaysia, American Express, and The Huffington Post.

Pharming attacks carried out by DNS spoofing cannot be detected by antivirus software or spyware removal software. DNS spoofing is eventually detected and corrected by domain registrars. Until corrections are in place, consumers have little defense against such attacks except to remain alert to any details that don't look quite right when visiting familiar Web sites.

Pharming attacks can also be carried out by malware that changes an IP address in a file called Hosts. This file contains URLs and their corresponding IP addresses, which override the mapping accessed from a domain name server. Malware that enters a device, perhaps in a trojan, seeks out the Hosts file and inserts a bogus URL. For example, the entry 34.123.67.999 www.facebook.com sets the IP address of Facebook to a look-alike hacker's site (Figure 7-44). Because malware is used to carry out this pharming technique, it may be detected by antivirus software.

QuickCheck

What is the difference between phishing and pharming?

a. Phishing is a social engineering exploit, but pharming is not.

b. Phishing can be blocked by antivirus software, but pharming cannot.

c. Phishing is based on fraudulent email, whereas pharming is based on fraudulent Web sites.

d. Phishing exploits spoof the DNS, whereas pharming exploits spoof email headers.

Figure 7-44: The hosts file can be hacked by injecting a bogus URL

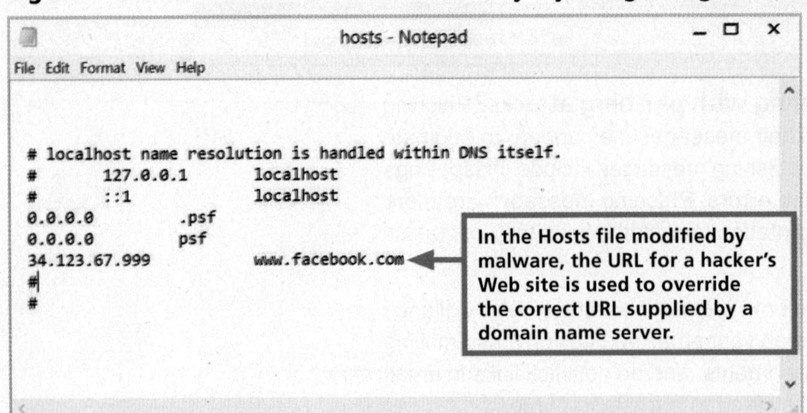

What is Safe Browsing? **Safe Browsing** is a service offered by Google that checks URLs against a list of suspicious Web site URLs. The list is used to generate warnings like the one in Figure 7-45.

Figure 7-45: Warning generated by Google Safe Browsing

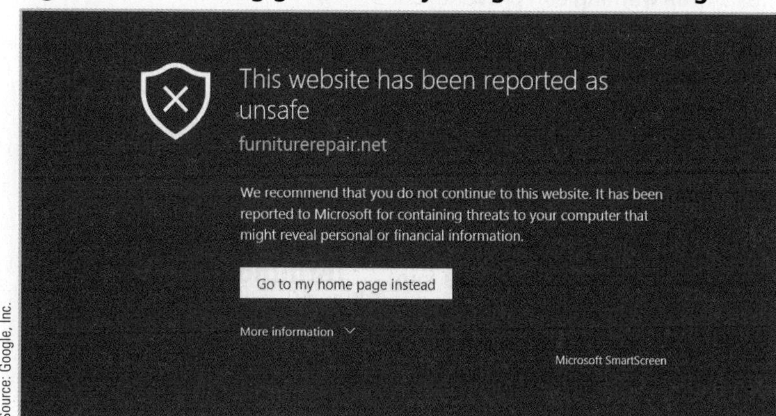

Source: Google, Inc.

Try It!

Safe Browsing and SmartScreen enhance security when you are browsing the Web. Is this service activated in the browser that you use?

How can I activate Safe Browsing? Chrome, Safari, and Firefox use Google's Safe Browsing service to alert users about sites to avoid. Microsoft offers a similar service called **SmartScreen**. Figure 7-46 illustrates how to activate safe browsing.

Figure 7-46: How to activate safe browsing

In Safari, access Preferences, choose Security, and then check the box for Fraudulent sites.

In Chrome, select Settings, go to "Privacy and security," select Security, and then choose the level of Safe Browsing you want to use.

In Microsoft Edge, select Settings, choose "privacy, search, and services," and then turn on Microsoft Defender SmartScreen.

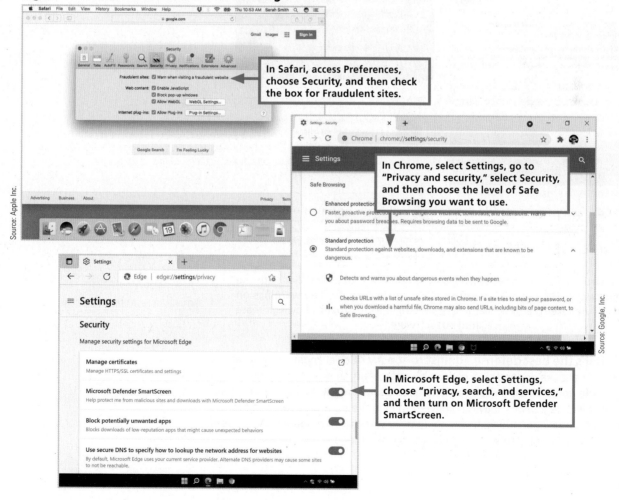

Source: Apple Inc.

Source: Google, Inc.

Rogue Antivirus

"WARNING! Your computer may be infected with spyware." When that window pops up, is it a warning generated by your antivirus software or a social engineering scam designed to prey on your desire to take precautions against malware? Knowing the difference between a real and a fake virus warning can prevent you from becoming a victim of fraud and identity theft.

What is a rogue antivirus exploit? Most consumers who own digital devices know the dangers of malware. Seeing a notification that your device has a virus makes you want to take immediate action to eradicate it before further damage is done. Social engineers use fake virus notifications to prey on consumers' aversion to malware and their sense of urgency to eradicate it.

A **rogue antivirus exploit** usually begins with a virus warning and an offer to disinfect the infected device. The goal of this exploit is to trick consumers into clicking a link that downloads malware. Some of these fraudulent alerts offer a free virus scan or download, which often doesn't work or actually infects devices with the dangerous malware it is supposed to protect against. Other rogue antivirus exploits charge consumers for bogus software, obtain personal information, or carry out malware attacks.

Terminology

Rogue antivirus exploits are sometimes referred to as *rogue AV* or *rogue security software*.

Fake virus alerts commonly appear when browsing the Web at slightly sketchy Web sites. These alerts appear as pop-up windows. Can you tell which alerts in Figure 7-47 are real and which are fake?

Figure 7-47: Malware alerts: which are fake?

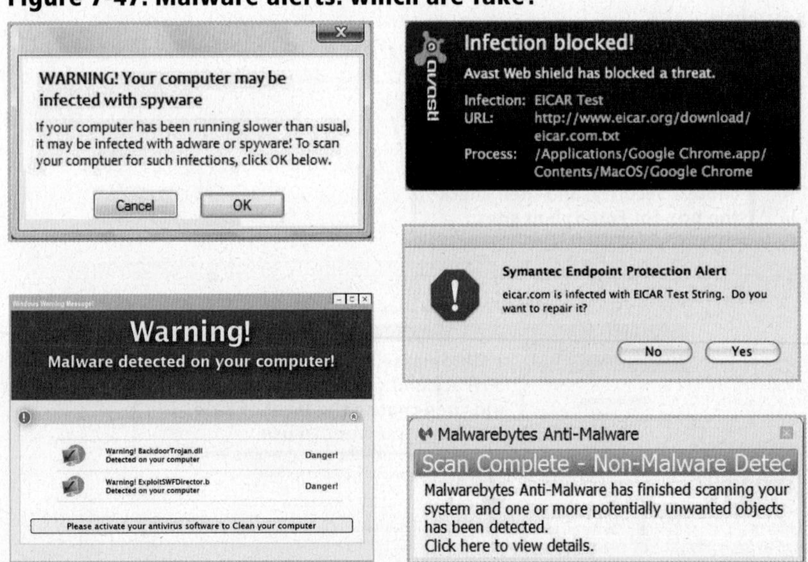

Fake virus alerts can look realistic, so it is important to be familiar with the legitimate alerts displayed by your antivirus software. The two warnings on the left are fake. The three warnings on the right were produced by legitimate antivirus software.

What's the best defense against rogue AV? Social engineers who launch rogue AV attacks depend on the victim's sense of urgency and ignorance about legitimate antivirus alerts. Your best defense against rogue AV is to protect your devices with legitimate antivirus software and make sure that you can identify the virus alerts it generates. If you are familiar with the alerts generated by your legitimate software, you will not be fooled by fake alerts.

PUAs

Some software is not exactly malware, but it is a nuisance. It takes up residence on a digital device and seems impossible to disable or remove. What's up with that?

What is this stuff? The acronym **PUP** stands for *potentially unwanted program*. A similar acronym, **PUA**, stands for *potentially unwanted application*. The terms are used interchangeably. The most common types of PUPs and PUAs are toolbars and alternative browsers. If you suddenly notice that an odd browser has become the default and your attempts to reset the default browser to Chrome, Edge, or Safari fail, your computer is likely to have a PUA.

How do PUAs end up on my devices? PUAs are installed using social engineering techniques. Knowing that consumers often speed through the installation process, social engineers insert an option for accepting an application that "enriches" or "enhances" a function such as Web browsing. If you fail to read the fine print and accept the application, the PUA is installed along with the application you've downloaded (Figure 7-48).

QuickCheck

PUPs and PUAs are most similar to ______________.

a. phishing scams
b. pharming attacks
c. pretexting
d. malware

7

Figure 7-48: When installing software, stay alert for PUAs

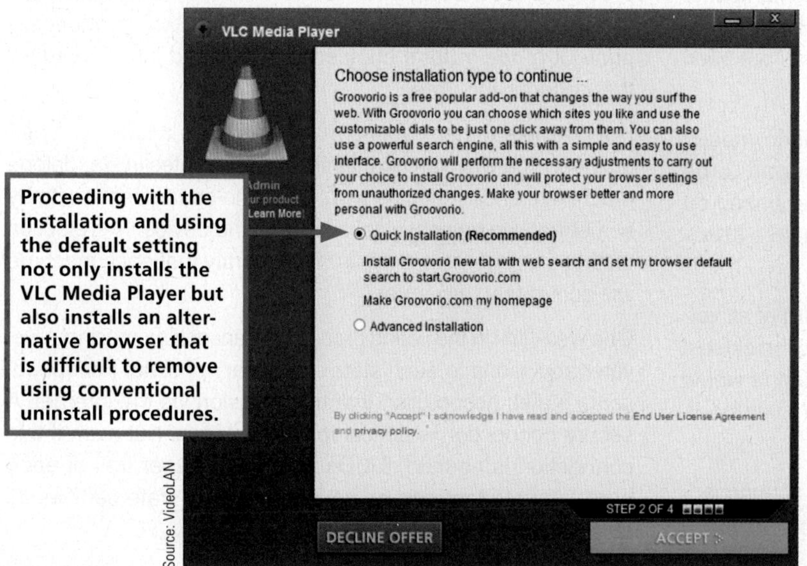

Try It!

Many antivirus utilities include PUP and PUA detection tools. Check the antivirus utility that you use to find out if it protects you from unwanted applications and make sure the detection feature is activated.

QuickQuiz Section E

1. Advance [ ] fraud and stranded traveler scams are two social engineering exploits that are delivered in spam.
2. Blacklist spam [ ] block mail that originates from IP addresses of known spammers.
3. A(n) [ ] attack usually begins with a fraudulent email message that appears to be from a legitimate company.
4. Many [ ] attacks use DNS spoofing to send victims to a fraudulent Web site.
5. A(n) [ ] antivirus exploit displays a fake virus warning.

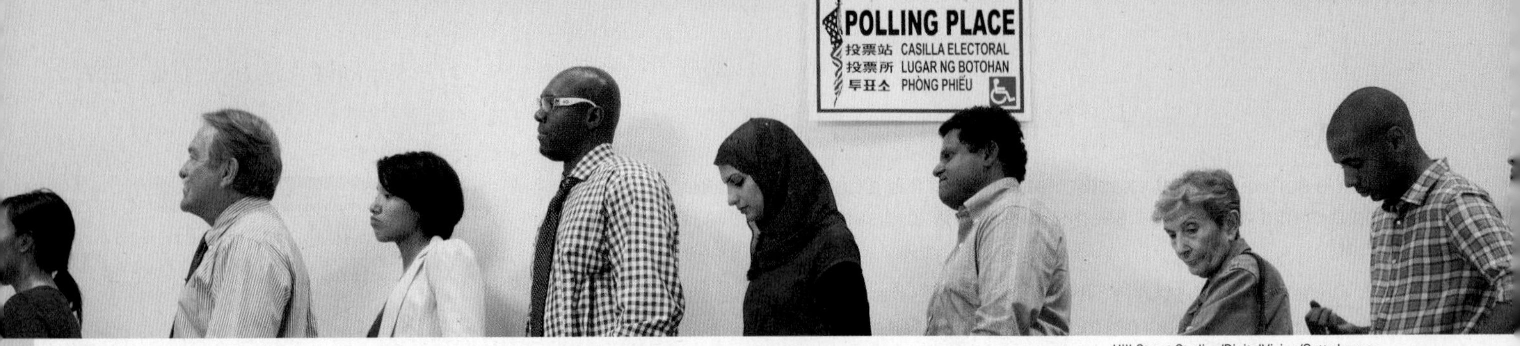

Hill Street Studios/DigitalVision/Getty Images

Issue: How Secure Is Democracy?

Russian hackers. The 2016 U.S. presidential election ended under a cloud of controversy with reports that Russian hackers influenced the vote. It was not the first time that election results were questioned, but it was the first time that a security breach was blamed.

The foundation of democracy is built upon the idea that "we the people" vote for our choice of candidates. In today's high-tech world, it might seem that touchscreen voting machines, ballot scanners, and even online voting might reduce the number of invalid ballots and fraudulent votes. Can technology assure free and fair elections? The track record so far has not been encouraging.

In the 1970s, when the country danced to disco music, cumbersome lever-operated voting booths began to be replaced by new technology. The new systems, based on IBM computer punch cards, required voters to use a stylus to punch through a card to select candidates.

For the 2000 presidential election, about one-third of all voters used these punch card voting systems. It was the closest election in the nation's history. The winner in Florida would become president, but the vote was too close to immediately call.

When a recount was conducted, the deficiencies of punched-card voting technology became clear. Some voters had failed to punch through the card, leaving "hanging chads." Those votes were rejected by the card reader, necessitating a manual recount. Teams of analysts examined each punched card, a process that stretched on for weeks. When the election results were finally certified, only 547 votes separated the winner from his opponent.

Determined to establish a voting system for subsequent elections that would be less prone to controversy, states adopted two emerging technology solutions: DRE voting machines and optical scan ballots.

DREs (direct recording electronic systems) are microprocessor-based voting machines that display candidates' names on a touchscreen. Votes are recorded on a memory card, which is later transferred to election headquarters where votes are tallied.

Optical scan technology requires voters to use a marker to fill in a circle next to the candidates of their choice. The paper ballots are tallied by an optical reader.

Unfortunately, DREs and optical scan ballots used in the 2004, 2008, and 2012 elections came with their own set of usability and security problems.

For the 2020 election, many states turned to yet another voting machine technology. Ballot marking devices (BMDs) provide a touchscreen for voters to select candidates, but that selection is not an actual vote. The BMD produces a printout of the voter's choices, which is fed into a scanner that records the vote.

Is it possible to hack voting machines? The answer is "yes," but not in the way you might think. To alter votes in standalone machines, each machine would need to be tampered with by someone who has physical access to the device. Pre-election testing procedures are designed to certify that each machine will accurately tally votes.

One weak link in the voting process is transmitting precinct-level vote tabulations to each state's secretary of state. For speed, some states accomplish that transmission via the Internet. A secure connection is critical for this process. But even if this connection is hacked, BMDs produce a paper trail of each person's vote that can be verified before a state certifies its election results.

Significant cases of voting machine tampering have not been discovered. Tampering with the vote tally requires physical access, so voting machines seem to be safe from remote intrusions by Russian, Chinese, or even U.S.-based hackers. Other aspects of the election process are less secure.

Voter registration data, campaign Web sites, email messages between campaign organizers, campaign files, fund-raising bank accounts, lists of campaign workers, and donor databases all flow over the Internet and are susceptible to attacks that steal, alter, or delete data. Security analysts warn that it is essential to reinforce security defenses to assure that future elections are accurate and fair.

Try It!

Try It! Our intuition might tell us that technology offers improvements to just about every aspect of life. But when it comes to voting, technological innovations come with a cloud of suspicion about reliability and accuracy. Here is your chance to explore the emerging issues of election technology and security.

1. Permission to vote is essentially granted by voter registration databases. If your name is in a voter registration database, you are allowed to vote. Critics of every political affiliation have cast doubt on the accuracy and security of voter registration databases. Search online articles and news reports to discover if hackers have attempted to access the voter registration database in your state. Were they successful? If so, were the hackers caught and did their interference affect election results?

2. In the United States, each state is responsible for selecting the technology that is used to conduct elections. How reliable and secure is the technology used to collect and tabulate votes in your state? Do the majority of other states use similar technology? Check Ballotpedia to discover the voting technology used by each state and to see how your state compares to others.

3. Ballot marking devices (BMDs) were the technology of choice for the 2020 U.S. presidential election. Explore the technology to answer the following questions:

   What is the cost of each BMD?

   Exactly how does a voter use a BMD?

   What is the configuration of a typical polling place that uses BMDs?

   How do poll workers certify each machine before voting takes place?

   How are results from each polling place transmitted to the state's secretary of state?

4. How secure was the most recent national election in your country? Search reliable online sources, such as the FBI Vault, National Intelligence Agency reports, and findings from congressional investigative committees, and then answer the following questions:

   Was there hacking of voting machines, voter rolls, campaign communications, or other aspects of the election process?

   If so, what type of attacks occurred and what was so damaging about the data that hackers collected?

   What level of confidence do investigators attach to their findings?

   How is the security of this election likely to affect the technology used in the next election?

What Do You Think?

Issue

1. Do you think that hacking is a top security threat facing the democratic process of free and fair elections?
2. Does it seem that technology has improved the electoral process?
3. Do you agree that paper ballots are the best defense against fraudulent elections?

Information Tools: Your Own Words

Plagiarism. Buying a term paper from a company or an individual and turning it in as your own. Copying words directly from someone else's print or online work. Paraphrasing without attribution. These are all forms of plagiarism.

Common knowledge. Whether you obtain information from an online or written source, to avoid plagiarism in your written work, you should include citations for any statements that are not common knowledge. Common knowledge includes ideas and facts that can be found in many places and are known by many people. Material that is based on the work, ideas, or statements of other people is not common knowledge and needs a citation for its source. Include a citation for:

- Any statement that refers to a research study or is based on its conclusions
- Any statement or graph that includes statistics
- Any word-for-word spoken or written quotations
- Any statement that restates or summarizes another person's original ideas

Paraphrasing. Citations are required even when you paraphrase. Changing the words of an original source is not sufficient. You must cite the source whenever you borrow ideas as well as words.

Acceptable paraphrasing should not be too similar to the original wording, yet you must be careful not to change the idea behind the original wording. Your paraphrase also requires a citation to the original source. Suppose you find this passage on Carla Charmer's blog that contains material you'd like to include in a mid-term report:

> A Michigan man who accessed his wife's email account while she was allegedly carrying on an affair faces up to five years in prison. He is being prosecuted for violating a state law typically used against hackers and identity thieves. It is shocking that a person could be charged with a felony for reading his spouse's email.

There are several ways in which you can use this material. Some ways are more ethical than others.

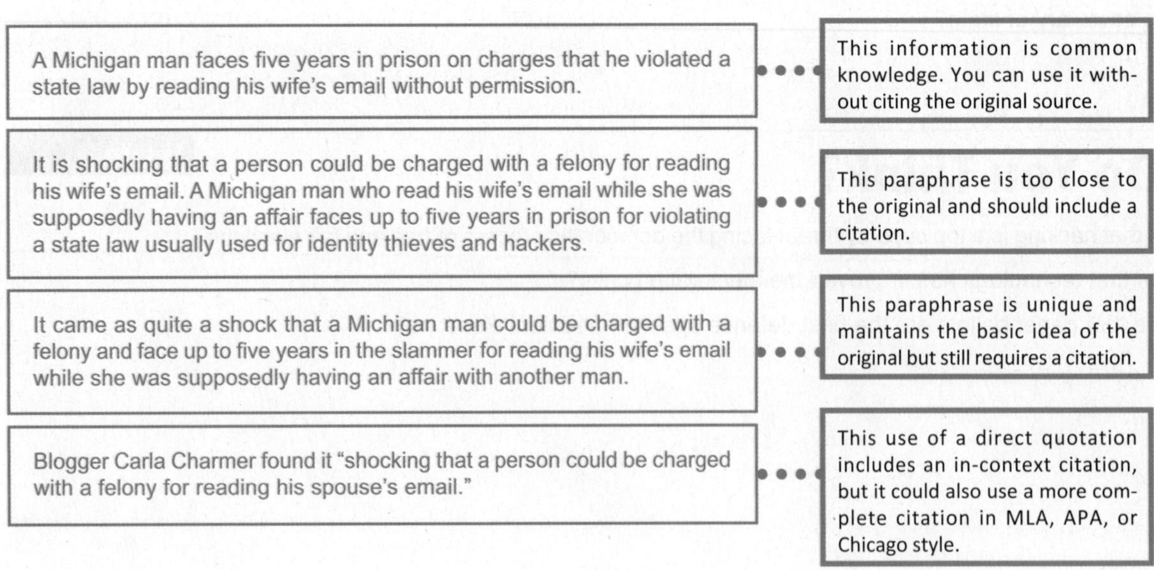

A Michigan man faces five years in prison on charges that he violated a state law by reading his wife's email without permission.
This information is common knowledge. You can use it without citing the original source.
It is shocking that a person could be charged with a felony for reading his wife's email. A Michigan man who read his wife's email while she was supposedly having an affair faces up to five years in prison for violating a state law usually used for identity thieves and hackers.
This paraphrase is too close to the original and should include a citation.
It came as quite a shock that a Michigan man could be charged with a felony and face up to five years in the slammer for reading his wife's email while she was supposedly having an affair with another man.
This paraphrase is unique and maintains the basic idea of the original but still requires a citation.
Blogger Carla Charmer found it "shocking that a person could be charged with a felony for reading his spouse's email."
This use of a direct quotation includes an in-context citation, but it could also use a more complete citation in MLA, APA, or Chicago style.

Try It! Explore the differences between original and plagiarized material by answering the following questions.

1. Which of these statements would not need a citation because it is common knowledge?
   a. While it is fairly uncomplicated to build a slow crawler that downloads one or a few pages per second for a short period of time, building a high-performance system that can download hundreds of millions of pages over several weeks presents a number of challenges in system design, I/O and network efficiency, and robustness and manageability.
   b. Search engines, such as Google, include software called a Web crawler that visits Web sites and indexes the material it finds there. This material can later be accessed by entering keywords at a search engine site.
   c. Experimental results show that a distributed Web crawler can more effectively visit Web pages than a single Web crawler.
2. Which of these statements would need a citation because it refers to statements based on statistics?
   a. The main problem search engines have to deal with is the size and rate of change of the Web, with no search engine indexing more than one-third of the publicly available Web.
   b. Back in 2004, the average working day consisted of dealing with 46 phone calls, 15 internal memos, 19 items of snail mail, and 22 email messages.
   c. Search engines deal with a vast amount of material. The process of collecting and organizing that material becomes ever greater as the Web expands.
3. Which of these statements should have citations because it refers to a research study or its conclusions?
   a. We ran a crawl of more than 100 million Web pages on about 5 million hosts. The crawl was performed over a period of 18 days; however, the crawler was not continuously in operation during this time. Of the 138 million pages cataloged, more than 400,000 produced a 403 error, indicating that access was forbidden.
   b. Given the current size of the Web, even large search engines cover only a portion of the publicly available part. A report from the Websonite Group indicates that large-scale search engines index no more than 40% to 70% of the indexable Web.
   c. You can study the Web all you want, but there will still be more to learn.
4. Use a search engine to find the boxed quotation below, and then do the following:

> "Can ordinary Americans like you and me sue the government for illegally spying on them? When it comes to the NSA surveillance program, the government itself says the answer is no. After all, since it's a secret program you don't really know if you're being spied on. And if you don't know you're being spied on, you have no standing to sue."

   a. Create an MLA citation for the original source.
   b. Create an acceptable paraphrase for the quotation using an in-context citation.
   c. Write at least two sentences on the same topic that would be common knowledge and not need a citation.
5. Plagiarism scanning services, such as Turnitin and Viper, make it easy for instructors to check the originality of your work. Before turning in a paper, you can make sure you've cited all relevant sources by running your document through the student version of Turnitin or a free plagiarism scanner such as Viper, Grammarly, Dustball, or Dupli Checker. Copy a page of text from one of your original documents and submit it to a plagiarism checker, and then do the same for a page that you copy out of Wikipedia. What are the results?

Comstock/Thinkstock

Technology in Context: Law Enforcement

Sirens wail. Blue lights flash. A speeding car slows and pulls off to the side of the road. It looks like a routine traffic stop, but the patrol car is outfitted with a mobile data computer. The police officers on this high-tech force have already checked the speeding car's license plate number and description against a database of stolen cars and vehicles allegedly used in kidnapping and other crimes.

Mounted in the dashboard of marked and unmarked police cars is a laptop computer with its flat-panel screen and compact keyboard. Unlike a consumer-grade laptop, however, the computers in police cruisers use hardened technology designed to withstand extreme conditions, such as high temperatures in parked vehicles. The dashboard-mounted computer communicates with an office-based server using a wireless link, such as short-range radio, mobile phone technology, or Wi-Fi. With this wireless link, police officers can access data from local, state, and national databases.

Comstock/Thinkstock

One national database, the National Crime Information Center (NCIC), is maintained by the FBI and can be accessed by authorized personnel in local, state, and federal law enforcement agencies. The system can process more than 12 million queries per day related to stolen vehicles, wanted criminals, missing persons, violent gang members, stolen guns, and members of terrorist organizations. The officers who pulled over the speeding car received information from the NCIC that the car was stolen, so they activate their body cameras and approach the vehicle with caution.

Technology for wearable body cameras has been available for several years, but police departments were slow to add these devices to officers' toolbelts. Costs and privacy concerns—for both the officers and the civilians they serve—prompted a wait-and-see attitude. In 2014, however, a disputed incident between a police officer and an unarmed civilian in Ferguson, Missouri, brought national attention to the need for documentary evidence of encounters between police and civilians.

Body cameras offered part of the solution to these disputes. A year-long pilot program in Rialto, California, showed a significant reduction in citizen complaints against police. The report concluded that filming improved the behavior of both the officers and the civilians they interacted with. Body cameras and the protocols that govern their use are still a work in progress to ensure that footage is not hacked, leaked, or tampered with.

Following protocol, the officers in our stolen car scenario arrest the car's occupant and take the suspect to the police station for booking.

At the police station, digital cameras flash and the suspect's mug shot is automatically entered into an automated warrants and booking system. The system stores the suspect's complete biographical and arrest information, such as name, aliases, addresses, Social Security number, charges, and arrest date. The system also checks for outstanding warrants against the suspect, such as warrants for other thefts. Booking agents can enter those charges into the system, assign a new inmate to a cell, log the perpetrator's personal items, and print a photo ID or wrist band.

Automated warrants and booking systems have been proven to increase police productivity. New York City's system handles more than 300,000 bookings per year, with gains in productivity that allow officers more time to investigate crimes and patrol neighborhoods.

As part of the booking process, suspects are fingerprinted. A standard fingerprint card, sometimes called a ten-print card, contains inked prints of the fingers on each hand, plus name, date of birth, and other arrest information. Now, however, instead of using ink, a biometric scanning device electronically captures fingerprints. Text information is entered using a keyboard and stored with digital fingerprint images.

The fingerprint information can be transmitted in digital format from local law enforcement agencies to the FBI's Next Generation Identification (NGI) system. This biometric identification system uses digital imaging technology and sophisticated algorithms to analyze fingerprints and other biometric data. Within an hour, NGI can match fingerprints with 99% accuracy from its database containing millions of records.

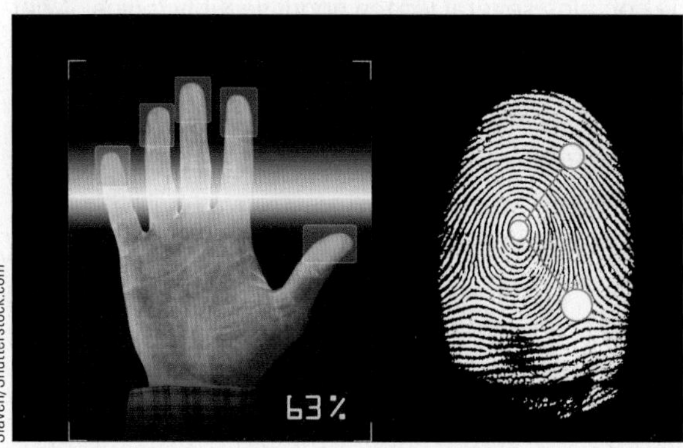

Slaven/Shutterstock.com

Conventional crimes, such as car theft, are often solved by using standard investigative techniques with information from computer databases. To solve cybercrimes, however, the special skills of computer forensic investigators are often required.

Computer forensics is the scientific examination and analysis of data located on computer storage media; it is conducted to offer evidence of computer crimes in court. Computer crimes can be separated into two categories. The first includes crimes that use computers, such as transmitting trade secrets to competitors, reproducing copyrighted material, and distributing child pornography. The second includes crimes targeted at computers, such as denial-of-service attacks on servers, Web site vandalism, data theft, and destructive viruses. Computer forensics can be applied to both categories.

Whether investigators suspect that a digital device is the origin of a cyber-attack or contains evidence, the first step in the forensic process is to use disk imaging software to make an exact replica of the information stored on the hard disk or SSD drive. The disk image is collected on a write-once medium that cannot be altered with planted evidence, and the forensic scientist begins analyzing the disk image data with basic search software that looks through files for keywords related to the crime.

In the case of the Gap-Toothed Bandit, who was twice convicted for robbing nine banks in Southern California, analysis of the disk image from his computer revealed word processing files containing notes he handed to tellers demanding money.

After a 2015 terrorist attack in San Bernardino, California, investigators were able to use data from the shooter's iPhone to track the activities of the shooter and his accomplice prior to the attack.

Criminals might attempt to delete files with incriminating evidence, but a good forensic scientist can retrieve data from deleted files with undelete software or data recovery software. Cloud storage, temporary Internet files, and cache files can also yield evidence that points law enforcement officers to Web sites the suspect visited that might be fronts for illegal activity.

When a network is the target of a cyber-attack, forensic investigators use three techniques to track the source. The first option is to make an immediate image of the server's hard disk and look through its log files for evidence of activity coming from unauthorized IP addresses. The second technique is to monitor the intruder by watching login attempts, changes to log files, and file access requests. Sophisticated intruders might be able to detect such monitoring, however, and cover their tracks. The third technique is to create a "honeypot"—an irresistible computer system or Web site containing fake information that allows investigators to monitor hackers until identification is possible.

Despite the many techniques and tools available to forensic investigators, they have three main constraints. First, they must adhere to privacy regulations and obtain warrants to set up wiretaps or gather information from ISPs about their customers. Second, investigators must scrupulously document their procedures so that the evidence they produce cannot be discredited in court as planted or fabricated. Third, forensic investigators must examine a wide range of alternatives pertaining to the crime, such as the chance that an IP address or email address used to commit a cybercrime might belong to an innocent bystander being spoofed by the real hacker.

Privacy, documentation, and evidentiary constraints cost forensic investigators time, and failure to adhere to strict standards can sometimes allow criminals to avoid conviction and penalties. But even within these constraints, careful forensic investigation is an important aspect of catching and convicting high-tech criminals.

Flipped Class Projects

Critical Thinking

What motivates hackers to create malware and launch cyber-attacks? Make a list of incentives, including financial and psychological, that might be the basis for attacks. Next, consider the types of cyber-attacks presented in Module 7. Classifying them according to severity may help you form some hypotheses about the incentives behind various attacks. Create a threat matrix with vertical headings for attack types and horizontal headings for incentives. When your matrix is complete, browse online to find out if your thoughts are in line with expert assessments.

Group Project

You see a similar scenario on television or in movies: a spy, hacker, or law enforcement agent needs to bypass a password. The password is cracked in three or four tries. How realistic is that? Work with a group of five classmates and try to guess one of the passwords used by a member of your group. You can ask questions such as "Is your password based on your dog's name? Your birthdate?" Does that sound risky? If someone can guess your password, it is very weak and you should change it immediately!

Cyberclassroom

One of the obstacles to distance education initiatives is securing the testing environment for students who are off-site in an unproctored environment. Several companies offer secure online testing products, but do they effectively prevent cheating? Work with a partner to brainstorm the requirements for exam security. Research an online exam monitoring product to determine its effectiveness. How could you defeat the security measures?

Multimedia Project

Envisioning how cybercrime exploits work can be difficult. YouTube contains several videos about security topics. What can they tell you? Choose a security topic from this module. You might choose a specific exploit, such as ransomware or IMSI catchers, or you might want to select a security product or a social engineering controversy. Describe the three best videos on the topic you selected.

Resume Builder

Job hunting can be stressful enough without worrying about scams, but con artists know that job seekers are particularly vulnerable to fake job offers and various head-hunting scams. When preparing for a job search, get your resume in order, but also get familiar with scams that circulate to job seekers. To begin, look for information on fake job phishing, reshipping, check-cashing, money laundering, and work-at-home scams. Next, locate guidelines on how to avoid job scams. Summarize what you find in a printed brochure, blog post, or Pinterest board.

Globalization

Because the Internet connects computers all over the globe, you might expect that malware and cybercrime exploits would be evenly spread among countries. That is far from the case. Search online for statistics about malware incidents by country. Which countries are hardest hit by malware? Also, examine the other side of the issue to gather statistics about which countries are the source of most malware attacks. You might be surprised by what you discover.

Key Terms

Interactive Summary

Section A: __________ transforms a message or data file in such a way that its contents are hidden from unauthorized readers. An original message or file that has not yet been encrypted is referred to as __________ or cleartext. An encrypted message or file is referred to as __________. Data can be encrypted one file at a time, or an entire storage volume can be encrypted. User __________ techniques, such as passwords, PINs, and fingerprint scanners, are the first line of defense against data thieves and snoopers. The single most effective security measure for digital devices is to password-protect access to them. A(n) __________ password is quite secure because it is difficult to hack. Conventional wisdom tells us that a secure password is at least __________ characters in length and includes one or more uppercase letters, numbers, and symbols. A(n) __________ force attack uses password-cracking software to generate every possible combination of letters, numerals, and symbols. A(n) __________ attack helps hackers guess your password by stepping through a dictionary containing word lists in common languages. Password __________ is a measure of a password's unpredictability. For example, the entropy of a four-digit iPhone passcode is 14 bits. The core function of a password __________ (sometimes called a keychain) is to store user IDs with their corresponding passwords. Passwords can be stored in the __________, locally, or on a USB drive.

Section B: Malware refers to any computer program designed to surreptitiously enter a digital device. The action carried out by malware code is referred to as a(n) __________ or payload. There are several types of malware. A computer __________ is a set of self-replicating program instructions that surreptitiously attaches itself to a legitimate __________ file on a host computer. This type of malware spreads when people exchange infected files on CDs, as email attachments, and via downloads. They can also be inadvertently obtained from unauthorized app stores. Through a process called side-__________, an app from a source other than an official app store is installed on a device. Modern __________ are used to hide malicious code by replacing parts of the operating system with modified code. A computer __________ is a self-replicating, self-distributing program designed to carry out unauthorized activity on a victim's device. They are usually __________ executable programs that can spread themselves from one device to another without any assistance from victims. __________ are a type of standalone malware that masquerades as useful utilities or applications, which victims download and install while unaware of their destructive nature. Antivirus software is a type of utility software that looks for and eradicates malware by watching for virus __________ or through a(n) __________ analysis that examines the behavior of suspicious files. When antivirus software detects malware, it can try to remove the infection, put the file into __________, or simply delete the file. Antivirus software is an essential security tool. It should be installed, properly configured, and updated regularly.

Section C: An online intrusion takes place when an unauthorized person gains access to a digital device by using an Internet connection and exploiting vulnerabilities in hardware or software. A(n) [ ] Access Trojan is malware that arrives in a trojan, disguised as legitimate software, and then sets up a(n) [ ] that provides unauthorized access to a victim's device. An exploit known as [ ] locks a device and then requests payment for an unlocking code. Malware with [ ] control capability is programmed for off-site control of the camera or microphone on a victim's device. Hackers who gain control over several computers can organize them into a client-server network known as a(n) [ ]. Such networks are cloaked from the victims, who continue to use their devices as usual and are unaware of illicit activities that may be taking place behind the scenes. A(n) [ ]-day attack exploits previously unknown vulnerabilities in software applications, hardware, and operating system program code. To defend against these attacks, consumers can use an on-[ ] scanner. Defense against intrusions is also offered by personal [ ], which block unauthorized access through open [ ]. A network router can be deployed as a hardware-based firewall.

Section D: There are several types of [ ] exploits that surreptitiously capture data. Any software that secretly gathers personal information without the victim's knowledge is classified as [ ]. [ ] monitors Web browsing activity to supply ad-serving sites with data used to generate targeted ads. A(n) [ ] records keystrokes and sends them to a hacker. The objective of an MITM attack is for a third party to intercept communications between two entities without their knowledge. An MITM exploit executed at Wi-Fi hotspots is called a(n) [ ]. MITM attacks are also carried out by [ ] the addresses in email messages, IP packets, [ ] servers, and ARP routing tables. Data sent over encrypted channels also falls victim to MITM attacks that use fake digital [ ]. An MITM attack that targets cellular data can intercept conversations using a(n) [ ] catcher.

Section E: In the context of cyber security, social engineering (SE) is a deceptive practice that exploits human [ ] by inducing victims to interact with a digital device in a way that is not in their best interest. Many of these attacks begin with [ ], which is defined as unsolicited messages that are usually sent in massive numbers using electronic mail systems. A spam filter uses a set of [ ] to examine email messages and blocks those that appear to be spam. There are four common types of spam filters. [ ] filters examine the content within a message for certain words or phrases commonly used in spam emails. [ ] filters review the email header for falsified information, such as spoofed IP addresses. [ ] filters block mail that originates from IP addresses of known spammers. [ ] filters block or allow mail based on the sender's address. [ ] is an email scam that masquerades as a message from a legitimate company or agency of authority, such as the IRS. [ ] redirects Web site traffic to fraudulent Web sites that distribute malware, collect personal data, sell counterfeit products, and perpetrate other scams. A rogue [ ] exploit usually begins with a virus warning and an offer to disinfect the infected device. Some software is not exactly malware, but it is a nuisance. A(n) [ ] (Hint: Use the acronym) takes up residence on a digital device and seems impossible to disable or remove.

Interactive Situation Questions

1. On your next vacation, you'll be traveling to India and taking your laptop. The device is protected by a login password, but for extra protection you decide to __________ the entire storage volume.

2. An urgent security update arrives for Java. You have to assume that hackers have discovered a vulnerability and carried out a(n) __________ -day attack, which the update is designed to fix.

3. You are fed up with receiving spam that offers free gift cards. To block such messages, you set up a(n) __________ spam filter.

4. While browsing the Web, you suddenly see a virus alert. Oddly, it doesn't look like the alerts that usually appear while you are browsing and downloading email. You don't click the alert because you assume it is a(n) __________ virus scan.

WARNING! Your computer may be infected with spyware

If your computer has been running slower than usual, it may be infected with adware or spyware! To scan your comptuer for such infections, click OK below.

Cancel OK

5. One day you dash into the library to check your email. Before you can complete the login process, your phone chimes and you see a text message from your email provider. The text message contains a code for two-factor __________.

6. You're installing a new security suite that includes antivirus software and a personal firewall. Is it true that leaving Windows Firewall on in addition to using the firewall from the new security suite will beef up your digital security? __________

7. You are between flights at the airport, and you want to check your email. Your wireless settings show two options: a) a free, unsecured site called TerminalAir and b) a pay-by-the-hour site called Boingo. Which one is likely to be the most secure? __________

8. One of your former classmates has just returned from a visit to China. She complains that while she was there, some of her Google searches led to meaningless sites. Your friend was probably the victim of an MITM attack using fake digital __________.

9. You're in the process of downloading some email messages when your antivirus software displays an alert. You assume the software has discovered malware in a(n) __________, which will be moved to quarantine.

10. You just finished installing a new media converter that lets you download YouTube videos and run them when you are not connected to the Internet. Now, however, your default browser seems to have changed. You have a(n) __________, so you immediately fire up an on-demand scanner to eliminate the unwanted browser.

Lab: Chrome Lockdown

Every Web site is a potential risk. You know the exploits: malware, infected downloads, spyware, fraudulent Web sites, rogue JavaScripts...the list goes on. Antivirus software, firewalls, and other security software help to block some of these exploits, but they may leave cracks that allow exploits to slip into digital devices. In this lab, you'll find out how to lock down the Google Chrome browser to help defend against common online attacks.

Requirements:

For this lab, you'll need a desktop or laptop computer with Google Chrome installed. Chrome is a free browser. If it is not currently installed on your device, take a moment to do so before proceeding. (Note: The instructions for this lab apply to the version of Chrome that was available when this book went to print. If these instructions seem not to apply, check for updated instructions at *support.google.com/*.)

Assignment:

❶ Perform a safety check.

Log in to your Google account. Select the three dots in the upper-right corner of the browser window and choose Settings. Scroll down to the "Safety check" and select the button for "Check now." Note the status of Updates, Passwords, Safe browsing, Extensions, and Device software.

Select the "Safe browsing" option. Use the arrows to expand the explanations for "Enhanced protection" and "Standard protection." Select the one you want.

❷ Block third-party cookies and turn on Do Not Track.

Return to the Settings menu and scroll down to "Privacy and security." Select "Cookies and other site data." Selecting "Block third-party cookies in incognito" blocks those cookies only when you browse in incognito mode. Selecting "Block third-party cookies" blocks all third-party cookies.

The option for "Clear cookies and site data when you quit Chrome" should be On.

The option for "Send a Do Not Track request with your browsing traffic" should be On. If there are sites displayed under "Sites that can always use cookies," make sure that there are no sites listed that might serve malicious cookies.

❸ Check Site Settings

Return to the "Privacy and security" menu and select "Site Settings." To ensure your privacy, make sure that Location, Camera, Microphone, and Notifications are set to "Ask before accessing" so that you will be alerted when a site wants to use these assets.

❹ Manage JavaScripts, pop-ups, and redirects.

Scroll down the "Site Settings" menu and note that JavaScript can be allowed. It is sometimes used to deliver malware, but it is required for most dynamic Web pages.

The options for "Pop-ups and redirects" and for Ads should be set to Blocked.

❺ Prevent download exploits.

Even trusted sites might get hacked so that malware is surreptitiously downloaded along with legitimate files.

From the main Settings menu, look in the Advanced section and select "Downloads." Activate the option "Ask where to save each file before downloading" so that you can verify that you want to accept each file to be downloaded.

❻ Explore Privacy Sandbox settings.

When this book went to press, Google was introducing a technology called Privacy Sandbox, which is designed to prevent sites from tracking you but provides marketers with advertising opportunities. Determine the current status of the Privacy Sandbox feature. If you have options for settings, configure the feature to provide the security and privacy that you desire.

❼ Screenshot and save your security settings.

Take a screenshot of the current content settings.

Select the Done button to complete the content Settings configuration.

Close the Settings tab at the top of the Chrome window.

PY Coding with Python

Module Contents

Writing computer code is increasingly a core competency for 21st-century workers. If you want to get on the career fast track, programming proficiency could be just the ticket. Get started coding today by following the step-by-step tutorials presented in this module.

Try It! Apply what you learn.

- Write, run, and save simple programs in Python.
- Use the Python debugger to find and correct errors in a program.
- Work with text strings to display user prompts and program output.
- Assign a value to a variable and then modify the contents of the variable.
- Use commands such as int() and str() to change data types.
- Create a Wacky Word Game program that uses variables, strings, and input.
- Set up calculations by loading values into variables to create formulas in your programs.
- Write the code for an airport kiosk that calculates airline baggage fees.
- Use *if* statements along with Boolean operators and the <, >, and == comparison operators to specify program logic.
- Manipulate input using the upper() and lower() methods.
- Use for-loops and while-loops to set up blocks of code that run multiple times.
- Use an import-random statement and the random.randint() command to generate random numbers.
- Write a program to pick lottery numbers.
- Work with Python lists to efficiently process key locations in an adventure game.
- Create an Ask the Fortune Teller program.
- Use the def command to create programmer-defined functions.
- Use object-oriented programming techniques, such as instantiation, methods, and polymorphism.

PY

Coding with Python

Pre-Check

Gauge your level of expertise. The answers are in the module.

"Pizza" "Pizza" is a(n) ________ .	== > != ________ operators	["Eva", "Mateo", "Jay"] In Python, a(n) ________ is enclosed in square brackets.
def printme(str): printme() is a(n) ________ .	"Hello" + "World!" The + sign is used here as a(n) ________ operator.	class Dog(Pet): Dog is a(n) ________ class.
sum = sum + number The variable "sum" is used here as a(n) ________ .	Print() A(n) ________ error	1.5, 5.0, -2.4 ________ numbers

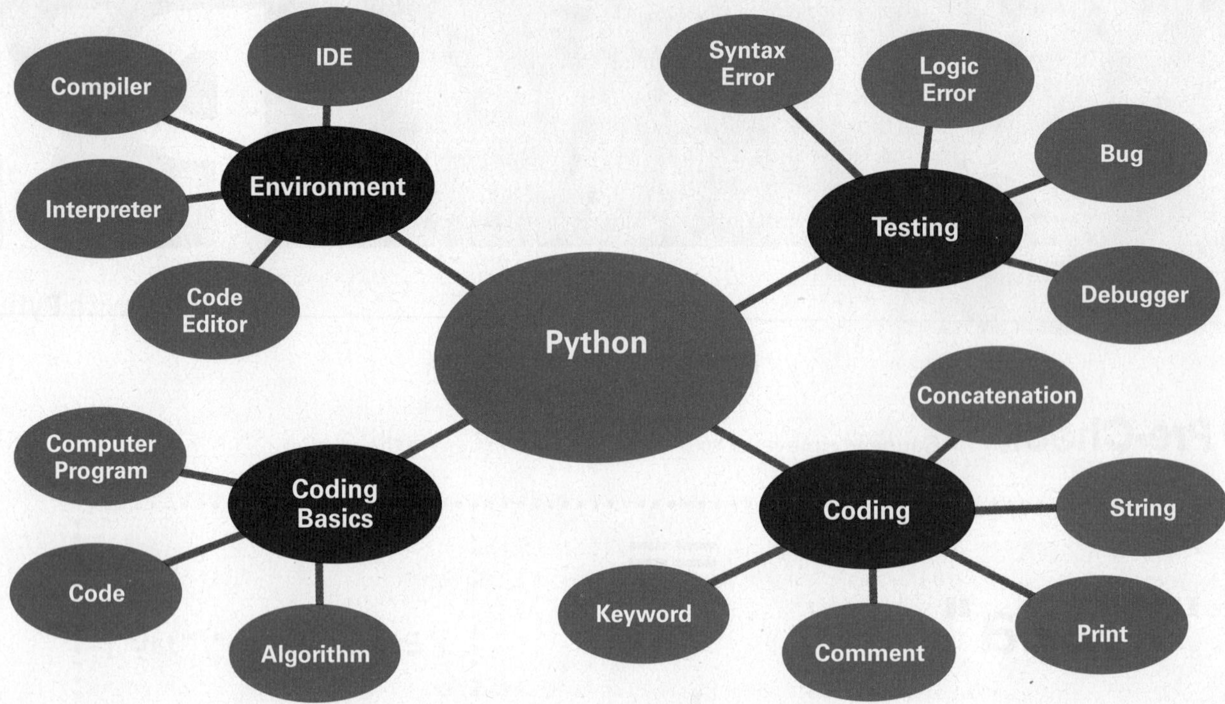

Section A "Hello World!"—Python Style

Objectives

- Identify the elements of a Python integrated development environment (IDE).
- Write a simple program using the Python programming language.
- Save a program you have written.
- Use the correct syntax for the print keyword.
- Use program comments effectively.
- Concatenate strings.
- Describe the vocabulary of Python keywords.
- Identify syntax and logic errors in a Python program.

Have you ever thought you could create your own computer programs? One of the great things about programming is that it is open to everyone who wants to try it. All you need is access to a computer. Even the programmers of the popular Subway Surfer game had to start somewhere. You will start by writing a simple program in this section and build up to creating more advanced programs as you work through the module.

Terminology

code
coding
algorithm
code editor
debugger
interpreter
compiler
IDE
syntax
comment
string
concatenation
concatenation operator
bug
debugging
syntax error
logic error

Python Basics

In today's digital age, almost everyone uses some type of computer program. You have probably used word processing software for school or played computer games at home. But do you know how to *write* a computer program? For writing code, you follow a set of rules and use logic to solve a problem. Section A is designed to get you coding quickly without requiring any prior experience.

What is a computer program? A computer program is a set of step-by-step instructions that tells the computer what to do. These instructions are sometimes referred to as **code**, and the process of writing the instructions is referred to as **coding**.

The code for a computer program is based on an **algorithm**, which is simply a sequence of steps for solving a problem or performing a task. You use algorithms every day. For example, you bake a cake by following the algorithm for a recipe.

Just as there are many spoken languages that people use to communicate with each other, there are also many programming languages that people can use to communicate with a computer. Some of these languages—such as C, C++, Java, C#, JavaScript, and Python—you may have heard of before.

What is Python? In this module, you will learn to use the Python programming language. Python was first released by its designer, Guido Van Rossum, in 1991. It was named not after a large snake, but after the British comedy television series *Monty Python's Flying Circus*.

Python is excellent for beginners, yet outstanding for experts. It is a language that is relatively easy to learn, but still powerful enough to be useful for solving real-life problems. There are several versions of Python, including versions 2 and 3. You will be using version 3 in this module.

How do I start writing code in Python? To write code using Python, you will need a code editor, a debugger, and an interpreter or a compiler.

- A **code editor** is a place to enter source code for a computer program.
- A **debugger** is a computer program that is used to find errors that may exist in a program.
- An **interpreter** is a program that reads your code in text form and translates the code, instruction by instruction, into a machine language the computer can understand.
- A **compiler** is a program that reads your source code and translates all of the code to a machine language before sending it to the computer to run. Some compilers are Web apps that can be accessed online using a browser.

An **IDE** (integrated development environment) provides an editor, debugger, and interpreter. Several IDEs are available for Python programming. Some IDEs—such as PyCharm, Wing IDE, IDLE, and PyDev—are local software that you install onto your computer's hard disk. Python online IDEs include Replit, Python Fiddle, Pynative, and Ideone.

PY

Terminology

Writing instructions or code for computers can be called programming or coding. Typically, *coding* is a term used for less formal programming. *Coding* is also a less intimidating term used for easy, basic, or fun programming tasks.

Terminology

Programmers can use a text editor, but not a word processor, to write program code. Program code cannot contain the formatting codes that a word processor embeds.

QuickCheck

Where is the best place to enter program code?

a. A code editor

b. A Word document

c. A browser

d. A debugger

Setting Up Your Python Environment

To create the programs in this module, you can use a local or online Python IDE. To get started:

1. Access the Python IDE of your choice or the one specified by your instructor.
2. To use some IDEs, you are required to sign up for an account by providing your name, entering your email address, and creating a password.
3. If your IDE gives you a choice of languages, select Python 3. If you are prompted to name your program, enter **Hello**.
4. A typical online IDE provides two programming panels. Figure PY-1 and other screenshots in this module illustrate the panels displayed by the Replit IDE.

Figure PY-1: The Replit IDE for Python programs

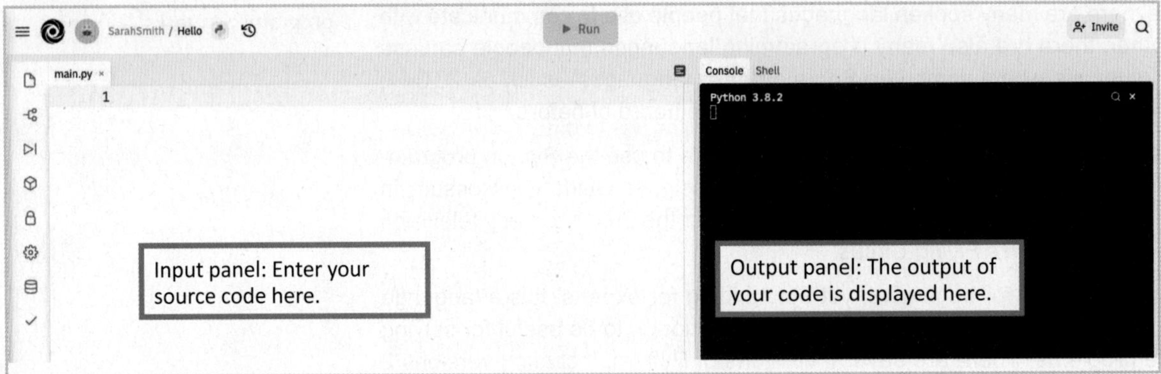

Source: Replit

Let's Start Coding

The most famous program in the world is a single line of code that prints "Hello World!" on the screen. It has been written millions of times in every programming language that exists and is frequently used to illustrate basic command structure.

Is it difficult to learn? Learning how to write code can be exciting and challenging. It is certainly an important skill to have in today's digital world, and it is fun to do. This could be the beginning of a new adventure for you, so let's get started!

Writing a "Hello World!" Program in Python

While viewing the input and output panels of your IDE, follow these steps to start writing your program:

1. Select the Clear option to delete any sample code that might appear in the input panel.
2. Select line 1.
3. Type the following code on line 1. (Hint: You can use the Backspace and Delete keys to correct typing errors.)

```
# My first program
```

4. Press the Enter key to move down to line 2, and then type the following code all on one line. (Hint: Be sure to include the spaces and punctuation marks exactly as they appear in the example.)

```
print("Hello World! This is my first Python program.")
```

5. Select the button that will run your program. Compare your program and output to Figure PY-2.

Figure PY-2: First "Hello World!" program

```
1  # My first program
2  print("Hello World! This is my first Python program.")
3
4
```

```
Hello World! This is my first Python program.
> 
```

Source: Replit

(Hint: If you receive an error message, make sure you have included the parentheses and quotation marks, and that the word *print* is in lowercase. Clear the output panel by selecting the Clear button, and then try to run the program again.)

6. When your program is running correctly, congratulations! You have just written your first program.

7. Some IDEs, such as Replit, automatically save your code. Other IDEs have a Save option. If your IDE does not provide a way to save your code, you can select it, copy it (with Ctrl+C), and then paste it into a text file, which you can then save.

Modifying a Saved Program

You can modify any of your saved code in the editor. Follow these steps to modify your first program:

1. Retrieve your saved code. To do this with Replit:
   a. Select your user name in the upper-right corner of the screen to display a list of repls. (A "repl" is Replit jargon for your program code.)
   b. Select Hello as the repl you want to open. Any code in the input panel will be replaced with code from your saved repl.

2. In the input panel, line 2, select the word "first" and then type **modified**.

   The code for line 2 should now look like this:

```
print("Hello World! This is my modified Python program.")
```

3. Run your program and compare the output to Figure PY-3.

Figure PY-3: Modified "Hello World!" program

```
1  # My first program
2  print("Hello World! This is my modified Python program.")
```

```
Hello World! This is my modified Python program.
> 
```

Source: Replit

Creating a Multi-Line Program

Most programs contain more than one line of code. The computer follows each line in the order it is written. For example, the code to display a "knock, knock" joke requires multiple lines. Let's try writing it.

1. Start a new program.

   If you're using Replit, select the menu in the upper-left corner and then select the Create Repl option.

   For other IDEs, be sure to clear the input and output panels.

2. Name your program **Joke**.
3. Type the following code on line 1:

```
# My second program
```

4. Press the Enter key to move down to line 2, and then type the following code on lines 2 through 6:

```
print("Knock, knock.")
print("Who's there?")
print("Tank.")
print("Tank who?")
print("You're welcome.")
```

5. Save and run the program. Compare your program and output to Figure PY-4.

Figure PY-4: Create a multi-line program

```
1  # My second program
2  print("Knock, knock.")
3  print("Who's there?")
4  print("Tank.")
5  print("Tank who?")
6  print("You're welcome.")
```

```
Knock, knock.
Who's there?
Tank.
Tank who?
You're welcome.
>
```

Source: Replit

Are there rules for writing Python code? The Python programming language has its own **syntax**, which is a set of rules that defines how it can be written. You will start by using a few of these rules in this section and expand on them as you learn more of the language.

What is the rule for using a comment? A **comment** in Python is used by programmers to explain what the code does. Comments do not show up when the program runs. Adding comments generally makes the code easier to understand and maintain.

An important rule to remember when coding in Python is that a comment must begin with the # character and end with the physical line on which the # character has been typed—that is, a comment ends when you move to the next line. If you need to include more than one line of comments, you must start each line with #.

For example, in your first program, line 1 contains this comment:

```
# My first program
```

Working with Strings

The first computers functioned without any programming languages. Instead, computers were rewired for each task they processed. Developers later created languages to process tasks more efficiently.

Python is considered a high-level programming language because it works by using command words and grammar based on human languages. This makes it easier for novice programmers to create code because it is similar to writing in their own language.

What is a string? When you write a sentence, you create a sequence of words that your reader will understand. Similarly, when writing code, you create a sequence of characters called a string. A **string** can contain words, letters, punctuation marks, and numerals.

For example, in your first program, line 2 contains this string:

```
"Hello World! This is my first Python program."
```

What is concatenation? The term **concatenation** is used by programmers any time two or more characters are connected. Several strings can be connected using a symbol, such as the + symbol, as a **concatenation operator**. Let's see how it works.

Concatenating a Simple String

You will concatenate two strings using the + symbol as the concatenation operator.

1. Start a new program. Enter **Strings** as the title for your program.
2. Type the following code in line 1:

```
# My first program
```

3. Type the following code in line 2, all on one line:

```
print("Hello World! " + "This is my first Python program.")
```

4. Save and run the program. The output should look exactly like the first program you created, which is shown in Figure PY-2. `"Hello World!"` is concatenated by the + symbol to `"This is my first Python program."`

Try It!

When concatenating strings, you must be careful about positioning spaces to separate words. Enter the following code and notice the different methods used to separate words:

```
# Add a space at the end of a word.
print("I'm " + "glad to see you.")
# Add a space between two quotation marks
print("This" + " " + "is" + " " + "fun.")
# Without a space,
# The strings combine without a space.
print("Me" + "ow!")
```

Your output should look like this:

I'm glad to see you.

This is fun.

Meow!

Duplicating a String

Python gives programmers a shortcut for working with repeated strings. To print the same word to the screen more than once, just use the * symbol and the number of times you want it duplicated. Let's try it.

Try It!

Using duplication, write a Python program that results in the following output:

```
****
****
****
****
```

1. Start a new program.
2. Enter **Judy** as the program name.
3. Type the following code as line 1:

```
# Duplicate one word
```

4. Type the following code on lines 2 through 6:

```
print("Judy" * 4)
# Duplicate a sentence
print("There's no place like home. " * 3)
# Duplication and concatenation
print("very,  " * 3 + "hot")
```

5. Save and run the program. Compare your program and output to Figure PY-5.

Figure PY-5: Duplication examples

```
1 # Duplicate one word
2 print("Judy" * 4)
3 # Duplicate a sentence
4 print("There's no place like home. " * 3)
5 # Duplication and concatenation
6 print("very, " * 3 + "hot")
```

```
JudyJudyJudyJudy
There's no place like home. There's no place like home. There's no
place like home.
very, very, very, hot
>
```

Source: Replit

Using Python Keywords

All programming languages have their own vocabulary, which is based on a set of keywords. The Python programming language has a small vocabulary of only 34 keywords. Of these, only about ten are frequently used.

How do programmers use keywords? In Python and other programming languages, each keyword has a predefined meaning. For example, you have already worked with the keyword *print*. In Python, using *print* means you want the computer to display something on the screen. You will work with many of the keywords listed in Figure PY-6 throughout this module.

Figure PY-6: Python keywords

False	class	finally	is	return
None	continue	for	lambda	try
True	def	from	nonlocal	while
and	del	global	not	with
as	elif	if	or	yield
assert	else	import	pass	print
break	except	in	raise	

PY

Debugging

Programs must be tested to see if they work correctly. A coding error is called a **bug**, and the process of tracking down bugs and correcting them is called **debugging**.

My program does not work—what now? A computer cannot read your mind. When running a program, the computer will only do exactly what you tell it to do—no more, no less. Any errors in the code that produce incorrect results are introduced by the programmer—you. This may seem to be a simple concept, but it is very important to keep in mind when devising algorithms for your programs.

What are coding errors? Several kinds of errors can occur in a program. Syntax errors and logic errors are the two most frequently encountered. It is useful to distinguish between them so you can track them down more quickly.

What are typical syntax errors? Python can only execute a program if the syntax is correct; otherwise, the process fails and the computer returns an error message. A **syntax error** occurs when an instruction does not follow the rules of the programming language.

The rules for coding syntax can be compared to the rules for English grammar. For example, in English, capitalization, word order, and punctuation are all important grammar elements. In Python, these elements are also important aspects of syntax. To avoid syntax errors, it is essential to follow the Python rules. You have already learned some of Python's syntax rules, including the following:

- Comments always start with a #.
- Python is case sensitive.
- Strings are delineated by quotation marks.
- Keywords can only be used for their intended purpose.

Debugging Syntax Errors

Let's introduce an error into a program and see how the Python debugger works.

1. Start a new program and use **Error** as the program name.
2. On line 1, type the following line of code, in which *Print* is incorrectly capitalized:

```
Print("Hello World! This is my first Python program.")
```

3. Run the program. Notice the error message in Figure PY-7, which indicates that *Print* (with a capital *P*) is not defined.

Figure PY-7: Syntax error output

```
Traceback (most recent call last):
  File "main.py", line 1, in <module>
    Print("Hello World! This is my first Python
 program.")
NameError: name 'Print' is not defined
> 
```

Source: Replit

How can I fix a syntax error? If there is a single syntax error anywhere in your program, Python prints an error message and quits. The error message displays the number of the last line the program was able to execute. Sometimes, however, the error occurs prior to that line, in which case you might have to look back a line or two to find the error.

To fix a syntax error, check the line carefully. If you are copying code from an example, start by comparing your code to the example's code very carefully. Be sure to check every character, space, and punctuation mark. When you find the error, you can modify the code and rerun your program.

How can I identify a logic error? Another type of error is a logic error. A program containing a **logic error** will run without displaying an error message, but it will not produce the expected result. The problem is that the program you wrote is not the program you intended to write because the logic of the program is incorrect.

Identifying logic errors can be tricky because it requires you to work backward by looking at the output of the program and trying to figure out what it is doing. An example of a logic error would be to enter the following code:

```
print("Hello World! + This is my first Python program.")
```

These are the results you wanted:

```
Hello World! This is my first Python program.
```

The program runs without error, but you do not get the expected results. These are the results you get:

```
Hello World! + This is my first Python program.
```

What happened? The program needs more matching quotation marks to produce the expected results. The code should be:

```
print("Hello World! " + "This is my first Python program.")
```

How do I find the program errors? One of the most important coding skills you can acquire is debugging. Debugging is like detective work. You are confronted with clues, and you have to figure out what led to the results you see. Once you have an idea of what is going wrong, you can modify your program and try again. Most coding errors are spelling mistakes and typos. Although it is sometimes frustrating, debugging is one of the most challenging and interesting parts of coding.

QuickCheck

A program that calculates the price for a store's sale produces the wrong amount. What kind of error did the programmer make?

a. A syntax error

b. A Python error

c. A logic error

d. An input error

QuickQuiz — Section A

1. The Python IDE provides an editor, a debugger, and a(n) ____________ that translates the code into machine language.
2. Python comments begin with a(n) ____________ symbol.
3. Programmers use the term ____________ to describe a sequence of letters, punctuation marks, and numerals.
4. In Python, using an uppercase keyword produces a(n) ____________ error.
5. The process of tracking down program errors and correcting them is called ____________.

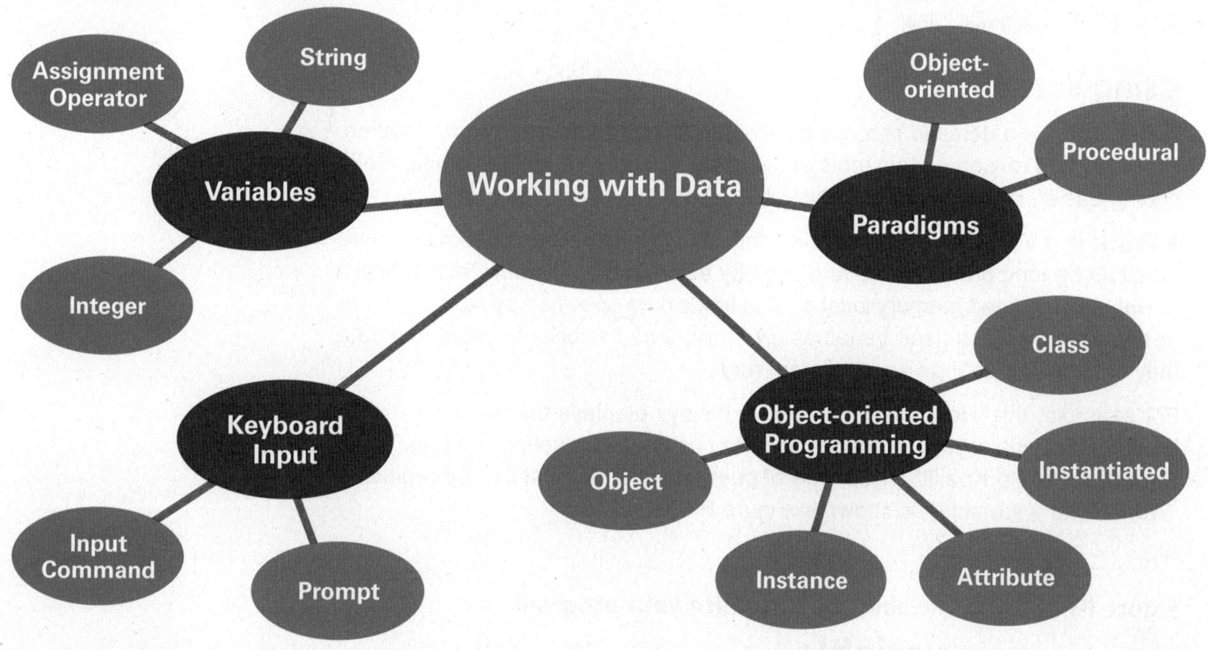

Section B The Wacky Word Game

Objectives

- Create variables using an assignment statement.
- List four rules for naming variables in Python.
- Provide examples of three data types commonly used in Python programs.
- Explain the significance of a data type error.
- Convert numbers to strings.
- Distinguish the difference between classes and objects.
- Instantiate an object from a class.
- Use the correct Python syntax to collect user input.
- Code the Wacky Word Game.
- Share your programs using a Share link, file, or screenshot.

You are off to a great start! You now have some basic coding experience. In this section, you will learn how to use variables to make your programs more efficient and easier to code. You'll also learn how to collect input from users as your programs run. You can then use this skill to build interactive programs such as the Wacky Word Game, which is based on word games such as Mad Libs.

Terminology

variable
assignment operator
data type
object-oriented paradigm
object-oriented programming
object
class
attribute
instance
instantiated
input command
prompt

Using Variables

Writing code is a detailed process that requires time and careful concentration. Programmers rely on certain tools of the trade, such as variables, to help make coding easier, faster, and more enjoyable.

What is a variable? Programmers think of variables as empty boxes where data can be temporarily stored and used by a computer program. Technically, a **variable** is a named memory location that holds data specified by a programmer or entered by an end user. Variables give programs flexibility because the data they contain can change as a program runs.

For example, the "Hello World!" program always displays the message "Hello World!"—but what if you wanted to display a customized greeting, such as "Hello Sarah!" or "Hello Khalil!"? This type of customization is possible by replacing "World" with a variable, as shown in Figure PY-8.

Figure PY-8: Using variables to customize your program

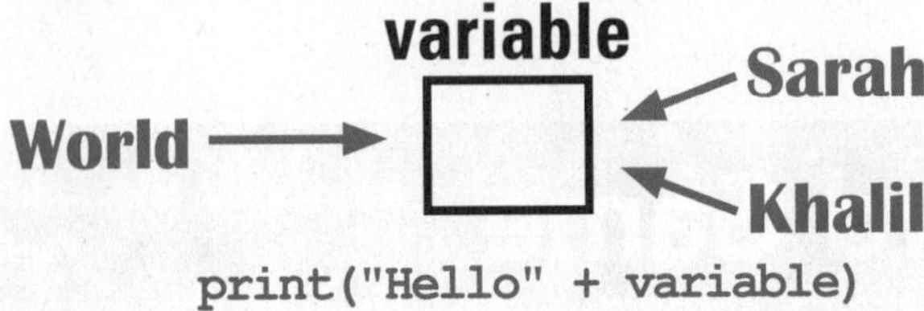

Are there rules for naming variables? A variable name should describe the information the variable is designed to store. For example, a good name for a variable that will contain a person's first name might be "firstname" or "first_name".

Here are some specific rules for naming variables in Python:

- The name must begin with a letter or an underscore character "_".
- The name can contain only letters, numbers, and the underscore character; no punctuation characters, special characters, or spaces are allowed.
- Python keywords, such as `print` and `class`, are not allowed as variable names.
- Every variable should have a unique name.

If you violate any one of the rules listed above, you will get a syntax error. Figure PY-9 shows some examples of invalid variable names.

Figure PY-9: Invalid variable names in Python

Invalid Name	Problem
`76trombones`	The name does not begin with a letter or an underscore.
`more$`	The name cannot contain a special character.
`last name`	The name cannot contain a space.
`class`	The name cannot be a Python keyword.

Terminology

In some programming languages, camel case or Pascal case is used when naming variables. *Camel case* capitalizes the second word of a two-word variable name: firstName. *Pascal case* capitalizes both words of a two-word variable name: FirstName. Camel case and Pascal case are used in Python programs, though they are not the standard.

Try It!

Type these lines in your Python IDE and run them to see what happens:

```
76trombones = "big parade"
more$ = 10000
class = "Computers 100"
```

How do I create a variable? The process of creating a variable is sometimes referred to as *declaring a variable*. Putting data in a variable is referred to as *assigning a value* to it. Although the term *value* is used, the data that is assigned can be a string, such as "Joe," or a numeric value, such as 145, as shown in Figure PY-10.

Figure PY-10: Assigning a value to a variable

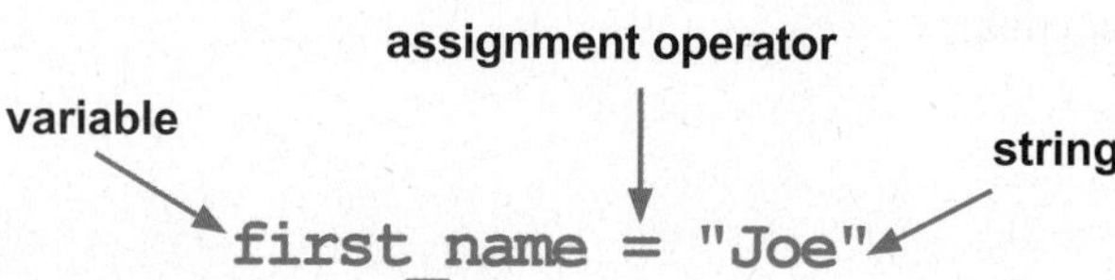

In Python, programmers can declare a variable and assign it a value using only one line of code. To store data in a variable, programmers use the = symbol, called the **assignment operator**.

Assigning a Value to a Variable

Let's assign the value `"Joe"` to the variable `first_name`.

1. Start a new program. Name it **Joe** and enter the following:

```
first_name = "Joe"
print(first_name)
```

2. Save and run the program. Compare your program and output to Figure PY-11.

Figure PY-11: Assigning the first_name variable

```
first_name = "Joe"
print(first_name)
```

```
Joe
>
```

Source: Replit

How do programmers use variables? Programmers use variables to store data that might change when the program runs. Data can be changed by program code, by calculations that are carried out by a program, or by data entered by end users.

Changing a Variable While a Program Runs

Try modifying the program called Joe to see how the contents of the variable first_name can change as a program runs.

1. Modify the code so that it contains the following four lines:

```
first_name = "Joe"
print("Hello " + first_name)
first_name = "Mary"
print("Hello " + first_name)
```

2. Save and run the program. Compare your program and output to Figure PY-12.

Figure PY-12: Changing a variable

```
first_name = "Joe"
print("Hello " + first_name)
first_name = "Mary"
print("Hello " + first_name)
```

```
Hello Joe
Hello Mary
>
```

Source: Replit

Can I assign any value to a variable? The type of data that a variable can hold is referred to as its **data type**. Every variable has a data type that limits the kind of data it can contain.

In Python, a variable automatically gets a data type based on the data stored in it by an assignment statement. If you assign a string such as "Joe" to a variable, its data type automatically becomes String. If you assign a number such as 20 to a variable, its data type automatically becomes Integer. The data types most frequently used in Python programs are listed in Figure PY-13.

Figure PY-13: Common data types

Data Type	Examples
Integers	-2, -1, 0, 1, 2, 3, 4, 5
Floating-point numbers	-1.0, -0.5, 0.0, 1.0, 1.25
Strings	"Joe", "Hello!", "11 cats"

What is the significance of data types? Once a variable has a data type, it can only hold data of that type. If you begin a program and assign a string such as "Joe" to first_name, the variable first_name can only hold strings unless you later code a new assignment statement, such as first_name = 123. This second assignment statement would give first_name an integer data type and allow it to store numeric data instead of text data.

Variables with different data types must be treated carefully. For example, string variables cannot be concatenated directly with integer variables.

PY

Encountering a Data Type Error

Let's see what happens if you try to combine string and integer data types.

1. Start a new program called **Age**, and then enter the following lines of code:

```
first_name = "Joe"
age = 22
info = first_name + age
print(info)
```

2. Save and run the program. The result is an error message, as shown in Figure PY-14. This message tells you that the string (str) variable first_name cannot be combined with the integer (int) variable age.

Figure PY-14: Data type error message

```
1  first_name = "Joe"
2  age = 22
3  info = first_name + age
4  print(info)
```

```
Traceback (most recent call last):
  File "main.py", line 3, in <module>
    info = first_name + age
TypeError: can only concatenate str (not "int") to str
>
```

Source: Replit

How can I avoid data type errors? Because Python does not like to combine different types of data, you may have to convert some of your data. For example, when trying to combine a person's age and name in a variable, you can convert age into a string so it matches the data type for the person's name.

Converting a Number to a String

1. Revise line 3 of the previous program so that your code reads as follows:

```
first_name = "Joe"
age = 22
info = first_name + " " + str(age)
print(info)
```

2. Save and run the program. It should now run without an error and produce `Joe 22` as the output.

When writing Python programs, keep in mind the data type for each variable. This requirement becomes more and more important as you write complex programs that combine variables and use them in calculations.

QuickCheck

In this code, what type of variable is zipcode?

```
zipcode = "60137"
```

a. Integer

b. Float

c. String

d. Number

Objects and Classes

Python is an object-oriented programming language, which is a language that enables you to use objects to accomplish a program's goals.

▸ What is the object-oriented paradigm? The **object-oriented paradigm** is based on objects and classes that can be defined and manipulated by program code. **Object-oriented programming** (OOP) is a style of programming that focuses on using objects to design and build applications.

▸ What is an object? An **object** is anything that can be seen, touched, or used. It can be a person, a place, or a thing, such as a car, a house, or a name.

▸ What is a class? Every object in an object-oriented program is created from a **class**, which is a description or template that the computer uses to create the object. A class is defined by attributes and methods. A class **attribute** defines the characteristics of a set of objects. You will learn more about methods in Section E.

▸ What is the difference between an object and a class? An object created from a class is called an **instance** of a class and is said to be **instantiated** (created) from the class. Think of a class as a cookie cutter. It is not a cookie itself—instead, it is a description or template of what a cookie looks like. The cookie cutter can be used to create many individual cookies. Each cookie can be thought of as an instance of the cookie cutter class. A cookie object can have different attributes, such as shape, color, and flavor. Figure PY-15 can help you visualize the difference between a class and objects.

Figure PY-15: Classes and objects

Class: Cookies
A class is similar to a template, mold, or cookie cutter.
Fortune cookie
Frosted cookie
Chocolate chip cookie
Objects
Objects are instances created by the template, mold, or cookie cutter.

Instantiating an Object from a Class

Consider the example of a dog object instantiated from the Pet class that has an attribute of having four legs. Let's instantiate an object of the Pet class. (Hint: Class names are generally capitalized in Python.)

1. Start a new program called **Fido**. Enter and run the following lines of code:

```
class Pet:
    number_of_legs = 0
dog = Pet()
dog.number_of_legs = 4
print("Dogs are pets with " + str(dog.number_of_legs) + " legs.")
```

Be sure to indent this line using spaces or the Tab key.

2. Save this program. Compare your program and output to Figure PY-16.

Figure PY-16: Pet class

```
1  class Pet:
2      number_of_legs = 0
3  dog = Pet()
4  dog.number_of_legs = 4
5  print("Dogs are pets with " + str
   (dog.number_of_legs) + " legs.")
```

```
Dogs are pets with 4 legs.
>
```

Source: Replit

The code `class Pet:` defines the Pet class. The Pet class has an attribute of the number of legs for the pet. The third line of code, `dog = Pet()`, instantiates a dog object of the Pet class. The fourth line, `dog.number_of_legs = 4`, assigns the number 4 to the number_of_legs attribute for a dog object in the Pet class.

Why use classes and objects? Classes and objects help programmers develop programs modeled on the real world. Classes help programmers think about the characteristics and structure of the data that a program manipulates. In contrast to standalone variables, classes enable programmers to build objects with multiple attributes and define ways for objects to interact with each other.

Try It!

Now, add a parrot object, assign the correct number of legs to the parrot, and print your results.

Input

Until now, you have only been able to assign strings and numbers to variables within your program. However, you might want a user to be able to interact with your program and enter input as it runs. This input can provide information that can be stored in your program's variables. Input can be accepted from a keyboard or a touchscreen.

◗ How does the computer accept input? Python uses the **input command** to get user input. The input command allows the program to display a message on the screen that asks a user to enter information. This message is often called a **prompt** because it prompts the user to enter something.

For example, suppose you want a program to gather the user's name. You could write the following code:

```
first_name = input("Please enter your name: ")
```

When this program runs, the prompt `Please enter your name:` is displayed on the screen. The program waits until the user enters a name and presses the Enter key. Whatever the user types after the prompt is stored as a string in the first_name variable.

Using the Input Command to Write Prompts

Writing prompts using the input command in Python is a great way to relay instructions to your program's user. These instructions help to make your program more user-friendly and accessible. The first step is to code the input command. Let's see how.

1. Start a new program called **Names**. Enter and run the following three lines of code:

```
# Getting keyboard input
first_name = input("What is your name? ")
print("Hi, " + first_name)
```

2. Run the program and enter your name when prompted.
3. Now, add the following code on lines 4 and 5:

```
answer = input("What did you have for breakfast? ")
print("You had " + answer + "! That sounds delicious!")
```

4. Save and run the program. Compare your program and output to Figure PY-17.

Try It!

Write a program that displays the prompt "Halt! Who goes there?" and waits for the user to enter a name. The program should produce the message "You may pass," plus the person's name, like this:

Halt! Who goes there? Jenna

You may pass, Jenna.

Figure PY-17: Using the input command

```
1  # Getting keyboard input
2  first_name = input("What is your name? ")
3  print("Hi, " + first_name)
4  answer = input("What did you have for
   breakfast? ")
5  print("You had " + answer + "! That
   sounds delicious!")
```

```
What is your name? Sasha
Hi, Sasha
What did you have for breakfast? eggs
You had eggs! That sounds delicious!
>
```

Source: Replit

PY

Wacky Word Game

You will now create a program that uses variables, strings, and input. This program produces a game that prompts a player for a list of words and then generates a nonsensical or comical story.

Creating the Wacky Word Game Program

1. Enter the following lines of code for a program called **Wacky**:

```
# Wacky Word Game program
# Part 1: request the input words
first_name = input("Type your name, and select enter. ")
print("")
print("Hello " + first_name + ". Let's play a game.")
print("")
adjective1 = input("Tell me an adjective, and select enter. ")
noun1 = input("Tell me a noun (plural), and select enter. ")
noun2 = input("Tell me another noun (plural), and select enter. ")
adjective2 = input("Tell me another adjective, and select enter. ")
# Part 2: print the poem
print(first_name + "'s Wacky Word Game")
print("")
print("Roses are " + adjective1)
print(noun1 + " are blue")
print(noun2 + " are " + adjective2)
print("And so are you!")
```

2. Save and run the program. Figure PY-18 shows a sample of output from the **Wacky Word Game** program.

Figure PY-18: Wacky Word Game

```
# Wacky Word Game program
# Part 1: request the input words
first_name = input("Type your name, and select enter. ")
print("")
print("Hello " + first_name + ". Let's play a game.")
print("")
adjective1 = input("Tell me an adjective, and select enter. ")
noun1 = input("Tell me a noun (plural), and select enter. ")
noun2 = input("Tell me another noun (plural), and select enter. ")
adjective2 = input("Tell me another adjective, and select enter. ")

# Part 2: print the poem
print(first_name + "'s Wacky Word Game")
print("")
print("Roses are " + adjective1)
print(noun1 + " are blue")
print(noun2 + " are " + adjective2)
print("and so are you!")
```

```
Type your name, and select enter. Annette

Hello Annette. Let's play a game.

Tell me an adjective, and select enter. smelly
Tell me a noun (plural), and select enter. dogs
Tell me another noun (plural), and select enter. cats
Tell me another adjective, and select enter. sleepy
Annette's Wacky Word Game

Roses are smelly
dogs are blue
cats are sleepy
and so are you!
> 
```

Source: Replit

Sharing Your Programs

You may want to share your program code. The procedure depends on your IDE. Some IDEs provide a Share button that you can use to enter the recipient's email address. You might be able to copy the URL for your program and send it via email. If you've saved your program as a file, you can attach it to an email message.

If none of those options are available in your IDE, you can take a screenshot of your code using the following steps:

Making a Screenshot on a PC

1. Click the window containing your program.
2. While holding down the Windows key, press the Print Screen key.
3. Open a new blank Microsoft Word document. Right-click and choose Paste. Save your document as **Wacky Word Game**.

Making a Screenshot on a Mac

1. Press Command (⌘)-Shift-3.
2. Locate the new .png file on your desktop. You can change the name to **Wacky Word Game**.

Try It!

Here's your chance to get creative! Suppose you know a small child who loves bedtime stories. You're having a hard time coming up with plots. Create a program that generates stories. We've started one for you. Collect the input for the words in red and insert them into the story to view the output. Add at least two more lines to the story to collect input for the ending.

```
Once upon a time, there was a noun named name who lived in
place. name was very adjective and decided to explore place.
All of name's friends said "proverb." But name went anyway.
The journey to place was very adverb. "exclamation!" said
name. "I must have been adjective2 to think of going to
place." So, name turned around and headed back home. Then...
```

QuickQuiz — Section B

1. Programmers think of a(n) ________ as a named memory location, which holds information that can change when a program is run.
2. In Python, the equal (=) symbol is known as the ________ operator.
3. Every ________ in an object-oriented program is created from a class.
4. A class ________ defines the characteristics of a set of objects.
5. Python uses the input command to get user input from a(n) ________ or a(n) ________.

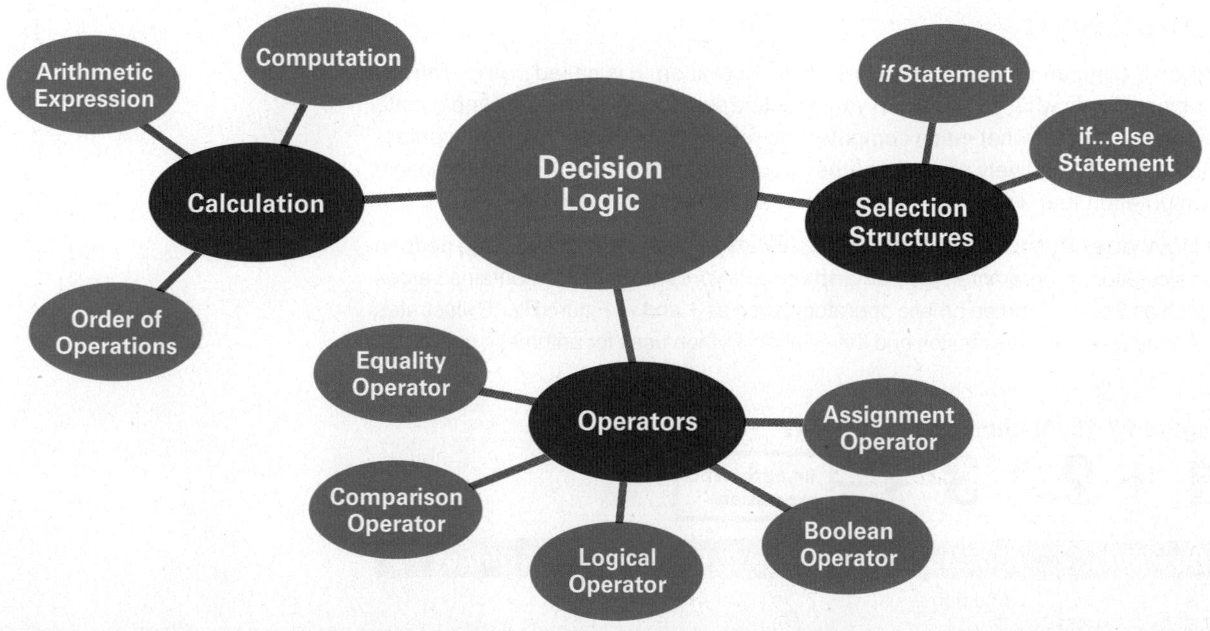

Section C Build Your Own Calculator

Objectives

- Identify the operators used in Python arithmetic expressions.
- Code calculations that store results in a variable.
- Collect user input to use in a calculation.
- Convert string input into integer values.
- Use the if and if...else commands along with comparison and logical operators to control program flow.
- List the comparison operators used in Python.
- Explain the difference between the = and == operators.
- Correctly use logical operators in Python statements.
- Convert strings to a known case.
- Code an interactive calculator program.

Computers are amazing machines. They can customize output based on user input and can even seem to make intelligent decisions. Programmers instruct computers to make decisions based on conditions that exist when a program runs. In this section, you will learn how to program calculations and how comparisons can help computers perform logical operations. Using these techniques, you will build a simple calculator program.

Terminology

computation
arithmetic expression
order of operations
selection control structure
comparison operator
equality operator
logical operators
Boolean operators

Calculations

When a computer calculates an arithmetic operation, it is called **computation**. Computation is what you do when you calculate something, such as a simple math problem. Much of what made computers so revolutionary in the mid-20th century was that in a relatively short time, they could perform a complex mathematical computation that would have taken a human many lifetimes to do.

How does Python perform calculations? To instruct the computer to perform a calculation, programmers use an **arithmetic expression**, which contains values (such as 2 and 3) and arithmetic operators (such as + and -). Figure PY-19 illustrates a simple arithmetic expression and the symbols Python uses for arithmetic operators.

Figure PY-19: Arithmetic expressions

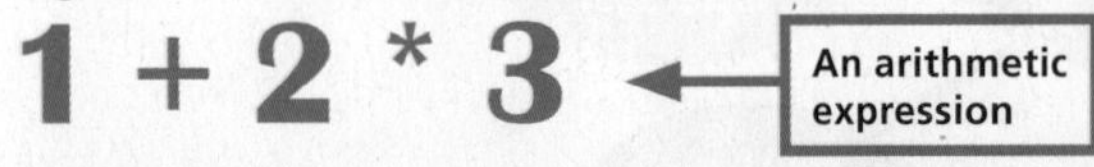

Operator	Operation	Example	Output
+	Addition	4+3	7
-	Subtraction	7-5	2
*	Multiplication	4*5	20
/	Division	19/5	3
%	Modulus (Remainder)	19%5	4
**	Exponent	2**3	8

Coding a Simple Calculation

When coding Python programs, arithmetic expressions can be used in a variety of ways. Typically, they are assigned to variables or used in print statements.

1. Enter the following lines of code for a program called **Math**:

```
# Is the output 9 or 7?
result = 1+2*3
print("The result is ", result)
```

2. Before you run the program, try to guess what it will output.
3. Save and run the program.

Why wasn't the result 9? The result of an arithmetic expression depends on the order in which Python performs the math. In this example, it performed the multiplication 2*3 before adding 1. Why? In mathematics, the **order of operations** is a collection of rules that dictate which procedures to perform first when calculating an arithmetic expression.

In Python, the order of operations follows these rules:

- Perform expressions in parentheses () first.
- Resolve exponential notations, such as 2**2, which means 2^2.
- Perform multiplication (*), division (/), and modulus (%) operations.
- Perform addition (+) and subtraction (-) last.

In your program, Python followed the order of operations and performed the multiplication before the addition. If you want the addition carried out before the multiplication, use parentheses to code the expression as `(1+2)*3`. Python will follow the order of operations and do the math in parentheses first.

Terminology

The order of operations is also referred to as *mathematical precedence*, or simply *precedence*.

PY

Try It!

Add parentheses to line 2 of the Math program so that Python performs the addition first and outputs 9 as the result.

Performing a Calculation

Programmers frequently set up calculations by loading values into variables and then writing formulas using variables instead of numbers. This technique allows you to modify the numbers used in a calculation or get the numbers as input when a program runs.

1. Enter the following lines of code for a program called **Discount** that uses the variables price and discount in an arithmetic expression:

```
price = 25
discount = 10
final_price = price - discount
print("Final price = ", final_price)
```

2. Save and run the program. Notice the code in line 4. You can print numbers and variables on the same line by using a comma to separate the string `"Final price = "` from the number represented by final_price.

3. Compare your program and output to Figure PY-20.

QuickCheck

How many variables are used in the program that calculates discounted prices?

a. 1

b. 2

c. 3

d. 4

Figure PY-20: Variables in expressions

```
1  price = 25
2  discount = 10
3  final_price = price - discount
4  print("Final price = ", final_price)
```

```
Final price =  15
> 
```

Source: Replit

▶ How do I get input values for calculations? Programs that perform calculations often use values that are input by the user as the program runs. For example, a bargain hunter might wonder if buying that supersized box of cereal or that gigantic package of chicken is really a better deal than buying the product in a smaller quantity. A program for a mobile app might ask shoppers to enter the number of ounces in the package and the price. It would then divide the price by the number of ounces to calculate the unit price.

Collecting Input for Calculations

1. Enter the following lines of code for a program called **Bargain Hunter**:

```
#Bargain Hunter
print("Enter the cost of the item: ")
cost = input()
print("Enter the quantity: ")
quantity = input()
print("The unit cost is ", cost/quantity)
```

2. Save and run the program, entering **20** as the item cost and **5** as the quantity.
3. It produces an error, as shown in Figure PY-21. Why?

QuickCheck

In the Bargain Hunter program, what are the names of the variables that collect input from the user?

a. input and cost

b. input and quantity

c. cost and quantity

d. input and input()

Figure PY-21: Output error

```
#Bargain Hunter
print("Enter the cost of the item: ")
cost = input()
print("Enter the quantity: ")
quantity = input()
print("The unit cost is ", cost/quantity)
```

```
Enter the cost of the item:
20
Enter the quantity:
5
Traceback (most recent call last):
  File "main.py", line 6, in <module>
    print("The unit cost is ", cost/quantity)
TypeError: unsupported operand type(s) for /: 'str
' and 'str'
> 
```

Source: Replit

▶ What is the trick to collecting values with an input statement? When users enter numbers via the keyboard or touchscreen, Python treats the input as a string rather than a value. The string input cannot be used for calculations. To fix this problem, you can use the int() command to convert the input data to an integer, or you can use the float() command to convert the input to a floating point number with decimal places.

Converting String Input to Integer Values

To correct the syntax error in the Bargain Hunter program, you can add the int() command to the two lines of code that assign the input to variables.

1. Change line 3 of the Bargain Hunter program to the following:

```
cost = int(input())
```

2. Change line 5 of the program to the following:

```
quantity = int(input())
```

3. Save and run the program.
4. Enter **20** for the cost and **5** for the quantity.
5. Compare your program and output to Figure PY-22. The program should now run without a syntax error.

QuickCheck

To convert an input string into a floating point number, programmers can use which of the following commands?

a. float()

b. int()

c. str()

d. convert()

PY

Figure PY-22: Collecting input values

```
1  #Bargain Hunter
2  print("Enter the cost of the item: ")
3  cost = int(input())
4  print("Enter the quantity: ")
5  quantity = int(input())
6  print("The unit cost is ", cost/quantity)
```

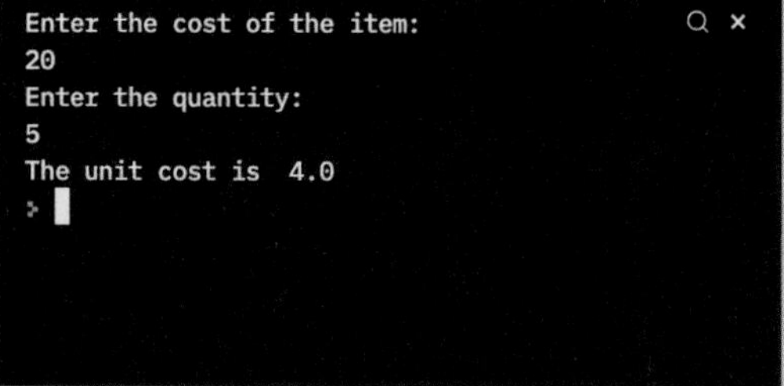
Enter the cost of the item:
20
Enter the quantity:
5
The unit cost is 4.0

Source: Replit

▸ Can I simplify the input code? Instead of using one line to display the input prompt and another line to convert the input to an integer, you can combine both tasks into one line of code, as shown in Figure PY-23.

Figure PY-23: Combined code for input, assignment, and integer conversion

Original Code

```
print("Enter the cost of the item: ")
cost = int(input())
```

Combined Code

```
cost = int(input("Enter the cost of the item: "))
```

An Alternative Method for Collecting Input Values

1. Modify the Bargain Hunter program to the following:

```
#Bargain Hunter
cost = int(input("Enter the cost of the item: "))
quantity = int(input("Enter the quantity: "))
print("The unit cost is ", cost/quantity)
```

2. Save and run the program to make sure that the revision works.

Selection Structures

So far, all the programs you've written have been executed line by line in sequence from beginning to end. Sometimes, however, programmers want parts of their code to be executed only when certain conditions are met. For example, an airport check-in kiosk might ask passengers to enter the number of bags they are checking. For passengers with more than one bag, the kiosk program would display a message indicating the charge for their baggage. For passengers without extra baggage, the program would not execute the lines that perform the calculation.

▶ Can I design a program that handles different conditions? Computer programs can be designed to execute sections of code based on specific conditions. These programs use selection control structures to determine which branch of code to execute. A **selection control structure** tells a computer what to do based on whether a condition is true or false. You can think of a selection control as one or more paths in a program. Figure PY-24 illustrates a simple branch.

Figure PY-24: A simple control structure creates two paths

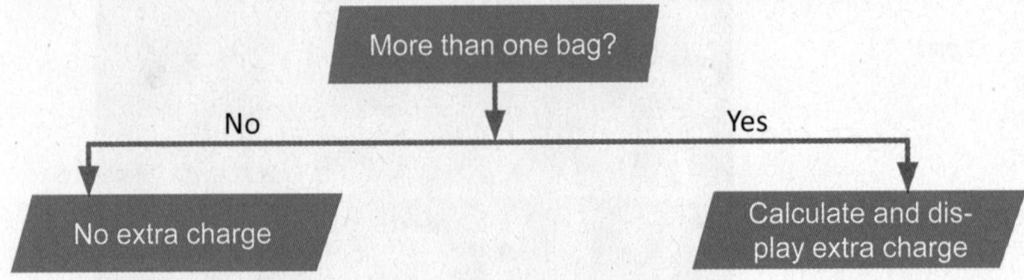

Using the *if* Command to Control Program Flow

An example of a selection control structure is the *if* command. You can use it to write the section of code for an airport check-in kiosk that calculates baggage fees.

1. Start a new program called **Airport Kiosk**.
2. Enter the following code. Use the Tab key, if necessary, to indent the last two lines.

```
#Airport Kiosk
print("How many bags are you checking?")
number_of_bags = int(input())
if number_of_bags >1:
    print("The first checked bag is free. Each
    additional bag is $25")
    print("Please pay $", (number_of_bags-1) * 25)
```

3. Save and run the program, entering **1** as the initial input. The program should end without displaying any charges.
4. Run the program again, entering **2** for the number of bags. The output should look like Figure PY-25 because this time, the *if* statement was true and the indented statements it contains were executed.

QuickCheck

In the Airport Kiosk program, why is -1 in the following calculation:

(number_of_bags-1) * 25?

a. Because the first bag is free
b. To designate the order of operations
c. To make the *if* statement true
d. Because it specified the end of the calculation

Figure PY-25: A simple if statement

```
#Airport Kiosk
print("How many bags are you checking?")
number_of_bags = int(input())
if number_of_bags >1:
  print("The first checked bag is free. Each
  additional bag is $25")
  print("Please pay $", (number_of_bags-1) * 25)
```

```
How many bags are you checking?
2
The first checked bag is free. Each additional bag is $25
Please pay $ 25
>
```

Source: Replit

Are there rules for creating *if* statements? Yes. The *if* command requires a colon as punctuation, and the statements in its execution path must be indented. It is standard in Python to use four spaces for indenting. You may also use the Tab key. To discontinue indents, simply press the Delete key or the left arrow key.

What is an if...else statement? Frequently, programmers want one thing to happen when a condition is true and something else to happen when it is false. To accomplish this, they use the if...else statement.

Using if...else Statements

1. Enter the following code for a program called **Weather**. (Hint: Include the colons in the if and else statements; be mindful of the indentation.)

```
temp = int(input("What is the outside temperature? "))
if temp > 70:
    print("Wear shorts ")
else:
    print("Wear jeans ")
print("when you go outside.")
```

2. Save and run the program, first using **50** as the input value and then using **80**. You should get different results depending on the input.
3. When you enter **80**, compare your program and output to Figure PY-26.

Figure PY-26: If...else statement

```
temp = int(input("What is the outside temperature? "))
if temp > 70:
    print("Wear shorts ")
else:
    print("Wear jeans ")
print("when you go outside.")
```

```
What is the outside temperature? 80
Wear shorts
when you go outside.
>
```

Source: Replit

What happens if I need to use more than two conditions? Sometimes there are more than two possible conditions. You can code multiple conditions using elif statements. The keyword *elif* is an abbreviation of "else if." There must be a colon after the elif condition.

Coding Multiple Conditions

1. Enter the following lines of code for a program called **Compare** that uses elif statements to deal with three conditions:

```
x = 8
y = 4
if x < y:
    print("x is less than y")
elif x > y:
    print("x is greater than y")
else:
    print("x and y are equal")
```

2. Save and run the program.
3. Compare your program and output to Figure PY-27.

QuickCheck

In the program shown in Figure PY-26, why is the last line not indented?

a. It is never supposed to be executed.
b. It is part of the *if* statement.
c. It is part of the *else* statement.
d. It is part of the main program and is always executed.

Figure PY-27: Multiple conditions

```
x = 8
y = 4
if x < y:
    print("x is less than y")
elif x > y:
    print("x is greater than y")
else:
    print("x and y are equal")
```

```
x is greater than y
>
```

Source: Replit

There is no limit on the number of elif statements that can follow an *if* statement. If there is an *else* clause, it must be at the end, but there doesn't have to be one.

Each condition is checked in order. If the first condition is false, the next is checked, and so on. If one of them is true, the code indented under the elif statement is executed, and then the sequence ends. Even if more than one condition is true, only the first true condition is executed.

QuickCheck

If x = 7 and y = 9, which line in Figure PY-27 prints?

a. x is less than y

b. x is greater than y

c. x and y are equal

d. That input produces an error.

Comparison and Logical Operators

In coding, an operator is a symbol that represents an action. You've used arithmetic operators (such as +, -, *, and /) to specify actions for calculations. Additional operators can be useful for a variety of coding tasks. When coding statements for control structures, it is handy to know the symbols for comparison and logical operators.

▶ What is a comparison operator? A **comparison operator** is used in an expression to compare two values. You have already used comparison operators, such as > and <, to write expressions such as `number_of_bags > 1` and `x < y`. Additional comparison operators are listed in Figure PY-28, where the example assumes that the variable x contains 10 and the variable y contains 20.

Figure PY-28: Comparison operators

Operator	Description	Example
==	If the values of two operands are equal, then the condition becomes true.	(x == y) is not true.
!=	If the values of two operands are not equal, then the condition becomes true.	(x != y) is true.
>	If the value of the left operand is greater than the value of the right operand, then the condition becomes true.	(x > y) is not true.
<	If the value of the left operand is less than the value of the right operand, then the condition becomes true.	(x < y) is true.
>=	If the value of the left operand is greater than or equal to the value of the right operand, then the condition becomes true.	(x >= y) is not true.
<=	If the value of the left operand is less than or equal to the value of the right operand, then the condition becomes true.	(x <= y) is true.

How do comparison operators work? Typically, expressions with comparison operators are used with commands, such as *if*, that form control structures.

Using Comparison Operators

The most commonly used comparison operators are >, <, and ==. Let's see how they can be used in a program that might operate a "smart" thermostat.

1. Enter the following lines of code for a program called **Temperature**:

```
room_temperature = 69
if room_temperature > 70:
    print("Turn on the fan!")
if room_temperature < 70:
    print("Turn on the heat!")
if room_temperature == 70:
    print("Perfect!")
```

2. Save and run the program. The expression `room_temperature < 70` is evaluated as true based on the value assigned to room_temperature. Therefore, the *if* statement containing this expression is executed.
3. Modify the value assigned to room_temperature so that the expression `room_temperature > 70` is evaluated as true. What is the output?
4. Modify the program again so that the expression `room_temperature == 70` is evaluated as true.

How does == differ from =? The == operator is the **equality operator**. It is used for comparisons such as `if room_temperature == 70`. The = symbol is the assignment operator. It is used to store values and strings in variables, as in `room_temperature = 70`.

Are there other rules for using comparison operators? Two rules come in handy when using comparison operators.

- First rule: If an expression contains more than one comparison operator, the operators are evaluated from left to right in the expression.
- Second rule: Comparison operators are evaluated after any arithmetic operators in an expression. For example, in 3 + 6 < 16 / 2, the two arithmetic operators will be evaluated first, and then the two resulting numbers will be compared.

What are logical operators? If...else statements can also contain **logical operators**. Python has three logical operators: AND, OR, and NOT. These are also known as **Boolean operators**, named after mathematician George Boole. You can use Boolean operators to formulate conditions, such as "if ticket is first class AND traveler is a frequent flyer then admit to airport lounge."

Expressions containing logical operators can be used in ways similar to expressions containing comparison operators. Python evaluates logical expressions as true or false, so they can be the basis for control structures that use *if* statements.

PY

QuickCheck

What is the result of this code?

```
num1 = 5
num2 = 10
num1 = num2
if num1 == num2:
    print("True")
else:
    print("False")
```

a. True
b. False
c. 15
d. 10

QuickCheck

What is the result of this code?

```
3 + 6 < 16 / 2
```

a. True
b. False
c. 17
d. Less than

Using Logical Operators

Python evaluates AND expressions differently than OR expressions. In the following program, can you understand why some statements evaluate to true, whereas others evaluate to false?

1. Enter the following lines of code for a program called **AndOr**:

```
print(1 < 2 and 4 > 2)
print(1 > 2 and 4 > 2)
print(1 < 2 or 4 > 2)
print(1 > 2 or 4 > 2)
print(not(1 > 2))
```

2. Save and run the program.
3. Can you change line 4 so that it evaluates to false?

QuickCheck

Using the variables

a = 1

b = 2

which of the following statements will evaluate to false?

a. if a == 1 and b == 1:
b. if a == 1 or b == 1:
c. if a == 2 or b == 2:
d. if a == 1 or b == 2:

Comparing Strings

When a program collects string input, such as a user's name, it can be used in expressions that become part of control structures. For example, a program might ask users if they know how to swim in order to enroll them in the appropriate swim class. This type of user interaction can make computers seem intelligent.

Strings in Python are case sensitive, which means the string "Yes" is not the same as either the string "YES" or the string "yes". However, programmers may not be able to anticipate whether users will enter upper- or lowercase strings.

How can you deal with case sensitivity? To avoid problems with case, you can use the upper() and lower() methods to convert string input to a known case.

Converting Strings to a Known Case

When converting input to a known case, programmers typically convert to uppercase. Let's see how that works.

1. Enter the following lines of code for a program called **Swim**:

```
answer = str(input("Can you swim? Enter Y for Yes or N for No. "))
if answer.upper() == "Y":
    print("Enroll in Swimming 2")
else:
    print("Enroll in Swimming for Beginners")
```

2. Save and run the program, entering a lowercase "n" as input.
3. Compare your program and output to Figure PY-29.

QuickCheck

In the swim class program, what prints if you enter **X**?

a. Enroll in Swimming 2
b. Enroll in Swimming for Beginners
c. Nothing

Figure PY-29: Comparing strings

```
answer = str(input("Can you swim? Enter Y for Yes or N for No. "))
if answer.upper() == "Y":
    print("Enroll in Swimming 2")
else:
    print("Enroll in Swimming for Beginners")
```

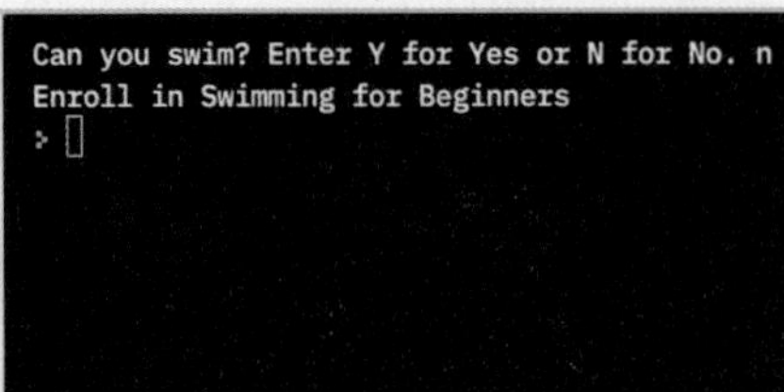

Source: Replit

Building an Interactive Calculator Program

Let's use the coding techniques you learned in this section to write a program that takes two numbers as input and then performs the mathematical operation selected by the user. The boxes indicate lines that have been left out. You'll need to add the code for those lines yourself.

1. Enter the following code for a program called **Simple Calculator**:

```
# Simple Calculator
num1 = int(input("Enter a number: "))
[                              ]
choice = input("Do you want to add, subtract, multiply, or divide?")
if choice.upper() == "ADD":
    answer = num1 + num2
    print(num1, "+", num2,"=",answer)
[                              ]
    answer = num1 - num2
    print(num1, "-", num2,"=",answer)
elif choice.upper() == "MULTIPLY":
    [                              ]
    print(num1, "*", num2,"=",answer)
elif choice.upper() == "DIVIDE":
    answer = num1 / num2
    print(num1, "/", num2,"=",answer)
[                              ]
    print("Invalid input. Sorry.")
```

2. Save and run the program.
3. Compare your output to Figure PY-30.

Figure PY-30: A simple calculator

```
>
Enter a number:  10
Enter another number:  25
Do you want to add, subtract, multiply, or divide? multiply
10 * 25 = 250

>
```

Source: Replit

PY

QuickQuiz Section C

1. An arithmetic expression contains [   ] and arithmetic operators.
2. The order of operations can be changed by using [   ] in an expression.
3. A(n) [   ] structure is a part of a computer program that tells the computer what to do, depending on whether a condition is true or false.
4. In Python, when you need to make multiple decisions in an *if* statement, use the [   ] keyword.
5. Logical operators are also known as [   ] operators.

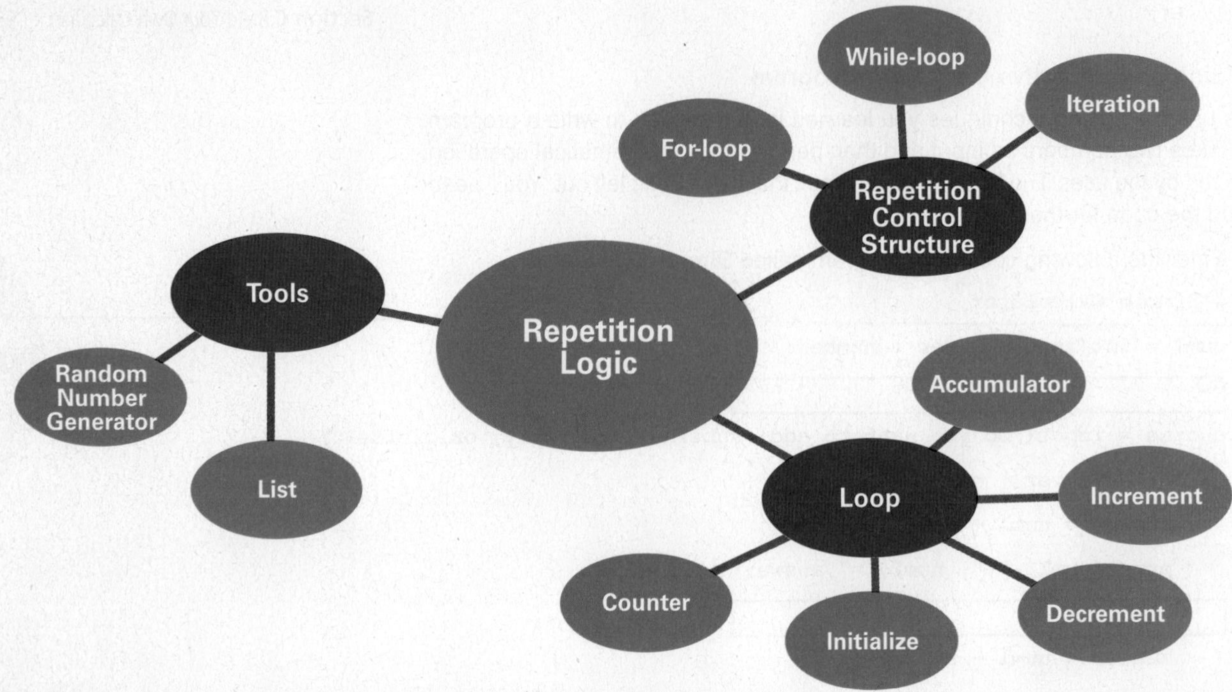

Section **D**

Ask the Fortune Teller

Objectives

- Code a basic for-loop.
- Determine the number of for-loop repetitions based on range parameters.
- Code a basic while-loop.
- Increment and decrement counters within loops.
- Use the import random command to generate random numbers.
- Incorporate random numbers in programs to roll dice, pick lottery numbers, and play a number guessing game.
- Use the correct Python syntax to create lists.
- Iterate through a list.
- Use an accumulator to combine the values in a list.
- Code the FortuneTeller program.

Repetition is part of your daily life. For example, you wash your clothes, dry them, and put them away—and then you repeat the cycle when your laundry basket fills up again. Computers can also perform repetitive tasks, such as calculating grades for every student in a college course. In this section, you will learn how to write a program that repeats multiple times. Using this new skill, you will create a number guessing game and a fun program that tells fortunes.

Terminology

repetition control structure
loop
iteration
increment
decrement
counter
initialize
random number generator
list
accumulator

Repetition Control Structures

Because applications often require the same tasks to be executed over and over again, all programming languages include repetition control structures. A **repetition control structure** allows programmers to write code that can repeatedly execute a statement or a series of statements.

The section of code that repeats is referred to as a **loop** or an **iteration**. Statements in the loop are executed repeatedly as long as a condition holds true. Python has two types of loops: the for-loop and the while-loop.

What is a for-loop? When you know in advance the number of times you want to execute a statement or statements, use a for-loop. The for-loop is known as a counter-controlled loop because the loop will be repeated a certain number of times. It is best to illustrate how a loop works by using a simple Python example.

PY

Try It!

Modify the program in Figure PY-31 to produce the following output using a for-loop:

1

Go, fight, win!

2

Go, fight, win!

3

Go, fight, win!

Coding a Basic For-Loop

Try entering this for-loop example that writes "Hello World!" four times.

1. Enter the following lines of code for a program called **Hello4**:

```
for repetitions in range(1,5):
    print(repetitions)
    print("Hello World!")
```

2. Save and run the program.
3. Compare your program and output to Figure PY-31.

Figure PY-31: For-loop

```
for repetitions in range(1,5):
  print(repetitions)
  print("Hello World!")
```

```
1
Hello World!
2
Hello World!
3
Hello World!
4
Hello World!
>
```

Source: Replit

What should I know about the syntax for a for-loop? The control statement for a for-loop begins with the command word *for*, which is followed by a variable and a range. In the program you wrote, the variable is called "repetitions."

The function "range()" is used to indicate how many times the loop will be repeated. The structure of the range function is *range(start value, upto value)*. The *start value* is optional. If it is not present, the range starts with 0. The *upto value* must always be specified. It means "up to but not including" the value.

The range for your program is range(1,5). Here's what happens:

- When the loop begins, Python loads 1 into a variable called "repetitions" and performs the indented statements.
- Python then adds 1 to the value of "repetitions." As long as "repetitions" is not 5, Python will do the loop again. Although the range is (1,5), the loop repeats only four times.
- When the value of "repetitions" becomes 5, the loop ends without executing the indented statements a fifth time.

QuickCheck

What does this code print?

```
for y in range(4):
    print(y)
```

a. The letter "y" four times

b. The numbers 0 to 3

c. The numbers 0 to 4

d. The numbers 1 to 3

What is a while-loop? When you do not know in advance the number of times you want to execute a statement or statements, use the while-loop. A while-loop repeats until a certain condition exists. You can specify the condition using many of the conditional expressions you learned in the previous section.

Using the While-Loop Control Structure

In a guess-the-number game, the programmer does not know how many times the program will have to loop before the user guesses the correct number. The following guessing game program uses a while-loop.

1. Enter the following lines of code for a program called **Guess** that uses the while-loop control structure:

```
secret_number = 7
guess = 0
while guess != secret_number:
    print("I'm thinking of a number between 1 and 10.")
    print("Can you guess it?")
    guess = int(input())
    if guess == secret_number:
        print("That's it!")
    else:
        print("That's not the number. Try again")
```

2. Save and run the program.
3. Enter **5** as the input. Because that is not the secret number, the program loops and asks you to guess again. Enter a few more guesses before you enter the secret number. When you've guessed correctly, the program outputs "That's it!"

PY

4. Compare your program and output to Figure PY-32.

Figure PY-32: While-loop

```
secret_number = 7
guess = 0
while guess != secret_number:
  print("I'm thinking of a number between 1 and 10.")
  print("Can you guess it?")
  guess = int(input())
  if guess == secret_number:
    print("That's it!")
  else:
    print("That's not the number. Try again")
```

```
I'm thinking of a number between 1 and 10.
Can you guess it?
5
That's not the number. Try again
I'm thinking of a number between 1 and 10.
Can you guess it?
7
That's it!
>
```

Source: Replit

Manual Loop Controls

Although for-loops make it relatively easy to specify the number of repetitions in a loop, some programmers like to set up loop counters within a while-loop. These loops use techniques referred to as incrementing and decrementing, which update a variable—where the new value of the variable depends on the old one.

Can I set up manual loop controls? To **increment** a variable means to add an amount to its current value. The statement `num = num + 1` takes the current value of num, adds 1, and then updates num with the new value. To **decrement** a variable, you subtract instead of add, as in `num = num - 1`.

In the above examples, the variable num is known as a counter. A **counter** is a numeric variable used for counting something, such as the total number of items purchased, the number of employees paid in a week, or the number of times to execute a loop.

Before you can increment or decrement a variable, you have to **initialize** it. To initialize a variable, you must give it a beginning value. This happens with a simple assignment:

```
num = 0
```

Controlling a Loop with a Counter

Here is a program that counts down from 5 and then prints "Blastoff!"

1. Enter the following lines of code for a program called **Blastoff**:

```
counter = 5    # initialize counter
while counter > 0:
    print(counter)
    counter = counter - 1   # decrement counter
print("Blastoff!")
```

2. Save and run the program.
3. Compare your program and output to Figure PY-33.

Figure PY-33: While-loop countdown

```
counter = 5    # initialize counter
while counter > 0:
  print(counter)
  counter = counter - 1   # decrement counter
print("Blastoff!")
```

```
5
4
3
2
1
Blastoff!
>
```

Source: Replit

Try It!

Use a while-loop to print the following sentence three times: "There's no place like home."

Python's Random Number Generator

Most programming languages provide a **random number generator** to create the random numbers that are needed for certain programs, and Python is no exception. Python provides a tool called a random module that implements the random number generator. Here are a few situations where you would use random numbers:

- To play a game of chance where the computer needs to throw dice, pick a number, pick lottery numbers, or flip a coin
- To shuffle a deck of playing cards randomly
- To make an enemy spaceship appear at a random location in a game

QuickCheck

In Python, random is a ________.

a. variable

b. function

c. module

d. counter

▸ How do I generate random numbers in Python? To have access to the random number generator, you need to include an `import random` statement at the beginning of your program. Then you can use the `random.randint()` command to generate a random number and place it in a variable.

Generating a Random Number

This example generates a random integer in the range 1 to 10 inclusive.

1. Enter the following lines of code for a program called **Random1**:

```
import random
x = random.randint(1, 10)
print(x)
```

2. Save and run the program several times. Each time you run the program, it should output a random number.

Generating Multiple Random Numbers

The original Mega Millions lottery was based on selecting five winning numbers ranging from 1 to 56. You can create a Python program to randomly choose lottery numbers.

1. Enter the following lines of code for a program called **Random2**:

```
import random
count = 0
while count < 5:
    # Get random number in range 1 through 56.
    n = random.randint(1,56)
    print(n)
    count = count + 1
```

2. Save and run the program.
3. Compare your program and output to Figure PY-34.

Figure PY-34: Generate lottery numbers

```
import random
count = 0
while count < 5:
  # Get random number in range 1 through 56.
  n = random.randint(1,56)
  print(n)
  count = count + 1
```

```
21
37
2
15
16
>
```

Source: Replit

Using the Random Number Generator to Simulate Rolling Two Dice

Let's try using the random number generator to simulate rolling two dice.

1. Enter the following lines of code for a program called **Dice**:

```
import random
roll_again = "y"
while roll_again.lower() == "y":
    print("Rolling the dice...")
    print("The first number is: ")
    print(random.randint(1, 6))
    print("The second number is: ")
    print(random.randint(1, 6))
    roll_again = input("Roll the dice again? y or n: ")
```

2. Save and run the program.
3. Compare your program and output to Figure PY-35. Your output should look similar to the figure.

Figure PY-35: Rolling dice simulation

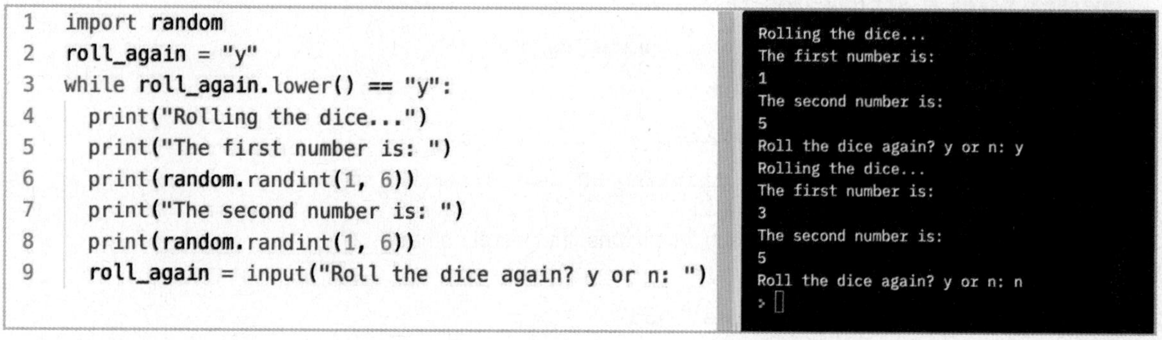

```
import random
roll_again = "y"
while roll_again.lower() == "y":
  print("Rolling the dice...")
  print("The first number is: ")
  print(random.randint(1, 6))
  print("The second number is: ")
  print(random.randint(1, 6))
  roll_again = input("Roll the dice again? y or n: ")
```

```
Rolling the dice...
The first number is:
1
The second number is:
5
Roll the dice again? y or n: y
Rolling the dice...
The first number is:
3
The second number is:
5
Roll the dice again? y or n: n
> 
```

Source: Replit

Revising the Guess the Number Game

You created a basic Guess the Number game earlier in this section. In that version, the secret number was hard-coded into the program. Now you can create the game using a random number, so each time the program runs, the secret number will be different. This more sophisticated program also limits users to five guesses.

1. Enter the following code for a program called **Secret Number** that asks the user's name, generates a random number, and starts the guessing game:

```
import random
guesses_taken = 0
print("Hello! What is your name?")
myName = input()
secret_number = random.randint(1, 20)
print(myName + ", I am thinking of a number between 1 and 20.")
```

2. Enter the following while-loop that collects the user's guesses and provides hints when the number is too high or too low:

```
while guesses_taken < 6:
    print("Try to guess the number.")
    guess = input()
    guess = int(guess)
    guesses_taken = guesses_taken + 1
    if guess < secret_number:
        print("Your guess is too low.")
    if guess > secret_number:
        print("Your guess is too high.")
    if guess == secret_number:
        guesses_taken = 6  # force the while-loop to end
```

3. Enter the following lines of code that display the guessing game results. (Hint: These lines are outside the loop, so do not indent the two lines that begin with *if*.)

```
if guess == secret_number:
    guesses_taken = str(guesses_taken)
    print("Good job, " + myName + "! You guessed my number!")
if guess != secret_number:
    secret_number = str(secret_number)
    print("Nope. The number I was thinking of was" + secret_number)
```

4. Save and run the program several times. Each time it runs, the secret number should be selected at random.

5. Compare your program and output to Figure PY-36.

Figure PY-36: Guess the Number game

```
import random
guesses_taken = 0
print("Hello! What is your name?")
myName = input()
secret_number = random.randint(1, 20)
print(myName + ", I am thinking of a number between 1 and 20.")
while guesses_taken < 6:
  print("Try to guess the number.")
  guess = input()
  guess = int(guess)
  guesses_taken = guesses_taken + 1
  if guess < secret_number:
    print("Your guess is too low.")
  if guess > secret_number:
    print("Your guess is too high.")
  if guess == secret_number:
    guesses_taken = 6 # force the while-loop to end
if guess == secret_number:
  guesses_taken = str(guesses_taken)
  print("Good job, " + myName + "! You guessed my number!")
if guess != secret_number:
  secret_number = str(secret_number)
  print("Nope. The number I was thinking of was" + secret_number)
```

```
Hello! What is your name?
Carlotta
Carlotta, I am thinking of a number between 1 and 20.
Try to guess the number.
10
Your guess is too high.
Try to guess the number.
5
Your guess is too high.
Try to guess the number.
3
Good job, Carlotta! You guessed my number!
>
```

Source: Replit

Python Lists

A **list** in Python is an ordered group of items that can be numbers or strings that are modifiable. Programs may need to hold a series of related values for various reasons, such as keeping a list of the days of the week, the months in a year, or the names of friends.

Creating a list is as simple as putting a series of comma-separated values between square brackets. The following are some examples of lists:

```
my_list = [1, 2, 3, 4, 5]

some_names = ["Bob", "Kumar", "Jay"]

fruit_list = ["apple", "banana", "cantaloupe"]
```


Why would I use a list in a Python program? Lists are tools that programmers use to make certain coding tasks straightforward when combined with repetition. For example, if you have a list of grocery items, you could use a loop to print the items or sort them into alphabetical order. Programmers can use a for-loop to process items in a list. The block of code in the for-loop is executed only once for each item in the list.

Printing the Items in a List

A very basic program for processing a list simply prints each item on a separate line.

1. Enter the following code for a program called **Basic List**:

```
my_list = [1, 2, 3, 4, 5]

for item in my_list:

    print(item)
```

2. Run your program.
3. Compare your program and output to Figure PY-37.

Figure PY-37: Print the number list

```
my_list = [1, 2, 3, 4, 5]
for item in my_list:
  print(item)

```

```
1
2
3
4
5
> 
```

Source: Replit

Inserting List Items into Output Strings

List items can be inserted into print statements. Let's invite friends to a party by using one print() command.

1. Enter and run this code for a program called **Friends**:

```
friend_list = ["Jasmin","Zoe","Brad","Zuki",\
"Thandi","Amir"]
for name in friend_list:
    print("Hi " + name + ". Come to my party!")
```

2. Compare your program and output to Figure PY-38.

Terminology

The \ symbol tells Python that a line of code is continued on the next line. It is handy when creating long lists that exceed the width of your IDE's entry area.

Figure PY-38: List items in output

```
friend_list = ["Jasmin","Zoe","Brad","Zuki",\
"Thandi","Amir"]
for name in friend_list:
  print("Hi " + name + ". Come to my party!")
```

```
Hi Jasmin. Come to my party!
Hi Zoe. Come to my party!
Hi Brad. Come to my party!
Hi Zuki. Come to my party!
Hi Thandi. Come to my party!
Hi Amir. Come to my party!
>
```

Source: Replit

▶ Can list items be used for mathematical operations? Yes. For example, you can total the items in a list and place the result in an accumulator. An **accumulator** is a numeric variable in which values are repetitively added. It works essentially like a hand calculator into which you enter a sequence of numbers.

QuickCheck

What is the value of sum after this code is run?

```
num_list = [1,3,-1,5]
sum = 0
for number in num_list:
    sum = sum + number
print("The sum is:", sum)
```

a. 9

b. 8

c. 5

d. 2

Totaling the Numbers in a List

Let's see how you can use an accumulator to calculate the sum of the values in a list.

1. Enter the following code for a program called **Accumulator**:

```
num_list = [2,4,6,8]
sum = 0
for number in num_list:
    sum = sum + number
print("The sum is:", sum)
```

2. Save and run the program.
3. Compare your program and output to Figure PY-39.

Figure PY-39: Print the sum of numbers in the list

```
num_list = [2,4,6,8]
sum = 0
for number in num_list:
  sum = sum + number
print("The sum is:", sum)
```

```
The sum is: 20
>
```

Source: Replit

Choosing Random Items from a List

The random number generator can be used to randomly choose items from a list. Using random.choice from the random module will pick a random item from a list.

1. Enter the following code for a program called **Pick**:

```
import random
# pick a random choice from a list
print(random.choice(["yes", "no", "maybe"]))
```

2. Save and run the program. Do you expect to get exactly the same results as in Figure PY-40?

Figure PY-40: Choose an item at random

```
import random
# pick a random choice from a list
print(random.choice(["yes", "no", "maybe"]))
```

```
maybe
> 
```

Source: Replit

Ask the Fortune Teller

Have you ever used the "fortune-telling" Magic 8 Ball toy? You can create a fortune-telling program that randomly produces a "fortune" in response to a question posed by a user. Your program will contain the following elements:

- A while-loop that allows the player to ask multiple questions
- A list to hold the "predictions"
- A random number generator to randomly select an answer from the list of predictions

Creating the Fortune Teller Program

1. Start a new program called **Fortune**. Enter the following code to begin the program and import the random module:

```
# The Fortune Teller
import random
```

2. Add the following code to populate a list with predictions. (Hint: Using a slash at the end of a line tells Python that the code continues on to the next line. So, you can press the Enter key after you type the slash.)

```
predictions = ["yes", "no", "maybe","certainly",\
"try again later", "my sources say no","very doubtful",\
"not now","outlook good","cannot predict now","most \
likely","reply hazy, try again","signs point to yes"]
```

3. Add the following code to display a message to the user and collect input in a variable called question.

```
print("Welcome to Ask the Fortune Teller.")
print("Ask the Fortune Teller a question.")
question = input()
```

4. Add the following code to create a while-loop that randomly selects a prediction and displays it:

```
# Loop that repeats until the user types "Quit"
while question.upper() != "QUIT":
    answer = random.choice(predictions)
    print("My answer is: " + answer + ".")
    print("Ask another question or type Quit to end!")
    question = input()
```

5. Save and run the program.
6. Compare your program and output to Figure PY-41.

Figure PY-41: Ask the Fortune Teller

```
# The Fortune Teller
import random
predictions = ["yes", "no", "maybe","certainly",\
"try again later", "my sources say no","very doubtful",\
"not now","outlook good","cannot predict now","most \
likely","reply hazy, try again","signs point to yes"]
print("Welcome to Ask the Fortune Teller.")
print("Ask the Fortune Teller a question.")
question = input()
# Loop that repeats until the user types "Quit"
while question.upper() != "QUIT":
    answer = random.choice(predictions)
    print("My answer is: " + answer + ".")
    print("Ask another question or type Quit to end!")
    question = input()
```

```
Welcome to Ask the Fortune Teller.
Ask the Fortune Teller a question.
Will it rain today?
My answer is: outlook good.
Ask another question or type Quit to end!
Will I ace my math test?
My answer is: signs point to yes.
Ask another question or type Quit to end!
Quit
>
```

Source: Replit

QuickQuiz — Section D

1. A(n) __________ structure enables you to write code that can repeatedly execute a statement or a series of statements.
2. Another name for a loop is a(n) __________.
3. Statements in a loop are executed repeatedly as long as a condition holds __________.
4. If the number of times that you execute a loop varies, use the __________ loop.
5. Use a(n) __________ to store the names of the days of the week or the months of the year.

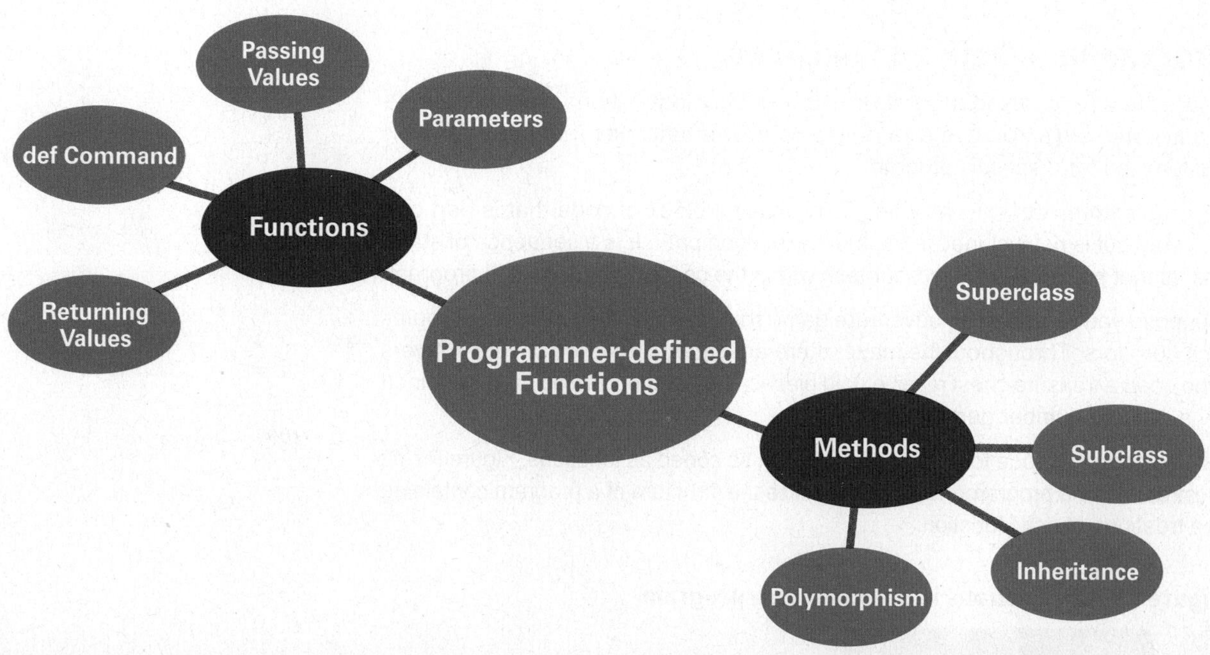

Section **E**

Dogs and Cats

Objectives

- Explain the advantages of using programmer-defined functions.
- Use the def command to code a function in a Python program.
- Pass values and strings to a function.
- Return values and strings from a function to the main program.
- Explain the purpose of a method used in an object-oriented program.
- Create methods for a class.
- Explain the efficiency of inheritance.
- Create a subclass that inherits attributes from a superclass.
- Describe the concept of polymorphism by providing an example in Python.

As you have worked through the sections in this module, the programs have become larger and more complex. Programmers use tools to make complex programs more manageable and understandable. In this section, you will learn how to use functions in an adventure game and how to use objects in a program about dogs and cats.

Terminology

programmer-defined function
parameters
method
inheritance
superclass
subclass
polymorphism

Programmer-Defined Functions

You have already used several of Python's built-in functions, such as print(), input(), and str(). You can also define your own functions that perform tasks customized for a specific program.

A **programmer-defined function** is typically a block of code that is part of a program but is not included in the main execution path. It is a sequence of statements that performs a distinct subtask within the context of the overall program.

Suppose you're writing an adventure game that takes place in a maze of rooms and corridors. Throughout the maze, there are several treasure chests. Players who open a treasure chest receive gold pieces, the number of which is determined by a random number generator.

The segments of code for treasure chests can be coded as functions. Figure PY-42 illustrates how a programmer would visualize the structure of a program containing the treasure_chest() function.

Figure PY-42: Functions in an adventure program

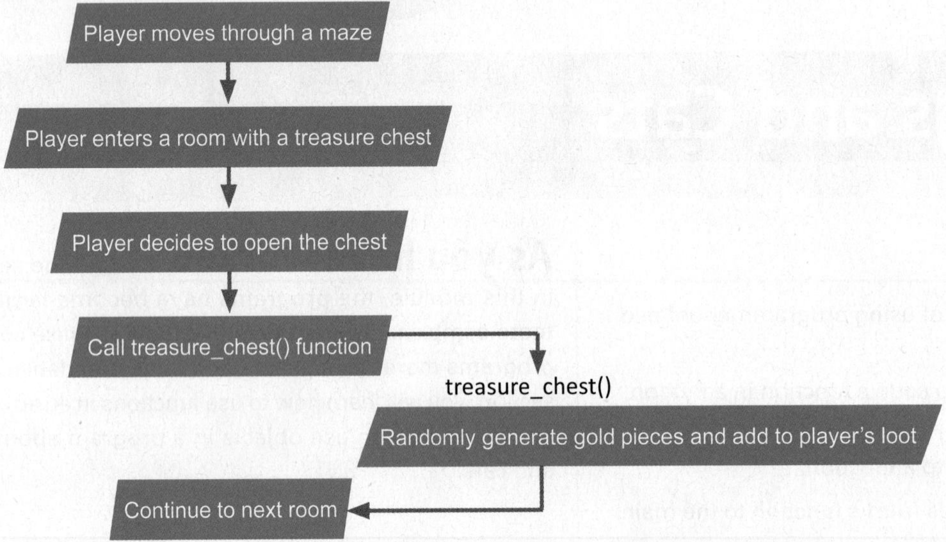

▶ What's the advantage of using programmer-defined functions? Once you've defined a function, it can be used over and over again, which saves you work. Functions eliminate the need to rewrite or copy code in order to reuse it. Using functions can also enhance the clarity and quality of a program by organizing subtasks into modules.

For the adventure game, the treasure_chest() function is written once, but it is used many times within the game whenever the player finds a treasure chest in the maze.

▶ How do I define a function? You can define functions in Python using the *def* command. The *def* command word is followed by the name of the function and a set of parentheses—for example, `def treasure_chest()`.

PY

Coding Your First Function

Let's start with a basic function that generates a random amount of gold and prints a corresponding message.

1. Start a new program called **Treasure**. Enter the following lines of code for the treasure_chest() function:

```
def treasure_chest():
    amount = random.randint(1,10)
    print("The treasure chest contains", amount, "pieces
    of gold.")
```

2. Look back at the code you have just written. The first line defines the name of the function as treasure_chest(), and it ends with a colon. The indented lines are the body of the function.

3. A function cannot run on its own. It requires a function call within the main execution path of a program. The main program will begin on line 4. Enter the following code for lines 4 through 8. (Hint: Make sure these lines are not indented.)

```
# Main program begins here
import random
player_gold = 5
print("There is a treasure chest here.")
treasure_chest() # This statement calls the treasure_chest
function
```

4. Save your program and run it.

5. Compare your program and output to Figure PY-43.

Terminology

Parameters are also called *arguments*.

Figure PY-43: A function that generates a random amount of gold

```
1 def treasure_chest():
2     amount = random.randint(1,10)
3     print("The treasure chest contains", amount, "pieces of gold.")
4 # Main program begins here
5 import random
6 player_gold = 5
7 print("There is a treasure chest here.")
8 treasure_chest() # This statement calls the treasure_chest function
```

```
There is a treasure chest here.
The treasure chest contains 9 pieces of gold.
> 
```

Source: Replit

▶ Can functions exchange values with the main program? Yes. You can put a number or a variable in the parentheses of a function call. You can use a corresponding number or a variable in the function definition. The contents within parentheses that are passed to a function are called **parameters** (Figure PY-44).

Figure PY-44: Passing a parameter

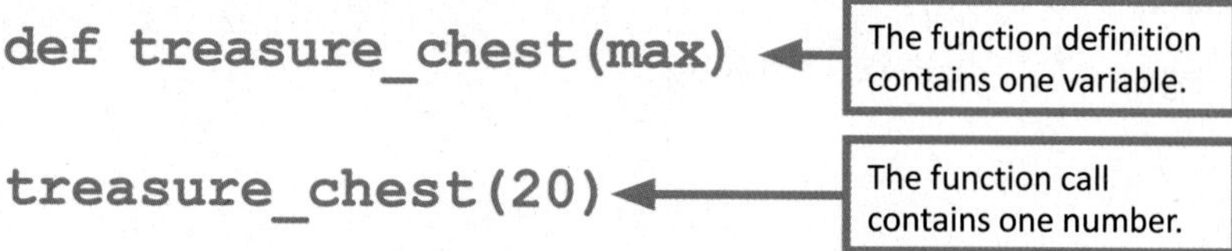
def treasure_chest(max)
The function definition contains one variable.
treasure_chest(20)
The function call contains one number.

QuickCheck

In the code for Figure PY-43, what is the maximum amount of gold that can be in a treasure chest?

a. None

b. One piece

c. Five pieces

d. Ten pieces

Passing Data into a Function

Some treasure chests contain more than 10 pieces of gold. Let's add a "max" parameter to the treasure_chest() function so we can specify the maximum number produced by the random number generator. In the following program, the number 20 is passed from the function call to the treasure_chest() function, where it is the maximum number used to generate the number of gold pieces in the chest.

1. Modify the Treasure program so it becomes the following:

```
def treasure_chest(max):
    amount = random.randint(1,max)
    print("The treasure chest contains", amount, "pieces of
    gold.")
# Main program begins here
import random
player_gold = 5
print("There is a treasure chest here.")
treasure_chest(20) # This statement calls the treasure_chest
function
```

2. Save the program and run it.
3. Compare your program and output to Figure PY-45.

Figure PY-45: Passing a value to a function

```
def treasure_chest(max):
    amount = random.randint(1,max)
    print("The treasure chest contains", amount, "pieces of gold.")
# Main program begins here
import random
player_gold = 5
print("There is a treasure chest here.")
treasure_chest(20) # This statement calls the treasure_chest function
```

```
There is a treasure chest here.
The treasure chest contains 19 pieces of gold.
>
```

Source: Replit

Is it possible to get a value out of a function and pass it to the main program? Yes. Here's the trick: Add a return command at the end of a function. When you do so, the function call takes on the value that was calculated in the function.

Using a Value Generated by a Function

Let's modify your program so that the gold generated by the treasure_chest() function is returned to the main program and placed in a variable called found_gold.

1. Add the line `return amount` to the end of the function, like this:

```
def treasure_chest(max):
    amount = random.randint(1,max)
    print("The treasure chest contains", amount, "pieces
    of gold.")
    return amount;
```

2 Modify the code in your main program to put the amount returned by the function call into a variable called found_gold, as follows:

```
# Main program begins here
import random
player_gold = 5
print("You are in a blue room. There is a treasure chest here.")
# The next statement calls the function and loads the result
into found_gold
found_gold = treasure_chest(20)
```

3 Now, add these two lines of code to the main program to add the found_gold to the amount of gold the player started with:

```
player_gold = found_gold + player_gold
print("Player gold =", player_gold)
```

4 Save and run the program.

5 Compare your program and output to Figure PY-46. Does the player now have the original five gold pieces plus the amount of gold in the treasure chest?

Figure PY-46: Returning a value from a function

```
def treasure_chest(max):
    amount = random.randint(1,max)
    print("The treasure chest contains", amount, "pieces of gold.")
    return amount;
# Main program begins here
import random
player_gold = 5
print("You are in a blue room. There is a treasure chest here.")
# The next statement calls the function and loads the result
into found_gold
found_gold = treasure_chest(20)
player_gold = found_gold + player_gold
print("Player gold =", player_gold)
```

```
You are in a blue room. There is a treasure chest here.
The treasure chest contains 13 pieces of gold.
Player gold = 18
>
```

Source: Replit

Can functions work with text strings? Yes. Text strings can be used as parameters in function calls. As you would expect, strings need to be enclosed in quotation marks in the call. They can be represented by a variable in the function definition.

Using Text Strings in Functions

In the adventure game, some treasure chests contain gems in addition to gold. Let's add parameters to the treasure_chest function to hold the name of the gem ("ruby") and its value (8 gold pieces).

1 Modify the function call in the adventure game program to the following:

```
found_gold = treasure_chest("ruby",8,20)
```

QuickCheck

What is the output of this program?

```
def say_hello():
    print("Hello World!")
say_hello()
say_hello()
```

a. Hello World!
   Hello World!

b. "Hello World!"
   "Hello World!"

c. Hello
   Hello

d. say_hello
   say_hello

❷ Modify the function definition as follows:

```
def treasure_chest(gem,value,max):
    amount = random.randint(1,max)
    print("The treasure chest contains", amount, "pieces of gold.")
    if gem != "none":
        print("The treasure chest contains a", gem, "worth ", value, "gold
        pieces.")
        amount = amount + value
    return amount;
```

❸ Save and run the program. Calculate the contents of the treasure chest in your head and compare your results to Figure PY-47 to make sure the program is producing the correct results.

Try It!

What happens if the function call contains "none" instead of "ruby"? Modify the program and find out!

Figure PY-47: Passing a string value to a function

```
def treasure_chest(gem,value,max):
  amount = random.randint(1,max)
  print("The treasure chest contains", amount, "pieces of gold.")
  if gem != "none":
    print("The treasure chest contains a", gem, "worth",
    value, "gold pieces.")
    amount = amount + value
  return amount;
# Main program begins here
import random
player_gold = 5
print("You are in a blue room. There is a treasure chest here.")
# The next statement calls the function and loads the result
into found_gold
found_gold = treasure_chest("ruby",8,20)
player_gold = found_gold + player_gold
print("Player gold =", player_gold)
```

```
You are in a blue room. There is a treasure chest here.
The treasure chest contains 13 pieces of gold.
The treasure chest contains a ruby worth 8 gold pieces.
Player gold = 26
>
```

Source: Replit

▸ What should I remember about functions? Now that you know how functions work, you can use them in your programs in place of blocks of code that perform specific repetitive tasks. Once a function is defined, it can be used over and over again. When using functions, keep the following rules in mind:

- Function blocks begin with the keyword def followed by the function name and parentheses ().
- The parentheses can hold parameters. Make sure that the function call and the function definition have the same number of parameters.
- The code block within every function starts with a colon (:) and is indented.
- The function terminates with the last indented line of code.
- The return statement passes data from the function to the main program.

Try It!

Add a red room to the maze. It contains a treasure chest with a diamond worth 50 pieces of gold. Add a print statement and a second function call to the main program. The output should look similar to the following:

You are in a blue room.

There is a treasure chest here.

The treasure chest contains 10 pieces of gold.

The treasure chest contains a ruby worth 8 pieces of gold.

You are in a red room.

There is a treasure chest here.

The treasure chest contains 15 pieces of gold.

The treasure chest contains a diamond worth 50 pieces of gold.

Player gold = 88

Methods

In Section B, you were introduced to classes and objects. As a review, every object in an object-oriented program is created from a class. A class attribute defines the characteristics of a set of objects. Classes can also include methods.

What is a method? A **method** is a segment of code that defines an action belonging to a class. In Python, methods are essentially functions, but they are defined slightly differently. A method must always have an argument called *self* within the parentheses.

When Python calls a method, it passes the current object to that method as the first parameter. Figure PY-48 explains how this works.

Figure PY-48: A method for the Pet class

```
class Pet: A
    number_of_legs = 0 B
    def sleep(self): C
        print ("zzz") D
    dog = Pet() E
    dog.sleep() F
```

A Class Pet: defines the Pet class.

B number_of_legs is an attribute of the Pet class. It is set to 0 when the program begins, but it can be changed according to the type of pet.

C The sleep() method is defined here. It must include (self) as the first parameter.

D print ("zzz") is the action the method performs.

E dog = Pet(): creates a dog object of the Pet class.

F dog.sleep: passes the dog object as an argument to the sleep() method, which prints out a message, "zzz".

Creating a Method in the Class

Let's create a Pet class with a method called sleep(), which prints "zzz" whenever it is called.

Try It!

Try running this program without the word *self* in line 3. What happens?

1. Start a new program called **Pets**. Enter the following:

```
class Pet:
    number_of_legs = 0
    def sleep(self):
        print("zzz")
```

2. Now, enter the following statement that creates a dog object:

```
dog = Pet()
```

3. Add the following statement that calls the sleep() method:

```
dog.sleep()
```

4. Save and run the program.
5. Compare your program and output to Figure PY-49.

Figure PY-49: The Pet class and its sleep() method

```
1 class Pet:
2   number_of_legs = 0
3   def sleep(self):
4     print("zzz")
5 dog = Pet()
6 dog.sleep()
```

```
zzz
> 
```

Source: Replit

▶ **Can a class have more than one method?** Yes. Each method begins with the def command and includes the word *self* as the parameter inside parentheses. Be sure to indent the code for each method and end the indent at the conclusion of the method.

Creating Another Method in the Class

Let's create a new method to print out how many legs a pet has. You will need to add the count_legs() method, an assignment statement that gives dogs four legs, and a statement that calls the count_legs() method.

1. Modify your program so that it contains the following lines of code:

```
class Pet:
    number_of_legs = 0
    def sleep(self):
        print("zzz")
    def count_legs(self):
        print("This pet has", self.number_of_legs, "legs.")
dog = Pet()
dog.sleep()
dog.number_of_legs = 4
dog.count_legs()
```

2. Save and run the program.

❸ Compare your program and output to Figure PY-50.

Figure PY-50: Sleep() and count_legs() methods

```
class Pet:
  number_of_legs = 0
  def sleep(self):
    print("zzz")
  def count_legs(self):
    print("This pet has", self.number_of_legs, "legs.")
dog = Pet()
dog.sleep()
dog.number_of_legs = 4
dog.count_legs()
```

```
zzz
This pet has 4 legs.
>
```

Source: Replit

Superclasses and Subclasses

A bark() method does not belong to the Pet class because not all pets bark. It makes sense, then, to create a Dog class that has a bark() method. But the Dog class also has other attributes common to all pets. You can combine attributes from the Pet class with special attributes for the Dog class using a technique called inheritance.

▶ What is inheritance? In object-oriented jargon, **inheritance** refers to passing certain characteristics from one class to other classes. For example, the Dog class can inherit attributes and methods of the Pet class and include methods that apply only to the Dog class.

The Pet class and the Dog class are related. The Pet class is known as the **superclass** because it is a class from which attributes and methods can be inherited. The Dog class is the **subclass** (or derived class) because it is a class that inherits attributes and methods from a superclass.

To designate that Dog is a subclass of Pet, you can define it using the statement `class Dog(Pet)`. That statement gives the Dog class all of the attributes of the Pet class, such as number_of_legs. For attributes specific to the Dog class, you can define methods. For example, you can add a bark() method, like this:

```
class Dog(Pet):
    def bark(self):
        print ("Woof")
```

Creating a Subclass from a Superclass

Let's modify the Pets program so that Dog is a subclass of Pet. The Dog class will have a bark() method that is unique for dogs.

❶ Delete the last four lines of the previous program.

❷ Add the following lines of code to define the Dog class:

```
class Dog(Pet):
    def bark(self):
        print("Woof")
```

❸ Create an object in the Dog class called spike, as follows:

```
spike = Dog()
```

4. Add this code to call the following methods that are defined in the Pet class and the Dog class:

```
spike.bark()
spike.sleep()
spike.number_of_legs = 4
spike.count_legs()
```

5. Save and run the program.

6. Compare your program and output to Figure PY-51. Notice that the spike object calls the bark(), sleep(), and count_legs() methods defined in the Dog class and inherited from the Pet class.

Figure PY-51: The Dog class inherits methods from the Pet class

```
class Pet:
    number_of_legs = 0
    def sleep(self):
        print("zzz")
    def count_legs(self):
        print("This pet has", self.number_of_legs, "legs.")
class Dog(Pet):
    def bark(self):
        print("woof")
spike = Dog()
spike.bark()
spike.sleep()
spike.number_of_legs = 4
spike.count_legs()
```

```
woof
zzz
This pet has 4 legs.
>
```

Source: Replit

How would a Cat class fit in? You can create a Cat subclass that inherits attributes from the Pet superclass. That should be easy.

Creating a Second Subclass

You can modify your program to add a Cat class and create a Cat object called Fluffy. While you're adding a Cat subclass, let's generalize the bark() method and rename it talk(). You'll find out why this is useful in a moment.

1. Modify your program to the following:

```
class Pet:
    number_of_legs = 0
    def sleep(self):
        print("zzz")
    def count_legs(self):
        print("This pet has",self.number_of_legs, "legs.")
class Dog(Pet):
    def talk(self):
        print("woof")
class Cat(Pet):
    def talk(self):
        print("meow")
spike = Dog()
spike.talk()
fluffy = Cat()
fluffy.talk()
```

2. Save and run the program.
3. Compare your program and output to Figure PY-52. Spike "woofs" and Fluffy "meows."

PY

QuickCheck

If the following statements are added to the Pets program, what is the output from the two statements?

```
spot = Cat()
spot.talk()
```

a. woof

b. meow

c. zzz

d. Nothing

Figure PY-52: Two talk() methods perform different tasks

```
class Pet:
  number_of_legs = 0
  def sleep(self):
    print("zzz")
  def count_legs(self):
    print("This pet has",self.number_of_legs, "legs.")
class Dog(Pet):
  def talk(self):
    print("woof")
class Cat(Pet):
  def talk(self):
    print("meow")
spike = Dog()
spike.talk()
fluffy = Cat()
fluffy.talk()
```

```
woof
meow
>
```

Source: Replit

How can the Dog and Cat classes both have a talk() method? An object-oriented concept called polymorphism makes it possible to assign more than one sound to the talk() method.

What is polymorphism? **Polymorphism**, sometimes called overloading, is the ability to redefine a method in a subclass. It enables programmers to create a single, more generic name for a method that behaves in unique ways for different classes.

An object of the Dog class will print "Woof" when using the talk() method because this talk() method is a part of the Dog class. An object of the Cat class will print "Meow" when using the talk() method because this talk() method is a part of the Cat class. Through polymorphism, subclasses tailor methods to fit their unique requirements.

QuickQuiz — Section E

1. Python functions begin with the keyword ______ followed by the function name and parentheses.
2. The contents between parentheses that are passed to a function are called ______.
3. In Python, functions contained within a class are called ______.
4. A(n) ______ is a class from which attributes and methods can be inherited.
5. Passing certain characteristics from one class to other classes is referred to as ______.

Flipped Class Projects

Critical Thinking

Think like a programmer and create a character that will perform a series of tasks in the videogame Minecraft. To get started, search online for *"minecraft hour of code"* at the code.org Web site. Select *Minecraft Voyage Aquatic* or the current project. Watch the video and then follow the instructions to select a character. Have your character follow the assigned tasks to complete each program. These assigned tasks will test your critical thinking with regard to how well you plan your moves so that your character successfully completes each mission. When you are finished going through all the tasks, answer the following questions: What coding techniques did you use to plan your character's actions? Was it easier to write programs using blocks of code? What difficulties, if any, did you experience?

Group Project

Working in a group of three students, develop a Python program that produces the average for a series of test scores using the steps below. The grading scale is 90–100 = A, 80–89 = B, 70–79 = C, 60–69 = D, <60 = F.

1. Use a loop to input a variable number of test scores.
2. Use a counter to keep track of how many scores are entered, and use an accumulator to store the test score total.
3. Calculate the average test score.
4. Print out the average test score.
5. After the program is running with no errors, add code to assign a letter grade to the grade average.
6. Print out the average test score and the letter grade.
7. Take a screenshot, print it out, and then submit the program and output to your instructor.

Cyberclassroom

There are a variety of free online classes to help you learn programming languages. Try at least three introductory Python tutorials, such as those you find at *Codecademy*, *W3Schools*, and *Coursera*. Write a short blog post comparing your experiences with the tutorials at each site.

Multimedia Project

Videos are a popular tutorial format. Search online for *MIT App Inventor*, scroll down the page to select *Tutorials*, and then select the *Talk To Me app* under *Beginner Tutorials*. Watch the videos and follow the instructions to create three starter apps. Were you able to build the apps based on the tutorial instructions? What are the apps used for? After completing this project, are you interested in trying to build your own app?

Resume Builder

In the job market of the 21st century, having the skills to perform technology-related tasks is essential. Make a list of careers you're interested in, and then search online to find out how coding skills might enhance your qualifications for each of these careers. Think outside of the box and into the future to come up with ideas about how coding might apply to the career fields you have selected.

Globalization

Which programming languages are used globally? Conduct research on the Web, and then create a list of the top ten most frequently used languages worldwide. Has this list changed since last year? Name your source(s) for this information. Most programming languages are written in English. Why do you think this is the case? Can you find three programming languages that are not written in English? List them and indicate what human language they are written in.

Key Terms

accumulator 560
algorithm 523
arithmetic expression 542
assignment operator 533
attribute 536
Boolean operators 549
bug 529
class 536
code 523
code editor 523
coding 523
comment 527
comparison operator 548
compiler 523
computation 542
concatenation 527
concatenation operator 527
counter 555
data type 534
debugger 523
debugging 529
decrement 555
equality operator 549
IDE 523
increment 555
inheritance 571
initialize 555
input command 538
instance 536
instantiated 536
interpreter 523
iteration 553
list 559
logic error 530
logical operators 549
loop 553
method 569
object 536
object-oriented paradigm 536
object-oriented programming 536
order of operations 543
parameters 565
polymorphism 574
programmer-defined function 564
prompt 538
random number generator 556
repetition control structure 553
selection control structure 546
string 527
subclass 571
superclass 571
syntax 527
syntax error 529
variable 532

Interactive Situation Questions

1. As an internship assignment, you are working with a team to modify a program that calculates employee wages. When employees work more than 40 hours per week, they get paid one and a half times their normal wages. The existing code shown below is supposed to calculate wages, but it is not working correctly:

```
1 if hours_worked > 40:
2       wages = (hours_worked - 40) * (pay_
        rate * 1.5) + (40 * pay_rate)
3 else:
4       wages = 40 * pay_rate
5 print(wages)
```

a. Based on the existing code, the input values for each employee are hours_worked and ________.

b. Which line of code should be changed so that it calculates wages for employees working 40 hours or less? ________

2. Your friend asks you for help with a coding assignment. She has written the following program:

```
1 def printMax(a, b):
2       if a > b:
3           print(a, "is maximum")
4       else if a == b:
5           print(a, "is greater than", b)
6       else
7           print(b, "is maximum")
8 printMax(3, 4)
```

a. What is the name of the function in your friend's program? ________

b. How many parameters are sent to the function? ________

c. There is a logic error in the program in line ________.

d. There is a syntax error in line ________.

3. Your internship team is also working on software for the company's accounting system. The team leader asks you to become familiar with the following code:

```
1 class Bank_account:
2       balance = 0
3       def withdraw(self, amount):
4           self.balance = self.balance -
            amount
5           print(self.balance)
6           return self.balance
7       def deposit(self, amount):
8           self.balance = self.balance +
            amount
9           print(self.balance)
10          return self.balance
11     def print_balance(self):
12          print("This account balance\
            is",self.balance)
13 acc101 = Bank_account()
14 acc101.deposit(100)
```

a. How many classes are defined in this segment of code? ________

b. In the program, withdraw(), deposit(), and print_balance() are ________.

c. What is the output of line 14 in the code shown above? ________

Interactive Situation Questions (cont.)

4. Skilled programmers are quite adept at visualizing program output. Walk through the three programs below to determine how many lines of text each one outputs.

```
x = 3
if x < 10:
    print ("Small")
```

a. The above program prints ______ line(s) of text.

```
food = "spam"
if food == "spam":
    print("Yummmm, my favorite!")
    print("food " *3)
```

b. The above program prints ______ line(s) of text.

```
food = "spam"
for x in range(1,5):
    print("food")
```

c. The above program prints ______ line(s) of text.

5. You are helping to develop a game that spins a wheel to determine how many times you can move your game piece. Review the following code:

```
1 import random
2 spin_again = "y"
3 while spin_again.upper() == "y":
4     print ("Spinning the wheel...")
5     print ("The number is: ")
6     print (random.randint(1, 5))
7     spin_again = input ("spin again? y or n: ")
```

a. There is a logic error in the program in line ______.

6. Review the following code:

```
1 value = "Car"
2 x = value.upper()
3 print(x)
4 # Lowercase the string.
5 y = value.lower()
6 print(y)
```

a. What is the output of line 3? ______

b. What is the output of line 6? ______

7. Review the following code:

```
1 import random
2 print (random.choice(["yesterday",\
  "today", "tomorrow"]))
```

a. In line 2, what is the term for (["yesterday", "today", "tomorrow"])? ______

b. In line 2, how many choices can print at one time? ______

8. Review the following code:

```
1 x ?? 8
2 if x ?? 8:
3     print ("It's 8!")
4 else:
5     print ("It's not 8!")
```

a. In the above program, what operator should be used in line 1 in place of the ?? (question marks)? ______

b. In the above program, what operator should be used in line 2 in place of the ?? (question marks)? ______

Lab: Adventure Game

The earliest computer games were text based. Using your Python knowledge, you can create your own text adventure game.

The game starts in a room of a house. The player wakes up in a locked room and must find the key to escape. The player must inspect items in the room to find the key and then use the key to open the door.

1. Start a new program called **Adventure**. Begin by entering a comment, substituting your full name for "your_name":

```
#Adventure Game your_name
```

2. Then enter the following commands to describe the start of the game:

```
print("Last night, you went to sleep in your own home.")
print("Now, you wake up in a locked room.")
print("Could there be a key hidden somewhere?")
print("In the room, you can see:")
```

3. Create a function to print a menu of the items in the room that could contain the key to open the door. In a Python list, each item has an index number. The first item's index is 0, the second item's index is 1, and so on. The code `list.index(item)` produces the index number.

   The first item in the items list, "backpack," has an index of 0. But when you display the list, the first item should be labeled 1, not 0. Therefore, you have to use the code `1 + list.index(item)` to display the number 1 in front of the backpack item.

   The code `print(1 + list.index(item), item)` will print "1 backpack" when the program runs.

   Enter the code for the menu() function:

```
#The menu function:
def menu(list, question):
    for item in list:
        print(1 + list.index(item), item)
    return int(input(question))
#This is a list of the items in the room:
items = ["backpack","painting","vase","bowl","door"]
```

4. Generate a random number for the location of the key among the first four items in the list. (The key is never located in the door.) Add the following statements to your program:

```
import random
keylocation = random.randint(1,4)
```

5. Now, add code that calls the menu() function using two parameters: items and the wording for a user prompt:

```
menu(items,"What do you want to inspect?")
```

6. Save the program and then test your code. Your program and output should look like this:

```
#Adventure Game
print("Last night, you went to sleep in your own home.")
print("Now, you wake up in a locked room.")
print("Could there be a key hidden somewhere?")
print("In the room, you can see:")
#The menu function:
def menu(list, question):
    for item in list:
        print(1 + list.index(item), item)
    return int(input(question))
#This is a list of the items in the room:
items = ["backpack","painting","vase","bowl","door"]
import random
keylocation = random.randint(1,4)
menu(items,"What do you want to inspect? ")
```

```
Last night, you went to sleep in your own home.
Now, you wake up in a locked room.
Could there be a key hidden somewhere?
In the room, you can see:
1 backpack
2 painting
3 vase
4 bowl
5 door
What do you want to inspect?
```

Source: Replit

7. Once the first part of the program is working without errors, delete the last line. We will call the menu later from within a loop. Delete the following line of code:

```
menu(items,"What do you want to inspect?")
```

8. Before you create the loop, you first need to add the following code to initialize variables:

```
#The key is not found:
keyfound = "No"
loop = 1
```

Lab: Adventure Game (cont.)

9 You can use a loop to display the menu and collect the user's selection until the key is found. Add the following code:

```
#Display the menu until the key is found:
while loop == 1:
    choice = menu(items,"What do you want to inspect?")
    print("")
    if choice < 5:
        if choice == keylocation:
            print("You found a small key in the", items[choice -1])
            keyfound = "Yes"
        else:
            print("You found nothing in the", items[choice -1])
```

The code `print("You found a small key in the", items[choice -1])` prints the name of the item chosen from the menu, based on the item's index number. But remember that the items in the index are numbered beginning with 0, not 1. If the user's choice is 3 for the vase, the index number of the vase is actually 2. Therefore, the code subtracts 1 from the variable choice to get the correct index number.

10 Save your program and then test your code. Your program and output should look similar to this:

```
#Adventure Game
print("Last night, you went to sleep in your own home.")
print("Now, you wake up in a locked room.")
print("Could there be a key hidden somewhere?")
print("In the room, you can see:")
#The menu function:
def menu(list, question):
  for item in list:
    print(1 + list.index(item), item)
  return int(input(question))
#This is a list of the items in the room:
items = ["backpack","painting","vase","bowl","door"]
import random
keylocation = random.randint(1,4)
#The key is not found:
keyfound = "No"
loop = 1
#Display the menu until the key is found:
while loop == 1:
  choice = menu(items,"What do you want to inspect? ")
  print("")
  if choice < 5:
    if choice == keylocation:
      print("You found a small key in the", items[choice -1])
      keyfound = "Yes"
    else:
      print("You found nothing in the", items[choice -1])
```

```
Last night, you went to sleep in your own home.
Now, you wake up in a locked room.
Could there be a key hidden somewhere?
In the room, you can see:
1 backpack
2 painting
3 vase
4 bowl
5 door
What do you want to inspect? 3

You found nothing in the vase
1 backpack
2 painting
3 vase
4 bowl
5 door
What do you want to inspect? 1

You found a small key in the backpack
1 backpack
2 painting
3 vase
4 bowl
5 door
What do you want to inspect?
```

Source: Replit

Lab: Adventure Game (cont.)

11 What if the player chooses the door? Once the player has found the key, the door can be selected. The following code handles three conditions for when the player selects 5 from the menu. (Hint: Make sure elif is indented four spaces.)

```
elif choice == 5:
    if keyfound == "Yes":
        loop = 0
        print("You insert the key in the keyhole and turn it.")
    else:
        print("The door is locked. You need to find a key.")
else:
    print("Choose a number less than 6.")
```

12 Players can exit the room when they have found the key and opened the door. Add the following line of code. (Hint: The line should not be indented.)

```
print("You open the door to your freedom.")
```

13 Save your program and test your code. Your program and output should look like that in the figure on the following page.

14 Now, get creative and modify the code to make it your own. You can modify the names of the items in the room or add a few extra items to the list. You can also change the game to have the player collect a coin or gem instead of a key to get out of the room.

15 After testing your adventure game to make sure it runs without errors, you can save it and then submit it by making a screenshot of the program or sharing it, according to your instructor's preference.

Lab: Adventure Game (cont.)

```
#Adventure Game
print("Last night, you went to sleep in your own home.")
print("Now, you wake up in a locked room.")
print("Could there be a key hidden somewhere?")
print("In the room, you can see:")
#The menu function:
def menu(list, question):
    for item in list:
        print(1 + list.index(item), item)
    return int(input(question))
#This is a list of the items in the room:
items = ["backpack","painting","vase","bowl","door"]
import random
keylocation = random.randint(1,4)
#The key is not found:
keyfound = "No"
loop = 1
#Display the menu until the key is found:
while loop == 1:
    choice = menu(items,"What do you want to inspect? ")
    print("")
    if choice < 5:
        if choice == keylocation:
            print("You found a small key in the", items[choice -1])
            keyfound = "Yes"
        else:
            print("You found nothing in the", items[choice -1])
    elif choice == 5:
        if keyfound == "Yes":
            loop = 0
            print("You insert the key in the keyhole and turn it.")
        else:
            print("The door is locked. You need to find a key.")
    else:
        print("Choose a number less than 6.")
print("You open the door to your freedom.")
```

```
Last night, you went to sleep in your own home.
Now, you wake up in a locked room.
Could there be a key hidden somewhere?
In the room, you can see:
1 backpack
2 painting
3 vase
4 bowl
5 door
What do you want to inspect? 2

You found nothing in the painting
1 backpack
2 painting
3 vase
4 bowl
5 door
What do you want to inspect? 3

You found a small key in the vase
1 backpack
2 painting
3 vase
4 bowl
5 door
What do you want to inspect? 5

You insert the key in the keyhole and turn it.
You open the door to your freedom.
>
```

Source: Replit

Glossary

@mention On Twitter, a method for referring to any user within the body of a tweet. 339

@username On Twitter, a unique identifier for each user. 339

 # hashtag A hashtag such as #ipadgames specifies a keyword that can be used to find and group social media posts by topic, both in Twitter and across other social media. 339

2-in-1 A personal computer form factor that can be used as a tablet or with its attached keyboard. 97

3D graphics A type of digital graphics format that displays a three-dimensional image in a two-dimensional space. 56

AAC (Advanced Audio Coding) A file format that provides highly compressed audio files with very little loss of sound quality and is promoted by Apple on its iTunes Web site. 32

AAX (Audible Enhanced Audio) A popular digital audio format used by Amazon to distribute audio books. 32

Absolute reference In a worksheet formula, a cell reference (usually preceded by a $ symbol) that cannot change as a result of a move or copy operation. 422

Accelerometer A device used in cell phones and other equipment to measure acceleration, or g-force. 143

Access time The estimated time for a storage device to locate data on a disk, usually measured in milliseconds. 120

Accumulator In the context of computer programming, a variable used to hold the results of multiple arithmetic operations. 560

Additive manufacturing An alternative term for 3D printing. 141

Address spoofing Using a fake IP or email address to conceal the origin of a packet or message. 491

Advance fee fraud A social engineering fraud that promises a large sum of money to a victim, but as an indication of good faith, the victim must first "forward" a small sum of money. 498

Adware Software that displays unwanted advertisements or analyzes user online behavior to create a profile used by advertisers. 489

AES (Advanced Encryption Standard) An encryption standard based on the Rijndael encryption algorithm that uses multiple steps to encrypt data. 455

AirDrop A built-in network utility for ad-hoc file sharing between devices using iOS and macOS. 202

Algorithm An abstract or general procedure for solving a problem, typically expressed as pseudocode, structured English, or a flowchart. 523

Alpha blending The process of combining a foreground color with background colors, as when an image is pasted onto a background and the edges are blended to look more natural. 48

ALU (Arithmetic Logic Unit) The part of the CPU that performs arithmetic and logical operations on the numbers stored in its registers. 102

Anaglyph A method of achieving 3D effects using two differently colored images. 50

Analog data Data that is measured or represented on a continuously varying scale, such as a dimmer switch or a watch with a sweep second hand. 19

Analog-to-digital converter Any device, such as a sound card, that converts analog data into digital data. 30

Android An open source operating system used primarily for tablet computers and smartphones. 401

Antivirus software A computer program used to identify, isolate, and eliminate viruses by scanning files as they arrive, leave, or are executed. 472

App Short for *application*; popularly used to refer to applications available for the iPhone, the iPad, and other mobile devices. 86

Application extensions Files, usually ending with .dll, containing program code that may be used by more than one software application. 409

Application software Computer programs that help users perform a specific task such as word processing. Also called application programs, applications, or programs. 86

Arithmetic expression A sequence, such as x + 5, that includes numbers, variables, and mathematical operators. 542

ARM A RISC-based instruction set used as the basis for microprocessors in tablet computers and smartphones. 105

ARPANET (Advanced Research Projects Agency Network) One of the first packet switching computer networks using TCP/IP, and the prototype for the Internet. 173

ASCII (American Standard Code for Information Interchange) A code that represents characters as a series of 1s and 0s. Most computers use ASCII code to represent text, making it possible to transfer data between computers. 22

ASCII text Text files that contain no embedded formatting codes. 23

ASF (Advanced Systems Format) Microsoft's proprietary container format for streaming digital multimedia; typically holds WMV and WMA files. 67

Aspect ratio The ratio of the width and height of an image or display screen. 63

Assignment operator The symbol (typically the equal sign =) used to place a value into a variable. 533

Asymmetric connection A network connection in which the download capacity is different from (usually faster than) the upload capacity. 188

Asynchronous In the context of communications, such as email and text messaging, both parties need not be online at the same time. 345

Attribute In the context of computer programming, any characteristic assigned to an object or class. 536

Audio compression Techniques used to reduce the size of files that contain audio data. 32

Audio interface The hardware and software that accept input from a microphone and feeds it into a digital device. 33

Automatic recalculation A feature found in spreadsheet software that automatically recalculates every formula after a user makes a change to any cell. 422

AVI (Audio Video Interleave) A video file format, developed by Microsoft, that was once the most common format for desktop video on the PC. 67

Backdoor A method typically used by hackers for surreptitiously accessing computers. 480

Backup A duplicate copy of a file, disk, or tape. Also refers to a Windows utility that allows you to create and restore backups. 125

Bandwidth The data transmission capacity of a communications channel. Digital signals are measured in bits per second; analog signals in hertz. 165

Bandwidth cap The maximum speed allowed by an Internet service provider, based on its system capacity or on the user's subscription plan. 188

Bandwidth throttling The process by which an Internet service provider intentionally slows service to regulate network traffic. 188

Bidirectional links In the context of the Web, links that allow two documents to refer to each other, rather than a link that contains only a one-way reference. 248

Binary The representation of data using two states, such as off-on or 1-0. 19

Binary adjacency matrix A representation in table format of the relationships among various people in a social network. 322

Binary number system A method for representing numbers using only two digits: 0 and 1. Contrast to the decimal number system, which uses ten digits: 0, 1, 2, 3, 4, 5, 6, 7, 8, and 9. 21

Bit The smallest unit of information handled by a computer. A bit is one of two values, either a 0 or a 1. Eight bits constitute a byte, which can represent a letter or a number. 20

Bit rate The number of bits that are transmitted or processed per unit of time (usually per second); usually measured as bps (bits per second). 65

Bitmap graphic An image, such as a digital photo, that is stored as a gridwork of colored dots. 39

BitTorrent A peer-to-peer technology in which pieces of files are distributed to and from a collection of networked computers; used for distributing music and movies over the Internet. 224

Blog (Web log) A publicly accessible personal journal posted on the Web. Blogs often reflect the views of the author and are periodically updated with new entries. 335

Blogging platform A platform that provides tools for creating blogs; it may also provide a Web site where blogs can be posted for access by the public. 336

Blogosphere The world of blogs and all their interconnections. 336

Bluetooth A short-range network technology, typically used to transmit data between a peripheral device and a computer or handheld digital device. 134

Bluetooth LE A low-power, short-range technology developed specifically for IoT networks. 212

BMP The native bitmap graphics file format of Microsoft Windows. 41

Bookmarks A feature of Web browsers that saves the URLs for selected Web sites. 259

Boolean operators Named after mathematician George Boole; AND, OR, and NOT are used to formulate database queries. 549`

Boot loader A program, usually stored in read-only memory, that starts the boot sequence, which loads the operating system into RAM. 114

Botnet A group of bots under the remote control of a botmaster, used to distribute spam and denial-of-service attacks. 482

Broadband A term used to refer to communications channels that have bandwidth that equals or exceeds 2 Mbps. 165

Browser cache The collection of HTML pages and images that is stored locally by a browser and used to quickly load pages that have been previously viewed without waiting for them to be downloaded again. 262

Browser extension A module of computer code that adds capabilities to a browser, such as the ability to block ads on Web pages. 260

Browser home page The first page displayed when a browser starts. 258

Browser tabs Graphical controls near the top of a browser window that allow users to hold open multiple Web pages and switch back and forth between them. 259

Brute force attack A method of breaking encryption code by trying all possible encryption keys. 460

BSD license (Berkeley Software Distribution license) An open source software license patterned on a license originally used by the University of California. 387

Buffers Memory that is temporarily used to store input or other data until the processor is ready to use it. 394

Bug In the context of programming, an error that must be found and corrected. 529

Bulletin board systems Early forms of online social networking in which user posts could be viewed asynchronously by other members of the bulletin board community. 326

Bus topology A network architecture in which devices connect sequentially to a main data link like birds on a telephone wire. 158

Byte An 8-bit unit of data that represents a single character. 166

Cable Internet service A type of Internet connection offered to subscribers by cable television companies. 192

CAN-SPAM Act The result of legislation passed by the U.S. Congress in 2003 to limit the dissemination of SPAM over email systems. 499

Capacitive technology A touchscreen technology coated with a thick layer of electrically conductive material, commonly used for smartphone screens. 138

Capacitors Electronic circuit components that store an electrical charge; in RAM, a charged capacitor represents an "on" bit, and a discharged one represents an "off" bit. 113

Card reader A device that can be used to read and record data on solid state storage devices, such as flash memory cards. 122

CCD (charge-coupled device) One of the components in a digital camera that captures light from an image and converts it into color data. 40

CDs (compact discs) A useful method of archival storage for documents, music, and photos. 121

Cell In spreadsheet terminology, the intersection of a column and a row. In cellular communications, a limited geographical area surrounding a cellular phone tower. 419

Cell references The column letter and row number that designate the location of a worksheet cell. For example, the cell reference C5 refers to a cell in column C, row 5. 421

Cell tower triangulation The process used to find the location of a cellular phone by gauging the strength of its signal from nearby cell towers. 320

Central processing unit (CPU) The main processing circuitry, or "chip," within a computer that contains the ALU, control unit, and registers. 85

CGI (Computer-generated imagery) The use of computer-based graphics to create realistic characters and scenery for films, videogames, and other motion graphics. 58

Character data Letters, symbols, or numerals that will not be used in arithmetic operations (name, Social Security number, etc.). 22

Chromebook A clamshell-style laptop computer that uses Chrome OS as an operating system and a thin client for Web access. 96

Chrome OS An operating system, developed by Google, that is used for Chromebooks. 402

Ciphertext An encrypted message. 455

Circuit switching The method used by the telephone network to temporarily connect one telephone with another for the duration of a call. 177

CISC (complex instruction set computer) A general-purpose microprocessor chip designed to handle a wider array of instructions than a RISC chip. 112

Class In object-oriented terminology, a group with specific characteristics to which an object belongs. 536

Client-side scripts Program code that is executed by a client's browser, as opposed to being executed by the server. 274

Clickbait Eye-catching content with a teaser headline designed to entice people to click a provided link and satisfy their curiosity. 497

Clipping path The outline of an object in a digital image that can be used to cut out the object from its background. 48

Cloning In the context of digital graphics, the process of replicating a section of an image, often used to cover blemishes or fill in backgrounds. 47

Cloud storage A storage area that is located on a remote server, usually on the Internet, rather than on a local storage device. 123

Cluster A group of sectors on a storage medium that, when accessed as a group, speeds up data access. 436

Code One or more statements written as part of a computer program. 523

Codec Short for compressor/decompressor; a hardware or software routine that compresses and decompresses digital graphics, sound, and video files. 66

Code editor A software tool, similar to a word processor, that can be used to write computer programs. 523

Code injection A method used by hackers to insert malicious code into otherwise legitimate files or data transmissions. 468

Coding The process of writing statements using a computer programming language. 523

Color depth The number of bits that determines the range of possible colors that can be assigned to each pixel. For example, an 8-bit color depth can create 256 colors. 42

Comment In the context of computer programming, an annotation placed in the code by a programmer that is not executed at runtime.527

Commercial software Copyrighted computer applications sold to consumers for profit. 385

Communication channel Any pathway between the sender and receiver; *channel* may refer to a physical medium or a frequency. 162

Communication network A collection of devices used to originate, send, route, and receive data transmissions. 161

Communication port In the context of computer networks, a virtual location for data that arrives or leaves the device; common ports include 21 for FTP, 110 for email, and 80 for Web data. 178

Communication protocol A set of rules that ensures the orderly and accurate transmission and reception of data. 170

Comparison operator A symbol, such as > <, ==, or =>, used in logical statements to determine equality or the difference between variables or values. 548

Compatible In the context of digital devices, the situation when two devices use interchangeable software and peripherals. 101

Compiler Software that translates a program written in a high-level language into low-level instructions before the program is executed. 523

Compression ratio A ratio such as 5:1 indicating the amount of compression that has been applied to a file. High compression ratios such as 35:1 indicate more compression so data can be contained in smaller files. 66

Computation The action of mathematical calculation. 542

Computer A device that accepts input, processes data, stores data, and produces output according to a stored program. 85

Computer graphics Images created using computers and stored in digital formats. 39

Computer program A detailed set of instructions that tells a computer how to solve a problem or carry out a task. 86

Computer virus A program designed to attach itself to a file, reproduce, destroy data, display an irritating message, or otherwise disrupt computer operations. 468

Computer worm A software program designed to enter a computer system, usually a network, through security "holes" and then replicate itself and spread to other devices. 470

Concatenation The process of combining two or more strings within a computer program. 527

Concatenation operator The symbol (typically a + sign) used to combine two or more strings in a computer program. 527

Connection speed A common term for the capacity of an Internet connection, usually measured in Mbps or Gbps. 187

Container formats The formats for files that hold multiple types of media files, such as video and audio. 66

Content aggregator A way to collect Web or media content and applications; it can be used to monitor blogs, collect current posts, and display them. 336

Content communities Social media sites where members post original content, such as stories, photos, music, or video. 325

Control unit The part of the microprocessor that directs and coordinates processing. 108

Cookie A message sent from a Web server to a browser and stored on a user's hard disk, usually containing information about the user. 281

Copyleft A modification of copyright practices, copyleft allows third-party copying and distribution as long as the copies have the same license as the original. 332

Copy protection The use of various technologies by music and video distributors to curtail unauthorized copying. 34

Copyright A form of legal protection that grants certain exclusive rights to the work's creator or the owner of the copyright. 330

Counter In the context of computer programming, a variable that is used to keep track of the number of repetitions in a loop. 555

CPU cache Special high-speed memory providing the CPU rapid access to data that would otherwise be accessed from disk or RAM. 112

Creative Commons license Licensing options that extend rights, such as creating derivatives, to someone other than the copyright owner. 331

Cross-site tracking A practice in which third-party cookies are often set by Web sites that have affiliations with wide-ranging ad-serving companies able to combine cookie data from multiple sites. 282

Crowdsourcing An activity in which a group of people contribute, usually online, to solving a problem or completing a task. 319

Cryptographic algorithm A specific procedure for encrypting and decrypting data. 455

Cryptographic key A specific word, number, or phrase that must be used to encrypt or decrypt data. 455

CSS (Cascading Style Sheets) Used in conjunction with HTML, a means of formatting the appearance of text and other elements of a Web page. 272

Cyberbullying The use of computers and online technology to harass others. 357

Dark Web A part of the deep Web accessible with special software that encrypts searches and anonymizes users; it has a reputation for illicit content and activities. 289

Data In the context of computing and data management, *data* refers to the symbols that a computer uses to represent facts and ideas. 19

Database A collection of information that might be stored in more than one file or in more than one record type. 423

Database software Software designed for entering, finding, organizing, updating, and reporting information stored in a database. 423

Data bus An electronic pathway or circuit that connects electronic components (such as the processor and RAM) on a computer's system board. 131

Data compression The process of shrinking the size of a file by removing data or recoding it more efficiently. 26

Data representation The use of electronic signals, marks, or binary digits to represent character, numeric, visual, or audio data. 19

Data transfer rate The amount of data that a storage device can move from a storage medium to computer memory in one time unit, such as one second. 120

Data type The characteristics of data that can be entered into a field in a data file; data types include character, numeric, date, logical, and memo. 534

DCE (data communication equipment) Devices, such as routers and hubs, that are used to manage data that flows over a communications network. 168

DDoS (distributed denial of service) An attack in which a target system, such as a Web server, is deliberately flooded with data from a malicious source, denying service to legitimate customers. 482

Debugger A programming utility that helps programmers locate and correct syntax and logic errors. 523

Debugging The process of testing and correcting a computer program. 529

Decrement The process of decreasing the value of a variable, as in counter = counter − 1. 555

Decryption The process of removing the encryption to produce clear text. 529

Dedicated graphics Circuitry for graphics that is supplied on an expansion card rather than integrated into the main system board of a digital device. 139

Deep Web Web pages that require password-protected logins and pages that are dynamically generated with server-side scripts; also called the "invisible Web." 289

Defamation The communication of false statements intended to harm the reputation of a person, business, product, religion, or organization. 357

Default application The software application that automatically runs when files of a particular file type are opened. 432

Default browser The browser that opens automatically when clicking links from email messages or other sources. 257

Delimiter A special character used to separate commands or formatting characters from the rest of the text in a file. 24

Demoware Software that is supplied for free, but is limited in some way until you pay for it. 386

Derivative work A work, such as a translation or adaptation, that contains major elements of a previously copyrighted work. 333

Desktop computer A computer that is small enough to fit on a desk, runs from a wall outlet, and is built around a single microprocessor chip. 96

Desktop operating system An operating system specifically designed for use on personal computers, such as Microsoft Windows or macOS. 391

Development tools A software classification used to create other software; examples include programming languages and scripting languages. 86

Device driver A type of system software that provides the computer with the means to control a peripheral device. 135

Device letter The letter of the alphabet, such as C:, used to label a storage device on a system running Windows. 428

DHCP (Dynamic Host Configuration Protocol) A set of rules that allows network client computers to find and use the Internet address that corresponds to a domain name. 180

Dial-up A connection that uses a phone line to establish a temporary Internet connection. 193

Dictionary attack A method of discovering a password by trying every word in an electronic dictionary. 460

Digital audio Music or voice that has been digitized into files using sampling techniques; sometimes referred to as waveform audio. 30

Digital audio extraction The process of copying files from an audio CD and converting them into a format that can be stored and accessed from a computer storage device, such as a hard disk; sometimes referred to as ripping. 33

Digital certificate A file that verifies the identity of a device, usually used in the context of network-based servers sending an encryption key to a client device. 492

Digital compositing Assembling parts from multiple digital images into a single image. 48

Digital data Text, numbers, graphics, or sound represented by discrete digits, such as 1s and 0s. 19

Digital rights management The use of various technologies by music and video distributors to curtail unauthorized copying. 34

Digital-to-analog converter A device that converts digital data, such as 1s and 0s, in an audio file into continuous data, such as audio sounds. 30

Digital video A series of still frames stored sequentially in digital format by assigning values to each pixel in a frame. 51

Digitization Converting non-digital information or media to a digital format through the use of a scanner, sampler, or other input device. 20

Directory In the context of computer file management, a list of files contained on a computer storage device. 429

Discharge rate In the context of battery life, the speed at which energy stored in the battery is released. 93

Disk image A bit-by-bit copy of the contents of a disk, created for backup, archiving, or duplication of data. 127

Disk partition An area of a hard disk created by dividing a large hard disk into several smaller virtual ones, such as when using two operating systems on a single computer. 428

DM In the context of Twitter, messages similar to email that are sent directly to followers. 339

DMG A container format used to deliver software applications to Macs. 412

DNS spoofing A malicious attack on the domain name system in which the IP address corresponding to a Web site is changed in order to redirect users to different locations. 184

Document formatting The specifications applied to fonts, spacing, margins, and other elements in a document created with word processing software. 418

Domain name Short for *fully qualified domain name*; an identifying name by which host computers on the Internet are familiarly known (for example, nike.com). 182

Domain name servers Computers that host the Domain Name System database. 183

Domain Name System (DNS) A large database of unique IP addresses that correspond to domain names. 182

Doppelgangers In the context of social media, two unrelated people whose online identities are so similar that they cause confusion. 357

DOS (Disk Operating System) The operating system software shipped with the first IBM PCs, then used on millions of computers until the introduction of Microsoft Windows. 396

Dot pitch (dp) The diagonal distance between colored dots on a display screen. Measured in millimeters, dot pitch helps to determine the quality of an image displayed on a monitor. 137

Download The process of transferring a copy of a file from a remote computer to a local computer's storage device. 33

Dropper A type of malware with a small footprint that is "dropped" into a computer to pave the way for more extensive malware. 471

DSL (digital subscriber line) A high-speed Internet connection that uses existing telephone lines, requiring close proximity to a switching station. 194

DTE (data terminal equipment) Computers and other devices connected to a network to send or receive data. 206

Dual band The capability of a communications device, such as a router, to use two communications frequencies. 198

DVDs (digital video discs) A useful method of archival storage for documents, music, and photos. 121

Dynamic IP addresses Temporarily assigned IP addresses usually provided by an ISP. 172

Dynamic RAM (DRAM) Random access memory that requires a power source to hold data; used as main memory on most computers. 113

Dynamic Web page A way of displaying customized content in response to keyboard or mouse actions, or based on information supplied directly or indirectly by the person viewing the page. 274

Editorial newsletter platform A spin-off of blogs that offers tools for creating and sending content directly to subscribers' inboxes; examples are Substack and Review. 337

Email A system for sending messages from one digital device to another using protocols such as SMTP, POP, and IMAP. 346

Email message A computer file containing a letter or memo that is transmitted electronically via a communications network. 346

Email server A computer that uses special software to store and send email messages over the Internet. 346

Email system The collection of computers and software that works together to provide email services. 346

Encryption The process of scrambling or hiding information so that it cannot be understood without the key necessary to change it back into its original form. 455

Equality operator A symbol (== in Python) used in statements that compare if two variables or values are equal. 549

Error correction The method a digital communications system uses to identify transmission errors and correct them. 163

Ethernet A popular network technology in which network nodes are connected by coaxial cable or twisted-pair wire. 203

Ethernet adapter A type of network interface card designed to support Ethernet protocols. 204

EULAs (end-user license agreements) A type of software license that appears on the computer screen when software is being installed and prompts the user to accept or decline. 384

Evil Twin A malicious wireless network or hotspot designed to look legitimate and ensnare unwary users looking for a free Internet connection. 490

Exabyte One billion gigabytes. 174

Executable file A file, usually with an .exe extension, containing instructions that tell a computer how to perform a specific task. 382

Expansion ports Sockets into which the user plugs a cable from a peripheral device, allowing data to pass between the computer and the peripheral device. 131

Extended ASCII Similar to ASCII but with 8-bit character representation instead of 7-bit, allowing for an additional 128 characters. 22

External CSS A cascading style sheet that is stored in a file separate from the HTML source document for a Web page. 272

Fair use The concept that copyrighted materials can be legally used in some specifically defined instances such as for critical reviews and teaching. 333

False positives In the context of antivirus software, reports of a virus infection when in fact no infection exists. 473

Field The smallest meaningful unit of information contained in a data file. 423

File A named collection of data (such as a computer program, document, or graphic) that exists on a storage medium, such as a hard disk or flash drive. 20

File format The method of organization used to encode and store data in a computer. Text formats include DOCX and TXT. Graphics formats include BMP, TIFF, GIF, and PNG. 20

File hosting services Companies that offer online space for a fee to companies and individuals who want to store files or establish a Web presence. 223

File management utilities Software, such as Finder and File Explorer, that helps users locate, rename, move, copy, and delete files. 430

File name extension The characters in a file name after the period, such as .exe and .txt. 20

File-naming conventions A set of rules, established by the operating system, that must be followed to create a valid file name. 427

File path The specification for a file's location that includes the device, folders, and file name (for example, C:\Documents\Homework\Assignment 1.DOCX). 429

File sharing The process of allowing access to document, photo, video, and other files from a computer other than the one on which they are stored. 215

File-sharing worm A type of malware that is distributed on file sharing networks, such as pirate music download sites. 470

File shredder software Software designed to overwrite sectors of a disk with a random series of 1s and 0s to ensure deletion of data. 437

File synchronization A method for backing up data by copying any additions, changes, or deletions made on one storage device to another storage device. 126

File system A method that is used by an operating system to keep track of the locations for all files stored on a device. 436

Firewall Software or hardware designed to analyze and control incoming and outgoing packets on a network; used to enhance security by filtering out potential intrusion attempts. 485

First-party cookie A cookie that is generated by the Web page that is shown in the browser. 282

Fixed Internet access Any Internet access service designed to be used from a fixed, non-portable location (for example, dial-up, DSL, and cable Internet service). 191

Folder The subdirectories, or subdivisions of a directory, that can contain files or other folders. 429

Follow A Twitter term that describes when people elect to see the tweets of another person. 339

Follow back The process of following someone who is following you on Twitter. 339

Follower A person who receives your tweets. 339

Font A typeface or style of lettering, such as Arial, Times New Roman, or Gothic. 418

Footer Text that appears in the bottom margin of each page of a document. 418

Forked In the context of open source programming, the process of deriving a new version of a software application from an already established version. 402

Formal tagging The process of adding tags to media files based on a standard set of identifiers. 328

Formatting The process of dividing a disk into sectors so that it can be used to store information. 436

Form factor The configuration of a computer's system unit; examples include tower, mini-tower, and cube. 89

Formula In spreadsheet terminology, a combination of numbers and symbols that tells the computer how to use the contents of cells in calculations. 420

Frame In the context of digital video, one of the sequential images that are combined to produce video footage. 58

Frame rate The number of frames that are displayed in a video per second. 62

Freeware Copyrighted software that is given away by the author or copyright owner. 386

FTP (File Transfer Protocol) A set of rules for uploading and downloading files between a client computer and a remote server. 222

FTTH (fiber-to-the-home) A communication link that connects subscribers' homes using fiber-optic cable. 194

Fully justified The horizontal alignment of text where the text terminates exactly at both margins of the document. 418

Function (1) In the context of spreadsheet software, a built-in formula for making a calculation. 421 (2) In the context of programming, a section of code that manipulates data, but is not included in the main sequential execution path of a program. 564

Game engine The software that controls the characters, background, and scoring for a computer game. 59

Generic profile image The photo or icon supplied to new subscribers by a social network service as a placeholder. 356

Geocoding Using informal information such as street addresses to derive more formal geolocational data, such as GPS coordinates. 320

Geosocial networking Social networking services, such as Yelp and Google Maps, that offer location-based interaction. 319

Geotagging Adding geographic data, such as GPS coordinates, to a file tag. 320

GIF (Graphics Interchange Format) A bitmap graphics file format, popularized by CompuServe, for use on the Web. 41

Gigabit (Gb or Gbit) Approximately 1 billion bits, exactly 1,024 megabits. 26

Gigabyte (GB) Approximately 1 billion bytes; exactly 1,024 megabytes (1,073,741,824 bytes). 26

Gigahertz (GHz) A measure of frequency equivalent to 1 billion cycles per second. 110

GPL (General Public License) A software license often used for freeware that ensures software will be distributed freely whether in its original form or as a derivative work. 387

GPS trilateration The process of determining the location of a person or thing based on GPS signals. 320

Grammar checker A feature of word processing software that coaches the user on correct sentence structure and word usage. 417

Graphics processing unit (GPU) A microprocessor dedicated to rendering and displaying graphics on personal computers, workstations, and videogame consoles. 139

Guest network A wireless LAN that allows access to the Internet, but not to other devices on the network. 209

Gyro sensor A device used in smartphones and other equipment to determine spatial orientation and direction of movement. 143

Handshaking A process where a protocol helps two network devices communicate. 170

Hard disk drive A storage device that contains a large-capacity magnetic storage surface sealed inside a drive case. Typically used as the primary storage device in desktop and laptop computers. 119

Hard disk platter The component of a hard disk drive on which data is stored. It is a flat, rigid disk made of aluminum or glass and coated with a magnetic oxide. 119

Hash value A number produced by a hash function to create a unique digital "fingerprint" that can be used to allow or deny access to a software application. 386

Head crash A collision between the read-write head and the surface of the hard disk platter, resulting in damage to some of the data on the disk. 120

Header Text that is placed in the top margin of each page of a document. 418

Heuristic analysis In the context of antivirus software, the process of identifying malware based not on a signature, but on other factors, such as context and behavior. 472

History list A file of recently visited Web sites maintained by a browser. 263

Hot-plugging The ability of a component, such as a USB flash drive, to connect to or disconnect from a computer while it is running; also referred to as hot-swapping. 133

Hotspot triangulation The process of locating a device based on its distance from various hotspot servers. 320

HTML conversion utility Utility software that converts documents, spreadsheets, and databases into HTML files that can be posted on the Web. 269

HTML document A plain text or ASCII document with embedded HTML tags that dictate formatting and are interpreted by a browser. 267

HTML tags A set of instructions, such as <B>, inserted into an HTML document to provide formatting and display information to a Web browser. 267

HTML5 The current version of HTML. 267

HTTP (Hypertext Transfer Protocol) The communications protocol used to transmit Web pages. HTTP:// is an identifier that appears at the beginning of Web URLs (for example, *http://www.fooyong.com*). 279

HTTP methods A set of commands, such as GET and POST, that are transmitted between Web servers and clients using the HTTP protocol. 279

HTTPS (HTTP Secure) The protocol used to create secure connections for ecommerce by adding a layer of encryption. 284

HTTP session The connection between a Web server and a client that begins with an HTTP request and ends when the response is complete. 280

HTTP status code A code that is sent in reply to a HTTP command. For example, 404 is the status code for Page not Found. 280

Hypertext A way of organizing a collection of documents by assigning an address to each and providing a way to link from one address to another. 244

Hypertext links Also referred to simply as links; words, phrases, or images on a Web page that, when clicked, take you to designated URLs. 247

ICANN (Internet Corporation for Assigned Names and Numbers) A global organization that coordinates the management of the Internet's domain name system, IP addresses, and protocol parameters. 174

IDE (integrated development environment) A set of programming tools, typically including editor, compiler, and debugger, packaged into an application for creating programs. 523

IEEE 802.3 The IEEE standard for Ethernet networks. 203

IEEE 802.11 The IEEE (Institute of Electrical and Electronics Engineers) standard for Wireless Wi-Fi networks. 205

Image compression Any technique that is used to reduce the size of a file that holds a graphic. 44

Image histogram An interactive graph that can be used to adjust the colors in a digital photo. 46

Image resolution The number of pixels in an image, usually expressed as horizontal pixels × vertical pixels. 43

Image stitching The process of combining two or more images together to produce a panoramic scene. 48

IMAP (Internet Message Access Protocol) A protocol similar to POP that is used to retrieve email messages from an email server, but offers additional features, such as choosing which emails to download from the server. 348

Impersonation Pretending to be someone you are not. 357

IMSI (International Mobile Subscriber Identity) A unique identifier used on mobile networks and sometimes intercepted by IMSI catchers. 494

Increment The process of increasing the value of a variable, as in counter = counter + 1. 555

Inheritance In object-oriented terminology, a method for defining new classes of objects based on the characteristics of existing classes. 571

Initialize To assign a value or condition to a variable. 555

Ink jet printer A non-impact printer that creates characters or graphics by spraying liquid ink onto paper or other media. 140

Inline CSS A Cascading Style Sheet that is embedded among the lines of HTML in a source document. 272

Inpainting The process of reconstructing missing parts of digital images, usually by means of an algorithm built into graphics software. 47

Input As a noun, the information that is conveyed to a computer. As a verb, to enter data into a digital device. 85

Input command The Python keyword that collects input from a keyboard or touchscreen. 538

Instance In object-oriented programming, a specific realization of an object. 536

Instantiated In programming, the creation of a real instance or a particular realization of an abstraction or template such as a class of objects or a computer process. 536

Instant messaging (IM) A private chat in which users can communicate with each other in real time using electronically transmitted text messages. 351

Instruction cycle The steps followed by a computer to process a single instruction: fetch, interpret, execute, then increment the instruction pointer. 108

Instruction pointer A component of the CPU that keeps track of sequential program execution. 109

Instruction set The collection of instructions that a CPU is designed to process. 107

Integrated circuit Electronic circuitry etched on a base of silicon to form a microchip. 87

Integrated graphics Circuitry for graphics processing that is integrated into the main board rather than as an expansion card. 139

Intellectual property A legal concept that refers to ownership of intangible information, such as ideas. 329

Interframe compression Shrinking the size of a video by removing redundant data that is the same in two successive frames. 66

Interlaced scan The way a display device builds an image by showing every other row of pixels, then going back and filling in the remaining rows. 63

Internal CSS A Cascading Style Sheet that is part of an HTML document, but located in a separate area (usually the head section). 264

Internet backbone The major communications links that form the core of the Internet. 175

Internet exchange points (IXPs) Nodes on the Internet where data from one service provider is transferred to a different service provider. 175

Internet governance The rules and standards that are the foundation for global operation of the Internet. 174

Internet infrastructure The communication channels and data communications equipment that are deployed as the foundation for the Internet. 175

Internet service providers (ISPs) Companies that provide Internet access to businesses, organizations, and individuals. 175

Internet worm A type of malware that spreads over the Internet, usually by sending itself to random IP addresses. 470

Interpreter A program that converts high-level instructions in a computer program into machine language instructions, one instruction at a time. 523

Intraframe compression In a digital video, compression that takes place within a single frame, similar to the compression used for still images. 66

Invisible Web Web sites that are not accessible to Web crawlers. 289

iOS The operating system used for iPhones, iPods, and iPads. 400

IP (Internet Protocol) One of the main protocols of TCP/IP; responsible for addressing packets so that they can be routed to their destinations; IPv4 offers 32-bit addresses whereas IPv6 offers 128-bit addresses. 179

IP address lookup Finding an IP address using a service such as What's My IP. 320

IPv4 (Internet Protocol version 4) Internet addresses that are 32-bit IP addresses. 179

IPv6 (Internet Protocol version 6) Internet addresses that are 128-bit IP addresses. 179

ISDN (Integrated Services Digital Network) A digital communications system used to access the Internet over the telephone system's copper wiring. 194

Iteration In the context of computer programming, a section of code that is repeated; also called a loop. 553

Jailbreak Making unauthorized changes to an iPod, iPhone, or iPad to get apps from a source other than the official iTunes App Store. 408

Jitter Deviations in the timing of a digital signal that can interfere with communications, especially voice over IP. 189

JPEG (Joint Photographic Experts Group) A format that uses lossy compression to store bitmap images. JPEG (pronounced "JAY-peg") files have a .jpg extension. 41

Kernel The core module of an operating system that typically manages memory, processes, tasks, and storage devices. 391

Keyframe In animation and video, the beginning frame of a transition or movement sequence. 58

Keylogger A program, sometimes part of a trojan, that records a person's keystrokes, saves them, and then sends them to a system administrator or remote hacker. 489

Kilobit (Kbit or Kb) 1,024 bits. 26

Kilobyte (KB) Approximately 1,000 bytes; exactly 1,024 bytes. 26

Label In the context of spreadsheets, any text used to describe data. 419

LAN (local area network) An interconnected group of computers and peripherals located within a relatively limited area, such as a building or campus. 161

Laptop computer A small, lightweight, portable computer that usually runs on batteries. Sometimes called a notebook computer. 96

Laser printer A printer that uses laser-based technology, similar to that used by photocopiers, to produce text and graphics. 140

Latency The elapsed time it takes for a packet of data to arrive at its destination. 188

LCD (liquid crystal display) Technology used for flat panel computer screens typically found on laptop computers. 136

Leading Also called line spacing, the vertical spacing between lines of text. 419

Lidar A technique for measuring distance to a target using laser light; a key component of autonomous vehicles. 145

Link popularity A metric used by some search engines to rank the sites that are relevant to a query. 290

Linkrot Web page links that no longer connect to active sites. 251

Linux An open source operating system commonly used for servers, and also available for desktop computers. 403

Linux distribution A bundle of software, such as Ubuntu or Fedora, that contains the Linux operating system, utilities, and a graphical desktop; also called *distros*. 403

List In computer science, an abstract data type that represents an ordered sequence of values, where the same value may occur more than once. 559

Lithium ion The type of battery technology used in many of today's portable devices. 92

Live stream Streaming data that carries an event happening in real time. 33

Local application Software that is stored on a local device and loaded from there into RAM when it runs. 409

Local email An email system that requires users to install email client software on their computer hard disk or flash drive; messages are held on a server until the client software downloads them to the local computer. 348

Local HTML editors Software for creating HTML pages that is stored on a local device. 269

Local storage Devices such as disk drives that store data within a computer or smartphone system unit, rather than on a network or in the cloud. 117

Logic error A runtime error in the logic or design of a computer program. 530

Logical operators AND, OR, and NOT. Included in program statements and evaluated at runtime as true or false. 549

Logical storage model A metaphor for the representation of stored files as, for example, a file cabinet containing folders. 436

Loop The section of program code that is repeated because of a repetition control structure; also called an iteration. 553

Lossless compression A compression technique that is able to reconstitute all of the data in the original file; hence lossless means that this compression technique does not lose data. 26

Lossy compression Any data compression technique in which some of the data is sacrificed to obtain more compression. 26

MAC address (Media Access Control address) A unique identifier similar to a serial number assigned to networking equipment at the time of manufacture. 202

Machine language A low-level language written in binary code that the computer can execute directly. 107

macOS An operating system used on Apple desktop and laptop computers; formerly OS X. 398

Magnetic storage A technology for recording data onto disks or tape by magnetizing particles of an oxide-based surface coating. 119

Magnetometer A device or component that measures magetism and is used as a compass in mobile devices. 143

Mainframe A large, fast, and expensive computer generally used by businesses or government agencies to provide centralized storage, processing, and management for large amounts of data. 95

Malware Programs such as viruses, worms, and bots designed to disrupt computer operations. 467

Malware exploit The actions carried out by malicious code supplied by viruses, worms, and bots. 467

Man-in-the-middle A malicious exploit in which messages between two people are intercepted without their knowledge. 489

Markup language A language that provides text and graphics formatting through the use of tags. Examples of markup languages include HTML, XML, and SGML. 267

Mass-mailing worm A worm that sends itself to every email address in the address book of an infected computer. 470

Megabit (Mb or Mbit) 1,048,576 bits. 26

Megabyte (MB) Approximately 1 million bytes; exactly 1,048,576 bytes. 26

Memory The computer circuitry that holds data waiting to be processed. 85

Memory card A small, flat, solid state storage medium, frequently used to store data on cameras and handheld devices. 122

Memory leak An undesirable state in which a program requests memory but never releases it, which can eventually prevent other programs from running. 393

Mesh topology A system for connecting nodes of a network in which devices connect to one another rather than to a central server. 166

Message header The section of an email file that contains address, subject, and file attachment information. 346

Metadata tag Data that contains information about other data; file tags are an example of metadata. 328

Method In the context of object-oriented programming, any action that an object can perform. 569

Microblogging service A social media service for posting short asynchronous messages such as tweets. 338

Microcontrollers Special-purpose microprocessors that are built into the device they control. 98

Microprocessor An integrated circuit that contains the circuitry for processing data. It is a single-chip version of the central processing unit (CPU) found in all computers. 85

Microprocessor clock A timing signal that sets the pace for executing instructions in a microprocessor. 110

Microsoft Windows An operating system, developed by Microsoft Corporation, that provides a graphical interface. 395

Microwaves Electromagnetic waves with a frequency of at least 1 gigahertz; one type of channel for transmitting data over communications networks. 164

MIDI (Musical Instrument Digital Interface) A standardized way in which sound and music are encoded and transmitted between digital devices that play music. 34

MIDI messages The commands that create MIDI music by specifying the note to play, its duration, and the instrument that plays it. 34

Mobile app An application designed to be downloaded to a handheld device, such as a smartphone or tablet computer. 408

Mobile broadband service High-bandwidth wireless technology that was developed for sending digital data over cell phone systems. 196

Mobile hotspot A wireless network that has a server that gets its Internet connection from a mobile network. 197

Mobile Internet access Any service that allows subscribers to access the Internet while on the go. 191

Mobile operating systems Operating systems used by handheld devices, such as smartphones or tablet computers. 391

Modem A device that modulates and demodulates a signal; typically used to send data from a computer to the Internet over telephone, cable television, or satellite networks. 168

Module In the context of software, a component or part of a software program or an office suite (for example, a word processing module). 415

Motion graphics Digital video and animation that create the illusion of motion; opposite of *still graphics*. 39

MOV A multimedia file format, popular for digital videos, that works with QuickTime software. 67

MP3 A file format that provides highly compressed audio files with very little loss of sound quality. 32

MPEG (Moving Picture Experts Group) A family of highly compressed container file formats and codecs for digital multimedia; MPEG-1, MPEG-2, and MPEG-4. 67

Multi-core processor A microprocessor that contains circuitry for more than one processing unit. 110

Multiple-user license Legal permission for more than one person to use a particular software package. 385

Multiprocessing The ability of a computer or an operating system to support dual-core processors or multiple processors. 393

Multitasking The ability of a computer, a processor, or an operating system to run more than one program, job, or task at the same time. 393

Multithreading A technology that allows multiple parts or threads from a program to run simultaneously. 393

MU-MIMO (multiple-user, multiple-input, multiple-output) A technology that transmits signals simultaneously to multiple devices that have one or more antennas 206

Narrowband A term that refers to communications channels that have low bandwidth. 165

NAT (network address translation) A security technique that allows a LAN to use one type of IP address for intra-network data and another type of address for data traveling to and from the Internet. 181

Network discovery A setting that when turned on allows a computer to see other computers on a network and to be seen by those other computers. 217

Network interface controller Circuitry, often on an expansion card mounted inside a computer, that transmits and receives data on a local area network. Also called a NIC, network card, or network adapter. 202

NFC (near field communication) A short-range wireless communication technology that allows two devices to exchange data by touching or being in very close proximity. 212

Node In a network, a connection point; in a hierarchical database, a segment or record type. 168

Non-volatile Any electronic component that does not require a constant supply of power to hold data. 122

NOR A Wikipedia policy that means "no original research." All material must be backed by references. 340

NPOV A Wikipedia policy that means "neutral point of view." 340

Numeric data Numbers that represent quantities and can be used in arithmetic operations. 21

Object In an object database or OO programming language, a discrete piece of code describing a person, place, thing, event, or type of information. 536

Object-oriented paradigm An approach to programming that focuses on the manipulation of objects rather than on the generation of procedure-based code. 536

Object-oriented programming A programming language model organized around objects rather than "actions" and organized around data rather than logic. 536

OCR (optical character recognition) The ability of a device or software to digitize text from printed sources. 25

Office suite A collection of productivity programs, typically word processing, spreadsheet, presentation, and database modules. 415

Ogg Theora A non-proprietary container format (Ogg) and video codec (Theora). 67

Ogg Vorbis An open source audio file format. 32

Oleophobic The characteristic of smartphone screens that resists oils. 92

On-access scan Virus scanning that automatically takes place in the background while the device is turned on. 483

On-demand scan Virus scanning that is manually initiated by a user. 483

On-demand stream Streaming media that starts and stops when requested, as opposed to a live stream. 33

One-way edges In a sociogram, the lines between two entities that go only one way. 321

Online HTML editor A Web app that provides tools for creating HTML pages. 269

Online identity The aggregation of a person's social media presence online. 317

Online intrusion Unauthorized access to a digital device that originates from the Internet. 479

Online reputation The perception formed by third parties of a person's online identity. 357

Online services A term used to describe pre-Internet social networking sites such as America Online, MySpace, and Prodigy. 316

Open source software Software that includes its source code, allowing programmers to modify and improve it. 387

Operating system The software that controls the computer's use of its hardware resources, such as memory and disk storage space. Also called an OS. 86

Optical storage A technology that records data as light and dark spots on a CD, DVD, or other optical media. 121

Order of operations A standard order for calculations involving more than one arithmetic operation. 543

Output The results produced by a computer (for example, reports, graphs, and music). 85

Packet A small unit of data transmitted over a network. 176

Packet loss A situation in which data bits are lost in transit, requiring them to be re-sent, which significantly increases the time required for an intact message to arrive at its destination. 189

Packet switching A technology used by data communications networks, such as the Internet, where a message is divided into smaller units called packets for transmission. 177

Page layout The physical positions of elements on a document page such as headers, footers, page numbering, and graphics. 418

PAN (personal area network) An interconnected group of personal digital devices located within a range of about 30 feet. 161

Paragraph alignment The horizontal position (left, right, justified, centered, for example) of the text in a document. 418

Paragraph style A specification for the format of a paragraph, which includes the alignment of text within the margins and line spacing. 418

Parallel processing The simultaneous use of more than one processor to execute a program. 111

Parameters In the context of programming, a keyword or variable used to specify variations of commands. 565

Password entropy A measure of a password's unpredictability and resistance to discovery. 462

Password manager Software that keeps track of sites at which a user has registered and the password that corresponds to each site. 464

PDA (personal digital assistant) A device or software that helps track appointments, contacts, and notes. 97

Peripheral devices Components or equipment, such as printers, that expand a computer's input, output, or storage capability. 130

Permissions In the context of file sharing, the activities that third parties are allowed to perform when accessing shared files. 219

Persistent cookies Cookies that are stored on a local device and remain there when a session ends. 282

Personal computer A microcomputer designed for use by an individual user for applications such as Web browsing and word processing. 96

Personal firewall A device or software controlled by an end user that is designed to block unauthorized intrusions. 485

Personally identifiable information (PII) Data pertaining to a person that can be used for purposes of identification or tracking. 360

Pharming An exploit that redirects users to fake Web sites. 504

Phishing An email-based scam that's designed to fool users into revealing confidential information. 503

Phoneme A unit of sound that is a basic component of words and is produced by speech synthesizers. 36

Photosites In digital photography, each photosite is a single point on an image capture chip, equivalent to one pixel. 40

Physical storage model A representation of data as it is physically stored. 436

Ping (Packet Internet Groper) A command on a TCP/IP network that sends a test packet to a specified IP address and waits for a reply. 188

Pipeline processing A technology that allows a processor to begin executing an instruction before completing the previous instruction. 111

Pirated software Software that is copied, sold, or distributed without permission from the copyright holder. 389

Pixel Short for *picture element*; the smallest unit in a graphic image. Computer display devices use a matrix of pixels to display text and graphics. 39

Pixelation Describes the effect of increasing the size of an image until smooth edges become jagged. 43

Pixel interpolation A process that is used by graphics software to average the color of adjacent pixels in an image, usually when the image is enlarged. 43

Plaintext An original, unencrypted message. 455

PNG (Portable Network Graphics) A type of graphics file format similar to but newer than GIF and JPEG. 41

Point size A unit of measure (1/72 of an inch) used to specify the height of characters in a font. 418

Point-to-point topology A network link that directly connects two devices. 166

Polymorphism In the context of object-oriented programming, the ability to redefine a method for a subclass. Also called overloading. 574

POP3 (Post Office Protocol version 3) A standard for retrieving email messages from an email server. 348

Portable computer Any type of computer, such as a laptop computer, that runs on batteries and is designed to be carried from one location to another; also called a mobile computer. 96

Portable Internet access Any type of Internet service, such as portable satellite, that can be moved from one place to another. 191

Port scan An exploit used by hackers to locate computer ports that can be used for surreptitious access; also called a port probe. 484

Predictive services In the context of browsers, search engines, and the Web, the ability of software to better locate information using accumulated historical queries. 258

Pre-rendering The process of rendering an animated sequence and saving it prior to displaying it; opposite of *real-time rendering*. 58

Presentation software Software that provides tools to combine text, graphics, graphs, animation, and sound into a series of electronic "slides" that can be output on a projector, or as overhead transparencies, or as paper copies. 425

Pretexting The use of some false pretext to trick victims into participating in a scam. 500

Privacy The right to be let alone or at least control the dissemination of personally identifiable information. 360

Privacy policy A set of statements describing how collected data will and will not be used by the Web site or other entity that collects it. 360

Private browsing A service offered by many browsers that deletes the browser cache and history list. 264

Private IP address An IP address that cannot be routed over the Internet. 180

Process data A systematic series of actions that a computer performs to manipulate data; typically represented on a data flow diagram by a rounded rectangle. 85

Processes Activities that are performed by the microprocessor. 392

Product activation The process of becoming a registered user of a software product; the process might include entering a validation code to unlock the software. 386

Productivity software Software that helps people work more efficiently; traditionally, word processing, spreadsheet, presentation, email, and database software. 415

Programmer-defined function A function that is named and defined as a block of code by the programmer. 564

Programming language A set of keywords and grammar (syntax) that allows a programmer to write instructions that a computer can execute. 107

Progressive scan A method for displaying motion graphics in which the lines of pixels are drawn in sequence; opposite of *interlaced scan*. 63

Promoted tweet Tweets purchased by advertisers. 339

Prompt One or more characters in a command line interface that indicate the computer is ready to accept typed input. 538

Proprietary software Software that carries restrictions on its use that are delineated by copyright, patents, or license agreements. 385

Protocol stack The collection of protocols used by a network (for example, TCP and IP). 170

PUA (potentially unwanted application) A program that is installed surreptitiously and is sometimes difficult to remove. 507

Public domain Material that is not subject to copyright restrictions on its use and distribution. 330

Public domain software Software that is available for public use without restriction except that it cannot be copyrighted. 385

Public IP address IP addresses that can be routed over the Internet (as opposed to private IP addresses that cannot). 181

Public key encryption An method of encryption that uses one key to encrypt data, but a different key to decrypt it. 285

PUP (potentially unwanted program) *See PUA*. 507

Quarantined file A file suspected to be infected with a virus that is moved to a special folder by antivirus software to prevent accidental access to it. 473

Query processor The component of a search engine that examines keywords entered by users and fetches results that match the query. 290

RAM (random access memory) Computer memory circuitry that holds data, program instructions, and the operating system while the computer is on. 113

Random number generator A routine that creates random numbers for use in computer programs. 556

Ransomware Malware that encrypts files as part of an exploit to extort money from victims who want to regain use of their files in unencrypted format. 481

Rasterization The process of superimposing a grid over a vector image and determining the color depth for each pixel. 56

RAT (Remote Access Trojan) Malware that creates a backdoor for unauthorized remote access. 480

RAW In the context of digital graphics, a file that contains unprocessed image data directly from a digital camera's sensors. 41

Ray tracing A technique by which light and shadows are added to a 3D image. 57

Readability formula A feature found in some word processing software that can estimate the reading level of a written document. 417

Read-only Storage media that can only be read from, but not recorded on. 121

Read-write head The mechanism in a disk drive that magnetizes particles on the storage disk surface to write data, or senses the bits that are present to read data. 119

Real-time rendering The process in which motion graphics are rendered as they are displayed; opposite of *pre-rendering*. 59

Record In the context of database management, the fields of data that pertain to a single entity in a database. 423

Recordable The devices and standards that allow computers to write data permanently on CDs and DVDs, but do not allow that data to be changed once it has been recorded. 121

Recovery drive A storage device containing all the operating system files and application software files necessary to restore a computer to its original state. 126

Registers A sort of "scratch pad" area of the microprocessor into which data or instructions are moved so that they can be processed. 108

Relative reference In a worksheet, a cell reference that can change if cells change position as a result of a move or copy operation. 422

Remote storage Any storage device that is not directly connected to a computer, but rather is accessed over a network. 123

Rendering In graphics software, the process of creating a 3D solid image by covering a wireframe drawing and applying computer-generated highlights and shadows. 56

Repetition control structure A component of a computer program that repeats one or more instructions until a certain condition is met (also called loop or iteration). 553

Resistive technology Touchscreen technology composed of multiple layers that when pressed contact each other and complete an electrical circuit. 138

Resolution dependent Graphics, such as bitmaps, in which the quality of the image is dependent on the number of pixels constituting the image. 43

Resource A component, either hardware or software, that is available for use by a computer's processor. 392

Response rate In the context of display technology, the time it takes for one pixel to change from black to white then back to black. 136

Retweet A tweet that is forwarded by someone other than the original tweeter. 339

Rewritable The devices and standards that allow users to write data on a storage medium and then change that data. 121

RFID (radio-frequency identification) A short-range wireless network technology commonly used to track products containing RFID tags. 212

RF signals (radio frequency signals) Data that is broadcast and received via radio waves with a transceiver. 164

RGB color model The use of red, green, and blue light that can be combined to create the full spectrum of colors. 42

RISC (reduced instruction set computer) A microprocessor designed for rapid and efficient processing of a small set of simple instructions. 112

Rogue antivirus exploit Fake virus alerts that warn of virus infections and then offer to remove them. 506

ROM (read-only memory) Refers to one or more integrated circuits that contain permanent instructions that the computer uses during the boot process. 114

Root directory The main directory of a disk. 429

Rooting A process that enables users to gain root access to Android mobile devices with the purpose of overcoming limitations imposed by mobile service providers. 408

Rootkit Software that conceals running processes; used by hackers to disguise security breaches and break-ins. 469

Router A device used to make wired or wireless connections and route data to its destination on a network. 168

Run-length encoding (RLE) A graphics file compression technique that looks for patterns of bytes and replaces them with messages that describe the patterns. 44

Safe Browsing A Google service that maintains a list of suspicious Web sites and warns users if they attempt to access those sites. 505

Sampling rate The number of times per second a sound is measured during the recording process. 31

SATA (Serial Advanced Technology Attachment) The interface that transfers data from a drive to the main circuit board. 120

Satellite Internet service A high-speed Internet service that uses a geosynchronous or low-earth orbit satellite to send data directly to satellite dishes owned by individuals. 195

Scanner A device that converts a printed image into a bitmap graphic. 40

Screen resolution The density of the grid used to display text or graphics on a display device; the greater the horizontal and vertical density, the higher the resolution. 137

Search and Replace A feature of document production software that allows the user to automatically locate all instances of a particular word or phrase and substitute another word or phrase. 416

Search engine indexer The component of a search engine that reviews the Web pages brought back by a crawler and creates pointers to them so that they can be quickly accessed. 289

Search engine optimization (SEO) Making modifications to a Web site to move it closer to the top of the list returned by search engines. 291

Search history A list of queries entered into a search engine and also stored by the search engine. 295

Search operator A logical operator such as AND, OR, or NOT used to formulate complex queries. 293

Search terms The words entered into a search engine or database to form a query. 292

Sectors Subdivisions of the tracks on a storage medium that provide storage areas for data. 436

Selection control structure A component of a computer program that tells a computer what to do, depending on whether a condition is true or false (also called decision structure or branch). 546

Semiconductors Substances, such as silicon or germanium, that can act as either a conductor or an insulator. Used in the manufacture of computer chips. 87

Sense-plan-act algorithms Artificial intelligence routines that make decisions and carry out activities in autonomous cars and other digital systems without human intervention. 144

Serial processing Processing data one instruction at a time, completing one instruction before beginning another. 111

Server A computer or software on a network that supplies the network with data and storage. 95

Server operating system A type of operating system, sometimes called a network operating system, that provides management tools for distributed networks, email servers, and Web hosting sites. 391

Server-side scripts Program code that is executed by a Web server in response to client data. 275

Session cookies Cookies that are deleted when the browser is closed. 282

Setup program A program module supplied with a software package for the purpose of installing the software. 410

Short URLs Web site addresses that have been shortened by services such as Bitly; commonly used in tweets where there is a character limit. 252

Side-loading Installing a mobile app by some means other than downloading it from an official app store. 469

Single-user license Legal permission for one person to use a particular software package. 385

Site license Legal permission for software to be used on any and all computers at a specific location (for example, within a corporate building or on a university campus). 385

Slate tablet A tablet computer form factor in which the screen covers most of the system unit and there is no physical keyboard. 97

Smart sensors Sensors that include processing capabilities. 142

Smartglasses Head-mounted wearable computers, such as Google Glass. 92

Smartphones Cellular phones that have a high-resolution color screen, a browser, and the ability to run apps. 97

SmartScreen A feature of Microsoft Edge that warns users of unsafe Web sites. 505

SMTP (Simple Mail Transfer Protocol) A communications protocol used to send email across a network or the Internet. 348

Social discovery Connecting with other nearby users on a geosocial network. 319

Social engineer Someone who uses psychology to encourage people to do something. 497

Social engineering Methods for tricking people into engaging in non-secure activities, such as clicking on links and downloading infected files. 497

Social media Online Web sites and services, such as Facebook, Twitter, and LinkedIn, that help users create content and share it with others. 313

Social Media Honeycomb A model or taxonomy for classifying social networking services. 313

Social media profile The basic, publicly viewable information about an online persona. 317

Social networking service Web-based services, such as Facebook and LinkedIn, for connecting with other users. 316

Sociogram edges The lines that connect entities in a sociogram. 321

Sociogram nodes The entities in a sociogram. 321

Sociograms A visual model of the links between entities in a social network. 321

Sockpuppets Fake online personas often used to bolster someone's real online presence. 355

Software The instructions that direct a computer to perform a task, interact with a user, or process data. 86

Software license A legal contract that defines the ways in which a user may use a computer program. 384

Software update A section of code or a program module designed to correct errors or enhance security on an already installed software product. 383

Software upgrade A new version of a software product containing new features and designed to replace the entire earlier version of the product. 383

Solid state drive A data storage device that utilizes erasable, rewritable circuitry. 123

Solid state storage A technology that records data and stores it in a microscopic grid of cells on a non-volatile, erasable, low-power chip. 122

Source document A file containing the HTML tags or scripts for a Web page. 268

Spam Unsolicited email typically sent as a bulk or mass mailing and often used for fraudulent or deceptive marketing. 499

Spam filter Software that identifies unsolicited and unwanted email messages and blocks them from the recipient's inbox. 502

Spear phishing A social engineering exploit in which email with links to malware is sent to one or more targets. 503

Speech recognition The process by which computers recognize voice patterns and words, and then convert them to digital data. 36

Speech synthesis The process by which computers produce sound that resembles spoken words. 36

Spelling checker A feature of document production software that checks each word in a document against an electronic dictionary of correctly spelled words, and then presents a list of alternatives for possible misspellings. 417

Spelling dictionary A data module that is used by a spelling checker as a list of correctly spelled words. 417

Sponsored links Links displayed by a search engine that have paid placements. 291

Spreadsheet A numerical model or representation of a real situation, presented in the form of a table. 419

Spreadsheet software Software for creating electronic worksheets that hold data in cells and perform calculations based on that data. 419

Spyware Any software that covertly gathers user information without the user's knowledge, usually for advertising purposes. 489

SSID (service set identifier) A code that identifies a network containing wireless connections and is attached to every packet that travels on that network. 208

Star topology An arrangement of network devices in which they connect to a central device such as a router. 166

Stateless protocol A protocol, such as HTTP, that allows one request and response per session. 280

Static IP addresses Permanently assigned and unique IP addresses used by hosts or servers. 179

Static Web page A Web page that does not change once it is displayed on the screen by a browser. 274

Stereo pair A set of two images that produce the sense of 3D when viewed one image per eye through a stereoscope. 49

Stereogram Two images from a stereo pair that are combined into a single slide. 49

Stereoscopic imaging A graphical technique used to produce the sense of three dimensions from the use of one or more 2D images. 49

Still images Photos and computer graphics that are not in motion. 39

Storage The area in a computer where data is retained on a permanent basis. 85

Store-and-forward A technology used by communications networks in which a message, such as an email, is temporarily held in storage on a server until it is requested by a client computer. 348

Stored program A set of instructions that resides on a storage device, such as a hard drive, and can be loaded into computer memory and executed. 86

Strength meter An indication of the strength of a password. 464

String In the context of computer programming, a sequence of characters, such as a word or a sentence, that can include letters, numerals, symbols, and punctuation marks. 527

Strong password A password that is difficult to guess or to discover using password-cracking software. 460

Style A feature in many desktop publishing and word processing programs that allows the user to apply numerous format settings with a single command. 418

Style rules Specifications for styles that are compiled into Cascading Style Sheets (CSS). 272

Subclass In object-oriented programming, subclass is derived from a superclass and inherits its attributes and methods.571

Subdirectory Any directory found under the root directory. 429

Superclass In object-oriented programming, a superclass can provide attributes and methods for subclasses. 571

Supercomputer The fastest and most expensive type of computer, capable of processing trillions of instructions per second. 95

SVG (Scalable Vector Graphics) A graphics format designed specifically for Web display that automatically resizes when displayed on different screens. 54

Symmetric connection Any connection to the Internet in which the upstream speed is the same as the downstream speed. 188

Synchronous A communications mode, such as VoIP, in which participants must be online at the same time. 345

Syntax In the context of programming languages, refers to the grammar rules that create valid program statements. 527

Syntax error An error that results when an instruction does not follow the syntax rules, or grammar, of the programming language. 529

Synthesized sound Artificially created sound, usually found in MIDI music or synthesized speech. 34

System board The main circuit board in a computer that houses chips and other electronic components. 88

System requirements The minimum hardware and operating system specifications required for a software application to operate correctly. 382

System software Computer programs, such as an operating system or utility software, that help the computer carry out essential operating tasks. 86

System unit The case or box that contains the computer's power supply, storage devices, main circuit board, processor, and memory. 89

Tablet computer A small, portable computer with a touch-sensitive screen that can be used as a writing or drawing pad. 97

Tagline In the context of social media, a short description of an online persona. 356

TCP (Transmission Control Protocol) The protocol within TCP/IP that is responsible for establishing a data connection between two hosts and breaking data into packets. 178

Tethering Connecting devices to a network server that has a mobile Internet connection. 197

Text-to-speech software Software that generates speech based on written text that is played back through a computer's sound card. 36

Thesaurus A feature of documentation software that provides synonyms. 417

Thin client A device or software that depends on software, storage, and other services provided by another device, such as a Web server. 402

Third-party cookie A cookie that is generated by an ad or an entity other than the Web page that is shown in the browser. 282

TIFF (Tagged Image File Format) A bitmap image file format with the .tif extension that automatically compresses the file data. 41

TLS (Transport Layer Security) An update of the Secure Sockets Layer (SSL) protocol for encrypting data before it is transmitted over a network. 492

Top-level domain A major domain category into which groups of computers on the Internet are divided, such as .com, .edu, .gov, .int, .mil, .net, and .org. 183

Topology The physical structure of a network including its devices and connections. 166

Touchscreen A display device that accepts input from being touched with a stylus or fingertip. 138

Traceroute A network utility that records a packet's path, the number of hops, and the time it takes for the packet to make each hop. 190

Tracks In the context of computer storage, a series of concentric or spiral storage areas created on a storage medium during the formatting process. 436

Trademark A logo symbol or word used to represent a business. 329

Transceiver A combination of a transmitter and a receiver used to send and receive data in the form of radio frequencies. 164

Transcoding The process of converting audio and video files from one digital format to another, such as converting an MOV file into a Flash video file. 67

Transformative work An image, video, or music that is based on someone else's work, but has been sufficiently transformed so as not to be a derivative work. 333

Trending Becoming noticed or popular. 339

Trojan A computer program that appears to perform one function while actually doing something else, such as inserting a virus into a computer system or stealing a password. 471

True Color A color image with a color depth of 24 bits or 32 bits. Each pixel in a True Color image can be displayed using any of 16.7 million different colors. 42

Tweets Short messages, sometimes called microblogs, posted on Twitter. 338

Twitter stream/timeline The succession of tweets displayed by Twitter. Also called a "feed." 339

Two-factor authentication The use of two identity validators, such as a password and a code sent to the user's cell phone. 456

Two-way edges In a sociogram, links between entities A and B that show relationships from A to B and from B to A. 321

UDP (User Datagram Protocol) A protocol used on the Internet as an alternative to TCP. 178

Unicode A 16-bit character-representation code that can represent more than 65,000 characters. 22

Unidirectional links Links between Web pages that go in one direction only, linking A to B, but not linking B back to A. 248

Uninstall utility A program that removes software files, references, and registry entries from a computer's hard disk. 413

Upconverting Adding pixel data to video frames to increase the resolution. 62

URL (Uniform Resource Locator) The address of a Web page. 249

USB flash drive A portable solid state storage device nicknamed "pen drive" or "keychain drive" that plugs directly into a computer's USB port. 123

USB hub A device that provides several auxiliary USB ports. 133

User authentication The process of verifying the identity of an entity that is attempting to access a device, network, or Web site. 456

User interface The software and hardware that enable people to interact with computers. 391

UTF-8 A variable-length coding scheme that uses seven bits for common ASCII characters, but uses 16-bit Unicode as necessary. 22

V A Wikipedia policy that requires information to be verifiable. 340

Value A number used in a calculation. 419

Variable A named storage location that is capable of holding data that can be modified during program execution. 532

Vector Lines and curves that form simple shapes. 52

Vector animation A series of vector images designed to be viewed sequentially to impart a vision of motion. 58

Vector graphic An image generated from descriptions that specify the position, length, and direction in which lines and shapes are drawn. 52

VFX (visual effects) The integration of computer-generated imagery (CGI) with live-action footage. 58

Viral An image, a video, or other content that spreads rapidly on social media sites. 326

Virtual keyboard A keyboard that is displayed on a touchscreen and used for input on smartphones and tablet computers. 138

Virtual machine Software that creates an operating environment that emulates another computer platform (for example, Parallels Desktop creates a virtual PC on an Intel Macintosh computer). 404

Virtual memory A computer's use of hard disk storage to simulate RAM. 114

Virus hoax A message, usually email, that makes claims about a virus problem that doesn't actually exist. 477

Virus signature The unique computer code contained in a virus that security software uses to identify it. 472

VOB (Video Object) An industry-standard video format for stand alone DVD players. 66

Voiceband modem The type of modem typically used to connect a computer to a telephone line. 193

VoIP (Voice over Internet Protocol) Hardware, software, and protocols used to make telephone-style calls over the Internet. Also referred to as Internet telephony. 352

Volatile A term that describes data (usually in RAM) that can exist only with a constant supply of power. 113

WAN (wide area network) An interconnected group of computers and peripherals that covers a large geographical area, such as multiple branches of a corporation. 161

WAN port A wired port on a router that is used to connect to an Internet modem. 207

WAV An audio file format with the .wav extension that was Windows' original "native" sound format. 32

Wearable computers Computers that are designed to be worn as clothing rather than to be carried. 98

Web application Application software that is accessed and used from within a browser. 406

Web browser A program that communicates with a Web server and displays Web pages. 243

Web crawler The component of a search engine that autonomously visits Web sites collecting Web page data that will be indexed and available for searching. 288

Web hosting service A company that offers Web server space for people or businesses that want to create Web sites. 276

Web page Information displayed by a Web browser that's produced from an HTML document or generated on the fly from data in a database. 246

Web search engine A program that uses keywords to find information on the Internet and returns a list of links to relevant documents. 287

Web server A computer that listens for queries from Web browsers and transmits HTML documents over the Internet. 246

Web site A group of Web pages accessible at a specific Web address that holds a collection of information identified by a common domain name, such as *www.cnn.com*. 246

WebM A multimedia container format designed for HTML5 projects. 67

Webmail An email system that allows users to access email messages using a browser. 347

WEP (Wired Equivalent Privacy) An encryption algorithm used to protect data on Wi-Fi networks. 200

What-if analysis The process of setting up a model in a spreadsheet and experimenting to see what happens when different values are entered. 419

Wi-Fi An Ethernet-compatible wireless connection that uses 802.11a, b, g, and n standards. 205

Wi-Fi adapter A type of network interface card that includes a transmitter and a receiver using Wi-Fi protocols. 206

Wi-Fi hotspot The geographical area in which you can connect to a Wi-Fi signal, such as a Wi-Fi equipped campus or coffeehouse. 198

Wiki Software that allows users to collaborate to create, change, and link Web pages. Used for applications such as Wikipedia and open source project management. 340

Wired channels Communication pathways that use copper, coaxial, or fiber cables to carry data. 162

Wireframe A representation of a 3D object using separate lines, which resemble wire, to create a model. 56

Wireless channels Communication pathways that travel through the air as radio frequencies or microwave signals. 162

Wireless encryption A security measure for networks containing wireless connections that scrambles data transmitted between network devices. 208

Wireless encryption key The basis for scrambling and unscrambling the data that travels over a wireless connection; sometimes called a network security key. 208

WMA (Windows Media Audio) A file format with the .wma extension that is promoted by Microsoft and provides highly compressed audio files with very little loss of sound quality. 32

Word processing software Computer programs that assist the user in producing documents, such as reports, letters, papers, and manuscripts. 416

Word size The number of bits that a CPU can manipulate at one time, which is dependent on the size of the registers in the CPU and the number of data lines in the bus. 112

Word wrap The ability of word processing software to automatically sense the right margin and stream text to the next line. 416

Worksheet A computerized, or electronic, spreadsheet. 419

World Wide Web An Internet-based collection of linked HTML documents identified by URLs and accessed using browsers and the HTTP protocol. 243

WPS (Wi-Fi Protected Setup) A standard for the easy and secure establishment of a wireless network. 208

WPA (Wi-Fi Protected Access) A method for encrypting data transmitted over wireless connections. 208

X86 A family of microprocessors manufactured by Intel Corporation that define the PC platform. 105

Zero-day attack A malicious attack that takes advantage of previously unknown vulnerabilities in a device, operating system, or application. 483

ZigBee A short-range, low-power network technology used for the Internet of Things. 212

Z-Wave A short-range, low-power network technology used for the Internet of Things. 212

Index

S

Answers

Introduction

QuickChecks

4. A
6. D
7a. B
7b. C
9. A
10. C
11. B
12. B

QuickQuiz

1. input
2. local
3. convergence
4. Internet
5. Cloud

Module 1

Pre-Check

1a. 110
1b. 00110110
2. sampling
3. Lossless
4. JPG, RAW, TIF, GIF, PNG, BMP
5. Phoneme
6. Violet
7. Vector
8. MPEG, VP8, DivX, H.264, Theora, WMV
9. Rendering

QuickChecks

19. D
20. C
21a. C
21b. B
22. 01001000, 01101001, 00100001
23a. B
23b. C
25. A
26a. C
26b. A
27. B
30. B
31. B
32. A
33. C
34. A
35. D
36. A
39. B
42. A
44a. C
44b. B
46. A
48. D
50. A
52a. D
52b. B
54. B
55. C
56. A
58. C
61. A
62. B
64. D
66a. A
66b. B

QuickQuizzes

Section A

1. bit
2. ASCII
3. delimiter
4. terabyte
5. lossy

Section B

1. Sampling
2. lossy
3. extraction
4. MIDI
5. concatenative

Section C

1. CCD
2. dependent
3. 24
4. stereogram
5. PNG

Section D

1. True
2. rasterization or rendering
3. SVG
4. wireframe
5. tracing

Section E

1. capture
2. codec
3. progressive
4. container
5. transcoding

Module 2

Pre-Check
1. Input, Process, Output, Storage
2. Lithium ion (Li-ion)
3. Processor (CPU), Video (Graphics) card
4. The smartphone
5. GHz (Gigahertz)
6. Boot loader
7. pipeline processing
8. USB 3.0
9. image

QuickChecks
85. B
86. C
87a. B
87b. A
89. C
90. C
91. C
92. A
93. B
99. C
100. B
101. B
102a. C
102b. B
105a. C
105b. B
107. B
108a. C
108b. A
109a. B
109b. D
110. D
111. A
112. B
113. B
114. A
119. C
120. A
121a. B
121b. D
122. D
123. A
124. A
126. A
127. B
130. A
131. C
132. A
133. B
134. B
135. D
136. A
137. D
138. A
140. B
143. A

QuickQuizzes
Section A
1. data
2. system
3. integrated
4. clamshell
5. oleophobic

Section B
1. servers
2. macOS
3. desktop
4. Smartphones
5. operating

Section C
1. GHz
2. x86
3. ALU
4. volatile
5. ROM

Section D
1. write
2. optical
3. remote
4. SSD
5. image

Section E
1. expansion
2. Bluetooth
3. GPU
4. capacitive
5. USB

Module 3

Pre-Check
1. Partial mesh
2. Packets
3. Latency
4. Cable, DSL, ISDN, Satellite, Fiber-to-the-home
5. WPA
6. LTE
7. .com
8. TCP/IP
9. file sharing

QuickChecks
161. D
162. B
163a. A
163b. B
164. A
165. C
166. B
168a. A
168b. C
169. C
170. C
173. B
174. C
175. B
176a. A
176b. A
177. C
178a. A
178b. B
179. B
180. A
181. C
182. B
183. C
184. A
185. D
187. B
188. B
189. C
190. B
191. B
192. C
193. D
194a. D
194b. B
195. B
196. B
197. C
198. A
199. C
201. C
202. D
203. A
204. A
205. B
206a. C
206b. C
208. C
209. C
212. C
213. A
216. D
217. C
218. A
219. A
220. C
221. D
222. B
224. A
225. D

QuickQuizzes
Section A
1. personal
2. channels
3. broadband
4. DCE
5. protocols

Section B
1. backbone
2. packet
3. TCP
4. IPv4
5. Private

Section C
1. capacity
2. jitter
3. Traceroute
4. latency
5. motion

Section D
1. router
2. MAC, media access control
3. Ethernet
4. encryption
5. IoT, Internet of Things

Section E
1. discovery
2. write
3. sharing
4. FTP
5. mesh

Module 4

Pre-Check
1. hyperlink, link, or hypertext link
2. refresh or reload
3. URL or Uniform Resource Locator
4. Cookies, HTTP cookies, or cookie
5. incognito or incognito mode
6. HTML, HTM
7. AND, OR, NOT
8. HTTPS
9. Public key encryption

QuickChecks
243. B
244. D
246. D
247. A
248. B
249. C
251. C
257. C
259. D
262. A
264. B
265. D
267. A
268. A
269. C
270. D
272a. A
272b. C
273. C
274. A
278. D
276. B
279a. B
279b. A
280. C
281a. A
281b. B
282. C
283. B
284. B
285. A
288. A
289. D
290. A
291. A
295. C
297. A

QuickQuizzes
Section A
1. Internet
2. hypertext
3. ? or question mark
4. domain
5. short

Section B
1. update
2. History
3. cache
4. Predictive, preload
5. extension

Section C
1. HTML or source
2. code, tags
3. links or hyperlinks
4. Style
5. scripts

Section D
1. stateless
2. third
3. session
4. status
5. public

Section E
1. indexer
2. query
3. operators
4. cookie
5. URL

Module 5

Pre-Check
1. profile or avatar
2. hashtag
3. sociogram or sociograph
4. POP3, IMAP, SMTP
5. trademark or registered trademark
6. Wikipedia
7. derivatives
8. doppelganger
9. Share Alike

QuickChecks
313. C
314. C
316. B
319a. A
319b. D
320. B
321. A
322. A
323. A
325. A
326. A
327. D
328. C
329. B
330. D
332. A
333. D
335. D
337. A
337b. D
338. A
339. D
340. A
342. A
345. B
346. C
348. C
349. D
350. B
351. A
352. B
355. C
356. A
358. A
360. C
361. D
362. B

QuickQuizzes
Section A
1. Honeycomb
2. crowdsourcing
3. triangulation
4. sociogram
5. adjacency

Section B
1. viral
2. generated
3. tagging
4. trademark
5. ND

Section C
1. platforms
2. content
3. # or hashtag
4. wiki
5. research

Section D
1. asynchronous
2. header or message header
3. IMAP
4. IM or instant messaging
5. synchronous

Section E
1. sockpuppet
2. identities
3. cyberbullying
4. identifiable
5. service

Module 6

Pre-Check
1. kernel
2. multitasking
3. thin
4. virtual
5. DMG
6. absolute
7. 256 characters
8. root
9. Windows File Explorer, macOS Finder

QuickChecks
381. B
382. C
384. A
385. C
386. A
387. B
391. B
392. B
393. B
395. B
396. B
398. A
400. B
401. D
402. C
403. D
404. C
406. A
408. B
409. A
410. D
411. B
412. C
416. B
417. A
418. D
419. A
420. D
421. B
422. A
423. B
424a. A
424b. C
427. A
428. B
429. C
434. B
436. A
437. C

QuickQuizzes
Section A
1. system
2. exe
3. intellectual
4. freemium
5. activation

Section B
1. False
2. kernel
3. iOS
4. Android
5. virtual

Section C
1. Web
2. setup
3. Registry
4. .dmg
5. uninstall

Section D
1. paragraph
2. Spreadsheet
3. absolute
4. table
5. fields

Section E
1. conventions
2. partition
3. root
4. cluster or block
5. system or systems

Module 7

Pre-Check
1. AES
2. password entropy
3. signature
4. Trojan
5. Stuxnet
6. Zero-day attack
7. ports
8. MITM
9. botnet

QuickChecks
456. D
459. C
460. B
461. C
462. C
464. A
468. B
469. D
470. D
471. A
472. C
473. D
475. C
476. B
479. C
482. A
483. B
484. C
485. A
487. C
489. A
490. A
491. B
492. D
495. A
497. D
499. A
501. B
502. C
503. A
504. C
507. D

QuickQuizzes
Section A
1. encrypt
2. authentication
3. dictionary
4. entropy
5. browser

Section B
1. worm
2. dropper
3. heuristic
4. positive
5. hoax

Section C
1. remote
2. denial
3. zero
4. port
5. firewall

Section D
1. Wi-Fi or wireless
2. DNS
3. TLS
4. True
5. IMSI

Section E
1. fee
2. filters
3. phishing or spear phishing
4. pharming
5. rogue

Module PY

Pre-Check

1. string
2. Comparison
3. list
4. function
5. concatenation
6. sub or derived
7. accumulator
8. syntax
9. Floating point or floating-point

QuickChecks

523. A
530. C
535. C
543. C
544. C
545. A
546. A
547. D
548. A
549a. A
549b. B
550a. A
550b. B
554. B
556. C
560. B
565. D
567. A
573. B

QuickQuizzes

Section A

1. interpreter
2. #, hashtag, or pound sign
3. string
4. syntax
5. debugging

Section B

1. variable
2. assignment
3. object
4. attribute
5. keyboard, touchscreen

Section C

1. values
2. parentheses
3. selection control
4. elif
5. Boolean

Section D

1. repetition control
2. iteration
3. true
4. while
5. list

Section E

1. def
2. parameters
3. methods
4. superclass
5. inheritance